SPECIAL INDIAN EDITION

Corporate Finance

THIRTEENTH EDITION

About the Authors

STEPHEN A. ROSS *Sloan School of Management, Massachusetts Institute of Technology* Stephen A. Ross was the Franco Modigliani Professor of Finance and Economics at the Sloan School of Management, Massachusetts Institute of Technology. One of the most widely published authors in finance and economics, Professor Ross was widely recognized for his work in developing the Arbitrage Pricing Theory and his substantial contributions to the discipline through his research in signaling, agency theory, option pricing, and the theory of the term structure of interest rates, among other topics. A past president of the American Finance Association, he also served as an associate editor of several academic and practitioner journals. He was a trustee of CalTech. He passed away unexpectedly in March of 2017.

RANDOLPH W. WESTERFIELD *Marshall School of Business, University of Southern California* Randolph W. Westerfield is Dean Emeritus of the University of Southern California's Marshall School of Business and is the Charles B. Thornton Professor of Finance Emeritus. Professor Westerfield came to USC from the Wharton School, University of Pennsylvania, where he was the chairman of the finance department and member of the finance faculty for 20 years. He is a member of the Board of Trustees of Oak Tree Capital Mutual Funds. His areas of expertise include corporate financial policy, investment management, and stock market price behavior.

JEFFREY F. JAFFE *Wharton School of Business, University of Pennsylvania* Jeffrey F. Jaffe has been a frequent contributor to the finance and economics literatures in such journals as the *Quarterly Economic Journal, The Journal of Finance, The Journal of Financial and Quantitative Analysis, The Journal of Financial Economics,* and *The Financial Analysts Journal.* His best-known work concerns insider trading, where he showed both that corporate insiders earn abnormal profits from their trades and that regulation has little effect on these profits. He also has made contributions concerning initial public offerings, regulation of utilities, the behavior of market makers, the fluctuation of gold prices, the theoretical effect of inflation on interest rates, the empirical effect of inflation on capital asset prices, the relationship between small-capitalization stocks and the January effect, and the capital structure decision.

BRADFORD D. JORDAN *Warrington College of Business, University of Florida* Bradford D. Jordan is Visiting Scholar at the University of Florida. He previously held the duPont Endowed Chair in Banking and Financial Services at the University of Kentucky, where he was department chair for many years. He specializes in corporate finance and securities valuation. He has published numerous articles in leading finance journals, and he has received a variety of research awards, including the Fama/DFA Award in 2010.

Dr. Jordan is coauthor of *Corporate Finance* 13e, *Corporate Finance: Core Principles and Applications* 6e, *Fundamentals of Corporate Finance* 13e, and *Essentials of Corporate Finance* 10e, which collectively are the most widely used business finance textbooks in the world, along with *Fundamentals of Investments: Valuation and Management* 9e, a popular investments text.

RAM KUMAR KAKANI *Indian Institute of Management (IIM), Raipur, India* Ram Kumar Kakani is currently Director at IIM, Raipur. He is a Professor in Accounting and Finance. Apart from academics, Professor Kakani has a rich experience in both the corporate sector and the public administration sector. He joined IIM Raipur in 2022. Earlier, he served as faculty for more than two decades in India, primarily at IIM Kozhikode (3 years), XLRI Jamshedpur (16 years) and LBSNAA Mussoorie (3 years). He had also worked as a residential academic in many international locations, including Denmark, Nigeria, Singapore, and the U.A.E. SSRN has ranked him as one of the top 1% authors (2007 onwards). He has been conferred the Best Young Teacher Award (2005) by the Association of Indian Management Schools. His areas of interest include Accounting & Financial Analysis, Corporate Finance, and Business Groups.

SPECIAL INDIAN EDITION

Corporate Finance

THIRTEENTH EDITION

Stephen A. Ross

Randolph W. Westerfield
Marshall School of Business
University of Southern California, Emeritus

Jeffrey Jaffe
Wharton School of Business
University of Pennsylvania

Bradford D. Jordan
University of Florida

Ram Kumar Kakani
Director
Indian Institute of Management, Raipur

With Special Contributor
Kelly Shue
Yale University

Mc Graw Hill

McGraw Hill Education (India) Private Limited

Published by McGraw Hill Education (India) Private Limited,
Registered Office: Anjana Complex No: 5/90A, Butt Road, St. Thomas Mount, Chennai - 600016

Published by arrangement with McGraw Hill LLC.

Special Indian Edition (SIE) 2025
This edition can be exported from India only by the publishers
Sales Territories: India, Pakistan, Nepal, Bangladesh, Sri Lanka and Bhutan

Print Edition:
ISBN (13) : 978-93-5532-981-3
ISBN (10) : 93-5532-981-4

E-Book Edition:
ISBN (13) : 978-93-5532-753-6
ISBN (10) : 93-5532-753-6

1 2 3 4 5 6 7 8 9 7093309 28 27 26 25 24

Printed and bound in India

Typeset at CoKrator Content Solutions Private Limited, Delhi-110092 & printed at Rajkamal Electric Press, Kundli, Haryana-131 028

Cover Image Source: Shutterstock
Cover Designer: Neeraj Dayal

Visit us at: www.mheducation.co.in
Write to us at: support.india@mheducation.com
CIN: U80302TN2010PTC111532
Toll Free Number: 1800 103 5875

To Stephen A. Ross and family

Our great friend, colleague, and coauthor Steve Ross passed away unexpectedly on March 3, 2017. Steve's influence on our textbook is seminal, deep, and enduring, and we miss him greatly. On the foundation of Steve's lasting and invaluable contributions, we pledge to continue our efforts to provide the best possible textbook for today–and tomorrow.

R.W.W. J.F.J B.D.J.

Preface

The teaching and the practice of corporate finance are more challenging and exciting than ever before. Among other things, the first two decades of the twenty-first century brought us the global financial crisis of 2008–2009 and the COVID-19 pandemic of 2020–2021. Both shocks led to major corporate restructurings, and we still routinely see announcements in the financial press about takeovers, junk bonds, financial restructuring, initial public offerings, bankruptcies, and derivatives. In addition, there are the new recognitions of "real" options, private equity and venture capital, subprime mortgages, bailouts, and credit spreads. As we have learned, the world's financial markets are more integrated than ever before. Both the theory and practice of corporate finance have been moving ahead with uncommon speed, and our teaching must keep pace.

These developments have placed new burdens on the teaching of corporate finance. On one hand, the changing world of finance makes it more difficult to keep materials up to date. On the other hand, the teacher must distinguish the permanent from the temporary and avoid the temptation to follow fads. Our solution to this problem is to emphasize the modern fundamentals of the theory of finance and make the theory come to life with contemporary examples. Increasingly, many of these examples are outside the United States.

All too often, the beginning student views corporate finance as a collection of unrelated topics that are unified largely because they are bound together between the covers of one book. We want our book to embody and reflect the main principle of finance: Namely, good financial decisions will add value to the firm and to shareholders and bad financial decisions will destroy value. The key to understanding how value is added or destroyed is cash flows. To add value, firms must generate more cash than they use. We hope this simple principle is manifest in all parts of this book.

The Intended Audience of This Book

This book has been written for the introductory courses in corporate finance at the MBA level and for the intermediate courses in many undergraduate programs. Some instructors will find our text appropriate for the introductory course at the undergraduate level as well.

We assume that most students either will have taken, or will be concurrently enrolled in, courses in accounting, statistics, and economics. This exposure will help students understand some of the more difficult material. However, the book is self-contained, and a prior knowledge of these areas is not essential. The only mathematics prerequisite is basic algebra.

New to the 13th Edition

There are five primary areas of change reflected in the 13th edition:

1. *Personal taxes.* Entities other than C corporations still face progressive taxation at the personal tax level. Discussion of marginal versus average tax rates is examined.
2. *COVID-19.* The 2020–2021 COVID-19 pandemic affected corporate operations in numerous ways, including capital budgeting, long-term and short-term financial planning, capital structure, supply chain management, and risk management. We have incorporated discussions around these shocks and their impact on different types of corporations.
3. *Discussion of levered versus unlevered beta.* We have added a more in-depth discussion of levering and unlevering beta, including a discussion of when to unlever beta and when not to do so.

4. *Venture capital.* We added a much updated and expanded discussion of entrepreneurship and venture capital, including the different venture capital funding stages.
5. *Comparables valuation for stocks.* We added an expanded discussion of comparable valuation for stocks, including price ratios for various industries.

With the 13th edition, we've also included coverage of:

- Tax advantages of share repurchases.
- Empirical evidence of behavioral challenges to market efficiency.
- Fintech.
- Updated discussion of executive stock options.
- More detailed discussion of the Change to WACC approach.
- Cross-selling, leveraged recapitalizations, and debt overhang.
- Using forward rates to implement the home currency approach.

In addition, each chapter has been updated and, where relevant, "internationalized." We try to capture the excitement of corporate finance with current examples, chapter vignettes, and openers. Spreadsheet applications are spread throughout.

Finally, perhaps the biggest change for the 13th edition is the addition, for the first time, of a special contributor, Professor Kelly Shue of Yale University. Kelly made a number of suggestions that led to more complete coverage, sharpened exposition, and new insights on a variety of subjects.

Publisher's Note

McGraw Hill Education (India) invites suggestions and comments from you, all of which can be sent to support.india@mheducation.com (kindly mention the title and author name in the subject line). Piracy-related issues may also be reported.

Supplemental Features

Instructor Resources

The Instructor Library in Connect contains all the necessary supplements–Instructor's Manual, Test Bank, Computerized Test Bank, and PowerPoint–all in one place. Go to connect.mheducation.com to find:

- **Instructor's Manual**

  Prepared for this edition by Joshua Spizman, Loyola Marymount University

  This is a great place to find new lecture ideas. The IM has three main sections. The first section contains a chapter outline and other lecture materials. The annotated outline for each chapter includes lecture tips, real-world tips, ethics notes, suggested PowerPoint slides, and, when appropriate, a video synopsis.

- **PowerPoint Presentations**

  Customize our content for your course. This presentation has been thoroughly revised to include more lecture-oriented slides, as well as exhibits and examples both from the book and from outside sources. Applicable slides have web links that take you directly to specific internet sites or a spreadsheet link to show an example in Excel. You also can go to the Notes Page function for more tips on presenting the slides. If you already have PowerPoint installed on your PC, you can edit, print, or rearrange the complete presentation to meet your specific needs.

- **Corporate Finance Videos**

  These brief and engaging conceptual videos (and accompanying questions) will help students to master the building blocks of the Corporate Finance course.

Student Support

- **Narrated Presentations**

  Each chapter's slides follow the chapter topics and provide steps and explanations showing how to solve key problems. Because each student learns differently, a quick click on each slide will "talk through" its contents with you!

- **Excel Templates**

  Corresponding to most end-of-chapter problems, each template allows the student to work through the problem using Excel. Each end-of-chapter problem with a template is indicated by an Excel icon in the margin beside it.

- **ExcelMaster**

  Developed by the authors for the RWJ franchise, this valuable and comprehensive supplement provides a tutorial for students in using Excel in finance that is broken out by chapter sections.

Acknowledgments

We are lucky to have had skilled and experienced instructors developing the supplement material for this edition. We greatly appreciate the contributions of Joe Smolira, Belmont University, who worked closely with us to develop the Solutions Manual, Excel Master, and to create Excel templates for many of the end-of-chapter problems. Thank you also to Heidi Toprac, University of Texas, for thoroughly updating, revising, and tagging of every problem in the test bank.

The following proofers did outstanding work on this edition of *Corporate Finance:* Emily Bello and Steve Hailey. To them fell the unenviable task of technical proofreading and, in particular, careful checking of each calculation throughout the text and Solutions Manual.

In every phase of this project, we have been privileged to have had the complete and unwavering support of a great organization, McGraw Hill. We especially thank the sales group. The suggestions they provide, their professionalism in assisting potential adopters, and the service they provide to current users have been a major factor in our success.

We are deeply grateful to the select group of professionals who served as our development team on this edition: Chuck Synovec, Director; Allison McCabe-Carroll, Senior Product Developer; Trina Maurer, Senior Marketing Manager; Matt Diamond, Senior Designer; and Susan Trentacosti, Lead Core Project Manager. Others at McGraw Hill, too numerous to list here, have improved the book in countless ways.

Finally, we thank our special contributor to this edition, Professor Kelly Shue of Yale University. Between her deep knowledge of the corporate finance literature and extensive experience teaching MBA-level corporate finance at University of Chicago and Yale, Kelly brings a lot to the table. She reviewed the entire book and suggested a number of changes and additions that we implemented. We look forward to working even more closely with Kelly on future projects.

Andras Danis
Georgia Institute of Technology

Sugata Das
Montana State University-Billings

Lowell D'Souza
Northeastern University

Eric Eller
Loras College

Melissa B. Frye
University of Central Florida

Melody J. Gunter
Florida State University

Atul Gupta
Bentley University

Janet Hamilton
Portland State University

John Hartman
University of California-Santa Barbara

Abu Jalai
Suffolk University

Robert James
Boston College

Victoria Javine
University of Alabama

Roger Klee
Cleveland State University

Wendy Liu
University of Kentucky

Jeremy Marcq
Tufts University and Harvard University

Narasimha Mohan
Baldwin Wallace University

Hongsong Neuhauser
Elizabethtown College

Francis Blaise Roncagli
Cleveland State University

Ronald M. Shapiro
Rutgers University

Stephen V. Smith
Drexel University

Mete Tepe
Virginia Tech

Gary P. Tripp
Southern New Hampshire University

Emre Unlu
University of Nebraska

Kainan Wang
University of Toledo

Arthur J. Wilson
George Washington University

A Kanagaraj
XLRI Jamshedpur

Abhilash S Nair
IIM Kozhikode

Ajay Kumar Garg
IIM Lucknow

Alok Dixit
IIM Lucknow

Ameet Kumar Banerjee
XLRI Jamshedpur

Amrinder Singh
IIM Sirmaur

Anirban Banerjee
IIM Ahmedabad

Arunima Haldar
SPJIMR Mumbai

Arvind Sampath
IIM Kozhikode

Ashok Banerjee
IIM Udaipur

Aswin Alora
IIM Kozhikode

Avinash Ghalke
SPJIMR Mumbai

Bhanu Pratap Singh
IIM Sirmaur

Debasish Maitra
IIM Indore

Deepak Kumar
IIM Ranchi

Devika Arumugam
IIM Indore

Divya Agarwal
MDI Gurgaon

Diwakar Nadar
IIM Sambalpur

Ekta Sikarwar
IIM Kozhikode

Gaurav Singh Chauhan
IIM Indore

H K Pradhan
XLRI Jamshedpur

Hariprasad B
IIM Indore

Hemant Manuj
Jindal School of Banking & Finance
Sonipat

Jagan Kumar Sur
IIM Ranchi

Jalaj Pathak
IIM Lucknow

Jiju Lukose P J
IIM Kozhikode

Jyothi Kumari
IBS Hyderabad

K Kiran Kumar
IIM Indore

K S Ranjani
IIM Mumbai

Kamlesh Thakkar
XLRI Jamshedpur

Kaveri Krishnan
IIM Visakhapatnam

Keyur Thaker
IIM Indore

Kousik Guhathakurta
IIM Indore

Kriti Saxena
IIM Sirmaur

L.V. Ramana
IIM Indore

M Kannadhasan
IIM Raipur

Madhumita Chakraborty
IIM Lucknow

Madhusudan Karmakar
IIM Lucknow

Malvika Chhatwani
XLRI Jamshedpur

Manoj Kumar
IIM Jammu

Mehul Raithatha
IIM Indore

Mohammad Shameem Jawed
IIM Visakhapatnam

Moonika
IIM Visakhapatnam

Mrityunjay Kumar Tiwary
IIM Lucknow

N Ramachandran
DCSMAT Vagamon

N Sivasankaran
XLRI Jamshedpur

Nemiraja Jadiyappa
IIM Kozhikode

Nidhi Sharma
IIM Raipur

P Sanjay
IIM Sirmaur

Pankaj Kumar Agarwal
XLRI Jamshedpur

Pankaj Kumar Baag
IIM Kozhikode

Pitabas Mohanty
XLRI Jamshedpur

Pooja Kumari
IIM Visakhapatnam

Prabhakar Patil
SEBI Mumbai

Pradip Banerjee
IIM Indore

Pradiptarathi Panda
IIM Raipur

Prakash Singh
IIM Lucknow

Pranith Kumar Roy
IIM Raipur

Prantik Ray
XLRI Jamshedpur

Prince Doliya
IIM Visakhapatnam

Qambar Abidi
IIM Kozhikode

Rachappa Shette
IIM Kozhikode

Radha Mukesh Ladkani
IIM Indore

Rajesh Kumar Sinha
XLRI Jamshedpur

Rajesh Pathak
IIM Raipur

Rajesh S P
IIM Raipur

Ramprasath L
IIM Kozhikode

Ranjan Dasgupta
IIM Raipur

Sabyasachi Sengupta
XLRI Jamshedpur

Santosh Kumar Sangem
XLRI Jamshedpur

Satish Kumar
IIM Nagpur

Satish Kumar
IBS Hyderabad

Saumya Ranjan Dash
IIM Indore

Seshadev Sahoo
IIM Lucknow

Shalini Agnihotri
IIM Visakhapatnam

Sony Thomas
IIM Kozhikode

Soumya Guha Deb
IIM Sambalpur

Sowmya Subramaniam
IIM Lucknow

SSS Kumar
IIM Kozhikode

Sudershan Kuntluru
IIM Kozhikode

Surya Bhushan Kumar
IIM Indore

Swamy Perumandla
IIM Nagpur

Trilochan Tripathy
XLRI Jamshedpur

Uday Damodaran
IIM Udaipur

Udayan Sharma
IIM Indore

V Gopal
IIM Trichy

V Nagi Reddy
IBS Hyderabad

Vaibhav Lalwani
XLRI Jamshedpur

Vasant Sivaraman
SPJIMR Mumbai

VG Sridharan
IIM Kozhikode

Vinit Singh Chauhan
IIM Lucknow

Yogesh Chauhan
IIM Raipur

Pedagogy

In this edition of *Corporate Finance*, we have updated and improved our features to present material in a way that makes it coherent and easy to understand. In addition, *Corporate Finance* is rich in valuable learning tools and support to help students succeed in learning the fundamentals of financial management.

Chapter Opening Vignettes

Each chapter begins with a contemporary vignette that highlights the concepts in the chapter and their relevance to real-world examples.

10

PART III: RISK

Lessons from Market History

Given the headlines in the spring of 2020 about the market crash caused by COVID-related lockdowns, you might be surprised to learn that 2020 was a great year for investors. With the S&P 500 index returning about 18 percent and the Nasdaq Composite index up about 43 percent in 2020, stock market performance overall was very good. For example, investors in bitcoin mining company Bit Digital had to be happy about the 3,688 percent gain in that stock, and investors in biotechnology company Novavax had to feel pretty good following that company's 2,889 percent gain. Of course, not all stocks increased in value during the year. Stock in Occidental Petroleum fell 58 percent, and stock in cruise ship operator Carnival Corp. sunk 57 percent.

These examples show that there were tremendous potential profits to be made during 2020, but there was also the risk of losing money—and lots of it. So what should you, as a stock market investor, expect when you invest your own money? In this chapter, we study more than eight decades of market history to find out.

Please visit us at **rwjcorporatefinance.blogspot.com** for the latest developments in the world of corporate finance.

10.1 Returns

RUPEE RETURNS

Excel Master coverage online

Suppose the Vashisht Concept Company has several thousand shares of stock outstanding and you are a shareholder. Further suppose that you purchased some of the shares of stock in the company at the beginning of the year; it is now year-end and you want to figure out how well you have done on your investment. The return you get on an investment in stocks, like that in bonds or any other investment, comes in two forms.

How did the market do today? Find out at **finance.yahoo.com**.

As the owner of stock in the Vashisht Concept Company, you are a part owner of the company. If the company is profitable, it generally could distribute some of its profits to the shareholders. Therefore, as the owner of shares of stock, you could receive some cash, called a *dividend*, during the year. This cash is the *income component* of your return. In addition to the dividends, the other part of your return is the *capital gain*—or, if it is negative, the *capital loss* (negative capital gain)—on the investment. Your *total Rupee return* is the sum of your dividend income and capital gain or loss.

313

ExcelMaster Icons

Topics covered in the comprehensive ExcelMaster supplement (in Connect) are indicated by an icon in the margin.

Why was there such a reward? Does it mean that it never pays to invest in T-bills and that someone who invested in them instead of in the stock market needs a course in finance? A complete answer to these questions lies at the heart of modern finance. However, part of the answer can be found in the variability of the various types of investments. There are many years when an investment in T-bills achieves higher returns than an investment in large common stocks. Also, we note that the returns from an investment in common stocks are frequently negative, whereas an investment in T-bills have only once had a negative return, −.02 percent in 1938. So, we now turn our attention to measuring the variability of returns and an introductory discussion of risk.

10.5 Risk Statistics

Excel Master coverage online

The second number that we use to characterize the distribution of returns is a measure of the risk in returns. There is no universally agreed-upon definition of risk. One way to think about the risk of returns on common stock is in terms of how spread out the frequency distribution in Figure 10.9 is. The spread, or dispersion, of a distribution is a measure of how much a particular return can deviate from the mean return. If the distribution is very spread out, the returns that will occur are very uncertain. By contrast, a distribution whose returns are all within a few percentage points of each other is tight, and the returns are less uncertain. The measures of risk we will discuss are variance and standard deviation.

VARIANCE

The **variance** and its square root, the **standard deviation,** are the most common measures of variability, or dispersion. We will use Var and σ^2 to denote the variance, and we will use SD and σ to represent the standard deviation. σ is, of course, the Greek letter sigma.

EXAMPLE 10.3

Volatility Suppose the returns on common stocks are (in decimals) .1370, .3580, .4514, and −.0888, respectively. As we calculated in Example 10.2, the average return is .2144. The variance of this sample is computed as follows:

$$\text{Var} = \frac{1}{T-1}[(R_1 - \bar{R})^2 + (R_2 - \bar{R})^2 + (R_3 - \bar{R})^2 + (R_4 - \bar{R})^2]$$

$$.0582 = \frac{1}{3}[(.1370 - .2144)^2 + (.3580 - .2144)^2 + (.4514 - .2144)^2 + (-.0888 - .2144)^2]$$

$$\text{SD} = \sqrt{.0582} = .2413, \text{ or } 24.13\%$$

Figures and Tables

This text makes extensive use of real data and presents them in various figures and tables. Explanations in the narrative, examples, and end-of-chapter problems will refer to many of these exhibits.

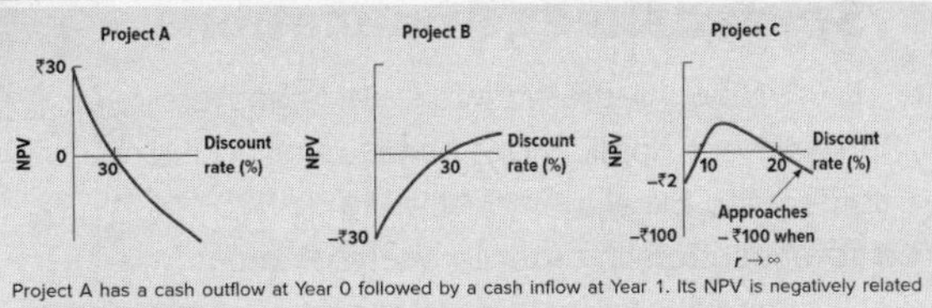

Project A has a cash outflow at Year 0 followed by a cash inflow at Year 1. Its NPV is negatively related to the discount rate.
Project B has a cash inflow at Year 0 followed by a cash outflow at Year 1. Its NPV is positively related to the discount rate.
Project C has two changes of sign in its cash flows. It has an outflow at Year 0, an inflow at Year 1, and an outflow at Year 2. Projects with more than one change of sign can have multiple rates of return.

Figure 5.5 NPV Profile for Projects A, B, and C

As with Project A, the internal rate of return is 30 percent. However, notice that the net present value is negative when the discount rate is below 30 percent. Conversely, the net present value is positive when the discount rate is above 30 percent. The decision rule is exactly the opposite of our previous result. For this type of project, the following rule applies:

Accept the project when the IRR is less than the discount rate. Reject the project when the IRR is greater than the discount rate.

This unusual decision rule follows from the NPV profile of Project B in Figure 5.5. The curve is upward sloping, implying that NPV is positively related to the discount rate.

Table 5.2 The Internal Rate of Return and Net Present Value

	Project A			Project B			Project C		
	0	1	2	0	1	2	0	1	2
Cash flows	–₹100	₹130		₹100	–₹130		–₹100	₹230	–₹132
IRR	30%			30%			10% and 20%		
NPV @10%	₹18.18			–₹18.18			₹ 0		
Accept if market rate	<30%			>30%			>10% but <20%		
Financing or investing	Investing			Financing			Mixture		

EXAMPLE 6.5

Allocated Costs The Vedakshya Consulting Company devotes one wing of its suite of offices to a library requiring a cash outflow of ₹100,000 a year in upkeep. A proposed capital budgeting project is expected to generate revenue equal to 5 percent of the overall firm's sales. An executive at the firm, Dayavan Pillai, argues that ₹5,000 (= .05 × ₹100,000) should be viewed as the proposed project's share of the library's costs. Is this appropriate for capital budgeting?

The answer is no. One must ask what the difference is between the cash flows of the entire firm with the project and the cash flows of the entire firm without the project. The firm will spend ₹100,000 on library upkeep whether or not the proposed project is accepted. Because acceptance of the proposed project does not affect this cash flow, the cash flow should be ignored when calculating the NPV of the project. Suppose the project has a positive NPV without the allocated costs but is rejected because of the allocated costs. In this case, the firm is losing potential value that it could have gained otherwise.

6.2 The Bhimsen Company: An Example

Excel Master coverage online

To forecast cash flows for a new project, we need to estimate operating cash flow less the needed investments. To illustrate this process, we next consider the example of a proposed investment in machinery and related items. Our example involves the Bhimsen Company and colored bowling balls.

Examples

Separate called-out examples are integrated throughout the chapters. Each example illustrates an intuitive or mathematical application in a step-by-step format. There is enough detail in the explanations so students don't have to look elsewhere for additional information.

"In Their Own Words" Boxes

Located throughout the chapters, this unique series consists of articles written by distinguished scholars or practitioners about key topics in the text. Boxes include essays by Edward I. Altman, Robert S. Hansen, Robert C. Higgins, Michael C. Jensen, Merton Miller, and Jay R. Ritter.

In Their Own Words

ROBERT C. HIGGINS ON SUSTAINABLE GROWTH

Most financial officers know intuitively that it takes money to make money. Rapid sales growth requires increased assets in the form of accounts receivable, inventory, and fixed plant, which, in turn, require money to pay for assets. They also know that if their company does not have the money when needed, it can literally "grow broke." The sustainable growth equation states these intuitive truths explicitly.

Sustainable growth is often used by bankers and other external analysts to assess a company's creditworthiness. They are aided in this exercise by several sophisticated computer software packages that provide detailed analyses of the company's past financial performance, including its annual sustainable growth rate.

Bankers use this information in several ways. Quick comparison of a company's actual growth rate to its sustainable rate tells the banker what issues will be at the top of management's financial agenda. If actual growth consistently exceeds sustainable growth, management's problem will be where to get the cash to finance growth. The banker thus can anticipate interest in loan products. Conversely, if sustainable growth consistently exceeds actual, the banker had best be prepared to talk about investment products because management's problem will be what to do with all the cash that keeps piling up in the till.

Bankers also find the sustainable growth equation useful for explaining to financially inexperienced small business owners and overly optimistic entrepreneurs that, for the long-run viability of their business, it is necessary to keep growth and profitability in proper balance.

Finally, comparison of actual to sustainable growth rates helps a banker understand why a loan applicant needs money and for how long the need might continue. In one instance, a loan applicant requested ₹100,000 to pay off several insistent suppliers and promised to repay in a few months when he collected some accounts receivable that were coming due. A sustainable growth analysis revealed that the firm had been growing at four to six times its sustainable growth rate and that this pattern was likely to continue in the foreseeable future. This alerted the banker that impatient suppliers were only a symptom of the much more fundamental disease of overly rapid growth, and that a ₹100,000 loan would likely prove to be only the down payment on a much larger, multiyear commitment.

SOURCE: Robert C. Higgins is Professor Emeritus of Finance at the Foster School of Business at the University of Washington. He pioneered the use of sustainable growth as a tool for financial analysis.

Spreadsheet Applications

Now integrated into select chapters, Spreadsheet Applications boxes reintroduce students to Excel, demonstrating how to set up spreadsheets in order to analyze common financial problems—a vital part of every business student's education. (For even more spreadsheet example problems, check out ExcelMaster in Connect.)

SPREADSHEET APPLICATIONS

Calculating NPVs with a Spreadsheet

Spreadsheets are commonly used to calculate NPVs. Examining the use of spreadsheets in this context also allows us to issue an important warning. Consider the following:

	A	B	C	D	E	F	G	H
1								
2	**Using a spreadsheet to calculate net present values**							
3								
4	A project's cost is ₹10,000. The cash flows are ₹2,000 per year for the first two years,							
5	₹4,000 per year for the next two years, and ₹5,000 in the last year. The discount rate is							
6	10 percent. What's the NPV?							
7								
8		Year	Cash flow					
9		0	–₹10,000		Discount rate =	10%		
10		1	2,000					
11		2	2,000		**NPV =**	**₹2,102.72**	*(wrong answer)*	
12		3	4,000		**NPV =**	**₹2,312.99**	*(right answer)*	
13		4	4,000					
14		5	5,000					
15								
16	The formula entered in cell F11 is =NPV(F9,C9:C14). However, this gives the wrong answer because the							
17	NPV function actually calculates present values, not *net* present values.							
18								
19	The formula entered in cell F12 is =NPV(F9,C10:C14) + C9. This gives the right answer because the							
20	NPV function is used to calculate the present value of the cash flows and then the initial cost is							
21	subtracted to calculate the answer. Notice that we added cell C9 because it is already negative.							

In our spreadsheet example, notice that we have provided two answers. The first answer is wrong even though we used the spreadsheet's NPV formula. What happened is that the "NPV" function in our spreadsheet is actually a PV function; unfortunately, one of the original spreadsheet programmers many years ago got the definition wrong, and subsequent programmers have copied it! Our second answer shows how to use the formula properly.

The example here illustrates the danger of blindly using calculators or computers without understanding what is going on; we shudder to think of how many capital budgeting decisions in the real world are based on incorrect use of this particular function.

Explanatory Website Links

These web links are specifically selected to accompany text material and provide students and instructors with a quick reference to additional information on the internet.

Liabilities are obligations of the firm that require a payout of cash within a stipulated period. Many liabilities involve contractual obligations to repay a stated amount plus interest over a period. Liabilities are debts and are frequently associated with fixed cash burdens, called *debt service*, that put the firm in default of a contract if they are not paid. *Stockholders' equity* is a claim against the firm's assets that is residual and not fixed. In general terms, when the firm borrows, it gives the bondholders first claim on the firm's cash flow.[1] Bondholders can sue the firm if the firm defaults on its bond contracts. This may lead the firm to declare itself bankrupt. Stockholders' equity is the difference between assets and liabilities:

$$\text{Assets} - \text{Liabilities} \equiv \text{Stockholders' equity}$$

This is the stockholders' share in the firm stated in accounting terms. The accounting value of stockholders' equity increases when retained earnings are added. This occurs when the firm retains part of its earnings instead of paying them out as dividends.

VALUE VERSUS COST

The accounting value of a firm's assets is frequently referred to as the *carrying value* or the *book value* of the assets.[2] Under **generally accepted accounting principles (GAAP)**, audited financial statements of firms in the United States carry assets at cost.[3] Similar is the case with India as well.[4] The terms *carrying value* and *book value* are misleading and cause many readers of financial statements to believe the firm's

The home page for the Financial Accounting Standards Board (FASB) is **www.fasb.org**.

[1]Bondholders are investors in the firm's debt. They are creditors of the firm. In this discussion, the term *bondholder* means the same thing as *creditor*.
[2]Confusion often arises because many financial accounting terms have the same meaning. For example, the following terms usually refer to the same thing: *assets minus liabilities*, *net worth*, *stockholders' equity*, *owners' equity*, *book equity*, and *equity capitalization*.
[3]Generally, the U.S. GAAP require assets to be carried at the lower of cost or market value. In most instances, cost is lower than market value. However, in some cases when a fair market value can be readily determined, the assets have their value adjusted to the fair market value.
[4]In the Indian context, cost consideration is used by the companies based on the Indian Accounting Standards (Ind AS) issued by the Central Government of India under the supervision and control of Accounting Standards Board (ASB) of ICAI and in consultation with National Advisory Committee on Accounting Standards (NACAS). NACAS was replaced by National Financial Reporting Authority (NFRA). NFRA has been constituted as a quasi-judicial body with larger remit than NACAS which only advised on accounting policies and standards.

Numbered Equations

Key equations are numbered and available for download.

MARKET VALUE MEASURES

Our final group of measures is based, in part, on information not necessarily contained in financial statements–the market price per share of the stock. Obviously, these measures can be calculated directly only for publicly traded companies.

We assume that Badrinath has 33 million shares outstanding and the stock sold for ₹88 per share at the end of the year. If we recall that Badrinath's net income was ₹363 million, then we can calculate that its earnings per share were:

$$\text{EPS} = \frac{\text{Net income}}{\text{Shares outstanding}} = \frac{₹363}{33} = ₹10.99 \quad \textbf{(3.17)}$$

Price-Earnings Ratio The first of our market value measures, the *price-earnings* or *PE ratio* (or multiple), is defined as:

$$\begin{aligned}\text{PE ratio} &= \frac{\text{Price per share}}{\text{Earnings per share}} \\ &= \frac{₹88}{₹10.99} = 8.01 \text{ times}\end{aligned} \quad \textbf{(3.18)}$$

In the vernacular, we would say that Badrinath shares sell for 8 times earnings, or we might say that Badrinath shares have, or "carry," a PE multiple of 8.

Because the PE ratio measures how much investors are willing to pay per Rupee of current earnings, higher PEs are often taken to mean that the firm has significant prospects for future growth. Of course, if a firm had no or almost no earnings, its PE would probably be quite large; so, as always, care is needed in interpreting this ratio.

Market-to-Book Ratio A second commonly quoted measure is the *market-to-book ratio*:

$$\begin{aligned}\text{Market-to-book ratio} &= \frac{\text{Market value per share}}{\text{Book value per share}} \\ &= \frac{₹88}{₹2{,}591/33} = \frac{₹88}{₹78.5} = 1.12 \text{ times}\end{aligned} \quad \textbf{(3.19)}$$

Notice that book value per share is total equity (not just common stock) divided by the number of shares outstanding.

The end-of-chapter material reflects and builds upon the concepts learned from the chapter and study features.

Summary and Conclusions

The summary provides a quick review of key concepts in the chapter.

Questions and Problems

Because solving problems is so critical to a student's learning, new questions and problems have been added and existing questions and problems have been revised. All problems also have been thoroughly reviewed and checked for accuracy. Problems have been grouped according to level of difficulty with the levels listed in the margin: Basic, Intermediate, and Challenge.

Additionally, we have tried to make the problems in the critical "concept" chapters, such as those on value, risk, and capital structure, especially challenging and interesting.

We provide answers to selected problems in Appendix B at the end of the book.

Summary and Conclusions

This chapter discussed a number of practical applications of capital budgeting.

1. Though NPV is the best capital budgeting approach conceptually, it has been criticized in practice for giving managers a false sense of security. Sensitivity analysis shows NPV under varying assumptions, giving managers a better feel for the project's risks. Unfortunately, sensitivity analysis modifies only one variable at a time, but many variables are likely to vary together in the real world. Scenario analysis examines a project's performance under different scenarios (such as war breaking out or oil prices skyrocketing). Finally, managers want to know how bad forecasts must be before a project loses money. Break-even analysis calculates the sales figure at which the project breaks even. Though break-even analysis is frequently performed on an accounting profit basis, we suggest that a net present value basis is more appropriate.
2. Monte Carlo simulation begins with a model of the firm's cash flows, based on both the interactions between different variables and the movement of each individual variable over time. Random sampling generates a distribution of these cash flows for each period, leading to a net present value calculation.
3. We analyzed the hidden options in capital budgeting, such as the option to expand, the option to abandon, and timing options.
4. Decision trees represent an approach for valuing projects with these hidden, or real, options.

Concept Questions

1. **Forecasting Risk** What is forecasting risk? In general, would the degree of forecasting risk be greater for a new product or a cost-cutting proposal? Why?
2. **Sensitivity Analysis and Scenario Analysis** What is the essential difference between sensitivity analysis and scenario analysis?
3. **Marginal Cash Flows** A co-worker claims that looking at so much marginal this and incremental that is a bunch of nonsense, and states, "Listen, if our average revenue doesn't exceed our average cost, then we will have a negative cash flow, and we will go broke!" How do you respond?
4. **Break-Even Point** As a shareholder of a firm that is contemplating a new project, would you be more concerned with the accounting break-even point, the cash break-even point (the point at which operating cash flow is zero), or the financial break-even point? Why?
5. **Break-Even Point** Assume a firm is considering a new typical project that requires an initial investment with sales, variable costs, and fixed costs over its life. Will the project usually reach the accounting, cash, or financial break-even point first? Which will it reach next? Last? Will this order always apply?
6. **Real Options** Why does traditional NPV analysis tend to underestimate the true value of a capital budgeting project?
7. **Real Options** The Mango Republic has liberalized its markets and is now permitting foreign investors. Tesla Manufacturing has analyzed starting a project in the country and has determined that the project has a negative NPV. Why might the company go ahead with the project? What type of option is most likely to add value to this project?
8. **Sensitivity and Break-Even Analysis** How does sensitivity analysis interact with break-even analysis?
9. **Option to Wait** An option often can have more than one source of value. Consider a logging company. The company can log the timber today or wait another year (or more) to log the timber. What advantages would waiting one year potentially have?

Excel Master It! Problem

Excel is a great tool for solving problems, but with many time value of money problems, you may still need to draw a time line. Consider a classic retirement problem. A friend is celebrating her birthday and wants to start saving for her anticipated retirement. She has the following years to retirement and retirement spending goals:

Excel Master coverage online

Years until retirement	30
Amount to withdraw each year	₹90,000
Years to withdraw in retirement	20
Investment rate	8%

Because your friend is planning ahead, the first withdrawal will not take place until one year after she retires. She wants to make equal annual deposits into her account for her retirement fund.

Excel Master It! Problems

Included in the end-of-chapter material are problems directly incorporating Excel, and new tips and techniques taught in the chapter's ExcelMaster supplement.

34. **Growing Annuity** Your job pays you only once a year for all the work you did over the previous 12 months. Today, December 31, you just received your salary of ₹48,000 and you plan to spend all of it. However, you want to start saving for retirement beginning next year. You have decided that one year from today you will begin depositing 9 percent of your annual salary in an account that will earn 10 percent per year. Your salary will increase at 3.5 percent per year throughout your career. How much money will you have on the date of your retirement 40 years from today?
35. **Present Value and Discount Rates** What is the relationship between the value of an annuity and the level of interest rates? Suppose you just bought an annuity with 13 annual payments of ₹10,000 per year at a discount rate of 10 percent per year. What happens to the value of your investment if the discount rate suddenly drops to 5 percent? What if the discount rate rate suddenly rises to 15 percent?
36. **Calculating the Number of Payments** You're prepared to make monthly payments of ₹225, beginning at the end of this month, into an account that pays an APR of 6.5 percent compounded monthly. How many payments will you have made when your account balance reaches ₹15,000?
37. **Calculating Annuity Present Values** You want to borrow ₹95,000 from your local bank to buy a new sailboat. You can afford to make monthly payments of ₹1,850, but no more. Assuming monthly compounding, what is the highest rate you can afford on a 60-month APR loan?

Excel Problems

Indicated by the Excel icon in the margin, these problems can be found at the end of almost all chapters. Located in Connect Finance for *Corporate Finance,* 13e, Excel templates have been created for each of these problems, where students can use the data in the problem to work out the solution using Excel skills.

Mini Case THE MBA DECISION

Ben Bates graduated from college six years ago with a finance undergraduate degree. Although he is satisfied with his current job, his goal is to become an investment banker. He feels that an MBA degree would allow him to achieve this goal. After examining schools, he has narrowed his choice to either Wilton University or Mount Perry College. Although internships are encouraged by both schools, to get class credit for the internship, no salary can be paid. Other than internships, neither school will allow its students to work while enrolled in its MBA program.

Ben currently works at the money management firm of Dewey and Louis. His annual salary at the firm is ₹69,000 per year, and his salary is expected to increase at 3 percent per year until retirement. He is currently 28 years old and expects to work for 40 more years. His current job includes a fully paid health insurance plan, and his current average tax rate is 26 percent. Ben has a savings account with enough money to cover the entire cost of his MBA program.

The Ritter College of Business at Wilton University is one of the top MBA programs in the country. The MBA degree requires two years of full-time enrollment at the university. The annual tuition is ₹75,000, payable at the beginning of each school year. Books and other supplies are estimated to cost ₹3,600 per year. Ben expects that after graduation from Wilton, he will receive a job offer for about ₹115,000 per year, with a ₹20,000 signing

End-of-Chapter Cases

Located at the end of almost every chapter, these mini cases focus on common company situations that embody important corporate finance topics. Each case presents a new scenario, data, and a dilemma. Several questions at the end of each case require students to analyze and focus on all of the material they learned in that chapter.

Brief Contents

Part I
OVERVIEW

Part II
VALUATION AND CAPITAL BUDGETING

Part III
RISK

Part IV
CAPITAL STRUCTURE AND DIVIDEND POLICY

Part V
LONG-TERM FINANCING

Part VI
OPTIONS, FUTURES, AND CORPORATE FINANCE

Part VII
SHORT-TERM FINANCE

Part VIII
SPECIAL TOPICS

Contents

PART I Overview

PART II Valuation and Capital Budgeting

CHAPTER 4

CHAPTER 5

CHAPTER 6

PART III Risk

CHAPTER 10

CHAPTER 11

CHAPTER 12
An Alternative View of Risk and Return 389

CHAPTER 13
Risk, Cost of Capital, and Valuation 412

PART IV Capital Structure and Dividend Policy

CHAPTER 14
Efficient Capital Markets and Behavioral Challenges 449

CHAPTER 15
Long-Term Financing 490

CHAPTER 16
Capital Structure: Basic Concepts 512

CHAPTER 17
Capital Structure: Limits to the Use of Debt 546

PART V Long-Term Financing

CHAPTER 20

CHAPTER 21

PART VI Options, Futures, and Corporate Finance

CHAPTER 22

CHAPTER 23

CHAPTER 27

CHAPTER 28

PART VIII Special Topics

CHAPTER 29
Mergers, Acquisitions, and Divestitures 927

CHAPTER 30
Financial Distress 971

1

PART I: OVERVIEW

Introduction to Corporate Finance

In 2010, Adam Neumann and a business partner opened the first WeWork space in New York's Little Italy. WeWork provided shared office space for businesses that would rent space as needed, sometimes only for a day. By 2019, WeWork operated in more than 111 cities in 29 countries. Revenues had grown to about $3 billion, but the company was still losing money. Early in 2019, the giant tech investor SoftBank made a major bet on WeWork, which valued the company at $47 billion.

Unfortunately, everything was not rosy at WeWork. In the middle of 2019, the company filed to go public in an IPO, but then changed its mind. In late 2019, Softbank agreed to another major investment, but it pulled the deal in 2020. What happened? Among other things, the COVID-19 pandemic hit, calling into question the company's entire business model of shared, face-to-face meeting spaces. But in a surprise to many, in July 2020, Marcelo Claure, who was brought in to revitalize WeWork, announced the company should be profitable by 2021.

Understanding WeWork's story as it progressed from a start-up to a multibillion-dollar enterprise and its subsequent struggles takes us into issues involving the corporate form of organization, corporate goals, and corporate control, all of which we discuss in this chapter.

Please visit us at **rwjcorporatefinance.blogspot.com** for the latest developments in the world of corporate finance.

1.1 What is Corporate Finance?

Suppose you decide to start a firm to make tennis balls. To do this you hire managers to buy raw materials and assemble a workforce that will produce and sell finished tennis balls. In the language of finance, you make an investment in assets such as inventory, machinery, land, and labor. The amount of cash you invest in assets must be matched by an equal amount of cash raised by financing. When you begin to sell tennis balls, your firm will generate cash. This is the basis of value creation. The purpose of the firm is to create value for you, the owner. The value is reflected in the framework of the simple balance sheet model of the firm.

THE BALANCE SHEET MODEL OF THE FIRM

Suppose we take a financial snapshot of the firm and its activities at a single point in time. Figure 1.1 shows a graphic conceptualization of the balance sheet and it will help introduce you to corporate finance.

The assets of the firm are on the left side of the balance sheet. These assets can be thought of as current and fixed. *Fixed assets* are those that will last a long time, like buildings. Some fixed assets are tangible,

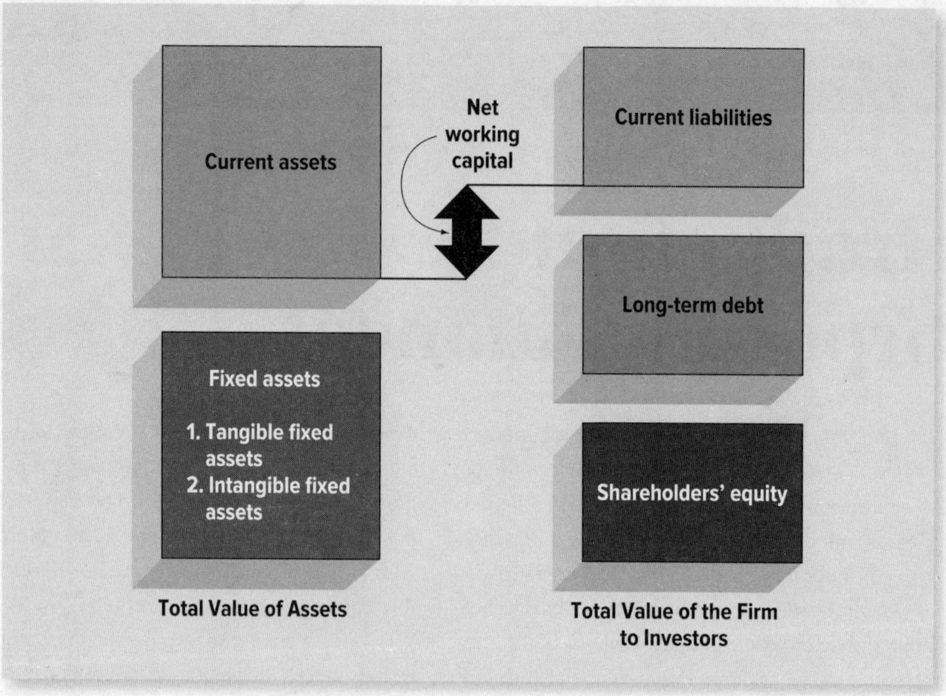

Figure 1.1 The Balance Sheet Model of the Firm

such as machinery and equipment. Other fixed assets are intangible, including patents and trademarks. The other category of assets, *current assets*, comprises those that have short lives, such as inventory. The tennis balls that your firm has made, but not yet sold, are part of its inventory. Unless you have overproduced, they will leave the firm shortly.

Before a company can invest in an asset, it first must obtain financing, which means that it must raise the money to pay for the investment. The forms of financing are represented on the right side of the balance sheet. A firm will issue (sell) pieces of paper called *debt* (loan agreements) or *equity shares* (stock certificates). Both assets and liabilities can be classified as long-lived or short-lived. A short-term debt is called a *current liability*. Short-term debt represents loans and other obligations that must be repaid within one year. Long-term debt is debt that does not have to be repaid within one year. Shareholders' equity represents the difference between the value of the assets and the debt of the firm. In this sense, it is a residual claim on the firm's assets.

From the balance sheet model of the firm, it is easy to see why finance can be thought of as the study of the following three questions:

1. In what long-lived assets should the firm invest? This question concerns the left side of the balance sheet. Of course, the types and proportions of assets the firm needs tend to be set by the nature of the business. We use the term **capital budgeting** to describe the process of making and managing expenditures on long-lived assets.
2. How can the firm raise cash for required capital expenditures? This question concerns the right side of the balance sheet. The answer to this question involves the firm's **capital structure**, which represents the proportions of the firm's financing from current and long-term debt and equity.
3. How should short-term operating cash flows be managed? This question concerns the upper portion of the balance sheet. There is often a mismatch between the timing of cash inflows and cash outflows

during operating activities. Furthermore, the amount and timing of operating cash flows are not known with certainty. Financial managers must attempt to manage the gaps in cash flow. From a balance sheet perspective, short-term management of cash flow is associated with a firm's **net working capital**. Net working capital is defined as current assets minus current liabilities. From a financial perspective, short-term cash flow problems come from the mismatching of cash inflows and outflows. This is the subject of short-term finance.

THE FINANCIAL MANAGER

For current issues facing CFOs, see **www.cfo.com**.

In large firms, the finance activity is usually associated with a top officer of the firm, such as the vice president or chief financial officer, and some lesser officers. Figure 1.2 depicts a general organizational structure emphasizing the finance activity

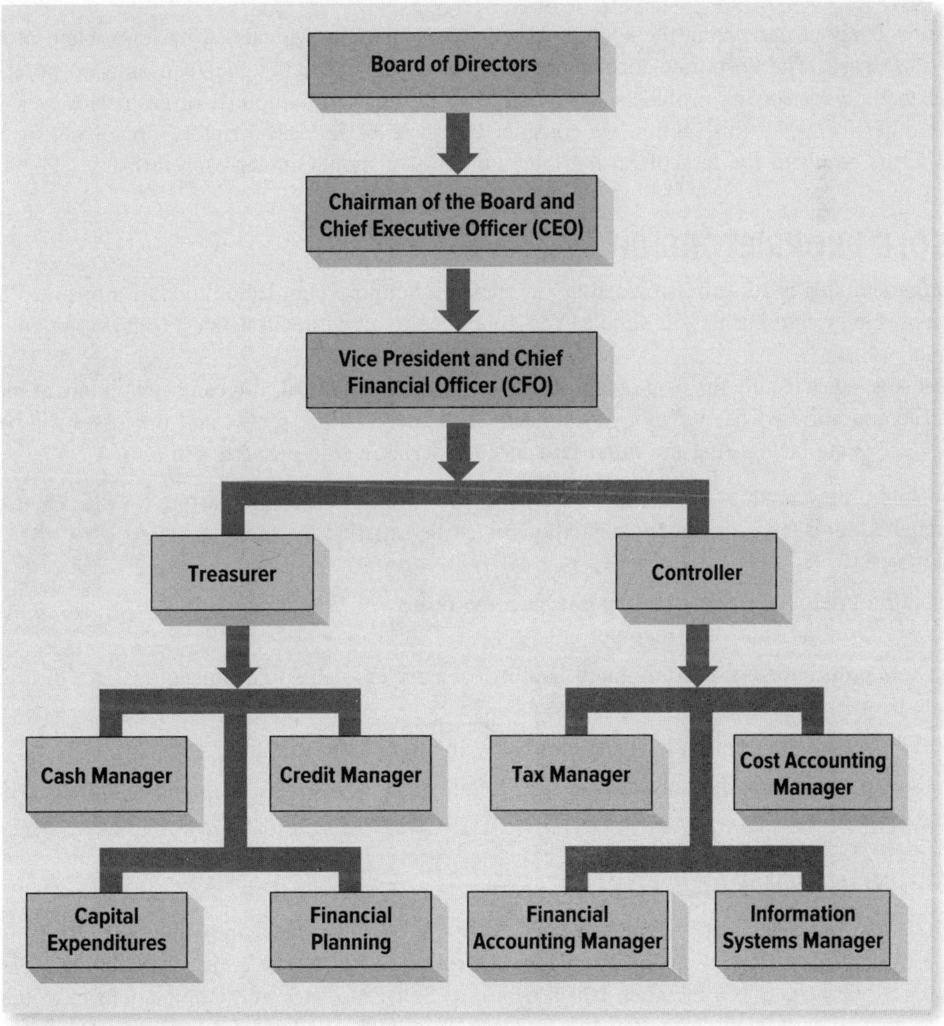

Figure 1.2 Hypothetical Organization Chart

within the firm. Reporting to the chief financial officer are the treasurer and the controller. The treasurer is responsible for handling cash flows, managing capital expenditure decisions, and making financial plans. The controller handles the accounting function, which includes taxes, cost and financial accounting, and information systems.

In the Indian context, the CFO is also popular as the *President (Finance)* or *Director (Finance)* or *Vice President (Finance)*. The designation largely depends on the size of the company and the designations of other heads. The controller is known as the *Head of Accounts* and the treasurer is known as the *Finance Head* or *Finance Controller*. In small firms, the *company secretary* classically dons the above two roles and hence does a three-in-one, i.e., he takes up the functions of a Treasurer and Controller combined with the role of a Principal Compliance officer with respect to the Indian Companies Act, 2013.

1.2 The Corporate Firm

The firm is a way of organizing the economic activity of many individuals. A basic problem of the firm is how to raise cash. The corporate form of business–that is, organizing the firm as a corporation–is the standard method for solving problems encountered in raising large amounts of cash. However, businesses can take other forms. In this section we consider the three basic legal forms of organizing firms, and we see how firms go about the task of raising large amounts of money under each form.

THE SOLE PROPRIETORSHIP

A **sole proprietorship** is a business owned by one person. Suppose you decide to start a business to produce mousetraps. Going into business is simple: You announce to all who will listen, "Today, I am going to build a better mousetrap."

Most large cities require that you obtain a business license. Afterward, you can begin to hire as many people as you need and borrow whatever money you need. At year-end all the profits and the losses will be yours.

Here are some factors that are important in considering a sole proprietorship:

1. The sole proprietorship is the cheapest business to form. No formal charter is required, and few government regulations must be satisfied for most industries.
2. A sole proprietorship pays no corporate income taxes. All profits of the business are taxed as individual income.
3. The sole proprietorship has unlimited liability for business debts and obligations. No distinction is made between personal and business assets.
4. The life of the sole proprietorship is limited by the life of the sole proprietor.
5. The sole proprietor is the only owner, so the equity available to the business is limited to her personal wealth.

For more about business types, see the "Launch your Business" section at **www.sba.gov**.

ONE-PERSON COMPANY (OPC)

As in the west, India has also introduced OPC. Section 2(62) of the Companies Act, 2013 introduces a new type of entity to the existing list. It enables the formation of a new entity, OPC, implying a company that has only one person as a member. It is a hybrid of Sole-Proprietor and Company form of business and has been provided with relaxed requirements under the Act. OPC is a legal entity separate from its members, offering limited liability protection to its sole members.

THE PARTNERSHIP

Any two or more people can get together and form a **partnership**. Partnerships fall into two categories: (1) general partnerships and (2) limited partnerships.

In a *general partnership*, all partners agree to provide some fraction of the work and cash and to share the profits and losses. Each partner is liable for all of the debts of the partnership. A partnership agreement specifies the nature of the arrangement. The partnership agreement may be an oral agreement or a formal document setting forth the understanding. In India, a partnership agreement specifying the nature of the arrangement such as the capital contributions, shares, rights, duties and obligations of the partners is covered under the Indian Partnership Act, 1932.[1] This legislation regulates the relationship between the partner's interest as well as the parties dealing with the partnership firm.

Limited partnerships permit the liability of some of the partners to be limited to the amount of cash each has contributed to the partnership. Limited partnerships usually require that (1) at least one partner be a general partner and (2) the limited partners do not participate in managing the business. In India, the Limited Liability Partnership Act, 2008 was notified in 2009. A case in point is Amarchand Shantilal & Associates LLP, registered in Telangana. Here are some things that are important when considering a partnership:

1. Partnerships are usually inexpensive and easy to form. Written documents are required in complicated arrangements. Business licenses and filing fees may be necessary.
2. General partners have unlimited liability for all debts. The liability of limited partners is usually limited to the contribution each has made to the partnership. If one general partner is unable to meet his or her commitment, the shortfall must be made up by the other general partners.
3. The general partnership is terminated when a general partner dies or withdraws (but this is not so for a limited partner). It is difficult for a partnership to transfer ownership without dissolving. Usually all general partners must agree. However, limited partners may sell their interest in a business.
4. It is difficult for a partnership to raise large amounts of cash. Equity contributions are usually limited to a partner's ability and desire to contribute to the partnership. Many companies start life as a proprietorship or partnership, but at some point they choose to convert to corporate form.
5. Income from a partnership is taxed as personal income to the partners.
6. Management control resides with the general partners. Usually a majority vote is required on important matters, such as the amount of profit to be retained in the business.

It is difficult for large business organizations to exist as sole proprietorships or partnerships. The main advantage to a sole proprietorship or partnership is the cost of getting started. Afterward, the disadvantages, which may become severe, are: (1) unlimited liability, (2) limited life of the enterprise, and (3) difficulty of transferring ownership. These three disadvantages lead to (4) difficulty in raising cash.

Hence, most small sized enterprises are either sole proprietorships or partnerships. M/s Lalumal Sons and M/s Meena Handicrafts are two examples of sole proprietorships. M/s Arul Dry Fish Stores, M/s Khusbhu Enterprises and M/s M. Muhammad Shafi & Company are three more examples of partnerships located in Colombo, Mumbai and Karachi, respectively.

THE CORPORATION

Of the forms of business enterprises, the **corporation** is by far the most important. It is a distinct legal entity. As such, a corporation can have a name and enjoy many of the legal powers of natural persons. For example,

[1]A partnership firm (including LLP) is taxable at 30% plus Surcharge and Cess.

corporations can acquire and exchange property. Corporations can enter contracts and may sue and be sued. For jurisdictional purposes, the corporation is a citizen of its state of incorporation (it cannot vote, however).

In India, the most significant business entity is a corporation and is commonly known as a joint stock company. It is an incorporated association and a distinct legal entity regulated by the Indian Companies Act, 2013. It is an Act of the Parliament of India which came into force on 12 September 2013. The Companies (Amendment) Act, 2020, an Act furthered to amend the Companies Act, 2013 got the assent on September 28, 2020.

Starting a corporation is more complicated than starting a proprietorship or partnership. The incorporators must prepare articles of incorporation and a set of bylaws. The articles of incorporation must include the following:

1. Name of the corporation.
2. Intended life of the corporation (it may be forever).
3. Business purpose.
4. Number of shares of stock that the corporation is authorized to issue, with a statement of limitations and rights of different classes of shares.
5. Nature of the rights granted to shareholders.
6. Number of members of the initial board of directors.

The bylaws are the rules to be used by the corporation to regulate its own existence, and they concern its shareholders, directors, and officers. Bylaws range from the briefest possible statement of rules for the corporation's management to hundreds of pages of text.

In its simplest form, the corporation comprises three sets of distinct interests: the shareholders (the owners), the directors, and the corporate officers (the top management). Traditionally, the shareholders control the corporation's direction, policies, and activities. The shareholders elect a board of directors, who in turn select top management. Members of top management serve as corporate officers and manage the operations of the corporation in the best interest of the shareholders. In closely held corporations with few shareholders, there may be a large overlap among the shareholders, the directors, and the top management. Even in larger corporations, top management usually own shares and often serve on the board of directors.

In the Indian context, firms can be divided into four types: (a) firms run by the state, i.e., public sector units (such as, NTPC and State Bank of India); (b) subsidiaries and firms owned by multinational corporations (such as, Hindustan Unilever and Siemens India); (c) affiliate firms of Indian business groups (such as, Godrej Consumer Products and Mahindra & Mahindra); and (d) firms run by private professionals (such as, Infosys Technologies and Matrimony.com). More than 70% of the Indian economy is run by business groups, owned and controlled by either families or trusts. Thus, to a large extent, these can be considered as closely held corporations.

While overlap between shareholders, directors, and corporate officers is common, the potential separation of ownership from management gives the corporation several advantages over proprietorships and partnerships:

1. Because ownership in a corporation is represented by shares of stock, ownership can be readily transferred to new owners. Because the corporation exists independently of those who own its shares, there is no limit to the transferability of shares as there is in partnerships.
2. The corporation has unlimited life. Because the corporation is separate from its owners, the death or withdrawal of an owner does not affect the corporation's legal existence. The corporation can continue after the original owners have withdrawn.

3. The shareholders' liability is limited to the amount invested in the ownership shares. If a shareholder purchased $1,000 in shares of a corporation, the potential loss would be $1,000. In a partnership, a general partner with a $1,000 contribution could lose the $1,000 plus any other indebtedness of the partnership.

Limited liability, ease of ownership transfer, and perpetual succession are the major advantages of the corporate form of business organization. These give the corporation an enhanced ability to raise cash.

There is one great disadvantage to incorporation. The federal government taxes corporate income (the states do as well). When corporate income is paid out to investors through a dividend, shareholders have to pay personal income tax on the dividend income. This is double taxation for shareholders when compared to taxation on sole proprietorships and partnerships. And, these points are equally applicable to business entities in India as well. Table 1.1 summarizes our discussion of partnerships and corporations.

The two most commonly used forms of companies in India are *public limited* and *private limited* companies. *Private limited companies* can be formed by having a minimum and maximum of 2 to 200 members. These companies are prohibited from invitation to public for capital issues. On the other hand, a minimum of 7 members are required to form a public limited company with no upper limit. In the case of *private limited companies*, there is a restriction on transfer of shares and the taxation rates are higher. On the other hand, shares of the *public limited companies* are freely transferable and their taxation rates are lower. These companies also have a wider coverage of the Companies Act, 2013. So, another main difference relates to certain provisions of the Companies Act that are not applicable to *private limited companies*. Some of these provisions include provisions as to the type of share capital, further issue of share capital, voting rights, and issue of shares with disproportionate rights; and provisions restricting the powers of the Board of Directors.

Today all 50 states in the U.S.A. have enacted laws allowing for the creation of a relatively new form of business organization, the limited liability company (LLC). An Indian LLC / Limited Liability Company is a popular platform for foreigners wishing to become 100% owners in an Indian company. The Companies Act of

Table 1.1 A Comparison of Partnerships and Joint Stock Companies (Corporations)

	Corporation	Partnership
Liquidity and marketability	Shares can be exchanged without termination of the corporation. Common stock can be listed on a stock exchange.	Units are subject to substantial restrictions on transferability. There is usually no established trading market for partnership units.
Voting rights	Usually each share of common stock entitles the holder to one vote per share on matters requiring a vote and on the election of the directors. Directors determine top management.	There are some voting rights by limited partners. However, general partners have exclusive control and management of operations.
Taxation	Corporations have double taxation: Corporate income is taxable, and dividends to shareholders are also taxable.	Partnerships are not taxable. Partners pay personal taxes on partnership profits.
Reinvestment and dividend payout	Corporations have broad latitude on dividend payout decisions.	Partnerships are generally prohibited from reinvesting partnership profits. All profits are distributed to partners.
Liability	Shareholders are not personally liable for obligations of the corporation.	Limited partners are not liable for obligations of partnerships. General partners may have unlimited liability.
Continuity of existence	Corporations may have perpetual lives.	Partnerships have limited lives.

2013 regulates LLC's along with how they are formed, allowable business activities, and dissolved. It obtains benefits like 100% foreign ownership, limited liability, two shareholders (who can be foreigners) are required, low minimum share capital. The goal of this entity is to operate and be taxed like a partnership but retain limited liability for owners, so an LLC is essentially a hybrid of partnership and corporation. Although states have differing definitions for LLCs, the more important scorekeeper is the Internal Revenue Service (IRS). The IRS will consider an LLC a corporation, thereby subjecting it to double taxation, unless it meets certain specific criteria. In essence, an LLC cannot be too corporation-like, or it will be treated as one by the IRS. LLCs have become common. For example, Goldman, Sachs and Co., one of Wall Street's last remaining partnerships, decided to convert from a private partnership to an LLC (it later "went public," becoming a publicly held corporation). Large accounting firms and law firms have largely converted to LLCs.

A CORPORATION BY ANOTHER NAME . . .

The corporate form of organization has many variations around the world. The exact laws and regulations differ from country to country, of course, but the essential features of public ownership and limited liability remain. These firms are often called *joint stock companies*, *public limited companies*, or *limited liability companies*, depending on the specific nature of the firm and the country of origin.

Table 1.2 gives the names of a few well-known international corporations, their countries of origin, and a translation of the abbreviation that follows each company name.

Table 1.2 International Corporations

		Type of Company	
Company	**Country of Origin**	**In Original Language**	**Interpretation**
Bayerische Motoren Werke (BMW) AG	Germany	Aktiengesellschaft	Corporation
Red Bull GmbH	Austria	Gesellschaft mit beschränkter Haftung	Limited liability company
Rolls-Royce PLC	United Kingdom	Public Limited Company	Public limited company
Shell UK Ltd.	United Kingdom	Limited	Corporation
Unilever NV	Netherlands	Naamloze Vennootschap	Joint stock company
Fiat SpA	Italy	Società per Azioni	Joint stock company
Volvo AB	Sweden	Aktiebolag	Joint stock company
Peugeot SA	France	Société Anonyme	Joint stock company
Reliance Industries Limited	India	Public limited company	Joint stock company
Google India Private Limited	India	Private limited company	Private limited company
Walmart Stores, Inc.	United States of America	Incorporated	Corporation

1.3 The Importance of Cash Flows

The most important job of a financial manager is to create value from the firm's capital budgeting, financing, and net working capital activities. How do financial managers create value? The answer is that the firm should:

1. Try to buy assets that generate more cash than they cost.
2. Sell bonds, stocks, and other financial instruments that raise more cash than they cost.

The firm must create more cash flow than it uses. The cash flows paid to bondholders and stockholders of the firm should be greater than the cash flows put into the firm by the bondholders and stockholders.

The interplay of the firm's activities with the financial markets is illustrated in Figure 1.3. The arrows in Figure 1.3 trace cash flow from the firm to the financial markets and back again. Suppose we begin with the firm's financing activities. To raise money, the firm sells debt and equity shares to investors in the financial markets. This results in cash flows from the financial markets to the firm (*A*). This cash is invested in the investment activities (assets) of the firm (*B*) by the firm's management. The cash generated by the firm (*C*) is paid to shareholders and bondholders (*F*). The shareholders receive cash in the form of dividends; the bondholders who lent funds to the firm receive interest and, when the initial loan is repaid, principal. Not all of the firm's cash is paid out. Some is retained (*E*), and some is paid to the government as taxes (*D*).

Over time, if the cash paid to shareholders and bondholders (*F*) is greater than the cash raised in the financial markets (*A*), value will be created.

IDENTIFICATION OF CASH FLOWS

Unfortunately, it is sometimes not easy to directly observe cash flows generated by the firm. Much of the information we obtain is in the form of accounting statements, and much of the work of financial analysis is to extract cash flow information from these statements. The following example illustrates how this is done.

TIMING OF CASH FLOWS

The value of an investment made by a firm depends on the timing of cash flows. One of the most important principles of finance is that individuals prefer to receive cash flows earlier rather than later. One rupee received today is worth more than one rupee received next year.

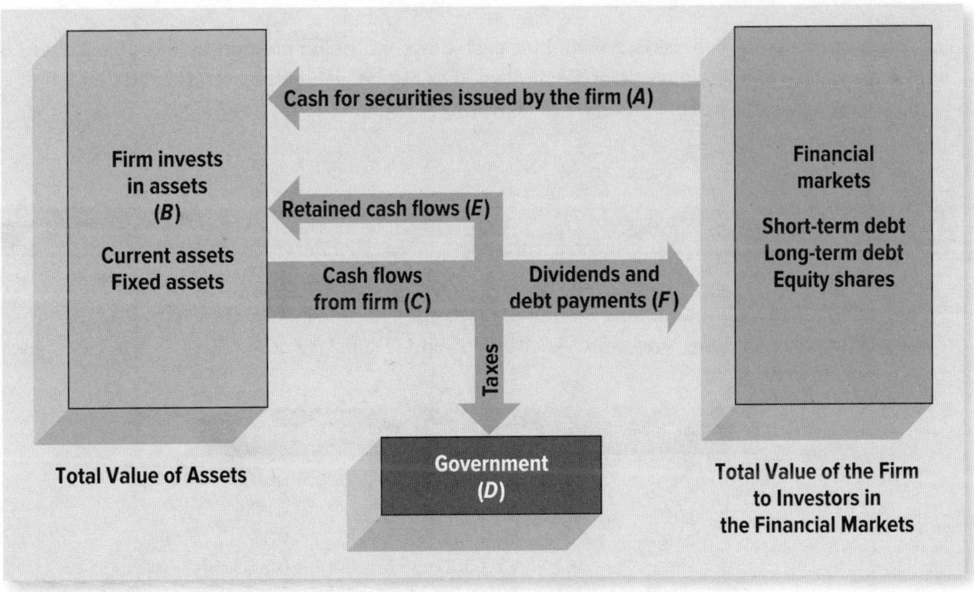

Figure 1.3 Cash Flows between the Firm and the Financial Markets

EXAMPLE 1.1

Accounting Profit versus Cash Flows The Meera Company refines and trades gold. At the end of the year, it sold 2,500 ounces of gold for ₹1 million. The company had acquired the gold for ₹900,000 at the beginning of the year. The company paid cash for the gold when it was purchased. Unfortunately, it has yet to collect from the customer to whom the gold was sold. The following is a standard accounting of Meera's financial circumstances at year-end.

The Meera Company
Accounting View Income Statement
Year Ended December 31

Sales	₹1,000,000
Costs	900,000
Profit	₹ 100,000

By generally accepted accounting principles (GAAP), the sale is recorded even though the customer has yet to pay. It is assumed that the customer will pay soon. From the accounting perspective, Meera seems to be profitable. The corporate finance perspective focuses on cash flows, as you can see in the following example.

The Meera Company
Financial View Income Statement
Year Ended December 31

Cash inflow	₹ 0
Cash outflow	900,000
	−₹900,000

The focus of corporate finance is on whether cash flows are being created by the gold trading operations of Meera. Value creation depends on cash flows. For Meera, value creation depends on whether and when it actually receives ₹1 million.

EXAMPLE 1.2

Cash Flow Timing The Meera Company is attempting to choose between two new products. Both products will provide additional cash flows over a four-year period and will initially cost ₹10,000. The cash flows from the products are as follows:

Year	New Product A	New Product B
1	₹ 0	₹ 4,000
2	0	4,000
3	0	4,000
4	20,000	4,000
Total	₹20,000	₹16,000

(continued)

At first, it appears that Product A would be best. However, the cash flows from Product B come earlier than those of A. Without more information, we cannot decide which set of cash flows would create the most value for the bondholders and shareholders. It depends on whether the value of getting cash from B up front outweighs the extra total cash from A.

RISK OF CASH FLOWS

The firm must consider risk. The amount and timing of cash flows are not usually known with certainty. Most investors have an aversion to risk.

EXAMPLE 1.3

Risk The Meera Company is considering expanding operations overseas. It is evaluating Europe and Japan as possible sites. Europe is considered to be relatively safe, whereas operating in Japan is seen as very risky. In both cases, the company would close down operations after one year.

After doing a complete financial analysis, Meera has come up with the following cash flows of the alternative plans for expansion under three scenarios—pessimistic, most likely, and optimistic.

	Pessimistic	Most Likely	Optimistic
Europe	₹75,000	₹100,000	₹125,000
Japan	0	150,000	200,000

If we ignore the pessimistic scenario, then Japan is the better alternative. When we take the pessimistic scenario into account, the choice is unclear. Japan is riskier because it may deliver zero cash flows under the pessimistic scenario. What is risk and how can it be defined? We must try to answer this important question. Corporate finance cannot avoid coping with risky alternatives and much of our book is devoted to developing methods for evaluating risky opportunities.

1.4 The Goal of Financial Management

Assuming that we restrict our discussion to for-profit businesses, the goal of financial management is to make money or add value for the owners. This goal is a little vague, of course, so we examine some different ways of formulating it to come up with a more precise definition. Such a definition is important because it leads to an objective basis for making and evaluating financial decisions.

POSSIBLE GOALS

If we were to consider possible financial goals, we might come up with some ideas like the following:

- Survive.
- Avoid financial distress and bankruptcy.
- Beat the competition.
- Maximize sales or market share.

- Minimize costs.
- Maximize profits.
- Maintain steady earnings growth.

These are only a few of the goals we could list. Furthermore, each of these possibilities presents problems as a goal for the financial manager.

For example, it's easy to increase market share or unit sales: All we have to do is lower our prices or relax our credit terms. Similarly, we can always cut costs by doing away with things such as research and development. We can avoid bankruptcy by never borrowing any money or never taking any risks, and so on. It's unclear whether any of these actions are in the shareholders' best interests.

Profit maximization would probably be the most commonly cited goal, but even this is not a precise objective. Do we mean profits this year? If so, then we should note that actions such as deferring maintenance, letting inventories run down, and taking other short-run, cost-cutting measures will tend to increase profits now, but these activities aren't necessarily desirable.

The goal of maximizing profits may refer to some sort of "long-run" or "average" profits, but it's still unclear exactly what this means. First, do we mean something like accounting net income or earnings per share? As we will see in more detail in the next chapter, these accounting numbers may have little to do with what is good or bad for the firm. We are actually more interested in cash flows. Second, what do we mean by the long run? As a famous economist once remarked, in the long run, we're all dead! More to the point, this goal doesn't tell us what the appropriate trade-off is between current and future profits.

The goals we've listed here are all different, but they tend to fall into two classes. The first of these relates to profitability. The goals involving sales, market share, and cost control all relate, at least potentially, to different ways of earning or increasing profits. The goals in the second group, involving bankruptcy avoidance, stability, and safety, relate in some way to controlling risk. Unfortunately, these two types of goals are somewhat contradictory. The pursuit of profit normally involves some element of risk, so it isn't really possible to maximize both safety and profit. What we need is a goal that encompasses both factors.

THE GOAL OF THE FINANCIAL MANAGER

The financial manager in a corporation makes decisions for the shareholders of the firm. So, instead of listing possible goals for the financial manager, we really need to answer a more fundamental question: From the shareholders' point of view, what is a good financial management decision?

If we assume that shareholders buy stock because they seek to gain financially, then the answer is obvious: Good decisions increase the value of the stock, and poor decisions decrease the value of the stock.

From our observations, it follows that the financial manager acts in the shareholders' best interests by making decisions that increase the value of the stock. The appropriate goal for the financial manager can be stated quite easily:

The goal of financial management is to maximize the current value of the existing stock.

The goal of maximizing the value of the stock avoids the problems associated with the different goals we listed earlier. There is no ambiguity in the criterion. There is no short-run versus long-run issue or safe versus risky issue. We explicitly mean that our goal is to maximize the *current* stock value.

If this goal seems a little strong or one-dimensional to you, keep in mind that the current stock value reflects the total value of owning a piece of the firm. shareholders are entitled to both the current and future cash flows of the firm. They also bear the costs of any risks associated with those cash flows. Therefore, the current stock value reflects how shareholders weigh the sometimes conflicting goals of getting cash flows sooner versus later, or increasing profits versus reducing risk. By maximizing the current value of the stock, managers are actually pursuing a broader set of goals in exactly the way that matters to shareholders.

By maximizing stock value, managers can also make the firm's other investors and stakeholders better off. This occurs because the shareholders in a firm are residual owners. By this we mean that they are entitled only to what is left after employees, suppliers, and creditors (and everyone else with legitimate claims) are paid what they are due. If any of these groups go unpaid, the shareholders get nothing. So if the shareholders are winning in the sense that the leftover, residual portion is growing, it is usually true that everyone else also is winning. As we will discuss in later chapters, an important exception occurs when the firm is at risk of bankruptcy. In those situations, creditors may prefer a safer strategy to guarantee that they will be paid, while shareholders may prefer a riskier strategy with upside potential.

Because the goal of financial management is usually to maximize the value of the stock, we need to learn how to identify investments and financing arrangements that favorably impact the value of the stock. This is precisely what we will be studying. In the previous section, we emphasized the importance of cash flows in value creation. In fact, we could have defined *corporate finance* as the study of the relationship between business decisions, cash flows, and the value of the stock in the business.

A MORE GENERAL GOAL

If our goal is as stated in the preceding section (to maximize the value of the stock), an obvious question comes up: What is the appropriate goal when the firm has no traded stock? Corporations are certainly not the only type of business; and the stock in many corporations rarely changes hands, so it's difficult to say what the value per share is at any particular time.

As long as we are considering for-profit businesses, only a slight modification is needed. The total value of the stock in a corporation is equal to the value of the owners' equity. Therefore, a more general way of stating our goal is as follows:

Maximize the value of the existing owners' equity.

With this in mind, we don't care whether the business is a sole proprietorship, partnership, or corporation. For each of these structures, good financial decisions increase the value of the owners' equity, and poor financial decisions decrease it. In fact, although we choose to focus on corporations in the chapters ahead, the principles we develop apply to all forms of business. Many of them even apply to the not-for-profit sector.

Finally, our goal does not imply that the financial manager should take illegal or unethical actions in the hope of increasing the value of the equity in the firm. What we mean is that the financial manager best serves the owners of the business by identifying goods and services that add value to the firm because they are desired, legal, and valued in the free marketplace.

Business ethics are considered at **www.business-ethics.com**.

1.5 The Agency Problem and Control of the Corporation

We've seen that the financial manager acts in the best interests of the stockholders by taking actions that increase the value of the stock. However, in large corporations, ownership can be spread over a huge number of shareholders. This dispersion of ownership arguably means that management effectively controls the firm. In this case, will management necessarily act in the best interests of the shareholders? Put another way, might not management pursue its own goals at the stockholders' expense? In the following pages, we briefly consider some of the arguments relating to this question.

Corporate governance represents rules and practices that ensure that management acts in the interests of shareholders and other groups with a claim to the firm's cash flows. It varies quite a bit around the world. For example, in most countries other than the United States and the United Kingdom, publicly traded companies are usually controlled by one or more large shareholders.[2] Moreover, in countries with limited shareholder protection, when compared to countries with strong shareholder protection like the United States and the United Kingdom, large shareholders may have a greater opportunity to take advantage of minority shareholders. Research shows that a country's investor protection framework is important to understanding a firm's cash holdings and dividend payouts. Studies find that shareholders do not highly value cash holdings of firms in countries with low investor protection because of the fear that cash held inside the firm will not be paid out to minority investors.

In the basic corporate governance setup, the shareholders elect the board of directors, who, in turn, appoint the top corporate managers, such as the CEO. The CEO is usually a member of the board of directors. One aspect of corporate governance that has received attention recently concerns the chair of a firm's board of directors. In a large number of U.S. corporations, the CEO and the board chair are the same person. An argument can be made that combining the CEO and board chair positions can contribute to poor corporate governance. When comparing corporate governance in the United States and the United Kingdom, an edge is often given to the United Kingdom, partly because more than 90 percent of U.K. companies are chaired by outside directors rather than the CEO. This is a contentious issue confronting many U.S. corporations. For example, in 2019, 34 percent of the S&P 500 companies had named an independent outsider as board chair, up from only 10 percent a few years earlier. An additional 19 percent of S&P 500 companies had split the board chair and CEO roles. One trend that is evident in S&P 500 board memberships is the growth in diversity. During 2019, 432 board members were added to S&P 500 boards. Of this number, 59 percent were women or minority men. Currently, more than 90 percent of S&P 500 boards have two or more women directors.

Business families and dispersed owners can give rise to principal-principal conflicts. Ladkani and Banerjee (2016) researched on the same and found that these conflicts exist in Indian firms, especially in bidding firms with very high ownership concentration. This transpires in the form of risk aversion when such companies seek to merge or acquire[3].

AGENCY RELATIONSHIPS

The relationship between shareholders and management is called an *agency relationship*. Such a relationship exists whenever someone (the principal) hires another (the agent) to represent his or her interests. For example, you might hire someone (an agent) to sell a car that you own while you are away at school. In all such relationships, there is a possibility of a conflict of interest between the principal and the agent. Such a conflict is called an **agency problem**.

Suppose you hire someone to sell your car and you agree to pay that person a flat fee when he or she sells the car. The agent's incentive in this case is to make the sale, not necessarily to get you the best price. If you offer a commission of, say, 10 percent of the sales price instead of a flat fee, then this problem might not exist. This example illustrates that the way in which an agent is compensated is one factor that affects agency problems.

[2]For a somewhat contrary view about the concentration of shareholder ownership in the United States and around the world, see Clifford G. Holderness, "The Myth of Diffuse Ownership in the United States," *The Review of Financial Studies* 22, no. 4 (April 2009).

[3]Reference: Ladkani, Radha M. and Ashok Banerjee; More than a Fair Share? Principal-Principal Conflicts in Emerging Markets: Evidence from India; *International Journal of Economics and Finance*, 8(7), 2016.

MANAGEMENT GOALS

To see how management and stockholder interests might differ, imagine that a firm is considering a new investment. The new investment is expected to favorably impact the share value, but it is also a relatively risky venture. The owners of the firm will wish to take the investment (because the stock value will rise), but management may not because there is the possibility that things will turn out badly and management jobs will be lost. If management does not take the investment, then the stockholders may lose a valuable opportunity. This is one example of an *agency cost*.

More generally, the term *agency costs* refers to the costs of the conflict of interest between stockholders and management. These costs can be indirect or direct. An indirect agency cost is a lost opportunity, such as the one we have just described.

Direct agency costs come in two forms. The first type is a corporate expenditure that benefits management but costs the stockholders. Perhaps the purchase of a luxurious and unneeded corporate jet would fall under this heading. The second type of direct agency cost is an expense that arises from the need to monitor management actions. Paying outside auditors to assess the accuracy of financial statement information is one example.

It is sometimes argued that, left to themselves, managers would tend to maximize the amount of resources over which they have control or, more generally, corporate power or wealth. This goal could lead to an overemphasis on corporate size or growth. For example, cases in which management is accused of overpaying to buy another company to increase the size of the business or to demonstrate corporate power are not uncommon. Obviously, if overpayment does take place, such a purchase does not benefit the stockholders of the purchasing company.

Our discussion indicates that management may overemphasize organizational survival to protect job security. Management may also dislike outside interference, and reject external oversight even when that would increase stockholder value.

DO MANAGERS ACT IN THE STOCKHOLDERS' INTERESTS?

Whether managers will, in fact, act in the best interests of stockholders depends on two factors. First, how closely are management goals aligned with stockholder goals? This question relates, at least in part, to the way managers are compensated. Second, can managers be replaced if they do not pursue stockholder goals? This issue relates to control of the firm. As we will discuss, managerial compensation structures and the threat of replacement can incentivize managers to act in the interests of stockholders.

Managerial Compensation Management will frequently have a significant economic incentive to increase share value for two reasons. First, managerial compensation, particularly at the top, is usually tied to financial performance in general and often to share value in particular. For example, managers are frequently given the option to buy stock at a certain price, known as the strike price. If the stock's value increases beyond the strike price, the option becomes more valuable. In fact, stock and option grants are often used to motivate employees of all types. For example, during 2020, Apple expensed about $12.2 billion in stock-related compensation, or about $63,200 per employee. In 2020, the total compensation for Tim Cook, CEO of Apple, was about $15 million. His base salary was $3 million with a bonus of $10.7 million, and $1 million for security and travel. He also owned restricted stock units totaling $281 million. Although there are many critics of the high level of CEO compensation, from the stockholders' point of view, sensitivity of compensation to firm performance is more important.

The second incentive managers have relates to job prospects. Better performers within the firm will tend to get promoted. More generally, managers who are successful in pursuing stockholder goals will be in greater demand in the labor market and command higher salaries.

In fact, managers who are successful in pursuing stockholder goals can reap enormous rewards. The best-paid executive in 2020 was Chad Richison, the founder and CEO of Paycom, who made about $211 million. By way of comparison, Kylie Jenner made $590 million, and Kanye West made about $170 million.[4]

In India, top managers and corporate honchos who have ownership over the firm have reaped enormous rewards. For example, some of the best-paid executives in 2023 were C Vijayakumar and Natarajan Chandrasekaran, the CEO and managing director of HCL Tech and Chairman of Tata Sons Ltd., respectively. They took home ₹120 crore average salary in a year. On the other hand, this is not true in the case of top executives of public sector giants having little ownership of the firm; for example, India's top power company, state-owned NTPC Limited, pays its chairman, Gurdeep Singh, a package of about ₹1.68 crore. In fact, the State Bank of India chairman, Dinesh Kumar Khara, is the least-paid Fortune 500 CEO.

While the appropriate level of executive compensation can be debated, bonuses and other payments made to executives who receive payments due to illegal or unethical behavior are a problem. Recently, "clawbacks" and deferred compensation have been introduced to combat such questionable payments. With a clawback, a bonus can be reclaimed by the company for specific reasons, such as fraud. For example, in 2019, Goldman Sachs said it was investigating the possibility of clawing back $14.2 million from former CEO Lloyd Blankfein and $15.4 million from Chief Executive David Solomon. The clawback was being considered after a Malaysian bribery scandal that caused the bank's value to tumble by half. The use of deferred compensation has also increased. Deferred compensation is money paid to an executive several years after it is earned. With a deferred compensation agreement, if circumstances warrant, the payment can be canceled.

Control of the Firm Control of the firm ultimately rests with stockholders. They elect the board of directors, who, in turn, hire and fire management.

An important mechanism by which unhappy stockholders can replace existing management is called a *proxy fight*. A proxy is the authority to vote someone else's stock. A proxy fight develops when a group solicits proxies in order to replace the existing board and thereby replace existing management. For example, in January 2019, activist hedge fund Elliott Management announced plans for a proxy fight with eBay. Elliott was joined by fellow activist investor Starboard Value. Elliott and Starboard wanted eBay to sell Stubhub and the company's Classifieds business. The funds eventually pushed for four seats on eBay's board. In response, eBay sold Stubhub for about $4 billion in November 2019. The proxy fight for four seats on the board ended in April 2020 when eBay hired Jamie Iannone as the new CEO of e-commerce. Even though the proxy fight had ended, eBay sold its Classifieds business in July 2020 for $9.2 billion. Such proxy fights have never been heard of in the Indian corporate circles.

Another way that management can be replaced is by takeover. Firms that are poorly managed are more attractive as acquisitions than well-managed firms because a greater profit potential exists from a change in management. For example, in July 2020, Eldorado completed its $17.3 billion acquisition of Caesars Entertainment, creating the largest gambling company in the United States. And, even though the new company kept the Caesars name and ticker symbol, the management of Caesars was let go, and Eldorado management took over the merged company. Avoiding a takeover by another firm gives management another incentive to act in the stockholders' interests. Unhappy prominent shareholders can suggest different business strategies to a firm's top management.

[4]This raises the issue of the level of top management pay and its relationship to other employees. According to the *Economic Policy Institute*, the average CEO compensation was greater than 221 times the average employee compensation in 2019 and only 30 times in 1978. However, there is no precise formula that governs the gap between top management compensation and that of employees. In 2018, large companies began reporting the pay ratio between the CEO compensation and the median compensation of other employees.

An illustration of such a takeover struggle in the Indian context was recently observed in the Information Technology sector, L&T's hostile takeover of Mindtree. The shareholding pattern of Mindtree facilitated this takeover. The founders collectively held only 13% of its equity shares. The acquisition of bankrupt Café Coffee Day founder V.G. Siddhartha's 20% stake was L&T's first move to add Mindtree to L&T Infotech Limited and L&T Technology Services Ltd. This was followed by an order to purchase a further 15% stake. It was followed by an open offer for buying 31% voting shares in consonance with the SEBI requirements.

STAKEHOLDERS

Our discussion thus far implies that management and stockholders are the only parties with an interest in the firm's decisions. This is an oversimplification, of course. Employees, customers, suppliers, and even the government all have a financial interest in the firm.

Taken together, these various groups are called **stakeholders** in the firm. In general, a stakeholder is someone who potentially has a claim on the cash flows of the firm. Stakeholder groups may have conflicting interests and compete to exert control over the firm.

1.6 Regulation

Until now, we have talked mostly about the actions that shareholders and boards of directors can take to reduce the conflicts of interest between themselves and management. We have not talked about regulation.[5] Until recently, the main thrust of federal regulation has been to require that companies disclose all relevant information to investors and potential investors. Disclosure of relevant information by corporations is intended to put all investors on a level information playing field and reduce conflicts of interest. Of course, regulation imposes costs on corporations and any analysis of regulation must include both benefits and costs.

THE SECURITIES CONTRACTS (REGULATION) ACT OF 1956 AND THE SEBI ACT OF 1992

The SCRA and SEBI Acts provide the basic regulatory framework in India for the public trading of securities. The Securities and Exchange Board of India (SEBI) is a statutory authority established in 1988. It acts as the supervisory body for the Indian securities market. It is a successor of the Controller of Capital Issues (*an erstwhile authority for issue of securities*). The SCRA Act focuses on the issuing of new securities. The SCRA Act require companies to file a registration statement that must be available to every buyer of a new security. The intent of the registration statement is to provide potential shareholders with all the necessary information to make a reasonable decision. The SEBI Act (along with its amendments) covers a large number of issues, including corporate reporting, tender offers and insider trading. It requires companies to file reports to the SEBI on an annual basis (such as, annual reports), on a quarterly basis (such as, quarterly ownerships) and on a timely basis (such as, insider trading requirement).

As mentioned, the Act deals with the key issue of insider trading. Illegal insider trading occurs when any person who has acquired nonpublic, special information (i.e., insider information) buys or sells securities based on that information. One section of the 1992 Act deals with insiders such as directors, officers, and large shareholders, while another deals with any person who has acquired inside information. The intent

[5]At this stage in our book, we focus on the regulation of corporate governance. We do not talk about many other regulators in financial markets, not to mention nonfinancial markets, such as the Federal Reserve Board. In Chapter 8, we discuss the nationally recognized statistical rating organizations (NRSROs) in the United States. These include Fitch Ratings, Moody's, and Standard & Poor's. Their ratings are used by market participants to help value securities such as corporate bonds. Many critics of the rating agencies blame the 2007–2009 subprime credit crisis on weak regulatory oversight of these agencies.

of these sections of the Act is to prevent insiders or persons with inside information from taking unfair advantage of this information when trading with outsiders.

A classic case of insider trading in India involved during the 1990s merger of Hindustan Lever Ltd. and Brooke Bond Lipton India Ltd., wherein R. Gopalakrishnan, a common director of both the firms, and others were involved. He was charged with (assisting) trading on privileged information during a meeting to decide the terms of the merger between the two entities. It was a classic fight, a unique one at that. On the one side was the capital market regulator SEBI, cracking down with India's first-ever 'guilty' verdict for an insider trading offence. On the other side was a Unilever subsidiary and its formidable corporate resources and its reputed directors to defend themselves.

In 2020, SEBI amended the Listing Obligations and Disclosure Requirements (LODR) regulation to address the gaps in the availability of information. Henceforth, listed companies are to make disclosures about initiation of forensic audit to stock exchanges. In 2015, SEBI extended the charge of insider trading to both, securities listed and proposed to be listed. Further, this Act has been widened to include persons associated with the company in a contractual (say, consultant), fiduciary (channel-partner) or employment relationship or having direct or indirect access to unpublished (intern under an auditor) price-sensitive information. To improve on corporate governance, SEBI also approved tougher eligibility criteria for Independent Directors, also requiring at least one woman Independent Director, and separation of CEO/MD and Chairperson roles.

CLAUSE 49 (THE SARBANES-OXLEY OF INDIA)

Clause 49 of the Listing Agreement to the Indian stock exchange, deals with corporate governance norms that a listed entity should follow. It was introduced in FY2001 based on the recommendations of the Kumar Mangalam Birla Committee. Global focus towards reducing scandals also forced India to come out with its own version of Sarbanes-Oxley Act. SEBI did the same in FY2006 by revising Clause 49 on the recommendation of the Narayan Murthy committee (after diluting them considerably). Most of its requirements are adapted from the Sarbanes-Oxley Act of USA (in a diluted version). Some of the important provisions are:

- A company with Executive Chairman to have 50% independent directors on Board. Otherwise, one-third of the directors should be independent.
- CEO/CFOs are required to assess internal controls and take corrective measures, if needed.
- CEO/CFOs are required to certify the financial statements.
- All the companies are required to submit quarterly compliance reports at stock exchanges.
- A Compliance Certificate from auditors is to be obtained and annexed with Directors' Report.
- Establishment of an audit committee is a must.
- Incorporated a wider definition of independent directors and increased their responsibility in audit committee.
- Whistle Blower Policy was set out to provide security to those who retaliate against wrong doers.
- Formal Code of Conduct was laid down for Board of Directors and Senior Management.
- Related party transactions are to be disclosed separately.

SEBI, together with the government organization, has been steadily increasing the corporate governance norms for Indian Corporate Sector with the reforms such as the continuous amendment in the Indian Companies Act, 2013 and implementation of IFRS vide Indian Accounting Standards (Ind. AS). The law brought discipline in the financial reporting process. The transparency boosted the investor's confidence that further helped build a strong capital market in the economy.

RESEARCH IN EMERGING MARKET CONTEXT

Large shareholders can hold a firm's management accountable, reducing the risk of excessive control and improving efficiency. Chacko and Padmakumari (2023) suggest that a balanced mix of large shareholders can mitigate the risk of excessive control and enhance efficient company monitoring. Financial health information safeguards investors' and stakeholders' interests and ensures long-term sustainability. Kanoujiya et al. (2023) found that Transparency and disclosure (T&D) have a U-curved association with a firm's Financial Distress (FD). Increasing T&D reduces the probability of FD at lower levels, but improving T&D increases the chances of FD after achieving a certain level of disclosure. In an interesting study, Chauhan et al. (2022) highlight the crucial role of informal institutions like societal trust in resolving agency issues arising from conflicts of interest between shareholders and managers.

References

Chauhan, Y., Jaiswall, M., & Goyal, V. (2022). Does societal trust affect corporate capital structure?. *Emerging Markets Review, 51,* 100845.

Jains, P Chacko & Lakshmi Padmakumari (2023). Does ownership structure affect the ex-ante cost of capital? *Investment Management and Financial Innovations, 20*(1), 112–126.

Kanoujiya, J., Abraham, R., Rastogi, S., & Bhimavarapu, V. M. (2023). Transparency and Disclosure and Financial Distress of Non-Financial Firms in India under Competition: Investors' Perspective. *Journal of Risk and Financial Management, 16*(4), 217.

Summary and Conclusions

This chapter introduced you to some of the basic ideas in corporate finance:

1. Corporate finance has three main areas of concern:
   a. *Capital budgeting*: What long-term investments should the firm take?
   b. *Capital structure*: Where will the firm get the long-term financing to pay for its investments? Also, what mixture of debt and equity should it use to fund operations?
   c. *Working capital management*: How should the firm manage its everyday financial activities?
2. The goal of financial management in a for-profit business is to make decisions that increase the value of the stock, or, more generally, increase the value of the equity.
3. The corporate form of organization is superior to other forms when it comes to raising money and transferring ownership interests, but it has the significant disadvantage of double taxation.
4. There is the possibility of conflicts between stockholders and management in a large corporation. We called these conflicts *agency problems* and discussed how they might be controlled and reduced.
5. The advantages of the corporate form are enhanced by the existence of financial markets.

Of the topics we've discussed thus far, the most important is the goal of financial management: maximizing the value of the stock. Throughout the text we will be analyzing many different financial decisions, but we will always ask the same question: How does the decision under consideration affect the value of the stock?

Concept Questions

1. **Agency Problems** Who owns a corporation? Describe the process whereby the owners control the firm's management. What is the main reason that an agency relationship exists in the corporate form of organization? In this context, what kinds of problems can arise?

2. **Not-for-Profit Firm Goals** Suppose you were the financial manager of a not-for-profit business (a not-for-profit hospital, perhaps). What kinds of goals do you think would be appropriate?
3. **Goal of the Firm** Evaluate the following statement: Managers should not focus on the current stock value because doing so will lead to an overemphasis on short-term profits at the expense of long-term profits.
4. **Ethics and Firm Goals** Can the goal of maximizing the value of the stock conflict with other goals, such as avoiding unethical or illegal behavior? In particular, do you think subjects like customer and employee safety, the environment, and the general good of society fit into this framework, or are they essentially ignored? Think of some specific scenarios to illustrate your answer.
5. **International Firm Goal** Would the goal of maximizing the value of the stock differ for financial management in a foreign country? Why or why not?
6. **Agency Problems** Suppose you own stock in a company. The current price per share is $25. Another company has just announced that it wants to buy your company and will pay $35 per share to acquire all the outstanding stock. Your company's management immediately begins fighting off this hostile bid. Is management acting in the shareholders' best interests? Why or why not?
7. **Agency Problems and Corporate Ownership** Corporate ownership varies around the world. Historically, individuals have owned the majority of shares in public corporations in the United States. In Germany and Japan, however, banks, other large financial institutions, and other companies own most of the stock in public corporations. Do you think agency problems are likely to be more or less severe in Germany and Japan than in the United States?
8. **Agency Problems and Corporate Ownership** In recent years, large financial institutions such as mutual funds and pension funds have become the dominant owners of stock in the United States, and these institutions are becoming more active in corporate affairs. What are the implications of this trend for agency problems and corporate control?
9. **Executive Compensation** Critics have charged that compensation to top managers in the United States is too high and should be cut back. For example, focusing on large corporations, Larry Culp of General Electric was one of the best-compensated CEOs in the United States during 2020, earning about $73 million. Are such amounts excessive? In answering, it might be helpful to recognize that superstar athletes such as Cristiano Ronaldo, top earners in the entertainment field such as Kanye West and Oprah Winfrey, and many others at the top of their respective fields earn at least as much, if not a great deal more.
10. **Goal of Financial Management** Why is the goal of financial management to maximize the current value of the company's stock? In other words, why isn't the goal to maximize the future value?
11. **Agency Problems**: Who owns a business group affiliate (say, TVS Motors or Tata Motors)? Describe the process whereby the owners control the firm's management. In this context, what kind of problems can arise? Will the scenario be different if the firm were to be state-owned (Indian Oil Corporation, perhaps) or privately held professional entity (Infosys Technologies, perhaps)? Discuss.
12. **Business-Group Affiliate Goal:** L&T Infotech is a subsidiary of Larsen and Toubro, with its activities focused towards information technology. PTC India Financial Services is a subsidiary of PTC India, with its activities focused towards financial services. During case discussion on this issue, a bright student of finance, Vasudha, asserts that 'L&T Infotech does not believe in maximizing its shareholder value.' Is Vasudha correct in her assessment? Comment on the same. Would this be the case in PTC India Financial Services as well? Comment further.
13. **CEO Compensation and Agency Perspective**: In 2023, the top ten pay packets of largest paid Indian CEOs ranged between ₹130 crore and ₹10 crore. Interestingly, all the names in the top ten of the list were CEOs managing affiliates of Indian business groups. In comparison, the top 100 list did not contain the name of any CEO from the large number of state-owned public sector units. What could be the reason for such a difference in the pay packets of CEOs of public sector units vis-à-vis CEOs of Indian business groups?

    In the latest list of India's top ten CEOs, there were some surprises. The list included a few professionals from the InfoTech and Banking space (say, CP Gurnani, CEO, Tech Mahindra CEO). What could be the reason?

2

Financial Statements and Cash Flow

The COVID-19 crisis in the early part of 2020 affected many industries, perhaps none more significantly than the airlines. For the industry as a whole, the International Air Transport Association (IATA) stated that global losses would be about ₹84 billion in 2020 and an additional ₹15 billion in 2021. United Airlines, for example, lost about ₹2 billion in the first quarter of 2020 alone and another ₹1.6 billion in the second quarter.

Of course, global pandemics aren't the only reason companies report losses. In mid-2020, Shell announced that it would write off ₹22 billion due to a decrease in the value of its assets, and BP announced a ₹17.5 billion write-off for the same reason. Both companies attributed the write-offs to an expected reduction in oil and gas prices in the coming decades, along with the transition to cleaner energy sources.

India's fuel demand also declined sharply as the government imposed lockdowns due to COVID-19. Indian Oil Corporation reported a surge in inventory losses following a sharp fall in crude oil prices. Indian aviation sector also got affected in 2020 and major airlines facing losses and challenging times laid off employees, sent them on leave without pay, or cut their salaries.

So did stockholders in the major airlines lose money because of the traffic reduction? Definitely. Did stockholders in Shell and BP lose money when the write-offs were announced? Probably not. Understanding why ultimately leads us to the main subject of this chapter: that all-important substance known as *cash flow*.

Please visit us at **rwjcorporatefinance.blogspot.com** for the latest developments in the world of corporate finance.

2.1 The Balance Sheet

Excel Master coverage online

The **balance sheet** is an accountant's snapshot of a firm's accounting value on a particular date, as though the firm stood momentarily still. The balance sheet has two sides: On the left are the *assets* and on the right are the *liabilities* and *stockholders' equity*. The balance sheet states what the firm owns and how it is financed. The accounting definition that underlies the balance sheet and describes the balance is:

$$\text{Assets} \equiv \text{Liabilities} + \text{Stockholders' equity}$$

We have put a three-line equality in the balance equation to indicate that it must always hold, by definition. In fact, the stockholders' equity is *defined* to be the difference between the assets and the liabilities of the firm. In principle, equity is what the stockholders would have if the firm were to discharge its obligations.

Table 2.1(a) The Balance Sheet of the Bharat Composite Company

BHARAT COMPOSITE COMPANY Balance Sheet 2021 and 2022 (in millions)					
Assets	**2021**	**2022**	**Liabilities (Debt) and Stockholders' Equity**	**2021**	**2022**
Current assets:			Current liabilities:		
Cash and equivalents	₹ 157	₹ 198	Accounts payable	₹ 455	₹ 490
Accounts receivable	270	294	Total current liabilities	₹ 455	₹ 490
Inventory	280	269	Long-term liabilities:		
Total current assets	₹ 707	₹ 761	Deferred taxes	₹ 104	₹ 113
Fixed assets:			Long-term debt*	458	471
Property, plant, and equipment	₹1,274	₹1,423	Total long-term liabilities	₹ 562	₹ 584
			Stockholders' equity:		
Less accumulated depreciation	460	550	Preferred stock	₹ 39	₹ 39
			Common stock (₹1 par value)	32	55
Net property, plant, and equipment	₹ 814	₹ 873	Capital surplus	327	347
			Accumulated retained earnings	347	390
Intangible assets and others	221	245	Less treasury stock†	20	26
Total fixed assets	₹1,035	₹1,118	Total equity	₹ 725	₹ 805
Total assets	₹1,742	₹1,879	Total liabilities and stockholders' equity‡	₹1,742	₹1,879

*Long-term debt rose by ₹471 million − 458 million = ₹13 million. This is the difference between ₹86 million new debt and ₹73 million in retirement of old debt.

†Treasury stock rose by ₹6 million. This reflects the repurchase of ₹6 million of Bharat Composite's company stock.

‡Bharat Composite reports ₹43 million in new equity. The company issued 23 million shares at a price of ₹1.87. The par value of common stock increased by ₹23 million, and capital surplus increased by ₹20 million.

The Indian Companies Act prescribes a slightly different format for reporting, known as Vertical Format. In this format, all the equity and liabilities are listed first, followed by all the assets. A sample is illustrated in Table 2.1(b).

Table 2.1(b) The Balance Sheet of the Heeralal Gadi Limited

HEERALAL GADI LIMITED Balance Sheet as on March 31, 2023 (₹ in crores)			
S No	**Particulars**	**As on March 31, 2023**	**As on March 31, 2022**
I	**EQUITIES AND LIABILITIES**		
	1. SHAREHOLDER'S FUNDS		
	(a) Equity Share Capital	40	40
	(b) Other Equity	16,616	15,807
	2. NON-CURRENT LIABILITIES		
	(a) Deferred Tax Liabilities [Net]	486	378
	(b) Other Long-Term Liabilities	436	407
	(c) Long-Term Provisions	202	181

(continued)

Table 2.1(b) The Balance Sheet of the Heeralal Gadi Limited *(concluded)*

HEERALAL GADI LIMITED Balance Sheet as on March 31, 2023 (₹ in crores)			
S No	**Particulars**	**As on March 31, 2023**	**As on March 31, 2022**
	3. CURRENT LIABILITIES		
	(a) Trade Payables	4,760	4,343
	(b) Other Current Liabilities	1,184	1,143
	(c) Short-Term Provisions	193	179
	TOTAL EQUITY AND LIABILITIES	**23,917**	**22,478**
II	**ASSETS**		
	1. NON-CURRENT ASSETS		
	(a) Tangible Assets	5,159	5,354
	(b) Right of use assets	481	518
	(c) Intangible Assets under development	851	689
	(d) Equity-accounted investments in associates	2,619	2,203
	(e) Capital Work-In-Progress	122	149
	(f) Non-Current Investments	4,600	2,455
	(g) Long-Term Loans and Advances	496	417
	(h) Other Non-Current Assets	154	121
	TOTAL NON-CURRENT ASSETS	**14,482**	**11,906**
	2. CURRENT ASSETS		
	(a) Current Investments	3,672	5,870
	(b) Inventories	1,756	1,472
	(c) Trade Receivables	2,719	2,158
	(d) Cash and Bank	447	324
	(e) Short-Term Loans and Advances	572	475
	(f) Other Current Assets	269	273
	TOTAL CURRENT ASSETS	**9,435**	**10,572**
	TOTAL ASSETS	**23,917**	**22,478**

Table 2.1(a) gives the 2021 and 2022 balance sheet for the fictitious Bharat Composite Company. The assets in the balance sheet are listed in order by the length of time it normally would take an ongoing firm to convert them into cash. The asset side depends on the nature of the business and how management chooses to conduct it. Management must make decisions about cash versus marketable securities, credit versus cash sales, whether to make or buy commodities, whether to lease or purchase items, the type of business in which to engage, and so on. The liabilities and the stockholders' equity are listed in the order in which they would typically be paid over time.

The liabilities and stockholders' equity side reflects the types and proportions of financing, which depend on management's choice of capital structure. Management will decide on which combination of debt and equity, and, for debt, which combination of short-term and long-term debt.

When analyzing a balance sheet, the financial manager should be aware of three concerns: liquidity, debt versus equity, and value versus cost.

Two excellent sources for company financial information are **finance.yahoo.com** and **money.cnn.com**.

LIQUIDITY

Liquidity refers to the ease and quickness with which assets can be converted to cash (without significant loss in value). *Current assets* are the most liquid and include cash and assets that will be turned into cash within a year from the date of the balance sheet. *Accounts receivable* are amounts not yet collected from customers for goods or services sold to them (after adjustment for potential bad debts). *Inventory* is composed of raw materials to be used in production, work in process, and finished goods. *Fixed assets* are the least liquid kind of assets. Tangible fixed assets include property, plant, and equipment. These assets do not convert to cash from normal business activity, and they are not usually used to pay expenses such as payroll.

Annual and quarterly financial statements for most public U.S. corporations can be found in the EDGAR database at **www.sec.gov**.

Annual and quarterly financial statements for listed Indian corporations can be found on the NSE and BSE website.

Some fixed assets are intangible. Intangible assets have no physical existence but can be very valuable. Examples of intangible assets are the value of a trademark or the value of a patent. The more liquid a firm's assets, the less likely the firm is to experience problems meeting short-term obligations. The probability that a firm will avoid financial distress can be linked to the firm's liquidity. Unfortunately, liquid assets frequently have lower rates of return than fixed assets; for example, cash generates no investment income. To the extent a firm invests in liquid assets, it sacrifices an opportunity to invest in potentially more profitable investment vehicles.

DEBT VERSUS EQUITY

Liabilities are obligations of the firm that require a payout of cash within a stipulated period. Many liabilities involve contractual obligations to repay a stated amount plus interest over a period. Liabilities are debts and are frequently associated with fixed cash burdens, called *debt service*, that put the firm in default of a contract if they are not paid. *Stockholders' equity* is a claim against the firm's assets that is residual and not fixed. In general terms, when the firm borrows, it gives the bondholders first claim on the firm's cash flow.[1] Bondholders can sue the firm if the firm defaults on its bond contracts. This may lead the firm to declare itself bankrupt. Stockholders' equity is the difference between assets and liabilities:

$$\text{Assets} - \text{Liabilities} \equiv \text{Stockholders' equity}$$

This is the stockholders' share in the firm stated in accounting terms. The accounting value of stockholders' equity increases when retained earnings are added. This occurs when the firm retains part of its earnings instead of paying them out as dividends.

VALUE VERSUS COST

The accounting value of a firm's assets is frequently referred to as the *carrying value* or the *book value* of the assets.[2] Under **generally accepted accounting principles (GAAP)**, audited financial statements of firms in the United States carry assets at cost.[3] Similar is the case with India as well.[4] The terms *carrying value* and *book value* are misleading and cause many readers of financial statements to believe the firm's

The home page for the Financial Accounting Standards Board (FASB) is **www.fasb.org**.

[1]Bondholders are investors in the firm's debt. They are creditors of the firm. In this discussion, the term *bondholder* means the same thing as *creditor*.

[2]Confusion often arises because many financial accounting terms have the same meaning. For example, the following terms usually refer to the same thing: *assets minus liabilities, net worth, stockholders' equity, owners' equity, book equity,* and *equity capitalization*.

[3]Generally, the U.S. GAAP require assets to be carried at the lower of cost or market value. In most instances, cost is lower than market value. However, in some cases when a fair market value can be readily determined, the assets have their value adjusted to the fair market value.

[4]In the Indian context, cost consideration is used by the companies based on the Indian Accounting Standards (Ind AS) issued by the Central Government of India under the supervision and control of Accounting Standards Board (ASB) of ICAI and in consultation with National Advisory Committee on Accounting Standards (NACAS). NACAS was replaced by National Financial Reporting Authority (NFRA). NFRA has been constituted as a quasi-judicial body with larger remit than NACAS which only advised on accounting policies and standards.

assets are recorded at true market values. *Market value* is the price at which willing buyers and sellers would trade the assets. It would be only a coincidence if accounting value and market value were the same. In fact, management's job is to create value for the firm that exceeds its cost.

Many people use the balance sheet, but the information each may wish to extract is different. A banker may look at a balance sheet for evidence of accounting liquidity and working capital, while a supplier also may note the size of accounts payable and the general promptness of payments. Many users of financial statements, including managers and investors, want to know the market value of the firm, not its cost. This information is not found on the balance sheet. In fact, many of the true resources of the firm do not appear on the balance sheet: good management, proprietary assets, favorable economic conditions, and so on. Henceforth, whenever we refer to the value of an asset or the value of the firm, we will normally mean its market value. So, when we say the goal of the financial manager is to increase the value of the stock, we usually mean the market value of the stock, not the book value.

With the increasing globalization of business, there has been a growing need to make accounting standards more comparable across countries. In recent years, U.S. accounting standards have become more closely tied to International Financial Reporting Standards (IFRS). In particular, the Financial Accounting Standards Board, which is in charge of GAAP policies, and the International Accounting Standards Board, in charge of IFRS polices, have been working toward convergence of policies. Although GAAP and IFRS have become similar in several areas, it appears that a full convergence of accounting policies is off the table, at least for now.

For more information about IFRS, check out the website **www.ifrs.org**.

With regard to India, to enable converge with the IFRS, the Ministry of Corporate Affairs issued Ind AS in 2015. The implementation of Ind AS has been steadily ramped up to include even banking and financial services sector, insurance sector, etc.

EXAMPLE 2.1

Market Value versus Book Value The Zaroon Company has fixed assets with a book value of ₹700 and an appraised market value of about ₹1,000. Net working capital is ₹400 on the books, but approximately ₹600 would be realized if all the current accounts were liquidated. Zaroon has ₹500 in long-term debt, In book value and market value terms. What is the book value of the equity? What is the market value?

We can construct two simplified balance sheets, one in accounting (book value) terms and one in economic (market value) terms:

ZAROON COMPANY
Balance Sheets
Market Value versus Book Value

Assets	Book	Market	Liabilities and Shareholders' Equity	Book	Market
Net working capital	₹ 400	₹ 600	Long-term debt	₹ 500	₹ 500
Net fixed assets	700	1,000	Shareholders' equity	600	1,100
	₹1,100	₹1,600		₹1,100	₹1,600

In this example, shareholders' equity is actually worth almost twice as much as what is shown on the books. The distinction between book and market values is important precisely because book values can be so different from market values.

2.2 The Income Statement

Excel Master coverage online

The **income statement** measures performance over a specific period–say a year. The accounting definition of income is:

$$\text{Revenue} - \text{Expenses} \equiv \text{Income}$$

If the balance sheet is like a snapshot, the income statement is like a video recording of what the company did between two snapshots. Table 2.2 gives the income statement for the Bharat Composite Company for 2022.

Table 2.2 The Income Statement of the Bharat Composite Company

BHARAT COMPOSITE COMPANY 2022 Income Statement (in millions)	
Total operating revenues	₹2,262
Cost of goods sold	1,715
Selling, general, and administrative expenses	327
Depreciation	90
Operating income	₹ 130
Other income	29
Earnings before interest and taxes (EBIT)	₹ 159
Interest expense	49
Pretax income	₹ 110
Taxes	24
Current: ₹15	
Deferred: 9	
Net income	₹ 86
Addition to retained earnings	₹ 43
Dividends	43

NOTE: There are 29 million shares outstanding. Earnings per share and dividends per share can be calculated as follows:

$$\text{Earnings per share} = \frac{\text{Net income}}{\text{Total shares outstanding}} = \frac{₹86}{29} = ₹2.97 \text{ per share}$$

$$\text{Dividends per share} = \frac{\text{Dividends}}{\text{Total shares outstanding}} = \frac{₹43}{29} = ₹1.48 \text{ per share}$$

The income statement usually includes several sections. The operations section reports the firm's revenues and expenses from principal operations. One number of particular importance is earnings before interest and taxes (EBIT), which summarizes earnings before taxes and financing costs. Among other things, the nonoperating section of the income statement includes all financing costs, such as interest expense. Usually a second section reports as a separate item the amount of taxes levied on income. The last item on the income statement is the bottom line, or net income. Net income is frequently expressed per share of common stock–that is, earnings per share.

When analyzing an income statement, the financial manager should keep in mind GAAP, noncash items, time, and costs.

GENERALLY ACCEPTED ACCOUNTING PRINCIPLES

Revenue is recognized on an income statement when the earnings process is virtually completed and an exchange of goods or services has occurred. Therefore, the unrealized appreciation from owning property will not be recognized as income. This provides a device for smoothing income by selling appreciated property at convenient times. For example, if the firm owns a tree farm that has doubled in value, then, in a year when its earnings from other businesses are down, it can raise overall earnings by selling some trees. The matching principle of GAAP dictates that revenues be matched with expenses. Income is reported when it is earned, or accrued, even though no cash flow has necessarily occurred (e.g., sales are reported at the time goods are sold, even if the goods are sold on credit).

NONCASH ITEMS

The economic value of assets is intimately connected to their future incremental cash flows. However, cash flow does not appear on an income statement. There are several **noncash items** that are expenses against revenues but do not affect cash flow. The most important of these is *depreciation*. Depreciation reflects the accountant's estimate of the cost of equipment used up in the production process. Suppose an asset with a five-year life and no resale value is purchased for ₹1,000. According to accountants, the ₹1,000 cost must be expensed over the useful life of the asset. If straight-line depreciation is used, there will be five equal installments, and ₹200 of depreciation expense will be incurred each year. From a finance perspective, the cost of the asset is the actual negative cash flow incurred when the asset is acquired (i.e., ₹1,000, *not* the accountant's smoothed ₹200-per-year depreciation expense).

Another noncash expense is *deferred taxes*. Deferred taxes result from differences between accounting income and true taxable income.[5] Notice that the accounting tax shown on the income statement for the Bharat Composite Company is ₹24 million. It can be broken down as current taxes and deferred taxes. The current tax portion is actually sent to the tax authorities (e.g., the Internal Revenue Service), while the deferred tax portion is not. However, the theory is that if taxable income is less than accounting income in the current year, it will be more than accounting income later on. Consequently, the taxes that are not paid today will have to be paid in the future, and they represent a liability of the firm. This shows up on the balance sheet as deferred tax liability. From the cash flow perspective, though, deferred tax is not a cash outflow.

Indian companies use the written down value method of depreciation for tax purposes, while for their published financial statements, they calculate depreciation based on the asset's useful life, cost, and residual value, in accordance with Indian Accounting Standards. As a result, the depreciation amounts under the Income Tax Act and the Companies Act differ.

In practice, the difference between cash flows and accounting income can be quite dramatic, so it is important to understand the difference. For example, in the second quarter of 2020, commercial graphics company Quad/Graphics announced a net loss in accounting income of ₹15 million. Sounds bad, but the company also reported a positive cash flow of ₹51 million, a difference of ₹66 million.

An Indian company in the technology engineering services sector, Olectra Greentech Ltd., for the financial year ending 31st March 2023, reported a net profit of ₹90 crores. However, Olectra Greentech also reported a *negative* cash flow of ₹10 crores, a difference of ₹100 crores.

[5] One situation in which taxable income may be lower than accounting income is when the firm uses accelerated depreciation expense procedures for the IRS but uses straight-line procedures allowed by GAAP for reporting purposes.

TIME AND COSTS

It is often useful to visualize all of future time as having two distinct parts, the *short run* and the *long run*. The short run is the period in which certain equipment, resources, and commitments of the firm are fixed; but the time is long enough for the firm to vary its output by using more labor and raw materials. The short run is not a precise period that will be the same for all industries. However, all firms making decisions in the short run have some fixed costs–that is, costs that will not change because of fixed commitments. Examples of fixed costs are bond interest, overhead, and property taxes. Costs that are not fixed are variable. Variable costs change as the output of the firm changes; some examples are raw materials and wages for laborers on the production line.

In the long run, all costs are variable. Financial accountants do not distinguish between variable costs and fixed costs. Instead, accounting costs usually fit into a classification that distinguishes product costs from period costs. Product costs are the total production costs incurred during a period–raw materials, direct labor, and manufacturing overhead–and are reported on the income statement as cost of goods sold. Both variable and fixed costs are included in product costs. Period costs are costs that are allocated to a time period; they are called *selling, general,* and *administrative expenses*. One period cost would be the company president's salary.

2.3 Taxes

Excel Master coverage online

Taxes can be one of the largest cash outflows a firm experiences. For example, for the fiscal year 2019, Southwest Airlines' earnings before taxes were about ₹2.96 billion. Its tax bill, including all taxes paid worldwide, was a whopping ₹657 million, or about 22 percent of its pretax earnings. Also for fiscal year 2019, Walmart had a taxable income of ₹20.12 billion, and the company paid ₹4.92 billion in taxes–an average tax rate of 24 percent. The size of the firm's tax bill is determined by the tax code, an often-amended set of rules. In this section, we examine corporate tax rates and how taxes are calculated.

If the various rules of taxation seem a little bizarre or convoluted to you, keep in mind that the tax code is the result of political, not economic, forces. As a result, there is no reason why it has to make economic sense.

CORPORATE AND PERSONAL TAX RATES

After the passage of the Tax Cuts and Jobs Act of 2017, the federal corporate tax rate in the United States became a flat 21 percent. However, tax rates on other forms of business such as proprietorships, partnerships, and LLCs did not become flat. To illustrate some important points about taxes for such entities, we take a look at personal tax rates in Table 2.3(a). As shown, in 2021, there are seven tax brackets, ranging from 10 percent to a high of 37 percent, down from 39.6 percent in 2017.

For a history of income taxes, listen to **tinyurl.com/y3rzqcx2**.

AVERAGE VERSUS MARGINAL TAX RATES

In making financial decisions, it is important to distinguish between average and marginal tax rates. Your **average tax rate** is your tax bill divided by your taxable income–in other words, the percentage of your income that goes to pay taxes. Your **marginal tax rate** is the tax you would pay (in percent) if you earned one more dollar. The percentage tax rates shown in Table 2.3 are all marginal rates. Put another way, the tax rates apply to the part of income in the indicated range only, not all income.

The difference between average and marginal tax rates can best be illustrated with a simple example. Suppose your personal taxable income is ₹100,000. What is your tax bill? Using Table 2.3, we can figure your tax bill like this:

.10 (₹9,950)	= ₹	995.00
.12 (₹40,525 − 9,950)	=	3,669.00
.22 (₹86,375 − 40,525)	=	10,087.00
.24 (₹100,000 − 86,375)	=	3,270.00
		₹18,021.00

The IRS and the Indian income tax department have great websites at **www.irs.gov** and **www.incometaxindia.gov.in.**

Your total tax is ₹18,021.

In our example, what is your average tax rate? You had a taxable income of ₹100,000 and a tax bill of ₹18,021, so your average tax rate is ₹18,021/₹100,000 = .1802, or 18.02%. What is your marginal tax rate? If you made one more dollar, the tax on that dollar would be 24 cents, so your marginal rate is 24 percent.

Table 2.3 (a) Personal Tax Rates for 2021 (Unmarried Individuals) in the U.S.A.

Taxable Income	Tax Rate
$ 0–9,950	10%
9,950–40,525	12%
40,525–86,375	22%
86,375–164,925	24%
164,925–209,425	32%
209,425–523,600	35%
523,600+	37%

Table 2.3 (b) Personal Tax Rates for FY2024 in India (New Tax Regime)

Taxable Income (in INR)	Tax Rate
0–3,00,000	Nil
3,00,001–6,00,000	5%
600,001–9,00,000	10%
9,00,001–1,200,000	15%
12,00,001–1,500,000	20%
1,500,000+	30%

EXAMPLE 2.2

Deep in the Heart of Taxes Manipuri Sangma, Inc., a small proprietorship owned by an unmarried individual, has a taxable income of ₹80,000. What is its tax bill? Its average tax rate? Its marginal tax rate?

From Table 2.3 (a), we see that the tax rate applied to the first ₹9,950 is 10 percent; the rate applied over that up to ₹40,525 is 12 percent; the rate applied after that up to our total of ₹80,000 is 22 percent. So Manipuri Sangma, Inc., must pay .10 × ₹9,950 + .12 × (₹40,525 − 9,950) + .22 × (₹80,000 − 40,525) = ₹13,348.50. The average tax rate is thus ₹13,348.50/₹80,000 = .1669, or 16.69%. The marginal rate is 22 percent because Manipuri Sangma's taxes would rise by 22 cents if it earned another dollar in taxable income.

Normally, the marginal tax rate will be relevant for financial decision making. The reason is that any new cash flows will be taxed at that marginal rate. Because financial decisions usually involve new cash flows or changes in existing ones, this rate will tell us the marginal effect of a decision on our tax bill.

With a flat-rate tax, such as the U.S. federal corporate tax (as of 2018), there is only one tax rate, so the rate is the same for all income levels. With such a tax system, the marginal tax rate is always the same as the average tax rate.

Before moving on, we should note that the tax rates we have discussed in this section relate to federal taxes only. Overall tax rates can be higher if state, local, and any other taxes are considered.

In the Indian context, earlier, there were a lot of incentives and exemptions such as tax benefits provided to the Indian companies engaged in export-oriented business, setting up a plant in a backward area, etc. However, the recent (optional) flat corporate tax rate of 25% change has been welcomed by most corporates (such as, Accelya Solutions India Ltd. and Deepak Nitrite Ltd.). In these companies, the marginal tax rate will be equal to the average tax rate.

2.4 Net Working Capital

Excel Master coverage online

Net working capital is current assets minus current liabilities. Net working capital is positive when current assets are greater than current liabilities. This means the cash that will become available over the next 12 months will be greater than the cash that must be paid out. The net working capital of the Bharat Composite Company is ₹252 million in 2021 and ₹271 million in 2022.

	Current assets (millions)	−	Current liabilities (millions)	=	Net working capital (millions)
2021	₹707	−	₹455	=	₹252
2022	761	−	490	=	271

In addition to investing in fixed assets (i.e., capital spending), a firm can invest in net working capital. This is called the **change in net working capital**. The change in net working capital in 2022 is the difference between the net working capital in 2022 and 2021–that is, ₹271 million − 252 million = ₹19 million. The change in net working capital is usually positive in a growing firm.[6]

2.5 Cash Flow of the Firm

Excel Master coverage online

Perhaps the most important item that can be extracted from financial statements is the actual **cash flow** of the firm. An official accounting statement called the *statement of cash flows* helps to explain the change in accounting cash and equivalents, which for Bharat Composite is ₹41 million in 2022. (See Section 2.6.) Notice in Table 2.1 that cash and equivalents increase from ₹157 million in 2021 to ₹198 million in 2022. However, we will look at cash flow from a different perspective: the perspective of finance. In finance, the value of the firm is its ability to generate financial cash flow. (We will talk more about financial cash flow in a later chapter.)

[6]A firm's current liabilities sometimes include short-term, interest-bearing debt usually referred to as *notes payable*. However, financial analysts often distinguish between interest-bearing, short-term debt and noninterest-bearing, short-term debt (such as accounts payable). When this distinction is made, only noninterest-bearing, short-term debt is usually included in the calculation of net working capital. This version of net working capital is called "operating" net working capital. The interest-bearing, short-term debt is not forgotten but instead is included in cash flow from financing activities, and the interest is considered a return on capital. Financial analysts also sometimes exclude "excess" cash and short-term investments from the calculation of net working capital because this excess could represent a temporary imbalance to a firm's cash flow and may not be directly related to a firm's normal operating or financing activities.

In India, the existing Companies Act, 2013 has made it mandatory for all companies (public and private) to prepare cash flow statement except One Person Company, Small Company and Dormant Company.

The first point we should mention is that cash flow is not the same as net working capital. For example, increasing inventory requires using cash. Because both inventories and cash are current assets, this does not affect net working capital. In this case, an increase in inventory purchased with cash is associated with a decrease in the cash balance.

As we established that the value of a firm's assets is always equal to the combined value of the liabilities and the value of the equity, the cash flows received from the firm's assets (i.e., its operating activities), CF(A), must equal the cash flows to the firm's creditors, CF(B), and equity investors, CF(S):

$$\text{CF}(A) \equiv \text{CF}(B) + \text{CF}(S)$$

The first step in determining cash flows of the firm is to figure out the *cash flow from operations*. As can be seen in Table 2.4, operating cash flow is the cash flow generated by business activities, including sales of goods and services. Operating cash flow reflects tax payments, but not financing, capital spending, or changes in net working capital:

	(in millions)
Earnings before interest and taxes	₹159
Depreciation	90
Current taxes	−15
Operating cash flow	₹234

Table 2.4 Financial Cash Flow of the Bharat Composite Company

BHARAT COMPOSITE COMPANY Cash Flow of the Firm 2022 (in millions)	
Cash flow of the firm	
Operating cash flow	₹234
(Earnings before interest and taxes plus depreciation minus taxes)	
Capital spending	−173
(Acquisitions of fixed assets minus sales of fixed assets)	
Additions to net working capital	−19
Total	₹ 42
Cash flow to investors in the firm	
Debt	₹ 36
(Interest plus retirement of debt minus long-term debt financing)	
Equity	6
(Dividends plus repurchase of equity minus new equity financing)	
Total	₹ 42

Another important component of cash flow involves *changes in fixed assets*. When Bharat Composite sold its power systems subsidiary in 2022, it generated ₹25 million in cash flow. The net change in fixed assets equals the acquisition of fixed assets minus the sales of fixed assets. The result is the cash flow used for capital spending:

Acquisition of fixed assets	₹198	
Sales of fixed assets	−25	
Capital spending	₹173	(₹149 + 24 = Increase in property, plant, and equipment + Increase in intangible assets)

We also can calculate capital spending as:

$$\begin{aligned}\text{Capital spending} &= \text{Ending net fixed assets} - \text{Beginning net fixed assets} \\ &\quad + \text{Depreciation} \\ &= ₹1{,}118 - 1{,}035 + 90 \\ &= ₹173\end{aligned}$$

Cash flows also are used for making investments in net working capital. In Bharat Composite Company in 2022, *additions to net working capital* are:

Additions to net working capital	₹19

Note that this ₹19 million is the change in net working capital we previously calculated.

Total cash flows generated by the firm's assets are then equal to:

Operating cash flow	₹234
Capital spending	−173
Additions to net working capital	− 19
Total cash flow of the firm	₹ 42

The total outgoing cash flow of the firm can be separated into cash flow paid to creditors and cash flow paid to stockholders. The cash flow paid to creditors represents a regrouping of the data in Table 2.4 and an explicit recording of interest expense. Creditors are paid an amount generally referred to as *debt service.* Debt service is interest payments plus repayments of principal (i.e., retirement of debt).

An important source of cash flow is the sale of new debt. Bharat Composite's long-term debt increased by ₹13 million (the difference between ₹86 million in new debt and ₹73 million in retirement of old debt).[7] An increase in long-term debt is the net effect of new borrowing and repayment of maturing obligations plus interest expense:

Cash Flow Paid to Creditors (in millions)	
Interest	₹ 49
Retirement of debt	73
Debt service	₹122
Proceeds from long-term debt sales	−86
Total	₹ 36

[7]New debt and the retirement of old debt are usually found in the "notes" to the balance sheet, footnoted in Table 2.1(a) in this case. This increase can also be seen from the increase in long-term debt on the balance sheet from ₹458 million to ₹471 million.

Cash flow paid to creditors also can be calculated as:

$$
\begin{aligned}
\text{Cash flow paid to creditors} &= \text{Interest paid} - \text{Net new borrowing} \\
&= \text{Interest paid} - (\text{Ending long-term debt} \\
&\quad - \text{Beginning long-term debt}) \\
&= ₹49 - (471 - 458) \\
&= ₹36
\end{aligned}
$$

Cash flow of the firm also is paid to the stockholders. It is the net effect of paying dividends plus repurchasing outstanding shares of stock and issuing new shares of stock:

Cash Flow to Stockholders (in millions)	
Dividends	₹43
Repurchase of stock	6
Cash to stockholders	₹49
Proceeds from new stock issue	−43
Total	₹ 6

In general, cash flow to stockholders can be determined as:

$$
\begin{aligned}
\text{Cash flow to stockholders} &= \text{Dividends paid} - \text{Net new equity raised} \\
&= \text{Dividends paid} - (\text{Stock sold} - \text{Stock repurchased})
\end{aligned}
$$

To determine stock sold, first notice that the common stock and capital surplus accounts went up by a combined ₹23 + 20 = ₹43, which implies that the company sold ₹43 million worth of stock. Second, treasury stock went up by ₹6, indicating that the company bought back ₹6 million worth of stock. Net new equity is ₹43 − 6 = ₹37. Dividends paid were ₹43 million, so the cash flow to stockholders was:

$$\text{Cash flow to stockholders} = ₹43 - (43 - 6) = ₹6$$

which is what we previously calculated.

Some important observations can be drawn from our discussion of cash flow:

1. Several types of cash flow are relevant to understanding the financial situation of the firm. **Operating cash flow**, defined as earnings before interest plus depreciation minus taxes, measures the cash generated from operations not counting capital spending or working capital requirements. It is usually positive; a firm is in trouble if operating cash flow is negative for a long time because the firm is not generating enough cash to pay operating costs. **Total cash flow of the firm** includes adjustments for capital spending and additions to net working capital. It will frequently be negative. When a firm is growing at a rapid rate, spending on inventory and fixed assets can be higher than operating cash flow.
2. Net income is not cash flow. The net income of the Bharat Composite Company in 2022 was ₹86 million, whereas cash flow was ₹42 million. The two numbers are not usually the same. In determining the economic and financial condition of a firm, cash flow is more revealing.

A firm's total cash flow sometimes goes by a different name, **free cash flow**. Of course, there is no such thing as "free" cash (we wish!). Instead, the name refers to cash that the firm is free to distribute to creditors and stockholders because it is not needed for working capital or fixed asset investments. For now, we will stick with "total cash flow of the firm" as our label for this important concept because, in practice, there is some variation in exactly how free cash flow is computed. Nonetheless, whenever you hear the phrase "free cash flow," you should understand that what is being discussed is cash flow from assets that can be distributed to investors.

2.6 The Accounting Statement of Cash Flows

Excel Master coverage online

As previously mentioned, there is an official accounting statement called the *statement of cash flows*. This statement helps explain the change in accounting cash, which for Bharat Composite is ₹41 million in 2022. It is very useful in understanding financial cash flow.

The first step in determining the change in cash is to figure out cash flow from operating activities. This is the cash flow that results from the firm's normal activities in producing and selling goods and services. The second step is to make an adjustment for cash flow from investing activities. The final step is to make an adjustment for cash flow from financing activities. Financing activities are the net payments to creditors and owners (excluding interest expense) made during the year.

The three components of the statement of cash flows are explained next.

CASH FLOW FROM OPERATING ACTIVITIES

To calculate cash flow from operating activities we start with net income. Net income can be found on the income statement and is equal to ₹86 million. We now need to add back noncash expenses and adjust for changes in current assets and liabilities (other than cash and notes payable). The result is cash flow from operating activities:

BHARAT COMPOSITE COMPANY Cash Flow from Operating Activities 2022 (in millions)	
Net income	₹ 86
Depreciation	90
Deferred taxes	9
Change in assets and liabilities	
Accounts receivable	−24
Inventories	11
Accounts payable	35
Cash flow from operating activities	₹207

CASH FLOW FROM INVESTING ACTIVITIES

Cash flow from investing activities involves changes in capital assets: acquisition of fixed assets and sales of fixed assets (i.e., net capital expenditures). The result for Bharat Composite is shown here:

BHARAT COMPOSITE COMPANY Cash Flow from Investing Activities 2022 (in millions)	
Acquisition of fixed assets	−₹198
Sales of fixed assets	25
Cash flow from investing activities	−₹173

CASH FLOW FROM FINANCING ACTIVITIES

Cash flows to and from creditors and owners include changes in equity and debt:

BHARAT COMPOSITE COMPANY Cash Flow from Financing Activities 2022 (in millions)	
Retirement of long-term debt	–₹73
Proceeds from long-term debt sales	86
Dividends	–43
Repurchase of stock	–6
Proceeds from new stock issue	43
Cash flow from financing activities	₹ 7

The statement of cash flows is the addition of cash flows from operations, cash flows from investing activities, and cash flows from financing activities, and is produced in Table 2.5(a). When we add all the cash flows together, we get the change in cash on the balance sheet of ₹41 million.

Table 2.5 (a) Statement of Consolidated Cash Flows of the Bharat Composite Company

Bharat Composite Company Statement of Cash Flows 2022 (in millions)	
Operations	
Net income	₹ 86
Depreciation	90
Deferred taxes	9
Changes in assets and liabilities	
Accounts receivable	–24
Inventories	11
Accounts payable	35
Total cash flow from operations	₹207
Investing activities	
Acquisition of fixed assets	–₹198
Sales of fixed assets	25
Total cash flow from investing activities	–₹173
Financing activities	
Retirement of long-term debt	–₹ 73
Proceeds from long-term debt sales	86
Dividends	–43
Repurchase of stock	–6
Proceeds from new stock issue	43
Total cash flow from financing activities	₹ 7
Change in cash (on the balance sheet)	₹ 41

The accounting statement of cash flows shown here is similar to the total cash flow of the firm used in finance that was discussed in the previous section (see Table 2.4). The biggest difference lies in the treatment of interest payments to debtholders, also known as interest expense. The statement of cash flows starts with net income, from which interest has already been deducted as an expense. Conceptually, interest paid to debtholders should actually go under financing activities, but that is not how the accounting is handled. Table 2.5(b) displays the statement of cash flow of an Indian company for FY2023. It complies with Indian Accounting Standard 7 (Ind AS 7)[8]. Notice the difference in the treatment of interest paid by Indian companies. Interest paid is included in financial activities. There are a few more minor differences in the accounting standards as per the US GAAP and the Indian GAAP.[9]

Table 2.5(b) Statement of Consolidated Cash Flows of the Heeralal Gadi Limited

HEERALAL GADI LIMITED
Statement of Consolidated Cash Flow for the year ended March 31, 2023
(₹ in crores)

PARTICULARS	Year ended March 31, 2023	Year ended March 31, 2022
A. CASH FLOW FROM OPERATING ACTIVITIES		
Profit after tax	**2,800**	**2,329**
Adjustments for:		
Add: Depreciation and amortisation expense	697	690
Tax expense	1,064	729
Loss on property, plant and equipment sold/discarded	5	10
Finance cost	105	53
Employee Stock Compensation Cost	16	10
Loss allowance on trade receivables and on advance to supplier	10	52
	1,897	**1,545**
Less: Interest income on financial assets carried at amortised cost	261	189
Dividend income	2	2
Profit on sale of investments	112	109
Gain on investments carried at fair value through profit or loss	189	224
Profit on sale of property, plant and equipment	6	1
Net Foreign Currency translation	34	–8
Share of profit in associates	3	–199
	607	**318**
Operating profit before working capital changes	**4,090**	**3,556**
Changes in working capital:		
Adjustment for (increase)/decrease in operating assets:		
Inventories	–284	317

(continued)

[8]Indian Accounting Standard 7 (Ind AS 7) and International Accounting Standard 7 (IAS 7) on 'Cash Flow Statements' are the corresponding accounting standards for ICAI's AS 3.

[9]Under Indian GAAP (AS 3) most unlisted companies escape the burden of providing cash flow statements as part of their financial statements. On the other hand, US GAAP (SFAS 95) mandates furnishing of cash flow statements for the latest 3 years, i.e., current year and 2 immediately preceding years irrespective of whether the company is listed or not. Cash flow statement is applicable for all companies (including Private Company); however, certain exemptions are provided to OPC, Dormant Companies and Small Companies in respect of Applicability of Cash Flow Statement. One difference in cash flow statements prepared under the Indian GAAP and International AS: In the case of other than financial entities, IAS 7 allows the option to classify interest paid, and interest and dividends received, as items of operating cash flows. In contrast, Ind AS 7 mandates that these items be classified as financing and investing activities, respectively. Additionally, while IAS 7 permits the classification of dividends paid as operating activities, Ind AS 7 requires them to be classified solely as financing activities.

Table 2.5(b) The Balance Sheet of the Heeralal Gadi Limited *(concluded)*

HEERALAL GADI LIMITED
Statement of Consolidated Cash Flow for the year ended March 31, 2023
(₹ in crores)

PARTICULARS	Year ended March 31, 2023	Year ended March 31, 2022
Trade receivables	–571	116
Loans	–3	–1
Other financial assets	–277	–67
Other current assets	4	-46
Other non–current assets	3	3
	–1,128	**322**
Adjustment for increase/(decrease) in operating liabilities:		
Trade payables	417	–921
Other financial liabilities–Current	5	4
Other current liabilities	66	–74
Current provisions	1	–4
Non-current provisions	–21	6
	509	**–990**
Cash generated from operations	**3,470**	**2,888**
Less: Direct tax paid (net of refund)	857	784
Net cash generated from operating activities	**2,614**	**2,104**
B. CASH FLOW FROM INVESTING ACTIVITIES		
Capital expenditure on property, plant & equipment, capital work-in-progress and intangible assets including capital advances	–604	–570
Proceeds from sale of property, plant & equipment	43	11
Deposits made	–80	–10
Sale of investments	45,336	42,436
Purchase of investments	–44,433	–42,105
Investment in associates	–963	150
Dividend income received from associates	-	5
Interest income on financial assets carried at amortised cost	277	157
Dividend income	2	2
Net cash generated/(used) in investing activities	**–422**	**–222**
C. CASH FLOW FROM FINANCING ACTIVITIES		
Interest paid	–105	–53
Payment of lease liabilities	–7	–31
Dividends paid	–1998	–1908
Proceeds from issue of equity share capital (including share premium)	3	5
(Repayment)/Proceeds of non-current borrowings	–16	–9
(Repayment)/Proceeds from non-current borrowings	–24	21
Net cash (used) in financing activities	**–2147**	**–1975**
D. INCREASE / (DECREASE) IN CASH AND CASH EQUIVALENTS (A+B+C)	**45**	**–94**
Cash and cash equivalents at the beginning of the year	**181**	**274**
Cash and cash equivalents at the end of the year	**226**	**181**

2.7 Cash Flow Management

One of the reasons cash flow analysis is popular is the difficulty in manipulating, or spinning, cash flows. GAAP allows for significant subjective decisions to be made regarding many key areas. The use of cash flow as a metric to evaluate a company comes from the idea that there is less subjectivity involved, and, therefore, it is harder to spin the numbers. But several well-known cases have shown that companies can still find ways to manipulate operating cash flow.

For example, security systems company Tyco used several ploys to alter cash flows. The company purchased more than ₹800 million of customer security alarm accounts from dealers. The cash flows from these transactions were reported in the financing activity section of the accounting statement of cash flows. When Tyco received payments from customers, the cash inflows were reported as operating cash flows. Another method used by Tyco was to have acquired companies prepay operating expenses. In other words, the company acquired by Tyco would pay vendors for items not yet received. In one case, the payments totaled more than ₹50 million. When the acquired company was consolidated with Tyco, the prepayments reduced Tyco's cash outflows, increasing the operating cash flows.

We also come across a number of similar examples in India, firms like Yes Bank, where the founder managed the bank and reported high quality of assets on a regular basis while not declaring related party transactions (in FY2020). The company showed inflated assets for years (similar to IL&FS in FY2018–19). Laxmi Vilas Bank was under Prompt Corrective Action (PCA) citing high bad loans, insufficient capital, negative return on assets and high leverage. Potential indicators can be a sudden increase in inventory/sales ratio, which means the assets are being inflated (e.g. Alok Industries). Reported earnings consistently being higher than cash flows could also be considered a warning signal as to why the operating earnings are not being converted into cash.

In a second case, Dynegy, the energy giant, was accused of engaging in a number of complex "round-trip trades." The round-trip trades essentially involved the sale of natural resources to a counterparty, with the repurchase of the resources from the same party at the same price. In essence, Dynegy would sell an asset for ₹100, and immediately repurchase it from the buyer for ₹100. The problem arose with the treatment of the cash flows from the sale. Dynegy treated the cash from the sale of the asset as an operating cash flow but classified the repurchase as an investing cash outflow. The total cash flows of the contracts traded by Dynegy in these round-trip trades totaled ₹300 million.

Adelphia Communications was another company that apparently manipulated cash flows. In Adelphia's case, the company capitalized the labor required to install cable. In other words, the company classified this labor expense as a fixed asset. While this practice is fairly common in the telecommunications industry, Adelphia capitalized a higher percentage of labor than is common. The effect of this classification was that the labor was treated as an investment cash flow, which increased the operating cash flow.

In each of these examples, the companies were trying to boost operating cash flows by shifting cash flows to a different heading. The important thing to notice is that these movements don't affect the total cash flow of the firm, which is why we recommend focusing on this number, not just operating cash flow.

RESEARCH IN EMERGING MARKET CONTEXT

Rao et al. (2022) explored the mandatory adoption of the Indian Accounting Standards (Ind AS) on energy companies' financial information reporting. They found that book value per share and net cash flow from investing activities significantly influence a company's market price. Profit after tax cannot explain the variability in share prices. Nagar and Raithatha (2016) found that operating cash flow manipulation increases with controlling ownership, and board diligence and audits fail to curb such manipulation. Another form of earnings management is classification shifting (CS), where managers misclassify income and cash flow statement items to report favourable operating performance. Bansal et al. (2021) found that Indian firms use revenue and cash flow misclassification to report inflated core earnings. However, involving Big-4 audit firms limits the extent of CS (Nagar et al., 2021; Mulchandani & Mulchandani, 2022).

References

Bansal, M., Kumar, A., & Badhani, K. N. (2021). Do Indian firms engage in classification shifting to report inflated core earnings?. *Managerial Finance*, 47(11), 1533–1552.

Mulchandani, K., & Mulchandani, K. (2022). Do independent directors and big-4 audit firms limit classification shifting: evidence from Indian firms. *Managerial Finance*, 48(12), 1754–1770.

Nagar, N., & Raithatha, M. (2016). Does good corporate governance constrain cash flow manipulation? Evidence from India. *Managerial Finance*, 42(11), 1034–1053.

Nagar, N., Desai, N., & Jacob, J. (2021). Do Big 4 auditors limit classification shifting? Evidence from India. *Journal of International Accounting, Auditing and Taxation*, 42, 100376.

Venugopala Rao, K. P., Ibrahim, F., & Phutela, N. (2022). The relevance of accounting information in the era of Ind AS: Evidence from a Nifty Energy Index. *Investment Management and Financial Innovations*, 19(2), 201–210.

Summary and Conclusions

Besides introducing you to corporate accounting, the purpose of this chapter has been to teach you how to determine cash flow from the accounting statements of a typical company.

1. Cash flow is generated by the firm and paid to creditors and shareholders. It can be classified as:
   a. Cash flow from operations.
   b. Cash flow from changes in fixed assets.
   c. Cash flow from changes in working capital.
2. Calculations of cash flow are not difficult, but they require care and particular attention to detail in properly accounting for noncash expenses such as depreciation and deferred taxes. It is especially important that you do not confuse cash flow with changes in net working capital and net income.

Concept Questions

1. **Liquidity** True or false: All assets are liquid at some price. Explain.
2. **Accounting and Cash Flows** Why might the revenue and cost figures shown on a standard income statement not represent the actual cash inflows and outflows that occurred during a period?

3. **Accounting Statement of Cash Flows** Looking at the accounting statement of cash flows, what does the bottom-line number mean? How useful is this number for analyzing a company?
4. **Cash Flows** How do financial cash flows and the accounting statement of cash flows differ? Which is more useful for analyzing a company?
5. **Book Values versus Market Values** Under standard accounting rules, it is possible for a company's liabilities to exceed its assets. When this occurs, the owners' equity is negative. Can this happen with market values? Why or why not?
6. **Cash Flow from Assets** Why is it not necessarily bad for the cash flow from assets to be negative for a particular period?
7. **Operating Cash Flow** Why is it not necessarily bad for the operating cash flow to be negative for a particular period?
8. **Net Working Capital and Capital Spending** Could a company's change in net working capital be negative in a given year? (*Hint*: Yes.) Explain how this might come about. What about net capital spending?
9. **Cash Flow to Stockholders and Creditors** Could a company's cash flow to stockholders be negative in a given year? (*Hint*: Yes.) Explain how this might come about. What about cash flow to creditors?
10. **Firm Values** In July 2020, Kraft Heinz announced that it was writing off ₹2.9 billion due to the loss in value of several of its well-known brands, including Oscar Meyer and Maxwell House. We would argue that Kraft Heinz's stockholders probably didn't suffer as a result of the reported loss. What do you think is the basis for our conclusion?
11. **Balance Sheet Format**: Why do you think the balance sheet format has been so suggested for the Indian companies?
12. **Tax Rates**: 'In India, the tax rates for corporates are same while there is a differential rate (i.e., slab system) for the personal income tax computation.' Do you agree with this statement? What could be the prime reasons for such a difference?
13. **Net Working Capital**: Referring back to the Heeralal Gadi example [see Table 2.1(b)], we observe that the net working capital has been positive for both the years with just 'cash & current investments', a component of *current assets,* being nearly equal to the *current liabilities*. Is that a common phenomenon for Indian companies? Explain how this could be justified for this giant.

Questions and Problems

BASIC (Questions 1–10)

1. **Building a Balance Sheet** Bing, Inc., has current assets of ₹5,400, net fixed assets of ₹28,100, current liabilities of ₹4,100, and long-term debt of ₹10,600. What is the value of the shareholders' equity account for this firm? How much is net working capital?
2. **Building an Income Statement** Gia, Inc., has sales of ₹497,000, costs of ₹276,000, depreciation expense of ₹43,000, interest expense of ₹24,000, and a tax rate of 21 percent. What is the net income for the firm? Suppose the company paid out ₹30,000 in cash dividends. What is the addition to retained earnings?
3. **Market Values and Book Values** Klingon Widgets, Inc., purchased new cloaking machinery three years ago for ₹6 million. The machinery can be sold to the Romulans today for ₹5.4 million. Klingon's current balance sheet shows net fixed assets of ₹3.5 million, current liabilities of ₹945,000, and net working capital of ₹275,000. If the current assets and current liabilities were liquidated today, the company would receive a total of ₹1.25 million cash. What is the book value of Klingon's total assets today? What is the sum of the market value of NWC and the market value of fixed assets?
4. **Calculating Taxes** Timmy Tappan is single and had ₹189,000 in taxable income. Using the rates from Table 2.3 in the chapter, calculate his income taxes. What is the average tax rate? What is the marginal tax rate?

5. **Calculating OCF** Graff, Inc., has sales of ₹49,800, costs of ₹23,700, depreciation expense of ₹2,300, and interest expense of ₹1,800. If the tax rate is 22 percent, what is the operating cash flow, or OCF?

6. **Calculating Net Capital Spending** Wallace Driving School's 2020 balance sheet showed net fixed assets of ₹2.3 million, and the 2021 balance sheet showed net fixed assets of ₹3.1 million. The company's 2021 income statement showed a depreciation expense of ₹327,000. What was net capital spending for 2021?

7. **Building a Balance Sheet** The following table presents the long-term liabilities and stockholders' equity of Information Control Corp. from one year ago:

Long-term debt	₹ 48,000,000
Preferred stock	3,100,000
Common stock (₹1 par value)	11,500,000
Accumulated retained earnings	108,000,000
Capital surplus	51,000,000

During the past year, the company issued 4.6 million shares of new stock at a total price of ₹61 million, and issued ₹34 million in new long-term debt. The company generated ₹7.9 million in net income and paid ₹1.9 million in dividends. Construct the current balance sheet reflecting the changes that occurred at the company during the year.

8. **Cash Flow to Creditors** The 2020 balance sheet of Osaka's Tennis Shop, Inc., showed long-term debt of ₹2.25 million, and the 2021 balance sheet showed long-term debt of ₹2.66 million. The 2021 income statement showed an interest expense of ₹305,000. What was the firm's cash flow to creditors during 2021?

9. **Cash Flow to Stockholders** The 2020 balance sheet of Osaka's Tennis Shop, Inc., showed ₹780,000 in the common stock account and ₹4.78 million in the additional paid-in surplus account. The 2021 balance sheet showed ₹965,000 and ₹5.04 million in the same two accounts, respectively. If the company paid out ₹654,000 in cash dividends during 2021, what was the cash flow to stockholders for the year?

10. **Calculating Cash Flows** Given the information for Osaka's Tennis Shop, Inc., in Problems 9 and 10, suppose you also know that the firm's net capital spending for 2021 was ₹1.5 million and that the firm reduced its net working capital investment by ₹55,000. What was the firm's 2021 operating cash flow, or OCF?

INTERMEDIATE
(Questions 11–22)

11. **Cash Flows** Ritter Corporation's accountants prepared the following financial statements for year-end 2021:

    a. Explain the change in cash during 2021.
    b. Determine the change in net working capital in 2021.
    c. Determine the cash flow generated by the firm's assets during 2021.

RITTER CORPORATION Income Statement 2021	
Revenue	₹781
Expenses	539
Depreciation	94
Net income	₹148
Dividends	₹115

RITTER CORPORATION Balance Sheet December 31		
Assets	**2020**	**2021**
Cash	₹ 65	₹ 87
Other current assets	177	195
Net fixed assets	400	420
Total assets	₹642	₹702
Liabilities and Equity		
Accounts payable	₹131	₹149
Long-term debt	157	166
Stockholders' equity	354	387
Total liabilities and equity	₹642	₹702

12. **Financial Cash Flows** The Stancil Corporation provided the following current information:

Proceeds from long-term borrowing	₹13,800
Proceeds from the sale of common stock	5,000
Purchases of fixed assets	27,500
Purchases of inventories	2,600
Payment of dividends	13,800

Determine the total cash flows spent on fixed assets and NWC. What are the cash flows to investors of the firm?

13. **Building an Income Statement** During the year, the Senbet Discount Tire Company had gross sales of ₹895,000. The firm's cost of goods sold and selling expenses were ₹461,000 and ₹215,000, respectively. The company also had notes payable of ₹685,000. These notes carried an interest rate of 4 percent. Depreciation was ₹108,000. The tax rate was 21 percent.

a. What was the company's net income?

b. What was the company's operating cash flow?

14. **Calculating Total Cash Flows** Nightwish Corp. shows the following information on its 2021 income statement: Sales = ₹336,000; Costs = ₹194,700; Other expenses = ₹9,800; Depreciation expense = ₹20,600; Interest expense = ₹14,200; Taxes = ₹21,275; Dividends = ₹21,450. In addition, you're told that the firm issued ₹7,100 in new equity during 2021 and redeemed ₹5,400 in outstanding long-term debt.

a. What is the 2021 operating cash flow?

b. What is the 2021 cash flow to creditors?

c. What is the 2021 cash flow to stockholders?

d. If net fixed assets increased by ₹53,200 during the year, what was the addition to net working capital (NWC)?

15. **Using Income Statements** Given the following information for Troiano Pizza Co., calculate the depreciation expense: Sales = ₹76,800; Costs = ₹36,900; Addition to retained earnings = ₹6,800; Dividends paid = ₹2,370; Interest expense = ₹5,300; Tax rate = 22 percent.

16. **Residual Claims** Polska, Inc., is obligated to pay its creditors ₹10,300 very soon.

 a. What is the market value of the shareholders' equity if assets have a market value of ₹11,600?

 b. What if assets equal ₹9,400?

17. **Net Income and OCF** During 2021, Raines Umbrella Corp. had sales of ₹865,000. Cost of goods sold, administrative and selling expenses, and depreciation expenses were ₹535,000, ₹125,000, and ₹170,000, respectively. In addition, the company had an interest expense of ₹90,000 and a tax rate of 25 percent. (Ignore any tax loss carryforward provisions and assume interest expense is fully deductible.)

 a. What is the company's net income for 2021?

 b. What is its operating cash flow?

 c. Explain your results in parts (a) and (b).

18. **Accounting Values versus Cash Flows** In Problem 17, suppose Raines Umbrella Corp. paid out ₹128,000 in cash dividends. Is this possible? If spending on net fixed assets and net working capital was zero, and if no new stock was issued during the year, what do you know about the firm's long-term debt account?

19. **Calculating Cash Flows** Martinez Industries had the following operating results for 2021: Sales = ₹38,072; Cost of goods sold = ₹27,168; Depreciation expense = ₹6,759; Interest expense = ₹3,050; Dividends paid = ₹2,170. At the beginning of the year, net fixed assets were ₹22,790, current assets were ₹8,025, and current liabilities were ₹4,511. At the end of the year, net fixed assets were ₹28,053, current assets were ₹9,904, and current liabilities were ₹5,261. The tax rate for 2021 was 22 percent.

 a. What is net income for 2021?

 b. What is the operating cash flow for 2021?

 c. What is the cash flow from assets for 2021? Is this possible? Explain.

 d. If no new debt was issued during the year, what is the cash flow to creditors? What is the cash flow to stockholders? Explain and interpret the positive and negative signs of your answers in parts (a) through (d).

20. **Calculating Cash Flows** Consider the following abbreviated financial statements for Parrothead Enterprises:

PARROTHEAD ENTERPRISES
Partial Balance Sheets

Assets	2020	2021	Liabilities and Owners' Equity	2020	2021
Current assets	₹1,327	₹1,438	Current liabilities	₹ 530	₹ 595
Net fixed assets	5,470	6,587	Long-term debt	2,891	3,075

PARROTHEAD ENTERPRISES
2021 Income Statement

Sales	₹16,831
Costs	7,849
Depreciation	1,499
Interest paid	427

 a. What is owners' equity for 2020 and 2021?

 b. What is the change in net working capital for 2021?

 c. In 2021, Parrothead Enterprises purchased ₹2,740 in new fixed assets. How much in fixed assets did Parrothead Enterprises sell? What is the cash flow from assets for the year? The tax rate is 21 percent.

 d. During 2021, Parrothead Enterprises raised ₹554 in new long-term debt. How much long-term debt must Parrothead Enterprises have paid off during the year? What is the cash flow to creditors?

Use the following information for Ingersoll, Inc., for Problems 21 and 22. Assume the tax rate is 21 percent.

	2020	2021
Sales	₹ 7,616	₹ 8,174
Depreciation	1,094	1,094
Cost of goods sold	2,621	2,975
Other expenses	621	519
Interest	510	587
Cash	3,994	5,058
Accounts receivable	4,387	5,955
Short-term notes payable	772	725
Long-term debt	13,083	15,601
Net fixed assets	33, 490	35,144
Accounts payable	4,195	4,068
Inventory	9,400	9,660
Dividends	929	1,022

21. **Financial Statements** Draw up an income statement and balance sheet for this company for 2020 and 2021.

22. **Calculating Cash Flow** For 2021, calculate the cash flow from assets, cash flow to creditors, and cash flow to stockholders.

CHALLENGE (Questions 23–24)

23. **Cash Flows** You are researching Time Manufacturing and have found the following accounting statement of cash flows for the most recent year. You also know that the company paid ₹81 million in current taxes and had an interest expense of ₹38 million. Use the accounting statement of cash flows to construct the financial statement of cash flows.

TIME MANUFACTURING Statement of Cash Flows (in millions)	
Operations	
Net income	₹187
Depreciation	74
Deferred taxes	11
Changes in assets and liabilities	
Accounts receivable	−12
Inventories	15
Accounts payable	11
Accrued expenses	−6
Other	2
Total cash flow from operations	₹282
Investing activities	
Acquisition of fixed assets	−₹194
Sale of fixed assets	19
Total cash flow from investing activities	−₹175

Financing activities	
Retirement of long-term debt	−₹145
Proceeds from long-term debt sales	110
Dividends	−67
Repurchase of stock	−32
Proceeds from new stock issue	39
Total cash flow from financing activities	−₹ 95
Change in cash (on balance sheet)	₹ 12

24. **Net Fixed Assets and Depreciation** On the balance sheet, the net fixed assets (NFA) account is equal to the gross fixed assets (FA) account (which records the acquisition cost of fixed assets) minus the accumulated depreciation (AD) account (which records the total depreciation taken by the firm against its fixed assets). Using the fact that NFA = FA − AD, show that the expression given in the chapter for net capital spending, $NFA_{end} - NFA_{beg} + D$ (where D is the depreciation expense during the year), is equivalent to $FA_{end} - FA_{beg}$.

Excel Master It! Problem

Using Excel to find the marginal tax rate can be accomplished using the VLOOKUP function. However, calculating the total tax bill is a little more difficult. Below we have shown a copy of the IRS tax table for an individual for 2021 (the income thresholds are indexed to inflation and change through time):

Excel Master coverage online

If taxable income is over —	But not over —	The tax is:
₹ 0	₹ 9,950	10% of the amount over ₹0
9,950	40,525	₹995.00 plus 12% of the amount over ₹9,950
40,525	86,375	₹4,664.00 plus 22% of the amount over ₹40,525
86,375	164,925	₹14,751.00 plus 24% of the amount over ₹86,375
164,925	209,425	₹33,603.00 plus 32% of the amount over ₹164,925
209,425	523,600	₹47,843.00 plus 35% of the amount over ₹209,425
523,600		₹157,804.50 plus 37% of the amount over ₹523,600

In reading this table, the marginal tax rate for taxable income less than ₹9,950 is 10 percent. If the taxable income is between ₹9,950 and ₹40,525, the tax bill is ₹995 plus the marginal taxes. The marginal taxes are calculated as the taxable income minus ₹9,950 times the marginal tax rate of 12 percent.

Below, we have the tax table for a married couple filing jointly:

If taxable income is over —	But less than —	Tax rate
₹ 0	₹ 19,900	10%
19,900	81,050	12
81,050	172,750	22
172,750	329,850	24
329,850	418,850	32
418,850	628,300	35
628,300		37

a. Create a tax table in Excel for a married couple similar to the individual tax table shown above. Your spreadsheet should then calculate the marginal tax rate, the average tax rate, and the tax bill for any level of taxable income input by a user.
b. For a taxable income of ₹265,000, what is the marginal tax rate?
c. For a taxable income of ₹265,000, what is the total tax bill?
d. For a taxable income of ₹265,000, what is the average tax rate?

Mini Case CASH FLOWS AT WARF COMPUTERS, INC.

Warf Computers, Inc., was founded 15 years ago by Nick Warf, a computer programmer. The small initial investment to start the company was made by Nick and his friends. Over the years, this same group has supplied the limited additional investment needed by the company in the form of both equity and short- and long-term debt. Recently the company has developed a virtual keyboard (VK). The VK uses sophisticated artificial intelligence algorithms that allow the user to speak naturally and have the computer input the text, correct spelling and grammatical errors, and format the document according to preset user guidelines. The VK even suggests alternative phrasing and sentence structure, and it provides detailed stylistic diagnostics. Based on a proprietary, very advanced software/hardware hybrid technology, the system is a full generation beyond what is currently on the market. To introduce the VK, the company will require significant outside investment.

Nick has made the decision to seek this outside financing in the form of new equity investments and bank loans. Naturally, new investors and the banks will require a detailed financial analysis. Your employer, Angus Jones & Partners, LLC, has asked you to examine the financial statements provided by Nick. Here are the balance sheets for the two most recent years and the most recent income statement:

WARF COMPUTERS BALANCE SHEETS
(in thousands)

	2021	2022		2021	2022
Current assets			Current liabilities		
Cash and equivalents	₹ 516	₹ 596	Accounts payable	₹ 645	₹ 685
Accounts receivable	883	945	Accrued expenses	529	329
Inventories	875	846	Total current liabilities	₹ 1,174	₹ 1,014
Other	103	121	Long-term liabilities		
Total current assets	₹2,377	₹2,508	Deferred taxes	₹ 210	₹ 282
Fixed assets			Long-term debt	1,517	1,557
Property, plant, and equipment	₹4,197	₹5,476	Total long-term liabilities	₹ 1,727	₹ 1,839
Less accumulated depreciation	1,441	1,777	Stockholders' equity		
Net property, plant, and equipment	₹2,756	₹3,699	Preferred stock	₹ 25	₹ 25
Intangible assets and others	936	1,047	Common stock	166	171
Total fixed assets	₹3,962	₹4,746	Capital surplus	1,027	1,044
			Accumulated retained earnings	2,116	3,414
			Less treasury stock	166	253
			Total equity	₹ 3,168	₹4,401
Total assets	₹6,069	₹7,254	Total liabilities and shareholders' equity	₹6,069	₹7,254

WARF COMPUTERS INCOME STATEMENT (in thousands)	
Sales	₹9,975
Cost of goods sold	5,882
Selling, general, and administrative expense	933
Depreciation	336
Operating income	₹2,824
Other income	98
EBIT	₹2,922
Interest expense	180
Pretax income	₹2,742
Taxes	687
Current: ₹615	
Deferred: ₹72	
Net income	₹2,055
Dividends: ₹757	
Retained earnings: ₹1,298	

Nick also has provided the following information: During the year the company raised ₹301,000 in new long-term debt and retired ₹261,000 in long-term debt. The company also sold ₹22,000 in new stock and repurchased ₹87,000 in stock. The company purchased ₹1,955,000 in fixed assets and sold ₹565,000 in fixed assets.

Angus has asked you to prepare the financial statement of cash flows and the accounting statement of cash flows. He also has asked you to answer the following questions:

1. How would you describe Warf Computers's cash flows?
2. Which cash flow statement more accurately describes the cash flows at the company?
3. In light of your previous answers, comment on Nick's expansion plans.

3

Financial Statements Analysis and Financial Models

The price of a share of common stock in home improvement company Lowe's closed at about ₹158 on August 17, 2020. At that price, Lowe's had a price-earnings (PE) ratio of 27. That is, investors were willing to pay ₹27 for every Rupee in income earned by Lowe's. At the same time, investors were willing to pay ₹9, ₹76, and ₹950 for each Rupee earned by Citigroup, Starbucks, and Tesla, respectively. At the other extreme were Walt Disney and Beyond Meat. Both had negative earnings for the previous year, but Walt Disney was priced at about ₹129 per share and Beyond Meat at about ₹125 per share. Because they had negative earnings, their PE ratios would have been negative, so they were not reported. At the time, the typical stock in the S&P 500 Index of large-company stocks was trading at a PE of about 28, or about 28 times earnings, as they say on Wall Street. Likewise, in India, the price of an equity share of Sun Pharmaceutical Industries closed at about ₹1,159 on September 29, 2023. At that price, Sun Pharma had a PE ratio of 117. That is, investors were willing to pay ₹117 for every rupee in income earned by Sun Pharma. At the same time, investors were willing to pay ₹88, ₹210, and ₹33 for each rupee earned by HCL Technologies, DLF and State Bank of India, respectively. At the other extreme were Delhivery Ltd. and Interglobe Aviation Ltd. Both had negative earnings for the previous year, but Delhivery Ltd. was priced at ₹412.70 per share and Interglobe Aviation Ltd. at ₹2381.70 per share. Because they had negative earnings, their PE ratios would have been negative, so they were not reported.

Price-earnings comparisons are examples of the use of financial ratios. As we will see in this chapter, there are a wide variety of financial ratios, all designed to summarize specific aspects of a firm's financial position. In addition to discussing how to analyze financial statements and interpret financial ratios, we will have quite a bit to say about who uses this information and why.

Please visit us at **rwjcorporatefinance.blogspot.com** for the latest developments in the world of corporate finance.

3.1 Financial Statements Analysis

Excel Master coverage online

In Chapter 2, we discussed some of the essential concepts of financial statements and cash flows. This chapter continues where our earlier discussion left off. Our goal here is to expand your understanding of the uses (and abuses) of financial statement information.

A good working knowledge of financial statements is desirable because such statements, and numbers derived from those statements, are the primary means of communicating financial information both within the firm and outside the firm. In short, much of the language of business finance is rooted in the ideas we discuss in this chapter.

Clearly, one important goal of the accountant is to report financial information to the user in a form useful for decision making. Ironically, the information frequently does not come to the user in such a form. In other words, financial statements don't come with a user's guide. This chapter is a first step in filling this gap.

STANDARDIZING STATEMENTS

One obvious thing we might want to do with a company's financial statements is to compare them to those of other, similar companies. We would immediately have a problem, however. It's almost impossible to directly compare the financial statements for two companies because of differences in size.

For example, Tesla and GM are obviously serious rivals in the auto market, but GM is larger, so it is difficult to compare them directly. For that matter, it's difficult even to compare financial statements from different points in time for the same company if the company's size has changed. The size problem is compounded if we try to compare GM and, say, Toyota. If Toyota's financial statements are denominated in yen, then we have size *and* currency differences.

To start making comparisons, one obvious thing we might try to do is to somehow standardize the financial statements. One common and useful way of doing this is to work with percentages instead of total rupees. The resulting financial statements are called **common-size statements**. We consider these next.

COMMON-SIZE BALANCE SHEETS

For easy reference, Badrinath Company's 2021 and 2022 balance sheets are provided in Table 3.1. Using these, we construct common-size balance sheets by expressing each item as a percentage of total assets. Badrinath's 2021 and 2022 common-size balance sheets are shown in Table 3.2.

Table 3.1

BADRINATH COMPANY Balance Sheets as of December 31, 2021 and 2022 (in millions)		
Assets	**2021**	**2022**
Current assets		
Cash	₹ 84	₹ 98
Accounts receivable	165	188
Inventory	393	422
Total	₹ 642	₹ 708
Fixed assets		
Net plant and equipment	₹2,731	₹2,880
Total assets	₹3,373	₹3,588
Liabilities and Owners' Equity		
Current liabilities		
Accounts payable	₹ 312	₹ 344
Notes payable	231	196
Total	₹ 543	₹ 540
Long-term debt	₹ 531	₹ 457
Owners' equity		
Common stock and paid-in surplus	₹ 500	₹ 550
Retained earnings	1,799	2,041
Total	₹2,299	₹2,591
Total liabilities and owners' equity	₹3,373	₹3,588

Table 3.2

BADRINATH COMPANY Common-Size Balance Sheets December 31, 2021 and 2022			
Assets	**2021**	**2022**	**Change**
Current assets			
Cash	2.5%	2.7%	+ .2%
Accounts receivable	4.9	5.2	+ .3
Inventory	11.7	11.8	+ .1
Total	19.0	19.7	+ .7
Fixed assets			
Net plant and equipment	81.0	80.3	− .7
Total assets	100.0%	100.0%	.0%
Liabilities and Owners' Equity			
Current liabilities			
Accounts payable	9.2%	9.6%	+ .3%
Notes payable	6.8	5.5	−1.4
Total	16.1	15.1	−1.0
Long-term debt	15.7	12.7	−3.0
Owners' equity			
Common stock and paid-in surplus	14.8	15.3	+ .5
Retained earnings	53.3	56.9	+3.5
Total	68.2	72.2	+4.1
Total liabilities and owners' equity	100.0%	100.0%	.0%

Notice that some of the totals don't check exactly because of rounding. Also notice that the total change has to be zero because the beginning and ending numbers must add up to 100 percent.

In this form, financial statements are relatively easy to read and compare. For example, looking at the two balance sheets for Badrinath, we see that current assets were 19.7 percent of total assets in 2022, up from 19.0 percent in 2021. Current liabilities declined from 16.1 percent to 15.1 percent of total liabilities and equity over that same time. Similarly, total equity rose from 68.2 percent of total liabilities and equity to 72.2 percent.

Overall, Badrinath's liquidity, as measured by current assets compared to current liabilities, increased over the year. Simultaneously, Badrinath's indebtedness diminished as a percentage of total assets. We might be tempted to conclude that the balance sheet has grown "stronger."

COMMON-SIZE INCOME STATEMENTS

Table 3.3 describes some commonly used measures of earnings. A useful way of standardizing the income statement shown in Table 3.4 is to express each item as a percentage of total sales, as illustrated for Badrinath in Table 3.5.

The common-size income statement tells us what happens to each rupee in sales. For Badrinath, interest expense eats up ₹.061 out of every sales rupee, and taxes take another ₹.042. When all is said and done, ₹.157 of each rupee flows through to the bottom line (net income), and that amount is split into ₹.105 retained in the business and ₹.052 paid out in dividends.

These percentages are useful in comparisons. For example, a relevant figure is the cost percentage. For Badrinath, ₹.621 of each ₹1.00 in sales goes to pay for goods sold. It would be interesting to compute the same percentage for Badrinath's main competitors to see how Badrinath stacks up in terms of cost control.

Table 3.3 Measures of Earnings

Investors and analysts look closely at the income statement for clues on how well a company has performed during a particular year. Here are some commonly used measures of earnings.

Net income	The so-called bottom line, defined as total revenue minus total expenses. Net income for Badrinath in the latest period is ₹363 million. Net income reflects differences in a firm's capital structure and taxes as well as operating income. Interest expense and taxes are subtracted from operating income in computing net income. Shareholders look closely at net income because dividends and retained earnings are closely linked to net income.
EPS	Net income divided by the number of shares outstanding. It expresses net income on a per share basis. Assuming Badrinath has 33 million shares of stock outstanding, EPS = Net income/Shares outstanding = ₹363/33 = ₹11.
EBIT	Earnings before interest expense and taxes. EBIT is often called "operating income" on the income statement and is income before unusual items, discontinued operations, or extraordinary items. To calculate EBIT, operating expenses are subtracted from total operations revenues. Analysts like EBIT because it removes the impact of differences in earnings from a firm's capital structure (interest expense) and taxes. For Badrinath, EBIT is ₹600 million.
EBITDA	Earnings before interest expense, taxes, depreciation, and amortization. EBITDA = EBIT + depreciation and amortization. Here, amortization refers to a noncash expense similar to depreciation except it applies to an intangible asset (such as a patent), rather than a tangible asset (such as a machine). The word *amortization* does not refer to the payment of debt in this context. There is no amortization in Badrinath's income statement. For Badrinath, EBITDA = ₹600 + 276 = ₹876 million. Analysts like to use EBITDA because it adds back two noncash items (depreciation and amortization) to EBIT and thus is a better measure of before-tax operating cash flow.

Sometimes these measures of earnings are preceded by the letters LTM, meaning the last 12 months. For example, LTM EPS is the last 12 months of EPS and LTM EBITDA is the last 12 months of EBITDA. At other times, the letters TTM are used, meaning trailing 12 months. Needless to say, LTM is the same as TTM.

Table 3.4

BADRINATH COMPANY 2022 Income Statement (in millions)		
Sales		₹2,311
Cost of goods sold		1,435
Depreciation		276
Earnings before interest and taxes		600
Interest paid		141
Taxable income		459
Taxes (21%)		96
Net income		₹ 363
Dividends	₹121	
Addition to retained earnings	242	

Table 3.5

BADRINATH COMPANY Common-Size Income Statement 2022		
Sales		100.0%
Cost of goods sold		62.1
Depreciation		11.9
Earnings before interest and taxes		26.0%
Interest paid		6.1
Taxable income		19.9%
Taxes (21%)		4.2
Net income		15.7%
Dividends	5.2%	
Addition to retained earnings	10.5	

3.2 Ratio Analysis

Excel Master coverage online

Another way of avoiding the problems involved in comparing companies of different sizes is to calculate and compare **financial ratios**. Such ratios are ways of comparing and investigating the relationships between different pieces of financial information. We cover some of the more common ratios next (there are many others we don't discuss here).

One problem with ratios is that different people and different sources frequently don't compute them in exactly the same way, and this leads to much confusion. The specific definitions we use here may or may not be the same as ones you have seen or will see elsewhere. If you are using ratios as tools for analysis, you should be careful to document how you calculate each one; and, if you are comparing your numbers to those of another source, be sure you know how their numbers are computed.

Go to **www.reuters.com**/finance/stocks and find the financial ratios link to examine comparative ratios for a huge number of companies.

We will defer much of our discussion of how ratios are used and some problems that come up with using them until later in the chapter. For now, for each ratio we discuss, several questions come to mind:

1. How is it computed?
2. What is it intended to measure, and why might we be interested?
3. What is the unit of measurement?
4. What might a high or low value be telling us? How might such values be misleading?
5. How could this measure be improved?

Go to **www.reuters.com**/finance/stocks and find the financial ratios link to examine comparative ratios for a huge number of U.S. companies.

Financial ratios are traditionally grouped into the following categories:

1. Short-term solvency, or liquidity, ratios.
2. Long-term solvency, or financial leverage, ratios.
3. Asset management, or turnover, ratios.
4. Profitability ratios.
5. Market value ratios.

Go to **www.screener.in** and find the important financial ratios of Indian companies along with the ratios of peers.

We will consider each of these in turn. In calculating these numbers for Badrinath, we will use the ending balance sheet (2022) figures unless we explicitly say otherwise.

SHORT-TERM SOLVENCY OR LIQUIDITY MEASURES

As the name suggests, short-term solvency ratios as a group are intended to provide information about a firm's liquidity, and these ratios are sometimes called *liquidity ratios*. The primary concern is the firm's ability to pay its bills over the short run without undue stress. Consequently, these ratios focus on current assets and current liabilities.

For obvious reasons, liquidity ratios are particularly interesting to short-term creditors. Because financial managers are constantly working with banks and other short-term lenders, an understanding of these ratios is essential.

One advantage of looking at current assets and liabilities is that their book values and market values are likely to be similar. Often (though not always), these assets and liabilities don't live long enough for the two to get seriously out of step. On the other hand, like any type of near-cash, current assets and liabilities can and do change fairly rapidly, so today's amounts may not be a reliable guide to the future.

Current Ratio One of the best-known and most widely used ratios is the *current ratio*. As you might guess, the current ratio is defined as:

$$\text{Current ratio} = \frac{\text{Current assets}}{\text{Current liabilities}} \tag{3.1}$$

For Badrinath, the 2022 current ratio is:

$$\text{Current ratio} = \frac{₹708}{₹540} = 1.31 \text{ times}$$

Because current assets and liabilities are, in principle, converted to cash over the following 12 months, the current ratio is a measure of short-term liquidity. The unit of measurement is either rupees or times. So, we could say Badrinath has ₹1.31 in current assets for every ₹1 in current liabilities, or we could say Badrinath has its current liabilities covered 1.31 times over. Absent some extraordinary circumstances, we would expect to see a current ratio of at least 1; a current ratio of less than 1 would mean that net working capital (current assets less current liabilities) is negative.

EXAMPLE 3.1

Current Events Suppose a firm were to pay off some of its suppliers and short-term creditors. What would happen to the current ratio? Suppose a firm buys some inventory. What happens in this case? What happens if a firm sells some merchandise?

The first case is a trick question. What happens is that the current ratio moves away from 1. If it is greater than 1, it will get bigger, but if it is less than 1, it will get smaller. To see this, suppose the firm has ₹4 in current assets and ₹2 in current liabilities, for a current ratio of 2. If we use ₹1 in cash to reduce current liabilities, the new current ratio is (₹4 – 1)/(₹2 – 1) = 3. If we reverse the original situation to ₹2 in current assets and ₹4 in current liabilities, the change will cause the current ratio to fall to 1/3 from 1/2.

The second case is not quite as tricky. Nothing happens to the current ratio because cash goes down while inventory goes up—total current assets are unaffected.

In the third case, the current ratio would usually rise because inventory is normally shown at cost and the sale would normally be at something greater than cost (the difference is the markup). The increase in either cash or receivables is therefore greater than the decrease in inventory. This increases current assets, and the current ratio rises.

The current ratio, like any ratio, is affected by various types of transactions. Suppose the firm borrows over the long term to raise money. The short-run effect would be an increase in cash from the issue proceeds and an increase in long-term debt. Current liabilities would not be affected, so the current ratio would rise.

Finally, note that an apparently low current ratio may not be a bad sign for a company with a large reserve of untapped borrowing power.

Quick (or Acid-Test) Ratio Inventory is often the least liquid current asset. It's also the one for which the book values are least reliable as measures of market value because the quality of the inventory isn't considered. Some of the inventory may later turn out to be damaged, obsolete, or lost.

More to the point, relatively large inventories are often a sign of short-term trouble. The firm may have overestimated sales and overbought or overproduced as a result. In this case, the firm may have a substantial portion of its liquidity tied up in slow-moving inventory.

To further evaluate liquidity, the *quick*, or *acid-test, ratio* is computed like the current ratio, except inventory is omitted:

$$\text{Quick ratio} = \frac{\text{Current assets} - \text{Inventory}}{\text{Current liabilities}} \tag{3.2}$$

Notice that using cash to buy inventory does not affect the current ratio, but it reduces the quick ratio. Again, the idea is that inventory is relatively illiquid compared to cash.

For Badrinath, this ratio in 2022 was:

$$\text{Quick ratio} = \frac{₹708 - 422}{₹540} = .53 \text{ times}$$

The quick ratio here tells a somewhat different story than the current ratio because inventory accounts for more than half of Badrinath's current assets. To exaggerate the point, if this inventory consisted of, say, unsold nuclear power plants, then this would be a cause for concern.

To give an example of current versus quick ratios, based on recent financial statements, Walmart and ManpowerGroup had current ratios of .80 and 1.44, respectively. However, ManpowerGroup carries no inventory to speak of, whereas Walmart's current assets are virtually all inventory. As a result, Walmart's quick ratio was only .23, and ManpowerGroup's was 1.44, the same as its current ratio.

Let us consider the case in the Indian context. Sobha Ltd. and National Hydroelectric Power Corporation Ltd. (NHPC) had a current ratio of 1.11 and 1.85, respectively, for FY23. However, NHPC carries no inventory worth speaking of, whereas Sobha's current assets (being a real estate player) are largely inventory. As a result, Sobha's quick ratio stood at 0.18, and NHPC's at 1.83, close to its current ratio.

Cash Ratio A very short-term creditor might be interested in the *cash ratio*:

$$\text{Cash ratio} = \frac{\text{Cash}}{\text{Current liabilities}} \tag{3.3}$$

You can verify that this works out to be .18 times for Badrinath.

LONG-TERM SOLVENCY MEASURES

Long-term solvency ratios are intended to address the firm's long-run ability to meet its obligations or, more generally, its financial leverage. These ratios are sometimes called *financial leverage ratios* or *leverage ratios*. We consider three commonly used measures and some variations.

Total Debt Ratio The *total debt ratio* takes into account all debts of all maturities to all creditors. It can be defined in several ways, the easiest of which is this:

$$\text{Total debt ratio} = \frac{\text{Total assets} - \text{Total equity}}{\text{Total assets}} = \frac{₹3{,}588 - 2{,}591}{₹3{,}588} = .28 \text{ times} \quad \textbf{(3.4)}$$

In this case, an analyst might say that Badrinath uses 28 percent debt.[1] Whether this is high or low or whether it even makes any difference depends on whether capital structure matters, a subject we discuss in a later chapter.

Badrinath has ₹.28 in debt for every ₹1 in assets. Therefore, there is ₹.72 in equity (= ₹1 − .28) for every ₹.28 in debt. With this in mind, we can define two useful variations on the total debt ratio, the *debt-equity ratio* and the *equity multiplier*:

The online U.S. Small Business Administration has more information about financial statements, ratios, and small business topics at **www.sba.gov**.

$$\text{Debt-equity ratio} = \text{Total debt/Total equity} = ₹.28/₹.72 = .38 \text{ times} \quad \textbf{(3.5)}$$

$$\text{Equity multiplier} = \text{Total assets/Total equity} = ₹1/₹.72 = 1.38 \text{ times} \quad \textbf{(3.6)}$$

The fact that the equity multiplier is 1 plus the debt-equity ratio is not a coincidence:

$$\begin{aligned}\text{Equity multiplier} &= \text{Total assets/Total equity} = ₹1/₹.72 = 1.38 \text{ times}\\ &= (\text{Total equity} + \text{Total debt})/\text{Total equity}\\ &= 1 + \text{Debt-equity ratio} = 1.38 \text{ times}\end{aligned}$$

The thing to notice here is that given any one of these three ratios, you can immediately calculate the other two, so they all say exactly the same thing.

Times Interest Earned Another common measure of long-term solvency is the *times interest earned* (TIE) *ratio*. Once again, there are several possible (and common) definitions, but we'll stick with the most traditional:

$$\text{Times interest earned ratio} = \frac{\text{EBIT}}{\text{Interest}} = \frac{₹600}{₹141} = 4.26 \text{ times} \quad \textbf{(3.7)}$$

As the name suggests, this ratio measures how well a company has its interest obligations covered, and it is often called the *interest coverage ratio*. For Badrinath, the interest bill is covered 4.26 times over.

Cash Coverage A problem with the TIE ratio is that it is based on EBIT, which is not really a measure of cash available to pay interest. The reason is that depreciation and amortization, both noncash expenses, have been deducted out. Because interest is most definitely a cash outflow (to creditors), one way to define the *cash coverage ratio* is:

$$\text{Cash coverage ratio} = \frac{\text{EBIT} + (\text{Depreciation and amortization})}{\text{Interest}} = \frac{₹600 + 276}{₹141} = \frac{₹876}{₹141} = 6.21 \text{ times} \quad \textbf{(3.8)}$$

[1]Total equity here includes preferred stock, if there is any. An equivalent numerator in this ratio would be (Current liabilities + Long-term debt).

The numerator here, EBIT plus depreciation and amortization, is often abbreviated EBITDA (earnings before interest, taxes, depreciation, and amortization). It is a basic measure of the firm's ability to generate cash from operations, and it is frequently used as a measure of cash flow available to meet financial obligations.

More recently, another long-term solvency measure is increasingly seen in financial statement analysis and in debt covenants. It uses EBITDA and interest-bearing debt. Specifically, for Badrinath:

$$\frac{\text{Interest-bearing debt}}{\text{EBITDA}} = \frac{₹196 \text{ million} + 457 \text{ million}}{₹876 \text{ million}} = .75 \text{ times}$$

Here we include notes payable (typically bank debt) and long-term debt in the numerator and EBITDA in the denominator. Values below 1 on this ratio are considered very strong and values above 5 are considered weak. However, a careful comparison with other comparable firms is necessary to properly interpret the ratio.

ASSET MANAGEMENT OR TURNOVER MEASURES

We next turn our attention to the efficiency with which Badrinath uses its assets. The measures in this section are sometimes called *asset management* or *utilization ratios*. The specific ratios we discuss all can be interpreted as measures of turnover. What they are intended to describe is how efficiently, or intensively, a firm uses the asset we are measuring. We first look at two important current assets: inventory and receivables.

Inventory Turnover and Days' Sales in Inventory During 2022, Badrinath had a cost of goods sold of ₹1,435. Inventory at the end of the year was ₹422. With these numbers, *inventory turnover* can be calculated as:

$$\begin{aligned}\text{Inventory turnover} &= \frac{\text{Cost of goods sold}}{\text{Inventory}} \\ &= \frac{₹1{,}435}{₹422} = 3.40 \text{ times}\end{aligned} \tag{3.9}$$

In a sense, we sold off, or turned over, the entire inventory 3.40 times during the year. As long as we are not running out of stock and thereby forgoing sales, the higher this ratio is, the more efficiently we are managing inventory. However, a high inventory turnover could indicate that we are paying for too many shipments.

If we know that we turned our inventory over 3.40 times during the year, we can immediately figure out how long it took us to turn it over, on average. The result is the average *days' sales in inventory*:

$$\begin{aligned}\text{Days' sales in inventory} &= \frac{365 \text{ days}}{\text{Inventory turnover}} \\ &= \frac{365}{3.40} = 107.34 \text{ days}\end{aligned} \tag{3.10}$$

This tells us that, roughly speaking, inventory sits about 107 days, on average, before it is sold. Alternatively, assuming we used the most recent inventory and cost figures, it will take about 107 days to work off our current inventory.

In practice, inventory levels can vary dramatically from optimal levels. To give an example, in March 2020, with sales dropping due to the COVID-19 pandemic, the U.S. automobile industry as a whole had a 116-day supply of cars, almost twice the 60-day supply considered normal. This figure means that at the then-current rate of sales, it would have taken 116 days to deplete the available supply. Of course, there

To see the ratio of auto inventory to sales, check out **fred.stlouisfed.org/series/AISRSA**.

was significant variation in models. For example, light truck sales exceeded sedan sales for the first time. As a result, there were only 400,000 light trucks in inventory and, when GM wanted to ramp up light truck production, it faced delays due to parts shortages.

Let us give you an example from India. The two Oil Marketing Companies (OMC) in India IOCL and BPCL reported inventory holding period of 59 and 32 days respectively, for FY23. The extra inventory worth 27 days' supply meant that ONGC had more money tied up in inventory - money that could have been used elsewhere.

Receivables Turnover and Days' Sales in Receivables Our inventory measures give some indication of how fast we can sell products. We now look at how fast we collect on those sales. Like inventory turnover, *receivables turnover* uses sales in the numerator:

$$\text{Receivables turnover} = \frac{\text{Sales}}{\text{Accounts receivable}} = \frac{₹2{,}311}{₹188} = 12.29 \text{ times} \quad \textbf{(3.11)}$$

Loosely speaking, we collected our outstanding credit accounts and lent the money again 12.29 times during 2022.[2]

This ratio makes more sense if we convert it to days, so the *days' sales in receivables* is:

$$\text{Days' sales in receivables} = \frac{365 \text{ days}}{\text{Receivables turnover}} = \frac{365}{12.29} = 29.69 \text{ days} \quad \textbf{(3.12)}$$

Therefore, on average, we collect on our credit sales in about 30 days. For obvious reasons, this ratio is frequently called the *average collection period* (ACP). Note that if we are using the most recent figures, we also can say that we have 30 days' worth of sales currently uncollected.

EXAMPLE 3.2

Payables Turnover Here is a variation on the receivables collection period. How long, on average, does it take for Badrinath Company to *pay* its bills? To answer, we need to calculate the accounts payable turnover ratio using cost of goods sold. We will assume that Badrinath purchases everything on credit.

The cost of goods sold is ₹1,435, and accounts payable are ₹344. The turnover is therefore ₹1,435/₹344 = 4.17 times. So, payables turned over about every 365/4.17 = 87.50 days. On average, then, Badrinath takes 88 days to pay. As a potential creditor, we might take note of this fact.

Total Asset Turnover Moving away from specific accounts like inventory or receivables, we can consider an important "big picture" ratio, the *total asset turnover* ratio. As the name suggests, total asset turnover is:

$$\text{Total asset turnover} = \frac{\text{Sales}}{\text{Total assets}} = \frac{₹2{,}311}{₹3{,}588} = .64 \text{ times} \quad \textbf{(3.13)}$$

In other words, for every rupee in assets, we generated ₹.64 in sales.

[2]Here we have implicitly assumed that all sales are credit sales. If they were not, we would use total credit sales in these calculations, not total sales.

EXAMPLE 3.3

More Turnover Suppose you find that a particular company generates ₹.40 in annual sales for every Rupee in total assets. How often does this company turn over its total assets?

The total asset turnover here is .40 times per year. It takes 1/.40 = 2.5 years to turn assets over completely.

PROFITABILITY MEASURES

The four measures we discuss in this section are probably the best-known and most widely used of all financial ratios. In one form or another, they are intended to measure how efficiently the firm uses its assets and how efficiently the firm manages its operations.

Profit Margin Companies pay a great deal of attention to their *profit margins*:

$$\text{Profit margin} = \frac{\text{Net income}}{\text{Sales}} = \frac{₹363}{₹2{,}311} = .1569, \text{ or } 15.69\% \tag{3.14}$$

This tells us that Badrinath, in an accounting sense, generates a little less than 16 cents in net income for every rupee in sales.

EBITDA Margin Another commonly used measure of profitability is the EBITDA margin. As mentioned, EBITDA is a measure of before-tax operating cash flow. It adds back noncash expenses and does not include taxes or interest expense. Therefore, EBITDA margin looks more directly at operating cash flows than does net income and does not include the effect of capital structure or taxes. For Badrinath, EBITDA margin is:

$$\frac{\text{EBITDA}}{\text{Sales}} = \frac{₹876}{₹2{,}311} = .3791, \text{ or } 37.91\%$$

All other things being equal, a relatively high margin is obviously desirable. This situation corresponds to low expense ratios relative to sales. However, we hasten to add that other things are often not equal.

For example, lowering our sales price usually will increase unit volume but normally will cause margins to shrink. Total profit (or, more importantly, operating cash flow) may go up or down, so the fact that margins are smaller isn't necessarily bad. After all, isn't it possible that, as the saying goes, "Our prices are so low that we lose money on everything we sell, but we make it up in volume"?[3]

Because profit margin measures how well a company makes money, it is a widely followed ratio. However, as with any ratio, there is significant variation between different industries. Table 3.6 shows the profit margins for various industries for a recent quarter.

As you can see, the average profit margin for a U.S. manufacturing company was 9.04 percent, but the scientific research industry experienced significant issues, with a negative profit margin. At the other extreme, broadcasting had a profit margin of about 23%.

There are similar instances in the Indian economy as well. In the year 2022-23, ITC Limited, the tobacco giant, had a margin of over 27% whereas in the same field, its competing peers, Godfrey Philips India, had a meager margin of 17% only.

[3]No, it's not.

Table 3.6 Profit Margins for Various Industries

Industry	Profit margin
All manufacturing	9.04%
Scientific research and development services	−22.54%
Management and technical consulting services	1.27%
Motion picture and sound recording industries	−4.78%
Computer systems design and related services	3.79%
Food	4.55%
Wood products	3.96%
Apparel and leather products	10.46%
Chemicals	16.34%
Pharmaceuticals and medicines	24.41%
Broadcasting, except internet	23.37%

SOURCE: U.S. Census Bureau, U.S. Manufacturing, Mining, Wholesale Trade, and Selected Service Industries, First Quarter 2020, author calculations.

Return on Assets *Return on assets* (ROA) is a measure of profit per rupee of assets. It can be defined several ways,[4] but the most common is:

$$\text{Return on assets} = \frac{\text{Net income}}{\text{Total assets}} = \frac{₹363}{₹3{,}588} = .1011, \text{ or } 10.11\% \tag{3.15}$$

Return on Equity *Return on equity* (ROE) is a measure of how the stockholders fared during the year. Because benefiting shareholders is our goal, ROE is, in an accounting sense, the true bottom-line measure of performance. ROE is usually measured as:

$$\text{Return on equity} = \frac{\text{Net income}}{\text{Total equity}} = \frac{₹363}{₹2{,}591} = .1399, \text{ or } 13.99\% \tag{3.16}$$

Therefore, for every rupee in equity, Badrinath generated 14 cents in profit; but, again, this is correct only in accounting terms.

Because ROA and ROE are such commonly cited numbers, we stress that it is important to remember they are accounting rates of return. For this reason, these measures should properly be called *return on book assets* and *return on book equity*. In addition, ROE is sometimes called *return on net worth*. Whatever it's called, it would be inappropriate to compare the result to, for example, an interest rate observed in the financial markets.

The fact that ROE exceeds ROA reflects Badrinath's use of financial leverage. We will examine the relationship between these two measures in the next section.

[4]For example, we might want a return on assets measure that is neutral with respect to capital structure (interest expense) and taxes. Such a measure for Badrinath would be:

$$\frac{\text{EBIT}}{\text{Total assets}} = \frac{₹600}{₹3{,}588} = .1672, \text{ or } 16.72\%$$

This measure has a very natural interpretation. If 16.72 percent exceeds Badrinath's borrowing rate, Badrinath will earn more money on its investments than it will pay out to its creditors. The surplus will be available to Badrinath's shareholders after adjusting for taxes.

MARKET VALUE MEASURES

Our final group of measures is based, in part, on information not necessarily contained in financial statements–the market price per share of the stock. Obviously, these measures can be calculated directly only for publicly traded companies.

We assume that Badrinath has 33 million shares outstanding and the stock sold for ₹88 per share at the end of the year. If we recall that Badrinath's net income was ₹363 million, then we can calculate that its earnings per share were:

$$\text{EPS} = \frac{\text{Net income}}{\text{Shares outstanding}} = \frac{₹363}{33} = ₹10.99 \tag{3.17}$$

Price-Earnings Ratio The first of our market value measures, the *price-earnings* or *PE ratio* (or multiple), is defined as:

$$\begin{aligned}\text{PE ratio} &= \frac{\text{Price per share}}{\text{Earnings per share}}\\ &= \frac{₹88}{₹10.99} = 8.01 \text{ times}\end{aligned} \tag{3.18}$$

In the vernacular, we would say that Badrinath shares sell for 8 times earnings, or we might say that Badrinath shares have, or "carry," a PE multiple of 8.

Because the PE ratio measures how much investors are willing to pay per Rupee of current earnings, higher PEs are often taken to mean that the firm has significant prospects for future growth. Of course, if a firm had no or almost no earnings, its PE would probably be quite large; so, as always, care is needed in interpreting this ratio.

Market-to-Book Ratio A second commonly quoted measure is the *market-to-book ratio*:

$$\begin{aligned}\text{Market-to-book ratio} &= \frac{\text{Market value per share}}{\text{Book value per share}}\\ &= \frac{₹88}{₹2{,}591/33} = \frac{₹88}{₹78.5} = 1.12 \text{ times}\end{aligned} \tag{3.19}$$

Notice that book value per share is total equity (not just common stock) divided by the number of shares outstanding.

Book value per share is an accounting number that reflects historical costs. In a loose sense, the market-to-book ratio therefore compares the market value of the firm's investments to their cost. A value less than 1 could mean that the firm has not been successful overall in creating value for its stockholders.

Market Capitalization The market capitalization of a public firm is equal to the firm's stock market price per share multiplied by the number of shares outstanding. For Badrinath, this is:

$$\text{Price per share} \times \text{Shares outstanding} = ₹88 \times 33 \text{ million} = ₹2{,}904 \text{ million}$$

This is a useful number for potential buyers of Badrinath. A prospective buyer of all of the outstanding shares of Badrinath (in a merger or acquisition) would need to come up with at least ₹2,904 million plus a premium.

Enterprise Value Enterprise value is a measure of firm value that is very closely related to market capitalization. Instead of focusing on only the market value of outstanding shares of stock, it measures the market value of outstanding shares of stock plus the market value of outstanding interest-bearing debt less cash on hand.

We know the market capitalization of Badrinath but we do not know the market value of its outstanding interest-bearing debt. In this situation, the common practice is to use the book value of outstanding interest-bearing debt less cash on hand as an approximation. For Badrinath, enterprise value is (in millions):

$$\begin{aligned} \text{EV} &= \text{Market capitalization} + \text{Market value of interest-bearing debt} - \text{Cash} \\ &= ₹2{,}904 + (196 + 457) - 98 = ₹3{,}459 \text{ million} \end{aligned} \quad \textbf{(3.20)}$$

The purpose of the EV measure is to better estimate how much it would take to buy all of the outstanding stock of a firm and also to pay off the debt. The adjustment for cash is to recognize that if we were a buyer, the cash could be used immediately to buy back debt or pay a dividend.

Enterprise Value Multiples Financial analysts use valuation multiples based upon a firm's enterprise value when the goal is to estimate the value of the firm's total business rather than focus on the value of its equity. To form an appropriate multiple, enterprise value is divided by EBITDA. For Badrinath, the enterprise value multiple is:

$$\text{EV multiple} = \frac{\text{EV}}{\text{EBITDA}} = \frac{₹3{,}459}{₹876} = 3.95 \text{ times} \quad \textbf{(3.21)}$$

The multiple is especially useful because it allows comparison of one firm with another when there are differences in capital structure (interest expense), taxes, or capital spending. The multiple is not directly affected by these differences.

Similar to PE ratios, we would expect a firm with high growth opportunities to have high EV multiples.

This completes our definition of some common ratios. We could tell you about more of them, but these are enough for now. We'll leave it here and discuss some ways of using these ratios. Table 3.7 summarizes some of the ratios we've discussed.

EXAMPLE 3.4 (A)

Enterprise Value Multiples Consider the following 2022 data for Atlantic Company, Inc., and Pacific Depot, Inc. (in billions except for price per share):

	Atlantic Company, Inc.	Pacific Depot, Inc.
Sales	₹53.4	₹78.8
EBIT	₹ 4.1	₹16.6
Net income	₹ 2.3	₹ 5.4
Cash	₹ .4	₹ 2.0
Depreciation	₹ 1.5	₹ 1.6
Interest-bearing debt	₹10.1	₹14.7
Total assets	₹32.7	₹40.5
Price per share	₹ 53	₹ 91
Shares outstanding	1.0	1.4
Shareholder equity	₹11.9	₹17.9

continued

1. Determine the profit margin, ROE, market capitalization, enterprise value, PE multiple, and EV multiple for both Atlantic Company and Pacific Depot.

	Atlantic Company, Inc.	Pacific Depot, Inc.
Equity multiplier	₹32.7/₹11.9 = 2.75	₹40.5/₹17.9 = 2.26
Total asset turnover	₹53.4/₹32.7 = 1.63	₹78.8/₹40.5 = 1.95
Profit margin	₹2.3/₹53.4 = .0431, or 4.31%	₹5.4/₹78.8 = .0685, or 6.85%
ROE	₹2.3/₹11.9 = .1933, or 19.33%	₹5.4/₹17.9 = .3017, or 30.17%
Market capitalization	1.0 × ₹53 = ₹53 billion	1.4 × ₹91 = ₹127.4 billion
Enterprise value	(1.0 × ₹53) + ₹10.1 − .4 = ₹62.7 billion	(1.4 × ₹91) + ₹14.7 − 2.0 = ₹140.1 billion
PE multiple	₹53/₹2.3 = 23.04	₹91/₹5.4 = 16.85
EBITDA	₹4.1 + 1.5 = ₹5.6	₹16.6 + 1.6 = ₹18.2
EV multiple	₹62.7/₹5.6 = 11.20	₹140.1/₹18.2 = 7.70

2. How would you describe these two companies from a financial point of view? Overall, they are similarly situated. In 2022, Pacific Depot had a higher ROE (partially because of a higher total asset turnover and a higher profit margin), but Atlantic had a higher EV multiple.

Table 3.7 Common Financial Ratios

I. Short-Term Solvency, or Liquidity, Ratios

$$\text{Current ratio} = \frac{\text{Current assets}}{\text{Current liabilities}}$$

$$\text{Quick ratio} = \frac{\text{Current assets} - \text{Inventory}}{\text{Current liabilities}}$$

$$\text{Cash ratio} = \frac{\text{Cash}}{\text{Current liabilities}}$$

II. Long-Term Solvency, or Financial Leverage, Ratios

$$\text{Total debt ratio} = \frac{\text{Total assets} - \text{Total equity}}{\text{Total assets}}$$

$$\text{Debt-equity ratio} = \frac{\text{Total debt}}{\text{Total equity}}$$

$$\text{Equity multiplier} = \frac{\text{Total assets}}{\text{Total equity}}$$

$$\text{Times interest earned ratio} = \frac{\text{EBIT}}{\text{Interest}}$$

$$\text{Cash coverage ratio} = \frac{\text{EBITDA}}{\text{Interest}}$$

III. Asset Utilization, or Turnover, Ratios

$$\text{Inventory turnover} = \frac{\text{Cost of goods sold}}{\text{Inventory}}$$

$$\text{Days' sales in inventory} = \frac{\text{365 days}}{\text{Inventory turnover}}$$

$$\text{Receivables turnover} = \frac{\text{Sales}}{\text{Accounts receivable}}$$

$$\text{Days' sales in receivables} = \frac{\text{365 days}}{\text{Receivables turnover}}$$

$$\text{Total asset turnover} = \frac{\text{Sales}}{\text{Total assets}}$$

$$\text{Capital intensity} = \frac{\text{Total assets}}{\text{Sales}}$$

IV. Profitability Ratios

$$\text{Profit margin} = \frac{\text{Net income}}{\text{Sales}}$$

$$\text{Return on assets (ROA)} = \frac{\text{Net income}}{\text{Total assets}}$$

$$\text{Return on equity (ROE)} = \frac{\text{Net income}}{\text{Total equity}}$$

$$\text{ROE} = \frac{\text{Net income}}{\text{Sales}} \times \frac{\text{Sales}}{\text{Assets}} \times \frac{\text{Assets}}{\text{Equity}}$$

V. Market Value Ratios

$$\text{Price-earnings ratio} = \frac{\text{Price per share}}{\text{Earnings per share}}$$

$$\text{Market-to-book ratio} = \frac{\text{Market value per share}}{\text{Book value per share}}$$

$$\text{EV multiple} = \frac{\text{Enterprise value}}{\text{EBITDA}}$$

EXAMPLE 3.4 (B)

Consider the following data of FY23 for the two textile giants, Arvind and Raymond (all figures are in billion except for price per share).

Item	Arvind	Raymond
Sales	₹76.36	₹ 82.15
EBDIT	₹ 9.29	₹ 12.29
Net income	₹ 9.28	₹ 5.37
Cash	₹ 0.88	₹ 3.26
Depreciation	₹ 2.61	₹ 3.80
Interest bearing debt	₹ 1.92	₹ 2.57
Total assets	₹68.98	₹ 81.86
Price per share	₹85.35	₹1221.60
Shares outstanding	0.26	0.06
Shareholders equity funds	₹33.62	₹ 28.99

1. Determine the profit margin, ROE, market capitalization, enterprise value, PE multiple, and EV multiple for both Arvind and Raymond.

Item	Arvind	Raymond
Equity multiplier	2.05	2.82
Total asset turnover	1.11	1.00
Profit margin	12%	7%
ROE	28%	19%
Market capitalization (in billion)	₹22.19	₹ 73.30
Enterprise value (in billion)	₹23.23	₹ 72.61
EPS	₹35.69	₹ 89.50
PE multiple	2.39x	13.65x
EBITDA (in billion)	₹11.90	₹ 16.09
EV multiple	1.95	4.51

2. How would you describe these two companies from a financial point of view?
   Overall, both the companies were not in great shape during the stated year. Arvind was better than Raymond. In spite of lower total asset turnover and lower equity multiplier, Arvind had a higher ROE – largely because of a higher profit margin.

3.3 The DuPont Identity

As we mentioned in discussing ROA and ROE, the difference between these two profitability measures reflects the use of debt financing or financial leverage. In this section, we illustrate the relationship between these measures by investigating a famous way of decomposing ROE into its component parts.

Excel Master coverage online

A CLOSER LOOK AT ROE

To begin, let's recall the definition of ROE:

$$\text{Return on equity} = \frac{\text{Net income}}{\text{Total equity}}$$

If we were so inclined, we could multiply this ratio by Assets/Assets without changing anything:

$$\begin{aligned}\text{Return on equity} &= \frac{\text{Net income}}{\text{Total equity}} = \frac{\text{Net income}}{\text{Total equity}} \times \frac{\text{Assets}}{\text{Assets}} \\ &= \frac{\text{Net income}}{\text{Assets}} \times \frac{\text{Assets}}{\text{Total equity}}\end{aligned}$$

Notice that we have expressed the ROE as the product of two other ratios–ROA and the equity multiplier:

$$\text{ROE} = \text{ROA} \times \text{Equity multiplier} = \text{ROA} \times (1 + \text{Debt-equity ratio})$$

Looking back at Badrinath, we see that the equity multiplier was 1.38 and ROA was 10.11 percent. Our work here implies that Badrinath's ROE, as we previously calculated, is:

$$\text{ROE} = .1011 \times 1.38 = .1399, \text{ or } 13.99\%$$

The difference between ROE and ROA can be substantial, particularly for certain businesses. For example, in 2019, Bank of America had an ROA of 2.61 percent, which is actually fairly typical for a bank. However, banks tend to borrow a lot of money, and, as a result, have relatively large equity multipliers. For Bank of America, ROE is about 22 percent, implying an equity multiplier of 8.43. In India, one of the largest private banks, Kotak Mahindra Bank, had an ROA of only 2.40% but a large debt-equity ratio of 6 times, resulting in an ROE of about 13.34%.

We can further decompose ROE by multiplying the top and bottom by total sales:

$$\text{ROE} = \frac{\text{Sales}}{\text{Sales}} \times \frac{\text{Net income}}{\text{Assets}} \times \frac{\text{Assets}}{\text{Total equity}}$$

If we rearrange things a bit, ROE is:

$$\begin{aligned}\text{ROE} &= \underbrace{\frac{\text{Net income}}{\text{Sales}} \times \frac{\text{Sales}}{\text{Assets}}}_{\text{Return on assets}} \times \frac{\text{Assets}}{\text{Total equity}} \\ &= \text{Profit margin} \times \text{Total asset turnover} \times \text{Equity multiplier}\end{aligned} \qquad \textbf{(3.22)}$$

What we have now done is to partition ROA into its two component parts, profit margin and total asset turnover. The last expression of the preceding equation is called the **DuPont identity** after the DuPont Corporation, which popularized its use.

We can check this relationship for Badrinath by noting that the profit margin was 15.69 percent and the total asset turnover was .64. ROE should be:

$$\begin{aligned} \text{ROE} &= \text{Profit margin} \times \text{Total asset turnover} \times \text{Equity multiplier} \\ &= .1569 \times .64 \times 1.38 \\ &= .1399, \text{ or } 13.99\% \end{aligned}$$

This 13.99 percent ROE is exactly what we had before.

The DuPont identity tells us that ROE is affected by three things:

1. Operating efficiency (as measured by profit margin).
2. Asset use efficiency (as measured by total asset turnover).
3. Financial leverage (as measured by the equity multiplier).

Weakness in either operating or asset use efficiency (or both) will show up in a diminished return on assets, which will translate into a lower ROE.

Considering the DuPont identity, it appears that the ROE could be leveraged up by increasing the amount of debt in the firm. However, notice that increasing debt also increases interest expense, which reduces profit margins, which acts to reduce ROE. So, ROE could go up or down, depending. More important, the use of debt financing has a number of other effects, and, as we discuss at some length in later chapters, the amount of leverage a firm uses is governed by its capital structure policy.

The decomposition of ROE we've discussed in this section is a convenient way of systematically approaching financial statement analysis. If ROE is unsatisfactory by some measure, then the DuPont identity tells you where to start looking for the reasons.[5]

DuPont analysis (and ratio analysis in general) can be used to compare two companies as well. Amazon and Alibaba are among the most important internet companies in the world. We will use them to illustrate how DuPont analysis can be useful in helping to ask the right questions about a firm's financial performance. The DuPont breakdowns for Amazon and Alibaba are summarized in Table 3.8.

Table 3.8 The DuPont Breakdown for Amazon and Alibaba

			Amazon				
	ROE	=	**Profit Margin**	×	**Total Asset Turnover**	×	**Equity Multiplier**
2019	18.7%	=	4.1%	×	1.245	×	3.63
2018	23.1	=	4.3	×	1.432	×	3.73
2017	10.9	=	1.7	×	1.355	×	4.74
			Alibaba				
	ROE	=	**Profit Margin**	×	**Total Asset Turnover**	×	**Equity Multiplier**
2019	34.9%	=	35.2%	×	.507	×	1.96
2018	16.6	=	21.3	×	.390	×	2.00
2017	16.8	=	24.5	×	.349	×	1.96

[5]Perhaps this is a time to mention Abraham Briloff, a well-known financial commentator, who famously remarked that "financial statements are like fine perfume; to be sniffed but not swallowed."

As shown, in 2019, Amazon had an ROE of 18.7 percent, down over 4 percent from the previous year. In contrast, in 2019, Alibaba had an ROE of 34.9 percent, more than double its ROE in 2018 of 16.6 percent. For two of the three years, Alibaba had a higher ROE than Amazon.

A closer inspection of the DuPont breakdown shows the divergence in how these two companies generate their respective ROE. Alibaba has consistently shown a profit margin above 20 percent, while Amazon's profit margin has been in the low single digits. However, Amazon has a much higher total asset turnover, as a well as an equity multiplier that is twice as large as Alibaba's. We can say that Alibaba has an advantage in that its operating efficiency is much higher than that of Amazon, but Amazon has an advantage in its asset utilization.

PROBLEMS WITH FINANCIAL STATEMENT ANALYSIS

We continue our chapter by discussing some additional problems that can arise in using financial statements. In one way or another, the basic problem with financial statement analysis is that there is no underlying theory to help us identify which quantities to look at and to guide us in establishing benchmarks.

As we discuss in other chapters, there are many cases in which financial theory and economic logic provide guidance in making judgments about value and risk, but little such help exists with financial statements. This is why we can't make a blanket statement about which ratios matter the most and what a high or low value might be.

One particularly severe problem is that many firms are conglomerates, owning more or less unrelated lines of business. *GE, Mahindra & Mahindra Limited* and *Larsen & Toubro Limited* are well-known examples. The consolidated financial statements for such firms don't really fit any neat industry category. More generally, the kind of peer group analysis we have been describing is going to work best when the firms are strictly in the same line of business, the industry is competitive, and there is only one way of operating.

Another problem that is becoming increasingly common is that major competitors and natural peer group members in an industry may be scattered around the globe. The automobile industry is an obvious example. The problem here is that financial statements from outside the United States do not necessarily conform to US GAAP. The existence of different standards and procedures makes it difficult to compare financial statements across national borders.

Even companies that are clearly in the same line of business may not be comparable. For example, electric utilities engaged primarily in power generation are all classified in the same group. This group often is thought to be relatively homogeneous. However, most utilities operate as regulated monopolies, so they don't compete much with each other, at least not historically. Many have stockholders, but many others are organized as cooperatives with no stockholders. There are several different ways of generating power, ranging from wind to hydroelectric to nuclear, so the operating activities of these utilities can differ quite a bit. Finally, profitability is strongly affected by the regulatory environment, so utilities in different locations can be similar but show different profits.

Several other general problems frequently crop up. First, different firms use different accounting procedures–for inventory, for example. This makes it difficult to compare statements. Second, different firms end their fiscal years at different times. For firms in seasonal businesses (such as a retailer with a large Christmas season), this can lead to difficulties in comparing balance sheets because of fluctuations in accounts during the year. Finally, for any particular firm, unusual or transient events, such as a one-time profit from an asset sale, may affect financial performance. Such events can give misleading signals as we compare firms.

3.4 Financial Models

Financial planning is another important use of financial statements. Most financial planning models use pro forma financial statements, where pro forma means "as a matter of form." In our case, this means that financial statements are the form we use to summarize the projected future financial status of a company.

Excel Master coverage online

A SIMPLE FINANCIAL PLANNING MODEL

We can begin our discussion of financial planning models with a relatively simple example. The Nagaland Pulp & Paper Company's financial statements from the most recent year are shown below.

Unless otherwise stated, the financial planners at Nagaland Pulp & Paper assume that all variables are tied directly to sales and current relationships are optimal. This means that all items will grow at exactly the same rate as sales. This is obviously oversimplified; we use this assumption only to make a point.

NAGALAND PULP & PAPER COMPANY
Financial Statements

Income Statement		Balance Sheet			
Sales	₹1,000	Assets	₹500	Debt	₹250
Costs	800			Equity	250
Net income	₹ 200	Total	₹500	Total	₹500

Suppose sales increase by 20 percent, rising from ₹1,000 to ₹1,200. Planners would then also forecast a 20 percent increase in costs, from ₹800 to ₹800 × 1.2 = ₹960. The pro forma income statement would look like this:

Pro Forma Income Statement

Sales	₹1,200
Costs	960
Net income	₹ 240

The assumption that all variables will grow by 20 percent lets us easily construct the pro forma balance sheet as well:

Pro Forma Balance Sheet

Assets	₹600 (+100)	Debt	₹300 (+50)
		Equity	300 (+50)
Total	₹600 (+100)	Total	₹600 (+100)

Notice we have increased every item by 20 percent. The numbers in parentheses are the rupee changes for the different items.

Now we have to reconcile these two pro forma statements. How, for example, can net income be equal to ₹240 and equity increase by only ₹50? The answer is that Nagaland Pulp & Paper must have paid out the difference of ₹240 – 50 = ₹190, possibly as a cash dividend. In this case, dividends are the "plug" variable.

Suppose Nagaland Pulp & Paper does not pay out the ₹190. Then, the addition to retained earnings would be the full ₹240. Nagaland Pulp & Paper's equity will grow to ₹250 (the starting amount) plus ₹240 (net income), or ₹490, and debt must be retired to keep total assets equal to ₹600.

With ₹600 in total assets and ₹490 in equity, debt will have to be ₹600 – 490 = ₹110. Because we started with ₹250 in debt, Nagaland Pulp & Paper will have to retire ₹250 – 110 = ₹140 in debt. The resulting pro forma balance sheet would look like this:

Pro Forma Balance Sheet			
Assets	₹600 (+100)	Debt	₹110 (+140)
		Equity	490 (+240)
Total	₹600 (+100)	Total	₹600 (+100)

In this case, debt is the plug variable used to balance projected total assets and liabilities.

This example shows the interaction between sales growth and financial policy. As sales increase, so do total assets. This occurs because the firm must invest in net working capital and fixed assets to support higher sales levels. Because assets are growing, total liabilities and equity, the right side of the balance sheet, will grow as well.

The thing to notice from our simple example is that the way the liabilities and owners' equity change depends on the firm's financing and dividend policies. The growth in assets requires the firm to decide on how to finance that growth. This is strictly a managerial decision. Note that in our example the firm needed no outside funds. This won't usually be the case, so we explore a more detailed situation in the next section.

THE PERCENTAGE OF SALES APPROACH

In the previous section, we described a simple planning model in which every item increased at the same rate as sales. This may be a reasonable assumption for some elements. For others, such as long-term borrowing, it probably is not, as the amount of long-term borrowing is set by management, and it does not necessarily relate directly to the level of sales.

In this section, we describe an extended version of our simple model. The basic idea is to separate the income statement and balance sheet accounts into two groups: those that vary directly with sales and those that do not. Given a sales forecast, we will then be able to calculate how much financing the firm will need to support the predicted sales level.

The financial planning model we describe next is based on the **percentage of sales approach**. Our goal here is to develop a quick and practical way of generating pro forma statements. We defer discussion of some "bells and whistles" to a later section.

The Income Statement We start out with the most recent income statement for the Mirza Company, as shown in Table 3.9. Notice that we have still simplified things by including costs, depreciation, and interest in a single cost figure.

Mirza has projected a 25 percent increase in sales for the coming year, so we are anticipating sales of ₹1,000 × 1.25 = ₹1,250. To generate a pro forma income statement, we assume that total costs will continue to run at ₹833/₹1,000 = .833, or 83.3 percent of sales. With this assumption, Mirza's pro forma income statement is as shown in Table 3.10. The effect here of assuming that costs are a constant percentage of sales is to assume that the profit margin is constant. To check this, notice that the profit margin was ₹132/₹1,000 = .132, or 13.2 percent. In our pro forma statement, the profit margin is unchanged at ₹165/₹1,250 = .132, or 13.2 percent.

Table 3.9

MIRZA COMPANY Income Statement		
Sales		₹1,000
Costs		833
Taxable income		₹ 167
Taxes (21%)		35
Net income		₹ 132
Dividends	₹44	
Addition to retained earnings	88	

Table 3.10

MIRZA COMPANY Pro Forma Income Statement	
Sales (projected)	₹1,250
Costs (83.3% of sales)	1,041
Taxable income	₹ 209
Taxes (21%)	44
Net income	₹ 165

Next, we need to project the dividend payment. This amount is up to Mirza's management. We will assume Mirza has a policy of paying out a constant fraction of net income in the form of a cash dividend. For the most recent year, the **dividend payout ratio** was:

$$\begin{aligned}\text{Dividend payout ratio} &= \text{Cash dividends/Net income} \\ &= ₹44/₹132 = .3333, \text{ or } 33.33\%\end{aligned} \tag{3.23}$$

We also can calculate the ratio of the addition to retained earnings to net income:

$$\text{Addition to retained earnings/Net income} = ₹88/₹132 = .6667, \text{ or } 66.67\%$$

This ratio is called the **retention ratio** or **plowback ratio**, and it is equal to 1 minus the dividend payout ratio because everything not paid out is retained. Assuming that the payout ratio is constant, the projected dividends and addition to retained earnings will be:

$$\begin{aligned}\text{Projected dividends paid to shareholders} &= ₹165 \times .3333 = ₹\ 55 \\ \text{Projected addition to retained earnings} &= ₹165 \times .6667 = \underline{\ 110} \\ &= \underline{\underline{₹165}}\end{aligned}$$

The Balance Sheet To generate a pro forma balance sheet, we start with the most recent statement, as shown in Table 3.11.

On our balance sheet, we assume that some items vary directly with sales and others do not. For those items that vary with sales, we express each as a percentage of sales for the year just completed. When an item does not vary directly with sales, we write "n/a" for "not applicable."

For example, on the asset side, inventory is equal to 60 percent of sales (= ₹600/₹1,000) for the year just ended. We assume this percentage applies to the coming year, so for each ₹1 increase in sales, inventory will rise by ₹.60. More generally, the ratio of total assets to sales for the year just ended is ₹3,000/₹1,000 = 3, or 300 percent.

This ratio of total assets to sales is sometimes called the **capital intensity ratio**. It tells us the amount of assets needed to generate ₹1 in sales; the higher the ratio, the more capital intensive is the firm. Notice also that this ratio is the reciprocal of the total asset turnover ratio we defined previously.

For Mirza, assuming that this ratio is constant, it takes ₹3 in total assets to generate ₹1 in sales (apparently Mirza is in a relatively capital-intensive business). Therefore, if sales are to increase by ₹100, Mirza will have to increase total assets by 3 times this amount, or ₹300.

Table 3.11

MIRZA COMPANY
Balance Sheet

Assets			Liabilities and Owners' Equity		
		Percentage of Sales			Percentage of Sales
Current assets			Current liabilities		
Cash	₹ 160	16%	Accounts payable	₹ 300	30%
Accounts receivable	440	44	Notes payable	100	n/a
Inventory	600	60	Total	₹ 400	n/a
Total	₹ 1,200	120	Long-term debt	₹ 800	n/a
Fixed assets			Owners' equity		
Net plant and equipment	₹ 1,800	180	Common stock and paid-in surplus	₹ 800	n/a
			Retained earnings	1,000	n/a
			Total	₹ 1,800	n/a
Total assets	₹ 3,000	300%	Total liabilities and owners' equity	₹ 3,000	n/a

On the liability side of the balance sheet, we show accounts payable varying with sales. The reason is that we expect to place more orders with our suppliers as sales volume increases, so payables will change "spontaneously" with sales. Notes payable, on the other hand, represents short-term debt such as bank borrowing. This will not vary unless we take specific actions to change the amount, so we mark this item as "n/a."

Similarly, we use "n/a" for long-term debt because it won't automatically change with sales. The same is true for common stock and paid-in surplus. The last item on the right side, retained earnings, will vary with sales, but it won't be a percentage of sales. Instead, we will explicitly calculate the change in retained earnings based on our projected net income and dividends.

We now can construct a partial pro forma balance sheet for Mirza. We do this by using the percentages we have calculated wherever possible to estimate the projected amounts. For example, net fixed assets are 180 percent of sales; so, with a new sales level of ₹1,250, the net fixed asset amount will be 1.80 × ₹1,250 = ₹2,250, representing an increase of ₹2,250 − 1,800 = ₹450 in plant and equipment. It is important to note that for items that don't vary directly with sales, we initially assume no change and write in the original amounts. The result is shown in Table 3.12. Notice that the change in retained earnings is equal to the ₹110 addition to retained earnings we calculated earlier.

Inspecting our pro forma balance sheet, we notice that assets are projected to increase by ₹750. However, without additional financing, liabilities and equity will increase by only ₹185, leaving a shortfall of ₹750 − 185 = ₹565. We label this amount *external financing needed* (EFN).

Rather than create pro forma statements, if we were so inclined, we could calculate EFN directly as follows:

$$\text{EFN} = \frac{\text{Assets}}{\text{Sales}} \times \Delta\text{Sales} - \frac{\text{Spontaneous liabilities}}{\text{Sales}} \times \Delta\text{Sales} - \text{PM} \times \text{Projected sales} \times (1 - d) \tag{3.24}$$

In this expression, "ΔSales" is the projected change in sales (in rupees). In our example projected sales for next year are ₹1,250, an increase of ₹250 over the previous year, so ΔSales = ₹250. By "Spontaneous liabilities," we mean liabilities that naturally move up and down with sales. For Mirza, the spontaneous liabilities are the ₹300 in accounts payable. Finally, PM and d are the profit margin and dividend payout ratios, which we previously calculated as 13.2 percent and 33.33 percent, respectively. Total assets and sales are ₹3,000 and ₹1,000, respectively, so we have

$$\text{EFN} = \frac{₹3{,}000}{₹1{,}000} \times ₹250 - \frac{₹300}{₹1{,}000} \times ₹250 - .132 \times ₹1{,}250 \times (1 - .3333) = ₹565$$

In this calculation, notice that there are three parts. The first part is the projected increase in assets, which is calculated using the capital intensity ratio. The second part is the spontaneous increase in liabilities. The third part is the product of profit margin and projected sales, which is projected net income, multiplied by the retention ratio. Thus, the third part is the projected addition to retained earnings.

Table 3.12

MIRZA COMPANY
Partial Pro Forma Balance Sheet

Assets	Next Year	Change from Current Year	Liabilities and Owners' Equity	Next Year	Change from Current Year
Current assets			Current liabilities		
Cash	₹ 200	₹ 40	Accounts payable	₹ 375	₹ 75
Accounts receivable	550	110	Notes payable	100	0
Inventory	750	150	Total	₹ 475	₹ 75
Total	₹1,500	₹300	Long-term debt	₹ 800	₹ 0
Fixed assets			Owners' equity		
Net plant and equipment	₹2,250	₹450	Common stock and paid-in surplus	₹ 800	₹ 0
			Retained earnings	1,110	110
			Total	₹1,910	₹110
Total assets	₹3,750	₹750	Total liabilities and owners' equity	₹3,185	₹185
			External financing needed	₹ 565	₹565

A Particular Scenario Our financial planning model now reminds us of one of those good news–bad news jokes. The good news is we're projecting a 25 percent increase in sales. The bad news is this isn't going to happen unless Mirza can somehow raise ₹565 in new financing.

This is a good demonstration of how the planning process can point out problems and potential conflicts. If, for example, Mirza has a goal of not borrowing any additional funds and not selling any new equity, then a 25 percent increase in sales is probably infeasible.

If we take the need for ₹565 in new financing as given, we know that Mirza has three possible sources: short-term borrowing, long-term borrowing, and new equity. The choice of some combination among these three is up to management; we will illustrate only one of the many possibilities.

Suppose Mirza decides to borrow the needed funds. In this case, the firm might choose to borrow some over the short term and some over the long term. Current assets increased by ₹300 whereas current liabilities rose by only ₹75. Mirza could borrow ₹300 − 75 = ₹225 in short-term notes payable and leave total net working capital unchanged. With ₹565 needed, the remaining ₹565 − 225 = ₹340 would have to come from long-term debt. Table 3.13 shows the completed pro forma balance sheet for Mirza.

We have used a combination of short- and long-term debt as the plug here, but we emphasize that this is just one possible strategy; it is not necessarily the best one by any means. We could (and should) investigate many other scenarios. The various ratios we discussed earlier come in handy here. With the scenario we looked at, we would surely want to examine the current ratio and the total debt ratio to see if we were comfortable with the new projected debt levels.

Table 3.13

MIRZA COMPANY
Pro Forma Balance Sheet

Assets			Liabilities and Owners' Equity		
	Next Year	Change from Current Year		Next Year	Change from Current Year
Current assets			Current liabilities		
Cash	₹ 200	₹ 40	Accounts payable	₹ 375	₹ 75
Accounts receivable	550	110	Notes payable	325	225
Inventory	750	150	Total	₹ 700	₹ 300
Total	₹ 1,500	₹ 300	Long-term debt	₹ 1,140	₹ 340
Fixed assets			Owners' equity		
Net plant and equipment	₹ 2,250	₹ 450	Common stock and paid-in surplus	₹ 800	₹ 0
			Retained earnings	1,110	110
			Total	₹ 1,910	₹ 110
Total assets	₹ 3,750	₹ 750	Total liabilities and owners' equity	₹ 3,750	₹ 750

3.5 External Financing and Growth

Excel Master coverage online

External financing needed and growth are obviously related. All other things staying the same, the higher the rate of growth in sales or assets, the greater will be the need for external financing. In the previous section, we took a growth rate as given, and then we determined the amount of external financing needed to support that growth. In this section, we turn things around a bit. We will take the firm's financial policy as given and then examine the relationship between that financial policy and the firm's ability to finance new investments and thereby to grow.

We emphasize that we are focusing on growth not because growth is an appropriate goal; instead, for our purposes, growth is a convenient means of examining the interactions between investment and financing decisions. In effect, we assume that the use of growth as a basis for planning is a reflection of the very high level of aggregation used in the planning process.

THE RELATIONSHIP BETWEEN EFN AND GROWTH

The first thing we need to do is establish the relationship between EFN and growth. To do this, we introduce the simplified income statement and balance sheet for the Gowri Company in Table 3.14. Notice that we have simplified the balance sheet by combining short-term and long-term debt into a single total debt figure. Effectively, we are assuming that none of the current liabilities vary spontaneously with sales. This assumption isn't as restrictive as it sounds. If any current liabilities (such as accounts payable) vary with sales, we can assume that any such accounts have been netted out by offsetting changes in current assets. Also, we continue to combine depreciation, interest, and costs on the income statement.

Suppose the Gowri Company is forecasting next year's sales level at ₹600, a ₹100 increase. Notice that the percentage increase in sales is ₹100/₹500 = .20, or 20 percent. Using the percentage of sales approach and the figures in Table 3.14, we can prepare a pro forma income statement and balance sheet as in Table 3.15. As Table 3.15 illustrates, at a 20 percent growth rate, Gowri needs ₹100 in new assets. The projected addition to retained earnings is ₹52.8, so the external financing needed, EFN, is ₹100 − 52.8 = ₹47.2.

Notice that the debt-equity ratio for Gowri was originally (from Table 3.14) equal to ₹250/₹250 = 1.0. We will assume that the Gowri Company does not wish to sell new equity. In this case, the ₹47.2 in EFN will have to be borrowed. What will the new debt-equity ratio be? From Table 3.15, we know that total owners' equity is projected at ₹302.8. The new total debt will be the original ₹250 plus ₹47.2 in new borrowing, or ₹297.2. The debt-equity ratio falls slightly from 1.0 to ₹297.2/₹302.8 = .98.

Table 3.14

GOWRI COMPANY
Income Statement and Balance Sheet

Income Statement

Sales		₹500.0
Costs		416.5
Taxable income		₹ 83.5
Taxes (21%)		17.5
Net income		₹ 66.0
Dividends	₹22	
Addition to retained earnings	44	

Balance Sheet

Assets			Liabilities and Owners' Equity		
		Percentage of Sales			**Percentage of Sales**
Current assets	₹ 200	40%	Total debt	₹250	n/a
Net fixed assets	300	60	Owners' equity	250	n/a
Total assets	₹3,750	100%	Total liabilities and owners' equity	₹500	n/a

Table 3.15

GOWRI COMPANY Pro Forma Income Statement and Balance Sheet		
Income Statement		
Sales (projected)		₹600.0
Costs (83.3% of sales)		499.8
Taxable income		₹ 100.2
Taxes (21%)		21.0
Net income		₹ 79.2
Dividends	₹26.4	
Addition to retained earnings	52.8	

Balance Sheet

Assets		Percentage of Sales	Liabilities and Owners' Equity		Percentage of Sales
Current assets	₹240.0	40%	Total debt	₹250.0	n/a
Net fixed assets	₹360.0	60	Owners' equity	₹302.8	n/a
Total assets	₹600.0	100%	Total liabilities and owners' equity	₹552.8	n/a
			External financing needed	₹ 47.2	n/a

Table 3.16 shows EFN for several different growth rates. The projected addition to retained earnings and the projected debt-equity ratio for each scenario also are given (you should probably calculate a few of these for practice). In determining the debt-equity ratios, we assumed that any needed funds were borrowed, and we also assumed any surplus funds were used to pay off debt. For the zero growth case, the debt falls by ₹44, from ₹250 to ₹206. In Table 3.16, notice that the increase in assets required is equal to the original assets of ₹500 multiplied by the growth rate. Similarly, the addition to retained earnings is equal to the original ₹44 plus ₹44 times the growth rate.

Table 3.16 shows that for relatively low growth rates, Gowri will run a surplus, and its debt-equity ratio will decline. Once the growth rate increases to about 10 percent, however, the surplus becomes a deficit. Furthermore, as the growth rate exceeds approximately 20 percent, the debt-equity ratio passes its original value of 1.0.

Table 3.16 Growth and Projected EFN for the Gowri Company

Projected Sales Growth	Increase In Assets Required	Addition to Retained Earnings	External Financing Needed, EFN	Projected Debt-Equity Ratio
0%	₹ 0	₹44.0	–₹44.0	.70
5	25	46.2	– 21.2	.77
10	50	48.4	1.6	.84
15	75	50.6	24.4	.91
20	100	52.8	47.2	.98
25	125	55.0	70.0	1.05

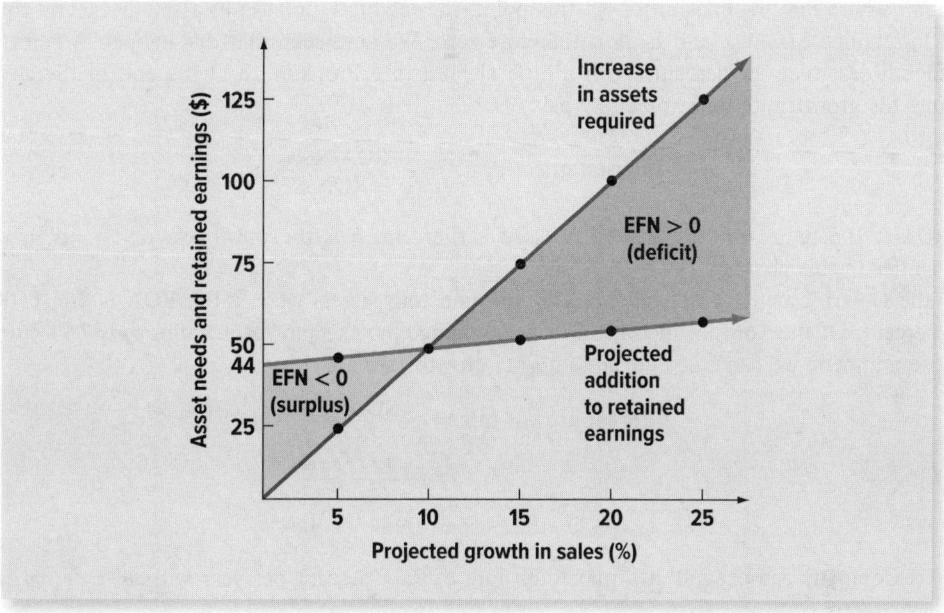

Figure 3.1 Growth and Related Financing Needed for the Gowri Company

Figure 3.1 illustrates the connection between growth in sales and external financing needed in more detail by plotting asset needs and additions to retained earnings from Table 3.16 against the growth rates. As shown, the need for new assets grows at a much faster rate than the addition to retained earnings, so the internal financing provided by the addition to retained earnings rapidly disappears.

As this discussion shows, whether a firm runs a cash surplus or deficit depends on growth. Microsoft is a good example. Its revenue growth in the 1990s was amazing, averaging well over 30 percent per year for the decade. Growth slowed noticeably over the 2000–2010 period. Nonetheless, Microsoft's combination of growth and substantial profit margins led to enormous cash surpluses. In part because Microsoft paid few dividends, the cash really piled up. In the middle of 2020, Microsoft's cash and short-term investments horde exceeded ₹136 billion.

The Indian IT behemoth Infosys Technologies saw exceptionally strong revenue growth in the decade around the dotcom boom, averaging over 100%. However, revenue growth slowed in the following decade, and Infosys kept a substantial cash balance to take advantage of acquisition opportunities, just like most other Indian IT companies. Despite a share buyback in the 2019–20 fiscal year, Infosys had cash that accounted for more than 20% of its balance sheet.

FINANCIAL POLICY AND GROWTH

Based on our preceding discussion, we see that there is a direct link between growth and external financing. In this section, we discuss two growth rates that are particularly useful in long-range planning.

The Internal Growth Rate The first growth rate of interest is the maximum growth rate that can be achieved with no external financing of any kind. We call this the **internal growth rate** because this is the rate the firm can maintain with internal financing only. In Figure 3.1, this internal growth rate is represented by the point where the two lines cross. At this point, the required increase in assets is exactly equal to the addition to retained earnings, and EFN is therefore zero. We have seen that this happens when the growth rate is slightly less than 10 percent. With a little algebra (see Problem 28 at the end of the chapter), we can define this growth rate more precisely as:

$$\text{Internal growth rate} = \frac{\text{ROA} \times b}{1 - \text{ROA} \times b} \tag{3.25}$$

where ROA is the return on assets we discussed earlier and b is the plowback, or retention, ratio, also defined earlier in this chapter.

For the Gowri Company, net income was ₹66 and total assets were ₹500. ROA is ₹66/₹500 = .132, or 13.2 percent. Of the ₹66 net income, ₹44 was retained, so the plowback ratio, b, is ₹44/₹66 = .6667. With these numbers, we can calculate the internal growth rate as:

$$\begin{aligned}\text{Internal growth rate} &= \frac{\text{ROA} \times b}{1 - \text{ROA} \times b}\\ &= \frac{.132 \times .6667}{1 - .132 \times .6667}\\ &= .0964, \text{ or } 9.64\%\end{aligned}$$

The Gowri Company can expand at a maximum rate of 9.64 percent per year without external financing.

The Sustainable Growth Rate We have seen that if the Gowri Company wishes to grow more rapidly than at a rate of 9.64 percent per year, external financing must be arranged. The second growth rate of interest is the maximum growth rate a firm can achieve with no external *equity* financing while it maintains a constant debt-equity ratio. This rate is commonly called the **sustainable growth rate** because it is the maximum rate of growth a firm can maintain without increasing its overall financial leverage.

There are various reasons a firm might wish to avoid equity sales. For example, new equity sales can be expensive because of the substantial fees that may be involved. Alternatively, the current owners may not wish to bring in new owners or contribute additional equity. Why a firm might view a particular debt-equity ratio as optimal is discussed in later chapters; for now, we will take it as given.

Based on Table 3.15, the sustainable growth rate for Gowri is approximately 20 percent because the debt-equity ratio is near 1.0 at that growth rate. The precise value can be calculated as follows (see Problem 28 at the end of the chapter):

$$\text{Sustainable growth rate} = \frac{\text{ROE} \times b}{1 - \text{ROE} \times b} \tag{3.26}$$

This is identical to the internal growth rate except that ROE, return on equity, is used instead of ROA.

For the Gowri Company net income was ₹66 and total equity was ₹250; ROE is ₹66/₹250 = .264, or 26.4 percent. The plowback ratio, b, is still .6667, so we can calculate the sustainable growth rate as:

$$\begin{aligned}\text{Sustainable growth rate} &= \frac{\text{ROE} \times b}{1 - \text{ROE} \times b}\\ &= \frac{.264 \times .6667}{1 - .264 \times .6667}\\ &= .2134, \text{ or } 21.34\%\end{aligned}$$

The Gowri Company can expand at a maximum rate of 21.34 percent per year without external equity financing.

EXAMPLE 3.5

Sustainable Growth Suppose Gowri grows at exactly the sustainable growth rate of 21.34 percent. What will the pro forma statements look like?

At a 21.34 percent growth rate, sales will rise from ₹500 to ₹606.7. The pro forma income statement will look like this:

GOWRI COMPANY Pro Forma Income Statement		
Sales (projected)		₹606.7
Costs (83.3% of sales)		505.4
Taxable income		₹ 101.3
Taxes (21%)		21.3
Net income		₹ 80.0
Dividends	₹26.7	
Addition to retained earnings	53.3	

We construct the balance sheet as we did before. Notice, in this case, that owners' equity will rise from ₹250 to ₹303.3 because the addition to retained earnings is ₹53.3.

GOWRI COMPANY Pro Forma Balance Sheet					
Assets			Liabilities and Owners' Equity		
		Percentage of Sales			Percentage of Sales
Current assets	₹242.7	40%	Total debt	₹250.0	n/a
Net fixed assets	364.0	60	Owners' equity	303.3	n/a
Total assets	₹606.7	100%	Total liabilities and owners' equity	₹553.3	n/a
			External financing needed	₹ 53.3	n/a

As illustrated, EFN is ₹53.3. If Gowri borrows this amount, total debt will rise to ₹303.3, and the debt-equity ratio will be exactly 1.0, which verifies our earlier calculation. At any other growth rate, something would have to change.

Determinants of Growth Earlier in this chapter, we saw that the return on equity, ROE, could be decomposed into its various components using the DuPont identity. Because ROE appears so prominently in the determination of the sustainable growth rate, it is obvious that the factors important in determining ROE are also important determinants of growth.

From our previous discussions, we know that ROE can be written as the product of three factors:

$$\text{ROE} = \text{Profit margin} \times \text{Total asset turnover} \times \text{Equity multiplier}$$

If we examine our expression for the sustainable growth rate, we see that anything that increases ROE will increase the sustainable growth rate by making the numerator bigger and the denominator smaller. Increasing the plowback ratio will have the same effect.

Putting it all together, what we have is that a firm's ability to sustain growth depends explicitly on the following four factors:

1. *Profit margin*: An increase in profit margin will increase the firm's ability to generate funds internally and thereby increase its sustainable growth.
2. *Dividend policy*: A decrease in the percentage of net income paid out as dividends will increase the retention ratio. This increases both internally generated equity and sustainable growth.
3. *Financial policy*: An increase in the debt-equity ratio increases the firm's financial leverage. Because this makes additional debt financing available, it increases the sustainable growth rate.
4. *Total asset turnover*: An increase in the firm's total asset turnover increases the sales generated for each Rupee in assets. This decreases the firm's need for new assets as sales grow and thereby increases the sustainable growth rate. Notice that increasing total asset turnover is the same thing as decreasing capital intensity.

The sustainable growth rate is a very useful planning number. What it illustrates is the explicit relationship between the firm's four major areas of concern: operating efficiency as measured by profit margin, dividend policy as measured by the retention ratio, financial policy as measured by the debt-equity ratio, and asset use efficiency as measured by total asset turnover.

EXAMPLE 3.6

Profit Margins and Sustainable Growth The Sundar Co. has a debt-equity ratio of .5, a profit margin of 3 percent, a dividend payout ratio of 40 percent, and a capital intensity ratio of 1. What is its sustainable growth rate? If Sundar desired a 10 percent sustainable growth rate and planned to achieve this goal by improving profit margins, what would you think?

ROE is $.03 \times 1 \times 1.5 = .045$, or 4.5%

The retention ratio is $1 - .40 = .60$.

Sustainable growth is thus $.045(.60)/[1 - .045(.60)] = .0277$, or 2.77%

For the company to achieve a 10 percent growth rate, the profit margin will have to rise. To see this, assume that sustainable growth is equal to 10 percent and then solve for profit margin, PM:

$$.10 = \text{PM}(1.5)(.6)/[1 - \text{PM}(1.5)(.6)]$$

$$\text{PM} = .1/.99 = .101, \text{ or } 10.1\%$$

For the plan to succeed, the necessary increase in profit margin is substantial, from 3 percent to about 10 percent. This may not be feasible.

Given values for all four measures, there is only one growth rate that can be achieved. This is an important point, so it bears restating:

If a firm does not wish to sell new equity and its profit margin, dividend policy, financial policy, and total asset turnover (or capital intensity) are all fixed, then there is only one possible growth rate.

Table 3.17 Summary of Internal and Sustainable Growth Rates

I.Internal Growth Rate

$$\text{Internal growth rate} = \frac{\text{ROA} \times b}{1 - \text{ROA} \times b}$$

where:

ROA = Return on assets = Net income/Total assets
b = Plowback (retention) ratio
= Addition to retained earnings/Net income

The internal growth rate is the maximum growth rate that can be achieved with no external financing of any kind.

II.Sustainable Growth Rate

$$\text{Sustainable growth rate} = \frac{\text{ROE} \times b}{1 - \text{ROE} \times b}$$

where:

ROA = Return on equity = Net income/Total equity
b = Plowback (retention) ratio
= Addition to retained earnings/Net income

The sustainable growth rate is the maximum growth rate that can be achieved with no external equity financing while maintaining a constant debt-equity ratio.

One of the primary benefits of financial planning is that it ensures internal consistency among the firm's various goals. The concept of the sustainable growth rate captures this element nicely. Also, we now see how a financial planning model can be used to test the feasibility of a planned growth rate. If sales are to grow at a rate higher than the sustainable growth rate, the firm must increase profit margins, increase total asset turnover, increase financial leverage, increase earnings retention, or sell new shares.

The two growth rates, internal and sustainable, are summarized in Table 3.17.

A NOTE ABOUT SUSTAINABLE GROWTH RATE CALCULATIONS

Commonly, the sustainable growth rate is calculated using the numerator in our expression, ROE × *b*. This causes some confusion, which we can clear up here. The issue has to do with how ROE is computed. Recall that ROE is calculated as net income divided by total equity. If total equity is taken from an ending balance sheet (as we have done consistently, and is commonly done in practice), then our formula is the correct one. However, if total equity is from the beginning of the period, then the simpler formula is the correct one.

In principle, you'll get exactly the same sustainable growth rate regardless of which way you calculate it (as long as you match up the ROE calculation with the correct formula). In reality, you may see some differences because of accounting-related complications. By the way, if you use the average of beginning and ending equity (as some advocate), yet another formula is needed. All of our comments here apply to the internal growth rate as well.

In Their Own Words

ROBERT C. HIGGINS ON SUSTAINABLE GROWTH

Most financial officers know intuitively that it takes money to make money. Rapid sales growth requires increased assets in the form of accounts receivable, inventory, and fixed plant, which, in turn, require money to pay for assets. They also know that if their company does not have the money when needed, it can literally "grow broke." The sustainable growth equation states these intuitive truths explicitly.

Sustainable growth is often used by bankers and other external analysts to assess a company's creditworthiness. They are aided in this exercise by several sophisticated computer software packages that provide detailed analyses of the company's past financial performance, including its annual sustainable growth rate.

Bankers use this information in several ways. Quick comparison of a company's actual growth rate to its sustainable rate tells the banker what issues will be at the top of management's financial agenda. If actual growth consistently exceeds sustainable growth, management's problem will be where to get the cash to finance growth. The banker thus can anticipate interest in loan products. Conversely, if sustainable growth consistently exceeds actual, the banker had best be prepared to talk about investment products because management's problem will be what to do with all the cash that keeps piling up in the till.

Bankers also find the sustainable growth equation useful for explaining to financially inexperienced small business owners and overly optimistic entrepreneurs that, for the long-run viability of their business, it is necessary to keep growth and profitability in proper balance.

Finally, comparison of actual to sustainable growth rates helps a banker understand why a loan applicant needs money and for how long the need might continue. In one instance, a loan applicant requested ₹100,000 to pay off several insistent suppliers and promised to repay in a few months when he collected some accounts receivable that were coming due. A sustainable growth analysis revealed that the firm had been growing at four to six times its sustainable growth rate and that this pattern was likely to continue in the foreseeable future. This alerted the banker that impatient suppliers were only a symptom of the much more fundamental disease of overly rapid growth, and that a ₹100,000 loan would likely prove to be only the down payment on a much larger, multiyear commitment.

SOURCE: Robert C. Higgins is Professor Emeritus of Finance at the Foster School of Business at the University of Washington. He pioneered the use of sustainable growth as a tool for financial analysis.

3.6 Some Caveats Regarding Financial Planning Models

Financial planning models do not always ask the right questions. A primary reason is that they tend to rely on accounting relationships and not financial relationships. In particular, the three basic elements of firm value tend to get left out–namely, cash flow size, risk, and timing.

Because of this, financial planning models sometimes do not produce output that gives the user many meaningful clues about what strategies will lead to increases in value. Instead, they divert the user's attention to questions concerning the association of, say, the debt-equity ratio and firm growth.

The financial model we used for the Gowri Company was simple–in fact, too simple. Our model, like many in use today, is really an accounting statement generator at heart. Such models are useful for pointing out inconsistencies and reminding us of financial needs, but they offer little guidance concerning what to do about these problems.

In closing our discussion, we should add that financial planning is an iterative process. Plans are created, examined, and modified over and over. The final plan will be a result negotiated between all the different parties to the process. In fact, long-term financial planning in most corporations relies on what might be called the Procrustes approach.[6] Upper-level management has a goal in mind, and it is up to the planning staff to rework and ultimately deliver a feasible plan that meets that goal.

The final plan therefore will implicitly contain different goals in different areas and also satisfy many constraints. For this reason, such a plan need not be a dispassionate assessment of what we think the future will bring. Rather, it may be a means of reconciling the planned activities of different groups and a way of setting common goals for the future.

However it is done, the important thing to remember is that financial planning should not become a purely mechanical exercise. If it does, it will probably focus on the wrong things. Nevertheless, the alternative to planning is stumbling into the future. Perhaps the immortal Yogi Berra (the baseball catcher, not the cartoon character) said it best: "Ya gotta watch out if you don't know where you're goin'. You just might not get there."[7]

[6] In Greek mythology, Procrustes is a giant who seizes travelers and ties them to an iron bed. He stretches them or cuts off their legs as needed to make them fit the bed.

[7] We're not *exactly* sure what this means, either, but we like the sound of it.

RESEARCH IN EMERGING MARKET CONTEXT

Kaur et al. (2022) found that external sources of finance positively impact MSMEs' innovative activities, leading to overall economic growth. External equity finance can be raised through IPOs. Yadav et al. (2023) developed an empirical model to study the relationship between key Financial Performance Indicators and IPO Offer Prices. They found that Net Asset Value (NAV), Return on Assets (RoA), Profit after Tax (PAT), and Return on Net Worth (RoNW) significantly impact IPO Offering Price. This study can help investors evaluate the value of IPO issues, allowing them to decide if the issue is worth investing in.

References

Kaur, P., Kaur, N., & Kanojia, P. (2022). Firm innovation and access to finance: firm-level evidence from India. *Journal of Financial Economic Policy*, 14(1), 93–112.

Yadav, A., Prosad, J. M., & Singh, S. (2023). Pre-IPO Financial Performance and Offer Price Estimation: Evidence from India. *Journal of Risk and Financial Management*, 16(2), 135.

Summary and Conclusions

This chapter focuses on working with information contained in financial statements. Specifically, we studied standardized financial statements, ratio analysis, and long-term financial planning.

1. We explained that differences in firm size make it difficult to compare financial statements, and we discussed how to form common-size statements to make comparisons easier and more meaningful.
2. Evaluating ratios of accounting numbers is another way of comparing financial statement information. We defined a number of the most commonly used financial ratios, and we discussed the famous DuPont identity.

3. We showed how pro forma financial statements can be generated and used to plan for future financing needs.

After studying this chapter, we hope that you have some perspective on the uses and abuses of financial statement information. You also should find that your vocabulary of business and financial terms has grown substantially.

Concept Questions

1. **Financial Ratio Analysis** A financial ratio by itself tells us little about a company because financial ratios vary a great deal across industries. There are two basic methods for analyzing financial ratios for a company: Time trend analysis and peer group analysis. In time trend analysis, you find the ratios for the company over some period, say five years, and examine how each ratio has changed over this period. In peer group analysis, you compare a company's financial ratios to those of its peers. Why might each of these analysis methods be useful? What does each tell you about the company's financial health?

2. **Industry-Specific Ratios** So-called same-store sales are a very important measure for companies as diverse as McDonald's and Target. As the name suggests, examining same-store sales means comparing revenues from the same stores or restaurants at two different points in time. Why might companies focus on same-store sales rather than total sales?

3. **Sales Forecast** Why do you think most long-term financial planning begins with sales forecasts? Put differently, why are future sales the key input?

4. **Sustainable Growth** In the chapter, we used Mirza Company to demonstrate how to calculate EFN. The ROE for Mirza is about 7.3 percent, and the plowback ratio is about 67 percent. If you calculate the sustainable growth rate for Mirza, you will find it is only 5.14 percent. In our calculation for EFN, we used a growth rate of 25 percent. Is this possible? (*Hint*: Yes. How?)

5. **EFN and Growth Rate** Broslofski Co. maintains a positive retention ratio and keeps its debt-equity ratio constant every year. When sales grow by 20 percent, the firm has a negative projected EFN. What does this tell you about the firm's sustainable growth rate? Do you know with certainty if the internal growth rate is greater than or less than 20 percent? Why? What happens to the projected EFN if the retention ratio is increased? What if the retention ratio is decreased? What if the retention ratio is zero?

6. **Common-Size Financials** One tool of financial analysis is common-size financial statements. Why do you think common-size income statements and balance sheets are used? Note that the accounting statement of cash flows is not converted into a common-size statement. Why do you think this is?

7. **Asset Utilization and EFN** One of the implicit assumptions we made in calculating the external funds needed was that the company was operating at full capacity. If the company is operating at less than full capacity, how will this affect the external funds needed?

8. **Comparing ROE and ROA** Both ROA and ROE measure profitability. Which one is more useful for comparing two companies? Why?

9. **Ratio Analysis** Consider the ratio EBITD/Assets. What does this ratio tell us? Why might it be more useful than ROA in comparing two companies?

10. **Return on Investment** A ratio that is becoming more widely used is return on investment. Return on investment is calculated as net income divided by the sum of long-term liabilities plus equity. What do you think return on investment is intended to measure? What is the relationship between return on investment and return on assets?

Use the following information to answer the next five questions: A small business called The Grandmother Calendar Company began selling personalized photo calendar kits. The kits were a hit, and sales soon sharply exceeded forecasts. The rush of orders created a huge backlog, so the company leased more space and expanded capacity, but it still could not keep up with demand. Equipment failed from overuse and quality suffered. Working capital was drained to expand production, and, at the same time, payments from customers were often delayed until the product was shipped. Unable to deliver on orders, the company became so strapped for cash that employee paychecks began to bounce. Finally, out of cash, the company ceased operations entirely three years later.

11. **Product Sales** Do you think the company would have suffered the same fate if its product had been less popular? Why or why not?
12. **Cash Flow** The Grandmother Calendar Company clearly had a cash flow problem. In the context of the cash flow analysis we developed in Chapter 2, what was the impact of customers not paying until orders were shipped?
13. **Corporate Borrowing** If the firm was so successful at selling, why wouldn't a bank or some other lender step in and provide it with the cash it needed to continue?
14. **Cash Flow** Which was the biggest culprit for the company's demise: too many orders, too little cash, or too little production capacity?
15. **Cash Flow** What are some actions a small company like The Grandmother Calendar Company can take (besides expansion of capacity) if it finds itself in a situation in which growth in sales outstrips production?
16. **Contingent Liability** What are contingent liabilities? Give a few illustrations of the same in a recent Indian context. Will contingent liability affect the share price of a company? Discuss.
17. **Contingent Assets** What are contingent assets? Give a few illustrations of the same in a recent Indian context. Will contingent asset affect the share price of a company? Discuss.

Questions and Problems

BASIC (Questions 1–10)

1. **DuPont Identity** If Rogers, Inc., has an equity multiplier of 1.43, total asset turnover of 1.87, and a profit margin of 6.05 percent, what is its ROE?
2. **Equity Multiplier and Return on Equity** Kodi Company has a debt-equity ratio of .63. Return on assets is 8.4 percent, and total equity is ₹645,000. What is the equity multiplier? Return on equity? Net income?
3. **Using the DuPont Identity** Y3K, Inc., has sales of ₹5,987, total assets of ₹2,532, and a debt-equity ratio of .57. If its return on equity is 11 percent, what is its net income?
4. **EFN** The most recent financial statements for Mixton, Inc., are shown here:

Income Statement		Balance Sheet			
Sales	₹20,300	Assets	₹47,000	Debt	₹26,900
Costs	17,100			Equity	20,100
Taxable income	₹ 3,200	Total	₹47,000	Total	₹ 47,000
Taxes (21%)	672				
Net income	₹ 2,528				

Assets and costs are proportional to sales; debt and equity are not. A dividend of ₹1,400 was paid, and the company wishes to maintain a constant payout ratio. Next year's sales are projected to be ₹23,345. What external financing is needed?

5. **Sales and Growth** The most recent financial statements for Anderson Co. are shown here:

Income Statement		Balance Sheet			
Sales	₹8,700	Current assets	₹ 4,200	Long-term debt	₹ 4,300
Costs	5,600	Fixed assets	10,400	Equity	10,300
Taxable income	₹ 3,100	Total	₹14,600	Total	₹14,600
Taxes (25%)	775				
Net income	₹2,325				

Assets and costs are proportional to sales. Long-term debt and equity are not. The company maintains a constant 40 percent dividend payout ratio and a constant debt-equity ratio. What is the maximum increase in sales that can be sustained assuming no new equity is issued?

6. **Sustainable Growth** If the Premier Corp. has an ROE of 14.1 percent and a payout ratio of 25 percent, what is its sustainable growth rate?

7. **Sustainable Growth** Assuming the following ratios are constant, what is the sustainable growth rate?

Total asset turnover = 3.20

Profit margin = 5.2%

Equity multiplier = .95

Payout ratio = 35%

8. **Calculating EFN** The most recent financial statements for Hu, Inc., are shown here (assuming no income taxes):

Income Statement		Balance Sheet			
Sales	₹9,400	Assets	₹20,300	Debt	₹ 8,400
Costs	6,730			Equity	11,900
Net income	₹2,670	Total	₹20,300	Total	₹20,300

Assets and costs are proportional to sales; debt and equity are not. No dividends are paid. Next year's sales are projected to be ₹11,092. What is the external financing needed?

9. **External Funds Needed** Dahlia Colby, CFO of Charming Florist Ltd., has created the firm's pro forma balance sheet for the next fiscal year. Sales are projected to grow by 16 percent to ₹320 million. Current assets, fixed assets, and accounts payable are 20 percent, 70 percent, and 15 percent of sales, respectively. Charming Florist pays out 30 percent of its net income in dividends. The company currently has ₹105 million of long-term debt and ₹45 million in common stock par value. The profit margin is 9 percent.

   a. Construct the current balance sheet for the firm using the projected sales figure.

   b. Based on Ms. Colby's sales growth forecast, how much does Charming Florist need in external funds for the upcoming fiscal year?

   c. Construct the firm's pro forma balance sheet for the next fiscal year and confirm the external funds needed that you calculated in part (b).

10. **Sustainable Growth Rate** The Iron River Company has an ROE of 11.05 percent and a payout ratio of 25 percent.

   a. What is the company's sustainable growth rate?

   b. Can the company's actual growth rate be different from its sustainable growth rate? Why or why not?

   c. How can the company increase its sustainable growth rate?

INTERMEDIATE (Questions 11–23)

11. **Return on Equity** Firm A and Firm B have debt-total asset ratios of 60 percent and 35 percent, respectively, and returns on total assets of 4.5 percent and 8 percent, respectively. Which firm has a greater return on equity?

12. **Ratios and Foreign Companies** Prince Albert Canning PLC had a net loss of £26,382 on sales of £315,650. What was the company's profit margin? Does the fact that these figures are quoted in a foreign currency make any difference? Why? In Rupees, sales were ₹385,815. What was the net loss in Rupees?

13. **External Funds Needed** The Optical Scam Company has forecast a sales growth rate of 15 percent for next year. The current financial statements are shown here:

Income Statement		
Sales		₹24,046,000
Costs		21,395,000
Taxable income		₹ 2,651,000
Taxes		662,750
Net income		₹ 1,988,250
Dividends	₹ 397,600	
Addition to retained earnings	1,590,650	

Balance Sheet			
Assets		**Liabilities and Owners' Equity**	
Current assets	₹ 7,245,000	Accounts payable	₹ 5,200,000
		Long-term debt	₹ 5,900,000
Fixed assets	19,380,000		
		Common stock	₹ 3,100,000
		Accumulated retained earnings	12,425,000
		Total equity	₹ 15,525,000
Total assets	₹26,625,000	Total liabilities and equity	₹26,625,000

   a. Using the equation from the chapter, calculate the external funds needed for next year.

   b. Construct the firm's pro forma balance sheet for next year and confirm the external funds needed that you calculated in part (a).

   c. Calculate the sustainable growth rate for the company.

   d. Can the company eliminate the need for external funds by changing its dividend policy? What other options are available to the company to meet its growth objectives?

14. **Days' Sales in Receivables** A company has net income of ₹213,700, a profit margin of 7.1 percent, and an accounts receivable balance of ₹126,385. Assuming 65 percent of sales are on credit, what is the company's days' sales in receivables?

15. **Ratios and Fixed Assets** The Mikado Company has a ratio of long-term debt to long-term debt plus equity of .35 and a current ratio of 1.45. Current liabilities are ₹1,140, sales are ₹8,370, profit margin is 8.3 percent, and ROE is 16.5 percent. What is the amount of the firm's net fixed assets?

16. **Calculating the Cash Coverage Ratio** Whipporwill, Inc.'s, net income for the most recent year was ₹19,382. The tax rate was 21 percent. The firm paid ₹3,681 in total interest expense and deducted ₹4,738 in depreciation expense. What was the cash coverage ratio for the year?

17. **DuPont Identity** The DuPont identity presented in the chapter is commonly referred to as the three-factor DuPont identity. Another way that the DuPont identity is expressed is the five-factor model, which is:

$$\text{ROE} = \frac{\text{Net income}}{\text{EBT}} \times \frac{\text{EBT}}{\text{EBIT}} \times \frac{\text{EBIT}}{\text{Sales}} \times \frac{\text{Sales}}{\text{Total assets}} \times \frac{\text{Total assets}}{\text{Equity}}$$

Derive the five-factor DuPont identity (EBT is earnings before tax, but after interest). What does each term measure?

18. **Common-Size and Common-Base Year Financial Statements** In addition to common-size financial statements, common-base year financial statements are often used. Common-base year financial statements are constructed by dividing the current year account value by the base year account value. The result shows the growth rate in the account. Using the following financial statements, construct the common-size balance sheet and common-base year balance sheet for the company. Use 2020 as the base year.

JARROW CORPORATION
2020 and 2021 Balance Sheets

Assets	2020	2021	Liabilities and Owners' Equity	2020	2021
Current assets			Current liabilities		
Cash	₹ 12,032	₹ 15,176	Accounts payable	₹ 61,407	₹ 64,385
Accounts receivable	30,709	34,969	Notes payable	26,228	24,735
			Total	₹ 87,635	₹ 89,120
Inventory	55,288	63,723	Long-term debt	₹ 37,500	₹ 43,500
Total	₹ 98,029	₹ 113,868	Owners' equity		
Fixed assets			Common stock and paid-in surplus	₹ 59,000	₹ 64,500
Net plant and equipment	₹362,374	₹423,995	Retained earnings	276,268	340,743
			Total	₹335,268	₹405,243
Total assets	₹460,403	₹ 537,863	Total liabilities and owners' equity	₹460,403	₹537,863

Use the following information for Problems 19, 20, and 22:

The discussion of EFN in the chapter implicitly assumed that the company was operating at full capacity. Often, this is not the case. Assume that Mirza was operating at 90 percent capacity. Full-capacity sales would be ₹1,000/.90 = ₹1,111. The balance sheet shows ₹1,800 in fixed assets. The capital intensity ratio for the company is:

Capital intensity ratio = Fixed assets/Full-capacity sales = ₹1,800/₹1,111 = 1.62

This means that Mirza needs ₹1.62 in fixed assets for every Rupee in sales when it reaches full capacity. At the projected sales level of ₹1,250, it needs ₹1,250 × 1.62 = ₹2,025 in fixed assets, which is ₹225 lower than our projection of ₹2,250 in fixed assets. So, EFN is ₹565 − 225 = ₹340.

19. **Full-Capacity Sales** Blue Sky Mfg., Inc., is currently operating at 90 percent of fixed asset capacity. Current sales are ₹575,000. How much can sales increase before any new fixed assets are needed?

20. **Fixed Assets and Capacity Usage** For the company in the previous problem, suppose fixed assets are ₹720,000 and sales are projected to grow to ₹665,000. How much in new fixed assets are required to support this growth in sales?

21. **Calculating EFN** The most recent financial statements for Crosby, Inc., follow. Sales for 2022 are projected to grow by 20 percent. Interest expense will remain constant; the tax rate and the dividend payout rate will also remain constant. Costs, other expenses, current assets, fixed assets, and accounts payable increase spontaneously with sales. If the firm is operating at full capacity and no new debt or equity is issued, what external financing is needed to support the 20 percent growth rate in sales?

CROSBY, INC.
2021 Income Statement

Sales		₹686,530
Costs		554,420
Other expenses		14,020
Earnings before interest and taxes		₹ 118,090
Interest expense		12,090
Taxable income		₹ 106,000
Taxes (21%)		22,260
Net income		₹ 83,740
Dividends	₹27,475	
Addition to retained earnings	56,265	

CROSBY, INC.
Balance Sheet as of December 31, 2021

Assets		Liabilities and Owners' Equity	
Current assets		Current liabilities	
Cash	₹ 20,940	Accounts payable	₹ 53,790
Accounts receivable	31,970	Notes payable	13,215
Inventory	71,320	Total	₹ 67,005
Total	₹124,230	Long-term debt	₹127,500
		Owners' equity	
Fixed assets		Common stock and paid-in surplus	₹105,000
Net plant and equipment	₹341,980	Retained earnings	166,705
Total assets	₹466,210	Total	₹271,705
		Total liabilities and owners' equity	₹466,210

22. **Capacity Usage and Growth** In the previous problem, suppose the firm was operating at only 80 percent capacity in 2021. What is EFN now?

23. **Calculating EFN** In Problem 21, suppose the firm wishes to keep its debt-equity ratio constant. What is EFN now?

CHALLENGE (Questions 24–30)

24. **EFN and Internal Growth** Redo Problem 21 using sales growth rates of 15 and 25 percent in addition to 20 percent. Illustrate graphically the relationship between EFN and the growth rate and use this graph to determine the relationship between them.

25. **EFN and Sustainable Growth** Redo Problem 23 using sales growth rates of 30 and 35 percent in addition to 20 percent. Assume the company wishes to keep its debt-equity ratio constant. Illustrate graphically the relationship between EFN and the growth rate and use this graph to determine the relationship between them.

26. **Constraints on Growth** Tinsley, Inc., wishes to maintain a growth rate of 12 percent per year and a debt-equity ratio of .55. The profit margin is 6.2 percent, and the ratio of total assets to sales is constant at 1.05. Is this growth rate possible? To answer, determine what the dividend payout ratio must be. How do you interpret the result?

27. **EFN** We define the following variables as:

$$\begin{aligned} S &= \text{Previous year's sales} \\ A &= \text{Total assets} \\ E &= \text{Total equity} \\ g &= \text{Projected growth in sales} \\ PM &= \text{Profit margin} \\ b &= \text{Retention (plowback) ratio} \end{aligned}$$

Assuming that all debt is constant, show that EFN can be written as:

$$\text{EFN} = -\ \text{PM(S)}b + [\text{A} - \text{PM(S)}b] \times g$$

[*Hint*: Asset needs will equal A × g. The addition to retained earnings will equal PM(S)b × (1 + g).]

28. **Sustainable Growth Rate** Based on the results in Problem 27, show that the internal and sustainable growth rates can be calculated as shown in Equations 3.25 and 3.26. (*Hint*: For the internal growth rate, set EFN equal to zero and solve for g.)

29. **Sustainable Growth Rate** In the chapter, we discussed one calculation of the sustainable growth rate as:

$$\text{Sustainable growth rate} = \frac{\text{ROE} \times b}{1 - \text{ROE} \times b}$$

In practice, probably the most commonly used calculation of the sustainable growth rate is ROE × b. This equation is identical to the sustainable growth rate equation presented in the chapter if the ROE is calculated using the beginning-of-period equity. Derive this equation from the equation presented in the chapter.

30. **Sustainable Growth Rate** Use the sustainable growth rate equations from the previous problem to answer the following questions. Simone, Inc., had total assets of ₹430,000 and equity of ₹260,000 at the beginning of the year. At the end of the year, the company had total assets of ₹470,000. During the year, the company sold no new equity. Net income for the year was ₹80,000 and dividends were ₹44,000. What is the sustainable growth rate for the company? What is the sustainable growth rate if you calculate ROE based on the beginning-of-period equity?

Excel Master It! Problem

Excel Master coverage online

Financial planning can be more complex than the percentage of sales approach indicates. Often, the assumptions behind the percentage of sales approach may be too simple. A more sophisticated model allows important items to vary without being a strict percentage of sales.

Consider a new model in which depreciation is calculated as a percentage of beginning fixed assets and interest expense depends directly on the amount of debt. Debt is still the plug variable. Note that because depreciation and interest now do not necessarily vary directly with sales, the profit margin is no longer constant. Also, for the same reason, taxes and dividends will no longer be a fixed percentage of sales. The parameter estimates used in the new model are:

Cost percentage = Costs/Sales

Depreciation rate = Depreciation/Beginning fixed assets

Interest rate = Interest paid/Total debt

Tax rate = Taxes/Net income

Payout ratio = Dividends/Net income

Capital intensity ratio = Fixed assets/Sales

Fixed assets ratio = Fixed assets/Total assets

The model parameters can be determined by whatever methods the company deems appropriate. For example, they might be based on average values for the last several years, industry standards, subjective estimates, or even company targets. Alternatively, sophisticated statistical techniques can be used to estimate them.

The Yasmin Company is preparing its pro forma financial statements for the next year using this model. The abbreviated financial statements are presented below.

Sales growth		20%
Tax rate		21%
Income Statement		
Sales		₹780,000
Costs		415,000
Depreciation		135,000
Interest		68,000
Taxable income		₹ 162,000
Taxes		55,080
Net income		₹ 106,920
Dividends	₹30,000	
Additions to retained earnings	76,920	

Balance Sheet

Assets		Liabilities and Equity	
Current assets	₹ 240,000	Total debt	₹ 880,000
Net fixed assets	1,350,000	Owners' equity	710,000
Total assets	₹1,590,000	Total debt and equity	₹1,590,000

a. Calculate each of the parameters necessary to construct the pro forma balance sheet.

b. Construct the pro forma balance sheet. What is the total debt necessary to balance the pro forma balance sheet?

c. In this financial planning model, show that it is possible to solve algebraically for the amount of new borrowing.

Mini Case

RATIOS AND FINANCIAL PLANNING AT EAST COAST YACHTS

Dan Ervin was recently hired by East Coast Yachts to assist the company with its short-term financial planning and also to evaluate the company's financial performance. Dan graduated from college five years ago with a finance degree, and he has been employed in the treasury department of a *Fortune* 500 company since then.

East Coast Yachts was founded 10 years ago by Larissa Warren. The company's operations are located near Hilton Head Island, South Carolina, and the company is structured as an LLC. The company has manufactured custom midsize, high-performance yachts for clients over this period, and its products have received high reviews for safety and reliability. The company's yachts also have recently received the highest award for customer satisfaction. The yachts are primarily purchased by wealthy individuals for pleasure use. Occasionally, a yacht is manufactured for purchase by a company for business purposes.

The custom yacht industry is fragmented with a number of manufacturers. As with any industry, there are market leaders, but the diverse nature of the industry ensures that no manufacturer dominates the market. The competition in the market, as well as the product cost, ensures that attention to detail is a necessity. For example,

EAST COAST YACHTS
2022 Income Statement

Sales		₹185,250,000
Cost of goods sold		136,125,000
Other expenses		22,169,000
Depreciation		6,054,000
Earnings before interest and taxes (EBIT)		₹ 20,902,000
Interest		3,336,000
Taxable income		₹ 17,566,000
Taxes (21%)		3,688,860
Net income		₹ 13,877,140
Dividends	₹6,340,000	
Additions to retained earnings	7,537,140	

EAST COAST YACHTS
Balance Sheet as of December 31, 2022

Assets		Liabilities & Equity	
Current assets		Current liabilities	
Cash	₹ 2,891,400	Accounts payable	₹ 5,582,200
Accounts receivable	5,201,500	Notes payable	12,621,500
Inventory	5,832,100	Total	₹ 18,203,700
Total	₹ 13,925,000		
Fixed assets		Long-term debt	₹ 32,100,000
Net plant and equipment	₹ 89,303,400		
		Shareholders' equity	
		Common stock	₹ 4,912,000
		Retained earnings	48,012,700
		Total equity	₹ 52,924,700
Total assets	₹103,228,400	Total liabilities and equity	₹103,228,400

Yacht Industry Ratios

	Lower Quartile	Median	Upper Quartile
Current ratio	.50	1.43	1.89
Quick ratio	.21	.38	.62
Total asset turnover	.68	.85	1.38
Inventory turnover	6.85	9.15	16.13
Receivables turnover	6.27	11.81	21.45
Debt ratio	.44	.52	.61
Debt-equity ratio	.79	1.08	1.56
Equity multiplier	1.79	2.08	2.56
Interest coverage	5.18	8.06	9.83
Profit margin	4.05%	6.98%	9.87%
Return on assets	6.05%	10.53%	15.83%
Return on equity	9.93%	16.54%	28.14%

East Coast Yachts will spend 80 to 100 hours on hand-buffing the stainless steel stem-iron, which is the metal cap on the yacht's bow that conceivably could collide with a dock or another boat.

To get Dan started with his analyses, Larissa has provided the financial statements. Dan has gathered the industry ratios for the yacht manufacturing industry.

1. Calculate all of the ratios listed in the industry table for East Coast Yachts.
2. Compare the performance of East Coast Yachts to the industry as a whole. For each ratio, comment on why it might be viewed as positive or negative relative to the industry. Suppose you create an inventory ratio calculated as inventory divided by current liabilities. How do you interpret this ratio? How does East Coast Yachts compare to the industry average?
3. Calculate the sustainable growth rate of East Coast Yachts. Calculate EFN and prepare pro forma income statements and balance sheets assuming growth at precisely this rate. Recalculate the ratios in the previous question. What do you observe?
4. East Coast Yachts is unlikely to be willing to raise external equity capital, in part because the owners don't want to dilute their existing ownership and control positions. However, East Coast Yachts is planning for a growth rate of 20 percent next year. What are your conclusions and recommendations about the feasibility of East Coast's expansion plans?
5. Most assets can be increased as a percentage of sales. For example, cash can be increased by any amount. However, fixed assets often must be increased in specific amounts because it is impossible to buy part of a new plant or machine. In this case, a company has a "staircase" or "lumpy" fixed cost structure. Assume that East Coast Yachts is currently producing at 100 percent of capacity. As a result, to expand production, the company must set up an entirely new line at a cost of ₹25 million. Calculate the new EFN with this assumption. What does this imply about capacity utilization for East Coast Yachts next year?

4

PART II: VALUATION AND CAPITAL BUDGETING

Discounted Cash Flow Valuation

The signing of big-name athletes is often accompanied by great fanfare, but the numbers can be misleading. For example, in late 2019, catcher Yasmani Grandal reached a deal with the Chicago White Sox, signing a contract with a reported value of ₹73 million. Not bad, especially for someone who makes a living using the "tools of ignorance" (jock jargon for a catcher's equipment). And, in 2020, the Miami Dolphins signed safety Byron Jones to an ₹82.5 million contract.

It looks like Yasmani and Byron did pretty well, but then there was quarterback Patrick Mahomes, who signed a 12-year contract to play for the Kansas City Chiefs. Patrick's contract had a value of ₹477.6 million, but this amount was actually payable over multiple years. The contract consisted of ₹10.825 million to be paid in 2020, plus ₹466.8 million to be paid in the years 2021 through 2031. Yasmani's and Byron's payments were similarly spread over time. Because all three contracts called for payments that are made at future dates, we must consider the time value of money, which means none of these players received the quoted amounts. How much did they really get? This chapter gives you the "tools of knowledge" to answer this question.

Please visit us at **rwjcorporatefinance.blogspot.com** for the latest developments in the world of corporate finance.

4.1 Valuation: The One-Period Case

Jivan Pandey is trying to sell a piece of raw land in Junagadh. Yesterday he was offered ₹10,000 for the property. He was ready to accept the offer when another individual offered him ₹11,424. However, the second offer was to be paid a year from now. Jivan has satisfied himself that both buyers are honest and financially solvent, so he has no fear that the offer he selects will fall through. These two offers are pictured as cash flows in Figure 4.1. Which offer should Jivan choose?

Sadanand Tiwari, Jivan's financial advisor, points out that if Jivan takes the first offer, he could invest the ₹10,000 in the bank at a rate of 12 percent. At the end of one year, he would have:

$$\underset{\text{Return of principal}}{₹10{,}000} + \underset{\text{Interest}}{(.12 \times ₹10{,}000)} = ₹10{,}000 \times 1.12 = ₹11{,}200$$

Because this is less than the ₹11,424 Jivan could receive from the second offer, Sadanand recommends that he take the latter offer. This analysis uses the concept of **future value (FV)** or **compound value**, which is the

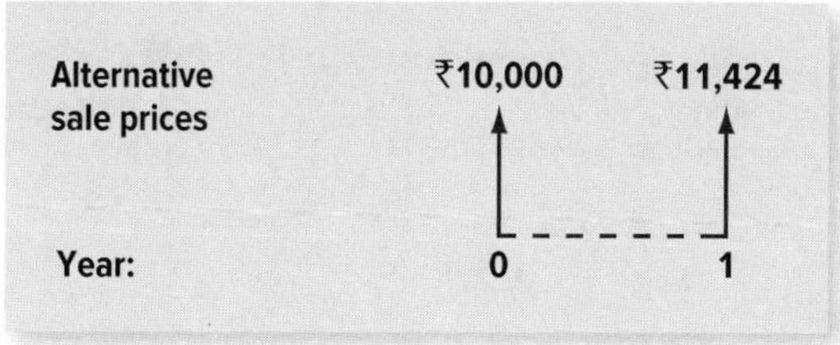

Figure 4.1 Cash Flow for Jivan Pandey's Sale

value of a sum after investing over one or more periods. The compound, or future, value of ₹10,000 at 12 percent is ₹11,200.

An alternative method employs the concept of **present value (PV)**. One can determine present value by asking the following question: How much money must Jivan put in the bank today so that he will have ₹11,424 next year? We can write this algebraically as:

$$\text{PV} \times 1.12 = ₹11{,}424$$

We want to solve for PV, the amount of money that yields ₹11,424 if invested at 12 percent today. Solving for PV, we have:

$$\text{PV} = \frac{₹11{,}424}{1.12} = ₹10{,}200$$

The formula for PV can be written as follows:

Present Value of Investment

$$\text{PV} = \frac{\text{FV}_1}{1 + r} \tag{4.1}$$

where FV_1 is future value at Year 1 and r is the rate of return that Jivan Pandey requires on his land sale. It is sometimes referred to as the *discount rate*.

Present value analysis tells us that a payment of ₹11,424 to be received next year has a present value of ₹10,200 today. In other words, at a 12 percent interest rate, Jivan is indifferent between ₹10,200 today or ₹11,424 next year. If you gave him ₹10,200 today, he could put it in the bank and receive ₹11,424 next year.

Because the second offer has a present value of ₹10,200, whereas the first offer is for ₹10,000, present value analysis also indicates that Jivan should take the second offer. In other words, both future value analysis and present value analysis lead to the same decision. As it turns out, present value analysis and future value analysis must always lead to the same decision.

As simple as this example is, it contains the basic principles that we will be working with over the next few chapters. We now use another example to develop the concept of net present value.

Frequently, financial analysts want to determine the exact *cost* or *benefit* of a decision. In Example 4.1, we evaluate the decision to buy this year and sell next year.

EXAMPLE 4.1

Present Value Dimpy Mishra, a financial analyst at Kolte Patil Developers, a leading real estate firm, is thinking about recommending that Kolte Patil Developers invest in a piece of land that costs ₹85,000. She is certain that next year the land will be worth ₹91,000, a sure ₹6,000 gain. Given that the interest rate in similar alternative investments is 10 percent, should Kolte Patil Developers undertake the investment in land? Dimpy's choice is described in Figure 4.2 with the cash flow timeline.

(continued)

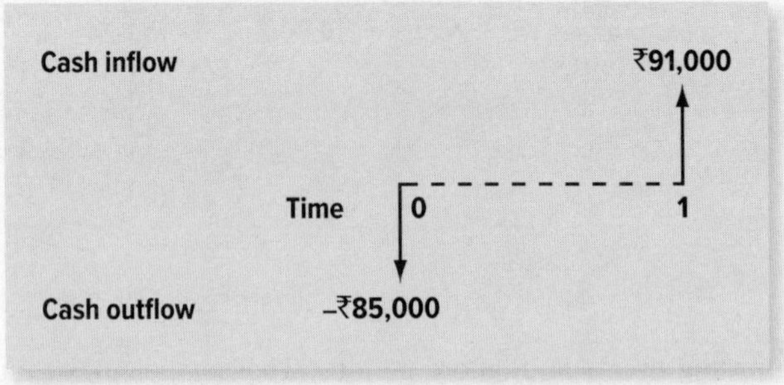

Figure 4.2 Cash Flows for Land Investment

A moment's thought should be all it takes to convince her that this is not an attractive business deal. By investing ₹85,000 in the land, she will have ₹91,000 available next year. Suppose, instead, that Kolte Patil Developers puts the same ₹85,000 into alternative investments. At the interest rate of 10 percent, this ₹85,000 would grow to:

$$(1 + .10) \times ₹85{,}000 = ₹93{,}500$$

next year.

It would be foolish to buy the land when investing the same ₹85,000 in similar alternative investments would produce an extra ₹2,500 (that is, ₹93,500 from the bank minus ₹91,000 from the land investment). This is a future value calculation.

Alternatively, she could calculate the present value of the sale price next year as:

$$\text{Present value} = \frac{₹91{,}000}{1.10} = ₹82{,}727.27$$

The benefit of the decision to purchase the land today is:

$$-₹2{,}273 \;=\; \underset{\substack{\text{Cost of land}\\ \text{today}}}{-₹85{,}000} \;+\; \underset{\substack{\text{Present value of}\\ \text{next year's sales price}}}{\frac{₹91{,}000}{1.10}}$$

Because the present value of next year's sales price is less than this year's purchase price of ₹85,000, present value analysis also indicates that she should not recommend purchasing the property.

The formula for net present value can be written as follows:

Net Present Value of Investment

$$\text{NPV} = -\text{Cost} + \text{PV} \tag{4.2}$$

Equation 4.2 says that the value of the investment is –₹2,273, after stating all the benefits and all the costs as of Year 0. We say that –₹2,273 is the **net present value (NPV)** of the investment. That is, NPV is the present value of future cash flows minus the present value of the cost of the investment. Because the net present value is negative, Dimpy should not recommend purchasing the land.

Both the Jivan and the Dimpy examples deal with a high degree of certainty. That is, Jivan knows with a high degree of certainty that he could sell his land for ₹11,424 next year. Similarly, Dimpy knows with a high degree of certainty that Kolte Patil Developers could receive ₹91,000 for selling its land. Unfortunately, businesspeople frequently do not know future cash flows. This uncertainty is addressed in the next example.

EXAMPLE 4.2

Uncertainty and Valuation Hindustan Artworks Ltd., is a firm that speculates in modern paintings. The manager is thinking of buying an original M F Hussain for ₹400,000 with the intention of selling it at the end of one year. The manager expects that the painting will be worth ₹480,000 in one year. The relevant cash flows are depicted in Figure 4.3.

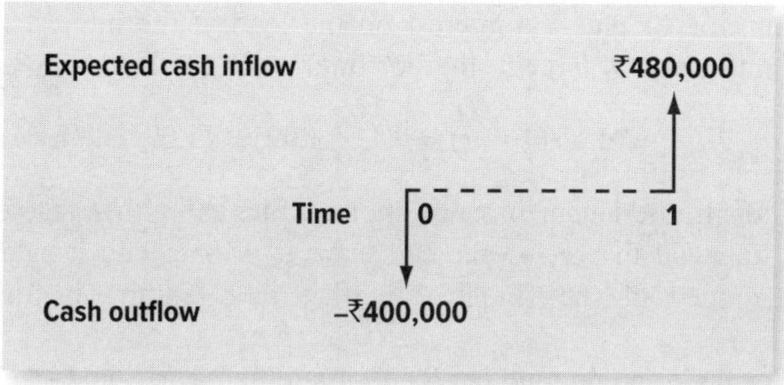

Figure 4.3 Cash Flows for Investment in Painting

Of course, this is only an expectation—the painting could be worth more or less than ₹480,000. Suppose the guaranteed interest rate granted by banks is 10 percent. Should the firm purchase the piece of art?

Our first thought might be to discount at the interest rate, yielding:

$$\frac{₹480,000}{1.10} = ₹436,364$$

Because ₹436,364 is greater than ₹400,000, it looks at first glance as if the painting should be purchased. However, 10 percent is the return one can earn on a riskless investment. Because the painting is quite risky, a higher discount rate is called for. The manager chooses a rate of 25 percent to reflect this risk. In other words, he argues that a 25 percent expected return is fair compensation for an investment as risky as this painting.

The present value of the painting becomes:

$$\frac{₹480,000}{1.25} = ₹384,000$$

At this interest rate, the painting is overpriced at ₹400,000 and the manager should not make the purchase.

The preceding analysis is typical of decision making in today's corporations, though real-world examples are, of course, much more complex. Unfortunately, any example with risk poses a problem not faced in a riskless example. Conceptually, the correct discount rate for an expected cash flow is the expected return available in the market on other investments of the same risk. This is the appropriate discount rate to apply because it represents an economic opportunity cost to investors. It is the expected return they will require before committing funding to a project. However, the selection of the discount rate for a risky investment is a difficult task. We don't know at this point whether the discount rate on the painting in Example 4.2 should be 10 percent, 15 percent, 25 percent, or some other percentage.

Because the choice of a discount rate is so difficult, we merely wanted to broach the subject here. We must wait until the specific material on risk and return is covered in later chapters before a risk-adjusted analysis can be presented.

4.2 The Multiperiod Case

The previous section presented the calculation of future value and present value for one period only. We will now perform the calculations for the multiperiod case.

FUTURE VALUE AND COMPOUNDING

Suppose an individual were to make a loan of ₹1. At the end of the first year, the borrower would owe the lender the principal amount of ₹1 plus the interest on the loan at the interest rate of r. For the specific case where the interest rate is, say, 9 percent, the borrower owes the lender:

$$₹1 \times (1 + r) = ₹1 \times 1.09 = ₹1.09$$

At the end of the year, though, the lender has two choices. She can either take the ₹1.09–or, more generally, $(1 + r)$–out of the financial market or she can leave it in and lend it again for a second year. The process of leaving the money in the financial market and lending it for another year is called **compounding**.

Suppose the lender decides to compound her loan for another year. She does this by taking the proceeds from her first one-year loan, ₹1.09, and lending this amount for the next year. At the end of next year, then, the borrower will owe her:

$$₹1 \times (1 + r) \times (1 + r) = ₹1 \times (1 + r)^2 = 1 + 2r + r^2$$
$$₹1 \times 1.09 \times 1.09 = ₹1 \times 1.09^2 = ₹1 + .18 + .0081 = ₹1.1881$$

This is the total she will receive two years from now by compounding the loan.

By providing a ready opportunity for lending, the capital market enables the investor to transform ₹1 today into ₹1.1881 at the end of two years. At the end of three years, the total cash will be ₹1 × 1.09^3 = ₹1.2950.

The most important point to notice is that the total amount the lender receives is not just the ₹1 that she lent plus two years' worth of interest on ₹1:

$$2 \times r = 2 \times ₹.09 = ₹.18$$

The lender also gets back an amount r^2, which is the interest in the second year on the interest that was earned in the first year. The term $2 \times r$ represents **simple interest** over the two years, and the term r^2 is referred to as the *interest on interest*. In our example, this latter amount is exactly:

$$r^2 = .09^2 = .0081, \text{ or } ₹.0081$$

When cash is invested at **compound interest**, each interest payment is reinvested. With simple interest, the interest is not reinvested. Benjamin Franklin's statement, "Money makes money and the money that money makes makes more money," is a colorful way of explaining compound interest. The difference between compound interest and simple interest is illustrated in Figure 4.4. In this example, the difference does not amount to much because the loan is for ₹1. If the loan were for ₹1 million, the lender would receive ₹1,188,100 in two years' time. Of this amount, ₹8,100 is interest on interest. The lesson is that those small numbers beyond the decimal point can add up to large rupee amounts when the transactions are for large amounts. In addition, the longer-lasting the loan or the greater the interest rate, the more important interest on interest becomes.

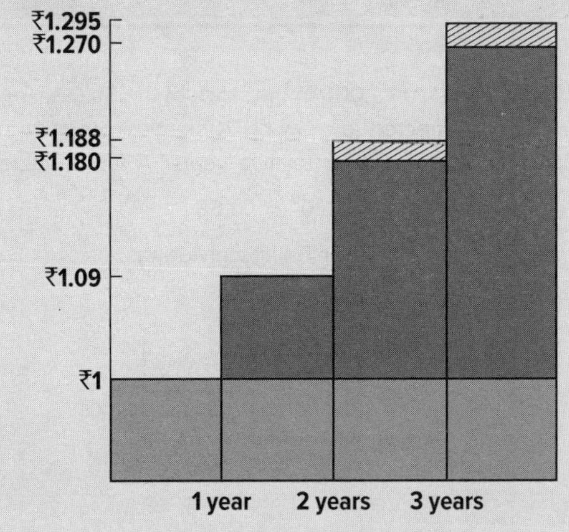

The area with slanting lines indicates the difference between compound and simple interest. The difference is substantial over a period of many years or decades.

Figure 4.4 Simple and Compound Interest

The general formula for an investment over many periods can be written as follows:

Future Value of an Investment

$$\text{FV} = \text{PV} \times (1 + r)^t \tag{4.3}$$

where PV is the present value, r is the interest rate per period, and t is the number of periods over which the cash is invested.

EXAMPLE 4.3

Interest on Interest Sarla Mistry has put ₹500 in a savings account at the Mussoorie Cooperative Bank. The account earns 7 percent, compounded annually. How much will she have at the end of three years? The answer is:

$$₹500 \times 1.07 \times 1.07 \times 1.07 = ₹500 \times 1.07^3 = ₹612.52$$

Figure 4.5 illustrates the growth of Sarla account.

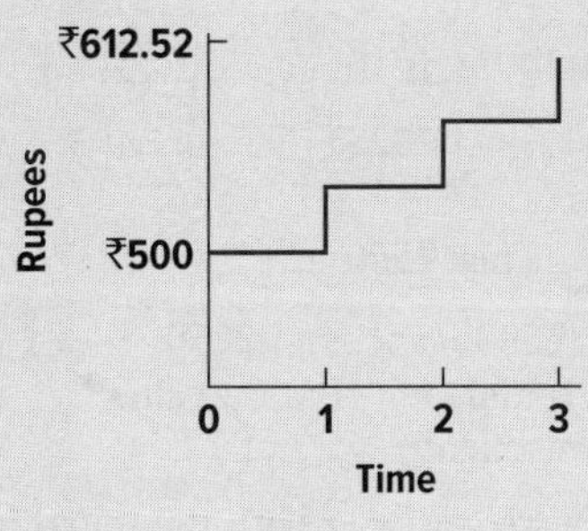

Figure 4.5 Sarla Mistry's Savings Account

EXAMPLE 4.4

Compound Growth Jaswant Gupta invested ₹1,000 in the stock of the Salasar Balaji Company. The company pays a current dividend of ₹2, which is expected to grow by 20 percent per year for the next two years. What will the dividend of the Salasar Balaji Company be after two years? A future value calculation gives:

$$₹2 \times 1.20^2 = ₹2.88$$

Figure 4.6 illustrates the increasing value of Salasar Balaji's dividends.

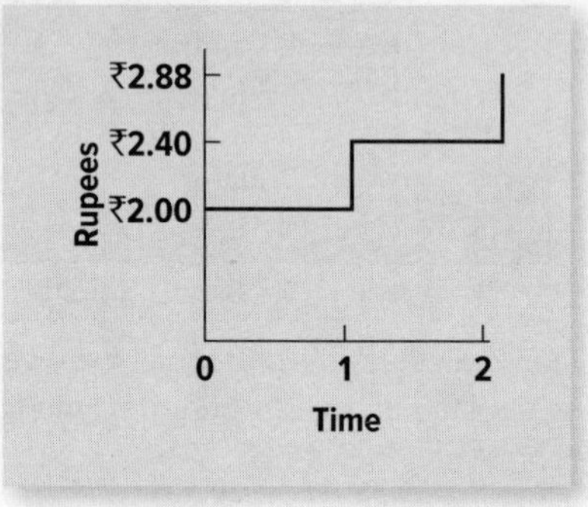

Figure 4.6 The Growth of the Salasar Balaji's Dividends

The two previous examples can be calculated several ways. The computations could be done by hand, by calculator, by spreadsheet, or with the help of a table. We will introduce spreadsheets shortly and we show how to use a calculator in Appendix 4B on the website. The appropriate table is Table A.3, which appears in the back of the text. This table shows the *future value of ₹1 at the end of* t *periods*. The table is used by locating the appropriate interest rate on the horizontal and the appropriate number of periods on the vertical. Sarla would look at the following portion of Table A.3:

	Interest Rate		
Period	6%	7%	8%
1	1.0600	1.0700	1.0800
2	1.1236	1.1449	1.1664
3	1.1910	1.2250	1.2597
4	1.2625	1.3108	1.3605

She could calculate the future value of her ₹500 as:

$$\underset{\text{Initial investment}}{₹500} \times \underset{\text{Future value of ₹1}}{1.2250} = ₹612.50$$

In the example concerning Sarla, we gave you both the initial investment and the interest rate and then asked you to calculate the future value. Alternatively, the interest rate could have been unknown, as shown in the following example.

EXAMPLE 4.5

Finding the Rate Fatimah, who recently won ₹20,000 in the lottery, wants to buy a car in five years. Fatimah Bilal estimates that the car will cost ₹32,210 at that time. His cash flows are displayed in Figure 4.7.

What interest rate must he earn to be able to afford the car?

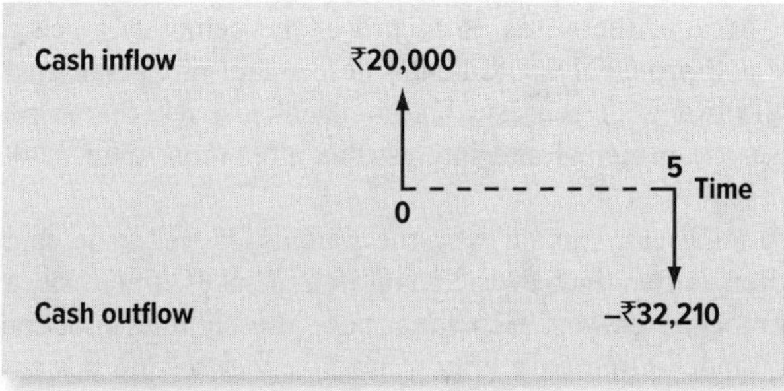

Figure 4.7 Cash Flows for Purchase of Car

The ratio of purchase price to initial cash is:

$$\frac{₹32{,}210}{₹20{,}000} = 1.6105$$

He must earn an interest rate that allows ₹1 to become ₹1.6105 in five years. Table A.3 tells us that an interest rate of 10 percent will allow him to purchase the car.

We can express the problem algebraically as:

$$₹20{,}000 \times (1 + r)^5 = ₹32{,}210$$

where r is the interest rate needed to purchase the car. Because ₹32,210/₹20,000 = 1.6105, we have:

$$(1 + r)^5 = 1.6105$$
$$r = .10, \text{ or } 10\%$$

The table, a spreadsheet, or a calculator can be used to solve for r.

THE POWER OF COMPOUNDING: A DIGRESSION

Most people who have had any experience with compounding are impressed with its power over long periods. We can show how by looking at the stock market. Ibbotson and Sinquefield calculated what the stock market returned as a whole from 1926 through 2020.[1] They find that ₹1 placed in large U.S. stocks at the beginning of 1926 would have been worth ₹10,944.66 at the end of 2020. This is 10.29 percent compounded annually for 95 years–that is, 1.1029^{95} = ₹10,944.66.

The example illustrates the great difference between compound and simple interest. At 10.29 percent, simple interest on ₹1 is 10.29 cents a year. Simple interest over 95 years is ₹10.77 (= ₹1 + 95 × ₹.1077). This is quite a bit below the ₹10,944.66 that was obtained by reinvestment of all dividends and capital gains.

[1] R. G. Ibbotson and R. A. Sinquefield, *Stocks, Bonds, Bills, and Inflation* [SBBI] (Charlottesville, VA: Financial Analysis Research Foundation, 1982). Updated by Morningstar, 2021.

The results are more impressive over even longer periods. A person with no experience in compounding might think that the value of ₹1 at the end of 190 years would be twice the value of ₹1 at the end of 95 years, if the yearly rate of return stayed the same. Actually the value of ₹1 at the end of 190 years would be the *square* of the value of ₹1 at the end of 95 years. That is, if the annual rate of return remained the same, a ₹1 investment in common stocks would be worth ₹119,785,582.52 (= ₹1 × 10,944.66 × 10,944.66).

A few years ago, an archaeologist unearthed a relic stating that Julius Caesar lent the Roman equivalent of one penny to someone. Because there was no record of the penny ever being repaid, the archaeologist wondered what the interest and principal would be if a descendant of Caesar tried to collect from a descendant of the borrower in the twentieth century. The archaeologist felt that a rate of 6 percent might be appropriate. To his surprise, the principal and interest due after more than 2,000 years was vastly greater than the entire wealth on earth.

The power of compounding can explain why the parents of well-to-do families frequently bequeath wealth to their grandchildren rather than to their children. That is, they skip a generation. The parents would rather make the grandchildren very rich than make the children moderately rich. We have found that in these families the grandchildren have a more positive view of the power of compounding than do the children.

EXAMPLE 4.6

Seward's Folly? U.S. Secretary of State William Seward negotiated the purchase of Alaska from Russia in 1867. The United States paid ₹7.2 million in exchange for 586,412 square miles of new land. Opponents of the deal mockingly labeled the transaction "Seward's Folly" because they believed the newly acquired land was a useless icebox. Did the United States really get a bad deal? If Russia had invested the ₹7.2 million at 5 percent (tax free), it would now, 155 years later, be worth about ₹13.9 billion. Today, Alaska, with its wealth of natural resources, is undoubtedly worth much more than ₹13.9 billion, so at a 5 percent rate of return, the Russians got the worst of the deal. If Russia had instead invested at 10 percent, the amount of money they received would be worth about:

$$₹7.2(1 + r)^t = ₹7.2 \times 1.1^{155} = ₹18.8 \text{ trillion}$$

This is a lot of money. In fact, ₹18.8 trillion is worth almost as much as the estimated combined value of all land in the contiguous United States today. However, note that no one in the history of the world has ever been able to find an investment yielding 10 percent every year for 155 years.

PRESENT VALUE AND DISCOUNTING

We now know that an annual interest rate of 9 percent enables the investor to transform ₹1 today into ₹1.1881 two years from now. In addition, we would like to know the following:

How much would an investor need to lend today so that she could receive ₹1 two years from today?

Algebraically, we can write this as:

$$\text{PV} \times 1.09^2 = ₹1$$

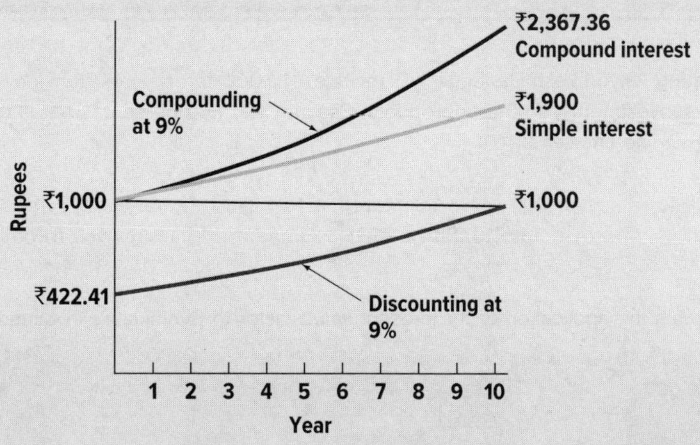

The top line shows the growth of ₹1,000 at compound interest with the funds invested at 9 percent: ₹1,000 × 1.09^{10} = ₹2,367.36. Simple interest is shown on the next line. It is ₹1,000 + [10 × (₹1,000 × .09)] = ₹1,900. The bottom line shows the discounted value of ₹1,000 if the interest rate is 9 percent.

Figure 4.8 Compounding and Discounting

In the preceding equation, PV stands for present value, the amount of money we must lend today to receive ₹1 in two years' time.

Solving for PV in this equation, we have:

$$\text{PV} = \frac{₹1}{1.1881} = ₹.84$$

This process of calculating the present value of a future cash flow is called **discounting**. It is the opposite of compounding. The difference between compounding and discounting is illustrated in Figure 4.8.

To be certain that ₹.84 is in fact the present value of ₹1 to be received in two years, we must check whether or not, if we lent ₹.84 today and rolled over the loan for two years, we would get exactly ₹1 back. If this were the case, the capital markets would be saying that ₹1 received in two years' time is equivalent to having ₹.84 today. Checking the exact numbers, we get:

$$₹.84168 \times 1.09 \times 1.09 = ₹1$$

In other words, when we have capital markets with a certain interest rate of 9 percent, we are indifferent between receiving ₹.84 today or ₹1 in two years. We have no reason to treat these two choices differently from each other because if we had ₹.84 today and lent it out for two years, it would return ₹1 to us at the end of that time. The value .84 [$= 1/1.09^2$] is called the **present value factor**. It is the factor used to calculate the present value of a future cash flow.

In the multiperiod case, the formula for PV can be written as follows:

Present Value of Investment

$$\text{PV} = \frac{\text{FV}_t}{(1 + r)^t} \tag{4.4}$$

Here, FV_t is the cash flow at Year t and r is the appropriate discount rate.

EXAMPLE 4.7

Multiperiod Discounting Byomkesh Banerjee will receive ₹10,000 three years from now. Byomkesh can earn 8 percent on his investments, so the appropriate discount rate is 8 percent. What is the present value of his future cash flow? The answer is:

$$\begin{aligned} PV &= ₹10{,}000 \times \left(\frac{1}{1.08}\right)^3 \\ &= ₹10{,}000 \times .7938 \\ &= ₹7{,}938 \end{aligned}$$

Figure 4.9 illustrates the application of the present value factor to Byomkesh's investment.

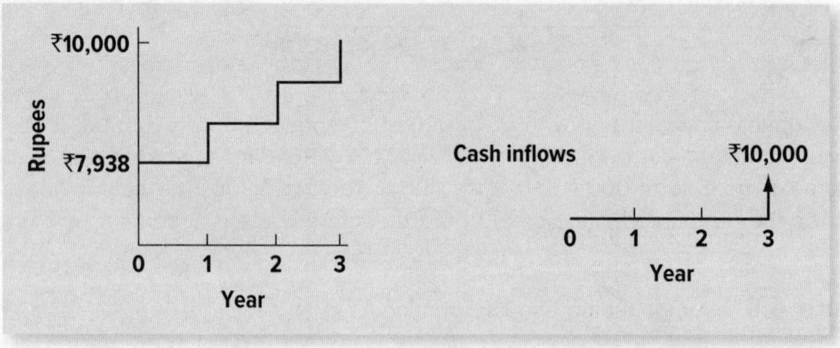

Figure 4.9 Discounting Byomkesh Banerjee's Opportunity

When his investments grow at an 8 percent rate of interest, Byomkesh is equally inclined toward receiving ₹7,938 now and receiving ₹10,000 in three years' time. After all, he could convert the ₹7,938 he receives today into ₹10,000 in three years by lending it at an interest rate of 8 percent.

Byomkesh could have reached his present value calculation in one of several ways. The computation could have been done by hand, by calculator, with a spreadsheet, or with the help of Table A.1, which appears in the back of the text. This table presents the *present value of ₹1 to be received after* t *periods*. We use the table by locating the appropriate interest rate on the horizontal and the appropriate number of periods on the vertical. Byomkesh would look at the following portion of Table A.1:

	INTEREST RATE		
Period	7%	8%	9%
1	.9346	.9259	.9174
2	.8734	.8573	.8417
3	.8163	.7938	.7722
4	.7629	.7350	.7084

The appropriate present value factor is .7938.

In the preceding example we gave both the interest rate and the future cash flow. Alternatively, the interest rate could have been unknown.

EXAMPLE 4.8

Finding the Rate Zulfikar Ali wants to buy a tugboat today. Rather than paying immediately, she offers to pay ₹150,000 in three years. It will cost Shriram Finance ₹115,830 to build the tugboat immediately. The relevant cash flows to Shriram Finance are displayed in Figure 4.10. What interest rate should Shriram Finance charge to neither gain nor lose on the sale?

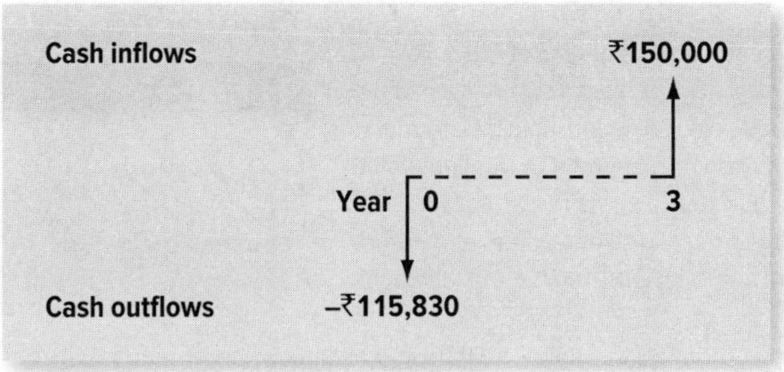

Figure 4.10 Cash Flows for Tugboat

The ratio of construction cost (present value) to sale price (future value) is:

$$\frac{₹115{,}830}{₹150{,}000} = .7722$$

We must determine the interest rate that allows ₹1 to be received in three years to have a present value of ₹.7722. Table A.1 tells us that 9 percent is that interest rate.

FINDING THE NUMBER OF PERIODS

Suppose we are interested in purchasing an asset that costs ₹50,000. We currently have ₹25,000. If we can earn 12 percent on this ₹25,000, how long until we have the ₹50,000? Finding the answer involves solving for the last variable in the basic present value equation: the number of periods. There is an easy way to get an approximate answer to this particular problem. Notice that we need to double our money. From the Rule of 72 (see Problem 74 at the end of the chapter), this will take about 72/12 = 6 years at 12 percent.

To come up with the exact answer, we can again manipulate the basic present value equation. The present value is ₹25,000, and the future value is ₹50,000. With a 12 percent discount rate, the basic equation takes one of the following forms:

$$₹25{,}000 = ₹50{,}000/1.12^t$$
$$₹50{,}000/₹25{,}000 = 1.12^t = 2$$

We have a future value factor of 2 for a 12 percent rate. We now need to solve for t. If you look down the column in Table A.3 that corresponds to 12 percent, you will see that a future value factor of 1.9738 occurs at six periods. It will take about six years, as we calculated. To get the exact answer, we have to explicitly solve for t (by using a financial calculator or the spreadsheet below). You will see that the answer is 6.1163 years, so our approximation was quite close in this case.

SPREADSHEET APPLICATIONS

Using a Spreadsheet for Time Value of Money Calculations

More and more, businesspeople from many different areas (not only finance and accounting) rely on spreadsheets to do all the different types of calculations that come up in the real world. In this section, we will show you how to use a spreadsheet to handle the various time value of money problems we present in this chapter. We will use Microsoft Excel, but the commands are similar for other types of software. We assume you are already familiar with basic spreadsheet operations.

As we have seen, you can solve for any one of the following four potential unknowns: future value, present value, the discount rate, or the number of periods. The following box lists formulas that can be used in Excel to solve for each input in the time value of money equation.

To Find	Enter This Formula
Future value	= FV(rate,nper,pmt,pv)
Present value	= PV(rate,nper,pmt,fv)
Discount rate	= RATE(nper,pmt,pv,fv)
Number of periods	= NPER(rate,pmt,pv,fv)

In these formulas, pv and fv are present value and future value; nper is the number of periods; and rate is the discount, or interest, rate.

Two things are a little tricky here. First, unlike a financial calculator, the spreadsheet requires that the rate be entered as a decimal. Second, as with most financial calculators, you have to put a negative sign on either the present value or the future value to solve for the rate or the number of periods. For the same reason, if you solve for a present value, the answer will have a negative sign unless you input a negative future value. The same is true when you compute a future value.

To illustrate how you might use these formulas, we will go back to an example in the chapter. If you invest ₹25,000 at 12 percent per year, how long until you have ₹50,000? You might set up a spreadsheet like this:

	A	B	C	D	E	F	G	H
1								
2	**Using a spreadsheet for time value of money calculations**							
3								
4	If we invest ₹25,000 at 12 percent, how long until we have ₹50,000? We need to solve							
5	for the unknown number of periods, so we use the formula NPER(rate,pmt,pv,fv).							
6								
7	Present value (pv):	₹25,000						
8	Future value (fv):	₹50,000						
9	Rate (rate):	.12						
10								
11	Periods:	**6.1162554**						
12								
13	The formula entered in cell B11 is =NPER(B9,0,-B7,B8); notice that pmt is zero and that pv							
14	has a negative sign on it. Also notice that rate is entered as a decimal, not a percentage.							

EXAMPLE 4.9

Waiting for Dhandapani You've been saving up to buy the Dhandapani Company. The total cost will be ₹10 million. You currently have about ₹2.3 million. If you can earn 5 percent on your money, how long will you have to wait? At 16 percent, how long must you wait?

At 5 percent, you'll have to wait a long time. From the present value equation:

$$₹2.3 \text{ million} = ₹10 \text{ million}/1.05^t$$
$$1.05^t = 4.35$$
$$t \approx 30 \text{ years}$$

At 16 percent, things are a little better. Verify for yourself that it will take about 10 years.

Frequently, an investor or a business will receive more than one cash flow. The present value of a set of cash flows is the sum of the present values of the individual cash flows. This is illustrated in the following two examples.

Learn more about using Excel for time value and other calculations at **www.studyfinance.com**.

EXAMPLE 4.10

Cash Flow Valuation Ahmed Abbas Maksood won the Punjab State Lottery and will receive the following set of cash flows over the next two years:

Year	Cash Flow
1	₹20,000
2	50,000

Ahmed can currently earn 6 percent in his money market account, so the appropriate discount rate is 6 percent. The present value of the cash flows is:

Year	Cash Flow × Present Value Factor = Present Value
1	$₹20{,}000 \times \frac{1}{1.06} = ₹18{,}867.92$
2	$₹50{,}000 \times \frac{1}{1.06^2} = \underline{44{,}499.82}$
	Total ₹63,367.75

In other words, Ahmed is indifferent between receiving ₹63,367.75 today or receiving ₹20,000 in one year and ₹50,000 in two years.

EXAMPLE 4.11

NPV **Classteacher.com** has an opportunity to invest in a new high-speed computer that costs ₹50,000. The computer will generate cash flows of ₹25,000 one year from now, ₹20,000 two years from now, and ₹15,000 three years from now. The computer will be worthless after three years, and no additional cash flows will occur. **Classteacher.com** has determined that the appropriate discount rate is 7 percent for this investment. Should **Classteacher.com** make this investment in a new high-speed computer? What is the net present value of the investment?

The cash flows and present value factors of the proposed computer are as follows:

Year	Cash Flows	Present Value Factor
0	−₹50,000	$1 = 1$
1	25,000	$\frac{1}{1.07} = .9346$
2	20,000	$\left(\frac{1}{1.07}\right)^2 = .8734$
3	15,000	$\left(\frac{1}{1.07}\right)^3 = .8163$

(continued)

The present value of the cash flows is:

Cash flows × Present value factor = Present value

Year			
0	−₹50,000 × 1	=	−₹50,000.00
1	25,000 × .9346	=	23,364.49
2	20,000 × .8734	=	17,468.77
3	15,000 × .8163	=	12,244.47
		Total:	₹ 3,077.73

Classteacher.com should invest in the new high-speed computer because the present value of its future cash flows is greater than its cost. The NPV is ₹3,077.73.

THE ALGEBRAIC FORMULA

To derive an algebraic formula for the net present value of a cash flow, recall that the PV of receiving a cash flow one year from now is:

$$\text{PV} = C_1/(1 + r)$$

and the PV of receiving a cash flow two years from now is:

$$\text{PV} = C_2/(1 + r)^2$$

We can write the NPV of a t-period project as:

$$\text{NPV} = -C_0 + \frac{C_1}{1+r} + \frac{C_2}{(1+r)^2} + \cdots + \frac{C_t}{(1+r)^t} = -C_0 + \sum_{i=1}^{t} \frac{C_i}{(1+r)^i} \tag{4.5}$$

The initial flow, $-C_0$, is assumed to be negative because it represents an investment. The $\sum$ is shorthand for the sum of the series.

We close this section by answering the question we posed at the beginning of the chapter concerning quarterback Patrick Mahomes' contract. Recall that the contract called for ₹10.825 million in 2020. The remaining ₹466.8 million was to be paid as ₹22,806,905 in 2021, ₹29.45 million in 2022, ₹40.45 million in 2023, ₹37.95 million in 2024, ₹41.95 million in 2025 and 2026, ₹59.95 million in 2027, ₹44.45 million in 2028, ₹44.95 million in 2029, ₹50.45 million in 2030, and ₹52.45 million in 2031. If 12 percent is the appropriate discount rate, how much money was really thrown at the Chiefs' quarterback?

To answer, we can calculate the present value by discounting each year's salary back to the present as follows (notice we assume that all the payments are made at year-end):

Year 0 (2020): ₹10,825,000 = ₹10,825,000.00

Year 1 (2021): ₹22,806,905 × $1/1.12^1$ = ₹20,363,308.04

Year 2 (2022): ₹29,450,000 × $1/1.12^2$ = ₹23,477,359.69

. . .

Year 11 (2031): ₹52,450,000 × $1/1.12^{11}$ = ₹15,078,121.66

If you fill in the missing rows and then add (do it for practice), you will see that Patrick's contract had a present value of about ₹245.2 million, or about half of the stated ₹477 million value (still pretty good!).

4.3 Compounding Periods

So far, we have assumed that compounding and discounting occur yearly. Sometimes, compounding may occur more frequently than once a year. Imagine that a bank pays a 10 percent interest rate "compounded semiannually." This means that a ₹1,000 deposit in the bank would be worth ₹1,000 × 1.05 = ₹1,050 after six months, and ₹1,050 × 1.05 = ₹1,102.50 at the end of the year.

The end-of-the-year wealth can be written as:

$$₹1{,}000\left(1+\frac{.10}{2}\right)^2 = ₹1{,}000 \times 1.05^2 = ₹1{,}102.50$$

Of course, a ₹1,000 deposit would be worth ₹1,100 (= ₹1,000 × 1.10) with yearly compounding. Note that the future value at the end of one year is greater with semiannual compounding than with yearly compounding. With yearly compounding, the original ₹1,000 remains the investment base for the full year. With semiannual compounding, the original ₹1,000 is the investment base only for the first six months. The base over the second six months is ₹1,050. Hence, one gets *interest on interest* with semiannual compounding.

Because ₹1,000 × 1.1025 = ₹1,102.50, 10 percent compounded semiannually is the same as 10.25 percent compounded annually. In other words, a rational investor is indifferent between being quoted a rate of 10 percent compounded semiannually or a rate of 10.25 percent compounded annually.

Quarterly compounding at 10 percent yields wealth at the end of one year of:

$$₹1{,}000\left(1+\frac{.10}{4}\right)^4 = ₹1{,}103.81$$

More generally, compounding an investment m times a year provides end-of-year wealth of:

$$C_0(1 + r/m)^m \qquad \textbf{(4.6)}$$

where C_0 is the initial investment and r is the **annual percentage rate (APR)**. The annual percentage rate is the annual interest rate without consideration of compounding. Banks and other financial institutions may use other names for the annual percentage rate.

EXAMPLE 4.12

EARs What is the end-of-year wealth if Raj Ranjan receives an APR of 24 percent compounded monthly on a ₹1 investment?

Using Equation 4.6, her wealth is:

$$₹1\left(1+\frac{.24}{12}\right)^{12} = ₹1 \times 1.02^{12}$$
$$= ₹1.2682$$

The annual rate of return is 26.82 percent. This annual rate of return is called either the **effective annual rate (EAR)** or the **effective annual yield (EAY)**. Due to compounding, the effective annual interest rate is greater than the APR of 24 percent. Algebraically, we can write the effective annual interest rate as follows:

$$\text{Effective annual rate} = (1 + r/m)^m - 1 \qquad \textbf{(4.7)}$$

Students are often bothered by the subtraction of 1 in Equation 4.7. Note that end-of-year wealth is composed of both the interest earned over the year and the original principal. We remove the original principal by subtracting 1 in Equation 4.7.

EXAMPLE 4.13

Compounding Frequencies If an 8 percent annual percentage rate is compounded quarterly, what is the effective annual rate?

Using Equation 4.7, we have:

$$\left(1+\frac{r}{m}\right)^m - 1 = \left(1+\frac{.08}{4}\right)^4 - 1 = .0824, \text{ or } 8.24\%$$

Referring back to our original example where C_0 = ₹1,000 and r = 10%, we can generate the following table:

C_0	Compounding Frequency (m)	C_1	Effective Annual Rate $=\left(1+\frac{r}{m}\right)^m - 1$
₹1,000	Yearly (m = 1)	₹1,100.00	.10
1,000	Semiannually (m = 2)	1,102.50	.1025
1,000	Quarterly (m = 4)	1,103.81	.10381
1,000	Daily (m = 365)	1,105.16	.10516

DISTINCTION BETWEEN ANNUAL PERCENTAGE RATE AND EFFECTIVE ANNUAL RATE

The distinction between the annual percentage rate, or APR, and the effective annual rate (EAR) is frequently troubling to students. We can reduce the confusion by noting that the APR becomes meaningful only if the compounding interval is given. For an APR of 10 percent, the future value at the end of one year with semiannual compounding is $[1 + (.10/2)]^2 = 1.1025$. The future value with quarterly compounding is $[1 + (.10/4)]^4 = 1.1038$. If the APR is 10 percent but no compounding interval is given, we cannot calculate future value. In other words, we do not know whether to compound semiannually, quarterly, or over some other interval.

By contrast, the EAR is meaningful without a compounding interval. An EAR of 10.25 percent means that a ₹1 investment will be worth ₹1.1025 in one year. We can think of this as an APR of 10 percent with semiannual compounding or an APR of 10.25 percent with annual compounding, or some other possibility.

There can be a big difference between an APR and an EAR when interest rates are large. For example, consider "payday loans." Payday loans are short-term loans made to consumers, often for less than two weeks. They are offered by companies such as Check Into Cash and AmeriCash Advance. The loans work like this: You write a check today that is postdated. When the check date arrives, you go to the store and pay the cash for the check, or the company cashes the check. For example, in one particular state, Check Into Cash allows you to write a check for ₹115 dated 14 days in the future, for which they give you ₹100 today. So what are the APR and EAR of this arrangement? First, we need to find the interest rate, which we can find by the FV equation as follows:

$$\text{FV} = \text{PV} \times (1 + r)^1$$
$$₹115 = ₹100 \times (1 + r)^1$$
$$1.15 = (1 + r)$$
$$r = .15, \text{ or } 15\%$$

That doesn't seem too bad until you remember this is the interest rate for *14 days*! The APR of the loan is:

$$\text{APR} = .15 \times 365/14$$
$$\text{APR} = 3.9107, \text{ or } 391.07\%$$

And the EAR for this loan is:

$$\text{EAR} = (1 + \text{Quoted rate}/m)^m - 1$$
$$\text{EAR} = (1 + .15)^{365/14} - 1$$
$$\text{EAR} = 37.2366, \text{ or } 3{,}723.66\%$$

Now that's an interest rate! To see what a difference a small change in fees can make, AmeriCash Advance will make you write a check for ₹117.50 for the same ₹100 today. Check for yourself that the APR of this arrangement is 456.25 percent and the EAR is 6,598.65 percent. Still not a loan we would like to take out!

By law, lenders are required to report the APR on all loans. In this text, we compute the APR as the interest rate per period multiplied by the number of periods in a year. According to federal law, the APR is a measure of the cost of consumer credit expressed as a yearly rate, and it includes interest and certain noninterest charges and fees. In practice, the APR can be much higher than the interest rate on the loan if the lender charges substantial fees that must be included in the federally mandated APR calculation.

These regulations are also existent in the Indian context.[2] For instance, APR for housing loans by Indian banks is shown around 8% in small fonts even though their bigger advertisements speak of less than 7%.

COMPOUNDING OVER MANY YEARS

Equation 4.6 applies for an investment over one year. For an investment over one or more (t) years, the formula becomes this:

$$\text{FV} = \text{PV}\left(1 + \frac{r}{m}\right)^{mt} \tag{4.8}$$

EXAMPLE 4.14

Multiyear Compounding Karunanidhy Thavaseelan is investing ₹5,000 at an annual percentage rate of 12 percent per year, compounded quarterly, for five years. What is his wealth at the end of five years?

Using Equation 4.8, his wealth is:

$$₹5{,}000 \times \left(1 + \frac{.12}{4}\right)^{4\times5} = ₹5{,}000 \times 1.03^{20} = ₹5{,}000 \times 1.8061 = ₹9{,}030.56$$

CONTINUOUS COMPOUNDING

The previous discussion shows that we can compound much more frequently than once a year. We could compound semiannually, quarterly, monthly, daily, hourly, each minute, or even more often. The limiting case would be to compound every infinitesimal instant, which is commonly called **continuous compounding**. Surprisingly, banks and other financial institutions sometimes quote continuously compounded rates, which is why we study them.

[2]The Reserve Bank of India is strict about the same - so much so, even microfinance organizations are required to state their APR (after the Andhra Pradesh microfinance scam in FY2011-12). Annual Percentage Return for Home Loans

Though the idea of compounding this rapidly may boggle the mind, a simple formula is involved. With continuous compounding, the value at the end of t years is expressed as:

$$C_0 \times e^{rt} \tag{4.9}$$

where C_0 is the initial investment, r is the APR, and t is the number of years over which the investment runs. The number e is a constant and is approximately equal to 2.718. It is not an unknown like C_0, r, and t.

EXAMPLE 4.15

Continuous Compounding Gayatri Krishnan invested ₹1,000 at a continuously compounded rate of 10 percent for one year. What is the value of her wealth at the end of one year?

From Equation 4.9 we have:

$$₹1{,}000 \times e^{.10} = ₹1{,}000 \times 1.1052 = ₹1{,}105.17$$

This number can easily be read from Table A.5. We merely set r, the value on the horizontal dimension, to 10 percent and t, the value on the vertical dimension, to 1. For this problem the relevant portion of the table is shown here:

	Continuously Compounded Rate (r)		
Period (t)	**9%**	**10%**	**11%**
1	1.0942	1.1052	1.1163
2	1.1972	1.2214	1.2461
3	1.3100	1.3499	1.3910

Note that a continuously compounded rate of 10 percent is equivalent to an annually compounded rate of 10.52 percent. In other words, Gayatri would not care whether her bank quoted a continuously compounded rate of 10 percent or a 10.52 percent rate, compounded annually.

EXAMPLE 4.16

Continuous Compounding, Continued Gayatri's husband, Jitendra, invested ₹1,000 at a continuously compounded rate of 10 percent for two years.

The appropriate formula here is:

$$₹1{,}000 \times e^{.10\times 2} = ₹1{,}000 \times e^{.20} = ₹1{,}221.40$$

Using the portion of the table of continuously compounded rates shown in the previous example, we find the value to be 1.2214.

Figure 4.11 illustrates the relationship among annual, semiannual, and continuous compounding. Semiannual compounding gives rise to both a smoother curve and a higher ending value than does annual compounding. Continuous compounding has both the smoothest curve and the highest ending value.

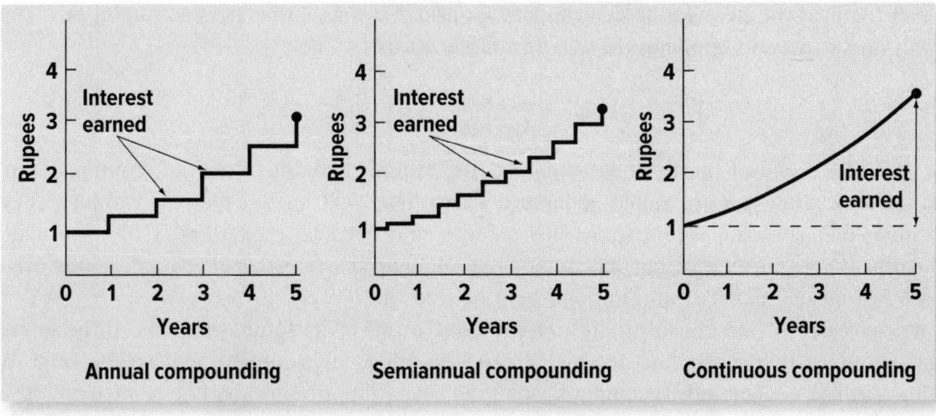

Figure 4.11 Annual, Semiannual, and Continuous Compounding

EXAMPLE 4.17

Present Value with Continuous Compounding The Kerala State Lottery is going to pay you ₹100,000 at the end of four years. If the annual continuously compounded rate of interest is 8 percent, what is the present value of this payment?

$$₹100{,}000 \times \frac{1}{e^{.08\times4}} = ₹100{,}000 \times \frac{1}{1.3771} = ₹72{,}614.90$$

4.4 Simplifications

The first part of this chapter has examined the concepts of future value and present value. Although these concepts allow us to answer a host of problems concerning the time value of money, the effort involved can be excessive. Consider a bank calculating the present value of a 20-year monthly mortgage. This mortgage has 240 (= 20 × 12) payments, so a lot of time is needed to perform a conceptually simple task.

Because many basic finance problems are potentially time-consuming, we search for simplifications in this section. We provide simplifying formulas for four classes of cash flow streams:

- Perpetuity
- Growing perpetuity
- Annuity
- Growing annuity

PERPETUITY

A **perpetuity** is a constant stream of cash flows without end. If you are thinking that perpetuities have no relevance to reality, it will surprise you that there is a well-known case of an unending cash flow stream: the British bonds called *consols*. An investor purchasing a consol is entitled to receive yearly interest from the British government forever.

How can the price of a consol be determined? Consider a consol that pays a coupon of C rupees each year and will do so forever. Applying the PV formula gives us:

$$\text{PV} = \frac{C}{1+r} + \frac{C}{(1+r)^2} + \frac{C}{(1+r)^3} + \cdots$$

where the dots at the end of the formula stand for the infinite string of terms that continues the formula. Series like the preceding one are called geometric series. It is well known that even though they have an infinite number of terms, the whole series has a finite sum because each term is only a fraction of the preceding term. Before turning to our calculus books, though, it is worth going back to our original principles to see if a bit of financial intuition can help us find the PV.

The present value of the consol is the present value of all of its future coupons. In other words, it is an amount of money that, if an investor had it today, would enable him to achieve the same pattern of expenditures that the consol and its coupons would achieve. Suppose an investor wanted to spend exactly C rupees each year. If he had the consol, he could do this. How much money must he have today to spend the same amount? Clearly, he would need exactly enough so that the interest on the money would be C rupees per year. If he had any more, he could spend more than C rupees each year. If he had any less, he would eventually run out of money spending C rupees per year.

The amount that will give the investor C rupees each year, and therefore the present value of the consol, is:

$$\text{PV} = \frac{C}{r} \tag{4.10}$$

To confirm that this is the right answer, notice that if we lend the amount C/r, the interest it earns each year will be:

$$\text{Interest} = \frac{C}{r} \times r = C$$

which is exactly the perpetuity payment. We have arrived at this formula for a perpetuity:

Formula for Present Value of Perpetuity

$$\begin{aligned} \text{PV} &= \frac{C}{1+r} + \frac{C}{(1+r)^2} + \frac{C}{(1+r)^3} + \cdots \\ &= \frac{C}{r} \end{aligned} \tag{4.11}$$

It is comforting to know how easily we can use a bit of financial intuition to solve this mathematical problem.

EXAMPLE 4.18

Perpetuities Consider a perpetuity paying ₹100 a year. If the relevant discount rate is 8 percent, what is the value of the perpetuity today?

Using Equation 4.10 we have:

$$\text{PV} = \frac{₹100}{.08} = ₹1{,}250$$

Now suppose that the discount rate falls to 6 percent. Using Equation 4.10 the value of the perpetuity is:

$$\text{PV} = \frac{₹100}{.06} = ₹1{,}666.67$$

Note that the value of the perpetuity rises with a drop in the discount rate. Conversely, the value of the perpetuity falls with a rise in the discount rate.

GROWING PERPETUITY

Imagine an apartment building where cash flows to the landlord after expenses will be ₹100,000 next year. These cash flows are expected to rise at a rate of 5 percent per year. If one assumes that this rise will continue indefinitely, the cash flow stream is termed a **growing perpetuity**. The relevant discount rate is 11 percent. Therefore, when the appropriate discount rate is 11 percent, the present value of the cash flows can be represented as:

$$\text{PV} = \frac{₹100{,}000}{1.11} + \frac{₹100{,}000(1.05)}{1.11^2} + \frac{₹100{,}000(1.05)^2}{1.11^3} + \cdots$$

$$+ \frac{₹100{,}000(1.05)^{N-1}}{1.11^N} + \cdots$$

Algebraically, we can write the formula as:

$$\text{PV} = \frac{C}{1+r} + \frac{C \times (1+g)}{(1+r)^2} + \frac{C \times (1+g)^2}{(1+r)^3} + \cdots + \frac{C \times (1+g)^{N-1}}{(1+r)^N} + \cdots$$

where C is the cash flow to be received in one period, g is the rate of growth per period, and r is the appropriate discount rate.

Fortunately, this formula reduces to the following simplification:

Formula for Present Value of Growing Perpetuity

$$\text{PV} = \frac{C}{r - g} \tag{4.12}$$

From Equation 4.12 the present value of the cash flows from the apartment building is:

$$\frac{₹100{,}000}{.11 - .05} = ₹1{,}666{,}667$$

There are three important points concerning the growing perpetuity formula:

1. *The numerator*: The numerator in Equation 4.12 is the cash flow in one period, not at Year 0. Consider the following example.

EXAMPLE 4.19

Paying Dividends Prajapati Company is about to pay a dividend of ₹3.00 per share. Investors anticipate that the annual dividend will rise by 6 percent a year forever. The applicable discount rate is 11 percent. What is the price of the stock today?

The numerator in Equation 4.12 is the cash flow to be received next period. Because the growth rate is 6 percent, the dividend next year is ₹3.18 (= ₹3.00 × 1.06). The price of the stock today is:

$$₹66.60 = ₹3.00 + \frac{₹3.18}{.11 - .06}$$

₹66.60	=	₹3.00	+	$\frac{₹3.18}{.11 - .06}$
		Imminent dividend		Present value of all dividends beginning a year from now

The price of ₹66.60 includes both the dividend to be received immediately and the present value of all dividends beginning a year from now. Equation 4.12 makes it possible to calculate only the present value of all dividends beginning a year from now. Be sure you understand this example; test questions on this subject always seem to trip up a few of our students.

2. *The discount rate and the growth rate*: The discount rate r must be greater than the growth rate g for the growing perpetuity formula to work. Consider the case in which the growth rate approaches the discount rate in magnitude. This would mean the denominator in the growing perpetuity formula gets infinitesimally small and the present value grows infinitely large. The present value is undefined when r is less than g.
3. *The timing assumption*: Cash generally flows into and out of real-world firms both randomly and nearly continuously. However, Equation 4.12 assumes that cash flows are received and disbursed at regular and discrete points in time. In the example of the apartment, we assumed that the net cash flows of ₹100,000 occurred only once a year. In reality, rent checks are commonly received every month. Payments for maintenance and other expenses may occur anytime within the year.

   We can apply the growing perpetuity formula of Equation 4.12 only by assuming a regular and discrete pattern of cash flow. Although this assumption is sensible because the formula saves so much time, the user should never forget that it is an assumption. This point will be mentioned again in the chapters ahead.

A few words should be said about terminology. Authors of financial textbooks generally use one of two conventions to refer to time. A minority of financial writers treat cash flows as being received on exact dates–for example Date 0, Date 1, and so forth. Under this convention, Date 0 represents the present time. However, the majority of authors refer to cash flows that occur at the end of a year (or alternatively, the end of a period). Under this end-of-year convention, the end of Year 0 is the present, the end of Year 1 occurs one period in the future, and so on.[3]

The interchangeability of the two conventions can be seen from the following chart:

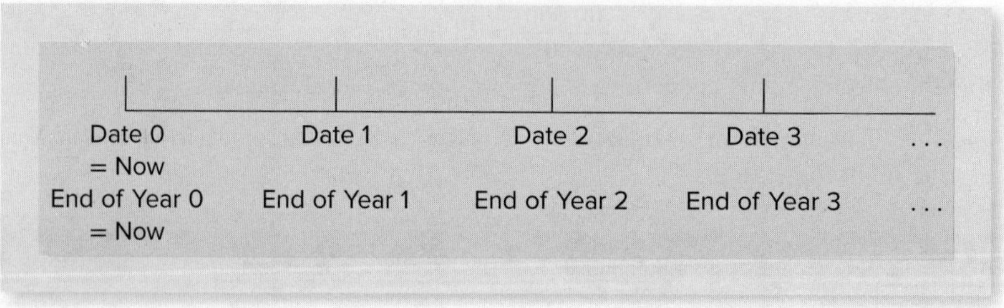

Our preference is for the end-of-year convention, but you may see the dates convention in later courses. For the sake of practice, you may see both conventions in this text.

ANNUITY

An **annuity** is a level stream of regular payments that lasts for a fixed number of periods. Not surprisingly, annuities are among the most common kinds of financial instruments. The pensions that people receive when they retire are often in the form of an annuity. Leases and mortgages are also often annuities.

To figure out the present value of an annuity, we need to evaluate the following equation:

$$PV = \frac{C}{1+r} + \frac{C}{(1+r)^2} + \frac{C}{(1+r)^3} + \cdots + \frac{C}{(1+r)^t}$$

[3]Sometimes, financial writers merely speak of a cash flow in Year x. Although this terminology is ambiguous, such writers generally mean the end of Year x.

The present value of receiving the coupons for only t periods must be less than the present value of a perpetuity, but how much less? To answer this, we have to look at perpetuities a bit more closely.

Consider the following timeline:

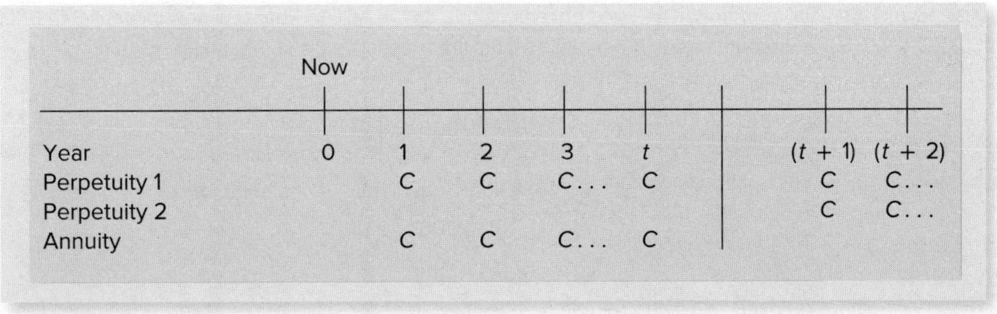

Perpetuity 1 is a normal perpetuity with its first payment at Year 1. The first payment of Perpetuity 2 occurs at Year $t + 1$.

The present value of having a cash flow of C at each of t periods is equal to the present value of Perpetuity 1 minus the present value of Perpetuity 2. The present value of Perpetuity 1 is given by:

$$\text{PV} = \frac{C}{r} \tag{4.13}$$

Perpetuity 2 is a perpetuity with its first payment at Year $t + 1$. From the perpetuity formula, this perpetuity will be worth C/r at Year t.[4] However, we do not want the value at Year t. We want the value now, in other words, the present value at Year 0. We must discount C/r back by t periods. Therefore, the present value of Perpetuity 2 is:

$$\text{PV} = \frac{C}{r}\left[\frac{1}{(1+r)^t}\right] \tag{4.14}$$

The present value of having cash flows for t years is the present value of a perpetuity with its first payment at Year 1 minus the present value of a perpetuity with its first payment at Year $t + 1$. The present value of an annuity is Equation 4.13 minus Equation 4.14. This can be written as:

$$\text{PV} = \frac{C}{r} - \frac{C}{r}\left[\frac{1}{(1+r)^t}\right]$$

This simplifies to the following:

Formula for Present Value of Annuity

$$\text{PV} = C\left[\frac{1}{r} - \frac{1}{r(1+r)^t}\right] \tag{4.15}$$

This also can be written as:

$$\text{PV} = C\left[\frac{1 - \frac{1}{(1+r)^t}}{r}\right]$$

[4]Students frequently think that C/r is the present value at Year $t + 1$ because the perpetuity's first payment is at Year $t + 1$. However, the formula values the perpetuity as of one period before the first payment.

EXAMPLE 4.20

Lottery Valuation Keshav Yadav has won the state lottery, paying ₹50,000 a year for 20 years. He is to receive his first payment a year from now. The state advertises this as the Million Rupee Lottery because ₹1,000,000 = ₹50,000 × 20. If the discount rate is 8 percent, what is the present value of the lottery? Equation 4.15 yields:

$$\text{Present value of Million Rupee Lottery} = ₹50{,}000 \times \left[\frac{1 - \frac{1}{1.08^{20}}}{.08}\right]$$

Periodic payment   Annuity factor

$$= ₹50{,}000 \times 9.8181$$

$$= ₹490{,}907$$

Rather than being overjoyed at winning, Keshav sues the state for misrepresentation and fraud. His legal brief states that he was promised ₹1 million but received only ₹490,907.

The term we use to compute the present value of the stream of level payments, C, for t years is called a *present value interest factor for annuities*. The present value interest factor for annuities in the current example is 9.8181. Because the present value interest factor for annuities is used so often in PV calculations, we have included it in Table A.2 in the back of this book. The table gives the values of these factors for a range of interest rates, r, and periods, t.

The present value interest factor for annuities as expressed in the brackets of Equation 4.15 is a complex formula. For simplification, we may from time to time refer to the annuity factor as:

$$\text{PVIFA}_{r,t}$$

This expression stands for the present value of ₹1 a year for t years at a discount rate of r.

We also can provide a formula for the future value of an annuity:

$$\text{FV} = C\left[\frac{(1+r)^t}{r} - \frac{1}{r}\right] = C\left[\frac{(1+r)^t - 1}{r}\right] \tag{4.16}$$

As with present value factors for annuities, we have compiled future value factors in Table A.4 in the back of this book.

EXAMPLE 4.21

Retirement Investing Suppose you put ₹3,000 per year into a LIC Investment Fund. The account earns 6 percent interest per year. How much will you have when you retire in 30 years?

This question asks for the future value of an annuity of ₹3,000 per year for 30 years at 6 percent, which we can calculate as follows:

$$\text{FV} = C\left[\frac{(1+r)^t - 1}{r}\right] = ₹3{,}000 \times \left[\frac{1.06^{30} - 1}{.06}\right]$$

$$= ₹3{,}000 \times 79.0582$$

$$= ₹237{,}174.56$$

So, you'll have close to a quarter million rupees in the account.

Our experience is that annuity formulas are not difficult, but tricky, for the beginning student. We present four tricks next.

SPREADSHEET APPLICATIONS

Annuity Present Values

We can use a spreadsheet to find the present value of an annuity as follows:

	A	B	C	D	E	F	G
1							
2	**Using a spreadsheet to find the present value of an annuity**						
3							
4	What is the present value of ₹500 per year for 3 years if the discount rate is 10 percent?						
5	We need to solve for the unknown present value, so we use the formula PV(rate,nper,pmt,fv).						
6							
7	Payment amount per period:	₹500					
8	Number of payments:	3					
9	Discount rate:	0.1					
10							
11	Annuity present value:	**₹1,243.43**					
12							
13	The formula entered in cell B11 is =PV(B9,B8,-B7,0); notice that fv is zero and that						
14	pmt has a negative sign on it. Also notice that rate is entered as a decimal, not a percentage.						
15							
16							
17							

Trick 1: A Delayed Annuity One of the tricks in working with annuities or perpetuities is getting the timing exactly right. This is particularly true when an annuity or perpetuity begins in the future. We have found that even the brightest beginning student can make errors here. Consider the following example.

EXAMPLE 4.22

Delayed Annuities Pratap Bogzi will receive a four-year annuity of ₹500 per year, with the first payment at Year 6. If the discount rate is 10 percent, what is the value of her annuity today? The timeline for the cash flows is:

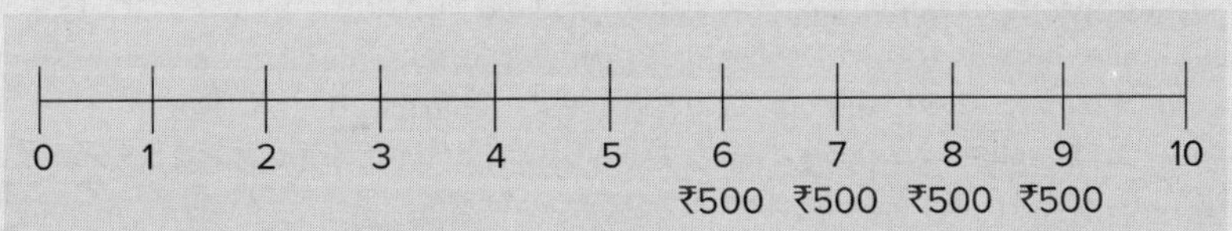

The analysis involves two steps:

1. Calculate the present value of the annuity using Equation 4.15:

Present Value of Annuity at Year 5

$$₹500 \left[\frac{1 - \frac{1}{1.10^4}}{.10}\right] = ₹500 \times \text{PVIFA}_{10,4}$$
$$= ₹500 \times 3.1699$$
$$= ₹1,584.93$$

Note that ₹1,584.93 represents the present value at Year 5.

(continued)

Students frequently think that ₹1,584.93 is the present value at Year 6 because the first payment is at Year 6. However, our formula values the annuity as of one period prior to the first payment. This can be seen in the most typical case where the first payment occurs at Year 1. The formula values the annuity as of Year 0 in that case.

2. Discount the present value of the annuity back to Year 0:

Present Value at Year 0

$$\frac{₹1{,}584.93}{1.10^5} = ₹984.12$$

Again, it is worthwhile mentioning that because the annuity formula brings Pratap's annuity back to Year 5, the second calculation must discount over the remaining five periods. The two-step procedure is shown in Figure 4.12.

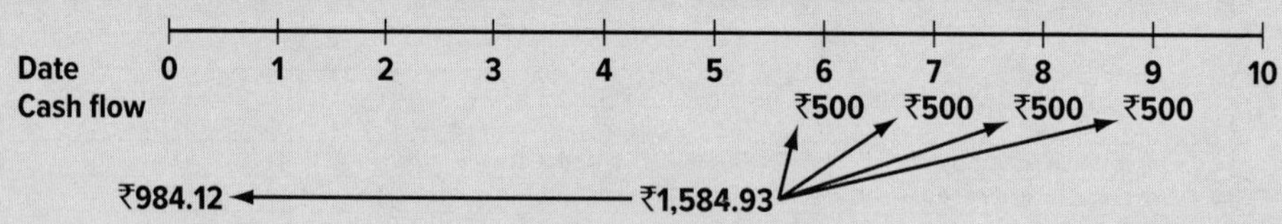

Step one: Discount the four payments back to Year 5 by using the annuity formula.
Step two: Discount the present value at Year 5 (₹1,584.93) back to present value at Year 0.

Figure 4.12 Discounting Pratap Bogzi's Annuity

Trick 2: Annuity Due The annuity formula of Equation 4.15 assumes that the first annuity payment begins a full period in the future. This type of annuity is sometimes called an *annuity in arrears* or an *ordinary annuity*. What happens if the annuity begins today–in other words, at Year 0?

EXAMPLE 4.23

Annuity Due In a previous example, Keshav Yadav received ₹50,000 a year for 20 years from the state lottery. In that example, he was to receive the first payment in one year. Let us now assume that the first payment occurs immediately. The total number of payments remains 20.

Under this new assumption, we have a 19-year annuity with the first payment occurring at Year 1—plus an extra payment at Year 0. The present value is:

$$\underset{\text{Payment at Year 0}}{₹50{,}000} \quad \underset{\text{19-year annuity}}{+ ₹50{,}000 \times \frac{[1 - 1/1.08^{19}]}{.08}}$$

$$= ₹50{,}000 + (₹50{,}000 \times 9.6036)$$

$$= ₹530{,}180$$

₹530,180, the present value in this example, is greater than ₹490,907, the present value in the earlier lottery example. This is to be expected because the annuity of the current example begins earlier. An annuity with an immediate initial payment is called an *annuity in advance* or, more commonly, an **annuity due**. Always remember that Equation 4.15 and Table A.2 in this book refer to an *ordinary annuity*.

Trick 3: The Infrequent Annuity The following example values an annuity with payments occurring less frequently than once a year.

EXAMPLE 4.24

Infrequent Annuities Sumi Sarkar receives an annuity of ₹450, payable once every two years. The annuity stretches out over 20 years. The first payment occurs at Year 2—that is, two years from today. The annual discount rate is 6 percent.

The trick is to determine the discount rate over a two-year period. The discount rate over two years is:

$$1.06^2 - 1 = .1236, \text{ or } 12.36\%$$

That is, ₹100 invested over two years will yield ₹112.36.

What we want is the present value of a ₹450 annuity over 10 periods, with a discount rate of 12.36 percent per period:

$$₹450 \left[\frac{1 - \frac{1}{1.1236^{10}}}{.1236} \right] = ₹450 \times \text{PVIFA}_{12.36\%,10} = ₹2,505.57$$

Trick 4: Equating Present Value of Two Annuities The following example equates the present value of inflows with the present value of outflows.

EXAMPLE 4.25

Working with Annuities Mamta and Mayavati Thakur are saving for the college education of their newborn daughter, Kejri. The Thakurs estimate that college expenses will run ₹30,000 per year when their daughter reaches college in 18 years. The annual discount rate over the next few decades will be 14 percent. How much money must they deposit in the bank each year so that their daughter will be completely supported through four years of college?

To simplify the calculations, we assume that Kejri is born today. Her parents will make the first of her four annual tuition payments on her 18th birthday. They will make equal bank deposits on each of her first 17 birthdays, but no deposit at Year 0. This is illustrated as follows:

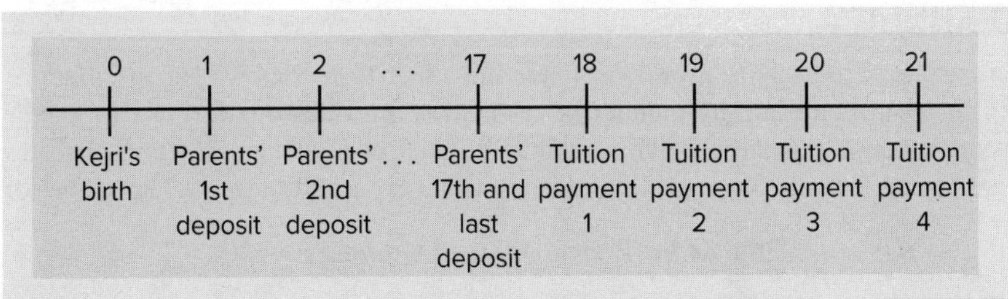

The Thakurs will be making deposits to the bank over the next 17 years. They will be withdrawing ₹30,000 per year over the following four years. We can be sure they will be able to withdraw fully ₹30,000 per year if the present value of the deposits is equal to the present value of the four withdrawals of ₹30,000.

This calculation requires three steps. The first two determine the present value of the withdrawals. The final step determines yearly deposits that will have a present value equal to that of the withdrawals.

(continued)

1. We calculate the present value of the four years at college using the annuity formula:

$$₹30{,}000 \times \left[\frac{1 - \dfrac{1}{1.14^4}}{.14}\right] = ₹30{,}000 \times \text{PVIFA}_{14,4}$$

$$= ₹30{,}000 \times 2.9137 = ₹87{,}411.37$$

We assume that Kejri enters college on her 18th birthday. Given our discussion in Trick 1, ₹87,411.37 represents the value at Year 17.

2. We calculate the present value of the college education at Year 0 as:

$$\frac{₹87{,}411.37}{1.14^{17}} = ₹9{,}422.92$$

3. Assuming that Mamta and Mayavati Thakur make deposits to the bank at the end of each of the 17 years, we calculate the annual deposit that will yield a present value of all deposits of ₹9,422.92. This is calculated as:

$$C \times \text{PVIFA}_{14\%,17} = ₹9{,}422.92$$

Because $\text{PVIFA}_{14\%,17} = 6.3729$:

$$C = \frac{₹9{,}422.92}{6.3729} = ₹1{,}478.60$$

Deposits of ₹1,478.60 made at the end of each of the first 17 years and invested at 14 percent will provide enough money to make tuition payments of ₹30,000 over the following four years.

An alternative method in Example 4.25 would be to (1) calculate the present value of the tuition payments at Kejri's 18th birthday and (2) calculate annual deposits so that the future value of the deposits at her 18th birthday equals the present value of the tuition payments at that date. Although this technique also can provide the right answer, we have found that it is more likely to lead to errors. Therefore, we equate only present values in our presentation.

GROWING ANNUITY

Cash flows in business are likely to grow over time, due either to real growth or to inflation. The growing perpetuity, which assumes an infinite number of cash flows, provides one formula to handle this growth. We now consider a **growing annuity**, which is a finite number of growing cash flows. Because perpetuities of any kind are rare, a formula for a growing annuity would be useful indeed. Here is the formula:

Formula for Present Value of Growing Annuity

$$\text{PV} = C\left[\frac{1}{r-g} - \frac{1}{r-g} \times \left(\frac{1+g}{1+r}\right)^t\right] = C\left[\frac{1 - \left(\dfrac{1+g}{1+r}\right)^t}{r-g}\right] \quad \textbf{(4.17)}$$

As before, C is the payment to occur at the end of the first period; r is the discount rate; g is the rate of growth per period, expressed as a percentage; and t is the number of periods for the annuity.

EXAMPLE 4.26

Growing Annuities Sonia Daruwala, a second-year MBA student, has been offered a job at ₹80,000 a year. He anticipates his salary will increase by 9 percent a year until his retirement in 40 years. Given a discount rate of 20 percent, what is the present value of his lifetime salary?

We simplify by assuming he will be paid his ₹80,000 salary exactly one year from now and that his salary will continue to be paid in annual installments. The appropriate discount rate is 20 percent. From Equation 4.17, the calculation is:

$$\text{Present value of Sonia's lifetime salary} = ₹80{,}000 \times \left[\frac{1 - \left(\frac{1.09}{1.20}\right)^{40}}{.20 - .09}\right] = ₹711{,}730.71$$

Though the growing annuity formula is quite useful, it is more tedious than the other simplifying formulas. Whereas most financial calculators have special programs for a perpetuity, a growing perpetuity, and an annuity, there is no special program for a growing annuity. Hence, we must calculate all the terms in Equation 4.17 directly.

EXAMPLE 4.27

More Growing Annuities In a previous example, Mayavati and Mamta Thakur planned to make 17 identical payments to fund the college education of their daughter, Kejri. Alternatively, imagine that they planned to increase their payments at 4 percent per year. What would their first payment be?

The first two steps of the previous Thakur family example showed that the value today of the college costs was ₹9,422.92. These two steps would be the same here. However, the third step must be altered. Now we must ask: How much should their first payment be so that if payments increase by 4 percent per year, the present value of all payments will be ₹9,422.92?

We set the growing annuity formula equal to ₹9,422.92 and solve for C:

$$C\left[\frac{1 - \left(\frac{1+g}{1+r}\right)^{t}}{r - g}\right] = C\left[\frac{1 - \left(\frac{1.04}{1.14}\right)^{17}}{.14 - .04}\right] = ₹9{,}422.92$$

Here, C = ₹1,192.75. The deposit on their daughter's first birthday is ₹1,192.75, the deposit on the second birthday is ₹1,240.46 (= 1.04 × ₹1,192.75), and so on.

4.5 Loan Amortization

Whenever a lender extends a loan, some provision will be made for repayment of the principal (the original loan amount). A loan might be repaid in equal installments, or it might be repaid in a single lump sum. Because the way that the principal and interest are paid is up to the parties involved, there are actually an unlimited number of possibilities.

In this section, we describe amortized loans. Working with these loans is a very straightforward application of the present value principles that we have already developed.

An amortized loan may require the borrower to repay parts of the loan amount over time. The process of providing for a loan to be paid off by making regular principal reductions is called amortizing the loan.

With an equal principal loan, the borrower pays the interest each period plus an equal principal amount. This approach is common with medium-term business loans. Suppose a business takes out a ₹5,000, five-year loan at 9 percent. The loan agreement calls for the borrower to pay the interest on the loan balance each year and to reduce the loan balance each year by ₹1,000. Because the loan amount declines by ₹1,000 each year, it is fully paid in five years.

In the case we are considering, notice that the total payment will decline each year. The reason is that the loan balance goes down, resulting in a lower interest charge each year, whereas the ₹1,000 principal reduction is constant. The interest in the first year will be ₹5,000 × .09 = ₹450. The total payment will be ₹1,000 + 450 = ₹1,450. In the second year, the loan balance is ₹4,000, so the interest is ₹4,000 × .09 = ₹360, and the total payment is ₹1,360. We can calculate the total payment in each of the remaining years by preparing an amortization schedule as follows:

Year	Beginning Balance	Total Payment	Interest Paid	Principal Paid	Ending Balance
1	₹5,000	₹1,450	₹ 450	₹1,000	₹4,000
2	4,000	1,360	360	1,000	3,000
3	3,000	1,270	270	1,000	2,000
4	2,000	1,180	180	1,000	1,000
5	1,000	1,090	90	1,000	0
Totals		₹6,350	₹1,350	₹5,000	

Notice that in each year, the interest paid is given by the beginning balance multiplied by the interest rate. Also notice that the beginning balance is given by the ending balance from the previous year.

Probably the most common way of amortizing a loan is an equal payment loan. In an equal payment loan, the borrower makes a single, fixed payment every period. Almost all consumer loans (such as car loans and student loans) and mortgages work this way. Suppose our five-year, 9 percent, ₹5,000 loan was amortized this way. How would the amortization schedule look?

We first need to determine the payment. From our discussion earlier in the chapter, we know that this loan's cash flows are in the form of an ordinary annuity. In this case, we can solve for the payment as follows:

$$\text{₹}5{,}000 = C \times \{[1 - (1/1.09^5)]/.09\}$$
$$= C \times [(1 - .6499)/.09]$$

This gives us:

$$C = \text{₹}5{,}000/3.8897$$
$$= \text{₹}1{,}285.46$$

The borrower will therefore make five equal payments of ₹1,285.46. Will this pay off the loan? We will check by filling in an amortization schedule.

In the fixed principal loan, we knew the principal reduction each year. We then calculated the interest owed to get the total payment. In the fixed payment loan, we know the total payment. We will calculate the interest and then subtract it from the total payment to calculate the principal portion in each payment.

In the first year, the interest is ₹450, as we calculated before. Because the total payment is ₹1,285.46, the principal paid in the first year must be:

$$\text{Principal paid} = \text{₹}1{,}285.46 - 450 = \text{₹}835.46$$

The ending loan balance is thus:

$$\text{Ending balance} = \text{₹}5{,}000 - 835.46 = \text{₹}4{,}164.54$$

The interest in the second year is ₹4,164.54 × .09 = ₹374.81, and the loan balance declines by ₹1,285.46−374.81 = ₹910.65. We can summarize all of the relevant calculations in the following schedule:

Year	Beginning Balance	Total Payment	Interest Paid	Principal Paid	Ending Balance
1	₹5,000.00	₹1,285.46	₹ 450.00	₹ 835.46	₹4,164.54
2	4,164.54	1,285.46	374.81	910.65	3,253.88
3	3,253.88	1,285.46	292.85	992.61	2,261.27
4	2,261.27	1,285.46	203.51	1,081.95	1,179.32
5	1,179.32	1,285.46	106.14	1,179.32	0.00
Totals		₹6,427.31	₹1,427.31	₹5,000.00	

Because the loan balance declines to zero, the five equal payments pay off the loan. Notice that the interest paid declines each period. This isn't surprising because the loan balance is going down. Given that the total payment is fixed, the principal paid must be rising each period.

If you compare the two loan amortizations in this section, you will see that the total interest is greater for the equal payment case: ₹1,427.31 versus ₹1,350. The reason for this is that the loan is repaid more slowly early on, so the interest is somewhat higher. This doesn't mean that one loan is better than the other; it means that one is effectively paid off faster than the other. For example, the principal reduction in the first year is ₹835.46 in the equal total payment case as compared to ₹1,000 in the first case.

EXAMPLE 4.28

Partial Amortization, or "Bite the Bullet" A common arrangement in real estate lending might call for a 5-year loan with, say, a 15-year amortization. What this means is that the borrower makes a payment every month of a fixed amount based on a 15-year amortization. However, after 60 months, the borrower makes a single, much larger payment called a "balloon" or "bullet" to pay off the loan. Because the monthly payments don't fully pay off the loan, the loan is said to be partially amortized.

Suppose we have a ₹100,000 commercial mortgage with a 12 percent APR and a 20-year (240-month) amortization. Further suppose the mortgage has a five-year balloon. What will the monthly payment be? How big will the balloon payment be?

The monthly payment can be calculated based on an ordinary annuity with a present value of ₹100,000. There are 240 payments and the interest rate is 1 percent per month. The monthly payment is:

$$\text{₹}100{,}000 = C \times [1 - (1/1.01^{240})]/.01$$
$$= C \times 90.8194$$
$$C = \text{₹}1{,}101.09$$

There is an easy way and a hard way to determine the balloon payment. The hard way is to actually amortize the loan for 60 months to see what the balance is at that time. The easy way is to recognize that after 60 months, we have a 240 − 60 = 180-month loan. The payment is still ₹1,101.09 per month, and the interest rate is still 1 percent per month. The loan balance is the present value of the remaining payments:

$$\text{Loan balance} = \text{₹}1{,}101.09 \times [1 - (1/1.01^{180})]/.01$$
$$= \text{₹}1{,}101.09 \times 83.3217$$
$$= \text{₹}91{,}744.33$$

The balloon payment is a substantial ₹91,744. Why is it so large? To get an idea, consider the first payment on the mortgage. The interest in the first month is ₹100,000 × .01 = ₹1,000. Your payment is ₹1,101.09, so the loan balance declines by only ₹101.09. Because the loan balance declines so slowly, the cumulative "pay down" over five years is not large.

We will close this section with an example that may be of particular relevance. Federal Stafford loans are an important source of financing for many college students, helping to cover the cost of tuition, books, new cars, condominiums, and many other things. Sometimes students do not seem to fully realize that Stafford loans have a serious drawback: They must be repaid in monthly installments, usually beginning six months after the student leaves school.

Some Stafford loans are subsidized, meaning that the interest does not begin to accrue until repayment begins (this is a good thing). If you are a dependent undergraduate student under this particular option, the maximum subsidized debt you can run up is ₹23,000. The interest rate in 2020–2021 is 2.75 percent, or 2.75/12 = .2292 percent per month. Under the "standard repayment plan," the loans are amortized over 10 years (subject to a minimum payment of ₹50 per month).

Suppose you max out borrowing under this program. Beginning six months after you graduate (or otherwise depart the ivory tower), how much is your monthly payment? How much will you owe after making payments for four years?

Given our earlier discussions, see if you don't agree that your monthly payment assuming a ₹23,000 total loan is ₹219.45 per month. Also, as explained in Example 4.28, after making payments for four years, you still owe the

SPREADSHEET APPLICATIONS

Loan Amortization Using a Spreadsheet

Loan amortization is a common spreadsheet application. To illustrate, we will set up the problem that we examined earlier: a five-year, ₹5,000, 9 percent loan with constant payments. Our spreadsheet looks like this:

	A	B	C	D	E	F	G	H
1								
2				Using a spreadsheet to amortize a loan				
3								
4			Loan amount:	₹5,000				
5			Interest rate:	0.09				
6			Loan term:	5				
7			Loan payment:	**₹1,285.46**				
8				Note: Payment is calculated using PMT(rate, nper, -pv, fv).				
9		*Amortization table:*						
10								
11		Year	Beginning	Total	Interest	Principal	Ending	
12			Balance	Payment	Paid	Paid	Balance	
13		1	₹5,000.00	₹1,285.46	₹450.00	₹835.46	₹4,164.54	
14		2	4,164.54	1,285.46	374.81	910.65	3,253.88	
15		3	3,253.88	1,285.46	292.85	992.61	2,261.27	
16		4	2,261.27	1,285.46	203.51	1,081.95	1,179.32	
17		5	1,179.32	1,285.46	106.14	1,179.32	0.00	
18		Totals		6,427.31	1,427.31	5,000.00		
19								
20		*Formulas in the amortization table:*						
21								
22		Year	Beginning	Total	Interest	Principal	Ending	
23			Balance	Payment	Paid	Paid	Balance	
24		1	=+D4	=₹D₹7	=+₹D₹5*C13	=+D13-E13	=+C13-F13	
25		2	=+G13	=₹D₹7	=+₹D₹5*C14	=+D14-E14	=+C14-F14	
26		3	=+G14	=₹D₹7	=+₹D₹5*C15	=+D15-E15	=+C15-F15	
27		4	=+G15	=₹D₹7	=+₹D₹5*C16	=+D16-E16	=+C16-F16	
28		5	=+G16	=₹D₹7	=+₹D₹5*C17	=+D17-E17	=+C17-F17	
29								
30		Note: Totals in the amortization table are calculated using the SUM formula.						
31								

present value of the remaining payments. There are 120 payments in all. After you make 48 of them (the first four years), you have 72 to go. By now, it should be easy for you to verify that the present value of ₹219.45 per month for 72 months at .2292 percent per month is about ₹14,550, so you still have a long way to go.

Of course, it is possible to rack up much larger debts. For example, the son of former Federal Reserve Chair Ben Bernanke graduated medical school with over ₹400,000 in student loans! In fact, according to the Association of American Medical Colleges, medical students who borrowed to attend medical school and graduated in 2019 had an average student loan balance of ₹201,490. Similarly, in India, the average student loan balance is ₹25 lakh per borrower who graduated in 2022. Ouch! How long will it take the average student to pay off her medical school loans?

To answer, let's say she makes a monthly payment of ₹1,400, and the loan has an interest rate of 7 percent per year, or .5833 percent per month. See if you agree that it will take about 315 months, or a little more than 26 years, to pay off the loan. Maybe MD really stands for "mucho debt"!

4.6 What Is a Firm Worth?

Suppose you are a business appraiser trying to determine the value of small companies. How can you determine what a firm is worth? One way to think about the question of how much a firm is worth is to calculate the present value of its future cash flows.

Let us consider the example of a firm that is expected to generate net cash flows (cash inflows minus cash outflows) of ₹5,000 at the end of the first year and ₹2,000 for each of the next five years. The firm can be sold for ₹10,000 seven years from now. After considering other investments available in the market with similar risks, the owners of the firm would like to be able to make 10 percent on their investment in the firm.

The value of the firm is the sum of the present values of the individual net cash flows. The present values of the firm's cash flows are:

The Present Value of the Firm

Year	Net Cash Flow of the Firm	Present Value Factor (10%)	Present Value of Net Cash Flows
1	₹ 5,000	.90909	₹ 4,545.45
2	2,000	.82645	1,652.89
3	2,000	.75131	1,502.63
4	2,000	.68301	1,366.03
5	2,000	.62092	1,241.84
6	2,000	.56447	1,128.95
7	10,000	.51316	5,131.58
		Present value of firm	₹16,569.38

Algebraically, we can write:

$$₹5{,}000/1.1 + 2{,}000/1.1^2 + \cdots + 2{,}000/1.1^6 + 10{,}000/1.1^7$$

We also can use the formula for an annuity:

$$\frac{₹5{,}000}{1.1} + \frac{₹2{,}000 \times \left(1 - 1/1.1^5\right)/.10}{1.1} + \frac{₹10{,}000}{1.1^7} = ₹16{,}569.38$$

Suppose you have the opportunity to acquire the firm for ₹12,000. Should you acquire the firm? The answer is yes because the NPV is positive:

$$\text{NPV} = \text{PV} - \text{Cost}$$

$$₹4{,}569.38 = ₹16{,}569.38 - 12{,}000$$

The incremental value (NPV) of acquiring the firm is ₹4,569.38.

EXAMPLE 4.29

Firm Valuation The Udipi Tiffins Company is contemplating investing ₹1 million in four new outlets in Hyderabad. Rahul Gandharv, the firm's chief financial officer (CFO), has estimated that the investments will pay out cash flows of ₹200,000 per year for nine years at the end of each year and nothing thereafter. Rahul has determined that the relevant discount rate for this investment is 15 percent. This is the rate of return that the firm can earn on comparable projects. Should the Udipi Tiffins Company make the investments in the new outlets?

The decision can be evaluated as follows:

$$\begin{aligned} \text{NPV} &= -₹1{,}000{,}000 + \frac{₹200{,}000}{1.15} + \frac{₹200{,}000}{1.15^2} + \cdots + \frac{₹200{,}000}{1.15^9} \\ &= -₹1{,}000{,}000 + ₹200{,}000 \times \text{PVIFA}_{15\%,9} \\ &= -₹1{,}000{,}000 + 954{,}316.78 \\ &= -₹45{,}683.22 \end{aligned}$$

The present value of the four new outlets is only ₹954,316.78. The outlets are worth less than they cost. The Udipi Tiffins Company should not make the investment because the NPV is −₹45,683.22. If the Udipi Tiffins Company requires a 15 percent rate of return, the new outlets are not a good investment.

SPREADSHEET APPLICATIONS

How to Calculate Present Values with Multiple Future Cash Flows Using a Spreadsheet

We can set up a basic spreadsheet to calculate the present values of the individual cash flows as follows. Notice that we have calculated the present values one at a time and added them up:

	A	B	C	D	E
1					
2	**Using a spreadsheet to value multiple future cash flows**				
3					
4	What is the present value of ₹200 in one year, ₹400 the next year, ₹600 the next year, and				
5	₹800 the last year if the discount rate is 12 percent?				
6					
7	Rate:	0.12			
8					
9	Year	Cash flows	Present values	Formula used	
10	1	₹200	₹178.57	=PV(₹B₹7,A10,0,–B10)	
11	2	₹400	₹318.88	=PV(₹B₹7,A11,0,–B11)	
12	3	₹600	₹427.07	=PV(₹B₹7,A12,0,–B12)	
13	4	₹800	₹508.41	=PV(₹B₹7,A13,0,–B13)	
14					
15		Total PV:	**₹1,432.93**	=SUM(C10:C13)	
16					
17	Notice the negative signs inserted in the PV formulas. These make the present value positive.				
18	The discount rate in cell B7 is entered as ₹B₹7 (an "absolute" reference) because we want to				
19	reference this cell every time we copy and paste this formula. We could have just entered ".12"				
20	instead, but our approach is more flexible.				
21					
22					

RESEARCH IN EMERGING MARKET CONTEXT

Anesten et al. (2020) found that the dividend discount model offers the most accurate valuation model when comparing several techniques for equity valuation based on projections of firm dividends, earnings, and/or equity book values for Scandinavian countries. But for valuation purposes, experts like to employ discounted cash flow (DCF) (Mukhlynina & Nyborg, 2020). However, they discovered that there is still a misunderstanding over the weighted average cost of capital (WACC) and the application of interest tax shielding. Using a survey technique, they discovered that professional education is less influential on valuing approaches than the profession, i.e., every profession applies the DCF approach while considering the particulars of that discipline.

References

Anesten, S., Möller, N., Skogsvik, K., & Skogsvik, S. (2020). The pricing accuracy of alternative equity valuation models: Scandinavian evidence. *Journal of International Financial Management & Accounting*, 31(1), 5–34.

Mukhlynina, L., & Nyborg, K. G. (2016). The choice of valuation techniques in practice: education versus profession. *Swiss Finance Institute Research Paper*, (16–36).

Summary and Conclusions

1. Two basic concepts, future value and present value, were introduced in the beginning of this chapter. With a 10 percent discount rate, an investor with ₹1 today can generate a future value of ₹1.10 in a year, ₹1.21 (= ₹1 × 1.10^2) in two years, and so on. Conversely, present value analysis places a current value on a future cash flow. With the same 10 percent rate, a rupee to be received in one year has a present value of ₹.909 (= ₹1/1.10) today. A rupee to be received in two years has a present value of ₹.826 (= ₹1/1.10^2) today.
2. We commonly express an interest rate as, say, 12 percent per year. However, we can speak of the interest rate as 3 percent per quarter. Although the annual percentage rate remains 12 percent (= 3 percent × 4), the effective annual interest rate is 12.55 percent (= $1.03^4 - 1$). In other words, the compounding process increases the future value of an investment. The limiting case is continuous compounding, where funds are assumed to be reinvested every infinitesimal instant.
3. A basic quantitative technique for financial decision making is net present value analysis. The net present value formula for an investment that generates cash flows (C_i) in future periods is:

$$\text{NPV} = -C_0 + \frac{C_1}{(1+r)} + \frac{C_2}{(1+r)^2} + \cdots + \frac{C_t}{(1+r)^t} = -C_0 + \sum_{i=1}^{t} \frac{C_i}{(1+r)^i}$$

   The formula assumes that the cash flow at Year 0 is the initial investment (a cash outflow) and r is the appropriate discount rate reflecting time and risk.
4. Frequently, the actual calculation of present value is long and tedious. The computation of the present value of a 30-year mortgage with monthly payments is a good example. We presented four simplifying formulas:

$$\text{Perpetuity: PV} = \frac{C}{r}$$

$$\text{Growing perpetuity: PV} = \frac{C}{r-g}$$

$$\text{Annuity: PV} = C\left[\frac{1 - \dfrac{1}{(1+r)^t}}{r}\right]$$

$$\text{Growing annuity: PV} = C\left[\frac{1 - \left(\dfrac{1+g}{1+r}\right)^t}{r-g}\right]$$

5. We stressed a few practical considerations in the application of these formulas:
   a. The numerator in each of the formulas, *C*, is the cash flow to be received in one period.
   b. Cash flows are generally irregular in practice. To avoid unwieldy problems, assumptions to create more regular cash flows are made both in this textbook and in the real world.
   c. A number of present value problems involve annuities (or perpetuities) beginning a few periods in the future. You should practice combining the annuity (or perpetuity) formula with the discounting formula to solve these problems.
   d. Annuities and perpetuities may have periods of every *n* years, rather than once a year. Using the effective rate for *n* years allows us to use the annuity or perpetuity formula.
   e. We frequently encounter problems where the present value of one annuity must be equated with the present value of another annuity.

Concept Questions

1. **Compounding Periods** As you increase the length of time involved, what happens to future values? What happens to present values?

2. **Interest Rates** What happens to the future value of an annuity if you increase the rate *r*? What happens to the present value?

3. **Present Value** Suppose two athletes each sign a 10-year contract for ₹80 million. In one case, we're told that the ₹80 million will be paid in 10 equal installments. In the other case, we're told that the ₹80 million will be paid in 10 installments, but the installments will increase by 5 percent per year. Who got the better deal?

4. **APR and EAR** Should lending laws be changed to require lenders to report EARs instead of APRs? Why or why not?

5. **Time Value** On subsidized Stafford loans, a common source of financial aid for college students, interest does not begin to accrue until repayment begins. Who receives a bigger subsidy: a freshman or a senior? Explain.

Use the following information to answer the next five questions:

Toyota Motor Credit Corporation (TMCC), a subsidiary of Toyota Motor Corporation, offered some securities for sale to the public on March 28, 2008. Under the terms of the deal, TMCC promised to repay the owner of one of these securities ₹100,000 on March 28, 2038, but investors would receive nothing until then. Investors paid TMCC ₹24,099 for each of these securities; so they gave up ₹24,099 on March 28, 2008, for the promise of a ₹100,000 payment 30 years later.

6. **Time Value of Money** Why would TMCC be willing to accept such a small amount today (₹24,099) in exchange for a promise to repay about four times that amount (₹100,000) in the future?

7. **Call Provisions** A feature of this particular deal is that TMCC has the right to buy back the securities on the anniversary date at a price established when the securities were issued. What impact does this feature have on the desirability of this security as an investment?

8. **Time Value of Money** Would you be willing to pay ₹24,099 today in exchange for ₹100,000 in 30 years? What would be the key considerations in answering yes or no? Would your answer depend on who is making the promise to repay?

9. **Investment Comparison** Suppose that when TMCC offered the security for ₹24,099, the U.S. Treasury had offered an essentially identical security. Do you think it would have had a higher or lower price? Why?

10. **Length of Investment** The TMCC security is bought and sold on the New York Stock Exchange. If you looked at the price today, do you think the price would exceed the ₹24,099 original price? Why? If you looked in the year 2025, do you think the price would be higher or lower than today's price? Why?

Questions and Problems

BASIC (Questions 1–20)

1. **Simple Interest versus Compound Interest** First City Bank pays 7.5 percent simple interest on its savings account balances, whereas Second City Bank pays 7.5 percent interest compounded annually. If you made a deposit of ₹8,600 in each bank, how much more money would you earn from your Second City Bank account at the end of eight years?

2. **Calculating Future Values** Compute the future value of ₹1,640 compounded annually for:

   a. 10 years at 5 percent.
   b. 10 years at 10 percent.
   c. 20 years at 5 percent.
   d. Why is the interest earned in part (c) not twice the amount earned in part (a)?

3. **Calculating Present Values** For each of the following, compute the present value:

Present Value	Years	Interest Rate	Future Value
	17	9%	₹ 16,832
	9	7	48,318
	23	13	886,073
	35	21	550,164

4. **Calculating Interest Rates** Solve for the unknown interest rate in each of the following:

Present Value	Years	Interest Rate	Future Value
₹ 181	8		₹ 317
335	13		1,080
48,000	11		185,382
40,353	25		531,618

5. **Calculating the Number of Periods** Solve for the unknown number of years in each of the following:

Present Value	Years	Interest Rate	Future Value
₹ 610		7%	₹ 1,389
940		8	1,821
26,350		9	289,715
43,500		11	430,258

6. **Calculating the Number of Periods** At 4.3 percent interest, how long does it take to double your money? To quadruple it?

7. **Calculating Present Values** Imprudential, Inc., has an unfunded pension liability of ₹450 million that must be paid in 20 years. To assess the value of the firm's stock, financial analysts want to discount this liability back to the present. If the relevant discount rate is 5.2 percent, what is the present value of this liability?

8. **Calculating Rates of Return** Although appealing to more refined tastes, art as a collectible has not always performed so profitably. During 2003, Sotheby's sold the Edgar Degas bronze sculpture *Petite Danseuse de Quatorze Ans* at auction for a price of ₹10,311,500. Unfortunately for the previous owner, he had purchased it in 1999 at a price of ₹12,377,500. What was his annual rate of return on this sculpture?

9. **Perpetuities** An investor purchasing a British consol is entitled to receive annual payments from the British government forever. What is the price of a consol that pays ₹50 annually if the next payment occurs one year from today? The market rate is 2.9 percent.

10. **Continuous Compounding** Compute the future value of ₹4,250 continuously compounded for:
    a. 9 years at an APR of 12 percent.
    b. 5 years at an APR of 8 percent.
    c. 17 years at an APR of 5 percent.
    d. 10 years at an APR of 9 percent.

11. **Present Value and Multiple Cash Flows** Mendez Co. has identified an investment project with the following cash flows. If the discount rate is 10 percent, what is the present value of these cash flows? What is the present value at 18 percent? At 24 percent?

Year	Cash Flow
1	₹470
2	610
3	735
4	920

12. **Present Value and Multiple Cash Flows** Investment X offers to pay you ₹5,300 per year for eight years, whereas Investment Y offers to pay you ₹7,300 per year for five years. Which of these cash flow streams has the higher present value if the discount rate is 5 percent? If the discount rate is 15 percent?

13. **Calculating Annuity Present Value** An investment offers ₹3,850 per year for 15 years, with the first payment occurring one year from now. If the required return is 6 percent, what is the value of the investment? What would the value be if the payments occurred for 40 years? For 75 years? Forever?

14. **Calculating Perpetuity Values** The Perpetual Life Insurance Co. is trying to sell you an investment policy that will pay you and your heirs ₹20,000 per year forever. If the required return on this investment is 3.4 percent, how much will you pay for the policy? Suppose the Perpetual Life Insurance Co. told you the policy costs ₹475,000. At what discount rate would this be a fair deal?

15. **Calculating EAR** Find the EAR in each of the following cases:

APR	Number of Times Compounded	EAR
7.8%	Quarterly	
15.3	Monthly	
12.4	Daily	
11.4	Infinite	

16. **Calculating APR** Find the APR in each of the following cases:

APR	Number of Times Compounded	EAR
	Semiannually	14.2%
	Monthly	18.4
	Weekly	11.1
	Infinite	8.9

17. **Calculating EAR** First National Bank charges 13.8 percent compounded monthly on its business loans. First United Bank charges 14.1 percent compounded semiannually. As a potential borrower, to which bank would you go for a new loan?

18. **Interest Rates** Well-known financial writer Andrew Tobias argues that he can earn 177 percent per year buying wine by the case. Specifically, he assumes that he will consume one ₹10 bottle of fine Bordeaux per week for the next 12 weeks. He can either pay ₹10 per week or buy a case of 12 bottles today. If he buys the case, he receives a 10 percent discount and, by doing so, earns the 177 percent. Assume he buys the wine and consumes the first bottle today. Do you agree with his analysis? Do you see a problem with his numbers?

19. **Calculating Number of Periods** One of your customers is delinquent on his accounts payable balance. You've mutually agreed to a repayment schedule of ₹500 per month. You will charge 1.8 percent per month interest on the overdue balance. If the current balance is ₹18,000, how long will it take for the account to be paid off?

20. **Calculating EAR** Friendly's Quick Loans, Inc., offers you "three for four or I knock on your door." This means you get ₹3 today and repay ₹4 when you get your paycheck in one week (or else). What's the EAR Friendly's earns on this lending business? If you were brave enough to ask, what APR would Friendly's say you were paying?

INTERMEDIATE (Questions 21–50)

21. **Future Value** What is the future value in 11 years of ₹1,200 invested in an account with an APR of 7.8 percent:

a. Compounded annually?
b. Compounded semiannually?
c. Compounded monthly?
d. Compounded continuously?
e. Why does the future value increase as the compounding period shortens?

22. **Simple Interest versus Compound Interest** First Simple Bank pays 6.4 percent simple interest on its investment accounts. If First Complex Bank pays interest on its accounts compounded annually, what rate should the bank set if it wants to match First Simple Bank over an investment horizon of 10 years?

23. **Calculating Annuities** You are planning to save for retirement over the next 30 years. To do this, you will invest ₹850 per month in a stock account and ₹250 per month in a bond account. The return of the stock account is expected to be 11 percent, and the bond account will return 6 percent. When you retire, you will combine your money into an account with a return of 5 percent. All interest rates are APRs with monthly compounding. How much can you withdraw each month from your account assuming a 25-year withdrawal period?

24. **Calculating Rates of Return** Suppose an investment offers to triple your money in 12 months (don't believe it). What rate of return per quarter are you being offered?

25. **Calculating Rates of Return** You're trying to choose between two different investments, both of which have up-front costs of ₹65,000. Investment G returns ₹125,000 in 6 years. Investment H returns ₹205,000 in 10 years. Which of these investments has the higher return?

26. **Growing Perpetuities** Mark Weinstein has been working on an advanced technology in laser eye surgery. His technology will be available in the near term. He anticipates his first annual cash flow

from the technology to be ₹225,000, received two years from today. Subsequent annual cash flows will grow at 3.2 percent in perpetuity. What is the present value of the technology if the discount rate is 10.1 percent?

27. **Perpetuities** A prestigious investment bank designed a new security that pays a quarterly dividend of ₹2.50 in perpetuity. The first dividend occurs one quarter from today. What is the price of the security if the APR is 3.7 percent compounded quarterly?

28. **Annuity Present Values** What is the value today of ₹5,100 per year, at a discount rate of 7.9 percent, if the first payment is received 6 years from today and the last payment is received 20 years from today?

29. **Annuity Present Values** What is the value today of a 15-year annuity that pays ₹950 a year? The annuity's first payment occurs 6 years from today. The discount rate is 7 percent for Years 1 through 5 and 10 percent thereafter.

30. **Balloon Payments** Amanda Rice has arranged to purchase a ₹775,000 vacation home in the Bahamas with a 20 percent down payment. The mortgage has a 4.9 APR compounded monthly and calls for equal monthly payments over the next 30 years. Her first payment will be due one month from now. However, the mortgage has an eight-year balloon payment, meaning that the balance of the loan must be paid off at the end of Year 8. There were no other transaction costs or finance charges. How much will Amanda's balloon payment be in eight years?

31. **Calculating Interest Expense** You receive a credit card application from Shady Banks Savings and Loan offering an introductory rate of 1.25 percent per year, compounded monthly for the first six months, increasing thereafter to 17.8 percent compounded monthly. Assuming you transfer the ₹9,000 balance from your existing credit card and make no subsequent payments, how much interest will you owe at the end of the first year?

32. **Perpetuities** M3 Pharmaceuticals is considering a drug project that costs ₹5.95 million today and is expected to generate end-of-year annual cash flows of ₹560,000 forever. At what discount rate would the company be indifferent between accepting or rejecting the project?

33. **Growing Annuity** Southern California Publishing Company is trying to decide whether to revise its popular textbook *Financial Psychoanalysis Made Simple*. The company has estimated that the revision will cost ₹325,000. Cash flows from increased sales will be ₹94,000 the first year. These cash flows will increase by 4 percent per year. The book will go out of print five years from now. Assume that the initial cost is paid now and revenues are received at the end of each year. If the company requires a return of 10 percent for such an investment, should it undertake the revision?

34. **Growing Annuity** Your job pays you only once a year for all the work you did over the previous 12 months. Today, December 31, you just received your salary of ₹48,000 and you plan to spend all of it. However, you want to start saving for retirement beginning next year. You have decided that one year from today you will begin depositing 9 percent of your annual salary in an account that will earn 10 percent per year. Your salary will increase at 3.5 percent per year throughout your career. How much money will you have on the date of your retirement 40 years from today?

35. **Present Value and Discount Rates** What is the relationship between the value of an annuity and the level of interest rates? Suppose you just bought an annuity with 13 annual payments of ₹10,000 per year at a discount rate of 10 percent per year. What happens to the value of your investment if the discount rate suddenly drops to 5 percent? What if the discount rate rate suddenly rises to 15 percent?

36. **Calculating the Number of Payments** You're prepared to make monthly payments of ₹225, beginning at the end of this month, into an account that pays an APR of 6.5 percent compounded monthly. How many payments will you have made when your account balance reaches ₹15,000?

37. **Calculating Annuity Present Values** You want to borrow ₹95,000 from your local bank to buy a new sailboat. You can afford to make monthly payments of ₹1,850, but no more. Assuming monthly compounding, what is the highest rate you can afford on a 60-month APR loan?

38. **Calculating Loan Payments** You need a 30-year, fixed-rate mortgage to buy a new home for ₹245,000. Your mortgage bank will lend you the money at an APR of 4.8 percent for this 360-month loan. However, you can afford monthly payments of only ₹900, so you offer to pay off any remaining loan balance at the end of the loan in the form of a single balloon payment. How large will this balloon payment have to be for you to keep your monthly payments at ₹900?

39. **Present and Future Values** The present value of the following cash flow stream is ₹8,200 when discounted at 9 percent annually. What is the value of the missing cash flow?

Year	Cash Flow
1	₹2,100
2	?
3	2,740
4	3,270

40. **Calculating Present Values** You just won the TVM Lottery. You will receive ₹1 million today plus another 10 annual payments that increase by ₹450,000 per year. Thus, in one year, you receive ₹1.45 million. In two years, you get ₹1.9 million, and so on. If the appropriate interest rate is 6.2 percent, what is the value of your winnings today?

41. **EAR versus APR** You have just purchased a new warehouse. To finance the purchase, you've arranged for a 30-year mortgage loan for 80 percent of the ₹2.6 million purchase price. The monthly payment on this loan will be ₹14,200. What is the APR on this loan? The EAR?

42. **Present Value and Break-Even Rate** Consider a firm with a contract to sell an asset for ₹175,000 four years from now. The asset costs ₹104,600 to produce today. Given a relevant discount rate of 11 percent per year, will the firm make a profit on this asset? At what rate does the firm just break even?

43. **Present Value and Multiple Cash Flows** You are buying a house and will borrow ₹265,000 on a 30-year fixed rate mortgage with monthly payments to finance the purchase. Your loan officer has offered you a mortgage with an APR of 4.6 percent. Alternatively, she tells you that you can "buy down" the interest rate to 4.25 percent if you pay points up front on the loan. A point on a loan is 1 percent (one percentage point) of the loan value. How many points, at most, would you be willing to pay to buy down the interest rate?

44. **Variable Discount Rates** A 15-year annuity pays ₹1,750 per month, and payments are made at the end of each month. If the APR is 9 percent compounded monthly for the first seven years, and APR of 6 percent compounded monthly thereafter, what is the value of the annuity today?

45. **Comparing Cash Flow Streams** You have your choice of two investment accounts. Investment A is a 13-year annuity that features end-of-month ₹1,600 payments and has an APR of 7.8 percent compounded monthly. Investment B is a 7 percent continuously compounded lump sum investment, also good for 13 years. How much money would you need to invest in Investment B today for it to be worth as much as Investment A 13 years from now?

46. **Calculating Present Value of a Perpetuity** Given a discount rate of 4.6 percent per year, what is the value at Date $t = 7$ of a perpetual stream of ₹7,300 payments with the first payment at Date $t = 15$?

47. **Calculating EAR** A local finance company quotes an interest rate of 18.4 percent on one-year loans. So, if you borrow ₹20,000, the interest for the year will be ₹3,680. Because you must repay a total of ₹23,680 in one year, the finance company requires you to pay ₹23,680/12, or ₹1,973.33, per month over the next 12 months. Is the interest rate on this loan 18.4 percent? What rate would legally have to be quoted? What is the effective annual rate?

48. **Calculating Present Values** A five-year annuity of 10 ₹5,500 semiannual payments will begin nine years from now, with the first payment coming nine and a half years from now. If the discount rate is 8 percent compounded monthly, what is the value of this annuity five years from now? What is the value three years from now? What is the current value of the annuity?

49. **Calculating Annuities Due** Suppose you are going to receive ₹14,500 per year for five years. The appropriate interest rate is 7.1 percent.

   a. What is the present value of the payments if they are in the form of an ordinary annuity? What is the present value if the payments are an annuity due?
   b. Suppose you plan to invest the payments for five years. What is the future value if the payments are an ordinary annuity? What if the payments are an annuity due?
   c. Which has the highest present value, the ordinary annuity or annuity due? Which has the highest future value? Will this always be true?

50. **Calculating Annuities Due** You want to buy a new sports car from Muscle Motors for ₹64,500. The contract is in the form of a 60-month annuity due at an APR of 5.4 percent. What will your monthly payment be?

CHALLENGE (Questions 51–75)

51. **Calculating Annuities Due** You want to lease a set of golf clubs from Pings Ltd. The lease contract is in the form of 24 equal monthly payments at an APR of 10.4 percent compounded monthly. Because the clubs cost ₹3,850 retail, the company wants the value today of the lease payments to equal ₹3,850. Suppose that your first payment is due immediately. What will your monthly lease payments be?

52. **Annuities** You are saving for the college education of your two children. They are two years apart in age; one will begin college 15 years from today and the other will begin 17 years from today. You estimate your children's college expenses to be ₹76,000 per year per child, payable at the beginning of each school year. The appropriate interest rate is 7.8 percent. How much money must you deposit in an account each year to fund your children's education? Your deposits begin one year from today. You will make your last deposit when your oldest child enters college. Assume four years of college for each child.

53. **Growing Annuities** Mateo has received a job offer from a large investment bank as a clerk to an associate banker. His base salary will be ₹83,000. He will receive his first annual salary payment one year from the day he begins to work. In addition, he will get an immediate ₹10,000 bonus for joining the company. His salary will grow at 3.8 percent each year. Each year he will receive a bonus equal to 10 percent of his salary. He is expected to work for 30 years. What is the present value of the offer if the discount rate is 7.1 percent?

54. **Calculating Annuities** You have recently won the super jackpot in the Washington State Lottery. After reading the fine print, you discover that you have the following two options:

   a. You will receive 31 annual payments of ₹300,000, with the first payment being delivered today. The income will be taxed at a rate of 28 percent. Taxes will be withheld when the checks are issued.
   b. You will receive ₹750,000 now, and you will not have to pay taxes on this amount. In addition, beginning one year from today, you will receive ₹250,000 each year for 30 years. The cash flows from this annuity will be taxed at 28 percent.

   Using a discount rate of 4.95 percent, which option should you select?

55. **Calculating Growing Annuities** You have 35 years left until retirement and want to retire with ₹4.5 million. Your salary is paid annually, and you will receive ₹91,000 at the end of the current year. Your salary will increase at 3 percent per year, and you can earn a return of 9.4 percent on the money you invest. If you save a constant percentage of your salary, what percentage of your salary must you save each year?

56. **Balloon Payments** On September 1, 2021, Susan Chao bought a motorcycle for ₹35,000. She paid ₹4,500 down and financed the balance with a five-year loan at an annual percentage rate of 6.8 percent compounded monthly. She started the monthly payments exactly one month after the purchase (i.e., October 1, 2021). Two years later, at the end of October 2023, she got a new job and decided to pay off the loan. If the bank charges her a 1 percent prepayment penalty based on the loan balance, how much must she pay the bank on November 1, 2023?

57. **Calculating Annuity Values** Bilbo Baggins wants to save money to meet three objectives. First, he would like to be able to retire 30 years from now with retirement income of ₹16,000 per month for 25 years, with the first payment received 30 years and 1 month from now. Second, he would like to purchase a cabin in Rivendell in 10 years at an estimated cost of ₹375,000. Third, after he passes on at the end of the 25 years of withdrawals, he would like to leave an inheritance of ₹1.5 million to his nephew Frodo. He can afford to save ₹2,150 per month for the next 10 years. If he can earn an EAR of 10 percent before he retires and an EAR of 7 percent after he retires, how much will he have to save each month in Years 11 through 30?

58. **Calculating Annuity Values** After deciding to acquire a new car, you can either lease the car or purchase it on a three-year loan. The car you wish to buy costs ₹49,000. The dealer has a special leasing arrangement where you pay ₹5,100 today and ₹545 per month for the next three years. If you purchase the car, you will pay it off in monthly payments over the next three years at an APR of 5.3 percent. You believe you will be able to sell the car for ₹32,000 in three years. Should you buy or lease the car? What break-even resale price in three years would make you indifferent between buying and leasing?

59. **Calculating Annuity Values** An All-Pro defensive lineman is in contract negotiations. The team has offered the following salary structure:

Time	Salary
0	₹7,900,000
1	4,500,000
2	5,300,000
3	6,100,000
4	6,700,000
5	7,700,000
6	9,300,000

All salaries are to be paid in lump sums. The player has asked you as his agent to renegotiate the terms. He wants a ₹10 million signing bonus payable today and a contract value increase of ₹2 million. He also wants an equal salary paid every three months, with the first paycheck three months from now. If the APR rate is 4.8 percent compounded daily, what is the amount of his quarterly check? Assume 365 days in a year.

60. **Discount Interest Loans** This question illustrates what is known as *discount interest*. Imagine you are discussing a loan with a somewhat unscrupulous lender. You want to borrow ₹20,000 for one year. The interest rate is 14.6 percent. You and the lender agree that the interest on the loan will be .146 × ₹20,000 = ₹2,920. So, the lender deducts this interest amount from the loan up front and gives you ₹17,080. In this case, we say that the discount is ₹2,920. What's wrong here?

61. **Calculating Annuity Values** You are serving on a jury. A plaintiff is suing the city for injuries sustained after a freak street sweeper accident. In the trial, doctors testified that it will be five years before the plaintiff is able to return to work. The jury has already decided in favor of the plaintiff. You are the foreperson of the jury and propose that the jury give the plaintiff an award to cover the following: (a) The present value of two years' back pay. The plaintiff's annual salary for the last two years would have been ₹43,000 and ₹46,000, respectively. (b) The present value of five years' future salary. You assume the salary will be ₹51,000 per year. (c) ₹150,000 for pain and suffering. (d) ₹20,000 for court costs. Assume that the salary payments are equal amounts paid at the end of each month. If the interest rate you choose is an EAR of 5.9 percent, what is the size of the settlement? If you were the plaintiff, would you like to see a higher or lower interest rate?

62. **Calculating EAR with Points** You are looking at a one-year loan of ₹10,000. The interest rate is quoted as 8 percent plus 3 points. A *point* on a loan is 1 percent (one percentage point) of the loan

amount. Quotes similar to this one are common with home mortgages. The interest rate quotation in this example requires the borrower to pay 3 points to the lender up front and repay the loan later with 8 percent interest. What rate would you actually be paying here? What is the EAR for a one-year loan with a quoted interest rate of 11 percent plus 2 points? Is your answer affected by the loan amount?

63. **EAR versus APR** Two banks in the area offer 30-year, ₹320,000 mortgages at 4.9 percent and charge a ₹5,500 loan application fee. However, the application fee charged by Insecurity Bank and Trust is refundable if the loan application is denied, whereas that charged by I.M. Greedy and Sons Mortgage Bank is not. The current disclosure law requires that any fees that will be refunded if the applicant is rejected be included in calculating the APR, but this is not required with nonrefundable fees (presumably because refundable fees are part of the loan rather than a fee). What are the EARs on these two loans? What are the APRs?

64. **Calculating EAR with Add-On Interest** This problem illustrates a deceptive way of quoting interest rates called *add-on interest*. Imagine that you see an advertisement for Crazy Judy's Stereo City that reads something like this: "₹1,500 Instant Credit! 18.4% Simple Interest! Three Years to Pay! Low, Low Monthly Payments!" You're not exactly sure what all this means and somebody has spilled ink over the APR on the loan contract, so you ask the manager for clarification.

Judy explains that if you borrow ₹1,500 for three years at 18.4 percent interest, in three years you will owe:

$$₹1{,}500 \times 1.184^3 = ₹1{,}500 \times 1.65980 = ₹2{,}489.70$$

Now, Judy recognizes that coming up with ₹2,489.70 all at once might be a strain, so she lets you make "low, low monthly payments" of ₹2,489.70/36 = ₹69.16 per month, even though this is extra bookkeeping work for her.

Is the interest rate on this loan 18.4 percent? Why or why not? What is the APR on this loan? What is the EAR? Why do you think this is called add-on interest?

65. **Calculating the Number of Periods** Your Christmas ski vacation was great, but it unfortunately ran a bit over budget. All is not lost: You just received an offer in the mail to transfer your ₹15,000 balance from your current credit card, which charges an annual rate of 18.6 percent, to a new credit card charging a rate of 9.2 percent. How much faster could you pay the loan off by making your planned monthly payments of ₹275 with the new card? What if there was a fee of 2 percent charged on any balances transferred?

66. **Future Value and Multiple Cash Flows** An insurance company is offering a new policy to its customers. Typically, the policy is bought by a parent or grandparent for a child at the child's birth. For this policy, the purchaser (say, the parent) makes the following six payments to the insurance company:

First birthday	₹ 800
Second birthday	₹ 800
Third birthday	₹ 900
Fourth birthday	₹ 900
Fifth birthday	₹1,000
Sixth birthday	₹1,000

After the child's sixth birthday, no more payments are made. When the child reaches age 65, he or she receives ₹350,000. If the relevant rate is 10 percent for the first six years and 7 percent for all subsequent years, is the policy worth buying?

67. **Annuity Present Values and Effective Rates** You have won the lottery. You will receive ₹5 million today, and then receive 40 payments of ₹2.1 million. These payments will start one year from now

and will be paid every six months. A representative from Greenleaf Investments has offered to purchase all the payments from you for ₹50 million. If the appropriate discount rate is an APR of 6 percent compounded daily, should you take the offer? Assume there are 12 months in a year, each with 30 days.

68. **Calculating Rates** A financial planning service offers a college savings program. The plan calls for you to make six annual payments of ₹15,000 each, with the first payment occurring today on your child's 12th birthday. Beginning on your child's 18th birthday, the plan will provide ₹32,000 per year for four years. What return is this investment offering?

69. **Break-Even Investment Returns** Your financial planner offers you two different investment plans. Plan X is an annual perpetuity of ₹35,000 per year. Plan Y is an annuity for 15 years and an annual payment of ₹47,000. Both plans will make their first payment one year from today. At what discount rate would you be indifferent between these two plans?

70. **Perpetual Cash Flows** What is the value of an investment that pays ₹75,000 every *other* year forever, if the first payment occurs one year from today and the discount rate is a 7 percent APR compounded daily? What is the value today if the first payment occurs four years from today? Assume 365 days per year.

71. **Ordinary Annuities and Annuities Due** As discussed in the text, an annuity due is identical to an ordinary annuity except that the periodic payments occur at the beginning of each period instead of at the end of the period. Show that the relationship between the value of an ordinary annuity and the value of an otherwise equivalent annuity due is:

$$\text{Annuity due value} = \text{Ordinary annuity value} \times (1 + r)$$

Show this for both present and future values.

72. **Calculating EAR** A check-cashing store is in the business of making personal loans to walk-up customers. The store makes only one-week loans at 6.3 percent interest per week.

   a. What APR must the store report to its customers? What is the EAR that the customers are actually paying?
   b. Now suppose the store makes one-week loans at 6.3 percent discount interest per week (see Question 60). What's the APR now? The EAR?
   c. The check-cashing store also makes one-month add-on interest loans at 6.3 percent discount interest per week. If you borrow ₹100 for one month (four weeks), the interest will be (₹100 × 1.063^4) – 100 = ₹27.68. Because this is discount interest, your net loan proceeds today will be ₹72.32. You must then repay the store ₹100 at the end of the month. To help you out, though, the store lets you pay off this ₹100 in installments of ₹25 per week. What is the APR of this loan? What is the EAR?

73. **Present Value of a Growing Perpetuity** What is the equation for the present value of a growing perpetuity with a payment of C one period from today if the payments grow by C each period?

74. **Rule of 72** A useful rule of thumb for the time it takes an investment to double with discrete compounding is the "Rule of 72." To use the Rule of 72, you divide 72 by the rate to determine the number of periods it takes for a value today to double. For example, if the rate is 6 percent, the Rule of 72 says it will take 72/6 = 12 years to double. This is approximately equal to the actual answer of 11.90 years. The Rule of 72 also can be applied to determine what rate is needed to double money in a specified period. This is a useful approximation for many rates and periods. At what rate is the Rule of 72 exact?

75. **Rule of 69.3** A corollary to the Rule of 72 is the Rule of 69.3. The Rule of 69.3 is exactly correct except for rounding when rates are compounded continuously. Prove the Rule of 69.3 for continuously compounded interest.

Excel Master It! Problem

Excel is a great tool for solving problems, but with many time value of money problems, you may still need to draw a time line. Consider a classic retirement problem. A friend is celebrating her birthday and wants to start saving for her anticipated retirement. She has the following years to retirement and retirement spending goals:

Excel Master coverage online

Years until retirement	30
Amount to withdraw each year	₹90,000
Years to withdraw in retirement	20
Investment rate	8%

Because your friend is planning ahead, the first withdrawal will not take place until one year after she retires. She wants to make equal annual deposits into her account for her retirement fund.

a. If she starts making these deposits in one year and makes her last deposit on the day she retires, what amount must she deposit annually to be able to make the desired withdrawals in retirement?

b. Suppose your friend has inherited a large sum of money. Rather than making equal annual payments, she has decided to make one lump-sum deposit today to cover her retirement needs. What amount does she have to deposit today?

c. Suppose your friend's employer will contribute to the account each year as part of the company's profit-sharing plan. In addition, your friend expects a distribution from a family trust several years from now. What amount must she deposit annually now to be able to make the desired withdrawals in retirement? The details are:

Employer's annual contribution	₹ 1,500
Years until trust fund distribution	20
Amount of trust fund distribution	₹25,000

Mini Case THE MBA DECISION

Ben Bates graduated from college six years ago with a finance undergraduate degree. Although he is satisfied with his current job, his goal is to become an investment banker. He feels that an MBA degree would allow him to achieve this goal. After examining schools, he has narrowed his choice to either Wilton University or Mount Perry College. Although internships are encouraged by both schools, to get class credit for the internship, no salary can be paid. Other than internships, neither school will allow its students to work while enrolled in its MBA program.

Ben currently works at the money management firm of Dewey and Louis. His annual salary at the firm is ₹69,000 per year, and his salary is expected to increase at 3 percent per year until retirement. He is currently 28 years old and expects to work for 40 more years. His current job includes a fully paid health insurance plan, and his current average tax rate is 26 percent. Ben has a savings account with enough money to cover the entire cost of his MBA program.

The Ritter College of Business at Wilton University is one of the top MBA programs in the country. The MBA degree requires two years of full-time enrollment at the university. The annual tuition is ₹75,000, payable at the beginning of each school year. Books and other supplies are estimated to cost ₹3,600 per year. Ben expects that after graduation from Wilton, he will receive a job offer for about ₹115,000 per year, with a ₹20,000 signing bonus. The salary at this job will increase at 4 percent per year. Because of the higher salary, his average income tax rate will increase to 31 percent.

The Bradley School of Business at Mount Perry College began its MBA program 16 years ago. The Bradley School is smaller and less well known than the Ritter College. Bradley offers an accelerated, one-year program, with a tuition cost of ₹90,000 to be paid upon matriculation. Books and other supplies for the program are expected to cost ₹5,400. Ben thinks that he will receive an offer of ₹96,000 per year upon graduation, with an ₹18,000 signing bonus. The salary at this job will increase at 3.5 percent per year. His average tax rate at this level of income will be 29 percent.

Both schools offer a health insurance plan that will cost ₹3,500 per year, payable at the beginning of the year. Ben also estimates that room and board expenses will cost ₹2,500 more per year at both schools than his current expenses, payable at the beginning of each year. The appropriate discount rate is 4.7 percent.

1. How does Ben's age affect his decision to get an MBA?
2. What other, perhaps nonquantifiable, factors affect Ben's decision to get an MBA?
3. Assuming all salaries are paid at the end of each year, what is the best option for Ben–from a strictly financial standpoint?
4. Ben believes that the appropriate analysis is to calculate the future value of each option. How would you evaluate this statement?
5. What initial salary would Ben need to receive to make him indifferent between attending Wilton University and staying in his current position?
6. Suppose, instead of being able to pay cash for his MBA, Ben must borrow the money. The current borrowing rate is 4.3 percent. How would this affect his decision?

Appendix 4A Net Present Value: First Principles of Finance

Appendix 4B Using Financial Calculators

To access the appendix for this chapter, please log on to www.mheducation.co.in.

5

Net Present Value and Other Investment Rules

When a company is deciding whether to invest in a new project, large sums of money can be at stake. For example, in May 2020, Taiwan Semiconductor Manufacturing Co. (TSMC) announced plans to build a ₹12 billion plant in Arizona. The plant was slated to produce the company's five-nanometer wafers, and production would begin in 2024. By the middle of July, TSMC had not only selected the land for the plant, but also had secured the area around the plant. TSMC hoped to entice suppliers to locate on this land.

Of course, not all investments are in new facilities. Earlier in 2020, GM announced that it was planning to invest ₹2.2 billion in its Detroit-Hamtramck Assembly plant. The investment would transform the plant to manufacture electric and self-driving cars. In India, Reliance Jio, launched by Reliance Industries Limited (RIL) to occupy the digital space, is one of the largest green field project with an investment of ₹3.3 trillion. Projects such as these, with price tags in the billions, are obviously major undertakings, and the risks and rewards must be carefully weighed. In this chapter, we discuss the basic tools used in making such decisions.

We will begin by introducing the net present value investment rule. If managers follow this simple rule, they will always choose investment projects that increase firm value. This chapter also considers a variety of other techniques that financial analysts routinely use. More importantly, we will show how many of these techniques can be misleading and explain why the net present value approach is the right one to use.

Please visit us at **rwjcorporatefinance.blogspot.com** for the latest developments in the world of corporate finance.

5.1 Why Use Net Present Value?

Excel Master coverage online

This chapter, as well as the next two, focuses on capital budgeting, the decision-making process for accepting or rejecting projects. This chapter develops the basic capital budgeting methods, leaving much of the practical application to subsequent chapters. But we don't have to develop these methods from scratch. In Chapter 4, we pointed out that a rupee received in the future is worth less than a rupee received today. The reason is that today's rupee can be reinvested, yielding a greater amount in the future. And we showed in Chapter 4 that the exact worth of a rupee to be received in the future is its present value. Furthermore, Section 4.1 suggested calculating the net

Find out more about capital budgeting for Indian companies at **www.projectsmonitor.com** and in the CMIE CAPEX database (https://capex.cmie.com/)

Find out more about capital budgeting for small U.S.A. businesses at **www.missouribusiness.net**

present value (NPV) of any project, which is the difference between the sum of the present values of the project's future cash flows and the initial cost of the project.

The NPV method is the first one to be considered in this chapter. We begin by reviewing the approach with an example. Then, we ask why the method leads to good decisions.

EXAMPLE 5.1

Net Present Value The Bajrang Company is considering investing in a riskless project costing ₹100. The project receives ₹107 in one year and has no other cash flows. The discount rate on riskless investments is 2 percent.

The NPV of the project can easily be calculated as:

$$₹4.90 = -₹100 + \frac{₹107}{1.02} \tag{5.1}$$

From Chapter 4, we know that the project should be accepted because its NPV is positive. This is true because the project generates ₹107 of future cash flows from a ₹100 investment, whereas comparable investments only generate ₹102, as we will show below.

The basic investment rule can be generalized to:

Accept a project if the NPV is greater than zero.

Reject a project if the NPV is less than zero.

We refer to this as the **NPV rule.**

Why does the NPV rule lead to good decisions? Consider the following two strategies available to the managers of Bajrang Company:

1. Use ₹100 of corporate cash to invest in the project. The ₹107 will be paid as a dividend in one year.
2. Forgo the project and pay the ₹100 of corporate cash to stockholders as a dividend today.

If Strategy 2 is employed, the stockholder might deposit the cash dividend in a bank for one year. With an interest rate of 2 percent, Strategy 2 would produce cash of ₹102 (= ₹100 × 1.02) at the end of the year. The stockholder would prefer Strategy 1 because Strategy 2 produces less than ₹107 at the end of the year.

Our general point is:

Accepting positive NPV projects benefits the stockholders.[1]

How do we interpret the exact NPV of ₹4.90? This is the increase in the value of the firm from the project. Imagine that the firm today has productive assets worth ₹V and has ₹100 of cash. If the firm forgoes the project, the value of the firm today would be:

$$₹V + ₹100$$

[1]In rare cases when the firm is at high risk of bankruptcy, a positive NPV project may benefit debtholders but fail to benefit stockholders. We will discuss this exception in Chapter 17. Regardless, accepting positive NPV projects will always increase the total value of the firm.

If the firm accepts the project, the firm will receive ₹107 in one year but will have no cash today. The firm's value today would be:

$$₹V + \frac{₹107}{1.02}$$

The difference between these equations is ₹4.90, the net present value of Equation 5.1. Thus:

The value of the firm rises by the NPV of the project.

Note that the value of the firm is merely the sum of the values of the different projects, divisions, or other entities within the firm. This property, called **value additivity**, is quite important. It implies that the contribution of any project to a firm's value is the NPV of the project. As we will see later, alternative methods discussed in this chapter do not generally have this property.

The NPV rule uses the correct discount rate.

One detail remains. We assumed that the project was riskless, a rather implausible assumption. Future cash flows of real-world projects are invariably risky. In other words, cash flows can only be estimated, rather than known. Imagine that the managers of Bajrang *expect* the cash flow of the project to be ₹107 next year. That is, the cash flow could be higher, say ₹117, or lower, say ₹97. With this slight change, the project is risky. Suppose the project is about as risky as the stock market as a whole, where the expected return this year is perhaps 10 percent. Then 10 percent becomes the discount rate, implying that the NPV of the project would be:

$$-₹2.73 = -₹100 + \frac{₹107}{1.10}$$

Because the NPV is negative, the project should be rejected. This makes sense: A stockholder of Bajrang receiving a ₹100 dividend today could invest it in the stock market, expecting a 10 percent return. Why accept a project with the same risk as the market but with an expected return of only 7 percent?

Conceptually, the discount rate on a risky project is the return that one can expect to earn on a financial asset of comparable risk. This discount rate is often referred to as an opportunity cost because corporate investment in the project takes away the stockholders' option to invest the dividend in other opportunities. Conceptually, we should look for the expected return of investments with similar risks available in the capital markets. The calculation of the discount rate is by no means impossible. We forgo the calculation in this chapter but will discuss it in detail in later chapters.

Having shown that NPV is a sensible approach, we will devote the rest of this chapter to showing why NPV is superior to other popular investment rules. The key to NPV is its three attributes:

1. *NPV uses cash flows.* Cash flows from a project can be used for other corporate purposes (such as dividend payments, other capital budgeting projects, or payments of corporate interest). By contrast, earnings are an artificial construct. Although earnings are useful to accountants, they should not be used in capital budgeting because they do not represent cash.
2. *NPV uses all the cash flows of the project.* Some alternative approaches ignore cash flows beyond a particular date; beware of these approaches.
3. *NPV discounts the cash flows properly.* Other approaches may ignore the time value of money when handling cash flows. Beware of these approaches, as well.

Calculating NPVs by hand can be tedious. The following *Spreadsheet Applications* box shows how to do it the easy way and also illustrates an important *caveat calculator.*

SPREADSHEET APPLICATIONS

Calculating NPVs with a Spreadsheet

Spreadsheets are commonly used to calculate NPVs. Examining the use of spreadsheets in this context also allows us to issue an important warning. Consider the following:

	A	B	C	D	E	F	G	H
1								
2	**Using a spreadsheet to calculate net present values**							
3								
4	A project's cost is ₹10,000. The cash flows are ₹2,000 per year for the first two years,							
5	₹4,000 per year for the next two years, and ₹5,000 in the last year. The discount rate is							
6	10 percent. What's the NPV?							
7								
8		Year	Cash flow					
9		0	–₹10,000	Discount rate =		10%		
10		1	2,000					
11		2	2,000		**NPV =**	**₹2,102.72**	(*wrong* answer)	
12		3	4,000		**NPV =**	**₹2,312.99**	(*right* answer)	
13		4	4,000					
14		5	5,000					
15								
16	The formula entered in cell F11 is =NPV(F9,C9:C14). However, this gives the wrong answer because the							
17	NPV function actually calculates present values, not *net* present values.							
18								
19	The formula entered in cell F12 is =NPV(F9,C10:C14) + C9. This gives the right answer because the							
20	NPV function is used to calculate the present value of the cash flows and then the initial cost is							
21	subtracted to calculate the answer. Notice that we added cell C9 because it is already negative.							

In our spreadsheet example, notice that we have provided two answers. The first answer is wrong even though we used the spreadsheet's NPV formula. What happened is that the "NPV" function in our spreadsheet is actually a PV function; unfortunately, one of the original spreadsheet programmers many years ago got the definition wrong, and subsequent programmers have copied it! Our second answer shows how to use the formula properly.

The example here illustrates the danger of blindly using calculators or computers without understanding what is going on; we shudder to think of how many capital budgeting decisions in the real world are based on incorrect use of this particular function.

5.2 The Payback Period Method

DEFINING THE RULE

Excel Master coverage online

One alternative to NPV is the **payback period**. Here is how payback works: Consider a project with an initial investment of –₹50,000. Cash flows are ₹30,000, ₹20,000, and ₹10,000 in the first three years, respectively. These flows are illustrated in Figure 5.1. A useful way of writing investments like the preceding is with the notation:

$$(-₹50{,}000,\ ₹30{,}000,\ ₹20{,}000,\ ₹10{,}000)$$

The minus sign in front of the ₹50,000 reminds us that this is a cash outflow for the investor, and the commas between the different numbers indicate that they are received–or if they are cash outflows, that they are paid out–at different times. In this example we are assuming that the cash flows occur one year apart, with the first one occurring the moment we decide to take on the investment.

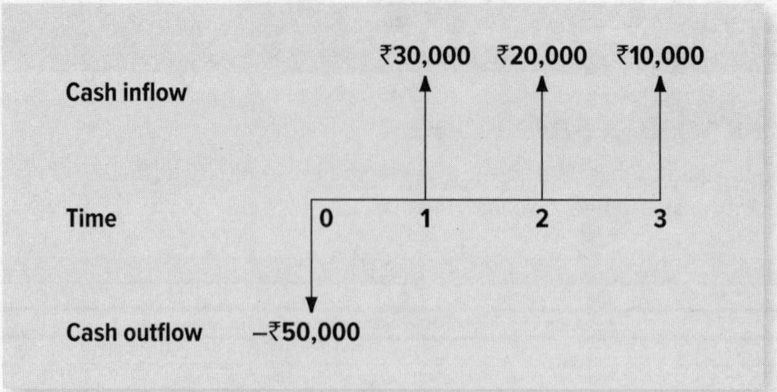

Figure 5.1 Cash Flows of an Investment Project

The firm receives cash flows of ₹30,000 and ₹20,000 in the first two years, which add up to the ₹50,000 original investment. This means that the firm has recovered its investment within two years. In this case, two years is the *payback period* of the investment.

Based on the *payback period rule*, a project is acceptable if its calculated payback is less than a prespecified number of years–say, two years. All projects that have payback periods of two years or less are accepted, and those that pay back in more than two years–if at all–are rejected.

PROBLEMS WITH THE PAYBACK METHOD

There are at least three problems with payback. To illustrate the first two problems, we consider the three projects in Table 5.1. All three projects have the same three-year payback period, so they should all be equally attractive–right?

Actually, they are not equally attractive, as can be seen by a comparison of different pairs of projects.

Problem 1: Timing of Cash Flows within the Payback Period Let us compare Project A with Project B. In Years 1 through 3, the cash flows of Project A rise from ₹20 to ₹50, while the cash flows of Project B fall from ₹50 to ₹20. Because the large cash flow of ₹50 comes earlier with Project B, its net present value must be higher. Nevertheless, we saw that the payback periods of the two projects are identical. A problem with the payback method is that it does not consider the timing of the cash flows within the payback period. This example shows that the payback method is inferior to NPV because, as we pointed out earlier, the NPV method discounts the cash flows properly.

Table 5.1 Expected Cash Flows for Projects A through C

Year	A	B	C
0	–₹100	–₹100	–₹100
1	20	50	50
2	30	30	30
3	50	20	20
4	60	60	100
Payback period (years)	3	3	3
NPV @ 10%	₹21.52	₹26.26	₹53.58

Problem 2: Payments after the Payback Period Now consider Projects B and C, which have identical cash flows within the payback period. However, Project C is clearly preferred because it has a cash flow of ₹100 in the fourth year. Another problem with the payback method is that it ignores all cash flows occurring after the payback period. Because of the short-term orientation of the payback method, some valuable long-term projects are likely to be rejected. The NPV method does not have this flaw because, as we pointed out earlier, this method uses all the cash flows of the project.

Problem 3: Arbitrary Standard for Payback Period We do not need to refer to Table 5.1 when considering a third problem with the payback method. Capital markets help us estimate the discount rate used in the NPV method. The riskless rate, perhaps proxied by the yield on a U.S. Treasury instrument, would be the appropriate rate for a riskless investment; a higher rate should be used for risky projects. Later chapters of this textbook show how to use historical returns in the capital markets to estimate the discount rate for a risky project. However, there is no comparable guide for choosing the payback cutoff date, so the choice is somewhat arbitrary.

To illustrate the payback period problems, consider Table 5.1. Suppose the expected return on comparable risky projects is 10 percent. Then we would use a discount rate of 10 percent for these projects. If so, the NPV would be ₹21.52, ₹26.26, and ₹53.58 for A, B, and C, respectively. When using the payback period, these projects are equal to one another because each has a payback period of three years. However, when considering all cash flows, B has a higher NPV than A because of the timing of cash flows within the payback period. And C has the highest NPV because of the ₹100 cash flow after the payback period.

MANAGERIAL PERSPECTIVE

The payback method is often used by large, sophisticated companies when making relatively small decisions. The decision to build a small warehouse or to pay for a tune-up for a truck is the sort of decision that often is made by lower-level management. Typically, a manager might reason that a tune-up would cost, say, ₹400, and if it saved ₹240 each year in reduced fuel costs, it would pay for itself in less than two years. On such a basis the decision would be made.

Although the treasurer of the company might not have made the decision in the same way, the company endorses such decision making. Why would upper management condone or even encourage such retrograde activity in its employees? One answer would be that it is easy to make decisions using payback. Multiply the tune-up decision into 50 such decisions a month, and the appeal of this simple method becomes clearer.

The payback method also has some desirable features for managerial control. As important as the investment decision itself is the company's ability to evaluate the manager's decision-making ability. Under the NPV method, a long time may pass before one decides whether a decision was correct. With the payback method we know in two years whether the manager's assessment of the cash flows was correct.

It also has been suggested that firms with good investment opportunities but no available cash may justifiably use payback. For example, the payback method could be used by small, privately held firms with good growth prospects but limited access to the capital markets. Quick cash recovery increases the reinvestment possibilities for such firms.

Finally, practitioners often argue that standard academic criticisms of the payback method overstate any real-world problems with the method. Textbooks typically make fun of payback by positing a project with low cash inflows in the early years but a huge cash inflow right after the payback cutoff date. This project is likely to be rejected under the payback method, though its acceptance would, in truth, benefit the firm. Project C in our Table 5.1 is an example of such a project. Practitioners point out that the pattern of cash flows in these textbook examples is much too stylized to mirror the real world. In fact, a number of executives have told us that for the overwhelming majority of real-world projects, both payback and NPV lead to the same decision. In addition, these executives indicate that if an investment like Project C were encountered in the real world, decision makers would almost certainly make ad hoc adjustments to the payback rule so that the project would be accepted.

Notwithstanding all of the preceding rationale, it is not surprising to discover that as the decisions grow in importance, which is to say when firms look at bigger projects, NPV becomes the order of the day. When questions of controlling and evaluating the manager become less important than making the right investment decision, payback is used less frequently. For big-ticket decisions, such as whether or not to buy a machine, build a factory, or acquire a company, the payback method is seldom used.

SUMMARY OF PAYBACK

The payback method differs from NPV and is therefore conceptually wrong. With its arbitrary cutoff date and its blindness to cash flows after that date, it can lead to some flagrantly foolish decisions if used too literally. Nevertheless, because of its simplicity, as well as its other mentioned advantages, companies often use it as a screen for making the myriad of minor investment decisions they continually face.

Although this means that you should be wary of trying to change approaches such as the payback method when you encounter them in companies, you should probably be careful not to accept the sloppy financial thinking they represent. You would do your company a disservice if you used payback instead of NPV for major decisions when you had a choice.

5.3 The Discounted Payback Period Method

Excel Master coverage online

Aware of the pitfalls of payback, some decision makers use a variant called the **discounted payback period**. Under this approach, we first discount the cash flows. Then we ask how long it takes for the discounted cash flows to equal the initial investment.

Suppose that the discount rate is 10 percent and the cash flows on a project are given by:

$$(-₹100, ₹50, ₹50, ₹20)$$

This investment has a payback period of two years because the investment is paid back in that time.

To compute the project's discounted payback period, we first discount each of the cash flows at the 10 percent rate. These discounted cash flows are:

$$[-₹100, ₹50/1.1, ₹50/1.1^2, ₹20/1.1^3] = (-₹100, ₹45.45, ₹41.32, ₹15.03)$$

The discounted payback period of the original investment is the payback period for these discounted cash flows. The payback period for the discounted cash flows is slightly less than three years (2.88 years, to be exact) because the discounted cash flows over the three years are ₹101.80 (= ₹45.45 + 41.32 + 15.03). As long as the cash flows and discount rate are positive, the discounted payback period will never be smaller than the payback period because discounting reduces the value of the cash flows.

At first glance, discounted payback may seem like an attractive alternative, but, on closer inspection, we see that it contains some of the same major flaws as the payback period method. Like payback, discounted payback first requires us to choose an arbitrary cutoff period, and then it ignores all cash flows after that date.

If we have already gone to the trouble of discounting the cash flows, we might as well add up all the discounted cash flows and use NPV to make the decision. Although discounted payback looks a bit like NPV, it is a poor compromise between the payback method and NPV.

5.4 The Internal Rate of Return

Excel Master coverage online

Now we come to the most important alternative to the NPV method: the internal rate of return, universally known as the IRR. The IRR is about as close as you can get to the NPV without actually being the NPV. The basic rationale behind the IRR method is that it provides a single number that summarizes the merits of a project. This number does not depend on the interest rate prevailing in the capital market. That is why it is called the internal rate of return: The number is internal or intrinsic to the project and does not depend on anything except the cash flows of the project.

For example, consider the simple project (–₹100, ₹110) in Figure 5.2. For a given rate, the net present value of this project can be described as:

$$\text{NPV} = -₹100 + \frac{₹110}{1+r}$$

where r is the discount rate. What discount rate will make the NPV of the project equal to zero?

We begin by using an arbitrary discount rate of 8 percent, which yields:

$$₹1.85 = -₹100 + \frac{₹110}{1.08}$$

Because the NPV in this equation is positive, we now try a higher discount rate, such as 12 percent. This yields:

$$-₹1.79 = -₹100 + \frac{₹110}{1.12}$$

Because the NPV in this equation is negative, we try lowering the discount rate to 10 percent. This yields:

$$0 = -₹100 + \frac{₹110}{1.10}$$

This trial-and-error procedure tells us that the NPV of the project is zero when r equals 10 percent.[2] Thus, we say that 10 percent is the project's **internal rate of return (IRR)**. The IRR is the interest rate that causes the NPV of the project to be zero. The implication of this exercise is very simple. The firm should be indifferent to the project if the discount rate is 10 percent. The firm should accept the project if the discount rate is below 10 percent. The firm should reject the project if the discount rate is above 10 percent.

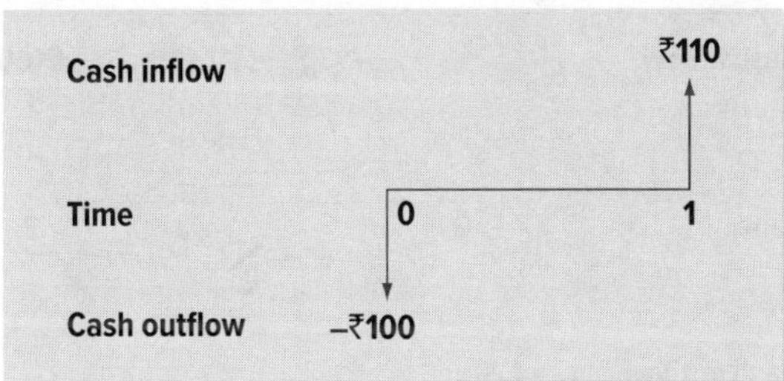

Figure 5.2 Cash Flows for a Simple Project

[2]We can derive the IRR directly for a problem with an initial cash outflow and up to four subsequent inflows. In the case of two subsequent inflows, the quadratic formula is needed. In general, only trial and error, a financial calculator, or spreadsheet will work for an outflow and five or more subsequent inflows.

The general rule for using the IRR is:

Accept the project if the IRR is greater than the discount rate. Reject the project if the IRR is less than the discount rate.

We refer to this as the *basic IRR rule.* Now we can try the more complicated example (−₹200, ₹100, ₹100, ₹100) in Figure 5.3.

As we did previously, let's use trial and error to calculate the IRR. We try 20 percent and 30 percent, yielding the following:

Discount Rate	NPV
20%	₹10.65
30	−18.39

After much more trial and error, we find that the NPV of the project is zero when the discount rate is 23.38 percent, which is the IRR. With a 20 percent discount rate, the NPV is positive and we would accept it. However, if the discount rate were 30 percent, we would reject it.

Algebraically, IRR is the unknown in the following equation:[3]

$$0 = -₹200 + \frac{₹100}{1 + \text{IRR}} + \frac{₹100}{(1 + \text{IRR})^2} + \frac{₹100}{(1 + \text{IRR})^3}$$

Figure 5.4 illustrates what the IRR of a project means. This figure, called the NPV profile, plots the NPV as a function of the discount rate. The curve crosses the horizontal axis at the IRR of 23.38 percent because this is where the NPV equals zero.

It also should be clear that the NPV is positive for discount rates below the IRR and negative for discount rates above the IRR. If we accept projects like this one when the discount rate is less than the IRR, we will be accepting positive NPV projects. Thus, the IRR rule coincides exactly with the NPV rule.

If this were all there were to it, the IRR rule would always coincide with the NPV rule. But the world of finance is not so kind. Unfortunately, the IRR rule and the NPV rule are consistent with each other only for projects with conventional cash flows, that is, projects with negative cash flows at the beginning and positive cash flows after. Several problems with the IRR approach occur in more complicated situations, which is a topic to be examined in the next section.

The IRR in the previous example was computed through trial and error. This laborious process can be averted through spreadsheets. A nearby *Spreadsheet Applications* box shows how.

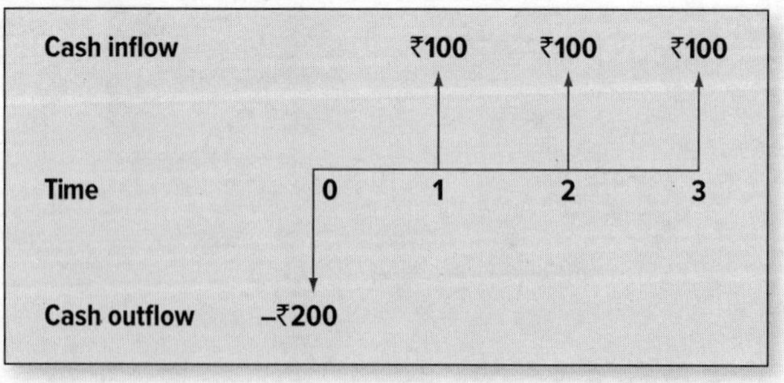

Figure 5.3 Cash Flows for a More Complex Project

[3]As mentioned, we can derive the IRR directly for a problem with an initial cash outflow and up to a couple of inflows. In the case of two subsequent inflows, for example, the quadratic formula is needed. In general, only a financial calculator or spreadsheet application will work.

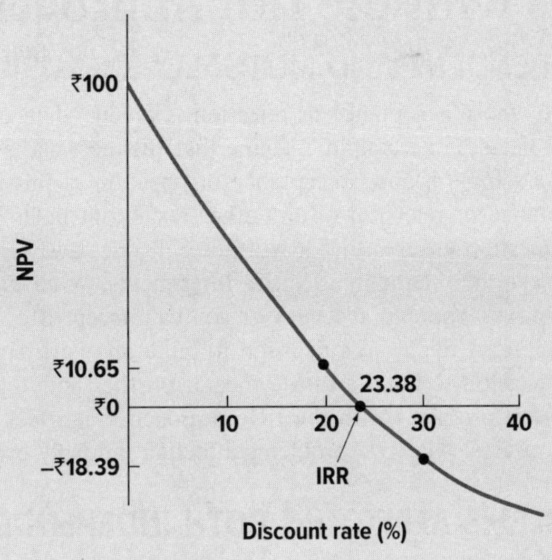

The NPV is positive for discount rates below the IRR and negative for discount rates above the IRR.

Figure 5.4 NPV Profile for a More Complex Project

SPREADSHEET APPLICATIONS

Calculating IRRs with a Spreadsheet

Because IRRs are so tedious to calculate by hand, financial calculators and, especially, spreadsheets are generally used. The procedures used by various financial calculators are too different for us to illustrate here, so we will focus on using a spreadsheet. As the following example illustrates, using a spreadsheet is very easy.

	A	B	C	D	E	F	G	H
1								
2	**Using a spreadsheet to calculate internal rates of return**							
3								
4	Suppose we have a 4-year project that costs ₹500. The cash flows over the 4-year life will be							
5	₹100, ₹200, ₹300, and ₹400. What is the IRR?							
6								
7		Year	Cash flow					
8		0	–₹500					
9		1	100		IRR =	27.3%		
10		2	200					
11		3	300					
12		4	400					
13								
14								
15	The formula entered in cell F9 is =IRR(C8:C12). Notice that the Year 0 cash flow has a negative							
16	sign representing the initial cost of the project.							
17								

5.5 Problems with the IRR Approach

DEFINITION OF INDEPENDENT AND MUTUALLY EXCLUSIVE PROJECTS

Excel Master coverage online

An **independent project** is one whose acceptance or rejection is independent of the acceptance or rejection of other projects. For example, imagine that Bikanerwala is considering putting a vada pav outlet on a remote island. Acceptance or rejection of this unit is likely to be unrelated to the acceptance or rejection of any other restaurant in its system. The remoteness of the outlet in question ensures that it will not pull sales away from other outlets.

Now consider the other extreme, **mutually exclusive investments**. What does it mean for two projects, A and B, to be mutually exclusive? You can accept A or you can accept B or you can reject both, but you cannot accept both. For example, A might be a decision to build an apartment house on a corner lot that you own, and B might be a decision to build a movie theater on the same lot.

We now present two general problems with the IRR approach that affect both independent and mutually exclusive projects. Then we deal with two problems affecting mutually exclusive projects only.

TWO GENERAL PROBLEMS AFFECTING BOTH INDEPENDENT AND MUTUALLY EXCLUSIVE PROJECTS

We begin our discussion with Project A, which has the following cash flows:

(–₹100, ₹130)

The IRR for Project A is 30 percent. Table 5.2 provides other relevant information about the project. The NPV profile for this project is shown in Figure 5.5. As you can see, the NPV declines as the discount rate rises.

Problem 1: Investing or Financing? Now consider Project B, with cash flows of:

(₹100, –₹130)

These cash flows are exactly the reverse of the flows for Project A. In Project B, the firm receives funds first and then pays out funds later. While unusual, projects of this type do exist. Consider a corporation conducting a seminar where the participants pay in advance. Because large expenses are frequently incurred at the seminar date, cash inflows precede cash outflows.

Consider our trial-and-error method to calculate IRR:

$$-\text{₹}4 = \text{₹}100 - \frac{\text{₹}130}{1.25}$$

$$\text{₹}3.70 = \text{₹}100 - \frac{\text{₹}130}{1.35}$$

$$\text{₹}0 = \text{₹}100 - \frac{\text{₹}130}{1.30}$$

Table 5.2 The Internal Rate of Return and Net Present Value

	Project A			Project B			Project C		
	0	1	2	0	1	2	0	1	2
Cash flows	–₹100	₹130		₹100	–₹130		–₹100	₹230	–₹132
IRR	30%			30%			10% and 20%		
NPV @10%	₹18.18			–₹18.18			₹ 0		
Accept if market rate	<30%			>30%			>10% but <20%		
Financing or investing	Investing			Financing			Mixture		

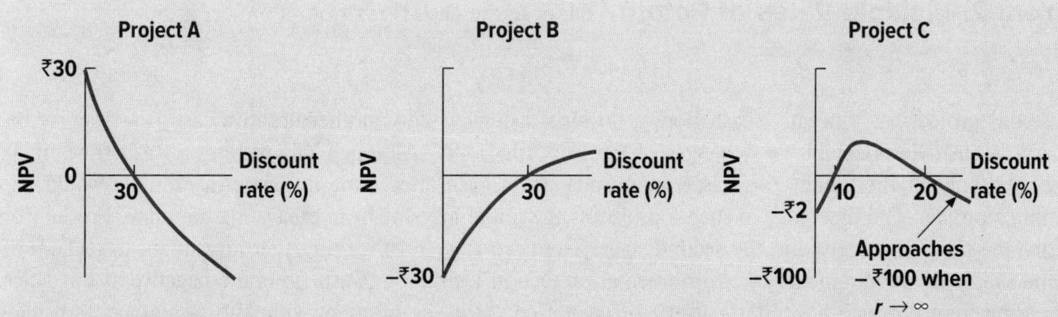

Project A has a cash outflow at Year 0 followed by a cash inflow at Year 1. Its NPV is negatively related to the discount rate.

Project B has a cash inflow at Year 0 followed by a cash outflow at Year 1. Its NPV is positively related to the discount rate.

Project C has two changes of sign in its cash flows. It has an outflow at Year 0, an inflow at Year 1, and an outflow at Year 2. Projects with more than one change of sign can have multiple rates of return.

Figure 5.5 NPV Profile for Projects A, B, and C

As with Project A, the internal rate of return is 30 percent. However, notice that the net present value is negative when the discount rate is below 30 percent. Conversely, the net present value is positive when the discount rate is above 30 percent. The decision rule is exactly the opposite of our previous result. For this type of project, the following rule applies:

Accept the project when the IRR is less than the discount rate. Reject the project when the IRR is greater than the discount rate.

This unusual decision rule follows from the NPV profile of Project B in Figure 5.5. The curve is upward sloping, implying that NPV is positively related to the discount rate.

The graph makes intuitive sense. Suppose the firm wants to obtain ₹100 immediately. It can either (1) accept Project B or (2) borrow ₹100 from a bank. This project is actually a substitute for borrowing. Because the IRR is 30 percent, taking on Project B is equivalent to borrowing at 30 percent. If the firm can borrow from a bank at 25 percent, it should reject the project. However, if a firm can borrow from a bank at 35 percent, it should accept the project. Project B will be accepted if and only if the discount rate is above the IRR.[4]

This should be contrasted with Project A. If the firm has ₹100 cash to invest, it can either (1) accept Project A or (2) lend ₹100 to the bank. The project is actually a substitute for lending. Because the IRR is 30 percent, taking on Project A is equivalent to lending at 30 percent. The firm should accept Project A if the lending rate is below 30 percent. Conversely, the firm should reject Project A if the lending rate is above 30 percent.

Because the firm initially pays out money with Project A but initially receives money with Project B, we refer to Project A as an *investing type project* and Project B as a *financing type project.* Investing type projects are the norm. Because the IRR rule is reversed for financing type projects, be careful when using it with this type of project.

[4]This paragraph implicitly assumes that the cash flows of the project are risk-free. In this way, we can treat the borrowing rate as the discount rate for a firm needing ₹100. With risky cash flows, another discount rate would be chosen. However, the intuition behind the decision to accept when the IRR is less than the discount rate would still apply.

Problem 2: Multiple Rates of Return Suppose the cash flows from a project are:

$$(-₹100,\ ₹230,\ -₹132)$$

Because this project has a negative cash flow, a positive cash flow, and another negative cash flow, we say that the project's cash flows exhibit two changes of sign, or "flip-flops." Although this pattern of cash flows might look a bit strange at first, many projects require outflows of cash after some inflows. An example would be a strip-mining project. The first stage in such a project is the initial investment in excavating the mine. Profits from operating the mine are received in the second stage. The third stage involves a further investment to reclaim the land and satisfy the requirements of environmental protection legislation. Cash flows are negative at this stage.

Leasing may produce a similar pattern of cash flows. Leases often provide substantial tax subsidies, generating cash inflows after an initial investment. However, these subsidies decline over time, frequently leading to negative cash flows in later years. (The details of leasing will be discussed in a later chapter.)

It is easy to verify that this project has not one but two IRRs, 10 percent and 20 percent.[5] In a case like this, the IRR does not make sense. Which IRR are we to use, 10 percent or 20 percent? Because there is no good reason to use one over the other, IRR cannot be used here.

Why does this project have multiple rates of return? Project C generates multiple internal rates of return because both an inflow and an outflow occur after the initial investment. In general, these changes in sign produce multiple IRRs. In theory, a cash flow stream with K changes in sign can have up to K sensible internal rates of return.[6] Therefore, because Project C has two changes in sign, it can have as many as two IRRs. As we pointed out, projects whose cash flows change sign repeatedly can occur in the real world.

NPV Rule Of course, we should not be too worried about multiple rates of return. After all, we can always fall back on the NPV rule. Figure 5.5 plots the NPV profile of Project C. As the figure shows, the NPV is zero at both 10 percent and 20 percent and negative outside the range. The NPV rule tells us to accept the project if the appropriate discount rate is between 10 percent and 20 percent. The project should be rejected if the discount rate lies outside this range.

THE MODIFIED INTERNAL RATE OF RETURN (MIRR)

To address some of the problems that can occur with the standard IRR, it is often proposed that a modified version be used. As we will see, there are several different ways of calculating a modified IRR, or MIRR, but the basic idea is to modify the cash flows first and then calculate an IRR using the modified cash flows.

To illustrate, let's look at Project D, which has the following cash flows:

$$(-₹60,\ ₹155,\ -₹100)$$

[5]The calculations are:

$$-₹100 + \frac{₹230}{1.1} - \frac{₹132}{1.1^2}$$

$$-₹100 + 209.09 - 109.09 = 0$$

and:

$$-₹100 + \frac{₹230}{1.2} - \frac{₹132}{1.2^2}$$

$$-₹100 + 191.67 - 91.67 = 0$$

Thus, we have multiple rates of return.

[6]To be more precise, the number of IRRs that are bigger than -100 percent is equal to the number of sign changes, or it differs from the number of sign changes by an even number. For example, if there are five sign changes, there are five IRRs, three IRRs, or one IRR. If there are two sign changes, there are either two IRRs or no IRRs.

Verify that the two IRRs for this project are 25 percent and 33.33 percent. We next illustrate three different MIRRs, all of which have the property that only one answer will result, thereby eliminating the multiple IRR problem.

Method 1: The Discounting Approach With the discounting approach, the idea is to discount all negative cash flows back to the present at the required return and add them to the initial cost. Then, calculate the IRR. Because only the first modified cash flow is negative, there will be only one IRR. The discount rate used might be the required return, or it might be some other externally supplied rate. We will use the project's required return.

If the required return on the project is 20 percent, then the modified cash flows look like this:

$$\text{Year 0: } -₹60 - \frac{₹100}{1.20^2} = -₹129.44$$

Year 1: ₹155

Year 2: ₹0

If you calculate the MIRR now, you should get 19.74 percent.

Method 2: The Reinvestment Approach With the reinvestment approach, we compound all cash flows (positive and negative), except the first, out to the end of the project's life and then calculate the IRR. In a sense, we are "reinvesting" the cash flows and not taking them out of the project until the very end. The rate we use could be the required return on the project, or it could be a separately specified "reinvestment rate." We will use the project's required return. When we do, here are the modified cash flows:

Year 0: −₹60

Year 1: ₹0

Year 2: −₹100 + (₹155 × 1.2) = ₹86

The MIRR on this set of cash flows is 19.72 percent, or slightly lower than we got using the discounting approach.

Method 3: The Combination Approach As the name suggests, the combination approach blends our first two methods. Negative cash flows are discounted back to the present, and positive cash flows are compounded to the end of the project. In practice, different discount or compounding rates might be used, but we again will stick with the project's required return.

With the combination approach, the modified cash flows are as follows:

$$\text{Year 0: } -₹60 - \frac{₹100}{1.20^2} = -₹129.44$$

Year 1: ₹0

Year 2: ₹155 × 1.2 = ₹186

See if you agree that the MIRR is 19.87 percent, the highest of the three.

MIRR or IRR: Which Is Better? MIRRs are controversial. At one extreme are those who claim that MIRRs are superior to IRRs, period. By design, they clearly don't suffer from the multiple rate of return problem.

At the other end, detractors say that MIRR should stand for "meaningless internal rate of return." As our example makes clear, one problem with MIRRs is that there are different ways of calculating them, and there is no clear reason to say one of our three methods is better than any other. The differences are small with our simple cash flows, but they could be much larger for a more complex project. Further, it's unclear how to interpret an MIRR. It may look like a rate of return, but it's a rate of return on a modified set of cash flows, not the project's actual cash flows.

We're not going to take sides. However, notice that calculating an MIRR requires discounting, compounding, or both, which leads to two obvious observations. First, if we have the relevant discount rate, why not calculate the NPV and be done with it? Second, because an MIRR depends on an externally supplied discount (or compounding) rate, the answer you get is not truly an "internal" rate of return, which, by definition, depends on only the project's cash flows.

We *will* take a stand on one issue that frequently comes up in this context. The value of a project does not depend on what the firm does with the cash flows generated by that project. A firm might use a project's cash flows to fund other projects, to pay dividends, or to buy an executive jet. It doesn't matter: How the cash flows are spent in the future does not affect their value today. As a result, there is generally no need to consider reinvestment of interim cash flows.

The Guarantee against Multiple IRRs If the first cash flow of a project is negative and if all of the remaining flows are positive, there can be only a single, unique IRR, no matter how many periods the project lasts. This is easy to understand by using the concept of the time value of money. We can verify that Project A in Table 5.2 has an IRR of 30 percent because using a 30 percent discount rate gives:

$$\begin{aligned} \text{NPV} &= -₹100 + ₹130/1.3 \\ &= ₹0 \end{aligned}$$

How do we know that this is the only IRR? Suppose we were to try a discount rate greater than 30 percent. In computing the NPV, changing the discount rate does not change the value of the initial cash flow of −₹100 because that cash flow is not discounted. Raising the discount rate lowers the present value of the future cash flows. In other words, because the NPV is zero at 30 percent, any increase in the rate will push the NPV into the negative range. Similarly, if we try a discount rate of less than 30 percent, the overall NPV of the project will be positive. Though this example has only one positive flow, the same reasoning still implies a single, unique IRR if there are many inflows (but no outflows) after the initial investment.

If the initial cash flow is positive–and if all of the remaining flows are negative–there can only be a single, unique IRR. This result follows from similar reasoning. Both these cases have only one change of sign in the cash flows. Thus, we are safe from multiple IRRs whenever there is one sign change in the cash flows.

General Rules The following chart summarizes our rules:

Flows	Number of IRRs	IRR Criterion	NPV Criterion
First cash flow is negative and all remaining cash flows are positive.	1	Accept if IRR > *r*. Reject if IRR < *r*.	Accept if NPV > 0. Reject if NPV < 0.
First cash flow is positive and all remaining cash flows are negative.	1	Accept if IRR < *r*. Reject if IRR > *r*.	Accept if NPV > 0. Reject if NPV < 0.
Some cash flows after first are positive and some cash flows after first are negative.	May be more than 1.	No valid IRR.	Accept if NPV > 0. Reject if NPV < 0.

Note that the NPV criterion is the same for each of the three cases. In other words, NPV analysis is always appropriate. Conversely, the IRR can be used only in certain cases. When it comes to NPV, the preacher's words, "You just can't lose with the stuff I use," clearly apply.

PROBLEMS SPECIFIC TO MUTUALLY EXCLUSIVE PROJECTS

As mentioned earlier, two or more projects are mutually exclusive if the firm can accept only one of them. We now present two problems dealing with the application of the IRR approach to mutually exclusive projects. These two problems are quite similar, though logically distinct.

The Scale Problem A professor we know motivates discussions of this topic with this statement: "Students, I am prepared to let one of you choose between two mutually exclusive 'business' propositions. Opportunity 1: You give me ₹1 now and I'll give you ₹1.50 back at the end of the class period. Opportunity 2: You give me ₹10 and I'll give you ₹11 back at the end of the class period. You can choose only one of the two opportunities, and you cannot choose either opportunity more than once. I'll pick the first volunteer."

Which would you choose? The correct answer is Opportunity 2.[7] To see this, look at the following chart:

	Cash Flow at Beginning of Class	Cash Flow at End of Class (90 Minutes Later)	NPV[8]	IRR
Opportunity 1	−₹1	₹ 1.50	₹ .50	50%
Opportunity 2	−10	11.00	1.00	10

As we have stressed earlier in the text, one should choose the opportunity with the highest NPV. This is Opportunity 2 in the example.

This business proposition illustrates a defect with the IRR criterion. The basic IRR rule indicates the selection of Opportunity 1 because the IRR is 50 percent. The IRR is only 10 percent for Opportunity 2.

Where does IRR go wrong? The problem with IRR is that it ignores issues of scale. Although Opportunity 1 has a greater IRR, the investment is much smaller. In other words, the high percentage return on Opportunity 1 is more than offset by the ability to earn at least a decent return on a much bigger investment under Opportunity 2.[9]

Because IRR seems to be misguided here, can we adjust or correct it? We illustrate how in the next example.

EXAMPLE 5.2

NPV versus IRR Santa Singh and Banta Singh have purchased the rights to *Corporate Finance: The Motion Picture.* They will produce this major motion picture on either a small budget or a large budget. Here are the estimated cash flows:

	Cash Flow at Year 0	Cash Flow at Year 1	NPV @25%	IRR
Small budget	−₹10 million	₹40 million	₹22 million	300%
Large budget	−25 million	65 million	27 million	160

(continued)

[7]The professor uses real money here. Though many students have done poorly on the professor's exams over the years, no student has ever chosen Opportunity 1. The professor claims that his students are "money players."

[8]We assume a zero rate of interest because his class lasted only 90 minutes; it just seemed like a lot longer.

[9]A 10 percent return is more than decent over a 90-minute interval!

Because of high risk, a 25 percent discount rate is considered appropriate. Banta wants to adopt the large budget because the NPV is higher. Santa wants to adopt the small budget because the IRR is higher. Who is right?

For the reasons explained in the classroom example, NPV is correct. Hence, Banta is right. However, Santa is very stubborn where IRR is concerned. How can Banta justify the large budget to Santa using the IRR approach?

This is where *incremental IRR* comes in. Banta calculates the incremental cash flows from choosing the large budget instead of the small budget as follows:

	Cash Flow at Year 0 (in millions)	Cash Flow at Year 1 (in millions)
Incremental cash flows from choosing large budget instead of small budget	−₹25 − (−10) = −₹15	₹65 − 40 = ₹25

This chart shows that the incremental cash flows are −₹15 million at Year 0 and ₹25 million at Year 1. Banta calculates incremental IRR as follows:

Formula for Calculating the Incremental IRR

$$0 = -₹15 \text{ million} + \frac{₹25 \text{ million}}{1 + \text{IRR}}$$

IRR equals 66.67 percent in this equation, implying that the **incremental IRR** is 66.67 percent. Incremental IRR is the IRR on the incremental investment from choosing the large project instead of the small project.

In addition, we can calculate the NPV of the incremental cash flows:

NPV of Incremental Cash lows

$$-₹15 \text{ million} + \frac{₹25 \text{ million}}{1.25} = ₹5 \text{ million}$$

We know the small-budget picture would be acceptable as an independent project because its NPV is positive. We want to know whether it is beneficial to invest an additional ₹15 million to make the large-budget picture instead of the small-budget picture. In other words, is it beneficial to invest an additional ₹15 million to receive an additional ₹25 million next year? First, our calculations show the incremental NPV to be positive. Second, the incremental IRR of 66.67 percent is higher than the discount rate of 25 percent. For both reasons, the incremental investment can be justified, so the large-budget movie should be made. The second reason is what Santa needed to hear to be convinced.

In review, we can handle this example (or any mutually exclusive example) in one of three ways:

1. *Compare the NPVs of the two choices.* The NPV of the large-budget picture is greater than the NPV of the small-budget picture. That is, ₹27 million is greater than ₹22 million.
2. *Calculate the incremental NPV from making the large-budget picture instead of the small-budget picture.* Because the incremental NPV equals ₹5 million, we choose the large-budget picture.
3. *Compare the incremental IRR to the discount rate.* Because the incremental IRR is 66.67 percent and the discount rate is 25 percent, we choose the large-budget picture.

All three approaches always give the same decision. However, we must not compare the IRRs of the two pictures. If we did, we would make the wrong choice. That is, we would accept the small-budget picture.

Although students frequently think that problems of scale are relatively unimportant, the truth is just the opposite. No real-world project comes in one clear-cut size. Rather, the firm has to determine the best size for the project. The movie budget of ₹25 million is not fixed in stone. Perhaps an extra ₹1 million to hire a bigger star or to film at a better location will increase the movie's gross. Similarly, an industrial firm must decide whether it wants a warehouse of, say, 500,000 square feet or 600,000 square feet. And, earlier in the chapter, we imagined Bikanerwala opening an outlet on a remote island. If it does this, it must decide how big the outlet should be. For almost any project, someone in the firm has to decide on its size, implying that problems of scale abound in the real world.

One final note here. Students often ask which project should be subtracted from the other in calculating incremental flows. Notice that we are subtracting the smaller project's cash flows from the bigger project's cash flows. This leaves an outflow at Year 0. We then use the basic IRR rule on the incremental flows.[10]

The Timing Problem Next we illustrate another, somewhat similar problem with the IRR approach to evaluating mutually exclusive projects.

EXAMPLE 5.3

Mutually Exclusive Investments Suppose that the Gitanjali Company has two alternative uses for a warehouse. It can store toxic waste containers (Project A) or electronic equipment (Project B). The cash flows are as follows:

	Cash Flow				NPV			
Year	0	1	2	3	@0%	@10%	@15%	IRR
Project A	−₹10,000	₹10,000	₹1,000	₹ 1,000	₹2,000	₹669	₹109	16.04%
Project B	−10,000	1,000	1,000	12,000	4,000	751	−484	12.94

We find that the NPV of Project B is higher with low discount rates, and the NPV of Project A is higher with high discount rates. This is not surprising if you look closely at the cash flow patterns. The larger cash flows of A occur early, whereas the larger cash flows of B occur later. With the time value of money, earlier cash flows are less affected by higher discount rates, so A's Year 1 cash flow is more valuable. Because Project B's cash flows are greater, B's value is relatively high with low discount rates because the cost of waiting on the larger cash flows is lower.

The NPV profiles for both projects appear in Figure 5.6. Project A has an NPV of ₹2,000 at a zero discount rate. This is calculated by adding up the cash flows without discounting them. Project B has an NPV of ₹4,000 at the zero discount rate. However, the NPV of Project B declines more rapidly as the discount rate increases than does the NPV of Project A. As we mentioned, this occurs because the cash flows of B occur later. Both projects have the same NPV at a discount rate of 10.55 percent. The IRR for a project is the rate at which the NPV equals zero. Because the NPV of B declines more rapidly, B actually has a lower IRR.

[10]Alternatively, we could have subtracted the larger project's cash flows from the smaller project's cash flows. This would have left an inflow at Year 0, making it necessary to use the IRR rule for financing situations. This would work, but we find it more confusing.

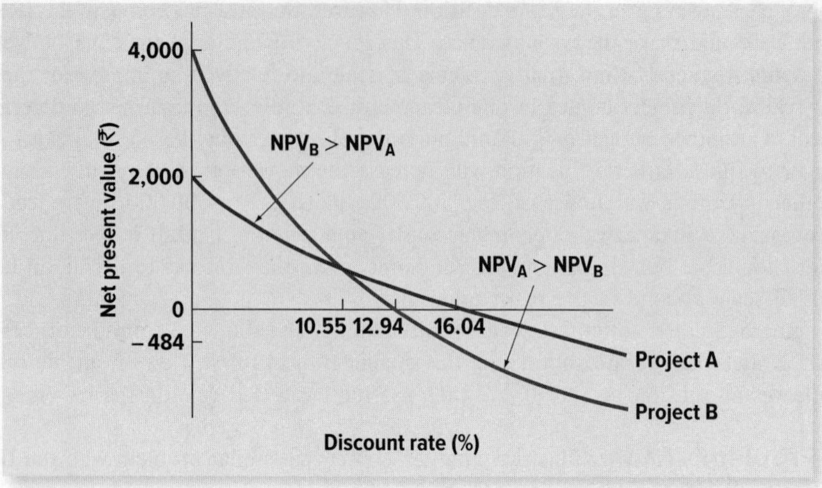

Figure 5.6 Net Present Value and the Internal Rate of Return for Mutually Exclusive Projects

As with the movie example, we can select the better project with one of three different methods:

1. *Compare the NPVs of the two projects.* Figure 5.6 aids our decision. If the discount rate is below 10.55 percent, we should choose Project B because B has a higher NPV. If the rate is above 10.55 percent, we should choose Project A because A has a higher NPV.
2. *Compare the incremental IRR to discount rate.* Another way of determining whether A or B is a better project is to subtract the cash flows of A from the cash flows of B and then calculate the IRR. This is the incremental IRR approach.

   The incremental cash flows are:

						NPV of Incremental Cash Flows		
Year	0	1	2	3	Incremental IRR	@0%	@10%	@15%
B − A	0	−₹9,000	0	₹11,000	10.55%	₹2,000	₹83	−₹593

This chart shows that the incremental IRR is 10.55 percent. In other words, the NPV on the incremental investment is zero when the discount rate is 10.55 percent. Thus, if the relevant discount rate is below 10.55 percent, Project B is preferred to Project A. If the relevant discount rate is above 10.55 percent, Project A is preferred to Project B.

Figure 5.6 shows that the NPVs of the two projects are equal when the discount rate is 10.55 percent. In other words, the *crossover rate* in the figure is 10.55 percent. The incremental cash flows chart shows that the incremental IRR is also 10.55 percent. It is not a coincidence that the crossover rate and the incremental IRR are the same; this equality must always hold. The incremental IRR is the rate that causes the incremental cash flows to have zero NPV. The incremental cash flows have zero NPV when the two projects have the same NPV.

3. *Calculate the NPV on incremental cash flows.* Finally, we could calculate the NPV on the incremental cash flows. The chart that appears with the previous method displays these NPVs. We find that the incremental NPV is positive when the discount rate is either 0 percent or 10 percent. The incremental NPV is negative if the discount rate is 15 percent. If the NPV is positive on the incremental flows, we should choose B. If the NPV is negative, we should choose A.

In summary, the same decision is reached whether we (1) compare the NPVs of the two projects, (2) compare the incremental IRR to the relevant discount rate, or (3) examine the NPV of the incremental cash flows. However, as mentioned earlier, we should *not* compare the IRR of Project A with the IRR of Project B.

We suggested earlier that we should subtract the cash flows of the smaller project from the cash flows of the larger project. What do we do here when the two projects have the same initial investment? Our suggestion in this case is to perform the subtraction so that the first nonzero cash flow is negative. In the Gitanjali Company example we achieved this by subtracting A from B. In this way, we can still use the basic IRR rule for evaluating cash flows.

The preceding examples illustrate problems with the IRR approach in evaluating mutually exclusive projects. Both the professor-student example and the motion picture example illustrate the problem that arises when mutually exclusive projects have different initial investments. The Gitanjali Company example illustrates the problem that arises when mutually exclusive projects have different cash flow timing. When working with mutually exclusive projects, it is unnecessary to determine whether it is the scale problem or the timing problem that exists. Very likely both occur in any real-world situation. Instead, the practitioner should use either an incremental IRR or an NPV approach.

REDEEMING QUALITIES OF IRR

IRR probably survives because it fills a need that NPV does not. People seem to want a rule that summarizes the information about a project in a single rate of return. This single rate gives people a simple way of discussing projects. For example, one manager in a firm might say to another, "Remodeling the north wing has a 20 percent IRR."

To their credit, however, companies that employ the IRR approach seem to understand its deficiencies. Companies frequently restrict managerial projections of cash flows to be negative at the beginning and strictly positive later. Perhaps both the ability of the IRR approach to capture a complex investment project in a single number and the ease of communicating that number explain the survival of the IRR.

A TEST

To test your knowledge, consider the following two statements:

1. You must know the discount rate to compute the NPV of a project, but you compute the IRR without referring to the discount rate.
2. The IRR rule is easier to apply than the NPV rule because you don't use the discount rate when applying IRR.

The first statement is true. The discount rate is needed to compute NPV. The IRR is computed by solving for the rate where the NPV is zero. No mention is made of the discount rate in the mere computation. However, the second statement is false. To apply IRR, you must compare the internal rate of return with the discount rate. Thus, the discount rate is needed for making a decision under either the NPV or IRR approach.

5.6 The Profitability Index

Another method used to evaluate projects is called the **profitability index**. It is the ratio of the present value of the future expected cash flows after initial investment divided by the amount of the initial investment. The profitability index can be calculated as:

Excel Master coverage online

$$\text{Profitability index (PI)} = \frac{\text{PV of cash flows subsequent to initial investment}}{\text{Initial investment}}$$

EXAMPLE 5.4

Profitability Index Hariram Fishing Industries (HFI), applies a 12 percent discount rate to two investment opportunities.

	Cash Flows (in millions)			PV @12% of Cash Flows Subsequent to Initial Investment (in millions)	Profitability Index	NPV @12% (in millions)
Project	C_0	C_1	C_2			
1	−₹20	₹70	₹10	₹70.47	3.52	₹50.47
2	−10	15	40	45.28	4.53	35.28

CALCULATION OF PROFITABILITY INDEX

The profitability index is calculated for Project 1 as follows. The present value of the cash flows *after* the initial investment is:

$$₹70.47 = \frac{₹70}{1.12} + \frac{₹10}{1.12^2}$$

The profitability index is calculated by dividing this result by the initial investment of ₹20. This yields:

$$3.52 = \frac{₹70.47}{₹20}$$

Application of the Profitability Index How do we use the profitability index? We consider three situations:

1. *Independent projects*: Assume that HFI's two projects are independent. According to the NPV rule, both projects should be accepted because NPV is positive in each case. The profitability index (PI) is greater than one whenever the NPV is positive. Thus, the PI *decision rule* is:
    - Accept an independent project if PI > 1.
    - Reject it if PI < 1.
2. *Mutually exclusive projects*: Let us now assume that HFI can only accept one of its two projects. NPV analysis says accept Project 1 because this project has the larger NPV. Because Project 2 has the higher PI, the profitability index leads to the wrong selection.

For mutually exclusive projects, the profitability index suffers from the scale problem that IRR also suffers from. Project 2 is smaller than Project 1. Because the PI is a ratio, it ignores Project 1's larger investment.

Like IRR, the flaw with the PI approach can be corrected using incremental analysis. We write the incremental cash flows after subtracting Project 2 from Project 1 as follows:

Project	Cash Flows (in millions) C_0	C_1	C_2	PV @12% of Cash Flows Subsequent to Initial Investment (in millions)	Profitability Index	NPV @ 12% (in millions)
1–2	–₹10	₹55	–₹30	₹25.19	2.52	₹15.19

Because the profitability index of the incremental cash flows is greater than 1.0, we should choose the larger project–that is, Project 1. This is the same decision we get with the NPV approach.

3. *Capital rationing*: The first two cases implicitly assumed that HFI could always attract enough capital to make any profitable investments. Now consider the case when the firm does not have enough capital to fund all positive NPV projects. This is the case of **capital rationing**.

   Imagine that the firm has a third project, as well as the first two. Project 3 has the following cash flows:

Project	Cash Flows (in millions) C_0	C_1	C_2	PV @12% of Cash Flows Subsequent to Initial Investment (in millions)	Profitability Index	NPV @ 12% (in millions)
3	–₹10	–₹5	₹60	₹43.37	4.34	₹33.37

   Further, imagine that (1) the projects of HFI are independent, but (2) the firm has only ₹20 million to invest. Because Project 1 has an initial investment of ₹20 million, the firm cannot select both this project and another one. Conversely, because Projects 2 and 3 have initial investments of ₹10 million each, both these projects can be chosen. In other words, the cash constraint forces the firm to choose either Project 1 or Projects 2 and 3.

   What should the firm do? Individually, Projects 2 and 3 have lower NPVs than Project 1 has. However, when the NPVs of Projects 2 and 3 are added together, the sum is higher than the NPV of Project 1. Common sense dictates that Projects 2 and 3 should be accepted.

What does our conclusion have to say about the NPV rule or the PI rule? In the case of limited funds, we cannot rank projects according to their NPVs. Under certain assumptions, we can rank them according to the ratio of present value to initial investment. This is the PI rule. Both Project 2 and Project 3 have higher PI ratios than does Project 1. Thus, they should be ranked ahead of Project 1 when capital is rationed.

The usefulness of the profitability index under capital rationing can be explained in military terms. The Pentagon speaks highly of a weapon with a lot of "bang for the buck." In capital budgeting, the profitability index measures the bang (the rupee return) for the buck invested. Hence, it is useful for capital rationing.

It should be noted that the profitability index does not work if funds are also limited beyond the initial time period. For example, if heavy cash outflows elsewhere in the firm were to occur at Year 1, Project 3, which also has a cash outflow at Year 1, might need to be rejected. In other words, the profitability index cannot handle capital rationing over multiple time periods.

In addition, what economists term *indivisibilities* may reduce the effectiveness of the PI rule. Imagine that HFI has ₹30 million available for capital investment, not ₹20 million. The firm now has enough cash for Projects 1 and 2. Because the sum of the NPVs of these two projects is greater than the sum of the NPVs of Projects 2 and 3, the firm would be better served by accepting Projects 1 and 2. But because Projects 2 and 3 still have the highest profitability indexes, the PI rule now leads to the wrong decision. Why does the PI rule lead us astray here? The key is that Projects 1 and 2 use up all of the ₹30 million, whereas Projects 2 and 3 have a combined initial investment of only ₹20 million (= ₹10 + 10). If Projects 2 and 3 are accepted, the remaining ₹10 million must be left in the bank.

This situation points out that care should be exercised when using the profitability index in the real world. Nevertheless, while not perfect, the profitability index goes a long way toward handling capital rationing.

5.7 The Practice of Capital Budgeting

So far this chapter has asked, "Which capital budgeting methods should companies be using?" An equally important question is this: Which methods *are* companies using? Tables 5.3(a) and 5.3(b) help answer this question. As can be seen from the table, approximately three-quarters of Indian, U.S. and Canadian companies use the IRR and NPV methods. This is not surprising given the theoretical advantages of these approaches. Over half of these companies use the payback method, a rather surprising result given the conceptual problems with this approach. And while discounted payback represents a theoretical improvement over regular payback, the usage here is far less. Perhaps companies are attracted to the user-friendly nature of payback. In addition, the flaws of

Table 5.3(a) Percentage of CFOs in the U.S.A. Who Always or Almost Use a Given Technique

	Always or Almost Always
Internal rate of return (IRR)	75.6%
Net present value (NPV)	74.9
Payback method	56.7
Discounted payback	29.5
Profitability index	11.9

SOURCE: Figure 2 from John R. Graham and Campbell R. Harvey, "The Theory and Practice of Corporate Finance: Evidence from the Field," *Journal of Financial Economics* 60 (2001). Based on a survey of 392 CFOs.

Table 5.3(b) Percentage of Finance Heads in India Who Always or Almost Always Use a Given Technique

Capital Budgeting Technique	Always / Often (Year 2002)	Always / Often (Year 2009)	Always / Often (Year 2017)
Internal rate of return (IRR)	85.0%	83.3%	79.3%
Payback period	67.5	93.3	85.8
Net present value (NPV)	66.3	76.7	83.2
Profitability index	35.1	63.3	41.6
Discounted payback	–	–	45.5
NPV adjusted with real options analysis	–	–	20.8

Further readings: Authors' compilations using (a) Batra, Roopali, and Satish Verma, "Capital budgeting practices in Indian companies," IIMB Management Review, Vol. 29, No. 1 (2017): 29–44; (b) Satish Verma, Sanjiv Gupta and Roopali Batra, "A Survey of Capital Budgeting Practices in Corporate India", *VISION–The Journal of Business Perspective*, Vol.13, No. 3, July–September 2009.; (c) Manoj Anand, "Corporate Finance Practices in India: A Survey", ***Vikalpa***, Vol. 27, No. 4, October–December 2002.

this approach, as mentioned in the current chapter, may be relatively easy to correct. While the payback method ignores all cash flows after the payback period, an alert manager can make ad hoc adjustments for a project with back-loaded cash flows. Table 5.3(b) also gives an idea of the changing criteria by Indian corporate CFOs in their project choice decisions with time. It is reassuring that NPV is widely used now as a capital budgeting technique than it was fifteen years ago. One might believe that the growing popularity of discounted payback stems from its *emphasis* on *early* investment *recovery* and *early adoption of risk mitigation strategies.*

One can also expect the capital budgeting methods to differ in India based on a firm's size, growth rate, and owners. Empirical works[11] on Indian companies state that large firms are more likely to use NPV than small firms. Small firms are more likely to use payback method than large firms. High growth firms are more likely to use IRR than the low growth firms. Public sector firms are more likely to use profitability index than the private sector firms. NPV adjusted for real options analysis, a technique explained in the next few chapters, seems to be increasingly used by large-sized firms having sales of ₹1,000 crore and above.

Capital expenditures by individual corporations can add up to enormous sums for the economy as a whole. For example, for 2020, ExxonMobil announced that it expected to have ₹33 to ₹35 billion in capital outlays during the year, up from ₹30 billion in 2019. The company's largest capital budget was ₹42.5 billion in 2013. About the same time, competitor Chevron announced planned investments of ₹18 to ₹20 billion in 2020, similar to the ₹19.8 billion it spent in 2019. Other companies with large capital spending budgets included Walmart, which projected capital spending of about ₹11 billion for 2020, and AT&T, which projected capital spending of about ₹20 billion for 2020.

Large-scale capital spending is often an industrywide occurrence. For example, in 2020, capital spending in the semiconductor industry was expected to reach ₹94.3 billion. This tidy sum was down from a record ₹105.9 billion spent in 2018.

According to information released by the Census Bureau in 2020, capital investment for the economy as a whole was ₹1.575 trillion in 2016, ₹1.683 trillion in 2017, and ₹1.698 trillion in 2018. The total for the three years was almost ₹5 trillion! Given the sums at stake, it is not too surprising that careful analysis of capital expenditures is something at which successful businesses seek to become adept.

One might expect the capital budgeting methods of large firms to be more sophisticated than the methods of small firms. After all, large firms have the financial resources to hire more sophisticated employees. Table 5.4 provides some support for this idea. Here firms indicate frequency of use of the various capital budgeting methods on a scale of 0 (never) to 4 (always). Both the IRR and NPV methods are used more frequently, and payback less frequently, in large firms than in small firms. Conversely, large and small firms employ the last two approaches about equally.

Table 5.4(a) Frequency of Use of Various Capital Budgeting Methods in the U.S.A.

	Large Firms	Small Firms
Internal rate of return (IRR)	3.41	2.87
Net present value (NPV)	3.42	2.83
Payback method	2.25	2.72
Discounted payback	1.55	1.58
Profitability index	.75	.88

Firms indicate frequency of use on a scale from 0 (never) to 4 (always). Numbers in table are averages across respondents.

SOURCE: Adapted from Table 2 from Graham and Harvey (2001), op. cit.

[11]Anand (2002); Verma, Gupta and Batra (2009); and Batra and Verma (2017), op. cit.

Table 5.4(b) Frequency of Use of Various Capital Budgeting Methods in India

Capital Budgeting Technique	Large Firms	Small Firms
Internal rate of return (IRR)	4.18	3.45
Net present value (NPV)	3.93	3.71
Payback period	3.68	3.10
Discounted payback	2.32	2.71
Profitability index	2.50	2.12
NPV adjusted with real options analysis	2.04	1.49

Firms indicate frequency of use on a scale of 0 (never) to 5 (always). Numbers in the table are averages across respondents.
REFERENCE: Table 5.3(b) from Batra and Verma (2017), op. cit.

The use of quantitative techniques in capital budgeting varies with the industry. As one would imagine, firms that are better able to estimate cash flows are more likely to use NPV. For example, estimation of cash flow in certain aspects of the oil business is quite feasible. Because of this, energy-related firms were among the first to use NPV analysis. Conversely, the cash flows in the motion picture business are very hard to project. The grosses of great hits like *Spiderman, Avatar, RRR, KGF, Pathaan, Harry Potter,* and *Star Wars* were far, far greater than anyone imagined. The big failures like *Alamo, Dhaakad, Laal Singh Chaddha, Adipurush* and *Waterworld* were unexpected as well. Because of this, NPV analysis is frowned upon in the movie business.

How does Hollywood perform capital budgeting? The information that a studio uses to accept or reject a movie idea comes from the pitch. An independent movie producer schedules an extremely brief meeting with a studio to pitch his or her idea for a movie. Consider the following four paragraphs of quotes concerning the pitch from the thoroughly delightful book *Reel Power*:[12]

> "They [studio executives] don't want to know too much," says Ron Simpson. "They want to know concept. . . . They want to know what the three-liner is, because they want it to suggest the ad campaign. They want a title. . . . They don't want to hear any esoterica. And if the meeting lasts more than five minutes, they're probably not going to do the project."
>
> "A guy comes in and says this is my idea: '*Jaws* on a spaceship,'" says writer Clay Frohman (*Under Fire*). "And they say, 'Brilliant, fantastic.' Becomes *Alien*. That is *Jaws* on a spaceship, ultimately . . . And that's it. That's all they want to hear. Their attitude is 'Don't confuse us with the details of the story.'"
>
> ". . . Some high-concept stories are more appealing to the studios than others. The ideas liked best are sufficiently original that the audience will not feel it has already seen the movie, yet similar enough to past hits to reassure executives wary of anything too far-out. Thus, the frequently used shorthand: It's *Flashdance* in the country (*Footloose*) or *High Noon* in outer space (*Outland*)."
>
> ". . . One gambit not to use during a pitch," says executive Barbara Boyle, "is to talk about big box-office grosses your story is sure to make. Executives know as well as anyone that it's impossible to predict how much money a movie will make, and declarations to the contrary are considered pure malarkey."

[12]Mark Litwak, *Reel Power: The Struggle for Influence and Success in the New Hollywood* (New York: William Morrow and Company, 1986), pp. 73, 74, and 77.

RESEARCH IN EMERGING MARKET CONTEXT

According to Kim et al. (2021), Korean companies' capital budgeting methods are competitive with those of developed market companies, as they are more likely to use recommended approaches like NPV and IRR. Nonetheless, they bemoan the reality that companies, particularly when it comes to foreign investments, neglect to modify project discount rates to consider varying levels of risk. Notwithstanding, Korean enterprises implement certain modifications, such as designating distinct national rates for multinational projects and modifying cash flows and discount rates in response to interest rates, commodity prices, foreign exchange, and inflationary risks.

References

Kim, T., Lee, H., Park, K., & Waggle, D. (2021). Capital budgeting practices: Evidence from Korea. *Managerial Finance, 47*(2), 189–208.

Summary and Conclusions

1. In this chapter, we covered different investment decision rules. We evaluated the most popular alternatives to NPV: the payback period, the discounted payback period, the internal rate of return, and the profitability index. In doing so, we learned more about the NPV.
2. While we found that the alternatives have some redeeming qualities, when all is said and done, they are not NPV; for those of us in finance, that makes them decidedly second-rate.
3. Of the competitors to NPV, IRR must be ranked above payback. In fact, IRR always reaches the same decision as NPV for an independent project with conventional cash flows.
4. We classified the flaws of IRR into two types. First, we considered the general case applying to both independent and mutually exclusive projects. There appeared to be two problems here:
   a. Some projects have cash inflows followed by one or more outflows. The IRR rule is inverted here: One should accept when the IRR is *below* the discount rate.
   b. Some projects have a number of changes of sign in their cash flows. Here, there are likely to be multiple internal rates of return. The practitioner must use NPV.
5. Next, we considered the specific problems with the IRR for mutually exclusive projects. We showed that, due to differences in either size or timing, the project with the highest IRR need not have the highest NPV. Hence, the IRR rule should not be applied. (Of course, NPV can still be applied.)

   However, we then calculated incremental cash flows. For ease of calculation, we suggested subtracting the cash flows of the smaller project from the cash flows of the larger project. In that way, the incremental initial cash flow is negative. One can always reach a correct decision by accepting the larger project if the incremental IRR is greater than the discount rate.
6. We described capital rationing as the case where funds are limited to a fixed rupee amount. With capital rationing, the profitability index is a useful method of adjusting the NPV.

Concept Questions

1. **Payback Period and Net Present Value** If a project with conventional cash flows has a payback period less than the project's life, can you definitively state the algebraic sign of the NPV? Why or why not? If you know that the discounted payback period is less than the project's life, what can you say about the NPV? Explain.

2. **Net Present Value** Suppose a project has conventional cash flows and a positive NPV. What do you know about its payback? Its discounted payback? Its profitability index? Its IRR? Explain.

3. **Comparing Investment Criteria** Define each of the following investment rules and discuss any potential shortcomings of each. In your definition, state the criterion for accepting or rejecting independent projects under each rule.

   a. Payback period.
   b. Internal rate of return.
   c. Profitability index.
   d. Net present value.

4. **Payback and Internal Rate of Return** A project has perpetual cash flows of C per period, a cost of I, and a required return of r. What is the relationship between the project's payback and its IRR? What implications does your answer have for long-lived projects with relatively constant cash flows?

5. **International Investment Projects** In March 2020, Ireland-based Kerry Group announced plans to spend ₹125 million to expand production at its Georgia plant. The new investment would allow Kerry to double production at the plant, especially in the seafood, poultry, and alternative protein markets. Also in 2020, German auto parts supplier GEDIA Automotive Group announced plans to build an ₹85 billion plant in Georgia, and Mercedes-Benz Vans announced plans to build a ₹500 billion plant in South Carolina. What are some of the reasons that foreign manufacturers of products as diverse as food, auto parts, and vans might arrive at the same conclusion to build plants in the United States?

6. **Capital Budgeting Problems** What are some of the difficulties that might come up in actual applications of the various criteria we discussed in this chapter? Which one would be the easiest to implement in actual applications? The most difficult?

7. **Capital Budgeting in Not-for-Profit Entities** Are the capital budgeting criteria we discussed applicable to not-for-profit corporations? How should such entities make capital budgeting decisions? What about the U.S. government? Should it evaluate spending proposals using these techniques?

8. **Net Present Value** The investment in Project A is ₹1 million, and the investment in Project B is ₹2 million. Both projects have a unique internal rate of return of 20 percent. Is the following statement true or false?

   For any discount rate from 0 percent to 20 percent, Project B has an NPV twice as great as that of Project A.

   Explain your answer.

9. **Net Present Value versus Profitability Index** Consider the following two mutually exclusive projects available to Global Investments, Inc.:

	C_0	C_1	C_2	Profitability Index	NPV
A	−₹1,000	₹1,000	₹500	1.32	₹322
B	−500	500	400	1.57	285

The appropriate discount rate for the projects is 10 percent. Global Investments chose to undertake Project A. At a luncheon for shareholders, the manager of a pension fund that owns a substantial amount of the firm's stock asks you why the firm chose Project A instead of Project B when Project B has a higher profitability index.

How would you, the CFO, justify your firm's action? Are there any circumstances under which Global Investments should choose Project B?

10. **Internal Rate of Return** Projects A and B have the following cash flows:

Year	Project A	Project B
0	−₹1,000	−₹2,000
1	C1A	C1B
2	C2A	C2B
3	C3A	C3B

a. If the cash flows from the projects are identical, which of the two projects would have a higher IRR? Why?
b. If C1B = 2C1A, C2B = 2C2A, and C3B = 2C3A, then does $IRR_A = IRR_B$?

11. **Net Present Value** You are evaluating Project A and Project B. Project A has a short period of future cash flows, while Project B has a relatively long period of future cash flows. Which project will be more sensitive to changes in the required return? Why?

12. **Modified Internal Rate of Return** One of the less flattering interpretations of the acronym MIRR is "meaningless internal rate of return." Why do you think this term is applied to MIRR?

13. **Net Present Value** It is sometimes stated that "the net present value approach assumes reinvestment of the intermediate cash flows at the required return." Is this claim correct? To answer, suppose you calculate the NPV of a project in the usual way. Next, suppose you do the following:

a. Calculate the future value (as of the end of the project) of all the cash flows other than the initial outlay assuming they are reinvested at the required return, producing a single future value figure for the project.
b. Calculate the NPV of the project using the single future value calculated in the previous step and the initial outlay. It is easy to verify that you will get the same NPV as in your original calculation only if you use the required return as the reinvestment rate in the previous step.

14. **Internal Rate of Return** It is sometimes stated that, "The internal rate of return approach assumes reinvestment of the intermediate cash flows at the internal rate of return." Is this claim correct? To answer, suppose you calculate the IRR of a project in the usual way. Next, suppose you do the following:

a. Calculate the future value (as of the end of the project) of all the cash flows other than the initial outlay assuming they are reinvested at the IRR, producing a single future value figure for the project.
b. Calculate the IRR of the project using the single future value calculated in the previous step and the initial outlay. It is easy to verify that you will get the same IRR as in your original calculation only if you use the IRR as the reinvestment rate in the previous step.

Questions and Problems

1. **Calculating Payback Period and NPV** Janina, Inc., has the following mutually exclusive projects.

BASIC (Questions 1–8)

Year	Project A	Project B
0	−₹20,000	−₹23,000
1	15,200	14,300
2	5,900	8,100
3	2,100	7,100

a. Suppose the company's payback period cutoff is two years. Which of these two projects should be chosen?

b. Suppose the company uses the NPV rule to rank these two projects. Which project should be chosen if the appropriate discount rate is 15 percent?

2. **Calculating Payback** An investment project provides cash inflows of ₹835 per year for eight years. What is the project payback period if the initial cost is ₹1,900? What if the initial cost is ₹3,600? What if it is ₹7,400?

3. **Calculating Discounted Payback** An investment project has annual cash inflows of ₹2,800, ₹3,700, ₹5,100, and ₹4,300, for the next four years, respectively. The discount rate is 9 percent. What is the discounted payback period for these cash flows if the initial cost is ₹5,200? What if the initial cost is ₹6,400? What if it is ₹10,400?

4. **Calculating Discounted Payback** An investment project costs ₹19,000 and has annual cash flows of ₹5,100 for six years. What is the discounted payback period if the discount rate is zero percent? What if the discount rate is 5 percent? If it is 19 percent?

5. **Calculating IRR** A firm evaluates all projects by applying the IRR rule. If the required return is 14 percent, should the firm accept the following project?

Year	Cash Flows
0	−₹41,000
1	20,000
2	23,000
3	14,000

6. **Calculating IRR** Compute the internal rate of return for the cash flows of the following two projects:

Year	Project A	Project B
0	−₹8,500	−₹4,870
1	4,250	2,360
2	3,860	2,530
3	2,890	1,920

7. **Calculating Profitability Index** Vince plans to open a self-serve grooming center in a storefront. The grooming equipment will cost ₹365,000, to be paid immediately. Vince expects aftertax cash inflows of ₹79,000 annually for 7 years, after which he plans to scrap the equipment and retire to the beaches of Nevis. The first cash inflow occurs at the end of the first year. Assume the required return is 13 percent. What is the project's PI? Should it be accepted?

8. **Calculating Profitability Index** Suppose the following two independent investment opportunities are available to a company. The appropriate discount rate is 8.5 percent.

Year	Project Alpha	Project Beta
0	−₹3,700	−₹4,300
1	1,900	1,500
2	1,800	3,100
3	1,400	2,400

a. Compute the profitability index for each of the two projects.
b. Which project(s) should the company accept based on the profitability index rule?

INTERMEDIATE (Questions 9–21)

9. Cash Flow Intuition A project has an initial cost of I, has a required return of R, and pays C annually for N years.

a. Find C in terms of I and N such that the project has a payback period equal to its life.
b. Find C in terms of I, N, and R such that this is a profitable project according to the NPV decision rule.
c. Find C in terms of I, N, and R such that the project has a benefit-cost ratio of 2.

10. Problems with IRR Suppose you are offered a project with the following cash flows:

Year	Cash Flows
0	₹ 9,800
1	−4,300
2	−3,300
3	−2,500
4	−2,300

a. What is the IRR of this project?
b. If the appropriate discount rate is 10 percent, should you accept this project?
c. If the appropriate discount rate is 20 percent, should you accept this project?
d. What is the NPV of the project if the appropriate discount rate is 10 percent? 20 percent?
e. Are the decisions under the NPV rule in part (d) consistent with those of the IRR rule?

11. NPV versus IRR Consider the following cash flows on two mutually exclusive projects for the Bahamas Recreation Corporation (BRC). Both projects require an annual return of 14 percent.

Year	Deepwater Fishing	New Submarine Ride
0	−₹875,000	−₹1,650,000
1	330,000	890,000
2	480,000	730,000
3	440,000	590,000

As a financial analyst for the company, you are asked the following questions:

a. If your decision rule is to accept the project with the greater IRR, which project should you choose?
b. Because you are fully aware of the IRR rule's scale problem, you calculate the incremental IRR for the cash flows. Based on your computation, which project should you choose?
c. To be prudent, you compute the NPV for both projects. Which project should you choose? Is it consistent with the incremental IRR rule?

12. Problems with Profitability Index Symon's Sausage Corporation is trying to choose between the following two mutually exclusive design projects:

Year	Project I	Project II
0	−₹65,000	−₹49,800
1	31,500	24,900
2	31,500	24,900
3	31,500	24,900

a. If the required return is 10 percent and the company applies the profitability index decision rule, which project should the firm accept?

b. If the company applies the NPV decision rule, which project should it take?
c. Explain why your answers in parts (a) and (b) are different.

13. **Problems with IRR** Howell Petroleum, Inc., is trying to evaluate a generation project with the following cash flows:

Year	Cash Flow
0	−₹52,000,000
1	74,000,000
2	−12,000,000

a. If the company requires a 12 percent return on its investments, should it accept this project? Why?
b. Compute the IRR for this project. How many IRRs are there? Using the IRR decision rule, should the company accept the project? What's going on here?

14. **Comparing Investment Criteria** Wii Brothers, a game manufacturer, has a new idea for an adventure game. It can market the game either as a traditional board game or as an interactive DVD, but not both. Consider the following cash flows of the two mutually exclusive projects for the company. Assume the discount rate for both projects is 10 percent.

Year	Board Game	DVD
0	−₹750	−₹1,500
1	640	1,180
2	480	670
3	80	320

a. Based on the payback period rule, which project should be chosen?
b. Based on the NPV, which project should be chosen?
c. Based on the IRR, which project should be chosen?
d. Based on the incremental IRR, which project should be chosen?

15. **Profitability Index versus NPV** Hanmi Group, a consumer electronics conglomerate, is reviewing its annual budget in wireless technology. It is considering investments in three different technologies to develop wireless communication devices. Consider the following cash flows of the three independent projects available to the company. Assume the discount rate for all projects is 10 percent. Further, the company has only ₹43 million to invest in new projects this year.

	Cash Flows (in millions)		
Year	CDMA	G4	Wi-Fi
0	−₹18	−₹25	−₹43
1	23	21	39
2	16	51	66
3	6	41	42

a. Based on the profitability index decision rule, rank these investments.
b. Based on the NPV, rank these investments.
c. Based on your findings in parts (a) and (b), what would you recommend to the CEO of the company and why?

16. **Comparing Investment Criteria** Consider the following cash flows of two mutually exclusive projects for AZ-Motorcars. Assume the discount rate for both projects is 10 percent.

Year	AZM Mini-SUV	AZF Full-SUV
0	−₹675,000	−₹930,000
1	403,000	415,000
2	274,000	467,000
3	238,000	319,000

a. Based on the payback period, which project should be accepted?
b. Based on the NPV, which project should be accepted?
c. Based on the IRR, which project should be accepted?
d. Based on this analysis, is incremental IRR analysis necessary? If yes, please conduct the analysis.

17. **Comparing Investment Criteria** The treasurer of Amaro Canned Fruits, Inc., has projected the cash flows of Projects A, B, and C as follows:

Year	Project A	Project B	Project C
0	−₹405,000	−₹810,000	−₹405,000
1	297,000	540,000	324,000
2	297,000	540,000	243,000

Suppose the relevant discount rate is 12 percent per year.

a. Compute the profitability index for each of the three projects.
b. Compute the NPV for each of the three projects.
c. Suppose these three projects are independent. Which project(s) should Amaro accept based on the profitability index rule?
d. Suppose these three projects are mutually exclusive. Which project(s) should Amaro accept based on the profitability index rule?
e. Suppose Amaro's budget for these projects is ₹810,000. The projects are not divisible. Which project(s) should Amaro accept?

18. **Comparing Investment Criteria** Consider the following cash flows of two mutually exclusive projects for Tokyo Rubber Company. Assume the discount rate for both projects is 8 percent.

Year	Dry Prepreg	Solvent Prepreg
0	−₹1,800,000	−₹715,000
1	1,080,000	380,000
2	840,000	627,000
3	870,000	396,000

a. Based on the payback period, which project should be taken?
b. Based on the NPV, which project should be taken?
c. Based on the IRR, which project should be taken?
d. Based on this analysis, is incremental IRR analysis necessary? If yes, please conduct the analysis.

19. **Comparing Investment Criteria** Consider two mutually exclusive new product launch projects that Nagano Golf is considering. Assume the discount rate for both products is 15 percent.

Project A: Nagano NP-30.
Professional clubs that will take an initial investment of ₹675,000 at Year 0.

For each of the next five years (Years 1–5), sales will generate a consistent cash flow of ₹224,000 per year.
Introduction of new product at Year 6 will terminate further cash flows from this project.

Project B: Nagano NX-20.
High-end amateur clubs that will take an initial investment of ₹430,000 at Year 0.
Cash flow at Year 1 is ₹125,000. In each subsequent year, cash flow will grow at 10 percent per year.
Introduction of new product at Year 6 will terminate further cash flows from this project.

Year	NP-30	NX-20
0	−₹675,000	−₹430,000
1	224,000	125,000
2	224,000	137,500
3	224,000	151,250
4	224,000	166,375
5	224,000	183,013

Please fill in the following table:

	NP-30	NX-20	Implications
Payback			
IRR			
PI			
NPV			

20. **MIRR** Duo Corp. is evaluating a project with the following cash flows:

Year	Cash Flow
0	−₹53,000
1	16,700
2	21,900
3	27,300
4	20,400
5	− 8,600

The company uses a discount rate of 10 percent on all of its projects. Calculate the MIRR of the project using all three methods.

21. **MIRR** Suppose the company in the previous problem uses a discount rate of 11 percent and a reinvestment rate of 8 percent on all of its projects. Calculate the MIRR of the project using all three methods using these interest rates.

CHALLENGE (Questions 22–30)

22. **NPV and Multiple IRRs** You are evaluating a project that costs ₹75,000 today. The project has an inflow of ₹155,000 in one year and an outflow of ₹65,000 in two years. What are the IRRs for the project? What discount rate results in the maximum NPV for this project? How can you determine that this is the maximum NPV?

23. **Payback and NPV** An investment under consideration has a payback of seven years and a cost of ₹745,000. If the required return is 11 percent, what is the worst-case NPV? The best-case NPV? Explain. Assume the cash flows are conventional.

24. **Multiple IRRs** This problem is useful for testing the ability of financial calculators and spreadsheets. Consider the following cash flows. How many different IRRs are there? (*Hint:* Search between 20 percent and 70 percent.) When should we take this project?

Year	Cash Flow
0	–₹ 3,024
1	17,172
2	– 36,420
3	34,200
4	– 12,000

25. **NPV Valuation** The Yurdone Corporation wants to set up a private cemetery business. According to the CFO, Barry M. Deep, business is "looking up." As a result, the cemetery project will provide a net cash inflow of ₹180,000 for the firm during the first year, and the cash flows are projected to grow at a rate of 4 percent per year forever. The project requires an initial investment of ₹2.2 million.

    a. If the company requires a return of 11 percent on such undertakings, should the cemetery business be started?

    b. The company is somewhat unsure about the assumption of a growth rate of 4 percent in its cash flows. At what constant growth rate would the company break even if it still required a return of 11 percent on investment?

26. **Calculating IRR** The Utah Mining Corporation is set to open a gold mine near Provo, Utah. According to the treasurer, Monty Goldstein, "This is a golden opportunity." The mine will cost ₹3.8 million to open and will have an economic life of 11 years. It will generate a cash inflow of ₹625,000 at the end of the first year, and the cash inflows are projected to grow at 8 percent per year for the next 10 years. After 11 years, the mine will be abandoned. Abandonment costs will be ₹750,000 at the end of Year 11.

    a. What is the IRR for the gold mine?

    b. The Utah Mining Corporation requires a return of 13 percent on such projects. Should the mine be opened?

27. **NPV and IRR** Anderson International Limited is evaluating a project in Erewhon. The project will create the following cash flows:

Year	Cash Flow
0	–₹1,785,000
1	610,000
2	707,000
3	580,000
4	483,000

All cash flows will occur in Erewhon and are expressed in rupees. In an attempt to improve its economy, the Erewhonian government has declared that all cash flows created by a foreign company are "blocked" and must be reinvested with the government for one year. The reinvestment rate for these funds is 4 percent. If Anderson uses a required return of 11 percent on this project, what are the NPV and IRR of the project? Is the IRR you calculated the MIRR of the project? Why or why not?

28. **Calculating IRR** Consider two streams of cash flows, A and B. Stream A's first cash flow is ₹11,600 and is received three years from today. Future cash flows in Stream A grow by 4 percent in perpetuity. Stream B's first cash flow is –₹13,000, is received two years from today, and will continue in perpetuity. Assume that the appropriate discount rate is 12 percent.

a. What is the present value of each stream?
b. Suppose that the two streams are combined into one project, called C. What is the IRR of Project C?
c. What is the correct IRR rule for Project C?

29. **Calculating Incremental Cash Flows** Darin Clay, the CFO of MakeMoney.com, has to decide between the following two projects:

Year	Project Million	Project Billion
0	−₹1,200	−₹I_0
1	I_0 + 160	I_0 + 400
2	960	1,200
3	1,200	1,600

The expected rate of return for either of the two projects is 12 percent. What is the range of initial investment (I_0) for which Project Billion is more financially attractive than Project Million?

30. **Problems with IRR** Mako Corp. has a project with the following cash flows:

Year	Cash Flow
0	₹25,000
1	−11,000
2	7,000

What is the IRR of the project? What is happening here?

Excel Master It! Problem

Excel Master coverage online

As you have already seen, Excel does not have a function to calculate the payback period. We have shown three ways to calculate the payback period, but there are numerous other methods as well. The cash flows for a project are shown below. You need to calculate the payback period using two different methods:

a. Calculate the payback period in a table. The first three columns of the table will be the year, the cash flow for that year, and the cumulative cash flow. The fourth column will show the whole year for the payback. In other words, if the payback period is three-plus years, this column will have a 3, otherwise it will be a zero. The next column will calculate the fractional part of the payback period, or else it will display zero. The last column will add the previous two columns and display the final payback period calculation. You also should have a cell that displays the final payback period by itself and a cell that returns the correct accept or reject decision based on the payback criteria.
b. Write a nested IF statement that calculates the payback period using only the project cash flow column. The IF statement should return a value of "Never" if the project has no payback period. In contrast to the example we showed previously, the nested IF function should test for the payback period starting with shorter payback periods and working toward longer payback periods. Another cell should display the correct accept or reject decision based on the payback criteria.

Year	Cash Flow
0	–₹250,000
1	41,000
2	48,000
3	63,000
4	79,000
5	88,000
6	64,000
7	41,000
Required payback:	5

Mini Case BULLOCK GOLD MINING

Seth Bullock, the owner of Bullock Gold Mining, is evaluating a new gold mine in South Dakota. Dan Dority, the company's geologist, has just finished his analysis of the mine site. He has estimated that the mine would be productive for eight years, after which the gold would be completely mined. Dan has taken an estimate of the gold deposits to Alma Garrett, the company's financial officer. Alma has been asked by Seth to perform an analysis of the new mine and present her recommendation on whether the company should open the new mine.

Alma has used the estimates provided by Dan to determine the revenues that could be expected from the mine. She also has projected the expense of opening the mine and the annual operating expenses. If the company opens the mine, it will cost ₹825 million today, and it will have a cash outflow of ₹75 million nine years from today in costs associated with closing the mine and reclaiming the area surrounding it. The expected cash flows each year from the mine are shown in the following table. Bullock Mining has a 12 percent required return on all of its gold mines.

Year	Cash Flow
0	–₹825,000,000
1	160,000,000
2	185,000,000
3	215,000,000
4	245,000,000
5	210,000,000
6	205,000,000
7	190,000,000
8	160,000,000
9	– 75,000,000

1. Construct a spreadsheet to calculate the payback period, internal rate of return, modified internal rate of return, profitability index, and net present value of the proposed mine.
2. Based on your analysis, should the company open the mine?
3. Bonus question: Most spreadsheets do not have a built-in formula to calculate the payback period. Write a VBA script that calculates the payback period for a project.

6

Making Capital Investment Decisions

Is there green in in outer space? Elon Musk certainly thinks so. Musk famously launched SpaceX, with the goal of commercializing space travel. What is less well-known is that SpaceX is also working on Starlink, which could eventually have as many as 30,000 interconnected satellites to provide broadband connections worldwide. The cost is expected to reach as much as ₹60 billion, with an additional ₹12 billion more each year to replace outdated satellites.

Of course, SpaceX is not alone: Famed Virgin Atlantic Airways owner Sir Richard Branson is also working on commercial space travel, and Amazon disclosed plans for more than 3,000 satellites to provide internet service.

As you no doubt recognize from your study of the previous chapter, SpaceX's decision to develop and market green technology represents a capital budgeting decision. In this chapter, we identify the relevant cash flows of a project, including initial investment outlays, requirements for net working capital, and operating cash flows. We also look at the effects of depreciation and taxes. Finally, we examine the impact of inflation and show how to evaluate a project when there is inflation.

The previous chapter discussed the basic principles behind capital budgeting approaches such as net present value, internal rate of return, and payback. We pointed out that these three approaches all use cash flows. We did not, however, indicate how cash flows are to be estimated in the real world. Chapter 6 addresses this task. We begin with the idea that one should estimate *incremental* cash flows.

Please visit us at **rwjcorporatefinance.blogspot.com** for the latest developments in the world of corporate finance.

6.1 Incremental Cash Flows: The Key to Capital Budgeting

CASH FLOWS—NOT ACCOUNTING INCOME

You may not have thought about it, but there is a big difference between corporate finance courses and financial accounting courses. Techniques in corporate finance generally use cash flows, whereas financial accounting generally stresses income or earnings numbers. Certainly our text follows this tradition: Our net present value techniques discount cash flows, not earnings. When considering a single project, we discount the cash flows that the firm receives from the project.

EXAMPLE 6.1

Relevant Cash Flows The Vidyut Industries Limited just paid ₹1 million in cash for a building as part of a new capital budgeting project. This entire ₹1 million is an immediate cash outflow. However, assuming straight-line depreciation over 20 years, only ₹50,000 (= ₹1 million/20) is considered an accounting expense in the current year. Current earnings are thereby reduced by only ₹50,000 (less the depreciation tax shield). The remaining ₹950,000 is expensed over the following 19 years. For capital budgeting purposes, the relevant cash outflow at Year 0 is the full ₹1 million, not the reduction in earnings of only ₹50,000.

Cash flows represent the change in the firm's cash that could be used to invest in future projects or pay out to the firm's investors. Always discount cash flows, not earnings, when performing a capital budgeting calculation. Earnings do not represent real money. You can't spend out of earnings, you can't eat out of earnings, and you can't pay dividends out of earnings. You can do these things only out of cash flows.

In calculating the NPV of a project, only cash flows that are incremental to the project should be used. These cash flows are the changes in the firm's cash flows that occur as a direct consequence of accepting the project. That is, we are interested in the difference between the cash flows of the firm with the project and the cash flows of the firm without the project.

The use of incremental cash flows sounds easy enough, but pitfalls abound in the real world. We describe how to avoid some of the pitfalls of determining incremental cash flows.

SUNK COSTS

A **sunk cost** is a cost that has already occurred. Because sunk costs are in the past, they cannot be changed by the decision to accept or reject the project. As we "let bygones be bygones," we should ignore such costs. Sunk costs are not incremental cash outflows.

EXAMPLE 6.2

Sunk Costs The Ghaziabad Milk Company (GMC) is currently evaluating the NPV of establishing a line of chocolate milk. As part of the evaluation, the company paid a consulting firm ₹100,000 last year for a test marketing analysis. Is this cost relevant for the capital budgeting decision now confronting GMC's management?

The answer is no. The ₹100,000 is not recoverable, so the ₹100,000 expenditure is a sunk cost, or spilled milk. In other words, one must ask, "What is the difference between the cash flows of the entire firm with the chocolate milk project and the cash flows of the entire firm without the project?" Because the ₹100,000 was already spent, acceptance of the project does not affect this cash flow. Therefore, the cash flow should be ignored for capital budgeting purposes.

Of course, the decision to spend ₹100,000 for a marketing analysis was a capital budgeting decision itself and was perfectly relevant before it was sunk. Our point is that once the company incurred the expense, the cost became irrelevant for any future decision.

Thinking about sunk costs the right way is important when making project continuation decisions. Suppose as CEO, you made a costly mistake last year when you decided to invest in a new manufacturing plant to produce a new product. The upfront investment was very expensive, and you now realize that you will never recoup the costs given updated forecasts of modest consumer demand for the new product.

However, you should be careful not to compound your original mistake by blindly canceling the project. As you consider whether to continue production, you should ignore the upfront cost of the manufacturing plant, because that is a sunk cost. Remember, "let bygones be bygones."

OPPORTUNITY COSTS

Your firm may have an asset that it is considering selling, leasing, or employing elsewhere in the business. If the asset is used in a new project, potential cash flows from alternative uses are lost. These lost cash flows can meaningfully be viewed as costs. They are called **opportunity costs** because, by taking the project, the firm forgoes other opportunities for using the assets.

EXAMPLE 6.3

Opportunity Costs Suppose the Wangdu Trading Company has an empty warehouse in Mumbai that can be used to store a new line of electronic pinball machines. The company hopes to sell these machines to affluent northeastern consumers. Should the warehouse be considered a cost in the decision to sell the machines?

The answer is yes. The company could sell the warehouse if the firm decides not to market the pinball machines. Thus, the sales price of the warehouse is an opportunity cost in the pinball machine decision.

SIDE EFFECTS

Another difficulty in determining incremental cash flows comes from the side effects of the proposed project on other parts of the firm. A side effect is classified as either **erosion** or **synergy**. Erosion occurs when a new product reduces the sales and, hence, the cash flows of existing products. For example, one of Walt Disney Company's concerns when it built Disneyland Paris was that the new park would drain visitors from the Florida park, a popular vacation destination for Europeans. Synergy occurs when a new project increases the cash flows of existing projects. While a shaving-supplies firm may appear to lose money on its new razor, the increase in sales of its new razor blades may make the razor an overall winner for the firm.

EXAMPLE 6.4

Erosion Suppose the Itanagar Motors Corporation (IMC) is determining the NPV of a new convertible sports car. Some of the would-be purchasers are owners of IMC's compact sedans. Are all cash flows from the new convertible sports car incremental?

The answer is no because some of the cash flow represents transfers from other elements of IMC's product line. This is erosion, which must be included in the NPV calculation. Without taking erosion into account, IMC might erroneously calculate the NPV of the sports car to be, say, ₹100 million. If half the customers are transfers from the sedan and lost sedan sales have an NPV of –₹150 million, the true NPV is –₹50 million (= ₹100 million – 150 million).

Synergy IMC is also contemplating the formation of a racing team. The team is forecast to lose money for the foreseeable future, with perhaps the best projection showing an NPV of –₹35 million for the operation. However, IMC's managers are aware that the team will likely generate great publicity for all of IMC's products. A consultant estimates that the increase in cash flows elsewhere in the firm has a present value of ₹65 million. Assuming that the consultant's estimates of synergy are accurate, the net present value of the team is ₹30 million (= ₹65 million – 35 million). The company should form the team.

ALLOCATED COSTS

Frequently a particular expenditure benefits a number of projects. Accountants allocate this cost across the different projects when determining income. However, for capital budgeting purposes, this **allocated cost** should be viewed as a cash outflow of a project only if it is an incremental cost of the project.

EXAMPLE 6.5

Allocated Costs The Vedakshya Consulting Company devotes one wing of its suite of offices to a library requiring a cash outflow of ₹100,000 a year in upkeep. A proposed capital budgeting project is expected to generate revenue equal to 5 percent of the overall firm's sales. An executive at the firm, Dayavan Pillai, argues that ₹5,000 (= .05 × ₹100,000) should be viewed as the proposed project's share of the library's costs. Is this appropriate for capital budgeting?

The answer is no. One must ask what the difference is between the cash flows of the entire firm with the project and the cash flows of the entire firm without the project. The firm will spend ₹100,000 on library upkeep whether or not the proposed project is accepted. Because acceptance of the proposed project does not affect this cash flow, the cash flow should be ignored when calculating the NPV of the project. Suppose the project has a positive NPV without the allocated costs but is rejected because of the allocated costs. In this case, the firm is losing potential value that it could have gained otherwise.

6.2 The Bhimsen Company: An Example

Excel Master coverage online

To forecast cash flows for a new project, we need to estimate operating cash flow less the needed investments. To illustrate this process, we next consider the example of a proposed investment in machinery and related items. Our example involves the Bhimsen Company and colored bowling balls.

The Bhimsen Company, originally established 16 years ago to make footballs, is now a leading producer of tennis balls, baseballs, footballs, and golf balls. Nine years ago, the company introduced "High Flite," its first line of high-performance golf balls. Bhimsen management has sought opportunities in whatever businesses seem to have some potential for cash flow. Recently K. S. Srinivas, vice president of the Bhimsen Company, identified another segment of the sports ball market that looked promising and that he felt was not adequately served by larger manufacturers. That market was for brightly colored bowling balls, and he believed many bowlers valued appearance and style above performance. He also believed that it would be difficult for competitors to take advantage of the opportunity because of both Bhimsen's cost advantages and its highly developed marketing skills.

As a result, the Bhimsen Company investigated the marketing potential of brightly colored bowling balls. Bhimsen sent a questionnaire to consumers in three markets: Mumbai, Bengaluru, and Kolkata. The results of the three questionnaires were much better than expected and supported the conclusion that the brightly colored bowling balls could achieve a 10 to 15 percent share of the market. Of course, some people at Bhimsen complained about the cost of the test marketing, which was ₹250,000. (As we discussed earlier, this is a sunk cost and should not be included in project evaluation.)

In any case, the Bhimsen Company is now considering investing in a machine to produce bowling balls. The bowling balls would be manufactured in a warehouse owned by the firm and located near Bengaluru. This warehouse, which is vacant, and the land can be sold for ₹150,000 after taxes.

Working with his staff, Srinivas is preparing an analysis of the proposed new product. He summarizes his assumptions as follows: The cost of the bowling ball machine is ₹100,000 and it is expected to last five years. At the end of five years, the machine will be sold at a price estimated to be ₹30,000. Production by year during the five-year life of the machine is expected to be as follows: 5,000 units, 8,000 units, 12,000 units, 10,000 units, and 6,000 units. The price of bowling balls in the first year will be ₹20. The bowling ball market is highly competitive, so Srinivas believes that the price of bowling balls will increase at only 2 percent per year, as compared to the anticipated general inflation rate of 5 percent. Conversely, the plastic used to produce bowling balls is rapidly becoming more expensive. Because of this, production cash outflows are expected to grow at 10 percent per year. First-year production costs will be ₹10 per unit. Srinivas has determined, based on Bhimsen's taxable income, that the appropriate incremental corporate tax rate in the bowling ball project is 21 percent.

Net working capital is defined as the difference between current assets and current liabilities. Like any other manufacturing firm, Bhimsen finds that it must maintain an investment in working capital. It will purchase raw materials before production and sale, giving rise to an investment in inventory. It will maintain cash as a buffer against unforeseen expenditures. And its credit sales will not generate cash until payment is made at a later date. Management determines that an initial investment (Year 0) in net working capital of ₹10,000 is required. Subsequently, net working capital at the end of each year will be equal to 10 percent of sales for that year. In the final year of the project, net working capital will decline to zero as the project is wound down. In other words, the investment in working capital is to be completely recovered by the end of the project's life.

Projections based on these assumptions and Srinivas's analysis appear in Tables 6.1 through 6.4. In these tables, all cash flows are assumed to occur at the end of the year. Because of the large amount of

Table 6.1 Worksheet for Cash Flows of the Bhimsen Company (in thousands) (All cash flows occur at the end of the year.)

	Year 0	Year 1	Year 2	Year 3	Year 4	Year 5
Investments:						
(1) Bowling ball machine	–₹100.00					₹ 24.91*
(2) Accumulated depreciation		₹ 20.00	₹ 52.00	₹ 71.20	₹ 82.72	94.24
(3) Adjusted basis of machine after depreciation (end of year)		80.00	48.00	28.80	17.28	5.76
(4) Opportunity cost (warehouse)	–150.00					150.00
(5) Net working capital (end of year)	10.00	10.00	16.32	24.97	21.22	
(6) Change in net working capital	–10.00		–6.32	–8.65	3.75	21.22
(7) Total cash flow of investment [(1) + (4) + (6)]	–260.00		–6.32	–8.65	3.75	196.13
Income:						
(8) Sales revenue		₹100.00	₹163.20	₹249.70	₹212.24	₹129.89
(9) Operating costs		50.00	88.00	145.20	133.10	87.85
(10) Depreciation		20.00	32.00	19.20	11.52	11.52
(11) Income before taxes [(8) + (9) + (10)]		₹ 30.00	₹ 43.20	₹ 85.30	₹ 67.62	₹ 30.53
(12) Tax (21%)		6.30	9.07	17.91	14.20	6.41
(13) Net income		₹ 23.70	₹ 34.13	₹ 67.38	₹ 53.42	₹ 24.12

*We assume that the ending market value of the capital investment at Year 5 is ₹30 (in thousands). The taxable amount is ₹24.24 (= ₹30 – 5.76). The aftertax salvage value is ₹30 – [.21 × (₹30 – 5.76)] = ₹24.91.

information in these tables, it is important to see how the tables are related. Table 6.1 shows the basic data for both investment and income. Supplementary schedules on operations and depreciation, as presented in Tables 6.2 and 6.3, help explain the numbers in Table 6.1. Our goal is to obtain projections of cash flow. The data in Table 6.1 are all that are needed to calculate the relevant cash flows, as shown in Table 6.4. We discuss each component of the analysis in detail in the next section.

Table 6.2 Operating Revenue and Costs of the Bhimsen Company

(1) Year	(2) Quantity Sold	(3) Price	(4) Sales Revenue	(5) Cost per Unit	(6) Operating Costs
1	5,000	₹20.00	₹100,000	₹10.00	₹ 50,000
2	8,000	20.40	163,200	11.00	88,000
3	12,000	20.81	249,696	12.10	145,200
4	10,000	21.22	212,242	13.31	133,100
5	6,000	21.65	129,892	14.64	87,846

Price rises at 2 percent per year. Unit cost rises at 10 percent per year. Price, revenue, cost per unit, and operating costs (Columns 3, 4, 5, and 6) are calculated using exact, i.e., nonrounded, prices and costs.

Table 6.3 Depreciation under Modified Accelerated Cost Recovery System (MACRS)

	Recovery Period Class					
Year	3 Years	5 Years	7 Years	10 Years	15 Years	20 Years
1	.3333	.2000	.1429	.1000	.0500	.03750
2	.4445	.3200	.2449	.1800	.0950	.07219
3	.1481	.1920	.1749	.1440	.0855	.06677
4	.0741	.1152	.1249	.1152	.0770	.06177
5		1152	.0893	.0922	.0693	.05713
6		.0576	.0892	.0737	.0623	.05285
7			.0893	.0655	.0590	.04888
8			.0446	.0655	.0590	.04522
9				.0656	.0591	.04462
10				.0655	.0590	.04461
11				.0328	.0591	.04462
12					.0590	.04461
13					.0591	.04462
14					.0590	.04461
15					.0591	.04462
16					.0295	.04461
17						.04462
18						.04461
19						.04462
20						.04461
21						.02231

Depreciation is expressed as a percentage of the asset's initial cost. These schedules are based on IRS Publication 946, entitled *How to Depreciate Property.* Details of depreciation are presented later in the chapter. Five-year depreciation actually carries over six years because the IRS assumes the purchase is made midyear.

Table 6.4 Incremental Cash Flows for the Bhimsen Company (in thousands)

	Year 0	Year 1	Year 2	Year 3	Year 4	Year 5
(1) Sales revenue [Line 8, Table 6.1]		₹100.00	₹163.20	₹249.70	₹212.24	₹129.89
(2) Operating costs [Line 9, Table 6.1]		−50.00	−88.00	−145.20	−133.10	−87.85
(3) Taxes [Line 12, Table 6.1]		−6.30	−9.07	−17.91	−14.20	−6.41
(4) Cash flow from operations [(1) + (2) + (3)]		₹ 43.70	₹ 66.13	₹ 86.58	₹ 64.94	₹ 35.64
(5) Total cash flow of investment [Line 7, Table 6.1]	−₹260.00		−6.32	−8.65	3.75	196.13
(6) Total cash flow of project [(4) + (5)]	−₹260.00	₹ 43.70	₹ 59.81	₹ 77.93	₹ 68.69	₹231.77

NPV @		
	4%	₹155.81
	10%	₹ 78.53
	15%	₹ 28.97
	18.54%	₹ 0.00
	20%	−₹ 10.68

AN ANALYSIS OF THE PROJECT

For most projects, cash flows follow a common pattern. First, firms invest at the beginning of the project, generating cash outflows. Second, product sales provide cash inflows over the life of the project. Third, plant and equipment are sold off at the end of the project, generating more cash inflow. We now discuss Bhimsen's cash flows for each of these three steps.

Investments The investment outlays for the project are summarized in the top segment of Table 6.1. They consist of three parts:

1. *The bowling ball machine*: The purchase requires an immediate (Year 0) cash outflow of ₹100,000. The firm realizes a cash inflow when the machine is sold in Year 5. These cash flows are shown in Line 1. As indicated in the footnote to the table, taxes are incurred when the asset is sold.
2. *The opportunity cost of not selling the warehouse*: If Bhimsen accepts the bowling ball project, it will use a warehouse and land that could otherwise be sold. The estimated aftertax sales price of the warehouse and land is therefore included as an opportunity cost in Year 0, as presented in Line 4. Opportunity costs are treated as cash outflows for purposes of capital budgeting. Note that if the project is accepted, management assumes that the warehouse will be sold for ₹150,000 (after taxes) in Year 5.

   The test marketing cost of ₹250,000 is not included. As stated earlier, the tests occurred in the past and should be viewed as sunk costs.
3. *The investment in working capital*: Required working capital appears in Line 5. Working capital rises over the early years of the project as expansion occurs. However, all working capital is assumed to be recovered at the end, a common assumption in capital budgeting. In other words, all inventory is sold by the end, the cash balance maintained as a buffer is liquidated, and all accounts receivable are collected.

   Increases in working capital in the early years must be funded by cash generated elsewhere in the firm. Hence, these increases are viewed as cash outflows. To reiterate, it is the increase in working capital over a year that leads to a cash outflow in that year. Even if working capital is at a high level, there will be no cash outflow over a year if working capital stays constant over that year. Conversely, decreases in working capital in the later years are viewed as cash inflows. All of these cash flows are presented in Line 6. A more complete discussion of working capital is provided later in this section.

To recap, there are three investments in this example: the bowling ball machine (Line 1), the opportunity cost of the warehouse (Line 4), and the changes in working capital (Line 6). The total cash flow from these three investments is shown in Line 7.

Income and Taxes Next, the determination of net income is presented in the bottom segment of Table 6.1. While we are ultimately interested in cash flow–not net income–we need the net income calculation to determine taxes. Lines 8 and 9 of Table 6.1 show sales revenues and operating costs, respectively. The projections in these lines are based on the sales revenues and operating costs computed in Columns 4 and 6 of Table 6.2. The estimates of revenues and costs follow from assumptions made by the corporate planning staff at Bhimsen. In other words, the estimates depend on the forecast that product prices will increase at 2 percent per year and costs per unit will increase at 10 percent per year.

Depreciation of the ₹100,000 capital investment is shown in Line 10 of Table 6.1. Where do these numbers come from? Depreciation for tax purposes for U.S. companies is based on the modified accelerated cost recovery system (MACRS). Each asset is assigned a useful life under MACRS, with an accompanying depreciation schedule as shown in Table 6.3. Under IRS rules, Bhimsen is to depreciate its capital investment over five years, so the second column of the table applies in this case. Because depreciation in the table is expressed as a percentage of the asset's cost, multiply the percentages in this column by ₹100,000 to arrive at depreciation in rupees. Notice that the percentages in each column of Table 6.3 sum to 100 percent, implying that the IRS allows the asset to be depreciated to zero.

While the Bhimsen illustration uses computations using the US tax rules, things will not be very different in India. In the Indian context, depreciation rates for tax purposes are prescribed under Schedule II of the Indian Companies Act, 2013.[1] The depreciation allowance as a percentage of *written-down value* is pre-specified by the tax authorities for different classes of assets and is treated based on a block of assets. Block of assets means a group of assets falling within a class of similar assets (say, machinery) in respect of which a pre-specified rate of depreciation is prescribed.

Income before taxes is calculated in Line 11 of Table 6.1. Taxes are provided in Line 12 of this table, and net income is shown in Line 13.

Salvage Value When selling an asset, one must pay taxes on the difference between the asset's sales price and its book value. We stated earlier that Bhimsen plans to sell the bowling ball machine at the end of Year 5, estimating the sales price at ₹30,000.

At the end of the fifth year, the book value of the machine would be ₹5,760, as shown in Line 3 of Table 6.1. If the company sold the machine for ₹30,000, it would pay taxes on the difference between this sales price and the book value of ₹5,760. With a 21 percent tax rate, the tax liability would be .21 × (₹30,000 − 5,760) = ₹5,090. The aftertax salvage value of the equipment, a cash inflow to the company, would be ₹30,000 − 5,090 = ₹24,910, as indicated in Line 1 of Table 6.1.

Alternatively, if the book value exceeds the market value, the difference is treated as a loss for tax purposes. If Bhimsen sold the machine for ₹4,000, the book value would exceed the market value by ₹1,760. In this case, taxes of .21 × ₹1,760 = ₹370 would be saved.

Cash Flow The total cash flow is determined in Table 6.4. We begin by reproducing Lines 8, 9, and 12 in Table 6.1 as Lines 1, 2, and 3 in Table 6.4. Cash flow from operations, which is sales minus both operating costs and taxes, is provided in Line 4 of Table 6.4. Total investment cash flow, taken from Line

---

[1]ICAI website and many standard accounting textbooks in India provide these rates. For detailed reference, see, for example, https://www.mca.gov.in/SearchableActs/Schedule2.htm

7 of Table 6.1, appears as Line 5 of Table 6.4. Cash flow from operations plus total cash flow of the investment equals total cash flow of the project, which is displayed as Line 6 of Table 6.4.[2]

Net Present Value The NPV of the Bhimsen bowling ball project can be calculated from the cash flows in Line 6. As can be seen at the bottom of Table 6.4, the NPV is ₹78,533 if 10 percent is the appropriate discount rate and –₹10,682 if 20 percent is the appropriate discount rate. If the discount rate is 18.54 percent, the project will have a zero NPV. In other words, the project's IRR is 18.54 percent. If the discount rate of the Bhimsen bowling ball project is above 18.54 percent, the project should be rejected because its NPV would be negative.

In the Indian context, till a few years back, the profit on a sale of an asset would have resulted in different types of income, resulting in differential tax treatment - as profit would be divided as *ordinary income* and *capital gain*.

WHICH SET OF BOOKS?

Corporations must provide a computation of profit or loss to both their own stockholders and tax authorities. While you might think that the numbers going to both parties would be the same, this is not the case. In actual fact, Indian and U.S. firms keep two sets of books, one for the Internal Revenue Service (IRS), i.e., income tax authorities, called *tax books*, and another for their annual reports (called *stockholders' books*), with the numbers differing across the two sets.

How can this be? The two sets of books differ because their rules were developed by two separate bodies. The tax books follow the rules of the IRS and the stockholders' books follow the rules of the *Financial Accounting Standards Board* (FASB) or *Indian Accounting Standards* (IndAS)[3], the respective governing bodies in accounting. For example, interest on municipal bonds is ignored for tax purposes while the FASB treats the interest as income. And companies typically use accelerated depreciation for their taxes and straight-line depreciation for their stockholders' books.

The differences almost always benefit the firm; the rules permit income on the stockholders' books to be higher than income on the tax books. Thus, the company can look profitable to its stockholders without having to pay taxes on all of the reported profit. In fact, plenty of large companies consistently report positive earnings to their stockholders while reporting losses to the IRS. A cynical interpretation is that Members of Indian Parliament *or* US Congress, who collectively make tax policy, develop favorable rules to help their constituents. Whether or not this interpretation is true, one thing is clear: Companies are following the law, not breaking the law, by creating two sets of books.

Indian businesses maintain two sets of records as well. The Indian Income Tax Act prescribes standards for one set of books kept by the tax authorities, while another set of books kept for shareholders basis their financial statements on Indian GAAP cum Ind AS (Accounting Standards) published by the ICAI. The differences can be illustrated by how product warranties (when an item is sold) are handled in the two books. Indian income tax authorities are unwilling to provide any provisions for warranties because they are afraid of manipulation, yet Indian GAAP recommends doing so to give shareholders a true view of the accounting.

Which set of books is relevant for the present chapter? The numbers in the tax books are the relevant ones because you can only calculate cash flows after subtracting taxes. While the stockholders' books are relevant for accounting and financial analysis, they are not used for capital budgeting.

---

[2]The total cash flow of the project is the same as the cash flow from assets that we calculated in Chapter 2 except that we are calculating the cash flow for the project rather than for the firm as a whole.

[3]*Indian Accounting Standards* (abbreviated as, *IndAS*) are a set of accounting standards notified by the Ministry of Corporate Affairs, Government of India. They are converged with *International Financial Reporting Standards* (IFRS).

Finally, while Indian and U.S. firms are allowed two sets of books, this is not the case in all, or perhaps even a majority, of other countries. Knowledge of local rules is needed before estimating international cash flows.

A NOTE ABOUT NET WORKING CAPITAL

Net working capital is the difference between current assets and current liabilities. Investment in net working capital is an important part of any capital budgeting analysis because it affects cash flows. While we considered net working capital in Lines 5 and 6 of Table 6.1, students may be wondering where the numbers in these lines came from. In capital budgeting, we are most interested in inventory, accounts receivable, accounts payable, and cash. An investment in net working capital arises whenever (1) inventory is purchased; (2) cash is kept in the project as a buffer against unexpected expenditures; and (3) sales are made on credit, generating accounts receivable rather than cash. This is reversed for credit purchases, which reduce net working capital and generate accounts payable. Such an investment in net working capital represents a cash outflow because cash generated elsewhere in the firm is tied up in the project.

To see how the investment in net working capital is built from its component parts, we focus on Year 1. We see in Table 6.1 that Bhimsen's managers predict sales in Year 1 to be ₹100,000 and operating costs to be ₹50,000. If both the sales and costs were cash transactions, the firm would receive ₹50,000 (= ₹100,000 − 50,000). As stated earlier, this cash flow would occur at the end of Year 1.

Now let's give you more information. The managers:

1. Forecast that ₹9,000 of the sales will be on credit, implying that cash receipts at the end of Year 1 will be ₹91,000 (= ₹100,000 − 9,000). The accounts receivable of ₹9,000 will be collected at the end of Year 2.
2. Believe that they can defer payment on ₹3,000 of the ₹50,000 of costs, implying that cash disbursements at the end of Year 1 will be ₹47,000 (= ₹50,000 − 3,000). Bhimsen will pay off the ₹3,000 of accounts payable at the end of Year 2.
3. Decide that inventory of ₹2,500 should be left on hand at the end of Year 1 to avoid stockouts, or running out of inventory.
4. Decide that cash of ₹1,500 should be earmarked for the project at the end of Year 1 to avoid running out of cash.

Thus, net working capital at the end of Year 1 is:

₹9,000	−	3,000	+	2,500	+	1,500	=	₹10,000
Accounts receivable		Accounts payable		Inventory		Cash		Net working capital

Because ₹10,000 of cash generated elsewhere in the firm must be used to offset this requirement for net working capital, Bhimsen's managers correctly view the investment in net working capital as a cash outflow of the project. As the project grows over time, needs for net working capital increase. Changes in net working capital from year to year represent further cash flows, as indicated by the negative numbers for the first few years on Line 6 of Table 6.1. However, in the declining years of the project, net working capital is reduced–ultimately to zero. That is, accounts receivable are finally collected, the project's cash buffer is returned to the rest of the corporation, and all remaining inventory is sold off. This frees up cash in the later years, as indicated by positive numbers in Years 4 and 5 on Line 6.

Typically, corporate worksheets (such as Table 6.1) treat net working capital as a whole. The individual components of working capital (receivables, inventory, and the like) do not generally appear in the worksheets.

However, the reader should remember that the working capital numbers in the worksheets are not pulled out of thin air. Rather, they result from a meticulous forecast of the components, as we illustrated for Year 1.

A NOTE ABOUT DEPRECIATION

The Bhimsen case made some assumptions about depreciation. Where did these assumptions come from? Depreciation rules are set forth in IRS Publication 946, entitled *How to Depreciate Property.* This publication sorts different property types into classes, thereby determining their depreciable lives for tax purposes. For example:

- The 3-year class includes certain specialized short-lived property. Tractor units and racehorses over two years old are among the few items fitting into this class.
- The 5-year class includes cars, trucks, computers and peripheral equipment, office machinery, and property used in research.
- The 7-year class includes office furniture and fixtures and agricultural machinery and equipment.
- The 10-year class includes vessels, barges and tugs, and some agricultural and horticultural structures.
- The 15-year class includes improvements to land, such as shrubbery, fences, roads, sidewalks, and bridges, and certain restaurant property.
- The 20-year class includes farm buildings and land improvements for electric utility plants.
- Real property is separated into two classes: residential and nonresidential. The cost of residential property is recovered over 27.5 years and nonresidential property over 39 years.

Items in the 3-, 5-, 7-, 10-, 15-, and 20-year classes are depreciated according to the schedules in Table 6.3. All real estate is depreciated on a straight-line basis.

Calculations of depreciation include a half-year convention, which treats all property as if it were placed in service at midyear. To be consistent, the IRS allows half a year of depreciation for the year in which property is disposed of or retired. The effect of this is to spread the deductions for property over one year more than the name of its class–for example, six tax years for five-year property.

In the Indian context, depreciation for tax purposes for Indian companies is calculated using the *Written-Down Value (WDV)* method. The depreciation allowance as a percentage of written-down value for some common asset classes is given below:

Assets	Depreciation allowance as a percentage of written-down value
Buildings used for residential classes	5
Buildings other than those used for residential purposes	10
Furniture and fittings	10
Machinery and plant	15
Motor cars other than those used in the business of running them	15
Computers, including computer software	60
Know-how, patents, copyrights, trademarks, licenses, franchises	25

For a number of years prior to 2018, various tax rules and regulations were enacted that allowed "bonus" depreciation. Based on the Protecting Americans from Tax Hikes (PATH) Act of 2015, the size of the bonus in 2017 was 50 percent. What this means is that a firm can take a depreciation deduction of 50 percent of the cost on an eligible asset in the first year and then depreciate the remaining 50 percent using the MACRS schedules as we have just described. Significantly, in late 2017, Congress passed the Tax Cuts and Jobs Act, which increased the bonus depreciation to 100 percent for 2018, lasting until the end of 2022. After that, it drops by 20 percent per year until it reaches zero after 2026. The implication is that most firms will not use the MACRS schedules until 2023 unless they wish to (taking the bonus depreciation is optional). Of course, future legislation may change things.

FINANCING COSTS

In our Bhimsen example, we did not consider financing costs such as interest expense. The reason is that in analyzing a proposed investment, we are interested in the cash flow generated by the assets of the project. As we mentioned in Chapter 2, interest paid, for example, is a component of cash flow to creditors, not cash flow from assets.

More generally, our goal in project evaluation is to compare the cash flow from a project to the cost of acquiring that project in order to estimate NPV. The particular mixture of debt and equity a firm actually chooses to use in financing a project is a managerial variable and primarily determines how project cash flow is divided between owners and creditors. This is not to say that financing arrangements are unimportant. They are just something to be analyzed separately. We will cover this in later chapters.

6.3 Alternative Definitions of Operating Cash Flow

As our Bhimsen example shows, project cash flow equals operating cash flow (OCF) minus investment. Proper calculation of OCF is essential to capital budgeting. A number of different definitions of OCF are in common usage, a fact frequently perplexing to corporate finance students. However, the good news is that these definitions are consistent with each other. That is, if used correctly, they will all lead to the same answer for a given problem. We now consider some of the common definitions, showing in the process that they are identical with each other.

In the discussion that follows, keep in mind that when we speak of cash flow, we literally mean rupees in less rupees out. This is all we are concerned with.

For a particular project and year under consideration, suppose we have the following estimates:

$$\text{Sales} = ₹1{,}500$$
$$\text{Cash costs} = ₹700$$
$$\text{Depreciation} = ₹600$$

With these estimates, earnings before taxes (EBT) is:

$$\begin{aligned} \text{EBT} &= \text{Sales} - \text{Cash costs} - \text{Depreciation} \\ &= ₹1{,}500 - 700 - 600 \\ &= ₹200 \end{aligned} \tag{6.1}$$

The taxes for the year will be:

$$\begin{aligned} \text{Taxes} &= \text{EBT} \times T_C \\ &= ₹200 \times .21 = ₹42 \end{aligned} \tag{6.2}$$

where T_C, the corporate tax rate, is 21 percent.

Now that we have calculated earnings before taxes in Equation 6.1 and taxes in Equation 6.2, how do we determine OCF? Below we show three different approaches, and all are consistent with each other.

THE TOP-DOWN APPROACH

Perhaps the most obvious way to calculate OCF is:

$$\begin{aligned} \text{OCF} &= \text{Sales} - \text{Cash costs} - \text{Taxes} \\ &= ₹1{,}500 - 700 - 42 \\ &= ₹758 \end{aligned} \tag{6.3}$$

We call this the *top-down* approach because we start at the top of the income statement and work our way down to cash flow by subtracting costs, taxes, and other expenses.

Along the way, we left out depreciation. Why? Because depreciation is not a cash outflow. While depreciation is an accounting concept, it is not a cash flow. Nevertheless, depreciation does play an indirect part in the cash flow calculation. Under current tax rules, depreciation is a deduction, lowering taxable income. A lower taxable income number leads to lower taxes, which in turn leads to higher cash flow.

THE BOTTOM-UP APPROACH

Because we are ignoring any financing expenses, such as interest, in our calculations of project OCF, we can write project net income as:

$$\begin{aligned} \text{Net income} &= \text{EBT} - \text{Taxes} \\ &= ₹200 - 42 \\ &= ₹158 \end{aligned}$$

Next, depreciation is added back, giving us:

$$\begin{aligned} \text{OCF} &= \text{Net income} + \text{Depreciation} \\ &= ₹158 + 600 \\ &= ₹758 \end{aligned} \tag{6.4}$$

Expressing net income in terms of its components, we could write OCF more completely as:

$$\begin{aligned} \text{OCF} &= (\text{Sales} - \text{Cash costs} - \text{Depreciation})(1 - T_C) + \text{Depreciation} \\ &= (₹1{,}500 - 700 - 600)(1 - .21) + ₹600 = ₹758 \end{aligned} \tag{6.4′}$$

This is the *bottom-up* approach, whether written as Equation 6.4 or Equation 6.4′. Here we start with the accountants' bottom line (net income) and add back any noncash deductions such as depreciation. It is crucial to remember that this definition of operating cash flow as net income plus depreciation is correct only if there is no interest expense subtracted in the calculation of net income.

Can we explain intuitively why one should add back depreciation as was done here? Accounting texts devote a lot of space explaining the intuition behind the bottom-up approach, and we don't want to duplicate their efforts in a finance text. However, let's give it a try in two sentences. As mentioned above, while depreciation reduces income, depreciation is not a cash outflow. Thus, one must add depreciation back when going from income to cash flow.

THE TAX SHIELD APPROACH

The tax shield approach is a variant of the top-down approach, as presented in Equation 6.3. One of the terms comprising OCF in Equation 6.3 is taxes, which is defined in Equation 6.2. If we plug the formula for taxes provided in Equation 6.2 into Equation 6.3, we get:

$$\text{OCF} = \text{Sales} - \text{Cash costs} - (\text{Sales} - \text{Cash costs} - \text{Depreciation}) \times T_C$$

which simplifies to:

$$\text{OCF} = (\text{Sales} - \text{Cash costs}) \times (1 - T_C) + \text{Depreciation} \times T_C \quad \textbf{(6.5)}$$

where T_C is again the corporate tax rate. Assuming that $T_C = 21$ percent, OCF works out to be:

$$\begin{aligned} \text{OCF} &= (₹1{,}500 - 700) \times .79 + ₹600 \times .21 \\ &= ₹632 + 126 \\ &= ₹758 \end{aligned}$$

This is what we had before.

This approach views OCF as having two components. The first part is what the project's cash flow would be if there were no depreciation expense. In our example, this would-have-been cash flow is ₹632.

The second part of OCF in this approach is the depreciation deduction multiplied by the tax rate. This is called the **depreciation tax shield**. We know that depreciation is a noncash expense. The only cash flow effect of deducting depreciation is to reduce our taxes, a benefit to us. At the current 21 percent corporate tax rate, every rupee in depreciation expense saves us 21 cents in taxes. So, in our example, the ₹600 depreciation deduction saves us ₹600 × .21 = ₹126 in taxes. In the Indian context, at the present corporate tax rate of 25% every 100 rupees in depreciation expense would saves ₹25 in taxes for Indian companies.

Students often think that the tax shield approach contradicts the bottom-up approach because depreciation is added back in Equation 6.4, but only the tax shield on depreciation is added back in Equation 6.5. However, the two formulas are perfectly consistent with each other, an idea most easily seen by comparing Equation 6.4′ to Equation 6.5. Depreciation is subtracted out in the first term on the right-hand side of Equation 6.4′. No comparable subtraction occurs on the right-hand side of Equation 6.5. We add the full amount of depreciation at the end of Equation 6.4′ (and at the end of its equivalent, Equation 6.4) because we subtracted out depreciation earlier in the equation.

CONCLUSION

Now that we've seen that all of these approaches are the same, you're probably wondering why everybody doesn't agree on one of them. One reason is that different approaches are useful in different circumstances. The best one to use is whichever happens to be the most convenient for the problem at hand.

6.4 Some Special Cases of Discounted Cash Flow Analysis

Let's now look at three common cases involving discounted cash flow analysis. The first case considers cost-cutting investments. The second case considers competitive bidding. The third case compares equipment with different lives.

Excel Master coverage online

There are many other special cases, but these three are particularly common. Also, they illustrate some diverse applications of cash flow analysis and discounted cash flow (DCF) valuation.

EVALUATING COST-CUTTING PROPOSALS

Firms frequently must decide whether to make existing facilities cost-effective. The issue is whether the cost savings are large enough to justify the necessary capital expenditure.

Suppose we are considering automating some part of an existing production process. The necessary equipment costs ₹80,000 to buy and install. The automation will save ₹22,000 per year (before taxes) by reducing labor and material costs. The equipment has a 5-year life and is depreciated to zero on a straight-line basis over that period. It can be sold for ₹20,000 in five years. Should we automate? The tax rate is 21 percent and the discount rate is 10 percent.

Let's begin by identifying the relevant cash flows. Determining the relevant capital spending is easy enough. The initial cost is ₹80,000. The aftertax salvage value is ₹20,000 × (1 − .21) = ₹15,800 because the book value will be zero in five years. There are no working capital consequences here, so we don't need to worry about changes in net working capital.

Operating cash flows also must be considered. Buying the new equipment affects our operating cash flows in three ways. First, we save ₹22,000 before taxes every year. In other words, the firm's operating income increases by ₹22,000, so this is the relevant incremental project operating income. Second, we have an additional depreciation deduction. In this case, the depreciation is ₹80,000/5 = ₹16,000 per year.

Because the project has an operating income of ₹22,000 and a depreciation deduction of ₹16,000, the project will increase the firm's earnings before interest and taxes (EBIT) by ₹22,000 − 16,000 = ₹6,000. In other words, ₹6,000 is the project's EBIT.

Third, because EBIT is rising for the firm, taxes will increase. This increase in taxes will be ₹6,000 × .21 = ₹1,260. With this information, we can compute operating cash flow as:

EBIT	₹ 6,000
+Depreciation	16,000
−Taxes	1,260
Operating cash flow	₹20,740

So, our aftertax operating cash flow is ₹20,740.

We also can calculate operating cash flow using a different approach. First, the cost savings increase our pretax income by ₹22,000. We have to pay taxes on this amount, so our tax bill increases by .21 × ₹22,000 = ₹4,620. In other words, the ₹22,000 pretax saving amounts to ₹22,000 × (1 − .21) = ₹17,380 after taxes.

Second, while the extra ₹16,000 in depreciation isn't a cash outflow, it does reduce our taxes by ₹16,000 × .21 = ₹3,360. The sum of these two components is ₹17,380 + 3,360 = ₹20,740, as we had before. Notice that the ₹3,360 is the depreciation tax shield we discussed earlier, and we have effectively used the tax shield approach here.

We now can finish our analysis. Based on our discussion, here are the relevant cash flows:

	Year					
	0	1	2	3	4	5
Operating cash flow		₹20,740	₹20,740	₹20,740	₹20,740	₹20,740
Capital spending	−₹80,000					15,800
Total cash flow	−₹80,000	₹20,740	₹20,740	₹20,740	₹20,740	₹36,540

At 10 percent, verify that the NPV here is ₹8,431, so we should go ahead and automate.

EXAMPLE 6.6

To Buy or Not to Buy We are considering the purchase of a ₹200,000 computer-based inventory management system. It will be depreciated straight-line to zero over its four-year life. It will be worth ₹30,000 at the end of that time. The system will save us ₹60,000 before taxes in inventory-related costs. The relevant tax rate is 21 percent. Because the new setup is more efficient than our existing one, we can carry less total inventory, thereby freeing up ₹45,000 in net working capital. What is the NPV at 16 percent? What is the IRR on this investment?

Let's first calculate the operating cash flow. The aftertax cost savings are ₹60,000 × (1 − .21) = ₹47,400 per year. The depreciation is ₹200,000/4 = ₹50,000 per year, so the depreciation tax shield is ₹50,000 × .21 = ₹10,500. Operating cash flow is ₹47,400 + 10,500 = ₹57,900 per year.

The system involves a ₹200,000 upfront cost to buy the system. The aftertax salvage is ₹30,000 × (1 − .21) = ₹23,700. Finally, and this is somewhat tricky, the initial investment in net working capital (NWC) is a ₹45,000 inflow because the system frees up working capital. Furthermore, we will have to put this back in at the end of the project's life. What this really means is that while the system is in operation, we have ₹45,000 to use elsewhere.

To finish our analysis, we can compute the total cash flows:

	Year				
	0	1	2	3	4
Operating cash flow		₹57,900	₹57,900	₹57,900	₹57,900
Change in NWC	₹ 45,000				−45,000
Capital spending	−200,000				23,700
Total cash flow	−₹155,000	₹57,900	₹57,900	₹57,900	₹36,600

At 16 percent, the NPV is −₹4,749, and the IRR is 14.36 percent, so the investment should be rejected.

SETTING THE BID PRICE

One generally uses the NPV approach to evaluate a new project. The NPV approach also can be used when submitting a competitive bid to win a job. Under such circumstances, the winner is whoever submits the lowest bid.

There is an old joke concerning this process: The low bidder is whoever makes the biggest mistake. This is called the winner's curse. In other words, if you win, there is a good chance you underbid. In this section, we look at how to go about setting the bid price to avoid the winner's curse. The procedure we describe is useful any time we have to set a price on a product or service.

As with any other capital budgeting project, we must be careful to account for all relevant cash flows. For example, industry analysts estimated that the materials in Microsoft's Xbox 360 cost ₹470 before assembly. Other items such as the power supply, cables, and controllers increased the materials cost by another ₹55. At a retail price of ₹399, Microsoft obviously loses a significant amount on each Xbox 360 it sells. Why would a manufacturer sell at a price well below break-even? A Microsoft spokesperson stated that the company believed that sales of its game software would make the Xbox 360 a profitable project.

To illustrate how to go about setting a bid price, imagine we are in the business of buying stripped-down truck platforms and then modifying them to customer specifications for resale. A local distributor has requested bids for five specially modified trucks each year for the next four years, for a total of 20 trucks in all.

We need to decide what price to bid per truck. The goal of our analysis is to determine the lowest price we can profitably charge. This maximizes our chances of being awarded the contract while guarding against the winner's curse.

Suppose we can buy the truck platforms for ₹15,000 each. The facilities we need can be leased for ₹36,000 per year. The labor and material for the modification cost about ₹7,000 per truck. Total cost per year will be ₹36,000 + 5 × (₹15,000 + 7,000) = ₹146,000.

We will need to invest ₹150,000 in new equipment. This equipment will be depreciated straight-line to a zero salvage value over the four years. It will be worth about ₹25,000 at the end of that time. We also will need to invest ₹50,000 in raw materials inventory and other working capital items. The relevant tax rate is 21 percent. What price per truck should we bid if we require a 20 percent return on our investment?

We start by looking at the capital spending and net working capital investment. We have to spend ₹150,000 today for new equipment. The aftertax salvage value is ₹25,000 × (1 − .21) = ₹19,750. We also will have to invest ₹50,000 today in working capital that we will get back in four years.

We can't determine the OCF yet because we don't know the sales price. If we draw a time line, here is what we have so far:

	Year				
	0	1	2	3	4
Operating cash flow		+OCF	+OCF	+OCF	+OCF
Change in NWC	−₹ 50,000				₹50,000
Capital spending	−150,000				19,750
Total cash flow	−₹200,000	+OCF	+OCF	+OCF	+OCF + ₹69,750

With this in mind, note that the key observation is the following: The lowest possible price we can profitably charge will result in a zero NPV at 20 percent. At that price, we earn exactly 20 percent on our investment.

Given this observation, we first need to determine what the operating cash flow must be for the NPV to equal zero. To do this, we calculate the present value of the ₹69,750 nonoperating cash flow from the last year and subtract it from the ₹200,000 initial investment:

$$₹200{,}000 - 69{,}750/1.20^4 = ₹200{,}000 - 33{,}637 = ₹166{,}363$$

Once we have done this, our time line is:

	Year				
	0	1	2	3	4
Total cash flow	−₹166,363	+OCF	+OCF	+OCF	+OCF

As the time line suggests, the operating cash flow is now an unknown ordinary annuity amount. The four-year annuity factor for 20 percent, $\text{PVIFA}_{20\%,4}$ is 2.58873, so we have:

$$\text{NPV} = 0 = -₹166{,}363 + \text{OCF} \times 2.58873$$

This implies that:

$$\text{OCF} = ₹166{,}363/2.58873 = ₹64{,}264$$

So, the operating cash flow needs to be ₹64,264 each year.

We're not quite finished. The final problem is to find out what sales price results in an operating cash flow of ₹64,264. The easiest way to do this is to recall that operating cash flow can be written as net income plus depreciation (the bottom-up definition). The depreciation here is ₹150,000/4 = ₹37,500. Given this, we can determine what net income must be:

$$\begin{aligned}\text{Operating cash flow} &= \text{Net income} + \text{Depreciation}\\ ₹64{,}264 &= \text{Net income} + ₹37{,}500\\ \text{Net income} &= ₹26{,}764\end{aligned}$$

From here, we work our way backward up the income statement. If net income is ₹26,764, then our income statement is as follows:

Sales	?
Costs	₹146,000
Depreciation	37,500
Taxes (21%)	?
Net income	₹ 26,764

We can solve for sales by noting that:

$$\begin{aligned}\text{Net income} &= (\text{Sales} - \text{Costs} - \text{Depreciation}) \times (1 - T_C)\\ ₹26{,}764 &= (\text{Sales} - ₹146{,}000 - 37{,}500) \times (1 - .21)\\ \text{Sales} &= ₹26{,}764/.79 + ₹146{,}000 + 37{,}500\\ \text{Sales} &= ₹217{,}379\end{aligned}$$

Sales per year must be ₹217,379. Because the contract calls for five trucks per year, the sales price has to be ₹217,379/5 = ₹43,476. If we round this up a bit, it looks as though we need to bid about ₹43,500 per truck. At this price, were we to get the contract, our return would be just over 20 percent.

INVESTMENTS OF UNEQUAL LIVES: THE EQUIVALENT ANNUAL COST METHOD

Suppose a firm must choose between two machines having unequal lives. Both machines can do the same job, but they have different operating costs and will last for different time periods. A simple application of the NPV rule suggests taking the machine whose costs have the lower present value. However, this choice might be a mistake because the lower-cost machine may need to be replaced before the other one.

Let's consider an example. The Dharavi Athletic Club must choose between two mechanical tennis ball throwers. Machine A costs less than Machine B but will not last as long. The aftertax cash flows from the two machines are shown here:

Machine	0	1	2	3	4
A	−₹500	−₹120	−₹120	−₹120	
B	−₹600	−₹100	−₹100	−₹100	−₹100

Machine A costs ₹500 and lasts three years. There will be aftertax maintenance expenses of ₹120 to be paid at the end of each of the three years. Machine B costs ₹600 and lasts four years. There will be aftertax maintenance expenses of ₹100 to be paid at the end of each of the four years. Revenues per year are assumed to be the same, regardless of machine, so they are not considered in the analysis.

To get a handle on the decision, let's take the present value of the costs of each of the two machines. Assuming a discount rate of 10 percent, we have:

$$\text{Machine A: } -₹798.42 = -₹500 - \frac{₹120}{1.1} - \frac{₹120}{1.1^2} - \frac{₹120}{1.1^3}$$

$$\text{Machine B: } -₹916.99 = -₹600 - \frac{₹100}{1.1} - \frac{₹100}{1.1^2} - \frac{₹100}{1.1^3} - \frac{₹100}{1.1^4}$$

Machine B has a higher present value of outflows. A naive approach would be to select Machine A because of its higher present value. However, Machine B has a longer life, so perhaps its cost per year is actually lower.

How might one properly adjust for the difference in useful life when comparing the two machines? Our approach is to calculate the equivalent annual cost of each machine. This approach puts costs on a per-year basis.

The previous equation for Machine A showed that payments of (₹500, ₹120, ₹120, ₹120) are equivalent to a single payment of ₹798.42 at Year 0. We now wish to equate the single payment of ₹798.42 at Year 0 with a three-year annuity. Using techniques of previous chapters, we have:

$$-₹798.42 = C \times \text{PVIFA}_{10\%,3}$$

C is the unknown–the annuity payment per year such that the present value of all payments equals –₹798.42. Because $\text{PVIFA}_{10\%,3}$ equals 2.4869, C equals –₹321.06 (= –₹798.42/2.4869). Thus, a payment stream of (₹500, ₹120, ₹120, ₹120) is equivalent to annuity payments of ₹321.06 made at the end of each year for three years. We refer to –₹321.06 as the equivalent annual cost (EAC) of Machine A.

This idea is summarized in the following chart:

	0	1	2	3
Cash outflows of Machine A	–₹500	–₹120	–₹120	–₹120
EAC of Machine A		–321.06	–321.06	–321.06

The Dharavi Athletic Club should be indifferent between cash outflows of (₹500, ₹120, ₹120, ₹120) and cash outflows of (₹0, ₹321.06, ₹321.06, ₹321.06). Alternatively, one can say that the purchase of the machine is financially equivalent to a rental agreement calling for annual lease payments of ₹321.06.

Now let's turn to Machine B. We calculate its equivalent annual cost from:

$$-₹916.99 = C \times \text{PVIFA}_{10\%,4}$$

Because $\text{PVIFA}_{10\%,4}$ equals 3.1699, C equals –₹916.99/3.1699, or –₹289.28.

As we did for Machine A, we can create the following chart for Machine B:

	0	1	2	3	4
Cash outflows of Machine B	–₹600	–₹100	–₹100	–₹100	–₹100
EAC of Machine B		–289.28	–289.28	–289.28	–289.28

The decision is easy once the charts of the two machines are compared. Would you rather make annual lease payments of ₹321.06 or ₹289.28? Put this way, the problem becomes a no-brainer: A rational person would rather pay the lower amount. Thus, Machine B is the preferred choice.

EAC only applies if one anticipates that both machines can be replaced indefinitely. The analysis would differ if no replacement were possible. Imagine that the only company that manufactured tennis ball throwers went out of business and no new producers are expected to enter the field. In this case, Machine B would generate revenues in the fourth year whereas Machine A would not. Here, a net present value analysis for mutually exclusive projects including both revenues and costs would be appropriate.

6.5 Inflation and Capital Budgeting

To finish our chapter, we look at the effect of inflation on capital budgeting. Inflation (or deflation) can affect both cash flows and discount rates in capital budgeting. We begin our examination of inflation by considering the relationship between interest rates and inflation.

Excel Master coverage online

INTEREST RATES AND INFLATION

Suppose a bank offers a one-year interest rate of 10 percent. This means that an individual who deposits ₹1,000 will receive ₹1,100 (= ₹1,000 × 1.10) in one year. Although 10 percent may seem like a handsome return, one can put it in perspective only after examining the rate of inflation.

Imagine that the rate of inflation is 6 percent over the year and it affects all goods equally. For example, a fast-food restaurant charging ₹1.00 for a vada pav today will charge ₹1.06 for the same vada pav at the end of the year. You can use your ₹1,000 to buy 1,000 vada pavs today (Year 0). Alternatively, if you put your money in the bank, you can buy 1,038 (= ₹1,100/₹1.06) vada pavs at Year 1. Lending increases your vada pav consumption by only 3.8 percent.

Because the prices of all goods rise at this 6 percent rate, lending lets you increase your consumption of any single good or any combination of goods by 3.8 percent. Thus, 3.8 percent is what you are really earning through your savings account, after adjusting for inflation. Economists refer to the 3.8 percent number as the *real interest rate.* Economists refer to the 10 percent rate as the *nominal interest rate* or the *interest rate.* This discussion is illustrated in Figure 6.1.

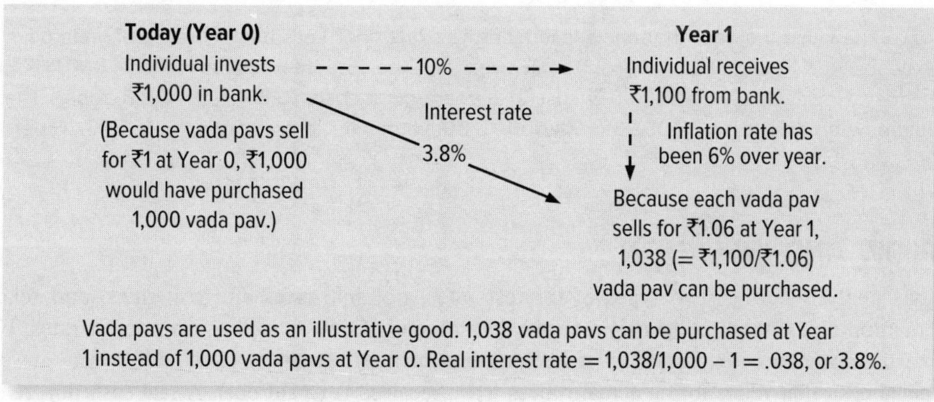

Figure 6.1 Calculation of Real Rate of Interest

We have used an example with a specific nominal interest rate and a specific inflation rate. In general, the formula between real and nominal interest rates can be written as follows:

$$1 + \text{Nominal interest rate} = (1 + \text{Real interest rate}) \times (1 + \text{Inflation rate})$$

Rearranging terms, we have:

$$\text{Real interest rate} = \frac{1 + \text{Nominal interest rate}}{1 + \text{Inflation rate}} - 1 \qquad \textbf{(6.6)}$$

The formula indicates that the real interest rate in our example is 3.8 percent (= 1.10/1.06 − 1).

Equation 6.6 determines the real interest rate precisely. The following formula is an approximation:

$$\text{Real interest rate} \cong \text{Nominal interest rate} - \text{Inflation rate} \qquad \textbf{(6.7)}$$

The symbol ≅ indicates that the equation is approximately true. This latter formula calculates the real rate in our example as:

$$4\% = 10\% - 6\%$$

You should be aware that although Equation 6.7 may seem more intuitive than Equation 6.6, Equation 6.7 is only an approximation. This approximation is reasonably accurate for low rates of interest and inflation. In our example, the difference between the approximate calculation and the exact one is only .2 percent (= 4 percent − 3.8 percent). Unfortunately, the approximation becomes poor when rates are higher.

EXAMPLE 6.7

Real and Nominal Rates The little-known monarchy of Gandharvlok recently had a nominal interest rate of 300 percent and an inflation rate of 280 percent. According to Equation 6.7, the real interest rate is:

$$300\% - 280\% = 20\% \text{ (Approximate formula)}$$

However, according to Equation 6.6, this rate is:

$$\frac{1 + 3}{1 + 2.8} - 1 = .0526, \text{ or } 5.26\% \text{ (Exact formula)}$$

How do we know that the second formula is indeed the exact one? Let's think in terms of vada pavs again. Had you deposited ₹1,000 in a Gandharvlok bank a year ago, the account would be worth ₹4,000 [= ₹1,000 × (1 + 3)] today. However, while a vada pav cost ₹1 a year ago, it costs ₹3.80 (= ₹1 + 2.8) today. Therefore, you would now be able to buy 1,052.6 (= ₹4,000/₹3.80) vada pavs, a real interest rate of 5.26 percent.

CASH FLOW AND INFLATION

The previous analysis defines two types of interest rates, nominal rates and real rates, and relates them through Equation 6.6. Capital budgeting requires data on cash flows as well as on interest rates. Like interest rates, cash flows can be expressed in either nominal or real terms.

A **nominal cash flow** refers to the actual rupees to be received (or paid out). A **real cash flow** refers to the cash flow's purchasing power in relation to a base year. These definitions are best explained by examples.

EXAMPLE 6.8

Nominal versus Real Cash Flow Ranga Publishers has purchased the rights to the next book of famed romantic novelist Jhumpa Lahiri. Still unwritten, the book should be available to the public in four years. Currently, romantic novels sell for ₹10 in softcover. The publishers believe that inflation will be 6 percent a year over the next four years. Because romantic novels are so popular, the publishers anticipate that their prices will rise about 2 percent per year more than the inflation rate over the next four years. Ranga Publishers plans to sell the novel at ₹13.60 $(= 1.08^4 \times ₹10)$ four years from now, anticipating sales of 100,000 copies.

The expected cash flow in the fourth year of ₹1.36 million (= ₹13.60 × 100,000) is a *nominal cash flow*. That is, the firm expects to receive ₹1.36 million at that time. In other words, a nominal cash flow refers to the actual rupees to be received in the future.

The purchasing power of ₹1.36 million in four years is:

$$₹1{,}077{,}635 = \frac{₹1{,}360{,}489}{1.06^4}$$

The figure of ₹1.078 million is a real cash flow because it is expressed in terms of purchasing power. Extending our vada pav example, the ₹1.36 million to be received in four years will only buy 1.078 million vada pavs because the price of a vada pav will rise from ₹1 to ₹1.26 $(= ₹1 \times 1.06^4)$ over the period.

EXAMPLE 6.9

Depreciation Chandamama Publishers, a competitor of Ranga, recently bought a printing press for ₹2,000,000 to be depreciated to zero by the straight-line method over five years. This implies yearly depreciation of ₹400,000 (= ₹2,000,000/5). Is this ₹400,000 figure a real or a nominal quantity?

Depreciation is a nominal quantity because ₹400,000 is the actual tax deduction over each of the next five years. Depreciation becomes a real quantity if it is adjusted for purchasing power. Assuming an annual inflation rate of 6 percent, depreciation in the fourth year expressed as a real quantity is ₹316,837 $(= ₹400{,}000/1.06^4)$.

DISCOUNTING: NOMINAL OR REAL?

Our previous discussion showed that interest rates can be expressed in either nominal or real terms. Similarly, cash flows can be expressed in either nominal or real terms. Given these choices, how should one express interest rates and cash flows when performing capital budgeting?

Financial practitioners correctly stress the need to maintain consistency between cash flows and discount rates. That is:

Nominal cash flows must be discounted at the nominal rate.

Real cash flows must be discounted at the real rate.

As long as one is consistent, either approach is correct. To minimize computational error, it is generally advisable in practice to choose the approach that is easiest. This idea is illustrated in the following two examples.

It is important to note that financial rates, such as interest rates, discount rates, and rates of return, are almost always quoted in nominal terms. To remind you of this, we will henceforth use the symbol *R* (nominal rate) instead of *r* (real rate) in most of our discussions about such rates.

EXAMPLE 6.10

Real and Nominal Discounting Sonparis Electric forecasts the following nominal cash flows on a particular project:

	0	1	2
Cash Flow	−₹1,000	₹600	₹650

The nominal discount rate is 14 percent, and the inflation rate is forecast to be 5 percent. What is the value of the project?

Using Nominal Quantities The NPV can be calculated as:

$$₹26.47 = -₹1{,}000 + \frac{₹600}{1.14} + \frac{₹650}{1.14^2}$$

The project should be accepted.

Using Real Quantities The real cash flows are:

	0	1	2
Cash Flow	−₹1,000	₹571.43 $= \frac{₹600}{1.05}$	₹589.57 $= \frac{₹650}{1.05^2}$

According to Equation 6.6, the real discount rate is 8.57143 percent (= 1.14/1.05 − 1). The NPV can be calculated as:

$$₹26.47 = -₹1{,}000 + \frac{₹571.43}{1.0857143} + \frac{₹589.57}{1.0857143^2}$$

The NPV is the same whether cash flows are expressed in nominal or in real quantities. It must always be the case that the NPV is the same under the two different approaches.

Because both approaches always yield the same result, which one should be used? Again, we should use the approach that is simpler because the simpler approach generally leads to fewer computational errors. The Sonparis Electric example begins with nominal cash flows, so nominal quantities produce a simpler calculation here.

EXAMPLE 6.11

Real and Nominal NPV Malabar Gold Limited, generated the following forecast for a capital budgeting project:

	Year 0	Year 1	Year 2
Capital expenditure	₹1,210		
Revenues (in real terms)		₹1,900	₹2,000
Cash expenses (in real terms)		950	1,000
Depreciation (straight-line)		605	605

The CEO, Shamlal Malabar, estimates inflation to be 10 percent per year over the next two years. In addition, he believes that the cash flows of the project should be discounted at the nominal rate of 15.5 percent. His firm's tax rate is 21 percent.

Shamlal forecasts all cash flows in nominal terms, leading to the following table and NPV calculation:

	Year 0	Year 1	Year 2
Capital expenditure	−₹1,210		
Revenues		₹2,090 (= ₹1,900 × 1.10)	₹2,420 (= ₹2,000 × 1.10^2)
Expenses		1,045 (= ₹950 × 1.10)	1,210 (= ₹1,000 × 1.10^2)
Depreciation		605 (= ₹1,210/2)	605
Taxable income		₹ 440	₹ 605
Taxes (21%)		92	127
Net income		₹ 348	₹ 478
Depreciation		605	605
Cash flow		₹ 953	₹1,083

$$\text{NPV} = -₹1{,}210 + \frac{₹953}{1.155} + \frac{₹1{,}083}{1.155^2} = ₹427$$

The firm's CFO, Ranjeeta Premarajan, prefers working in real terms. She first calculates the real rate to be 5 percent (= 1.155/1.10 − 1). Next, she generates the following table in real quantities:

	Year 0	Year 1	Year 2
Capital expenditure	−₹1,210		
Revenues		₹1,900	₹2,000
Expenses		950	1,000
Depreciation		550 (= ₹605/1.10)	500 (= ₹605/1.10^2)
Taxable income		₹ 400	₹ 500
Taxes (21%)		84	105
Net income		₹ 316	₹ 395
Depreciation		550	500
Cash flow		₹ 866	₹ 895

Ranjeeta calculates the value of the project as:

$$\text{NPV} = -₹1{,}210 + \frac{₹866}{1.05} + \frac{₹895}{1.05^2} = ₹427$$

(continued)

In explaining her calculations to Shamlal, Ranjeeta points out these facts:

1. The capital expenditure occurs at Year 0, so its nominal value and its real value are equal.
2. Because yearly depreciation of ₹605 is a nominal quantity, one converts it to a real quantity by discounting at the inflation rate of 10 percent.

It is no coincidence that both Shamlal and Ranjeeta arrive at the same NPV number. Both methods must always generate the same NPV.

RESEARCH IN EMERGING MARKET CONTEXT

Managers frequently have personal biases that cloud their judgment when applying the decision rules to choose which initiatives to pursue. Martin (2021) discovered that even in the face of conflicting financial incentives and societal norms, managers' preferences for CSR investments can impact behavior. According to Jeremias and Hoi Hu (2020), managers who are allowed the freedom to select their own projects have higher levels of confidence in the success of those projects than the projects assigned to managers by their superiors. Internal audit reports and accountability are also useful tools for lessening the impact of past choices on managers' reluctance to give up on unsuccessful projects. Fehrenbacher et al. (2020) discovered that the emotive responses of independent reviewers to a manager's capital project proposal might skew their decisions. Holding the reviewers accountable will help to lessen this bias.

References

Fehrenbacher, D. D., Kaplan, S. E., & Moulang, C. (2020). The role of accountability in reducing the impact of affective reactions on capital budgeting decisions. *Management Accounting Research*, *47*, 100650.

Jermias, J., & Hoi Hu, B. K. (2020). Overconfidence and resistance to abandoning unprofitable capital budgeting projects: The effects of autonomy, internal audit, and accountability. *Accounting Perspectives*, *19*(2), 49–71.

Martin, P. R. (2021). Corporate social responsibility and capital budgeting. *Accounting, Organizations and Society*, *92*, 101236.

Summary and Conclusions

This chapter discussed a number of practical applications of capital budgeting.

1. Capital budgeting must be evaluated on an incremental basis. This means that sunk costs must be ignored, whereas both opportunity costs and side effects must be considered.
2. In the Bhimsen case, we computed NPV using the following two steps:
   a. Calculate the net cash flow from all sources for each period.
   b. Calculate the NPV using these cash flows.

3. The discounted cash flow approach can be applied to many areas of capital budgeting. In this chapter we applied the approach to cost-cutting investments, competitive bidding, and choices between equipment of different lives.
4. Operating cash flow (OCF) can be computed in a number of different ways. We presented three different methods for calculating OCF: the top-down approach, the bottom-up approach, and the tax shield approach. The three approaches are consistent with each other.
5. Inflation must be handled consistently. One approach is to express both cash flows and the discount rate in nominal terms. The other approach is to express both cash flows and the discount rate in real terms. Because both approaches yield the same NPV calculation, the simpler method should be used. The simpler method will generally depend on the type of capital budgeting problem.

Concept Questions

1. **Opportunity Cost** In the context of capital budgeting, what is an opportunity cost?
2. **Incremental Cash Flows** Which of the following should be treated as an incremental cash flow when computing the NPV of an investment?
   a. A reduction in the sales of a company's other products caused by the investment.
   b. An expenditure on plant and equipment that has not yet been made and will be made only if the project is accepted.
   c. Costs of research and development undertaken in connection with the product during the past three years.
   d. Annual depreciation expense from the investment.
   e. Dividend payments by the firm.
   f. The resale value of plant and equipment at the end of the project's life.
   g. Salary and medical costs for production personnel who will be employed only if the project is accepted.
3. **Incremental Cash Flows** Your company currently produces and sells steel shaft golf clubs. The board of directors wants you to consider the introduction of a new line of titanium bubble woods with graphite shafts. Which of the following costs are irrelevant?
   a. Land you already own that will be used for the project, but otherwise will be sold for its market value of ₹700,000.
   b. A ₹300,000 drop in your sales of steel shaft clubs if the titanium woods with graphite shafts are introduced.
   c. ₹200,000 spent on research and development last year on graphite shafts.
4. **Depreciation** Given the choice, would a firm prefer to use MACRS depreciation or straight-line depreciation? Why?
5. **Net Working Capital** In our capital budgeting examples, we assumed that a firm would recover all of the working capital it invested in a project. Is this a reasonable assumption? When might it not be valid?
6. **Stand-Alone Principle** Suppose a financial manager is quoted as saying, "Our firm uses the stand-alone principle. Since we treat projects like minifirms in our evaluation process, we include financing costs because they are relevant at the firm level." Critically evaluate this statement.
7. **Equivalent Annual Cost** When is EAC analysis appropriate for comparing two or more projects? Why is this method used? Are there any implicit assumptions required by this method that you find troubling? Explain.

8. **Cash Flow and Depreciation** "When evaluating projects, we're only concerned with the relevant incremental aftertax cash flows. Therefore, because depreciation is a noncash expense, we should ignore its effects when evaluating projects." Critically evaluate this statement.

9. **Capital Budgeting Considerations** A major college textbook publisher has an existing finance textbook. The publisher is debating whether to produce an "essentialized" version, meaning a shorter (and lower-priced) book. What are some of the considerations that should come into play?

To answer the next three questions, refer to the following example. In 2003, Porsche unveiled its new sports utility vehicle (SUV), the Cayenne. With a price tag of over ₹40,000, the original Cayenne went from zero to 62 mph in 8.5 seconds. Porsche's decision to enter the SUV market was in response to the runaway success of other high-priced SUVs such as the Mercedes-Benz M class. Vehicles in this class had generated years of very high profits. The Cayenne certainly spiced up the market, and, in 2006, Porsche introduced the Cayenne Turbo S, which goes from zero to 60 mph in 3.9 seconds and has a top speed of 177 mph. The base price for the Cayenne Turbo in 2020? Almost ₹128,000!

Some analysts questioned Porsche's entry into the luxury SUV market. The analysts were concerned because not only was Porsche a late entry into the market, but also the introduction of the Cayenne might damage Porsche's reputation as a maker of high-performance automobiles.

10. **Erosion** In evaluating the Cayenne, would you consider the possible damage to Porsche's reputation as erosion?

11. **Capital Budgeting** Porsche was one of the last manufacturers to enter the sports utility vehicle market. Why would one company decide to proceed with a product when other companies, at least initially, decide not to enter the market?

12. **Capital Budgeting** In evaluating the Cayenne, what do you think Porsche needs to assume regarding the substantial profit margins that exist in this market? Do you think they were able to maintain this profit margin as the market became more competitive, or would Porsche be able to maintain the profit margin because of its image and the performance of the Cayenne?

Questions and Problems

BASIC (Questions 1–2)

1. **Calculating Project NPV** Chauhan Restaurant is considering the purchase of a soufflé maker that costs ₹8,600. The soufflé maker has an economic life of five years and will be fully depreciated by the straight-line method. The machine will produce 1,100 soufflés per year, with each costing ₹2.15 to make and priced at ₹5.95. The discount rate is 14 percent and the tax rate is 21 percent. Should the company make the purchase?

2. **Calculating Project NPV** The Fancy Manufacturing Company is considering a new investment. Financial projections for the investment are tabulated here. The corporate tax rate is 22 percent. Assume all sales revenue is received in cash, all operating costs and income taxes are paid in cash, and all cash flows occur at the end of the year. All net working capital is recovered at the end of the project.

	Year 0	Year 1	Year 2	Year 3	Year 4
Investment	₹32,400				
Sales revenue		₹14,900	₹16,300	₹17,800	₹13,700
Operating costs		3,200	3,400	4,500	3,100
Depreciation		8,100	8,100	8,100	8,100
Net working capital spending	350	220	250	150	?

a. Compute the incremental net income of the investment for each year.
b. Compute the incremental cash flows of the investment for each year.
c. Suppose the appropriate discount rate is 12 percent. What is the NPV of the project?

3. **Calculating Project NPV** Esfandairi Enterprises is considering a new three-year expansion project that requires an initial fixed asset investment of ₹2.18 million. The fixed asset will be depreciated straight-line to zero over its three-year tax life, after which time it will be worthless. The project is estimated to generate ₹1.645 million in annual sales, with costs of ₹610,000. The required return is 12 percent. If the tax rate is 21 percent, what is the project's NPV?

4. **Calculating Project Cash Flow from Assets** In the previous problem, suppose the project requires an initial investment in net working capital of ₹250,000 and the fixed asset will have a market value of ₹180,000 at the end of the project. What is the project's Year 0 net cash flow? Year 1? Year 2? Year 3? What is the new NPV?

5. **NPV and Modified ACRS** In the previous problem, suppose the fixed asset actually falls into the three-year MACRS class. All the other facts are the same. What is the project's Year 1 net cash flow now? Year 2? Year 3? What is the new NPV?

6. **NPV and Bonus Depreciation** In the previous problem, suppose the fixed asset actually qualifies for 100 percent bonus depreciation. All the other facts are the same. What is the project's Year 1 net cash flow now? Year 2? Year 3? What is the new NPV?

7. **Project Evaluation** Your firm is contemplating the purchase of a new ₹535,000 computer-based order entry system. The system will be depreciated straight-line to zero over its five-year life. It will be worth ₹30,000 at the end of that time. You will save ₹165,000 before taxes per year in order processing costs, and you will be able to reduce working capital by ₹60,000 (this is a one-time reduction). If the tax rate is 24 percent, what is the IRR for this project?

8. **Project Evaluation** Dog Up! Franks is looking at a new sausage system with an installed cost of ₹385,000. This cost will be depreciated straight-line to zero over the project's five-year life, at the end of which the sausage system can be scrapped for ₹60,000. The sausage system will save the firm ₹135,000 per year in pretax operating costs, and the system requires an initial investment in net working capital of ₹35,000. If the tax rate is 21 percent and the discount rate is 10 percent, what is the NPV of this project?

9. **NPV and Bonus Depreciation** In the previous problem, suppose the fixed asset actually qualifies for 100 percent bonus depreciation. All the other facts are the same. What is the new NPV?

10. **Calculating Salvage Value** An asset used in a four-year project falls in the five-year MACRS class for tax purposes. The asset has an acquisition cost of ₹5.7 million and will be sold for ₹1.8 million at the end of the project. If the tax rate is 21 percent, what is the aftertax salvage value of the asset?

11. **Calculating NPV** Medavoy Co. is considering a new project that complements its existing business. The machine required for the project costs ₹3.7 million. The marketing department predicts that sales related to the project will be ₹2.65 million per year for the next four years, after which the market will cease to exist. The machine will be depreciated to zero over its four-year economic life using the straight-line method. Cost of goods sold and operating expenses related to the project are predicted to be 40 percent of sales. The company also needs to add net working capital of ₹175,000 immediately. The additional net working capital will be recovered in full at the end of the project's life. The corporate tax rate is 25 percent and the required return for the project is 13 percent. Should the company proceed with the project?

12. **Calculating EAC** You are evaluating two different silicon wafer milling machines. The Techron I costs ₹265,000, has a three-year life, and has pretax operating costs of ₹74,000 per year. The Techron II costs ₹445,000, has a five-year life, and has pretax operating costs of ₹47,000 per year. For both

milling machines, use straight-line depreciation to zero over the project's life and assume a salvage value of ₹35,000. If your tax rate is 22 percent and your discount rate is 10 percent, compute the EAC for both machines. Which do you prefer? Why?

INTERMEDIATE (Questions 13–31)

13. **Cost-Cutting Proposals** Tanaka Machine Shop is considering a four-year project to improve its production efficiency. Buying a new machine press for ₹445,000 is estimated to result in ₹160,000 in annual pretax cost savings. The press falls in the MACRS five-year class, and it will have a salvage value at the end of the project of ₹40,000. The press also requires an initial investment in spare parts inventory of ₹20,000, along with an additional ₹2,800 in inventory for each succeeding year of the project. If the shop's tax rate is 22 percent and its discount rate is 9 percent, should the company buy and install the machine press?

14. **NPV and Bonus Depreciation** In the previous problem, suppose the fixed asset actually qualifies for 100 percent bonus depreciation. All the other facts are the same. What is the new NPV?

15. **Comparing Mutually Exclusive Projects** Rust Industrial Systems Company is trying to decide between two different conveyor belt systems. System A costs ₹295,000, has a four-year life, and requires ₹77,000 in pretax annual operating costs. System B costs ₹355,000, has a six-year life, and requires ₹83,000 in pretax annual operating costs. Both systems are to be depreciated straight-line to zero over their lives and will have zero salvage value. Whichever project is chosen, it will *not* be replaced when it wears out. If the tax rate is 21 percent and the discount rate is 8 percent, which project should the firm choose?

16. **Comparing Mutually Exclusive Projects** Suppose in the previous problem that the company always needs a conveyor belt system; when one wears out, it must be replaced. Which system should the firm choose now?

17. **NPV and Bonus Depreciation** Eggz, Inc., is considering the purchase of new equipment that will allow the company to collect loose hen feathers for sale. The equipment will cost ₹525,000 and will be eligible for 100 percent bonus depreciation. The equipment can be sold for ₹35,000 at the end of the project in five years. Sales would be ₹348,000 per year, with annual fixed costs of ₹56,000 and variable costs equal to 35 percent of sales. The project would require an investment of ₹40,000 in NWC that would be returned at the end of the project. The tax rate is 22 percent and the required return is 9 percent. What is the project's NPV?

18. **Comparing Mutually Exclusive Projects** Vandelay Industries is considering the purchase of a new machine for the production of latex. Machine A costs ₹2.1 million and will last for six years. Variable costs are 35 percent of sales, and fixed costs are ₹315,000 per year. Machine B costs ₹4.8 million and will last for nine years. Variable costs for this machine are 30 percent of sales and fixed costs are ₹355,000 per year. The sales for each machine will be ₹10 million per year. The required return is 10 percent, and the tax rate is 24 percent. Both machines will be depreciated on a straight-line basis. If the company plans to replace the machine when it wears out on a perpetual basis, which machine should it choose?

19. **Capital Budgeting with Inflation** Consider the following cash flows on two mutually exclusive projects:

Year	Project A	Project B
0	−₹53,000	−₹59,000
1	24,000	27,000
2	22,000	26,000
3	20,000	25,000

The cash flows of Project A are expressed in real terms, whereas those of Project B are expressed in nominal terms. The appropriate nominal discount rate is 11 percent and the inflation rate is 3 percent. Which project should you choose?

20. **Inflation and Company Value** Sparkling Water, Inc., expects to sell 3.8 million bottles of drinking water each year in perpetuity. This year each bottle will sell for ₹1.52 in real terms and will cost ₹.87 in real terms. Sales income and costs occur at year-end. Revenues will rise at a real rate of 1.3 percent annually, while real costs will rise at a real rate of .9 percent annually. The real discount rate is 6 percent. The corporate tax rate is 21 percent. What is the company worth today?

21. **Calculating Nominal Cash Flow** Shado, Inc., is considering an investment of ₹750,000 in an asset with an economic life of five years. The firm estimates that the nominal annual cash revenues and expenses at the end of the first year will be ₹320,000 and ₹125,000, respectively. Both revenues and expenses will grow thereafter at the annual inflation rate of 3 percent. The company will use the straight-line method to depreciate its asset to zero over five years. The salvage value of the asset is estimated to be ₹65,000 in nominal terms at that time. The one-time net working capital investment of ₹20,000 is required immediately and will be recovered at the end of the project. The corporate tax rate is 21 percent. What is the project's total nominal cash flow from assets for each year?

22. **Cash Flow Valuation** Phillips Industries runs a small manufacturing operation. For this fiscal year, it expects real net cash flows of ₹295,000. The company is an ongoing operation, but it expects competitive pressures to erode its real cash flows at 3.5 percent per year in perpetuity. The appropriate real discount rate for the company is 4 percent. All cash flows are received at year-end. What is the present value of the cash flows from the company's operations?

23. **Equivalent Annual Cost** Sheep Ranch Golf Academy is evaluating new golf practice equipment. The "Dimple-Max" equipment costs ₹135,000, has a three-year life, and costs ₹15,700 per year to operate. The relevant discount rate is 12 percent. Assume that the straight-line depreciation method is used and that the equipment is fully depreciated to zero. Furthermore, assume the equipment has a salvage value of ₹19,500 at the end of the project's life. The relevant tax rate is 23 percent. All cash flows occur at the end of the year. What is the equivalent annual cost (EAC) of this equipment?

24. **Calculating Project NPV** Market Top Investors, Inc., is considering the purchase of a ₹425,000 computer with an economic life of five years. The computer will be fully depreciated over five years using the straight-line method, at which time it will be worth ₹35,000. The computer will replace two office employees whose combined annual salaries are ₹95,000. The machine also will immediately lower the firm's required net working capital by ₹40,000. This amount of net working capital will need to be replaced once the machine is sold. The corporate tax rate is 22 percent. Is it worthwhile to buy the computer if the appropriate discount rate is 9 percent?

25. **Calculating NPV and IRR for a Replacement** A firm is considering an investment in a new machine with a price of ₹10.9 million to replace its existing machine. The current machine has a book value of ₹3.8 million and a market value of ₹2.8 million. The new machine is expected to have a four-year life, and the old machine has four years left in which it can be used. If the firm replaces the old machine with the new machine, it expects to save ₹4.4 million in operating costs each year over the next four years. Both machines will have no salvage value in four years. If the firm purchases the new machine, it also will need an investment of ₹250,000 in net working capital. The required return on the investment is 10 percent and the tax rate is 21 percent. The company uses straight-line depreciation. What are the NPV and IRR of the decision to replace the old machine?

26. **Project Analysis and Inflation** Shinoda Manufacturing, Inc., has been considering the purchase of a new manufacturing facility for ₹780,000. The facility is to be fully depreciated on a straight-line basis over seven years. It is expected to have no resale value at that time. Operating revenues from the facility are expected to be ₹595,000, in nominal terms, at the end of the first year. The revenues are expected to increase at the inflation rate of 5 percent. Production costs at the end of the first year will be ₹355,000, in nominal terms, and they are expected to increase at 4 percent per year. The real discount rate is 7 percent. The corporate tax rate is 24 percent. Should the company accept the project?

27. **Calculating Project NPV** With the growing popularity of casual surf print clothing, two recent MBA graduates decided to broaden this casual surf concept to encompass a "surf lifestyle for the home."

With limited capital, they decided to focus on surf print table and floor lamps to accent people's homes. They projected unit sales of these lamps to be 10,000 in the first year, with growth of 8 percent each year. Production of these lamps will require ₹95,000 in net working capital to start. Total fixed costs are ₹150,000 per year, variable production costs are ₹34 per unit, and the units are priced at ₹73 each. The equipment needed to begin production will cost ₹485,000. The equipment will be depreciated using the straight-line method over a five-year life and is not expected to have a salvage value. The tax rate is 21 percent and the required rate of return is 18 percent. What is the NPV of this project?

28. **Calculating Project NPV** You have been hired as a consultant for Pristine Urban-Tech Zither, Inc. (PUTZ), manufacturers of fine zithers. The market for zithers is growing quickly. The company bought some land three years ago for ₹1.9 million in anticipation of using it as a toxic waste dump site but has recently hired another company to handle all toxic materials. Based on a recent appraisal, the company believes it could sell the land for ₹2.2 million on an aftertax basis. In four years, the land could be sold for ₹2.4 million after taxes. The company also hired a marketing firm to analyze the zither market, at a cost of ₹275,000. An excerpt of the marketing report is as follows:

> The zither industry will have a rapid expansion in the next four years. With the brand name recognition that PUTZ brings to bear, we feel that the company will be able to sell 5,200, 5,900, 6,500, and 4,800 units each year for the next four years, respectively. Again, capitalizing on the name recognition of PUTZ, we feel that a premium price of ₹435 can be charged for each zither. Because zithers appear to be a fad, we feel at the end of the four-year period, sales should be discontinued.

PUTZ feels that fixed costs for the project will be ₹375,000 per year, and variable costs are 20 percent of sales. The equipment necessary for production will cost ₹2.85 million and will be depreciated according to a three-year MACRS schedule. At the end of the project, the equipment can be scrapped for ₹405,000. Net working capital of ₹150,000 will be required immediately. PUTZ has a tax rate of 22 percent and the required return on the project is 13 percent. What is the NPV of the project?

29. **NPV and Bonus Depreciation** In the previous problem, suppose the fixed asset actually qualifies for 100 percent bonus depreciation. What is the new NPV?

30. **Calculating Project NPV** Calligraphy Pens is deciding when to replace its old machine. The machine's current salvage value is ₹2.8 million. Its current book value is ₹1.6 million. If not sold, the old machine will require maintenance costs of ₹855,000 at the end of the year for the next five years. Depreciation on the old machine is ₹320,000 per year. At the end of five years, it will have a salvage value of ₹140,000 and a book value of ₹0. A replacement machine costs ₹4.5 million now and requires maintenance costs of ₹350,000 at the end of each year during its economic life of five years. At the end of the five years, the new machine will have a salvage value of ₹900,000. It will be fully depreciated by the straight-line method. In five years, a replacement machine will cost ₹3.4 million. The company will need to purchase this machine regardless of what choice it makes today. The corporate tax rate is 21 percent and the appropriate discount rate is 8 percent. The company is assumed to earn sufficient revenues to generate tax shields from depreciation. Should the company replace the old machine now or at the end of five years?

31. **Project Analysis and Inflation** Yang Brothers, Inc., is considering investing in a machine to produce computer keyboards. The price of the machine will be ₹1.5 million, and its economic life is five years. The machine will be fully depreciated by the straight-line method. The machine will produce 40,000 keyboards each year. The price of each keyboard will be ₹49 in the first year and will increase by 3 percent per year. The production cost per keyboard will be ₹19 in the first year and will increase by 4 percent per year. The project will have an annual fixed cost of ₹450,000 and require an immediate investment of ₹650,000 in net working capital. The corporate tax rate for the company is 21 percent. If the appropriate discount rate is 11 percent, what is the NPV of the investment?

CHALLENGE (Questions 32–42)

32. **Project Evaluation** Aria Acoustics, Inc. (AAI), projects unit sales for a new seven-octave voice emulation implant as follows:

Year	Unit Sales
1	71,000
2	84,000
3	103,000
4	95,000
5	64,000

Production of the implants will require ₹2.3 million in net working capital to start and additional net working capital investments each year equal to 15 percent of the projected sales increase for the following year. Total fixed costs are ₹2.9 million per year, variable production costs are ₹285 per unit, and the units are priced at ₹410 each. The equipment needed to begin production has an installed cost of ₹14.8 million. Because the implants are intended for professional singers, this equipment is considered industrial machinery and thus qualifies as seven-year MACRS property. In five years, this equipment can be sold for about 20 percent of its acquisition cost. The tax rate is 21 percent and the required return is 18 percent. Based on these preliminary project estimates, what is the NPV of the project? What is the IRR?

33. **Calculating Required Savings** A proposed cost-saving device has an installed cost of ₹905,000. The device will be used in a five-year project but is classified as three-year MACRS property for tax purposes. The required initial net working capital investment is ₹65,000, the tax rate is 22 percent, and the project discount rate is 9 percent. The device has an estimated Year 5 salvage value of ₹125,000. What level of pretax cost savings do we require for this project to be profitable?

34. **Calculating a Bid Price** Martin Enterprises needs someone to supply it with 110,000 cartons of machine screws per year to support its manufacturing needs over the next five years, and you've decided to bid on the contract. It will cost you ₹940,000 to install the equipment necessary to start production; you'll depreciate this cost straight-line to zero over the project's life. You estimate that, in five years, this equipment can be salvaged for ₹75,000. Your fixed production costs will be ₹850,000 per year, and your variable production costs should be ₹21.43 per carton. You also need an initial investment in net working capital of ₹90,000. If your tax rate is 21 percent and you require a return of 12 percent on your investment, what bid price should you submit?

35. **Financial Break-Even Analysis** The technique for calculating a bid price can be extended to many other types of problems. Answer the following questions using the same technique as setting a bid price; that is, set the project NPV to zero and solve for the variable in question.

    a. In the previous problem, assume that the price per carton is ₹33 and find the project NPV. What does your answer tell you about your bid price? What do you know about the number of cartons you can sell and still break even? How about your level of costs?

    b. Solve the previous problem again with the price still at ₹33–but find the quantity of cartons per year that you can supply and still break even. (*Hint*: It's less than 110,000.)

    c. Repeat part (b) with a price of ₹33 and a quantity of 110,000 cartons per year, and find the highest level of fixed costs you could afford and still break even. (*Hint*: It's more than ₹850,000.)

36. **Calculating a Bid Price** Your company has been approached to bid on a contract to sell 5,000 voice recognition (VR) computer keyboards per year for four years. Due to technological improvements, beyond that time they will be outdated and no sales will be possible. The equipment necessary for the production will cost ₹3.4 million and will be depreciated on a straight-line basis to a zero salvage value. Production will require an initial investment in net working capital of ₹395,000 that will be returned at the end of the project, and the equipment can be sold for ₹325,000 at the end of production. Fixed costs are ₹595,000 per year, and variable costs are ₹85 per unit. In addition to the contract, you feel your company can sell 12,300, 14,600, 19,200, and 11,600 additional units to companies in other countries over the next four years, respectively, at a price of ₹180. This price is fixed. The tax rate is 23 percent, and the required return is 10 percent. Additionally, the president of the company will undertake the project only if it has an NPV of ₹100,000. What bid price should you set for the contract?

37. **Replacement Decisions** Suppose we are thinking about replacing an old computer with a new one. The old one cost us ₹1.4 million; the new one will cost ₹1.7 million. The new machine will be depreciated straight-line to zero over its five-year life. It will probably be worth about ₹325,000 after five years.

The old computer is being depreciated at a rate of ₹281,000 per year. It will be completely written off in three years. If we don't replace it now, we will have to replace it in two years. We can sell it now for ₹450,000; in two years, it will probably be worth ₹130,000. The new machine will save us ₹315,000 per year in operating costs. The tax rate is 22 percent, and the discount rate is 12 percent.

a. Suppose we recognize that if we don't replace the computer now, we will be replacing it in two years. Should we replace now or should we wait? (*Hint*: What we effectively have here is a decision either to "invest" in the old computer–by not selling it–or to invest in the new one. Notice that the two investments have unequal lives.)

b. Suppose we consider only whether we should replace the old computer now without worrying about what's going to happen in two years. What are the relevant cash flows? Should we replace it or not? (*Hint*: Consider the net change in the firm's aftertax cash flows if we do the replacement.)

38. **Project Analysis** Hardwick Enterprises is evaluating alternative uses for a three-story manufacturing and warehousing building that it has purchased for ₹1.75 million. The company can continue to rent the building to the present occupants for ₹80,000 per year. The present occupants have indicated an interest in staying in the building for at least another 15 years. Alternatively, the company could modify the existing structure to use for its own manufacturing and warehousing needs. The company's production engineer feels the building could be adapted to handle one of two new product lines. The cost and revenue data for the two product alternatives are as follows:

	Product A	Product B
Initial cash outlay for building modifications	₹135,000	₹175,000
Initial cash outlay for equipment	360,000	275,000
Annual pretax cash revenues (generated for 15 years)	295,000	310,000
Annual pretax expenditures (generated for 15 years)	125,000	145,000

The building will be used for only 15 years for either Product A or Product B. After 15 years, the building will be too small for efficient production of either product line. At that time, the company plans to rent the building to firms similar to the current occupants. To rent the building again, the company will need to restore the building to its present layout. The estimated cash cost of restoring the building if Product A has been undertaken is ₹80,000. If Product B has been manufactured, the cash cost will be ₹95,000. These cash costs can be deducted for tax purposes in the year the expenditures occur.

The company will depreciate the original building shell over a 30-year life to zero, regardless of which alternative it chooses. The building modifications and equipment purchases for either product are estimated to have a 15-year life. They will be depreciated by the straight-line method. The firm's tax rate is 21 percent and its required rate of return on each alternative is 12 percent.

Assume all cash flows occur at the end of the year. The initial outlays for modifications and equipment will occur today and the restoration outlays will occur at the end of Year 15. Which use of the building would you recommend to management?

39. **Project Analysis and Inflation** The Biological Insect Control Corporation (BICC) has hired you as a consultant to evaluate the NPV of its proposed toad ranch. The company plans to breed toads and sell them as ecologically desirable insect control mechanisms. They anticipate that the business will continue into perpetuity. Following the negligible start-up costs, the company expects the following nominal cash flows at the end of the year:

Revenues	₹385,000
Labor costs	197,000
Other costs	77,000

The company will lease machinery for ₹175,000 per year. The lease payments start at the end of Year 1 and are expressed in nominal terms. Revenues will increase by 4 percent per year in real terms. Labor costs will increase by 3 percent per year in real terms. Other costs will increase by 1 percent per year in real terms. The rate of inflation is expected to be 3.8 percent per year. The required rate of return for this project is 7 percent in real terms. The company has a tax rate of 22 percent. All cash flows occur at year-end. What is the NPV of the proposed toad ranch today?

40. **Project Analysis and Inflation** Kopperud Electronics has an investment opportunity to produce a new HDTV. The required investment on January 1 of this year is ₹125 million. The firm will depreciate the investment to zero using the straight-line method over four years. The investment has no resale value after completion of the project. The firm is in the 21 percent tax bracket. The price of the product will be ₹435 per unit, in real terms, and will not change over the life of the project. Labor costs for Year 1 will be ₹16.25 per hour, in real terms, and will increase at 2 percent per year in real terms. Energy costs for Year 1 will be ₹4.35 per physical unit, in real terms, and will increase at 3 percent per year in real terms. The inflation rate is 5 percent per year. Revenues are received and costs are paid at year-end. Refer to the following table for the production schedule:

	Year 1	Year 2	Year 3	Year 4
Physical production, in units	150,000	160,000	170,000	145,000
Labor input, in hours	1,250,000	1,450,000	1,560,000	1,150,000
Energy input, physical units	205,000	230,000	260,000	195,000

The real discount rate for the project is 4 percent. Calculate the NPV of this project.

41. **Project Analysis and Inflation** After extensive medical and marketing research, Pill, Inc., believes it can penetrate the pain reliever market. It is considering two alternative products. The first is a medication for headache pain. The second is a pill for headache and arthritis pain. Both products would be introduced at a price of ₹6.25 per package in real terms. The headache-only medication is projected to sell 5.5 million packages a year, whereas the headache and arthritis remedy would sell 7.1 million packages a year. Cash costs of production in the first year are expected to be ₹3.40 per package in real terms for the headache-only brand. Production costs are expected to be ₹4.15 in real terms for the headache and arthritis pill. All prices and costs are expected to rise at the general inflation rate of 3 percent.

Either product requires further investment. The headache-only pill could be produced using equipment costing ₹29 million. That equipment would last three years and have no resale value. The machinery required to produce the broader remedy would cost ₹34 million and last three years. The firm expects that equipment to have a ₹1 million resale value (in real terms) at the end of Year 3.

The firm uses straight-line depreciation and has a tax rate of 22 percent. The appropriate real discount rate is 5 percent. Which pain reliever should the firm produce?

42. **Calculating Project NPV** J. Smythe, Inc., manufactures fine furniture. The company is deciding whether to introduce a new mahogany dining room table set. The set will sell for ₹6,000, including a set of eight chairs. The company feels that sales will be 1,900, 2,250, 2,750, 2,450, and 2,300 sets per year for the next five years, respectively. Variable costs will amount to 42 percent of sales and fixed costs are ₹2.15 million per year. The new tables will require inventory amounting to 10 percent of sales, produced and stockpiled in the year prior to sales. It is believed that the addition of the new table will cause a loss of 260 tables per year of the oak tables the company produces. These tables sell for ₹4,400 and have variable costs of 40 percent of sales. The inventory for this oak table is also 10 percent of sales. The sales of the oak table will continue indefinitely. J. Smythe currently has excess production capacity. If the company buys the necessary equipment today, it will cost ₹17 million. However, the excess production capacity means the company can produce the new table without buying the new

equipment. The company controller has said that the current excess capacity will end in two years with current production. This means that if the company uses the current excess capacity for the new table, it will be forced to spend the ₹17 million in two years to accommodate the increased sales of its current products. In five years, the new equipment will have a market value of ₹3 million if purchased today and ₹4.9 million if purchased in two years. The equipment is depreciated on a seven-year MACRS schedule. The company has a tax rate of 21 percent and the required return for the project is 11 percent.

a. Should J. Smythe undertake the new project?

b. Can you perform an IRR analysis on this project? How many IRRs would you expect to find?

c. How would you interpret the profitability index?

Excel Master It! Problems

For this Master It! assignment, refer to the Goodweek Tires, Inc., case at the end of this chapter. For your convenience, we have entered the relevant values such as the price and variable costs in the case on the next page. For this project, answer the following questions:

Excel Master coverage online

a. What is the profitability index of the project?

b. What is the IRR of the project?

c. At what OEM price would Goodweek Tires be indifferent to accepting the project? Assume the replacement market price is constant.

d. At what level of variable costs per unit would Goodweek Tires be indifferent to accepting the project?

Mini Case BETHESDA MINING COMPANY

Bethesda Mining is a midsized coal mining company with 20 mines located in Ohio, Pennsylvania, West Virginia, and Kentucky. The company operates deep mines as well as strip mines. Most of the coal mined is sold under contract, with excess production sold on the spot market.

The coal mining industry, especially high-sulfur coal operations such as Bethesda, has been hard-hit by environmental regulations. Recently, however, a combination of increased demand for coal and new pollution reduction technologies has led to an improved market demand for high-sulfur coal. Bethesda has been approached by Mid-Ohio Electric Company with a request to supply coal for its electric generators for the next four years. Bethesda Mining does not have enough excess capacity at its existing mines to guarantee the contract. The company is considering opening a strip mine in Ohio on 5,000 acres of land purchased 10 years ago for ₹4.2 million. Based on a recent appraisal, the company feels it could receive ₹6.7 million on an aftertax basis if it sold the land today.

Strip mining is a process where the layers of topsoil above a coal vein are removed and the exposed coal is removed. Some time ago, the company would remove the coal and leave the land in an unusable condition. Changes in mining regulations now force a company to reclaim the land; that is, when the mining is completed, the land must be restored to near its original condition. The land can then be used for other purposes. Because it is currently operating at full capacity, Bethesda will need to purchase additional necessary equipment, which will cost ₹105 million. The equipment will be depreciated on a seven-year MACRS schedule. The contract runs for only four years. At that time the coal from the site will be entirely mined. The company feels that the equipment can be sold for 60 percent of its initial purchase price in four years. However, Bethesda plans to open another strip mine at that time and will use the equipment at the new mine.

The contract calls for the delivery of 500,000 tons of coal per year at a price of ₹89 per ton. Bethesda Mining feels that coal production will be 660,000 tons, 720,000 tons, 760,000 tons, and 620,000 tons, respectively, over the next four years. The excess production will be sold in the spot market at an average of ₹77 per ton. Variable costs amount to ₹30 per ton, and fixed costs are ₹4.1 million per year. The mine will require a net working capital investment of 5 percent of sales. The NWC will be built up in the year prior to the sales.

Bethesda will be responsible for reclaiming the land at termination of the mining. This will occur in Year 5. The company uses an outside company for reclamation of all the company's strip mines. It is estimated the cost of reclamation will be ₹2.4 million. In order to get the necessary permits for the strip mine, the company agreed to donate the land after reclamation to the state for use as a public park and recreation area. This will occur in Year 6 and result in a charitable expense deduction of ₹7 million. Bethesda faces a 25 percent tax rate and has a 12 percent required return on new strip mine projects. Assume that a loss in any year will result in a tax credit.

You have been approached by the president of the company with a request to analyze the project. Calculate the payback period, profitability index, net present value, and internal rate of return for the new strip mine. Should Bethesda Mining take the contract and open the mine?

GOODWEEK TIRES, INC.

After extensive research and development, Goodweek Tires, Inc., has recently developed a new tire, the SuperTread, and must decide whether to make the investment necessary to produce and market it. The tire would be ideal for drivers doing a large amount of wet weather and off-road driving in addition to normal freeway usage. The research and development costs so far have totaled about ₹10 million. The SuperTread would be put on the market beginning this year, and Goodweek expects it to stay on the market for a total of four years. Test marketing costing ₹5 million has shown that there is a significant market for a SuperTread-type tire.

As a financial analyst at Goodweek Tires, you have been asked by your CFO, Adam Smith, to evaluate the SuperTread project and provide a recommendation on whether to go ahead with the investment. Except for the initial investment that will occur immediately, assume all cash flows will occur at year-end.

Goodweek must initially invest ₹185 million in production equipment to make the SuperTread. This equipment can be sold for ₹75 million at the end of four years. Goodweek intends to sell the SuperTread to two distinct markets:

1. *The original equipment manufacturer (OEM) market*: The OEM market consists primarily of the large automobile companies (like General Motors) that buy tires for new cars. In the OEM market, the SuperTread is expected to sell for ₹43 per tire. The variable cost to produce each tire is ₹31.
2. *The replacement market*: The replacement market consists of all tires purchased after the automobile has left the factory. This market allows higher margins; Goodweek expects to sell the SuperTread for ₹64 per tire there. Variable costs are the same as in the OEM market.

Goodweek Tires intends to raise prices at 1 percent above the inflation rate; variable costs also will increase at 1 percent above the inflation rate. In addition, the SuperTread project will incur ₹53 million in marketing and general administration costs the first year. This cost is expected to increase at the inflation rate in the subsequent years.

Goodweek's corporate tax rate is 23 percent. Annual inflation is expected to remain constant at 3.25 percent. The company uses a 13.4 percent discount rate to evaluate new product decisions. Automotive industry analysts expect automobile manufacturers to produce 8.5 million new cars this year and for production to grow at 2.5 percent per year thereafter. Each new car needs four tires (the spare tires are undersized and are in a different category). Goodweek Tires expects the SuperTread to capture 11 percent of the OEM market.

Industry analysts estimate that the replacement tire market size will be 35 million tires this year and that it will grow at 2 percent annually. Goodweek expects the SuperTread to capture an 8 percent market share.

The appropriate depreciation schedule for the equipment is the 7-year MACRS depreciation schedule. The immediate initial working capital requirement is ₹10 million. Thereafter, the net working capital requirements will be 15 percent of sales. What are the NPV, payback period, discounted payback period, IRR, and PI on this project?

7

Risk Analysis, Real Options, and Capital Budgeting

Even in the best of times, movies often bomb at the box office. In the summer of 2019, the movie *Dark Phoenix*, starring Jennifer Lawrence and James McAvoy, flew into theaters with the slogan, "The Phoenix will rise." But the film's box office never rose from the ashes. Critics were harsh, saying the movie was "a thoughtless and mechanical descent into nonsense" and calling it a "stupendously dull series-ender without a shred of wit, narrative thrust, or genuine emotional force." Ouch!

Looking at the numbers, *Dark Phoenix*'s losses were epic. After production, distribution, and marketing costs, moviemaker Twentieth Century Studios and its partners were estimated to have lost as much as ₹120 million on the film. In fact, about 4 of 10 movies lose money in theaters, though streaming and DVD and Bluray sales often help the final tally. In 2020, the box office numbers for most movies were effectively zero due to COVID-19. In fact, one source estimated that box office tallies worldwide were reduced by more than ₹10 billion through May 2020 alone. Of course, there are movies that do quite well. Also in 2020, the Lucasfilm movie *Star Wars: The Rise of Skywalker* raked in over ₹1 billion worldwide at a production cost of ₹275 million. Fortunately for Lucasfilm, this movie was released in late December 2019, so its box office run ended before many COVID-19 lockdowns.

Obviously, Twentieth Century Studios didn't *plan* to lose ₹120 million or so on *Dark Phoenix*, but it happened. As this flop shows, projects don't always go as companies think they will. Likewise, big budget Indian films ranging from *Baahubali 2: The Conclusion* (₹250 crore, Telugu), *2.0* (₹570 crore, Tamil), *RRR* (₹550 crore, Telugu) *Saaho* (₹350 crore, Telugu), *Thugs of Hindostan* (₹310 crore, Hindi), *Sye Raa Narasimha Reddy* (₹300 crore, Telugu), and *Adipurush* (₹700 crore, Hindi) were never planned to lose money. As the box office spun out, new collection records were broken by *Baahubali 2: The Conclusion* (₹1,810 crore), *2.0* (₹800 crore), *RRR* (₹1387 crore) and *Saaho* (₹433 crore); yet, movies like Thugs of Hindostan (₹170 crore), *Sye Raa Narasimha Reddy* (₹240 crore) and *Adipurush* (₹350 crore) were losing ventures.

This chapter explores how this can happen, and what companies can do to analyze and possibly avoid these situations.

Please visit us at **rwjcorporatefinance.blogspot.com** for the latest developments in the world of corporate finance.

7.1 Sensitivity Analysis, Scenario Analysis, and Break–Even Analysis

Excel Master coverage online

One main point of this text is that NPV analysis is a superior capital budgeting technique. In fact, because the NPV approach uses cash flows rather than profits, uses all the cash flows, and discounts the cash flows properly, it is hard to find any theoretical fault with it.

NPV analysis can account for project risk, as long as we forecast expected cash flows rather than optimistic cash flows, and discount riskier cash flows more than safe cash flows. However, in our conversations with practical businesspeople, we hear the phrase "a false sense of security" frequently. These people point out that the documentation for capital budgeting proposals is often quite impressive. Cash flows are projected down to the last thousand rupees (or even the last rupee) for each year (or even each month). Opportunity costs and side effects are handled properly. Sunk costs are ignored–also properly. When a high net present value appears at the bottom, one is tempted to say yes immediately. Nevertheless, the projected cash flow often goes unmet in practice and the firm ends up with a money loser.

SENSITIVITY ANALYSIS AND SCENARIO ANALYSIS

How can the firm get the net present value technique to live up to its potential? One approach is **sensitivity analysis**, which examines how sensitive a particular NPV calculation is to changes in underlying assumptions. Sensitivity analysis is also known as *what-if* analysis and *bop* (best, optimistic, and pessimistic) analysis.

Consider the following example. Surya Electronics Corporation (SEC) has recently developed a surya-powered jet engine and wants to go ahead with full-scale production. The initial (Year 1)[1] investment is ₹1,500 million, followed by production and sales over the next five years. The preliminary cash flow projection appears in Table 7.1. Should SEC go ahead with investment in and production of the jet engine, the NPV (in millions) at a discount rate of 15 percent is:

$$\begin{aligned} \text{NPV} &= -₹1{,}500 + \sum_{t=1}^{5}\frac{₹900}{1.15^t} \\ &= -₹1{,}500 + ₹900 \times \text{PVIFA}_{15\%,5} \\ &= ₹1{,}518 \end{aligned}$$

Table 7.1 Cash Flow Forecasts for Surya Electronics Corporation's Jet Engine: Base Case (in millions)*

	Year 1	Years 2–6
Revenue		₹ 6,000
Variable costs		3,000
Fixed costs		1,940
Depreciation		300
Pretax profit		₹ 760
Tax (21%)		160
Net income		₹ 600
Cash flow		₹ 900
Initial investment costs	₹1,500	

*Assumptions: (1) Investment is depreciated in Years 2 through 6 using the straight-line method; (2) tax rate is 21 percent; and (3) the company receives no tax benefits for initial development costs.

[1]Financial custom generally designates Year 0 as "today." However, we use Year 1 as today in this example because later in this chapter we will consider another decision made a year earlier. That decision will have occurred at Year 0.

Because the NPV is positive, basic financial theory implies that SEC should accept the project. However, is this all there is to say about the venture? Before actual funding, we ought to check out the project's underlying assumptions about revenue and costs.

Revenue Let's assume that the marketing department has projected annual sales to be:

Number of jet engines sold per year	=	Market share	×	Size of jet engine market per year
3,000	=	.30	×	10,000

Annual sales revenues	=	Number of jet engines sold	×	Price per engine
₹6,000 million	=	3,000	×	₹2 million

Thus, it turns out that the revenue estimates depend on three assumptions:

1. Market share.
2. Size of jet engine market.
3. Price per engine.

Costs Financial analysts frequently divide costs into two types: variable costs and fixed costs. **Variable costs** change as the output changes, and they are zero when production is zero. Costs of direct labor and raw materials are usually variable. It is common to assume that a variable cost is constant per unit of output, implying that total variable costs are proportional to the level of production. For example, if direct labor is variable and one unit of final output requires ₹10 of direct labor, then 100 units of final output should require ₹1,000 of direct labor.

Fixed costs are not dependent on the amount of goods or services produced during the period. Fixed costs are usually measured as costs per unit of time, such as rent per month or salaries per year. Fixed costs are not fixed forever; they are fixed only over a predetermined time period.

The engineering department has estimated variable costs to be ₹1 million per engine. Fixed costs are ₹1,940 million per year. The cost breakdowns are:

Variable cost per year	=	Variable cost per unit	×	Number of jet engines sold per year
₹3,000 million	=	₹1 million	×	3,000

Total cost before taxes per year	=	Variable cost per year	+	Fixed cost per year
₹4,940 million	=	₹3,000 million	+	1,940 million

These estimates for market size, market share, price, variable cost, and fixed cost, as well as the estimate of initial investment, are presented in the middle column of Table 7.2. These figures represent the firm's expectations or best estimates of the different parameters. By best estimates, we mean the firm's best guess for each variable's expected value, not the best-case scenario. For comparison, the firm's analysts also prepared both optimistic and pessimistic forecasts for each of the different variables. These forecasts are provided in the table, as well.

Table 7.2 Different Estimates for Surya Electronics' Surya Jet Engine

Variable	Pessimistic	Expected or Best	Optimistic
Market size (per year)	5,000	10,000	20,000
Market share	20%	30%	50%
Price	₹1.9 million	₹2 million	₹2.2 million
Variable cost (per engine)	₹1.2 million	₹1 million	₹.8 million
Fixed cost (per year)	₹2,000 million	₹1,940 million	₹1,740 million
Investment	₹1,900 million	₹1,500 million	₹1,000 million

Standard sensitivity analysis calls for an NPV calculation for all three possibilities of a single variable, along with the expected forecast for all other variables. This procedure is illustrated in Table 7.3. Consider the NPV calculation of ₹9,463 million provided in the upper right corner of this table. This NPV occurs when the optimistic forecast of 20,000 units per year is used for market size while all other variables are set at their expected forecasts from Table 7.2. Note that each row of the middle column of Table 7.3 shows a value of ₹1,518 million. This occurs because the expected forecast is used for the variable that was singled out, as well as for all other variables.

Table 7.3 can be used for a number of purposes. First, taken as a whole, the table can indicate whether NPV analysis should be trusted. In other words, it reduces the false sense of security we spoke of earlier. Suppose that NPV is positive when the expected forecast for each variable is used. Further suppose that every number in the pessimistic column is highly negative and every number in the optimistic column is highly positive. A change in a single forecast greatly alters the NPV estimate, making one leery of the net present value approach. A conservative manager might well scrap the entire NPV analysis in this situation. Fortunately, the surya jet engine does not exhibit this wide dispersion because all but three of the numbers in Table 7.3 are positive. Managers viewing the table will likely consider NPV analysis to be useful for the surya-powered jet engine.

Second, sensitivity analysis shows where more information is needed. An error in the estimate of investment appears to be relatively unimportant because, even under the pessimistic scenario, the NPV of ₹1,175 million is still highly positive. By contrast, the pessimistic forecast for market share leads to an NPV of −₹1,130 million, and a pessimistic forecast for market size leads to an NPV of −₹2,454 million. Because

Table 7.3 NPV Calculations (in millions) for the Surya Jet Engine Using Sensitivity Analysis

	Pessimistic	Expected or Best	Optimistic
Market size	−₹2,454*	₹1,518	₹9,463
Market share	− 1,130*	1,518	6,815
Price	724	1,518	3,107
Variable cost	− 71	1,518	3,106
Fixed cost	1,359	1,518	2,048
Investment	1,175	1,518	1,948

Under sensitivity analysis, one input is varied while all other inputs are assumed to meet their expectation. For example, an NPV of −₹2,454 occurs when the pessimistic forecast of 5,000 is used for market size, while all other variables are set at their expected forecasts from Table 7.2.

*We assume that the other divisions of the firm are profitable, implying that a loss on this project can offset income elsewhere in the firm, thereby reducing the overall taxes of the firm.

the effect of incorrect estimates on revenue is so much greater than the effect of incorrect estimates on costs, more information about the factors determining revenue might be needed.

Because of these advantages, sensitivity analysis is widely used in practice. Graham and Harvey[2] report that slightly over 50 percent of the 392 firms in their sample subject their capital budgeting calculations to sensitivity analysis. This number is particularly large when one considers that only about 75 percent of the firms in their sample use NPV analysis.

Unfortunately, sensitivity analysis also suffers from some drawbacks. Sensitivity analysis may unwittingly increase the false sense of security among managers. Suppose all pessimistic forecasts yield positive NPVs. A manager might feel that there is no way the project can lose money. Of course, the forecasters may have an optimistic view of a pessimistic forecast. To combat this, some companies do not treat optimistic and pessimistic forecasts subjectively. Rather, their pessimistic forecasts are always, say, 20 percent less than expected. Unfortunately, the cure in this case may be worse than the disease: A deviation of a fixed percentage ignores the fact that some variables are easier to forecast than others.

In addition, sensitivity analysis treats each variable in isolation when, in reality, the different variables are likely to be related. If ineffective management allows costs to get out of control, it is likely that variable costs, fixed costs, and investment all will rise above expectation at the same time. If the market is not receptive to a surya jet engine, both market share and price should decline together.

Managers frequently perform **scenario analysis**, a variant of sensitivity analysis, to minimize this problem. This approach examines a number of different likely scenarios, where each scenario involves a confluence of factors. As an example, consider the effect of a few airline crashes. These crashes are likely to reduce flying in total, thereby limiting the demand for any new engines. Furthermore, even if the crashes do not involve surya-powered aircraft, the public could become more averse to any innovative and controversial technologies. Hence, SEC's market share might fall, as well. Perhaps the cash flow calculations would look like those in Table 7.4 under the scenario of a plane crash. Given the calculations in the table, the NPV (in millions) would be:

$$-₹2,719 = -₹1,500 - ₹364 \times \text{PVIFA}_{15\%,5}$$

Table 7.4 Cash Flow Forecast (in millions) under the Scenario of a Plane Crash*

	Year 1	Years 2–6
Revenue		₹2,800
Variable costs		1,400
Fixed costs		1,940
Depreciation		300
Pretax profit		–₹ 840
Tax (21%)†		– 176
Net income		–₹ 664
Cash flow		–₹ 364
Initial investment cost	₹1,500	

*Assumptions are:

Market size: 7,000 (70 percent of expectation)

Market share: 20% (2⁄3 of expectation)

Forecasts for all other variables are the expected forecasts as given in Table 7.2.

† We are assuming the loss is offset by income elsewhere in the firm.

[2]See Figure 2 of John Graham and Campbell Harvey, "The Theory and Practice of Corporate Finance: Evidence from the Field," *Journal of Financial Economics* (May/June 2001).

A series of scenarios like this might illuminate issues concerning the project better than the standard application of sensitivity analysis would.

Unfortunately, in practice, even the worst-case scenarios may be overly optimistic. Two recent examples involving the Berlin Brandenburg Airport and Boeing 737 MAX demonstrate this point.

Planning for the Berlin Brandenburg Airport started in 1996, with a targeted opening date of 2006. The original budget was for €2.86 billion (₹3.1 billion). A number of issues arose and construction didn't even begin until 2006, with the opening date announced for late 2011. Pre-opening inspections in 2011 found lights that wouldn't turn off, escalators that were too short, and misnumbered rooms. More importantly, the fire suppression system didn't work.

When the grand opening was delayed until the spring of 2012, airline tickets were issued, and the train station below the terminal was fully operational. But this opening date was missed as well, so all tickets had to be canceled. This delay also introduced an additional construction cost because a train now had to be run at least weekly to keep the tracks operational.

The opening date was pushed back to 2014, then 2016. When 2016 came around, an audit determined that the airport was only 57 percent usable. And the fire suppression system was still not working properly. Officials stopped making opening date estimates after this as six opening dates had been canceled. Finally, 24 years from the start of planning, the Brandenburg airport opened on October 31, 2020, but new issues had arisen. Because of reduced air traffic due to COVID-19, it is likely that the airport will operate at a loss until air travel increases. Although the final tally is not in, it has been reported that the cost of Brandenburg Airport is €10.3 billion (₹11.2 billion), more than 3.5 times the original budget.

Another example is the Boeing 737 MAX, which was involved in two crashes within five months of being introduced. The fleet of 387 aircraft had flown 8,600 weekly flights for 59 airlines. Because of the crashes, aviation authorities around the globe grounded the new jet. During the second quarter of 2019, Boeing stated that it was taking a ₹4.9 billion charge to cover compensation to airlines that had been forced to cancel flights. Southwest, which is known for its all-737 fleet, reportedly lost out on ₹175 million in income during the second quarter due to the continued grounding of the 737 MAX. As a result, there was speculation that Southwest would acquire another airline to diversify its fleet to include Airbus jets, an opportunity cost for Boeing. In aviation circles, it became a running (and sardonic) joke in 2020 that the first jet that landed at Brandenburg Airport would be a Boeing 737 MAX.

BREAK-EVEN ANALYSIS

Our discussion of sensitivity analysis and scenario analysis suggests that there are many ways to examine variability in forecasts. We now present another approach, **break-even analysis**. As its name implies, this approach determines the sales needed to break even. The approach is a useful complement to sensitivity analysis because it also sheds light on the severity of incorrect forecasts. We calculate the break-even point in terms of both accounting profit and present value.

Accounting Profit Annual net profits under four different sales forecasts are as follows:

Annual Unit Sales	Net Profit (in millions)
0	−₹1,770
1,000	− 980
3,000	600
10,000	6,130

Table 7.5 Revenue and Costs of Project under Different Sales Assumptions (in millions, except unit sales)

Year 1	Years 2–6								
Initial Investment	Annual Unit Sales	Revenue	Variable Costs	Fixed Costs	Depreciation	Taxes* (21%)	Net Income	Operating Cash Flows	NPV (evaluated Year 1)
₹1,500	0	₹ 0	₹ 0	₹1,940	₹300	−₹470	−₹1,770	−₹1,470	−₹6,426
1,500	1,000	2,000	1,000	1,940	300	− 260	− 980	− 680	− 3,778
1,500	3,000	6,000	3,000	1,940	300	160	600	900	1,518
1,500	10,000	20,000	10,000	1,940	300	1,630	6,130	6,430	20,056

*Loss is incurred in the first two rows. For tax purposes, this loss offsets income elsewhere in the firm.

A more complete presentation of costs and revenue appears in Table 7.5.

We plot the revenue, costs, and profits under the different assumptions about sales in Figure 7.1. The revenue and cost curves cross at 2,240 jet engines. This is the break-even point–that is, the point where the project generates no profits or losses. As long as annual sales are above 2,240 jet engines, the project will make a profit.

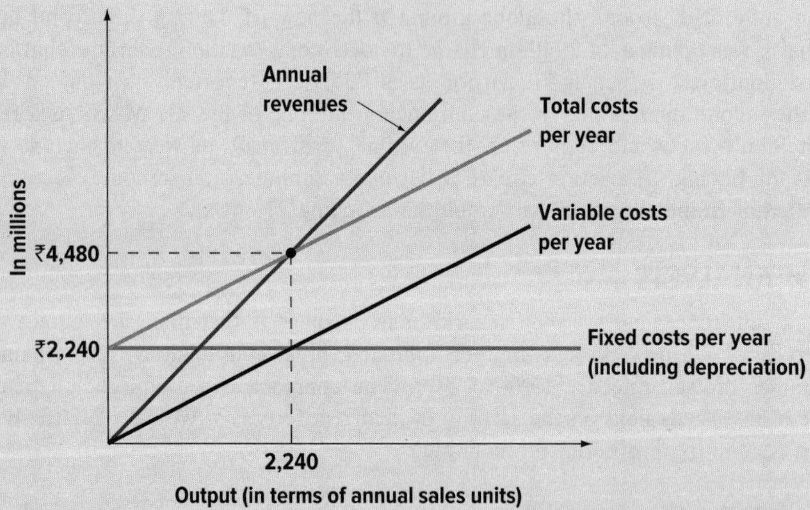

The pretax contribution margin per engine is ₹1 million. The firm can recover its annual fixed costs of ₹2,240 million by selling 2,240 engines. Hence, the break-even point occurs with annual sales of 2,240 engines.

Figure 7.1 Break-Even Point Using Accounting Numbers

This break-even point can be calculated very easily. Because the sales price is ₹2 million per engine and the variable cost is ₹1 million per engine,[3] the difference between sales price and variable cost per engine is

$$\begin{aligned}\text{Sales price} - \text{Variable cost} &= ₹2 \text{ million} - 1 \text{ million}\\ &= ₹1 \text{ million}\end{aligned}$$

This difference is called the pretax **contribution margin** because each additional engine contributes this amount to pretax profit.

Fixed costs are ₹1,940 million and depreciation is ₹300 million, implying that the sum of these costs is:

$$\begin{aligned}\text{Fixed costs} + \text{Depreciation} &= ₹1{,}940 \text{ million} + 300 \text{ million}\\ &= ₹2{,}240 \text{ million}\end{aligned}$$

That is, the firm incurs costs of ₹2,240 million per year, regardless of the number of sales. Because each engine contributes ₹1 million, annual sales must reach the following level to offset the costs:

Accounting Profit Break-Even Point

$$\frac{\text{Fixed costs} + \text{Depreciation}}{\text{Sales price} - \text{Variable costs}} = \frac{₹2{,}240 \text{ million}}{₹1 \text{ million}} = 2{,}240$$

The break-even point required for an accounting profit is 2,240 engines.

The astute reader might be wondering why taxes have been ignored in the calculation of break-even accounting profit. The reason is that a firm with a pretax profit of ₹0 also will have an aftertax profit of ₹0 because no taxes are paid if no pretax profit is reported. Thus, the number of units needed to break even on a pretax basis must be equal to the number of units needed to break even on an aftertax basis.

Financial Break-Even As we have stated many times in the text, we are more interested in present value than we are in profit. Therefore, we should calculate break-even in terms of present value, or the *financial break-even.* Given a discount rate of 15 percent, the surya jet engine has the following net present values for different levels of annual sales:

Annual Unit Sales	NPV (in millions)
0	−₹6,426
1,000	− 3,778
3,000	1,518
10,000	20,056

These NPV calculations are reproduced from the last column of Table 7.5.

Figure 7.2 relates the net present value of both the revenue and the costs to output. There are at least two differences between Figure 7.2 and Figure 7.1, one of which is quite important and the other is much

[3]Though the previous section considered both optimistic and pessimistic forecasts for sales price and variable cost, break-even analysis uses the expected or best estimates of these variables.

Break Even Point of Indian Toll Operator

The Indian Toll Operator Company Ltd. (ITOCL) was promoted by Infrastructure Leasing and Financial Services Ltd. (IL&FS) as a special purpose vehicle (SPV) to develop, construct, operate and maintain the Fast Flyway on a Build Own Operate Transfer (BOOT) basis. ITOCL is a public listed company, incorporated in Uttar Pradesh, India.

Fast Flyway grew out of a need to bridge the growing population of Delhi with its neighbours across the Yamuna. We took a few figures from the annual reports of the company. The fixed costs and depreciation work out to ₹27 crore per year. On an average, the company earns a toll of ₹12 per vehicle. Variable charges per vehicle work out to ₹3 per vehicle.

Using the above data, we decided to compute accounting profit break even point of the Indian Toll Operator company. The figure below displays the relative movement of sales and expenses.

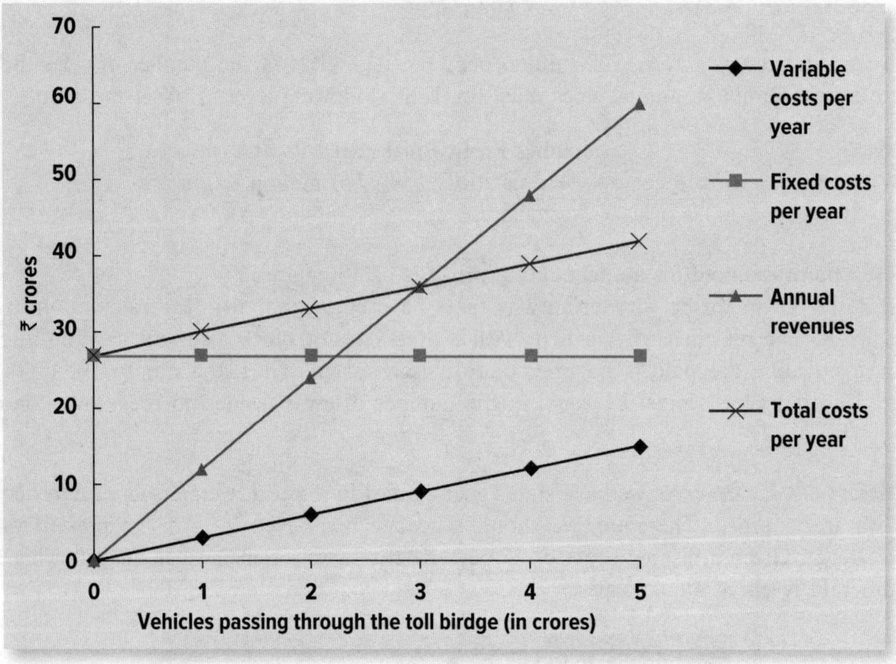

Figure Break Even Point for Indian Toll Operator

The annual revenues become equal to total costs at the point of 3 crore vehicles passing through the bridge. Based on the above observations, one can state that the accounting break even point of the project will happen when 82,200 vehicles would cross the bridge and pay the toll per day.

less so. First, the less important point: The rupee amounts on the vertical dimension of Figure 7.2 are greater than those on the vertical dimension of Figure 7.1 because the net present values are calculated over five years. More important, accounting break-even occurs when 2,240 engines are sold annually, whereas financial break-even occurs when 2,427 engines are sold annually.

The NPV break-even point can be calculated directly. The firm originally invested ₹1,500 million. This initial investment can be expressed as a five-year equivalent annual cost (EAC), determined by dividing the initial investment by the appropriate five-year annuity factor:

$$\text{EAC} = \frac{\text{Initial investment}}{\text{5-year annuity factor at 15\%}} = \frac{\text{Initial investment}}{\text{PVIFA}_{15\%,5}}$$

$$= \frac{₹1{,}500 \text{ million}}{3.3522} = ₹447.5 \text{ million}$$

Note that the EAC of ₹447.5 million is greater than the yearly depreciation of ₹300 million. This must occur because the calculation of EAC implicitly assumes that the ₹1,500 million investment could have been invested at 15 percent.

Aftertax costs, regardless of output, can be viewed like this:

$$\begin{array}{c} ₹1{,}917.1 \\ \text{million} \end{array} = \begin{array}{c} ₹447.5 \\ \text{million} \end{array} + \begin{array}{c} ₹1{,}940 \\ \text{million} \end{array} \times .79 - ₹300 \text{ million} \times .21$$

$$= \text{EAC} + \text{Fixed costs} \times (1 - T_C) - \text{Depreciation} \times T_C$$

That is, in addition to the initial investment's equivalent annual cost of ₹447.5 million, the firm pays fixed costs each year and receives a depreciation tax shield each year. The depreciation tax shield is written as

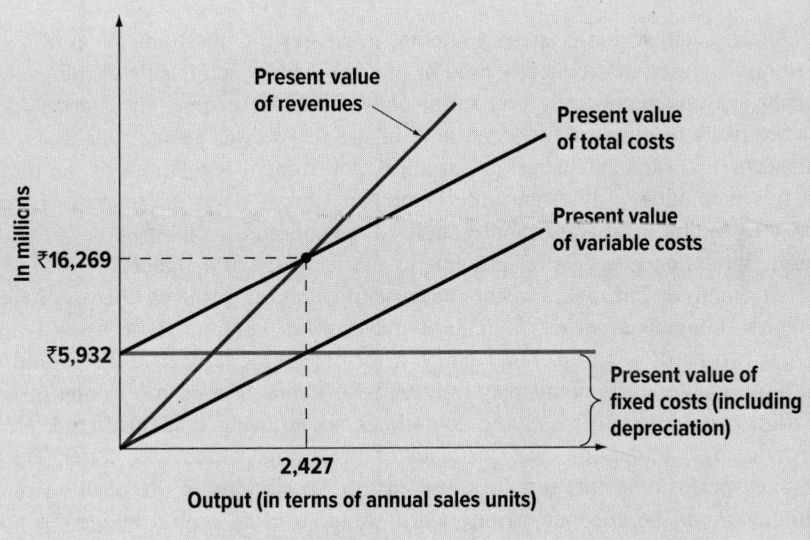

Break-even in terms of NPV occurs at a higher level of sales than does break-even for accounting income. Companies that just break even on an accounting basis are not recovering the opportunity cost of the initial investment.

Figure 7.2 Break-Even Point Using Net Present Value

a negative number because it offsets the costs in the equation. Each engine contributes ₹.79 million to aftertax profit, so it will take the following sales to offset the costs:

Financial Break-Even Point

$$\frac{\text{EAC} + \text{Fixed costs} \times (1 - T_C) - \text{Depreciation} \times T_C}{(\text{Sales price} - \text{Variable costs}) \times (1 - T_C)} = \frac{₹1{,}917.1 \text{ million}}{₹.79 \text{ million}} = 2{,}426.68$$

About 2,427 engines must be sold to reach the financial break-even point.

Why is the accounting break-even point different from the financial break-even point? When we use accounting profit as the basis for the break-even calculation, we subtract depreciation. Depreciation for the surya jet engines project is ₹300 million per year. If 2,240 surya jet engines are sold per year, SEC will generate sufficient revenue to cover the ₹300 million depreciation expense plus other costs. Unfortunately, at this level of sales, SEC will not cover the economic opportunity costs of the ₹1,500 million laid out for the investment. If we take into account that the ₹1,500 million could have been invested at 15 percent, the true annual cost of the investment is ₹447.5 million, not ₹300 million. Depreciation understates the true costs of recovering the initial investment. Companies that break even on an accounting basis are really losing money. They are losing the opportunity cost of the initial investment.

Is break-even analysis important? Very much so: All corporate executives fear losses. Break-even analysis determines how far sales can fall before the project is losing money, either in an accounting sense or an NPV sense.

7.2 Monte Carlo Simulation

Excel Master coverage online

Both sensitivity analysis and scenario analysis attempt to answer the question "What if?" However, while both analyses are frequently used in the real world, each has its own limitations. Sensitivity analysis allows only one variable to change at a time. By contrast, many variables are likely to move at the same time in the real world. Scenario analysis follows specific scenarios, such as changes in inflation, government regulation, or the number of competitors. Although this methodology is often quite helpful, it cannot cover all sources of variability. In fact, projects are likely to exhibit a lot of variability under one economic scenario.

Monte Carlo simulation is a further attempt to model real-world uncertainty. This approach takes its name from the famous European casino because it analyzes projects the way one might analyze gambling strategies. Imagine a serious blackjack player who wonders if he should take a third card whenever his first two cards total 16. Most likely, a formal mathematical model would be too complex to be practical here. However, he could play thousands of hands in a casino, sometimes drawing a third card when his first two cards add to 16 and sometimes not drawing that third card. He could compare his winnings (or losings) under the two strategies to determine which was better. He would probably lose a lot of money performing this test in a real casino, so simulating the results from the two strategies on a computer might be cheaper. Monte Carlo simulation of capital budgeting projects is in this spirit.

Imagine that Brindavan Bhojnalaya Industries (BBI), a manufacturer of both charcoal and gas grills, has a blueprint for a new grill that cooks with compressed hydrogen. The CFO, Tenzing Loden Lepcha, dissatisfied with simpler capital budgeting techniques, wants a Monte Carlo simulation for this new grill. A consultant specializing in the Monte Carlo approach, Srikanth Mani, takes her through the five basic steps of the method.

STEP 1: SPECIFY THE BASIC MODEL

Srikanth breaks up cash flow into three components: annual revenue, annual costs, and initial investment. The revenue in any year is viewed as:

$$\begin{matrix}\text{Number of grills sold} \\ \text{by entire industry}\end{matrix} \times \begin{matrix}\text{Market share of BBI's} \\ \text{hydrogen grill (in percent)}\end{matrix} \times \begin{matrix}\text{Price per} \\ \text{hydrogen grill}\end{matrix} \quad \mathbf{(7.1)}$$

The cost in any year is viewed as:

$$\text{Fixed manufacturing costs} + \text{Variable manufacturing costs} + \text{Marketing costs} + \text{Selling costs}$$

The initial investment is viewed as:

$$\text{Cost of patent} + \text{Test marketing costs} + \text{Cost of production facility}$$

STEP 2: SPECIFY A DISTRIBUTION FOR EACH VARIABLE IN THE MODEL

Here comes the hard part. Let's start with revenue, which has three components in Equation 7.1. The consultant first models overall market size–that is, the number of grills sold by the entire industry. The trade publication *Outdoor Food (OF)* reported that 10 million grills of all types were sold in the India last year, and it forecasts sales of 10.5 million next year. Srikanth, using *OF*'s forecast and his own intuition, creates the following distribution for next year's sales of grills by the entire industry:

Probability	20%	60%	20%
Next year's industrywide unit sales	10 million	10.5 million	11 million

The tight distribution here reflects the slow but steady historical growth in the grill market. This probability distribution is graphed in Panel A of Figure 7.3.

Srikanth realizes that estimating the market share of BBI's hydrogen grill is more difficult. Nevertheless, after a great deal of analysis, he determines the distribution of next year's market share is:

Probability	10%	20%	30%	25%	10%	5%
Market share of BBI's hydrogen grill next year	1%	2%	3%	4%	5%	8%

Whereas the consultant assumed a symmetrical distribution for industrywide unit sales, he believes a skewed distribution makes more sense for the project's market share. In his mind, there is always the small possibility that sales of the hydrogen grill will really take off. This probability distribution is graphed in Panel B of Figure 7.3.

These forecasts assume that unit sales for the overall industry are unrelated to the project's market share. In other words, the two variables are independent of each other. Srikanth reasons that although an economic boom might increase industrywide grill sales and a recession might decrease them, the project's market share is unlikely to be related to economic conditions.

Srikanth must determine the distribution of price per grill. Tenzing informs him that the price will be in the area of ₹200 per grill, given what other competitors are charging. However, the consultant believes that the price per hydrogen grill will almost certainly depend on the size of the overall market for grills. As in any business, you can usually charge more if demand is high.

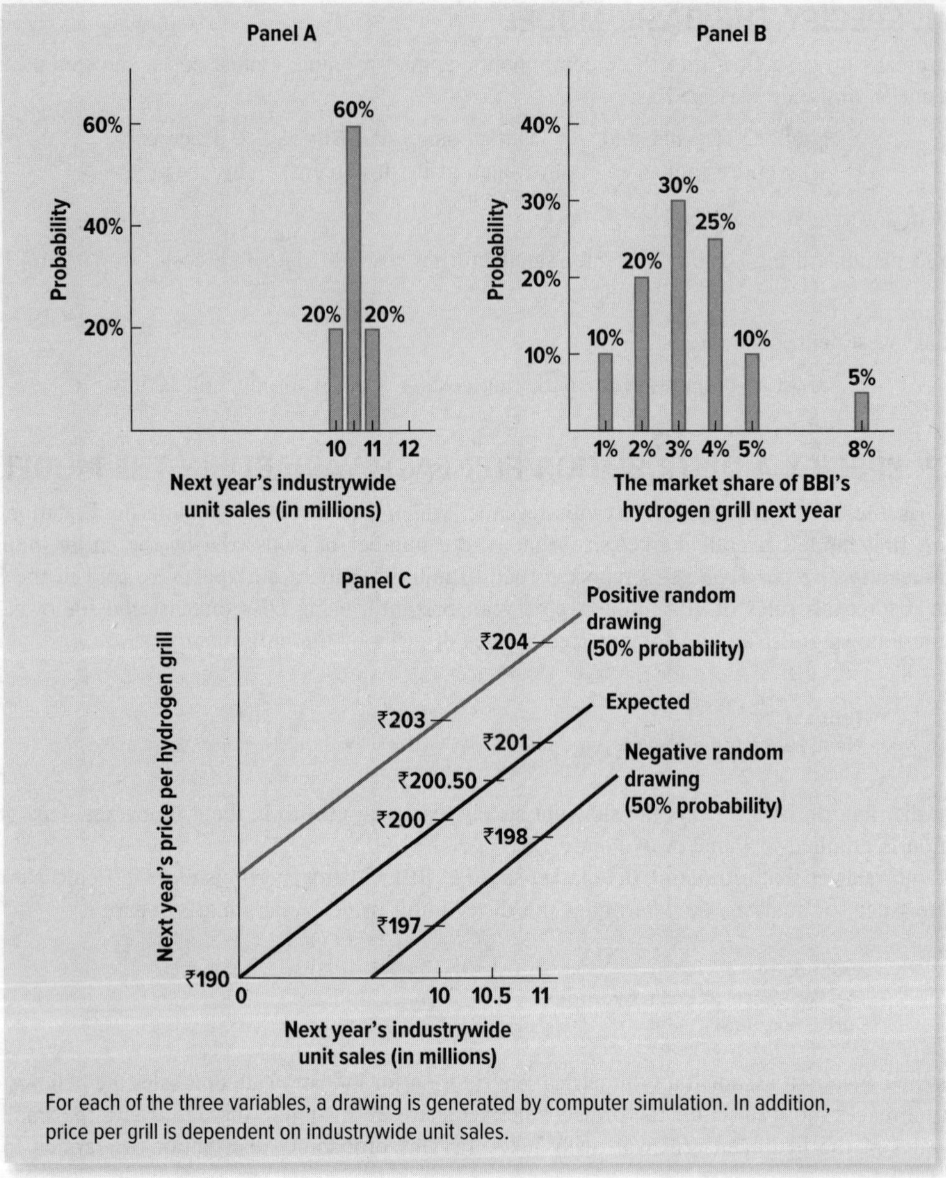

Figure 7.3 Probability Distributions for Industrywide Unit Sales, Market Share of BBI's Hydrogen Grill, and Price of Hydrogen Grill

After rejecting a number of complex models for price, Srikanth settles on the following specification:

$$\begin{matrix}\text{Next year's price} \\ \text{per hydrogen grill}\end{matrix} = ₹190 + ₹1 \times \begin{matrix}\text{Industrywide unit sales} \\ \text{(in millions)} + /-₹3\end{matrix} \qquad \textbf{(7.2)}$$

The grill price in Equation 7.2 depends on the unit sales of the industry. In addition, random variation is modeled via the term " + /–₹3," where a drawing of +₹3 and a drawing of –₹3 each occurs 50 percent of the time. If industrywide unit sales are 11 million, the price per share would be either of the following:

$$₹190 + 11 + 3 = ₹204 \quad (50\% \text{ probability})$$
$$₹190 + 11 - 3 = ₹198 \quad (50\% \text{ probability})$$

The relationship between the price of a hydrogen grill and industrywide unit sales is graphed in Panel C of Figure 7.3.

The consultant now has distributions for each of the three components of next year's revenue. However, he needs distributions for future years, as well. Using forecasts from *Outdoor Food* and other publications, Srikanth forecasts the following distribution of growth rates for the entire industry over the second year:

Probability	20%	60%	20%
Growth rate of industrywide unit sales in second year	1%	3%	5%

Given both the distribution of next year's industrywide unit sales and the distribution of growth rates for this variable over the second year, we can generate the distribution of industrywide unit sales for the second year. A similar extension should give Srikanth a distribution for later years, as well, though we won't go into the details here. And as the consultant extended the first component of revenue (industrywide unit sales) to later years, he would want to do the same thing for market share and unit price.

The preceding discussion shows how the three components of revenue can be modeled. Step 2 would be complete once the components of cost and investment are modeled in a similar way. Special attention must be paid to the interactions between variables here because ineffective management will likely allow the different cost components to rise together. However, you are probably getting the idea now, so we will skip the rest of this step.

STEP 3: THE COMPUTER DRAWS ONE OUTCOME

As we said, next year's revenue in our model is the product of three components. Imagine that the computer randomly picks industrywide unit sales of 10 million, a market share for BBI's hydrogen grill of 2 percent, and a +₹3 random price variation. Given these drawings, next year's price per hydrogen grill will be:

$$₹190 + 10 + 3 = ₹203$$

and next year's revenue for BBI's hydrogen grill will be:

$$10 \text{ million} \times .02 \times ₹203 = ₹40.6 \text{ million}$$

Of course, we are not done with the entire outcome yet. We would have to perform drawings for revenue in each future year. In addition, we would perform drawings for costs in each future year. Finally, a drawing for initial investment would have to be made, as well. In this way, a single outcome, made up of a drawing for each variable in the model, would generate a cash flow from the project in each future year.

How likely is it that the specific outcome discussed would be drawn? We can answer this because we know the probability of each component. Because industry sales of 10 million units has a 20 percent probability, a market share of 2 percent also has a 20 percent probability, and a random price variation of +₹3 has a 50 percent probability, the probability of these three drawings together in the same outcome is:

$$.02 = .20 \times .20 \times .50$$

Of course, the probability would get even smaller once drawings for future revenues, future costs, and the initial investment are included in the outcome.

This step generates the cash flow for each year from a single outcome. What we are ultimately interested in is the distribution of cash flows each year across many outcomes. We ask the computer to randomly draw over and over again to give us this distribution, which is what is done in the next step.

STEP 4: REPEAT THE PROCEDURE

The first three steps generate one outcome, but the essence of Monte Carlo simulation is repeated outcomes. Depending on the situation, the computer may be called on to generate thousands or even millions of outcomes. The result of all these drawings is a distribution of cash flow for each future year. This distribution is the basic output of Monte Carlo simulation.

Consider Figure 7.4. Here, repeated drawings have produced the simulated distribution of the third year's cash flow. There would be, of course, a distribution like the one in this figure for each future year. This leaves us with one more step.

STEP 5: CALCULATE NPV

Given the distribution of cash flow for the third year in Figure 7.4, one can determine the expected cash flow for this year. In a similar manner, one also can determine the expected cash flow for each future year and then calculate the net present value of the project by discounting these expected cash flows at an appropriate rate.

Monte Carlo simulation is often viewed as a step beyond either sensitivity analysis or scenario analysis. Interactions between the variables are explicitly specified in Monte Carlo; so (at least in theory) this methodology provides a more complete analysis. And, as a by-product, having to build a precise model deepens the forecaster's understanding of the project.

Because Monte Carlo simulations have been around since at least the 1940s, you might think that most firms would be performing them by now. Surprisingly, this does not seem to be the case. In our experience,

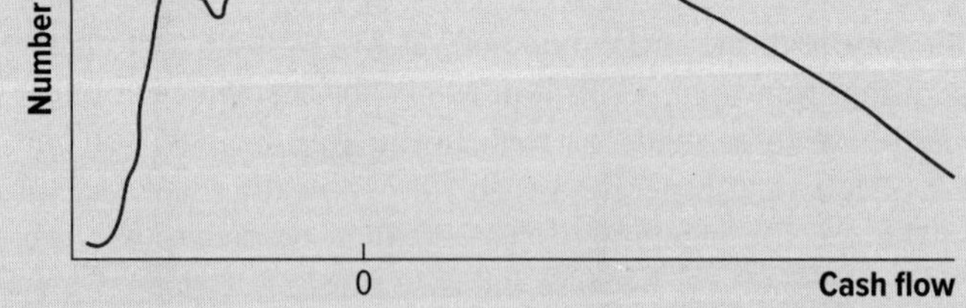

In Monte Carlo simulations, repeated sampling of all the variables from a specific model generates a statistical distribution.

Figure 7.4 Simulated Distribution of the Third Year's Cash Flow for BBI's New Hydrogen Grill executives are frequently skeptical of the complexity. It is difficult to model either the distributions of each variable or the interactions between variables. In addition, the computer output is often devoid of economic intuition. Thus, while Monte Carlo simulations are used in certain real-world situations,[4] the approach is not likely to be "the wave of the future." In fact, Graham and Harvey[5] report that only about 15 percent of the firms in their sample use capital budgeting simulations.

7.3 Real Options

In Chapter 5, we stressed the superiority of net present value (NPV) analysis over other approaches when valuing capital budgeting projects. When conducting NPV analysis, we should be careful to factor in the option to expand and the option to abandon in response to market conditions and new information. However, traditional real-world applications of NPV often ignore the adjustments that a firm can make after a project is initiated. These adjustments are called **real options**. In this respect, NPV underestimates the true value of a project if we fail to adjust for real options.

THE OPTION TO EXPAND

Esha Wangdu, an entrepreneur, recently learned of a chemical treatment causing water to freeze at 100 degrees Fahrenheit rather than 32 degrees. Of all the many practical applications for this treatment, Esha liked the idea of hotels made of ice more than anything else. Esha estimated the annual cash flows from a single ice hotel to be ₹2 million, based on an initial investment of ₹12 million. She felt that 20 percent was an appropriate discount rate, given the risk of this new venture. Believing that the cash flows would be perpetual, Esha determined the NPV of the project to be:

$$-₹12{,}000{,}000 + ₹2{,}000{,}000/.20 = -₹2{,}000{,}000$$

Most entrepreneurs would have rejected this venture, given its negative NPV. But Esha was not your typical entrepreneur. She reasoned that the current NPV analysis missed a hidden source of value. While she was pretty sure that the initial investment would cost ₹12 million, there was some uncertainty concerning annual cash flows. Her cash flow estimate of ₹2 million per year actually reflected her belief that there was a 50 percent probability that annual cash flows will be ₹3 million and a 50 percent probability that annual cash flows will be ₹1 million.

The NPV calculations for the two forecasts are given here:

Optimistic forecast: $-₹12{,}000{,}000 + ₹3{,}000{,}000/.20 = ₹3{,}000{,}000$
Pessimistic forecast: $-₹12{,}000{,}000 + ₹1{,}000{,}000/.20 = -₹7{,}000{,}000$

On the surface, this new calculation doesn't seem to help Esha much. An average of the two forecasts yields an NPV for the project of:

$$.50 \times ₹3{,}000{,}000 + .50 \times (-₹7{,}000{,}000) = -₹2{,}000{,}000$$

which is the value she calculated in the first place.

However, if the optimistic forecast turns out to be correct, Esha would want to expand. If she believes that there are, say, 10 locations in the country that can support an ice hotel, the true NPV of the venture would be:

$$.50 \times 10 \times ₹3{,}000{,}000 + .50 \times (-₹7{,}000{,}000) = ₹11{,}500{,}000$$

[4]Perhaps more than any other industry, the pharmaceutical industry has pioneered applications of this methodology. For example, see Nancy A. Nichols, "Scientific Management at Merck: An Interview with CFO Judy Lewent," *Harvard Business Review* (January/February 1994)
[5]See Figure 2 of Graham and Harvey, op. cit.

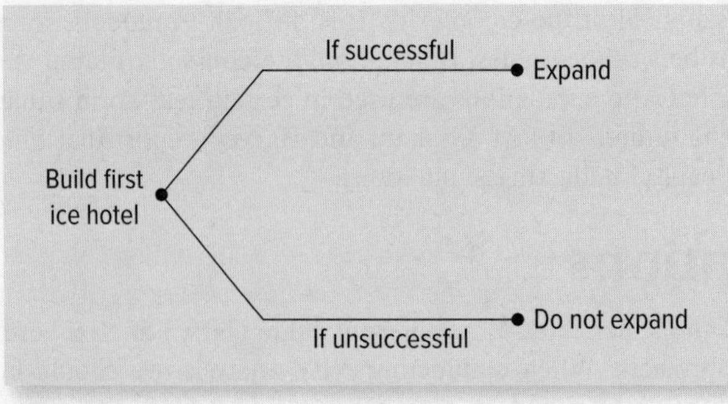

Figure 7.5 Decision Tree for Ice Hotel

Figure 7.5, which represents Esha's decision, is often called a decision tree. The idea expressed in the figure is both basic and universal. The entrepreneur has the option to expand if the pilot location is successful. For example, think of all the people who start restaurants, most of them ultimately failing. These individuals are not necessarily overly optimistic. They may realize the likelihood of failure but go ahead anyway because of the small chance of starting the next McDonald's or Burger King.

In India, most companies going in for Greenfield projects acquire a higher quantity of land that they would require for their new project requirement (example: Jindal Group, Mukesh Reliance Group, Tata Group and Vedanta Group). The idea behind the acquisition is to capture the real option to expand, i.e., take up the Brownfield project if the initial Greenfield project were to be successful (by paying a small sum).[6] CK Mehta's Deepak Nitrite and Dr Reddy Laboratories often use this tactic while setting up their chemical and pharmaceutical plants, respectively, by ensuring that it can expand production if conditions become favourable.

THE OPTION TO ABANDON

Managers also have the option to abandon existing projects. Abandonment may seem cowardly, but it often can save companies a great deal of money. Because of this, the option to abandon increases the value of any potential project.

The example of ice hotels, which illustrated the option to expand, also can illustrate the option to abandon. To see this, imagine that Esha now believes that there is a 50 percent probability that annual cash flows will be ₹6 million and a 50 percent probability that annual cash flows will be –₹2 million. The NPV calculations under the two forecasts become:

$$\textbf{Optimistic forecast: } -₹12{,}000{,}000 + ₹6{,}000{,}000/.2 = ₹18{,}000{,}000$$
$$\textbf{Pessimistic forecast: } -₹12{,}000{,}000 - ₹2{,}000{,}000/.2 = -₹22{,}000{,}000$$

yielding an NPV for the project of:

$$.50 \times ₹18{,}000{,}000 + .50 \times (-₹22{,}000{,}000) = -₹2{,}000{,}000 \qquad \textbf{(7.3)}$$

Now imagine that Esha wants to own, at most, only one ice hotel, implying that there is no option to expand. Because the NPV in Equation 7.3 is negative, it looks as if she will not build the hotel.

[6]There also exists the option of unlocking value due to the high land and real estate prices in the nearby areas (after the Greenfield industrial project is successful). Jaiprakash Gaur Group owned Yamuna Expressway from Greater Noida to Agra is a perfect example of the same.

But things change when we consider the abandonment option. As of Year 1, she will know which forecast has come true. If cash flows equal those under the optimistic forecast, Esha will keep the project alive. If, however, cash flows equal those under the pessimistic forecast, she will abandon the hotel. If Esha knows these possibilities ahead of time, the NPV of the project becomes:

$$.50 \times ₹18{,}000{,}000 + .50 \times (-₹12{,}000{,}000 - ₹2{,}000{,}000/1.20) = ₹2{,}166{,}667$$

Because Esha abandons after experiencing the cash flow of −₹2 million at Year 1, she does not have to endure this outflow in any of the later years. The NPV is now positive, so Esha will accept the project.

The example here is clearly a stylized one. Whereas many years may pass before a project is abandoned in the real world, our ice hotel was abandoned after one year. And, while salvage values generally accompany abandonment, we assumed no salvage value for the ice hotel. Nevertheless, abandonment options are pervasive in the real world.

Consider the moviemaking industry. As shown in Figure 7.6, movies begin with either the purchase or development of a script. A completed script might cost a movie studio a few million rupees and potentially lead to actual production. However, the great majority of scripts (perhaps well in excess of 80 percent) are abandoned. Why would studios abandon scripts that they commissioned in the first place? The studios know ahead of time that only a few scripts will be promising, but they don't know which ones. Thus, they cast a wide net, commissioning many scripts to get a few good ones. The studios must be ruthless with the bad scripts because the expenditure here pales in comparison to the huge losses from producing a bad movie.

The few lucky scripts then move into production, where costs might be budgeted in the tens of millions of rupees, if not much more. At this stage, the dreaded phrase is that on-location production gets "bogged down," creating cost overruns, but the studios are equally ruthless here. Should these overruns become excessive, production is likely to be abandoned midstream. Interestingly,

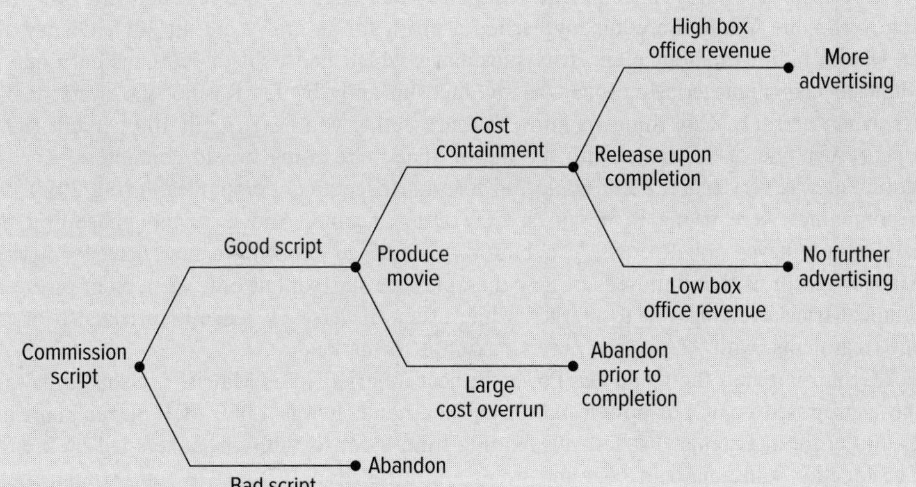

Movie studios have abandonment options throughout the production of a movie.

Figure 7.6 The Abandonment Option in the Movie Industry

abandonment almost always occurs due to high costs, not due to the fear that the movie won't be able to find an audience. Little information on that score will be obtained until the movie is actually released.

Release of the movie is accompanied by significant advertising expenditures, with an average budget for U.S. advertising of ₹40 million. However, for global event movies, the advertising budget can exceed ₹300 million. Advertising will continue following strong ticket sales, but it likely will be abandoned after a few weeks of poor box office performance.

Moviemaking is one of the riskiest businesses around, with studios receiving hundreds of millions of rupees in a matter of weeks from a blockbuster while receiving practically nothing during this period from a flop. The abandonment options contain costs that might otherwise bankrupt the industry.

To illustrate some of these ideas, consider the case of Euro Disney, now Disnelyand Paris. The deal to open Euro Disney occurred in 1987, and the park opened its doors outside Paris in 1992. Disney's management thought Europeans would go goofy over the new park, but trouble soon began. The number of visitors never met expectations, in part because the company priced tickets too high. Disney also decided not to serve alcohol in a country that was accustomed to wine with meals. French labor inspectors fought Disney's strict dress codes, and so on.

After several years of operations, the park began serving wine in its restaurants, lowered ticket prices, and made other adjustments. In other words, management exercised its option to reformulate the product. The park began to make a small profit. Then the company exercised the option to expand by adding a "second gate," which was another theme park next to Euro Disney named Walt Disney Studios. The second gate was intended to encourage visitors to extend their stays. But the new park flopped. The reasons ranged from high ticket prices, attractions geared toward Hollywood rather than European filmmaking, labor strikes in Paris, and a summer heat wave.

By the summer of 2003, Euro Disney was close to bankruptcy again. Executives discussed an array of options. These options ranged from letting the company go broke (the option to abandon) to pulling the Disney name from the park. In 2005, the company finally agreed to a restructuring with the help of the French government. While the company earned a profit for several years, in 2017, Disney announced a €1 billion (₹1.25 billion) bailout plan of its subsidiary, which had debt of 15 times earnings.

The whole idea of managerial options was summed up aptly by Jay Rasulo, the overseer of Disney's theme parks, when he said, "One thing we know for sure is that you never get it 100 percent right the first time. We open every one of our parks with the notion that we're going to add content."

Abandonment was very much a consideration for pharmaceutical companies during 2020. Most pharmaceutical companies were trying to design a COVID-19 vaccine. And even though several made it to market, many others never did. It costs ₹2.6 billion, on average, to bring a new drug to market, a huge expense. A major reason is that hundreds of new therapies are started, but only 12 percent of the new drugs that start clinical trials ever make it to market, while others never even make it to trials. It is even worse for oncology treatments, with 97 percent never making it to market.

Abhijeet Group initiated the Chandwa Power Project, referred to as Matrishri Usha Jayaswal Thermal Power Plant, a proposed coal-fired power station in Jharkhand. It was 1,080 MW power plant involving a capex of ₹5,000 crore in Latehar district with lending from a consortium of bankers led by the State Bank of India. The location had abundant coal and water and a rail track was set to run through the premises. However, the construction work had to be suspended due to strong public opposition. In 2018, the project was abandoned. Similarly, the Coca Cola Company had to shut down (or abandon) their bottling plants in Rajasthan, Uttar Pradesh, Tamil Nadu and Uttarakhand due to community protests and shortage of natural resources. Recently, villagers in Kerala protested to halt the construction of $900 million Vizhinjam port project by India's Adani Group.

TIMING OPTIONS

One often finds urban land that has been vacant for many years. Yet this land is bought and sold from time to time. Why would anyone pay a positive price for land that has no source of revenue? Certainly, one could not arrive at a positive price through NPV analysis. The paradox can easily be explained in terms of real options.

Suppose that the land's highest and best use is as an office building. Total construction costs for the building are estimated to be ₹1 million. Currently, net rents (after all costs) are estimated to be ₹90,000 per year in perpetuity, and the discount rate is 10 percent. The NPV of this proposed building would be:

$$-₹1 \text{ million} + ₹90{,}000/.10 = -₹100{,}000$$

Because this NPV is negative, one would not currently want to build. However, suppose that the federal government is planning various urban revitalization programs for the city. Office rents will likely increase if the programs succeed. In this case, the property's owner might want to erect the office building after all. Conversely, office rents will remain the same, or even fall, if the programs fail. The owner will not build in this case.

We say that the property owner has a *timing option*. Although she does not currently want to build, she will want to build in the future should rents in the area rise substantially. This timing option explains why vacant land often has value. There are costs, such as taxes, from holding raw land, but the value of an office building after a substantial rise in rents may more than offset these holding costs. Of course, the exact value of the vacant land depends on both the probability of success in the revitalization program and the extent of the rent increase. Figure 7.7 illustrates this timing option.

Mining operations almost always provide timing options, as well. Suppose you own a copper mine where the cost of mining each ton of copper exceeds the sales revenue. It's a no-brainer to say that you would not want to mine the copper currently. And because there are costs of ownership such as property taxes, insurance, and security, you actually might want to pay someone to take the mine off your hands. However, we would caution you not to do so hastily. Copper prices in the future might increase enough so that production is profitable. Given that possibility, you could likely find someone who would pay a positive price for the property today.

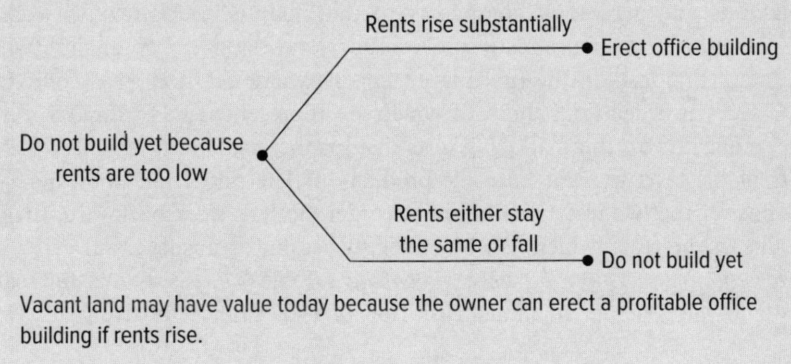

Vacant land may have value today because the owner can erect a profitable office building if rents rise.

Figure 7.7 Decision Tree for Vacant Land

The Indian power sector has a plethora of examples, both classic and recent. For instance, SJVN, a state-owned hydel power player, has about eight approved hydel power plant proposals, including a few in cross-border nations (Bhutan and Nepal), as per its FY2020 annual report. These long-due projects are stuck due to lack of viability clarity. Since 2010, the Indian government has cleared numerous super thermal power plants. Like most power projects, the project involving SREI group's 450 MW thermal power project in West Bengal had been inordinately delayed due to the promoters using the timing option, i.e., the option to abandon. Similarly, most of the approved super thermal power projects of many private operators are yet to see the light of day for the same reason. Of course, all investors have the right to reconsider their investments, and finally, entrepreneurial capitalism is also about picking up such smart timing options by investing the minor sunk costs in picking up the real option.

7.4 Decision Trees

Excel Master coverage online

As shown in the previous section, managers adjust their decisions on the basis of new information. For example, a project may be expanded if early experience is promising, whereas the same project might be abandoned in the wake of bad results. As we said earlier, the choices available to managers are called *real options* and an individual project often can be viewed as a series of real options, leading to valuation approaches beyond the basic present value methodology of earlier chapters.

Earlier in this chapter, we considered Surya Electronics Corporation's (SEC's) surya-powered jet engine project, with cash flows as shown in Table 7.1. In that example, SEC planned to invest ₹1,500 million at Year 1 and expected to receive ₹900 million per year in each of the next five years. Our calculations showed an NPV of ₹1,518 million, so the firm would presumably want to go ahead with the project.

To illustrate decision trees in more detail, let's move back one year to Year 0, when SEC's decision was more complicated. At that time, the engineering group had developed the technology for a surya-powered jet engine, but test marketing had not begun. The marketing department proposed that SEC develop some prototypes and conduct test marketing of the engine. A corporate planning group, including representatives from production, marketing, and engineering, estimated that this preliminary phase would take a year and cost ₹100 million. Furthermore, the group believed there was a 75 percent chance that the marketing tests would prove successful. After completion of the marketing tests, SEC would decide whether to engage in full-scale production, necessitating the investment of ₹1,500 million.

The marketing tests add a layer of complexity to the analysis. Our previous work on the example assumed that the marketing tests had already proved successful. How do we analyze whether we want to go ahead with the marketing tests in the first place? This is where decision trees come in.

To recap, SEC faces two decisions, both of which are represented in Figure 7.8. First, the firm must decide whether to go ahead with the marketing tests. And if the tests are performed, the firm must decide whether the results of the tests warrant full-scale production. The important point here, as we will see, is that decision trees answer the two questions in reverse order. So let's work backward, first considering what to do with the results of the tests, which can be either successful or unsuccessful.

Assume tests have been successful (75 percent probability). Table 7.1 tells us that full-scale production will cost ₹1,500 million and will generate an annual cash flow of ₹900 million for five years, yielding an NPV of:

$$\begin{aligned} \text{NPV} &= -₹1{,}500 + \sum_{t=1}^{5} \frac{₹900}{1.15^t} \\ &= -₹1{,}500 + ₹900 \times \text{PVIFA}_{15\%,5} \\ &= ₹1{,}518 \end{aligned}$$

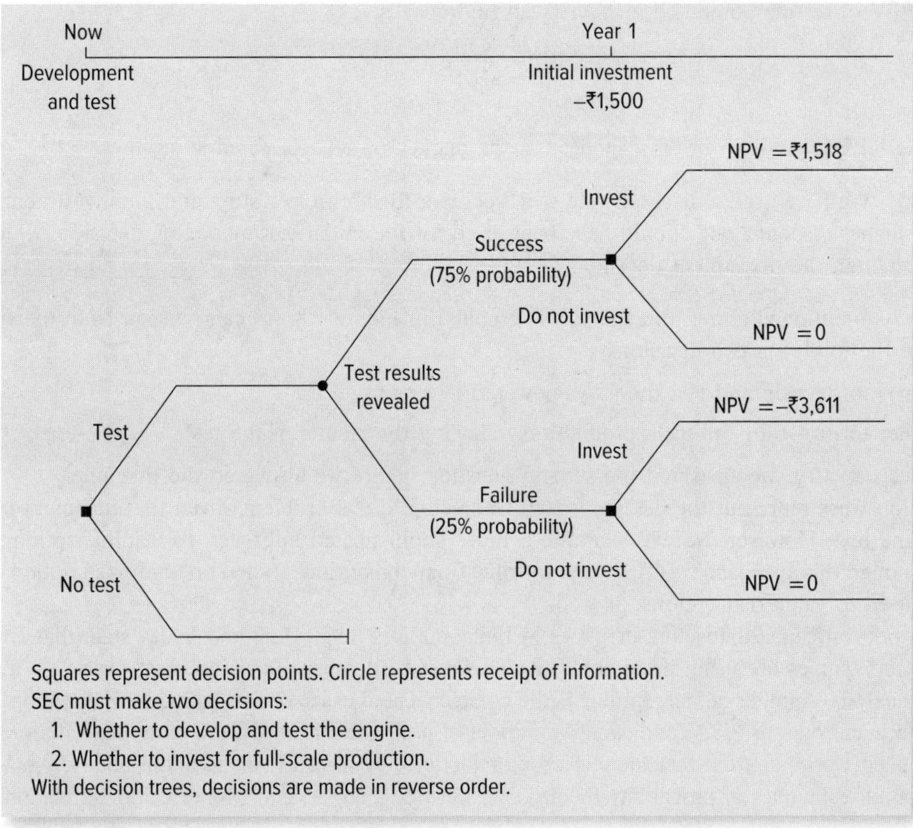

Figure 7.8 Decision Tree for SEC (in millions)

Because the NPV is positive, successful marketing tests should lead to full-scale production. (Note that the NPV is calculated as of Year 1, the time at which the investment of ₹1,500 million is made. Later we will discount this number back to Year 0, when the decision on test marketing is to be made.)

Assume tests have not been successful (25 percent probability). Here, SEC's ₹1,500 million investment would produce an NPV of −₹3,611 million, calculated as of Year 1. (To save space, we will not provide the raw numbers leading to this calculation.) Because the NPV here is negative, SEC will not want full-scale production if the marketing tests are unsuccessful.

Decision on marketing tests. Now we know what to do with the results of the marketing tests. Let's use these results to move back one year. That is, we now want to figure out whether SEC should invest ₹100 million for the test marketing costs in the first place.

The expected payoff evaluated at Year 1 (in millions) is:

$$\frac{\text{Expected}}{\text{payoff}} = \left(\begin{array}{c}\text{Probability}\\\text{of}\\\text{success}\end{array} \times \begin{array}{c}\text{Payoff}\\\text{if}\\\text{successful}\end{array}\right) + \left(\begin{array}{c}\text{Probability}\\\text{of}\\\text{failure}\end{array} \times \begin{array}{c}\text{Payoff}\\\text{if}\\\text{failure}\end{array}\right)$$

$$= (.75 \times ₹1{,}518) + (.25 \times ₹0)$$

$$= ₹1{,}139$$

The NPV of testing computed at Year 0 (in millions) is:

$$\text{NPV} = -₹100 + \frac{₹1{,}139}{1.15}$$
$$= ₹890$$

Because the NPV is positive, the firm should test the market for surya-powered jet engines.

Warning We have used a discount rate of 15 percent for both the testing and the investment decisions. Perhaps a higher discount rate should have been used for the initial test marketing decision, which is likely to be riskier than the investment decision.

Recap As mentioned above, the analysis is graphed in Figure 7.8. As can be seen from the figure, SEC must make the following two decisions:

1. Whether to develop and test the surya-powered jet engine.
2. Whether to invest for full-scale production following the results of the test.

Using a decision tree, we answered the second question before we answered the first one.

Decision trees represent the best approach to solving SEC's problem, given the information presented so far in the text. However, we will examine a more sophisticated approach to valuing options in a later chapter. Though this approach was first used to value financial options traded on organized option exchanges, it can be used to value real options, as well.

In a work[7] on capital budgeting practices in India, authors Singh, Jain and Yadav state that an increasing number of companies are using more sophisticated DCF techniques. To assess risk, over 96% make use of sensitivity analysis. Another notable finding is the emergence and usage of new techniques of real options (50%) and abandonment options (18%), indicating high level of professionalism. On the other hand, Batra and Verma (2017)[8] in their work point out that there is strong reluctance by Indian firms to adopt relatively new and theoretically sound techniques of probability theory, decision tree analysis, and Monte Carlo simulation.

[7]Shveta Singh, P.K. Jain, & Surendra S. Yadav (2012). "Capital budgeting decisions: evidence from India", *Journal of Advances in Management Research,* Vol. 9, Iss: 1, pp.96-112.

[8]Batra, Roopali, & Satish Verma. "Capital budgeting practices in Indian companies." *IIMB Management Review,* 29.1 (2017): 29-44.

RESEARCH IN EMERGING MARKET CONTEXT

According to Singh et al. (2012), a study on capital budgeting methods in India, more businesses are utilizing advanced DCF approaches. More than 96% of respondents employ sensitivity analysis to evaluate risk. Developing and applying novel real options (50%) and abandoning options (18%) procedures, demonstrating a high degree of expertise, is another noteworthy learning. However, Batra and Verma (2017) note in their research that Indian businesses are hesitant to embrace theoretically sound, relatively new methodologies in probability theory, decision tree analysis, and Monte Carlo simulation.

References

Batra, Roopali, and Satish Verma, (2017), Capital budgeting practices in Indian companies, *IIMB Management Review* 29.1 (2017): 29–44.

Shveta Singh, P.K. Jain, Surendra S. Yadav, (2012) "Capital budgeting decisions: evidence from India", *Journal of Advances in Management Research*, Vol. 9 Iss: 1, pp. 96–112.

Summary and Conclusions

This chapter discussed a number of practical applications of capital budgeting.

1. Though NPV is the best capital budgeting approach conceptually, it has been criticized in practice for giving managers a false sense of security. Sensitivity analysis shows NPV under varying assumptions, giving managers a better feel for the project's risks. Unfortunately, sensitivity analysis modifies only one variable at a time, but many variables are likely to vary together in the real world. Scenario analysis examines a project's performance under different scenarios (such as war breaking out or oil prices skyrocketing). Finally, managers want to know how bad forecasts must be before a project loses money. Break-even analysis calculates the sales figure at which the project breaks even. Though break-even analysis is frequently performed on an accounting profit basis, we suggest that a net present value basis is more appropriate.
2. Monte Carlo simulation begins with a model of the firm's cash flows, based on both the interactions between different variables and the movement of each individual variable over time. Random sampling generates a distribution of these cash flows for each period, leading to a net present value calculation.
3. We analyzed the hidden options in capital budgeting, such as the option to expand, the option to abandon, and timing options.
4. Decision trees represent an approach for valuing projects with these hidden, or real, options.

Concept Questions

1. **Forecasting Risk** What is forecasting risk? In general, would the degree of forecasting risk be greater for a new product or a cost-cutting proposal? Why?
2. **Sensitivity Analysis and Scenario Analysis** What is the essential difference between sensitivity analysis and scenario analysis?
3. **Marginal Cash Flows** A co-worker claims that looking at so much marginal this and incremental that is a bunch of nonsense, and states, "Listen, if our average revenue doesn't exceed our average cost, then we will have a negative cash flow, and we will go broke!" How do you respond?
4. **Break-Even Point** As a shareholder of a firm that is contemplating a new project, would you be more concerned with the accounting break-even point, the cash break-even point (the point at which operating cash flow is zero), or the financial break-even point? Why?
5. **Break-Even Point** Assume a firm is considering a new typical project that requires an initial investment with sales, variable costs, and fixed costs over its life. Will the project usually reach the accounting, cash, or financial break-even point first? Which will it reach next? Last? Will this order always apply?
6. **Real Options** Why does traditional NPV analysis tend to underestimate the true value of a capital budgeting project?
7. **Real Options** The Mango Republic has liberalized its markets and is now permitting foreign investors. Tesla Manufacturing has analyzed starting a project in the country and has determined that the project has a negative NPV. Why might the company go ahead with the project? What type of option is most likely to add value to this project?
8. **Sensitivity and Break-Even Analysis** How does sensitivity analysis interact with break-even analysis?
9. **Option to Wait** An option often can have more than one source of value. Consider a logging company. The company can log the timber today or wait another year (or more) to log the timber. What advantages would waiting one year potentially have?

10. **Project Analysis** You are discussing a project analysis with a co-worker. The project involves real options, such as expanding the project if successful or abandoning the project if it fails. Your co-worker makes the following statement: "This analysis is ridiculous. We looked at expanding or abandoning the project in two years, but there are many other options we should consider. For example, we could expand in one year and expand further in two years. Or we could expand in one year and abandon the project in two years. There are too many options for us to examine. Because of this, anything this analysis would give us is worthless." How would you evaluate this statement? Considering that with any capital budgeting project there are an infinite number of real options, when do you stop the option analysis on an individual project?

Questions and Problems

BASIC (Questions 1–10)

1. **Sensitivity Analysis and Break-Even Point** We are evaluating a project that costs ₹845,000, has an eight-year life, and has no salvage value. Assume that depreciation is straight-line to zero over the life of the project. Sales are projected at 51,000 units per year. Price per unit is ₹53, variable cost per unit is ₹27, and fixed costs are ₹950,000 per year. The tax rate is 22 percent, and we require a return of 10 percent on this project.
   a. Calculate the accounting break-even point.
   b. Calculate the base-case cash flow and NPV. What is the sensitivity of NPV to changes in the sales figure? Explain what your answer tells you about a 500-unit decrease in projected sales.
   c. What is the sensitivity of OCF to changes in the variable cost figure? Explain what your answer tells you about a ₹1 decrease in estimated variable costs.

2. **Scenario Analysis** In the previous problem, suppose the projections given for price, quantity, variable costs, and fixed costs are all accurate to within ±10 percent. Calculate the best-case and worst-case NPV figures.

3. **Calculating Break-Even** In each of the following cases, find the unknown variable.

Accounting Break-Even	Unit Price	Unit Variable Cost	Fixed Costs	Depreciation
143,286	₹39	₹30	₹ 820,000	?
104,300	?	27	2,320,000	₹975,000
24,640	92	?	237,000	128,700

4. **Financial Break-Even** Ayden's Toys, Inc., purchased a ₹485,000 machine to produce toy cars. The machine will be fully depreciated by the straight-line method over its five-year economic life. Each toy sells for ₹19. The variable cost per toy is ₹6 and the firm incurs fixed costs of ₹310,000 per year. The corporate tax rate for the company is 24 percent. The appropriate discount rate is 12 percent. What is the financial break-even point for the project?

5. **Option to Wait** Your company is deciding whether to invest in a new machine. The new machine will increase cash flow by ₹485,000 per year. You believe the technology used in the machine has a 10-year life; in other words, no matter when you purchase the machine, it will be obsolete 10 years from today. The machine is currently priced at ₹2.95 million. The cost of the machine will decline by ₹315,000 per year until it reaches ₹1.375 million, where it will remain. If your required return is 8 percent, should you purchase the machine? If so, when should you purchase it?

6. **Decision Trees** Ang Electronics, Inc., has developed a new mesh network. If successful, the present value of the payoff (when the product is brought to market) is ₹29 million. If the mesh network fails, the present value of the payoff is ₹9.2 million. If the product goes directly to market, there is a 50 percent chance of success. Alternatively,

the company can delay the launch by one year and spend ₹2.1 million to test market the mesh network. Test marketing would allow the firm to improve the product and increase the probability of success to 80 percent. The appropriate discount rate is 11 percent. Should the firm conduct test marketing?

7. **Decision Trees** The manager for a growing firm is considering the launch of a new product. If the product goes directly to market, there is a 50 percent chance of success. For ₹175,000 the manager can conduct a focus group that will increase the product's chance of success to 65 percent. Alternatively, the manager has the option to pay a consulting firm ₹375,000 to research the market and refine the product. The consulting firm successfully launches new products 80 percent of the time. If the firm successfully launches the product, the payoff will be ₹2.3 million. If the product is a failure, the NPV is zero. Which action will result in the highest expected payoff to the firm?

8. **Decision Trees** B&B has a new baby powder ready to market. If the firm goes directly to market with the product, there is only a 55 percent chance of success. However, the firm can conduct customer segment research, which will take a year and cost ₹945,000. By going through research, B&B will be able to better target potential customers and will increase the probability of success to 70 percent. If successful, the baby powder will bring a present value profit (at time of initial selling) of ₹17.1 million. If unsuccessful, the present value payoff is ₹7.9 million. Should the firm conduct customer segment research or go directly to market? The appropriate discount rate is 13 percent.

9. **Financial Break-Even Analysis** You are considering investing in a company that cultivates abalone to sell to local restaurants. Use the following information:

Sales price per abalone	= ₹45
Variable costs per abalone	= ₹10.95
Fixed costs per year	= ₹475,000
Depreciation per year	= ₹135,000
Tax rate	= 21%

The discount rate for the company is 15 percent, the initial investment in equipment is ₹945,000, and the project's economic life is seven years. Assume the equipment is depreciated on a straight-line basis over the project's life and has no salvage value.

a. What is the accounting break-even level for the project?
b. What is the financial break-even level for the project?

10. **Financial Break-Even** Martinez, Inc., has purchased a brand new machine to produce its High Flight line of shoes. The machine has an economic life of five years. The depreciation schedule for the machine is straight-line with no salvage value. The machine costs ₹480,000. The sales price per pair of shoes is ₹71, while the variable cost is ₹28. Fixed costs of ₹295,000 per year are attributed to the machine. The corporate tax rate is 21 percent and the appropriate discount rate is 8 percent. What is the financial break-even point?

INTERMEDIATE (Questions 11–25)

11. **Break-Even Intuition** Consider a project with a required return of R percent that costs ₹I and will last for N years. The project uses straight-line depreciation to zero over the N-year life; there are no salvage value or net working capital requirements.

a. At the accounting break-even level of output, what is the IRR of this project? The payback period? The NPV?
b. At the cash break-even level of output, what is the IRR of this project? The payback period? The NPV?
c. At the financial break-even level of output, what is the IRR of this project? The payback period? The NPV?

12. **Sensitivity Analysis** Consider a project with the following information: Initial fixed asset investment = ₹655,000; straight-line depreciation to zero over the four-year life; zero salvage value; price = ₹28; variable costs = ₹16; fixed costs = ₹245,000; quantity sold = 61,000 units; tax rate = 21 percent. How sensitive is OCF to changes in quantity sold?

13. **Project Analysis** You are considering a new product launch. The project will cost ₹1.675 million, have a four-year life, and have no salvage value; depreciation is straight-line to zero. Sales are projected at 195 units per year; price per unit will be ₹16,300; variable cost per unit will be ₹9,400; and fixed costs will be ₹550,000 per year. The required return on the project is 12 percent and the relevant tax rate is 21 percent.

   a. Based on your experience, you think the unit sales, variable cost, and fixed cost projections given here are probably accurate to within ±10 percent. What are the upper and lower bounds for these projections? What is the base-case NPV? What are the best-case and worst-case scenarios?
   b. Evaluate the sensitivity of your base-case NPV to changes in fixed costs.
   c. What is the accounting break-even level of output for this project?

14. **Project Analysis** McGilla Golf has decided to sell a new line of golf clubs. The clubs will sell for ₹815 per set and have a variable cost of ₹365 per set. The company has spent ₹150,000 for a marketing study that determined the company will sell 55,000 sets per year for seven years. The marketing study also determined that the company will lose sales of 10,000 sets of its high-priced clubs. The high-priced clubs sell at ₹1,345 and have variable costs of ₹730. The company will also increase sales of its cheap clubs by 12,000 sets. The cheap clubs sell for ₹445 and have variable costs of ₹210 per set. The fixed costs each year will be ₹9.45 million. The company has also spent ₹1 million on research and development for the new clubs. The plant and equipment required will cost ₹39.2 million and will be depreciated on a straight-line basis. The new clubs will also require an increase in net working capital of ₹1.85 million that will be returned at the end of the project. The tax rate is 25 percent, and the cost of capital is 10 percent. Calculate the payback period, the NPV, and the IRR.

15. **Scenario Analysis** In the previous problem, you feel that the values are accurate to within only ±10 percent. What are the best-case and worst-case NPVs? (*Hint*: The price and variable costs for the two existing sets of clubs are known with certainty; only the sales gained or lost are uncertain.)

16. **Sensitivity Analysis** McGilla Golf would like to know the sensitivity of NPV to changes in the price of the new clubs and the quantity of new clubs sold. What is the sensitivity of the NPV to each of these variables?

17. **Abandonment Value** We are examining a new project. We expect to sell 7,400 units per year at ₹59 net cash flow apiece for the next 10 years. In other words, the annual operating cash flow is projected to be ₹59 × 7,400 = ₹436,600. The relevant discount rate is 14 percent and the initial investment required is ₹1.9 million.

   a. What is the base-case NPV?
   b. After the first year, the project can be dismantled and sold for ₹1.1 million. If expected sales are revised based on the first year's performance, when would it make sense to abandon the investment? In other words, at what level of expected sales would it make sense to abandon the project?
   c. Explain how the ₹1.1 million abandonment value can be viewed as the opportunity cost of keeping the project in one year.

18. **Abandonment** In Problem 17, suppose you think it is likely that expected sales will be revised upward to 11,400 units if the first year is a success and revised downward to 3,500 units if the first year is not a success.

   a. If success and failure are equally likely, what is the NPV of the project? Consider the possibility of abandonment in answering.
   b. What is the value of the option to abandon?

19. **Abandonment and Expansion** In Problem 18, suppose the scale of the project can be doubled in one year in the sense that twice as many units can be produced and sold. Naturally, expansion would be desirable only if the project were a success. This implies that if the project is a success, projected sales after expansion will be 22,800. Again assuming that success and failure are equally likely, what is the NPV of the project? Note that abandonment is still an option if the project is a failure. What is the value of the option to expand?

20. **Break-Even Analysis** Your buddy comes to you with a sure-fire way to make some quick money and help pay off your student loans. His idea is to sell T-shirts with the words "I get" on them. "You get it?" He says, "You see all those bumper stickers and T-shirts that say 'got milk' or 'got surf.' So this says, 'I get.' It's funny! All we have to do is buy a used silk screen press for ₹8,900 and we are in business!" Assume there are no fixed costs and you depreciate the ₹8,900 in the first period. The tax rate is 21 percent.

    a. What is the accounting break-even point if each shirt costs ₹3.75 to make and you can sell them for ₹16 apiece?

    Now assume one year has passed and you have sold 5,000 shirts! You find out that the Dairy Farmers of America have copyrighted the "got milk" slogan and are requiring you to pay ₹25,000 to continue operations. You expect this craze will last for another three years and that your discount rate is 12 percent.

    b. What is the financial break-even point for your enterprise now?

21. **Decision Trees** Young screenwriter Carl Draper has just finished his first script. It has action, drama, and humor, and he thinks it will be a blockbuster. He takes the script to every motion picture studio in town and tries to sell it but to no avail. Finally, ACME studios offers to buy the script for either ₹30,000 today or 1.25 percent of the movie's profits. There are two decisions the studio will have to make. The first is to decide if the script is good or bad; the second is to decide if the movie is good or bad. First, there is a 90 percent chance that the script is bad. If it is bad, the studio does nothing more and throws the script out. If the script is good, it will shoot the movie. After the movie is shot, the studio will review it, and there is a 60 percent chance that the movie is bad. If the movie is bad, the movie will not be promoted and will not turn a profit. If the movie is good, the studio will promote it heavily; the average profit for this type of movie is ₹55 million. Carl rejects the ₹30,000 and says he wants the 1.25 percent of profits. Was this a good decision by Carl?

22. **Option to Wait** Hickock Mining is evaluating when to open a gold mine. The mine has 34,400 ounces of gold left that can be mined and mining operations will produce 4,300 ounces per year. The required return on the gold mine is 12 percent and it will cost ₹18.2 million to open the mine. When the mine is opened, the company will sign a contract that will guarantee the price of gold for the remaining life of the mine. If the mine is opened today, each ounce of gold will generate an aftertax cash flow of ₹1,025 per ounce. If the company waits one year, there is a 60 percent probability that the contract price will generate an aftertax cash flow of ₹1,350 per ounce and a 40 percent probability that the aftertax cash flow will be ₹940 per ounce. What is the value of the option to wait?

23. **Abandonment Decisions** Halloween, Inc., is considering a new product launch. The firm expects to have an annual operating cash flow of ₹6.9 million for the next 10 years. The discount rate for this project is 13 percent. The initial investment is ₹31 million. Assume that the project has no salvage value at the end of its economic life.
    a. What is the NPV of the new product?
    b. After the first year, the project can be dismantled and sold for ₹24 million. If the estimates of remaining cash flows are revised based on the first year's experience, at what level of expected cash flows does it make sense to abandon the project?

24. **Expansion Decisions** Herjavec Enterprises is thinking about introducing a new surface cleaning machine. The marketing department has come up with the estimate that the company can sell 20 units per year at ₹195,000 net cash flow per unit for the next five years. The engineering department has come up with the estimate that developing the machine will take a ₹14.5 million initial investment. The finance department has estimated that a discount rate of 11 percent should be used.
    a. What is the base-case NPV?
    b. If unsuccessful, after the first year, the project can be dismantled and will have an aftertax salvage value of ₹10.4 million. Also, after the first year, expected cash flows will be revised up to 30 units per year or down to 0 units with equal probability. What is the revised NPV?

25. **Scenario Analysis** You are the financial analyst for a tennis racket manufacturer. The company is considering using a graphitelike material in its tennis rackets. The company has estimated the information in the following table about the market for a racket with the new material. The company expects to sell the racket for six years. The equipment required for the project will be depreciated on a straight-line basis and has no salvage value. The required return for projects of this type is 13 percent and the company has a 21 percent tax rate. Should you recommend the project?

	Pessimistic	Expected	Optimistic
Market size	90,000	100,000	112,000
Market share	20%	23%	25%
Selling price	₹ 149	₹ 153	₹ 157
Variable costs per unit	₹ 82	₹ 78	₹ 75
Fixed costs per year	₹ 980,000	₹ 925,000	₹ 885,000
Initial investment	₹2,200,000	₹2,050,000	₹1,950,000

CHALLENGE (Questions 26–30)

26. **Scenario Analysis** Consider a project to supply Detroit with 20,000 tons of machine screws annually for automobile production. You will need an initial ₹3.1 million investment in threading equipment to get the project started; the project will last for five years. The accounting department estimates that annual fixed costs will be ₹925,000 and that variable costs should be ₹185 per ton; accounting will depreciate the initial fixed asset investment straight-line to zero over the five-year project life. It also estimates a salvage value of ₹400,000 after dismantling costs. The marketing department estimates that the automakers will let the contract at a selling price of ₹295 per ton. The engineering department estimates you will need an initial net working capital investment of ₹380,000. You require a return of 13 percent and face a tax rate of 22 percent on this project.

    a. What is the estimated OCF for this project? The NPV? Should you pursue this project?

    b. Suppose you believe that the accounting department's initial cost and salvage value projections are accurate only to within ±15 percent; the marketing department's price estimate is accurate only to within ±10 percent; and the engineering department's net working capital estimate is accurate only to within ±5 percent. What is your worst-case scenario for this project? Your best-case scenario? Do you still want to pursue the project?

27. **Sensitivity Analysis** In Problem 26, suppose you're confident about your own projections, but you're a little unsure about Detroit's actual machine screw requirements. What is the sensitivity of the project OCF to changes in the quantity supplied? What about the sensitivity of NPV to changes in quantity supplied? Given the sensitivity number you calculated, is there some minimum level of output below which you wouldn't want to operate? Why?

28. **Abandonment Decisions** Consider the following project of Hand Clapper, Inc. The company is considering a four-year project to manufacture clap-command garage door openers. This project requires an initial investment of ₹12 million that will be depreciated straight-line to zero over the project's life. An initial investment in net working capital of ₹900,000 is required to support spare parts inventory; this cost is fully recoverable whenever the project ends. The company believes it can generate ₹9.1 million in pretax revenues with ₹3.7 million in total pretax operating costs. The tax rate is 21 percent and the discount rate is 13 percent. The market value of the equipment over the life of the project is as follows:

Year	Market Value (in millions)
1	₹8.1
2	6.2
3	4.8
4	0

a. Assuming the company operates this project for four years, what is the NPV?

b. Now compute the project NPVs assuming the project is abandoned after only one year, after two years, and after three years. What economic life for this project maximizes its value to the firm? What does this problem tell you about not considering abandonment possibilities when evaluating projects?

29. Abandonment Decisions M.V.P. Games, Inc., has hired you to perform a feasibility study of a new video game that requires an initial investment of ₹8.9 million. The company expects a total annual operating cash flow of ₹1.6 million for the next 10 years. The relevant discount rate is 10 percent. Cash flows occur at year-end.

a. What is the NPV of the new video game?

b. After one year, the estimate of remaining annual cash flows will be revised either upward to ₹2.81 million or downward to ₹385,000. Each revision has an equal probability of occurring. At that time, the video game project can be sold for ₹2.9 million. What is the revised NPV given that the firm can abandon the project after one year?

30. Financial Break-Even The Cornchopper Company is considering the purchase of a new harvester. Cornchopper has hired you to determine the break-even purchase price in terms of present value of the harvester. This break-even purchase price is the price at which the project's NPV is zero. Base your analysis on the following facts:

- The new harvester is not expected to affect revenue, but pretax operating expenses will be reduced by ₹13,000 per year for 10 years.
- The old harvester is now 5 years old, with 10 years of its scheduled life remaining. It was originally purchased for ₹65,000 and has been depreciated by the straight-line method.
- The old harvester can be sold for ₹21,000 today.
- The new harvester will be depreciated by the straight-line method over its 10-year life.
- The corporate tax rate is 22 percent.
- The firm's required rate of return is 15 percent.
- The initial investment, the proceeds from selling the old harvester, and any resulting tax effects occur immediately.
- All other cash flows occur at year-end.
- The market value of each harvester at the end of its economic life is zero.

Excel Master It! Problem

Dahlia Simmons, CFO of Ulrich Enterprises, is analyzing a new project to sell surya-powered batteries for cell phones. Dahlia has estimated the following probability distributions for the variables in the project:

Excel Master coverage online

Probability	10%	30%	40%	20%		
Industry demand	80,000,000	95,000,000	108,000,000	124,000,000		
Probability	5%	20%	20%	25%	20%	10%
Ulrich market share	1%	2%	3%	4%	5%	6%
Probability	20%	70%	10%			
Initial cost	₹60,000,000	₹65,000,000	₹72,000,000			
Probability	20%	65%	15%			
VC per unit	₹24	₹26	₹29			
Probability	15%	25%	40%	20%		
Fixed costs	₹20,000,000	₹24,000,000	₹27,000,000	₹31,000,000		

The unit price depends on the industry demand because a greater demand will result in a higher price. Dahlia determines that the price per unit will be given by this equation:

Price = Industry demand/2,000,000 +/−₹2

The random "+/−₹2" term represents an increase or decrease in price according to the following distribution:

Probability	45%	55%
Price randomness	−₹2	₹2

The length of the project, tax rate, and required return are:

Project length (years)	6
Tax rate	21%
Required return	14%

Mini Case BUNYAN LUMBER, LLC

a. Create a Monte Carlo simulation for the project with at least 500 runs. Calculate the IRR for each run. Note that the IRR function in Excel will return an error if the IRR of the project is too low. For example, what is the IRR if both the initial cash flow and the operating cash flow are negative? The IRR is less than −100 percent. This is not a problem when you are calculating the IRR one time because you can see the IRR is too low, but when you are running 500 or more iterations, it can create a problem trying to summarize the results. Because of this issue, you should create an IF statement that tests if the operating cash flow divided by the absolute value of the initial investment is less than .1. If this is the case, the cell will return an IRR of −99.99 percent, or else the cell will calculate the IRR.

b. Create a graph of the distribution of the IRRs from the Monte Carlo simulation for different ranges of IRR.

c. Create a graph for the cumulative probability function for the IRR distribution.

Bunyan Lumber, LLC, harvests timber and delivers logs to timber mills for sale. The company was founded 70 years ago by Pete Bunyan. The current CEO is Paula Bunyan, the granddaughter of the founder. The company is currently evaluating a 5,000-acre forest it owns in Oregon. Paula has asked Steve Boles, the company's finance officer, to evaluate the project. Paula's concern is when the company should harvest the timber.

Lumber is sold by the company for its "pond value." Pond value is the amount a mill will pay for a log delivered to the mill location. The price paid for logs delivered to a mill is quoted in rupees per thousands of board feet (MBF), and the price depends on the grade of the logs. The forest Bunyan Lumber is evaluating was planted by the company 20 years ago and is made up entirely of Douglas fir trees. The table here shows the current price per MBF for the three grades of timber the company feels will come from the stand:

Timber Grade	Price per MBF
1P	₹645
2P	620
3P	605

Steve believes that the pond value of lumber will increase at the inflation rate. The company is planning to thin the forest today, and it expects to realize a positive cash flow of ₹1,200 per acre from thinning. The thinning is done to increase the growth rate of the remaining trees, and it is always done 20 years following a planting.

The major decision the company faces is when to log the forest. When the company logs the forest, it will immediately replant saplings, which will allow for a future harvest. The longer the forest is allowed to grow, the larger the harvest becomes per acre. Additionally, an older forest has a higher grade of timber. Steve has compiled the following table with the expected harvest per acre in thousands of board feet, along with the breakdown of the timber grades:

Years from Today to Begin Harvest	Harvest (MBF) per Acre	Timber Grade		
		1P	2P	3P
20	15.1	14%	32%	54%
25	17.4	20	44	36
30	18.2	22	46	32
35	18.9	24	47	29

The company expects to lose 5 percent of the timber it cuts due to defects and breakage.

The forest will be clear-cut when the company harvests the timber. This method of harvesting allows for faster growth of replanted trees. All of the harvesting, processing, replanting, and transportation are to be handled by subcontractors hired by Bunyan Lumber. The cost of the logging is expected to be ₹145 per MBF. A road system has to be constructed and is expected to cost ₹50 per MBF, on average. Sales preparation and administrative costs, excluding office overhead costs, are expected to be ₹18 per MBF.

As soon as the harvesting is complete, the company will reforest the land. Reforesting costs include the following:

	Cost per Acre
Excavator piling	₹155
Broadcast burning	305
Site preparation	150
Planting costs	230

All costs are expected to increase at the inflation rate.

Assume all cash flows occur at the year of harvest. For example, if the company begins harvesting the timber 20 years from today, the cash flow from the harvest will be received 20 years from today. When the company logs the land, it will immediately replant the land with new saplings. The harvest period chosen will be repeated for the foreseeable future. The company's nominal required return is 10 percent and the inflation rate is expected to be 3.7 percent per year. Bunyan Lumber has a 21 percent tax rate.

Clear-cutting is a controversial method of forest management. To obtain the necessary permits, Bunyan Lumber has agreed to contribute to a conservation fund every time it harvests the lumber. If the company harvested the forest today, the required contribution would be ₹500,000. The company has agreed that the required contribution will grow by 3.2 percent per year. When should the company harvest the forest?

8

Interest Rates and Bond Valuation

Generally, when you make an investment, you expect to get back more money in the future than you invested today. In 2019 and 2020, that wasn't the case for many bond investors. In May 2020, the U.K. sold €3.75 billion in three-year bonds with a yield of negative .003 percent. And, in August 2019, the German government sold 30-year bonds that had a yield of negative .11 percent. Investors bought €824 million of these bonds, yet would only get back €795 million in 2050. In fact, more than ₹15 trillion of government debt had negative yields at that time. And negative yields were not restricted to government bonds, as more than ₹1 trillion of corporate bonds also had negative yields. For example, German industrial conglomerate Siemens sold €1.5 billion worth of two-year bonds with a yield of negative .315 percent.

The 10-year government bonds, yield decreased from about 8% in September 2018 (before the IL&FS episode) to about 5.8% in June 2020 (COVID-19 pandemic), indicating a decline of 2.2% or 220 basis points. The period had a lot of negative news of corporate debt market defaults, i.e., IL&FS, DHFL, IndiaBulls Housing Finance and Yes Bank. The trend suggested elevated risk perception and implied heightened risk aversion. Even while this happened, lowering yields resulted in better returns for investors holding bonds. Returns from debt mutual funds, which hold a portfolio of debt securities, ranged in the midteens during this period.

This chapter introduces you to bonds. We first use the techniques shown in Chapter 4 to value bonds. We then discuss bond features and how bonds are bought and sold. One important point is that bond values depend, in large part, on interest rates. We therefore cover the behavior of interest rates in the last section of the chapter.

Please visit us at **rwjcorporatefinance.blogspot.com** for the latest developments in the world of corporate finance.

8.1 Bonds and Bond Valuation

Excel Master coverage online

Corporations (and governments) frequently borrow money by issuing or selling debt securities called bonds. In this section, we describe the various features of corporate bonds. We then discuss the cash flows associated with a bond and how bonds can be valued using our discounted cash flow procedure.

BOND FEATURES AND PRICES

A bond is normally an interest-only loan, meaning that the borrower will pay the interest every period, but none of the principal will be repaid until the end of the loan. A corporate bond is a debt claim issued by firms to raise cash. Corporate bonds have priority over stock, because the firm must first pay interest to its bondholders before it can pay dividends to its stockholders. For this reason, corporate bonds and other forms of debt are considered senior claims and stock is considered the most junior claim.

Suppose the Banaras Corporation wants to borrow ₹1,000 for 30 years. The interest rate on similar debt issued by similar corporations is 12 percent will pay .12 × ₹1,000 = ₹120 in interest every year for 30 years. At the end of 30 years, Banaras will repay the ₹1,000. As this example suggests, a bond is a fairly simple financing arrangement. There is, however, a rich jargon associated with bonds.

In our example, the ₹120 regular interest payments are called the bond's **coupons**. Because the coupon is constant and paid every year, this type of bond is sometimes called a *level coupon bond.* The amount repaid at the end of the loan is called the bond's **face value**, or **par value**. In our example, this par value is ₹1,000, and a bond that sells for its par value is called a *par value bond.* Historically, U.S. corporate bonds had par values of ₹1,000, but par values of ₹2,000 have become common in recent years. Government bonds frequently have much larger face, or par, values. Finally, the annual coupon divided by the face value is called the **coupon rate** on the bond. Because ₹120/₹1,000 = .12, or 12 percent, the Banaras bond has a 12 percent coupon rate.

The number of years until the face value is paid is called the bond's time to **maturity**. A corporate bond will frequently have a maturity of 30 years when it is originally issued, but this varies. Once the bond has been issued, the number of years to maturity declines as time passes.

BOND VALUES AND YIELDS

As time passes, interest rates change in the marketplace. Because the cash flows from a bond stay the same, the value of the bond fluctuates. When interest rates rise, the present value of the bond's remaining cash flows declines, and the bond is worth less. When interest rates fall, the bond is worth more.

To determine the value of a bond at a particular point in time, we need to know the number of periods remaining until maturity, the face value, the coupon, and the market interest rate for bonds with similar features. The interest rate required in the market on a bond is called the bond's **yield to maturity (YTM)**. This rate is sometimes called the bond's *yield* for short. Given all this information, we can calculate the present value of the cash flows as an estimate of the bond's current market value.

Suppose the Gangotri Co. were to issue a bond with 10 years to maturity. The Gangotri bond has an annual coupon of ₹80, implying the bond will pay ₹80 per year for the next 10 years in coupon interest. In addition, Gangotri will pay ₹1,000 to the bondholder in 10 years. The cash flows from the bond are shown in Figure 8.1. As illustrated in the figure, the cash flows have an annuity component (the coupons) and a lump sum (the face value paid at maturity).

Year	0	1	2	3	4	5	6	7	8	9	10
Coupon		₹80	₹80	₹80	₹80	₹80	₹80	₹80	₹80	₹80	₹ 80
Face value											1,000
		₹80	₹80	₹80	₹80	₹80	₹80	₹80	₹80	₹80	₹1,080

The Gangotri bond has an annual coupon of ₹80 and a face, or par, value of ₹1,000 paid at maturity in 10 years.

Figure 8.1 Cash Flows for Gangotri Co. Bond

Assuming similar bonds have a yield of 8 percent, what will this bond sell for? We estimate the market value of the bond by calculating the present value of the two components separately and adding the results together. First, at the going rate of 8 percent, the present value of the ₹1,000 paid in 10 years is:

$$\text{Present value} = ₹1{,}000/1.08^{10} = ₹1{,}000/2.1589 = ₹463.19$$

Second, the bond offers ₹80 per year for 10 years. The present value of this annuity stream is:

$$\begin{aligned}\text{Annuity present value} &= ₹80 \times (1 - 1/1.08^{10})/.08\\ &= ₹80 \times (1 - 1/2.1589)/.08\\ &= ₹80 \times 6.7101\\ &= ₹536.81\end{aligned}$$

We add the values for the two parts together to get the bond's value:

$$\text{Bond value} = ₹463.19 + 536.81 = ₹1{,}000$$

This bond sells for exactly its face value. This is not a coincidence. The going interest rate in the market is 8 percent. Considered as an interest-only loan, what interest rate does this bond have? With an ₹80 coupon, this bond pays exactly 8 percent interest only when it sells for ₹1,000.

To illustrate what happens as interest rates change, suppose that a year has gone by. The Gangotri bond now has 9 years to maturity. If the interest rate in the market has risen to 10 percent, what will the bond be worth? To find out, we repeat the present value calculations with 9 years instead of 10, and a 10 percent yield instead of an 8 percent yield. First, the present value of the ₹1,000 paid in 9 years at 10 percent is:

$$\text{Present value} = ₹1{,}000/1.10^{9} = ₹1{,}000/2.3579 = ₹424.10$$

Second, the bond now offers ₹80 per year for 9 years. The present value of this annuity stream at 10 percent is:

$$\begin{aligned}\text{Annuity present value} &= ₹80 \times (1 - 1/1.10^{9})/.10\\ &= ₹80 \times (1 - 1/2.3579)/.10\\ &= ₹80 \times 5.7590\\ &= ₹460.72\end{aligned}$$

We add the values for the two parts together to get the bond's value:

$$\text{Bond value} = ₹424.10 + 460.72 = ₹884.82$$

Therefore, the bond should sell for about ₹885. In the vernacular, we say that this bond, with its 8 percent coupon, is priced to yield 10 percent at ₹885.

The Gangotri Co. bond now sells for less than its ₹1,000 face value. Why? The market interest rate is 10 percent. Considered as an interest-only loan of ₹1,000, this bond pays only 8 percent, its coupon rate. Because the bond pays less than the going rate, investors are willing to lend only something less than the ₹1,000 promised repayment. Because the bond sells for less than face value, it is said to be a *discount bond.*

A good bond site to visit is **www.bloomberg.com/markets/rates-bonds**, which has loads of useful information.

The only way to get the interest rate up to 10 percent is to lower the price to less than ₹1,000 so that the purchaser, in effect, has a built-in gain. For the Gangotri bond, the price of ₹885 is ₹115 less than the face value, so an investor who purchased and kept the bond would get ₹80 per year and would have a ₹115 gain at maturity as well. This gain compensates the lender for the below-market coupon rate.

Another way to see why the bond is discounted by ₹115 is to note that the ₹80 coupon is ₹20 below the coupon on a newly issued par value bond, based on current market conditions. The bond would be worth

₹1,000 only if it had a coupon of ₹100 per year. In a sense, an investor who buys and keeps the bond gives up ₹20 per year for nine years. At 10 percent, this annuity stream is worth:

$$\begin{aligned}\text{Annuity present value} &= ₹20 \times (1 - 1/1.10^9)/.10 \\ &= ₹20 \times 5.7590 \\ &= ₹115.18\end{aligned}$$

This is the amount of the discount.

What would the Gangotri bond sell for if interest rates had dropped by 2 percent instead of rising by 2 percent? As you might guess, the bond would sell for more than ₹1,000. Such a bond is said to sell at a *premium* and is called a *premium bond.*

This case is the opposite of a discount bond. The Gangotri bond now has a coupon rate of 8 percent when the market rate is only 6 percent. Investors are willing to pay a premium to get this extra coupon amount. In this case, the relevant discount rate is 6 percent and there are nine years remaining. The present value of the ₹1,000 face amount is:

> Online bond calculators are available at **gpi.fidelity.com/ftgw/interfaces/pyc/**; interest rate information is available at **money.cnn.com/data/bonds**, and **www.bankrate.com**.

$$\text{Present value} = ₹1{,}000/1.06^9 = ₹1{,}000/1.6895 = ₹591.90$$

The present value of the coupon stream is:

$$\begin{aligned}\text{Annuity present value} &= ₹80 \times (1 - 1/1.06^9)/.06 \\ &= ₹80 \times (1 - 1/1.6895)/.06 \\ &= ₹80 \times 6.8017 \\ &= ₹544.14\end{aligned}$$

We add the values for the two parts together to get the bond's value:

$$\text{Bond value} = ₹591.90 + 544.14 = ₹1{,}136.03$$

The total bond value is therefore about ₹136 in excess of par value. Once again, we can verify this amount by noting that the coupon is now ₹20 too high based on current market conditions. The present value of ₹20 per year for nine years at 6 percent is:

$$\begin{aligned}\text{Annuity present value} &= ₹20 \times (1 - 1/1.06^9)/.06 \\ &= ₹20 \times 6.8017 \\ &= ₹136.03\end{aligned}$$

This is as we calculated.

Based on our examples, we can now write the general expression for the value of a bond. If a bond has (1) a face value of F paid at maturity, (2) a coupon of C paid per period, (3) t periods to maturity, and (4) a yield of R per period, its value is:

$$\text{Bond value} = C \times \left[1 - 1/(1 + R)^t\right]/R + F/(1 + R)^t$$

$$\text{Bond value} = \begin{array}{c}\text{Present value of the}\\\text{coupons}\end{array} + \begin{array}{c}\text{Present value of}\\\text{the face amount}\end{array} \qquad \textbf{(8.1)}$$

EXAMPLE 8.1

Semiannual Coupons In practice, bonds issued in India and the United States usually make coupon payments twice a year. So, if an ordinary bond has a coupon rate of 14 percent, the owner will receive a total of ₹140 per year, but this ₹140 will come in two payments of ₹70 each.

(continued)

Suppose the yield to maturity on our bond is quoted at 16 percent. Bond yields are quoted as annual percentage rates (APRs); the quoted rate is equal to the actual rate per period multiplied by the number of periods. With a 16 percent quoted yield and semiannual payments, the true yield is 8 percent per six months. If our bond matures in seven years, what is the bond's price? What is the effective annual yield on this bond?

Based on our discussion, we know the bond will sell at a discount because it has a coupon rate of 7 percent every six months when the market requires 8 percent every six months. So, if our answer exceeds ₹1,000, we know that we have made a mistake.

To get the exact price, we first calculate the present value of the bond's face value of ₹1,000 paid in seven years. This seven-year period has 14 periods of six months each. At 8 percent per period, the value is:

$$\text{Present value} = ₹1{,}000/1.08^{14} = ₹1{,}000/2.9372 = ₹340.46$$

The coupons can be viewed as a 14-period annuity of ₹70 per period. At an 8 percent discount rate, the present value of such an annuity is:

$$\begin{aligned}\text{Annuity present value} &= ₹70 \times (1 - 1/1.08^{14})/.08\\ &= ₹70 \times (1 - 1/2.9372)/.08\\ &= ₹70 \times 8.2442\\ &= ₹577.10\end{aligned}$$

The total present value is the bond's price:

$$\text{Bond value} = ₹340.46 + 577.10 = ₹917.56$$

To calculate the effective yield on this bond, note that 8 percent every six months is equivalent to:

$$\text{Effective annual rate} = (1 + .08)^2 - 1 = .1664, \text{ or } 16.64\%$$

The effective yield, therefore, is 16.64 percent.

As we have illustrated in this section, bond prices and interest rates always move in opposite directions. When interest rates rise, a bond's value, like any other present value, declines. Similarly, when interest rates fall, bond values rise. Even if the borrower is certain to make all payments, there is still risk in owning a bond. We discuss this next.

Learn more about bonds at **investorguide.com.**

INTEREST RATE RISK

The risk that arises for bond owners from fluctuating interest rates is called *interest rate risk.* How much interest rate risk a bond has depends on how sensitive its price is to interest rate changes. This sensitivity directly depends on two things: the time to maturity and the coupon rate. As we will see momentarily, you should keep the following in mind when looking at a bond:

1. All other things being equal, the longer the time to maturity, the greater the interest rate risk.
2. All other things being equal, the lower the coupon rate, the greater the interest rate risk.

We illustrate the first of these two points in Figure 8.2. As shown, we compute and plot prices under different interest rate scenarios for 10 percent coupon bonds with maturities of 1 year and 30 years. Notice how the slope of the line connecting the prices is much steeper for the 30-year maturity than it is for the 1-year maturity. This steepness tells us that a relatively small change in interest rates will lead to a

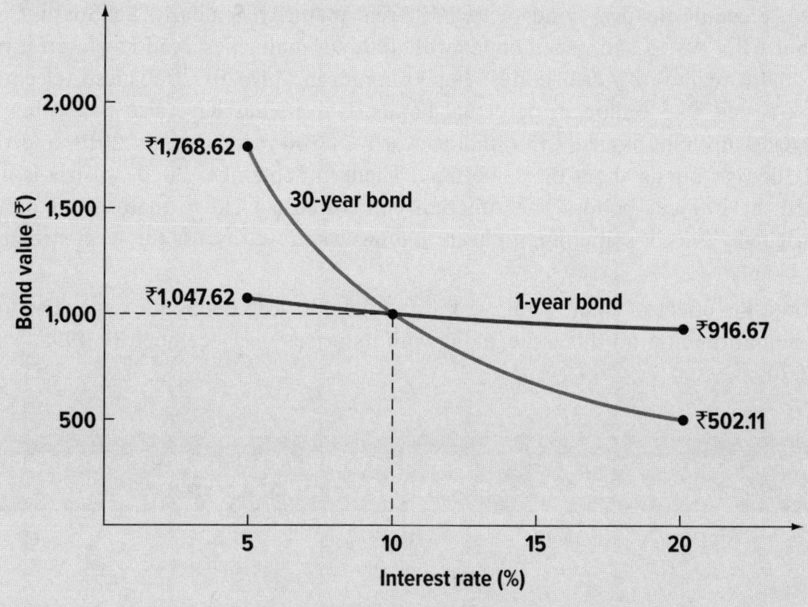

Value of a Bond with a 10 Percent Coupon Rate for Different Interest Rates and Maturities

	Time to Maturity	
Interest Rate	1 Year	30 Years
5%	₹1,047.62	₹1,768.62
10	1,000.00	1,000.00
15	956.52	671.70
20	916.67	502.11

Figure 8.2 Interest Rate Risk and Time to Maturity

substantial change in the bond's value. In comparison, the one-year bond's price is relatively insensitive to interest rate changes.

Intuitively, shorter-term bonds have less interest rate sensitivity because the ₹1,000 face amount is received so quickly. The present value of this amount isn't greatly affected by a small change in interest rates if the amount is received in, say, one year. However, even a small change in the interest rate, once compounded for, say, 30 years, can have a significant effect on present value. As a result, the present value of the face amount will be much more volatile with a longer-term bond.

The other thing to know about interest rate risk is that, like many things in finance and economics, it increases at a decreasing rate. A 10-year bond has much greater interest rate risk than a 1-year bond has. However, a 30-year bond has only slightly greater interest rate risk than a 10-year bond.

The reason that bonds with lower coupons have greater interest rate risk is essentially the same. As we discussed earlier, the value of a bond depends on the present value of both its coupons and its face amount. If two bonds with different coupon rates have the same maturity, the value of the lower-coupon bond is proportionately more dependent on the face amount to be received at maturity. As a result, its value will fluctuate more as interest rates change. Put another way, the bond with the higher coupon has a larger cash flow early in its life, so its value is less sensitive to changes in the discount rate.

Bonds are rarely issued with maturities longer than 30 years, though there are exceptions. In the 1990s, Walt Disney issued "Sleeping Beauty" bonds with a 100-year maturity. Similarly, BellSouth, Coca-Cola, and Dutch banking giant ABN AMRO all issued bonds with 100-year maturities. And low interest rates in recent years have led to more really long-term bonds. For example, in July 2017, Japanese telecommunications company SoftBank issued ₹4.5 billion in perpetual bonds. Universities have also issued long-term bonds. For example, Rutgers University issued ₹330 million worth of 100-year bonds in 2019, and the University of Virginia issued 100-year bonds about the same time. Then, in September 2020, Austria issued €2 billion (₹2.3 billion) worth of 100-year bonds. The Austrian bonds had a yield to maturity of only .88 percent when they were originally issued, something to keep in mind when we discuss the term structure of interest rates later in this chapter.

We can illustrate the effect of interest rate risk using the 100-year BellSouth issue. The following table provides some basic information on this issue, along with its prices on December 31, 1995, March 6, 2009, and August 21, 2020:

Maturity	Coupon Rate	Price on 12/31/95	Price on 3/6/09	Percentage Change in Price 1995–2009	Price on 8/21/20	Percentage Change in Price 2009–2020
2095	7.00%	₹1,000	₹803.43	−19.66%	₹1,529.36	+90.35%

Several things emerge from this table. First, interest rates apparently rose between December 31, 1995, and March 6, 2009 (Why?). The bond first lost 19.66 percent and then gained 90.35 percent.

FINDING THE YIELD TO MATURITY: MORE TRIAL AND ERROR

Frequently, we will know a bond's price, coupon rate, and maturity date, but not its yield to maturity. Suppose we are interested in a six-year, 8 percent coupon bond. A broker quotes a price of ₹955.14. What is the yield on this bond?

We've seen that the price of a bond can be written as the sum of its annuity and lump-sum components. Knowing that there is an ₹80 coupon for six years and a ₹1,000 face value, we can say that the price is:

$$₹955.14 = ₹80 \times \left[1 - 1/\left(1 + R\right)^6\right]/R + ₹1{,}000/(1 + R)^6$$

where R is the unknown discount rate, or yield to maturity. We have one equation here and one unknown, but we cannot solve for R directly without using a financial calculator or a spreadsheet application. Instead, we must use trial and error.

We can speed up the trial-and-error process by using what we know about bond prices and yields. In this case, the bond has an ₹80 coupon and is selling at a discount. We know that the yield is greater than 8 percent. If we calculate the price at 10 percent:

$$\begin{aligned}\text{Bond value} &= ₹80 \times (1 - 1/1.10^6)/.10 + ₹1{,}000/1.10^6 \\ &= ₹80 \times 4.3553 + ₹1{,}000/1.7716 \\ &= ₹912.89\end{aligned}$$

Table 8.1 Summary of Bond Valuation

I. Finding the Value of a Bond

Bond value $= C \times [1 - 1/(1 + R)^t]/R + F/(1 + R)^t$

where
C = Coupon paid each period
R = Discount rate per period
t = Number of periods
F = Bond's face value

II. Finding the Yield on a Bond

Given a bond value, coupon, time to maturity, and face value, one can find the implicit discount rate, or yield to maturity, by trial and error. To do this, try different discount rates until the calculated bond value equals the given value (or let a spreadsheet do it for you). Remember that increasing the rate decreases the bond value.

At 10 percent, the value is lower than the actual price, so 10 percent is too high. The true yield must be somewhere between 8 and 10 percent. At this point, it's "plug and chug" to find the answer. You would probably want to try 9 percent next. If you did, you would see that this is in fact the bond's yield to maturity.

Current market rates are available at **www.bankrate.com**.

A bond's yield to maturity should not be confused with its **current yield**, which is a bond's annual coupon divided by its price. In the present example, the bond's annual coupon is ₹80 and its price is ₹955.14. Given these numbers, we see that the current yield is ₹80/₹955.14 = .0838, or 8.38 percent, which is less than the yield to maturity of 9 percent. The reason the current yield is too low is that it only considers the coupon portion of your return; it doesn't consider the built-in gain from the price discount. For a premium bond, the reverse is true, meaning the current yield would be higher because it ignores the built-in loss.

Our discussion of bond valuation is summarized in Table 8.1. A nearby *Spreadsheet Applications* box shows how to find prices and yields the easy way.

EXAMPLE 8.2

Current Events A bond has a quoted price of ₹1,080.42. It has a face value of ₹1,000, a semiannual coupon of ₹30, and a maturity of five years. What is its current yield? What is its yield to maturity? Which is bigger? Why?

Notice that this bond makes semiannual payments of ₹30, so the annual payment is ₹60. The current yield is ₹60/₹1,080.42 = .0555, or 5.55 percent. To calculate the yield to maturity, refer back to Example 8.1. Now, in this case, the bond pays ₹30 every six months and it has 10 six-month periods until maturity. So, we need to find R as follows:

$$₹1{,}080.42 = ₹30 \times [1 - 1/(1 + R)^{10}]/R + ₹1{,}000/(1 + R)^{10}$$

After some trial and error, we find that R is equal to 2.1 percent. But the tricky part is that this 2.1 percent is the yield per six months. We have to double it to get the yield to maturity, so the yield to maturity is 4.2 percent, which is less than the current yield. Why is the yield to maturity less than the current yield? The reason is that the current yield ignores the built-in loss of the premium between now and maturity.

SPREADSHEET APPLICATIONS

How to Calculate Bond Prices and Yields Using a Spreadsheet

Most spreadsheets have fairly elaborate routines available for calculating bond values and yields; many of these routines involve details that we have not discussed. However, setting up a spreadsheet to calculate prices or yields is straightforward, as our next two spreadsheets show:

	A	B	C	D	E	F	G	H
1								
2	**Using a spreadsheet to calculate bond values**							
3								
4	Suppose we have a bond with 22 years to maturity, a coupon rate of 8 percent, and a yield to							
5	maturity of 9 percent. If the bond makes semiannual payments, what is its price today?							
6								
7	Settlement date:	1/1/20						
8	Maturity date:	1/1/42						
9	Annual coupon rate:	.08						
10	Yield to maturity:	.09						
11	Face value (% of par):	100						
12	Coupons per year:	2						
13	Bond price (% of par):	**90.49**						
14								
15	The formula entered in cell B13 is =PRICE(B7,B8,B9,B10,B11,B12); notice that face value and bond							
16	price are given as a percentage of face value.							

	A	B	C	D	E	F	G	H
1								
2	**Using a spreadsheet to calculate bond yields**							
3								
4	Suppose we have a bond with 22 years to maturity, a coupon rate of 8 percent, and a price of							
5	₹960.17. If the bond makes semiannual payments, what is its yield to maturity?							
6								
7	Settlement date:	1/1/20						
8	Maturity date:	1/1/42						
9	Annual coupon rate:	.08						
10	Bond price (% of par):	96.017						
11	Face value (% of par):	100						
12	Coupons per year:	2						
13	Yield to maturity:	**.084**						
14								
15	The formula entered in cell B13 is =YIELD(B7,B8,B9,B10,B11,B12); notice that face value and bond							
16	price are entered as a percentage of face value.							
17								

In our spreadsheets, notice that we had to enter two dates, a settlement date and a maturity date. The settlement date is the date you actually pay for the bond and the maturity date is the day the bond actually matures. In most of our problems, we don't explicitly have these dates, so we have to make them up. Because our bond has 22 years to maturity, we picked 1/1/2020 (January 1, 2020) as the settlement date and 1/1/2042 (January 1, 2042) as the maturity date. Any two dates would do as long as they are exactly 22 years apart, but these are particularly easy to work with. Finally, notice that we had to enter the coupon rate and yield to maturity in annual terms and then explicitly provide the number of coupon payments per year.

EXAMPLE 8.3

Bond Yields You're looking at two bonds identical in every way except for their coupons and, of course, their prices. Both have 12 years to maturity. The first bond has a 10 percent coupon rate and sells for ₹935.08. The second has a 12 percent coupon rate. What do you think it would sell for?

Because the two bonds are very similar, we assume they will be priced to yield about the same rate. We first need to calculate the yield on the 10 percent coupon bond. Proceeding as before, we know that the yield must be greater than 10 percent because the bond is selling at a discount. The bond has a fairly long maturity of 12 years. We've seen that long-term bond prices are relatively sensitive to interest rate changes, so the yield is probably close to 10 percent. A little trial and error reveals that the yield is actually 11 percent:

$$\begin{aligned}\text{Bond value} &= ₹100 \times (1 - 1/1.11^{12})/.11 + ₹1{,}000/1.11^{12}\\ &= ₹100 \times 6.4924 + ₹1{,}000/3.4985\\ &= ₹649.24 + 285.84\\ &= ₹935.08\end{aligned}$$

With an 11 percent yield, the second bond will sell at a premium because of its ₹120 coupon. Its value is:

$$\begin{aligned}\text{Bond value} &= ₹120 \times (1 - 1/1.11^{12})/.11 + ₹1{,}000/1.11^{12}\\ &= ₹120 \times 6.4924 + ₹1{,}000/3.4985\\ &= ₹779.08 + 285.84\\ &= ₹1{,}064.92\end{aligned}$$

ZERO COUPON BONDS

A bond that pays no coupons at all must be offered at a price much lower than its face value. Such bonds are called **zero coupon bonds**, or zeroes.[1]

EXAMPLE 8.4

Yield to Maturity on a Zero under Annual Compounding Suppose that the Gandhari Electronics Co. issues a ₹1,000 face value, eight-year zero coupon bond. What is the yield to maturity on the bond if the bond is offered at ₹627? Assume annual compounding.

The yield to maturity, *R*, can be calculated from the equation:

$$\frac{₹1{,}000}{(1+R)^8} = ₹627$$

Solving the equation, we find that *R* equals about 6 percent. The yield to maturity is 6 percent.

The example expresses the yield as an effective annual yield. However, even though no interest payments are made on the bond, zero coupon bond calculations use semiannual periods in practice to be consistent with the calculations for coupon bonds. We illustrate this practice in the next example.

[1]A bond issued with a very low coupon rate (as opposed to a zero coupon rate) is an original-issue discount (OID) bond.

EXAMPLE 8.5

Yield on a Zero under Real-World Convention of Semiannual Compounding Suppose the Phalana-Dhimka Company issues a ₹1,000 face value, five-year zero coupon bond. The initial price is set at ₹508.35. What is the yield to maturity using semiannual compounding?

The yield can be expressed as:

$$\frac{₹1{,}000}{(1 + R)^{10}} = ₹508.35$$

The exponent in the denominator is 10 because five years contain 10 semiannual periods. The yield equals 7 percent. Because the yield is expressed as a return per six-month interval, the yield to maturity, expressed as an annual percentage rate, is 14 percent.

Lately, Indian companies have preferred the issue of zero-coupon bonds, as issuers realize the higher appetite of Indian retail investors (for the same). They are also increasingly targeting foreign investors who would want to save withholding tax.

8.2 Government and Corporate Bonds

The previous section investigated the basic principles of bond valuation without much discussion of the differences between government and corporate bonds. In this section, we discuss the differences.

GOVERNMENT BONDS

The biggest borrower in the world–by a wide margin–is everybody's favorite family member, Uncle Sam. In the middle of 2020, the total debt of the U.S. government was about ₹26.7 *trillion,* or over ₹80,000 per citizen (and growing!). When the government wishes to borrow money for more than one year, it sells what are known as Treasury notes and bonds to the public (in fact, it does so every month). Currently, outstanding Treasury notes and bonds have original maturities ranging from 2 to 30 years.

If you're nervous about the level of debt piled up by the U.S. government, *don't* go to **www.usdebtclock.org/**. Learn all about government bonds at **www.newyorkfed.org**.

While most U.S. Treasury issues are ordinary coupon bonds, there are two important things to keep in mind. First, U.S. Treasury issues, unlike essentially all other bonds, have virtually no default risk because (we hope) the Treasury can always come up with the money to make the payments. Second, Treasury issues are exempt from state income taxes (though not federal income taxes). In other words, the coupons you receive on a Treasury note or bond are only taxed at the federal level.

For the history of government bonds, listen to **tinyurl.com/y2duldoh**.

State and local governments also borrow money by selling notes and bonds. Such issues are called *municipal* notes and bonds, or *munis.* Unlike Treasury issues, munis have varying degrees of default risk. The most intriguing thing about munis is that their coupons are exempt from federal income taxes (though not necessarily state income taxes), which makes them very attractive to high-income, high-tax-bracket investors. Because of this enormous tax break, the yields on municipal bonds are much lower than the yields on taxable bonds.

Another good bond market site is **money.cnn.com**.

EXAMPLE 8.6

Aftertax Yield Comparison Imagine that a long-term municipal bond selling at par is yielding 4.21 percent while a long-term Treasury bond selling at par yields 6.07 percent.[2] Further suppose an investor is in the 24 percent tax bracket. Ignoring any difference in default risk, would the investor prefer the Treasury bond or the muni?

To answer, we need to compare the aftertax yields on the two bonds. Ignoring state and local taxes, the muni pays 4.21 percent on both a pretax and an aftertax basis. The Treasury issue pays 6.07 percent before taxes, but it pays $.0607 \times (1 - .24) = .0461$, or 4.61 percent, once we account for the 24 percent tax bite. Given this, the Treasury bond still has a better yield.

EXAMPLE 8.7

Taxable versus Municipal Bonds Suppose taxable bonds are currently yielding 8 percent, while at the same time, munis of comparable risk and maturity are yielding 6 percent. Which is more attractive to an investor in a 35 percent tax bracket? What is the break-even tax rate? How do you interpret this rate?

For an investor in a 35 percent tax bracket, a taxable bond yields $.08 \times (1 - .35) = .052$, or 5.2 percent after taxes, so the muni is more attractive. The break-even tax rate is the tax rate at which an investor would be indifferent between a taxable and a nontaxable issue. If we let T^* stand for the break-even tax rate, we can solve for this tax rate as follows:

$$.08 \times (1 - T^*) = .06$$
$$1 - T^* = .06/.08 = .75$$
$$T^* = .25, \text{ or } 25\%$$

An investor in a 25 percent tax bracket would make 6 percent after taxes from either bond.

CORPORATE BONDS AND DEBENTURES

We pointed out that, while U.S. Treasury issues are virtually default-free, municipal bonds face the possibility of default. Corporate bonds also face the possibility of default. This possibility generates a wedge between the *promised yield* and the *expected return* on a bond.

To understand these two terms, imagine a one-year corporate bond with a par value of ₹1,000 and an annual coupon of ₹80. Further assume that fixed-income analysts believe that this bond has a 10 percent chance of default and, in the event of default, each bondholder will receive ₹800. Bondholders will likely receive something following default because the proceeds from any liquidation or reorganization go to the bondholders first. The stockholders typically receive a payoff only after the bondholders get paid in full. Because there is a 90 percent probability that the bond will pay off in full and a 10 percent probability that the bond will default, the expected payoff from the bond at maturity is:

$$.90 \times ₹1{,}080 + .10 \times ₹800 = ₹1{,}052$$

Assuming that the discount rate on risky bonds such as this one is 9 percent, the bond's value becomes:

$$\frac{₹1{,}052}{1.09} = ₹965.14$$

[2] Capital gains on municipal bonds are taxed, complicating the analysis somewhat. We avoid capital gains by assuming both bonds are priced at par.

What is the expected return on the bond? The expected return is clearly 9 percent because 9 percent is the discount rate in the previous equation. In other words, an investment of ₹965.14 today provides an expected payoff at maturity of ₹1,052, implying a 9 percent expected return.

What is the promised yield? The corporation is promising ₹1,080 in one year because the coupon is ₹80. Because the price of the bond is ₹965.14, the promised yield can be calculated from the following equation:

$$₹965.14 = \frac{₹1,080}{1 + R} \qquad \textbf{(8.2)}$$

In this equation, R, which is the promised yield, is 11.9 percent. Why is the promised yield above the expected return? The promised yield calculation assumes that the bondholder will receive the full ₹1,080. In other words, the promised yield calculation ignores the probability of default. By contrast, the expected return calculation specifically takes the probability of default into account. What about in a risk-free security? The promised yield and the expected return are equal here because the probability of default is zero, by definition, in a risk-free bond.

Now the promised yield on a corporate bond, as calculated in Equation 8.2, is the yield to maturity of the previous section. The promised yield can be calculated for any bond, be it corporate or government. All we need is the coupon rate, par value, and maturity. We do not need to know anything about the probability of default. Calculating the promised yield on a corporate bond is as easy as calculating the yield to maturity on a government bond. In fact, the two calculations are the same. However, the promised yield, or, equivalently, the yield to maturity, on a corporate bond is somewhat misleading. Our promised yield of 11.9 percent implies only that the bondholder will receive a return of 11.9 percent if the bond does not default. The promised yield does not tell us what the bondholder expects to receive.

For example, the Vanguard Intermediate-Term Treasury Bond Fund (TB Fund), a mutual fund composed of intermediate-term government bonds, had a yield of .27 percent in August 2020. The Vanguard High Yield Corporate Bond Fund (HY Fund), a mutual fund composed of intermediate-term corporate bonds with high default probabilities, had a yield of 4.00 percent on the same day. The yield on the HY Fund was 14.8 (= 4.00/.27) times as great as the yield on the TB Fund. Does that mean that an investor in the HY Fund expects a return about 14.8 times the return an investor in the TB Fund expects? Absolutely not. The yields quoted above are promised yields. They do not take into account any chance of default.

A professional analyst might very well find that, because of the high probability of default, the expected return on the HY Fund is actually below that expected on the TB Fund. However, we don't know this one way or the other. Calculation of the expected return on a corporate bond is quite difficult because one must assess the probability of default. However, this number, if it can be calculated, would be very meaningful. As its name implies, it tells us what rate of return the bondholder actually expects to receive.

In the Indian corporate bond market, JM Financial issued Zero coupon bonds in September 2019 at a face value of ₹1000, raising a total capital of ₹8.3 crore. The bonds had a maturity period of 7 years. At maturity in September 2026, the redemption price is fixed at ₹2000. The yield to maturity, in this case, works out to 10.41%. These zero coupon bonds (ISIN code INE523H07AQ1) are listed on the Bombay Stock Exchange.

EXAMPLE 8.8

Yields on Government and Corporate Bonds Both a default-free, two-year government bond and a two-year corporate bond pay a 7 percent coupon. However, the government bond sells at par (or ₹1,000) and the corporate bond sells at ₹982.16. What are the yields on these two bonds? Why is there a difference in yields? Are these yields promised yields? Assume annual coupon payments.

(continued)

Both bonds pay a coupon of ₹70 per year. The yield on the government bond can be calculated from the following equation:

$$₹1{,}000 = \frac{₹70}{1 + R} + \frac{₹1{,}070}{(1 + R)^2}$$

The yield on the government bond is 7 percent.

The yield on the corporate bond can be calculated from the following equation:

$$₹982.16 = \frac{₹70}{1 + R} + \frac{₹1{,}070}{(1 + R)^2}$$

The yield on the corporate bond is 8 percent.

The yield on the government bond is below that on the corporate bond because the corporate bond has default risk, while the government bond does not.

For both bonds, the yields we calculated are promised yields because the coupons are promised coupons. These coupons will not be paid in full if there is a default. The promised yield is equal to the expected return on the government bond because there is no chance of default. However, the promised yield is greater than the expected return on the corporate bond because default is a possibility.

While our previous discussion on corporate bonds depended heavily on the concept of default probability, estimation of default probabilities is well beyond the scope of this chapter. However, bond ratings provide an easy way to obtain a qualitative appreciation of a bond's default risk.

BOND RATINGS

Firms frequently pay to have their debt rated. The two leading bond-rating firms are Moody's and Standard & Poor's (S&P). The debt ratings are an assessment of the creditworthiness of the corporate issuer. The definitions of creditworthiness used by Moody's and S&P are based on how likely the firm is to default and the protection creditors have in the event of a default.

It is important to recognize that bond ratings are concerned only with the possibility of default. Earlier, we discussed interest rate risk, which we defined as the risk of a change in the value of a bond resulting from a change in interest rates. Bond ratings do not address this issue. As a result, the price of a highly rated bond can still be quite volatile.

Bond ratings are constructed from information supplied by the corporation and other sources. The rating classes and some information concerning them are shown in the following table:

	Investment-Quality Bond Ratings				Low-Quality, Speculative, and/or "Junk" Bond Ratings					
	High Grade		Medium Grade		Low Grade		Very Low Grade			
Standard & Poor's	AAA	AA	A	BBB	BB	B	CCC	CC	C	D
Moody's	Aaa	Aa	A	Baa	Ba	B	Caa	Ca	C	

Moody's	S&P	
Aaa	AAA	Debt rated Aaa and AAA has the highest rating. Capacity to pay interest and principal is extremely strong.
Aa	AA	Debt rated Aa and AA has a very strong capacity to pay interest and repay principal. Together with the highest rating, this group comprises the high-grade bond class.

(continued)

		Investment-Quality Bond Ratings				Low-Quality, Speculative, and/or "Junk" Bond Ratings					
		High Grade		Medium Grade		Low Grade		Very Low Grade			
Standard & Poor's		AAA	AA	A	BBB	BB	B	CCC	CC	C	D
Moody's		Aaa	Aa	A	Baa	Ba	B	Caa	Ca	C	
A	A	Debt rated A has a strong capacity to pay interest and repay principal, although it is somewhat more susceptible to the adverse effects of changes in circumstances and economic conditions than debt in higher-rated categories.									
Baa	BBB	Debt rated Baa and BBB is regarded as having an adequate capacity to pay interest and repay principal. Whereas it normally exhibits adequate protection parameters, adverse economic conditions or changing circumstances are more likely to lead to a weakened capacity to pay interest and repay principal for debt in this category than in higher-rated categories. These bonds are medium-grade obligations.									
Ba; B Caa Ca C	BB; B CCC CC C	Debt rated in these categories is regarded, on balance, as predominantly speculative with respect to capacity to pay interest and repay principal in accordance with the terms of the obligation. BB and Ba indicate the lowest degree of speculation, and Ca, CC, and C the highest degree of speculation. Although such debt is likely to have some quality and protective characteristics, these are outweighed by large uncertainties or major risk exposures to adverse conditions. Issues rated C by Moody's are typically in default.									
	D	Debt rated D is in default, and payment of interest and/or repayment of principal is in arrears.									

NOTE: At times, both Moody's and S&P use adjustments (called notches) to these ratings. S&P uses plus and minus signs: A+ is the strongest A rating and A– is the weakest. Moody's uses a 1, 2, or 3 designation, with 1 being the highest.

The highest rating a firm's debt can have is AAA or Aaa. Such debt is judged to be the best quality and to have the lowest degree of risk. For example, as of August 2020, Microsoft and Johnson & Johnson were the only U.S.-based nonfinancial companies with a AAA credit rating. AA or Aa ratings indicate very good quality debt and are much more common.

To hear why companies do not worry about a AAA rating, listen to **tinyurl.com/y4lw39qp**.

A large part of corporate borrowing takes the form of low-grade, or "junk," bonds. If these low-grade corporate bonds are rated at all, they are rated below investment grade by the major rating agencies. Investment-grade bonds are bonds rated at least BBB by S&P or Baa by Moody's.

Want to know what criteria are commonly used to rate corporate and municipal bonds? Go to **www.standardandpoors.com**, **www.moodys.com**, or **www.fitchratings.com**.

Rating agencies don't always agree. To illustrate, some bonds are known as "crossover" or "5B" bonds. The reason is that they are rated BBB (or Baa) by one rating agency and BB (or Ba) by another, a "split rating."

A bond's credit rating can change as the issuer's financial strength improves or deteriorates. For example, in February 2020, S&P Global Ratings cut the bond rating on ketchup-maker Kraft Heinz from BBB– to BB+, lowering the company's bond rating from investment grade to junk bond status. Bonds that drop into junk territory like this are called *fallen angels.* S&P was concerned about declining profitability and cash flow generation at Kraft Heinz. Note, this was before the COVID-19 lockdown in the United States. By May 2020, there were 24 fallen angels in the United States for the year and 111 fallen angels worldwide.

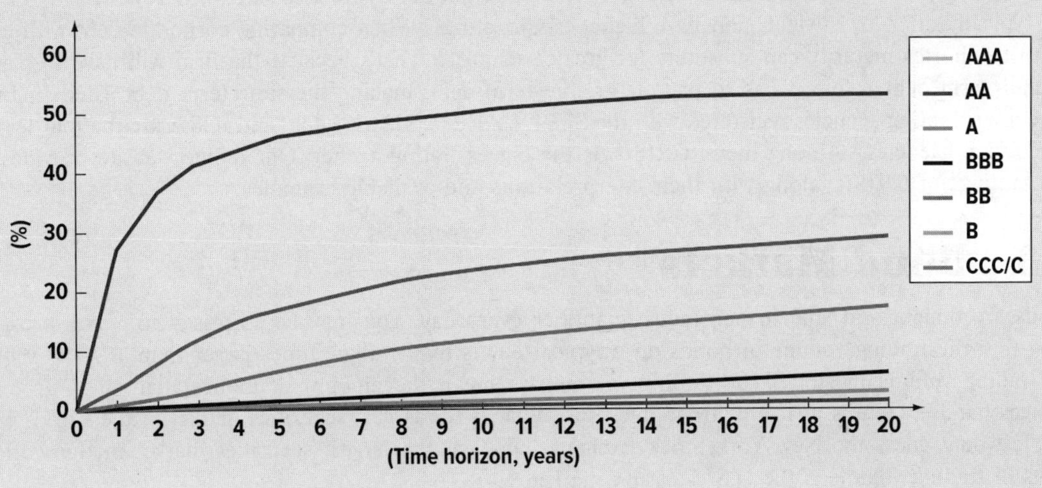

Figure 8.3 Default Rate by Bond Rating

SOURCE: 2019 Annual Global Corporate Default and Rating Transition Study, S&P Global Ratings.

Credit ratings are important because defaults really do occur. Consider Figure 8.3, which shows the default rate by bond rating. For example, about 30 percent of CCC/C rated bonds default within 1 year, and about 50 percent default within 9 years. By contrast, only about 1 to 2 percent of AAA and AA rated bonds default within 20 years. To show the importance of an investment grade rating, the default rate for BB bonds is more than twice the default rate for BBB bonds after 10 years.

When using credit ratings to assess risk, it is important to recognize that each rating reflects the default risk of a specific corporate bond rather than the risk of the firm as a whole. It is not uncommon for U.S. corporations to issue multiple types of bonds and other forms of debt that differ in seniority and maturity. Senior debt must

Listen to NPR's junk bond journey at **tinyurl.com/y4lzybtk**.

Junk Bond in India: Case of Sardar Sarovar Narmada Nigam Bonds

One classic example of a Junk bond in India is a bond issued by the Sardar Sarovar Narmada Nigam Ltd. (SSNNL) in 1993. The 20-year deep discount bonds were issued at ₹3,600 each and promised to give an investor a mouth-watering ₹1.11 lakh on maturity in 2014.

Since this was a long-term bond, there were periodic exit windows for investors. SSNNL bonds could be redeemed at the end of the seventh, eleventh or fifteenth years. However, given the high interest rate offered by the bond, a few people wanted to exit. By 2000, only 6% of the bonds were redeemed prematurely. In 2004, SSNNL dropped a bombshell when it announced its decision to pre-pay the deep discount bonds. The move would have saved the PSU ₹6,100 crore in interest costs. Within a week, the price of an SSNNL bond crashed from ₹40,200 to around ₹25,500— very close to the promised yield.

At a meeting of investors called by the PSU, bondholders rejected the buyback plan outright. When the SSNNL tried to push its way through, the investors moved court. After a six-month-long legal tussle, the Delhi High Court ruled in 2005 that the SSNNL must pay the sum on maturity. The ruling pushed the secondary market price of the bonds from ₹31,000 to ₹36,000.

be repaid before junior or subordinated debt. Therefore, senior bonds are associated with lower risk of default and typically offer lower yields and have higher credit ratings. When comparing corporate debt with equal seniority, shorter maturity can substitute for greater seniority. That's because the firm will have to pay off its short-term debt before it has to pay off its long-term debt, making the short-term debt safer. In India, there are six rating agencies registered with the SEBI. CARE, CRISIL, Fitch, and ICRA are the four leading bond-rating agencies.[3] Among them, CRISIL is the biggest rating agency. Our online website provides the bond ratings of CRISIL along with their interpretations and available examples.

8.3 Bond Markets

Excel Master coverage online

Bonds are bought and sold in enormous quantities every day. You may be surprised to learn that the trading volume in bonds on a typical day is many, many times larger than the trading volume in stocks (by trading volume, we mean the amount of money that changes hands). Here is a finance trivia question: What is the largest securities market in the world? Most people would guess the New York Stock Exchange. In fact, the largest securities market in the world in terms of trading volume is the U.S. Treasury market.

HOW BONDS ARE BOUGHT AND SOLD

Most trading in bonds takes place over the counter, or OTC, which means that there is no particular place where buying and selling occur. Instead, dealers around the country (and around the world) stand ready to buy and sell. The various dealers are connected electronically.

One reason the bond markets are so big is that the number of bond issues far exceeds the number of stock issues. There are two reasons for this. First, a corporation would typically have only one common stock issue outstanding, though there are exceptions. However, a single large corporation could easily have a dozen or more note and bond issues outstanding. Beyond this, federal, state, and local borrowing is enormous. Even a small city would usually have a wide variety of notes and bonds outstanding, representing money borrowed to pay for items like roads, sewers, and schools. When you think about how many small cities there are in the United States, you begin to get the picture!

Because the bond market is almost entirely OTC, it has historically had little or no *transparency*. A financial market is transparent if its prices and trading volume are easily observed. On the New York Stock Exchange, for example, one can see the price and quantity for every single transaction. In contrast, it is often not possible to observe either in the bond market. Transactions are privately negotiated between parties, and there is little or no centralized reporting of transactions.

Although the total volume of trading in bonds far exceeds that in stocks, only a very small fraction of the total outstanding bond issues actually trades on a given day. This fact, combined with the lack of transparency in the bond market, means that getting up-to-date prices on individual bonds can be difficult or impossible, particularly for smaller corporate or municipal issues. Instead, a variety of sources are commonly used for estimated prices.

BOND PRICE REPORTING

To learn more about the Indian bond market, visit **www.fimmda.org** and **www.crisil.com**

In 2002, transparency in the corporate bond market began to improve dramatically. Under new regulations, corporate bond dealers are now required to report trade information through what is known as the Trade Reporting and Compliance Engine (TRACE).

[3]CARE stands for Credit Analysis and Research Limited; CRISIL stands for Credit Rating Information Services of India Limited; ICRA stands for Investment Information and Credit Rating Agency of India Limited.

Issuer Name	Symbol	Callable	Sub-Product Type	Coupon	Maturity	Ratings		Last Sale	
						Moody's®	S&P	Price	Yield
CISCO SYS INC	CSCO.GD	Yes	Corporate Bond	5.900	02/15/2039	A1	AA-	154.354	2.278
CISCO SYS INC	CSCO.GG	Yes	Corporate Bond	5.500	01/15/2040	A1	AA-	149.968	2.293
CISCO SYS INC	CSCO4100888	Yes	Corporate Bond	2.900	03/04/2021	A1	AA-	101.320	0.394
CISCO SYS INC	CSCO4101281	Yes	Corporate Bond	3.625	03/04/2024	A1	AA-	111.190	0.421
CISCO SYS INC	CSCO4257979	Yes	Corporate Bond	3.000	06/15/2022	A1	AA-	105.112	0.159
CISCO SYS INC	CSCO4257977	Yes	Corporate Bond	3.500	06/15/2025	A1	AA-	114.694	0.409
CISCO SYS INC	CSCO4337807	Yes	Corporate Bond	2.200	02/28/2021	A1	AA-	101.030	0.161
CISCO SYS INC	CSCO4337700	Yes	Corporate Bond	2.600	02/28/2023	A1	AA-	105.699	0.315
CISCO SYS INC	CSCO4337813	No	Corporate Bond	2.950	02/28/2026	A1	AA-	112.998	0.550

SOURCE: FINRA reported TRACE prices, August 24, 2020.

TRACE bond quotes are available at finra-markets.morningstar.com/BondCenter/Default.jsp. We went to the site and entered "Cisco" to find bonds issued by tech giant Cisco Systems. We found a total of 20 bond issues outstanding. Below is a partial list of Cisco's bonds.

To learn more about TRACE, visit **www.finra.org**.

If you go to the website and click on a particular bond, you will get a lot of information about the bond, including the credit rating, original issue information, and trade information.

As shown in Figure 8.4, the Financial Industry Regulatory Authority (FINRA) provides a daily snapshot of the data from TRACE by reporting the most active issues. The information in the figure is largely self-explanatory. Notice that the price of the Noble Energy bond dropped by .294 percentage points on this day. What do you think happened to the yield to maturity for this bond? Figure 8.4 focuses on the most active bonds with investment grade ratings, but the most active high-yield and convertible bonds are also available on the website.

The Federal Reserve Bank of St. Louis maintains dozens of online files containing macroeconomic data as well as rates on U.S. Treasury issues. Go to **fred.stlouis.org**.

Most Active Investment Grade Bonds

Issuer Name	Symbol	Coupon	Maturity	Moody's®/S&P	High	Low	Last	Change	Yield%
T-MOBILE USA INC	DTEGF4973664	3.500%	04/15/2025	Baa3/BBB–	110.65400	11 0.48536	110.52438	0.038382	1.123563
LILLY ELI & CO	LLY5033675	2.500%	09/15/2060	/A+	99.08400	97.34300	99.02200	1.136000	
NOBLE ENERGY INC	NBL4529193	4.950%	08/15/2047	Baa3/BBB–	134.13900	133.22100	133.59300	–0.294000	3.083999
BA T CAPCORP	BTI4772648	2.764%	08/15/2022	Baa2/	104.02600	103.89600	103.91800	–0.016000	0.673166
PACIFIC GAS & ELEC CO	PCG5002762	3.300%	08/01/2040	Baa3/BBB–	94.69900	93.59900	93.78100	–1.622000	3.745012
INTERCONTINENTAL EXCHANGE INC	ICE5031638	1.850%	09/15/2032	A3/BBB+	100. 71100	100.34900	100.71100	0.366000	1.734055
LILLY ELI & CO	LLY4980390	2.250%	05/15/2050	WR/A+	98.31000	97.53200	97.70006	–0.083943	2.357977
NORTHROP GRUMMAN CORP	NOC4969026	5.150%	05/01/2040	Baa2/BBB	138.88000	138.16924	138.16924	0.371240	2.608102
APPLE INC	AAPL4336433	4.650%	02/23/2046	Aa1/AA+	138.59300	137.65000	138.41400	0.386000	2.559854
TJX COS INC NEW	TJX4972595	4.500%	04/15/2050	A2/A	131.09000	129.71500	131.09000	1.165000	2.910003

Figure 8.4 Sample TRACE Bond Quotations

SOURCE: FINRA reported TRACE prices, August 24, 2020.

Figure 8.4a Sample Corporate Bond traded in India

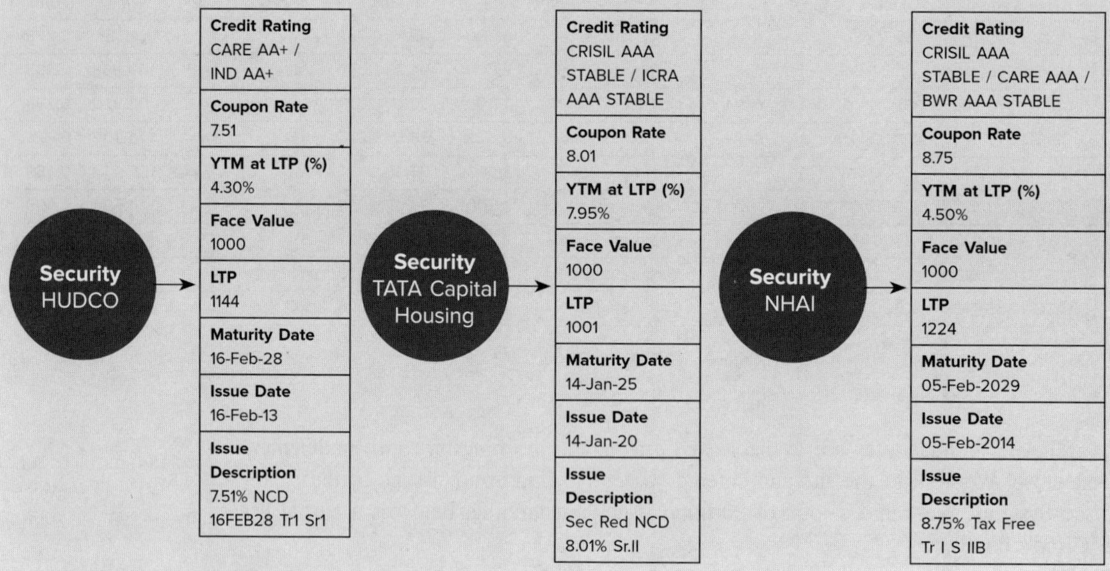

As we mentioned before, the U.S. Treasury market is the largest securities market in the world. As with bond markets in general, it is an OTC market, so there is limited transparency. However, unlike the situation with bond markets in general, trading in Treasury issues, particularly recently issued ones, is very heavy. Each day, representative prices for outstanding Treasury issues are reported.

Figure 8.5 shows a portion of the daily Treasury bond listings from the website **wsj.com**. Examine the entry that begins "8/15/2028." Reading from left to right, the 8/15/2028 tells us that the bond's maturity is August 15, 2028. The 2.875 is the bond's coupon rate.

The next two pieces of information are the **bid** and **asked prices**. In general, in any OTC or dealer market, the bid price represents what a dealer is willing to pay for a security, and the asked price, or "ask" price, is what a dealer is willing to take for it. The difference between the two prices is called the **bid-ask spread**, or "spread," and it represents the dealer's profit.

Treasury prices are quoted as a percentage of face value. The bid price, or what a dealer is willing to pay, on the 8/15/2028 bond is 118.116. With a ₹1,000 face value, this quote represents a Rupee price of ₹1,181.16. The asked price, or the price at which the dealer is willing to sell the bond, is 118.126, or ₹1,181.26.

The next number quoted is the change in the asked price from the previous day, measured as a percentage of face value, so this issue's asked price decreased by .03 percent, or ₹.30, in value from the previous day. Finally, the last number reported is the yield to maturity, based on the asked price. Notice that this is a premium bond because it sells for more than its face value. Not surprisingly, its yield to maturity (.517 percent) is less than its coupon rate (2.875 percent).

> Current and historical Treasury yield information is available at **www.treasurydirect.gov**.

The last bond listed, the 8/15/2050, is often called the "bellwether" bond. This bond's yield is the one that is usually reported in the evening news. So, when you hear that long-term interest rates rose, what is really being said is that the yield on this bond went up (and its price went down). Beginning in 2001, the Treasury announced that it would no longer sell 30-year bonds, leaving the 10-year note as the longest maturity issue sold. However, in 2006, the 30-year bond was resurrected and once again assumed bellwether status.

If you examine the yields on the various issues in Figure 8.5, you will clearly see that they vary by maturity. Why this occurs and what it might mean is one of the issues we discuss in our next section. Government, referred to as "sovereign," bond yields also vary by country of origin. Here we show the 10-year bond yields for several countries. The yields vary according to default risks and foreign exchange risks (to be discussed later in the text).

Maturity	Coupon	Bid	Asked	Chg	Asked Yld
7/15/2021	2.625	102.062	102.066	–0.002	0.134
2/28/2022	1.125	101.146	101.152	–0.004	0.15
1/15/2023	1.5	103.056	103.062	–0.016	0.159
8/15/2024	2.375	108.162	108.166	–0.022	0.219
9/30/2025	3	113.214	113.22	–0.042	0.293
7/31/2026	1.875	108.262	108.266	–0.03	0.368
1/31/2027	1.5	106.282	106.286	–0.002	0.412
8/15/2028	2.875	118.116	118.126	–0.03	0.517
2/15/2029	5.25	139.054	139.064	–0.03	0.515
5/15/2030	0.625	99.316	100.006	–0.72	0.623
8/15/2030	0.625	99.246	99.256	–0.046	0.645
2/15/2031	5.375	148.094	148.104	–0.086	0.606
2/15/2036	4.5	153.074	153.094	–0.062	0.824
5/15/2038	4.5	158.102	158.122	–0.082	0.922
11/15/2039	4.375	158.036	158.056	–0.068	1.031
8/15/2040	1.125	99.266	99.286	–0.016	1.131
11/15/2041	3.125	137.004	137.024	–0.032	1.151
8/15/2042	2.75	129.304	130.004	–0.718	1.193
5/15/2043	2.875	132.136	132.156	–0.01	1.231
5/15/2044	3.375	143.092	143.112	–0.008	1.256
8/15/2045	2.875	133.186	133.206	–0.006	1.294
11/15/2046	2.875	134.234	134.254	0.02	1.304
2/15/2047	3	137.286	137.306	0.016	1.301
5/15/2049	2.875	136.314	137.014	0.018	1.321
8/15/2050	1.375	100.202	100.222	0.02	1.347

Figure 8.5 Sample *Wall Street Journal* U.S. Treasury Bond Prices

SOURCE: www.wsj.com, August 24, 2020.

SELECTED INTERNATIONAL GOVERNMENT 10-YEAR BOND YIELDS	
	Yield (%)
United States	.65
United Kingdom	.21
Japan	.02
Germany	−.49
Australia	.85
Greece	1.07
Spain	.32
India	6.14
Brazil	7.14

SOURCE: www.bloomberg.com, August 24, 2020.

EXAMPLE 8.9

Treasury Quotes Locate the Treasury bond in Figure 8.5 maturing in July 2026. What is its coupon rate? What is its bid price? What was the previous day's asked price?

The bond's coupon rate is 1.875, or 1.875 percent of face value. The bid price is 108.262, or 108.262 percent of face value. The ask price is 108.266, which is down by .03 percent from the previous day. This means that the ask price on the previous day was equal to 108.266 + .03 = 108.296.

A NOTE ON BOND PRICE QUOTES

If you buy a bond between coupon payment dates, the price you pay is usually more than the price you are quoted. The reason is that standard convention in the bond market is to quote prices net of *accrued interest*, meaning that accrued interest is deducted to arrive at the quoted price. This quoted price is called the **clean price**. The price you actually pay, however, includes the accrued interest. This price is the **dirty price**, also known as the *full* or *invoice* price.

An example is the easiest way to understand these issues. Suppose you buy a bond with a 12 percent annual coupon, payable semiannually. You actually pay ₹1,080 for this bond, so ₹1,080 is the dirty, or invoice, price. Further, on the day you buy it, the next coupon is due in four months, so you are between coupon dates. Notice that the next coupon will be ₹60.

The accrued interest on a bond is calculated by taking the fraction of the coupon period that has passed, in this case two months out of six, and multiplying this fraction by the next coupon, ₹60. So, the accrued interest in this example is 2/6 × ₹60 = ₹20. The bond's quoted price, or clean price, would be ₹1,080 – 20 = ₹1,060.[4]

[4]The calculation of accrued interest differs slightly between Treasury bonds and corporate bonds. The difference involves the calculation of the fractional coupon period. In our example above, we implicitly treated the months as having exactly the same length (i.e., 30 days each, 360 days in a year), which is consistent with the way corporate bonds are quoted. In contrast, actual day counts are used for Treasury bonds. For more on counting the days between coupon payments, check out Excel Master for this chapter.

8.4 Inflation and Interest Rates

So far in this chapter, we have not considered the impact of inflation on interest rates. However, we did cover this relationship in Section 6.5. We briefly review our previous discussion before considering additional ideas on the topic.

REAL VERSUS NOMINAL RATES

Suppose the one-year interest rate is 15.5 percent so that anyone depositing ₹100 in a bank today will end up with ₹115.50 next year. Further imagine a pizza costs ₹5 today, implying that ₹100 can buy 20 pizzas. Finally, assume that the inflation rate is 5 percent, leading to the price of pizza being ₹5.25 next year. How many pizzas can you buy next year if you deposit ₹100 today? Clearly, you can buy ₹115.50/₹5.25 = 22 pizzas. This is up from 20 pizzas, implying a 10 percent increase in purchasing power. Economists say that, while the *nominal* rate of interest is 15.5 percent, the *real* rate of interest is only 10 percent.

The difference between nominal and real rates is important and bears repeating:

The nominal rate on an investment is the percentage change in the number of Rupees you have. The real rate on an investment is the percentage change in how much you can buy with your Rupees. In other words, the real rate is the percentage change in your buying power.

We can generalize the relationship between nominal rates, real rates, and inflation as:

$$1 + R = (1 + r) \times (1 + h)$$

where R is the nominal rate, r is the real rate, and h is the inflation rate.

In the preceding example, the nominal rate was 15.50 percent and the inflation rate was 5 percent. What was the real rate? We can determine it by plugging in these numbers:

$$\begin{aligned} 1 + .1550 &= (1 + r) \times (1 + .05) \\ 1 + r &= 1.1550/1.05 = 1.10 \\ r &= .10, \text{ or } 10\% \end{aligned}$$

This real rate is the same as we had before.

We can rearrange things a little as follows:

$$\begin{aligned} 1 + R &= (1 + r) \times (1 + h) \\ R &= r + h + r \times h \end{aligned} \tag{8.3}$$

What this tells us is that the nominal rate has three components. First, there is the real rate on the investment, r. Next, there is the compensation for the decrease in the value of the money originally invested because of inflation, h. The third component represents compensation for the fact that the Rupees earned on the investment are also worth less because of inflation.

For a discussion of inflation and deflation, listen to **tinyurl.com/y5r5gr8x**.

This third component is usually small, so it is often dropped. The nominal rate is then approximately equal to the real rate plus the inflation rate:

$$R \approx r + h \tag{8.4}$$

EXAMPLE 8.10

Nominal versus Real Rates If investors require a 10 percent real rate of return, and the inflation rate is 8 percent, what must be the approximate nominal rate? The exact nominal rate?

First of all, the nominal rate is approximately equal to the sum of the real rate and the inflation rate: 10percent + 8percent = 18percent. From Equation 8.3, we have:

$$\begin{aligned} 1 + R &= (1 + r) \times (1 + h) \\ &= 1.10 \times 1.08 \\ &= 1.1880 \end{aligned}$$

Therefore, the nominal rate will actually be closer to 19 percent.

It is important to note that financial rates, such as interest rates, discount rates, and rates of return, are almost always quoted in nominal terms. As we said before, we use the symbol R instead of r in most of our discussions about such rates.

INFLATION RISK AND INFLATION-LINKED BONDS

Consider a 20-year Treasury bond with an 8 percent coupon. If the par value or the principal amount is ₹1,000, the holder will receive ₹80 a year for each of the next 20 years and, in addition, will receive ₹1,000 in 20 years. Because the U.S. government has never defaulted, the bondholder is essentially guaranteed to receive these promised payments. Therefore, one can make the case that this is a riskless bond.

But is the bond really riskless after all? That depends on how you define risk. Suppose there is no chance of inflation, meaning that pizzas will always cost ₹5. We can be sure that the ₹1,080 (₹1,000 of principal and ₹80 of interest) at maturity will allow us to buy ₹1,080/₹5 = 216 pizzas. Alternatively, suppose that, over the next 20 years, there is a 50 percent probability of no inflation and a 50 percent probability of an annual inflation rate of 10 percent. With a 10 percent inflation rate, a pizza will cost ₹5 × 1.10^{20} = ₹33.64 in 20 years. The ₹1,080 payment will now allow the holder to buy only ₹1,080/₹33.64 = 32.1 pizzas, not the 216 pizzas we calculated for a world of no inflation. Given the uncertain inflation rate, the investor faces **inflation risk;** while he knows that he will receive ₹1,080 at maturity, he doesn't know whether he will be able to afford 216 or 32.1 pizzas.

Let's now speak in terms of nominal and real quantities. The *nominal value* of the payment at maturity is ₹1,080 because this is the actual cash the investor will receive. Assuming an inflation rate of 10 percent, the *real value* of this payment is only ₹1,080/1.10^{20} = ₹160.54. The real value measures the purchasing power of the payment. Because bondholders care about the purchasing power of their bond payments, they are ultimately concerned with real values, not nominal values. Inflation can erode the real value of the payments, implying that inflation risk is a serious concern, particularly in a time of high and variable inflation.

Do any bonds avoid inflation risk? As a matter of fact, yes. The U.S. government issues Treasury inflation-protected securities (TIPS), with promised payments specified in real terms, not nominal terms. A number of other countries also issue inflation-linked bonds. Imagine that a particular inflation-linked bond matures in two years, has a par value of ₹1,000, and pays a 2 percent coupon, where both the par value and the coupon are specified in real terms. Assuming annual payments, the bondholder will receive the following real payments:

End of Year 1	End of Year 2
₹20	₹1,020

Thus, the issuer is promising payments in real terms.

What amounts will the bondholder receive, expressed in nominal terms? Suppose the inflation rate over the first year is 3 percent and the inflation rate over the second year is 5 percent. The bondholder will receive the following nominal payments:[5]

End of Year 1	End of Year 2
₹20 × 1.03 = ₹20.60	₹1,020 × 1.03 × 1.05 = ₹1,103.13

While the bondholder knows the size of the payments in real terms when he buys the bond, he doesn't know the size of the payments in nominal terms until the inflation numbers are announced each period. Because TIPS and other inflation-linked bonds guarantee payments in real terms, we say that these bonds eliminate inflation risk.

Inflation-linked bonds are quoted in real yields. Suppose the bond trades at ₹971.50. The yield, y, would be solved by the following equation:

$$₹971.50 = \frac{₹20}{1 + y} + \frac{₹1{,}020}{(1 + y)^2}$$

In this example, y turns out to be 3.5 percent. Thus, we say that the real yield of the bond is 3.5 percent.

Are the yields on regular Treasury bonds related to the yields on TIPS? As of August 2020, the real yield on a 20-year TIPS was about −.52 percent and the nominal yield on a 20-year Treasury bond was about 1.08 percent. As a first approximation, one could argue that the differential of 1.60 percent [= 1.08 − (−.52)] implies that the market expects an annual rate of inflation of 1.60 percent over the next 20 years.[6]

You would expect that investors would always require a positive real return because a primary purpose of investing is to be able to spend more in the future than you could today. This means that the only time investors would accept a negative yield on a bond would be if there was deflation, or negative inflation. Going back to our discussion at the beginning of the chapter about negative yields, while inflation rates were low at the time, they were not negative, so investors were willing to accept a negative real return. Why? After all, just holding cash has a zero real return, which is better. One answer is that holding a huge amount of cash is both expensive and difficult to do, so investors were willing to accept a real return slightly below zero, at what amounts to a storage cost.

THE FISHER EFFECT

Imagine a world where, initially, there is no inflation and the nominal interest rate is 2 percent. Suppose that something, an action by the Federal Reserve or the RBI or a change in the foreign exchange rate, unexpectedly triggers an inflation rate of 5 percent. What do you think will happen to the nominal interest rate? Your first thought might be that the interest rate will rise because if the rate stays at 2 percent, the real rate would become negative. That is, a bank deposit of ₹100 today will still turn into ₹102 at the end of the year. However, if a hamburger priced at ₹1 today costs ₹1.05 next year, the ₹102 will only buy about 97 hamburgers (= ₹102/₹1.05) next year. Because the initial ₹100 allows one to buy 100 hamburgers today, there is a reduction in purchasing power.

[5]This example is simplified. Actual payment calculations are often complex and differ across countries. For example, TIPS have semiannual payments with a lag in the inflation adjustment.

[6]As mentioned earlier, regular Treasury bonds are subject to inflation risk while TIPS are not subject to this risk. Because the risks of the two bonds are not equivalent, this approach should be viewed only as a first-pass estimate of anticipated inflation.

How much should the interest rate rise? A well-known economist, Irving Fisher, conjectured many decades ago that the nominal interest rate should rise enough to keep the real interest rate constant. That is, the real rate should stay at 2 percent in our example. We can use Equation 8.4 to determine that the new nominal rate will be (approximately):

$$2\% + 5\% \cong 7\%$$

Fisher's thinking is that investors are not foolish. They know that inflation reduces purchasing power and, therefore, they will demand an increase in the nominal rate before lending money. Fisher's hypothesis, typically called the **Fisher effect**, can be stated as:

A rise in the rate of inflation causes the nominal rate to rise enough so that the real rate of interest is unaffected. In other words, the real rate is invariant to the rate of inflation.

While Fisher's reasoning makes sense, it's important to point out that the claim that the nominal rate will rise to 7 percent is only a hypothesis. It may be true and it may be false in any real-world situation. If investors are foolish after all, the nominal rate could stay at 2 percent, even in the presence of inflation. Alternatively, even if investors understand the impact of inflation, the nominal rate may not rise all the way to 7 percent. That is, there may be some unknown force preventing a full rise.

How can one test the Fisher effect empirically? While a precise empirical test is beyond the scope of this chapter, Figure 8.6 gives at least a hint of the evidence. The figure plots two curves, one showing annualized

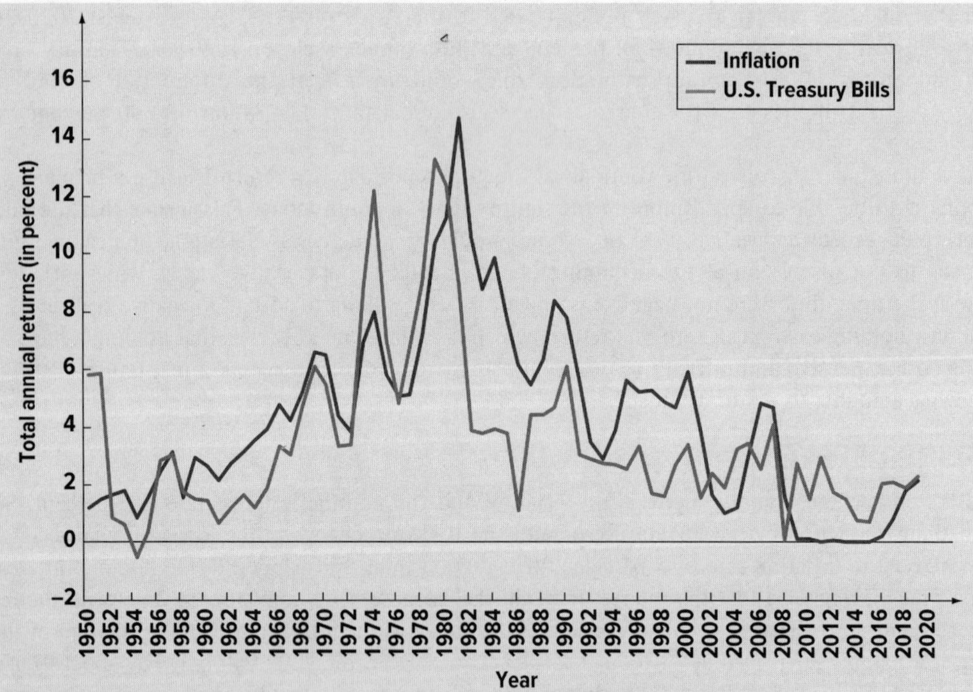

The figure plots both annualized returns on one-month Treasury bills and inflation rates in the United States. The two series appear to move together, implying that the inflation rate is an important determinant of the short-term interest rate.

Figure 8.6 The Relationship between Annualized One-Month Treasury Bill Returns and Inflation

SOURCE: Morningstar, 2020, author calculations.

returns on one-month Treasury bills over the last 60 years and the other showing inflation rates over the same period. It is apparent that the two curves move together. Both interest rates and inflation rates rose from the 1950s to the early 1980s while falling in the decades after. While statistical work is needed to establish a precise relationship, the figure suggests that inflation is an important determinant of the nominal interest rate.

In a research on the Inflation Indexed Bonds in India, Vaibhav Jain compared it with the "Normal Bond" on various parameters. They found that Inflation Indexed Bond value increases with an increase in inflation and vice-versa but for a normal bond, it remains unaffected by the rising inflation levels (keeping interest/reinvestment rate as constant for both the bonds).[7]

8.5 Determinants of Bond Yields

We are now in a position to discuss the determinants of a bond's yield. As we will see, the yield on any particular bond is a reflection of a variety of factors.

Excel Master coverage online

THE TERM STRUCTURE OF INTEREST RATES

At any point in time, short-term and long-term interest rates generally differ. Sometimes short-term rates are higher, sometimes lower. Figure 8.7 provides a long-range perspective on this by showing about two centuries of short- and long-term interest rates. The difference between short- and long-term rates in the figure has ranged from essentially zero to several percentage points, both positive and negative.

The relationship between short- and long-term interest rates is known as the **term structure of interest rates**. To be a little more precise, the term structure of interest rates tells us the nominal interest rates on

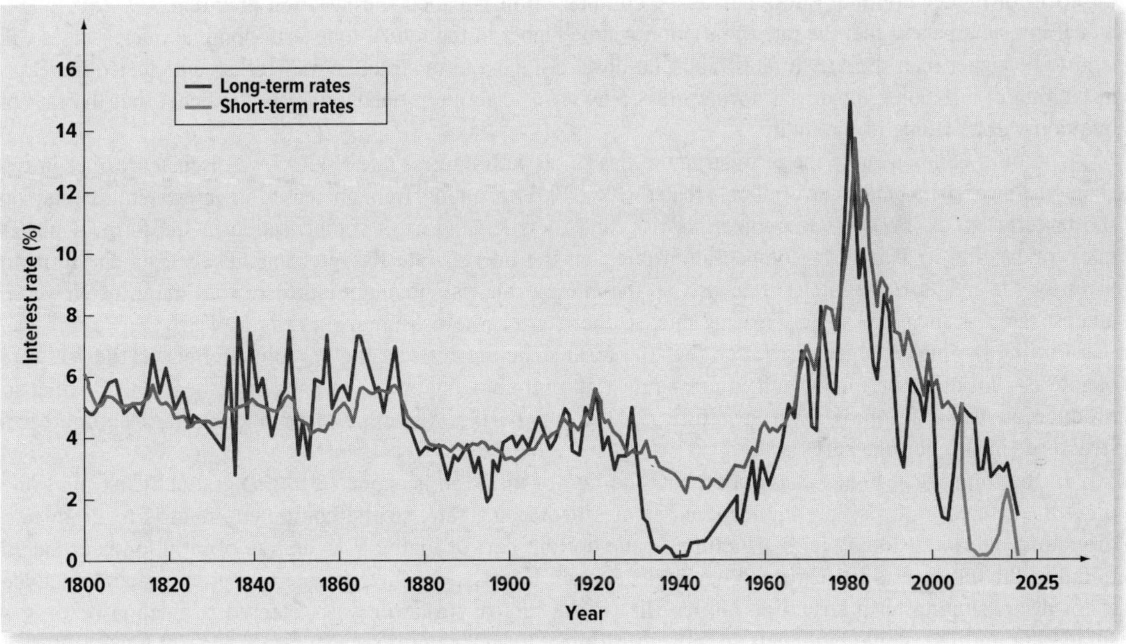

Figure 8.7 U.S. Interest Rates: 1800 to mid-2020

SOURCE: Jeremy J. Siegel, *Stocks for the Long Run,* 5th ed. (New York: McGraw-Hill, 2014), updated by the authors.

[7]Further reading: Vaibhav Jain, "A Study of Inflation Indexed Bonds in the Indian Debt Market", *International Journal of Economics and Finance*, Vol. 4(10), 2012.

default-free, pure discount bonds of all maturities. These rates are, in essence, "pure" interest rates because they contain no risk of default and involve a single, lump-sum future payment. In other words, the term structure tells us the pure time value of money for different lengths of time.

When long-term rates are higher than short-term rates, we say that the term structure is upward sloping, and when short-term rates are higher, we say it is downward sloping. The term structure also can be "humped." When this occurs, it is usually because rates increase at first but then decline at longer-term maturities. The most common shape of the term structure, particularly in modern times, is upward sloping. However, in March 2019, the yield curve became partially inverted when the yield on the 10-year U.S. Treasury note fell below the yield on the three-month U.S. Treasury bill.

What determines the shape of the term structure? There are three basic components. The first two are the ones we discussed in our previous section, the real rate of interest and the rate of inflation. The real rate of interest is the compensation investors demand for forgoing the use of their money. You can think of the real rate as the pure time value of money after adjusting for the effects of inflation.

The real rate of interest is a function of many factors. Consider expected economic growth. High expected growth is likely to raise the real rate and low expected growth is likely to lower it. The real rate of interest may differ across maturities, due to varying growth expectations among other factors. The real rate may be low for short-term bonds and high for long-term ones because the market expects lower economic growth in the short term than in the long term. However, the real rate of interest appears to have only a minor impact on the shape of the term structure.

In contrast, the prospect of future inflation very strongly influences the shape of the term structure. Investors thinking about loaning money for various lengths of time recognize that future inflation erodes the value of the Rupees that will be returned. As a result, investors demand compensation for this loss in the form of higher nominal rates. This extra compensation is called the **inflation premium**.

If investors believe that the rate of inflation will be higher in the future, long-term nominal interest rates will tend to be higher than short-term rates. Thus, an upward-sloping term structure may reflect anticipated increases in the rate of inflation. Similarly, a downward-sloping term structure probably reflects the belief that the rate of inflation will be falling in the future.

The third component of the term structure has to do with interest rate risk. As we discussed earlier in the chapter, longer-term bonds have much greater risk of loss resulting from increases in interest rates than do shorter-term bonds. Investors recognize this risk, and they demand extra compensation in the form of higher rates for bearing it. This extra compensation is called the **interest rate risk premium**. The longer the term to maturity, the greater is the interest rate risk, so the interest rate risk premium increases with maturity. However, interest rate risk increases at a decreasing rate, so the interest rate risk premium does as well.[8]

Putting the pieces together, we see that the term structure reflects the combined effect of the real rate of interest, inflation premium, and interest rate risk premium. Figure 8.8 shows how these can interact to produce an upward-sloping term structure (in the top part of Figure 8.8) or a downward-sloping term structure (in the bottom part).

In the top part of Figure 8.8, notice how the rate of inflation is expected to rise gradually. At the same time, the interest rate risk premium increases at a decreasing rate, so the combined effect is to produce a pronounced upward-sloping term structure. In the bottom part of Figure 8.8, the rate of inflation is expected to fall in the future, and the expected decline is enough to offset the interest rate risk premium and produce a downward-sloping term structure. Notice that if the rate of inflation was expected to decline by only a small amount, we could still get an upward-sloping term structure because of the interest rate risk premium.

[8]Many years ago, the interest rate risk premium was called a "liquidity" premium. Today, the term *liquidity premium* has an altogether different meaning, which we explore in our next section. Also, the interest rate risk premium is sometimes called a maturity risk premium. Our terminology is consistent with the modern view of the term structure.

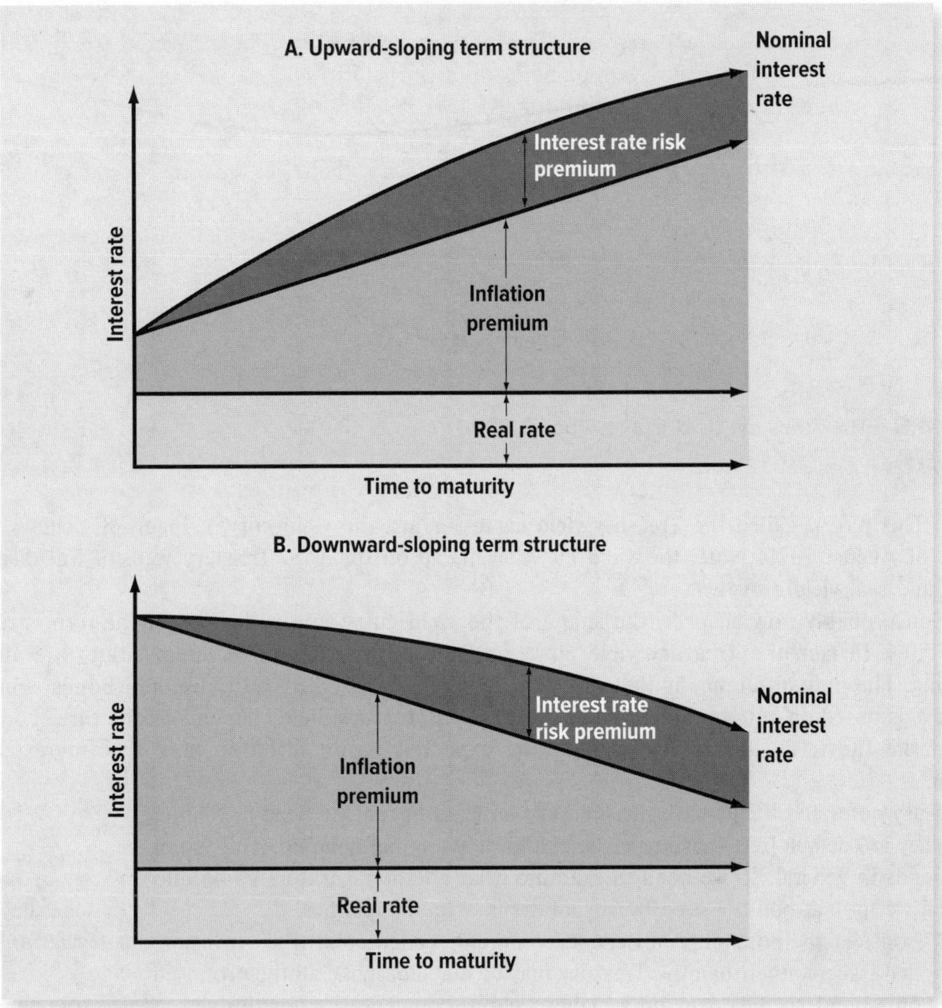

Figure 8.8 The Term Structure of Interest Rates

We assumed in drawing Figure 8.8 that the real rate would remain the same. However, as stated earlier, expected future real rates could be larger or smaller than the current real rate. Also, for simplicity, we used straight lines to show expected future inflation rates as rising or declining, but they do not necessarily have to look like this. They could, for example, rise and then fall, leading to a humped yield curve.

BOND YIELDS AND THE YIELD CURVE: PUTTING IT ALL TOGETHER

Online yield curve information is available at **www.bloomberg.com/markets**.

Going back to Figure 8.5, recall that the yields on Treasury notes and bonds differ across maturities. Each day, in addition to the Treasury prices and yields shown in Figure 8.5, *The Wall Street Journal* provides a plot of Treasury yields relative to

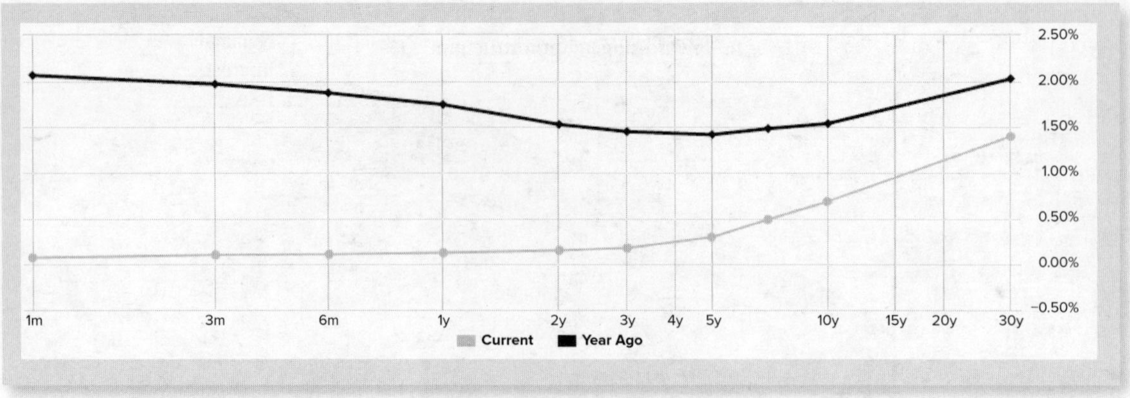

Figure 8.9 The Treasury Yield Curve: August 2020

SOURCE: www.wsj.com, August 25, 2020.

maturity. This plot is called the **Treasury yield curve** (or just the yield curve). Figure 8.9 shows the yield curve as of August 2020. Note, the yield curve available on the U.S. Treasury website will display both nominal and real yield curves.

As you probably now suspect, the shape of the yield curve is a reflection of the term structure of interest rates. In fact, the Treasury yield curve and the term structure of interest rates are almost the same thing. The only difference is that the term structure is based on pure discount bonds, whereas the yield curve is based on coupon bond yields. As a result, Treasury yields depend on the three components that underlie the term structure–the real rate, expected future inflation, and the interest rate risk premium.

Treasury notes and bonds have three important features that we need to remind you of: They are default-free, they are taxable, and they are highly liquid. This is not true of bonds in general, so we need to examine what additional factors come into play when we look at bonds issued by corporations or municipalities.

To hear about the dangers of an inverted yield curve, listen to **tinyurl .com/yyezatb5**.

First, consider the possibility of default, commonly called credit risk. Investors recognize that issuers other than the Treasury may or may not make all the promised payments on a bond, so they demand a higher yield as compensation for this risk. This extra compensation is called the **default risk premium**. Earlier in the chapter, we saw how bonds were rated based on their credit risk. What you will find if you start looking at bonds of different ratings is that lower-rated bonds have higher yields.

We stated earlier in this chapter that a bond's yield is calculated assuming that all the promised payments will be made. As a result, it is really a promised yield, and it may or may not be what you will earn. In particular, if the issuer defaults, your actual yield will be lower, probably much lower. This fact is particularly important when it comes to junk bonds. Thanks to a clever bit of marketing, such bonds are now commonly called high-yield bonds (which has a much nicer ring to it), but now you recognize that these are really high-promised-yield bonds.

Next, recall that we discussed earlier how municipal bonds are free from most taxes and, as a result, have much lower yields than taxable bonds. Investors demand the extra yield on a taxable bond as compensation for the unfavorable tax treatment. This extra compensation is the **taxability premium**.

Finally, bonds have varying degrees of liquidity. As we discussed earlier, there are an enormous number of bond issues, most of which do not trade on a regular basis. As a result, if you wanted to sell quickly, you would probably not get as high a price as you could otherwise. Investors prefer liquid assets to illiquid ones, so they demand a **liquidity premium** on top of all the other premiums we have discussed. As a result, all else being the same, less-liquid bonds will have higher yields than more-liquid bonds.

In a research paper on the understanding of market dynamics of the Indian corporate bond market, Rudra Sensarma and Indranil Bhattacharyya demonstrate that while monetary policy tightening impacts the level of the term structure, it has a stronger impact at the shorter end. Furthermore, given that banks in India try to hold more of government bonds not only from a risk-return perspective but also because it entails lower provisioning for capital adequacy, the authors state that policy tightening leads to a distinct preference for safe assets by market participants.[9]

CONCLUSION

If we combine everything we have discussed, we find that bond yields represent the combined effect of no fewer than six factors. The first is the real rate of interest. On top of the real rate are five premiums representing compensation for (1) expected future inflation, (2) interest rate risk, (3) default risk, (4) taxability, and (5) lack of liquidity. As a result, determining the appropriate yield on a bond requires careful analysis of each of these factors.

[9]Further reading: Sensarma, Rudra, and Indranil Bhattacharyya. "The impact of monetary policy on corporate bonds in India." *Journal of Policy modeling*, 38.3 (2016): 587–602.

RESEARCH IN EMERGING MARKET CONTEXT

According to Huang et al. (2022), firms' financial performance is negatively impacted and the possibility of default increases when exposed to increasing climate risk. Because of this, businesses have to pay higher interest rates and adhere to stricter covenant and collateral requirements when they borrow money from banks.

According to Chen and Sakouba (2021), bond investors believe that a portfolio with more bonds has a little lower exposure to interest rate risk. Salisu and Sikiru (2023) examine whether interest rate differentials—positive or negative—affect stock returns for equity investors. They present data that differs for the two interest rate scenarios. For the periods with low-interest rates, the association is negative; however, for the periods with high-interest rates, a positive correlation is observed.

References

Chen, Z., & Sakouba, I. (2021). Impact of the number of bonds on bond portfolio exposure to interest rate risk. *International Journal of Finance & Economics*, *26*(3), 4777–4797.

Huang, H. H., Kerstein, J., Wang, C., & Wu, F. (2022). Firm climate risk, risk management, and bank loan financing. *Strategic Management Journal*, *43*(13), 2849–2880.

Salisu, A. A., & Sikiru, A. A. (2023). Stock returns and interest rate differential in high and low interest rate environments. *International Journal of Finance & Economics*, *28*(2), 1713–1728.

Summary and Conclusions

This chapter has explored bonds, bond yields, and interest rates. We saw that:

1. Determining bond prices and yields is an application of basic discounted cash flow principles.
2. Bond values move in the direction opposite that of interest rates, leading to potential gains or losses for bond investors.
3. Bonds are rated based on their default risk. Some bonds, such as Treasury bonds, have no risk of default, whereas so-called junk bonds have substantial default risk.
4. Almost all bond trading is OTC, with limited transparency in many cases. As a result, bond price and volume information can be difficult to find for some types of bonds.
5. Bond yields and interest rates reflect six different factors: the real interest rate and five premiums, which investors demand as compensation for inflation, interest rate risk, default risk, taxability, and lack of liquidity.

In closing, we note that bonds are a vital source of financing to governments and corporations. Bond prices and yields are a rich subject, and our one chapter, necessarily, touches on only the most important concepts and ideas.

Concept Questions

1. **Treasury Bonds** Is it true that a U.S. Treasury security is risk-free?
2. **Interest Rate Risk** Which has greater interest rate risk, a 30-year Treasury bond or a 30-year BB corporate bond?
3. **Treasury Pricing** With regard to bid and ask prices on a Treasury bond, is it possible for the bid price to be higher? Why or why not?
4. **Yield to Maturity** Treasury bid and ask quotes are sometimes given in terms of yields, so there would be a bid yield and an ask yield. Which do you think would be larger? Explain.
5. **Coupon Rate** How does a bond issuer decide on the appropriate coupon rate to set on its bonds? Explain the difference between the coupon rate and the required return on a bond.
6. **Real and Nominal Returns** Are there any circumstances under which an investor might be more concerned about the nominal return on an investment than the real return?
7. **Bond Ratings** Companies pay rating agencies such as Moody's and S&P to rate their bonds, and the costs can be substantial. However, companies are not required to have their bonds rated in the first place; doing so is strictly voluntary. Why do you think they do it?
8. **Bond Ratings** U.S. Treasury bonds are not rated. Why? Often, junk bonds are not rated. Why?
9. **Term Structure** What is the difference between the term structure of interest rates and the yield curve?
10. **Crossover Bonds** Looking back at the crossover bonds we discussed in the chapter, why do you think split ratings such as these occur?
11. **Municipal Bonds** Why is it that municipal bonds are not taxed at the federal level but are taxable across state lines? Why is it that U.S. Treasury bonds are not taxable at the state level? (You may need to dust off the history books for this one.)
12. **Bond Market** What are the implications for bond investors of the lack of transparency in the bond market?

13. **Treasury Market** Take a look back at Figure 8.5. Notice the wide range of coupon rates. Why are they so different?

14. **Rating Agencies** A controversy erupted regarding bond-rating agencies when some agencies began to provide unsolicited bond ratings. Why do you think this is controversial?

15. **Bonds as Equity** The 100-year bonds we discussed in the chapter have something in common with junk bonds. Critics charge that, in both cases, the issuers are really selling equity in disguise. What are the issues here? Why would a company want to sell "equity in disguise"?

16. **Bond Prices versus Yields**

    a. What is the relationship between the price of a bond and its YTM?
    b. Explain why some bonds sell at a premium over par value while other bonds sell at a discount. What do you know about the relationship between the coupon rate and the YTM for premium bonds? What about for discount bonds? For bonds selling at par value?
    c. What is the relationship between the current yield and YTM for premium bonds? For discount bonds? For bonds selling at par value?

17. **Interest Rate Risk** All else being the same, which has more interest rate risk: a long-term bond or a short-term bond? What about a low coupon bond compared to a high coupon bond? What about a long-term, high coupon bond compared to a short-term, low coupon bond?

Questions and Problems

BASIC (Questions 1–16)

1. **Valuing Bonds** What is the price of a 25-year, zero coupon bond paying ₹1,000 at maturity, assuming semiannual compounding, if the YTM is:

    a. 6 percent?
    b. 8 percent?
    c. 10 percent?

2. **Valuing Bonds** Microhard has issued a bond with the following characteristics:

    Par: ₹1,000
    Time to maturity: 18 years
    Coupon rate: 7 percent
    Semiannual payments

    Calculate the price of this bond if the YTM is:

    a. 7 percent
    b. 9 percent
    c. 5 percent

3. **Bond Yields** Ashburn Corp. issued 25-year bonds two years ago at a coupon rate of 5.6 percent. The bonds make semiannual payments. If these bonds currently sell for 97 percent of par value, what is the YTM?

4. **Coupon Rates** Draiman Corporation has bonds on the market with 14.5 years to maturity, a YTM of 5.3 percent, a par value of ₹1,000, and a current price of ₹987. The bonds make semiannual payments. What must the coupon rate be on these bonds?

5. **Valuing Bonds** Even though most corporate bonds in the United States make coupon payments semiannually, bonds issued elsewhere often have annual coupon payments. Suppose a German company issues a bond with a par value of €1,000, 27 years to maturity, and a coupon rate of 3.6 percent paid annually. If the yield to maturity is 3.2 percent, what is the current price of the bond in euros?

6. **Bond Yields** A Japanese company has a bond outstanding that sells for 96.318 percent of its ¥100,000 par value. The bond has a coupon rate of 3.4 percent paid annually and matures in 16 years. What is the yield to maturity of this bond?

7. **Zero Coupon Bonds** You find a zero coupon bond with a par value of ₹10,000 and 24 years to maturity. If the yield to maturity on this bond is 4.2 percent, what is the Rupee price of the bond? Assume semiannual compounding periods.

8. **Valuing Bonds** Yan Yan Corp. has a ₹2,000 par value bond outstanding with a coupon rate of 4.7 percent paid semiannually and 13 years to maturity. The yield to maturity of the bond is 5.05 percent. What is the Rupee price of the bond?

9. **Valuing Bonds** Union Local School District has a bond outstanding with a coupon rate of 2.9 percent paid semiannually and 16 years to maturity. The yield to maturity on this bond is 2.7 percent, and the bond has a par value of ₹5,000. What is the Rupee price of the bond?

10. **Calculating Real Rates of Return** If Treasury bills are currently paying 4.6 percent and the inflation rate is 1.9 percent, what is the approximate real rate of interest? The exact real rate?

11. **Inflation and Nominal Returns** Suppose the real rate is 1.8 percent and the inflation rate is 2.7 percent. What rate would you expect to see on a Treasury bill?

12. **Nominal and Real Returns** An investment offers a total return of 11.7 percent over the coming year. Janice Yellen thinks the total real return on this investment will be only 9 percent. What does Janice believe the inflation rate will be over the next year?

13. **Nominal versus Real Returns** Say you own an asset that had a total return last year of 14.1 percent. If the inflation rate last year was 2.83 percent, what was your real return?

14. **Using Treasury Quotes** Locate the Treasury bond in Figure 8.5 maturing in January 2027. What is its coupon rate? What is its bid price? What was the previous day's asked price? Assume a par value of ₹10,000.

15. **Using Treasury Quotes** Locate the Treasury bond in Figure 8.5 maturing in November 2041. Is this a premium or a discount bond? What is its current yield? What is its yield to maturity? What is the bid-ask spread in Rupees? Assume a par value of ₹10,000.

16. **Zero Coupon Bonds** You buy a zero coupon bond at the beginning of the year that has a face value of ₹1,000, a YTM of 5.3 percent, and 25 years to maturity. If you hold the bond for the entire year, how much in interest income will you have to declare on your tax return? Assume semiannual compounding.

INTERMEDIATE (Questions 17–28)

17. **Bond Price Movements** Bond X is a premium bond making semiannual payments. The bond pays a coupon rate of 6.8 percent, has a YTM of 6.2 percent, and has 13 years to maturity. Bond Y is a discount bond making semiannual payments. This bond pays a coupon rate of 6.2 percent, has a YTM of 6.8 percent, and also has 13 years to maturity. The bonds have a par value of ₹1,000. What is the price of each bond today? If interest rates remain unchanged, what do you expect the price of these bonds to be 1 year from now? In 3 years? In 8 years? In 12 years? In 13 years? What's going on here? Illustrate your answers by graphing bond prices versus time to maturity.

18. **Interest Rate Risk** Both Bond Sam and Bond Dave have 7.1 percent coupons, make semiannual payments, and are priced at par value. Bond Sam has three years to maturity, whereas Bond Dave has 20 years to maturity. If interest rates suddenly rise by 2 percent, what is the percentage change in the price of Bond Sam? Of Bond Dave? If rates were to suddenly fall by 2 percent instead, what would the percentage change in the price of Bond Sam be then? Of Bond Dave? Illustrate your answers by graphing bond prices versus YTM. What does this problem tell you about the interest rate risk of longer-term bonds?

19. **Interest Rate Risk** Bond J has a coupon rate of 3 percent. Bond K has a coupon rate of 9 percent. Both bonds have 18 years to maturity, make semiannual payments, and have a YTM of 6 percent. If interest rates suddenly rise by 2 percent, what is the percentage price change of these bonds? What if rates

suddenly fall by 2 percent instead? What does this problem tell you about the interest rate risk of lower-coupon bonds?

20. **Bond Yields** Williams Software has 6.4 percent coupon bonds on the market with 18 years to maturity. The bonds make semiannual payments and currently sell for 106.32 percent of par. What is the current yield on the bonds? The YTM? The effective annual yield?

21. **Bond Yields** Uliana Co. wants to issue new 20-year bonds for some much-needed expansion projects. The company currently has 6 percent coupon bonds on the market with a par value of ₹1,000 that sell for ₹967, make semiannual payments, and mature in 20 years. What coupon rate should the company set on its new bonds if it wants them to sell at par?

22. **Accrued Interest** You purchase a bond with an invoice price of ₹1,053 and a par value of ₹1,000. The bond has a coupon rate of 5.3 percent, and there are four months to the next semiannual coupon date. What is the clean price of the bond?

23. **Accrued Interest** You purchase a bond with a coupon rate of 6.4 percent, a par value of ₹1,000, and a clean price of ₹1,027. If the next semiannual coupon payment is due in two months, what is the invoice price?

24. **Finding the Bond Maturity** Milton Corp. has 8 percent coupon bonds making annual payments with a YTM of 7.2 percent. The current yield on these bonds is 7.55 percent. How many years do these bonds have left until they mature?

25. **Using Bond Quotes** Suppose the following bond quote for IOU Corporation appears in the financial page of today's newspaper. Assume the bond has a face value of ₹1,000, it makes semiannual coupon payments, and the current date is April 15, 2022. What is the yield to maturity of the bond? What is the current yield?

Company (Ticker)	Coupon	Maturity	Last Price	Last Yield	EST Vol (000s)
IOU (IOU)	6.18	Apr 15, 2031	96.412	??	1,827

26. **Finding the Maturity** You found a 10 percent coupon bond on the market that sells for par value. What is the maturity on this bond?

27. **Interest on Zeroes** Imagination Dragons Corporation needs to raise funds to finance a plant expansion, and it has decided to issue 25-year zero coupon bonds with a par value of ₹1,000 each to raise the money. The required return on the bonds will be 5.3 percent. Assume semiannual compounding periods.
    a. What will these bonds sell for at issuance?
    b. Using the IRS amortization rule, what interest deduction can the company take on these bonds in the first year? In the last year?
    c. Repeat part (b) using the straight-line method for the interest deduction.
    d. Based on your answers in (b) and (c), which interest deduction method would the company prefer? Why?

28. **Zero Coupon Bonds** Suppose your company needs to raise ₹65 million and you want to issue 20-year bonds for this purpose. Assume the required return on your bond issue will be 4.9 percent, and you're evaluating two issue alternatives: a semiannual coupon bond with a coupon rate of 4.9 percent, and a zero coupon bond. The tax rate is 21 percent. Both bonds will have a par value of ₹1,000.
    a. How many of the coupon bonds would you need to issue to raise the ₹65 million? How many of the zeroes would you need to issue?
    b. In 20 years, what will your company's repayment be if you issue the coupon bonds? What if you issue the zeroes?
    c. Based on your answers in parts (a) and (b), why would you ever want to issue the zeroes? To answer, calculate the firm's aftertax cash outflows for the first year under the two different scenarios. Assume the IRS amortization rules apply for the zero coupon bonds.

CHALLENGE (Questions 29–35)

29. **Components of Bond Returns** Bond P is a premium bond with a coupon rate of 9 percent. Bond D has a coupon rate of 5 percent and is currently selling at a discount. Both bonds make annual payments, have a par value of ₹1,000, a YTM of 7 percent, and 15 years to maturity. What is the current yield for Bond P? For Bond D? If interest rates remain unchanged, what is the expected capital gains yield over the next year for Bond P? For Bond D? Explain your answers and the interrelationships among the various types of yields.

30. **Holding Period Yield** The YTM on a bond is the interest rate you earn on your investment if interest rates don't change. If you actually sell the bond before it matures, your realized return is known as the *holding period yield* (HPY).
    a. Suppose that today you buy a bond with an annual coupon of 7 percent for ₹1,050. The bond has 17 years to maturity. What rate of return do you expect to earn on your investment?
    b. Two years from now, the YTM on your bond has declined by 1 percent and you decide to sell. What price will your bond sell for? What is the HPY on your investment? Compare this yield to the YTM when you first bought the bond. Why are they different?

31. **Valuing Bonds** Cookie Dough Corporation has two different bonds currently outstanding. Bond M has a face value of ₹20,000 and matures in 20 years. The bond makes no payments for the first six years, then pays ₹900 every six months over the subsequent eight years, and finally pays ₹1,300 every six months over the last six years. Bond N also has a face value of ₹20,000 and a maturity of 20 years; it makes no coupon payments over the life of the bond. If the required return on both these bonds is 4.7 percent compounded semiannually, what is the current price of Bond M? Of Bond N?

32. **Treasury Bonds** The following Treasury bond quote appeared in *The Wall Street Journal* on May 11, 2004:

5/15/2009	9.125	100.09375	100.12500	0	−2.15

Why would anyone buy this Treasury bond with a negative yield to maturity? How is this possible?

33. **Real Cash Flows** When Marilyn Monroe died, ex-husband Joe DiMaggio vowed to place fresh flowers on her grave every Sunday as long as he lived. The week after she died in 1962, a bunch of fresh flowers that the former baseball player thought appropriate for the star cost about ₹7. Based on actuarial tables, "Joltin' Joe" could expect to live for 30 years after the actress died. Assume that the EAR is 6.8 percent. Also, assume that the price of the flowers will increase at 3.5 percent per year, when expressed as an EAR. Assuming that each year has exactly 52 weeks, what is the present value of this commitment? Joe began purchasing flowers the week after Marilyn died.

34. **Real Cash Flows** You are planning to save for retirement over the next 30 years. To save for retirement, you will invest ₹700 per month in a stock account in real Rupees and ₹300 per month in a bond account in real Rupees. The effective annual return of the stock account is expected to be 11 percent, and the bond account will earn 7 percent. When you retire, you will combine your money into an account with an effective return of 9 percent. The returns are stated in nominal terms. The inflation rate over this period is expected to be 4 percent. How much can you withdraw each month from your account in real terms assuming a 25-year withdrawal period? What is the nominal Rupee amount of your last withdrawal?

35. **Real Cash Flows** Paul Adams owns a health club in downtown Los Angeles. He charges his customers an annual fee of ₹500 and has an existing customer base of 720. Paul plans to raise the annual fee by 5 percent every year and expects the club membership to grow at a constant rate of 3 percent for the next five years. The overall expenses of running the health club are ₹145,000 a year and are expected to grow at the inflation rate of 2 percent annually. After five years, Paul plans to buy a luxury boat for ₹500,000, close the health club, and travel the world in his boat for the rest of his life. What is the annual amount that Paul can spend while on his world tour if he will have no money left in the bank when he dies? Assume Paul has a remaining life of 25 years after he retires and earns 9 percent on his savings.

36. **Deep Discount Bonds** Mahindra Bhoomiputra issued a series of bonds in 2006 called the Millionaire Bonds. Issued at ₹10,000 as a deep discount bond, it matures in 2041 and will be redeemed at ₹1 million. It is currently trading in BSE at ₹163,000. Based on this data, answer the following: [a] Estimate the returns to Kaikeyi for investing in the bond initially and holding it till maturity. [b] Estimate the returns to Kamala for investing in the bond initially and exiting in 2021. [c] Estimate the yield to maturity to Nidhi for investing in the bond in 2021 and holding it till maturity.

37. **Non-Convertible Debentures** Jindal Metals issued a non-convertible debenture in February 15, 2018, at a face value of ₹20 and at 14 percent, payable semi-annually. The bond would be redeemed in equal installments of ₹5 on August 15, 2025, 2026, 2027, and 2028. The bond is rated 'default' grade but is well-traded at the NSE with a market price of ₹6.50 in August 16, 2020. The bond has fallen steadily from ₹11 in February 16, 2019. Given the above information, [a] Compute the YTM if invested initially and sold in February 16, 2019. [b] What was the YTM rate for a person who invested in February 16, 2019, and quit in August 16, 2020? [c] What is the YTM for someone who invested initially and held it to maturity? [d] Compute the YTM if invested in February 16, 2019 and held to maturity. [e] What is the YTM for someone who invested in August 16, 2020 and held it to maturity?

Note: Perform all calculations for YTM assuming that the bond will not default.

38. **Perpetual Bonds** Axis Bank issued perpetual Tier-I bonds aggregating ₹7,000 crore on June 28, 2017. It received a CRISIL credit rating of AAA (Stable). The instrument has a fixed coupon rate of 8.75%. If it got traded at ₹100.42 on November 8, 2021, then what is its yield-to-maturity?

39. **Debt Instrument Trading** Identify any single corporate bond OR debt instrument that is publicly traded from the local stock exchange, i.e., BSE/NSE. Do share brief details of when it was last traded. Is the bond investment grade? Is the bond having a fixed coupon rate?

Excel Master It! Problem

Excel Master coverage online

Companies often buy bonds to meet a future liability or cash outlay. Such an investment is called a dedicated portfolio because the proceeds of the portfolio are dedicated to the future liability. In such a case, the portfolio is subject to reinvestment risk. Reinvestment risk occurs because the company will be reinvesting the coupon payments it receives. If the YTM on similar bonds falls, these coupon payments will be reinvested at a lower interest rate, which will result in a portfolio value that is lower than desired at maturity. Of course, if interest rates increase, the portfolio value at maturity will be higher than needed.

Suppose Ice Cubes, Inc., has the following liability due in five years. The company is going to buy five-year bonds today in order to meet the future obligation. The liability and current YTM are below:

Amount of liability	₹100,000,000
Current YTM	8%

a. At the current YTM, what is the face value of the bonds the company has to purchase today in order to meet its future obligation? Assume that the bonds in the relevant range will have the same coupon rate as the current YTM and these bonds make semiannual coupon payments.

b. Assume that the interest rates remain constant for the next five years. Thus, when the company reinvests the coupon payments, it will reinvest at the current YTM. What will be the value of the portfolio in five years?

c. Assume that immediately after the company purchases the bonds, interest rates either rise or fall by 1 percent. What will be the value of the portfolio in five years under these circumstances?

One way to eliminate reinvestment risk is called immunization. Rather than buying bonds with the same maturity as the liability, the company instead buys bonds with the same duration as the liability. If you think about the dedicated portfolio, if the interest rate falls, the future value of the reinvested coupon payments decreases. However, as interest rates fall, the price of the bond increases. These effects offset each other in an immunized portfolio.

Another advantage of using duration to immunize a portfolio is that the duration of a portfolio is the weighted average of the duration of the assets in the portfolio. In other words, to find the duration of a portfolio, you take the weight of each asset multiplied by its duration and then sum the results.

d. What is the duration of the liability for Ice Cubes, Inc.?

e. Suppose the two bonds shown below are the only bonds available to immunize the liability. What face amount of each bond will the company need to purchase to immunize the portfolio?

	Bond A	Bond B
Settlement	1/1/2020	1/1/2020
Maturity	1/1/2023	1/1/2028
Coupon rate	7.00%	8.00%
YTM	7.50%	9.00%
Coupons per year	2	2

Mini Case

FINANCING EAST COAST YACHTS' EXPANSION PLANS WITH A BOND ISSUE

After Dan's EFN analysis for East Coast Yachts (see the Mini Case in Chapter 3), Larissa has decided to expand the company's operations. She has asked Dan to enlist an underwriter to help sell ₹60 million in new 20-year bonds to finance new construction. Dan has entered into discussions with Kendahl Shoemaker, an underwriter from the firm of Crowe & Mallard, about which bond features East Coast Yachts should consider and also what coupon rate the issue will likely have. Although Dan is aware of bond features, he is uncertain as to the costs and benefits of some of them, so he isn't clear on how each feature would affect the coupon rate of the bond issue.

1. You are Kendahl's assistant and she has asked you to prepare a memo to Dan describing the effect of each of the following bond features on the coupon rate of the bond. She also would like you to list any advantages or disadvantages of each feature.
   a. The security of the bond, that is, whether or not the bond has collateral.
   b. The seniority of the bond.
   c. The presence of a sinking fund.
   d. A call provision with specified call dates and call prices.
   e. A deferred call accompanying the above call provision.
   f. A make-whole call provision.
   g. Any positive covenants. Also, discuss several possible positive covenants East Coast Yachts might consider.
   h. Any negative covenants. Also, discuss several possible negative covenants East Coast Yachts might consider.

i. A conversion feature (note that East Coast Yachts is not a publicly traded company).
j. A floating-rate coupon.

Dan is also considering whether to issue coupon-bearing bonds or zero coupon bonds. The YTM on either bond issue will be 5.8 percent. The coupon bond would have a 5.8 percent coupon rate. The company's tax rate is 21 percent.

2. How many of the coupon bonds must East Coast Yachts issue to raise the ₹60 million? How many of the zeroes must it issue?
3. In 20 years, what will be the principal repayment due if East Coast Yachts issues the coupon bonds? What if it issues the zeroes?
4. What are the company's considerations in issuing a coupon bond compared to a zero coupon bond?
5. Suppose East Coast Yachts issues the coupon bonds with a make-whole call provision. The make-whole call rate is the Treasury rate plus .40 percent. If East Coast calls the bonds in seven years when the Treasury rate is 4.3 percent, what is the call price of the bond? What if the Treasury rate is 6.7 percent?
6. Are investors really made whole with a make-whole call provision?
7. After considering all the relevant factors, would you recommend a zero coupon issue or a regular coupon issue? Why? Would you recommend an ordinary call feature or a make-whole call feature? Why?

9

Stock Valuation

When the stock market closed on August 26, 2020, the common stock of cell phone company Verizon was going for ₹59.46 per share. On that same day, stock in industrial giant DuPont de Nemours closed at ₹56.91, while stock in pet supply company Chewy closed at ₹58.28. Because the stock prices of these three companies were so similar, you might expect that they would be offering similar dividends to their stockholders, but you would be wrong. In fact, Verizon's annual dividend was ₹2.46 per share, DuPont de Nemours' was ₹1.20 per share, and Chewy was paying no dividend at all!

The Indian stock markets had a similar story to offer. On October 16, 2020, the equity shares of SJVN, a hydroelectric power producer, were selling for ₹21.40 per share. PTC India closed at ₹47.20 per share, while Adani Power closed at ₹36.05. However, regarding dividends, SJVN's annual dividend was ₹2.20 per share; PTC India paid an attractive dividend of ₹5.50 per share, whereas Adani Power has no track record of dividend at all!!

As we will see in this chapter, the current dividend is one of the primary factors in valuing common stocks. However, it is obvious from looking at Chewy that current dividends are not the end of the story. This chapter explores dividends, stock values, and the connection between the two.

In our previous chapter, we introduced you to bonds and bond valuation. In this chapter, we turn to the other major source of external financing for corporations: common stock. We first describe the cash flows associated with a share of stock and then develop a well-known result, the dividend growth model. Next, we point out that stocks are frequently priced using comparables, as well. We also show that the discounted cash flow approach introduced in Chapters 5 and 6 works for entire firms and shares of stock as well as for projects. We close out the chapter with a discussion of how shares of stock are traded and how stock prices and other important information are reported in the financial press.

Please visit us at **rwjcorporatefinance.blogspot.com** for the latest developments in the world of corporate finance.

9.1 The Present Value of Common Stocks

DIVIDENDS VERSUS CAPITAL GAINS

Excel Master coverage online

Our goal in this section is to value common stocks. We learned in previous chapters that an asset's value is determined by the present value of its future cash flows. A stock provides two kinds of cash flows. First, many stocks pay dividends on a regular basis. Second, the stockholder receives the sale price when she sells the stock. In order to value common stocks, we need to answer an important question: Is the price of a share of stock equal to:

1. The present value of the sum of next period's dividend plus next period's stock price, or:

2. The present value of all future dividends?

This is the kind of question that students would love to see on a multiple-choice exam because both (1) and (2) are correct.

To see that (1) and (2) are the same, let's start with an individual who will buy the stock and hold it for one year. In other words, she has a one-year holding period. In addition, she is willing to pay P_0 for the stock today. That is, she calculates:

$$P_0 = \frac{D_1}{1 + R} + \frac{P_1}{1 + R} \tag{9.1}$$

D_1 is the expected dividend paid at year's end and P_1 is the expected price at year's end. P_0 is the present value of the common stock investment. The term in the denominator, R, is the appropriate discount rate for the stock and represents the expected return that investors require in order to commit funds to the stock (or the required return).

That seems easy enough, but where does P_1 come from? P_1 is not pulled out of thin air. Rather, there must be a buyer at the end of Year 1 who is willing to purchase the stock for P_1. This buyer determines the price by:

$$P_1 = \frac{D_2}{1 + R} + \frac{P_2}{1 + R} \tag{9.2}$$

Substituting the value of P_1 from Equation 9.2 into Equation 9.1 yields:

$$\begin{aligned} P_0 &= \frac{1}{1 + R}\left[D_1 + \left(\frac{D_2 + P_2}{1 + R}\right)\right] \\ &= \frac{D_1}{1 + R} + \frac{D_2}{(1 + R)^2} + \frac{P_2}{(1 + R)^2} \end{aligned} \tag{9.3}$$

We can ask a similar question for Equation 9.3: Where does P_2 come from? An investor at the end of Year 2 is willing to pay P_2 because of the dividend and stock price at Year 3. This process can be repeated *ad nauseam.*[1] At the end, we are left with:

$$P_0 = \frac{D_1}{1 + R} + \frac{D_2}{(1 + R)^2} + \frac{D_3}{(1 + R)^3} + \cdots = \sum_{t=1}^{\infty} \frac{D_t}{(1 + R)^t} \tag{9.4}$$

Thus, the price of a share of common stock to the investor is equal to the present value of all of the expected future dividends.

This is a very useful result. A common objection to applying present value analysis to stocks is that investors are too shortsighted to care about the long-run stream of dividends. These critics argue that an investor will generally not look past his or her time horizon. Prices in a market dominated by short-term investors will reflect only near-term dividends. However, our discussion shows that a long-run dividend discount model holds even when investors have short-term time horizons. Although an investor may want to cash out early, she must find another investor who is willing to buy. The price this second investor pays is dependent on dividends after his date of purchase.

VALUATION OF DIFFERENT TYPES OF STOCKS

The preceding discussion shows that the price of a share of stock is the present value of its future dividends. How do we apply this idea in practice? Equation 9.4 represents a general model that is applicable whether

[1]This procedure reminds us of the physicist lecturing on the origins of the universe. He was approached by an elderly gentleman in the audience who disagreed with the lecture. The attendee said that the universe rests on the back of a huge turtle. When the physicist asked what the turtle rested on, the gentleman said another turtle. Anticipating the physicist's objections, the attendee said, "Don't tire yourself out, young fellow. It's turtles all the way down."

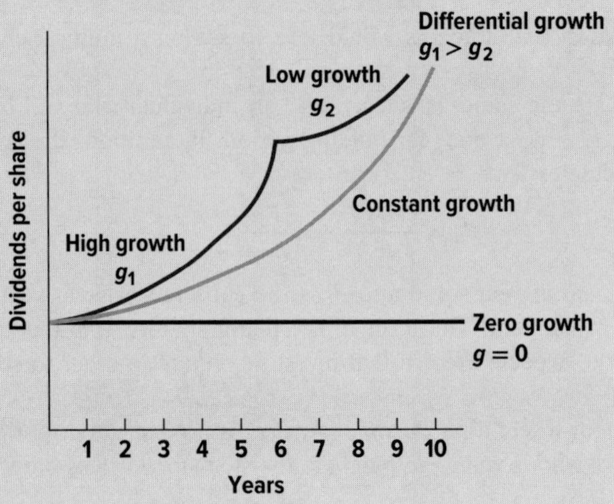

Dividend growth models:

$$\text{Zero growth: } P_0 = \frac{D}{R}$$

$$\text{Constant growth: } P_0 = \frac{D}{R-g}$$

$$\text{Differential growth: } P_0 = \sum_{t=1}^{T} \frac{D(1+g_1)^t}{(1+R)^t} + \frac{D_{T+1}}{R-g_2} \times \frac{1}{(1+R)^T}$$

Figure 9.1 Zero Growth, Constant Growth, and Differential Growth Patterns

dividends are expected to grow, decline, or stay the same. The general model can be simplified if dividends are expected to follow some basic patterns: (1) zero growth, (2) constant growth, and (3) differential growth. These cases are illustrated in Figure 9.1.

Case 1 (Zero Growth) The price of a share of stock with a constant dividend is given by:

$$P_0 = \frac{D_1}{1+R} + \frac{D_2}{(1+R)^2} + \cdots = \frac{D}{R}$$

Here it is assumed that $D_1 = D_2 = \cdots = D$. This is an application of the perpetuity formula from Chapter 4 and is useful in valuing preferred stocks where the dividends paid out are constant.

Case 2 (Constant Growth) Dividends are expected to grow at rate g, as follows:

End of Year	1	2	3	4	. . .
Dividend	D_1	$D_1(1+g)$	$D_1(1+g)^2$	$D_1(1+g)^3$	. . .

Note that D_1 is the dividend at the end of the first period.

EXAMPLE 9.1

Projected Dividends Humty Sharma Products will pay a dividend of ₹4 per share a year from now. Financial analysts believe that dividends will rise at 6 percent per year for the foreseeable future. What is the dividend per share at the end of each of the first five years?

End of Year	1	2	3	4	5
Dividend	₹4.00	₹4 × 1.06 = ₹4.24	₹4 × 1.06^2 = ₹4.4944	₹4 × 1.06^3 = ₹4.7641	₹4 × 1.06^4 = ₹5.0499

If dividends are expected to grow at a constant rate, the price of a share of stock is:

$$P_0 = \frac{D_1}{1+R} + \frac{D_1(1+g)}{(1+R)^2} + \frac{D_1(1+g)^2}{(1+R)^3} + \frac{D_1(1+g)^3}{(1+R)^4} + \cdots = \frac{D_1}{R-g}$$

where g is the growth rate and D_1 is the dividend on the stock at the end of the first period. This is the formula for the present value of a growing perpetuity, which we introduced in Chapter 4.

EXAMPLE 9.2

Stock Valuation Suppose an investor is considering the purchase of a share of the Mizoram Mining Company. The stock will pay a ₹3 dividend a year from today. This dividend is expected to grow at 10 percent per year (g = 10%) for the foreseeable future. The investor thinks that the required return (R) on this stock is 15 percent, given her assessment of Mizoram Mining's risk. (We also refer to R as the discount rate of the stock.) What is the price of a share of Mizoram Mining Company's stock?

Using the constant growth formula, we calculate the price to be ₹60:

$$₹60 = \frac{₹3}{.15 - .10}$$

Today's price, P_0, is quite dependent on the value of g. If g had been estimated to be 12.5 percent, the value of the share would have been:

$$₹120 = \frac{₹3}{.15 - .125}$$

The stock price doubles (from ₹60 to ₹120) when g only increases 25 percent (from 10 percent to 12.5 percent). Because of P_0's dependency on g, one should maintain a healthy sense of skepticism when using this constant growth of dividends model.

Furthermore, note that P_0 is equal to infinity when the growth rate, g, equals the discount rate, R. Because stock prices are never infinite, an estimate of g equal to or greater than R implies an error in estimation. More will be said of this point later.

EXAMPLE 9.2A

Chambal Fertilizers & Chemicals Limited (CFCL), listed on BSE, has an expected growth rate of 8%. Each equity share just received an annual ₹1.80 dividend per share. The appropriate required return is 12%. Using these figures, we compute the intrinsic value of the CFCL shares:

Expected dividend at the end of the year = Div_1 = ₹1.80 × (1 + 0.08)

Using the constant growth formula, we expect the value to be =
(Div_1) ÷ (k_e – g) = 1.80 ÷ (0.12 – 0.08) = ₹48.6

The assumption of steady dividend growth might strike you as peculiar. Why would the dividend grow at a constant rate? The reason is that, for many companies, steady growth in dividends is an explicit goal. For example, in April 2020, Procter & Gamble, the Cincinnati-based maker of personal care and household products, increased its dividend by 6 percent to ₹3.16 per share; this was notable because it was the 64th increase in a row. Similarly, in FY2020, MRF, India's largest tyre company, paid a dividend of ₹100 per equity share; this was its nearly seventh decade of steadily increasing shareholder rewards. The subject of dividend growth falls under the general heading of dividend policy, so we will defer further discussion of it to a later chapter.

You might wonder what would happen with the dividend growth model if the growth rate, g, were greater than the discount rate, R. It looks like we would get a negative stock price because $R - g$ would be less than zero, but this is not what would happen.

Instead, if the constant growth rate exceeds the discount rate, then the stock price is infinitely large. Why? If the growth rate is bigger than the discount rate, the present value of the dividends keeps getting bigger. Essentially the same is true if the growth rate and the discount rate are equal. In both cases, the simplification that allows us to replace the infinite stream of dividends with the dividend growth model is invalid, so the answers we get from the dividend growth model are nonsense unless the growth rate is less than the discount rate.

Case 3 (Differential Growth) In this case, an algebraic formula would be unwieldy. Instead, we present examples.

EXAMPLE 9.3

Differential Growth Euphoria Drug Company is expected to enjoy rapid growth from the introduction of its new back-rub ointment. The dividend for a share of Euphoria's stock a year from today is expected to be ₹1.15. During the next four years, the dividend is expected to grow at 15 percent per year (g_1 = 15%). After that, growth (g_2) will be equal to 10 percent per year. Calculate the present value of a share of stock if the required return (R) is 15 percent.

Figure 9.2 displays the growth in Euphoria's dividends. We need to apply a two-step process to discount these dividends. We first calculate the present value of the dividends growing at 15 percent per year. That is, we first calculate the present value of the dividends at the end of each of the first five years. Second, we calculate the present value of the dividends beginning at the end of Year 6.

(continued)

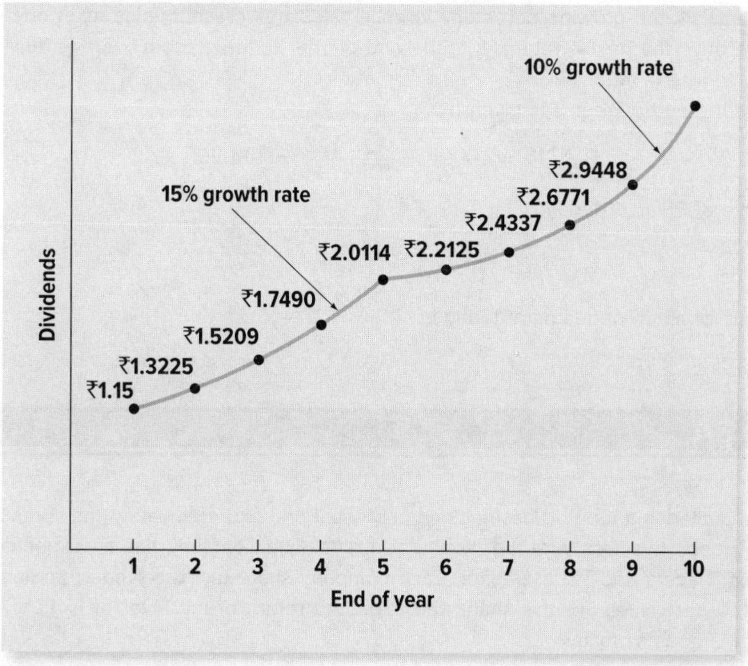

Figure 9.2 Growth in Dividends for Euphoria Drug Company

Present Value of First Five Dividends The present values of dividend payments in Years 1 through 5 are calculated as follows:

Future Year	Growth Rate (g_1)	Expected Dividend	Present Value
1	.15	₹1.1500	₹1
2	.15	1.3225	1
3	.15	1.5209	1
4	.15	1.7490	1
5	.15	2.0114	1
Years 1–5		The present value of dividends =	₹5

The growing annuity formula from the previous chapter could normally be used in this step. However, note that dividends grow at 15 percent per year, which is also the discount rate. Because $g = R$, the growing annuity formula cannot be used in this example.

Present Value of Dividends Beginning at End of Year 6 We use the procedure for deferred perpetuities and deferred annuities presented in Chapter 4. The dividends beginning at the end of Year 6 are:

End of Year	6	7	8	9	. . .
Dividend	$D_5 \times (1 + g_2)$	$D_5 \times (1 + g_2)^2$	$D_5 \times (1 + g_2)^3$	$D_5 \times (1 + g_2)^4$	. . .
	₹2.0114 × 1.10	2.0114 × 1.10^2	2.0114 × 1.10^3	2.0114 × 1.10^4	. . .
	= ₹2.2125	= ₹2.4337	= ₹2.6771	= ₹2.9448	

(continued)

As stated in Chapter 4, the growing perpetuity formula calculates present value as of one year prior to the first payment. Because the payment begins at the end of Year 6, the present value formula calculates present value as of the end of Year 5.

The price at the end of Year 5 is given by:

$$P_5 = \frac{D_6}{R - g_2} = \frac{₹2.2125}{.15 - .10} = ₹44.25$$

The present value of P_5 as of today is:

$$\frac{P_5}{(1 + R)^5} = \frac{₹44.25}{1.15^5} = ₹22$$

The present value of all dividends as of today is ₹27 (= ₹22 + 5).

EXAMPLE 9.3A

Kohinoor Foods Limited is a reputed basmati rice processor and exporter. Lately, the company ventured into the ready-to-eat foods business with the 'Kohinoor' brand. The company has an expected growth rate of 50% for the next 3 years and 7% thereafter. Each company share just received an annual ₹1.00 dividend per share (on ₹10 par value). For this share, the expected return of the investor is 12%. We compute the value of Kohinoor Foods as follows:

We start by determining the annual dividends to be paid by the company:
Div_0 = ₹1.00 (this has been paid already)
$Div_1 = Div_0 \times (1 + g_1)^1$ = ₹1.00 × $(1.5)^1$ = ₹1.50
$Div_2 = Div_0 \times (1 + g_1)^2$ = ₹1.00 × $(1.5)^2$ = ₹2.25
$Div_3 = Div_0 \times (1 + g_1)^3$ = ₹1.00 × $(1.5)^3$ = ₹3.37
$Div_4 = Div_0 \times (1 + g_2)^1$ = ₹.3.37 × $(1.07)^1$ = ₹3.61

$P_3 = 3.61/(12\% - 7\%)$

Using the constant dividend growth model, we find the stock price in the third year as ₹72.22/-. We then find the present value of the expected cash flows from holding this stock. Finally, we calculate the intrinsic value by summing up all the cash flow present values as follows:

The present value of all dividends today is = ₹1.3 + ₹1.8 + ₹2.4 + ₹51.4

9.2 Estimates of Parameters in the Dividend Discount Model

The value of the firm is a function of its growth rate, *g*, and its discount rate, *R*. How does one estimate these variables?

WHERE DOES *g* COME FROM?

The previous discussion assumed that dividends grow at the rate *g*. We now want to estimate this rate of growth. Consider a business whose earnings next year are expected to be the same as earnings this year unless a net investment is made. This situation is quite plausible because net investment is equal to gross, or total, investment less depreciation. A net investment of zero occurs when total investment equals depreciation. If total investment is equal to depreciation, the firm's physical plant is just maintained, consistent with no growth in earnings.

Net investment will be positive only if some earnings are not paid out as dividends, that is, only if some earnings are retained.[2] This leads to the following equation:

$$\underset{\text{year}}{\overset{\text{Earnings}}{\text{next}}} = \underset{\text{year}}{\overset{\text{Earnings}}{\text{this}}} + \underbrace{\underset{\text{this year}}{\overset{\text{Retained}}{\text{earnings}}} \times \underset{\text{earnings}}{\overset{\text{Return on}}{\text{retained}}}}_{\text{Increase in earnings}} \tag{9.5}$$

The increase in earnings is a function of both the retained earnings and the return on the retained earnings.

We now divide both sides of Equation 9.5 by earnings this year, yielding:

$$\frac{\text{Earnings next year}}{\text{Earnings this year}} = \frac{\text{Earnings this year}}{\text{Earnings this year}} + \left(\frac{\text{Retained earnings this year}}{\text{Earnings this year}}\right) \times \text{Return on retained earnings} \tag{9.6}$$

The left-hand side of Equation 9.6 is one plus the growth rate in earnings, which we write as $1 + g$. The ratio of retained earnings to earnings is called the **retention ratio**. We can write:

$$1 + g = 1 + \text{Retention ratio} \times \text{Return on retained earnings} \tag{9.7}$$

It is difficult for a financial analyst to determine the return expected on currently retained earnings because the details on forthcoming projects are not generally public information. However, it is frequently assumed that projects selected in the current year have an anticipated return equal to returns from past projects. Here, we can estimate the anticipated return on current retained earnings by the historical **return on equity**, or ROE. After all, ROE is the return on the firm's entire equity, which is the return on the cumulation of all the firm's past projects.

From Equation 9.7, we have a way to estimate growth in earnings:

$$g = \text{Retention ratio} \times \text{Return on retained earnings (ROE)} \tag{9.8}$$

The estimate for the growth rate in earnings, g, is also the estimate for the growth rate in dividends under the common assumption that the ratio of dividends to earnings is held constant.[3]

EXAMPLE 9.4

Earnings Growth Pushpanjali Enterprises just reported earnings of ₹2 million. The firm plans to retain 40 percent of its earnings in all years going forward. We also could say that 60 percent of earnings will be paid out as dividends. The ratio of dividends to earnings is often called the **payout ratio**, so the payout ratio for

(continued)

[2]We ignore the issuance of new shares or the buyback of existing shares of stock. The dividend discount model is valid under both situations. These possibilities are considered in later chapters.

[3]In Chapter 3, we also discussed methods for g's calculation.

Pushpanjali is 60 percent. The historical return on equity (ROE) has been 16 percent, which is expected to continue into the future. How much will earnings grow over the coming year?

We first perform the calculation without reference to Equation 9.8. Then we use Equation 9.8 as a check.

Calculation without Reference to Equation 9.8 The firm will retain ₹800,000 (= .40 × ₹2 million). Assuming that historical ROE is an appropriate estimate for future returns, the anticipated increase in earnings is:

$$₹800{,}000 \times .16 = ₹128{,}000$$

The percentage growth in earnings is:

$$\frac{\text{Change in earnings}}{\text{Total earnings}} = \frac{₹128{,}000}{₹2 \text{ million}} = .064, \text{ or } 6.4\%$$

This implies that earnings in one year will be ₹2,128,000 (= ₹2,000,000 × 1.064).

Check Using Equation 9.8 Using g = Retention ratio × ROE, we have:

$$g = .4 \times .16 = .064, \text{ or } 6.4\%$$

Because Pushpanjali's payout ratio is constant going forward, the growth rate of both earnings and dividends is 6.4 percent.

EXAMPLE 9.4A

Hindustan Unilever Limited just reported earnings per share of ₹29. It plans to have a dividend payout of 85% of its earnings. The historical return on equity (ROE) has been 70%, which is expected to continue into the future. How much will the earnings grow over the coming year?

We use, Growth Rate = ROE X Retention Ratio = 70% × 0.15 = 10.50%

WHERE DOES *R* COME FROM?

We have taken the required return or discount rate, R, as given. Conceptually, the required return is the return on assets with the same risk as the firm's shares. We show how to estimate R in Chapter 13. For now, we want to examine the implications of the dividend growth model for this required return. Earlier, we calculated the price of the stock today, P_0, as:

$$P_0 = \frac{D_1}{R - g}$$

Rearranging the equation to solve for R, we get:

$$R - g = \frac{D_1}{P_0}$$

$$R = \frac{D_1}{P_0} + g \qquad \textbf{(9.9)}$$

Equation 9.9 tells us that the required return, R, has two components. The first of these, D_1/P_0, is called the **dividend yield**. Because this is calculated as the expected cash dividend divided by the current price, it is conceptually similar to the current yield on a bond.

The second part of the total return is the expected growth rate, g. As we will verify shortly, the dividend growth rate is also the stock price's growth rate. Thus, this growth rate can be interpreted as the **capital gains yield**–that is, the rate at which the value of the investment grows.

To illustrate the components of the required return, suppose we observe a stock selling for ₹20 per share. The next dividend is expected to be ₹1 per share. You think that the dividend will grow by 10 percent per year more or less indefinitely. What expected return does this stock offer you?

The dividend growth model calculates total return as:

$$R = \text{Dividend yield} + \text{Capital gains yield}$$

$$R = \frac{D_1}{P_0} + g$$

In this case, total return works out to be:

$$\begin{aligned} R &= ₹1/₹20 + .10 \\ &= .05 + .10 \\ &= .15, \text{ or } 15\% \end{aligned}$$

This stock has an expected return of 15 percent.

We can verify this answer by calculating the price in one year, P_1, using 15 percent as the required expected return. Because the dividend expected to be received in one year is ₹1 and the expected growth rate of dividends is 10 percent, the dividend expected to be received in two years, D_2, is ₹1.10. Based on the dividend growth model, the stock price in one year will be:

$$\begin{aligned} P_1 &= D_2/(R - g) \\ &= ₹1.10/(.15 - .10) \\ &= ₹1.10/.05 \\ &= ₹22 \end{aligned}$$

Notice that this ₹22 is ₹20 × 1.1, so the stock price has grown by 10 percent, as it should. This means the capital gains yield is 10 percent, which equals the growth rate in dividends.

What is the investor's total expected return? If you pay ₹20 for the stock today, you will get a ₹1 dividend at the end of the year, and you will have a ₹22 – 20 = ₹2 gain. Your dividend yield is ₹1/₹20 = .05, or 5 percent. Your capital gains yield is ₹2/₹20 = .10, or 10 percent, so your total expected return would be 5 percent + 10 percent = 15 percent, as we calculated above.

To get a feel for actual numbers in this context, consider that, according to the 2020 Value Line *Investment Survey*, Procter & Gamble's dividends were expected to grow by 6.5 percent over the next five or so years, compared to a historical growth rate of 4 percent over the preceding 5- and 10-year periods. In 2020, the projected dividend for the coming year was given as ₹3.20. The stock price at that time was ₹138.39 per share. What is the expected return investors require on P&G? Here, the dividend yield is 2.3 percent (= ₹3.20/₹138.39) and the capital gains yield is 6.5 percent, giving a total required return of 8.8 percent on P&G stock.

EXAMPLE 9.5

Calculating the Required Return Pushpanjali Enterprises, the company examined in Example 9.4, has 1,000,000 shares of stock outstanding. The stock is selling at ₹10. What is the required return on the stock?

The payout ratio is the ratio of dividends/earnings. Because Pushpanjali's retention ratio is 40 percent, the payout ratio, which is 1 – Retention ratio, is 60 percent. Recall both that Pushpanjali reported earnings of ₹2,000,000 and that the firm's growth rate is 6.4 percent.

(continued)

Earnings a year from now will be ₹2,128,000 (= ₹2,000,000 × 1.064), implying that dividends will be ₹1,276,800 (= .60 × ₹2,128,000). Dividends per share will be ₹1.28 (= ₹1,276,800/1,000,000). Given that $g = .064$, we calculate R from Equation 9.9 as follows:

$$.192 = \frac{₹1.28}{₹10.00} + .064$$

A HEALTHY SENSE OF SKEPTICISM

It is important to emphasize that our approach merely estimates g; our approach does not determine g precisely. We mentioned earlier that our estimate of g is based on a number of assumptions. We assumed that the return on reinvestment of future retained earnings is equal to the firm's past ROE and that the future retention ratio is equal to the past retention ratio. Our estimate for g will be off if these assumptions prove to be wrong.

Unfortunately, the determination of R is highly dependent on g. For example, if g for Pushpanjali is estimated to be 0, R equals 12.8 percent (= ₹1.28/₹10.00). If g is estimated to be 12 percent, R equals 24.8 percent (= ₹1.28/₹10.00 + .12). Thus, one should view estimates of R with a healthy sense of skepticism.

Because of this, some financial economists generally argue that the estimation error for R for a single security is too large to be practical. Therefore, they suggest calculating the average R for an entire industry. This R would then be used to discount the dividends of a particular stock in the same industry.

One should be particularly skeptical of two polar cases when estimating R for individual securities. First, consider a firm not currently paying a dividend. If the firm initiates a dividend at some point, its dividend growth rate over the interval becomes infinite. Equation 9.9 must be used with extreme caution here, if at all–a point we emphasize later in this chapter.

Second, we mentioned earlier that share price is infinite when g is equal to R. Because stock prices are never infinite in the real world, an analyst whose estimate of g for a particular firm is equal to or above R must have made a mistake. Most likely, the analyst's high estimate for g is correct for the next few years. However, firms cannot maintain an abnormally high growth rate forever. The analyst's error was to use a short-run estimate of g in a model requiring a perpetual growth rate.

DIVIDENDS OR EARNINGS: WHICH TO DISCOUNT?

This chapter applied the growing perpetuity formula to the valuation of stocks. In our application, we discounted dividends, not earnings. This is sensible because investors select a stock for the cash they can get out of it. They only get two things out of a stock: dividends and the ultimate sales price, which is determined by what future investors expect to receive in dividends.

The calculated stock price would usually be too high were earnings to be discounted instead of dividends. As we saw in our estimation of a firm's growth rate, only a portion of earnings goes to the stockholders as dividends. The remainder is retained to generate future dividends. In our model, retained earnings are equal to the firm's investment. To discount earnings instead of dividends would be to ignore the investment that a firm must make today in order to generate future earnings and dividends.

THE NO-DIVIDEND FIRM

Students frequently ask the following question: If the dividend discount model is correct, why aren't no-dividend stocks selling at zero? This is a good question and gets at the goals of the firm. A firm with many growth opportunities is faced with a dilemma. The firm can pay out dividends now or it can forgo dividends now so that it can make investments that will generate even greater dividends in the future.[4] This is often a painful choice because a strategy of dividend deferment may be optimal yet unpopular among certain stockholders.

Many firms choose to pay no dividends–and these firms sell at positive prices. For example, most internet firms, such as Amazon, Alphabet, Twitter, and Facebook, pay no dividends. Alike, most Indian small-scale Bio-technological firms, such as Adinath Bio-Labs and ABL Biotechnologies, pay no dividends. Rational shareholders believe that they either will receive dividends at some point or will receive something just as good. That is, the firm will be acquired in a merger, with the stockholders receiving either cash or shares of stock at that time.

Of course, actual application of the dividend discount model is difficult for no-dividend firms. Clearly, the model for constant growth of dividends does not apply. Though the differential growth model can work in theory, the difficulties of estimating the date of the first dividend, the growth rate of dividends after that date, and the ultimate merger price make application of the model quite difficult in reality.

Empirical evidence suggests that firms with high growth rates are likely to pay lower dividends, a result consistent with the above analysis. Consider eBay. The company started in 1998 and grew rapidly for many years. It paid its first dividend in 2019, though it was a multibillion-rupee company (in both sales and market value of stockholders' equity) prior to that date. Identically, Bharti Airtel and Infosys Technologies did not pay any dividends for over a decade.[5] Why did it wait so long to pay a dividend? It waited because it had so many positive growth opportunities, such as new acquisitions, to fund.

9.3 Comparables

So far in this chapter, we have valued stocks by discounting dividends. Practitioners often value by comparables, as well. The comparables approach is similar to valuation in real estate. If your neighbor's home just sold for ₹250,000 and it has similar size and amenities to your home, your home is probably worth around ₹250,000 also. In the stock market, comparable firms are assumed to have similar *multiples.* To see how the comparables approach works, let's look at perhaps the most common multiple, the price-earnings (PE) multiple, or PE ratio.

PRICE-EARNINGS RATIO

A stock's price-earnings ratio is, as the name suggests, the ratio of the stock's price to its earnings per share. If the stock of Sun Aerodynamic Systems (SAS) is selling at ₹27.00 per share and its earnings per share over the last year was ₹4.50, SAS's PE ratio would be 6 (= ₹27/₹4.50).

It is generally assumed that similar firms have similar PE ratios. For example, imagine the average PE ratio across all publicly traded companies in the specialty retail industry is 12 and a particular company in the industry has earnings of ₹10 million. If this company is judged to be similar to the rest of the industry, one might estimate the company's value to be ₹120 million (= 12 × ₹10 million).

Valuation via PE certainly looks easier than valuation via discounted dividends because the discounted dividend approach calls for estimates of yearly dividends. But is the PE approach better? That depends on the similarity across comparables.

On August 28, 2020, *The Wall Street Journal* reported Alphabet's PE ratio to be 37. On that same day, IBM's PE was 15, HP's was 11, Apple's was 38, and Microsoft's was 40. Why would different stocks in the

[4]A third alternative is to issue stock so that the firm has enough cash both to pay dividends and to invest. This possibility is explored in a later chapter.

[5]Bharti Airtel's first dividend was in FY2009 (established in 1995) and Infosys Technologies' was in FY2000 (established in 1981).

same industry trade at different PE ratios? Do the differences imply that HP was underpriced and Apple was overpriced? Or are there rational reasons for the differences?

Equally, on a particular trading day in October 2020 at the Bombay Stock Exchange (BSE), Tata Consultancy Services (TCS) was trading at ₹2,762 and its EPS was ₹78, implying a PE ratio slightly above 35. On the same day, HCL Tech's PE was 24, Hexaware Tech's PE was 27, and Geometric Software's PE was 16.50. 63 Moons Technologies (earlier known as Financial Technologies) traded at a price of 72 but had negative EPS. Why would the stocks in the same sector trade at different PE ratios? What could explain the differences in the stock price?

The dividend discount model in Equations 9.1 and 9.4 implies that a firm's PE ratio is related to the value of its future projects. Consider two firms, each having just reported earnings per share of ₹1. However, one firm has many new projects, each with a positive net present value (NPV), while the other firm has no new projects at all. The firm with the valuable projects should sell at a higher price because an investor is buying both current income of ₹1 and the new projects.

Suppose that the firm with the projects sells for ₹16 and the other firm sells for ₹8. The ₹1 earnings per share number appears in the denominator of the PE ratio for both firms. Thus, the PE ratio is 16 for the firm with the valuable projects, but only 8 for the firm without the projects.

This explanation seems to hold fairly well in the real world. Electronics and other high-tech stocks generally sell at high PE ratios because they are perceived to have many vaulable projects. In fact, some technology stocks sell at high prices even though the companies have never earned a profit. The PE ratios of these companies are infinite. Conversely, railroads, utilities, and steel companies sell at lower PE ratios because of fewer valuable projects. Table 9.1(a) contains PE ratios in 2017 for some well-known US companies and the S&P 500 Index. Table 9.1(b) contains PE ratios in 2020 for some well-known Indian companies and the S&P BSE Sensex Index. Notice the variations across industries.

Table 9.1(a) Selected PE Ratios, 2020

Company	Industry	PE Ratio
Chubb	Insurance	26
Pepsico	Beverages	29
General Motors	Automotive	28
Goldman Sachs	Financial services	16
Whirlpool	Home appliances	14
Facebook	Technology	36
S&P 500 average	n/a	30

Table 9.1(b) Selected PE Ratios for Indian companies, 2024

Company	Industry	PE Ratio
Bajaj Auto	Automobiles	34
Dr. Reddy's Laboratories	Pharmaceuticals	20.42
Hindustan Unilever	Personal Care	54.69
ICICI Bank	Banking	17
Larsen & Toubro	Infrastructure	30.74
Tata Steel	Steel	42.86
S&P BSE SENSEX	n/a	25

There are at least two additional factors explaining the PE ratio. The first is the discount rate, *R*. Because *R* appears in the denominator of the dividend discount model (in Equation 9.1), the formula implies that the PE ratio is negatively related to the firm's discount rate. We have already suggested that the discount rate is positively related to the stock's risk or variability. Thus, the PE ratio is negatively related to the stock's risk. To see that this is a sensible result, consider two firms, A and B, where the stock market expects both firms to have annual earnings of ₹1 per share forever. However, the earnings of Firm A are known with certainty while the earnings of Firm B are quite variable. A rational stockholder is likely to pay more for a share of Firm A because of the absence of risk. If a share of Firm A sells at a higher price and both firms have the same EPS, the PE ratio of Firm A must be higher.

The second additional factor concerns the firm's choice of accounting methods. Consider two identical firms, C and D. Firm C uses LIFO and reports earnings of ₹2 per share. Firm D uses the less conservative accounting assumptions of FIFO and reports earnings of ₹3 per share. The market knows that both firms are identical and prices both at ₹18 per share. The price-earnings ratio is 9 (= ₹18/₹2) for firm C and 6 (= ₹18/₹3) for Firm D. Thus, the firm with the more conservative principles has the higher PE ratio.

In conclusion, we have argued that a stock's PE ratio is likely a function of three factors:

1. *Investment opportunities.* Companies with opportunities to invest in projects with large, positive NPVs are likely to have high PE ratios.
2. *Risk.* Low-risk stocks are likely to have high PE ratios.
3. *Accounting practices.* Firms following conservative accounting practices will likely have high PE ratios.

Which of these factors is most important in the real world? The consensus among finance professionals is that investment opportunities typically have the biggest impact on PE ratios. For example, high-tech companies generally have higher PE ratios than, say, utilities because utilities have fewer valuable investment opportunities, even though utilities typically have lower risk. And, within industries, differences in investment opportunities also generate the biggest differences in PE ratios.

Correspondingly, Tata Consultancy Services' (TCS) high PE is almost certainly due to its growth opportunities, not due to its low risk or its accounting conservatism. Geometric Software's PE is lower than TCS's PE because Geometric Software's growth opportunities are a small fraction of its existing business lines. However, Geometric Software had a much higher PE 7–8 years ago, when it had huge growth opportunities but little in the way of existing business.

While multiples such as the PE ratio can be used to price stocks, care must be taken. Firms in the same industry are likely to have different multiples if they have different investment opportunities, risk levels, and accounting treatments. Average multiples should not be calculated across all firms in any industry. Rather, an average multiple should be calculated only across those firms in an industry with similar characteristics.

There are a number of ways to calculate the price-earnings ratio, with perhaps the biggest difference involving the denominator. Imagine that a company's stock is selling at ₹20 today, with the company reporting earnings per share (EPS) of ₹2 for the last year. However, the consensus among analysts is that the firm will report earnings next year of ₹2.50. Some sources calculate the PE ratio as the ratio of current price to the EPS over the last 12 months. The TTM (for "trailing twelve months") earnings would be ₹2 in this example, and the trailing PE ratio would be 10 (= ₹20/₹2). Other sources use forward earnings–that is, earnings forecasted over the next year–to calculate a PE ratio. The forward PE would be 8 (= ₹20/₹2.50) here. Going back to our earlier example, Microsoft had a TTM EPS of ₹5.76, which is part of why its PE ratio was so high. The company's projected earnings for next year were ₹7.34, which resulted in a PE ratio of 31, still high, but more realistic.

Which approach is correct? There is no right answer. On the one hand, investors should discount future cash flows, not past cash flows, to value stocks, implying that the forward PE is more meaningful. On the other hand, trailing earnings reflect what actually happened, while forward earnings are merely forecasts. So, while we can't say which variant of the PE ratio is more appropriate in a particular situation, you should always be aware of how a particular PE has been calculated.

To hear more on the PE, go to **tinyurl.com/rebs43n**.

Often we will be interested in valuing newer companies that both don't pay dividends and are not yet profitable, meaning that earnings are negative. What do we do then? One answer is to use the price-sales ratio. As the name suggests, this ratio is the price per share of the stock divided by sales per share. You use this ratio like you use the PE ratio, except you use sales per share instead of earnings per share. As with PE ratios, price-sales ratios vary depending on company age and industry. Typical values are in the .8–2.0 range, but they can be much higher for younger, faster-growing companies. A drawback of the price-sales ratio is that it does not account for the amount of debt on the firm's balance sheet. When comparing two otherwise identical firms with the same sales, the firm with more debt will have a lower price-sales ratio because that firm will ultimately use part of its sales to service its debt rather than to pay dividends to its stockholders.

ENTERPRISE VALUE RATIOS

The PE ratio is an equity ratio. That is, the numerator is the price per share of stock and the denominator is the earnings per share of stock. In addition, practitioners often use ratios involving both equity and debt. Perhaps the most common is the enterprise value (EV) to EBITDA ratio. Enterprise value is equal to the market value of the firm's equity plus the market value of the firm's debt minus cash. Recall, EBITDA stands for earnings before interest, taxes, depreciation, and amortization.

Suppose the Irfan Food Products Co. (IFPC) has equity worth ₹800 million, debt worth ₹300 million, and cash of ₹100 million. The enterprise value here is ₹1 billion (= ₹800 + 300 − 100). The firm has the following income statement (in millions):

Revenue	₹700
Cost of goods sold	500
Earnings before interest, taxes, depreciation, and amortization (EBITDA)	₹200
Depreciation and amortization	100
Interest	24
Pretax income	₹ 76
Taxes (21%)	16
Net income	₹ 60

The EV to EBITDA ratio is 5 (= ₹1 billion/₹200 million). Note that all the items in the income statement below EBITDA are ignored when calculating this ratio.

As with PE ratios, it is generally assumed that similar firms have similar EV/EBITDA ratios. Assume the average EV/EBITDA ratio in an industry is 6. If Vadodara Corporation, a firm in the industry with EBITDA of ₹50 million, is judged to be similar to the rest of the industry, its enterprise value might be estimated at ₹300 million (= 6 × ₹50 million). We also find that Vadodara has ₹75 million of debt and ₹25 million of cash. Given our estimate of Vadodara's enterprise value, Vadodara's stock would be worth ₹250 million (= ₹300 − 75 + 25).

A number of questions arise with value ratios:

1. *Is there any advantage to the EV/EBITDA ratio over the PE ratio?* Yes. Companies in the same industry may differ by leverage–that is, the ratio of debt to equity. As you will learn in Chapter 16, leverage increases the risk of equity, impacting the discount rate, R. Thus, while firms in the same industry may be otherwise comparable, they are likely to have different PE ratios if they have different degrees of leverage. Because enterprise value includes debt and equity, the impact of leverage on the EV/EBITDA ratio is less.[6]
2. *Why is EBITDA used in the denominator?* The numerator and denominator of a ratio should be consistent. Because the numerator of the PE ratio is the price of a share of stock, it makes sense that the denominator is the earnings per share (EPS) of stock. That is, interest is specifically subtracted before EPS is calculated. By contrast, because EV involves the sum of debt and equity, it is sensible that the denominator is unaffected by interest payments. This is the case with EBITDA because, as its name implies, earnings are calculated before interest is taken out.
3. *Why does the denominator ignore depreciation and amortization?* Many practitioners argue that because depreciation and amortization are not cash flows, earnings should be calculated before taking out depreciation and amortization. In other words, depreciation and amortization merely reflect the sunk cost of a previous purchase. However, this view is by no means universal. Others point out that depreciable assets will eventually be replaced in an ongoing business. Because depreciation charges can reflect the cost of future replacement, it can be argued that these charges should be considered in a calculation of income.
4. *What other denominators are used in value ratios?* Among others, practitioners may use EBIT (earnings before interest and taxes), EBITA (earnings before interest, taxes, and amortization), and free cash flow.
5. *Why is cash subtracted out?* Many firms seem to hold amounts of cash well in excess of what is needed. For example, Microsoft held about ₹137 billion of cash and short-term investments in late 2020, far more than many analysts believed was optimal. Because an enterprise value ratio should reflect the ability of productive assets to create earnings or cash flow, cash should be subtracted out when calculating the ratio. The viewpoint that all cash should be ignored can be criticized. Some cash holdings are necessary to run a business, and this amount of cash should be included in EV.

If the firm has negative or very low EBITDA, you can instead compute the enterprise value to sales ratio by substituting revenue for EBITDA in the denominator. For IFPC in the example above, the EV to sales ratio is 1.43 (= ₹1 billion/₹700 million). If Vadodara has sales of ₹210 and we use IFPC as the comparable firm, Vadodara's enterprise value can be estimated as ₹300 million (= 1.43 × ₹210 million). We can then adjust for Vadodara's ₹75 million of debt and ₹25 million of cash to estimate that Vadodara's stock should be worth ₹250 million (= ₹300 − 75 + 25). Note that the enterprise value to sales ratio is similar to the price-sales ratio introduced earlier. However, the enterprise value to sales ratio has the advantage that it takes into account the amount of debt held by the firm.

9.4 Valuing Stocks Using Free Cash Flows

In Chapters 5 and 6, we valued corporate projects by discounting the projects' cash flows. Cash flows were determined by a top-down approach beginning with estimates of revenues and expenses. So far in this chapter, we have discounted dividends to value a single share of stock. As an alternative, one can value an entire firm by discounting its free cash flows in a manner similar to the project valuation in Chapters 5 and 6.

[6]Leverage does impact the ratio of EV to EBITDA to some extent. As we discuss in Chapter 16, leverage creates a tax shield, increasing EV. Because leverage should not impact EBITDA, the ratio should increase with leverage.

Consider Ganguly Harmonic Control Systems (GHCS). Revenue, which is forecast to be ₹500 million in one year, is expected to grow at 10 percent per year for the two years after that, 8 percent per year for the next two years, and 6 percent per year after that. Expenses including depreciation are 60 percent of revenues. Net investment, including net working capital and capital spending less depreciation, is 10 percent of revenues. Because all costs are proportional to revenue, free cash flow grows at the same rate as does revenue. GHCS is an all-equity firm with 12 million shares outstanding. A discount rate of 16 percent is appropriate for a firm of GHCS's risk.

The relevant numbers (in millions) for the first five years, rounded to two decimals, are:

	1	2	3	4	5
Revenue	₹500.00	₹550.00	₹605.00	₹653.40	₹705.67
Expenses	300.00	330.00	363.00	392.04	423.40
Earnings before taxes	₹200.00	₹220.00	₹242.00	₹261.36	₹282.27
Taxes (21%)	42.00	46.20	50.82	54.89	59.28
Earnings after taxes	₹158.00	₹173.80	₹191.18	₹206.47	₹222.99
Net investment	50.00	55.00	60.50	65.34	70.57
Free cash flow	₹108.00	₹118.80	₹130.68	₹141.13	₹152.43

Because free cash flow grows at 6 percent per year after Year 5, net cash flow in Year 6 is forecast to be ₹161.57 (= ₹152.43 × 1.06). Using the growing perpetuity formula, we can calculate the present value as of Year 5 of all future cash flows to be ₹1,615.71 million [= ₹161.57/(.16 – .06)].

The present value as of today of that terminal value is:

$$₹769.26 \text{ million} = ₹1{,}615.71 \times \frac{1}{1.16^5}$$

The present value of the free cash flows during the first five years is:

$$₹415.63 \text{ million} = \frac{₹108}{1.16} + \frac{₹118.80}{1.16^2} + \frac{₹130.68}{1.16^3} + \frac{₹141.13}{1.16^4} + \frac{₹152.43}{1.16^5}$$

Adding in the terminal value, today's value of the firm is ₹1,184.89 million (= ₹415.63 + 769.26). Given the number of shares outstanding, the price per share is ₹98.74 (= ₹1,184.89/12).

The above calculation assumes a growing perpetuity after Year 5. As we pointed out in the previous section, stocks are often valued by multiples. An investor might estimate the terminal value of GHCS via a multiple, rather than the growing perpetuity formula. Suppose that the price-earnings ratio for comparable firms in GHCS's industry is 7.

Because earnings after tax in Year 5 are ₹222.99, using the PE multiple of 7, the value of the firm at Year 5 would be estimated as ₹1,560.95 million (= ₹222.99 × 7).

The firm's value today is:

$$₹1{,}158.82 \text{ million} = \frac{₹108}{1.16} + \frac{₹118.80}{1.16^2} + \frac{₹130.68}{1.16^3} + \frac{₹141.13}{1.16^4} + \frac{₹152.43}{1.16^5} + \frac{₹1{,}560.95}{1.16^5}$$

With 12 million shares outstanding, the price per share of GHCS would be ₹96.57 (= ₹1,158.82/12).

Now we have two estimates of the value of a share of equity in GHCS. The different estimates reflect the different ways of calculating terminal value. Using the constant growth discounted cash flow method for terminal value, our estimate of the equity value per share of GHCS is ₹98.74, and using the PE comparable method, our estimate is ₹96.57. There is no best method. If the comparable firms were all identical to GHCS, perhaps the PE method would be best. Unfortunately, firms are not identical. On the other hand, if we were very sure of the terminal date and the growth in subsequent cash flows, perhaps the constant growth method would be best. In practice, both methods are used.

Conceptually, the dividend discount model, comparables method, and free cash flow model are mutually consistent and can be used to determine the value of a share of stock. In practice, the dividend discount model is especially useful for firms paying steady dividends and the comparables method is useful for firms with similar investment opportunities. The free cash flow model is helpful for non-dividend-paying firms with external financing needs.

9.5 The Stock Markets in General, Focus on US Markets

Excel Master coverage online

The stock market consists of a **primary market** and a **secondary market**. In the primary, or new-issue market, shares of stock are first brought to the market and sold to investors. In the secondary market, existing shares are traded among investors. In the primary market, companies sell securities to raise money. We will discuss this process in detail in a later chapter. We therefore focus mainly on secondary market activity in this section. We conclude with a discussion of how stock prices are quoted in the financial press.

DEALERS AND BROKERS

Because most securities transactions involve dealers and brokers, it is important to understand exactly what is meant by the terms *dealer* and *broker.* A **dealer** maintains an inventory and stands ready to buy and sell at any time. In contrast, a **broker** brings buyers and sellers together but does not maintain an inventory. When we speak of used car dealers and real estate brokers, we recognize that the used car dealer maintains an inventory, whereas the real estate broker does not.

In the securities markets, a dealer stands ready to buy securities from investors wishing to sell them and to sell securities to investors wishing to buy them. The price the dealer is willing to pay is called the *bid price.* The price at which the dealer will sell is called the *ask price* (sometimes called the *asked, offered,* or *offering price*). The difference between the bid and ask prices is called the *spread,* and it is the basic source of dealer profits.

Dealers exist in all areas of the economy, not just the stock markets. Your college bookstore is probably both a primary and a secondary market textbook dealer. If you buy a new book, this is a primary market transaction. If you buy a used book, this is a secondary market transaction, and you pay the store's ask price. If you sell the book back, you receive the store's bid price, often half of the ask price. The bookstore's spread is the difference between the two prices.

How big is the bid-ask spread on your favorite stock? Check out the latest quotes at **www.bloomberg.com**.

In contrast, a securities broker arranges transactions between investors, matching those wishing to buy securities with those wishing to sell securities. The distinctive characteristic of security brokers is that they do not buy or sell securities for their own accounts. Facilitating trades by others is their business.

ORGANIZATION OF THE NYSE

The New York Stock Exchange, or NYSE, popularly known as the Big Board, recently celebrated its bicentennial. It has occupied its current location on Wall Street since the turn of the twentieth century. Measured in terms of rupee volume of activity and the total value of shares listed, it is the largest stock market in the world.

Members The NYSE has 1,366 exchange **members**. Prior to 2006, the exchange members were said to own "seats" on the exchange, and, collectively, the members of the exchange were also the owners. For this and other reasons, seats were valuable and were bought and sold fairly regularly. Seat prices reached a record ₹4 million in 2005.

In 2006, all of this changed when the NYSE became a publicly owned corporation. Naturally, its stock is listed on the NYSE. Now, instead of purchasing seats, exchange members must purchase trading licenses, the number of which is still limited to 1,366. In 2020, a license cost ₹50,000 a year. Having a license entitles you to buy and sell securities on the floor of the exchange. Different members play different roles in this regard.

On April 4, 2007, the NYSE grew even larger when it merged with Euronext to form NYSE Euronext. Euronext was a stock exchange in Amsterdam, with subsidiaries in Belgium, France, Portugal, and the United Kingdom. With the merger, NYSE Euronext became the world's "first global exchange." Further expansion occurred in 2008 when NYSE Euronext merged with the American Stock Exchange. Then, in November 2013, the acquisition of the NYSE by the Intercontinental Exchange (ICE) was completed. ICE, which was founded in May 2000, was originally a commodities exchange, but its rapid growth gave it the necessary ₹8.2 billion for the acquisition of the NYSE.

As we briefly describe how the NYSE operates, keep in mind that other markets owned by NYSE Euronext and ICE may function differently. What makes the NYSE somewhat unique is that it is a *hybrid market.* In a hybrid market, trading takes place both electronically and face-to-face.

With electronic trading, orders to buy and orders to sell are submitted to the exchange. Orders are compared by a computer and whenever there is a match, the orders are executed with no human intervention. Most trades on the NYSE occur this way. For orders that are not handled electronically, the NYSE relies on its license holders. There are three different types of license holders: **designated market makers (DMMs)**, **floor brokers**, and **supplemental liquidity providers (SLPs)**.

The DMMs, formerly known as *specialists*, act as dealers in particular stocks. Typically, each stock on the NYSE is assigned to a single DMM. As a dealer, a DMM maintains a two-sided market, meaning that the DMM continually posts and updates bid and ask prices. By doing so, the DMM ensures that there is always a buyer or seller available, thereby promoting market liquidity.

Floor brokers execute trades for customers, trying to get the best price possible. Floor brokers are generally employees of large brokerage firms such as Merrill Lynch, the wealth management division of Bank of America. The interaction between floor brokers and DMMs is the key to nonelectronic trading on the NYSE. We discuss this interaction in detail in a moment.

The SLPs are essentially investment firms that agree to be active participants in stocks assigned to them. Their job is to regularly make a one-sided market (i.e., offering to either buy or sell). They trade purely for their own accounts (using their own money), so they do not represent customers. They are given a small rebate on their buys and sells, thereby encouraging them to be more aggressive. The NYSE's goal is to generate as much liquidity as possible, which makes it easier for ordinary investors to quickly buy and sell at prevailing prices. Unlike DMMs and floor brokers, SLPs do not operate on the floor of the stock exchange.

In recent years, floor brokers have become less important on the exchange floor because of the efficient Pillar system, which allows orders to be transmitted electronically directly to the DMM. Additionally, the NYSE has an electronic platform called Arca, which accounts for a substantial percentage of all trading on the NYSE, particularly for smaller orders. The average time for a trade on the NYSE Arca is less than one second.

Finally, a small number of NYSE members are floor traders who independently trade for their own accounts. Floor traders try to anticipate temporary price fluctuations and profit from them by buying low and selling high. In recent decades, the number of floor traders has declined substantially, suggesting that it has become increasingly difficult to profit from short-term trading on the exchange floor.

Operations Now that we have a basic idea of how the NYSE is organized and who the major players are, we turn to the question of how trading actually takes place. Fundamentally, the business of the NYSE is to attract and process **order flow**. The term *order flow* means the flow of customer orders to buy and sell stocks. The customers of the NYSE are the millions of individual investors and tens of thousands of institutional investors who place their orders to buy and sell shares in NYSE-listed companies. The NYSE has been quite successful in attracting order flow. Currently, it is common for well over a billion shares to change hands in a single day.

Floor Activity It is quite likely that you have seen footage of the NYSE trading floor on television, or you may have visited the NYSE and viewed exchange floor activity from the visitors' gallery. Either way, you would have seen a big room, about the size of a basketball gym. This big room is called, technically, "the Big Room." There are a couple of other, smaller rooms that you normally don't see, one of which is called "the Garage" because that is literally what it was before it was taken over for trading.

On the floor of the exchange are a number of stations, each with a roughly figure-eight shape. These stations have multiple counters with numerous terminal screens above and on the sides. People operate behind and in front of the counters in relatively stationary positions.

Other people move around on the exchange floor, frequently returning to the many telephones positioned along the exchange walls. In all, you may be reminded of worker ants moving around an ant colony. It is natural to wonder, "What are all those people doing down there (and why are so many wearing funny-looking coats)?"

As an overview of exchange floor activity, here is a quick look at what goes on. Each of the counters is a **DMM's post**. DMMs normally operate in front of their posts to monitor and manage trading in the stocks assigned to them. Clerical employees working for the DMMs operate behind the counter. Moving from the many workstations lining the walls of the exchange out to the exchange floor and back again are swarms of floor brokers, receiving customer orders, walking out to DMMs' posts where the orders can be executed, and returning to confirm order executions and receive new customer orders.

To better understand activity on the NYSE trading floor, imagine yourself as a floor broker. Your phone clerk has handed you an order to sell 20,000 shares of Walmart for a customer of the brokerage company that employs you. The customer wants to sell the stock at the best possible price as soon as possible. You immediately walk (running violates exchange rules) to the DMM's post where Walmart stock is traded.

As you approach the DMM's post where Walmart is traded, you check the terminal screen for information on the current market price. The screen reveals that the last executed trade was at ₹140.10 per share and that the DMM is bidding ₹140 per share. You could immediately sell to the DMM at ₹140 per share, but that would be too easy.

Instead, as the customer's representative, you are obligated to get the best possible price. It is your job to "work" the order, and your job depends on providing satisfactory order execution service. So, you look around for another broker who represents a customer who wants to buy Walmart stock. Luckily, you quickly find another broker at the DMM's post with an order to buy 20,000 shares. Noticing that the DMM is asking ₹140.10 per share, you both agree to execute your orders with each other at a price of ₹140.05 per share. This price is exactly halfway between the DMM's bid and ask prices, and it saves each of your customers ₹.05 × 20,000 = ₹1,000 as compared to dealing at the posted prices.

For a very actively traded stock, there may be many buyers and sellers around the DMM's post, and most of the trading will be done directly between brokers. This is called trading in the "crowd." In such cases, the DMM's responsibility is to maintain order and to make sure that all buyers and sellers receive a fair price. In other words, the DMM essentially functions as a referee.

More often, however, there will be no crowd at the DMM's post. Going back to our Walmart example, suppose you are unable to quickly find another broker with an order to buy 20,000 shares. Because you have an order to sell immediately, you may have no choice but to sell to the DMM at the bid price of ₹140 per share. In this case, the need to execute an order quickly takes priority, and the DMM provides the liquidity necessary to allow immediate order execution.

Finally, note that colored coats are worn by many of the people on the floor of the exchange. The color of the coat indicates the person's job or position. Clerks, runners, visitors, exchange officials, and so on wear particular colors to identify themselves. Also, things can get a little hectic on a busy day, with the result that good clothing doesn't last long; the cheap coats offer some protection.

TYPES OF ORDERS

The preceding example involving Walmart stock considers how trades are executed on the NYSE. We now want to discuss a related issue: What sort of trades can an investor make? In the Walmart example, we said that the customer placing the order to sell 20,000 shares of Walmart "wants to sell the stock at the best possible price as soon as possible." An order such as this is called a *market order* because the stock will be sold at or near the current market price. Another investor might want to buy 10,000 shares of, say, Apple under the same terms. This order is termed a market order to buy.

Are these the only orders that a customer can place? No. Consider an investor who, for whatever reason, wants to own Walmart stock but is not willing to pay as much as ₹140 per share for it. He might place a *limit order* to buy for, say, ₹135. This means that the customer is directing his broker only to buy the stock at a price of ₹135 or less. Because the customer's trade will only get filled at a price of ₹135 or less, the customer will never get to buy the stock if the price stays above ₹135. Conversely, if another investor would like to sell her Walmart stock, but not for a price as low as ₹140, she might place a limit order to sell for, say, ₹155, meaning that her trade will get executed only at a price of ₹155 or more.

Another type of trade is a *stop order.* Suppose an owner of Walmart stock who, while generally optimistic about Walmart's business prospects, is, nevertheless, worried about the possibility of a big price decline. He might place a *stop order* to sell at, say, ₹130. Here, the order will be executed as a market order to sell once the trigger price of ₹130 is reached. This means that, once another trade occurs at ₹130 or below, the broker will try to sell the stock at the best possible price as soon as possible. Does this mean that the customer is guaranteed a price of at least ₹130? Unfortunately, no. In a rapidly falling market, once the price of ₹130 is reached, the next price might be significantly below ₹130, implying that the customer might receive a price well below ₹130. Conversely, another customer might want to execute a stop order to buy at, say ₹140, implying her stop order will be converted to a market order to buy once the price of ₹140 is reached.

One more thing is worth mentioning. There is a time dimension to limit and stop orders. That is, one can place, for example, a *day order*, meaning that the limit or stop order will be canceled if it is not executed by the end of the trading day. Conversely, a *good-til-canceled order*, as its name suggests, remains open until the customer specifically cancels it.[7]

NASDAQ OPERATIONS

In terms of total rupee volume of trading, the second largest stock market in the United States is Nasdaq (say "Naz-dak"). The somewhat odd name originally was an acronym for the National Association of Securities Dealers Automated Quotations system, but Nasdaq is now a name in its own right.

[7]A more detailed discussion of these and other orders can be found in Bradford Jordan, Thomas Miller, and Steve Dolvin, *Fundamentals of Investments*, 9th ed. (New York: McGraw-Hill, 2021).

Introduced in 1971, the Nasdaq market is a computer network of securities dealers and others that disseminates timely security price quotes to computer screens worldwide. Nasdaq dealers act as market makers for securities listed on Nasdaq. As market makers, Nasdaq dealers post bid and ask prices at which they accept sell and buy orders, respectively. With each price quote, they also post the number of shares that they obligate themselves to trade at their quoted prices.

Like NYSE DMMs, Nasdaq market makers trade on an inventory basis–that is, using their inventory as a buffer to absorb buy and sell order imbalances. Unlike the NYSE DMM system, Nasdaq features multiple market makers for actively traded stocks. There are two key differences between the NYSE and Nasdaq:

1. Nasdaq is a computer network and has no physical location where trading takes place.
2. Nasdaq has a multiple market maker system rather than a DMM system.

Traditionally, a securities market largely characterized by dealers who buy and sell securities for their own inventories is called an **over-the-counter (OTC) market**. Consequently, Nasdaq is often referred to as an OTC market. However, in their efforts to promote a distinct image, Nasdaq officials prefer that the term *OTC* not be used when referring to the Nasdaq market. Nevertheless, old habits die hard, and many people still refer to Nasdaq as an OTC market.

The Nasdaq network operates with three levels of information access. Level 1 is designed to provide a timely, accurate source of price quotations. These prices are freely available over the internet. Level 2 allows users to view price quotes from all Nasdaq market makers. In particular, this level allows access to **inside quotes**. Inside quotes are the highest bid quotes and the lowest ask quotes for a Nasdaq-listed security. Level 2 is now available for a small fee. Level 3 is for the use of market makers only. This access level allows Nasdaq dealers to enter or change their price quote information.

Nasdaq is actually made up of three separate markets: the Nasdaq Global Select Market, the Nasdaq Global Market, and the Nasdaq Capital Market. As the market for Nasdaq's larger and more actively traded securities, the Global Select Market lists about 1,200 companies (as of 2020), including some of the best-known companies in the world, such as Microsoft and Intel. Global Market companies are somewhat smaller in size, and Nasdaq lists about 1,450 of these. Finally, the smallest companies listed on Nasdaq are in the Nasdaq Capital Market; about 550 are currently listed. Of course, as Capital Market companies become more established, they may move up to the Global Market or Global Select Market.

ECNs In a very important development in the late 1990s, the Nasdaq system was opened to so-called **electronic communications networks (ECNs)**. ECNs are basically websites that allow investors to trade directly with one another. Investor buy and sell orders placed on ECNs are transmitted to the Nasdaq and displayed along with market maker bid and ask prices. The ECNs open up the Nasdaq by essentially allowing individual investors, not just market makers, to enter orders. As a result, the ECNs act to increase liquidity and competition.

STOCK MARKET REPORTING

In recent years, stock price quotes and related information have increasingly moved from traditional print media, such as *The Wall Street Journal*, to various websites. Yahoo! Finance (finance.yahoo.com) is a good example. We went there and requested a stock quote on wholesale club Costco, which is listed on Nasdaq. Here is a portion of what we found:

You can get real-time stock quotes on the web. See **finance.yahoo.com** for details.

Costco Wholesale Corporation (COST)
NasdaqGS - NasdaqGS Delayed Price. Currency in USD

Add to watchlist | Visitors trend 2W ↑ 10W ↑ 9M ↑

346.89 -1.48 (-0.43%)
As of 2:35PM EDT. Market open.

Summary | Company Outlook | Chart | Conversations | Statistics | Historical Data | Profile | Financials | Analysis | Options

Previous Close	348.37	Market Cap	153.158B
Open	346.85	Beta (5Y Monthly)	0.69
Bid	346.83 x 1000	PE Ratio (TTM)	41.50
Ask	346.90 x 800	EPS (TTM)	8.36
Day's Range	344.29 - 347.94	Earnings Date	Sep 24, 2020
52 Week Range	271.28 - 349.06	Forward Dividend & Yield	2.80 (0.80%)
Volume	871,172	Ex-Dividend Date	Jul 30, 2020
Avg. Volume	2,301,985	1y Target Est	340.58

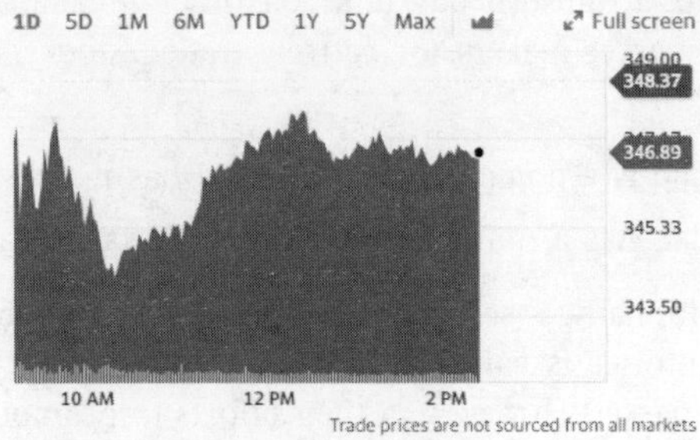

SOURCE: finance.yahoo.com, August 31, 2020.

Most of this information is self-explanatory. The price ₹346.89 is the real-time price of the last trade. The reported change is from the previous day's closing price. The opening price is the first trade of the day. We see the bid and ask prices of ₹346.83 and ₹346.90, respectively, along with the market "depth," which is the number of shares sought at the bid price and offered at the ask price. Next, we have the range of prices for this day, followed by the range over the previous 52 weeks. Volume is the number of shares traded today, followed by average daily volume over the last three months.

Moving to the second column, market cap is the number of shares outstanding (from the most recent quarterly financial statements) multiplied by the current price per share. The PE Ratio is the ratio we discussed earlier in this chapter. The earnings per share (EPS) used in the calculation is "TTM," meaning "trailing twelve months." Finally, we have the forward dividend on the stock, which is the estimated dividend over the next four quarters, and the dividend yield. Notice that the yield is the reported dividend divided by the previous close: ₹2.80/₹348.37 = .008, or .8 percent. The "1y Target Est" is the average estimated stock price one year ahead based on estimates from security analysts who follow the stock.

9.6 The Stock Markets in India

In India, the equity shares of almost all the firms trade in organized auction markets. In these markets, buyers enter competitive bids, and sellers enter competitive offers simultaneously. In other words, it is an organized market in which buyers and sellers gather to transact business through announced bids and ask prices. India has two large auction exchanges: the Bombay Stock Exchange (BSE) and the National Stock Exchange (NSE). These two control nearly the whole auction market. BSE was established in 1875. Until its corporatization and demutualization in 2007, brokerages owned and operated the exchange, similar to NYSE. On the other hand, the NSE was one of the first demutualized exchanges in the world right from its inception in 1992.[8]

[8] In addition, many companies also raise money from foreign markets. Outside the United States financial markets, there are other large and important financial markets (such as, Amsterdam Stock Exchange, London Stock Exchange and the Singapore Stock Exchange) and Indian corporations look to these markets to raise cash.

The Indian stock markets have been early adopters of technology. This has allowed them to usher in quicker settlement cycles. The settlement date refers to the actual day the stock ownership is transferred from the seller to buyer, typically later than the day the transactions happen on the exchange. Faster settlement cycles safeguard investors from potential fraudulent activities and provide investors with faster liquidity. India moved to a T+2 settlement cycle in April 2003, while in January 2023, India moved to a T+1 settlement cycle. In December 2023, SEBI began consultations to move to a T+0 settlement cycle. In contrast, the US SEC moved to the T+2 cycle in 2017 and plans to move to the T+1 settlement by May 2024.

RESEARCH IN EMERGING MARKET CONTEXT

Sakariyahu et al. (2023) look into adding sentiment measures as a risk component to asset pricing since existing models may not be sufficient to explain price or market anomalies. According to their analysis, investors' emotions are a significant systematic risk factor that contains valuable information.

Due to decreased funding costs and increased operating cash flows, Chauhan and Kumar (2018) conclude that nonfinancial disclosure has favourable value implications. Additionally, they note that independent businesses benefit more from nonfinancial transparency than do business group companies. However, Khandelwal et al. (2023) discovered a negative ESG disclosure premium, meaning that companies who disclose more information than others receive worse profits.

References

Chauhan, Y., & Kumar, S. B. (2018). Do investors value the nonfinancial disclosure in emerging markets?. *Emerging Markets Review*, *37*, 32–46.

Khandelwal, V., Sharma, P., & Chotia, V. (2023). ESG Disclosure and Firm Performance: An Asset-Pricing Approach. *Risks*, *11*(6), 112.

Sakariyahu, R., Paterson, A., Chatzivgeri, E., & Lawal, R. (2023). Chasing noise in the stock market: an inquiry into the dynamics of investor sentiment and asset pricing. *Review of Quantitative Finance and Accounting*, 1–35.

Summary and Conclusions

This chapter has covered the basics of stocks and stock valuations. The key points include:

1. A stock can be valued by discounting its dividends. We discuss three situations:
   a. The case of zero growth of dividends.
   b. The case of constant growth of dividends.
   c. The case of differential growth.
2. An estimate of the growth rate of dividends is needed for the dividend discount model. A useful estimate of the growth rate is:

$$g = \text{Retention ratio} \times \text{Return on retained earnings (ROE)}$$

   As long as the firm holds its ratio of dividends to earnings constant, g represents the growth rate of both dividends and earnings.

To learn more about the Indian exchanges, visit **www.bseindia.com** and **www.nseindia.com.**

3. From accounting, we know that earnings are divided into two parts: dividends and retained earnings. Most firms continually retain earnings in order to create future dividends. One should not discount earnings to obtain price per share because part of earnings must be reinvested. Only dividends reach the stockholders and only they should be discounted to obtain share price.
4. Some analysts value stock via multiples, such as the price-earnings ratio. However, we caution that one must apply the same multiple only to similar companies.
5. We suggest that a firm's price-earnings ratio is a function of three factors:
   a. The per-share amount of the firm's valuable investment opportunities.
   b. The risk of the stock.
   c. The type of accounting method used by the firm.
6. As an alternative to discounting dividends or valuing via comparables, one can value an entire firm by discounting its cash flows.
7. The two biggest stock markets in the United States are the NYSE and Nasdaq. We discussed the organization and operation of these two markets and saw how stock price information is reported.

Concept Questions

1. **Stock Valuation** Why does the value of a share of stock depend on dividends?
2. **Stock Valuation** A substantial percentage of the companies listed on the NYSE and Nasdaq don't pay dividends, but investors are nonetheless willing to buy shares in them. How is this possible given your answer to the previous question?
3. **Dividend Policy** Referring to the previous questions, under what circumstances might a company choose not to pay dividends?
4. **Dividend Growth Model** Under what two assumptions can we use the dividend growth model presented in the chapter to determine the value of a share of stock? Comment on the reasonableness of these assumptions.
5. **Common versus Preferred Stock** Suppose a company has a preferred stock issue and a common stock issue. Both have just paid a ₹2 dividend. Which do you think will have a higher price: a share of the preferred or a share of the common?
6. **Dividend Growth Model** Based on the dividend growth model, what are the two components of the total return on a share of stock? Which do you think is typically larger?
7. **Growth Rate** In the context of the dividend growth model, is it true that the growth rate in dividends and the growth rate in the price of the stock are identical?
8. **Price-Earnings Ratio** What are the three factors that determine a company's price-earnings ratio?
9. **Corporate Ethics** Is it unfair or unethical for corporations to create classes of stock with unequal voting rights?
10. **Stock Valuation** Evaluate the following statement: Managers should not focus on the current stock value because doing so will lead to an overemphasis on short-term profits at the expense of long-term profits.

Questions and Problems

BASIC (Questions 1–10)

1. **Stock Values** The RLX Co. just paid a dividend of ₹3.20 per share on its stock. The dividends are expected to grow at a constant rate of 4 percent per year indefinitely. If investors require a return of 10.5 percent on the company's stock, what is the current price? What will the price be in three years? In 15 years?

2. **Stock Values** The next dividend payment by Im, Inc., will be ₹1.87 per share. The dividends are anticipated to maintain a growth rate of 4.3 percent forever. If the stock currently sells for ₹37 per share, what is the required return?

3. **Stock Values** For the company in the previous problem, what is the dividend yield? What is the expected capital gains yield?

4. **Stock Values** Five Star Corporation will pay a dividend of ₹3.04 per share next year. The company pledges to increase its dividend by 3.75 percent per year indefinitely. If you require a return of 11 percent on your investment, how much will you pay for the company's stock today?

5. **Stock Valuation** Caccamise Co. is expected to maintain a constant 3.4 percent growth rate in its dividends indefinitely. If the company has a dividend yield of 5.3 percent, what is the required return on the company's stock?

6. **Stock Valuation** Suppose you know that a company's stock currently sells for ₹78 per share and the required return on the stock is 10.9 percent. You also know that the total return on the stock is evenly divided between a capital gains yield and a dividend yield. If it's the company's policy to always maintain a constant growth rate in its dividends, what is the current dividend per share?

7. **Stock Valuation** Hailey Corp. pays a constant ₹9.45 dividend on its stock. The company will maintain this dividend for the next 13 years and will then cease paying dividends forever. If the required return on this stock is 10.7 percent, what is the current share price?

8. **Valuing Preferred Stock** Fegley, Inc., has an issue of preferred stock outstanding that pays a ₹3.80 dividend every year in perpetuity. If this issue currently sells for ₹93 per share, what is the required return?

9. **Growth Rate** The newspaper reported last week that Chen Enterprises earned ₹19.2 million this year. The report also stated that the firm's return on equity is 12 percent. The firm retains 80 percent of its earnings. What is the firm's earnings growth rate? What will next year's earnings be?

10. **Stock Valuation and PE** The Dahlia Flower Co. has earnings of ₹3.64 per share. The benchmark PE for the company is 18. What stock price would you consider appropriate? What if the benchmark PE were 21?

INTERMEDIATE (Questions 11–28)

11. **Stock Valuation** Quinoa Farms just paid a dividend of ₹2.95 on its stock. The growth rate in dividends is expected to be a constant 3.4 percent per year indefinitely. Investors require a return of 15 percent for the first three years, a return of 13 percent for the next three years, and a return of 11 percent thereafter. What is the current share price?

12. **Nonconstant Growth** Metallica Bearings, Inc., is a young start-up company. No dividends will be paid on the stock over the next nine years because the firm needs to plow back its earnings to fuel growth. The company will pay a dividend of ₹14 per share 10 years from today and will increase the dividend by 3.9 percent per year thereafter. If the required return on this stock is 11.5 percent, what is the current share price?

13. **Nonconstant Dividends** Premier, Inc., has an odd dividend policy. The company has just paid a dividend of ₹3.75 per share and has announced that it will increase the dividend by ₹5 per share for each of the next five years and then never pay another dividend. If you require a return of 11 percent on the company's stock, how much will you pay for a share today?

14. **Nonconstant Dividends** McCabe Corporation is expected to pay the following dividends over the next four years: ₹15, ₹11, ₹9, and ₹2.95. Afterward, the company pledges to maintain a constant 4 percent growth rate in dividends forever. If the required return on the stock is 10.3 percent, what is the current share price?

15. **Differential Growth** Synovec Co. is growing quickly. Dividends are expected to grow at a rate of 30 percent for the next three years, with the growth rate falling off to a constant 4 percent thereafter. If the required return is 10 percent, and the company just paid a dividend of ₹2.65, what is the current share price?

16. **Differential Growth** Orkazana Corp. is experiencing rapid growth. Dividends are expected to grow at 25 percent per year during the next three years, 15 percent over the following year, and then 6 percent per year indefinitely. The required return on this stock is 10 percent, and the stock currently sells for ₹86 per share. What is the projected dividend for the coming year?

17. **Negative Growth** Antiques R Us is a mature manufacturing firm. The company just paid a dividend of ₹12.40, but management expects to reduce the payout by 4 percent per year, indefinitely. If you require a return of 9.5 percent on this stock, what will you pay for a share today?

18. **Finding the Dividend** Matterhorn Corporation stock currently sells for ₹49 per share. The market requires a return of 11 percent on the firm's stock. If the company maintains a constant 3.5 percent growth rate in dividends, what was the most recent dividend per share paid on the stock?

19. **Valuing Preferred Stock** E-Eyes.com just issued some new 20/20 preferred stock. The issue will pay an annual dividend of ₹20 in perpetuity, beginning 20 years from now. If the market requires a return of 5.4 percent on this investment, how much does a share of preferred stock cost today?

20. **Using Stock Quotes** You have found the following stock quote for RWJ Enterprises, Inc., in the financial pages of today's newspaper. What was the closing price for this stock that appeared in *yesterday's* paper? If the company currently has 25 million shares of stock outstanding, what was net income for the most recent four quarters?

HI	LO	Stock (DIV)	SYM	YLD%	PE	VOL 100s	CLOSE	Net Chg
95.13	63.17	RWJ 1.85	RWJ	2.15	19	17652	??	.27

21. **Nonconstant Growth and Quarterly Dividends** Mitchell Mineral Water, Inc., will pay a quarterly dividend per share of ₹.95 at the end of each of the next 12 quarters. Thereafter, the dividend will grow at a quarterly rate of 1 percent, forever. The appropriate rate of return on the stock is 11 percent, compounded quarterly. What is the current stock price?

22. **Finding the Dividend** Sorenson, Inc., is expected to pay equal dividends at the end of each of the next two years. Thereafter, the dividend will grow at a constant annual rate of 3.2 percent, forever. The current stock price is ₹75. What is next year's dividend payment if the required rate of return is 11 percent?

23. **Finding the Required Return** Mercury Satellite Corporation earned ₹25 million for the fiscal year ending yesterday. The firm's policy is to pay out 40 percent of its earnings as dividends. The remaining 60 percent of earnings is retained by the company for use in projects. The company has 2.9 million shares of common stock outstanding. The current stock price is ₹109. The historical return on equity (ROE) of 11 percent is expected to continue in the future. What is the required rate of return on the stock?

24. **Dividend Growth** Four years ago, Bling Diamond, Inc., paid a dividend of ₹1.95 per share. The company paid a dividend of ₹2.75 per share yesterday. Dividends will grow over the next five years at the same rate they grew over the last four years. Thereafter, dividends will grow at 4.5 percent per year. What will the company's dividend be in seven years?

25. **Price-Earnings Ratio** Consider Pacific Energy Company and Atlantic Energy, Inc., both of which reported earnings of ₹790,000. Without new projects, both firms will continue to generate earnings of ₹790,000 in perpetuity. Assume that all earnings are paid as dividends and that both firms require a return of 11 percent.
   - **a.** What is the current PE ratio for each company?
   - **b.** Pacific Energy Company has a new project that will generate additional earnings of ₹175,000 each year in perpetuity. Calculate the new PE ratio of the company.
   - **c.** Atlantic Energy has a new project that will increase earnings by ₹350,000 in perpetuity. Calculate the new PE ratio of the firm.

26. **Stock Valuation and PE** Meadow Dew Corp. currently has an EPS of ₹4.05, and the benchmark PE for the company is 21. Earnings are expected to grow at 4.9 percent per year.

   a. What is your estimate of the current stock price?
   b. What is the target stock price in one year?
   c. Assuming the company pays no dividends, what is the implied return on the company's stock over the next year? What does this tell you about the implicit stock return using PE valuation?

27. **Stock Valuation and EV** FFDP Corp. has yearly sales of ₹43 million and costs of ₹14 million. The company's balance sheet shows debt of ₹58 million and cash of ₹19 million. There are 1.85 million shares outstanding and the industry EV/EBITDA multiple is 6.4. What is the company's enterprise value? What is the stock price per share?

28. **Stock Valuation and Cash Flows** Full Boat Manufacturing has projected sales of ₹95 million next year. Costs are expected to be ₹52 million and net investment is expected to be ₹9 million. Each of these values is expected to grow at 14 percent the following year, with the growth rate declining by 2 percent per year until the growth rate reaches 5 percent, where it is expected to remain indefinitely. There are 6.5 million shares of stock outstanding and investors require a return of 13 percent on the company's stock. The corporate tax rate is 21 percent.

   a. What is your estimate of the current stock price?
   b. Suppose instead that you estimate the terminal value of the company using a PE multiple. The industry PE multiple is 11. What is your new estimate of the company's stock price?

CHALLENGE (Questions 29–32)

29. **Capital Gains versus Income** Consider four different stocks, all of which have a required return of 12 percent and a most recent dividend of ₹3.45 per share. Stocks W, X, and Y are expected to maintain constant growth rates in dividends for the foreseeable future of 10 percent, 0 percent, and −5 percent per year, respectively. Stock Z is a growth stock that will increase its dividend by 20 percent for the next two years and then maintain a constant 5 percent growth rate thereafter. What is the dividend yield for each of these four stocks? What is the expected capital gains yield? Discuss the relationship among the various returns that you find for each of these stocks.

30. **Stock Valuation** Most corporations pay quarterly dividends on their common stock rather than annual dividends. Barring any unusual circumstances during the year, the board raises, lowers, or maintains the current dividend once a year and then pays this dividend out in equal quarterly installments to its shareholders.

   a. Suppose a company currently pays an annual dividend of ₹3.60 on its common stock in a single annual installment and management plans on raising this dividend by 3.4 percent per year, indefinitely. If the required return on this stock is 10.5 percent, what is the current share price?
   b. Now suppose that the company actually pays its annual dividend in equal quarterly installments; thus, this company has just paid a dividend of ₹.90 per share, as it has for the previous three quarters. What is your value for the current share price now? (*Hint:* Find the equivalent annual end-of-year dividend for each year.) Comment on whether you think that this model of stock valuation is appropriate.

31. **Nonconstant Growth** Storico Co. just paid a dividend of ₹3.65 per share. The company will increase its dividend by 20 percent next year and will then reduce its dividend growth rate by 5 percentage points per year until it reaches the industry average of 5 percent dividend growth, after which the company will keep a constant growth rate forever. If the required return on the company's stock is 12 percent, what will a share of stock sell for today?

32. **Nonconstant Growth** This one's a little harder. Suppose the current share price for the firm in the previous problem is ₹67.25 and all the dividend information remains the same. What required return must investors be demanding on the company's stock? (*Hint:* Set up the valuation formula with all the relevant cash flows, and use trial and error to find the unknown rate of return.)

33. **Stock Valuation** Divyashakti Granites' investors have an expected rate of return of 10.5%. Divyashakti's past dividend track record is shared below:

FY →	20	19	18	17	16	15	14	13	12	11	10	9	8	7	6	5
DPS	1.81	1.81	1.81	1.81	1.81	1.81	1.81	1.81	1.81	1.81	1.81	1.81	1.81	1.81	1.81	1.81
EPS	7.28															

a. Compute the stock's intrinsic value using a zero growth dividend model.

b. Given additional information on Divyashakti's FY20, i.e., book value per share is 104.6 and earnings per share is 7.28. Is there a better way to arrive at its intrinsic value? Compute the same.

34. **Constant Dividend** The Government of Himachal Pradesh owned hydroelectric power firm, SJVN has a policy of constant dividend per share. The par value of the equity share is ₹10. Last year's dividend was 22%. Given an expected rate of return of 10% by investors, compute its intrinsic value. If it is known that SJVN's latest book value per share is 29.97 and earnings per share is 4.23, then what will be the stock's revised intrinsic value?

35. **Dividend Growth** Hindustan Unilever's investors have an expected rate of return of 8.5%. The essential numbers of the company for the past few years are provided below:

For the year	2020	2019	2018	2017	2016
EPS (Rs)	31.2	27.9	24.2	20.8	19.1
BVPS (Rs)	38.2	36.5	33.8	31.3	30.5
DPS (Rs)	34.5	22.0	20.0	17.0	16.0

Use a dividend growth model to compute Hindustan Unilever's intrinsic price.

36. **Stock Valuation** Barak Valley Cements' investors have an expected rate of return of 14%. Barak's per share indicators are:

FY →	2020	2019	2018	2017	2016
DPS	0.0	0.0	0.0	0.0	0.0
EPS	2.7	0.2	−1.0	−1.2	−3.9
BVPS	52.1	49.4	49.2	50.3	21.8

The firm is owned by the Prithwi Group. The factory and its key operations are located in the Karimgunj district of Assam, popularly known as Barak Valley. Make a few assumptions about the firm's future and compute its stock value using dividend growth model.

37. **Stock Valuation** CK Mehta group owned Deepak Nitrite's key numbers on a per equity share basis are shared below:

FY →	2020	2019	2018	2017	2016
EPS (Rs)	44.8	12.7	6.0	8.2	5.9
BVPS (Rs)	115.2	77.6	69.2	56.0	40.9
DPS (Rs)	4.5	2.0	1.3	1.2	1.2

Deepak Nitrite manufactures chemical intermediates selling products such as Acetone, Agrochemicals, Detergents, Dyes, Pigments, Personal Care, Pharmaceutical Intermediates, Phenol, and Water Treatment. Chinese manufacturers were its biggest competitors. Given the product demand, it has been expanding aggressively. A seven-year growth phase could be considered given its expansion plans.

We seek your inputs in building its story, brick by brick:

a. In August 2019, before the pandemic, compute the intrinsic value of Deepak Nitrite given a growth rate of 30% in the growth phase and investors' expected rate of return of 13%.

b. In February 2020, the firm roped in Professional Board Members. Compute the intrinsic value of Deepak Nitrite given a growth rate of 30% in the growth phase and investors' expected rate of return of 12%.

c. In April 2020, with COVID-19 pandemic in full force, the demand for Deepak's products, cleaning chemicals, jumped. Compute the intrinsic value of Deepak Nitrite given a growth rate of 40% in the growth phase and investors' expected rate of return of 12%.

d. In July 2020, sentiment turned negative against Chinese goods (including chemicals). Compute the intrinsic value of Deepak Nitrite given a growth rate of 50% in the growth phase and investors' expected rate of return of 12%.

e. In September 2020, credit rating agencies increased the credit rating of the company to AA from A. Compute the intrinsic value of Deepak Nitrite given a growth rate of 50% in the growth phase and investors' expected rate of return of 11%.

f. Identify a few lessons from the stock valuation computations over a timeline.

Excel Master It! Problem

Excel Master coverage online

In practice, the use of the dividend discount model is refined from the method we presented in the textbook. Many analysts will estimate the dividend for the next five years and then estimate a perpetual growth rate at some point in the future, typically 10 years. Rather than have the dividend growth fall dramatically from the fast growth period to the perpetual growth period, linear interpolation is applied. That is, the dividend growth is projected to fall by an equal amount each year. For example, if the high-growth period is 15 percent for the next five years and the dividends are expected to fall to a 4 percent perpetual growth rate five years later, the dividend growth rate would decline by 2 percent each year. Assume the required return is 11 percent.

The *Value Line Investment Survey* provides information for investors. Below, you will find information for AbbVie from the 2020 edition of *Value Line*:

2020 dividend	₹4.72
5-year dividend growth rate	16.5%

a. Assume that a perpetual growth rate of 5 percent begins 11 years from now and use linear interpolation between the high growth rate and perpetual growth rate. Construct a table that shows the dividend growth rate and dividend each year. What is the stock price at Year 10? What is the stock price today?

b. How sensitive is the current stock price to changes in the perpetual growth rate? Graph the current stock price against the perpetual growth rate in 11 years to find out.

Instead of applying the constant dividend growth model to find the stock price in the future, analysts often will combine the dividend discount method with mutiples valuation, often with the PE ratio. Remember that the PE ratio is the price per share divided by the earnings per share. So, if we know what the PE ratio is, we can solve for the stock price. Suppose we also have the following information about AbbVie:

Payout ratio	45%
PE ratio at constant growth rate	15

c. Use the PE ratio to calculate the stock price when AbbVie reaches a perpetual growth rate in dividends. Now find the value of the stock today by finding the present value of the dividends during the supernormal growth rate and thc price you calculated using the PE ratio.

d. How sensitive is the current stock price to changes in PE ratio when the stock reaches the perpetual growth rate? Graph the current stock price against the PE ratio in 11 years to find out.

Mini Case STOCK VALUATION AT RAGAN ENGINES

Larissa has been talking with the company's directors about the future of East Coast Yachts. To this point, the company has used outside suppliers for various key components of the company's yachts, including engines. Larissa has decided that East Coast Yachts should consider the purchase of an engine manufacturer to allow East Coast Yachts to better integrate its supply chain and get more control over engine features. After investigating several possible companies, Larissa feels that the purchase of Ragan Engines, Inc., is a possibility. She has asked Dan Ervin to analyze Ragan's value.

Ragan Engines, Inc., was founded nine years ago by a brother and sister–Carrington and Genevieve Ragan–and has remained a privately owned company. The company manufactures marine engines for a variety of applications. Ragan has experienced rapid growth because of a proprietary technology that increases the fuel efficiency of its engines with very little sacrifice in performance. The company is equally owned by Carrington and Genevieve. The original agreement between the siblings gave each 50,000 shares of stock.

Larissa has asked Dan to determine a value per share of Ragan stock. To accomplish this, Dan has gathered the following information about some of Ragan's competitors that are publicly traded:

	EPS	DPS	Stock Price	ROE	R
Blue Ribband Motors Corp.	₹ .81	₹ .20	₹14.18	10.00%	10.00%
Bon Voyage Marine, Inc.	1.38	.62	11.87	13.00	13.00
Nautilus Marine Engines	−.46	.38	13.21	14.00	12.00
Industry average	₹ .58	₹.404	₹13.09	12.33%	11.67%

Nautilus Marine Engines's negative earnings per share (EPS) were the result of an accounting write-off last year. Without the write-off, EPS for the company would have been ₹1.60. Last year, Ragan had an EPS of ₹4.54 and paid a dividend to Carrington and Genevieve of ₹60,000 each. The company also had a return on equity of 18 percent. Larissa tells Dan that a required return for Ragan of 18 percent is appropriate.

1. Assuming the company continues its current growth rate, what is the value per share of the company's stock?
2. Dan has examined both the company's financial statements and those of its competitors. Although Ragan currently has a technological advantage, Dan's research indicates that Ragan's competitors are investigating other methods to improve efficiency. Given this, Dan believes that Ragan's technological advantage will last only for the next five years. After that period, the company's growth will likely slow to the industry average. Additionally, Dan believes that the required return the company uses is too high. He believes the industry average required return is more appropriate. Under Dan's assumptions, what is the estimated stock price?
3. What is the industry average price-earnings ratio? What is Ragan's price-earnings ratio? Comment on any differences and explain why they may exist.
4. Assume the company's growth rate declines to the industry average after five years. What percentage of the stock's value is attributable to growth opportunities?
5. Assume the company's growth rate slows to the industry average in five years. What future return on equity does this imply?
6. Carrington and Genevieve are not sure if they should sell the company. If they do not sell the company outright to East Coast Yachts, they would like to try and increase the value of the company's stock. In this case, they want to retain control of the company and do not want to sell stock to outside investors. They also feel that the company's debt is at a manageable level and do not want to borrow more money. What steps can they take to try to increase the price of the stock? Are there any conditions under which this strategy would not increase the stock price?

10

PART III: RISK

Lessons from Market History

Given the headlines in the spring of 2020 about the market crash caused by COVID-related lockdowns, you might be surprised to learn that 2020 was a great year for investors. With the S&P 500 index returning about 18 percent and the Nasdaq Composite index up about 43 percent in 2020, stock market performance overall was very good. For example, investors in bitcoin mining company Bit Digital had to be happy about the 3,688 percent gain in that stock, and investors in biotechnology company Novavax had to feel pretty good following that company's 2,889 percent gain. Of course, not all stocks increased in value during the year. Stock in Occidental Petroleum fell 58 percent, and stock in cruise ship operator Carnival Corp. sunk 57 percent.

These examples show that there were tremendous potential profits to be made during 2020, but there was also the risk of losing money—and lots of it. So what should you, as a stock market investor, expect when you invest your own money? In this chapter, we study more than eight decades of market history to find out.

Please visit us at **rwjcorporatefinance.blogspot.com** for the latest developments in the world of corporate finance.

10.1 Returns

RUPEE RETURNS

Suppose the Vashisht Concept Company has several thousand shares of stock outstanding and you are a shareholder. Further suppose that you purchased some of the shares of stock in the company at the beginning of the year; it is now year-end and you want to figure out how well you have done on your investment. The return you get on an investment in stocks, like that in bonds or any other investment, comes in two forms.

Excel Master coverage online

As the owner of stock in the Vashisht Concept Company, you are a part owner of the company. If the company is profitable, it generally could distribute some of its profits to the shareholders. Therefore, as the owner of shares of stock, you could receive some cash, called a *dividend*, during the year. This cash is the *income component* of your return. In addition to the dividends, the other part of your return is the *capital gain*—or, if it is negative, the *capital loss* (negative capital gain)—on the investment. Your *total Rupee return* is the sum of your dividend income and capital gain or loss.

How did the market do today? Find out at **finance.yahoo.com**.

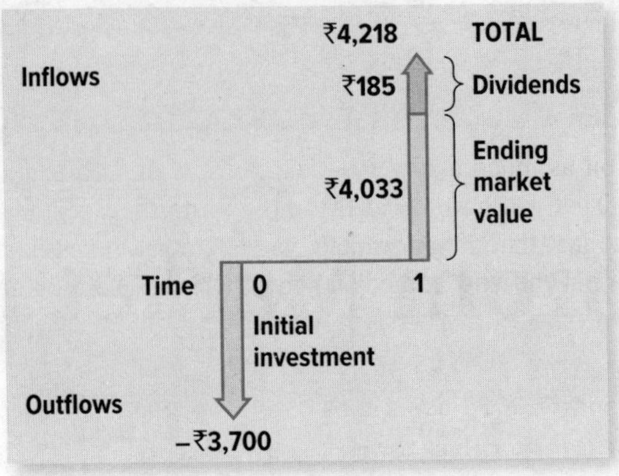

Figure 10.1 Rupee Returns

Suppose we are considering the cash flows of the investment in Figure 10.1, showing that you purchased 100 shares of stock at the beginning of the year at a price of ₹37 per share. Your total investment, then, was:

$$C_0 = ₹37 \times 100 = ₹3{,}700$$

Suppose that, over the year, the stock paid a dividend of ₹1.85 per share. During the year, then, you received income of:

$$\text{Dividend income} = ₹1.85 \times 100 = ₹185$$

Suppose that, at the end of the year, the market price of the stock is ₹40.33 per share. Because the stock increased in price, you had a capital gain of:

$$\text{Capital gain} = (₹40.33 - 37) \times 100 = ₹333$$

The capital gain, like the dividend, is part of the return that shareholders require to maintain their investment in the Vashisht Concept Company. Of course, if the price of Vashisht Concept stock had dropped in value to, say, ₹34.78, you would have recorded this capital loss:

$$\text{Capital loss} = (₹34.78 - 37) \times 100 = -₹222$$

The total Rupee return on your investment is the sum of the dividend income and the capital gain or loss on the investment:

$$\text{Total Rupee return} = \text{Dividend income} + \text{Capital gain (or loss)}$$

In our first example, the total Rupee return is given by:

$$\text{Total Rupee return} = ₹185 + 333 = ₹518$$

Notice that if you sold the stock at the end of the year, your total amount of cash would be the initial investment plus the total Rupee return. In the preceding example you would have:

$$\begin{aligned}\text{Total cash if stock is sold} &= \text{Initial investment} + \text{Total Rupee return}\\ &= ₹3{,}700 + 518\\ &= ₹4{,}218\end{aligned}$$

As a check, notice that this is the same as the proceeds from the sale of stock plus the dividends:

$$\begin{aligned}\text{Proceeds from stock sale} + \text{Dividends} &= ₹40.33 \times 100 + 185\\ &= ₹4{,}033 + 185\\ &= ₹4{,}218\end{aligned}$$

Suppose, however, that you hold your Vashisht Concept stock and don't sell it at year-end. Should you still consider the capital gain as part of your return? Does this violate our previous present value rule that only cash matters?

The answer to the first question is a strong yes; the answer to the second question is an equally strong no. The capital gain is every bit as much a part of your return as the dividend and you certainly should count it as part of your total return. That you have decided to hold on to the stock and not sell, or *realize* the gain or the loss, in no way changes the fact that, if you wanted, you could get the cash value of the stock. After all, you could always sell the stock at year-end and immediately buy it back. The total amount of cash you would have at year-end would be the ₹518 gain plus your initial investment of ₹3,700. You would not lose this return when you bought back 100 shares of stock. In fact, you would be in exactly the same position as if you had not sold the stock (assuming, of course, that there are no tax consequences and no brokerage commissions from selling the stock).

PERCENTAGE RETURNS

It is more convenient to summarize the information about returns in percentage terms than in Rupees because the percentages apply to any amount invested. The question we want to answer is this: How much return do we get for each Rupee invested? To find this out, let t stand for the year, let P_t be the price of the stock at the beginning of the year, and let D_{t+1} be the dividend paid on the stock during the year. Consider the cash flows in Figure 10.2.

In our example, the price at the beginning of the year was ₹37 per share and the dividend paid during the year on each share was ₹1.85. Hence, the percentage income return, sometimes called the *dividend yield*, is:

$$\begin{aligned}\text{Dividend yield} &= D_{t+1}/P_t \\ &= ₹1.85/₹37 \\ &= .05, \text{ or } 5\%\end{aligned}$$

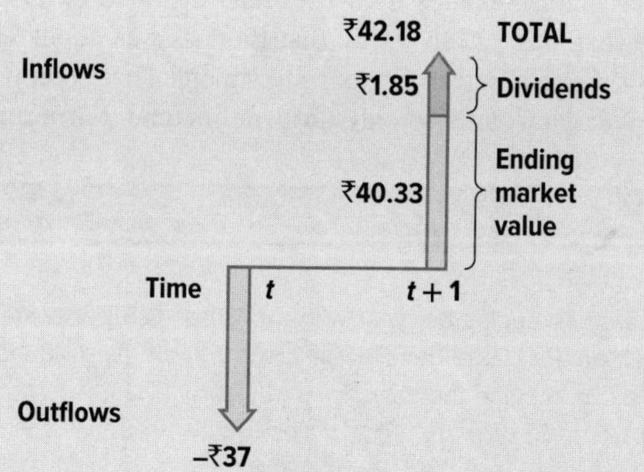

$$\text{Percentage return} = \frac{\text{Dividends paid at end of period} + \text{Change in market value over period}}{\text{Beginning market value}}$$

$$1 + \text{Percentage return} = \frac{\text{Dividends paid at end of period} + \text{Market value at end of period}}{\text{Beginning market value}}$$

Figure 10.2 Percentage Returns

The **capital gain** (or loss) is the change in the price of the stock divided by the initial price. Letting P_{t+1} be the price of the stock at year-end, we can compute the capital gain as follows:

$$\begin{aligned}\text{Capital gain} &= (P_{t+1} - P_t)/P_t \\ &= (₹40.33 - 37)/₹37 \\ &= ₹3.33/₹37 \\ &= .09, \text{ or } 9\%\end{aligned}$$

Go to **finviz.com/map.ashx?t=sec_all** for a Java applet that shows today's returns by market sector. **https://in.tradingview.com/heatmap/stock/** also gives the heatmap for different indices around the globe, including the Indian indices

Combining these two results, we find that the *total return* on the investment in Vashisht Concept stock over the year, which we will label R_{t+1}, was:

$$\begin{aligned}R_{t+1} &= \frac{D_{t+1}}{P_t} + \frac{(P_{t+1} - P_t)}{P_t} \\ &= .05 + .09 \\ &= .14, \text{or } 14\%\end{aligned}$$

From now on, we will refer to returns in percentage terms.

To give a more concrete example, stock in Microsoft began 2020 at ₹157.70 per share. Microsoft paid dividends of ₹2.09 during 2020 and the stock price at the end of the year was ₹221.68. What was the return on Microsoft for the year? For practice, see if you agree that the answer is 41.90 percent. Of course, negative returns occur as well. For example, again in 2020, Chevron's stock price at the end of the year was ₹85.33 per share and dividends of ₹5.16 were paid. The stock began the year at ₹120.51 per share. Verify that the loss was 24.91 percent for the year.

On corresponding lines, recently, Coal India, the world's largest coal-producing company and a Maharatna public sector's stock price at the beginning of the year was ₹183 per share, and dividends of ₹15 per share were paid. The stock ended the year at ₹214 per share. For practice, see if you agree that it is about 25 percent. Of course, negative returns occur as well, for example, the stock of Reliance Industries, the largest company in India, began 2023 at ₹2641 per share. Reliance Industries paid dividend of ₹9 per share during 2023, and the stock price at the end of the year was ₹2331. Verify that the loss was about 11 percent for the year.

As an investor, you care about the total return on your investment. Therefore, you should be cautious when interpreting charts that report only capital gains or only dividend income. For example, the very popular S&P

EXAMPLE 10.1

Calculating Returns Suppose a stock begins the year with a price of ₹25 per share and ends with a price of ₹35 per share. During the year, it paid a ₹2 dividend per share. What are its dividend yield, capital gains yield, and total return for the year? We can imagine the cash flows in Figure 10.3.

$$\begin{aligned}R_1 &= \frac{D_1}{P_0} + \frac{P_1 - P_0}{P_0} \\ &= \frac{₹2}{₹25} + \frac{₹35 - 25}{₹25} \\ &= .08 + .40 \\ &= .48, \text{ or } 48\%\end{aligned}$$

Thus, the stock's dividend yield, capital gains yield, and total return are 8 percent, 40 percent, and 48 percent, respectively.

Suppose you had ₹5,000 invested. The total Rupee return you would have received on an investment in the stock is ₹5,000 × .48 = ₹2,400. If you know the total Rupee return on the stock, you do not need to know

(continued)

how many shares you would have had to purchase to figure out how much money you would have made on the ₹5,000 investment; you use the total Rupee return.

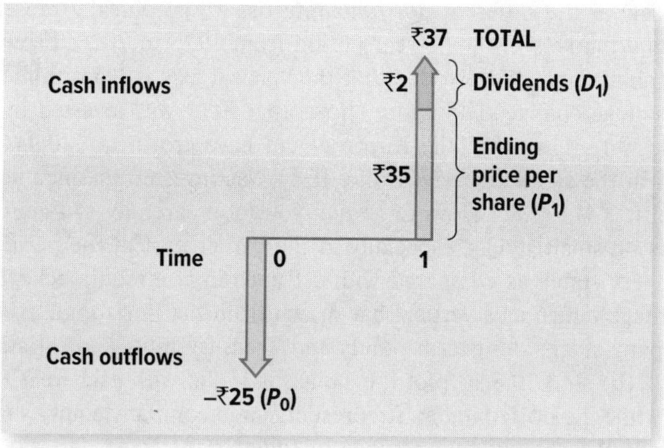

Figure 10.3 Cash Flow: An Investment Example

500 index is a capital gains index because it tracks the price changes of the stocks included in the index. It does not account for regular dividends. (A separate S&P 500 total return index does exist and is often used for research purposes such as the calculations and figures in this book, but that is not the version reported in the popular press.) The return of the S&P 500 index as reported in the media can be quite misleading, because S&P 500 firms are usually the biggest dividend payers in the U.S. economy. If you actually invested in these firms for a year, you would earn a substantially higher total return than the reported return of the index. You should also be skeptical when a fund manager brags about beating the S&P 500 last year because the fund manager might be comparing her fund's total return to the S&P's return excluding dividends.

10.2 Holding Period Returns

Roger Ibbotson and Rex Sinquefield conducted a famous set of studies dealing with rates of return in U.S. financial markets.[1] It presents year-by-year historical rates of total return on five important types of financial instruments in the United States. The returns can be interpreted as what you would have earned if you had held portfolios of the following:

Excel Master coverage online

1. *Large-company common stocks.* This common stock portfolio is based on the Standard & Poor's (S&P) 500, which contains the 500 largest (in terms of market value) companies in the United States.
2. *Small-company common stocks.* This is a portfolio composed of the stock corresponding to the smallest 20 percent of the companies listed on the New York Stock Exchange, again as measured by market value of outstanding stock.
3. *Long-term corporate bonds.* This is a portfolio of high-quality corporate bonds with 20-year maturities.
4. *Long-term U.S. government bonds.* This is based on U.S. government bonds with maturities of 20 years.
5. *U.S. Treasury bills.* This is based on Treasury bills (T-bills for short) with a one-month maturity.

[1] Ibbotson, Roger G., and Rex A. Sinquefield. 1982. *Stocks, Bonds, Bills, and Inflation [SBBI].* Charlottesville, VA: Financial Analysis Research Foundation.

None of the returns are adjusted for taxes or transaction costs. In addition to the year-by-year returns on financial instruments, the year-to-year change in the consumer price index is computed. This is a basic measure of inflation. We can calculate year-by-year real returns by subtracting annual inflation.

Before looking closely at the different portfolio returns, we graphically present the returns and risks available from U.S. capital markets in the 95-year period from 1926 to 2020. Figure 10.4 shows the growth of ₹1 invested at the beginning of 1926. Notice that the vertical axis is logarithmic, so that equal distances measure the same percentage change. The figure shows that if ₹1 was invested in large-company common stocks and all dividends were reinvested, the Rupee would have grown to ₹10,944.66 by the end of 2020. The biggest growth was in the small stock portfolio. If ₹1 was invested in small stocks in 1926, the investment would have grown to ₹41,977.83. However, when you look carefully at Figure 10.4, you can see great variability in the returns on small stocks, especially in the earlier part of the period. A Rupee in long-term government bonds was very stable as compared with a Rupee in common stocks. Figures 10.5 to 10.8 plot each year-to-year percentage return as a vertical bar drawn from the horizontal axis for large-company common stocks, small-company stocks, long-term bonds and Treasury bills, and inflation, respectively.

Figures 10.5(b), 10.7(b), and 10.8(b) plot the same for India, with each year to year percentage return as a vertical bar drawn while the horizontal axis represents large company equity shares, bank fixed deposits, and inflation, respectively. We observe that a rupee in Indian bank fixed deposits was very stable as compared to a rupee in Indian equity stocks.

Figure 10.4 gives the growth of a Rupee investment in the stock market from 1926 through 2020. In other words, it shows what the value of the investment would have been if the Rupee had been left in the

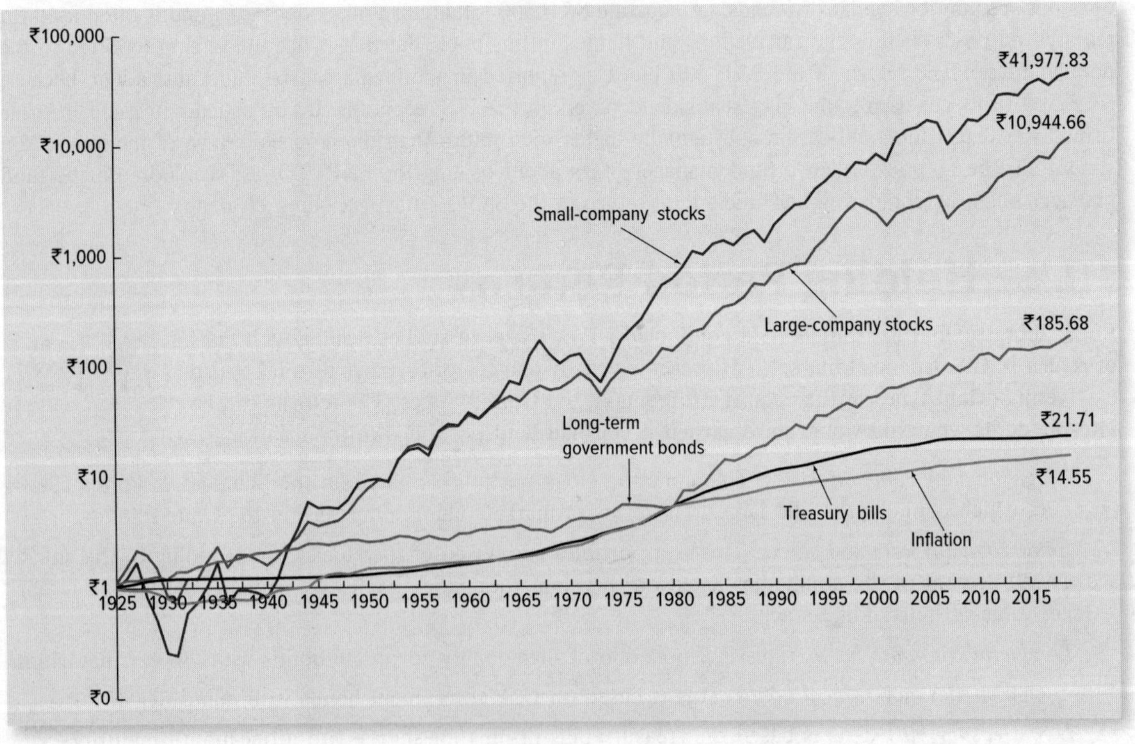

Figure 10.4(a) Wealth Indexes of Investments in the U.S. Capital Markets (Year-End 1925 = ₹1.00)

SOURCE: 2021 SBBI Yearbook. Duff & Phelps.

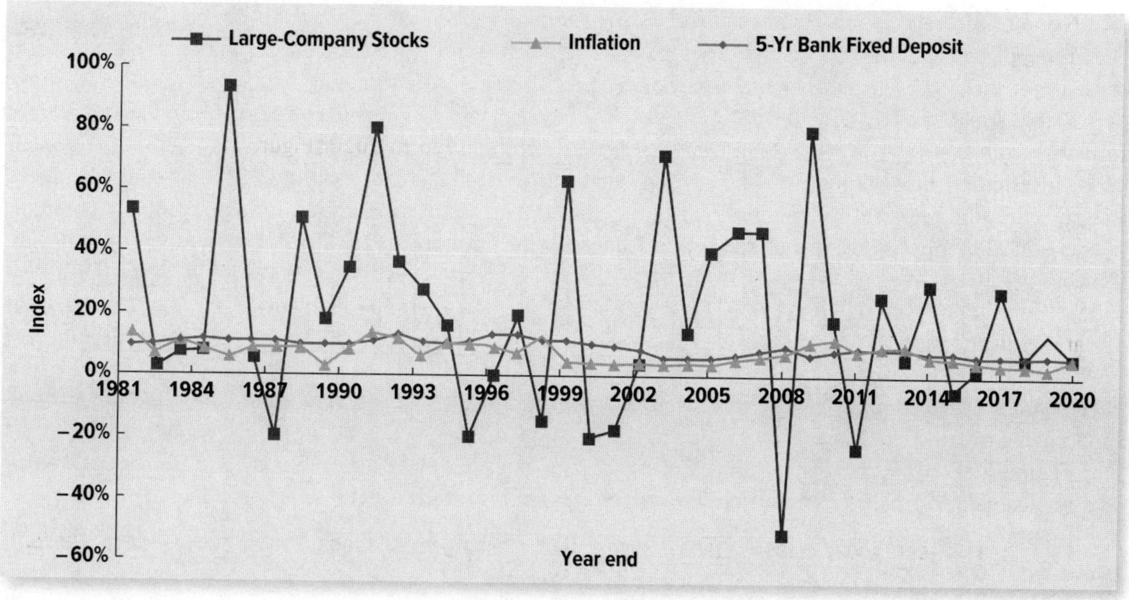

Figure 10.4(b) Wealth Indexes of Investments along with Inflation in Indian Markets, 1980–2020 (Year-End 1980 = ₹1)

SOURCE: Author(s) compilation based on data obtained and compiled from BSE, RBI, and other sources.

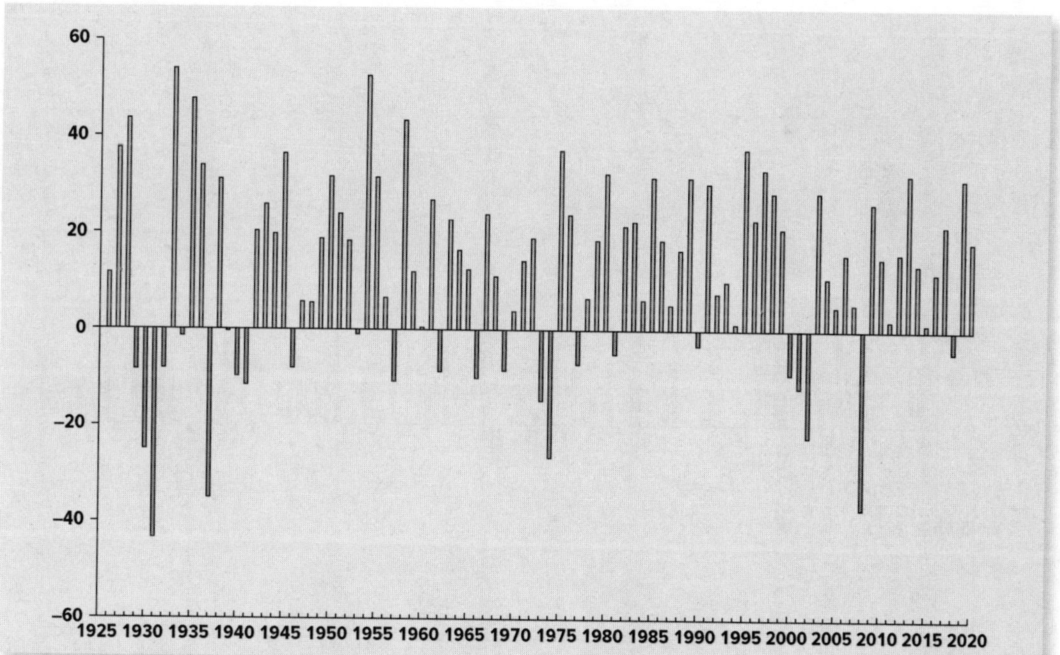

Figure 10.5(a) Year-by-Year Total Returns on Large Company Common Stocks in the U.S.A.

SOURCE: 2021 SBBI Yearbook. Duff & Phelps.

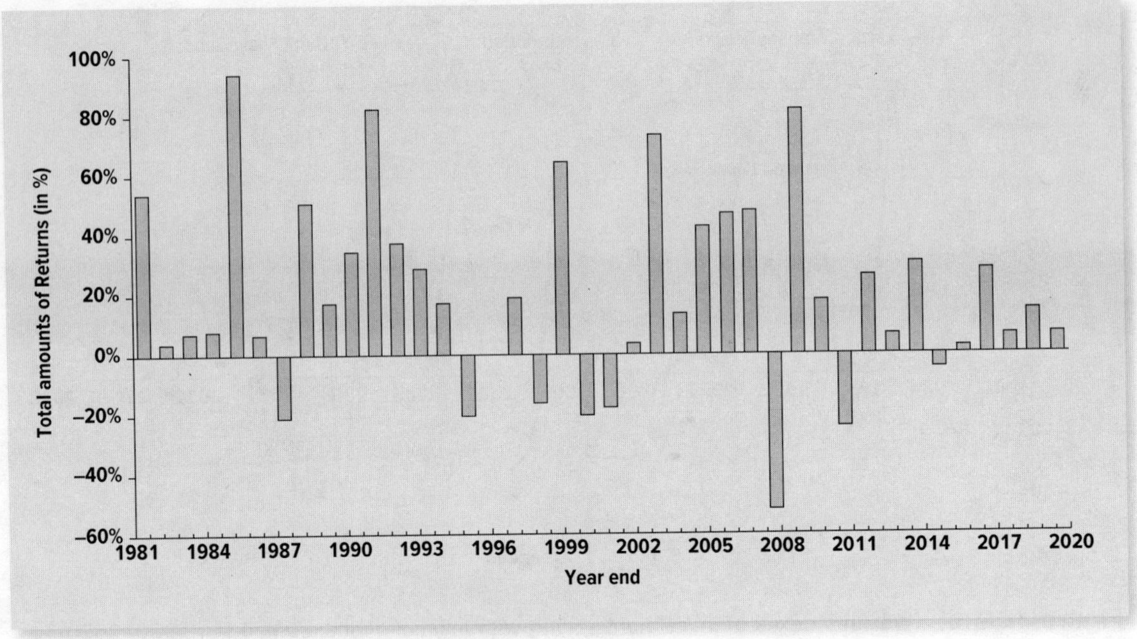

Figure 10.5(b) Year-by-year Total Returns on Large-company stocks of India (Period: 1980–2020)

SOURCE: Author(s) compilation based on the data obtained from BSE.

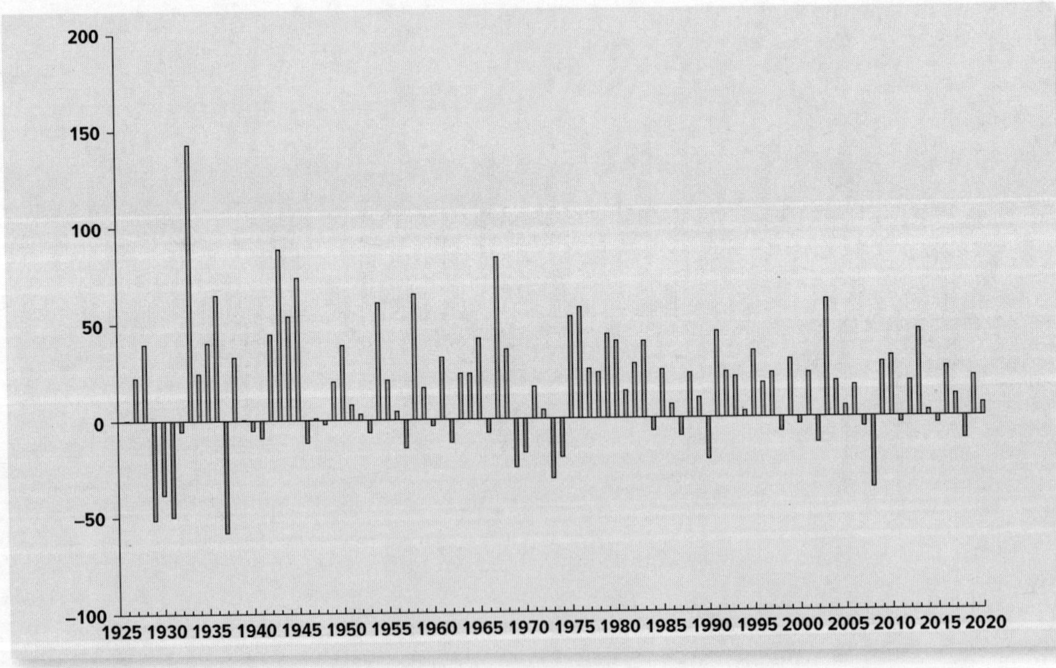

Figure 10.6 Year-by-Year Total Returns on Small-Company Common Stocks in the U.S.A.

SOURCE: 2021 SBBI Yearbook. Duff & Phelps.

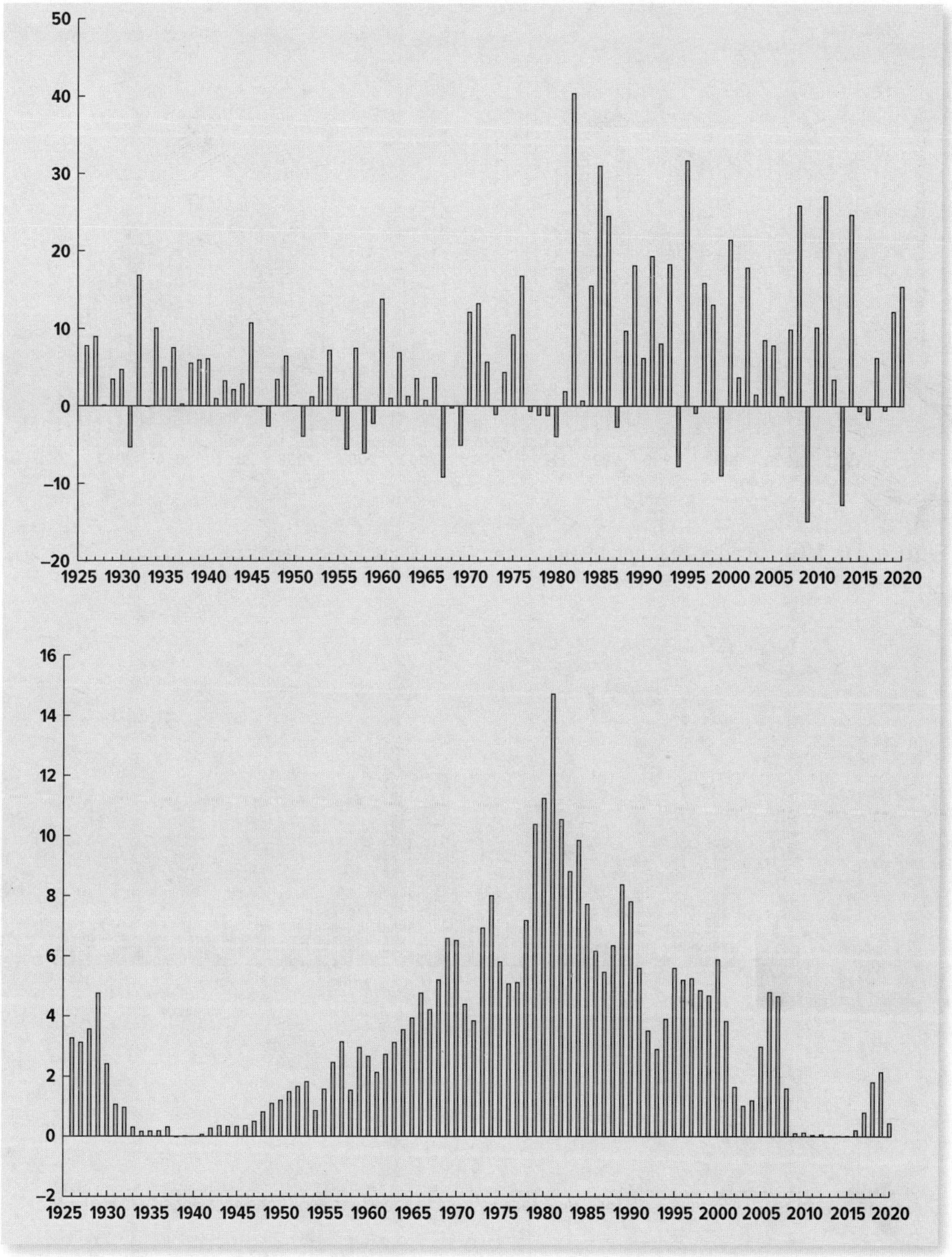

Figure 10.7(a) Year-by-Year Total Returns on U.S. Bonds and U.S. Treasury Bills

SOURCE: 2021 SBBI Yearbook. Duff & Phelps.

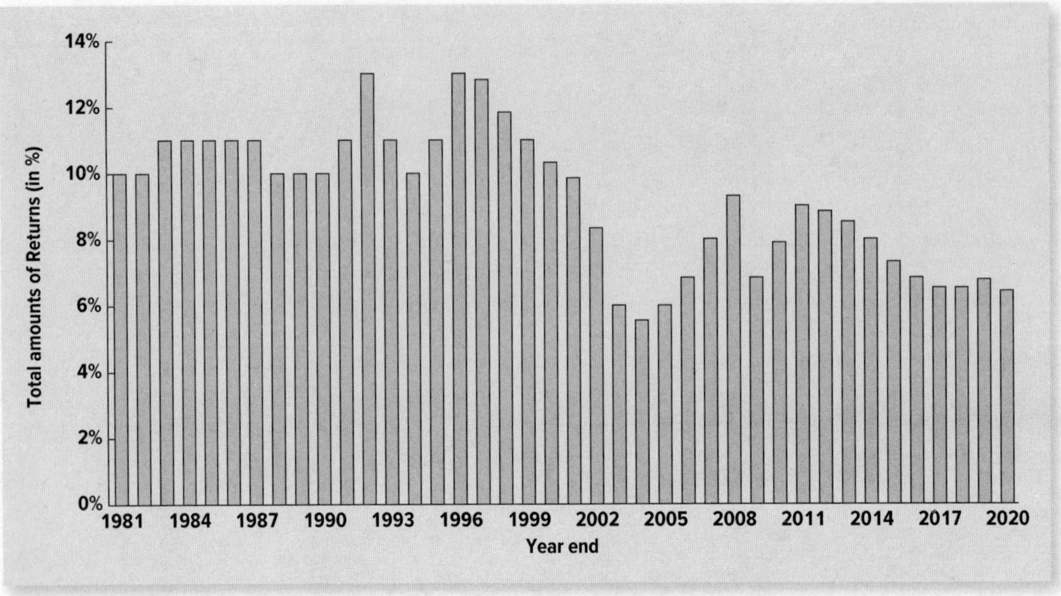

Figure 10.7(b) Year-by-Year Total Returns on 5 Year Bank Fixed Deposit Rate in India, 1980–2020

SOURCE: Author(s) compilation based on the data obtained from RBI.

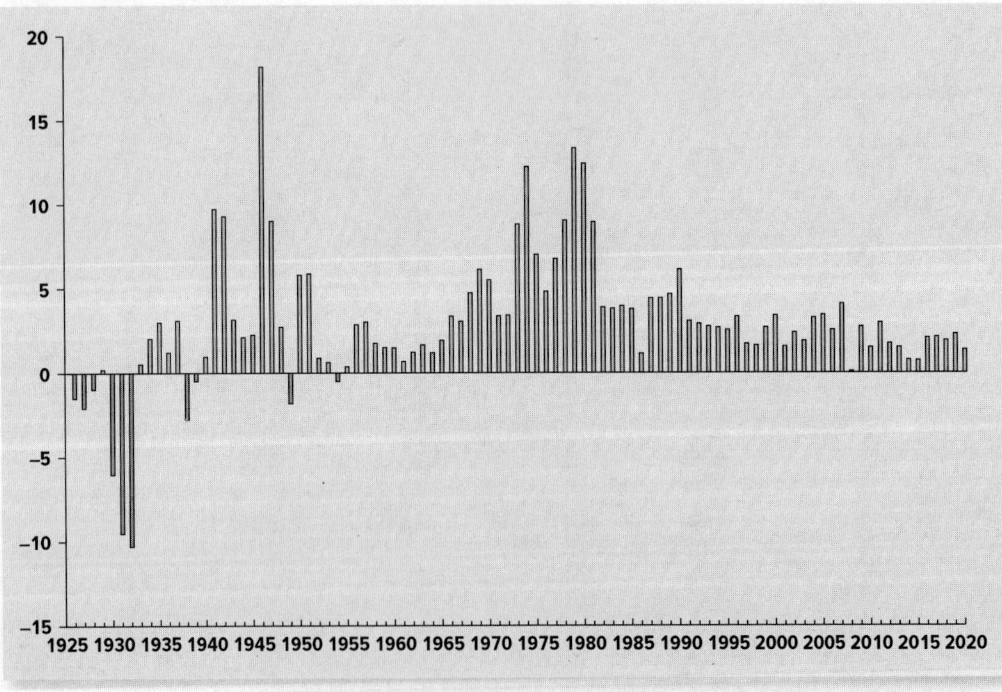

Figure 10.8(a) Year-by-Year Inflation in the U.S.A.

SOURCE: 2021 SBBI Yearbook. Duff & Phelps.

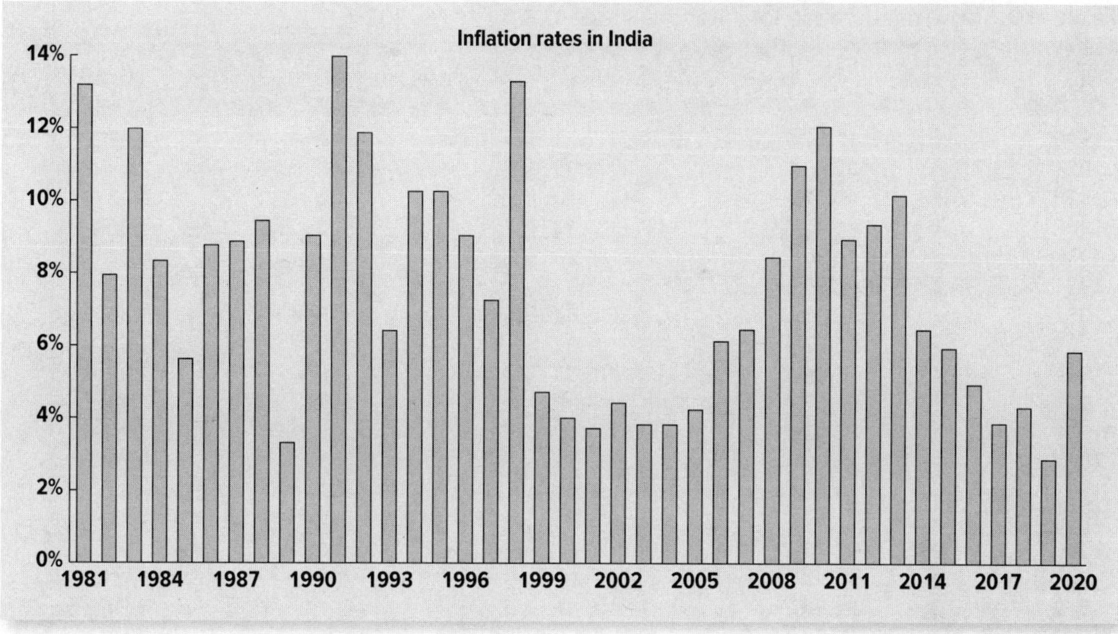

Figure 10.8(b) Year-by-Year Inflation in India

SOURCE: Author(s) compilation of Inflation, Consumer Price Index based on the data obtained from the World Bank, 1980–2020.

stock market and if each year the dividends from the previous year had been reinvested in more stock. If R_t is the return in Year t (expressed in decimals), the value you would have at the end of Year T is the product of 1 plus the return in each of the years:

$$\text{Value} = (1 + R_1) \times (1 + R_2) \times \cdots \times (1 + R_t) \times \cdots \times (1 + R_T)$$

For example, if the returns were 11 percent, −5 percent, and 9 percent in a three-year period, an investment of ₹1 at the beginning of the period would be worth:

Go to **bigcharts .marketwatch.com** to see both intraday and long-term charts.

$$\begin{aligned}(1 + R_1) \times (1 + R_2) \times (1 + R_3) &= ₹1 \times (1 + .11) \times (1 - .05) \times (1 + .09)\\ &= ₹1 \times 1.11 \times .95 \times 1.09\\ &= ₹1.15\end{aligned}$$

at the end of the three years. Notice that .15, or 15 percent, is the total return. This includes the return from reinvesting the first-year dividends in the stock market for two more years and reinvesting the second-year dividends for the final year. The 15 percent is called a three-year **holding period return**. Table 10.1 gives the annual returns each year for selected investments from 1926 to 2020. From this table, you can determine holding period returns for any combination of years.

In the Indian context, we present similar year-by-year historical rates of return for the following two types of financial instruments along with inflation:

1. Large-company common stocks: The common stock portfolio is based on the S&P BSE Sensitive Index of 30 stocks. It includes the largest stocks in the Indian markets.
2. Bank fixed deposit index: We created a bank fixed deposit index using the five-year fixed deposit rates given by the national banks in consonance with the Reserve Bank of India.

Table 10.1(a) Year-by-Year Total Returns in the U.S.A., 1926–2020

Year	Large-Company Stocks	Long-Term Government Bonds	U.S. Treasury Bills	Consumer Price Index
1926	11.62%	7.77%	3.27%	−1.49%
1927	37.49	8.93	3.12	−2.08
1928	43.61	.10	3.56	−.97
1929	−8.42	3.42	4.75	.20
1930	−24.90	4.66	2.41	−6.03
1931	−43.34	−5.31	1.07	−9.52
1932	−8.19	16.84	.96	−10.30
1933	53.99	−.07	.30	.51
1934	−1.44	10.03	.16	2.03
1935	47.67	4.98	.17	2.99
1936	33.92	7.52	.18	1.21
1937	−35.03	.23	.31	3.10
1938	31.12	5.53	−.02	−2.78
1939	−.41	5.94	.02	−.48
1940	−9.78	6.09	.00	.96
1941	−11.59	.93	.06	9.72
1942	20.34	3.22	.27	9.29
1943	25.90	2.08	.35	3.16
1944	19.75	2.81	.33	2.11
1945	36.44	10.73	.33	2.25
1946	−8.07	−.10	.35	18.16
1947	5.71	−2.62	.50	9.01
1948	5.50	3.40	.81	2.71
1949	18.79	6.45	1.10	−1.80
1950	31.71	.06	1.20	5.79
1951	24.02	−3.93	1.49	5.87
1952	18.37	1.16	1.66	.88
1953	−.99	3.64	1.82	.62
1954	52.62	7.19	.86	−.50
1955	31.56	−1.29	1.57	.37
1956	6.56	−5.59	2.46	2.86
1957	−10.78	7.46	3.14	3.02
1958	43.36	−6.09	1.54	1.76
1959	11.96	−2.26	2.95	1.50
1960	.47	13.78	2.66	1.48
1961	26.89	.97	2.13	.67
1962	−8.73	6.89	2.73	1.22
1963	22.80	1.21	3.12	1.65
1964	16.48	3.51	3.54	1.19
1965	12.45	.71	3.93	1.92
1966	−10.06	3.65	4.76	3.35
1967	23.98	−9.18	4.21	3.04
1968	11.06	−.26	5.21	4.72
1969	−8.50	−5.07	6.58	6.11
1970	3.86	12.11	6.52	5.49

(continued)

Table 10.1(a) Year-by-Year Total Returns in the U.S.A., 1926–2020 *(continued)*

Year	Large-Company Stocks	Long-Term Government Bonds	U.S. Treasury Bills	Consumer Price Index
1971	14.30	13.23	4.39	3.36
1972	19.00	5.69	3.84	3.41
1973	−14.69	−1.11	6.93	8.80
1974	−26.47	4.35	8.00	12.20
1975	37.23	9.20	5.80	7.01
1976	23.93	16.75	5.08	4.81
1977	−7.16	−.69	5.12	6.77
1978	6.57	−1.18	7.18	9.03
1979	18.61	−1.23	10.38	13.31
1980	32.50	−3.95	11.24	12.40
1981	−4.92	1.86	14.71	8.94
1982	21.55	40.36	10.54	3.87
1983	22.56	.65	8.80	3.80
1984	6.27	15.48	9.85	3.95
1985	31.73	30.97	7.72	3.77
1986	18.67	24.53	6.16	1.13
1987	5.25	−2.71	5.47	4.41
1988	16.61	9.67	6.35	4.42
1989	31.69	18.11	8.37	4.65
1990	−3.10	6.18	7.81	6.11
1991	30.47	19.30	5.60	3.06
1992	7.62	8.05	3.51	2.90
1993	10.08	18.24	2.90	2.75
1994	1.32	−7.77	3.90	2.67
1995	37.58	31.67	5.60	2.54
1996	22.96	−.93	5.21	3.32
1997	33.36	15.85	5.26	1.70
1998	28.58	13.06	4.86	1.61
1999	21.04	−8.96	4.68	2.68
2000	−9.10	21.48	5.89	3.39
2001	−11.89	3.70	3.83	1.55
2002	−22.10	17.84	1.65	2.38
2003	28.68	1.45	1.02	1.88
2004	10.88	8.51	1.20	3.26
2005	4.91	7.81	2.98	3.42
2006	15.79	1.19	4.80	2.54
2007	5.49	9.88	4.66	4.08
2008	−37.00	25.87	1.60	.09
2009	26.46	−14.90	.10	2.72
2010	15.06	10.14	.12	1.50
2011	2.11	27.10	.04	2.96
2012	16.00	3.43	.06	1.74
2013	32.39	−12.78	.02	1.51
2014	13.69	24.71	.02	.76
2015	1.38	−.65	.02	.73

(continued)

Table 10.1(a) Year-by-Year Total Returns in the U.S.A., 1926–2020 *(concluded)*

Year	Large-Company Stocks	Long-Term Government Bonds	U.S. Treasury Bills	Consumer Price Index
2016	11.96	−1.75	.20	2.07
2017	21.83	6.24	.80	2.11
2018	−4.38	−.57	1.81	1.91
2019	31.49	12.16	2.14	2.29
2020	18.40	15.40	.44	1.36

SOURCE: 2021 SBBI Yearbook. Duff & Phelps.

The graphs and figures carry a similar set of assumptions as done for the U.S. markets. Figure 10.4(b) graphically presents the growth of ₹1 invested at the beginning of 1981 and continued upto 2020 (40 years) in Indian markets. The figure shows that ₹1 invested at the beginning of 1981 would have grown to ₹430 by the end of 2020. If the same ₹1 were invested for the same period in bank fixed deposits, it would have grown to ₹9 only. However, when you look carefully at Figure 10.4(b), you can see great variability in returns on large-company stocks, especially in the later part of the period.

Table 10.1(b) gives the annual returns each year for selected investments in the Indian economy from 1980 to 2020. From this table, you can determine holding period returns for any combination of years for these investments in India.

Table 10.1(b) Year-by-Year Total Returns in India, 1981–2023

Year	Large-Company Stocks	5-Yr Bank Fixed Deposit	Inflation
1981	53.6%	10.0%	13.1%
1982	3.6%	10.0%	7.9%
1983	7.2%	11.0%	11.9%
1984	7.5%	11.0%	8.3%
1985	94.0%	11.0%	5.6%
1986	6.4%	11.0%	8.7%
1987	−21.2%	11.0%	8.8%
1988	50.7%	10.0%	9.4%
1989	16.9%	10.0%	3.3%
1990	34.6%	10.0%	9.0%
1991	82.1%	11.0%	13.9%
1992	37.0%	13.0%	11.8%
1993	28.6%	11.0%	6.4%
1994	16.9%	10.0%	10.2%
1995	−20.9%	11.0%	10.2%
1996	−0.8%	13.0%	9.0%
1997	18.6%	12.8%	7.2%
1998	−16.5%	11.8%	13.2%

(continued)

Table 10.1(b) Year-by-Year Total Returns in India, 1981–2023 *(concluded)*

Year	Large-Company Stocks	5-Yr Bank Fixed Deposit	Inflation
1999	63.8%	11.0%	4.7%
2000	–20.6%	10.3%	4.0%
2001	–17.9%	9.8%	3.7%
2002	3.5%	8.3%	4.4%
2003	72.9%	6.0%	3.8%
2004	13.1%	5.5%	3.8%
2005	42.3%	6.0%	4.2%
2006	46.7%	6.8%	6.1%
2007	47.1%	8.0%	6.4%
2008	–52.4%	9.3%	8.4%
2009	81.0%	6.8%	10.9%
2010	17.4%	7.9%	12.0%
2011	–24.6%	9.0%	8.9%
2012	25.7%	8.8%	9.3%
2013	6.2%	8.5%	10.1%
2014	29.9%	8.0%	6.4%
2015	–5.0%	7.3%	5.9%
2016	2.0%	6.8%	4.94%
2017	28%	6.5%	3.89%
2018	22%	7%	4.28%
2019	34%	6%	2.86%
2020	32%	5.25%	5.84%
2021	19%	6.75%	5.59%
2022	8%	6.70%	5.72%
2023	1%	6.75%	5.69%

SOURCE: Author(s) compilation based on the data obtained from BSE, RBI and other sources.

10.3 Return Statistics

Excel Master coverage online

The history of U.S. capital market returns is too complicated to be handled in its undigested form. To use the history, we must first find some manageable ways of describing it, dramatically condensing the detailed data into a few simple statements.

This is where two important numbers summarizing the history come in. The first and most natural number is some single measure that best describes the past annual returns on the stock market. In other words, what is our best estimate of the return that an investor could have realized in a particular year over the 1926 to 2020 period? This is the *arithmetic average return.*

Figure 10.9 plots the histogram of the yearly stock market returns given in Table 10.1(a). This plot is the **frequency distribution** of the numbers. The height of the graph gives the number of sample observations in the range on the horizontal axis.

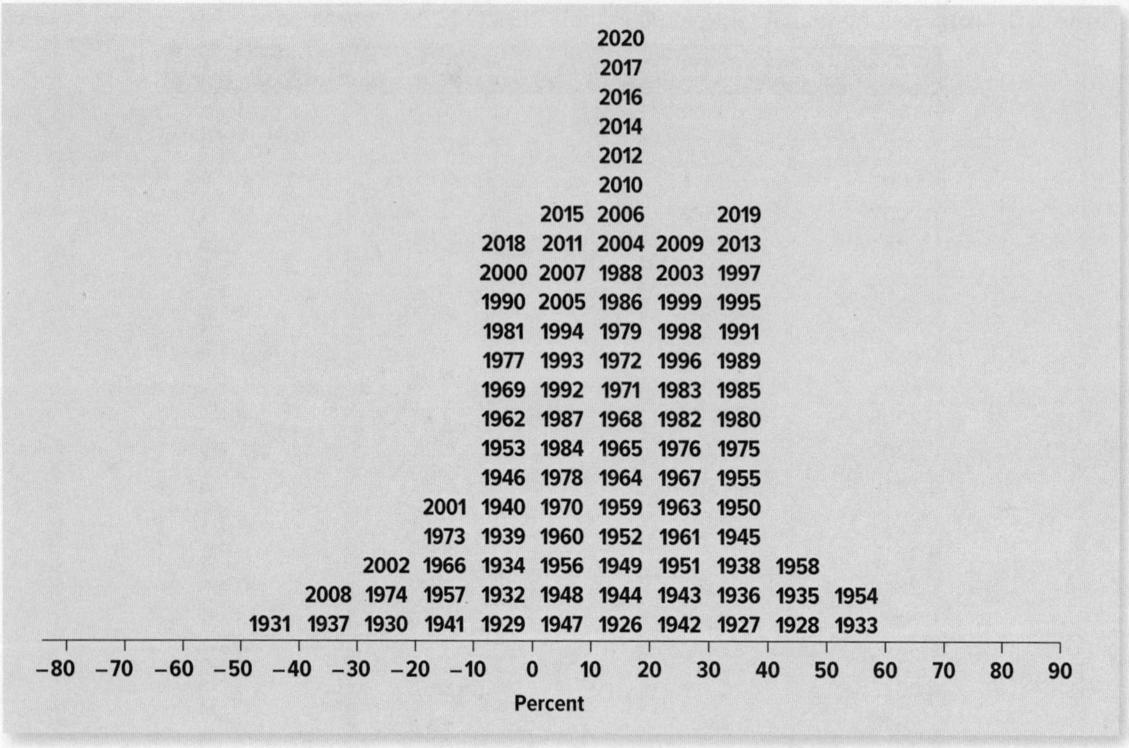

Figure 10.9(a) Histogram of Returns on Large-Company Stocks: 1926–2020

SOURCE: 2021 SBBI Yearbook. Duff & Phelps.

Given a frequency distribution like that in Figure 10.9, we can calculate the **average** or **mean** of the distribution. To compute the average of the distribution, we add up all of the values and divide by the total (T) number (95 in our case because we have 95 years of data). The bar over the R is used to represent the mean, and the formula is the ordinary formula for calculating an average:

$$\text{Mean} = \overline{R} = \frac{(R_1 + \cdots + R_T)}{T}$$

The mean of the 95 annual large-company stock returns from 1926 to 2020 is 12.2 percent.

EXAMPLE 10.2

Calculating Average Returns Suppose the returns on common stock over a four-year period are .1370, .3580, .4514, and −.0888, respectively. The average, or mean, return over these four years is:

$$\overline{R} = \frac{.1370 + .3580 + .4514 - .0888}{4} = .2144, \text{ or } 21.44\%$$

10.4 Average Stock Returns and Risk-Free Returns

Now that we have computed the average return on the U.S. stock market, it seems sensible to compare it with the returns on other securities. The most obvious comparison is with the low-variability returns in the U.S. government bond market. These are free of most of the volatility we see in the stock market.

An interesting comparison, then, is between the virtually risk-free return on T-bills and the very risky return on common stocks. This difference between risky returns and risk-free returns often is called the *excess return on the risky asset.* Of course, in any particular year, the excess return might be positive or negative.

Table 10.2 shows the average stock return, bond return, T-bill return, and inflation rate for the period from 1926 through 2020. From this we can derive average excess returns. The average excess return from

Table 10.2 Total Annual Returns in the U.S.A., 1926–2020

Series	Arithmetic Mean (%)	Standard Deviation (%)	Distribution (%)
Small-company stocks*	16.2	31.3	
Large-company stocks	12.2	19.7	
Long-term corporate bonds	6.5	8.5	
Long-term government bonds	6.1	9.8	
Intermediate-term government bonds	5.3	5.6	
U.S. Treasury bills	3.3	3.1	
Inflation	2.9	4.0	

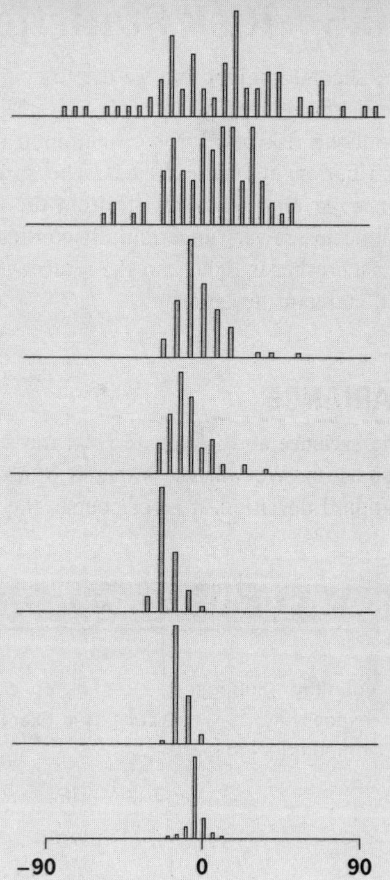

*The 1933 small-company stock total return was 142.9 percent.

SOURCE: 2021 SBBI Yearbook. Duff & Phelps.

large-company common stocks relative to T-bills for the entire period was 8.9 percent (= 12.2% − 3.3%). The average excess return on common stocks is called the historical *equity risk premium* because it is the additional return from bearing risk.

One of the most significant observations of stock market data is this long-term excess of the stock return over the risk-free return. An investor for this period was rewarded for investment in the stock market with an extra, or excess, return over what would have been achieved by investing in T-bills.

Why was there such a reward? Does it mean that it never pays to invest in T-bills and that someone who invested in them instead of in the stock market needs a course in finance? A complete answer to these questions lies at the heart of modern finance. However, part of the answer can be found in the variability of the various types of investments. There are many years when an investment in T-bills achieves higher returns than an investment in large common stocks. Also, we note that the returns from an investment in common stocks are frequently negative, whereas an investment in T-bills have only once had a negative return, −.02 percent in 1938. So, we now turn our attention to measuring the variability of returns and an introductory discussion of risk.

10.5 Risk Statistics

Excel Master coverage online

The second number that we use to characterize the distribution of returns is a measure of the risk in returns. There is no universally agreed-upon definition of risk. One way to think about the risk of returns on common stock is in terms of how spread out the frequency distribution in Figure 10.9 is. The spread, or dispersion, of a distribution is a measure of how much a particular return can deviate from the mean return. If the distribution is very spread out, the returns that will occur are very uncertain. By contrast, a distribution whose returns are all within a few percentage points of each other is tight, and the returns are less uncertain. The measures of risk we will discuss are variance and standard deviation.

VARIANCE

The **variance** and its square root, the **standard deviation,** are the most common measures of variability, or dispersion. We will use Var and σ^2 to denote the variance, and we will use SD and σ to represent the standard deviation. σ is, of course, the Greek letter sigma.

EXAMPLE 10.3

Volatility Suppose the returns on common stocks are (in decimals) .1370, .3580, .4514, and −.0888, respectively. As we calculated in Example 10.2, the average return is .2144. The variance of this sample is computed as follows:

$$\text{Var} = \frac{1}{T-1}\left[(R_1-\bar{R})^2 + (R_2-\bar{R})^2 + (R_3-\bar{R})^2 + (R_4-\bar{R})^2\right]$$

$$.0582 = \frac{1}{3}\left[(.1370-.2144)^2 + (.3580-.2144)^2 + (.4514-.2144)^2 + (-.0888-.2144)^2\right]$$

$$\text{SD} = \sqrt{.0582} = .2413, \text{ or } 24.13\%$$

The formula in Example 10.3 tells us just what to do: Take the T individual returns (R_1, R_2, ...) and subtract the average return $\bar{R}$, square the result, and add them up. Finally, this total must be divided by the number of returns less one ($T - 1$). The standard deviation is always the square root of the variance.

Using the stock returns for the 95-year period from 1926 through 2020 in this formula, the resulting standard deviation of large-company stock returns is 19.7 percent. The standard deviation is the standard statistical measure of the spread of a sample, and it will be the measure we use most of the time. Its interpretation is facilitated by a discussion of the normal distribution.

Standard deviations are widely reported for mutual funds. For example, the Fidelity Magellan Fund is a large mutual fund. How volatile is it? To find out, we went to www.morningstar.com, entered the ticker symbol FMAGX, and hit the "Risk" link. Here is what we found:

Risk & Volatility Measures ⓘ

Trailing	Fund	Category	Index
Alpha	2.77	5.26	7.24
Beta	0.95	1.02	1.04
R^2	93.75	92.02	95.44
Sharpe Ratio	0.85	0.95	1.07
Standard Deviation	18.50	20.11	19.92

SOURCE: www.morningstar.com, January 27, 2021.

Over the last three years, the standard deviation of the returns on the Fidelity Magellan Fund was 18.50 percent. When you consider the average stock has a standard deviation of about 50 percent, this seems like a low number. But the Magellan Fund is a relatively well-diversified portfolio, so this is an illustration of the power of diversification, a subject we will discuss in detail later. Also under the Volatility Measures section, you will see the **Sharpe ratio**. The Sharpe ratio is calculated as the risk premium of the asset divided by the standard deviation. As such, it is a measure of return to the level of risk taken (as measured by the standard deviation). The "beta" for the Fidelity Magellan Fund is .95. We will have more to say about this number–lots more–in the next chapter.

EXAMPLE 10.4

Sharpe Ratio The Sharpe ratio is the average equity risk premium over a period of time divided by the standard deviation. From 1926 to 2020 the average risk premium (relative to Treasury bills) for large-company stocks was 8.9 percent while the standard deviation was 19.7 percent. The Sharpe ratio of this sample is computed as:

$$\text{Sharpe ratio} = .089/.197 = .452$$

The Sharpe ratio is sometimes referred to as the reward-to-risk ratio where the reward is the average excess return and the risk is the standard deviation.

NORMAL DISTRIBUTION AND ITS IMPLICATIONS FOR STANDARD DEVIATION

A large enough sample drawn from a **normal distribution** looks like the bell-shaped curve drawn in Figure 10.10. As you can see, this distribution is *symmetric* about its mean, not *skewed*, and has a much cleaner shape than the actual distribution of yearly returns drawn in Figure 10.9. Of course, if we had been able to observe stock market returns for 1,000 years, we might have filled in a lot of the jumps and jerks in Figure 10.9 and had a smoother curve.

In classical statistics, the normal distribution plays a central role, and the standard deviation is the usual way to represent the spread of a normal distribution. For the normal distribution, the probability of having a return that is above or below the mean by a certain amount depends only on the standard deviation. For example, the probability of having a return that is within one standard deviation of the mean of the distribution is approximately .68, or 2/3, and the probability of having a return that is within two standard deviations of the mean is approximately .95.

The 19.7 percent standard deviation we found for stock returns from 1926 through 2020 can now be interpreted in the following way: If stock returns are roughly normally distributed, the probability that a yearly return will fall within 19.7 percent of the mean of 12.2 percent will be approximately 2/3. That is, about 2/3 of the yearly returns will be between −7.5 percent and 31.9 percent. (Note that −7.5% = 12.2% − 19.7% and 31.9% = 12.2% + 19.7%.) The probability that the return in any year will fall within two standard deviations is about .95. That is, about 95 percent of yearly returns will be between −27.2 percent and 51.6 percent.

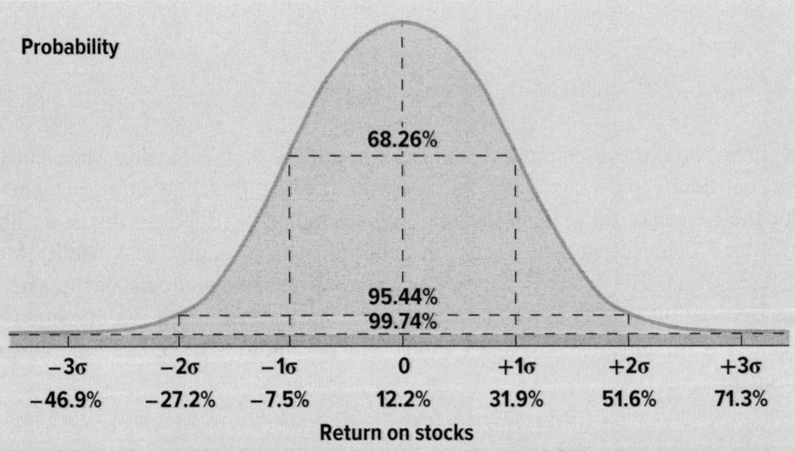

In the case of a normal distribution, there is a 68.26 percent probability that a return will be within one standard deviation of the mean. In this example, there is a 68.26 percent probability that a yearly return will be between −7.5 percent and 31.9 percent.

There is a 95.44 percent probability that a return will be within two standard deviations of the mean. In this example, there is a 95.44 percent probability that a yearly return will be between −27.2 percent and 51.6 percent.

Finally, there is a 99.74 percent probability that a return will be within three standard deviations of the mean. In this example, there is a 99.74 percent probability that a yearly return will be between −46.9 percent and 71.3 percent.

Figure 10.10 The Normal Distribution

10.6 More on Average Returns

Thus far in this chapter we have looked closely at simple average returns. But there is another way of computing an average return. The fact that average returns are calculated two different ways leads to some confusion, so our goal in this section is to explain the two approaches and also the circumstances under which each is most appropriate.

Excel Master coverage online

ARITHMETIC VERSUS GEOMETRIC AVERAGES

Let's start with a simple example. Suppose you buy a particular stock for ₹100. Unfortunately, the first year you own it, it falls to ₹50. The second year you own it, it rises back to ₹100, leaving you where you started (no dividends were paid).

What was your average return on this investment? Common sense seems to say that your average return must be exactly zero because you started with ₹100 and ended with ₹100. But if we calculate the returns year-by-year, we see that you lost 50 percent the first year (you lost half of your money). The second year, you made 100 percent (you doubled your money). Your average return over the two years was thus (−50 percent + 100 percent)/2 = 25 percent!

So which is correct, 0 percent or 25 percent? The answer is that both are correct; they answer different questions. The 0 percent is called the **geometric average return**. The 25 percent is called the **arithmetic average return**. The geometric average return answers the question, *"What was your average compound return per year over a particular period?"* The arithmetic average return answers the question, *"What was your return in an average year over a particular period?"*

Notice that in previous sections, the average returns we calculated were all arithmetic averages, so we already know how to calculate them. What we need to do now is (1) learn how to calculate geometric averages and (2) learn the circumstances under which average is more meaningful than the other.

CALCULATING GEOMETRIC AVERAGE RETURNS

First, to illustrate how we calculate a geometric average return, suppose a particular investment had annual returns of 10 percent, 12 percent, 3 percent, and −9 percent over the last four years. The geometric average return over this four-year period is calculated as $(1.10 \times 1.12 \times 1.03 \times .91)^{1/4} - 1 = .0366$, or 3.66 percent. In contrast, the average arithmetic return we have been calculating is $(.10 + .12 + .03 - .09)/4 = .040$, or 4.0 percent.

In general, if we have T years of returns, the geometric average return over these T years is calculated using this formula:

$$\text{Geometric average return} = [(1 + R_1) \times (1 + R_2) \times \cdots \times (1 + R_T)]^{1/T} - 1 \qquad \textbf{(10.1)}$$

This formula tells us that four steps are required:

1. Take each of the T annual returns $R_1, R_2, \ldots, R_T$ and add 1 to each (after converting them to decimals).
2. Multiply all the numbers from Step 1 together.
3. Take the result from Step 2 and raise it to the power of $1/T$.
4. Finally, subtract 1 from the result of Step 3. The result is the geometric average return.

EXAMPLE 10.5

Calculating the Geometric Average Return Calculate the geometric average return for S&P 500 large-cap stocks for a five-year period using the numbers given here.

First, convert percentages to decimal returns, add 1, and then calculate their product:

S&P 500 Returns	Product
13.75%	1.1375
35.70	× 1.3570
45.08	× 1.4508
−8.80	× .9120
−25.13	× .7487
	1.5291

Notice that the number 1.5291 is what our investment is worth after five years if we started with a ₹1 investment. The geometric average return is then calculated as:

$$\text{Geometric average return} = 1.5291^{1/5} - 1 = .0887, \text{ or } 8.87\%$$

Thus, the geometric average return is about 8.87 percent in this example. Here is a tip: If you are using a financial calculator, you can put −₹1 in as the present value, ₹1.5291 as the future value, and 5 as the number of periods. Then solve for the unknown rate. You should get the same answer we did.

You may have noticed in our examples thus far that the geometric average returns seem to be smaller. It turns out that this will always be true (as long as the returns are not all identical, in which case the two "averages" would be the same). To illustrate, Table 10.3 shows the arithmetic averages and standard deviations from Table 10.2, along with the geometric average returns.

As shown in Table 10.3, the geometric averages are all smaller, but the magnitude of the difference varies quite a bit. The reason is that the difference is greater for more volatile investments. In fact, there is a useful approximation. Assuming all the numbers are expressed in decimals (as opposed to percentages), the geometric average return is approximately equal to the arithmetic average return minus half the variance. For example, looking at the large-company stocks, the arithmetic average is 12.2 percent and the standard deviation is .197, implying that the variance is .0388. The approximate geometric average is thus $.122 - \frac{.0388}{2} = .103$, or 10.3 percent, which is the same as the actual value in this case.

Table 10.3 Geometric versus Arithmetic Average Returns in the U.S.A.: 1926–2020

Series	Geometric Mean	Arithmetic Mean	Standard Deviation
Small-company stocks	11.9%	16.2%	31.3%
Large-company stocks	10.3	12.2	19.7
Long-term corporate bonds	6.2	6.5	8.5
Long-term government bonds	5.7	6.1	9.8
Intermediate-term government bonds	5.1	5.3	5.6
U.S. Treasury bills	3.3	3.3	3.1
Inflation	2.9	2.9	4.0

SOURCE: 2021 SBBI Yearbook. Duff & Phelps.

EXAMPLE 10.6

More Geometric Averages Take a look back at Figure 10.4. There we showed the value of a ₹1 investment after 95 years. Use the value for the large-company stock investment to check the geometric average in Table 10.3.

In Figure 10.4, the large-company investment grew to ₹10,944.66 over 95 years. The geometric average return is thus:

$$\text{Geometric average return} = ₹10{,}944.66^{1/95} - 1 = .103, \text{ or } 10.3\%$$

This 10.3 percent is the value shown in Table 10.3. For practice, check some of the other numbers in Table 10.3 the same way.

ARITHMETIC AVERAGE RETURN OR GEOMETRIC AVERAGE RETURN?

When we look at historical returns, the difference between the geometric and arithmetic average returns isn't too hard to understand. To put it slightly differently, the geometric average tells you what you actually earned per year on average, compounded annually. The arithmetic average tells you what you earned in a typical year and is an unbiased estimate of the true mean of the distribution. The geometric average is very useful in describing the actual historical investment experience. The arithmetic average is useful in making estimates of the future.[2]

10.7 The U.S. Equity Risk Premium: Historical and International Perspectives

So far, in this chapter, we have studied the United States in the period from 1926 to 2020. As we have discussed, the historical U.S. stock market risk premium has been substantial. Of course, anytime we use the past to predict the future, there is a danger that the past period isn't representative of what the future will hold. Perhaps U.S. investors got lucky over this period and earned particularly large returns. Data from earlier years for the United States is available, though it is not of the same quality. With that caveat in mind, researchers have tracked returns back to 1802, and the U.S. equity risk premium in the pre-1926 era was smaller. Using the U.S. return data from 1802, the historical equity risk premium was 5.4 percent.[3]

Also, we have not looked at other major countries. Actually, more than half of the value of tradable stock is not in the United States. From Table 10.4, we can see that while the total world stock market capitalization was about ₹69 trillion in 2019, only about 44 percent was in the United States. Thanks to Dimson, Marsh, and Staunton, data from earlier periods and other countries are now available to help us take a closer look at equity risk premiums. Table 10.5 and Figure 10.11 show the historical stock market risk premiums for 17 countries around the world in the period from 1900 to 2010. Looking at the numbers, the U.S. historical equity risk premium is the seventh highest at 7.2 percent (which differs from our earlier estimate because of the different time periods examined). The overall world average risk

[2]Another way of thinking about estimating an investment's return over a particular future horizon is to recall from your statistics class that the arithmetic average is a "sample" mean. As such, it provides an unbiased estimate of the underlying true mean. To use the arithmetic average to estimate the future returns, we must make sure the historical returns are measured using the same interval as the future forecasting period. For example, we could use yearly (annual) returns to estimate next year's return. The arithmetic average would be a good basis for forecasting the next two-year returns if two-year holding period returns were used. We also must be confident that the past distribution of returns is the same as that of the future.

[3]Siegel, Jeremy J. 2008. *Stocks for the Long Run,* 4th ed. New York: McGraw-Hill.

Table 10.4 Estimate of World Tradable Stock Market Capitalization, 2019

Country	In Trillions	Percent
United States	₹30.44	44.3%
Euro area	7.3	10.6
China	9.3	13.5
Japan	5.0	7.3
Hong Kong	3.2	4.7
Saudi Arabia	2.0	2.9
India	1.6	2.3
World	**68.7**	**85.6**

SOURCE: https://data.worldbank.org/indicator/CM.MKT.LCAP.CD, April 22, 2021. Numbers do not sum due to excluded countries.

premium is 6.9 percent. It seems clear that U.S. investors did well, but not exceptionally so relative to many other countries. The top-performing countries according to the Sharpe ratio were the United States, Australia, South Africa, and France, while the worst performers were Belgium, Norway, and Denmark. Germany, Japan, and Italy might make an interesting case study because they have the highest stock returns over this period (despite World Wars I and II), but also the highest risk.

So what is a good estimate of the U.S. equity risk premium going forward? Unfortunately, nobody can know for sure what investors expect in the future. If history is a guide, the expected U.S. equity risk premium could be 7.2 percent based upon estimates from 1900–2010. We also should be mindful that the average

Table 10.5 Annualized Equity Risk Premiums and Sharpe Ratios for 17 Countries, 1900–2010

Country	Historical Equity Risk Premiums (%) (1)	Standard Deviation (%) (2)	Sharpe Ratio (1)/(2)
Australia	8.3%	17.6%	.47
Belgium	5.5	24.7	.22
Canada	5.6	17.2	.33
Denmark	4.6	20.5	.22
France	8.7	24.5	.36
Germany*	9.8	31.8	.31
Ireland	5.3	21.5	.25
Italy	9.8	32.0	.31
Japan	9.0	27.7	.32
Netherlands	6.5	22.8	.29
Norway	5.9	26.5	.22
South Africa	8.3	22.1	.38
Spain	5.4	21.9	.25
Sweden	6.6	22.1	.30
Switzerland	5.1	18.9	.27
United Kingdom	6.0	19.9	.30
United States	7.2	19.8	.36
Average	**6.9**	**23.0**	**.30**

*Germany omits 1922–1923.

SOURCE: Dimson, Elroy, Paul Marsh, and Michael Staunton. 2011. Credit Suisse Global Investment Returns Sourcebook. Credit Suisse Research Institute. The Dimson-Marsh-Staunton data set is distributed by Morningstar, Inc.

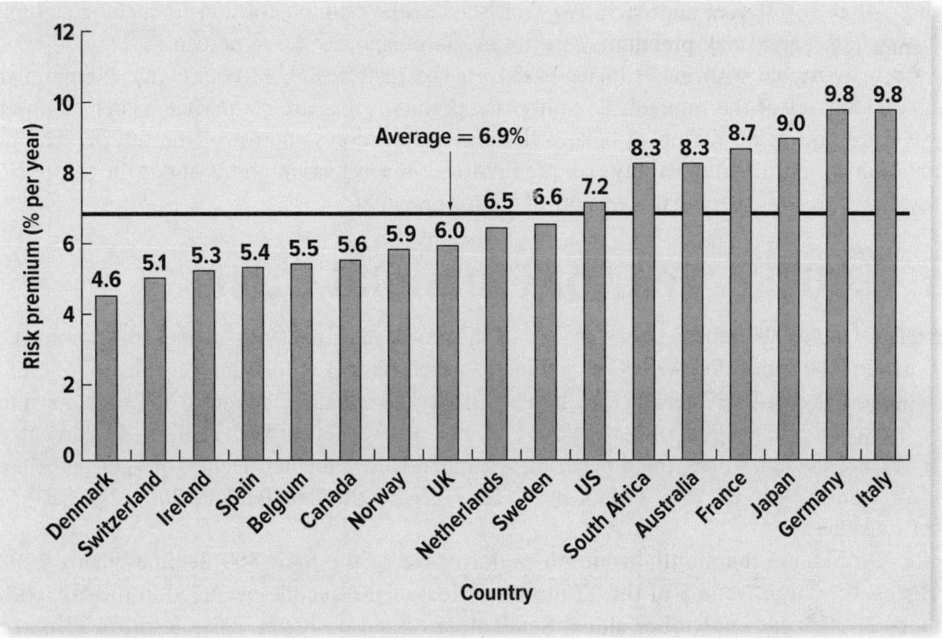

Figure 10.11 Stock Market Risk Premiums for 17 Countries: 1900–2010

SOURCE: Dimson, Elroy, Paul Marsh, and Michael Staunton. 2007. "The Worldwide Equity Premium: A Smaller Puzzle." In *Handbook of the Equity Risk Premium,* edited by Rajnish Mehra, 467–514. Elsevier.

world equity risk premium was 6.9 percent over this same period. On the other hand, the more recent periods (1926–2020) suggest higher estimates of the U.S. equity risk premium, and earlier periods going back to 1802 suggest lower estimates.

The standard error (SE) helps with the issue of how much confidence we can have in our historical average of 7.2 percent. The SE is the standard deviation of the historical risk premium and is given by the following formula:

$$\text{SE} = \text{SD}\,(\bar{R}) = \frac{\text{SD}\,(R)}{\sqrt{\text{The number of observations}}}$$

If we assume that the distribution of returns is normal and that each year's return is independent of all the others, we know there is a 95.4 percent probability that the true mean return is within two standard errors of the historical average.

More specifically, the 95.4 percent confidence interval for the true equity risk premium is the historical average return $\pm(2 \times$ standard error). As we have seen from 1900 to 2010, the historical equity risk premium of U.S. stocks was 7.2 percent and the standard deviation was 19.8 percent. Therefore, 95.4 percent of the time, the true equity risk premium should be within 3.44 and 10.96 percent:

$$7.2 \pm 2\left(\frac{19.8}{\sqrt{111}}\right) = 7.2 \pm 2\left(\frac{19.8}{10.5}\right) = 7.2 \pm 3.76$$

In other words, we can be 95.4 percent confident that our estimate of the U.S. equity risk premium from historical data is in the range from 3.44 percent to 10.96 percent.

Taking a slightly different approach, Ivo Welch asked the opinions of 226 financial economists regarding the future U.S. equity risk premium, and the median response was 7 percent.[4]

We are comfortable with an estimate based on the historical U.S. equity risk premium of about 7 percent, but estimates of the future U.S. equity risk premium that are somewhat higher or lower could be reasonable if we have good reason to believe the past is not representative of the future.[5] The bottom line is that any estimate of the future equity risk premium will involve assumptions about the future risk environment as well as the amount of risk aversion of future investors.

10.8 2008: A Year of Financial Crisis

The year 2008 entered the record books as one of the worst years for stock market investors in U.S. history. How bad was it? The widely followed S&P 500 index, which tracks the total market value of 500 of the largest U.S. corporations, decreased 37 percent for the year. Of the 500 stocks in the index, 485 were down for the year.

Over the period 1926-2008, only the year 1931 had a lower return than 2008 (−43 percent versus −37 percent). Making matters worse, the downdraft continued with a further decline of 8.43 percent in January 2009. In all, from November 2007 (when the decline began) through January 2009, the S&P 500 lost 45 percent of its value.

Figure 10.12 shows the month-by-month performance of the S&P 500 decline during 2008. As indicated, returns were negative in 8 of the 12 months. Most of the decline occurred in the fall, with investors losing almost 17 percent in October alone. Small stocks fared no better. They also fell 37 percent for the year (with a 21 percent drop in October), their worst performance since losing 58 percent in 1937.

As Figure 10.12 suggests, stock prices were highly volatile at the end of the year–more than has been generally true historically. Oddly, the S&P had 126 up days and 126 down days (remember the markets are closed weekends and holidays). Of course, the down days were much worse, on average.

The drop in stock prices was a global phenomenon, and many of the world's major markets declined by much more than the S&P. China, India, and Russia, for example, all experienced declines of more than 50 percent. Tiny Iceland saw share prices drop by more than 90 percent for the year. Trading on the Icelandic exchange was temporarily suspended on October 9. In what has to be a modern record for a single day, stocks fell by 76 percent when trading resumed on October 14.

Did any types of securities perform well in 2008? The answer is yes because, as stock values declined, bond values increased, particularly U.S. Treasury bonds. In fact, long-term Treasury bonds *gained* 20 percent, while shorter-term Treasury bonds were up 13 percent. Higher-quality, long-term corporate bonds did less well but still managed to achieve a positive return of about 9 percent. These returns were especially impressive considering that the rate of inflation, as measured by the CPI, was very close to zero.

Of course, stock prices can be volatile in both directions. From March 2009 through February 2011, a period of about 700 days, the S&P 500 doubled in value. This climb was the fastest doubling since 1936, when the S&P did it in only 500 days. So, what lessons should investors take away from this recent, and very turbulent, bit of capital market history? First, and most obviously, stocks have significant risk! But there is a second, equally important lesson. Depending on the mix, a diversified portfolio of stocks and bonds might have suffered in 2008, but the losses would have been much smaller than those experienced by an all-stock portfolio. In other words, diversification matters, a point we will examine in detail in our next chapter.

[4]For example, Welch, Ivo. 2000. "Views of Financial Economists on the Equity Premium and on Professional Controversies." *Journal of Business* 73, no. 4: 501-37. Pratt, Shannon P., and Roger J. Grabowski. 2010. *Cost of Capital: Applications and Examples.* John Wiley: Hoboken, NJ, conclude, after reviewing a variety of evidence, that the equity risk premium is in the 3.5 to 6 percent range.

[5]In Dimson, Elroy, Paul Marsh, and Michael Staunton. 2007. "The Worldwide Equity Premium: A Smaller Puzzle." In *Handbook of the Equity Risk Premium,* edited by Rajnish Mehra, 467-514. Amsterdam. The authors argue that a good estimate of the world equity risk premium going forward should be about 5 percent, largely because of nonrecurring factors that positively affected worldwide historical returns. However, it could be argued that the global financial crisis of 2008-2009 was a negative shock to the stock market that has increased the equity risk premium from its historical levels.

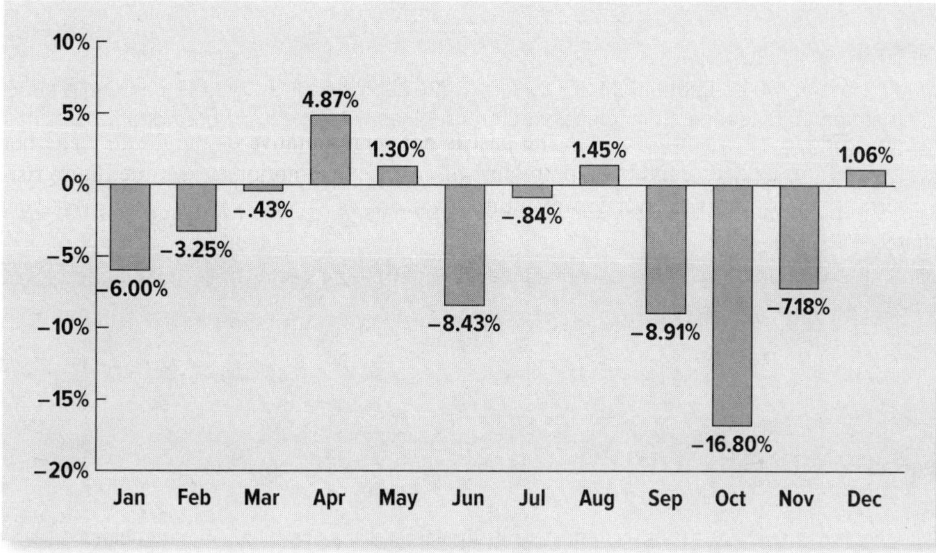

Figure 10.12 S&P 500 Monthly Returns, 2008

Another year with volatile stock prices was 2020. As we mentioned at the beginning of the chapter, overall, it was a good year for investors, but because of the COVID-19 lockdowns, it was a wild ride. On February 19, 2020, the S&P 500 closed at an all-time high, before it began a downward slide. The middle of March was particularly painful. From the close on Friday, March 6, until the close on Monday, March 23, the S&P 500 lost almost 25 percent. And by March 23, the S&P 500 was down 34 percent from its February 19 closing. Ouch! As investors began to better understand the economic implications of the COVID pandemic, the stock market began to rebound, and the S&P 500 recovered all of its losses by August 18. By the end of the year, the S&P 500 had increased 67 percent from its March low. And the S&P 500 had very high volatility during the early days of the pandemic. Eight of the 10 worst days of the year occurred between February 27 and April 1, while all 10 of the best days occurred between March 2 and April 8.

RESEARCH IN EMERGING MARKET CONTEXT

Peswani and Joshipura (2022) have conducted a study on an interesting phenomenon called the low-risk effect, where a portfolio of low-risk stocks outperforms the portfolio of high-risk stocks and market portfolios on a risk-adjusted basis. They have found that both sector and stock-level bets contribute to the return of the low-risk investing strategy, but the stock-level effect is dominant. They suggest launching sector-specific low-volatility indices for relevant sectors to allow investors to benefit from this strategy. Joshipura and Joshipura (2020) have also documented that the low-risk effect is independent of size, value, and momentum effects, and it is robust even after controlling for variables like liquidity and ticket-size of stocks. They have further documented that the low-risk effect is a combination of stock and sector-level effects, and it cannot be captured fully by concentrated sector exposure.

Dharani et al. (2022) have found that ethical Investments offer better risk-adjusted returns for investors. Compared to regular sectoral indices, they have found that Shariah sectoral indices offer higher returns with low risk, even during the Covid-19 global pandemic.

(continued)

References

Dharani, M., Hassan, M. K., Rabbani, M. R., & Huq, T. (2022). Does the Covid-19 pandemic affect faith-based investments? Evidence from global sectoral indices. *Research in International Business and Finance*, 59, 101537.

Joshipura, M., & Joshipura, N. (2020). Low-risk effect: evidence, explanations and approaches to enhancing the performance of low-risk investment strategies. *Investment Management and Financial Innovations*, 17(2), 128–145.

Peswani, S., & Joshipura, M. (2022). Low-risk investment strategy: sector bets or stock bets?. *Managerial Finance*, 48(3), 521–539.

Summary and Conclusions

1. This chapter presented returns for a number of different asset classes. The general conclusion is that stocks have outperformed bonds over most of the 20th century, though stocks also have exhibited more risk.
2. The statistical measures in this chapter are necessary building blocks for the material of the next three chapters. In particular, standard deviation and variance measure the variability of the returns on an individual security and on portfolios of securities. In the next chapter, we will argue that standard deviation and variance are appropriate measures of the risk of an individual security if an investor's portfolio is composed of that security only.

Concept Questions

1. **Investment Selection** Given that Bit Digital was up by about 3,688 percent for 2020, why didn't all investors hold Bit Digital?
2. **Investment Selection** Given that Occidental Petroleum was down by about 58 percent for 2020, why did some investors hold the stock? Why didn't they sell out before the price declined so sharply?
3. **Risk and Return** We have seen that over long periods, stock investments have tended to substantially outperform bond investments. However, it is not at all uncommon to observe investors with long horizons holding their investments entirely in bonds. Are such investors irrational?
4. **Stocks versus Gambling** Critically evaluate the following statement: Playing the stock market is like gambling. Such speculative investing has no social value, other than the pleasure people get from this form of gambling.
5. **Effects of Inflation** Look at Table 10.1 and Figure 10.7 in the text. When were T-bill rates at their highest over the period from 1926 through 2020? Why do you think they were so high during this period? What relationship underlies your answer?
6. **Risk Premiums** Is it possible for the risk premium to be negative before an investment is undertaken? Can the risk premium be negative after the fact? Explain.
7. **Returns** Two years ago, General Materials' and Standard Fixtures' stock prices were the same. During the first year, General Materials' stock price increased by 10 percent while Standard Fixtures' stock price decreased by 10 percent. During the second year, General Materials' stock price decreased by 10 percent and Standard Fixtures' stock price increased by 10 percent. Do these two stocks have the same price today? Explain.

8. **Returns** Two years ago, the Lake Minerals and Small Town Furniture stock prices were the same. The average annual return for both stocks over the past two years was 10 percent. Lake Minerals' stock price increased 10 percent each year. Small Town Furniture's stock price increased 25 percent in the first year and lost 5 percent last year. Do these two stocks have the same price today?

9. **Arithmetic versus Geometric Returns** What is the difference between arithmetic and geometric returns? Suppose you have invested in a stock for the last 10 years. Which number is more important to you, the arithmetic or geometric return?

10. **Historical Returns** The historical asset class returns presented in the chapter are not adjusted for inflation. What would happen to the estimated risk premium if we did account for inflation? The returns also are not adjusted for taxes. What would happen to the returns if we accounted for taxes? What would happen to the volatility?

Questions and Problems

BASIC (Questions 1–18)

1. **Calculating Returns** Suppose a stock had an initial price of ₹74 per share, paid a dividend of ₹1.65 per share during the year, and had an ending share price of ₹83. Compute the percentage total return.

2. **Calculating Yields** In Problem 1, what was the dividend yield? The capital gains yield?

3. **Calculating Returns** Rework Problems 1 and 2 assuming the ending share price is ₹61.

4. **Calculating Returns** Suppose you bought a bond with a 6 percent coupon rate one year ago for ₹1,010. The bond sells for ₹1,025 today.

   a. Assuming a ₹1,000 face value, what was your total Rupee return on this investment over the past year?
   b. What was your total nominal rate of return on this investment over the past year?
   c. If the inflation rate last year was 3 percent, what was your total real rate of return on this investment?

5. **Nominal versus Real Returns** What was the arithmetic average annual return on large-company stocks from 1926 through 2020?

   a. In nominal terms?
   b. In real terms?

6. **Bond Returns** What is the historical real return on long-term government bonds? On long-term corporate bonds?

7. **Calculating Returns and Variability** Using the following returns, calculate the arithmetic average returns, the variances, and the standard deviations for X and Y:

	Returns	
Year	X	Y
1	13%	27%
2	26	36
3	7	11
4	−5	−29
5	11	16

8. **Risk Premiums** Refer to Table 10.1 in the text and look at the period from 1973 through 1978.

   a. Calculate the arithmetic average returns for large-company stocks and T-bills over this period.
   b. Calculate the standard deviation of the returns for large-company stocks and T-bills over this period.

c. Calculate the observed risk premium in each year for the large-company stocks versus the T-bills. What was the arithmetic average risk premium over this period? What was the standard deviation of the risk premium over this period?

9. **Calculating Returns and Variability** You've observed the following returns on Pine Computers's stock over the past five years: 8 percent, −12 percent, 14 percent, 21 percent, and 16 percent.

   a. What was the arithmetic average return on the company's stock over this 5-year period?
   b. What was the variance of the company's returns over this period? The standard deviation?

10. **Calculating Real Returns and Risk Premiums** In Problem 9, suppose the average inflation rate over this period was 3.1 percent and the average T-bill rate over the period was 3.9 percent.

    a. What was the average real return on the company's stock?
    b. What was the average nominal risk premium on the company's stock?

11. **Calculating Real Rates** Given the information in Problem 10, what was the average real risk-free rate over this time period? What was the average real risk premium?

12. **Holding Period Return** A stock has had returns of 12.79, 9.21, 14.68, 21.83, and −10.34 percent over the past five years, respectively. What was the holding period return for the stock?

13. **Calculating Returns** You purchased a zero coupon bond one year ago for ₹286.40. The market interest rate is now 6.1 percent. If the bond had 21 years to maturity when you originally purchased it, what was your total return for the past year? Assume semiannual compounding.

14. **Calculating Returns** You bought a share of 3.1 percent preferred stock for ₹91.86 last year. The market price for your stock is now ₹95.63. What was your total return for last year?

15. **Calculating Returns** You bought a stock three months ago for ₹74.83 per share. The stock paid no dividends. The current share price is ₹82.65. What is the APR of your investment? The EAR?

16. **Calculating Real Returns** Refer to Table 10.1. What was the average real return for Treasury bills from 1926 through 1932?

17. **Return Distributions** Refer back to Table 10.2. What range of returns would you expect to see 68 percent of the time for long-term corporate bonds? What about 95 percent of the time?

18. **Return Distributions** Refer back to Table 10.2. What range of returns would you expect to see 68 percent of the time for large-company stocks? What about 95 percent of the time?

INTERMEDIATE (Questions 19–26)

19. **Calculating Returns and Variability** You find a certain stock that had returns of 18 percent, −23 percent, 16 percent, and 9 percent for four of the last five years. If the average return of the stock over this period was 10.5 percent, what was the stock's return for the missing year? What is the standard deviation of the stock's returns?

20. **Arithmetic and Geometric Returns** A stock has had returns of 6 percent, 29 percent, 13 percent, −3 percent, 22 percent, and −17 percent over the last six years. What are the arithmetic and geometric average returns for the stock?

21. **Arithmetic and Geometric Returns** A stock has had the following year-end prices and dividends:

Year	Price	Dividend
1	₹73.20	—
2	81.27	₹1.05
3	90.37	1.15
4	86.18	1.26
5	95.68	1.39
6	112.32	1.53

What are the arithmetic and geometric average returns for the stock?

22. **Calculating Returns** Refer to Table 10.1 in the text and look at the period from 1973 through 1980.
    a. Calculate the arithmetic average return for Treasury bills and the average annual inflation rate (consumer price index) for this period.
    b. Calculate the standard deviation of Treasury bill returns and inflation over this period.
    c. Calculate the real return for each year. What is the average real return for Treasury bills?
    d. Many people consider Treasury bills to be risk-free. What do these calculations tell you about the potential risks of Treasury bills?

23. **Calculating Investment Returns** You bought one of Cobalt Co.'s 4.9 percent coupon bonds one year ago for ₹1,008.50. These bonds make annual payments and mature six years from now. Suppose you decide to sell your bonds today when the required return on the bonds is 4.25 percent. If the inflation rate was 2.7 percent over the past year, what would be your total real return on the investment?

24. **Using Return Distributions** Suppose the returns on long-term government bonds are normally distributed. Based on the historical record, what is the approximate probability that your return on these bonds will be less than −3.7 percent in a given year? What range of returns would you expect to see 95 percent of the time? What range would you expect to see 99 percent of the time?

25. **Using Return Distributions** Assuming that the returns from holding small-company stocks are normally distributed, what is the approximate probability that your money will double in value in a single year? Triple in value?

26. **Distributions** In the previous problem, what is the probability that the return is less than −100 percent? (Think.) What are the implications for the distribution of returns?

CHALLENGE (Questions 27–28)

27. **Using Probability Distributions** Suppose the returns on large-company stocks are normally distributed. Based on the historical record, use the NORMDIST function in Excel to determine the probability that in any given year you will lose money by investing in common stock.

28. **Using Probability Distributions** Suppose the returns on long-term corporate bonds and T-bills are normally distributed. Based on the historical record, use the NORMDIST function in Excel to answer the following questions:
    a. What is the probability that in any given year, the return on long-term corporate bonds will be greater than 10 percent? Less than 0 percent?
    b. What is the probability that in any given year, the return on T-bills will be greater than 10 percent? Less than 0 percent?
    c. In 1979, the return on long-term corporate bonds was −4.18 percent. How likely is it that a return at least this low will recur at some point in the future? T-bills had a return of 10.38 percent in this same year. How likely is it that a return at least this high on T-bills will recur at some point in the future?

Excel Master It! Problem

Excel Master coverage online

As we have seen, over the 1926–2020 period, small-company stocks had the highest return and the highest risk, while U.S. Treasury bills had the lowest return and the lowest risk. While we certainly hope you have a 95-year holding period, it is likely your investment horizon will be somewhat shorter. One way risk and return are examined over a shorter investment period is by using rolling returns and standard deviations. Suppose you have a series of annual returns and you want to calculate a three-year rolling average return. You would calculate the first rolling average at Year 3 using the returns for the first three years. The next rolling average would be calculated using the returns from Years 2, 3, and 4, and so on.

a. Using the annual returns for large-company stocks and Treasury bills, calculate both the 5- and 10-year rolling average returns and standard deviations.
b. Over how many five-year periods did Treasury bills outperform large-company stocks? Over how many 10-year periods?
c. Over how many five-year periods did Treasury bills have a larger standard deviation than large-company stocks? Over how many 10-year periods?
d. Graph the rolling 5-year and 10-year average returns for large-company stocks and Treasury bills.
e. What conclusions do you draw from the above results?

Mini Case A JOB AT EAST COAST YACHTS

You recently graduated from college and your job search led you to East Coast Yachts. Because you felt the company's business was seaworthy, you accepted a job offer. The first day on the job, while you are finishing your employment paperwork, Dan Ervin, who works in Finance, stops by to inform you about the company's 401(k) plan.

A 401(k) plan is a retirement plan offered by many companies. Such plans are tax-deferred savings vehicles, meaning that any deposits you make into the plan are deducted from your current pretax income, so no current taxes are paid on the money. For example, assume your salary will be ₹50,000 per year. If you contribute ₹3,000 to the 401(k) plan, you will pay taxes on only ₹47,000 in income. There are also no taxes paid on any capital gains or income while you are invested in the plan, but you do pay taxes when you withdraw money at retirement. As is fairly common, the company also has a 5 percent match. This means that the company will match your contribution up to 5 percent of your salary, but you must contribute the amount that you want matched, up to the maximum.

The 401(k) plan has several options for investments, most of which are mutual funds. A mutual fund is a portfolio of assets. When you purchase shares in a mutual fund, you are actually purchasing partial ownership of the fund's assets. The return of the fund is the weighted average of the return of the assets owned by the fund, minus any expenses. The largest expense is typically the management fee, paid to the fund manager. The management fee is compensation for the manager, who makes all of the investment decisions for the fund.

East Coast Yachts uses Bledsoe Financial Services as its 401(k) plan administrator. Here are the investment options offered for employees:

Company Stock One option in the 401(k) plan is stock in East Coast Yachts. The company is currently privately held. However, when you interviewed with the owner, Larissa Warren, she informed you the company was expected to go public in the next three to four years. Until then, a company stock price is set each year by the board of directors.

Bledsoe S&P 500 Index Fund This mutual fund tracks the S&P 500. Stocks in the fund are weighted exactly the same as the S&P 500. This means the fund return is approximately the return on the S&P 500, minus expenses. Because an index fund purchases assets based on the composition of the index it is following, the fund manager is not required to research stocks and make investment decisions. The result is that the fund expenses are usually low. The Bledsoe S&P 500 Index Fund charges expenses of .15 percent of assets per year.

Bledsoe Small-Cap Fund This fund primarily invests in small-capitalization stocks. As such, the returns of the fund are more volatile. The fund also can invest 10 percent of its assets in companies based outside the United States. This fund charges 1.70 percent in expenses.

Bledsoe Large-Company Stock Fund This fund invests primarily in large-capitalization stocks of companies based in the United States. The fund is managed by Evan Bledsoe and has outperformed the market in six of the last eight years. The fund charges 1.50 percent in expenses.

Bledsoe Bond Fund This fund invests in long-term corporate bonds issued by U.S.-domiciled companies. The fund is restricted to investments in bonds with an investment-grade credit rating. This fund charges 1.40 percent in expenses.

Bledsoe Money Market Fund This fund invests in short-term, high-credit quality debt instruments, which include Treasury bills. As such, the return on the money market fund is only slightly higher than the return on Treasury bills. Because of the credit quality and short-term nature of the investments, there is only a very slight risk of negative return. The fund charges .60 percent in expenses.

1. What advantages do the mutual funds offer compared to the company stock?
2. Assume that you invest 5 percent of your salary and receive the full 5 percent match from East Coast Yachts. What EAR do you earn from the match? What conclusions do you draw about matching plans?
3. Assume you decide you should invest at least part of your money in large-capitalization stocks of companies based in the United States. What are the advantages and disadvantages of choosing the Bledsoe Large-Company Stock Fund compared to the Bledsoe S&P 500 Index Fund?
4. The returns on the Bledsoe Small-Cap Fund are the most volatile of all the mutual funds offered in the 401(k) plan. Why would you ever want to invest in this fund? When you examine the expenses of the mutual funds, you will notice that this fund also has the highest expenses. Does this affect your decision to invest in this fund?
5. A measure of risk-adjusted performance that is often used is the Sharpe ratio. The Sharpe ratio is calculated as the risk premium of an asset divided by its standard deviation. The standard deviations and returns of the funds over the past 10 years are listed here. Calculate the Sharpe ratio for each of these funds. Assume that the expected return and standard deviation of the company stock will be 16 percent and 58 percent, respectively. Calculate the Sharpe ratio for the company stock. How appropriate is the Sharpe ratio for these assets? When would you use the Sharpe ratio? Assume a 3.2 percent risk-free rate.

	10-Year Annual Return	Standard Deviation
Bledsoe S&P 500 Index Fund	11.04%	18.45%
Bledsoe Small-Cap Fund	16.14	29.18
Bledsoe Large-Company Stock Fund	12.15	24.43
Bledsoe Bond Fund	6.93	9.96

6. What portfolio allocation would you choose? Why? Explain your thinking carefully.

11

Return, Risk, and the Capital Asset Pricing Model

Expected returns on common stocks can vary quite a bit. One important determinant is the industry in which a company operates. For example, according to recent estimates from NYU professor Aswath Damodaran, the average expected return for the soft drink industry, which includes companies such as Coca-Cola and PepsiCo, is 8.26 percent, whereas air transportation companies such as Delta and Southwest have an average expected return of 9.38 percent. Steel companies such as Nucor and United States Steel have an average expected return of 10.34 percent.

These estimates raise some obvious questions. First, why do these industry expected returns differ so much, and how are these specific numbers calculated? Also, does the higher return offered by steel industry stocks mean that investors should prefer these to, say, air transportation companies? As we will see in this chapter, the Nobel Prize-winning answers to these questions form the basis of our modern understanding of risk and return.

Please visit us at **rwjcorporatefinance.blogspot.com** for the latest developments in the world of corporate finance.

11.1 Individual Securities

In the first part of Chapter 11, we will examine the characteristics of individual securities. In particular, we will discuss:

For industry expected returns (and more), check out Professor Damodaran's website at **pages.stern.nyu.edu/~adamodar/**.

1. *Expected return*: This is the return that an individual expects a stock to earn over the next period. Of course, because this is only an expectation, the actual return may be either higher or lower. An individual's expectation may be the average return per period a security has earned in the past. Alternatively, the expectation may be based on a detailed analysis of a firm's prospects, on some computer-based model, or on special (or inside) information.
2. *Variance and standard deviation*: There are many ways to assess the volatility of a security's return. One of the most common is variance, which is a measure of the squared deviations of a security's return from its expected return. Standard deviation is the square root of the variance.
3. *Covariance and correlation*: Returns on individual securities are related to one another. Covariance is a statistic measuring the interrelationship between two securities. Alternatively, this relationship can

be restated in terms of the correlation between the two securities. Covariance and correlation are building blocks to an understanding of the beta coefficient.

11.2 Expected Return, Variance, and Covariance

EXPECTED RETURN AND VARIANCE

Suppose financial analysts believe that there are four equally likely states of the economy: depression, recession, normal, and boom. The returns on the Supertech Company are expected to follow the economy closely, while the returns on the Slowpoke Company are not. The return predictions are as follows:

Excel Master coverage online

	Supertech Returns R_{Super}	Slowpoke Returns R_{Slow}
Depression	−20%	5%
Recession	10	20
Normal	30	−12
Boom	50	9

Variance can be calculated in four steps. An additional step is needed to calculate standard deviation. The steps are:

1. Calculate the expected return:

$$E(R_{Super}) = \frac{-.20 + .10 + .30 + .50}{4} = .175, \text{ or } 17.5\%$$

$$E(R_{Slow}) = \frac{.05 + .20 - .12 + .09}{4} = .055, \text{ or } 5.5\%$$

2. For each company, calculate the deviation of each possible return from the company's expected return given previously. This is presented in the third column of Table 11.1.
3. The deviations we have calculated are indications of the dispersion of returns. However, because some are positive and some are negative, it is difficult to work with them in this form.
   To make the deviations more meaningful, we multiply each one by itself. Now all the numbers are positive, implying that their sum must be positive as well. The squared deviations are presented in the last column of Table 11.1.
4. For each company, calculate the average squared deviation, which is the variance:[1]

$$\sigma^2_{Super} = \frac{.140625 + .005625 + .015625 + .105625}{4} = .066875$$

[1]In this example, the four states give rise to four equally likely possible outcomes. The expected return is calculated by taking a probability weighted average of the possible outcomes. For Supertech:

$$.25 \times (-.20) + .25 \times .10 + .25 \times .30 + .25 \times .50 = .175, \text{ or } 17.5\%$$

Because the four possible outcomes are equally likely, we can simplify by adding up the possible outcomes and dividing by 4. If outcomes are not equally likely, this simplification does not work.

The same type of calculation is required for variance. We take a probability weighted average of the squared deviations. For Supertech:

$$.25 \times .140625 + .25 \times .005625 + .25 \times .015625 + .25 \times .105625 = .066875$$

This is the same as adding up the possible squared deviations and dividing by 4. If we use past data (as in Chapter 10), the divisor is always the number of historical observations less 1.

Table 11.1 Calculating Variance and Standard Deviation

(1) State of Economy	(2) Rate of Return	(3) Deviation from Expected Return	(4) Squared Value of Deviation
	Supertech	(Expected return = .175)	
	R_{Super}	$R_{Super} - E(R_{Super})$	$[R_{Super} - E(R_{Super})]^2$
Depression	−.20	−.375 (= −.20 − .175)	.140625 $[= (-.375)^2]$
Recession	.10	−.075	.005625
Normal	.30	.125	.015625
Boom	.50	.325	.105625
	Slowpoke	(Expected return = .055)	
	R_{Slow}	$R_{Slow} - E(R_{Slow})$	$[R_{Slow} - E(R_{Slow})]^2$
Depression	.05	−.005 (= .05 − .055)	.000025 $[= (-.005)^2]$
Recession	.20	.145	.021025
Normal	−.12	−.175	.030625
Boom	.09	.035	.001225

$$\sigma^2_{Slow} = \frac{.000025 + .021025 + .030625 + .001225}{4} = .013225$$

The variance of Supertech is .066875 and the variance of Slowpoke is .013225.

5. Calculate standard deviation by taking the square root of the variance:

$$\sigma_{Super} = \sqrt{.066875} = .2586, \text{ or } 25.86\%$$

$$\sigma_{Slow} = \sqrt{.013225} = .1150, \text{ or } 11.50\%$$

Algebraically, the formula for variance can be expressed as:

$$\text{Var}(R) = \sigma^2 = \sum [R - \text{E}(R)]^2 \tag{11.1}$$

where E(R) is the security's expected return and R is the actual return.

A look at the four-step calculation for variance makes it clear why it is a measure of the spread of the sample of returns. For each observation, we square the difference between the actual return and the expected return. We then take an average of these squared differences. Squaring the differences makes them all positive. If we used the differences between each return and the expected return and then averaged these differences, we would get zero because the returns that were above the mean would cancel the ones below.

Because the variance is still expressed in squared terms, it is difficult to interpret. Standard deviation has a much simpler interpretation, which was provided in Section 10.5. Standard deviation is the square root of the variance. The general formula for the standard deviation is:

$$\text{SD}(R) = \sigma = \sqrt{\text{Var}(R)}$$

COVARIANCE AND CORRELATION

Variance and standard deviation measure the variability of individual stocks. We now wish to measure the relationship between the return on one stock and the return on another. Enter **covariance** and **correlation**.

Covariance and correlation measure how two random variables are related. We explain these terms by extending the Supertech and Slowpoke example.

EXAMPLE 11.1

Calculating Covariance and Correlation We have already determined the expected returns and standard deviations for both Supertech and Slowpoke. In addition, we calculated the deviation of each possible return from the expected return for each firm. Using this data, we can calculate covariance in two steps. An extra step is needed to calculate correlation.

1. For each state of the economy, multiply Supertech's deviation from its expected return by Slowpoke's deviation from its expected return. Supertech's rate of return in a depression is −.20, which is −.375 (= −.20 − .175) from its expected return. Slowpoke's rate of return in a depression is .05, which is −.005 (= .05 − .055) from its expected return. Multiplying the two deviations together yields .001875 [= (−.375) × (−.005)]. The actual calculations are given in the last column of Table 11.2. This procedure can be written algebraically as:

$$[R_{Super} - E(R_{Super})] \times [R_{Slow} - E(R_{Slow})] \tag{11.2}$$

   where R_{Super} and R_{Slow} are the returns on Supertech and Slowpoke in that state of the economy. $E(R_{Super})$ and $E(R_{Slow})$ are the expected returns on the two securities.

2. Calculate the average value of the four states in the last column. This average is the covariance. That is:[2]

$$\sigma_{Super,Slow} = Cov(R_{Super}, R_{Slow}) = \frac{-.0195}{4} = -.004875$$

Note that we represent the covariance between Supertech and Slowpoke as either $Cov(R_{Super}, R_{Slow})$ or $\sigma_{Super,Slow}$. Equation 11.2 illustrates the intuition of covariance. Suppose Supertech's return is generally above its average when Slowpoke's return is above its average, and Supertech's return is generally below its average when Slowpoke's return is below its average. This shows a positive dependency or a positive relationship between the two returns. Note that the term in Equation 11.2 will be positive in any state where both returns are above their averages. In addition, Equation 11.2 will still be positive in any state

(continued)

Table 11.2 Calculating Covariance and Correlation

State of Economy	Rate of Return of Supertech R_{Super}	Deviation from Expected Return $[R_{Super} - E(R_{Super})]$	Rate of Return of Slowpoke R_{Slow}	Deviation from Expected Return $[R_{Slow} - E(R_{Slow})]$	Product of Deviations $[R_{Super} - E(R_{Super})] \times [R_{Slow} - E(R_{Slow})]$
		(Expected return = .175)		(Expected return = .055)	
Depression	−.20	−.375 (= −.20 − .175)	.05	−.005 (= .05 − .055)	.001875 (= −.375 × −.005)
Recession	.10	−.075	.20	.145	−.010875 (= −.075 × .145)
Normal	.30	.125	−.12	−.175	−.021875 (= .125 × −.175)
Boom	.50	.325	.09	.035	.011375 (= .325 × .035)
					−.0195

[2]As with variance, we divided by N (4 in this example) because the four states give rise to four equally likely possible outcomes.

where both terms are below their averages. A positive relationship between the two returns will give rise to a positive value for covariance.

Conversely, suppose Supertech's return is generally above its average when Slowpoke's return is below its average, and Supertech's return is generally below its average when Slowpoke's return is above its average. This demonstrates a negative dependency or a negative relationship between the two returns. Note that the term in Equation 11.2 will be negative in any state where one return is above its average and the other return is below its average. A negative relationship between the two returns will give rise to a negative value for covariance.

Finally, suppose there is no relationship between the two returns. In this case, knowing whether the return on Supertech is above or below its expected return tells us nothing about the return on Slowpoke. In the covariance formula, then, there will be no tendency for the deviations to be positive or negative together. On average, they will tend to offset each other and cancel out, making the covariance zero.

Of course, even if the two returns are unrelated to each other, the covariance formula will not equal zero exactly in any actual history. This is due to sampling error; randomness alone will make the calculation positive or negative. But for a historical sample that is long enough, if the two returns are not related to each other, we should expect the covariance to come close to zero.

The covariance formula seems to capture what we are looking for. If the two returns are positively related to each other, they will have a positive covariance, and if they are negatively related to each other, the covariance will be negative. Last, and very important, if they are unrelated, the covariance should be zero.

The formula for covariance can be written algebraically as:

$$\sigma_{\text{Super,Slow}} = \text{Cov}(R_{\text{Super}}, R_{\text{Slow}}) = \sum\{[R_{\text{Super}} - \text{E}(R_{\text{Super}})] \times [R_{\text{Slow}} - \text{E}(R_{\text{Slow}})]\}$$

where $E(R_{\text{Super}})$ and $\text{E}(R_{\text{Slow}})$ are the expected returns on the two securities and R_{Super} and R_{Slow} are the actual returns. The ordering of the two variables is unimportant. That is, the covariance of Supertech with Slowpoke is equal to the covariance of Slowpoke with Supertech. This can be stated more formally as $\text{Cov}(R_A, R_B) = \text{Cov}(R_B, R_A)$ or $\sigma_{AB} = \sigma_{BA}$.

The covariance we calculated is −.004875. A negative number like this implies that the return on one stock is likely to be above its average when the return on the other stock is below its average, and vice versa. However, the size of the number is difficult to interpret. Like the variance figure, the covariance is in squared deviation units. Until we can put it in perspective, we don't know what to make of it.

We solve the problem by computing the correlation.

3. To calculate the correlation, divide the covariance by the product of the standard deviations of both of the two securities. For our example, we have:

$$\rho_{\text{Super,Slow}} = \text{Corr}(R_{\text{Super}}, R_{\text{Slow}}) = \frac{\text{Cov}(R_{\text{Super}}, R_{\text{Super}})}{\sigma_{\text{Super}} \times \sigma_{\text{Slow}}} = \frac{-.004875}{.2586 \times .1150} = -.1639 \qquad \textbf{(11.3)}$$

where σ_{Super} and σ_{Slow} are the standard deviations of Supertech and Slowpoke, respectively. Note that we represent the correlation between Supertech and Slowpoke either as $\text{Corr}(R_{\text{Super}}, R_{\text{Slow}})$ or $\rho_{\text{Super,Slow}}$. As with covariance, the ordering of the two variables is unimportant. That is, the correlation of A with B is equal to the correlation of B with A. More formally, $\text{Corr}(R_A, R_B) = \text{Corr}(R_B, R_A)$ or $\rho_{AB} = \rho_{BA}$.

Because the standard deviation is always positive, the sign of the correlation between two variables must be the same as that of the covariance between the two variables. If the correlation is positive, we say

(continued)

that the variables are *positively correlated*; if it is negative, we say that they are *negatively correlated*; and if it is zero, we say that they are *uncorrelated.* Furthermore, it can be proven that the correlation is always between +1 and −1. This is due to the standardizing procedure of dividing by the product of the two standard deviations.

We also can compare the correlation between different *pairs* of securities. For example, it turns out that the correlation between General Motors and Ford is much higher than the correlation between General Motors and IBM. On similar lines in India, the correlation between Infosys and TCS is much higher than that between TCS and Coal India. Hence, we can state that the first pair of securities is more interrelated than the second pair.

Figure 11.1 shows the three benchmark cases for two assets, A and B. The figure shows two assets with return correlations of +1, −1, and 0. This implies perfect positive correlation, perfect negative correlation, and no correlation, respectively. The graphs in the figure plot the separate returns on the two securities through time.

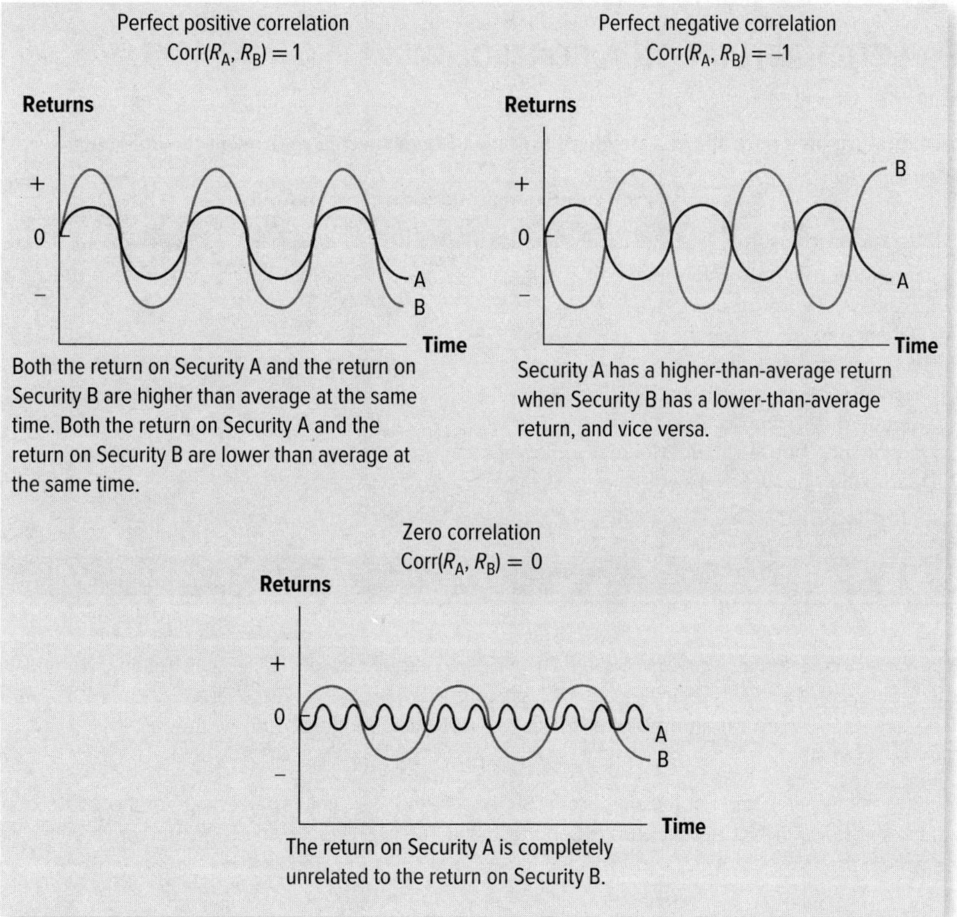

Figure 11.1 Examples of Different Correlation Coefficients: Graphs Plotting the Separate Returns on Two Securities through Time

11.3 The Return and Risk for Portfolios

Suppose an investor has estimates of the expected returns and standard deviations on individual securities and the correlations between securities. How does the investor choose the best combination or **portfolio** of securities to hold? Obviously, the investor would like a portfolio with a high expected return and a low standard deviation of return. It is therefore worthwhile to consider:

Excel Master coverage online

1. The relationship between the expected returns on individual securities and the expected return on a portfolio made up of these securities.
2. The relationship between the standard deviations of individual securities, the correlations between these securities, and the standard deviation of a portfolio made up of these securities.

To analyze these two relationships, we will use the same example of Supertech and Slowpoke. The relevant calculations follow.

THE EXPECTED RETURN ON A PORTFOLIO

The formula for expected return on a portfolio is:

The expected return on a portfolio is a weighted average of the expected returns on the individual securities.

Relevant Data from Example of Supertech and Slowpoke

Item	Symbol	Value
Expected return on Supertech	$E(R_{\text{Super}})$	.175, or 17.5%
Expected return on Slowpoke	$E(R_{\text{Slow}})$	.055, or 5.5%
Variance of Supertech	σ^2_{Super}	.066875
Variance of Slowpoke	σ^2_{Slow}	.013225
Standard deviation of Supertech	σ_{Super}	.2586, or 25.86%
Standard deviation of Slowpoke	σ_{Slow}	.1150, or 11.50%
Covariance between Supertech and Slowpoke	$\sigma_{\text{Super, Slow}}$	−.004875
Correlation between Supertech and Slowpoke	$\rho_{\text{Super, Slow}}$	−.1639

EXAMPLE 11.2

Portfolio Expected Returns Consider Supertech and Slowpoke. From our earlier calculations, we find that the expected returns on these two securities are 17.5 percent and 5.5 percent, respectively.

The expected return on a portfolio of these two securities alone can be written as:

$$E(R_P) = X_{\text{Super}}(.175) + X_{\text{Slow}}(.055)$$

where X_{Super} is the percentage of the portfolio in Supertech and X_{Slow} is the percentage of the portfolio in Slowpoke. If the investor with ₹100 invests ₹60 in Supertech and ₹40 in Slowpoke, the expected return on the portfolio can be written as:

$$E(R_P) = .6 \times .175 + .4 \times .055 = .127, \text{or } 12.7\%$$

Algebraically, we can write:

$$E(R_P) = X_A E(R_A) + X_B E(R_B) \tag{11.4}$$

where X_A and X_B are the proportions of the total portfolio in the assets A and B, respectively. (Because our investor can invest in only two securities, $X_A + X_B$ must equal 1, or 100 percent.) $E(R_A)$ and $E(R_B)$ are the expected returns on the two securities.

Now consider two stocks, each with an expected return of 10 percent. The expected return on a portfolio composed of these two stocks must be 10 percent, regardless of the proportions of the two stocks held. This result may seem obvious at this point, but it will become important later. The result implies that you do not reduce or dissipate your expected return by investing in a number of securities. Rather, the expected return on your portfolio is a weighted average of the expected returns on the individual assets in the portfolio.

VARIANCE AND STANDARD DEVIATION OF A PORTFOLIO

The Variance The formula for the variance of a portfolio composed of two securities, A and B, is:

$$\sigma_P^2 = X_A^2\sigma_A^2 + 2X_AX_B\sigma_{A,B} + X_B^2\sigma_B^2 \tag{11.5}$$

Note that there are three terms on the right side of the equation. The first term involves the variance of Security A (σ_A^2), the second term involves the covariance between the two securities ($\sigma_{A,B}$), and the third term involves the variance of Security B (σ_B^2). (Remember, $\sigma_{A,B} = \sigma_{B,A}$. That is, the ordering of the variables is irrelevant when we are expressing the covariance between two securities.)

The formula indicates an important point. The variance of a portfolio depends on both the variances of the individual securities and the covariance between the two securities. The variance of a security measures the variability of an individual security's return. Covariance measures the relationship between the two securities. For given variances of the individual securities, a positive relationship or covariance between the two securities increases the variance of the entire portfolio. A negative relationship or covariance between the two securities decreases the variance of the entire portfolio. This important result seems to square with common sense. If one of your securities tends to go up when the other goes down, or vice versa, your two securities are offsetting each other. You are achieving what we call a *hedge* in finance, and the risk of your entire portfolio will be low. However, if both your securities rise and fall together, you are not hedging at all. Hence, the risk of your entire portfolio will be higher.

The variance formula for our two securities, Super and Slow, is:

$$\sigma_P^2 = X_{Super}^2\sigma_{Super}^2 + 2X_{Super}X_{Slow}\sigma_{Super,\ Slow} + X_{Slow}^2\sigma_{Slow}^2 \tag{11.5$'$}$$

Given our earlier assumption that an individual with ₹100 invests ₹60 in Supertech and ₹40 in Slowpoke, $X_{Super} = .6$ and $X_{Slow} = .4$. Using this assumption and the relevant data from our previous calculations, the variance of the portfolio is:

$$.023851 = .36 \times .066875 + 2 \times [.6 \times .4 \times (-.004875)] + .16 \times .013225 \tag{11.5$''$}$$

The Matrix Approach Alternatively, Equation 11.5′ can be expressed in the following matrix format:

	Supertech	Slowpoke
Supertech	$X_{Super}^2\sigma_{Super}^2$ $.024075 = .36 \times .066875$	$X_{Super}X_{Slow}\sigma_{Super,\ Slow}$ $-.00117 = .6 \times .4 \times (-.004875)$
Slowpoke	$X_{Super}X_{Slow}\sigma_{Super,\ Slow}$ $-.00117 = .6 \times .4 \times (-.004875)$	$X_{Slow}^2\sigma_{Slow}^2$ $.002116 = .16 \times .013225$

There are four boxes in the matrix. We can add the terms in the boxes to obtain Equation 11.5′, the variance of a portfolio composed of the two securities. The term in the upper left corner involves the variance of Supertech. The term in the lower right corner involves the variance of Slowpoke. The other two boxes contain the term involving the covariance. These two boxes are identical, indicating why the covariance term is multiplied by two in Equation 11.5′.

At this point, students often find the box approach to be more confusing than Equation 11.5″. However, the box approach is easily generalized to more than two securities, a task we perform later in this chapter.

Standard Deviation of a Portfolio Given Equation 11.5″, we can now determine the standard deviation of the portfolio's return. This is:

$$\begin{aligned}\sigma_P &= \sqrt{\text{Var(portfolio)}} = \sqrt{.023851} \\ &= .1544, \text{ or } 15.44\%\end{aligned} \quad \textbf{(11.6)}$$

The interpretation of the standard deviation of the portfolio is the same as the interpretation of the standard deviation of an individual security. The expected return on our portfolio is 12.7 percent. A return of −2.74 percent (= 12.7% − 15.44%) is one standard deviation below the mean, and a return of 28.14 percent (= 12.7% + 15.44%) is one standard deviation above the mean. If the return on the portfolio is normally distributed, a return between −2.74 percent and +28.14 percent occurs about 68 percent of the time.[3]

The Diversification Effect It is instructive to compare the standard deviation of the portfolio with the standard deviation of the individual securities. The weighted average of the standard deviations of the individual securities is:

$$\begin{aligned}\text{Weighted average of standard deviations} &= X_{\text{Super}}\sigma_{\text{Super}} + X_{\text{Slow}}\sigma_{\text{Slow}} \\ .2012 &= .6 \times .2586 + .4 \times .115\end{aligned} \quad \textbf{(11.7)}$$

One of the most important results in this chapter concerns the difference between Equations 11.6 and 11.7. In our example, the standard deviation of the portfolio is less than a weighted average of the standard deviations of the individual securities.

We pointed out earlier that the expected return on the portfolio is a weighted average of the expected returns on the individual securities. Thus, we get a different type of result for the standard deviation of a portfolio than we do for the expected return on a portfolio.

Our result for the standard deviation of a portfolio is due to diversification. In our example, Supertech and Slowpoke are slightly negatively correlated ($\rho = -.1639$). Supertech's return is likely to be a little below average if Slowpoke's return is above average. Similarly, Supertech's return is likely to be a little above average if Slowpoke's return is below average. Thus, the standard deviation of a portfolio composed of the two securities is less than a weighted average of the standard deviations of the two securities.

The securities in our example have a negative correlation. Clearly, there will be less benefit from diversification if the two securities exhibit positive correlation. How high must the positive correlation be before all diversification benefits vanish?

To answer this question, let us rewrite Equation 11.5′ in terms of correlation rather than covariance. The covariance can be rewritten as:[4]

$$\sigma_{\text{Super,Slow}} = \rho_{\text{Super,Slow}}\sigma_{\text{Super}}\sigma_{\text{Slow}} \quad \textbf{(11.8)}$$

[3]There are only four equally probable returns for Supertech and Slowpoke, so neither security possesses a normal distribution. Thus, probabilities would be slightly different in our example.

[4]As with covariance, the ordering of the two securities is irrelevant when we express the correlation between the two securities. That is, $\rho_{\text{Super,Slow}} = \rho_{\text{Slow,Super}}$.

This formula states that the covariance between any two securities is the correlation between the two securities multiplied by the standard deviations of each. In other words, covariance incorporates both (1) the correlation between the two assets and (2) the variability of each of the two securities as measured by standard deviation.

From our calculations earlier in this chapter we know that the correlation between the two securities is −.1639. Given the variances used in Equation 11.5″, the standard deviations are .2586 and .115 for Supertech and Slowpoke, respectively. The variance of a portfolio can be expressed as follows:

$$\begin{aligned}\sigma_P^2 &= X_{\text{Super}}^2 \sigma_{\text{Super}}^2 + 2X_{\text{Super}}X_{\text{Slow}}\rho_{\text{Super, Slow}}\sigma_{\text{Super}}\sigma_{\text{Slow}} + X_{\text{Slow}}^2\sigma_{\text{Slow}}^2 \\ &= .36 \times .066875 + 2 \times [.6 \times .4 \times (-.1639) \times .2586 \times .115] + .16 \times .013225 \\ &= .023851\end{aligned} \tag{11.9}$$

The middle term on the right side is now written in terms of correlation, ρ, not covariance.

Suppose $\rho_{\text{Super, Slow}} = 1$, the highest possible value for correlation. Assume all the other parameters in the example are the same. The variance of the portfolio is:

$$\begin{aligned}\sigma_P^2 &= .36 \times .066875 + 2 \times (.6 \times .4 \times 1 \times .2586 \times .115) + .16 \times .013225 \\ &= .040466\end{aligned}$$

The standard deviation is:

$$\sigma_P = \sqrt{.040466} = .2012, \text{ or } 20.12\% \tag{11.9′}$$

Note that Equations 11.9′ and 11.7 are equal. That is, the standard deviation of a portfolio's return is equal to the weighted average of the standard deviations of the individual returns when $\rho = 1$. Inspection of Equation 11.9 indicates that the variance and hence the standard deviation of the portfolio must fall as the correlation drops below 1. This leads to the following result:

As long as ρ < 1, the standard deviation of a portfolio of two securities is less than the weighted average of the standard deviations of the individual securities.

In other words, the diversification effect applies as long as there is less than perfect correlation (as long as $\rho < 1$). Our Supertech-Slowpoke example is a case of overkill. We illustrated diversification by an example with negative correlation. We could have illustrated diversification by an example with positive correlation—as long as it was not perfect positive correlation.

An Extension to Many Assets The preceding insight can be extended to the case of many assets. That is, as long as correlations between pairs of securities are less than 1, the standard deviation of a portfolio of many assets is less than the weighted average of the standard deviations of the individual securities.

Now consider Table 11.3(a), which shows the standard deviation of the Standard & Poor's 500 Index and the standard deviations of some of the individual securities listed in the index over a recent five-year period. In Table 11.3(b), we have provided the standard deviation of the S&P BSE Sensex Index for the Indian markets and the standard deviations of some of the individual securities in the Indian markets from diverse sectors using monthly returns data from the Bombay Stock Exchange over a recent 10-year period, 2013–2023. Note that all of the individual securities in the table have higher standard deviations than that of the index. In general, the standard deviations of most of the individual securities in an index will be above the standard deviation of the index itself, though a few of the securities could have lower standard deviations than that of the index.

Table 11.3(a) Standard Deviations for Standard & Poor's 500 Index and for Selected Stocks in the Index, 2015–2020

Asset	Standard Deviation
S&P 500	15.12%
Johnson & Johnson	16.06
Microsoft	18.92
Facebook	27.77
Amazon	29.17
Bank of America	30.66
Delta	34.53
Boeing	37.16
Tesla	63.96

Note: As long as the correlations between pairs of securities are less than 1, the standard deviation of an index is less than the weighted average of the standard deviations of the individual securities within the index.

Table 11.3(b) Standard Deviations for S&P BSE Sensex Index and for Selected Stocks in the Index, 2013–2023

Asset	Standard Deviation
S&P BSE Sensex Index	4.07%
Hindustan Unilever	5.92%
Dr. Reddy's Laboratories	7.23%
Hero MotoCorp	8.14%
NTPC	7.56%
Tata Consultancy Services	6.14%
Asian Paints	7.20%
Axis Bank	10.39%

SOURCE: bseindia.com.

11.4 The Efficient Set for Two Assets

Our results for expected returns and standard deviations are graphed in Figure 11.2. The figure shows a dot labeled Slowpoke and a dot labeled Supertech. Each dot represents both the expected return and the standard deviation for an individual security. As can be seen, Supertech has both a higher expected return and a higher standard deviation.

The box, or "□," in the graph represents a portfolio with 60 percent invested in Supertech and 40 percent invested in Slowpoke. You will recall that we previously calculated both the expected return and the standard deviation for this portfolio.

The choice of 60 percent in Supertech and 40 percent in Slowpoke is one of an infinite number of portfolios that can be created. The set of portfolios is sketched by the curved line in Figure 11.3.

Consider Portfolio 1. This is a portfolio composed of 90 percent Slowpoke and 10 percent Supertech. Because the portfolio is weighted so heavily toward Slowpoke, it appears close to the Slowpoke point on the graph. Portfolio 2 is higher on the curve because it is composed of 50 percent Slowpoke and 50 percent Supertech. Portfolio 3 is close to the Supertech point on the graph because it is composed of 90 percent Supertech and 10 percent Slowpoke.

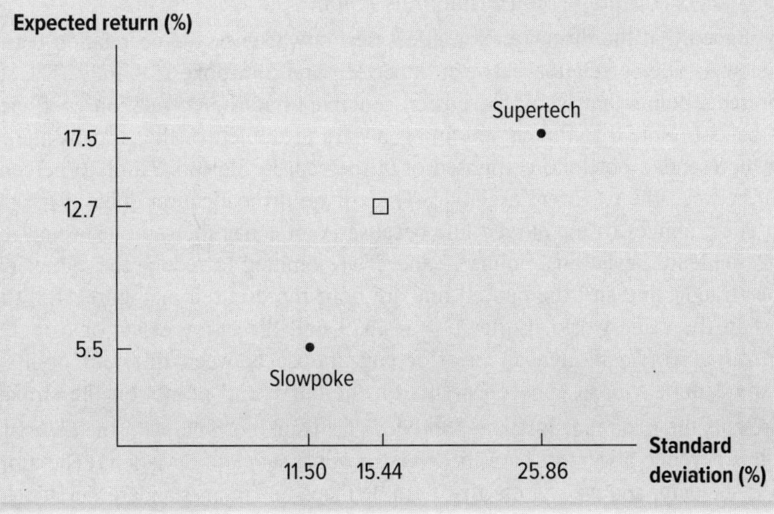

Figure 11.2 Expected Returns and Standard Deviations for Supertech, Slowpoke, and a Portfolio Composed of 60 Percent in Supertech and 40 Percent in Slowpoke

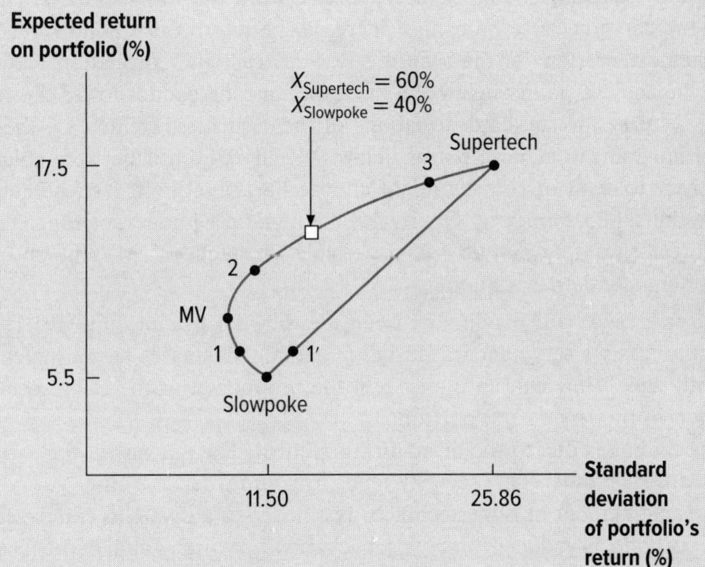

Portfolio 1 is composed of 90 percent Slowpoke and 10 percent Supertech ($\rho = -.1639$).
Portfolio 2 is composed of 50 percent Slowpoke and 50 percent Supertech ($\rho = -.1639$).
Portfolio 3 is composed of 10 percent Slowpoke and 90 percent Supertech ($\rho = -.1639$).
Portfolio 1′ is composed of 90 percent Slowpoke and 10 percent Supertech ($\rho = 1$).
Point MV denotes the minimum variance portfolio. This is the portfolio with the lowest possible variance. By definition, the same portfolio also must have the lowest possible standard deviation.

Figure 11.3 Set of Portfolios Composed of Holdings in Supertech and Slowpoke (correlation between the two securities is –.1639)

There are a few important points concerning this graph:

1. We previously argued that the diversification effect occurs whenever the correlation between two securities is below 1. The correlation between Supertech and Slowpoke is −.1639. The straight line in the graph represents points that would have been generated had the correlation coefficient between the two securities been 1. Note that the curved line is always to the left of the straight line. Consider Point 1′. This point represents a portfolio composed of 90 percent in Slowpoke and 10 percent in Supertech if the correlation between the two were exactly 1. There is no diversification effect if $\rho = 1$. However, the diversification effect applies to the curved line because Point 1 has the same expected return as Point 1′ but has a lower standard deviation. (Points 2′ and 3′ are omitted to reduce the clutter of Figure 11.3.)

   Though the straight line and the curved line are both represented in Figure 11.3, they do not simultaneously exist in the same world. Either $\rho = -.1639$ and the curve exists or $\rho = 1$ and the straight line exists. In other words, though an investor can choose between different points on the curve if $\rho = -.1639$, she cannot choose between points on the curve and points on the straight line.

2. Point MV represents the minimum variance portfolio. This is the portfolio with the lowest possible variance. By definition, this portfolio also must have the lowest possible standard deviation. (The term minimum variance portfolio is standard, and we will use that term. Perhaps minimum standard deviation would actually be better because standard deviation, not variance, is measured on the horizontal axis of Figure 11.3.)

3. An individual contemplating an investment in a portfolio of Slowpoke and Supertech faces an **opportunity set**, or **feasible set**, represented by the curved line in Figure 11.3. That is, he can achieve any point on the curve by selecting the appropriate mix between the two securities. He cannot achieve any point above the curve because he cannot increase the return on the individual securities, decrease the standard deviations of the securities, or decrease the correlation between the two securities. Neither can he achieve points below the curve because he cannot lower the returns on the individual securities, increase the standard deviations of the securities, or increase the correlation. (Of course, he would not want to achieve points below the curve, even if he were able to do so.)

   Were he relatively tolerant of risk, he might choose Portfolio 3. (In fact, he could even choose the end point by investing all his money in Supertech.) An investor with less tolerance for risk might choose Portfolio 2. An investor wanting as little risk as possible would choose MV, the portfolio with minimum variance or minimum standard deviation.

4. Note that the curve is backward bending between the Slowpoke point and MV. This indicates that, for a portion of the feasible set, standard deviation actually decreases as we increase expected return. Students frequently ask, "How can an increase in the proportion of the risky security, Supertech, lead to a reduction in the risk of the portfolio?"

   This surprising finding is due to the diversification effect. The returns on the two securities are negatively correlated with each other. One security tends to go up when the other goes down and vice versa. An addition of a small amount of Supertech acts as a hedge to a portfolio composed only of Slowpoke. The risk of the portfolio is reduced, implying backward bending. Actually, backward bending always occurs if $\rho \leq 0$. It may or may not occur when $\rho > 0$. Of course, the curve bends backward only for a portion of its length. As we continue to increase the percentage of Supertech in the portfolio, the high standard deviation of this security eventually causes the standard deviation of the entire portfolio to rise.

5. No investor would want to hold a portfolio with an expected return below that of the minimum variance portfolio. For example, no investor would choose Portfolio 1. This portfolio has less expected return but more standard deviation than the minimum variance portfolio has. We say that portfolios such as Portfolio 1 are dominated by the minimum variance portfolio. Though the entire curve from Slowpoke to Supertech is called the feasible set, investors consider only the curve from MV to Supertech. Hence, the curve from MV to Supertech is called the **efficient set**, or the **efficient frontier**.

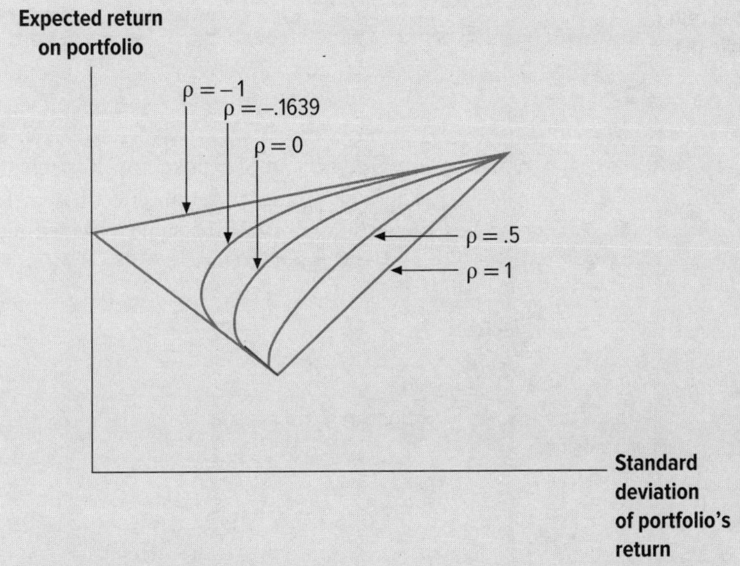

Each curve represents a different correlation. The lower the correlation, the more bend in the curve.

Figure 11.4 Opportunity Sets Composed of Holdings in Supertech and Slowpoke

Figure 11.3 represents the opportunity set where $\rho = -.1639$. It is worthwhile to examine Figure 11.4, which shows different curves for different correlations. As can be seen, the lower the correlation, the more the curve bends. This indicates that the diversification effect rises as ρ declines. The greatest bend occurs in the limiting case where $\rho = -1$. This is perfect negative correlation. While this extreme case where $\rho = -1$ seems to fascinate students, it has little practical importance. Most pairs of securities exhibit positive correlation. Very high negative correlations are unusual occurrences.[5]

Note that there is only one correlation between a pair of securities. We stated earlier that the correlation between Slowpoke and Supertech is −.1639. The curve in Figure 11.4 representing this correlation is the correct one, and the other curves should be viewed as merely hypothetical.

The graphs we examined are not mere intellectual curiosities. Rather, efficient sets can easily be calculated in the real world. As mentioned earlier, data on returns, standard deviations, and correlations are generally taken from past observations, though subjective notions can be used to determine the values of these parameters as well. Once the parameters have been determined, any one of a whole host of software packages can be purchased to generate the efficient set. However, the choice of the preferred portfolio within the efficient set is up to you. As with other important decisions like what job to choose, what house or car to buy, and how much time to allocate to this course, there is no computer program to choose the preferred portfolio.

An efficient set can be generated where the two individual assets are portfolios themselves. For example, the two assets in Figure 11.5 are a diversified portfolio of American stocks and a diversified portfolio of foreign stocks.[6] Expected returns, standard deviations, and the correlation coefficient were calculated over the recent

[5]A major exception occurs with derivative securities. For example, the correlation between a stock and a put on the stock is generally very strongly negative. Puts will be discussed later in the text.

[6]Similarly, one can construct a diversified portfolio of Indian stocks and a diversified portfolio of foreign stocks.

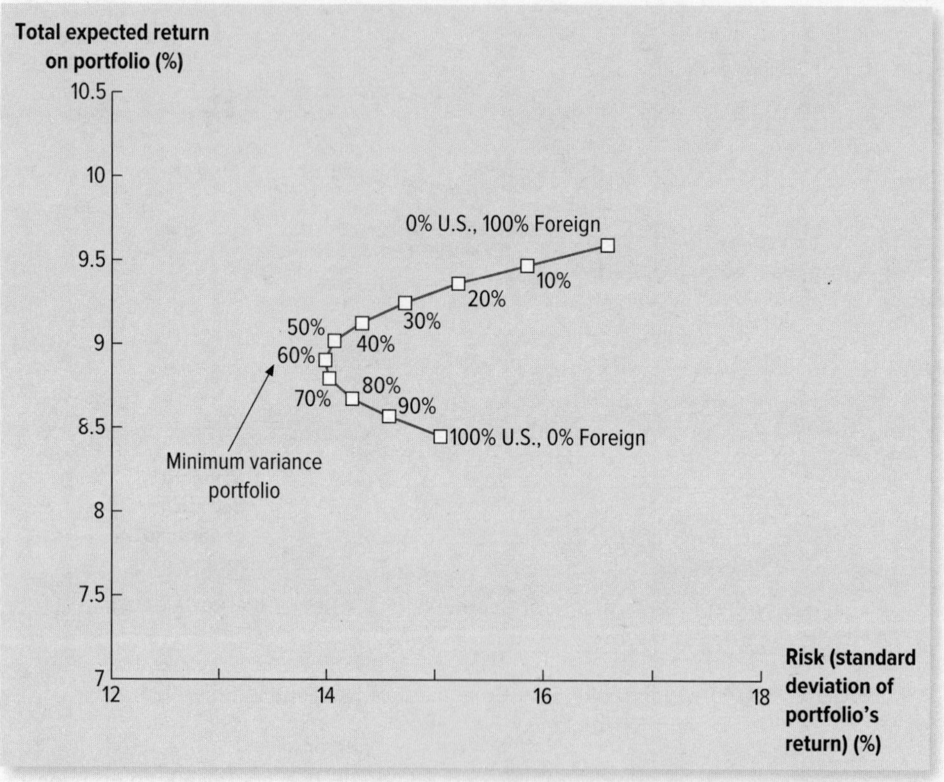

Figure 11.5 Return/Risk Trade-off for World Stocks: Portfolio of U.S. and Foreign Stocks

past. No subjectivity entered the analysis. The U.S. stock portfolio with a standard deviation of about .151 is less risky than the foreign stock portfolio, which has a standard deviation of about .166. However, combining a small percentage of the foreign stock portfolio with the U.S. portfolio actually reduces risk, as can be seen by the backward-bending nature of the curve. In other words, the diversification benefits from combining two different portfolios more than offset the introduction of a riskier set of stocks into our holdings. The minimum variance portfolio occurs with about 60 percent of our funds in American stocks and about 40 percent in foreign stocks. Addition of foreign securities beyond this point increases the risk of the entire portfolio. The backward-bending curve in Figure 11.5 is important information that has not bypassed American institutional investors. In recent years, pension funds and other institutions in the United States have sought investment opportunities overseas. Identically, Indian institutional investors, in recent years, especially big business groups, insurance companies, and other similar institutions in India, have sought investment opportunities overseas.

11.5 The Efficient Set for Many Securities

The previous discussion concerned two securities. We found that a simple curve sketched out all the possible portfolios. Because investors generally hold more than two securities, we should look at the same graph when more than two securities are held. The shaded area in Figure 11.6 represents the opportunity set or feasible set when many securities are considered. The shaded area represents all the possible combinations of expected returns and standard deviations for a portfolio. In a universe of 100 securities, Point 1 might represent a portfolio of, say, 40 securities. Point 2 might represent a portfolio of 80 securities. Point

3 might represent a different set of 80 securities, or the same 80 securities held in different proportions, or something else. Obviously, the combinations are virtually endless. However, note that all possible combinations fit into a confined region. No security or combination of securities can fall outside the shaded region. That is, no one can choose a portfolio with an expected return above that given by the shaded region. Furthermore, no one can choose a portfolio with a standard deviation below that given in the shaded area. Perhaps more surprisingly, no one can choose an expected return below that given in this area. In other words, the capital markets actually prevent a self-destructive person from taking on a guaranteed loss.[7]

So far, Figure 11.6 is different from the earlier graphs. When only two securities are involved, all the combinations lie on a single curve. Conversely, with many securities, the combinations cover an entire area. However, notice that an individual will want to be somewhere on the upper edge between MV and X. The upper edge, which we indicate in Figure 11.6 by a thick curve, is called the efficient set. Any point below the efficient set would receive less expected return and the same standard deviation as a point on the efficient set. Consider R on the efficient set and W directly below it. If W contains the risk level you desire, you should choose R instead to receive a higher expected return.

In the final analysis, Figure 11.6 is quite similar to Figure 11.3. The efficient set in Figure 11.3 runs from MV to Supertech. It contains various combinations of the securities Supertech and Slowpoke. The efficient set in Figure 11.6 runs from MV to X. It contains various combinations of many securities. The fact that a whole shaded area appears in Figure 11.6 but not in Figure 11.3 is not an important difference; no informed investor would choose any point below the efficient set in Figure 11.6 anyway.

We mentioned before that an efficient set for two securities can be traced out easily in the real world. The task becomes more difficult when additional securities are included because the number of observations grows. Using analysis to estimate expected returns and standard deviations for, say, 100 or 500 securities

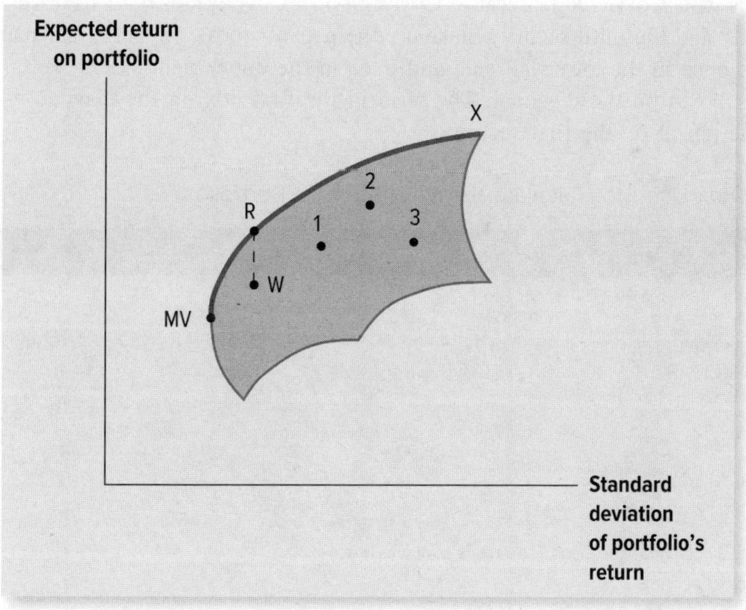

Figure 11.6 The Feasible Set of Portfolios Constructed from Many Securities

[7]Of course, someone dead set on parting with his money can do so. For example, he can trade frequently without purpose so that commissions more than offset the positive expected returns on the portfolio.

may very well become overwhelming, and the difficulties with correlations may be greater still. There are almost 5,000 correlations between pairs of securities from a universe of 100 securities.

Though much of the mathematics of efficient set computation had been derived in the 1950s,[8] the high cost of computer time restricted application of the principles. In recent years, this cost has been drastically reduced. A number of software packages allow the calculation of an efficient set for portfolios. By all accounts these packages sell quickly, implying that our discussion is important in practice.

VARIANCE AND STANDARD DEVIATION IN A PORTFOLIO OF MANY ASSETS

Earlier, we calculated the formulas for variance and standard deviation in the two-asset case. Because we considered a portfolio of many assets in Figure 11.6, it is worthwhile to calculate the formulas for variance and standard deviation in the many-asset case. The formula for the variance of a portfolio of many assets can be viewed as an extension of the formula for the variance of two assets.

To develop the formula, we employ the same type of matrix that we used in the two-asset case. This matrix is displayed in Table 11.4. Assuming that there are N assets, we write the numbers 1 through N on both the horizontal axis and the vertical axis. This creates a matrix of $N \times N = N^2$ boxes. The variance of the portfolio is the sum of the terms in all the boxes.

Consider the box in the second row and the third column. The term in the box is $X_2X_3\text{Cov}(R_2, R_3)$. X_2 and X_3 are the percentages of the entire portfolio that are invested in the second asset and the third asset, respectively. If an individual with a portfolio of ₹1,000 invests ₹100 in the second asset, $X_2 = .10$, or 10 percent (= ₹100/₹1,000). $\text{Cov}(R_2,R_3)$ is the covariance between the returns on the second asset and the returns on the third asset. Next, note the box in the third row and the second column. The term in this box is $X_3X_2\ \text{Cov}(R_3,R_2)$. Because $\text{Cov}(R_3,R_2) = \text{Cov}(R_2,R_3)$, both boxes have the same value. The second security and the third security make up one pair of stocks. In fact, every pair of stocks appears twice in the table: once in the lower left side and once in the upper right side.

Now consider boxes on the diagonal. The term in the first box on the diagonal is $X_1^2\sigma_1^2$. Here, σ_1^2 is the variance of the return on the first security.

Table 11.4 Matrix Used to Calculate the Variance of a Portfolio

Stock	1	2	3	. . .	N
1	$X_1^2\sigma_1^2$	$X_1X_2\text{Cov}(R_1,R_2)$	$X_1X_3\text{Cov}(R_1,R_3)$		$X_1X_N\text{Cov}(R_1,R_N)$
2	$X_2X_1\text{Cov}(R_2,R_1)$	$X_2^2\sigma_2^2$	$X_2X_3\text{Cov}(R_2,R_3)$		$X_2X_N\text{Cov}(R_2,R_N)$
3	$X_3X_1\text{Cov}(R_3,R_1)$	$X_3X_2\text{Cov}(R_3,R_2)$	$X_3^2\sigma_3^2$		$X_3X_N\text{Cov}(R_3,R_N)$
.					
.					
.					
N	$X_NX_1\text{Cov}(R_N,R_1)$	$X_NX_2\text{Cov}(R_N,R_2)$	$X_NX_3\text{Cov}(R_N,R_3)$		$X_N^2\sigma_N^2$

Note: The variance of the portfolio is the sum of the terms in all the boxes.

σ_i is the standard deviation of Stock i.

$\text{Cov}(R_i,R_j)$ is the covariance between Stock i and Stock j.

Terms involving the standard deviation of a single security appear on the diagonal. Terms involving covariance between two securities appear off the diagonal.

[8]The classic treatise is Harry Markowitz, *Portfolio Selection* (New York: John Wiley & Sons, 1959). Markowitz won the Nobel Prize in Economics in 1990 for his work on modern portfolio theory.

Table 11.5 Number of Variance and Covariance Terms as a Function of the Number of Stocks in the Portfolio

Number of Stocks in Portfolio	Total Number of Terms	Number of Variance Terms (number of terms on diagonal)	Number of Covariance Terms (number of terms off diagonal)
1	1	1	0
2	4	2	2
3	9	3	6
10	100	10	90
100	10,000	100	9,900
.	.	.	.
.	.	.	.
.	.	.	.
N	N^2	N	$N^2 - N$

Note: In a large portfolio, the number of terms involving covariance between two securities is much greater than the number of terms involving variance of a single security.

The diagonal terms in the matrix contain the variances of the different stocks. The off-diagonal terms contain the covariances. Table 11.5 relates the numbers of diagonal and off-diagonal elements to the size of the matrix. The number of diagonal terms (number of variance terms) is always the same as the number of stocks in the portfolio. The number of off-diagonal terms (number of covariance terms) rises much faster than the number of diagonal terms. A portfolio of 100 stocks has 9,900 covariance terms. Because the variance of a portfolio's return is the sum of all the boxes, we have the following:

The variance of the return on a portfolio with many securities is more dependent on the covariances between the individual securities than on the variances of the individual securities.

11.6 Diversification

So far in this chapter, we have examined how the risks and returns of individual assets impact the risk and return of the portfolio. We also touched on one aspect of this impact: diversification. To give a recent example, the Dow Jones Industrial Average (DJIA), which contains 30 large, well-known U.S. stocks, rose about 6.9 percent in 2020. The biggest individual gainers in that year were Apple (up 82 percent), Microsoft (up 43 percent), and Nike (up 41 percent), while the biggest losers were Boeing (down 34 percent), Walgreens Boots (down 29 percent), and Chevron (down 26 percent). Looking at the Indian equity markets, the Bombay Stock Exchange's sensitive index (S&P BSE Sensex), which contains 30 large well-known Indian stocks, rose around 22% during 2023. The biggest individual gainers in that year were Tata Motors (up 116 percent), NTPC (up 99 percent), and Power Grid (up 80 percent), while the biggest losers were HDFC Bank (down 11 percent), HUL (down 3 percent) and Kotak Mahindra Bank (down 0.02 percent). As can be seen, variation among these individual stocks was reduced through diversification. While this example shows that diversification is good, we now want to examine why it is good. And how good is it?

THE ANTICIPATED AND UNANTICIPATED COMPONENTS OF NEWS

We begin the discussion of diversification by focusing on the stock of one company, which we will call Godavari. What will determine this stock's return in, say, the coming year?

The return on any stock consists of two parts. First, the normal, or expected, return from the stock is the part of the return that shareholders in the market predict or expect. It depends on all of the information shareholders have that bears on the stock, and it uses all of our understanding of what will influence the stock in the next year.

The second part of the return is the uncertain, or risky, part. This is the portion that comes from unexpected information revealed within the year. The list of such information is endless, but here are some examples:

- News about Godavari' research.
- Government figures released for the gross national product (GNP).
- Results of the latest arms control talks.
- Discovery that a rival's product has been tampered with.
- News that Godavari' sales figures are higher than expected.
- A sudden drop in interest rates.
- The unexpected retirement of Godavari' founder and president.

A way to write the return on Godavari' stock in the coming year would be:

$$R = \text{E}(R) + U$$

where R stands for the actual total return in the year, $\text{E}(R)$ stands for the expected part of the return, and U stands for the unexpected part of the return. What this says is that the actual return, R, differs from the expected return, $\text{E}(R)$, because of surprises that occur during the year. In any given year, the unexpected return will be positive or negative, but, through time, the average value of U will be zero. This means that, on average, the actual return equals the expected return.

RISK: SYSTEMATIC AND UNSYSTEMATIC

The unanticipated part of the return–that portion resulting from surprises–is the true risk of any investment. After all, if we got what we had expected, there would be no risk and no uncertainty.

There are important differences among various sources of risk. Look at our previous list of news stories. Some of these stories are directed specifically at Godavari and some are more general. Which of the news items are of specific importance to Godavari?

Announcements about interest rates or GNP are clearly important for nearly all companies, whereas the news about Godavari' president, its research, its sales, or the affairs of a rival company are of specific interest to Godavari. We will divide these two types of announcements and the resulting risk, then, into two components: a systematic portion, called *systematic risk*, and the remainder, which we call *firm-specific* or *unsystematic risk*. The following definitions describe the difference:

- A **systematic risk** is any risk that affects a large number of assets, each to a greater or lesser degree.
- An **unsystematic risk** is a risk that specifically affects a single asset or a small group of assets.

Uncertainty about general economic conditions, such as GNP, interest rates, or inflation, are examples of systematic risk. These conditions affect nearly all stocks to some degree. An unanticipated or surprise increase in inflation affects wages and the costs of the supplies that companies buy, the value of the assets that companies own, and the prices at which companies sell their products. These forces to which all companies are susceptible are the essence of systematic risk. The "COVID crash" in the spring of 2020 is a particularly recent and vivid example of such a risk.

In contrast, the announcement of a small oil strike by a company may affect that company alone or a few other companies. Certainly, it is unlikely to have an effect on the world oil market. To stress that such information is unsystematic and affects only some specific companies, we sometimes call it an *idiosyncratic risk*.

This distinction permits us to break down the risk of Godavari' stock return into its two components: the systematic and the unsystematic. As is traditional, we will use the Greek epsilon, ε, to represent the unsystematic risk and write:

$$\begin{aligned} R &= \mathrm{E}(R) + U \\ &= \mathrm{E}(R) + m + \varepsilon \end{aligned} \tag{11.10}$$

where we have used the letter m to stand for the systematic risk. Sometimes systematic risk is referred to as *market risk*. This emphasizes the fact that m influences all assets in the market to some extent. E(R) is the Godavari' stock expected return.

The important point about the way we have broken the total risk, U, into its two components, m and ε, is that ε, because it is specific to the company, is unrelated to the specific risk of most other companies. The unsystematic risk on Godavari' stock, ε_F, is unrelated to the unsystematic risk of, say, General Electric's stock, ε_{GE}. The risk that Godavari' stock will go up or down because of a discovery by its research team–or its failure to discover something–probably is unrelated to any of the specific uncertainties that affect General Electric's stock. This means that the unsystematic risks of Godavari' stock and General Electric's stock are unrelated to each other, or uncorrelated.

THE ESSENCE OF DIVERSIFICATION

Now what happens when we combine Godavari' stock with another stock in a portfolio? Because the unsystematic risks or epsilons of the two stocks are uncorrelated, the epsilon may be positive for one stock when the epsilon of the other is negative. Because the epsilons can offset each other, the unsystematic risk of the portfolio will be lower than the unsystematic risk of either of the two securities. In other words, we see the beginnings of diversification. If we add a third security to our portfolio, the unsystematic risk of the portfolio will be lower than the unsystematic risk of the two-security portfolio. The effect continues when we add a fourth, a fifth, or a sixth security. In fact, if we were able, hypothetically, to combine an infinite number of securities, the unsystematic risk of the portfolio would disappear.

Now let's consider what happens to the portfolio's systematic risk when we add a second security. If the return on the second security is also modeled by Equation 11.10, the systematic risk of the portfolio will not be reduced. Suppose inflation turns out to be higher than previously anticipated, or GNP turns out to be lower than anticipated. Both stocks will likely decline, implying a decline in the portfolio. And we would get the same result with three securities, four securities, or more. In fact, suppose the portfolio had an infinite number of securities. Bad news for the economy would impact all of these securities negatively, implying a negative impact for the portfolio. Unlike unsystematic risk, systematic risk cannot be diversified away.

This insight can be illustrated in Figure 11.7. The graph, relating the standard deviation of a portfolio to the number of securities in the portfolio, shows a high standard deviation for one security. We often speak of standard deviation as the *total risk*, or the *risk*, of the portfolio. The addition of a second security reduces standard deviation, or risk, as does the addition of a third security, and so on. The total risk of the portfolio steadily falls with diversification.

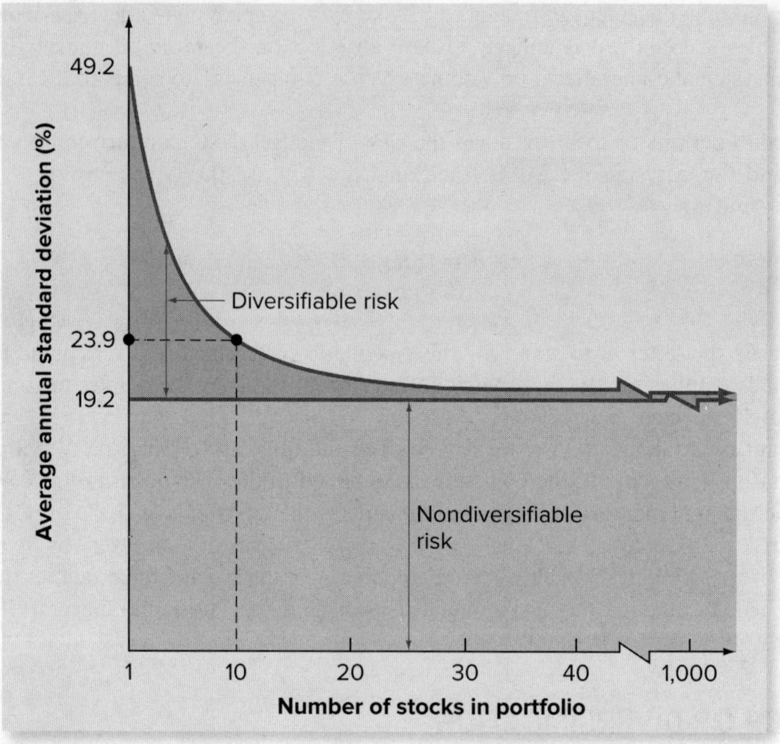

Figure 11.7 Portfolio Diversification

THE EFFECT OF DIVERSIFICATION: ANOTHER LESSON FROM MARKET HISTORY

To illustrate the relationship between portfolio size and portfolio risk, Table 11.6 illustrates typical average annual standard deviations for equally weighted portfolios that contain different numbers of randomly selected NYSE securities.

In Column 2 of Table 11.6, we see that the standard deviation for a "portfolio" of one security is about 49 percent. What this means is that if you randomly selected a single NYSE stock and put all your money into it, your standard deviation of return would typically be a substantial 49 percent per year. If you were to randomly select two stocks and invest half your money in each, your standard deviation would be about 37 percent on average, and so on.

The important thing to notice in Table 11.6 is that the standard deviation declines as the number of securities is increased. By the time we have 100 randomly chosen stocks, the portfolio's standard deviation has declined by about 60 percent, from 49 percent to about 20 percent. With 500 securities, the standard deviation is 19.27 percent, similar to the 19.7 percent we saw in our previous chapter for the large-company stock portfolio. The small difference exists because the portfolio securities and time periods examined are not identical.

Figure 11.7 plots the standard deviation of return versus the number of stocks in the portfolio. The figure illustrates two key points. First, some of the riskiness associated with individual assets can be eliminated by forming portfolios. The process of spreading an investment across assets (and thereby forming a

Table 11.6 Standard Deviations of Annual Portfolio Returns

(1) Number of Stocks in Portfolio	(2) Average Standard Deviation of Annual Portfolio Returns	(3) Ratio of Portfolio Standard Deviation to Standard Deviation of a Single Stock
1	49.24%	1.00
2	37.36	.76
4	29.69	.60
6	26.64	.54
8	24.98	.51
10	23.93	.49
20	21.68	.44
30	20.87	.42
40	20.46	.42
50	20.20	.41
100	19.69	.40
200	19.42	.39
300	19.34	.39
400	19.29	.39
500	19.27	.39
1,000	19.21	.39

SOURCE: Table 1 in M. Statman, "How Many Stocks Make a Diversified Portfolio?" *Journal of Financial and Quantitative Analysis* 22 (September 1987): 353–63. They were derived from E. J. Elton and M. J. Gruber, "Risk Reduction and Portfolio Size: An Analytical Solution," *Journal of Business* 50 (October 1977): 415–37.

portfolio) is called *diversification.* The **principle of diversification** tells us that spreading an investment across many assets will eliminate some of the risk. The darker shaded area in Figure 11.7, labeled "diversifiable risk," is the part that can be eliminated by diversification. Notice that the benefit in terms of risk reduction from adding securities drops off as we add more and more securities. Some investors mistakenly believe that they must hold portfolios of hundreds of stocks in order to reap the benefits of diversification. In reality, by the time we have 10 securities, most of the diversification effect is already realized; and by the time we get to 30 or so, there is little remaining benefit.

The second point is equally important. There is a minimum level of risk that cannot be eliminated by diversifying. This minimum level is labeled "nondiversifiable risk" in Figure 11.7. Taken together, these two points are another important lesson from capital market history: Diversification reduces risk, but only up to a point. Put another way, some risk is diversifiable and some is not.

The previous discussion implicitly assumed that all securities have the same level of systematic risk. While essentially all securities have some systematic risk, certain securities have more of this risk than others. The amount of systematic risk is measured by something called *beta*, a concept that will be explained in Section 11.8. But first we must consider the impact of riskless borrowing and lending.

11.7 Riskless Borrowing and Lending

Figure 11.6 assumes that all the securities in the efficient set are risky. Alternatively, an investor could combine a risky investment with an investment in a riskless, or risk-free, security, such as U.S. Treasury bills. This is illustrated in the following example.

EXAMPLE 11.3

Riskless Lending and Portfolio Risk Mohanlal Sharma is considering investing in the common stock of Shankar Enterprises. In addition, Mohanlal will either borrow or lend at the risk-free rate. The relevant parameters are:

	Common Stock of Shankar	Risk-Free Asset
Expected return	14%	10%
Standard deviation	20	0

Suppose Mara chooses to invest a total of ₹1,000, ₹350 of which is to be invested in Shankar Enterprises and ₹650 will be invested in the risk-free asset. The expected return on her total investment is a weighted average of the two returns:

$$E(R_P) = .35 \times .14 + .65 \times .10 = .114, \text{ or } 11.4\%$$

Because the expected return on the portfolio is a weighted average of the expected return on the risky asset (Shankar Enterprises) and the risk-free return, the calculation is analogous to the way we treated two risky assets. In other words, Equation 11.4 applies here.

Using Equation 11.5, the formula for the variance of the portfolio can be written as:

$$\sigma_P^2 = X_{\text{Shankar}}^2 \sigma_{\text{Shankar}}^2 + 2X_{\text{Shankar}} X_{\text{Risk-free}} \sigma_{\text{Shankar,Risk-free}} + X_{\text{Risk-free}}^2 \sigma_{\text{Risk-free}}^2$$

However, by definition, the risk-free asset has no variability. Both $\sigma_{\text{Shankar,Risk-free}}$ and $\sigma_{\text{Risk-free}}^2$ are equal to zero, reducing the above expression to:

$$\begin{aligned}\sigma_P^2 &= X_{\text{Shankar}}^2 \sigma_{\text{Shankar}}^2 \\ &= .35^2 \times .20^2 \\ &= .0049\end{aligned} \quad \textbf{(11.11)}$$

The standard deviation of the portfolio is:

$$\begin{aligned}\sigma_P &= X_{\text{Shankar}} \sigma_{\text{Shankar}} \\ &= .35 \times .20 \\ &= .07\end{aligned} \quad \textbf{(11.12)}$$

The relationship between risk and expected return for portfolios composed of one risky asset and the riskless asset can be seen in Figure 11.8. Mara's choice of portfolio between the two assets is represented by a straight line between the risk-free rate and a pure investment in Shankar Enterprises. Unlike the case of two risky assets, the opportunity set is straight, not curved.

Suppose that, alternatively, Mara borrows ₹200 at the risk-free rate. Combining this with her original sum of ₹1,000, she invests a total of ₹1,200 in Shankar. Her expected return would be:

$$E(R_P) = 1.20 \times .14 + (-.2 \times .10) = .148, \text{ or } 14.8\%$$

Here, she invests 120 percent of her original investment of ₹1,000 by borrowing 20 percent of her original investment. Note that the return of 14.8 percent is greater than the 14 percent expected return on Shankar Enterprises. This occurs because she is borrowing at 10 percent to invest in a security with an expected return greater than 10 percent.

The standard deviation is:

$$\sigma_P = 1.20 \times .2 = .24, \text{ or } 24\%$$

(continued)

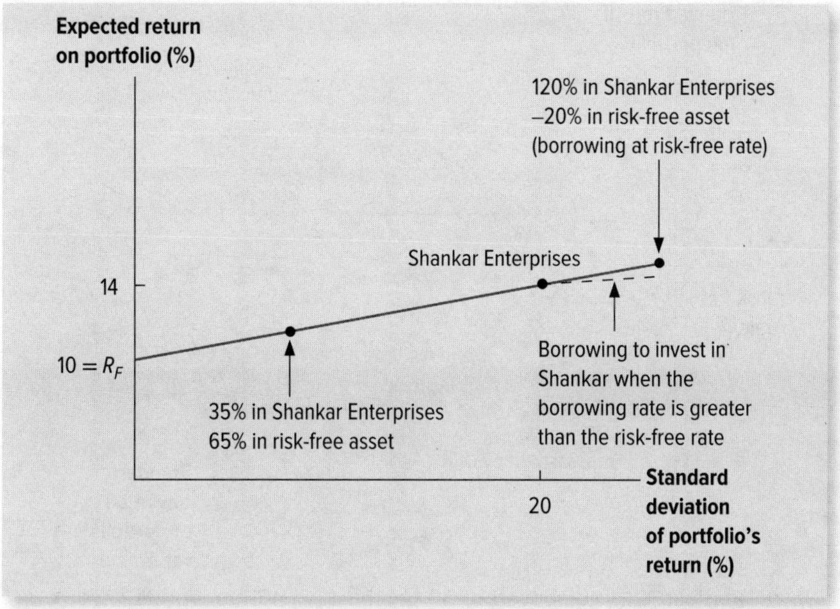

Figure 11.8 Relationship between Expected Return and Risk for Portfolios Composed of the Riskless Asset and One Risky Asset

The standard deviation of 24 percent is greater than 20 percent, the standard deviation of the Shankar investment, because borrowing increases the variability of the investment. This investment also appears in Figure 11.8.

So far, we have assumed that Mara is able to borrow at the same rate at which she can lend.[9] Now let us consider the case where the borrowing rate is above the lending rate. The dotted line in Figure 11.8 illustrates the opportunity set for borrowing opportunities in this case. The dotted line is below the solid line because a higher borrowing rate lowers the expected return on the investment.

THE OPTIMAL PORTFOLIO

The previous section concerned a portfolio formed between the riskless asset and one risky asset. In reality, an investor is likely to combine an investment in the riskless asset with a portfolio of risky assets. This is illustrated in Figure 11.9.

Consider Point Q, representing a portfolio of securities. Point Q is in the interior of the feasible set of risky securities. Let us assume the point represents a portfolio of 30 percent in ITC, 45 percent in Reliance Industries Limited (RIL), and 25 percent in Wipro. Individuals combining investments in Q with investments in the riskless asset would achieve points along the straight line from R_F to Q. We refer to this as Line I. For example, Point 1 on the line represents a portfolio of 70 percent in the riskless asset and 30 percent in stocks represented by Q. An investor with ₹100 choosing Point 1 as his portfolio would put ₹70 in the risk-free asset and ₹30 in Q. This can be restated as ₹70 in the riskless asset, ₹9 (= .3 × ₹30) in ITC, ₹13.50 (= .45 × ₹30) in RIL, and ₹7.50 (= .25 × ₹30) in Wipro. Point 2 also represents a portfolio of the risk-free asset and Q, with more (65%) being invested in Q.

[9]Surprisingly, this appears to be a decent approximation because many investors can borrow from a stockbroker (called *going on margin*) when purchasing stocks. The borrowing rate here is very near the riskless rate of interest, particularly for large investors. More will be said about this in a later chapter.

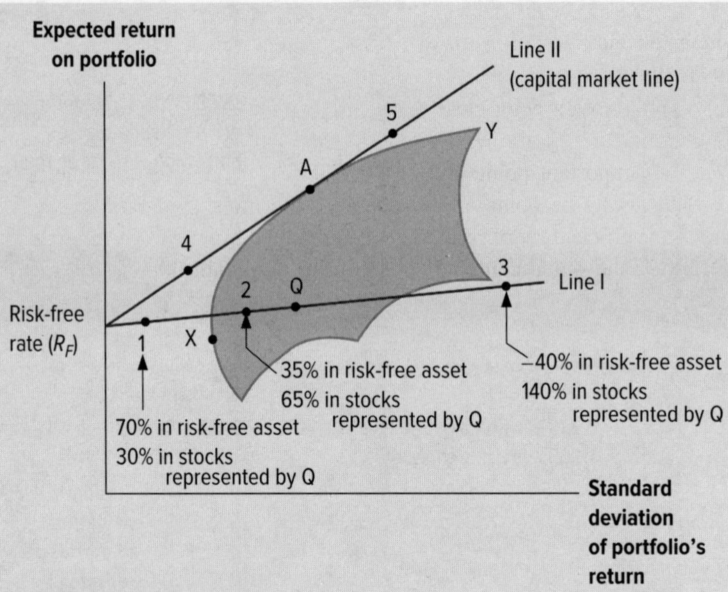

Portfolio Q is composed of 30 percent ITC, 45 percent RIL, and 25 percent Wipro.

Figure 11.9 Relationship between Expected Return and Standard Deviation for an Investment in a Combination of Risky Securities and the Riskless Asset

Point 3 is obtained by borrowing to invest in Q. For example, an investor with ₹100 of her own would borrow ₹40 from the bank or broker to invest ₹140 in Q. This can be stated as borrowing ₹40 and contributing ₹100 of her money to invest ₹42 (= .3 × ₹140) in ITC, ₹63 (= .45 × ₹140) in RIL, and ₹35 (= .25 × ₹140) in Wipro.

These investments can be summarized as follows:

	Point Q	Point 1 (Lending ₹70)	Point 3 (Borrowing ₹40)
ITC	₹ 30	₹ 9.00	₹ 42
RIL	45	13.50	63
Wipro	25	7.50	35
Risk-free	0	70.00	−40
Total investment	₹100	₹ 100	₹100

Though any investor can obtain any point on Line I, no point on the line is optimal. To see this, consider Line II, a line running from R_F through A. Point A represents a portfolio of risky securities. Line II represents portfolios formed by combinations of the risk-free asset and the securities in A. Points between R_F and A are portfolios in which some money is invested in the riskless asset and the rest is placed in A. Points past A are achieved by borrowing at the riskless rate to buy more of A than we could with our original funds alone.

As drawn, Line II is tangent to the efficient set of risky securities. Whatever point an individual can obtain on Line I, he can obtain a point with the same standard deviation and a higher expected return on Line II. In fact, because Line II is tangent to the efficient set of risky assets, it provides the investor with the best possible opportunities. In other words, Line II can be viewed as the efficient set of all assets, both risky and riskless. An investor with a fair degree of risk aversion might choose a point between R_F and A, perhaps Point 4. An individual with less risk aversion might choose a point closer to A or even beyond A. For example, Point 5 corresponds to an individual borrowing money to increase investment in A.

The graph illustrates an important point. With riskless borrowing and lending, the portfolio of risky assets held by any investor would always be Point A. Regardless of the investor's tolerance for risk, she would never choose any other point on the efficient set of risky assets (represented by Curve XAY) nor any point in the interior of the feasible region. Rather, she would combine the securities of A with the riskless asset if she had high aversion to risk. She would borrow the riskless asset to invest more funds in A if she had low aversion to risk.

This result establishes what financial economists call the **separation principle**. That is, the investor's investment decision consists of two separate steps:

1. After estimating the expected returns and variances of individual securities, and the covariances between pairs of securities, the investor calculates the efficient set of risky assets, represented by Curve XAY in Figure 11.9. She then determines Point A, the tangency between the risk-free rate and the efficient set of risky assets (Curve XAY). Point A represents the portfolio of risky assets that the investor will hold. This point is determined solely from her estimates of returns, variances, and covariances. No personal characteristics, such as degree of risk aversion, are needed in this step.
2. The investor must now determine how she will combine Point A, her portfolio of risky assets, with the riskless asset. She might invest some of her funds in the riskless asset and some in Portfolio A. She would end up at a point on the line between R_F and A in this case. Alternatively, she might borrow at the risk-free rate and contribute some of her own funds as well, investing the sum in Portfolio A. She would end up at a point on Line II beyond A. Her position in the riskless asset–that is, her choice of where on the line she wants to be–is determined by her internal characteristics, such as her ability to tolerate risk.

11.8 Market Equilibrium

DEFINITION OF THE MARKET EQUILIBRIUM PORTFOLIO

Excel Master coverage online

The preceding analysis concerns one investor. Her estimates of the expected returns and variances for individual securities and the covariances between pairs of securities are hers and hers alone. Other investors would obviously have different estimates of these variables. However, the estimates might not vary much because all investors would be forming expectations from the same data about past price movements and other publicly available information.

Financial economists often imagine a world where all investors possess the same estimates of expected returns, variances, and covariances. Though this is never literally true, it is a useful simplifying assumption in a world where investors have access to similar sources of information. This assumption is called **homogeneous expectations.**[10]

If all investors had homogeneous expectations, Figure 11.9 would be the same for all individuals. That is, all investors would sketch out the same efficient set of risky assets because they would be working with the same inputs. This efficient set of risky assets is represented by the Curve XAY. Because the same risk-free rate would apply to everyone, all investors would view Point A as the portfolio of risky assets to be held.

[10]The assumption of homogeneous expectations states that all investors have the same beliefs concerning returns, variances, and covariances. It does not say that all investors have the same aversion to risk.

This Point A takes on great importance because all investors would purchase the risky securities that it represents. Investors with a high degree of risk aversion might combine A with an investment in the riskless asset, achieving Point 4, for example. Others with low aversion to risk might borrow to achieve Point 5. Because this is a very important conclusion, we restate it:

In a world with homogeneous expectations, all investors would hold the portfolio of risky assets represented by Point A.

If all investors choose the same portfolio of risky assets, one can determine what that portfolio is. Common sense tells us that it is a market-value-weighted portfolio of all existing securities. It is the **market portfolio**.

In practice, economists use a broad-based index such as the S&P 500 as a proxy for the market portfolio. In the case of the Indian equity markets, most analysts make use of the popular indices such as S&P BSE Sensex or S&P CNX Nifty as a surrogate for market portfolio.[11] A few also use broader indices such as S&P BSE 500 or S&P CNX 500. Of course all investors do not hold the same portfolio in practice. However, we know that many investors hold diversified portfolios, particularly when mutual funds or pension funds are included. A broad-based index is a good proxy for the highly diversified portfolios of many investors.

DEFINITION OF RISK WHEN INVESTORS HOLD THE MARKET PORTFOLIO

Earlier in this chapter we pointed out that the risk or standard deviation of a stock could be broken down into systematic and unsystematic risk. Unsystematic risk can be diversified away in a large portfolio, but systematic risk cannot. Thus, a diversified investor holding the market portfolio must worry about the systematic risk, but not the unsystematic risk, of every security in a portfolio. Is there a way to measure the systematic risk of a security? Yes, it turns out that *beta* is the best measure of the risk of an individual security from the point of view of a diversified investor, which we illustrate with an example.

EXAMPLE 11.4

Beta Consider the following possible returns both on the stock of Hamdard (Wakf) Ltd., and on the market:

State	Type of Economy	Return on Market	Return on Hamdard (Wakf) Ltd.
I	Bull	15%	25%
II	Bull	15	15
III	Bear	−5	−5
IV	Bear	−5	−15

Though the return on the market has only two possible outcomes (15% and −5%), the return on Hamdard (Wakf) has four possible outcomes. It is helpful to consider the expected return on a security for a given return on the market. Assuming each state is equally likely, we have:

Type of Economy	Return on Market	Expected Return on Hamdard (Wakf) Ltd.
Bull	15%	.25 × .50 + .15 × .50 = .20, or 20%
Bear	−5%	−.05 × .50 + (−.15) × .50 = −.10, or − 10%

(continued)

[11]It is observed that large foreign institutional investors (FIIs) and hedge funds having exposure in large company stocks as part of their emerging market portfolio make use of the *MSCI Emerging Markets* Index as a replica of their market portfolio; MSCI standing for Morgan Stanley Capital International. Think, what makes them use this benchmark!!

Hamdard (Wakf) Ltd., responds to market movements because its expected return is greater in bullish states than in bearish states. We now calculate exactly how responsive the security is to market movements. The market's return in a bullish economy is 20percent [= 15% – (–5%)] greater than the market's return in a bearish economy. However, the expected return on Hamdard (Wakf) in a bullish economy is 30percent [= 20% – (–10%)] greater than its expected return in a bearish state. Thus, Hamdard (Wakf) Ltd., has a responsiveness coefficient of 1.5 (= 30%/20%).

This relationship appears in Figure 11.10. The returns for both Hamdard (Wakf) and the market in each state are plotted as four points. In addition, we plot the expected return on the security for each of the two possible returns on the market. These two points, each of which we designate by an X, are joined by a line called the **characteristic line** of the security. The slope of the line is 1.5, the number calculated in the previous paragraph. This responsiveness coefficient of 1.5 is the **beta** of Hamdard (Wakf).

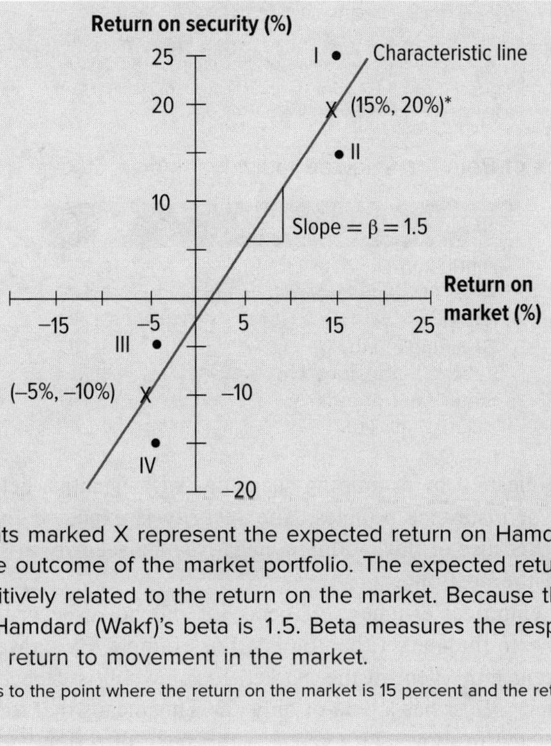

The two points marked X represent the expected return on Hamdard (Wakf) for each possible outcome of the market portfolio. The expected return on Hamdard (Wakf) is positively related to the return on the market. Because the slope is 1.5, we say that Hamdard (Wakf)'s beta is 1.5. Beta measures the responsiveness of the security's return to movement in the market.

*(15%, 20%) refers to the point where the return on the market is 15 percent and the return on the security is 20 percent.

Figure 11.10 Performance of Hamdard (Wakf) Ltd., and the Market Portfolio

The interpretation of beta from Figure 11.10 is intuitive. The graph tells us that the returns of Hamdard (Wakf) are magnified 1.5 times over those of the market. When the market does well, Hamdard (Wakf)'s stock is expected to do even better. When the market does poorly, Hamdard (Wakf)'s stock is expected to do even worse. Now imagine an individual with a portfolio near that of the market who is considering the addition of Hamdard (Wakf) to her portfolio. Because of Hamdard (Wakf)'s magnification factor of 1.5, she will view this stock as contributing much to the risk of the portfolio. (We will show shortly that the beta of the average security in the market is 1.) Hamdard (Wakf) contributes more to the risk of a large, diversified portfolio than does an average security because Hamdard (Wakf) is more responsive to movements in the market.

Table 11.7(a) Estimates of Beta for Selected Individual U.S. Stocks

Stock	Beta
Consolidated Edison	.29
Johnson & Johnson	.69
Pfizer	.73
3M Company	.96
Alphabet	1.04
Southwest Airlines	1.07
Anheuser-Busch InBev	1.14
ExxonMobil	1.30
Citigroup	1.77

SOURCE: finance.yahoo.com, September 2, 2020.

Note: The beta is defined as $\text{Cov}(R_i, R_M)/\text{Var}(R_M)$, where $\text{Cov}(R_i, R_M)$ is the covariance of the return on an individual stock, R_i, and the return on the market, R_M. $\text{Var}(R_M)$ is the variance of the return on the market, R_M.

Table 11.7(b) Estimates of Beta for Selected Individual Indian Stocks

Stock	Beta
Hindustan Unilever Ltd.	0.57
Tata Consultancy Services Ltd.	0.88
ITC Ltd.	0.77
GAIL (India) Ltd.	1.18
Reliance Industries Ltd.	1.21
State Bank of India	1.19
HDFC Bank Ltd.	1.27

Further insight can be gleaned by examining securities with negative betas. One should view these securities as either hedges or insurance policies. The security is expected to do well when the market does poorly and vice versa. Because of this, adding a negative-beta security to a large, diversified portfolio actually reduces the risk of the portfolio.[12]

Table 11.7(a) presents empirical estimates of betas for individual securities. As can be seen, some securities are more responsive to the market than others. For example, ExxonMobil has a beta of 1.30. This means that for every 1 percent movement in the market, ExxonMobil is expected to move 1.30 percent in the same direction. Conversely, Pfizer has a beta of only .73. This means that for every 1 percent movement in the market, Pfizer is expected to move .73 percent in the same direction.[13]

Similarly, we present estimates of betas for individual securities from Indian equity markets in Table 11.7(b). As can be seen, some securities are more responsive to the market than others. For example, HDFC Bank Ltd. has a beta of 1.27. This means that for every 2 percent movement in the market[14], HDFC Bank Ltd. is expected to move 2.54 percent in the same direction. Conversely, HUL has a beta of only 0.57. This means that for every 2 percent movement in the market, HUL is expected to move 1.14 percent in the same direction.

We can summarize our discussion of beta by saying:

Beta measures the responsiveness of a security to movements in the market portfolio.

[12]Unfortunately, empirical evidence shows that few, if any, stocks have negative betas.

[13]In Table 11.7(b), we use the Standard & Poor's 500 Index as a proxy for the market portfolio.

[14]In Table 11.6(b), we use the S&P BSE 500 as a proxy for the market portfolio.

THE FORMULA FOR BETA

Our discussion so far has stressed the intuition behind beta. The actual definition of beta is:

$$\beta_i = \frac{\text{Cov}(R_i, R_M)}{\sigma^2(R_M)} \tag{11.13}$$

where $\text{Cov}(R_i, R_M)$ is the covariance between the return on Asset i and the return on the market portfolio, and $\sigma^2(R_M)$ is the variance of the market.

One useful property is that the average beta across all securities, when weighted by the proportion of each security's market value to that of the market portfolio, is 1. That is:

$$\sum_{i=1}^{N} X_i \beta_i = 1 \tag{11.14}$$

where X_i is the proportion of Security i's market value to that of the entire market and N is the number of securities in the market.

Equation 11.14 is intuitive, once you think about it. If you weight all securities by their market values, the resulting portfolio is the market. By definition, the beta of the market portfolio is 1. That is, for every 1 percent movement in the market, the market must move 1 percent–by definition.

A TEST

We have put these questions on past corporate finance examinations:

1. What sort of investor rationally views the variance (or standard deviation) of an individual security's return as the security's proper measure of risk?
2. What sort of investor rationally views the beta of a security as the security's proper measure of risk?

A good response answering both questions might be something like the following:

> A rational, risk-averse investor views the variance (or standard deviation) of her portfolio's return as the proper measure of the portfolio's risk. If, for some reason, the investor can hold only one security, the variance of that security's return becomes the variance of the portfolio's return. Hence, the variance of the security's return is the security's proper measure of risk. Examples of such undiversified investors include start-up founders and family firm owners who must invest heavily in a single firm. Likewise, managers of large public firms are sometimes contractually obligated to own a large portion of stock in the firm they work for.
>
> If an individual instead holds a diversified portfolio, she still views the variance (or standard deviation) of her portfolio's return as the proper measure of the risk of her portfolio. However, she is no longer interested in the variance of each individual security's return. Rather, she is interested in the contribution of an individual security to the variance of the portfolio. The contribution of a security to the variance of a diversified portfolio is best measured by beta. Therefore, beta is the proper measure of the risk of an individual security for a diversified investor.
>
> Beta measures the systematic risk of a security. Diversified investors pay attention to the systematic risk of each security; however, they ignore the unsystematic risks of individual securities because unsystematic risks are diversified away in a large portfolio.

11.9 Relationship between Risk and Expected Return (CAPM)

It is commonplace to argue that the expected return on an asset should be positively related to its risk. That is, individuals will hold a risky asset only if its expected return compensates for its risk. In this section, we first estimate the expected return on the stock market as a whole. Next, we estimate expected returns on individual securities.

EXPECTED RETURN ON THE MARKET

Economists frequently argue that the expected return on the market can be represented as:

$$E(R_M) = R_F + \text{Risk premium}$$

In words, the expected return on the market is the sum of the risk-free rate plus some compensation for the risk inherent in the market portfolio. Note that the equation refers to the expected return on the market, not the actual return in a particular month or year. Because stocks have risk, the actual return on the market over a particular period can, of course, be below R_F or even negative.

Because investors want compensation for risk, the risk premium is presumably positive. But exactly how positive is it? It is generally argued that the place to start looking for the risk premium in the future is the average risk premium in the past. As reported in Chapter 10, Dimson, Marsh, and Staunton found the average excess annual return of U.S. common stocks over the risk-free rate (i.e., one-year Treasury bills) was 7.2 percent over 1900–2010. We referred to 7.2 percent as the historical U.S. equity risk premium. The average historical worldwide equity premium was 6.9 percent. Taking into account a number of factors, we find 7 percent to be a reasonable, but not definitive, estimate of the future U.S. equity risk premium.

If the risk-free rate is 1 percent, the expected return on the market is 8 percent (= 1% + 7%).

For Indian equity markets, Prof. Damodaran[15] applies an equity risk premium of 7.81 percent. Looking at the recent literature and considering the same, we find 6 percent to be a reasonable estimate of the future Indian equity risk premium.

For example, if the risk-free rate of return, estimated by the current yield on a one-year Treasury Bill of India, is 7 percent, the expected return on the Indian market would be:

$$14.81\% = 7.81\% + 7\%$$

Of course, the future equity risk premium could be higher or lower than the historical equity risk premium. This could be true if future risk is higher or lower than past risk or if individual risk aversions are higher or lower than those of the past.

EXPECTED RETURN ON AN INDIVIDUAL SECURITY

Now that we have estimated the expected return on the market as a whole, what is the expected return on an individual security? We have argued that the beta of a security is the appropriate measure of its risk in a large, diversified portfolio. Because most investors are diversified, the expected return on a security should be positively related to its beta. This idea is illustrated in Figure 11.11.

Actually, economists can be more precise about the relationship between expected return and beta. They posit that under plausible conditions, the relationship between expected return and beta can be represented by the following equation:[16]

[15]See, https://pages.stern.nyu.edu/~adamodar/New_Home_Page/datafile/ctryprem.html Prof Aswath Damodaran provides equity risk premium for different countries.

[16]This relationship was first proposed independently by John Lintner and William F. Sharpe.

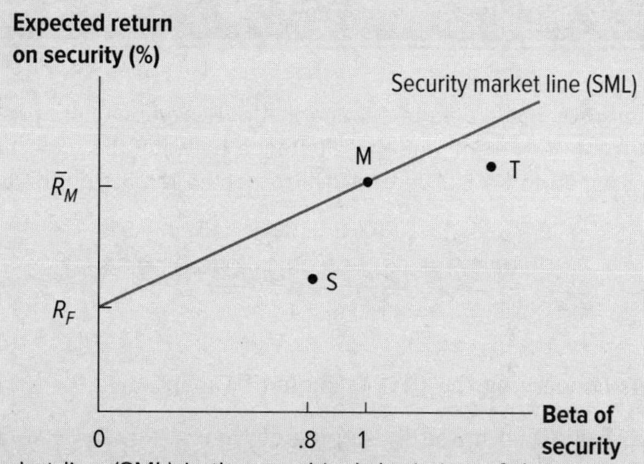

The security market line (SML) is the graphical depiction of the capital asset pricing model (CAPM).

The expected return on a stock with a beta of 0 is equal to the risk-free rate.

The expected return on a stock with a beta of 1 is equal to the expected return on the market.

Figure 11.11 Relationship between Expected Return on an Individual Security and Beta of the Security

$$\text{E}(R) = R_F + \beta \times [\text{E}(R_M) - R_F] \qquad \textbf{(11.15)}$$

Expected return on a security	=	Risk-free rate	+	Beta of the security	×	Difference between expected return on market and risk-free rate

This formula, which is called the **capital asset pricing model (CAPM)**, implies that the expected return on a security is linearly related to its beta. Because the average return on the market has been higher than the average risk-free rate over long periods of time, $\text{E}(R_M) - R_F$ is presumably positive. The CAPM implies that the expected return on a security is positively related to its beta. The formula can be illustrated by assuming a few special cases:

- *Assume* $\beta = 0$. In this case, $\text{E}(R) = R_F$. Because a security with zero beta has no relevant risk, its expected return should equal the risk-free rate.
- *Assume* $\beta = 1$. Equation 11.15 reduces to $\text{E}(R) = \text{E}(R_M)$. The expected return on the security is equal to the expected return on the market. This makes sense because the beta of the market portfolio is also 1.

Equation 11.15 can be represented graphically by the upward-sloping line in Figure 11.11. Note that the line begins at R_F and rises to $\text{E}(R_M)$ when beta is 1. This line is frequently called the **security market line (SML)**.

As with any line, the SML has both a slope and an intercept. R_F, the risk-free rate, is the intercept. Because the beta of a security is the horizontal axis, $\text{E}(R_M) - R_F$ is the slope. The line will be upward sloping as long as the expected return on the market is greater than the risk-free rate. Because the market portfolio is a risky asset, theory suggests that its expected return is above the risk-free rate, a result consistent with the empirical evidence of the previous chapter.

EXAMPLE 11.5

The stock of Kannagi Enterprises has a beta of 1.5 and that of Basavappa Enterprises has a beta of .7. The risk-free rate is assumed to be 3 percent, and the difference between the expected return on the market and the risk-free rate is assumed to be 8.0 percent. The expected returns on the two securities are:

$$E(R_{\text{Aardvark}}) = .03 + 1.5(.08) = .15, \text{ or } 15\%$$
$$E(R_{\text{Zebra}}) = .03 + .7(.08) = .086, \text{ or } 8.6\%$$

Three additional points concerning the CAPM should be mentioned:

1. *Linearity*: The intuition behind an upwardly sloping curve is clear. Because beta is the appropriate measure of risk, high-beta securities should have an expected return above that of low-beta securities. However, both Figure 11.11 and Equation 11.15 show something more than an upwardly sloping curve: The relationship between expected return and beta corresponds to a straight line.

   It is easy to show that the line of Figure 11.11 is straight. To see this, consider Security S with, say, a beta of .8. This security is represented by a point below the security market line in the figure. Any investor could duplicate the beta of Security S by buying a portfolio with 20 percent in the risk-free asset and 80 percent in a security with a beta of 1. However, the homemade portfolio would itself lie on the SML. In other words, the portfolio dominates Security S because the portfolio has a higher expected return and the same beta.

   Now consider Security T with a beta greater than 1. This security is also below the SML in Figure 11.11. Any investor could duplicate the beta of Security T by borrowing to invest in a security with a beta of 1. This portfolio also must lie on the SML, thereby dominating Security T.

   Because no one would hold either S or T, their stock prices would drop. This price adjustment would raise the expected returns on the two securities. The price adjustment would continue until the two securities lie on the security market line. The preceding example considered two overpriced stocks and a straight SML. Securities lying above the SML are underpriced. Their prices must rise until their expected returns lie on the line. If the SML is itself curved, many stocks would be mispriced. In equilibrium, all securities would be held only when prices changed so that the SML became straight. In other words, linearity would be achieved.

2. *Portfolios as well as securities*: Our discussion of the CAPM considered individual securities. Does the relationship in Figure 11.11 and Equation 11.15 hold for portfolios as well?

   Yes. To see this, consider a portfolio formed by investing equally in our two securities from Example 11.5, Kannagi and Basavappa. The expected return on the portfolio is:

$$E(R_P) = .5 \times .15 + .5 \times .086 = .118, \text{ or } 11.8\%$$

   The beta of the portfolio is a weighted average of the betas of the two securities. Thus, we have:

$$\beta_P = .5 \times 1.5 + .5 \times .7 = 1.1$$

   Under the CAPM, the expected return on the portfolio is:

$$E(R_P) = .03 + 1.1 \times .08 = .118, \text{ or } 11.8\%$$

Because the expected return of the portfolio using the sum of the weighted average of the returns of each asset is the same as the expected return of the portfolio using the CAPM, the CAPM holds for portfolios as well as for individual securities.

3. *A potential confusion*: Students often confuse the SML in Figure 11.11 with Line II in Figure 11.9. Actually, the lines are quite different. Line II traces the efficient set of portfolios formed from both risky assets and the riskless asset. Each point on the line represents an entire portfolio. Point A is a portfolio composed entirely of risky assets. Every other point on the line represents a portfolio of the securities in A combined with the riskless asset. The axes on Figure 11.9 are the expected return on a portfolio and the standard deviation of a portfolio. Individual securities do not lie along Line II.

   The SML in Figure 11.11 relates expected return to beta. Figure 11.11 differs from Figure 11.9 in at least two ways. First, beta appears in the horizontal axis of Figure 11.11, but standard deviation appears in the horizontal axis of Figure 11.9. Second, the SML in Figure 11.11 holds both for all individual securities and for all possible portfolios, whereas Line II in Figure 11.9 holds only for efficient portfolios.

We stated earlier that, under homogeneous expectations, Point A in Figure 11.9 becomes the market portfolio. In this situation, Line II is referred to as the **capital market line (CML)**.

RESEARCH IN EMERGING MARKET CONTEXT

Shetty et al. (2021) conducted a study on Indian BSE 30 stocks using a modified CAPM that incorporated rolling regression and cross-sectional regression techniques to analyze risk-return. According to their findings, beta is a reliable predictor for stock returns.

Jain (2022) investigated the impact of the COVID 19 pandemic on the Indian financial market and firm betas. The study revealed that betas increased during the first wave of COVID-19 in 2020, but not during the second wave in 2021. The consumer goods, infrastructure, insurance, and information technology industries experienced a more significant increase in betas, unlike the energy industries such as oil and gas, power, and mining.

Mittal et al. (2021) used behavioural models instead of conventional mean-variance models to analyze the tradeoffs that investors make. The study showed that asset allocations generated by the behavioural portfolio theory (BPT) had higher risks and returns compared to a typical Markowitz optimal portfolio.

References

Jain, S. (2021). Betas in the time of corona: a conditional CAPM approach using multivariate GARCH model for India. *Managerial Finance*, *48*(2), 243–257.

Mittal, S., Bhattacharya, S., & Mandal, S. (2022). Characteristics analysis of behavioural portfolio theory in the Markowitz portfolio theory framework. *Managerial finance*, *48*(2), 277–288.

Shetty, S., Dsouza, J. J., & Hawaldar, I. T. (2021). Rolling regression technique and cross-sectional regression: A tool to analyze capital asset pricing model. *Investment Management and Financial Innovations*, *18*(4), 241–251.

Summary and Conclusions

This chapter set forth the fundamentals of modern portfolio theory. Our basic points are these:

1. This chapter showed us how to calculate the expected return and variance for individual securities, and the covariance and correlation for pairs of securities. Given these statistics, the expected return and variance for a portfolio of two securities A and B can be written as:

$$\text{Expected return on portfolio} = X_A \mathrm{E}(R_A) + X_B \mathrm{E}(R_B)$$

$$\text{Var(portfolio)} = X_A^2 \sigma_A^2 + 2X_A X_B \sigma_{AB} + X_B^2 \sigma_B^2$$

2. In our notation, X stands for the proportion of a security in a portfolio. By varying X we can trace out the efficient set of portfolios. We graphed the efficient set for the two-asset case as a curve, pointing out that the degree of curvature or bend in the graph reflects the diversification effect: The lower the correlation between the two securities, the greater the bend. The same general shape of the efficient set holds in a world of many assets.
3. As the formula for variance in the two-asset case is computed from a 2×2 matrix, the variance formula is computed from an $N \times N$ matrix in the N-asset case. We showed that with a large number of assets, there are many more covariance terms than variance terms in the matrix. In fact, the variance terms are effectively diversified away in a large portfolio, but the covariance terms are not. Thus, a diversified portfolio can eliminate some, but not all, of the risk of the individual securities.
4. The efficient set of risky assets can be combined with riskless borrowing and lending. In this case, a rational investor will always choose to hold the portfolio of risky securities represented by Point A in Figure 11.9. Then he can either borrow or lend at the riskless rate to achieve any desired point on Line II in the figure.
5. The contribution of a security to the risk of a large, well-diversified portfolio is proportional to the covariance of the security's return with the market's return. This contribution, when standardized, is called the beta. The beta of a security also can be interpreted as the responsiveness of a security's return to that of the market.
6. The CAPM states that:

$$\mathrm{E}(R) = R_F + \beta[\mathrm{E}(R_M) - R_F]$$

In other words, the expected return on a security is positively (and linearly) related to the security's beta.

Concept Questions

1. **Diversifiable and Nondiversifiable Risks** In broad terms, why is some risk diversifiable? Why are some risks nondiversifiable? Does it follow that an investor can control the level of unsystematic risk in a portfolio, but not the level of systematic risk?
2. **Systematic versus Unsystematic Risk** Classify the following events as mostly systematic or mostly unsystematic. Is the distinction clear in every case?
   a. Short-term interest rates increase unexpectedly.
   b. The interest rate a company pays on its short-term debt borrowing is increased by its bank.
   c. Oil prices unexpectedly decline.
   d. An oil tanker ruptures, creating a large oil spill.
   e. A manufacturer loses a multimillion-rupee product liability suit.
   f. A Supreme Court decision substantially broadens producer liability for injuries suffered by product users.
3. **Expected Portfolio Returns** If a portfolio has a positive investment in every asset, can the expected return on the portfolio be greater than that on every asset in the portfolio? Can it be less than that on every asset in the portfolio? If you answer yes to one or both of these questions, give an example to support your answer.

4. **Diversification** True or false: The most important characteristic in determining the expected return of a well-diversified portfolio is the variances of the individual assets in the portfolio. Explain.

5. **Portfolio Risk** If a portfolio has a positive investment in every asset, can the standard deviation on the portfolio be less than that on every asset in the portfolio? What about the portfolio beta?

6. **Beta and CAPM** Is it possible that a risky asset could have a beta of zero? Explain. Based on the CAPM, what is the expected return on such an asset? Is it possible that a risky asset could have a negative beta? What does the CAPM predict about the expected return on such an asset? Can you give an explanation for your answer?

7. **Covariance** Briefly explain why the covariance of a security with the rest of a well-diversified portfolio is a more appropriate measure of the risk of the security than the security's variance.

8. **Beta** Consider the following quote from a leading investment manager: "The shares of Midwest Co. have traded close to ₹12 for most of the past three years. Since Midwest's stock has demonstrated very little price movement, the stock has a low beta. Tennessee Instruments, on the other hand, has traded as high as ₹150 and as low as its current ₹75. Since Tennessee Instrument's stock has demonstrated a large amount of price movement, the stock has a very high beta." Do you agree with this analysis? Explain.

9. **Risk** A broker has advised you not to invest in oil industry stocks because they have high standard deviations. Is the broker's advice sound for a risk-averse investor like yourself? Why or why not?

10. **Security Selection** Is the following statement true or false? A risky security cannot have an expected return that is less than the risk-free rate because no risk-averse investor would be willing to hold this asset in equilibrium. Explain.

Questions and Problems

BASIC (Questions 1–19)

1. **Determining Portfolio Weights** What are the portfolio weights for a portfolio that has 145 shares of Stock A that sell for ₹47 per share and 200 shares of Stock B that sell for ₹21 per share?

2. **Portfolio Expected Return** You own a portfolio that has ₹4,450 invested in Stock A and ₹9,680 invested in Stock B. If the expected returns on these stocks are 8 percent and 11 percent, respectively, what is the expected return on the portfolio?

3. **Portfolio Expected Return** You own a portfolio that is invested 15 percent in Stock X, 35 percent in Stock Y, and 50 percent in Stock Z. The expected returns on these three stocks are 9 percent, 15 percent, and 12 percent, respectively. What is the expected return on the portfolio?

4. **Portfolio Expected Return** You have ₹10,000 to invest in a stock portfolio. Your choices are Stock X with an expected return of 12.4 percent and Stock Y with an expected return of 10.1 percent. If your goal is to create a portfolio with an expected return of 10.85 percent, how much money will you invest in Stock X? In Stock Y?

5. **Calculating Returns and Standard Deviations** Based on the following information, calculate the expected return and standard deviation for Stock A and Stock B:

State of Economy	Probability of State of Economy	Rate of Return if State Occurs	
		Stock A	Stock B
Recession	.15	.04	−.17
Normal	.55	.09	.12
Boom	.30	.17	.27

6. **Calculating Returns and Standard Deviations** Based on the following information, calculate the expected return and standard deviation:

State of Economy	Probability of State of Economy	Rate of Return if State Occurs
Depression	.15	−.184
Recession	.30	.029
Normal	.45	.173
Boom	.10	.372

7. **Calculating Expected Returns** A portfolio is invested 45 percent in Stock G, 40 percent in Stock J, and 15 percent in Stock K. The expected returns on these stocks are 11 percent, 9 percent, and 15 percent, respectively. What is the portfolio's expected return? How do you interpret your answer?

8. **Returns and Variances** Consider the following information:

State of Economy	Probability of State of Economy	Rate of Return if State Occurs		
		Stock A	Stock B	Stock C
Boom	.75	.07	.18	.27
Bust	.25	.12	−.08	−.21

a. What is the expected return on an equally weighted portfolio of these three stocks?
b. What is the variance of a portfolio invested 20 percent each in A and B and 60 percent in C?

9. **Returns and Standard Deviations** Consider the following information:

State of Economy	Probability of State of Economy	Rate of Return if State Occurs		
		Stock A	Stock B	Stock C
Boom	.15	.35	.40	.28
Good	.45	.16	.17	.09
Poor	.30	−.01	−.03	.01
Bust	.10	−.10	−.12	−.09

a. Your portfolio is invested 30 percent each in A and C and 40 percent in B. What is the expected return of the portfolio?
b. What is the variance of this portfolio? The standard deviation?

10. **Calculating Portfolio Betas** You own a stock portfolio invested 15 percent in Stock Q, 20 percent in Stock R, 30 percent in Stock S, and 35 percent in Stock T. The betas for these four stocks are .79, 1.23, 1.13, and 1.36, respectively. What is the portfolio beta?

11. **Calculating Portfolio Betas** You own a portfolio equally invested in a risk-free asset and two stocks. If one of the stocks has a beta of 1.34 and the total portfolio is equally as risky as the market, what must the beta be for the other stock in your portfolio?

12. **Using CAPM** A stock has a beta of 1.15, the expected return on the market is 11.3 percent, and the risk-free rate is 3.6 percent. What must the expected return on this stock be?

13. **Using CAPM** A stock has an expected return of 11.4 percent, the risk-free rate is 3.9 percent, and the market risk premium is 6.8 percent. What must the beta of this stock be?

14. **Using CAPM** A stock has an expected return of 11.85 percent, its beta is 1.08, and the risk-free rate is 3.9 percent. What must the expected return on the market be?

15. **Using CAPM** A stock has an expected return of 10.45 percent, its beta is .85, and the expected return on the market is 11.8 percent. What must the risk-free rate be?

16. **Using CAPM** A stock has a beta of 1.19 and an expected return of 12.4 percent. A risk-free asset currently earns 2.7 percent.

a. What is the expected return on a portfolio that is equally invested in the two assets?
b. If a portfolio of the two assets has a beta of .92, what are the portfolio weights?
c. If a portfolio of the two assets has an expected return of 10 percent, what is its beta?
d. If a portfolio of the two assets has a beta of 2.38, what are the portfolio weights? How do you interpret the weights for the two assets in this case? Explain.

17. **Using the SML** Asset W has an expected return of 8.8 percent and a beta of .85. If the risk-free rate is 2.6 percent, complete the following table for portfolios of Asset W and a risk-free asset. Illustrate the relationship between portfolio expected return and portfolio beta by plotting the expected returns against the betas. What is the slope of the line that results?

Percentage of Portfolio in Asset W	Portfolio Expected Return	Portfolio Beta
0%		
25		
50		
75		
100		
125		
150		

18. **Reward-to-Risk Ratios** Stock Y has a beta of 1.2 and an expected return of 11.5 percent. Stock Z has a beta of .80 and an expected return of 8.5 percent. If the risk-free rate is 3.2 percent and the market risk premium is 6.8 percent, are these stocks correctly priced?

19. **Reward-to-Risk Ratios** In the previous problem, what would the risk-free rate have to be for the two stocks to be correctly priced?

INTERMEDIATE (Questions 20–32)

20. **Portfolio Returns** Using information from the previous chapter about capital market history, determine the return on a portfolio that is equally invested in large-company stocks and long-term government bonds. What is the return on a portfolio that is equally invested in small-company stocks and Treasury bills?

21. **CAPM** Using the CAPM, show that the ratio of the risk premiums on two assets is equal to the ratio of their betas.

22. **Portfolio Returns and Deviations** Consider the following information about three stocks:

State of Economy	Probability of State of Economy	Rate of Return if State Occurs		
		Stock A	Stock B	Stock C
Boom	.25	.13	.29	.60
Normal	.60	.08	.11	.13
Bust	.15	.02	−.18	−.45

a. If your portfolio is invested 40 percent each in A and B and 20 percent in C, what is the portfolio expected return? The variance? The standard deviation?
b. If the expected T-bill rate is 3.70 percent, what is the expected risk premium on the portfolio?

c. If the expected inflation rate is 3.30 percent, what are the approximate and exact expected real returns on the portfolio? What are the approximate and exact expected real risk premiums on the portfolio?

23. **Analyzing a Portfolio** You want to create a portfolio equally as risky as the market and you have ₹1 million to invest. Given this information, fill in the rest of the following table:

Asset	Investment	Beta
Stock A	₹195,000	.80
Stock B	₹365,000	1.09
Stock C		1.23
Risk-free asset		

24. **Analyzing a Portfolio** You have ₹100,000 to invest in a portfolio containing Stock X and Stock Y. Your goal is to create a portfolio that has an expected return of 12.1 percent. If Stock X has an expected return of 10.28 percent and a beta of 1.20, and Stock Y has an expected return of 7.52 percent and a beta of .80, how much money will you invest in Stock Y? How do you interpret your answer? What is the beta of your portfolio?

25. **Covariance and Correlation** Based on the following information, calculate the expected return and standard deviation of each of the following stocks. Assume each state of the economy is equally likely to happen. What are the covariance and correlation between the returns of the two stocks?

State of Economy	Return on Stock A	Return on Stock B
Bear	.073	−.094
Normal	.134	.142
Bull	.062	.321

26. **Covariance and Correlation** Based on the following information, calculate the expected return and standard deviation for each of the following stocks. What are the covariance and correlation between the returns of the two stocks?

State of Economy	Probability of State of Economy	Return on Stock J	Return on Stock K
Bear	.30	−.063	.014
Normal	.55	.109	.081
Bull	.15	.293	.104

27. **Portfolio Standard Deviation** Security F has an expected return of 9 percent and a standard deviation of 43 percent per year. Security G has an expected return of 12 percent and a standard deviation of 76 percent per year.

a. What is the expected return on a portfolio composed of 40 percent of Security F and 60 percent of Security G?

b. If the correlation between the returns of Security F and Security G is .25, what is the standard deviation of the portfolio described in part (a)?

28. **Portfolio Standard Deviation** Suppose the expected returns and standard deviations of Stocks A and B are $E(R_A) = .10$, $E(R_B) = .12$, $\sigma_A = .39$, and $\sigma_B = .72$.

a. Calculate the expected return and standard deviation of a portfolio that is composed of 40 percent A and 60 percent B when the correlation between the returns on A and B is .5.

b. Calculate the standard deviation of a portfolio with the same portfolio weights as in part (a) when the correlation coefficient between the returns on A and B is −.5.

c. How does the correlation between the returns on A and B affect the standard deviation of the portfolio?

29. **Correlation and Beta** You have been provided the following data about the securities of three firms, the market portfolio, and the risk-free asset:

Security	Expected Return	Standard Deviation	Correlation*	Beta
Firm A	.10	.38	(i)	.90
Firm B	.14	(ii)	.45	1.35
Firm C	.15	.74	.32	(iii)
The market portfolio	.12	.18	(iv)	(v)
The risk-free asset	.04	(vi)	(vii)	(viii)

*Correlation with the market.

a. Fill in the missing values in the table.

b. Is the stock of Firm A correctly priced according to the capital asset pricing model (CAPM)? What about the stock of Firm B? Firm C? If these securities are not correctly priced, what is your investment recommendation for someone with a well-diversified portfolio?

30. **CML** The market portfolio has an expected return of 11.3 percent and a standard deviation of 18 percent. The risk-free rate is 4.5 percent.

a. What is the expected return on a well-diversified portfolio with a standard deviation of 14 percent?

b. What is the standard deviation of a well-diversified portfolio with an expected return of 19 percent?

31. **Beta and CAPM** A portfolio that combines the risk-free asset and the market portfolio has an expected return of 9 percent and a standard deviation of 14 percent. The risk-free rate is 4.3 percent and the expected return on the market portfolio is 11.5 percent. Assume the capital asset pricing model holds. What expected rate of return would a security earn if it had a .29 correlation with the market portfolio and a standard deviation of 55 percent?

32. **Beta and CAPM** Suppose the risk-free rate is 3.9 percent and the market portfolio has an expected return of 11.4 percent. The market portfolio has a variance of .0315. Portfolio Z has a correlation coefficient with the market of .32 and a variance of .3192. According to the capital asset pricing model, what is the expected return on Portfolio Z?

CHALLENGE (Questions 33–38)

33. **Systematic versus Unsystematic Risk** Consider the following information about Stocks I and II:

State of Economy	Probability of State of Economy	Rate of Return if State Occurs	
		Stock I	Stock II
Recession	.15	.05	−.21
Normal	.70	.18	.10
Irrational exuberance	.15	.07	.39

The market risk premium is 7 percent and the risk-free rate is 3.5 percent. Which stock has more systematic risk? Which one has more unsystematic risk? Which stock is "riskier"? Explain.

34. **SML** Suppose you observe the following situation:

Security	Beta	Expected Return
Pete Corp.	1.25	.108
Repete Co.	.87	.082

Assume these securities are correctly priced. Based on the CAPM, what is the expected return on the market? What is the risk-free rate?

35. **Covariance and Portfolio Standard Deviation** There are three securities in the market. The following chart shows their possible payoffs:

State	Probability of Outcome	Return on Security 1	Return on Security 2	Return on Security 3
1	.15	.20	.20	.05
2	.35	.15	.10	.10
3	.35	.10	.15	.15
4	.15	.05	.05	.20

a. What are the expected return and standard deviation of each security?
b. What are the covariances and correlations between the pairs of securities?
c. What are the expected return and standard deviation of a portfolio with half of its funds invested in Security 1 and half in Security 2?
d. What are the expected return and standard deviation of a portfolio with half of its funds invested in Security 1 and half in Security 3?
e. What are the expected return and standard deviation of a portfolio with half of its funds invested in Security 2 and half in Security 3?
f. What do your answers in parts (a), (c), (d), and (e) imply about diversification?

36. **SML** Suppose you observe the following situation:

State of Economy	Probability of State	Return if State Occurs	
		Stock A	Stock B
Bust	.15	−.08	−.10
Normal	.60	.11	.09
Boom	.25	.30	.27

a. Calculate the expected return on each stock.
b Assuming the capital asset pricing model holds and Stock A's beta is greater than Stock B's beta by .35, what is the expected market risk premium?

37. **Standard Deviation and Beta** There are two stocks in the market, Stock A and Stock B. The price of Stock A today is ₹68. The price of Stock A next year will be ₹56 if the economy is in a recession, ₹78 if the economy is normal, and ₹86 if the economy is expanding. The probabilities of recession, normal times, and expansion are .2, .6, and .2, respectively. Stock A pays no dividends and has a correlation of .65 with the market portfolio. Stock B has an expected return of 13 percent, a standard deviation of 44 percent, a correlation with the market portfolio of .20, and a correlation with Stock A of .38. The market portfolio has a standard deviation of 19 percent. Assume the CAPM holds.

a. If you are a typical, risk-averse investor with a well-diversified portfolio, which stock would you prefer? Why?
b. What are the expected return and standard deviation of a portfolio consisting of 70 percent of Stock A and 30 percent of Stock B?
c. What is the beta of the portfolio in part (b)?

38. **Minimum Variance Portfolio** Assume Stocks A and B have the following characteristics:

Stock	Expected Return	Standard Deviation
A	11%	43%
B	15	65

The covariance between the returns on the two stocks is .003.

a. Suppose an investor holds a portfolio consisting of only Stock A and Stock B. Find the portfolio weights, X_A and X_B, such that the variance of her portfolio is minimized. (*Hint*: Remember that the sum of the weights must equal 1.)

b. What is the expected return on the minimum variance portfolio?

c. If the covariance between the returns on the two stocks is −.05, what are the minimum variance weights?

d. What is the variance of the portfolio in part (c)?

Excel Master It! Problem

The CAPM is one of the most thoroughly researched models in financial economics. When beta is estimated in practice, a variation of CAPM called the market model is often used. To derive the market model, we start with the CAPM:

Excel Master coverage online

$$E(R_i) = R_f + \beta[E(R_M) - R_f]$$

Because CAPM is an equation, we can subtract the risk-free rate from both sides, which gives us:

$$E(R_i) - R_f = \beta[E(R_M) - R_f]$$

This equation is deterministic, that is, exact. In a regression, we realize that there is some indeterminate error. We need to formally recognize this in the equation by adding epsilon, which represents this error:

$$E(R_i) - R_f = \beta[E(R_M) - R_f] + \varepsilon$$

Finally, think of the above equation in a regression. Because there is no intercept in the equation, the intercept is zero. However, when we estimate the regression equation, we can add an intercept term, which we will call alpha:

$$E(R_i) - R_f = \alpha_i + \beta[E(R_M) - R_f] + \varepsilon$$

This equation, known as the market model, is generally the model used for estimating beta. The intercept term is known as Jensen's alpha, and it represents the excess return. If CAPM holds exactly, this intercept should be zero. If you think of alpha in terms of the SML, if the alpha is positive, the stock plots above the SML and if alpha is negative, the stock plots below the SML.

a. You want to estimate the market model for an individual stock and a mutual fund. First, go to finance.yahoo.com and download the adjusted prices for the last 61 months for an individual stock, a mutual fund, and the S&P 500. Next, go to the St. Louis Federal Reserve website at www.stlouisfed.org. You should find the FRED® database there. Look for the 1-Month Treasury Constant Maturity Rate and download this data. This series will be the proxy for the risk-free rate. When using this rate, you should be aware that this interest rate is the annualized interest rate, so while we are using monthly stock returns, you will need to adjust the one-month T-bill rate. For the stock and mutual fund you select, estimate the beta and alpha using the market model. When you estimate the regression model, find the box that says "Residuals" and check this box when you do each regression. Because you are saving the residuals, you may want to save the regression output in a new worksheet.

1. Are the alpha and beta for each regression statistically different from zero?
2. How do you interpret the alpha and beta for the stock and the mutual fund?
3. Which of the two regression estimates has the highest *R*-squared? Is this what you would have expected? Why?

b. In part (a), you asked Excel to return the residuals of the regression, which is the epsilon in the regression equation. If you remember back to basic statistics, the residuals are the linear distance from each observation to the regression line. In this context, the residuals are the part of the monthly return that is not explained by the market model estimate. The residuals can be used to calculate the appraisal ratio, which is the alpha divided by the standard deviation of the residuals.

1. What do you think the appraisal ratio is intended to measure?
2. Calculate the appraisal ratios for the stock and the mutual fund. Which has a better appraisal ratio?
3. Often, the appraisal ratio is used to evaluate the performance of mutual fund managers. Why do you think the appraisal ratio is used more often for mutual funds, which are portfolios, than for individual stocks?

Mini Case A JOB AT EAST COAST YACHTS, PART 2

You are discussing your 401(k) with Dan Ervin when he mentions that Sarah Brown, a representative from Bledsoe Financial Services, is visiting East Coast Yachts today. You decide that you should meet with Sarah, so Dan sets up an appointment for you later in the day.

When you sit down with Sarah, she discusses the various investment options available in the company's 401(k) account. You mention to Sarah that you researched East Coast Yachts before you accepted your new job. You are confident in management's ability to lead the company. Analysis of the company has led to your belief that the company is growing and will achieve a greater market share in the future. You also feel you should support your employer. Given these considerations, along with the fact that you are a conservative investor, you are leaning toward investing 100 percent of your 401(k) account in East Coast Yachts stock.

Assume the risk-free rate is 3.2 percent. The correlation between the Bledsoe bond fund and large-cap stock fund is .15. Note that the spreadsheet graphing and "solver" functions may assist you in answering the following questions.

1. Considering the effects of diversification, how should Sarah respond to the suggestion that you invest 100 percent of your 401(k) account in East Coast Yachts stock?
2. Sarah's response to investing your 401(k) account entirely in East Coast Yachts stock has convinced you that this may not be the best alternative. Because you are a conservative investor, you tell Sarah that a 100 percent investment in the bond fund may be the best alternative. Is it?
3. Using the returns for the Bledsoe Large-Cap Stock Fund and the Bledsoe Bond Fund, graph the opportunity set of feasible portfolios.
4. After examining the opportunity set, you notice that you can invest in a portfolio consisting of the bond fund and the large-cap stock fund that will have exactly the same standard deviation as the bond fund. This portfolio also will have a greater expected return. What are the portfolio weights and expected return of this portfolio?
5. Examining the opportunity set, notice there is a portfolio that has the lowest standard deviation. This is the minimum variance portfolio. What are the portfolio weights, expected return, and standard deviation of this portfolio? Why is the minimum variance portfolio important?
6. A measure of risk-adjusted performance that is often used is the Sharpe ratio. The Sharpe ratio is calculated as the risk premium of an asset divided by its standard deviation. The portfolio with the highest possible Sharpe ratio on the opportunity set is called the Sharpe optimal portfolio. What are the portfolio weights, expected return, and standard deviation of the Sharpe optimal portfolio? How does the Sharpe ratio of this portfolio compare to the Sharpe ratios of the bond fund and the large-cap stock fund? Do you see a connection between the Sharpe optimal portfolio and the CAPM? What is the connection?

Appendix 11A Is Beta Dead?

To access the appendix for this chapter, please log on to www.mheducation.co.in.

12

An Alternative View of Risk and Return

THE ARBITRAGE PRICING THEORY

In early 2020, Boeing, Norwegian Cruise Lines, and Tencent all made major announcements. Boeing announced that its sales were about 2 percent lower than analysts' estimates and that EPS was about 6 percent lower than analysts' estimates. Norwegian Cruise Lines announced EPS of –₹.99, compared to analysts' estimates of –₹.28 and the previous year's EPS of ₹.83. For Chinese internet giant Tencent, the company announced that its first quarter revenue and profit beat analysts' estimates. You might expect that these three cases represent good news for Tencent and bad news for Boeing and Norwegian Cruise Lines, and usually you would be right. But here, Tencent's stock fell about 5 percent, Boeing's stock price jumped about 6 percent, and Norwegian Cruise Lines' stock rose by about 1.6 percent.

For these companies, good news seemed to be bad news (and vice versa). So when is good news really good news? The answer is fundamental to understanding risk and return, and—the good news is—this chapter explores it in some detail.

Please visit us at **rwjcorporatefinance.blogspot.com** for the latest developments in the world of corporate finance.

12.1 Systematic Risk and Betas

In the previous chapter, we introduced the CAPM. The CAPM shows that if the market portfolio is mean-variance efficient, then the best way to measure the systematic risk of a security is with the beta coefficient. The CAPM implies that the expected return on a security is linearly related to beta. We emphasized the important role of diversification in eliminating unsystematic risks.

In this chapter, we take a closer look at where betas come from and the important role of arbitrage in asset pricing.

As we have learned, the return of any stock can be written as:

$$R = \mathrm{E}(R) + U$$

where R is the actual return, $\mathrm{E}(R)$ is the expected return, and U stands for the unexpected part of the return. The U is the surprise and constitutes the risk.

We also know that the risk of any stock can be further broken down into two components: systematic and unsystematic. So, we can write:

$$R = \text{E}(R) + m + \varepsilon$$

where we have used the letter m to represent systematic risk and the Greek letter epsilon, ε, to represent unsystematic risk.

The fact that the unsystematic parts of the returns on two companies are unrelated to each other does not mean that the systematic portions are unrelated. On the contrary, because both companies are influenced by the same systematic risks, individual companies' systematic risks, and therefore their total returns, will be related.

For example, a surprise about inflation will influence almost all companies to some extent. How sensitive is a particular stock return to unanticipated changes in inflation? If the stock tends to go up on news that inflation is exceeding expectations, we would say that it is positively related to inflation. If the stock goes down when inflation exceeds expectations and up when inflation falls short of expectations, it is negatively related. In the unusual case where a stock's return is uncorrelated with inflation surprises, inflation has no effect on it.

We capture the influence of a systematic risk like inflation on a stock by using the **beta coefficient**. The beta coefficient, β, tells us the response of the stock's return to a systematic risk. In the previous chapter, beta measured the responsiveness of a security's return to a specific risk factor, the return on the market portfolio. We used this type of responsiveness to develop the capital asset pricing model. Because we now consider many types of systematic risks, our current work can be viewed as a generalization of our work in the previous chapter.

If a company's stock is positively related to the risk of inflation, that stock has a positive inflation beta. If it is negatively related to inflation, its inflation beta is negative; and if it is uncorrelated with inflation, its inflation beta is zero.

It's not hard to imagine some stocks with positive inflation betas and other stocks with negative inflation betas. The stock of a company owning gold mines will probably have a positive inflation beta because an unanticipated rise in inflation is usually associated with an increase in gold prices. On the other hand, an automobile company facing stiff foreign competition might find that an increase in inflation means that the wages it pays are higher, but that it cannot raise its prices to cover the increase. This profit squeeze, as the company's expenses rise faster than its revenues, would give its stock a negative inflation beta.

Companies that have few assets and that act as brokers–buying items in competitive markets and reselling them in other markets–might be relatively unaffected by inflation because their costs and their revenues would rise and fall together. Their stock would have an inflation beta of zero.

Some structure is useful at this point. Suppose we have identified three systematic risks on which we want to focus. We may believe that these three are sufficient to describe the systematic risks that influence stock returns. Three likely candidates are inflation, GNP, and interest rates. Every stock will have a beta associated with each of these systematic risks: an inflation beta, a GNP beta, and an interest rate beta. We can write the return on the stock, then, in the following form:

$$\begin{aligned} R &= \text{E}(R) + U \\ &= \text{E}(R) + m + \varepsilon \\ &= \text{E}(R) + \beta_I F_I + \beta_{\text{GNP}} F_{\text{GNP}} + \beta_r F_r + \varepsilon \end{aligned}$$

where we have used the symbol β_I to denote the stock's inflation beta, β_{GNP} for its GNP beta, and β_r to stand for its interest rate beta. In the equation, F stands for the surprise, whether it be in inflation, GNP, or interest rates.

We will go through an example to see how the surprises and the expected return add up to produce the total return, R, on a given stock. To make it more familiar, suppose that the return is over a horizon of a year and not a month. At the beginning of the year, inflation is forecast to be 5 percent for the year, GNP is forecast to increase by 2 percent, and interest rates are not expected to change. The stock we are looking at has the following betas:

$$\beta_I = 2$$
$$\beta_{GNP} = 1$$
$$\beta_r = -1.8$$

The magnitude of the beta describes how great an impact a systematic risk has on a stock's return. A beta of +1 indicates that the stock's return rises and falls one for one with the systematic factor. In our example, because the stock has a GNP beta of 1, it experiences a 1 percent increase in return for every 1 percent surprise increase in GNP. If its GNP beta were −2, it would fall by 2 percent when there was an unanticipated increase of 1 percent in GNP, and it would rise by 2 percent if GNP experienced a surprise 1 percent decline.

During the year, the following events occur: inflation rises by 7 percent, GNP rises by only 1 percent, and interest rates fall by 2 percent. Suppose we learn some good news about the company, perhaps that it is succeeding quickly with some new business strategy, and that this unanticipated development contributes 5 percent to its return. In other words:

$$\varepsilon = 5\%$$

We can assemble all of this information to find what return the stock had during the year.

First, we must determine what news or surprises took place in the systematic factors. From our information, we know that:

$$\text{Expected inflation} = 5\%$$
$$\text{Expected GNP change} = 2\%$$
$$\text{Expected change in interest rates} = 0\%$$

This means that the market had discounted these changes and the surprises will be the difference between what actually takes place and these expectations:

$$\begin{aligned} F_I &= \text{Surprise in inflation} \\ &= \text{Actual inflation} - \text{Expected inflation} \\ &= 7\% - 5\% \\ &= 2\% \end{aligned}$$

Similarly:

$$\begin{aligned} F_{GNP} &= \text{Surprise in GNP} \\ &= \text{Actual GNP} - \text{Expected GNP} \\ &= 1\% - 2\% \\ &= -1\% \end{aligned}$$

and:

$$\begin{aligned} F_r &= \text{Surprise in change in interest rates} \\ &= \text{Actual change} - \text{Expected change} \\ &= -2\% - 0\% \\ &= -2\% \end{aligned}$$

The total effect of the systematic risks on the stock return, then, is:

$$\begin{aligned} m &= \text{Systematic risk portion of return} \\ &= \beta_I F_I + \beta_{\text{GNP}} F_{\text{GNP}} + \beta_r F_r \\ &= [2 \times 2\%] + [1 \times (-1\%)] + [(-1.8) \times (-2\%)] \\ &= 6.6\% \end{aligned}$$

Combining this with the unsystematic risk portion, the total risky portion of the return on the stock is:

$$m + \varepsilon = 6.6\% + 5\% = 11.6\%$$

Last, if the expected return on the stock for the year was, say, 4 percent, the total return from all three components will be:

$$\begin{aligned} R &= \text{E}(R) + m + \varepsilon \\ &= 4\% + 6.6\% + 5\% \\ &= 15.6\% \end{aligned}$$

The model we have been looking at is called a **factor model** and the systematic sources of risk, designated F, are called the *factors.* To be perfectly formal, a *k-factor model* is a model where each stock's return is generated by:

$$R = \text{E}(R) + \beta_1 F_1 + \beta_1 F_2 + \cdots + \beta_k F_k + \varepsilon$$

where ε is specific to a particular stock and uncorrelated with the ε term for other stocks. In our preceding example, we had a three-factor model. We used inflation, GNP, and the change in interest rates as examples of systematic sources of risk, or factors. Researchers have not settled on what is the correct set of factors. Like so many other questions, this might be one of those matters that is never laid to rest.

In practice, researchers frequently use a one-factor model for returns. They do not use all of the sorts of economic factors we used previously as examples; instead, they use an index of stock market returns–like the S&P 500, or even a more broadly based index with more stocks in it–as the single factor. Using the single-factor model, we can write returns like this:

$$R = \text{E}(R) + \beta[R_{\text{S\&P 500}} - \text{E}(R_{\text{S\&P 500}})] + \varepsilon$$

When there is only one factor (the returns on the S&P 500 Index), we do not need to put a subscript on the beta. In this form (with minor modifications), the factor model is called a **market model**. This term is employed because the index that is used for the factor is an index of returns on the whole (stock) market. The market model is written as:

$$R = \text{E}(R) + \beta[R_M - \text{E}(R_M)] + \varepsilon$$

where $\text{E}(R_M)$ is the expected return on the market portfolio.[1] The single β is called the *beta coefficient.*

12.2 Portfolios and Factor Models

Now let us see what happens to portfolios of stocks when each of the stocks follows a one-factor model. For purposes of discussion, we will take the coming one-month period and examine returns. We could have used a day or a year or any other period. If the period represents the time between decisions, we would rather it be short than long, and a month is a reasonable time frame to use.

[1]Alternatively, the market model could be written as:

$$R = \alpha + \beta R_M + \varepsilon$$

Here, alpha (α) is an intercept term equal to $\text{E}(R) - \beta\text{E}(R_M)$.

We will create portfolios from a list of N stocks, using a one-factor model to capture the systematic risk. The ith stock in the list will therefore have returns:

$$R_i = \mathrm{E}(R_i) + \beta_i F + \varepsilon_i \tag{12.1}$$

where we have subscripted the variables to indicate that they relate to the ith stock. Notice that the factor F is not subscripted. The factor that represents systematic risk could be a surprise in GNP, or we could use the market model and let the difference between the S&P 500 return and what we expect that return to be, $R_{\text{S\&P 500}} - \mathrm{E}(R_{\text{S\&P 500}})$, be the factor. In either case, the factor applies to all of the stocks.

The β_i is subscripted because it represents the unique way the factor influences the ith stock. To review our discussion of factor models, if β_i is zero, the returns on the ith stock are:

$$R_i = \mathrm{E}(R_i) + \varepsilon_i$$

In other words, the ith stock's returns are unaffected by the factor F if β_i is zero. If β_i is positive, positive changes in the factor raise the ith stock's returns and negative changes lower them. Conversely, if β_i is negative, its returns and the factor move in opposite directions.

Figure 12.1 illustrates the relationship between a stock's excess returns, $R_i - \mathrm{E}(R_i)$, and the factor F for different betas, where $\beta_i > 0$. The lines in Figure 12.1 plot Equation 12.1 on the assumption that there has been no unsystematic risk. That is, $\varepsilon_i = 0$. Because we are assuming positive betas, the lines slope upward, indicating that the return on the stock rises with F. Notice that if the factor is zero ($F = 0$), the line passes through zero on the y-axis.

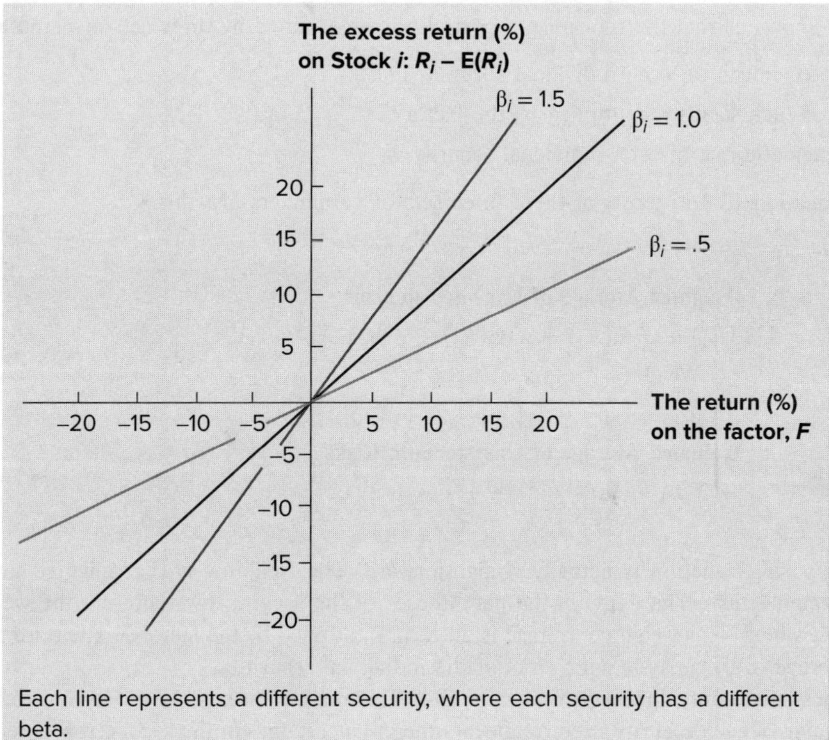

Figure 12.1 The One-Factor Model

Now let us see what happens when we create stock portfolios where each stock follows a one-factor model. Let X_i be the proportion of Security i in the portfolio. That is, if an individual with a portfolio of ₹100 wants ₹20 in Grasim Industries, we say $X_{GI} = 20$ percent. Because the Xs represent the proportions of wealth we are investing in each of the stocks, we know that they must add up to 100 percent, or 1:

$$X_1 + X_2 + X_3 + \cdots + X_N = 1$$

We know that the portfolio return is the weighted average of the returns on the individual assets in the portfolio. Algebraically, this can be written as follows:

$$R_P = X_1 R_1 + X_2 R_2 + X_3 R_3 + \cdots + X_N R_N \tag{12.2}$$

We saw from Equation 12.1 that each asset, in turn, is determined by both the factor F and the unsystematic risk of ε_i. By substituting Equation 12.1 for each R_i in Equation 12.2, we have:

$$\begin{aligned} R_P = {} & \underbrace{X_1[\text{E}(R_1) + \beta_1 F + \varepsilon_1]}_{\text{(Return on Stock 1)}} + \underbrace{X_2[\text{E}(R_2) + \beta_2 F + \varepsilon_2]}_{\text{(Return on Stock 2)}} \\ & + \underbrace{X_3[\text{E}(R_3) + \beta_3 F + \varepsilon_3]}_{\text{(Return on Stock 3)}} + \cdots + \underbrace{X_N[\text{E}(R_N) + \beta_N F + \varepsilon_N]}_{\text{(Return on Stock } N\text{)}} \end{aligned} \tag{12.3}$$

Equation 12.3 shows us that the return on a portfolio is determined by three sets of parameters:

1. The expected return on each individual security, $\text{E}(R_i)$.
2. The beta of each security multiplied by the factor F.
3. The unsystematic risk of each individual security, ε_i.

We express Equation 12.3 in terms of these three sets of parameters like this:

$$\begin{aligned} & \textbf{Weighted Average of Expected Returns} \\ R_P = {} & X_1\text{E}(R_1) + X_2\text{E}(R_2) + X_3\text{E}(R_3) + \cdots + X_N\text{E}(R_N) \\ & \textbf{Weighted Average of Betas} \times \textbf{F} \\ & + (X_1\beta_1 + X_2\beta_2 + X_3\beta_3 + \cdots + X_N\beta_N)F \\ & \textbf{Weighted Average of Unsystematic Risks} \\ & + X_1\varepsilon_1 + X_2\varepsilon_2 + X_3\varepsilon_3 + \cdots + X_N\varepsilon_N \end{aligned} \tag{12.4}$$

This rather imposing equation is actually straightforward. The first row is the weighted average of each security's expected return. The items in the parentheses of the second row represent the weighted average of each security's beta. This weighted average is, in turn, multiplied by the factor F. The third row represents a weighted average of the unsystematic risks of the individual securities.

Where does uncertainty appear in Equation 12.4? There is no uncertainty in the first row because only the expected value of each security's return appears there. Uncertainty in the second row is reflected by only one item, F. That is, while we know that the expected value of F is zero, we do not know what its value will be over a particular period. Uncertainty in the third row is reflected by each unsystematic risk, ε_i.

PORTFOLIOS AND DIVERSIFICATION

Because investors generally hold diversified portfolios, we now want to know what Equation 12.4 looks like in a large or diversified portfolio.[2]

As it turns out, something unusual occurs to Equation 12.4: The third row actually disappears in a large portfolio. To see this, consider a gambler who divides ₹1,000 by betting on red over many spins of the roulette wheel. He may participate in 1,000 spins, betting ₹1 at a time. Though we do not know ahead of time whether a particular spin will yield red or black, we can be confident that red will win about 50 percent of the time. Ignoring the house take, the investor can be expected to end up with about his original ₹1,000.

Though we are concerned with stocks, not roulette wheels, the same principle applies. Each security has its own unsystematic risk, where the surprise for one stock is unrelated to the surprise of another stock. By investing a small amount in each security, we bring the weighted average of the unsystematic risks close to zero in a large portfolio.[3]

Although the third row completely vanishes in a large portfolio, nothing unusual occurs in either Row 1 or Row 2. Row 1 remains a weighted average of the expected returns on the individual securities as securities are added to the portfolio. Because there is no uncertainty at all in the first row, there is no way for diversification to cause this row to vanish. The terms inside the parentheses of the second row remain a weighted average of the betas. They do not vanish, either, when securities are added. Because the factor F is unaffected when securities are added to the portfolios, the second row does not vanish.

Why does the third row vanish while the second row does not, though both rows reflect uncertainty? The key is that there are many unsystematic risks in Row 3. Because these risks are independent of each other, the effect of diversification becomes stronger as we add more assets to the portfolio. The resulting portfolio becomes less and less risky, and the return becomes more certain. However, the systematic risk, F, affects all securities because it is outside the parentheses in Row 2. Because we cannot avoid this factor by investing in many securities, diversification does not occur in this row.

EXAMPLE 12.1

Diversification and Unsystematic Risk The preceding material can be further explained by the following example. We keep our one-factor model here but make three specific assumptions:

1. All securities have the same expected return of 10 percent. This assumption implies that the first row of Equation 12.4 also must equal 10 percent because this row is a weighted average of the expected returns of the individual securities.
2. All securities have a beta of 1. The sum of the terms inside the parentheses in the second row of Equation 12.4 must equal 1 because these terms are a weighted average of the individual betas. Because the terms inside the parentheses are multiplied by F, the value of the second row is $1 \times F = F$.
3. In this example, we focus on the behavior of one individual, Ram Vikas Paswan, Ram Vikas decides to hold an equally weighted portfolio. That is, the proportion of each security in his portfolio is $1/N$.

(continued)

[2]Technically, we can think of a large portfolio as one where an investor keeps increasing the number of securities without limit. In practice, effective diversification would occur if at least a few dozen securities were held.

[3]More precisely, we say that the weighted average of the unsystematic risk approaches zero as the number of equally weighted securities in a portfolio approaches infinity.

We can express the return on Ram Vikas's portfolio as follows:

Return on Ram Vikas Paswan's Portfolio

$$R_p = \underset{\substack{\text{From}\\ \text{Row 1 of}\\ \text{Equation 12.4}}}{10\%} + \underset{\substack{\text{From}\\ \text{Row 2 of}\\ \text{Equation 12.4}}}{F} + \underbrace{\left(\frac{1}{N}\varepsilon_1 + \frac{1}{N}\varepsilon_2 + \frac{1}{N}\varepsilon_3 + \cdots + \frac{1}{N}\varepsilon_N\right)}_{\substack{\text{From Row 3 of}\\ \text{Equation 12.4}}} \quad \textbf{(12.4')}$$

We mentioned before that as N increases without limit, Row 3 of Equation 12.4 becomes equal to zero.[4] The return on Ram Vikas's portfolio when the number of securities is very large is:

$$R_P = 10\% + F \quad \textbf{(12.4'')}$$

The key to diversification is exhibited in Equation 12.4″. The unsystematic risk of Row 3 vanishes while the systematic risk of Row 2 remains.

This is illustrated in Figure 12.2. Systematic risk, captured by variation in the factor F, is not reduced through diversification. Conversely, unsystematic risk diminishes as securities are added, vanishing as the number of securities becomes infinite. Our result is analogous to the diversification example of the previous chapter. In that chapter, we said that undiversifiable or systematic risk arises from positive covariances between securities. In this chapter, we say that systematic risk arises from a common factor, F. Because a common factor causes positive covariances, the arguments of the two chapters are parallel.

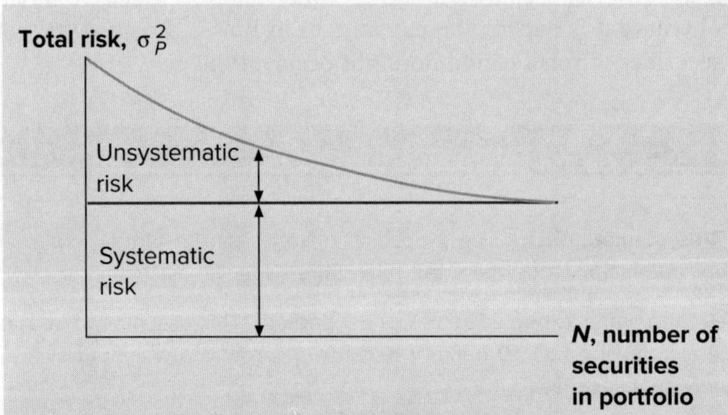

Total risk decreases as the number of securities in the portfolio rises. This drop occurs only in the unsystematic risk component. Systematic risk is unaffected by diversification.

Figure 12.2 Diversification and the Portfolio Risk for an Equally Weighted Portfolio

[4]Our presentation on this point has not been rigorous. The student interested in more rigor should note that the variance of Row 3 is:

$$\frac{1}{N^2}\sigma_\varepsilon^2 + \frac{1}{N^2}\sigma_\varepsilon^2 + \frac{1}{N^2}\sigma_\varepsilon^2 + \ldots + \frac{1}{N^2}\sigma_\varepsilon^2 = \frac{1}{N^2}N\sigma_\varepsilon^2$$

where σ_ε^2 is the variance of each ε. This can be rewritten as σ_ε^2/N, which tends to 0 as N goes to infinity.

12.3 Betas, Arbitrage, and Expected Returns

THE LINEAR RELATIONSHIP

We have argued many times that the expected return on a security compensates for its risk. In the previous chapter, we showed that market beta (the standardized covariance of the security's returns with those of the market) was the appropriate measure of risk under the assumptions of homogeneous expectations and riskless borrowing and lending. The capital asset pricing model, which posited these assumptions, implied that the expected return on a security was positively (and linearly) related to its beta. We will find a similar relationship between risk and return in the one-factor model of this chapter.

We begin by noting that the relevant risk in large and well-diversified portfolios is all systematic because unsystematic risk is diversified away. An implication is that when a well-diversified shareholder considers changing her holdings of a particular stock, she can ignore the security's unsystematic risk.

Notice that we are not claiming that stocks, like portfolios, have no unsystematic risk. Nor are we saying that the unsystematic risk of a stock will not affect its returns. Stocks do have unsystematic risk and their actual returns do depend on the unsystematic risk. Because this risk washes out in a well-diversified portfolio, however, shareholders can ignore this unsystematic risk when they consider whether to add a stock to their portfolio. Therefore, if shareholders are ignoring the unsystematic risk, only the systematic risk of a stock can be related to its expected return.

This relationship is illustrated in the security market line of Figure 12.3. Points P, C, A, and L all lie on the line emanating from the risk-free rate of 10 percent. The points representing each of these four assets can be created by combinations of the risk-free asset and any of the other three assets. Because A has a beta of 2.0 and P has a beta of 1.0, a portfolio of 50 percent in Asset A and 50 percent in the riskless asset has the same beta as Asset P. The risk-free rate is 10 percent and the expected return on Security A is 35 percent, implying that the combination's return of 22.5 percent [= (.10 + .35)/2] is identical to Security P's expected return. Because Security P has both the same beta and the same expected return as a combination of the riskless asset and Security A, an individual is equally inclined to add a small amount

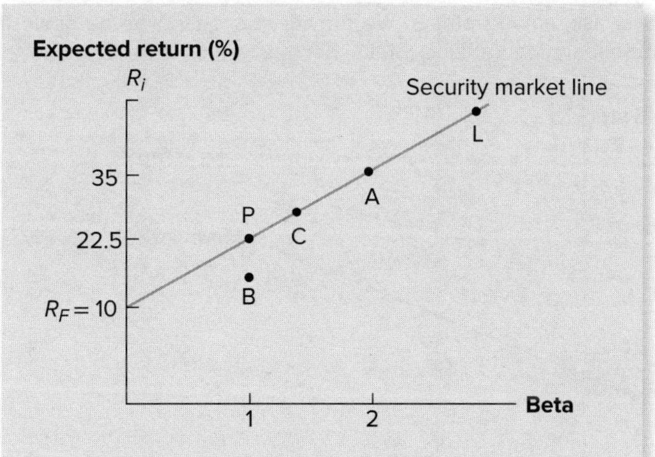

Figure 12.3 A Graph of Beta and Expected Return for Individual Stocks Under the One-Factor Model

of Security P and a small amount of this combination to her portfolio. However, the unsystematic risk of Security P need not be equal to the unsystematic risk of the combination of Security A and the risk-free asset because unsystematic risk is diversified away in a large portfolio.

Of course, the potential combinations of points on the security market line are endless. We can duplicate P by combinations of the risk-free asset and either C or L (or both of them). We can duplicate C (or A or L) by borrowing at the risk-free rate to invest in P. The infinite number of points on the security market line that are not labeled can be used as well.

Now consider Security B. Because its expected return is below the line, no investor would hold it. Instead, the investor would prefer Security P, a combination of Security A and the riskless asset, or some other combination. Thus, Security B's price is too high. Its price will fall in a competitive market, forcing its expected return back up to the line in equilibrium. Investors who try to spot situations where securities of the same risk have different expected returns are called arbitrageurs. The arbitrage trade here is to sell short Security B and buy Security P. The profit would be the difference in the market prices of Security B and Security P. The idea of arbitrage, and its significance in asset pricing, is referred to as the arbitrage pricing theory (APT).

The preceding discussion allows us to provide an equation for the security market line of Figure 12.3. We know that a line can be described algebraically from two points. It is perhaps easiest to focus on the risk-free asset and Security P because the risk-free asset has a beta of 0 and P has a beta of 1.

Because we know that the return on any zero-beta asset is R_F and the expected return on Security P is $E(R_P)$, it can be shown that:

$$E(R) = R_F + \beta[(E(R_P) - R_F] \tag{12.5}$$

In Equation 12.5, $E(R)$ can be thought of as the expected return on any security or portfolio lying on the security market line. β is the beta of that security or portfolio.

The Security Market Line Can Change with Time

We have argued many times that the security market line depends on inflation, GNP, change in interest rates, and socio-political risk, among others. We provide a scenario of the same from the Indian equity markets. Observe the Security Market Line (SML) changes in the figure below:

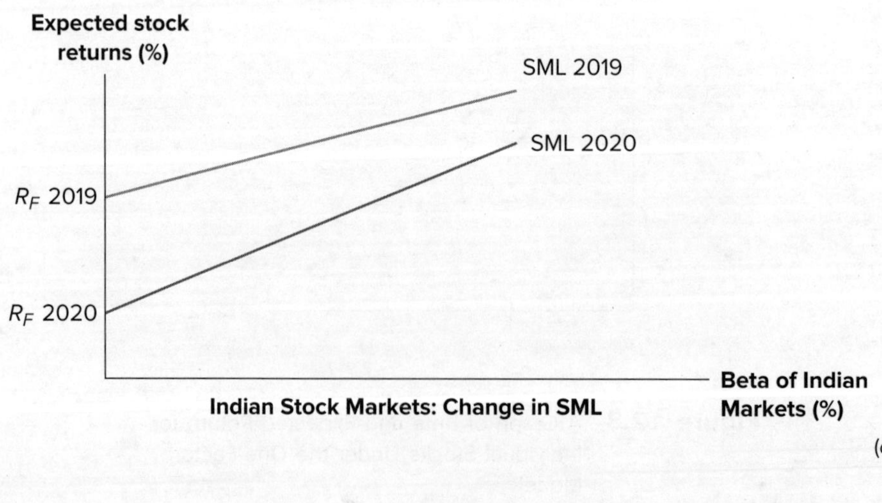

Indian Stock Markets: Change in SML

(continued)

All these factors have changed in the Indian equity markets over the last two decades, i.e., from what they were during the peak period COVID-19 pandemic (March-June 2020) to post-pandemic (October-December 2020). We provide below some logical arguments on the same:

- During the calendar year 2019, the interest rates were on the higher side influenced by the cost of demonetization. The global markets were also on the rise and there was less volatility in the markets. All this led to the SML to have a lower slope and a higher intercept.
- During the calendar year 2020, COVID-19 pandemic saw the markets extremely volatile. Interest rates were lowered to support the economy in the post - covid period. The sharp movements in the market implied a greater systematic risk in the market. This meant a lower intercept and a steeper slope for the SML in Indian equity markets.

THE MARKET PORTFOLIO AND THE SINGLE FACTOR

In the CAPM, the beta of a security measures the security's responsiveness to movements in the market portfolio. In the one-factor model of the arbitrage pricing theory, the beta of a security measures its responsiveness to the factor. We now relate the market portfolio to the single factor.

A large, diversified portfolio has no unsystematic risk because the unsystematic risks of the individual securities are diversified away. Assuming enough securities so that the market portfolio is fully diversified and assuming that no security has a disproportionate market share, this portfolio is fully diversified and contains no unsystematic risk.[5] In other words, the market portfolio is perfectly correlated with the single factor, implying that the market portfolio is really a scaled-up or scaled-down version of the factor. After scaling properly, we can treat the market portfolio as the factor itself.

The market portfolio, like every security or portfolio, lies on the security market line. When the market portfolio is the factor, the beta of the market portfolio is 1 by definition. This is shown in Figure 12.4. (We

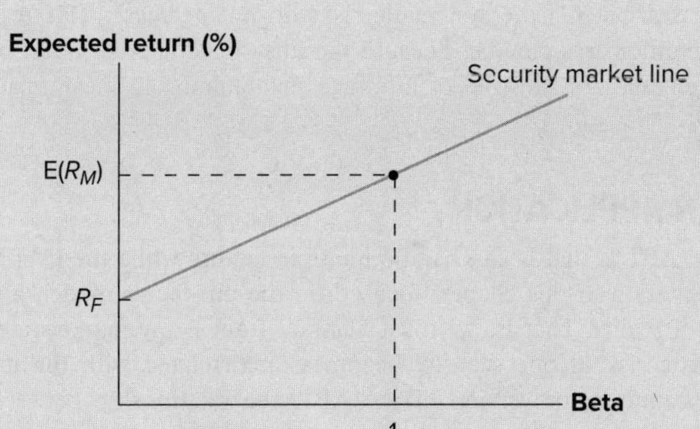

The factor is scaled so that it is identical to the market portfolio. The beta of the market portfolio is 1.

Figure 12.4 A Graph of Beta and Expected Return for Market Portfolio under the One-Factor Model

[5]This assumption is plausible in the real world. For example, even the market value of Apple in late 2020, at over ₹2 trillion, was only about 7 percent of the market value of the S&P 500 Index.

deleted the securities and the specific expected returns from Figure 12.3 for clarity. The two graphs are otherwise identical.) With the market portfolio as the factor, Equation 12.5 becomes:

$$E(R) = R_F + \beta[E(R_M) - R_F]$$

where $E(R_M)$ is the expected return on the market. This equation shows that the expected return on any asset, $E(R)$, is linearly related to the security's beta. The equation is identical to that of the CAPM, which we developed in the previous chapter.

12.4 The Capital Asset Pricing Model and the Arbitrage Pricing Theory

The CAPM and the APT are alternative models of risk and return. It is worthwhile to consider the differences between the two models, both in terms of the model and in terms of application.

DIFFERENCES IN PEDAGOGY

We feel that the CAPM has at least one strong advantage from the student's point of view. The derivation of the CAPM necessarily brings the reader through a discussion of efficient sets. This treatment–beginning with the case of two risky assets, moving to the case of many risky assets, and finishing when a riskless asset is added to the many risky ones–is of great intuitive value. This sort of presentation is not as easily accomplished with the APT.

However, the APT has some offsetting advantages. The model adds factors until the unsystematic risk of any security is uncorrelated with the unsystematic risk of every other security. Under this formulation, it is easily shown that (1) unsystematic risk steadily falls (and ultimately vanishes) as the number of securities in the portfolio increases, but (2) the systematic risks do not decrease. This result also was shown in the CAPM, though the intuition was cloudier because the unsystematic risks could be correlated across securities. Also, the APT emphasizes the role of arbitrage in obtaining a linear relationship between expected returns and betas.

DIFFERENCES IN APPLICATION

One advantage of the APT is that it can handle multiple factors while the CAPM ignores them. Although the bulk of our presentation in this chapter focused on the one-factor model, a multifactor model is probably more reflective of reality. That is, we must abstract from many marketwide and industrywide factors before the unsystematic risk of one security becomes uncorrelated with the unsystematic risks of other securities. Under this multifactor version of the APT, the relationship between risk and return can be expressed as:

$$\begin{aligned} E(R) = R_F &+ [E(R_1) - R_F]\beta_1 + [E(R_2) - R_F]\beta_2 \\ &+ [E(R_3) - R_F]\beta_3 + \cdots + [E(R_K) - R_F]\beta_K \end{aligned} \tag{12.6}$$

In this equation, β_1 stands for the security's beta with respect to the first factor, β_2 stands for the security's beta with respect to the second factor, and so on. If the first factor is GNP, β_1 is the security's GNP beta. The term $E(R_1)$ is the expected return on a security (or portfolio) whose beta with respect to the first factor is one and whose beta with respect to all other factors is zero. Because the market compensates for risk,

$[E(R_1) - R_F]$ will be positive in the normal case.[6] (An analogous interpretation can be given to $E(R_2)$, $E(R_3)$, and so on.)

The equation states that the security's expected return is related to the security's factor betas. The intuition in Equation 12.6 is straightforward. Each factor represents risk that cannot be diversified away. The higher a security's beta is with regard to a particular factor, the higher the risk that the security bears. In a rational world, the expected return on the security should compensate for this risk. Equation 12.6 states that the expected return is a summation of the risk-free rate plus the compensation for each type of risk that the security bears.

As an example, consider a study where the factors were monthly growth in industrial production (IP), change in expected inflation (ΔEI), unanticipated inflation (UI), unanticipated change in the risk premium between risky bonds and default-free bonds (URP), and unanticipated change in the difference between the return on long-term government bonds and the return on short-term government bonds (UBR).[7] Using the period 1958–1984, the empirical results of the study indicated that the expected monthly return on any stock, $E(R_S)$, can be described as:

$$E(R_S) = .0041 + .0136\,\beta_{IP} - .0001\,\beta_{\Delta EI} - .0006\,\beta_{UI} + .0072\,\beta_{URP} - .0052\,\beta_{UBR}$$

Suppose a particular stock had the following betas: $\beta_{IP} = 1.1$, $\beta_{\Delta EI} = 2$, $\beta_{UI} = 3$, $\beta_{URP} = .1$, $\beta_{UBR} = 1.6$. The expected monthly return on that security would be:

$$\begin{aligned} E(R_S) &= .0041 + .0136 \times 1.1 - .0001 \times 2 - .0006 \times 3 + .0072 \times .1 \\ &\quad - .0052 \times 1.6 \\ &= .0095 \end{aligned}$$

Assuming that a firm is unlevered and that one of the firm's projects has risk equivalent to that of the firm, this value of .0095 (i.e., .95%) can be used as the monthly discount rate for the project. (Because annual data are often supplied for capital budgeting purposes, the effective annual rate of 12 percent $[= 1.0095^{12} - 1]$ might be used instead.)

Because many factors appear on the right side of Equation 12.6, the APT formulation has the potential to measure expected returns more accurately than does the CAPM. However, as we mentioned earlier, we cannot easily determine which are the appropriate factors. The factors in the preceding study were included for reasons of both common sense and convenience. They were not derived from theory.

By contrast, the use of the market index in the CAPM formulation is implied by the theory of the previous chapter. We suggested in earlier chapters that the S&P 500 index reflects overall U.S. stock market movements. Using the Ibbotson-Sinquefield results showing that from 1926 to 2020 the yearly return on the S&P 500 Index was, on average, about 8.9 percent greater than the risk-free rate, the last chapter showed how to calculate expected returns on different securities using the CAPM.[8]

For Indian equity markets, the most popular barometer, the Bombay Stock Exchange's Sensitive Index (popularly known as S&P BSE Sensex), mirrors the stock market movements quite well. Doing quick computations using approximately 45 years of data (1979–2023) from the RBI and BSE shows us that the yearly

---

[6]Actually, $[E(R_i) - R_F]$ could be negative in the case where Factor i is perceived as a hedge of some sort.

[7]N. Chen, R. Roll, and S. Ross, "Economic Forces and the Stock Market," *The Journal of Business* (July 1986).

[8]Going back to 1900, the S&P 500 was, on average, 7.2 percent greater than the risk-free rate. Though many researchers assume that surrogates for the market portfolio are easily found, Richard Roll, "A Critique of the Asset Pricing Theory's Tests," *Journal of Financial Economics* (March 1977), argues that the absence of a universally acceptable proxy for the market portfolio seriously impairs application of the theory. After all, the market must include real estate, racehorses, and other assets that are not in the stock market.

return on the BSE Sensex was, on an average, 8.7 percent greater than the local risk-free rate. Doing similar computations using approximately 28 years of data (1996–2023) from the NSE shows us that the yearly return on the NSE Nifty was, on an average, 4.6 percent greater than the local risk-free rate.

12.5 Empirical Approaches to Asset Pricing

EMPIRICAL MODELS

Excel Master coverage online

The CAPM and the APT by no means exhaust the models and techniques used in practice to measure the expected return on risky assets. Both the CAPM and the APT are *risk-based models.* Each measures the risk of a security by its beta(s) on some systematic factor(s) and each argues that the expected excess return must be proportional to the beta(s). Although we have seen that this is intuitively appealing and has a strong basis in theory, there are alternative approaches.

Most of these alternatives can be lumped under the broad heading of parametric or **empirical models.** The word *empirical* refers to the fact that these approaches are based less on some theory of how financial markets work and more on looking for regularities and relations in the history of market data. In these approaches, the researcher specifies some parameters or attributes associated with the securities in question and then examines the data directly for a relation between these attributes and expected returns. For example, an extensive amount of research has been done on whether the expected return on a firm is related to its size. Is it true that small firms have higher average returns than large firms? Researchers also have examined a variety of accounting measures such as the ratio of the price of a stock to its accounting earnings, its PE ratio, and the closely related ratio of the market value of the stock to the book value of the company, the M/B ratio. Here it might be argued that companies with low PEs or low M/Bs are *undervalued* and can be expected to have higher returns in the future.

To use the empirical approach to determine the expected return, we would estimate the following equation:

$$E(R_i) = R_F + k_{PE}(PE)_i + k_{M/B}(M/B)_i + k_{size}(size)_i$$

where $E(R_i)$ is the expected return of Firm *i* and the *k*'s are coefficients that we estimate from stock market data. Notice that this is the same form as Equation 12.6 with the firm's attributes in place of betas and with the *k*'s in place of the excess factor portfolio returns.

When tested with data, these parametric approaches seem to do quite well. In fact, when comparisons are made between using parameters and using betas to predict stock returns, the parameters, such as PE and M/B, seem to work better. There are a variety of possible explanations for these results, and the issues have certainly not been settled. Critics of the empirical approach are skeptical of what they call *data mining.* The particular parameters that researchers work with are often chosen because they have been shown to be related to returns. Suppose that you were asked to explain the change in XAT test scores over the past 40 years in some particular state. To do this, you searched through all of the data series you could find. After much searching, you might discover, for example, that the change in the scores was directly related to the elephant's population in the state of Kerala. We know that any such relation is purely accidental; but if you search long enough and have enough choices, you will find something even if it is not really there. It's a bit like staring at clouds. After a while, you will see clouds that look like anything you want–clowns, bears, or whatever–but all you are really doing is data mining.

Needless to say, the researchers on these matters defend their work by arguing that they have not mined the data and have been very careful to avoid such traps by not snooping at the data to see what will work.

Of course, as a matter of pure theory, because anyone in the market can easily look up the PE ratio of a firm, we would certainly not expect to find that firms with low PEs did better than firms with high PEs because they were undervalued. In an efficient market, such public measures of undervaluation would be quickly exploited and would not last.

Perhaps a better explanation for the success of empirical approaches lies in a synthesis of the risk-based approaches and the empirical methods. In an efficient market, risk and return are related; so perhaps the parameters or attributes that appear to be related to returns are also better measures of risk. If we were to find that low PE firms outperformed high PE firms and that this was true even for firms that had the same beta(s), then we would have at least two possible explanations. First, we could discard the risk-based theories as incorrect. Furthermore, we could argue that markets are inefficient and that buying low PE stocks provides us with an opportunity to make higher-than-predicted returns. Second, we could argue that both views of the world are correct and that the PE is really just a better way to measure systematic risk–that is, beta(s)–than directly estimating beta from the data.

STYLE PORTFOLIOS

In addition to their use as a platform for estimating expected returns, stock attributes also are widely used as a way of characterizing money management styles. A portfolio that has a PE ratio much in excess of the market average might be characterized as a high PE portfolio or a **growth stock portfolio**. Similarly, a portfolio made up of stocks with an average PE less than that of a market index might be characterized as a low PE portfolio or a **value portfolio**.

To evaluate how well portfolio managers are doing, their performance is often compared with the performance of some basic indexes. For example, the portfolio returns of managers who purchase large Indian stocks might be compared to the performance of the S&P BSE 500 Index. In such a case, the S&P BSE 500 is said to be the **benchmark** against which their performance is measured. Similarly, an international manager might be compared against some common index of international stocks. In choosing an appropriate benchmark, care should be taken to identify a benchmark that contains only those types of stocks that the manager targets as representative of his style and that are also available to be purchased. A manager who was told not to purchase any stocks in the S&P 500 Index would not consider it legitimate to be compared against the S&P 500.

Increasingly, too, managers are compared not only against an index but also against a peer group of similar managers. The performance of a fund that advertises itself as a growth fund might be measured against the performance of a large sample of similar funds. For instance, the performance over some period is commonly assigned to quartiles. The top 25 percent of the funds are said to be in the first quartile, the next 25 percent in the second quartile, the next 25 percent in the third quartile, and the worst-performing 25 percent of the funds in the last quartile. If the fund we are examining happens to have a performance that falls in the second quartile, then we speak of its manager as a second-quartile manager.

Similarly, we call a fund that purchases low M/B stocks a value fund and would measure its performance against a sample of similar value funds. These approaches to measuring performance are relatively new, and they are part of an active and exciting effort to refine our ability to identify and use investment skills.

In Their Own Words

KENNETH FRENCH ON THE FAMA-FRENCH THREE-FACTOR MODEL

The Fama-French (1993) three-factor model is an empirically motivated implementation of Ross's (1976) arbitrage pricing theory. When we developed the model, researchers had identified two dominant patterns in the cross-section of average stock returns. Small companies, with relatively little market equity, tend to have higher average stock returns than big companies (Banz, 1981). And value companies, which are often defined as those with a high ratio of book equity to market equity, tend to have higher average returns than growth companies (Fama and French, 1992). Our goal was a simple model that captures these patterns in stock returns.

The three-factor model predicts that the expected excess return on Portfolio i, $E(R_i) - R_F$, is determined by its loadings on, well, three factors:

$$E(R_i) - R_F = \beta_i[E(R_M) - R_F] + s_i E(SMB) + h_i E(HML)$$

The excess return on the market, $E(R_M) - R_F$, plays much the same role here as it does in the capital asset pricing model. The expected compensation investors receive for bearing market risk equals the quantity of market risk, β_i, times the price per unit, $E(R_M) - R_F$.

The second and third factors are aimed at the size and value effects. The size factor, SMB (small minus big), is the difference between the returns on a portfolio of small stocks and a portfolio of big stocks. The value factor, HML (high minus low), is the difference between the returns on a portfolio of high book-to-market stocks and a portfolio of low book-to-market stocks. Because small stocks tend to outperform big stocks and value stocks tend to outperform growth stocks, the expected values of SMB and HML are positive. Thus, the three-factor model predicts that the expected return on a portfolio increases linearly with s_i, its loading on SMB, and with h_i, its loading on HML. A portfolio of small-value stocks, for example, is likely to have positive loadings on SMB and HML, so the model predicts the portfolio has a high expected return.

You can estimate a portfolio's loadings on $R_M - R_F$, SMB, and HML by regressing its excess return on the three factors:

$$R_{it} - R_{Ft} = \alpha_i + \beta_i(R_{Mt} - R_{Ft}) + s_i SMB_t + h_i HML_t + \varepsilon_{it}$$

The model predicts the intercept α_i in this time series regression is zero. I provide daily, monthly, quarterly, and annual returns for the three factors on my website, **www.dartmouth.edu/~kfrench**. People typically use monthly returns when estimating the model because they offer a good compromise between market microstructure issues that become important as the interval gets shorter and the loss of observations that occurs as the interval gets longer.

The three-factor model is not perfect, but it does a reasonable job explaining the returns on a wide range of stock portfolios. There is controversy, however, about whether the average premiums on SMB and HML are compensation for risk or the result of mispricing. (For what it is worth, I think they are the result of both risk and mispricing.) Fortunately, the answer to this question is irrelevant for many applications of the model. When evaluating a portfolio manager, for example, we can interpret SMB and HML as the returns to passive benchmark portfolios.

SOURCE: Kenneth R. French is the Roth Family Distinguished Professor of Finance at the Tuck School of Business at Dartmouth College. He is an expert on the behavior of security prices and investment strategies.

RESEARCH IN EMERGING MARKET CONTEXT

A study conducted by Pandey & Sehgal (2017) analyzed the volatility patterns in stock returns for 493 companies. They found that high-volatility stocks outperformed low-volatility stocks and that cash flow variability played a significant role in explaining these patterns. Pati et al. (2019) conducted a study of the volatility index using Indian data and found strong evidence of side effects but relatively weak

(continued)

value-growth and momentum effects. Adding the volatility risk factor improved the standard asset-pricing models, explaining the variation in stock returns.

Lalwani and Chakraborty (2020) compared the performance of various multifactor asset pricing models across ten emerging and developed markets. They reported that the Fama-French five-factor model improved the pricing performance for stocks in Australia, Canada, China, and the USA. For other markets, the parsimonious three-factor model or its four-factor variants appeared to be more suitable.

References

Lalwani, V., & Chakraborty, M. (2020). Multi-factor asset pricing models in emerging and developed markets. *Managerial Finance,* 46(3), 360–380.

Pandey, A., & Sehgal, S. (2017). Volatility effect and the role of firm quality factor in returns: Evidence from the Indian stock market. *IIMB Management Review,* 29(1), 18–28.

Pati, P. C., Rajib, P., & Barai, P. (2019). The role of the volatility index in asset pricing: The case of the Indian stock market. *The Quarterly Review of Economics and Finance,* 74, 336–346.

Summary and Conclusions

The previous chapter developed the capital asset pricing model (CAPM). As an alternative, this chapter developed the arbitrage pricing theory (APT).

1. The APT assumes that stock returns are generated according to factor models. For example, we might describe a stock's return as:

$$R = \mathrm{E}(R) + \beta_I F_I + \beta_{\mathrm{GNP}} F_{\mathrm{GNP}} + \beta_r F_r + \varepsilon$$

where I, GNP, and r stand for inflation, gross national product, and the interest rate, respectively. The three factors F_I, F_{GNP}, and F_r represent systematic risk because these factors affect many securities. The term ε is considered unsystematic risk because it is unique to each individual security.

2. For convenience, we frequently describe a security's return according to a one-factor model:

$$R = \mathrm{E}(R) + \beta F + \varepsilon$$

3. As securities are added to a portfolio, the unsystematic risks of the individual securities offset each other. A fully diversified portfolio has no unsystematic risk but still has systematic risk. This result indicates that diversification can eliminate some, but not all, of the risk of individual securities.
4. Because of this, the expected return on a stock is positively related to its systematic risk. In a one-factor model, the systematic risk of a security is the beta of the CAPM. Thus, the implications of the CAPM and the one-factor APT are identical. However, each security has many risks in a multifactor model. The expected return on a security is positively related to its beta with each factor.
5. Empirical or parametric models that capture the relationships between returns and stock attributes such as PE or M/B ratios can be estimated directly from the data without any appeal to theory. These ratios also are used to measure the styles of portfolio managers and to construct benchmarks and samples against which they are measured.

Concept Questions

1. **Systematic versus Unsystematic Risk** Describe the difference between systematic risk and unsystematic risk.
2. **APT** Consider the following statement: For the APT to be useful, the number of systematic risk factors must be small. Do you agree or disagree with this statement? Why?
3. **APT** Maneet Gupta, the CFO of Ultra Bread, has decided to use an APT model to estimate the required return on the company's stock. The risk factors she plans to use are the risk premium on the stock market, the inflation rate, and the price of wheat. Because wheat is one of the biggest costs Ultra Bread faces, she feels this is a significant risk factor for Ultra Bread. How would you evaluate her choice of risk factors? Are there other risk factors you might suggest?
4. **Systematic and Usystematic Risk** You own stock in the Lewis-Striden Drug Company. You expected the following events to occur last month:

   a. The government would announce that real GNP had grown 1.2 percent during the previous quarter. The returns of Lewis-Striden are positively related to real GNP.
   b. The government would announce that inflation over the previous quarter was 3.7 percent. The returns of Lewis-Striden are negatively related to inflation.
   c. Interest rates would rise 2.5 percentage points. The returns of Lewis-Striden are negatively related to interest rates.
   d. The president of the firm would announce her retirement. The retirement would be effective six months from the announcement day. The president is well-liked and she is considered an asset to the firm.
   e. Research data would conclusively prove the efficacy of an experimental drug. Completion of the efficacy testing means the drug will be on the market soon.

   Suppose the following events actually occurred:

   a. The government announced that real GNP grew 2.3 percent during the previous quarter.
   b. The government announced that inflation over the previous quarter was 3.7 percent.
   c. Interest rates rose 2.1 percentage points.
   d. The president of the firm died suddenly of a heart attack.
   e. Research results in the efficacy testing were not as strong as expected. The drug must be tested for another six months and the efficacy results must be resubmitted to the FDA.
   f. Lab researchers had a breakthrough with another drug.
   g. A competitor announced that it will begin distribution and sale of a medicine that will compete directly with one of Lewis-Striden's top-selling products.

   Discuss how each of the actual occurrences affects the return on your Lewis-Striden stock. Which events represent systematic risk? Which events represent unsystematic risk?
5. **Market Model versus APT** What are the differences between a *k*-factor model and the market model?
6. **APT** In contrast to the CAPM, the APT does not indicate which factors are expected to determine the risk premium of an asset. How can we determine which factors should be included? For example, one risk factor suggested is the company size. Why might this be an important risk factor in an APT model?
7. **CAPM versus APT** What is the relationship between the one-factor model and the CAPM?
8. **Factor Models** How can the return on a portfolio be expressed in terms of a factor model?
9. **Data Mining** What is data mining? Why might it overstate the relationships between some stock attribute and returns?
10. **Factor Selection** What is wrong with measuring the performance of a U.S. growth stock manager against a benchmark composed of British stocks?

Questions and Problems

BASIC (Questions 1–4)

1. **Factor Models** A researcher has determined that a two-factor model is appropriate to determine the return on a stock. The factors are the percentage change in GNP and an interest rate. GNP is expected to grow by 2.8 percent and the interest rate is expected to be 2.6 percent. A stock has a beta of 1.25 on the percentage change in GNP and a beta of −.47 on the interest rate. If the expected rate of return on the stock is 11.1 percent, what is the revised expected return on the stock if GNP actually grows by 2.4 percent and the interest rate is 2.7 percent?

2. **Factor Models** Suppose a three-factor model is appropriate to describe the returns of a stock. Information about those three factors is presented in the following chart:

Factor	β	Expected Value	Actual Value
GDP	.0000615	₹22,432	₹23,187
Inflation	−.90	2.3%	2.6%
Interest rates	−.32	2.8%	3.1%

   a. What is the systematic risk of the stock return?
   b. Suppose unexpected bad news about the firm was announced that causes the stock price to drop by 1.25 percent. If the expected return on the stock is 11.5 percent, what is the total return on this stock?

3. **Factor Models** Suppose a factor model is appropriate to describe the returns on a stock. The current expected return on the stock is 12.2 percent. Information about those factors is presented in the following chart:

Factor	β	Expected Value	Actual Value
Growth in GNP	1.35	2.1%	2.4%
Inflation	−.87	3.3	3.6

   a. What is the systematic risk of the stock return?
   b. The firm announced that its market share had unexpectedly increased from 12 percent to 15 percent. Investors know from past experience that the stock return will increase by .75 percent for every 1 percent increase in its market share. What is the unsystematic risk of the stock?
   c. What is the total return on this stock?

4. **Multifactor Models** Suppose stock returns can be explained by the following three-factor model:

$$R_i = R_F + \beta_1 F_1 + \beta_2 F_2 - \beta_3 F_3$$

Assume there is no firm-specific risk. The information for each stock is presented here:

	β_1	β_2	β_3
Stock A	1.45	.85	.10
Stock B	.87	1.35	−.30
Stock C	.76	−.26	1.19

The risk premiums for the factors are 5.3 percent, 4.1 percent, and 5.9 percent, respectively. If you create a portfolio with 20 percent invested in Stock A, 20 percent invested in Stock B, and the remainder in Stock C, what is the expression for the return on your portfolio? If the risk-free rate is 3.2 percent, what is the expected return on your portfolio?

INTERMEDIATE (Questions 5–7)

5. **Multifactor Models** Suppose stock returns can be explained by a two-factor model. The firm-specific risks for all stocks are independent. The following table shows the information for two diversified portfolios:

	β_1	β_2	E(*R*)
Portfolio A	.85	1.15	16%
Portfolio B	1.45	−.25	12

If the risk-free rate is 4 percent, what are the risk premiums for each factor in this model?

6. **Market Model** The following three stocks are available in the market:

	E(*R*)	β
Stock A	10.5%	1.20
Stock B	13.0	.98
Stock C	15.7	1.37
Market	14.2	1.00

Assume the market model is valid.

a. Write the market model equation for each stock.
b. What is the return on a portfolio with weights of 30 percent Stock A, 45 percent Stock B, and 25 percent Stock C?
c. Suppose the return on the market is 15 percent and there are no unsystematic surprises in the returns. What is the return on each stock? What is the return on the portfolio?

7. **Portfolio Risk** You are forming an equally weighted portfolio of stocks. Many stocks have the same beta of .84 for Factor 1 and the same beta of 1.69 for Factor 2. All stocks also have the same expected return of 11 percent. Assume a two-factor model describes the return on each of these stocks.

a. Write the equation of the returns on your portfolio if you place only five stocks in it.
b. Write the equation of the returns on your portfolio if you place in it a very large number of stocks that all have the same expected returns and the same betas.

CHALLENGE (Questions 8–10)

8. **APT** There are two stock markets, each driven by the same common force, *F*, with an expected value of zero and standard deviation of 10 percent. There are many securities in each market; you can invest in as many stocks as you wish. Due to restrictions, however, you can invest in only one of the two markets. The expected return on every security in both markets is 10 percent.

The returns for each security, *i*, in the first market are generated by the relationship:

$$R_{1i} = .10 + 1.5F + \varepsilon_{1i}$$

where ε_{1i} is the term that measures the surprises in the returns of Stock *i* in Market 1. These surprises are normally distributed; their mean is zero. The returns on Security *j* in the second market are generated by the relationship:

$$R_{2j} = .10 + .5F + \varepsilon_{2j}$$

where ε_{2j} is the term that measures the surprises in the returns of Stock *j* in Market 2. These surprises are normally distributed; their mean is zero. The standard deviation of ε_{1i} and ε_{2j} for any two stocks, *i* and *j*, is 20 percent.

a. If the correlation between the surprises in the returns of any two stocks in the first market is zero and if the correlation between the surprises in the returns of any two stocks in the second market is zero, in which market would a risk-averse person prefer to invest? (*Note*: The correlation between ε_{1i} and ε_{1j} for any i and j is zero, and the correlation between ε_{2i} and ε_{2j} for any i and j is zero.)

b. If the correlation between ε_{1i} and ε_{1j} in the first market is .9 and the correlation between ε_{2i} and ε_{2j} in the second market is zero, in which market would a risk-averse person prefer to invest?

c. If the correlation between ε_{1i} and ε_{1j} in the first market is zero and the correlation between ε_{2i} and ε_{2j} in the second market is .5, in which market would a risk-averse person prefer to invest?

d. In general, what is the relationship between the correlations of the disturbances in the two markets that would make a risk-averse person equally willing to invest in either of the two markets?

9. **APT** Assume that the following market model adequately describes the return-generating behavior of risky assets:

$$R_{it} = \alpha_i + \beta_i R_{Mt} + \varepsilon_{it}$$

Where:

R_{it} = The return on the ith asset at Time t.
R_{Mt} = The return on a portfolio containing all risky assets in some proportion at Time t.
R_{Mt} and ε_{it} are statistically independent.

Short selling (i.e., negative positions) is allowed in the market. You are given the following information:

Asset	β_i	E(R_i)	Var(ε_i)
A	.7	8.41%	.0100
B	1.2	12.06	.0144
C	1.5	13.95	.0225

The variance of the market is .0121, and there are no transaction costs.

a. Calculate the standard deviation of returns for each asset.

b. Calculate the variance of return of three portfolios containing an infinite number of asset types A, B, or C, respectively.

c. Assume the risk-free rate is 3.3 percent and the expected return on the market is 10.6 percent. Which asset will not be held by rational investors?

d. What equilibrium state will emerge such that no arbitrage opportunities exist? Why?

10. **APT** Assume that the returns on individual securities are generated by the following two-factor model:

$$R_{it} = \mathrm{E}(R_{it}) + \beta_{ij}F_{1t} + \beta_{i2}F_{2t}$$

Here:

R_{it} is the return on Security i at Time t.
F_{1t} and F_{2t} are market factors with zero expectation and zero covariance.

In addition, assume that there is a capital market for four securities and the capital market for these four assets is perfect in the sense that there are no transaction costs and short sales (i.e., negative positions) are permitted. The characteristics of the four securities follow:

Security	β_1	β_2	E(R)
1	1.0	1.5	20%
2	.5	2.0	20
3	1.0	.5	10
4	1.5	.75	10

a. Construct a portfolio containing (long or short) Securities 1 and 2, with a return that does not depend on the market factor, F_{1t}, in any way. (*Hint:* Such a portfolio will have $\beta_1 = 0$.) Compute the expected return and β_2 coefficient for this portfolio.
b. Following the procedure in part (*a*), construct a portfolio containing Securities 3 and 4 with a return that does not depend on the market factor, F_{1t}. Compute the expected return and β_2 coefficient for this portfolio.
c. There is a risk-free asset with an expected return equal to 5 percent, $\beta_1 = 0$, and $\beta_2 = 0$. Describe a possible arbitrage opportunity in such detail that an investor could implement it.
d. What effect would the existence of these kinds of arbitrage opportunities have on the capital markets for these securities in the short run and long run? Graph your analysis.

Excel Master It! Problem

Excel Master coverage online

The Fama-French three-factor model has become a popular APT model. However, another model, called the Carhart four-factor model, also has been proposed (Mark Carhart, "On Persistence in Mutual Fund Performance," *Journal of Finance* 52 (1997): 57–82). In the four-factor model, the first three factors are the same as in the Fama-French three-factor model. The fourth factor is momentum. The momentum factor is constructed by the monthly return difference between the returns on the high and low prior return portfolios.

The factors for the four-factor model are available on Kenneth French's website (**www.dartmouth.edu/~kfrench**). Note that there is a file for the three-factor model as well as a separate file for the momentum factor.

1. The data files are zipped. You will need to open the Zip file, save the text file, and then open the text file in Excel. Make sure you download the monthly factors. The Text Import Wizard in Excel will walk you through the steps necessary to import the text files into columns. When you get the data table set up, estimate the four-factor model and answer the following questions for the stock and mutual fund you selected in the previous chapter.
   a. Would you expect the explanatory power of the four-factor regression to be higher or lower than the market model regression from the previous chapter? Why?
   b. Are the alpha and betas for each regression statistically different from zero?
   c. How do you interpret the betas for each independent variable for the stock and the mutual fund?
   d. Which of the two regression estimates has the highest R squared? Is this what you would have expected? Why?

Mini Case

THE FAMA-FRENCH MULTIFACTOR MODEL AND MUTUAL FUND RETURNS

Tashiro Shinji, an investment broker, has been approached by client Jack Thomas about the risk of his investments. Tashiro has recently read several articles concerning the risk factors that can potentially affect asset returns, and she has decided to examine Jack's mutual fund holdings. Jack is currently invested in the Fidelity Magellan Fund (FMAGX), the Fidelity Low-Priced Stock Fund (FLPSX), and the Baron Small Cap Fund (BSCFX).

Tashiro would like to apply the well-known multifactor model proposed by Eugene Fama and Ken French to determine the risk of each mutual fund. The regression equation for the multifactor model she proposes to use is:

$$R_{it} - R_{Ft} = \alpha_i + \beta_1(R_{Mt} - R_{Ft}) + \beta_2(\text{SMB}_t) + \beta_3(\text{HML}_t) + \varepsilon_t$$

In the regression equation, R_{it} is the return on Asset i at Time t, R_{Ft} is the risk-free rate at Time t, and R_{Mt} is the return on the market at Time t. The first risk factor in the Fama-French regression is the market factor often used with the CAPM.

The second risk factor, SMB, or "small minus big," is calculated by taking the difference in the returns on a portfolio of small-cap stocks and a portfolio of large-cap stocks. This factor is intended to pick up the so-called small-firm effect. Similarly, the third factor, HML, or "high minus low," is calculated by taking the difference in the returns between a portfolio of "value" stocks and a portfolio of "growth" stocks. Stocks with low market-to-book ratios are classified as value stocks and vice versa for growth stocks. This factor is included because of the historical tendency for value stocks to earn a higher return.

In models such as the one Tashiro is considering, the alpha (α) term is of particular interest. It is the regression intercept; but more important, it is also the excess return the asset earned. In other words, if the alpha is positive, the asset earned a return greater than it should have given its level of risk; if the alpha is negative, the asset earned a return lower than it should have given its level of risk. This measure is called "Jensen's alpha," and it is a widely used tool for mutual fund evaluation.

1. For a large-company stock mutual fund, would you expect the betas to be positive or negative for each of the factors in a Fama-French multifactor model?
2. The Fama-French factors and risk-free rates are available at Ken French's website: **www.dartmouth.edu/~kfrench**. Download the monthly factors and save the most recent 60 months for each factor. The historical prices for each of the mutual funds can be found on various websites, including **finance.yahoo.com**. Find the prices of each mutual fund for the same time as the Fama-French factors and calculate the returns for each month. Be sure to include dividends. For each mutual fund, estimate the multifactor regression equation using the Fama-French factors. How well do the regression estimates explain the variation in the return of each mutual fund?
3. What do you observe about the beta coefficients for the different mutual funds? Comment on any similarities or differences.
4. If the market is efficient, what value would you expect for alpha? Do your estimates support market efficiency?
5. Which fund has performed best considering its risk? Why?

13

Risk, Cost of Capital, and Valuation

With more than 117,000 employees on five continents, Germany-based BASF is a major international business. The company operates in a variety of industries, including agriculture, oil and gas, chemicals, and plastics. BASF uses value-based management, a comprehensive plan that includes all functions within the company and challenges and encourages all employees to act in an entrepreneurial manner. The major financial component of the strategy is that the company expects to earn its weighted average cost of capital, or WACC, plus a premium. So, what exactly is the WACC?

The WACC is the minimum return a company needs to earn to satisfy all of its investors, including stockholders, bondholders, and preferred stockholders. In 2021, for example, BASF pegged its cost of capital at 9 percent, the same value that is used in 2020, but slightly lower than the 10 percent WACC that it used during 2019. In this chapter, we learn how to compute a firm's cost of capital and find out what it means to the firm and its investors. We also will learn when to use the firm's cost of capital and, perhaps more important, when not to use it.

Please visit us at **rwjcorporatefinance.blogspot.com** for the latest developments in the world of corporate finance.

13.1 The Cost of Capital

Whenever a firm has extra cash, it can take one of two actions. It can pay out the cash directly to its investors, or it can invest the extra cash in a project, paying out the future cash flows of the project. Which action would the investors prefer? If investors can reinvest the cash in a financial asset (a stock or bond) with the same risk as that of the project, the investors would desire the alternative with the higher expected return. In other words, the project should be undertaken only if its expected return is greater than that of a financial asset of comparable risk. This idea is illustrated in Figure 13.1.

Our discussion implies a simple capital budgeting rule:

The discount rate for a project should be the expected return on a financial asset of comparable risk.

It is a common error to forget this crucial point and fall into the trap of thinking that the discount rate for an investment depends primarily on how and where the capital is raised.

There are various synonyms for the discount rate, often called the *required return* on the project. This is an appropriate name because the project should be accepted only if the project generates an

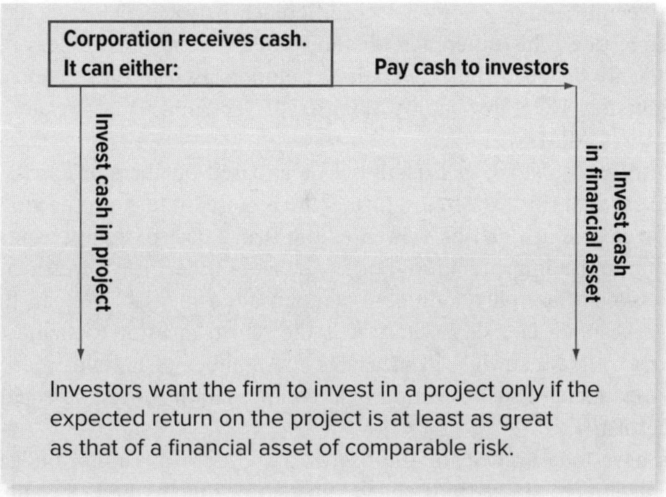

Figure 13.1 Choices of a Firm with Extra Cash

expected return above what is required. Alternatively, the discount rate for a project is said to be its *cost of capital.* This name is also appropriate because the project must earn enough to pay its suppliers of capital. Our book will use these three terms–the discount rate, the required return, and the cost of capital–synonymously.

The appropriate discount rate for any project should reflect the project's risks. In some cases, it is reasonable to assume that a new project will have the same risk properties as the firm as a whole, for example, when the firm is considering an expansion of its existing operations. If so, the discount rate for the project should equal the cost of capital for the firm as a whole. And, if the firm is all equity, the discount rate is also equal to the firm's cost of equity capital.

13.2 Estimating the Cost of Equity Capital with the CAPM

In this section, we will discuss how to compute the cost of equity capital, which is the required return on a stockholder's investment in the firm. For the simple case in which a firm is 100 percent equity financed, and we are valuing a project that is similar in risk to the firm's existing operations, the firm's cost of equity capital is also the project's cost of capital. In later sections, we will discuss how to estimate the project's cost of capital if leverage is involved or if the project differs in risk from the firm's existing operations.

The problem with estimating the cost of equity capital is that stockholders do not tell the firm what their required returns are. What can we do instead? Luckily, the capital asset pricing model (CAPM) can be used to estimate the required return.

Under the CAPM, the expected return on stock can be written as:

$$R_S = R_F + \beta \times (R_M - R_F) \qquad \textbf{(13.1)}$$

where R_F is the risk-free rate and $R_M - R_F$ is the difference between the expected return on the market portfolio and the risk-free rate. This difference is often called the expected excess market return or market risk premium. Note that we dropped the expectations notation used in the version of the CAPM that was first introduced in Equation 11.15 to simplify things, but remember that we are always thinking about expected returns with the CAPM.

The expected return on the stock in Equation 13.1 is based on the stock's risk, as measured by beta. Alternatively, we could say that this expected return is the required return on the stock, based on the stock's risk. Similarly, this expected return can be viewed as the firm's cost of equity capital.

The CAPM has an intuitive interpretation. For any stock or other risky investment, investors will require a return equal to the risk-free rate plus additional compensation for risk. We can think of the market risk premium, $R_M - R_F$, as the price of risk, because it is the return investors demand above the risk-free rate for one "unit" of market risk. Meanwhile, β measures the number of units of market risk associated with the specific stock or investment. Thus, the additional compensation for risk is equal to the amount of risk multiplied by the price of risk.

While academics have long argued for the use of the CAPM in capital budgeting, how prevalent is this approach in practice? One study finds that almost three-fourths of U.S. companies use the CAPM in capital budgeting, indicating that industry has largely adopted this approach. Likewise, this is the case in India.[1]

We now have the tools to estimate a firm's cost of equity capital. To do this, we need to know three things:

- The risk-free rate, R_F
- The market risk premium, $R_M - R_F$
- The stock beta, β

EXAMPLE 13.1

Cost of Equity Suppose the stock of the Charminar Company, a publisher of college textbooks, has a beta of 1.3. The firm is 100 percent equity financed. Charminar is considering a number of capital budgeting projects that will double its size. Because these new projects are similar to the firm's existing ones, the average beta on the new projects is assumed to be equal to Charminar's existing beta. The risk-free rate is 5 percent. What is the appropriate discount rate for these new projects if the market risk premium is 8.4 percent?

We estimate the cost of equity, R_S, for Charminar as:

$$\begin{aligned} R_S &= .05 + 1.3 \times .084 \\ &= .05 + .1092 \\ &= .1592, \text{ or } 15.92\% \end{aligned}$$

Two key assumptions were made in this example: (1) The beta risk of the new projects is the same as the risk of the firm and (2) the firm is all-equity financed. Given these assumptions, it follows that the cash flows of the new projects should be discounted at 15.92 percent.

[1]Refer: (a) Manoj Anand, "Corporate Finance Practices in India: A Survey", *Vikalpa,* Vol. 27, No. 4, October–December 2002; (b) Komera, Surenderrao, and P. J. Jijo Lukose, "Heterogeneity and asymmetry in speed of leverage adjustment: The Indian experience," Review of Pacific Basin Financial Markets and Policies, 19.03 (2016): 1650019;

EXAMPLE 13.2

Project Evaluation and Beta Suppose Garuda Air Freight is an all-equity firm with a beta of 1.21. The market risk premium is 9.5 percent and the risk-free rate is 5 percent. We can determine the expected return on the common stock of Garuda Air Freight from Equation 13.1. We find that the expected return is:

$$.05 + 1.21 \times .095 = .16495, \text{ or } 16.495\%$$

Because this is the return that shareholders can expect in the financial markets on a stock with a β of 1.21, it is the return they expect on Garuda Air Freight's stock.

Suppose Garuda is evaluating the following independent projects:

Project	Project's Beta (β)	Project's Expected Cash Flows Next Year	Project's Internal Rate of Return	Project's NPV When Cash Flows Are Discounted at 16.495%	Accept or Reject
A	1.21	₹140	40%	₹20.2	Accept
B	1.21	120	20	3.0	Accept
C	1.21	110	10	−5.6	Reject

Each project initially costs ₹100. All projects are assumed to have the same risk as the firm as a whole. Because the cost of equity capital is 16.495 percent, projects in an all-equity firm are discounted at this rate. Projects A and B have positive NPVs and Project C has a negative NPV, so only A and B will be accepted. This result is illustrated in Figure 13.2.

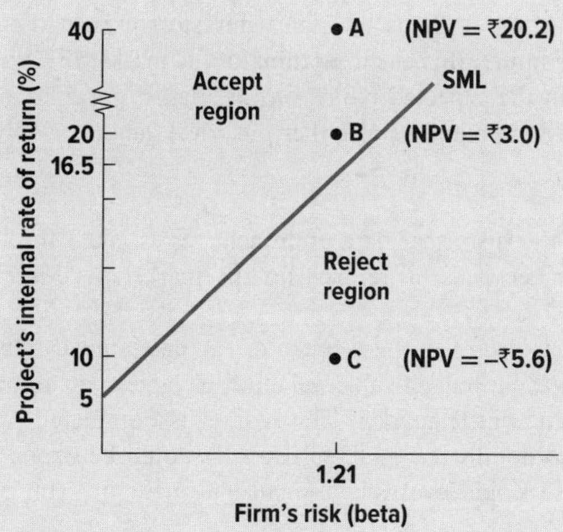

The diagonal line, called the security market line, is a graphical depiction of the CAPM and represents the relationship between the cost of equity capital and the firm's beta. An all-equity firm should accept a project whose internal rate of return is greater than the cost of equity capital and should reject a project whose internal rate of return is less than the cost of equity capital. This graph assumes that all projects are as risky as the firm.

Figure 13.2 Using the Security Market Line to Estimate the Risk-Adjusted Discount Rate for Risky Projects

In the above two examples, the values for the risk-free rate, the market risk premium, and the firm's beta were assumed. How would we go about estimating these parameters in practice? We will investigate each of these parameters in turn.

THE RISK-FREE RATE

The risk-free rate, R_F, is the first term in the CAPM equation. It should ideally be the current prevailing yield on a risk-free security with the same maturity as the cash flows of the stock or investment being valued. In practice, we will try to get as close as possible to this ideal using available data on traded safe securities.

While no bond is completely free of the risk of default, U.S. Treasury bills and bonds in India and the United States are very close to risk-free. No Indian and U.S. Treasury instrument has ever defaulted and, at the present time, no instrument is considered to be in danger of a future default. If you are doing international valuations, it is common practice to use a government (sovereign) bond in the local currency for a risk-free rate. Of course, some foreign government bonds are not actually risk-free, so the approximation will be less exact in those situations.

To estimate the risk-free rate, we first need to find a traded safe security whose maturity approximately matches the maturity of the cash flows of the firm or project being valued. For example, if we are trying to apply the CAPM to the equity of a long-lived U.S. firm or project, we would use the yield on a 20- or 30-year U.S. Treasury bond. Second, we need to be careful to use the bond's current prevailing yield, rather than its historical average yield. The first R_F in the CAPM equation represents the risk-free return investors expect to earn in the future, and this expectation is better represented by the current prevailing yield than by historical averages.

Yields for Treasury bills and bonds can be found under the data link at **www.treasury.gov/resource-center/data-chart-center/interest-rates/pages/textview.aspx?data=yield.**

MARKET RISK PREMIUM

As mentioned in Chapter 10, the market risk premium, $R_M - R_F$, is the return investors expect to earn on the market portfolio in excess of the risk-free rate in the future. It is useful to think of the market risk premium as a single quantity representing the difference between the expected return on the market portfolio and the risk-free rate. In practice, we can estimate the market risk premium using either historical data or the dividend discount model.

Method 1: Using Historical Data Under the historical data approach, we estimate the market risk premium using the historical average difference between the returns on the market portfolio and a risk-free security.

To estimate the historical average market return, we can use the average of the past annual returns of a market-value-weighted or large-company portfolio. Why a market-value-weighted or large-company portfolio? We are interested in a proxy for the return of the entire market. The market is dominated by large firms, so we need the return of a portfolio that is also dominated by large firms. It would be wrong to use an equally weighted portfolio because such a portfolio would overweight small and medium firms relative to their true weights in the market.

We also need to consider whether to use a long or short time series to compute the historical average. A longer time series gives us more data, but a shorter and more recent time series may give us a better approximation of what to expect in the future. In practice, it is common to use the return of firms in the S&P 500 (a large-company index) over the past 50 or more years.

Ultimately, we care about the historical average difference between the returns on the market portfolio and a risk-free security, so we need to compute the average risk-free return over the same historical period. For example, if we used the past 50 years of data to compute the market return, we should estimate the average risk-free rate over the same time period.

Note that when using this historical data approach, our estimates for the two R_F values in the CAPM equation will not be the same. As a reminder, the first R_F is the expected risk-free rate in the future, and for that we should use the current prevailing yield. The second R_F is part of the market risk premium, which we estimate as a single quantity representing the difference between the expected market return in excess of the risk-free rate. When we estimate the market risk premium using historical data, we estimate the second R_F using historical average yields.

To apply the historical data approach, we can refer to Chapter 10, which presented data for historical market and risk-free returns over various horizons. At the end of that chapter, we mentioned that 7 percent is a reasonable estimate of the market risk premium relative to the one-year Treasury bill. If we are instead valuing a long-term project or firm, we are comfortable with a market risk premium of about 6 percent (this is the difference in average historical returns on large-company stocks relative to long-term government bonds in Table 10.2). These numbers are only meant to be a rough guide. Your own estimate of the market risk premium may be higher or lower depending on how much historical data you choose to use and your choice of maturity for the risk-free asset.

Method 2: Using the Dividend Discount Model (DDM) We can also estimate the market risk premium using the dividend discount model. In Chapter 9, we pointed out that the price of a share of stock is equal to the present value of all of its future dividends. We then noted that if the firm's dividends are expected to grow at a constant rate, g, the current price of a share of stock, P_0, can be written as:

$$P_0 = \frac{D_1}{R_S - g}$$

where D_1 is the dividend per share expected next year, R_S is the discount rate or cost of equity, and g is the constant annual rate of expected growth in dividends. This equation can be rearranged, yielding:

$$R_S = \frac{D_1}{P_0} + g$$

In words, the annual expected return on a stock is the sum of the dividend yield ($= D_1/P_0$) over the next year plus the annual expected growth rate in dividends.

Just as this formula can be used to estimate the total expected return on a stock, it can be used to estimate the total expected return on the market as a whole. The first term on the right-hand side is easy to estimate because a number of print and internet services calculate the dividend yield for the market. For example, in late 2020, the average dividend yield for the S&P 500 Index as a whole was about 1.8 percent. Similarly, the average dividend yield across all stocks in the S&P BSE 500 Index was about 1.12 percent. We will use this number in our estimates.

Next, we need an estimate of the per-share growth rate in dividends across all companies in the market. Value Line (VL) is one well-known supplier of such estimates. Suppose the numbers in the VL *Investment Survey* in the U.S. imply a five-year growth rate in dividends for VL's Industrial Composite Index of about 6 percent per year. With a dividend yield of 1.8 percent, the expected return on the market becomes 1.8% + 6% = 7.8%. Of course, Value Line is just one source for forecasts. More likely, a firm would either rely on a consensus of many forecasts or use its own growth estimate.

Next, we need to subtract out the risk-free rate to estimate the market return over the risk-free rate. Unlike the historical data approach, the DDM approach is forward looking. Instead of using the historical average risk-free rate, we should use the current prevailing yield on a risk-free asset of similar maturity to the cash flows of the asset being valued. Thus, under the DDM approach, we can use the same risk-free estimate for both R_F variables in the CAPM equation. If we are valuing a long-lived project, and the current prevailing yield on 30-year U.S. Treasury bonds is 1.4 percent, the market risk premium would be 7.8% − 1.4% = 6.4%.

For a firm with a beta of 1.5, the cost of capital becomes:

$$.014 + 1.5 \times .064 = .11, \text{ or } 11\%$$

Similarly, in India, the 2 year consensus for growth rate in dividends for NSE 50 index is about 14–16 percent per year. Assuming a lower number of 14 percent and a dividend yield of 1.5 percent, the expected return on the market becomes 1.5% + 14% = 15.5%. Given our anticipated average one-year yield on Indian Treasury bills of 7 percent, the Indian market risk premium would be 15.5% − 7% = 8.5%.

For our Indian firm with a beta of 1.5, the cost of capital becomes:

$$7\% + (1.5 \times 8.5\%) = 19.75\%$$

Academics have long preferred the historical estimated market risk premium for its statistical objectivity. By contrast, estimation of future dividend growth in the DDM seems more error-prone. However, DDM can help to discipline our estimates of the market risk premium because returns in the long run can only come from the current dividend yield and future dividend growth. Anyone who thinks that long-run stock returns will exceed the sum of these two components is fooling herself.[2]

13.3 Estimation of Beta

In the previous section, we assumed that the beta of the company was known. Of course, beta must be estimated in the real world. We pointed out earlier that the beta of a security is the standardized covariance of a security's return with the return on the market portfolio. As we have seen, the formula for Security i is:

$$\text{Beta of Security } i = \frac{\text{Cov}(R_i, R_M)}{\text{Var}(R_M)} = \frac{\sigma_{i,M}}{\sigma_M^2} \tag{13.2}$$

In words, the beta is the covariance of a security with the market, divided by the variance of the market.

To estimate beta, it is standard practice to use data on the stock's monthly total returns for the past five years along with the monthly total returns of the S&P 500 Index as a proxy for the return of the market portfolio. The choice of interval length and time period is flexible. Some practitioners instead use weekly returns over the past one or two years. This latter approach may be preferred if we are considering a stock that has only recently started trading or if we believe that the stock's beta is changing over time, so more recent data would offer a better estimate of future beta.

Once we have assembled the data, we can estimate beta in two ways. First, we can directly compute the covariance of the stock's return with market returns and divide by the variance of market return. Alternatively, we can estimate a stock's beta by regressing its returns on the returns of the market portfolio. The regression coefficient on the market returns gives us an estimate of beta.

REAL-WORLD BETAS

It is helpful to see how betas are determined for actual real-world companies. Figure 13.3 plots monthly returns for four large firms against monthly returns on the S&P 500 Index. Using a standard regression technique, we fit a straight line through the data points. The result is called the *characteristic line* for the

[2]For example, see Jay R. Ritter, "The Biggest Mistakes We Teach," *Journal of Financial Research* 25, no. 2 (June 2002): 159–68; Eugene F. Fama and Kenneth R. French, "The Equity Premium," *Journal of Finance* 57, no. 2 (April 2002): 637–59; Ravi Jagannathan, Ellen R. McGrattan, and Anna Scherbina, "The Declining U.S. Equity Premium," *Federal Reserve Bank of Minneapolis Quarterly Review* 24, no. 4 (Fall 2000): 3–19.

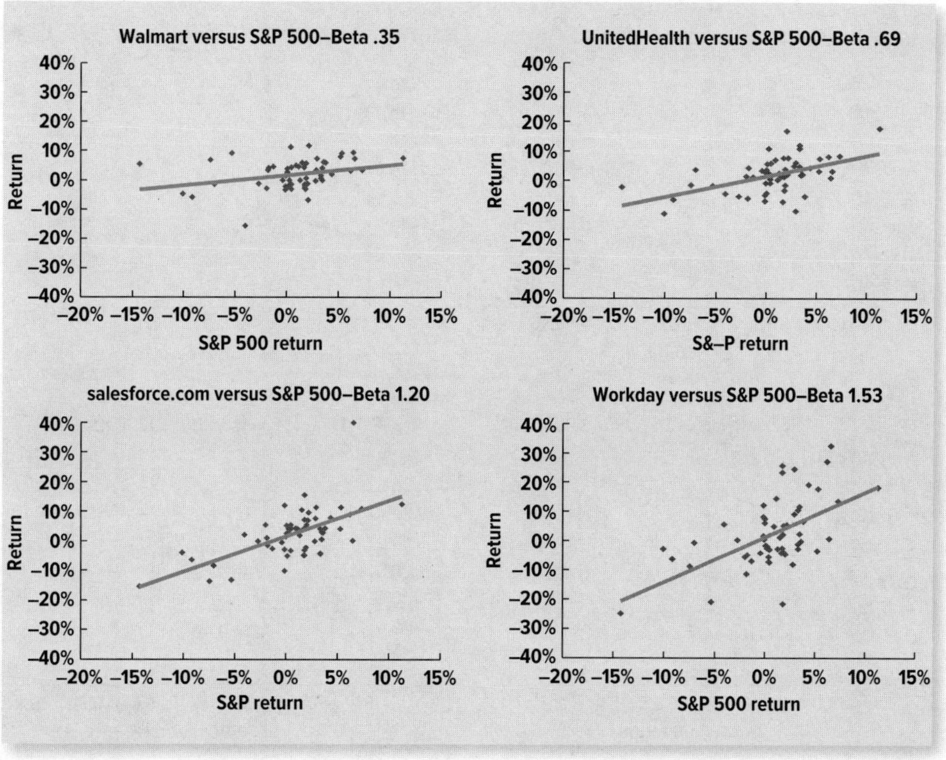

Figure 13.3 Plots of Five Years of Monthly Returns (2016–2020) on Four Individual Securities against Five Years of Monthly Returns on the S&P 500 Index

security. The slope of the characteristic line is the regression coefficient on the market return, and it gives us the estimate of beta. Though we have not shown it in the table, we also can determine the intercept, commonly called Garuda, of the characteristic line by regression.

We use five years of monthly data for each plot. Although this choice is arbitrary, it is in line with calculations performed in the real world. Practitioners know that the accuracy of the beta coefficient is suspect when too few observations are used. Conversely, because firms may change their business strategies over time, observations from the distant past are out of date.

We know that the average value-weighted beta across all stocks should equal 1. Of course, the beta of any individual stock could be higher or lower. Of the four securities in our figure, two have betas above 1 and two have betas below 1. Because beta is a measure of the risk of a single security for someone holding a large, diversified portfolio, our results indicate that Hindustan Unilever and Procter & Gamble have relatively lower risk and SJVN and Karnataka Bank have relatively high risk.

STABILITY OF BETA

A firm's beta may change over time, as its business strategies evolve, leading to changes in how its returns covary with the market. Figure 13.4 plots the returns on Microsoft against the returns on the S&P 500 for four consecutive five-year periods. As the figure shows, Microsoft's beta varies from period to period. Microsoft's beta was high in the first period, dropped to just above 1 in the second period, and became stable around .88 over the past decade.

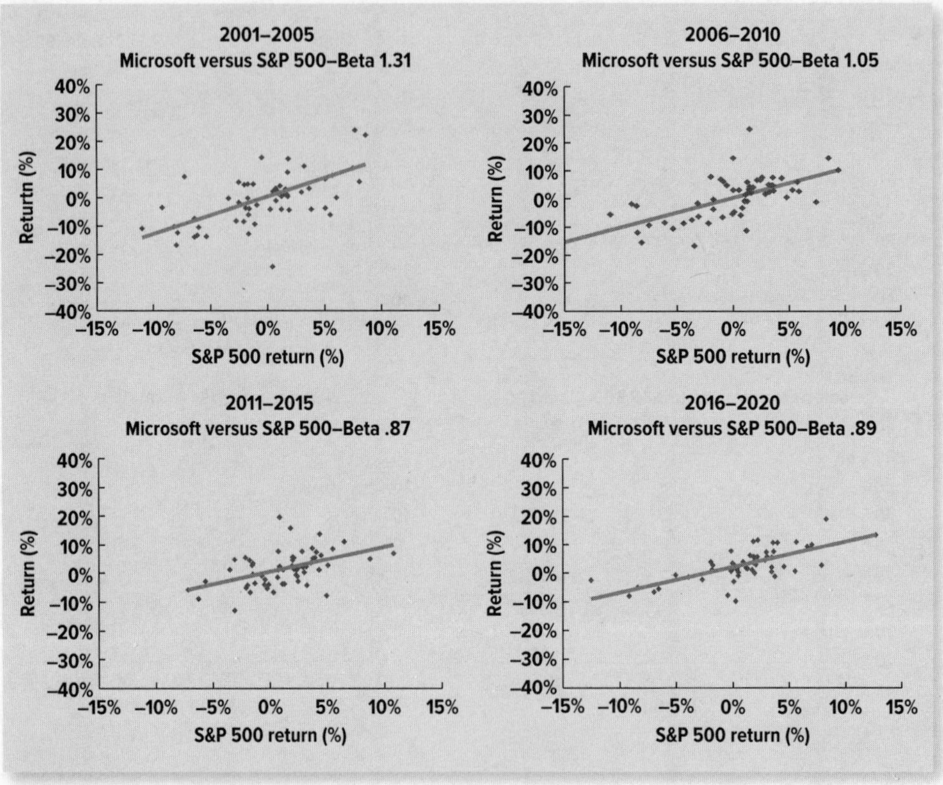

Figure 13.4 Plots of Monthly Returns on Microsoft against Returns on the S&P 500 Index for Four Consecutive Five-Year Periods

Some of this movement in beta is probably just random variation. However, this is not to say that a firm's beta will never change. Changes in product line, changes in technology, or changes in the market may affect a firm's beta. Furthermore, as we will show in a later section, an increase in a firm's leverage (i.e., the amount of debt in its capital structure) will increase the firm's beta.

Reliance Industries Limited (RIL) is an excellent example of a change in industry structure and market leading to a change in beta. The beta for RIL in 2009-12, 2013-16 and 2017-20 were 0.61, 0.45 and 0.34, respectively. The changes in the beta values can be attributed to the changing business mix of RIL over the years, as it added retail, telecom and digital services under its fold. For example, retail business accounted for 1 percent of RIL revenues in 2007-08. By 2015-16, the retail business contributed 6 percent of revenue, which further jumped to 27 percent by 2020-21.

13.4 Determinants of Beta

Why do some firms have higher betas than others? Of course, the beta of a stock does not come out of thin air. Rather, it is determined by the characteristics of the firm. Here we consider two factors, the cyclical nature of revenues and operating leverage, which depend on the firm's real operations (the set of projects on the asset side of a firm's balance sheet). In the next section, we will show how two firms with identical operations can still differ in their betas due to differences in the amount of debt on the liabilities side of the balance sheet.

CYCLICALITY OF REVENUES

The revenues of some firms are quite cyclical. These firms do well in the expansion phase of the business cycle and poorly in the contraction phase. Empirical evidence suggests high-tech firms, retailers, and automotive firms fluctuate with the business cycle. Firms in industries such as utilities, railroads, and food are less dependent on the cycle. Because beta measures the responsiveness of a stock's return to the market's return, it is not surprising that highly cyclical stocks have high betas.

It is worthwhile to point out that cyclicality is not the same as variability. A moviemaking firm has highly variable revenues because hits and flops are not easily predicted. However, because the revenues of a studio are more dependent on the quality of its releases than the phase of the business cycle, motion picture companies are not particularly cyclical. In other words, stocks with high standard deviations need not have high betas, a point we have stressed before.

OPERATING LEVERAGE

We distinguished fixed costs from variable costs in Chapter 7. We mentioned that fixed costs do not change as quantity changes. Conversely, variable costs increase as the quantity of output rises. Firms often face a trade-off between fixed and variable costs. A firm can build its own factory, incurring a high level of fixed costs in the process. Alternatively, the firm can outsource production to a supplier, typically generating lower fixed costs but higher variable costs. Fixed costs tend to magnify the impact of sales cyclicality. Fixed costs must be paid, even at a low level of sales, leaving the firm with the possibility of large losses. And with fixed costs replacing variable costs, any additional sales generate low marginal costs, leaving the firm with a substantial increase in profit.

Firms with high fixed costs and low variable costs are generally said to have high **operating leverage**. Conversely, firms with low fixed costs and high variable costs have low operating leverage. For example, among automakers, BMW loses ₹.43 for every rupee of lost sales, which of course means that the company gains ₹.43 for every increased rupee of sales. In contrast, Fiat Chrysler's operating leverage is about 18 percent, GM's is about 20 percent, and Ford's is about 25 percent. As a result, we would expect BMW's earnings to be more volatile when compared to other auto companies. Operating leverage magnifies the effect of the cyclicality of a firm's revenues on beta. That is, a firm with a given sales cyclicality will increase its beta if fixed costs replace variable costs in its production process.

FINANCIAL LEVERAGE AND BETA

When people talk about a firm's beta, they typically mean the firm's equity beta, which represents the beta of the firm's stock. We follow that convention in this book. In this section, we will introduce the notion of a beta for assets and show how it relates to the equity beta. Suppose two firms have identical sets of projects on the asset sides of their balance sheets. Given that the two firms have identical assets, they would also have the same **asset beta**. An asset beta measures the sensitivity of the value of a firm's assets to changes in the value of the market portfolio.

Holding the firm's assets constant, the firm's equity beta will increase with its financial leverage (the amount of debt on the liabilities side of its balance sheet). Financial leverage increases the firm's equity beta because debt has higher seniority in the capital structure than equity. A firm must make interest payments to its debtholders before it can make any dividend payments to its stockholders. When cash flows are low, interest payments must still be paid, leaving less cash that can be paid to stockholders. When cash flows are high, interest payments remain fixed, so the cash flows left for stockholders increase. Thus, financial leverage amplifies the return fluctuations of the equity, and it thereby increases the equity beta.

Note that financial leverage and operating leverage (which we introduced in Section 13.3) are similar concepts. Operating leverage refers to the firm's fixed costs of production. Financial leverage is the extent to which a firm relies on debt, and a levered firm is a firm with some debt in its capital structure. Because a levered firm must make interest payments regardless of the firm's sales, financial leverage refers to the firm's fixed costs of finance. Increases in operating leverage and increases in financial leverage both act to increase a firm's equity beta.

To see exactly how financial leverage affects the firm's equity beta, consider a firm with some debt and some equity in its capital structure. Imagine an individual who owns all the firm's debt and all its equity. In other words, this individual owns the entire firm. What is the beta of her portfolio of the firm's debt and equity?

As with any portfolio, the beta of this portfolio is a weighted average of the betas of the individual items in the portfolio. Let B stand for the market value of the firm's debt and S stand for the market value of the firm's equity. We have:

$$\beta_{\text{Portfolio}} = \beta_{\text{Asset}} = \frac{S}{B+S} \times \beta_{\text{Equity}} + \frac{B}{B+S} \times \beta_{\text{Debt}} \tag{13.3}$$

where β_{Equity} is the beta of the stock of the levered firm, that is, its equity beta. Notice that the debt beta, β_{Debt}, is multiplied by $B/(B + S)$, the percentage of debt in the capital structure. Similarly, the equity beta is multiplied by the percentage of equity in the capital structure. Because the portfolio contains both the debt of the firm and the equity of the firm, the portfolio is a claim to all the assets of the firm. Thus, the portfolio beta is the asset beta, and its value is dependent only on the assets of the firm.

The debt beta is very low in practice because debt has seniority over equity in the firm's capital structure, so the returns to debt are relatively stable and less sensitive to changes in the market portfolio. If we make the common assumption that the debt beta is zero (or very close to zero), we have:

$$\beta_{\text{Asset}} = \beta_{\text{Equity}} \times \frac{S}{B+S} \tag{13.4}$$

Because $S/(B + S)$ must be below 1 for a levered firm, it follows that $\beta_{\text{Asset}} < \beta_{\text{Equity}}$. Rearranging this equation, we have:

$$\beta_{\text{Equity}} = \beta_{\text{Asset}}\left(1 + \frac{B}{S}\right) \tag{13.5}$$

If the firm is 100 percent equity financed, the equity beta is the same as the asset beta. As the *debt-equity ratio* (B/S) increases, the equity beta will always be greater than the asset beta (assuming the asset beta is positive). In other words, the equity beta of a levered firm will always be greater than the equity beta of an otherwise identical all-equity firm.

Which beta does regression analysis estimate: the asset beta or the equity beta? A regression of stock returns on the market return, as performed in Section 13.3 and also in the real world, provides us with an equity beta because the technique uses stock returns as inputs. We must transform this equity beta using Equation 13.4 to arrive at the asset beta. Of course, the two betas are the same for an all-equity firm.

EXAMPLE 13.3

Asset versus Equity Betas Consider a floriculture company, Rewanchal Hariyali Limited, that is currently all equity and has a beta of .8. The firm has decided to move to a capital structure of one part debt to two parts equity. Because the firm does not plan to change its business operations, its asset beta should remain at .8. Assuming a zero beta for its debt, its equity beta would become:

$$\beta_{\text{Equity}} = \beta_{\text{Asset}}\left(1 + \frac{B}{S}\right)$$

$$1.2 = .8\left(1 + \frac{1}{2}\right)$$

(continued)

If the firm had one part debt to one part equity in its capital structure, its equity beta would be:

$$1.6 = .8(1 + 1)$$

However, as long as it does not change its business operations, its asset beta would remain at .8. The effect of leverage is to increase the equity beta.

BETA IN A WORLD WITH TAXES

In a world with corporate taxes, financing with debt changes the project's value because interest payments are usually tax deductible, which reduces taxes owed and increases overall project cash flow. This is a concept that we will cover in greater detail in later chapters. For now, we introduce an alternative formula for the relation between asset and equity betas. In a world with corporate taxes T_C, in which we assume the tax savings have the same risk as the debt, the relation among the asset, equity, and debt betas can be expressed as:

$$\beta_{\text{Portfolio}} = \beta_{\text{Asset}} = \frac{S}{B \times (1 - T_C) + S} \times \beta_{\text{Equity}} + \frac{B \times (1 - T_C)}{B \times (1 - T_C) + S} \times \beta_{\text{Debt}} \tag{13.6}$$

If we again assume that the debt beta is zero, we have:

$$\beta_{\text{Equity}} = \beta_{\text{Asset}}\left[1 + (1 - T_C)\frac{B}{S}\right] \tag{13.7}$$

In most examples in this book, we will use Equations 13.6 and 13.7 to describe the relation between equity and asset betas in a world with corporate taxes. However, our readers should be aware that some firms continue to use Equations 13.3 and 13.4 despite operating in a world with corporate taxes. These firms are not necessarily wrong in doing so. It is correct to use the previous set of equations if the firm assumes that the tax savings are approximately as risky as the assets.

13.5 The Dividend Discount Model Approach

In Section 13.2, we showed how the CAPM could be used to determine a firm's cost of capital. Among other inputs, we needed an estimate of the market risk premium. One approach used the dividend discount model (DDM) to forecast the expected return on the market as a whole, leading to an estimate of this risk premium. We now use the DDM to estimate the expected return on an individual stock directly.

Our discussion in Section 13.2 on the DDM led to the following formula:

$$R_S = \frac{D_1}{P_0} + g$$

where P_0 is the current price per share of a stock, D_1 is the dividend per share to be received next year, R_S is the discount rate, and g is the expected annual growth rate in dividends per share. The equation tells us that the discount rate on a stock is equal to the sum of the stock's dividend yield ($= D_1/P_0$) and its expected growth rate of dividends. In order to apply the DDM to a particular stock, we must estimate both the dividend yield and the expected growth rate.

The dividend yield is relatively easy to forecast. Security analysts routinely provide forecasts of next year's dividend for many stocks. Alternatively, we can set next year's dividend as the product of last year's dividend and $1 + g$, using approaches to estimate g that we describe below. The price per share of any publicly traded stock can be found at various websites.

The expected growth rate of dividends can be estimated in one of three ways. First, we can calculate the firm's historical growth rate in dividends from past data. For some firms, this historical growth rate may be an acceptable, though clearly imperfect, estimate of the future growth rate. Second, in Chapter 9, we showed the growth rate in dividends can be expressed as:

$$g = \text{Retention ratio} \times \text{ROE}$$

where the retention ratio is the ratio of retained earnings to earnings and ROE stands for return on equity. Return on equity is the ratio of earnings to the accounting book value of the firm's equity. All the variables needed to estimate both the retention ratio and ROE can be found on a firm's income statement and balance sheet. Third, security analysts commonly provide forecasts of future growth. However, analysts' estimates are generally for five-year growth rates in earnings, while the DDM requires long-term growth rates in dividends.

As an example of the third approach, the consensus five-year forecast for annual earnings growth for Procter & Gamble reported on **finance.yahoo.com** in late 2020 was 7.7 percent. Assuming a constant payout ratio, this indicates a 7.7 percent expected growth rate for dividends. The company's dividend yield was 3.06 percent, implying an expected rate of return, and therefore a cost of equity capital, of 3.06% + 7.7% = 10.76% for P&G. On the same lines, the consensus five-year forecast for annual earnings growth was 7.75 percent for the Indian tobacco giant, ITC Limited. The company's dividend yield was 3.75 percent for the year 2023, implying an expected rate of return for ITC, and therefore a cost of equity capital, of 7.75% + 3.75% = 11.50% for ITC Limited.

The above discussion shows how one can use the DDM to estimate a firm's cost of capital. How accurate is this approach compared to the CAPM? We examine this question in the section below.

COMPARISON OF DDM AND CAPM

Both the dividend discount model and the capital asset pricing model are internally consistent models. Nevertheless, academics have generally favored the CAPM over the DDM. In addition, one study reported that slightly fewer than three-fourths of companies use the CAPM to estimate the cost of equity capital, while slightly fewer than one-sixth of companies use the dividend discount model to do so.[3] Why has the pendulum swung over to the CAPM? The CAPM has three primary advantages. First, it explicitly adjusts for risk. Second, it is applicable to companies that pay no dividends or whose dividend growth is difficult to estimate. Third, the CAPM can be used to estimate discount rates for projects or divisions that differ from the firm as a whole, as we will discuss in the next section. The primary advantage of the DDM is its simplicity. Unfortunately, the DDM does not explicitly consider risk and is only applicable to firms that pay steady dividends. Another drawback of the DDM is that it cannot be used to estimate discount rates for projects or divisions that differ from the firm as a whole.

While no one, to our knowledge, has done a systematic comparison of the two approaches, the DDM appears to contain more measurement error than does the CAPM. The problem is that estimating the growth rate in dividends for an individual company is prone to error regardless of which of our three approaches is used. In contrast, consider the calculation of the beta for the CAPM. Though there is clearly measurement error here as well, it is probably less than for *g*. While we have been critical of the DDM's practical application, it provides some important intuition and can be a useful check on the CAPM estimates.

[3]John R. Graham and Campbell R. Harvey, "How Do CFOs Make Capital Budgeting and Capital Structure Decisions?" *Journal of Applied Corporate Finance* 15, no. 1 (Spring 2002): 8–23.

BETA VARIES IN THE SAME SECTOR, BETA CHANGES WITH TIME

We present below the estimated betas in the Indian IT sector for select companies using two different time periods as mentioned below.

Company Name	Beta computed using daily 1-year return	Beta computed using weekly 5-year return
Birlasoft	1.10	1.21
Infosys Technologies	0.87	0.63
Mastek Limited	0.72	0.75
Sasken Technologies	0.74	1.37
Sonata Software	0.70	1.49
Tata Consultancy Services	0.73	0.71

Source: Authors' tabulations as on March 2024

We observe that Beta values are lower, reflecting in general the defensive nature of industry. For most companies, these values are different for different time periods. In practice, it is observed that Beta values have three asset-specific drivers (in our case, company-specific drivers) – namely, degree of operating leverage, degree of financial leverage, and the business risk. With time, many of these factors change. For example, the increasing resistance in the United States towards liberal H1-B visa policies reflects changed business risk perception for the top two IT giants (Infosys and TCS) in the list above. Overall, we also see the sector risk being less than one level compared to the rest of Indian businesses. This is due to highly stable business fortunes and near zero financial leverage. We also observe that Beta values vary for companies within the same industry. These differences are apparent for smaller companies above (namely, Sasken, Birlasoft and Sonata) compared to large sized players (Infosys and TCS).

13.6 Cost of Capital for Projects

Previous sections of this chapter considered the simple case when the risk of a project is equal to the risk of the existing firm. How should we estimate the discount rate for a project whose risk differs from that of the firm? The answer is that each project should be discounted at a rate commensurate with its own risk.

Let's assume that we use the CAPM to determine the discount rate. If a project's beta differs from that of the firm, the project's cash flows should be discounted at a rate commensurate with the project's own beta. This is an important point because firms frequently speak of a *corporate discount rate* or *hurdle rate.* (As mentioned earlier, discount rate, required return, and cost of capital are frequently used synonymously.) Unless all projects in the corporation are of the same risk, using the same discount rate for all projects is incorrect.

In this section, we'll discuss how to compute a project-specific discount rate, assuming the project is financed with 100 percent equity. If the firm plans to finance the project partly with debt, we will need to make further adjustments as explained later in this chapter.

EXAMPLE 13.4

Project Risk HT Media is a conglomerate firm with operations in publishing and computer software. It is considering whether to accept a new project in computer software. Noting that publishing is a low-beta business while computer software is a high-beta business, the conglomerate firm realizes it should discount the project at a rate commensurate with the risk of computer software. Instead, if all projects in HT Media were discounted at the same rate, a bias would result. The firm would accept too many high-risk projects (software ventures) and reject too many low-risk projects (books and magazines). This point is illustrated in Figure 13.5.

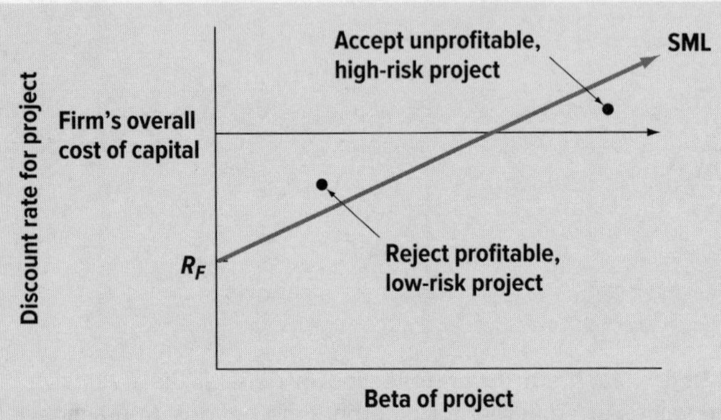

A single cost of capital for all projects in a firm, as indicated by the horizontal line in the figure, may lead to incorrect capital budgeting decisions. Projects with high risk, such as the software venture for HT Media, should be discounted at a high rate. By using the firm's cost of capital, the firm is likely to accept too many high-risk projects. Projects with low risk should be discounted at a low rate. By using the firm's cost of capital, the firm is likely to reject too many low-risk projects.

Figure 13.5 Relationship between the Firm's Cost of Capital and the Security Market Line (SML)

THE COMPARABLES METHOD

The HT Media (HT) example illustrates why we should discount a project at a rate commensurate with the risk of the project's cash flows. To estimate a project-specific discount rate, practitioners often use the *comparables method* or *twins method* described below:

1. We begin by finding one or more comparable firms that specialize in projects similar to the project being considered. The ideal comparable firm is a *pure play*–that is, a company that specializes only in projects similar to the project we are considering. Often, the perfect comparable firm does not exist, and we instead use firms in the same industry as the project. The comparable firm must also be publicly traded because we will need to calculate its equity beta.
2. Next, we calculate the equity beta of each comparable firm using its stock return data following the methods described in Section 13.4.

3. If the comparable firm has debt, its equity beta will be too large to represent the risk of its projects. We need to find the comparable firm's debt-equity ratio over the time period used to estimate its equity beta. Since debt-equity ratios fluctuate frequently, it is common to use an approximation or average. With the comparable firm's debt-equity ratio in hand, we can apply either Equation 13.5 or 13.7 to calculate the comparable firm's asset beta as appropriate. We assume the asset beta of the comparable firm is a reasonable proxy for the risk of our project. If we used more than one comparable firm, we would take the equal-weighted average of the asset betas across the comparable firms.
4. Using the estimated asset beta, we can apply the CAPM from Equation 13.1 to estimate the cost of capital for our project.

Note that this process becomes much simpler if the project under consideration is an extension of the firm's existing operations. If so, the parent firm can serve as the comparable for its own project, so the parent firm's discount rate would be the right discount rate for the project.

USING INDUSTRY COMPARABLES

To see the comparables method in action, let us return to the example of HT, a conglomerate firm that is considering a new project in computer software. Since HT is not a pure play specializing in computer software, it is not a good comparable for the project. Instead, HT decides to use firms in the computer software industry as comparables for the project.

Table 13.1 shows a list of comparable firms in the computer software industry (remember, comparables need to be publicly traded so that HT can compute their equity betas). The table also reports each comparable's approximate debt-equity ratio (B/S) over the time period used to measure its equity beta. Assuming that the corporate tax rate is 21 percent and that debt betas are zero, HT estimates each comparable firm's asset beta by unlevering its equity beta. HT's analysts use Equation 13.7.

Also assuming that HT identified a reasonable set of comparable firms for its project, HT converts the equity betas to asset betas and then takes the average of the asset betas, resulting in an asset beta for the project of 1.39.

Finally, HT applies the CAPM. Assuming a risk-free rate of 1 percent and a market risk premium of 6 percent, it might estimate its cost of capital for the project as:

$$.01 + 1.39 \times .06 = .0934, \text{ or } 9.34 \text{ percent}$$

So far, we have considered the discount rates for individual projects. The same message applies for discount rates for whole divisions. If a corporation has a number of divisions, each in a different industry, it would be a mistake to assign the same discount rate to each. Instead, we could apply the comparables method to find a discount rate for each division.

Likewise, we can use the comparables method to estimate the discount rate for a private firm or a firm that has recently gone public. Such a firm would not have past trading data, so we cannot compute its equity beta. Instead, we could find comparable publicly traded firms to estimate its discount rate.

Table 13.1 Equity and Asset Betas for Various Companies

	β_S	B/S	β_A
Omnisoft	1.42	0	1.42
CrystalTech	1.83	.35	1.43
Pinnacle Software	1.62	.29	1.32
Average			1.39

13.7 Cost of Fixed Income Securities

In this section, we examine the cost of two types of fixed income securities: debt and preferred stock. We consider the cost of debt first.

COST OF DEBT

The cost of equity is often difficult to estimate. The task generally involves a fair amount of data gathering and the end result is often measured with error. In general, the cost of debt is easier to determine. For bonds with a small risk of defaulting, the current yield to maturity is a good estimate of investor expected returns and the cost of borrowing. The firm can generally obtain this information either by checking the yield on publicly traded bonds or by talking to commercial and investment bankers.

Imagine that two years ago, the Rajan Manufacturing Corp. (RMC) issued ₹100 million of debt with a 7 percent coupon. While the bonds were initially issued at par, rising interest rates over the last two years have caused them to sell at a discount. The yield on the bonds is currently 8 percent. In order to finance expansion, RMC is considering another large issue of bonds. What is the cost of the new debt?

The cost of the new debt should be around 8 percent. If the old bonds are selling at 8 percent, the new debt will not sell at a lower yield. The 7 percent is a historical number, often called the embedded cost of the debt, with no relevance today.

Alternatively, perhaps a firm is issuing debt for the first time. Here, the firm's investment banker can generally indicate to the firm's managers what the yield on the prospective bonds will be. That yield is the cost of debt. Or perhaps the company will take out a loan with a commercial bank. Again, the borrowing rate on the prospective loan is the cost of debt.

There is only one complication that needs to be discussed. We have mostly ignored taxes so far, obviously an assumption at odds with reality. Financing with debt means the firm makes interest payments. Interest payments can be deducted from earnings, resulting in tax savings which lower the aftertax cost of debt.

The Tax Cuts and Jobs Act of 2017 placed limitations on the amount of interest that can be deducted in certain situations. Throughout this chapter, we will assume all interest can be deducted. We will discuss this issue in greater detail in a subsequent chapter.

Consider the following example where two firms, Unlevered Corp. and Levered Corp., differ only in debt. Unlevered Corp. has no debt and Levered Corp. has ₹100 of debt with an interest rate of 10 percent.

Unlevered Corp.		Levered Corp.	
Revenue	₹180.0	Revenue	₹180
Expenses	70.0	Expenses	70
Pretax earnings	₹110.0	Earnings before interest and taxes	₹110
Taxes (21%)	23.1	Interest (10% on ₹100 borrowed)	10
Aftertax earnings	₹ 86.9	Pretax earnings	₹100
		Taxes (21%)	21
		Aftertax earnings	₹ 79

While the Levered Corp. must pay ₹10 of interest per year, its aftertax earnings are only ₹7.9 (= ₹86.9 − 79) less than those of the Unlevered Corp. Why? Because the interest payments are tax deductible. That is, while Levered Corp.'s pretax earnings are ₹10 (= ₹110 − 100) less than those of Unlevered Corp., Levered Corp. pays ₹2.1 (= ₹23.1 − 21) less in taxes than does Unlevered Corp.

The ₹7.9 reduction of aftertax earnings is 7.9 percent of the ₹100 that Levered Corp. borrowed. Thus, the aftertax cost of debt is 7.9 percent. In general, the aftertax cost of debt can be written as:

$$\text{Aftertax cost of debt} = (1 - T_C) \times \text{Borrowing rate}$$
$$.079, \text{ or } 7.9\% = (1 - .21) \times .10$$

Why have we tax-adjusted the cost of debt while we did not tax-adjust the cost of equity? Because, while firms can deduct their interest payments before paying taxes, dividends are not tax deductible.

COST OF PREFERRED STOCK

The name *preferred stock* is misleading because preferred stock is probably more similar to bonds than to common stock. Preferred stock pays a constant dividend in perpetuity. Interest payments on bonds are similar to dividends on preferred stock, though almost all bonds have a finite maturity. By contrast, dividends on common stock are not constant over time.

Preferred stock is junior to debt and senior to common stock. This means that the firm must make promised interest payments to debt before it can make dividend payments to preferred stock. In addition, the firm must pay promised dividends to preferred stock before it can pay dividends to common stock.

Suppose a share of the preferred stock of Govindam Rubber Limited, is selling at ₹17.16 and pays a dividend of ₹1.50 per year. Because preferred stocks are perpetuities, they should be priced by the perpetuity formula, $P = D/R_P$, where P is the price; D is the dividend to be received each year; and R_P is the yield, or rate of return. Rearranging, we have:

$$R_P = D/P$$

For this preferred issue, the rate of return is .087, or 8.7 percent (= ₹1.50/₹17.16). The cost of preferred stock is this rate of return.

Why don't we tax-adjust the cost of preferred stock the way we did the cost of debt? We don't tax-adjust here because dividend payments on preferred stock are not tax deductible.

13.8 The Weighted Average Cost of Capital

So far, we have discussed how to compute the discount rate for a firm or project, assuming the firm or project is financed with 100 percent equity. In this section, we will introduce a powerful tool known as the weighted average cost of capital. The weighted average cost of capital can be used to calculate the discount rate for any firm, division, or project, financed with any mix of debt and equity. Our previous examples can be viewed as special cases that build up to this more general concept.

COST OF LEVERED EQUITY

In Section 13.2, we showed how to estimate the cost of equity capital for an all-equity firm, and in Section 13.5, we showed how to estimate the cost of equity for an all-equity-financed project. In the case of *levered equity*—that is, equity in a firm or project that is partially financed with debt—we need to make a further adjustment to compute the cost of equity. The adjustment occurs because equity is junior to debt, so an increase in financial leverage makes the equity more risky, raising the cost of equity.

Consider a public firm that maintains a constant target debt-equity ratio. Computing the cost of levered equity for this firm is simple because its equity beta already reflects the heightened risk of its equity due to the seniority of debt. Therefore, we can follow the method described in Sections 13.2 and 13.4 to estimate the firm's equity beta, apply the CAPM, and estimate the firm's cost of equity capital.

For example, consider Costco, for which we estimate an equity beta of .69 using data on monthly returns from 2016 to 2020. Over this time period, Costco maintained a target market debt-equity ratio and plans to maintain a similar mix of debt and equity going forward. Assuming a risk-free rate of 1 percent and a market risk premium of 6 percent, Costco's cost of equity is $.01 + .69 \times .06 = .0514$, or 5.14 percent.

More generally, to estimate the cost of equity for a project that is partially financed with debt, we could apply the comparables method to estimate the project's asset beta. Once we have the project's asset beta, we can compute the project's equity beta using Equation 13.7 and the appropriate debt-equity ratio for the project. Applying the CAPM to the project's equity beta, we can then estimate the project's cost of equity.

To see this in action, let's return to the example in Section 13.6. Suppose HT plans to finance its new software project using a debt-equity ratio of .5. The asset beta for the project is 1.34, as calculated previously. The corporate tax rate is 21 percent. HT applies the common assumption that its debt beta is equal to zero. Thus, the project's equity beta is $\beta_{\text{Asset}} \times [1 + B(1 - T_C)/S] = 1.39 \times [1 + .5(1 - .21)] = 1.94$. Assuming a risk-free rate of 1 percent and a market risk premium of 6 percent, the project's cost of equity is $.01 + 1.94 \times .06 = .1264$, or 12.64 percent.

FINANCING WITH A MIX OF DEBT AND EQUITY

Suppose a firm plans to use both debt and equity to finance a project. If the cost of debt for the project is R_{B^P} and the cost of equity for the project is R_{S^P}, what is the overall or average cost of its capital?

We can calculate the cost of equity for the project, R_{S^P} as described previously. Without considering the tax benefits of debt, the cost of debt for the project is the firm's expected borrowing cost for the project, R_{B^P} as described in Section 13.7. If there are tax benefits of debt, the aftertax cost of debt is:

$$\text{Cost of debt (after corporate tax)} = R_{B^P} \times (1 - T_C)$$

where T_C is the corporation's tax rate.

If a firm plans to finance the project using a mix of debt and equity, the cost of capital would be a weighted average of the cost of equity and the aftertax cost of debt. This works out to be:[4]

$$\text{WACC} = \frac{S_P}{S_P + B_P} \times R_{S^P} + \frac{B_P}{S_P + B_P} \times R_{B^P} \times (1 - T_C) \tag{13.8}$$

The weights in the formula are, respectively, the proportion of total project value that will be financed with equity:

$$\frac{S_P}{S_P + B_P}$$

[4]For simplicity, Equation 13.5 ignores preferred stock financing. With the addition of preferred stock, the formula becomes:

$$\text{Average cost of capital} = \frac{S}{S + B + P} \times R_S + \frac{B}{S + B + P} \times R_B \times (1 - T_C) + \frac{P}{S + B + P} \times R_P$$

where P is the amount of preferred stock in the firm's capital structure and R_P is the cost of preferred stock.

and the proportion that will be financed with debt:

$$\frac{B_P}{S_P + B_P}$$

This is only natural. If the firm plans to finance the project with only equity, its average cost of capital would equal its cost of equity, R_S. At the other extreme, if the firm plans to finance the project with only debt, the project's average cost of capital would be its aftertax cost of debt, $R_{B^P} \times (1 - T_C)$.

Intuitively, the WACC method accounts for the tax benefits of debt through a reduction in the project's discount rate. Without tax benefits, the portion of the project that is financed with debt would have to return R_{B^P} to investors to compensate them for their investment. With tax benefits, the project only has to return $R_{B^P} \times (1 - T_C)$ to investors through direct project cash flows because it will deliver an extra $R_{B^P} \times T_C$ as tax savings.

Because the average cost of capital weighs the cost of equity and the cost of debt, it is usually referred to as the **weighted average cost of capital**, or **WACC**, and from now on we will use this term.

The weights in the WACC are market value weights. Market value weights are more appropriate than book value weights because the market values of the securities are closer to the actual rupees that would be received from their sale. In the case of debt, it is common to approximate the market value of debt using its book value, since the two values are likely to be similar except in situations where the debt is close to default. In addition, it is useful to think in terms of target market weights. These are the market weights expected to prevail over the life of the project being valued.

Notice that many of the terms in the WACC formula contain a *P* superscript. The *P* indicates that we should use values that are specific to the project being valued. R_{S^P} and R_{B^P} should reflect the cost of equity and debt for the project, which may differ from those of the firm. Likewise, $\frac{S_P}{S_P + B_P}$ and $\frac{B_P}{S_P + B_P}$ should reflect the target mixture of equity and debt for the type of project under consideration.

To see the WACC method in action, let's return to our example of the conglomerate firm HT considering a new investment project in software. Recall that we estimated that the software project has a cost of equity of 12.64 percent. Suppose HT believes that the appropriate financing mix for this type of software investment is a debt-equity ratio $B/S = .5$, implying that $\frac{S_P}{S_P + B_P} \equiv 2/3$ and $\frac{B_P}{S_P + B_P} \equiv 1/3$. Assuming a pretax cost of debt of 5 percent and a corporate tax rate of 21 percent, the project's WACC is then $2/3 \times .1264 + 1/3 \times .05 \times (1 - .21) = .09748$, or 9.75 percent.

APPLYING THE WACC

The WACC is a powerful tool because it can be used to estimate the discount rate for any project, and we can define what we mean by project very broadly. The project could be a specific project considered by a conglomerate firm, as in the case of HT's investment project in software. The project could also be a division within a conglomerate firm, so we can use the WACC to estimate the discount rate for a division. Finally, the project could be the firm itself, so the WACC can be used to estimate the appropriate discount rate to value an entire firm.

It is common to compute the WACC for the firm as a whole, and then to use that WACC as a firmwide discount rate or hurdle rate when valuing the firm's specific projects. However, as we have discussed, this practice is only correct if the firm is valuing projects that are similar in risk to the firm as a whole. In addition, using the firmwide WACC to value individual projects is appropriate only if the firm targets a constant long-run debt-equity ratio, which implies that projects would be financed with a similar mix of debt and equity as the firm overall. For projects that differ from the firm as a whole, we should calculate a project-specific WACC. We would just need to know the project's cost of equity and aftertax cost of debt, and the project's target mix of debt and equity financing.

EXAMPLE 13.5

WACC Consider a firm in the USA, whose debt has a market value of ₹40 million and whose stock has a market value of ₹60 million. The firm pays a 5 percent rate of interest on its new debt and has a beta of 1.41. The corporate tax rate is 21 percent. Assume that the CAPM holds, the risk premium on the market is 9.5 percent, and the current Treasury bill rate is 1 percent. What is this firm's WACC?

To compute the WACC using Equation 13.8, we must know (1) the aftertax cost of debt, $R_B \times (1 - T_C)$; (2) the cost of equity, R_S; and (3) the weights of debt and equity used by the firm. These three values are determined next:

1. The pretax cost of debt is 5 percent, implying an aftertax cost of 3.95 percent [= .05 × (1 − .21)].
2. We calculate the cost of equity capital by using the CAPM:

$$R_S = R_F + \beta \times (R_M - R_F)$$
$$= .01 + 1.41 \times .095$$
$$= .1440, \text{ or } 14.40\%$$

3. We compute the proportions of debt and equity from the market values of debt and equity. Because the market value of the firm is ₹100 million (= ₹40 million + 60 million), the proportions of debt and equity are 40 and 60 percent, respectively.

The cost of equity, R_S, is 14.40 percent and the aftertax cost of debt, $R_B \times (1 - T_C)$, is 3.95 percent. B is ₹40 million and S is ₹60 million. Therefore:

$$\text{WACC} = \frac{S}{S+B} \times R_S + \frac{B}{S+B} \times R_B \times \left(1 - T_C\right)$$
$$= \left(\frac{₹60}{₹100} \times .1440\right) + \left(\frac{₹40}{₹100} \times .0395\right) = .1022, \text{ or } 10.22\%$$

The above calculations are presented in table form below:

(1) Financing Components	(2) Market Values	(3) Weight	(4) Cost of Capital (after taxes)	(5) Weighted Cost of Capital
Debt	₹ 40,000,000	.40	.05 × (1 − .21) = .0395, or 3.95%	1.58%
Equity	60,000,000	.60	.01 + 1.41 × .095 = .1440, or 14.40%	8.64
	₹100,000,000	1.00		10.22%

While the WACC is a general method that can be used to compute the discount rate for any project, we can sometimes take a shortcut. First, if the project is appropriately financed with only equity, the WACC will be equal to the project's cost of equity, which we discussed in a previous section. Second, it is common for firms to choose to finance a new project with a similar debt-equity mix as the project's comparable firms. As we will discuss in later chapters, it is difficult to know the exact optimal mix of debt and equity financing for a project, so some firms choose to mimic the debt-equity ratio of the project's comparable firms, under the assumption that other firms have chosen a debt-equity ratio that is close to optimal. If so, the project's cost of equity and debt, as well as weights for equity and debt, will be similar to that of the comparable firms. Therefore, the project's WACC should be the same as the comparable firms' WACCs.

13.9 Valuation with WACC

Now we are in a position to use the weighted average cost of capital to value both projects and entire firms. The WACC represents the return that investors could earn on an alternative investment with similar risk and a similar debt-equity ratio. Thus, the WACC is the appropriate discount rate when calculating the NPV of a project or firm. If valuation using the WACC discount rate yields a negative NPV, investors would be better off financing the alternative investment.

VALUING A FINITE-HORIZON PROJECT

When valuing a project, we start by determining the correct discount rate and use discounted cash flows to determine NPV.

Suppose a firm has both a current and a target debt-equity ratio for a project of .6, a pretax cost of debt of 5.15 percent, and a cost of equity of 10 percent. The corporate tax rate is 21 percent. What is the firm's weighted average cost of capital?

Our first step calls for transforming the debt-equity (B/S) ratio to a debt-value ratio. A B/S ratio of .6 implies 6 parts debt for 10 parts equity. Because value is equal to the sum of the debt plus the equity, the debt-value ratio is $6/(6 + 10) = .375$. Similarly, the equity-value ratio is $10/(6 + 10) = .625$. The WACC will then be:

$$\begin{aligned}\text{WACC} &= \left(\frac{S}{S+B}\right) \times R_S + \left(\frac{B}{S+B}\right) \times R_B \times (1 - T_C)\\ &= .625 \times .10 + .375 \times .0515 \times .79 = .0778, \text{ or } 7.78\%\end{aligned}$$

Suppose the firm is considering taking on a warehouse renovation costing ₹60 million that is expected to yield additional cash flows of ₹12 million a year for six years. The warehouse has a finite horizon and is expected to be worthless after Year 6. If we assume the warehouse renovation project has the same risk as the firm, we can use the firm's WACC to value the project.

Note that the expected cash flows in a WACC valuation should be the incremental aftertax cash flows associated with the project, assuming no interest deduction for debt financing. The tax benefits of financing the project partially with debt will be recognized by using the WACC as the project's discount rate. Do not also add tax savings into the estimates of cash flows as that would double-count the tax benefits of debt.

Using the NPV equation and discounting the six years of expected cash flows from the renovation at the WACC, we have:

$$\begin{aligned}\text{NPV} &= -₹60 + \frac{₹12}{(1 + \text{WACC})} + \cdots + \frac{₹12}{(1 + \text{WACC})^6}\\ &= -₹60 + ₹12 \times \frac{\left[1 - \left(\frac{1}{1.0778}\right)^6\right]}{.0778}\\ &= -₹60 + ₹12 \times 4.6545\\ &= -₹4.15\end{aligned}$$

Should the firm take on the warehouse renovation? The project has a negative NPV using the firm's WACC. This means that the financial markets offer superior investments in the same risk class, namely, the firm's risk class. The answer is clear: The firm should reject the project.

TERMINAL VALUE AND THE WACC

In our previous example, we assumed that the warehouse project had a finite life span of six years. In reality, many projects and firms have indefinite life spans. We may only be able to forecast expected cash flows in each period for a certain number of years, after which our best guess is that cash flows will continue to grow at a certain rate.

Suppose we are interested in using the WACC to value a firm with a potentially infinite horizon. We use the firm's weighted average cost of capital as our discount rate, and we set up the usual discounted cash flow model by forecasting the firm's entire cash flow (sometimes called cash flow from assets, distributable cash flow, free cash flow, or total cash flow of the firm) up to a horizon, along with a terminal value of the firm:

$$\mathrm{PV}_0 = \frac{\mathrm{CFA}_1^*}{1 + \mathrm{WACC}} + \frac{\mathrm{CFA}_2^*}{(1 + \mathrm{WACC})^2} + \frac{\mathrm{CFA}_3^*}{(1 + \mathrm{WACC})^3} + \cdots + \frac{\mathrm{CFA}_t^* + TV_t}{(1 + \mathrm{WACC})^t}$$

The terminal value (TV) is estimated by assuming a constant perpetual growth rate for cash flows beyond the horizon, *t*, so that:[5]

$$\mathrm{TV}_t = \frac{\mathrm{CFA}_{t+1}^*}{\mathrm{WACC} - g_{CF}} = \frac{\mathrm{CFA}_t^*(1 + g_{CF})}{\mathrm{WACC} - g_{CF}}$$

where CFA* is the net cash flows and is equal to earnings before interest and taxes (EBIT) plus depreciation, minus taxes, minus increases in net working capital, minus capital spending.[6] Here, g_{CF} is the growth rate of cash flows beyond *t*, and WACC is the weighted average cost of capital. To calculate CFA*, we need to first calculate what the firm's tax bill would have been if it had not used debt financing. To do that, we take EBIT and multiply it by the firm's tax rate (T_C) to get the firm's "would-have-been" tax bill, which we will call the "adjusted" taxes and label Taxes* in our next example. This adjustment is necessary because we have already accounted for the tax benefits of debt financing by using WACC as the discount rate, and, as we discussed, we don't want to double count it.

Consider the Good Food Corporation, a public company headquartered in Barstow, California, that is currently a leading global food service retailer. It operates about 10,000 restaurants in 100 countries. Good Food serves a value-based menu focused on hamburgers and french fries. The company has ₹4 billion in market-valued debt and ₹2 billion in market-valued common stock. Its tax rate is 20 percent. Good Food has estimated its cost of debt as 5 percent and its cost of equity as 10 percent. Its weighted average cost of capital can be calculated as:

Financial Component	Market Values	Weights	Cost of Capital	Weighted Average Cost of Capital
Debt	₹4 billion	.6667	.05(1 − .2) = .04, or 4%	.6667 × .04
Equity	2 billion	.3333	10%	.3333 × .10
	₹6 billion			.06, or 6%

Good Food is seeking to grow by acquisition and the investment bankers of Good Food have identified a potential acquisition candidate, Happy Meals, Inc. Happy Meals is currently a private firm with no publicly

[5]The terminal date is often referred to as the horizon. In general, we choose a horizon whenever we can assume cash flow grows at a constant rate perpetually thereafter. By using the word *terminal*, we do not rule out the firm continuing to exist. Instead, we are attempting to simplify the cash flow estimation process.

[6]This definition of cash flow is the same one we used to determine the NPV of capital investments in Chapter 6.

tradable common stock but has about the same product mix as Good Food and is a direct competitor to Good Food in many markets. It operates about 4,000 restaurants, mostly in North America and Europe. Happy Meals has ₹1,318.8 million of debt outstanding with its market value approximately the same as the book value.[7] It has 12.5 million shares outstanding. Because Happy Meals is a private firm, we have no stock market price to rely on for our valuation. Happy Meals expects its EBIT to grow 10 percent a year for the next five years. Increases in capital spending and net working capital are both expected to be 24 percent of EBIT. Depreciation will be 8 percent of EBIT. The perpetual growth rate in cash flow after five years is estimated to be 2 percent.

If Good Food acquires Happy Meals, Good Food analysts estimate the net cash flows from Happy Meals (in millions) would be (rounding to one decimal):

Year	1	2	3	4	5
Earnings before interest and taxes (EBIT)	₹150	₹165	₹181.5	₹199.7	₹219.6
− Taxes* (20%)	30	33	36.3	39.9	43.9
= Earnings after taxes	₹120	₹132	₹145.2	₹159.7	₹175.7
+ Depreciation	12	13.2	14.5	16	17.6
− Capital spending	36	39.6	43.6	47.9	52.7
− Increases in net working capital	36	39.6	43.6	47.9	52.7
= Net cash flows (*CF*)	₹ 60	₹ 66	₹ 72.6	₹ 79.9	₹ 87.8

We start our calculations by computing a terminal value of Happy Meals as:

$$\text{TV}_5 = \frac{₹87.8 \times 1.02}{.06 - .02} = ₹2,240.1$$

Next, we compute the present value of Happy Meals to be:

$$\text{PV}_0 = \frac{₹60}{1.06} + \frac{₹66}{1.06^2} + \frac{₹72.6}{1.06^3} + \frac{₹79.9}{1.06^4} + \frac{₹87.8 + 2,240.1}{1.06^5} = ₹1,979.1$$

so the total value of the company is ₹1,979.1.

To find the value of equity, we subtract the value of debt, which gives us ₹1,979.1 − 1,318.8 = ₹660.3. To find the equity value per share, we divide the value of equity by the number of shares outstanding: ₹660.3/12.5 = ₹52.83. Good Food will find Happy Meals an attractive acquisition candidate at a price of less than ₹52.83 per share (the less the better).

In doing our valuation of Happy Meals, Inc., it is important to remember that we have assumed that Good Food is a comparable firm for Happy Meals. Our weighted average cost of capital method only works if Happy Meals has the same business risks as Good Food.

The above calculations assume a growing perpetuity after Year 5 (i.e., the horizon). However, we pointed out in Chapter 3 and Chapter 9 that firms as a whole are often valued by multiples. The most common multiple for overall firm valuation is the enterprise value to the EBITDA multiple (EV/EBITDA). Suppose the analysts at Good Food estimate the terminal value of Happy Meals via an EV/EBITDA multiple, rather than as a growing perpetuity. To see how this might work, suppose the EV/EBITDA multiple for comparable

[7]Sometimes analysts refer to a firm's net debt, which is the market value of debt minus excess cash. Neither Good Food nor Happy Meals has excess cash.

firms in the food service industry is 10. The EBITDA for Happy Meals in Year 5 will be equal to EBIT + depreciation, or ₹237.2 (= ₹219.6 + 17.6). Using the EV/EBITDA multiple of 10, the value of Happy Meals in Year 5 can be estimated as ₹2,371.8. The present value of Happy Meals using the EV/EBITDA multiple for terminal value would be:

$$\text{PV}_0 = \frac{₹60}{1.06} + \frac{₹66}{1.06^2} + \frac{₹72.6}{1.06^3} + \frac{₹79.9}{1.06^4} + \frac{₹87.8 + 2{,}371.8}{1.06^5} = ₹2{,}077.6$$

The value of the equity of Happy Meals can be estimated as:

$$\text{PV (of entire firm) less debt} = ₹2{,}077.6 - 1{,}318.8 = ₹758.8$$

With 12.5 million shares outstanding, the value of a share of equity would be:

$$₹758.8/12.5 = ₹60.70$$

Now we have two estimates of the value of a share of equity in Happy Meals. The different estimates reflect the different ways of calculating terminal value. Using the constant growth discounted cash flow method for terminal value, our estimate of the equity value per share of Happy Meals is ₹52.83 and using the EV/EBITDA comparable firm method, our estimate is ₹60.70. As mentioned in Chapter 9, there is no perfect method. If the comparable firms were all identical to Happy Meals, perhaps the EV/EBITDA method would be best. Unfortunately, firms are not identical. On the other hand, if we were very sure of the terminal date and the growth in subsequent cash flows, perhaps the constant growth method would be best. Both methods are often used in practice.

13.10 Estimating Eastman Chemical's Cost of Capital

In our previous sections, we calculated the cost of capital for hypothetical examples. We will now calculate the cost of capital for a real company, Eastman Chemical Co., a leading international chemical company and maker of plastics for soft drink containers and other uses. It was created in 1993 when its former parent company, Eastman Kodak, split off the division as a separate company.

Eastman's Cost of Equity Our first stop for Eastman is **www.reuters.com** (ticker: EMN). In September 2020, the website reported the market capitalization of EMN's equity, which is share price times number of shares outstanding, as ₹10.509 billion. To estimate Eastman's cost of equity, we will assume a market risk premium of 6 percent. We could calculate Eastman's equity beta by regressing five years of monthly stock returns for Eastman on the market return. A common shortcut is to look up a company's equity beta online.[8] Eastman's beta on Reuters was 1.59. Our estimate of the risk-free rate is the then-current Treasury rate of .97 percent.

Using Eastman's beta in the CAPM to estimate the cost of equity, we find:

$$R_S = .0097 + 1.59 \times .06 = .1051, \text{ or } 10.51\%$$

[8]The company's equity beta as reported on financial websites may differ depending on how it is calculated–for example, the sample period, choice of weekly or monthly returns, and choice of the market portfolio.

Eastman's Cost of Debt Eastman has nine bond issues that account for essentially all of its debt. To calculate the cost of debt, we will have to combine these nine issues and compute a weighted average. We go to **finra-markets.morningstar.com/BondCenter/** to find quotes on the bonds. We should note here that finding the yield to maturity for all of a company's outstanding bond issues on a single day is unusual. In our previous discussion on bonds, we found that the bond market is not as liquid as the stock market, and on many days, individual bond issues may not trade. To find the book value of the bonds, we can look up the information on each bond at **finra-markets.morningstar.com/BondCenter/** or go to **www.sec.gov** and find the most recent 10-K report. The basic information is as follows:

Coupon Rate	Maturity	Book Value (Face Value in Millions)	Price (% of Par)	Yield to Maturity
3.50%	2021	₹298	118.528%	.70%
3.60	2022	742	104.642	.82
7.25	2024	198	117.193	2.00
7.625	2024	43	121.650	2.07
3.80	2025	701	111.967	2.12
7.60	2027	195	123.062	2.23
4.50	2028	493	108.875	2.57
4.80	2042	493	121.522	3.38
4.65	2044	874	103.420	3.39

To calculate the weighted average cost of debt, we take the percentage of the total debt represented by each issue and multiply by the yield on the issue. We then add to get the overall weighted average debt cost. We use both book values and market values here for comparison. The results of the calculations are as follows:

Coupon Rate	Book Value (Face Value, Millions)	Percentage of Total	Market Value (Millions)	Percentage of Total	Yield to Maturity	Book Value	Market Value
3.50	₹298	7.38%	₹353.21	7.89%	.70	.05	.05
3.60	742	18.38	776.44	17.34	.82	.15	.14
7.25	198	4.90	232.04	5.18	2.00	.10	.10
7.625	43	1.07	52.31	1.17	2.07	.02	.02
3.80	701	17.36	784.89	17.53	2.12	.37	.37
7.60	195	4.83	239.97	5.36	2.23	.11	.12
4.50	493	12.21	536.75	11.98	2.57	.31	.31
4.80	493	12.21	599.10	13.38	3.38	.41	.45
4.65	874	21.65	903.89	20.18	3.39	.73	.68
	₹4,037	100.00%	₹4,478.62	100.00%		2.26%	2.26%

As these calculations show, Eastman's cost of debt is 2.26 percent on a book value basis and 2.26 percent on a market value basis. For Eastman's debt, whether market values or book values are used makes no difference. The reason is that the market values and book values are similar. This will often be the case and explains why companies frequently use book values for debt in WACC calculations. However, we will use market values in our calculations because the market reflects current values.

Eastman's WACC We now have the various pieces necessary to calculate Eastman's WACC. First, we need to calculate the capital structure weights. We will assume that Eastman's capital structure represents its target mix of debt and equity.

The market values of Eastman's debt and equity are ₹4.479 billion and ₹10.509 billion, respectively. The total value of the firm is ₹14.987 billion, implying that the debt and equity percentages are ₹4.479/₹14.987 = .299 and ₹10.509/₹14.987 = .701, respectively. Assuming a tax rate of 21 percent, Eastman's WACC is:

$$\text{WACC} = .299 \times .0226 \times (1 - .21) + .701 \times .1051 = .0790, \text{ or } 7.90\%$$

13.11 Flotation Costs and the Weighted Average Cost of Capital

So far, we have not included issue costs in our discussion of the weighted average cost of capital. When projects are funded by stocks and bonds, the firm will incur these costs, which are commonly called *flotation costs.*

Sometimes it is suggested that the firm's WACC should be adjusted upward to reflect flotation costs. This is really not the best approach because the required return on an investment depends on the risk of the investment, not the source of the funds. This is not to say that flotation costs should be ignored. Because these costs arise as a consequence of the decision to undertake a project, they are relevant cash flows. We therefore briefly discuss how to include them in project analysis.

THE BASIC APPROACH

We start with a simple case. The Spatt Company, an all-equity firm, has a cost of equity of 20 percent. Because this firm is 100 percent equity, its WACC and its cost of equity are the same. Spatt is contemplating a large-scale ₹100 million expansion of its existing operations. The expansion would be funded by selling new stock.

Based on conversations with its investment banker, Spatt believes its flotation costs will run 10 percent of the amount issued. This means that Spatt's proceeds from the equity sale will be only 90 percent of the amount sold. When flotation costs are considered, what is the cost of the expansion?

Spatt needs to sell enough equity to raise ₹100 million after covering the flotation costs. In other words:

$$₹100 \text{ million} = (1 - .10) \times \text{Amount raised}$$
$$\text{Amount raised} = ₹100 \text{ million}/.90 = ₹111.11 \text{ million}$$

Spatt's flotation costs are thus ₹11.11 million and the true cost of the expansion is ₹111.11 million including flotation costs.

Things are only slightly more complicated if the firm uses both debt and equity. Suppose Spatt's target capital structure is 60 percent equity and 40 percent debt. The flotation costs associated with equity are still 10 percent, but the flotation costs for debt are less–say, 5 percent.

Earlier, when we had different capital costs for debt and equity, we calculated a weighted average cost of capital using the target capital structure weights. Here, we can calculate an overall or weighted average flotation cost, f_A, by multiplying the flotation cost for stock, f_S, by the percentage of stock (S/V) and the flotation cost for bonds, f_B, by the percentage of bonds (B/V) and then adding the two together:

$$\begin{aligned} f_A &= (S/V) \times f_S + (B/V) \times f_B \\ &= .60 \times .10 + .40 \times .05 \\ &= .08, \text{ or } 8\% \end{aligned} \tag{13.9}$$

The weighted average flotation cost is 8 percent. What this tells us is that for every rupee in outside financing needed for new projects, the firm must actually raise ₹1/(1 − .08) = ₹1.087. In our example, the project cost is ₹100 million when we ignore flotation costs. If we include them, then the true cost is ₹100 million/(1 − f_A) = ₹100 million/.92 = ₹108.7 million.

In taking issue costs into account, the firm must be careful not to use the wrong weights. The firm should use the target weights, even if it can finance the entire cost of the project with either debt or equity. The fact that a firm can finance a specific project with debt or equity is irrelevant. If a firm has a target debt-equity ratio of 1 but chooses to finance a particular project with all debt, it will have to raise additional equity later on to maintain its target debt-equity ratio. To take this into account, the firm should always use the target weights in calculating the flotation cost.

EXAMPLE 13.6

Calculating the Weighted Average Flotation Cost The Thoinu Singha Company has a target capital structure of 80 percent equity and 20 percent debt. The flotation costs for equity issues are 20 percent of the amount raised; the flotation costs for debt issues are 6 percent. If Thoinu Singha needs ₹65 million for a new manufacturing facility, what is the true cost including flotation costs?

We first calculate the weighted average flotation cost, f_A:

$$\begin{aligned} f_A &= S/V \times f_S + B/V \times f_B \\ &= .80 \times .20 + .20 \times .06 \\ &= .172, \text{ or } 17.2\% \end{aligned}$$

The weighted average flotation cost is 17.2 percent. The project cost is ₹65 million without flotation costs. If we include them, then the true cost is ₹65 million/(1 − f_A) = ₹65 million/.828 = ₹78.5 million, again illustrating that flotation costs can be a considerable expense.

FLOTATION COSTS AND NPV

To illustrate how flotation costs can be included in an NPV analysis, suppose the Utkal Printing Company is currently at its target debt-equity ratio of 100 percent. It is considering building a new ₹500,000 printing plant in Banaras. This new plant is expected to generate aftertax cash flows of ₹73,150 per year forever. The tax rate is 21 percent. There are two financing options:

1. A ₹500,000 new issue of common stock: The issuance costs of the new common stock would be about 10 percent of the amount raised. The required return on the company's new equity is 20 percent.

2. A ₹500,000 issue of 30-year bonds: The issuance costs of the new debt would be 2 percent of the proceeds. The company can raise new debt at 10 percent.

What is the NPV of the new printing plant?

To begin, because printing is the company's main line of business, we will use the company's weighted average cost of capital, WACC, to value the new printing plant:

$$\begin{aligned} \text{WACC} &= S/V \times R_S + B/V \times R_B \times (1 - T_C) \\ &= .50 \times .20 + .50 \times .10 \times (1 - .21) \\ &= .1395, \text{ or } 13.95\% \end{aligned}$$

Because the cash flows are ₹73,150 per year forever, the PV of the cash flows at 13.95 percent per year is:

$$\text{PV} = \frac{₹73{,}150}{.1395} = ₹524{,}373$$

If we ignore flotation costs, the NPV is:

$$\text{NPV} = ₹524{,}373 - 500{,}000 = ₹24{,}373$$

With no flotation costs, the project generates an NPV that is greater than zero, so it should be accepted.

What about financing arrangements and issue costs? Because new financing must be raised, the flotation costs are relevant. From the information given, we know that the flotation costs are 2 percent for debt and 10 percent for equity. Because Utkal uses equal amounts of debt and equity, the weighted average flotation cost, f_A, is:

$$\begin{aligned} f_A &= S/V \times f_S + B/V \times f_B \\ &= .50 \times .10 + .50 \times .02 \\ &= .06, \text{ or } 6\% \end{aligned}$$

Remember, the fact that Utkal can finance the project with all debt or all equity is irrelevant. Because Utkal needs ₹500,000 to fund the new plant, the true cost, once we include flotation costs, is ₹500,000/(1 − f_A) = ₹500,000/.94 = ₹531,915. Because the PV of the cash flows is ₹524,373, the plant has an NPV of ₹524,373 − 531,915 = −₹7,542, so it is no longer a good investment.

INTERNAL EQUITY AND FLOTATION COSTS

Our discussion of flotation costs to this point implicitly assumed that firms always finance new investments using external sources. However, firms can also finance their investments with internal equity, that is, with internally generated cash flows. In reality, most firms finance all or at least the equity portion of their capital spending with internal equity. They rarely sell equity because of the high flotation costs.

The use of internal equity doesn't change our approach. However, we now assign a value of zero to the flotation cost of equity because there is no such cost. In our Utkal example, the weighted average flotation cost would therefore be:

$$\begin{aligned} f_A &= S/V \times f_S + B/V \times f_B \\ &= .50 \times 0 + .50 \times .02 \\ &= .01, \text{ or } 1\% \end{aligned}$$

Notice that whether equity is generated internally or externally makes a big difference because external equity has a relatively high flotation cost.

RESEARCH IN EMERGING MARKET CONTEXT

Chauhan and Kumar's (2018) research found that firms disclosing more non-financial information have lower costs of funds and higher operating profits. They also report positive valuation effects associated with the nonfinancial disclosure, with the valuation effects weaker for business group firms compared to similar standalone firms.

Prasad et al. (2022) found that higher CSR performance leads to a decrease in the costs of debt and an increase in the costs of equity. However, mandatory CSR legislation moderates these relationships, resulting in an increase in both the costs of debt and equity. Eliwa et al. (2021) discovered that lenders value ESG performance and disclosure, leading to a lowering of the cost of debt capital for these firms. The impact of ESG performance and disclosure on the cost of debt is more dominant in stakeholder-oriented countries where the community is more prevalent.

References

Chauhan, Y., & Kumar, S. B. (2018). Do investors value the nonfinancial disclosure in emerging markets?. *Emerging Markets Review, 37,* 32–46.

Eliwa, Y., Aboud, A., & Saleh, A. (2021). ESG practices and the cost of debt: Evidence from EU countries. *Critical Perspectives on Accounting, 79,* 102097.

Prasad, K., Kumar, S., Devji, S., Lim, W. M., Prabhu, N., & Moodbidri, S. (2022). Corporate social responsibility and cost of capital: The moderating role of policy intervention. *Research in International Business and Finance, 60,* 101620.

Summary and Conclusions

This chapter discussed the cost of capital, which is the discount rate used for capital budgeting projects. The firm's WACC should be used only for projects that have the same risk as the firm's overall risk. Otherwise, the cost of capital depends on the riskiness of the project, not the riskiness of the firm. Proper capital budgeting will utilize this adjustment for risk.

1. A firm with excess cash can either pay a dividend or make a capital expenditure. Because stockholders can reinvest the dividend in risky financial assets, the expected return on a capital budgeting project should be at least as great as the expected return on a financial asset of comparable risk.
2. The expected return on any asset is dependent on its beta. We showed how to estimate the beta of a stock. The appropriate procedure employs regression analysis on historical returns.
3. We considered the case of a project with beta risk equal to that of the firm. If the project and firm are financed with only equity, the discount rate on the project is equal to:

$$R_F + \beta \times (R_M - R_F)$$

   where R_M is the expected return on the market portfolio and R_F is the risk-free rate. In words, the discount rate on the project is equal to the CAPM's estimate of the expected return on the security. Conceptually, a dividend growth model could also be used to estimate the cost of equity, though it is less popular in practice.
4. An asset beta measures the sensitivity of the firm's assets to changes in the value of the market portfolio. Holding the firm's assets constant, the firm's equity beta will increase with its financial leverage.

5. If the project's beta differs from that of the firm, the discount rate should be based on the project's beta. We can estimate the project's beta by using the comparables method.
6. If a project is partially financed with debt, the discount rate to use is the WACC. To calculate the WACC, we must estimate the cost of equity and the cost of debt applicable to a project.
7. New projects are often funded by issues of new bonds and stock. The costs of issuance, generally called flotation costs, should be included in any NPV analysis.

Concept Questions

1. **Project Risk** If you can borrow all the money you need for a project at 6 percent, doesn't it follow that 6 percent is your cost of capital for the project?
2. **WACC and Taxes** Why do we use an aftertax figure for cost of debt but not for cost of equity?
3. **SML Cost of Equity Estimation** If you use the stock beta and the security market line to compute the discount rate for a project, what assumptions are you implicitly making?
4. **SML Cost of Equity Estimation** What are the advantages of using the SML approach to finding the cost of equity capital? What are the disadvantages? What are the specific pieces of information needed to use this method? Are all of these variables observable, or do they need to be estimated? What are some of the ways in which you could get these estimates?
5. **Cost of Debt Estimation** How do you determine the appropriate cost of debt for a company? Does it make a difference if the company's debt is privately placed as opposed to being publicly traded? How would you estimate the cost of debt for a firm whose only debt issues are privately held by institutional investors?
6. **Cost of Capital** Suppose Tom O'Bedlam, president of Bedlam Products, Inc., has hired you to determine the firm's cost of debt and cost of equity capital.
   a. The stock currently sells for ₹50 per share and the dividend per share will probably be about ₹5. Tom argues, "It will cost us ₹5 per share to use the stockholders' money this year, so the cost of equity is equal to 10 percent (= ₹5/₹50)." What's wrong with this conclusion?
   b. Based on the most recent financial statements, Bedlam Products's total liabilities are ₹8 million. Total interest expense for the coming year will be about ₹1 million. Tom therefore reasons, "We owe ₹8 million and we will pay ₹1 million interest. Therefore, our cost of debt is obviously 12.5 percent (= ₹1,000,000/₹8,000,000)." What's wrong with this conclusion?
   c. Based on his own analysis, Tom is recommending that the company increase its use of equity financing because "debt costs 12.5 percent, but equity only costs 10 percent; thus, equity is cheaper." Ignoring all the other issues, what do you think about the conclusion that the cost of equity is less than the cost of debt?
7. **Company Risk versus Project Risk** Both Dow Chemical Company, a large natural gas user, and Superior Oil, a major natural gas producer, are thinking of investing in natural gas wells near Houston. Both are all-equity-financed companies. Dow and Superior are looking at identical projects. They've analyzed their respective investments, which would involve a negative cash flow now and positive expected cash flows in the future. These cash flows would be the same for both firms. No debt would be used to finance the projects. Both companies estimate that their projects would have net present values of ₹1 million at an 18 percent discount rate and a −₹1.1 million NPV at a 22 percent discount rate. Dow has a beta of 1.25, whereas Superior has a beta of .75. The expected risk premium on the market is 8 percent and risk-free bonds are yielding 12 percent. Should either company proceed? Explain.
8. **Divisional Cost of Capital** Under what circumstances would it be appropriate for a firm to use different costs of capital for its different operating divisions? If the overall firm WACC was used as the hurdle rate

for all divisions, would the riskier divisions or the more conservative divisions tend to get most of the investment projects? Why? If you were to try to estimate the appropriate cost of capital for different divisions, what problems might you encounter? What are two techniques you could use to develop a rough estimate for each division's cost of capital?

9. **Leverage** Consider a levered firm's projects that have similar risks to the firm as a whole. Is the discount rate for the projects higher or lower than the rate computed using the security market line? Why?

10. **Beta** What factors determine the beta of a stock? Define and describe each.

Questions and Problems

BASIC (Questions 1–15)

1. **Calculating Cost of Equity** The Swanson Corporation's common stock has a beta of 1.07. If the risk-free rate is 3.4 percent and the expected return on the market is 11 percent, what is the company's cost of equity capital?

2. **Calculating Cost of Debt** Sunrise, Inc., is trying to determine its cost of debt. The firm has a debt issue outstanding with 23 years to maturity that is quoted at 96 percent of face value. The issue makes semiannual payments and has an embedded cost of 5 percent annually. What is the company's pretax cost of debt? If the tax rate is 21 percent, what is the aftertax cost of debt?

3. **Calculating Cost of Debt** Jiminy's Cricket Farm issued a 30-year, 4.5 percent semiannual bond three years ago. The bond currently sells for 104 percent of its face value. The company's tax rate is 22 percent.
   - **a.** What is the pretax cost of debt?
   - **b.** What is the aftertax cost of debt?
   - **c.** Which is more relevant, the pretax or the aftertax cost of debt? Why?

4. **Calculating Cost of Debt** For the firm in the previous problem, suppose the book value of the debt issue is ₹75 million. In addition, the company has a second debt issue on the market, a zero coupon bond with eight years left to maturity; the book value of this issue is ₹30 million, and the bonds sell for 81 percent of par. What is the company's total book value of debt? The total market value? What is your best estimate of the aftertax cost of debt now?

5. **Calculating WACC** Mullineaux Corporation has a target capital structure of 70 percent common stock and 30 percent debt. Its cost of equity is 11.3 percent and the cost of debt is 5.9 percent. The relevant tax rate is 23 percent. What is the company's WACC?

6. **Taxes and WACC** Brannan Manufacturing has a target debt-equity ratio of .35. Its cost of equity is 11 percent, and its pretax cost of debt is 6 percent. If the tax rate is 21 percent, what is the company's WACC?

7. **Finding the Capital Structure** Fama's Llamas has a weighted average cost of capital of 8.4 percent. The company's cost of equity is 11 percent, and its pretax cost of debt is 5.8 percent. The tax rate is 25 percent. What is the company's target debt-equity ratio?

8. **Book Value versus Market Value** Dani Corp. has 5.5 million shares of common stock outstanding. The current share price is ₹83, and the book value per share is ₹5. The company also has two bond issues outstanding. The first bond issue has a face value of ₹80 million, a coupon rate of 5.5 percent, and sells for 109 percent of par. The second issue has a face value of ₹45 million, a coupon rate of 5.8 percent, and sells for 108 percent of par. The first issue matures in 21 years, the second in 6 years. Both bonds make semiannual coupon payments.
   - **a.** What are the company's capital structure weights on a book value basis?
   - **b.** What are the company's capital structure weights on a market value basis?
   - **c.** Which are more relevant, the book or market value weights? Why?

9. **Calculating the WACC** In the previous problem, suppose the most recent dividend was ₹3.85 and the dividend growth rate is 5 percent. Assume that the overall cost of debt is the weighted average of that implied by the two outstanding debt issues. The tax rate is 21 percent. What is the company's WACC?

10. **WACC** Ursala, Inc., has a target debt-equity ratio of .65. Its WACC is 10.4 percent, and the tax rate is 23 percent.

    a. If the company's cost of equity is 14 percent, what is its pretax cost of debt?
    b. If instead you know that the aftertax cost of debt is 5.8 percent, what is the cost of equity?

11. **Finding the WACC** Given the following information for Huntington Power Co., find the WACC. Assume the company's tax rate is 21 percent.

Debt:	20,000 5.1 percent coupon bonds outstanding, ₹2,000 par value, 20 years to maturity, selling for 105 percent of par; the bonds make semiannual payments.
Common stock:	900,000 shares outstanding, selling for ₹77 per share; the beta is .95.
Market:	7 percent market risk premium and 3.5 percent risk-free rate.

12. **Finding the WACC** Titan Corporation has 5.4 million shares of common stock outstanding and 125,000 5.8 percent semiannual bonds outstanding, with a par value of ₹1,000 each. The common stock currently sells for ₹53 per share and has a beta of 1.15; the bonds have 25 years to maturity and sell for 103 percent of par. The market risk premium is 6.8 percent, T-bills are yielding 2.9 percent, and the company's tax rate is 22 percent.

    a. What is the firm's market value capital structure?
    b. If the company is evaluating a new investment project that has the same risk as the firm's typical project, what rate should the firm use to discount the project's cash flows?

13. **CAPM and WACC** An all-equity firm is considering the following projects:

Project	Beta	IRR
W	.83	9.4%
X	.92	11.6
Y	1.09	12.9
Z	1.35	14.1

    The T-bill rate is 4 percent and the expected return on the market is 12 percent.

    a. Which projects have a higher expected return than the firm's 12 percent cost of capital?
    b. Which projects should be accepted?
    c. Which projects would be incorrectly accepted or rejected if the firm's overall cost of capital was used as a hurdle rate?

14. **Calculating Flotation Costs** Suppose your company needs ₹43 million to build a new assembly line. Your target debt-equity ratio is .75. The flotation cost for new equity is 6 percent, but the flotation cost for debt is only 2 percent. Your boss has decided to fund the project by borrowing money because the flotation costs are lower and the needed funds are relatively small.

    a. What do you think about the rationale behind borrowing the entire amount?
    b. What is your company's weighted average flotation cost, assuming all equity is raised externally?
    c. What is the true cost of building the new assembly line after taking flotation costs into account? Does it matter in this case that the entire amount is being raised from debt?

15. **Calculating Flotation Costs** Shinedown Company needs to raise ₹95 million to start a new project and will raise the money by selling new bonds. The company will generate no internal equity for the foreseeable future. The company has a target capital structure of 65 percent common stock, 5 percent preferred stock, and 30 percent debt. Flotation costs for issuing new common stock are 7 percent, for new preferred stock are 4 percent, and for new debt are 2 percent. What is the true initial cost figure the company should use when evaluating its project?

INTERMEDIATE (Questions 16–21)

16. **WACC and NPV** Lebleu, Inc., is considering a project that will result in initial aftertax cash savings of ₹2.9 million at the end of the first year, and these savings will grow at a rate of 2 percent per year indefinitely. The firm has a target debt-equity ratio of .75, a cost of equity of 10 percent, and an aftertax cost of debt of 4.6 percent. The cost-saving proposal is somewhat riskier than the usual project the firm undertakes; management uses the subjective approach and applies an adjustment factor of +3 percent to the cost of capital for such risky projects. Under what circumstances should the company take on the project?

17. **Preferred Stock and WACC** The Saunders Investment Bank has the following financing outstanding. What is the WACC for the company?

Debt:	50,000 bonds with a coupon rate of 5.1 percent and a current price quote of 104.5; the bonds have 15 years to maturity and a par value of ₹1,000. 30,000 zero coupon bonds with a price quote of 23.6, 30 years until maturity, and a par value of ₹10,000. Both bonds have semiannual compounding.
Preferred stock:	235,000 shares of 3.6 percent preferred stock with a current price of ₹87 and a par value of ₹100.
Common stock:	2,100,000 shares of common stock; the current price is ₹79 and the beta of the stock is 1.08.
Market:	The corporate tax rate is 23 percent, the market risk premium is 7 percent, and the risk-free rate is 3.6 percent.

18. **Flotation Costs** Cookies 'n Cream, Inc., recently issued new securities to finance a new TV show. The project cost ₹45 million, and the company paid ₹2.2 million in flotation costs. In addition, the equity issued had a flotation cost of 7 percent of the amount raised, whereas the debt issued had a flotation cost of 2 percent of the amount raised. If the company issued new securities in the same proportion as its target capital structure, what is the company's target debt-equity ratio?

19. **Calculating the Cost of Equity** Ginger Industries stock has a beta of 1.08. The company just paid a dividend of ₹.85, and the dividends are expected to grow at 4 percent. The expected return on the market is 11.3 percent, and Treasury bills are yielding 3.4 percent. The most recent stock price for the company is ₹72.

    a. Calculate the cost of equity using the DDM.
    b. Calculate the cost of equity using the CAPM.
    c. Why do you think your estimates in (a) and (b) are so different?

20. **Firm Valuation** Orca Industries is considering the purchase of Shark Manufacturing. Shark is currently a supplier for Orca and the acquisition would allow Orca to better control its material supply. The current cash flow from assets for Shark is ₹6.8 million. The cash flows are expected to grow at 11 percent for the next five years before leveling off to 4 percent for the indefinite future. The costs of capital for Orca and Shark are 12 percent and 10 percent, respectively. Shark currently has 2.3 million shares of stock outstanding and ₹50 million in debt outstanding. What is the maximum price per share Orca should pay for Shark?

21. **Firm Valuation** Happy Times, Inc., wants to expand its party stores into the Southeast. In order to establish an immediate presence in the area, the company is considering the purchase of the privately held Joe's Party Supply. Happy Times currently has debt outstanding with a market value of ₹135 million and a YTM

of 5 percent. The company's market capitalization is ₹390 million and the required return on equity is 11 percent. Joe's currently has debt outstanding with a market value of ₹55 million. The EBIT for Joe's next year is projected to be ₹18.4 million. EBIT is expected to grow at 10 percent per year for the next five years before slowing to 3 percent in perpetuity. Net working capital, capital spending, and depreciation as a percentage of EBIT are expected to be 9 percent, 15 percent, and 8 percent, respectively. Joe's has 2.45 million shares outstanding and the tax rate for both companies is 21 percent.

a. Based on these estimates, what is the maximum share price that Happy Times should be willing to pay for Joe's?

b. After examining your analysis, the CFO of Happy Times is uncomfortable using the perpetual growth rate in cash flows. Instead, she feels that the terminal value should be estimated using the EV/EBITDA multiple. If the appropriate EV/EBITDA multiple is 9, what is your new estimate of the maximum share price for the purchase?

CHALLENGE (Questions 22–24)

22. **Flotation Costs and NPV** Landman Corporation (LC) manufactures time series photographic equipment. It is currently at its target debt-equity ratio of .60. It's considering building a new ₹73 million manufacturing facility. This new plant is expected to generate aftertax cash flows of ₹9.4 million in perpetuity. The company raises all equity from outside financing. There are three financing options:

1. *A new issue of common stock*: The flotation costs of the new common stock would be 6 percent of the amount raised. The required return on the company's new equity is 13 percent.
2. *A new issue of 20-year bonds*: The flotation costs of the new bonds would be 3 percent of the proceeds. If the company issues these new bonds at an annual coupon rate of 7 percent, they will sell at par.
3. *Increased use of accounts payable financing*: Because this financing is part of the company's ongoing daily business, it has no flotation costs and the company assigns it a cost that is the same as the overall firm WACC. Management has a target ratio of accounts payable to long-term debt of .15. (Assume there is no difference between the pretax and aftertax accounts payable cost.)

What is the NPV of the new plant? Assume that LC has a 21 percent tax rate.

23. **Flotation Costs** Chauhan Corp. has a debt-equity ratio of .65. The company is considering a new plant that will cost ₹55 million to build. When the company issues new equity, it incurs a flotation cost of 6 percent. The flotation cost on new debt is 2.4 percent. What is the initial cost of the plant if the company raises all equity externally? What if it typically uses 60 percent retained earnings? What if all equity investment is financed through retained earnings?

24. **Project Evaluation** This is a comprehensive project evaluation problem bringing together much of what you have learned in this and previous chapters. Suppose you have been hired as a financial consultant to Defense Electronics, Inc. (DEI), a large, publicly traded firm that is the market share leader in radar detection systems (RDSs). The company is looking at setting up a manufacturing plant overseas to produce a new line of RDSs. This will be a five-year project. The company bought some land three years ago for ₹3.9 million in anticipation of using it as a toxic dump site for waste chemicals, but it built a piping system to safely discard the chemicals instead. The land was appraised last week for ₹4.1 million on an aftertax basis. In five years, the aftertax value of the land will be ₹4.4 million, but the company expects to keep the land for a future project. The company wants to build its new manufacturing plant on this land; the plant and equipment will cost ₹37 million to build. The following market data on DEI's securities is current:

Debt:	205,000 bonds with a coupon rate of 5.8 percent outstanding, 25 years to maturity, selling for 106 percent of par; the bonds have a ₹1,000 par value each and make semiannual payments.
Common stock:	8,600,000 shares outstanding, selling for ₹67 per share; the beta is 1.15.
Preferred stock:	500,000 shares of 4 percent preferred stock outstanding, selling for ₹83 per share; the stock has a par value of ₹100.
Market:	7 percent expected market risk premium; 3.1 percent risk-free rate.

DEI uses G.M. Wharton as its lead underwriter. Wharton charges DEI spreads of 7 percent on new common stock issues, 5 percent on new preferred stock issues, and 3 percent on new debt issues. Wharton has included all direct and indirect issuance costs (along with its profit) in setting these spreads. Wharton has recommended to DEI that it raise the funds needed to build the plant by issuing new shares of common stock. DEI's tax rate is 25 percent. The project requires ₹1.5 million in initial net working capital investment to get operational. Assume DEI raises all equity for new projects externally.

a. Calculate the project's initial Year 0 cash flow, taking into account all side effects.

b. The new RDS project is somewhat riskier than a typical project for DEI, primarily because the plant is being located overseas. Management has told you to use an adjustment factor of +2 percent to account for this increased riskiness. Calculate the appropriate discount rate to use when evaluating DEI's project.

c. The manufacturing plant has an eight-year tax life and DEI uses straight-line depreciation. At the end of the project (i.e., the end of Year 5), the plant and equipment can be scrapped for ₹4.9 million. What is the aftertax salvage value of this plant and equipment?

d. The company will incur ₹6.9 million in annual fixed costs. The plan is to manufacture 8,500 RDSs per year and sell them at ₹13,450 per machine; the variable production costs are ₹10,600 per RDS. What is the annual operating cash flow (OCF) from this project?

e. DEI's comptroller is primarily interested in the impact of DEI's investments on the bottom line of reported accounting statements. What will you tell her is the accounting break-even quantity of RDSs sold for this project?

f. Finally, DEI's president wants you to throw all your calculations, assumptions, and everything else into the report for the chief financial officer; all he wants to know is what the RDS project's internal rate of return (IRR) and net present value (NPV) are. What will you report?

Excel Master It! Problem

You want to calculate the WACC for auto parts retailer AutoZone (AZO). Complete the following steps to construct a spreadsheet that can be updated.

Excel Master coverage online

a. Using an input for the ticker symbol, create hyperlinks to the web pages that you will need to find all of the information necessary to calculate the cost of equity. Use a market risk premium of 7 percent when using CAPM.

b. Create hyperlinks to go to the FINRA bond quote website and the SEC EDGAR database and find the information for the company's bonds. Create a table that calculates the cost of debt for the company. Assume the tax rate is 21 percent.

c. Finally, calculate the market value weights for debt and equity. What is the WACC for AutoZone?

Mini Case COST OF CAPITAL FOR MASTER TOOLS

You have recently been hired by Master Tools (MT) in its relatively new treasury management department. MT was founded eight years ago by Martha Masters. Martha found a method to streamline the manufacturing process, resulting in a cheaper tool. The tools manufactured by MT are designed for the mass market and sold primarily through retail. The company is privately owned by Martha and her family, and it had sales of ₹97 million last year.

MT primarily sells to do-it-yourself (DIY) customers who use the tools for personal projects, although it does sell through various online marketplaces. As a result, the company's sales are price sensitive. When the company had sufficient capital, it would expand production. Relatively little formal analysis has been used in its capital budgeting process. Martha has just read about capital budgeting techniques and has come to you for help. For starters, the company has never attempted to determine its cost of capital, and Martha would like you to perform the analysis. Because the company is privately owned, it is difficult to determine the cost of equity for the company. Martha wants you to use the pure play approach to estimate the cost of capital for MT, and she has chosen Snap-On Incorporated as a representative company. The following questions will lead you through the steps to calculate this estimate.

1. Most publicly traded corporations are required to submit 10-Q (quarterly) and 10-K (annual) reports to the SEC detailing their financial operations over the previous quarter or year, respectively. These corporate filings are available on the SEC website at **www.sec.gov**. Go to the SEC website, follow the "Search SEC.gov" box, and search for SEC filings made by Snap-On (SNA). Find the most recent 10-Q or 10-K, and download the form. Look at the balance sheet to find the book value of debt and the book value of equity.
2. To estimate the cost of equity for SNA, go to **finance.yahoo.com** and enter the ticker symbol "SNA." Follow the links to answer the following questions: What is the most recent stock price listed for SNA? What is the market value of equity, or market capitalization? How many shares of stock does SNA have outstanding? What is the forward annual dividend? Analysts have estimated a 6 percent growth rate for dividends. What is the cost of equity for SNA using the DDM? What is the beta for SNA? Now go back to finance.yahoo.com and follow the "Bonds" link. What is the yield on three-month Treasury bills? Using the historical market risk premium, what is the cost of equity for SNA using CAPM? What is your final estimate for the cost of equity?
3. Go to **www.reuters.com** and find the list of competitors in the industry. Find the beta for each of these competitors and then calculate the industry average beta. Using the industry average beta, what is the cost of equity? Does it matter if you use the beta for SNA or the beta for the industry in this case?
4. You now need to calculate the cost of debt for SNA. Go to **finra-markets.morningstar.com/BondCenter**, enter SNA as the company, and find the yield to maturity for each of SNA's bonds. What is the weighted average cost of debt for SNA using the book value weights and using the market value weights? Does it make a difference in this case if you use book value weights or market value weights?
5. You now have all the necessary information to calculate the weighted average cost of capital for SNA. Calculate the WACC using book value weights and market value weights. SNA has a 21 percent tax rate. Which number is more relevant?
6. You used SNA as a pure play company to estimate the cost of capital for MT. Are there any potential problems with this approach in this situation? What improvements might you suggest?

Appendix 13A Economic Value Added and the Measurement of Financial Performance

To access the appendix for this chapter, please log on to www.mheducation.co.in.

14

PART IV: CAPITAL STRUCTURE AND DIVIDEND POLICY

Efficient Capital Markets and Behavioral Challenges

The Nasdaq stock market was raging in the late 1990s, gaining about 23 percent, 14 percent, 35 percent, and 87 percent from 1996 to 1999, respectively. That spectacular run came to a jarring halt, and the Nasdaq lost about 40 percent in 2000, followed by another 30 percent in 2001. The ISDEX, an index of internet-related stocks, rose from 100 in January 1996 to 1,100 in February 2000, a gain of about 1,000 percent! It then fell like a rock to 600 by May 2000.

A bubble can exist in a single asset, as well. For example, many investors saw a tech bubble echo in Tesla Motors, which increased in value more than 590 percent from March 22, 2013, to February 26, 2014. In fact, one analysis of the company's valuation indicated that the stock could be overvalued by about 150 percent. Tesla's stock evidently ran out of juice as it gained only about 39 percent over the next four years. Of course, Tesla then had another run. The stock jumped 811 percent from October 4, 2019, to September 14, 2020.

Nowhere was the tech bubble more evident than in the initial public offering (IPO) market. In the IPO market, companies offer stock for sale for the first time, and large initial gains are not uncommon. However, during 1999 to 2000, stupendous gains became commonplace. For example, stock in VA Linux shot up 698 percent in the first day of trading! Over this period, a total of 194 IPOs doubled, or more than doubled, in value on the first day. In contrast, only 39 companies had done so in the preceding 24 years.

The performance of the Nasdaq over this period, and particularly the rise and fall of internet stocks, has been described by many as one of the greatest market "bubbles" in history. The argument is that prices were inflated to economically ridiculous levels before investors came to their senses, which then caused the bubble to pop and prices to plunge. Debate over whether the stock market of the late 1990s really was a bubble has generated much controversy. In this chapter, we discuss the competing ideas, present some evidence on both sides, and then examine the implications for financial managers.

Please visit us at **rwjcorporatefinance.blogspot.com** for the latest developments in the world of corporate finance.

14.1 Can Financing Decisions Create Value?

Earlier parts of the book showed how to evaluate projects according to the net present value criterion. The real world is a competitive one where projects with positive net present value are not always easy to come by. However, through hard work or through good fortune, a firm can identify winning projects. To create value from capital budgeting decisions, the firm is likely to:

1. Locate an unsatisfied demand for a particular product or service.
2. Create a barrier to make it more difficult for other firms to compete.
3. Produce products or services at a lower cost than the competition.
4. Be the first to develop a new product.

The next eight chapters concern various aspects of *financing* decisions. Typical financing decisions include how much and what types of debt and equity to sell and when to sell them. Just as the net present value criterion was used to evaluate capital budgeting projects, we now want to use the same criterion to evaluate financing decisions.

Though the procedure for evaluating financing decisions is identical to the procedure for evaluating projects, the results are different. It turns out that the typical firm has many more capital expenditure opportunities with positive net present values than financing opportunities with positive net present values. In fact, we later show that some plausible financial models imply that no valuable financial opportunities exist at all.

Though this dearth of profitable financing opportunities will be examined in detail later, a few remarks are in order now. We maintain that there are basically three ways to create valuable financing opportunities:

1. *Fool investors.* Assume that a firm can raise capital either by issuing stock or by issuing a more complex security–say, a combination of stock and warrants. Suppose that, in truth, 100 shares of stock are worth the same as 50 units of our complex security. If investors have a misguided, overly optimistic view of the complex security, perhaps the 50 units can be sold for more than the 100 shares of stock. Clearly, this complex security provides a valuable financing opportunity because the firm is getting more than fair value for it.

   Financial managers try to package securities to receive the greatest value. A cynic might view this as attempting to fool investors.

   However, the theory of efficient capital markets implies that investors cannot easily be fooled. It says that securities are appropriately priced at all times, implying that the market as a whole is shrewd indeed. In our example, 50 units of the complex security would sell for the same price as 100 shares of stock. Thus, corporate managers cannot attempt to create value by fooling investors. Instead, managers must create value in other ways.
2. *Reduce costs or increase subsidies.* We show later in the book that certain forms of financing have greater tax advantages than other forms. Clearly, a firm packaging securities to minimize taxes can increase firm value. In addition, any financing technique involves other costs. For example, investment bankers, lawyers, and accountants must be paid. A firm packaging securities to minimize these costs also can increase its value.

EXAMPLE 14.1

Valuing Financial Subsidies Suppose Veerabhadraiah Electronics Company is thinking about relocating its plant to Bihar, where labor costs are lower. In the hope that it can stay in Veerabhadraiah, the company has submitted an application to the state of Veerabhadraiah to issue ₹2 million in five-year, tax-exempt industrial bonds. The coupon rate on industrial revenue bonds in Veerabhadraiah is currently 5 percent. This is an attractive rate because

(continued)

the normal cost of debt capital for Veerabhadraiah Electronics Company is 10 percent. The firm will pay annual interest of ₹100,000 (= ₹2 million × .05), rather than annual interest of ₹200,000 (= ₹2 million × .10). What is the NPV of this potential financing transaction?

If the application is accepted and the industrial revenue bonds are issued by the Veerabhadraiah Electronics Company, the NPV (ignoring corporate taxes) is:

$$\begin{aligned} \text{NPV} &= ₹2{,}000{,}000 - \left[\frac{₹100{,}000}{1.1} + \frac{₹100{,}000}{1.1^2} + \frac{₹100{,}000}{1.1^3} + \frac{₹100{,}000}{1.1^4} + \frac{₹2{,}100{,}000}{1.1^5}\right] \\ &= ₹2{,}000{,}000 - 1{,}620{,}921 \\ &= ₹379{,}079 \end{aligned}$$

This transaction has a positive NPV. The Veerabhadraiah Electronics Company obtains subsidized financing where the value of the subsidy is ₹379,079. Notice that we discounted the interest and principal payments at the normal cost of debt of 10 percent. Remember, the discount rate should always reflect the risk of the cash flows being discounted, not the subsidized borrowing rate.

3. *Create a new security.* There has been a surge in financial innovation in recent decades. In a speech on financial innovation, Nobel laureate Merton Miller asked the rhetorical question, "Can any 20-year period in recorded history have witnessed even a tenth as much new development? Where corporations once issued only straight debt and straight common stock, they now issue zero coupon bonds, adjustable rate notes, floating-rate notes, putable bonds, credit-enhanced debt securities, receivable-backed securities, adjusted-rate preferred stock, convertible adjustable preferred stock, auction rate preferred stock, single-point adjustable rate stock, convertible exchangeable preferred stock, adjustable-rate convertible debt, zero coupon convertible debt, debt with mandatory common stock purchase contracts–to name just a few!"[1] And financial innovation has occurred even more rapidly in the years following Miller's speech.

   Though the advantages of each instrument are different, one general theme is that these new securities cannot easily be duplicated by combinations of existing securities. A previously unsatisfied clientele may pay extra for a specialized security catering to its needs. For example, putable bonds let the purchaser sell the bond at a fixed price back to the firm. This innovation creates a price floor, allowing the investor to reduce her downside risk. Perhaps risk-averse investors or investors with little knowledge of the bond market would find this feature particularly attractive.

   Corporations gain by issuing these unique securities at high prices. However, the value captured by the innovator may well be small in the long run because the innovator usually cannot patent or copyright an idea. Soon many firms are issuing securities of the same kind, forcing prices down as a result.

This brief introduction sets the stage for the next several chapters of the book. Most of the rest of this chapter examines how efficient capital markets work. We show that if capital markets are efficient, corporate managers cannot create value by fooling investors. This is quite important because managers must create value in other, perhaps more difficult, ways. We also describe behavioral challenges to the notion of perfectly efficient capital markets.

[1]Merton H. Miller, "Financial Innovation: The Last Twenty Years and the Next," *Journal of Financial and Quantitative Analysis* 21, no. 4 (December 1986): 459–71.

14.2 A Description of Efficient Capital Markets

An efficient capital market for stocks is one in which stock prices fully reflect available information about the underlying value of the stock. To illustrate how an efficient market works, suppose the Firozabad Camera Corporation (FCC) is attempting to develop a camera that will double the speed of the auto-focusing system now available. FCC believes this research has a positive NPV.

Now consider a share of stock in FCC. What determines the willingness of investors to hold shares of FCC at a particular price? One important factor is the probability that FCC will be the first company to develop the new auto-focusing system. In an efficient market, we would expect the price of the shares of FCC to increase if this probability increases.

Suppose FCC hires a well-known engineer to develop the new auto-focusing system. In an efficient market, what will happen to FCC's share price when this is announced? If the engineer is paid a salary that fully reflects his contribution to the firm, the price of the stock will not necessarily change. Suppose instead that hiring the engineer is a positive NPV transaction. In this case, the price of shares in FCC will increase because the firm can pay the engineer a salary below his true value to the company.

When will the increase in the price of FCC's shares occur? Assume that the hiring announcement is made in a press release on Wednesday morning. In an efficient market, the price of shares in FCC will *immediately* adjust to this new information. Investors should not be able to buy the stock on Wednesday afternoon and make a profit on Thursday. This would imply that it took the stock market a day to realize the implication of the FCC press release. The efficient market hypothesis predicts that the price of shares of FCC stock on Wednesday afternoon will already reflect the information contained in the Wednesday morning press release.

The **efficient market hypothesis (EMH)** has implications for investors and for firms:

- Because information is reflected in prices immediately, investors should only expect to obtain a normal rate of return. Awareness of information when it is released does an investor no good. The price adjusts before the investor has time to trade on it.
- Firms should expect to receive fair value for securities that they sell. *Fair* means that the price they receive from issuing securities is the present value. Thus, valuable financing opportunities that arise from fooling investors are unavailable in efficient capital markets.

Figure 14.1 presents several possible adjustments in stock prices. The solid line represents the stock's price path in an efficient market. In this case, the price adjusts immediately to the new information with no further price changes. The dotted line depicts a slow reaction. Here it takes the market 30 days to fully absorb the information. Finally, the broken line illustrates an overreaction and subsequent correction back to the true price. The broken line and the dotted line show the paths that the stock price might take in an inefficient market. If the price of the stock takes several days to adjust, trading profits would be available to investors who suitably timed their purchases and sales.[2]

[2]Now you should appreciate the following short story. A student was walking down the hall with her finance professor when they both saw a ₹20 bill on the ground. As the student bent down to pick it up, the professor shook his head slowly and, with a look of disappointment on his face, said patiently to the student, "Don't bother. If it was really there, someone else would have already picked it up."

The moral of the story reflects the logic of the efficient market hypothesis: If you think you have found a pattern in stock prices or a simple device for picking winners, you probably have not. If there was such a simple way to make money, someone else would have found it before. Furthermore, if people tried to exploit the information, their efforts would become self-defeating and the pattern would disappear.

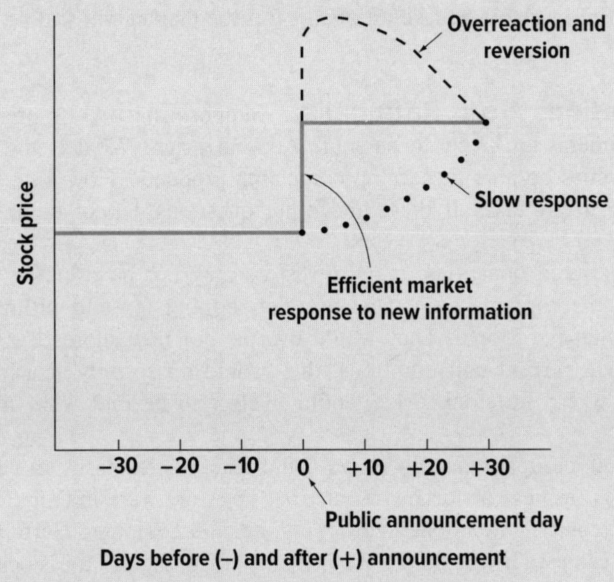

Efficient market response: The price instantaneously adjusts to and fully reflects new information; there is no tendency for subsequent increases and decreases.
Slow response: The price adjusts slowly to the new information; 30 days elapse before the price completely reflects the new information.
Overreaction: The price overadjusts to the new information; there is a bubble in the price sequence.

Figure 14.1 Reaction of Stock Price to New Information in Efficient and Inefficient Markets

FOUNDATIONS OF MARKET EFFICIENCY

Figure 14.1 shows the consequences of market efficiency. But what are the conditions that cause market efficiency? Andrei Shleifer argues that there are three conditions, any one of which will lead to efficiency: (1) rationality, (2) independent deviations from rationality, and (3) arbitrage.[3] A discussion of these conditions follows.

Rationality Imagine that all investors are rational. When new information is released in the marketplace, all investors will adjust their estimates of stock prices in a rational way. In our example, investors will use the information in FCC's press release, in conjunction with existing information about the firm, to determine the NPV of FCC's new venture. If the information in the press release implies that the NPV of the venture is ₹10 million and there are 2 million shares, investors will calculate that the NPV is ₹5 per share. While FCC's old price might be, say, ₹40, no one would now transact at that price. Anyone interested in selling would sell only at a price of at least ₹45 (= ₹40 + 5). And anyone interested in buying would now be willing to pay up to ₹45. In other words, the price would rise by ₹5. And the price would rise immediately because rational investors would see no reason to wait before trading at the new price.

[3]Andrei Shleifer, *Inefficient Markets: An Introduction to Behavioral Finance* (Oxford: Oxford University Press, 2000).

Of course, we all know times when individuals seem to behave less than perfectly rationally. Perhaps it is too much to ask that all investors behave rationally. But the market will still be efficient if the following scenario holds.

Independent Deviations from Rationality Suppose that FCC's press release is not all that clear. How many new cameras are likely to be sold? At what price? What is the likely cost per camera? Will other camera companies be able to develop competing products? How long will the development of these competing products likely take? If these and other questions cannot be answered easily, it will be difficult to estimate NPV.

With so many unanswered questions, many investors may not be thinking clearly. Some investors might get caught up in the romance of a new product, hoping for and ultimately believing in sales projections well above what is rational. They would overpay for new shares. And if they needed to sell shares (perhaps to finance current consumption), they would do so only at a high price. If these individuals dominate the market, the stock price would likely rise beyond what market efficiency would predict.

However, due to emotional resistance, investors could react just as easily to new information in a pessimistic manner. After all, business historians tell us that investors were initially quite skeptical about the benefits of the telephone, copier, automobile, motion picture, and computer. Certainly, they could be overly skeptical about this new camera. If investors were primarily of this type, the stock price would likely rise less than market efficiency would predict.

But suppose that about as many individuals were irrationally optimistic as were irrationally pessimistic. Prices would likely rise in a manner consistent with market efficiency, even though most investors would be classified as less than fully rational. Market efficiency does not require rational individuals–only countervailing irrationalities.

However, this assumption of offsetting irrationalities at all times may be unrealistic. Perhaps at certain times most investors are swept away by excessive optimism and at other times are caught in the throes of extreme pessimism. But even here there is an assumption that will produce efficiency.

Arbitrage Imagine a world with two types of individuals: the irrational amateurs and the rational professionals. The amateurs get caught up in their emotions, at times believing irrationally that a stock is undervalued and at other times believing the opposite. If the passions of the different amateurs do not cancel each other out, these amateurs, by themselves, would tend to carry stocks either above or below their efficient prices.

Now let's bring in the professionals. Suppose professionals go about their business methodically and rationally. They study companies thoroughly, evaluate the evidence objectively, estimate stock prices coldly and clearly, and act accordingly. If a stock is underpriced, they would buy it. If it is overpriced, they would sell it. And their confidence would likely be greater than that of the amateurs. Whereas an amateur might risk only a small sum, these professionals might risk large ones, knowing as they do that the stock is mispriced. Furthermore, they would be willing to rearrange their entire portfolio in search of a profit. If they find that UltraTech Cements is underpriced, they might sell the Ambuja Cements stock they own to buy Ultratech *Arbitrage* is the word that comes to mind here because arbitrage generates profit from the simultaneous purchase and sale of different, but substitute, securities. If the arbitrage of professionals dominates the speculation of amateurs, markets would still be efficient.

Short Sales Someone who engages in arbitrage is called an arbitrageur. An arbitrageur often will want to make a bet that the price of a stock or other asset will decrease. If the arbitrageur owns the asset in question, he can just sell it. But what if he does not own it? No problem; he can do what is known as a **short sale**. With the help of his broker, the short seller borrows the asset and then sells it, thereby creating a "short" position. At a future date, he buys it back and returns it.

A short seller profits if the price he pays to buy the asset back is less than what he got from selling it in the first place. Note that it is very important that the short seller "close" the short position by buying it back and returning it. In fact, as they say on Wall Street, "He who sells what isn't his'n, must buy it back or go to pris'n." The same is true for "She who sells what isn't hers'n," but it doesn't rhyme as well.

14.3 The Different Types of Efficiency

In our previous discussion, we assumed that the market responds immediately to all available information. In actuality, certain information may affect stock prices more quickly than other information. To handle differential response rates, researchers separate information into different types. The most common classification system identifies three types: information about past prices, publicly available information, and all information. The effect of these three information sets on prices is examined next.

THE WEAK FORM

Imagine a trading strategy that recommends buying a stock after it has gone up three days in a row and recommends selling a stock after it has gone down three days in a row. This strategy uses information based only on past prices. It does not use any other information, such as earnings forecasts, merger announcements, or money supply figures. A capital market is said to be *weakly efficient*, or to satisfy **weak form efficiency**, if it fully incorporates the information in past stock prices. The preceding strategy would not be able to generate profits if weak form efficiency holds.

Often, weak form efficiency is represented mathematically as:

$$P_t = P_{t-1} + \text{Expected return} + \text{Random error}_t \qquad \textbf{(14.1)}$$

Equation 14.1 states that the price today is equal to the sum of the last observed price plus the expected return on the stock (in rupees) plus a random component occurring over the interval. The last observed price could have occurred yesterday, last week, or last month, depending on the sampling interval. The expected return is a function of a security's risk and would be based on the models of risk and return in previous chapters. The random component is due to new information about the stock. It could be either positive or negative and has an expectation of zero. The random component in any period is unrelated to the random component in any past period. Hence, this component is not predictable from past prices. If stock prices follow Equation 14.1, they are said to follow a **random walk**.[4]

Weak form efficiency is the weakest type of efficiency that we would expect a financial market to display because historical price information is the easiest kind of information about a stock to acquire. If it were possible to make extraordinary profits by finding patterns in stock price movements, everyone would do it, and any profits would disappear in the scramble.

This effect of competition can be seen in Figure 14.2. Suppose the price of a stock displays a cyclical pattern, as indicated by the wavy curve. Shrewd investors would buy at the low points, forcing those prices up. Conversely, they would sell at the high points, forcing prices down. Via competition, cyclical regularities would be eliminated, leaving only random fluctuations.

[4]For purposes of this text, the random walk can be considered synonymous with weak form efficiency. Technically, the random walk is a slightly more restrictive hypothesis because it assumes that stock returns are identically distributed through time.

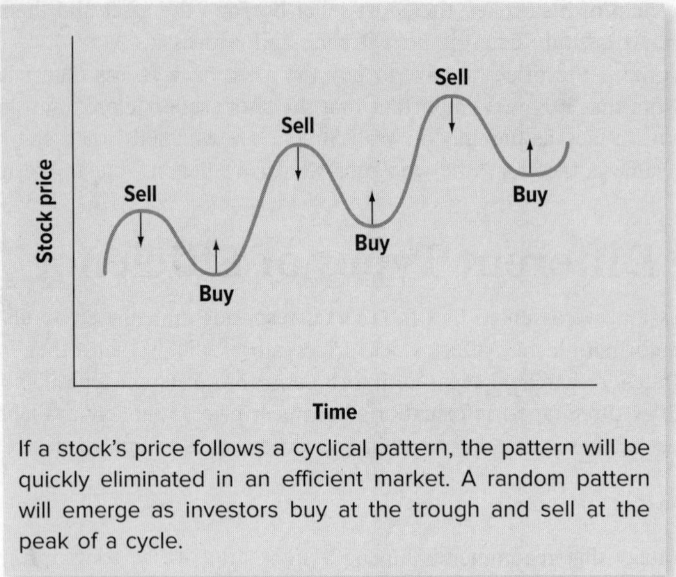

Figure 14.2 Investor Behavior Tends to Eliminate Cyclical Patterns

THE SEMISTRONG AND STRONG FORMS

If weak form efficiency is controversial, even more contentious are the two stronger types of efficiency, **semistrong form efficiency** and **strong form efficiency**. A market is semistrong form efficient if prices reflect, or incorporate, all publicly available information, including information such as published accounting statements for the firm, as well as historical price information. A market is strong form efficient if prices reflect all information, public or private.

The information set of past prices is a subset of the information set of publicly available information, which in turn is a subset of all information. This is shown in Figure 14.3. Strong form efficiency implies semistrong form efficiency, and semistrong form efficiency implies weak form efficiency. The reverse is not true. The distinction between semistrong form efficiency and weak form efficiency is that semistrong form efficiency requires not only that the market be efficient with respect to historical price information, but also that all of the information available to the public be reflected in prices.

To illustrate the different forms of efficiency, imagine an investor who always sold a particular stock after its price had risen. A market that was only weak form efficient and not semistrong form efficient would still prevent such a strategy from generating excess or abnormal positive profits. According to weak form efficiency, a recent price rise does not imply that the stock is overvalued.

Now consider a firm reporting increased earnings. An individual might consider investing in the stock after reading the news release providing this information. However, if the market is semistrong form efficient, the price should rise immediately upon the news release. The investor would end up paying the higher price, eliminating all chance for an abnormal return.

At the furthest end of the spectrum is strong form efficiency. This form says that anything that is pertinent to the value of the stock and that is known to at least one investor is, in fact, fully incorporated

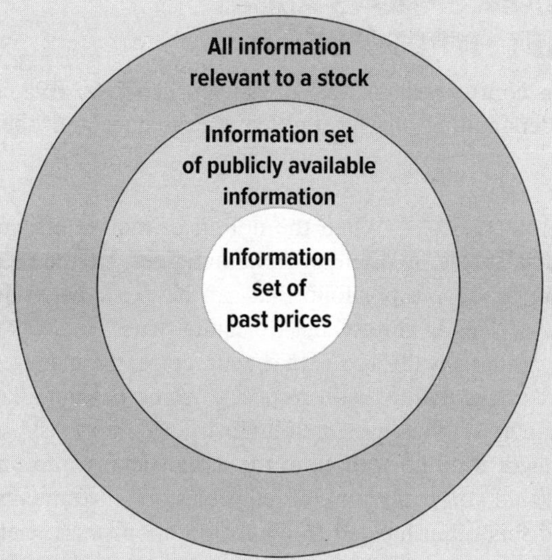

The information set of past prices is a subset of the set of all publicly available information, which in turn is a subset of all information. If today's price reflects only information about past prices, the market is weak form efficient. If today's price reflects all publicly available information, the market is semistrong form efficient. If today's price reflects all information, both public and private, the market is strong form efficient.

Semistrong form efficiency implies weak form efficiency, and strong form efficiency implies semistrong form efficiency.

Figure 14.3 Relationship among Three Different Information Sets

into the stock price. A strict believer in strong form efficiency would deny that an insider who knew whether a company mining operation had struck gold could profit from that information. Such a devotee of the strong form efficient market hypothesis might argue that as soon as the insider tried to trade on his information, the market would recognize what was happening and the price would shoot up before he could buy any of the stock. Alternatively, believers in strong form efficiency argue that there are no secrets, and as soon as the gold is discovered, the secret gets out.

One reason to expect that markets are weak form efficient is that it is so cheap and easy to find patterns in stock prices. Anyone who can program a computer and knows a little bit of statistics can search for such patterns. Proponents of weak form efficiency argue that if there were such patterns, people would find and exploit them, in the process causing them to disappear.

Semistrong form efficiency, though, implies more sophisticated investors than does weak form efficiency. An investor must be skilled at economics and statistics and steeped in the idiosyncrasies of individual industries and companies. Furthermore, to acquire and use such skills requires talent, ability, and time. In the jargon of the economist, such an effort is costly, and the ability to be successful at it is probably in scarce supply.

As for strong form efficiency, this is further down the road than semistrong form efficiency. It is difficult to believe that the market is so efficient that someone with valuable inside information cannot prosper from it. And empirical evidence tends to be unfavorable to this form of market efficiency.

SOME COMMON MISCONCEPTIONS ABOUT THE EFFICIENT MARKET HYPOTHESIS

No idea in finance has been as controversial as that of efficient markets. To a certain extent, the controversy can be attributed to a misunderstanding of what the hypothesis does and does not say. We illustrate three misconceptions next.

The Efficacy of Dart Throwing When the notion of market efficiency was first publicized and debated in the popular financial press, it often was characterized by the following quote: ". . . throwing darts at the financial page will produce a portfolio that can be expected to do as well as any managed by professional security analysts."[5,6] This is almost, but not quite, true.

All the efficient market hypothesis really says is that, on average, the manager cannot achieve an abnormal or excess return. The excess return is defined with respect to some benchmark expected return, such as that from the CAPM model of Chapter 11. The investor still must decide how risky a portfolio she wants. In addition, a random dart thrower might wind up with all of the darts sticking into one or two high-risk stocks that deal in genetic engineering. Would you really want all of your stock investments in two such stocks?

The failure to understand this often has led to confusion about market efficiency. For example, sometimes it is wrongly argued that market efficiency means that it does not matter what you do because the efficiency of the market will protect the unwary. However, someone once remarked, "The efficient market protects the sheep from the wolves, but nothing can protect the sheep from themselves."

What efficiency does say is that the price investors pay when they buy a share of stock is a fair price in the sense that it reflects the value of that stock given the information that is available about it. Investors need not worry that they are paying too much for a stock with a low dividend or some other characteristic because the market has already incorporated it into the price. However, investors still have to worry about such things as their level of risk exposure and their degree of diversification.

Price Fluctuations Much of the public is skeptical of efficiency because stock prices fluctuate from day to day. However, daily price movement is in no way inconsistent with efficiency; a stock in an efficient market adjusts to new information by changing price. A great deal of new information comes into the stock market each day. In fact, the absence of daily price movements in a changing world might suggest an inefficiency.

Stockholder Disinterest Many laypeople are skeptical that the market price can be efficient if only a fraction of the outstanding shares changes hands on any given day. However, the number of traders in a stock on a given day is generally far less than the number of people following the stock. This is true because an individual will trade only when his appraisal of the value of the stock differs enough from the market price to justify incurring brokerage commissions and other transaction costs. Furthermore, even if the number of traders following a stock is small relative to the number of outstanding shareholders, the stock can be expected to be efficiently priced as long as a number of interested traders use the publicly available information. That is, the stock price can reflect the available information even if many stockholders never follow the stock and are not considering trading in the near future.

[5] Burton Malkiel, *A Random Walk Down Wall Street: The Time-Tested Strategy for Successful Investing* (New York: W.W. Norton & Company, 2019).

[6] Older articles often referred to the benchmark of "dart-throwing monkeys." As government involvement in the securities industry grew, the benchmark often was restated as "dart-throwing congressional representatives."

14.4 The Evidence

The evidence for and against the efficient market hypothesis is extensive. In this section, we will review studies covering the broad categories of weak form, semistrong form, and strong form efficiency.

THE WEAK FORM

Weak form efficiency implies that a stock's past price movement is unrelated to the stock's future price movement. The work of Chapter 11 allows us to test this implication. In that chapter, we discussed the concept of correlation between the returns on two different stocks. The correlation between the return on UltraTech Cements and the return on Ambuja Cements is likely to be relatively high because both stocks are in the same industry. Conversely, the correlation between the return on UltraTech Cements and the return on the stock of, say, a European fast-food chain is likely to be low.

Financial economists frequently speak of **serial correlation**, which involves only one security. This is the correlation between the current return on a security and the return on the same security over a later period. A positive coefficient of serial correlation for a particular stock indicates a tendency toward *continuation*, also referred to as *momentum*. That is, a higher-than-average return in the past is likely to be followed by higher-than-average returns in the future. Similarly, a lower-than-average return in the past is likely to be followed by lower-than-average returns in the future.

A negative coefficient of serial correlation for a particular stock indicates a tendency toward *reversal*. A higher-than-average return in the past is likely to be followed by lower-than-average returns in the future. Similarly, a lower-than-average return in the past is likely to be followed by higher-than-average returns in the future. Both significantly positive and significantly negative serial correlation coefficients are indications of market inefficiencies; in either case, past returns can be used to predict future returns.

Serial correlation coefficients for stock returns near zero would be consistent with weak form efficiency. A current stock return that is higher than average is as likely to be followed by lower-than-average returns as by higher-than-average returns. Similarly, a current stock return that is lower than average is as likely to be followed by higher-than-average returns as by lower-than-average returns.

Table 14.1 shows the serial correlation coefficients for daily price changes for seven large U.S. companies. These coefficients indicate whether there are relationships between yesterday's return and today's return. As can be seen, five of the coefficients are negative, implying that a higher-than-average return yesterday makes a lower-than-average return today more likely. Conversely, two of the coefficients are positive, implying that a higher-than-average return yesterday makes a higher-than-average return today more likely.

Table 14.1 Serial Correlation Coefficients for Selected Companies

Company	Serial Correlation Coefficient in 2020
Tesla	.0095
Kellogg's	.0054
UltraTech	−.0087
JM Smucker	−.0099
Albemarle	−.0201
Equifax	−.0237
Clorox	−.0565

Kellogg's coefficient of .0054 is slightly positive, implying that a positive return today makes a positive return tomorrow slightly more likely. JM Smucker's coefficient is negative, implying that a positive return today makes a negative return tomorrow slightly more likely. However, the coefficients are so small relative to estimation error and transaction costs that the results are generally considered to be consistent with weak form efficient capital markets.

Because correlation coefficients vary between -1 and $+1$, the coefficients in this table are small. Given both estimation errors and transaction costs, numbers with these magnitudes would generally be considered consistent with weak form efficiency.

When these serial correlation tests are applied to large historical data samples, a different picture emerges. Researchers have found evidence of long-run and short-run reversals as well as medium-run momentum. The empirical evidence supports the existence of reversals at the one- to three-year horizon (the long run) as well as the one- to four-week horizon (the short run). For example, the long run reversal phenomenon predicts that stocks that have outperformed in the past one to three years will underperform in the next one to three years. In between the very long and short horizons, stocks appear to exhibit momentum, in which past performance persists instead of reversing.

Overall, evidence of reversals and momentum imply that past returns can predict future returns, leading proponents of behavioral finance to argue that the market is not weak form efficient. However, skeptics of this line of research are quick to point out that these conclusions could result from data mining our limited set of historical trading data. These patterns could be a mere coincidence, and the same patterns may not replicate in the future. These skeptics also point out that trading strategies that bet on momentum in stock markets are prone to devastating crashes.[7]

Regardless of whether you believe the evidence based on large historical data samples, we caution that you should not draw conclusions from patterns in a single price series. People may be inclined to see patterns in stock prices when none exist. The work of both psychologists and statisticians suggests that most people do not know what randomness looks like. Consider Figure 14.4. The top graph was generated by a computer using random numbers and Equation 14.1. Yet we have found that people examining the chart generally see patterns. Different people see different patterns and forecast different future price movements. However, in our experience, viewers are all quite confident of the patterns they see.

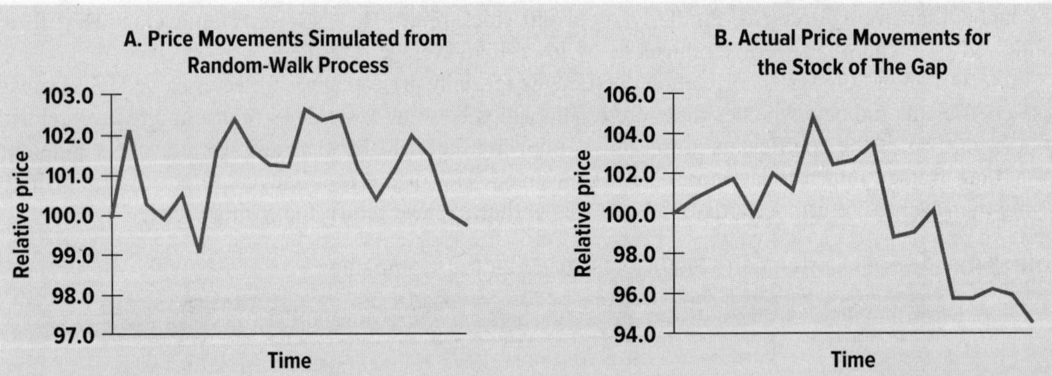

Although stock price movements simulated from a random-walk process are random by definition, people often see patterns. People also may see patterns in The Gap's price movements. However, the price patterns of The Gap are quite similar to those of the randomly simulated series.

Figure 14.4 Simulated and Actual Stock Price Movements

[7]For example, market patterns during the 2020 COVID-19 pandemic led to a dramatic momentum crash. www.wsj.com/articles/markets-vaccine-euphoria-was-bad-news-for-momentum-funds-11605695400.

Next, consider the bottom graph, which tracks actual movements in The Gap's stock price. This graph may look quite nonrandom to some, suggesting weak form inefficiency. However, it also bears a close visual resemblance to the simulated series, and statistical tests indicate that it indeed behaves like a purely random series. In our opinion, people claiming to see patterns in stock price data are probably seeing optical illusions.

THE SEMISTRONG FORM

The semistrong form of the efficient market hypothesis implies that prices should reflect all publicly available information. We present two types of tests of this form.

Event Studies The *abnormal return* (AR) on a given stock for a particular day can be calculated by subtracting the market's return on the same day (R_m)–as measured by a broad-based index such as the S&P Composite Index–from the actual return (R) on the stock for that day.[8] We write this difference algebraically as:

$$\text{AR} = R - R_m$$

The following system will help us understand tests of the semistrong form:

$$\begin{aligned}&\text{Information released on day } t-1 \rightarrow \text{AR}_{t-1}\\&\text{Information released on day } t \qquad\ \rightarrow \text{AR}_{t}\\&\text{Information released on day } t+1 \rightarrow \text{AR}_{t+1}\end{aligned}$$

The arrows indicate that the abnormal return in any time period is related only to the information released during that period.

According to the efficient market hypothesis, a stock's abnormal return at Day t, AR_t, should reflect the release of information at the same day, t. Any information released before then should have no effect on abnormal returns in this period because all of its influence should have been felt before. In other words, an efficient market would already have incorporated previous information into prices. Because a stock's return today cannot depend on what the market does not yet know, information that will be known only in the future cannot influence the stock's return either. Hence, the arrows point in the direction that is shown, with information in any period affecting only that period's abnormal return. *Event studies* are statistical studies that examine whether the arrows are as shown or whether the release of information influences returns on other days.

These studies also speak of *cumulative abnormal returns* (CARs), as well as abnormal returns. Consider a firm with ARs of 1 percent, −3 percent, and 6 percent for Dates −1, 0, and 1, respectively, relative to a corporate announcement. The CARs for Dates −1, 0, and 1 would be 1 percent, −2 percent [= 1% + (−3%)], and 4 percent [= 1% + (−3%) + 6%], respectively.

As an example, consider the study by Szewczyk, Tsetsekos, and Zantout on dividend omissions.[9] Figure 14.5 shows the plot of CARs for a sample of companies announcing dividend omissions. Because dividend omissions are generally considered to be bad events, we would expect abnormal returns to be negative around the time of the announcements. They are negative, as evidenced by a drop in the CAR on both the day before

[8] We also can measure the abnormal return by using the market model. In this case, the abnormal return is:

$$\text{AR} = R - (\alpha + \beta R_m)$$

[9] Samuel H. Szewczyk, George P. Tsetsekos, and Zaher Z. Zantout, "Do Dividend Omissions Signal Future Earnings or Past Earnings?" *Journal of Investing* 6, no. 1 (Spring 1997): 40–53.

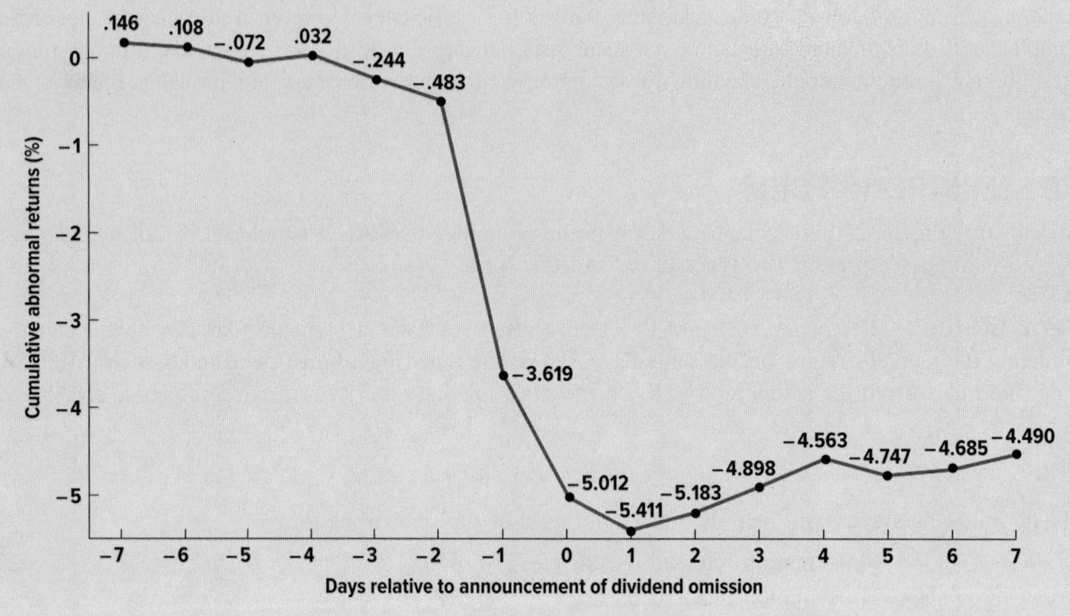

Cumulative abnormal returns (CARs) fall on both the day before the announcement and the day of the announcement of dividend omissions. CARs have little movement after the announcement date. This pattern is consistent with market efficiency.

Figure 14.5 Cumulative Abnormal Returns for Companies Announcing Dividend Omissions

SOURCE: From Exhibit 2 in Samuel H. Szewczyk, George P. Tsetsekos, and Zaher Z. Zantout, "Do Dividend Omissions Signal Future Earnings or Past Earnings?" *Journal of Investing*, Spring 1997.

the announcement (Day −1) and the day of the announcement (Day 0).[10] However, note that there is virtually no movement in the CARs in the days following the announcement. This implies that the bad news is fully incorporated into the stock price by the announcement day, a result consistent with market efficiency.

Over the years, this type of methodology has been applied to many events. Announcements of dividends, earnings, mergers, capital expenditures, and new issues of stock are a few examples of the vast literature in the area. The early event study tests generally supported the view that the market is semistrong form (and therefore also weak form) efficient. However, a number of more recent studies present evidence that the market does not incorporate all relevant information immediately. Some conclude from this that the market is not efficient. Others argue that this conclusion is unwarranted given statistical and methodological problems in the studies. This issue will be addressed in more detail later in the chapter.

[10]An astute reader may wonder why the abnormal return is negative on Day −1 as well as on Day 0. To see why, first note that the announcement date is generally taken in academic studies to be the publication date of the story in *The Wall Street Journal (WSJ)*. Then consider a company announcing a dividend omission via a press release at noon on Tuesday. The stock should fall on Tuesday. The announcement will be reported in the *WSJ* on Wednesday because the Tuesday edition of the *WSJ* has already been printed. For this firm, the stock price falls on the day before the announcement in the *WSJ*.

Alternatively, imagine another firm announcing a dividend omission via a press release on Tuesday at 8 P.M. Because the stock market is closed at that late hour, the stock price will fall on Wednesday. Because the *WSJ* will report the announcement on Wednesday, the stock price falls on the day of the announcement in the *WSJ*.

Firms may make announcements either during trading hours or after trading hours, so stocks should fall on both Day −1 and Day 0 relative to publication in the *WSJ*.

The Record of Mutual Funds If the market is efficient in the semistrong form, then no matter what publicly available information mutual fund managers rely on to pick stocks, their average returns should be the same as those of the average investor in the market as a whole. We can test market efficiency, then, by comparing the performance of actively managed mutual funds to index funds. Actively managed mutual funds try to use publicly available information and certain analytical skills to perform better than the market as a whole. Index funds are passively managed and try to replicate the performance of certain stock market indexes. The Vanguard 500 Index Fund is a well-known example of an index fund that mimics the Standard and Poor's 500 index. Figure 14.6 is a bar chart that shows the percentage of managed equity funds that beat the Vanguard 500 Index Fund in each year from 1989 to 2018. In only 12 of the 30 years did more than half of the professional money managers beat the Vanguard 500 Index Fund.

Perhaps nothing rankles successful stock market investors more than to have some professor tell them that they are not necessarily smart, just lucky. However, while Figure 14.6 represents only one study, there have been many papers on mutual funds. The overwhelming evidence here is that mutual funds, on average, do not beat broad-based indexes.

By and large, mutual fund managers rely on publicly available information. The finding that they do not outperform market indexes is consistent with semistrong form and weak form efficiency.

However, this evidence does not imply that mutual funds are bad investments for individuals. Though these funds fail to achieve better returns than some indexes of the market, they permit the investor to buy a portfolio of many stocks (the phrase "a well-diversified portfolio" is often used) that is tailored to the investor's preferences.

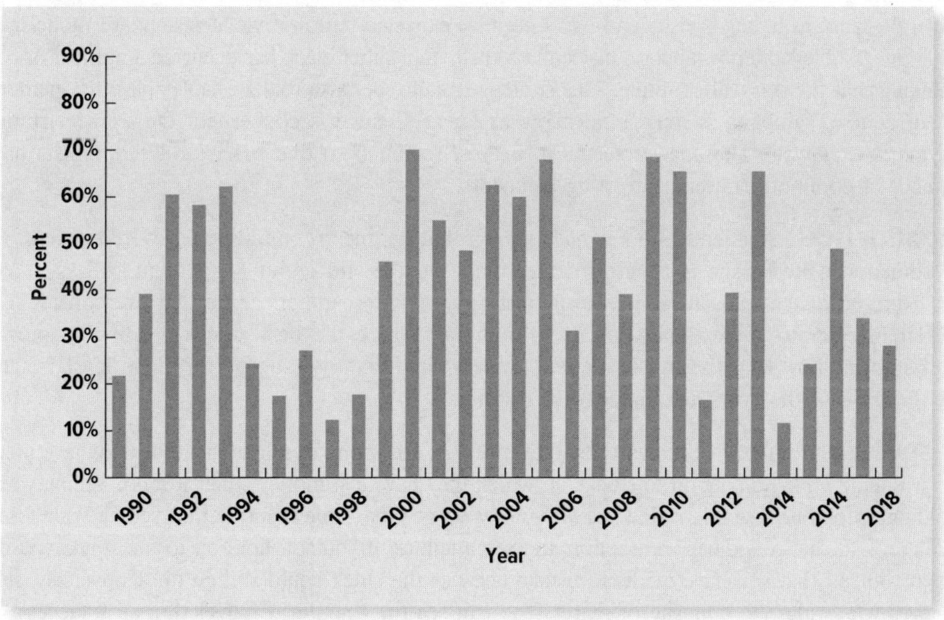

Figure 14.6 Percentage of Managed Equity Funds Beating the Vanguard 500 Index Fund, One-Year Returns

SOURCE: Bradford Jordan, D. Thomas W. Miller, and Steven D. Dolvin, *Fundamentals of Investments*, 9th ed. (New York: McGraw Hill, 2020).

THE STRONG FORM

Even the strongest adherents to the efficient market hypothesis would not be surprised to find that markets are inefficient in the strong form. After all, if an individual has information that no one else has, it is likely that she can profit from it.

One group of studies of strong form efficiency investigates insider trading. Insiders in firms have access to information that is not generally available. But if the strong form of the efficient market hypothesis holds, they should not be able to profit by trading on their information. A U.S. government agency, the Securities and Exchange Commission, requires insiders in companies to report trades they make in their own company's stock. By examining records of such trades, we can see whether they made abnormal returns. A number of studies support the view that these trades were abnormally profitable. Thus, strong form efficiency does not seem to be substantiated by the evidence.

14.5 The Behavioral Challenge to Market Efficiency

In Section 14.2, we presented three conditions, rationality, independent deviations from rationality, and arbitrage, any one of which will lead to market efficiency. However, some members of the academic community argue that none of the three conditions is likely to hold in reality. This point of view is based on what is called *behavioral finance.* Let us examine the behavioral view of each of these three conditions.

To hear a podcast on market efficiency and psychological biases, listen to **tinyurl.com/y3j4k5f6**.

RATIONALITY

Are people really rational? Not always. Just travel to Atlantic City or Las Vegas or locally to Goan Casinos to see people gambling, sometimes with large sums of money. The casino's take implies a negative expected return for the gambler. Because gambling is risky and has a negative expected return, it violates standard models of rationality. In addition, gamblers often will bet on black at a roulette table after black has occurred a number of consecutive times, thinking that the run will continue. This strategy is faulty because roulette tables have no memory.

But, of course, gambling is only a sideshow as far as finance is concerned. Do we see irrationality in financial markets as well? The answer seems to be yes, so much so that behavioral economists have names for a number of common irrational investing behaviors.

Overconfidence Academic studies have shown that people are, on average, overconfident. For example, ask someone if he or she is a better driver than average and about 80 percent will say, "Yes." How does this overconfidence translate to investing performance? Researchers argue that overconfidence is likely to cause an investor to overestimate his or her ability to pick the best stocks, leading to more trading. Empirical studies show that the most frequent traders significantly underperform the least frequent ones, primarily because of the costs associated with trading.

The Disposition Effect Studies show that investors are prone to sell stocks that they have made money on (their winners) while holding on to stocks on which they have lost money (their losers). Selling your winners while holding onto your losers is called the *disposition effect.* One explanation is that selling your losers causes regret. You look at that round-trip transaction and see a failure. If you still hold on to the stock, you don't have to admit to yourself that you have made a mistake because the stock could still go up. Conversely, selling your winners gives you pride, the opposite of regret. You can see the round-trip transaction as a success.

The disposition effect is irrational because your wealth depends on the current market value of your portfolio, regardless of whether you sell (to realize your gains or losses). Unfortunately, the disposition effect hurts investors. First, it has bad tax consequences. You have to pay taxes on the capital gains from your winners while not being able to take the tax deductions from your losers. Second, research on momentum has shown that stocks that have done well over the past six months tend to keep doing well over the next six months and vice versa. Given this pattern, investors should hold on to their winners and sell their losers, the exact opposite of the disposition effect behavior.

Familiarity and Home Bias Why do most people root for their home-town football team, rather than a football team a thousand miles away? Psychologists tell us that people are often guilty of *familiarity.* That is, we like what we are familiar with. Familiarity is a rather innocuous trait in most areas of life, but it can lead to something unfortunate in investing: under diversification. A number of studies show that individuals overinvest in their own country, reducing their level of international diversification. The investor's attitude appears to be "I live in a particular country, I'm familiar with that country, and, doggone it, I'm going to invest in that country." This overinvestment in the stock market of one's home country is often called *home bias.* And there is even domestic home bias. Research shows that individuals often overinvest in stocks headquartered in their home town. Other studies report that employees typically overweight their employer's stock in their 401(k) employer-based savings plan.

Representativeness (also called Overreacction) This attribute can be illustrated with the gambling example we used earlier. Gamblers believing a run of black will continue are in error because the probability of a black spin is still only about 50 percent. These gamblers are guilty of *representativeness* because they draw conclusions from insufficient data, generally from the recent past. During the great bull market between 1995 and 1999, many investors thought the market would continue its big gains for a long time, forgetting that bear markets also occur.

Conservatism (also called Underreaction) As representativeness is another word for overreaction, conservatism is another word for *underreaction.* Human beings often underreact, as was the case with the Telegraph Company, which later became Western Union. The firm was not worried about Alexander Graham Bell's invention of the telephone, as indicated by the following statement the firm released in 1876:

> *The "Telephone purports" to transmit the speaking voice over telegraph wires. We found that the voice is very weak and indistinct, and grows even weaker when long wires are used between the sender and receiver. . . . Furthermore, why would any person want to use this ungainly and impractical device when he can send a messenger to the local telegraph office and have a clear written message sent to any large city in the United States?*[11]

To hear about the emotions of investing, listen to **tinyurl.com/y6zhznw6**.

Underreaction can also occur if we fail to pay attention. There are only so many hours in a day, and investors may lack the time or focus necessary to process every piece of news. Studies have shown that investors underreact to firm news that is released on Friday evenings, over holidays, or during popular sporting events, when investors may not be paying attention to financial news. Investors also underreact to less salient news releases, such as information presented in the footnotes of corporate disclosure documents.

Does underreaction affect the stock market? In the next section, we'll discuss evidence that prices seem to adjust slowly to the information contained in earnings announcements. These findings suggest that an investor can profit from a strategy of buying a stock after an announcement of a surprisingly high earnings number and selling a stock after an announcement of a surprisingly low earnings number.

Risk-Taking Following Gains or Losses

House Money Effect How do individuals adjust their risk-taking following gains? A number of studies show that, on average, individuals increase their risk following gains. Las Vegas casinos find that gamblers are more likely to take big risks after winning money from casinos because they are no longer playing with their own money but with the *house's money.*

[11]Prof. R. Levine, Electrical Engineering Department, Southern Methodist University, EETS8302 (NTU TC716-N) Digital Telephony, Fall 2001.

Snakebite Effect and Get-Evenitis How do individuals adjust their risk-taking following losses? Here the evidence is two-sided. Some studies show that individuals reduce their level of risk following losses. In other words, they get *snakebit.* Getting snakebit is quite understandable. Imagine yourself after the stock market fell 22 percent on October 19, 1987. You might never have seen such an extreme drop. In response, you might have reduced your equity holdings, or have made the decision to get out of the stock market completely, behavior in line with the expression "Once bitten, twice shy."

But that is not the only way to react to losses. A number of studies show that people increase their level of risk in order to get even. In other words, they acquire a case of *get-evenitis.*

INDEPENDENT DEVIATIONS FROM RATIONALITY

The previous list of behavioral traits suggests that investors can be irrational much of the time. Are the deviations from rationality generally random, thereby likely to cancel out in a large population of investors? To the contrary, because psychologists conclude that the above irrational traits are rather pervasive across individuals, behavioral economists argue that these deviations from rationality cannot be expected to cancel each other out.

Rather than go through all of the traits we discussed, let's work with two, representativeness and conservatism, where the case can be made that deviations from rationality across individuals do not cancel each other out. We said that individuals have a tendency to overreact to information, particularly if it is recent. Some researchers suggest that this representativeness can cause bubbles. People may see a sector of the stock market with a short history of high revenue growth and extrapolate that the high revenue growth will continue forever, leading to high price-earnings and price-book multiples for these stocks. When the revenue growth inevitably slows, investors reduce these multiples, implying that stock prices will fall.

Other research suggests that the market often underreacts to new information, implying that conservatism dominates the market at times. We mentioned earlier that prices adjust slowly to the information in earnings announcements. This is an example where investors as a whole appear to underreact to information, so that the slowness to respond to new information by some investors is not canceled out by rapid reaction to the same information by other investors.

ARBITRAGE

As discussed above, behavioral economists do not believe that deviations from rationality must be independent across individuals. However, in Section 14.2 we suggested that professional investors, knowing that securities are mispriced, could buy the underpriced ones while selling correctly priced (or even overpriced) substitutes. This might undo any mispricing caused by emotional amateurs.

Trading of this sort is likely to be more risky than it appears at first glance. Suppose professionals generally believed that SBI's stock was underpriced. They would buy it while selling their holdings in, say, HDFC Bank (owned by Restaurant Brands International) and ICICI Bank's. However, if amateurs were taking opposite positions, prices would adjust to correct levels only if the positions of amateurs were small relative to those of the professionals. In a world of many amateurs, a few professionals would have to take big positions to bring prices into line, perhaps even engaging heavily in short selling. Buying large amounts of one stock and short selling large amounts of other stocks is quite risky, even if the two stocks are in the same industry. Here, unanticipated bad news about SBI's and unanticipated good news about the other two stocks would cause the professionals to register large losses.

In addition, if amateurs mispriced SBI's today, what is to prevent SBI's from being even more mispriced tomorrow? As the great economist John Maynard Keynes once remarked, "Markets can remain irrational longer than you can remain solvent."[12]

[12]This quote is often attributed to Lord Keynes, but there is no evidence that we can find that he ever said it.

This risk of further mispricing, even in the presence of no new information, makes this type of arbitrage risky. Imagine a shrewd professional who believed internet stocks were overpriced in 1998. Had he bet on a decline at that time, he would have lost a lot in the near term because prices rose tremendously through March 2000. While his position would have eventually made money because prices later fell, short-term losses may have forced him to close the position before that happened.

In conclusion, the arguments presented here suggest that the theoretical underpinnings of the efficient capital markets hypothesis, presented in Section 14.2, might not hold in reality. That is, investors may be irrational, irrationality may be related across investors rather than canceling out across investors, and arbitrage strategies may involve too much risk to eliminate market inefficiencies.

14.6 Empirical Challenges to Market Efficiency

Section 14.4 gave an overview of the evidence for and against the three forms of market efficiency. We now discuss some additional empirical challenges to market efficiency. Adherents of market efficiency generally refer to results of this type as *anomalies.*

1. *Limits to arbitrage*: Royal Dutch Petroleum and Shell Transport agreed to merge their interests in 1907, with all subsequent cash flows being split on a 60 percent–40 percent basis between the two companies. However, both companies continued to be publicly traded. You might imagine that the market value of Royal Dutch would always be 1.5 (= 60/40) times that of Shell. That is, if Royal Dutch ever became overpriced, rational investors would buy Shell instead of Royal Dutch. If Royal Dutch were underpriced, investors would buy Royal Dutch. In addition, arbitrageurs would go further by buying the underpriced security and selling the overpriced security short.

   However, Figure 14.7 shows that Royal Dutch and Shell rarely traded at parity (i.e., 60/40) between 1962 and 2005, at which time the two companies merged. Why would these deviations occur? As stated in the previous section, behavioral finance suggests that there are limits to arbitrage. That is, an investorbuying the overpriced asset and selling the underpriced asset does not have a sure thing. Deviations from parity could actually increase in the short run, implying losses for the arbitrageur. Thus, risk considerations may force arbitrageurs to take positions that are too small to move prices back to parity. Academics have documented a number of these deviations from parity. Froot and Dabora show similar results both for the twin companies of Unilever N.V. and Unilever PLC and for two classes of SmithKline Beecham stock.[13] Lamont and Thaler present similar findings for 3Com and its subsidiary Palm, Inc. (see Example 14.2 for more about 3Com and Palm).[14] Other researchers find price behavior in closed-end mutual funds suggestive of parity deviations.

2. *Earnings surprises*: Common sense suggests that prices should rise when earnings are reported to be higher than expected and prices should fall when the reverse occurs. However, market efficiency implies that prices will adjust immediately to the announcement, while behavioral finance would predict another pattern. Kolasinski and Li rank companies by the extent of their *earnings surprise*–that is, the difference between current quarterly earnings and an estimate of earnings for that quarter anticipated by the market.[15] The authors form a portfolio of companies with the most extreme positive surprises and another portfolio of companies with the most extreme negative surprises.

[13]Kenneth A. Froot and Emil M. Dabora, "How Are Stock Prices Affected by the Location of Trade?" *Journal of Financial Economics* 53, no. 2 (August 1999): 189–216.

[14]Owen A. Lamont and Richard H. Thaler, "Can the Market Add and Subtract? Mispricing in Tech Stock Carve Outs," *Journal of Political Economy* 111, no. 2 (April 2003): 227–68.

[15]Adam Kolasinski and Xu Li, "Can Rational Learning Explain Underreaction Anomalies? Evidence from Insider Trading after Earnings Announcements," University of Washington unpublished paper, 2011. The authors estimated anticipated earnings by a seasonal random walk model.

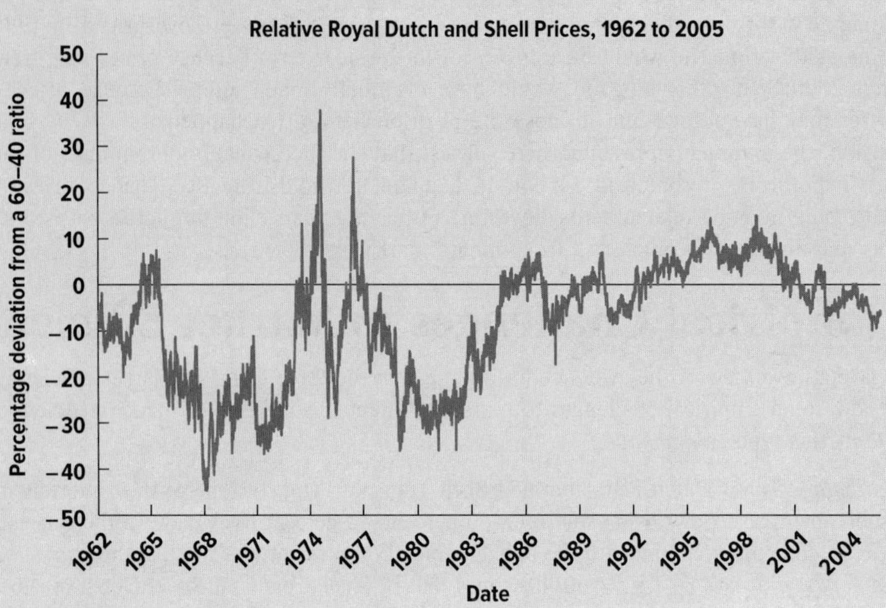

Apparently arbitrage is unable to keep the ratio of the market value of Royal Dutch to the market value of Shell at parity.

Figure 14.7 Deviations of the Ratio of the Market Value of Royal Dutch to the Market Value of Shell from Parity

SOURCE: Stephen Ross, Randolph Westerfield, and Bradford Jordan, *Fundamentals of Corporate Finance,* 12th ed., Alternate ed. (New York: McGraw Hill, 2021): 752.

EXAMPLE 14.2

Can Stock Market Investors Add and Subtract? On March 2, 2000, 3Com, a profitable provider of computer networking products and services, sold 5 percent of one of its subsidiaries, Palm, to the public via an initial public offering (IPO). 3Com planned to distribute the remaining Palm shares to 3Com shareholders at a later date. Under the plan, if you owned one share of 3Com, you would receive 1.5 shares of Palm. So after 3Com sold part of Palm via the IPO, investors could buy Palm shares directly or indirectly by purchasing shares of 3Com and waiting.

What makes this case interesting is what happened in the days that followed the Palm IPO. If you owned one 3Com share, you would be entitled, eventually, to 1.5 shares of Palm. Therefore, each 3Com share should be worth at least 1.5 times the value of each Palm share. We say at least because the other parts of 3Com were profitable. As a result, each 3Com share should have been worth much more than 1.5 times the value of one Palm share. But as you might guess, things did not work out this way.

The day before the Palm IPO, shares in 3Com sold for ₹104.13. After the first day of trading, Palm closed at ₹95.06 per share. Multiplying ₹95.06 by 1.5 results in ₹142.59, which is the minimum value we would expect to pay for 3Com. But the day Palm closed at ₹95.06, 3Com shares closed at ₹81.81, more than ₹60 lower than the price implied by Palm.

(continued)

A 3Com price of ₹81.81 when Palm was selling for ₹95.06 implies that the market valued the rest of 3Com's businesses (per share) at ₹81.81 − 142.59 = −₹60.78. Given the number of 3Com shares outstanding at the time, this means the market placed a *negative* value of about ₹22 billion on the rest of 3Com's businesses. Of course, a stock price cannot be negative. This means that the price of Palm relative to 3Com was much too high.

To profit from this mispricing, investors would purchase shares of 3Com and sell shares of Palm. This trade was a no-brainer. In a well-functioning market, arbitrage traders would force the prices into alignment quickly. What happened?

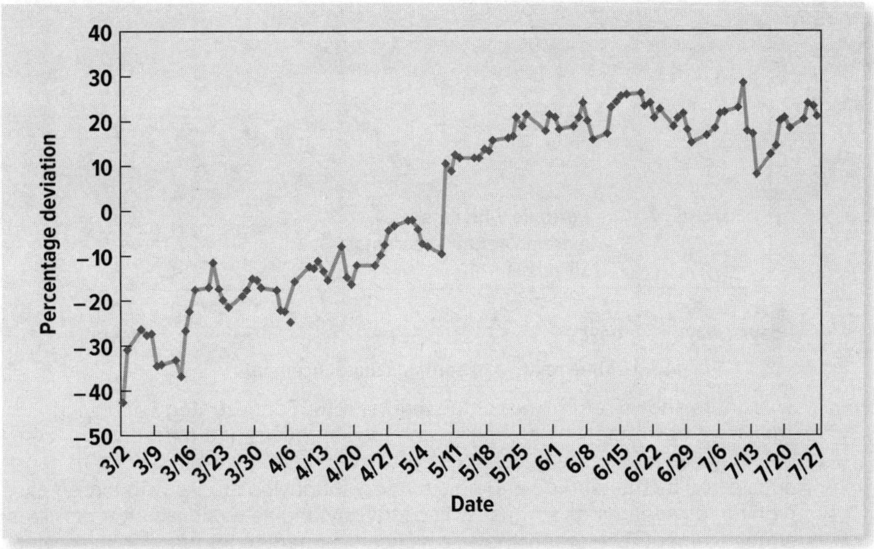

Figure 14.8 The Percentage Difference between One Share of 3Com and One and One-Half Shares of Palm, March 2, 2000, to July 27, 2000

As you can see in Figure 14.8, the market valued 3Com and Palm shares in such a way that the non-Palm part of 3Com had a negative value for about two months from March 2, 2000, until May 8, 2000. Thus, the pricing error was corrected by market forces, but not instantly, which is consistent with the existence of limits to arbitrage.

Figure 14.9 shows returns from buying the two portfolios, net of the return on the overall market. As can be seen, prices adjust slowly to earnings announcements, with the portfolio with the positive surprises outperforming the portfolio with the negative surprises over the next 275 days. Many other researchers obtain similar results.

Why do prices adjust slowly? Behavioral finance suggests that investors exhibit conservatism because they are slow to adjust to the information contained in the announcements.

3. *Size*: In 1981, two important papers presented evidence that in the United States, the returns on stocks with small market capitalizations were greater than the returns on stocks with large market capitalizations over most of the 20th century.[16] The studies have since been replicated over different

[16] See Rolt Banz, "The Relationship between Return and Market Value of Common Stocks," *Journal of Financial Economics* (March 1981); Marc R. Reinganum, "Misspecification of Capital Asset Pricing: Empirical Anomalies Based on Earnings' Yields and Market Values," *Journal of Financial Economics* 9, no. 1 (1981): 19–46.

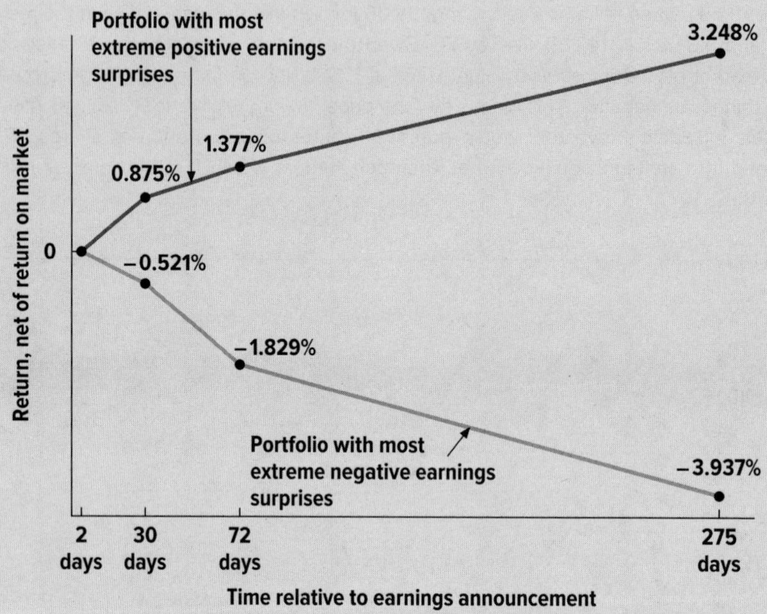

This figure shows returns net of the market return on a strategy of buying stocks with extremely high positive earnings surprises (the difference between current quarterly earnings and an estimate of earnings for that quarter anticipated by the market) and on a strategy of buying stocks with extremely high negative earnings surprises. The strategy begins two days after earnings announcement. The graph shows a slow adjustment to information in earnings announcements.

Figure 14.9 Returns on Two Investment Strategies Based on Earnings Surprise

SOURCE: Adapted from Table 1 of Adam Kolasinski and Xu Li, "Can Rational Learning Explain Underreaction Anomalies? Evidence from Insider Trading after Earnings Announcements," University of Washington unpublished paper, 2011.

periods and in different countries. Figure 14.10 shows average returns over the period from 1926 to 2013 for 10 portfolios of U.S. stocks ranked by size. As can be seen, over this period, the average return on small stocks is higher than the average return on large stocks, though the effect appears to have become smaller in more recent years. Although much of the differential performance is probably compensation for the extra risk of small stocks, researchers have generally argued that not all of it can be explained by risk differences. For example, it appears that most of the difference in performance occurs in the month of January.[17]

4. *Value versus growth*: A number of papers have argued that stocks with high book-value-to-stock-price ratios and/or high earnings-to-price ratios (generally called *value stocks*) outperform stocks with low ratios (*growth stocks*). Fama and French found higher average returns for value stocks than for

[17]The first paper to document this "January effect" was Donald B. Keim "Size-Related Anomalies and Stock Return Seasonality: Further Empirical Evidence," *Journal of Financial Economics* 12, no. 1 (June 1983): 13–32.

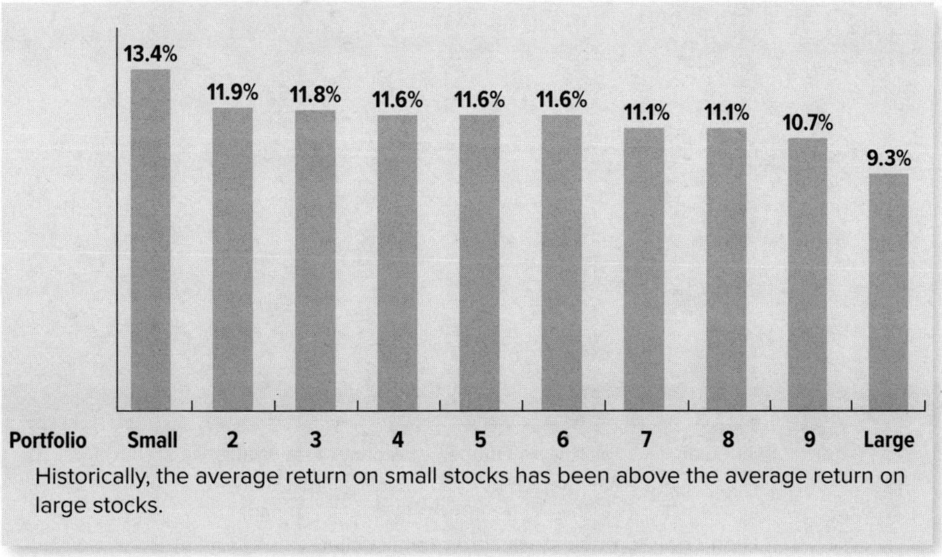

Figure 14.10 Annual Stock Returns on Portfolios Sorted by Size (Market Capitalization) from 1926 to 2013

SOURCE: Calculated from index values provided in Table 7.3 of *Ibbotson SBBI® 2014 Classic Yearbook* (Chicago: Morningstar, 2014).

growth stocks around the world.[18] Figure 14.11 shows the average monthly return differential between value and growth stocks in different geographical regions.

Because the return difference is so large and because these ratios can be obtained so easily for individual stocks, the results may constitute strong evidence against market efficiency. However, a number of papers suggest that the unusual returns are due to differences in risk, not to a true inefficiency.[19] Also, as with the size effect, the value effect appears to have become weaker or disappeared altogether in more recent years. Because the debate revolves around arcane statistical points, we will not pursue the issue further. However, it is safe to say that no conclusion is warranted at this time. As with so many other topics in finance and economics, further research is needed.

5. *Crashes and bubbles*: The stock market crash of October 19, 1987, is extremely puzzling. The market dropped between 20 and 25 percent on a Monday following a weekend during which little surprising news was released. A drop of this magnitude for no apparent reason is inconsistent with market efficiency. Because the somewhat similar crash of October 1929 is still an enigma, it is doubtful that the more recent 1987 debacle will be explained anytime soon–not to mention the crash of 2008, which we discussed in Chapter 10. The comments of an eminent historian are apt here: When asked what, in his opinion, the effect of the French Revolution of 1789 was, he replied that it was too early to tell.

   Perhaps stock market crashes are evidence consistent with the **bubble theory** of speculative markets. That is, security prices sometimes move wildly above their true values. Eventually, prices fall back to their original level, causing great losses for investors. Consider the behavior of internet stocks of the late 1990s. Figure 14.12

[18]Taken from Table I of Eugene F. Fama and Kenneth R. French, "Size, Value, and Momentum in International Stock Returns," *Journal of Financial Economics* 105, no. 3 (September 2012): 457–72.

[19]For example, see Eugene F. Fama and Kenneth R. French, "Multifactor Explanations of Asset Pricing Anomalies," *Journal of Finance* 51, no. 1 (March 1996): 55–84; Hengjie Ai and Dana Kiku, "Growth to Value: Option Exercise and the Cross Section of Equity Returns," *Journal of Financial Economics* 107, no. 2 (February 2013): 325–49.

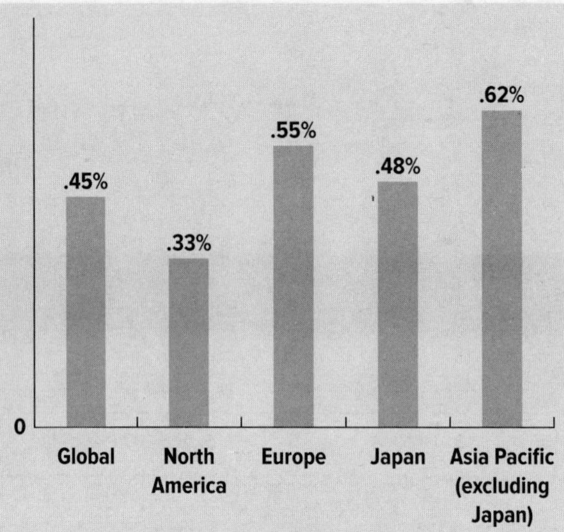

High book-to-price stocks (frequently called value stocks) outperform low book-to-price (growth) stocks in different countries.

Figure 14.11 Monthly Return Difference between High Book-to-Price Stocks (Value Stocks) and Low Book-to-Price Stocks (Growth Stocks) around the World

SOURCE: Eugene F. Fama and Kenneth R. French, "Size, Value, and Momentum in International Stock Returns," *Journal of Financial Economics* 105, no. 3 (September 2012): 457–72, Table 1.

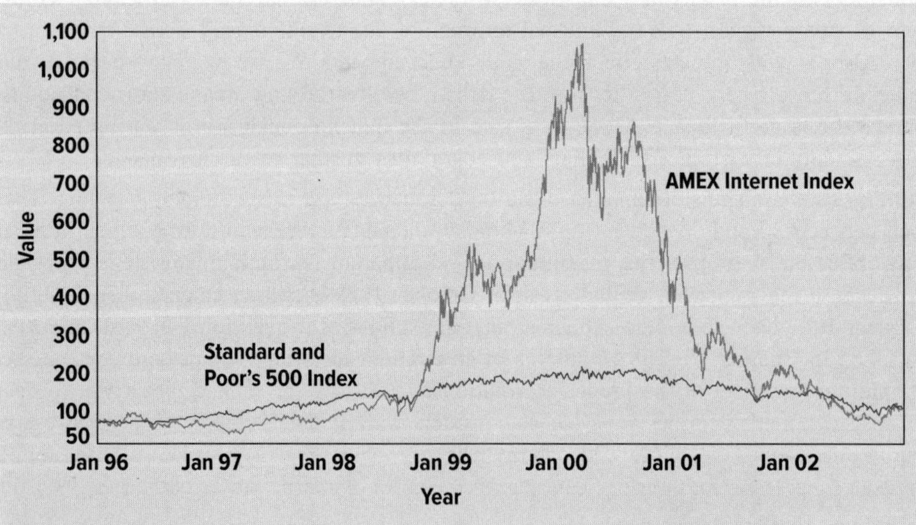

The index of Internet stocks rose over tenfold from the beginning of 1996 to its high in March 2000 before falling to approximately its original level in 2002.

Figure 14.12 Value of Index of Internet Stocks

shows values of an index of internet stocks from 1996 through 2002. The index rose over tenfold from January 1996 to its high in March 2000 before retreating to approximately its original level in 2002. For comparison, the figure also shows price movement for the S&P 500 Index. While this index rose and fell over the same period, the price movement was quite muted relative to that of internet stocks.

Many commentators describe the rise and fall of internet stocks as a bubble. Is it correct to do so? Unfortunately, there is no precise definition of the term. Some academics argue that the price movement in the figure is consistent with rationality. Prices rose initially, they say, because it appeared that the internet would soon capture a large chunk of international commerce. Prices fell when later evidence suggested this would not occur quite so quickly. However, others argue that the initial rosy scenario was never supported by the facts. Rather, prices rose due to nothing more than "irrational exuberance."

14.7 Reviewing the Differences

It is fair to say that the controversy over efficient capital markets has not yet been resolved. Rather, academic financial economists have sorted themselves into three camps, with some adhering to market efficiency, some believing in behavioral finance, and others (perhaps the majority) convinced of a combination of the two approaches. This state of affairs is certainly different from, say, 40 years ago, when market efficiency went unchallenged. We think that the evidence suggests security prices in most large capital markets around the world reflect a lot of information. However, it seems it is clear that from time to time behavioral forces can be significant. In any case, the controversy here is one of the most contentious of any area of financial economics.

Adherents of behavioral finance point out, as discussed in Section 14.5, that the three theoretical foundations of market efficiency appear to be violated in the real world. Second, they stress that there are too many anomalies, with a number of them having been replicated in out-of-sample tests. Critics of behavioral finance generally make three points in rebuttal:

1. *The file drawer problem*: Scholars generally submit their papers to academic journals, where independent referees judge whether the work is deserving of publication. Papers either get accepted in a journal, leading to potential influence in the field, or get rejected, leaving the author to, as the phrase goes, bury the paper "in the file drawer." It has been frequently suggested that, holding quality of research constant, referees are more likely to accept a paper with unusual and interesting results. Critics of behavioral finance argue that, because market efficiency has been the received paradigm in finance, any paper challenging efficiency has a higher probability of acceptance than one supporting efficiency. Thus, the publication process may inadvertently favor behavioral finance research.
2. *Risk*: As indicated in Chapter 11, investors try to maximize expected return per unit of risk. However, risk is not always easy to estimate. Efficient market adherents often suggest that some anomalies might disappear if more sophisticated adjustments for risk were made. As an example, we mentioned in the previous section that a number of researchers have argued that the high returns on value stocks can be explained by their higher risk.
3. *Behavioral finance and market prices*: Critics of behavioral finance often argue that, even if the data support certain anomalies, it is not clear that these anomalies support behavioral finance. Consider representativeness and conservatism, two psychological principles mentioned earlier in this chapter.

   Representativeness implies overweighting the results of small samples, as with the gambler who thinks a few consecutive spins of black on the roulette wheel make black a more likely outcome than red on the next spin. Financial economists argue that representativeness can lead to overreaction in stock returns. We mentioned earlier that financial bubbles are likely overreactions to news. Internet companies showed great revenue growth for a short time in the late 1990s, causing many to believe that this growth would continue indefinitely. Stock prices rose (too much) at this point. When at last investors realized that this growth could not be sustained, prices plummeted.

Conservatism states that individuals adjust their beliefs too slowly to new information. A market composed of this type of investor would likely lead to stock prices that underreact in the presence of new information. The example concerning earnings surprises may illustrate this underreaction. Prices rose slowly following announcements of positive earnings surprises. Announcements of negative surprises had a similar, but opposite, reaction.

Efficient market believers stress that representativeness and conservatism have opposite implications for stock prices. Which principle, they ask, should dominate in any particular situation? In other words, why should investors overreact to news about internet stocks but underreact to earnings news? Proponents of market efficiency say that unless behaviorists can answer these two questions satisfactorily, we should not reject market efficiency in favor of behavioral finance.[20]

Clearly, the jury is still out with respect to market efficiency. We have tried to present the arguments and evidence from both sides. However, it does not appear that our textbook, or any textbook, can easily resolve the differing points of view.

14.8 Implications for Corporate Finance

So far this chapter has examined both theoretical arguments and empirical evidence concerning efficient markets. We now ask whether market efficiency has any relevance for corporate financial managers. The answer is that it does. Next, we consider four implications of efficiency for managers.

1. ACCOUNTING CHOICES, FINANCIAL CHOICES, AND MARKET EFFICIENCY

The accounting profession provides firms with a significant amount of leeway in their reporting practices. For example, companies may choose between the last-in, first-out (LIFO) or the first-in, first-out (FIFO) method of valuing inventories. They may choose either the percentage-of-completion or the completed-contract method for construction projects. They may depreciate physical assets by either accelerated or straight-line depreciation.

Managers clearly prefer high stock prices to low stock prices. Should managers use the leeway in accounting choices to report the highest possible income? Not necessarily. That is, accounting choices should not affect the stock price if two conditions hold. First, enough information must be provided in the annual report so that financial analysts can construct earnings under the alternative accounting methods. This appears to be the case for many, though not necessarily all, accounting choices. Second, the market must be efficient in the semistrong form. In other words, the market must appropriately use all of this accounting information in determining the market price.

Of course, the issue of whether accounting choices affect stock prices is ultimately an empirical matter. A number of academic papers have addressed this issue. Kaplan and Roll found that the switch from accelerated to straight-line depreciation did not affect stock prices.[21] Kaplan and Roll also looked at changes

[20]See, for example, Eugene F. Fama, "Market Efficiency, Long-Term Returns, and Behavioral Finance," *Journal of Financial Economics* 49, no. 3 (September 1998): 283–306.

[21]Robert S. Kaplan and Richard Roll, "Investor Evaluation of Accounting Information: Some Empirical Evidence," *Journal of Business* 45, no. 2 (April 1972): 225–57.

from the deferral method of accounting for the investment tax credit to the flow-through method.[22] They found that a switch would increase accounting earnings but had no effect on stock prices.

Several other accounting procedures have been studied. Hong, Kaplan, and Mandelker found no evidence that the stock market was affected by the artificially higher earnings reported using the pooling method, compared to the purchase method, for reporting mergers and acquisitions.[23] Biddle and Lindahl found that firms switching to the LIFO method of inventory valuation experienced an increase in stock price.[24] This is to be expected in inflationary environments because LIFO valuation can reduce taxes compared to FIFO. They found that the larger the tax decrease resulting from the use of LIFO, the greater was the increase in stock price.

While the studies described above suggest that accounting changes do not affect financial markets as long as all information is public, there is also evidence to the contrary. Hirshleifer and Teoh summarize evidence suggesting that the form of disclosure, whether items are recognized as part of earnings or merely disclosed as a footnote, affects stock prices and returns.[25] Shue and Townsend show that regulatory changes requiring the transparent expensing of the grant-date value of executive stock options, instead of merely disclosing the number of options granted in the footnotes, led to a decline in the growth of CEO pay.[26]

Overall, the evidence on whether the market can see through accounting tricks remains mixed. A further caveat relates to accounting fraud. So far, our discussion specifically assumed that financial analysts can construct earnings under the alternative accounting methods. However, companies like Satyam Computers, Silverline Industries, Enron, WorldCom, Global Crossing, and Xerox simply reported fraudulent numbers in the past. There was no way for financial analysts to construct alternative earnings numbers because these analysts were unaware how the reported numbers were determined. So it was not surprising that the prices of these stocks initially rose well above fair value. Yes, managers can boost prices in this way–as long as they are willing to serve time once they are caught!

Is there anything else that investors can be expected to see through in an efficient market? Consider stock splits and stock dividends. Today, Amrapalli Constructions has 1 million shares outstanding and reports ₹10 million of earnings. In the hopes of boosting the stock price, the firm's chief financial officer (CFO), Ms. Shabnam, recommends to the board of directors that Amrapalli have a 2-for-1 stock split. That is, a shareholder with 100 shares prior to the split would have 200 shares after the split. The CFO contends that each investor would feel richer after the split because he would own more shares.

However, this thinking runs counter to market efficiency. A rational investor knows that he would own the same proportion of the firm after the split as before the split. Our investor with 100 shares owns 1/10,000 (= 100/1 million) of Amrapalli's shares prior to the split. His share of the earnings would be ₹1,000 (= ₹10 million/10,000). Although he would own 200 shares after the split, there would now be 2 million shares outstanding. Thus, he still would own 1/10,000 of the firm. His share of the earnings would still be ₹1,000 because the stock split would not affect the earnings of the entire firm.

[22]Before 1987, U.S. tax law allowed a 10 percent tax credit on the purchase of most kinds of capital equipment.

[23]Harrison Hong, Robert S. Kaplan, and Gershon Mandelker, "Pooling vs. Purchase: The Effects of Accounting for Mergers on Stock Prices," *Accounting Review* 53, no. 1 (January 1978): 31–47. The pooling method for mergers is no longer allowed under generally accepted accounting principles.

[24]Gary C. Biddle and Frederick W. Lindahl, "Stock Price Reactions to LIFO Adoptions: The Association between Excess Returns and LIFO Tax Savings," *Journal of Accounting Research* 20, no. 2 (Autumn 1982): 551–88.

[25]David Hirshleifer and Siew Hong Teoh, "Limited Attention, Information Disclosure, and Financial Reporting," *Journal of Accounting and Economics* 36, no. 1-3 (2003): 337–86.

[26]Kelly Shue and Richard R. Townsend, "Growth through Rigidity: An Explanation for the Rise in CEO Pay," *Journal of Financial Economics* 123, no. 1 (2017): 1–21.

2. THE TIMING DECISION

Imagine a firm whose managers are contemplating the date to issue equity. This decision is frequently called the timing decision. If managers believe that their stock is overpriced, they are likely to issue equity immediately. Here, they are creating value for their current stockholders because they are selling stock for more than it is worth. Conversely, if the managers believe that their stock is underpriced, they are more likely to wait to issue equity, hoping that the stock price eventually will rise to its true value.

However, if markets are strong form efficient, managers have no inside information and securities are always correctly priced. Efficiency implies that stock is sold for its true worth, so the timing decision becomes unimportant. On the other hand, managers may have more information about the firm's prospects than outside investors. Using this inside information, they may be able to time equity issues to benefit their current shareholders. Figure 14.13 shows three possible stock price adjustments to the issuance of new stock.

Of course, market efficiency is ultimately an empirical issue. Recent research suggests managers have some timing ability. Prof. Jay Ritter's website presents evidence that annual stock returns over the five years following an initial public offering (IPO) are about 1.9 percent less for the issuing company than the returns on a nonissuing company with a similar book-to-market ratio.[27] Annual stock returns over this period following a seasoned equity offering (SEO) are about 3.4 percent less for the issuing company than for a comparable nonissuing company. A company's first public offering is called an IPO and all subsequent offerings are termed SEOs. The upper half of Figure 14.14 shows average annual returns of both IPOs and their control group, and the lower half of the figure shows average annual returns of both SEOs and their control group.

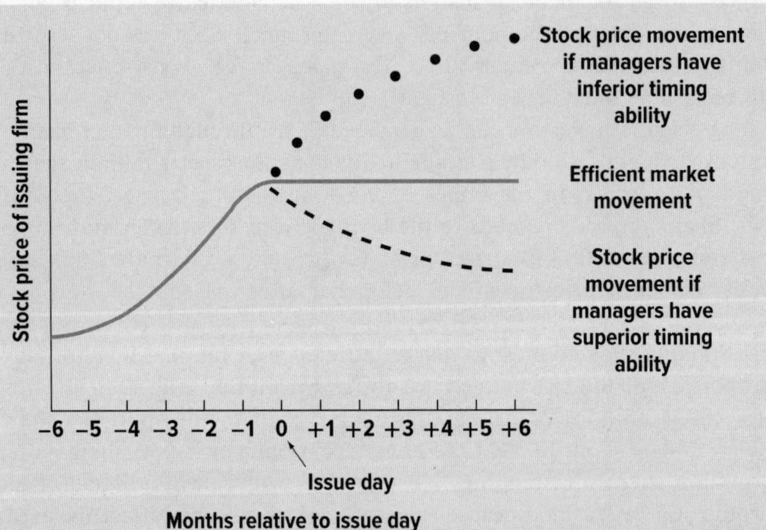

Studies show that stock is more likely to be issued after stock prices have increased. No inferences about market efficiency can be drawn from this result. Rather, market efficiency implies that the stock price of the issuing firm, on average, neither rises nor falls (relative to stock market indexes) after issuance of stock.

Figure 14.13 Three Stock Price Adjustments after Issuing Equity

[27] https://site.warrington.ufl.edu/ritter/.

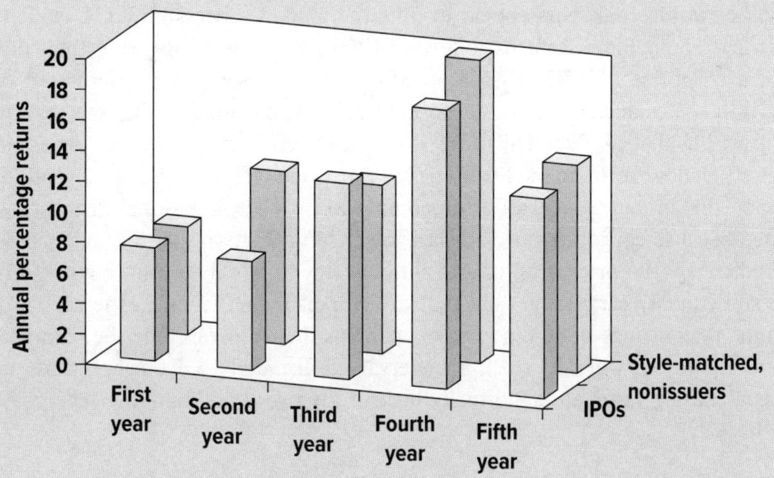

The figure shows the average raw returns for 8,397 IPOs from 1970 to 2012 and their matching nonissuing firms during the five years after the issue. The first-year return does not include the return on the day of issue. On average, IPOs underperform their control groups by about 1.9% per year in the five years following issuance.

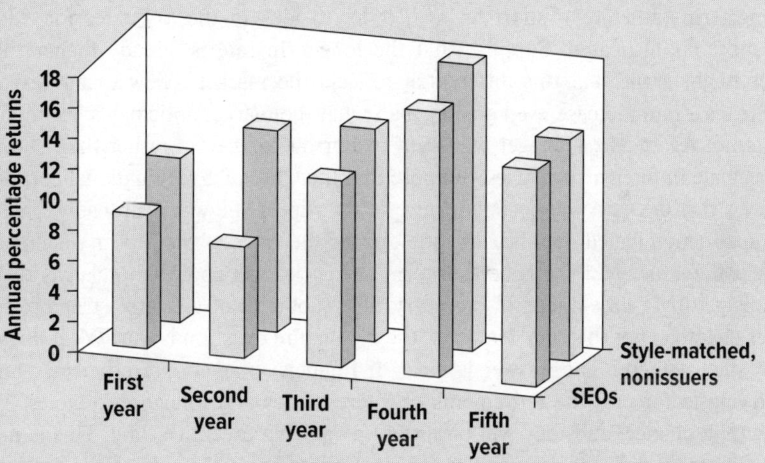

The figure shows the average raw returns for 10,208 SEOs from 1970 to 2012 and their matching nonissuing firms during the five years after the issue. The first-year return does not include the return on the day of issue. On average, SEOs underperform by about 3.4% per year.

Figure 14.14 Returns on Initial Public Offerings (IPOs) and Seasoned Equity Offerings (SEOs) in Years Following Issue

SOURCE: Jay Ritter, site.warrington.ufl.edu/ritter/.

The evidence in Ritter's work suggests that corporate managers issue SEOs when the company's stock is overpriced. In other words, managers appear to time the market successfully. The evidence that managers time their IPOs is less compelling: Returns following IPOs are closer to those of their control group.

The ability of a corporate official to issue an SEO when the security is overpriced contradicts strong form efficiency. Given that managers are likely to have special information that the rest of us do not have, it is perhaps unsurprising that markets fail to be strong form efficient. Is the evidence still consistent with semistrong market efficiency? If the market were truly semistrong efficient, the price would drop immediately and completely upon the announcement of an upcoming SEO. That is, rational investors would realize that stock is being issued because corporate officials have special information that the stock is overpriced. Indeed, many empirical studies report a price drop on the announcement date. However, Figure 14.14 shows a further price drop in the subsequent years, suggesting that the market is inefficient in the semistrong form.

If firms can time the issuance of common stock, perhaps they also can time the repurchase of stock. Here a firm would like to repurchase when its stock is undervalued. Ikenberry, Lakonishok, and Vermaelen find that stock returns of repurchasing firms are abnormally high in the two years following repurchase, suggesting that timing is effective here.[28]

3. SPECULATION AND EFFICIENT MARKETS

We normally think of individuals and financial institutions as the primary speculators in financial markets. However, industrial corporations speculate as well. For example, many companies make interest rate bets. If the managers of a firm believe that interest rates are likely to rise, they have an incentive to borrow because the present value of the liability will fall with the rate increase. In addition, these managers will have an incentive to borrow long term rather than short term in order to lock in the low rates for a longer period. The thinking can get more sophisticated. Suppose that the long-term rate is already higher than the short-term rate. The manager might argue that this differential reflects the market's view that rates will rise. However, perhaps she anticipates a rate increase even greater than what the market anticipates, as implied by the upward-sloping term structure. Again, the manager will want to borrow long term rather than short term.

Firms also speculate in foreign currencies. Suppose that the CFO of a multinational corporation based in the United States believes that the euro will decline relative to the rupee. She would probably issue euro-denominated debt rather than rupee-denominated debt because she expects the value of the foreign liability to fall. Conversely, she would issue debt domestically if she believes foreign currencies will appreciate relative to the rupee.

We are perhaps getting a little ahead of our story: The subtleties of the term structure and exchange rates are treated in other chapters, not this one. However, the big picture question is this: What does market efficiency have to say about such activity? The answer is clear. If financial markets are efficient, managers should not waste their time trying to forecast the movements of interest rates and foreign currencies. Their forecasts will likely be no better than chance, and they will be using up valuable executive time. This is not to say, however, that firms should flippantly pick the maturity or the denomination of their debt in a random fashion. A firm must choose these parameters carefully. However, the choice should be based on other rationales, not on an attempt to beat the market. For example, a firm with a project lasting five years might decide to issue five-year debt. A firm might issue yen-denominated debt because it anticipates expanding into Japan in a big way.

The same thinking applies to acquisitions. Many corporations buy other firms because they think these targets are underpriced. Unfortunately, the empirical evidence suggests that the market is too efficient for this type of speculation to be profitable. And the acquirer never pays just the current market price. The bidding firm must pay a premium above market value to induce a majority of shareholders of the target

[28]David Ikenberry, J. Lakonishok, and T. Vermaelen, "Market Underreaction to Open Market Share Repurchases," *Journal of Financial Economics* (October–November 1995).

firm to sell their shares. However, this is not to say that firms should never be acquired. Rather, managers should consider an acquisition if there are benefits (synergies) from the union. Improved marketing, economies in production, replacement of bad management, and even tax reduction are typical synergies. These synergies are distinct from the perception that the acquired firm is underpriced.

One final point should be mentioned. We talked earlier about empirical evidence suggesting that SEOs are timed to take advantage of overpriced stock. This makes sense–managers are likely to know more about their own firms than the market does. However, while managers may have special information about their own firms, it is unlikely that they have special information about interest rates, foreign currencies, and other firms. There are too many participants in these markets, many of whom are devoting all of their time to forecasting. Managers typically spend most of their effort running their own firms, with only a small amount of time devoted to studying financial markets.

4. INFORMATION IN MARKET PRICES

The previous section argued that it is quite difficult to forecast future market prices. However, the current and past prices of any asset are known–and of great use. Consider Becher's study of bank mergers.[29] The author finds that stock prices of acquired banks rise about 23 percent, on average, upon the first announcement of a merger. This is not surprising because companies are generally bought at a premium above the current stock price. However, the same study shows that prices of acquiring banks fall almost 5 percent, on average, upon the same announcement. This is pretty strong evidence that bank mergers do not benefit, and may even hurt, acquiring companies. The reason for this result is unclear, though perhaps acquirers overpay for acquisitions. Regardless of the reason, the implication is clear: A bank should think deeply before acquiring another bank.

Furthermore, suppose you are the CFO of a company whose stock price drops significantly upon announcement of an acquisition. The market is telling you that the merger is bad for your firm. Serious consideration should be given to canceling the merger even if, prior to the announcement, you thought the merger was a good idea.

Of course, mergers are only one type of corporate event. Managers should pay attention to the stock price reaction to any of their announcements, whether it concerns a new venture, a divestiture, a restructuring, or something else.

This is not the only way in which corporations can use the information in market prices. Suppose you are on the board of directors of a company whose stock price has declined precipitously since the CEO was hired. In addition, the stock prices of competitors have risen over the same time. Though there may be extenuating circumstances, this can be viewed as evidence that the CEO is doing a poor job. Perhaps he should be fired. If this seems harsh, consider that Warner, Watts, and Wruck find a strong negative correlation between managerial turnover and prior stock performance.[30] Figure 14.15 shows that stocks fall, on average, about 40 percent in price (relative to market movements) in the three years prior to the forced departure of a top manager.

If managers are fired for bad stock price performance, perhaps they are rewarded for stock price appreciation. Hall and Liebman state:

> Our main empirical finding is that CEO wealth often changes by millions of rupees for typical changes in firm value. For example, the median total compensation for CEOs is about ₹1 million if their firm's stock has a 30th percentile annual return (−7.0 percent) and is ₹5 million if the firm's stock has a 70th percentile annual return (20.5 percent). Thus, there is a difference of about ₹4 million in compensation for achieving a moderately above average performance relative to a moderately below average performance.[31]

[29]David A. Becher, "The Valuation Effects of Bank Mergers," *Journal of Corporate Finance* 6, no. 2 (July 2000): 189–214.

[30]Jerold B. Warner, Ross L. Watts, and Karen H. Wruck, "Stock Prices and Top Management Changes," *Journal of Financial Economics* 20 (January-March, 1988): 461–92.

[31]Brian J. Hall and Jeffrey B. Liebman, "Are CEOs Really Paid Like Bureaucrats?" *Quarterly Journal of Economics* 113, no. 3 (August 1998): 653–91.

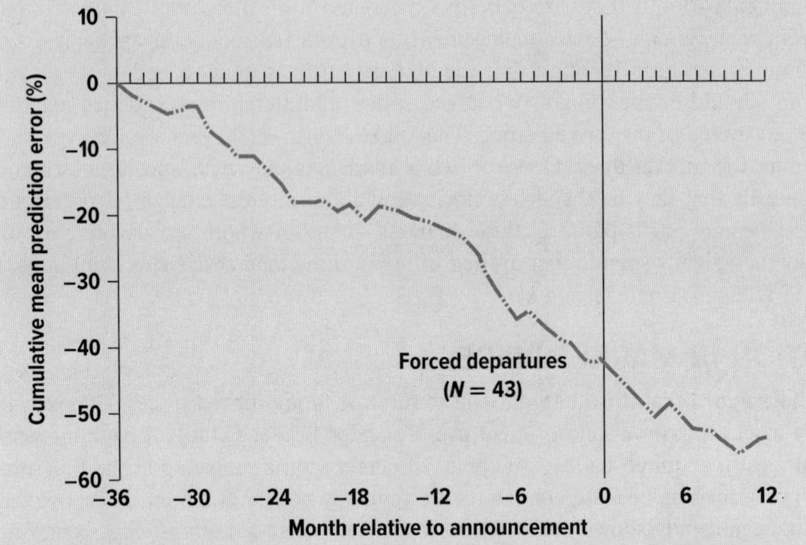

Stock prices decline, on average, by more than 40% (adjusted for market performance) in the three years prior to forced departures of management.

Figure 14.15 Stock Performance Prior to Forced Departures of Management

SOURCE: Adapted from Figure 1 of Jerold B. Warner, Ross L. Watts, and Karen H. Wruck, "Stock Prices and Top Management Changes," *Journal of Financial Economics* 20 (January–March 1988): 461–92.

Even if markets are not fully efficient, market prices are likely to contain a lot of information. We recommend using this information as much as possible in corporate decisions. And at least with respect to executive firings and executive compensation, it looks as if, in the real world, corporations do pay attention to market prices.

RESEARCH IN EMERGING MARKET CONTEXT

Pandey et al. (2020) tested the efficient market hypothesis using share buyback announcements. They found that predicting buyback announcements could result in extra-normal returns before the announcement. The study confirmed that Indian stock markets operate in the semi-strong form of efficiency and suggested insider trading as a possible explanation for abnormal returns in the pre-event window.

A study by Lalwani, Sharma and Chakraborty (2019) found that Indian stock markets tend to overreact to both negative and positive news. This suggests that investors in India exhibit significant behavioral and psychological biases, such as negativity bias and myopic loss aversion bias. Ghalke et al. (2023) explored a specific behavioral bias in the Indian markets. They found that on a Friday new moon day, the markets generate a significant negative return, whereas on the Muhurat trading day, they produce a significant positive return. The authors also proposed a trading strategy that takes advantage of the impact of the new moon day, which could potentially lead to profits.

References

Ghalke, A., Kumar, S., Kakani, R. K., & Modekurti, K. R. V. (2023). New moon day anomalies of Amavasya and Muhurat trading: Gestalting the role of culture and institutions. *IIMB Management Review, 35*(2), 137–148.

Lalwani, V., Sharma, U., & Chakraborty, M. (2019). Investor reaction to extreme price shocks in stock markets: A cross country examination. *IIMB Management Review, 31*(3), 258–267.

Pandey, A., Bhama, V., & Mohapatra, A. K. (2020). Trading strategy using share buybacks: evidence from India. *Investment Management and Financial Innovations, 17*(2), 169–182.

Summary and Conclusions

1. An efficient securities market processes the information available to investors about the underlying economic value of the securities and incorporates it into the prices of securities. Market efficiency has two general implications. First, in any given time period, a security's abnormal return depends on information or news received by the market in that period. Second, an investor who uses the same information as the market cannot expect to earn abnormal returns. In other words, systems for playing the market are doomed to fail.
2. What information does the market use to determine stock prices?
   a. The weak form of the efficient market hypothesis says that the market uses the history of stock prices and is therefore efficient with respect to these past prices. This implies that stock selection based on patterns of past stock price movements is no better than random stock selection.
   b. The semistrong form states that the market uses all publicly available information in setting prices.
   c. Strong form efficiency states that the market uses all of the information that anybody knows about stocks, even inside information.
3. Behavioral finance states that the market is not always efficient. Adherents argue that:
   a. Investors are irrational.
   b. Deviations from rationality are similar across investors.
   c. Arbitrage, being costly, does not eliminate inefficiencies.
4. Behaviorists point to empirical anomalies that contradict the notion of efficient markets, including studies showing that:
   a. Past returns predict future returns.
   b. Small stocks outperform large stocks.
   c. Value stocks outperform growth stocks.
   d. Stock prices adjust slowly to earnings surprises.
5. Four implications of market efficiency for corporate finance are:
   a. Managers cannot fool the market through creative accounting.
   b. Firms cannot successfully time issues of debt and equity.
   c. Managers cannot profitably speculate in foreign currencies and other instruments.
   d. Managers can reap many benefits by paying attention to market prices.

The following box summarizes some key issues in the efficient markets debate:

Efficient Market Hypothesis: A Summary

Does Not Say:

- Prices are uncaused.
- Investors are foolish and too stupid to be in the market.
- All shares of stock have the same expected returns.
- Investors should throw darts to select stocks.
- There is no upward trend in stock prices.

Does Say:

- Prices reflect underlying value.
- Financial managers cannot time stock and bond sales.
- Managers cannot profitably speculate in foreign currencies.
- Managers cannot boost stock prices through creative accounting.

Three Forms:

Weak form: Current prices reflect past prices; chartism (technical analysis) is useless.
Semistrong form: Prices reflect all public information; most financial analysis is useless.
Strong form: Prices reflect all that is knowable; nobody consistently makes superior profits.

Concept Questions

1. **Firm Value** What rule should a firm follow when making financing decisions? How can firms create valuable financing opportunities?
2. **Efficient Market Hypothesis** Define the three forms of market efficiency.
3. **Efficient Market Hypothesis** Which of the following statements are true about the efficient market hypothesis?
   a. It implies perfect forecasting ability.
   b. It implies that prices reflect all available information.
   c. It implies an irrational market.
   d. It implies that prices do not fluctuate.
   e. It results from keen competition among investors.
4. **Market Efficiency Implications** Explain why a characteristic of an efficient market is that investments in that market have zero NPVs.
5. **Efficient Market Hypothesis** A stock market analyst is able to identify mispriced stocks by comparing the average price for the last 10 days to the average price for the last 60 days. If this is true, what do you know about the market?
6. **Semistrong Efficiency** If a market is semistrong form efficient, is it also weak form efficient? Explain.
7. **Efficient Market Hypothesis** What are the implications of the efficient market hypothesis for investors who buy and sell stocks in an attempt to "beat the market"?

8. **Stocks versus Gambling** Critically evaluate the following statements: Playing the stock market is like gambling. Such speculative investing has no social value other than the pleasure people get from this form of gambling.

9. **Efficient Market Hypothesis** Several celebrated investors and stock pickers frequently mentioned in the financial press have recorded huge returns on their investments over the past two decades. Does the success of these particular investors invalidate the EMH? Explain.

10. **Efficient Market Hypothesis** For each of the following scenarios, discuss whether profit opportunities exist from trading in the stock of the firm under the conditions that (1) the market is not weak form efficient, (2) the market is weak form but not semistrong form efficient, (3) the market is semistrong form but not strong form efficient, and (4) the market is strong form efficient.
    a. The stock price has risen steadily each day for the past 30 days.
    b. The financial statements for a company were released three days ago, and you believe you've uncovered some anomalies in the company's inventory and cost control reporting techniques that are causing the firm's true liquidity strength to be understated.
    c. You observe that the senior management of a company has been buying a lot of the company's stock on the open market over the past week.

Use the following information for the next two questions:

Technical analysis is a controversial investment practice. Technical analysis covers a wide array of techniques, which are all used in an attempt to predict the direction of a particular stock or the market. Technical analysts look at two major types of information: historical stock prices and investor sentiment. A technical analyst would argue these two information sets provide information about the future direction of a particular stock or the market as a whole.

11. **Technical Analysis** What would a technical analyst say about market efficiency?

12. **Investor Sentiment** A technical analysis tool that is sometimes used to predict market movements is an investor sentiment index. AAII, the American Association of Individual Investors, publishes an investor sentiment index based on a survey of its members. In the following table, you will find the percentage of investors who were bullish, bearish, or neutral during a four-week period:

Week	Bullish	Bearish	Neutral
1	37%	25%	38%
2	52	14	34
3	29	35	36
4	43	26	31

What is the investor sentiment index intended to capture? How might it be useful in technical analysis?

13. **Performance of the Pros** In the middle to late 1990s, the performance of the pros was unusually poor–on the order of 90 percent of all equity mutual funds underperformed a passively managed index fund. What does this tell us about the issue of market efficiency?

14. **Efficient Markets** A hundred years ago or so, companies did not compile annual reports. Even if you owned stock in a particular company, you were unlikely to be allowed to see the balance sheet and income statement for the company. Assuming the market is semistrong form efficient, what does this say about market efficiency then compared to now?

15. **Efficient Market Hypothesis** Aerotech, an aerospace technology research firm, announced this morning that it has hired the world's most knowledgeable and prolific space researchers. Before today, Aerotech's stock had been selling for ₹100. Assume that no other information is received over the next week and the stock market as a whole does not move.

a. What do you expect will happen to Aerotech's stock?

b. Consider the following scenarios:

i. The stock price jumps to ₹118 on the day of the announcement. In subsequent days it floats up to ₹123, then falls back to ₹116.

ii. The stock price jumps to ₹116 and remains at that level.

iii. The stock price gradually climbs to ₹116 over the next week.

Which scenario(s) indicate market efficiency? Which do not? Why?

16. **Efficient Market Hypothesis** When the 56-year-old founder of Gulf & Western, Inc., died of a heart attack, the stock price immediately jumped from ₹18.00 a share to ₹20.25, a 12.5 percent increase. This is evidence of market inefficiency because an efficient stock market would have anticipated his death and adjusted the price beforehand. Assume that no other information is received and the stock market as a whole does not move. Is this statement about market efficiency true or false? Explain.

17. **Efficient Market Hypothesis** Today, the following announcement was made: "Early today the Justice Department reached a decision in the Universal Product Care (UPC) case. UPC has been found guilty of discriminatory practices in hiring. For the next five years, UPC must pay ₹2 million each year to a fund representing victims of UPC's policies." Assuming the market is efficient, should investors not buy UPC stock after the announcement because the litigation will cause an abnormally low rate of return? Explain.

18. **Efficient Market Hypothesis** Newtech Corp. is going to adopt a new chip-testing device that can greatly improve its production efficiency. Do you think the lead engineer can profit from purchasing the firm's stock before the news release on the device? After reading the announcement in *The Wall Street Journal*, should you be able to earn an abnormal return from purchasing the stock if the market is efficient?

19. **Efficient Market Hypothesis** TransTrust Corp. has changed how it accounts for inventory. Taxes are unaffected, although the resulting earnings report released this quarter is 20 percent higher than what it would have been under the old accounting system. There is no other surprise in the earnings report and the change in the accounting treatment was publicly announced. If the market is efficient, will the stock price be higher when the market learns that the reported earnings are higher?

20. **Efficient Market Hypothesis** The Durkin Investing Agency has been the best stock picker in the country for the past two years. Before this rise to fame occurred, the Durkin newsletter had 200 subscribers. Those subscribers beat the market consistently, earning substantially higher returns after adjustment for risk and transaction costs. Subscriptions have skyrocketed to 10,000. Now, when the Durkin Investing Agency recommends a stock, the price instantly rises several points. The subscribers currently earn only a normal return when they buy recommended stocks because the price rises before anybody can act on the information. Briefly explain this phenomenon. Is Durkin's ability to pick stocks consistent with market efficiency?

21. **Efficient Market Hypothesis** Your broker commented that well-managed firms are better investments than poorly managed firms. As evidence, your broker cited a recent study examining 100 small manufacturing firms that eight years earlier had been listed in an industry magazine as the best-managed small manufacturers in the country. In the ensuing eight years, the 100 firms listed have not earned more than the normal market return. Your broker continued to say that if the firms were well managed, they should have produced better-than-average returns. If the market is efficient, do you agree with your broker?

22. **Efficient Market Hypothesis** A famous economist just announced in *The Wall Street Journal* his findings that the recession is over and the economy is again entering an expansion. Assume market efficiency. Can you profit from investing in the stock market after you read this announcement?

23. **Efficient Market Hypothesis** Suppose the market is semistrong form efficient. Can you expect to earn excess returns if you make trades based on:

    a. Your broker's information about record earnings for a stock?
    b. Rumors about a merger of a firm?
    c. Yesterday's announcement of a successful new product test?

24. **Efficient Market Hypothesis** Imagine that a particular macroeconomic variable that influences your firm's net earnings is positively serially correlated. Assume market efficiency. Would you expect price changes in your stock to be serially correlated? Why or why not?

25. **Efficient Market Hypothesis** The efficient market hypothesis implies that all mutual funds should obtain the same expected risk-adjusted returns. Therefore, we can pick mutual funds at random. Is this statement true or false? Explain.

26. **Efficient Market Hypothesis** Assume that markets are efficient. During a trading day American Golf, Inc., announces that it has lost a contract for a large golfing project that, prior to the news, it was widely believed to have secured. If the market is efficient, how should the stock price react to this information if no additional information is released?

27. **Efficient Market Hypothesis** Prospectors, Inc., is a publicly traded gold prospecting company in Alaska. Although the firm's searches for gold usually fail, the prospectors occasionally find a rich vein of ore. What pattern would you expect to observe for Prospectors' cumulative abnormal returns if the market is efficient?

28. **Evidence on Market Efficiency** Some people argue that the efficient market hypothesis cannot explain the 1987 market crash or the high price-earnings ratios of internet stocks during the late 1990s. What alternative hypothesis is currently used for these two phenomena?

Questions and Problems

BASIC (Questions 1–4)

1. **Cumulative Abnormal Returns** Delta, United, and American Airlines announced purchases of planes on July 18 (7/18), February 12 (2/12), and October 7 (10/7), respectively. Given the following information, calculate the cumulative abnormal return (CAR) for these stocks as a group. Graph the result and provide an explanation. All of the stocks have a beta of 1 and no other announcements are made.

Delta			United			American		
Date	Market Return	Company Return	Date	Market Return	Company Return	Date	Market Return	Company Return
7/12	−.3	−.5	2/8	−.9	−1.1	10/1	.5	.3
7/13	.0	.2	2/9	−1.0	−1.1	10/2	.4	.6
7/16	.5	.7	2/10	.4	.2	10/3	1.1	1.1
7/17	−.5	−.3	2/11	.6	.8	10/6	.1	−.3
7/18	−2.2	1.1	2/12	−.3	−.1	10/7	−2.2	−.3
7/19	−.9	−.7	2/15	1.1	1.2	10/8	.5	.5
7/20	−1.0	−1.1	2/16	.5	.5	10/9	−.3	−.2
7/23	.7	.5	2/17	−.3	−.2	10/10	.3	.1
7/24	.2	.1	2/18	.3	.2	10/13	.0	−.1

2. **Cumulative Abnormal Returns** The following diagram shows the cumulative abnormal returns (CARs) for 386 oil exploration companies announcing oil discoveries between 1950 and 1980. Month 0 in the diagram is the announcement month. Assume that no other information is received and the stock market as a whole does not move. Is the diagram consistent with market efficiency? Why or why not?

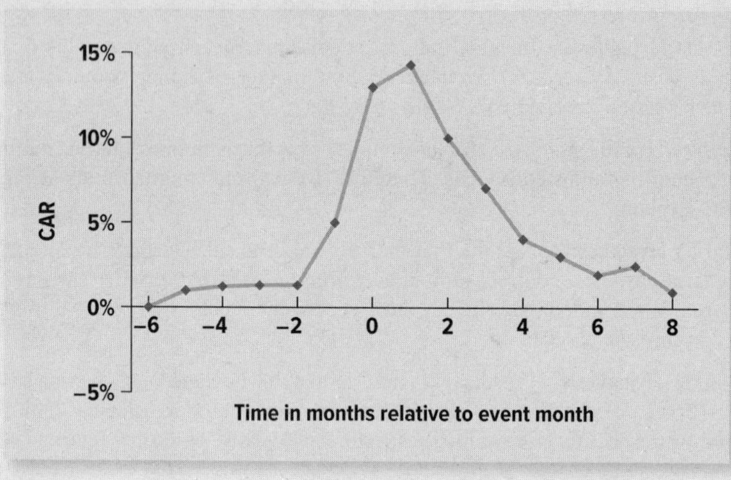

3. **Cumulative Abnormal Returns** The following figures present the results of four cumulative abnormal returns (CARs) studies. Indicate whether the results of each study support, reject, or are inconclusive about the semistrong form of the efficient market hypothesis. In each figure, Time 0 is the date of an event.

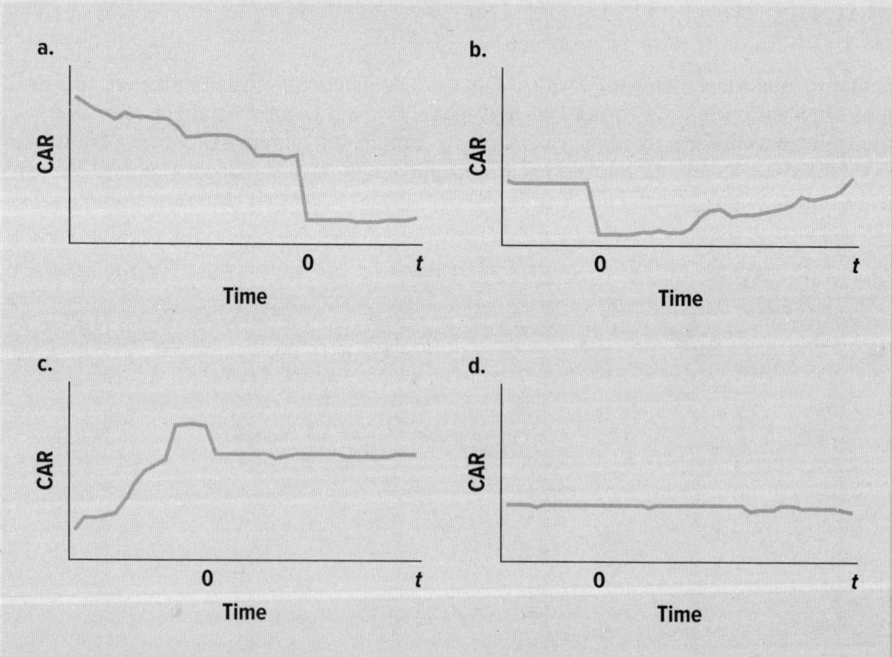

4. **Cumulative Abnormal Returns** A study analyzed the behavior of the stock prices of firms that had lost antitrust cases. Included in the diagram are all firms that lost the initial court decision, even if the decision was later overturned on appeal. The event at Time 0 is the initial, pre-appeal court decision. Assume no other information was released, aside from that disclosed in the initial trial. The stock prices all have a beta of 1. Is the diagram consistent with market efficiency? Why or why not?

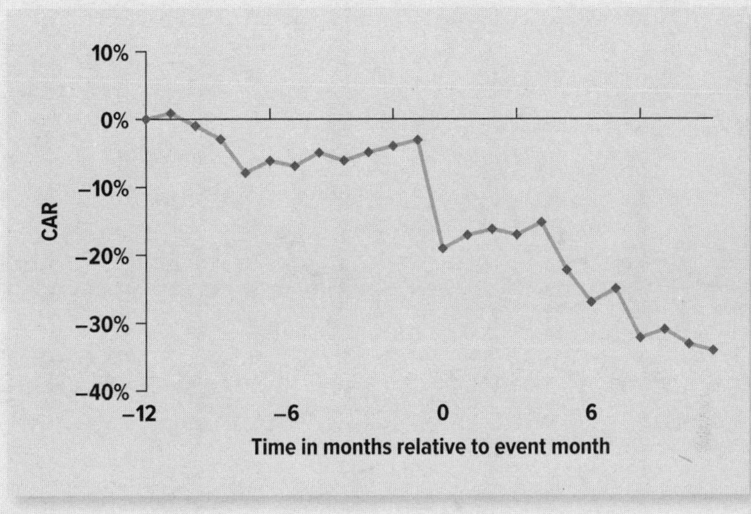

Mini Case

YOUR 401(k) ACCOUNT AT EAST COAST YACHTS

You have been at your job with East Coast Yachts for a week now and have decided you need to sign up for the company's 401(k) plan. Even after your discussion with Sarah Brown, the Bledsoe Financial Services representative, you are still unsure which investment option you should choose. Recall that the options available to you are stock in East Coast Yachts, the Bledsoe S&P 500 Index Fund, the Bledsoe Small-Cap Fund, the Bledsoe Large-Company Stock Fund, the Bledsoe Bond Fund, and the Bledsoe Money Market Fund. You have decided that you should invest in a diversified portfolio, with 70 percent of your investment in equities, 25 percent in bonds, and 5 percent in the money market fund. You also have decided to focus your equity investment in large-cap stocks, but you are debating whether to select the S&P 500 Index Fund or the Large-Company Stock Fund.

In thinking it over, you understand the basic difference in the two funds. One is a purely passive fund that replicates a widely followed large-cap index, the S&P 500, and has low fees. The other is actively managed with the intention that the skill of the portfolio manager will result in improved performance relative to an index. Fees are higher in the latter fund. You're not certain which way to go, so you ask Dan Ervin, who works in the company's finance area, for advice.

After discussing your concerns, Dan gives you some information comparing the performance of equity mutual funds and the Vanguard 500 Index Fund. The Vanguard 500 is the world's largest equity index mutual fund. It replicates the S&P 500 and its return is only negligibly different from the S&P 500. Fees are very low. As a result, the Vanguard 500 is essentially identical to the Bledsoe S&P 500 Index Fund offered in the 401(k) plan, but it has been in existence for much longer, so you can study its track record for over two decades. The graph below summarizes Dan's comments by showing the percentage of equity mutual funds that outperformed

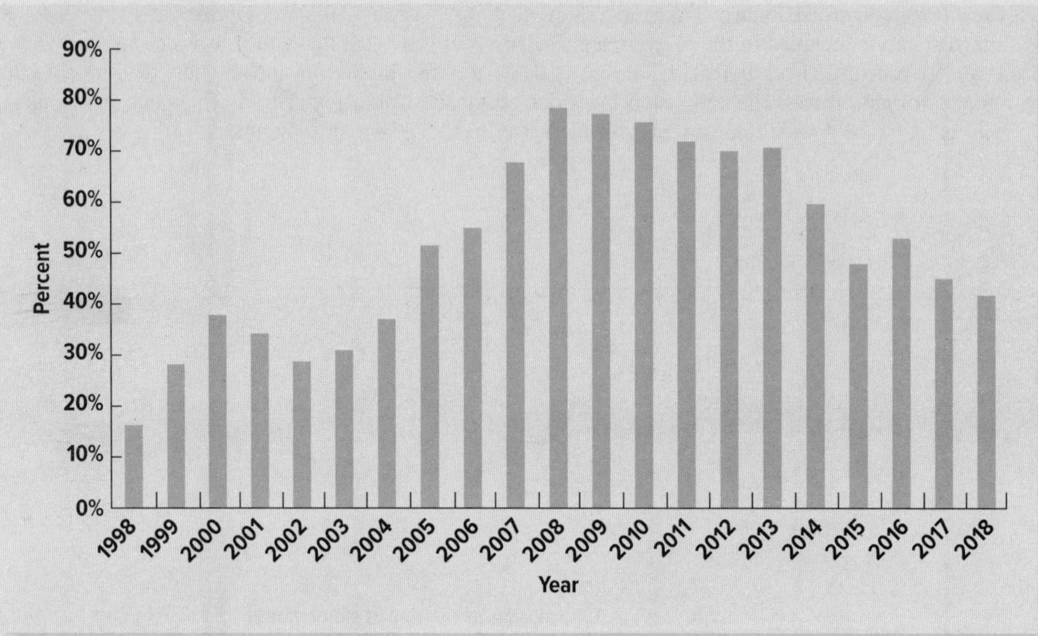

SOURCE: Bradford Jordan, Thomas Miller, and Steven Dolvin, *Fundamentals of Investments*, 9th ed. (New York: McGraw-Hill, 2021).

the Vanguard 500 Fund over 10-year periods.[32] For the 20 investment periods shown (1998–2007 through 2009–2018), in only 11 of these periods did more than 50 percent of mutual fund managers beat the Vanguard 500 Index Fund. Dan suggests that you study the graph and answer the following questions:

1. What implications do you draw from the graph for mutual fund investors?
2. Is the graph consistent or inconsistent with market efficiency? Explain carefully.
3. What investment decision would you make for the equity portion of your 401(k) account? Why?

MARKET INEFFICIENCY VS KNOWLEDGE DEFICIENCY?

In articles discussing the latest results of Reliance Industries Limited in the pink papers, views of various analysts were covered. Select excerpts by some of them are shared below:

ICICI Securities Analyst
"RIL's premium over Singapore complex could expand to ₹1–2/bbl, but gross refining margins (GRM) could still decline to ₹6–8/bbl (down 4% QoQ)."

Bonanza Portfolio Limited Analyst
The stock is consolidating in broad range of 1,765–2,030 in medium term. Recovering from lower levels means that the stock has strength; however, still it has not been able to cross above 2,030 level decisively. Last few sessions are indicating that the stock is facing resistance from 1,870–1,890 levels. So, this is a bearish signal.

[32]Note that this graph is not hypothetical; it reflects the actual performance of the Vanguard 500 Index Fund relative to a very large population of diversified equity mutual funds. Specialty funds, such as international funds, are excluded. All returns are net of management fees but do not include sales charges (which are known as "loads"), if any. As a result, the performance of actively managed funds is overstated.

Deen Dayal Investments Proprietary Trader & Technical Analyst
Investors are shy of the sector due to government's regulatory concerns and volatility in forex and oil prices. During the quarter, RIL and its refining partner BP received approval from DGH to invest ₹8.2 billion in the Z-series gas field. The production from KG-D6 block had declined to 28 Million Metric Standard Cubic Meter Per Day (mmscmd) compared to its target to reach over 60 mmscmd.

The stock's upside has been capped due to lower production from KG-D6 basin over the last few years. Results are expected to be under pressure due to slower demand but a rise in GRMs could induce some bit of optimism in the stock.

Latin Manharlal Securities Analyst
On the weekly chart, prices are trading in a triangle formation with the resistance of triangle level at 1,921 and support at 1,780. The break of 1,927 (previous high) can take the index in the two thousand plus mark. The indicator like MACD (Moving Average Convergence Divergence) is trading near the integer line. Prices are hovering near the 60 EMA (Exponential Moving Average) at 1,851.80.

Based on the four views in the above write-up, answer the following two questions:

1. **Type of Analysis**: Identify the views of each Analyst as either *technical analysis or fundamental analysis.* Provide appropriate reasoning for your answers.
2. **Level of Efficiency**: What *market efficiency level* would each of the four analysts must have assumed Indian markets (particularly, Reliance Industries' equity shares) to be while writing the above article (i.e., weak-form, or semi-strong form, or strong form, or none of them)? Do you agree with her assumption of the level of efficiency of Indian equity markets? Discuss.

15

Long-Term Financing

When a company with a low credit rating issues bonds, the bonds are referred to as high yield, or "junk," bonds. While junk bonds are more likely to default, they also have higher yields. In 2020, with the prevailing low interest rates, investors had an appetite for high-yield bonds to improve returns. In August 2020, ₹52.9 billion in junk bonds were issued, the second highest monthly issuance on record, far more than the ₹9.7 billion issued in August 2019. And the monthly record occurred in June 2020, with ₹59.9 billion in junk bonds issued. Through September 2020, ₹339 billion in junk bonds were issued, just ₹5 billion less than the full-year record.

Globally, the bond issuers with a rating between BB and B totalled ₹134 billion in 2023, up from ₹77 billion in the same period during 2022. Mirroring a similar trend, India saw a doubling in the issuance of junk corporate bonds (rated lower than BBB-) through October 2023 over the previous year.

Please visit us at **rwjcorporatefinance.blogspot.com** for the latest developments in the world of corporate finance.

15.1 Some Features of Equity and Preference Shares

In this chapter, we examine specific features of both stocks and bonds. We begin with stocks, both equity shares (also known as common stock) and preference shares (also known as preferred stock). In discussing equity share features, we focus on shareholder rights and dividend payments. For preference share we explain what "preference" means, and we also debate whether preference share, is really debt or equity.

Companies incorporated or registered in India are governed by the Companies Act 1956, 2013 and other allied Acts, Bills and Rules. Shares must be expressed in a fixed amount. Indian laws do not permit the issue of "no par value" or "bearer" shares. Shares to be subscribed must be expressed in Indian rupees and usually the par value of shares in India is ₹10.

EQUITY SHARE FEATURES

The term **equity share** means different things to different people, but it is usually applied to stock that has no special preference either in receiving dividends or in bankruptcy.

Shareholder Rights A company's shareholders elect directors who, in turn, hire management to carry out their directives. Shareholders, therefore, control the company through the right to elect the directors. Generally, only shareholders have this right.

Directors are elected each year at an annual meeting. Although there are exceptions (discussed next), the general idea is "one share, one vote" (not one shareholder, one vote). Corporate democracy is thus very different from our political democracy. With corporate democracy, the "golden rule" prevails absolutely.

Directors are elected at an annual shareholders' meeting by a vote of the holders of a majority of shares who are present and entitled to vote. However, the exact mechanism for electing directors differs across companies. The most important difference is whether shares must be voted cumulatively or voted straight.

To illustrate the two different voting procedures, imagine that a company has two shareholders: Shabbir with 20 shares and Prasad with 80 shares. Both want to be a director. Prasad does not want Shabbir to be one, however. We assume there are a total of four directors to be elected.

The effect of **cumulative voting** is to allow minority participation. If cumulative voting is permitted, the total number of votes that each shareholder may cast is determined first. This is usually calculated as the number of shares owned or controlled multiplied by the number of directors to be elected.

With cumulative voting, the directors are elected all at once. In our example, this means that the top four vote getters will be the new directors. A shareholder can distribute votes however she wishes.

Will Shabbir get a seat on the board? If we ignore the possibility of a five-way tie, then the answer is yes. Shabbir will cast $20 \times 4 = 80$ votes, and Prasad will cast $80 \times 4 = 320$ votes. If Shabbir gives all his votes to himself, he is assured of a directorship. The reason is that Prasad can't divide 320 votes among four candidates in such a way as to give all of them more than 80 votes, so Shabbir will finish fourth at worst.

In general, if there are N directors up for election, then $1/(N + 1)$ percent of the stock plus one share will guarantee you a seat. In our current example, this is $1/(4 + 1) = .20$, or 20 percent. So the more seats that are up for election at one time, the easier (and cheaper) it is to win one.

EXAMPLE 15.1

Buying the Election Stock in Babu Jagjeevan Ram Company sells for ₹20 per share and features cumulative voting. There are 10,000 shares outstanding. If three directors are up for election, how much does it cost to ensure yourself a seat on the board?

The question here is how many shares of stock it will take to get a seat. The answer is 2,501, so the cost is 2,501 × ₹20 = ₹50,020. Why 2,501? Because there is no way the remaining 7,499 votes can be divided among three people to give all of them more than 2,501 votes. Suppose two people receive 2,502 votes and the first two seats. A third person can receive, at most, 10,000 − 2,502 − 2,502 − 2,501 = 2,4 95, so the third seat is yours.

With **straight voting**, the directors are elected one at a time. Each time, Shabbir can cast 20 votes and Prasad can cast 80. As a consequence, Prasad will elect all of the candidates. The only way to guarantee a seat is to own 50 percent plus one share. This also guarantees that you will win every seat, so it's really all or nothing. This is the case in India, i.e., directors are elected by straight voting.

As we've illustrated, straight voting can "freeze out" minority shareholders, which is why many states have mandatory cumulative voting. However, in states where cumulative voting is mandatory, companies have ways to minimize its impact.

One such way is to stagger the voting for the board of directors. With staggered elections, only a fraction of the directorships are up for election at a particular time. If only two directors are up for election at any one time, it will take $1/(2 + 1) = .3333$, or 33.33 percent of the stock plus one share to guarantee a seat. Staggered boards are often called *classified* boards because directors are placed into different classes with terms that expire at different times. In recent years, companies have come under pressure to declassify their boards, meaning that all directors would stand for election every year, and many have done so.

Overall, staggering has two basic effects:

1. Staggering makes it more difficult for a minority to elect a director under cumulative voting because fewer directors are elected at one time.
2. Staggering deters takeover attempts because of the difficulty of voting in a majority of new directors.

However, staggering also can serve a beneficial purpose. It provides *institutional memory* from continuity on the board of directors. Continuity may be important for companies with significant long-range plans and projects.

Proxy Voting At the annual meeting, shareholders can vote in person, or they can transfer their right to vote to another party. A **proxy** is the grant of authority by a shareholder to someone else to vote her shares. For convenience, much of the voting in large public companies is actually done by proxy.

Obviously, management wants to accumulate as many proxies as possible. However, an outside group of shareholders can try to obtain proxies in an attempt to replace management by electing enough directors. The resulting battle is called a *proxy fight.*

Classes of Stock While allowed by Indian law, some firms outside India have more than one class of equity share. Often, the classes are created with unequal voting rights. For example, Ford Motor Company's Class B equity share is held by Ford family interests and trusts and is not publicly traded. This class has 40 percent of the voting power, even though it represents less than 10 percent of the total number of shares outstanding.

There are many other cases of companies with different classes of stock. At one time, Hindustan Motors had its "HM Classic" shares (the original) and two additional classes, Class E (HME) and Class H (HMH). These classes were created to help pay for two large acquisitions, Electronic Data Systems and Hughes Aircraft. Another good example is Alphabet, which initially created two classes of equity share, A and B. The Class A shares are held by the public, and each share has one vote. The Class B shares are held by company insiders, and each Class B share has 10 votes. Then, in 2014, the company had a stock split of its Class B shares, creating Class C shares, which have no vote at all. As a result, Alphabet's founders and managers control the company. As another example, when Palantir Industries went public in 2020, the three co-founders were granted 49.99 percent of the voting power in perpetuity, regardless of how many shares they owned.

Historically, the New York Stock Exchange did not allow companies to create classes of publicly traded equity share with unequal voting rights. However, exceptions (e.g., Ford) appear to have been made. In addition, many non-NYSE companies have dual classes of equity share. Limited-voting stock allows management of a firm to raise equity capital while maintaining control.

The subject of unequal voting rights is allowed in India[1] and controversial in the United States, and the idea of one share, one vote has a strong following and a long history. Interestingly, however, shares with unequal voting rights are quite common around the world. In India, differential voting rights (DVR) shares

[1]In India, only one class of common equity shares are permitted, thereby reducing the complexity of unequal voting rights for different class of common equity shares.

are a class of shares that carry voting rights different from one share one vote policy. These DVR shares carry lesser voting rights than common equity shares. Tata Motors issued DVR shares in 2008 to raise funds for the JLR acquisition. In July 2023, Tata Motors announced that they would be converting the DVR shares to ordinary shares. A few more DVRs that exist in India are Future Enterprises DVR, Jain Irrigation Systems DVR and Stampede Captial DVR.

Other Rights The value of a share of equity share in a company is directly related to the general rights of shareholders. In addition to the right to vote for directors, shareholders usually have the following rights:

1. The right to share proportionally in dividends.
2. The right to share proportionally in assets remaining after liabilities have been paid in a liquidation.
3. The right to vote on stockholder matters of great importance, such as a merger. Voting usually occurs at the annual meeting or a special meeting.

In addition, companies sometimes give a *preemptive right* to their stockholders. A preemptive right forces a company to sell stock to its existing stockholders before offering the stock to the general public. The right lets each stockholder protect his proportionate ownership in the company.

Dividends Companies are legally authorized to pay **dividends** to their shareholders. The payment of dividends is at the discretion of the board of directors.

Some important characteristics of dividends include the following:

1. Unless a dividend is declared by the board of directors of a company, it is not a liability of the company. A company cannot default on an undeclared dividend. As a consequence, companies cannot become bankrupt because of nonpayment of dividends. The amount of the dividend and even whether it is paid are decisions based on the business judgment of the board of directors.
2. Dividends are paid out of the companies aftertax cash flow. They are not business expenses and are not deductible for corporate tax purposes.
3. Dividends received by individual shareholders are taxable. However, companies that own stock in other companies are permitted to exclude 50 percent (or more) of the dividend amounts they receive and are taxed on only the remaining 30 percent.[2]
4. In India, there have been a few policy changes. Before FY2003, dividends were taxed in the hands of the recipient as any other income. However, from FY2003 to FY2020, all domestic companies were liable to pay a dividend distribution tax on the profits distributed as dividends. This move resulted in a smaller net dividend to the recipients. The rate of taxation was around 20 percent. This move also resulted in no taxation at the hands of the recipients. The policy makers have again moved towards the tax policy akin to pre-2003 period. In other words, the dividend distribution tax has been made redundant from FY2021 onwards. This move also implies that all dividends received on or after 1 April 2020 are taxable in the hands of the investor/shareholder.

PREFERENCE SHARE FEATURES

Preference share pays a cash dividend expressed in terms of rupees per share. Preference share has a preference over equity share in the payment of dividends and in the distribution of company assets in the event of liquidation. *Preference* means only that holders of preference shares must receive a dividend (in the case

[2]More specifically, the 50 percent exclusion applies when the recipient owns less than 20 percent of the outstanding stock in a company. If a company owns more than 20 percent but less than 65 percent, the exclusion is 65 percent. If more than 65 percent is owned, the company can file a single consolidated return and the exclusion is effectively 100 percent.

of an ongoing firm) before holders of common shares are entitled to anything. Preference share typically has no maturity date.

Preference share is a form of equity from a legal and tax standpoint. It is important to note, however, that holders of preference share usually have no voting privileges.

Stated Value Preference shares have a stated liquidating value, usually ₹100 per share. For example, Hindustan Motors' "₹5 preference," paying an annual dividend of ₹5, translates into a dividend yield of 5 percent of stated value.

Cumulative and Noncumulative Dividends A preference dividend is not like interest on a bond. The decision of the board of directors not to pay the dividends on preference shares may have nothing to do with the current net income of the company.

Dividends payable on preference share are either *cumulative* or *noncumulative*; most are cumulative. If preference dividends are cumulative and are not paid in a particular year, they will be carried forward as an *arrearage.* Usually, both the accumulated (past) preference dividends and the current preference dividends must be paid before the common shareholders can receive anything.

Unpaid preference dividends are not debts of the firm. Directors elected by the common shareholders can defer preference dividends indefinitely. However, in such cases, common shareholders also must forgo dividends. In addition, holders of preference shares are sometimes granted voting and other rights if preference dividends have not been paid for some time. For example, at one point, US Airways had failed to pay dividends on one of its preference share issues for six quarters. As a consequence, the holders of the shares were allowed to nominate two people to represent their interests on the airline's board. Because preferred shareholders receive no interest on the accumulated dividends, some have argued that firms have an incentive to delay paying preferred dividends. However, as with US Airways, this may mean giving voting rights to preferred shareholders.

Is Preference Share Really Debt? A good case can be made that preference share is really debt in disguise. Preference share pays out stated dividends that resemble interest payments to debt. Like debt, preference share does not benefit from upside growth in the firm's value above and beyond the firm's ability to pay the stated dividends. Often, preference shares carry credit ratings much like those of bonds. Preference share is sometimes convertible into equity share. In addition, preference share are often callable, which allows the issuer to repurchase, or *call*, part or all of the issue at a stated price. More will be said about the call feature in the next section.

Though preference share typically has no maturity date, many issues have obligatory sinking funds. A sinking fund requires a company to retire a portion of its preference share each year. A sinking fund effectively creates a final maturity because the entire issue ultimately will be retired. More will be said on sinking funds in the next section. For these reasons, preference share seems to be a lot like debt. However, for tax purposes, preference dividends are treated like equity share dividends.

In the 1990s, firms began to sell securities that looked a lot like preference share but were treated as debt for tax purposes. The new securities were given interesting acronyms like TOPrS (trust-originated preference securities, or toppers), MIPS (monthly income preference securities), and QUIPS (quarterly income preference securities), among others. Because of various specific features, these instruments can be counted as debt for tax purposes, making the interest payments tax deductible. Payments made to investors in these instruments are treated as interest for personal income taxes for individuals. Until 2003, interest payments and dividends were taxed at the same marginal tax rate. When the tax rate on dividend payments was reduced, these instruments were not included, so individuals still must pay their higher income tax rate on dividend payments received from these instruments. In India, there are no incentives for institutional, corporate, or other investors to hold preference shares issued by firms. Hence, preference shares become less of an obvious option for obtaining long-term finance for firms. However, in 2013, SEBI approved a new regulation on primary issues and listing non-convertible, redeemable preference shares. This provides a comprehensive regulatory framework for public issuance of non-convertible redeemable preference shares (NCPRS) and listing of privately placed NCPRS. However, things have not improved on this end. For example, Tata Capital Ltd. has lately been active in issuing cumulative redeemable preference shares (CRPS) in the last few years.

15.2 Corporate Long-Term Debt

In this section, we describe in some detail the basic terms and features of a typical long-term corporate bond. We discuss additional issues associated with long-term debt in subsequent sections.

Securities issued by companies may be classified roughly as *equity securities* or *debt securities.* A debt represents something that must be repaid; it is the result of borrowing money. When companies borrow, they generally promise to make regularly scheduled interest payments and to repay the original amount borrowed (i.e., the principal). The person or firm making the loan is called the *creditor* or *lender.* The company borrowing the money is called the *debtor* or *borrower.*

From a financial point of view, the main differences between debt and equity are:

Information for bond investors can be found at **www.investinginbonds.com**.

1. Debt is not an ownership interest in the firm. Creditors generally do not have voting power.
2. The company's payment of interest on debt is considered a cost of doing business and is tax deductible up to the 30 percent limit of the Tax Cuts and Jobs Act. Dividends paid to stockholders are not tax deductible.
3. Unpaid debt is a liability of the firm. If it is not paid, the creditors can legally claim the assets of the firm. This action can result in liquidation or reorganization, two of the possible consequences of bankruptcy. Thus, one of the costs of issuing debt is the possibility of financial failure. This possibility does not arise when only equity is issued.

IS IT DEBT OR EQUITY?

Sometimes it is not clear if a particular security is debt or equity. Suppose a company issues a perpetual bond with interest payable solely from corporate income if, and only if, earned. Whether or not this is really a debt is hard to say and is primarily a legal and semantic issue. Courts and taxing authorities would have the final say.

Companies are adept at creating exotic, hybrid securities that have many features of equity but are treated as debt. Obviously, the distinction between debt and equity is very important for tax purposes. One reason that companies try to create a debt security that is really equity is to obtain the tax benefits of debt and the bankruptcy benefits of equity.

As a general rule, equity represents an ownership interest and is a residual claim. This means that equityholders are paid after debtholders. As a result, the risks and benefits associated with owning debt and equity are different. To give an example, note that the maximum reward for owning a debt security is ultimately fixed by the amount of the loan, whereas there is no upper limit to the potential reward from owning an equity interest.

Equity versus Debt

Feature	Equity	Debt
Income	Dividends	Interest
Tax status	Dividends are taxed as personal income, although currently capped at 23.8 percent at the U.S. federal level. Dividends are not a business expense.	Interest is taxed as personal income. Interest is a business expense, and companies can deduct interest up to 30 percent of EBIT when computing their corporate tax liability.
Control	Equity share usually has voting rights.	Control is exercised with loan agreement.
Default	Firms cannot be forced into bankruptcy for nonpayment of dividends.	Unpaid debt is a liability of the firm. Nonpayment results in default and possible bankruptcy.

Bottom line: Tax status favors debt, but default favors equity. Control features of debt and equity are different, but one is not better than the other.

LONG-TERM DEBT: THE BASICS

Ultimately, all long-term debt securities are promises made by the issuing firm to pay principal when due and to make timely interest payments on the unpaid balance. Beyond this, a number of features distinguish these securities from one another. We discuss some of these features next.

The maturity of a long-term debt instrument is the length of time the debt remains outstanding with some unpaid balance. Debt securities can be short term (with maturities of one year or less) or long term (with maturities of more than one year).[3] Short-term debt is sometimes referred to as *unfunded debt.*[4]

Debt securities are typically called *notes, debentures*, or *bonds*. Strictly speaking, a bond is a secured debt, meaning that certain property is pledged as security for repayment of the debt, while a debenture is unsecured debt. However, in common usage, the word *bond* refers to all kinds of secured and unsecured debt. We will therefore continue to use the term generically to refer to long-term debt. Also, usually, the only difference between a note and a bond is the original maturity. Issues with an original maturity of 10 years or less are often called notes. Longer-term issues are called bonds.

Long-term debt can be issued to the public or privately placed. Privately placed debt is issued to a lender and not offered to the public. Because this is a private transaction, the specific terms are up to the parties involved. We concentrate on public-issue bonds. However, most of what we say about them holds true for private-issue, long-term debt, as well.

Information on individual bonds can be found at **www.bseindia.com** and **https://www.nseindia.com**

There are many other aspects to long-term debt, including such terms as security, call features, sinking funds, ratings, and protective covenants. The following table illustrates these features for a bond issued by Home Depot. If some of these terms are unfamiliar, have no fear. We will discuss them all in this chapter.

[3]There is no universally agreed-upon distinction between short-term and long-term debt. In addition, people often refer to intermediate-term debt, which has a maturity of more than 1 year and less than 3 to 5, or even 10, years.

[4]The word *funding* is part of the jargon of finance. It generally refers to the long term. Thus, a firm planning to fund its debt requirements may be replacing short-term debt with long-term debt.

Features of a Home Depot Bond		
Term		**Explanation**
Amount of issue	₹1.5 billion	The company issued ₹1.5 billion worth of bonds.
Date of issue	3/30/2020	The bonds were sold on 3/30/2020.
Maturity	4/15/2050	The bonds mature on 4/15/2050.
Face value	₹2,000	The denomination of the bonds is ₹2,000.
Annual coupon	3.35%	Each bondholder will receive ₹67 per bond per year (3.35% of face value).
Offer price	98.858	The offer price will be 98.858% of the ₹2,000 face value, or ₹1,977.16, per bond.
Coupon payment dates	04/15, 10/15	Coupons of ₹67/2 = ₹33.50 will be paid on these dates.
Security	None	The bonds are not secured by specific assets.
Sinking fund	None	The bonds have no sinking fund.
Call provision	At any time	The bonds do not have a deferred call.
Call price	Treasury rate plus .30%.	The bonds have a "make-whole" call price.
Rating	Moody's A2, S&P A	The bonds have a good-quality credit rating.

Many of these features will be detailed in the bond indenture, so we discuss this first.

THE INDENTURE

The **indenture** is the written agreement between the company (the borrower) and its creditors. It is sometimes referred to as the *deed of trust.*[5] Usually, a trustee (a bank perhaps) is appointed by the company to represent the bondholders. The trust company must (1) make sure the terms of the indenture are obeyed; (2) manage the sinking fund (described in the following pages); and (3) represent the bondholders in default, that is, if the company defaults on its payments to them.

The bond indenture is a legal document. It can run several hundred pages and generally makes for very tedious reading. It is an important document, however, because it generally includes the following provisions:

1. The basic terms of the bonds.
2. A description of property used as security.
3. Seniority.
4. The repayment arrangements.
5. The call provisions.
6. Details of the protective covenants.

We discuss these features next.

[5]The phrases *loan agreement* and *loan contract* are usually used for privately placed debt and term loans.

Terms of a Bond Corporate bonds have historically had a face value (that is a denomination of ₹1,000 or ₹1,000, as the issue of currency may be) although par values of ₹2,000 like the Home Depot bond have become relatively common. Other par values also exist. For example, municipal bonds often have par values of ₹5,000, and Treasury bonds with par values of ₹10,000 or ₹100,000 are often sold. This principal value is stated on the bond certificate. So, if a company wanted to borrow ₹10 million, 5,000 bonds with a ₹2,000 par value would have to be sold. The par value (i.e., the initial accounting value) of a bond is almost always the same as the face value, and the terms are used interchangeably in practice.

Corporate bonds are usually in **registered form**. The indenture might read as follows:

Interest is payable semiannually on July 1 and January 1 of each year to the person in whose name the bond is registered at the close of business on June 15 or December 15, respectively.

This means that the company has a registrar who will record the initial ownership of each bond, as well as any changes in ownership. The company will pay the interest and principal directly to the owner of record.

At one time, corporate bond certificates had attached coupons, where each coupon represented a payment. To receive a payment, the bond owner had to physically separate a coupon from the bond certificate and send it to the company registrar (the paying agent), who would then send the payment. This activity was referred to as "clipping coupons."

Alternatively, the bond could be in **bearer form**. This means that the certificate is the basic evidence of ownership, and the company will "pay the bearer." Ownership is not otherwise recorded, and, as with a registered bond with attached coupons, the holder of the bond certificate detaches the coupons and presents them to the company's agent at the appropriate time to receive payment.

There are two drawbacks to bearer bonds. First, they are difficult to recover if they are lost or stolen. Second, because the company does not know who owns its bonds, it cannot notify bondholders of important events. Bearer bonds were once the dominant type in India (and even in the United States), primarily used for funding the net working capital. In India, some of the popular bearer bonds include the state-backed Certificates of Deposit known as Indira Vikas Patra (IVP), Kisan Vikas Patra (KVP), and National Savings Scheme (NSS).[6] Both Kisan Vikas Patra (KVP) and Indira Vikas Patra (IVP) double the amount deposited in 9.5 years.

Security Debt securities are classified according to the collateral and mortgages used to protect the bondholder.

Collateral is a general term that frequently means securities (e.g., bonds and stocks) that are pledged as security for payment of debt. For example, collateral trust bonds often involve a pledge of equity share held by the company. However, the term *collateral* is commonly used to refer to any asset pledged on a debt.

Mortgage securities are secured by a mortgage on the real property of the borrower. The property involved is usually real estate, such as land or buildings. The legal document that describes the mortgage is called a *mortgage trust indenture* or *trust deed.*

Sometimes mortgages are on specific property, such as a railroad car. More often, blanket mortgages are used. A blanket mortgage pledges all the real property owned by the company.[7]

Bonds frequently represent unsecured obligations of the company. As we noted above, a **debenture** is an unsecured bond for which no specific pledge of property is made. The term **note** is generally used for such instruments if the maturity of the unsecured bond is less than 10 years from the date when the bond was originally issued. Debenture holders have a claim only on property not otherwise pledged–in other

[6] One finance professor, Dr. Ramachandran says that these instruments have been aptly named! In other words, the professor intended to convey that these instruments are primarily used to save '*black money*'.

[7] Real property includes land and things "affixed thereto." It does not include cash or inventories.

words, the property that remains after mortgages and collateral trusts are taken into account. The Home Depot bonds discussed earlier are an example of such an issue.

The terminology that we use here and elsewhere in this chapter is standard in (most of) India and the United States. Outside these contexts, these same terms can have different meanings. For example, bonds issued by the British government (*gilts*) are called *treasury stock*. Also, in the United Kingdom, a debenture is a *secured* obligation.

At the current time, public bonds issued in the United States by industrial and financial companies are typically debentures. However, most utility and railroad bonds are secured by a pledge of assets.

Seniority In general terms, *seniority* indicates preference in position over other lenders, and debts are sometimes labeled as *senior* or *junior* to indicate seniority. Some debt is *subordinated*, as in, for example, a subordinated debenture.

In the event of default, holders of subordinated debt must give preference to other specified creditors. Usually, this means that the subordinated lenders will be paid off only after the specified creditors have been compensated. However, debt cannot be subordinated to equity.

The Securities Industry and Financial Markets Association (SIFMA) site is **www.sifma.org**.

Repayment Bonds can be repaid entirely at maturity, at which time the bondholder receives the stated, or face, value of the bond, or they may be repaid in part or in entirety before maturity. Early repayment in some form is more typical and is often handled through a sinking fund.

A **sinking fund** is an account managed by the bond trustee for the purpose of repaying the bonds. The company makes annual payments to the trustee, who then uses the funds to retire a portion of the debt. The trustee does this by either buying some of the bonds in the market or calling in a fraction of the outstanding bonds. This second option is discussed in the next section.

There are many different kinds of sinking fund arrangements, and the details are spelled out in the indenture. For example:

1. Some sinking funds start about 10 years after the initial issuance.
2. Some sinking funds establish equal payments over the life of the bond.
3. Some high-quality bond issues establish payments to the sinking fund that are insufficient to redeem the entire issue. As a consequence, there may be a large *balloon payment* at maturity.

The Call Provision A **call provision** allows the company to repurchase, or *call*, part or all of the bond issue at stated prices over a specific period. Corporate bonds are usually callable.

Generally, the call price is above the bond's stated value (i.e., the par value). The difference between the call price and the stated value is the **call premium**. The amount of the call premium may become smaller over time. One arrangement is to initially set the call premium equal to the annual coupon payment and then make it decline to zero as the call date moves closer to the time of maturity.

Call provisions are often not operative during the first part of a bond's life, making the call provision less of a worry for bondholders in the bond's early years. For example, a company might be prohibited from calling its bonds for the first 10 years. This is a **deferred call** provision. During the period of prohibition, the bond is said to be **call protected**.

Another type of call provision, a *make-whole* call, has become widespread in the corporate bond market. With such a feature, bondholders receive approximately what the bonds are worth if they are called. Because bondholders don't suffer a loss in the event of a call, they are "made whole."

To determine the make-whole call price, we calculate the present value of the remaining interest and principal payments at a rate specified in the indenture. Looking at our Home Depot issue, we see that the discount rate is "Treasury rate plus .30%." What this means is that we determine the discount rate by first finding a U.S. Treasury issue with the same maturity. We calculate the yield to maturity on the Treasury issue and then add on an additional .30 percent to get the discount rate we use.

Notice that, with a make-whole call provision, the call price is higher when interest rates are lower and vice versa (why?). Also notice that, as is common with a make-whole call, the Home Depot issue does not have a deferred call feature. Why might investors not be too concerned about the absence of this feature?

EXAMPLE 15.2

Callable Bonds

A call provision permits a company to repurchase or call an entire bond issue at some price during a predetermined period. Common sense tells us that a call provision has positive value to the company and negative value to the creditor. If interest rates fall and bond prices go up, the option to buy back the bonds at a call price that is lower than would be true otherwise is valuable. Of course, bond investors know this and take into account the call provision.

Suppose Venture Capital Corp. (VCC) has an outstanding 30-year bond that pays semiannual coupons. It is a 7 percent bond with a ₹1,000 par value and is currently selling at par. Further suppose that because of potential changes in interest rates, the price of the VCC bond could be ₹700 or ₹1,300 at the end of the year with equal odds.

1. What is the expected value of the VCC bonds after one year?
   (.5 × ₹700) + (.5 × ₹1,300) = ₹1,000
2. What is the expected value of the VCC bonds if they are callable at ₹1,000?
   (.5 × ₹700) + (.5 × ₹1,000) = ₹850

If the bonds are callable, the expected bond value can be less than if the bonds are not callable. If the actual bond value rises above the call price, the company will call it. Therefore, other things equal, the bondholder will not pay as much for a callable bond.

Protective Covenants A **protective covenant** in the indenture or loan agreement affects certain corporate actions. Protective covenants can be classified into two types: *negative covenants* and *positive covenants.*

A *negative covenant* is a "thou shalt not" type of covenant. It limits or prohibits actions that the company might take. For example, the firm must limit the amount of dividends it pays according to some formula.

A *positive covenant* is a "thou shalt" type of covenant. It specifies an action that the company must take or a condition that the company must abide by. For example, the company must maintain its working capital at or above some specified minimum level.

A particular indenture may feature many different negative and positive covenants.

Want detailed information on the amount and terms of the debt issued by a particular firm? Check out its latest financials at **www.nseindia.com** or **www.bseindia.com.**

15.3 Some Different Types of Bonds

Thus far, we have considered only "plain vanilla" corporate bonds. In this section, we look at corporate bonds with unusual features.

FLOATING-RATE BONDS

The conventional bonds we have discussed in this chapter have fixed-rupee obligations because the coupon rate is set as a fixed percentage of the par value and the principal is set equal to the par value. With *floating-rate bonds (floaters)*, the coupon payments are adjustable. The adjustments are tied to an interest rate index such as the Treasury bill interest rate or the 30-year Treasury bond rate.

The value of a floating-rate bond depends on how the coupon payment adjustments are defined. In most cases, the coupon adjusts with a lag to some base rate. Suppose a coupon rate adjustment is made on June 1. The adjustment might be based on the simple average of Treasury bond yields during the previous three months.

In addition, the majority of floaters have the following features:

1. The holder has the right to redeem her note at par on the coupon payment date after some specified amount of time. This is called a *put* provision; it is discussed in the following section.
2. The coupon rate has a floor and a ceiling, meaning that the coupon is subject to a minimum and a maximum. In this case, the coupon rate is said to be *capped*, and the upper and lower rates are sometimes called the *collar.*

In the 1990s, the State Bank of India issued one of the first floating rate bonds in the Indian debt market. Another example of a popular floating rate bond in the India market was by IDBI. IDBI issued a five-year floating rate bond, in 1997, with the rates being reset semi-annually with reference to the 10-year yield on the central government securities and 50-basis points up mark. Currently, floating rate bonds are quite common in the housing loan markets. Companies also introduce many innovations in the floating rate bonds. Many Indian companies such as JSW steel, Maithon Power and Piramal Enterprises have raised funds through issue of floaters.

A particularly interesting type of floating-rate bond is an *inflation-linked* bond. Such bonds have coupons that are adjusted according to the rate of inflation (the principal amount may be adjusted as well). The U.S. Treasury began issuing such bonds in January of 1997. The issues are sometimes called "TIPS," or Treasury Inflation-Protected Securities. Other countries, including Canada, Israel, and Britain, have issued similar securities.

OTHER TYPES OF BONDS

Many bonds have unusual or exotic features. One such feature is called a *warrant.* A warrant gives the buyer of a bond the right to purchase shares of stock in the company at a fixed price. Such a right would be very valuable if the stock price climbed substantially. (A later chapter discusses this subject in greater depth.) Because of the value of this feature, bonds with warrants are often issued at a very low coupon rate.

So-called catastrophe, or cat, bonds are an interesting type. In June 2019, Hamilton Insurance Group issued ₹60 million in cat bonds. These cat bonds covered U.S.-named storms and earthquakes. If one of these triggering events occurs, investors would lose some or all of their money.

The largest single cat bond issue to date is a series of six bonds sold by Merna Reinsurance in 2007 (reinsurance companies sell insurance to insurance companies). The six bond issues were to cover various catastrophes the company might face due to its reinsurance of State Farm. The six bonds totaled about ₹1.2 billion in par value. Overall, during 2020, there was about ₹42 billion par value in cat bonds outstanding.

Of course, the term *catastrophe* has a broad definition. In 2020, investors in a ₹320 million bond issued by the World Bank lost ₹132.5 million in principal when a bond linked to a global pandemic was triggered by COVID-19. Investors in the less risky tranche, which paid 6.9 percent, lost 16.7 percent of their principal.

Investors in the riskier tranche, which paid 11.5 percent, lost all of their principal. The investors' principal was to be sent to dozens of poor countries, including Ethiopia, Ghana, Bangladesh, and Cambodia.

In 2019, Conservation Capital issued rhino impact bonds (RIB). The bonds are designed to increase the population of black rhinos in Kenya and South Africa, which has fallen from 65,000 in the 1970s to about 5,500 today. Bondholders receive payments based on the "outcome payments" model. In this case, payments will be based on the population of black rhinos in five years. An independent evaluator will determine whether the RIB target has been achieved, and bondholders will receive a return relative to the RIB target. Depending on how successful these bonds are, look for more bonds based on environmental goals.

During the COVID-19 pandemic, a new bond type, coronavirus bonds, came to market. The proceeds of the bonds were to go toward work linked to the pandemic. Between February and May 2020, over ₹150 billion of these bonds were issued. For example, Bank of America issued ₹1 billion in coronavirus bonds that would be used to support the health care industry. Of course, what is or isn't a coronavirus bond is a gray area. Pfizer issued ₹1.25 billion in bonds that were classified as coronavirus bonds by an outside agency. Pfizer disagreed with the categorization, preferring instead to market the bonds as sustainability bonds.

Bond features are really only limited by the imaginations of the parties involved. Unfortunately, there are far too many variations for us to cover in detail here. We therefore close out this section by mentioning only a few of the more common types.

Income bonds are similar to conventional bonds, except that coupon payments are dependent on company income. Specifically, coupons are paid to bondholders only if the firm's income is sufficient. This would appear to be an attractive feature, but income bonds are not very common.

A *convertible bond* can be swapped for a fixed number of shares of stock anytime before maturity at the holder's option. Convertibles are relatively common, but the number has been decreasing in recent years.

A *put bond* allows the *holder* to force the issuer to buy the bond back at a stated price. For example, International Paper Co. has bonds outstanding that allow the holder to force International Paper to buy the bonds back at 100 percent of face value if certain risk events happen. One such event is a change in credit rating from investment grade to lower than investment grade by Moody's or S&P. The put feature is therefore the reverse of the call provision.

The *reverse convertible* is a relatively new item. One type generally offers a high coupon rate, but the redemption at maturity can be paid in cash at par value or paid in shares of stock. For example, one Hindustan Motors (HM) reverse convertible had a coupon rate of 16 percent, which is a very high coupon rate in today's interest rate environment. However, at maturity, if HM's stock declined sufficiently, bondholders would receive a fixed number of HM shares that were worth less than par value. So, while the income portion of the bond return would be high, the potential loss in par value could easily erode the extra return.

Perhaps the most unusual bond (and certainly the most ghoulish) is the "death bond." Companies such as Stone Street Financial purchase life insurance policies from individuals who are expected to die within the next 10 years. They then sell bonds that are paid off from the life insurance proceeds received when the policyholders pass away. The return on the bonds to investors depends on how long the policyholders live. A major risk is that if medical treatment advances quickly, it will raise the life expectancy of the policyholders, thereby decreasing the return to the bondholder.

Structured notes are bonds that are based on stocks, bonds, commodities, or currencies. One particular type of structured note has a return based on a stock market index. At expiration, if the stock index has declined, the bond returns the principal. However, if the stock index has increased, the bond will return a portion of the stock index return–say, 80 percent. Another type of structured note will return twice the stock index return, but with the potential for loss of principal.

A given bond may have many unusual features. Two of the most recent exotic bonds are CoCo bonds, which have a coupon payment, and NoNo bonds, which are zero coupon bonds. CoCo and NoNo bonds are contingent convertible, putable, callable, subordinated bonds. The contingent convertible clause is similar to the normal conversion feature, except the contingent feature must be met. For example, a contingent feature may require that the company stock trade at 110 percent of the conversion price for 20 out of the most recent 30 days. Valuing a bond of this sort can be quite complex, and the yield to maturity calculation is often meaningless.

SUKUK Worldwide demand for assets that comply with sharia, or Islamic law and cultural tradition, has grown dramatically. Assets, including deposits at Islamic financial institutions, totaled about ₹1.8 trillion in 2019, up from ₹1.3 trillion in 2011. One of the major differences between Western financial practices and sharia is that Islamic law does not permit charging or paying *riba*, or interest. Given our current discussion about bonds, this means that anyone following sharia cannot buy or issue conventional bonds.

To accommodate the restriction on interest payments, Islamic bonds, or *sukuk*, have been created. There are many possible structures to sukuk, such as partial ownership in a debt (sukuk al-murabaha) or an asset (sukuk al-ijara). In the case of a sukuk al-ijara, there is a binding promise to repurchase a certain asset by the issuer at maturity. Before the sukuk matures, rent is paid on the asset. While we have noted that traditional bonds can be relatively illiquid, most sukuk are bought and held to maturity. As a result, secondary markets in sukuk are extremely illiquid.

Masala Bonds Rupee denominated bonds are informally known as Masala Bond. The term "Masala", meaning spices, was used by International Finance Corporation (IFC) to evoke the culture and cuisine of India. The most important feature of Masala Bond is that the Indian corporates can raise money in the overseas market in Indian currency, thus mitigating currency risk. IFC issued the first Masala Bond to raise 1,000 crore to fund infrastructure projects in India. In 2019, the state-owned Kerala Infrastructure Investment Fund Board (KIIFB) debuted its 'masala bond' issue of ₹2,150 crore on the London Stock Exchange. After this, KIIFB became the first sub-sovereign entity in India to tap the offshore rupee international bond market.

The secured bond has a five-year tenure with a 9.723% fixed coupon. The proceeds from this issue was used to part-finance the infrastructure rebuilding after 2018 floods.

Green Bonds Green bonds are a form of debt issued by public or private entities to finance projects, with a unique commitment: the funds raised are dedicated specifically to environmental initiatives or climate change-related projects, distinguishing them from other credit instruments. They are issued to mobilize resources for green infrastructure. The proceeds will be directed towards public sector projects aimed at reducing the carbon intensity of the economy.

Indian green bond issuances have reached a total of ₹21 billion as of February 2023. Greenko Group, India's largest green bond issuer, is using the proceeds to finance hydro, solar, and wind power projects across various states. Ghaziabad Nagar Nigam, a civic body in Uttar Pradesh, became the first Indian local government to issue a green bond (USD 20 million in 2021). Following suit, Indore Municipal Corporation issued green bonds worth USD 87 million in 2023.

15.4 Bank Loans

In addition to issuing bonds, a firm may borrow from a bank. Two important features of bank loans are lines of credit and syndication.

Lines of Credit Banks often provide a business customer with a line of credit, setting the maximum amount that the bank is willing to lend to the business. The business can then borrow the money according to its need for funds. If the bank is legally obligated, the credit line is generally referred to as a revolving line of credit, or a *revolver.* As an example, imagine a revolver for ₹75 million with a three-year commitment, implying that the business could borrow part or all of the ₹75 million anytime within the next three years. A commitment fee is generally charged on the unused portion of the revolver. Suppose the commitment fee is .20 percent and the company borrows ₹25 million in a particular year, leaving ₹50 million unborrowed. The rupee commitment fee would be ₹100,000 (= .002 × ₹50 million) for that year, in addition to the interest on the ₹25 million actually borrowed.

Syndicated Loans Very large banks such as Citigroup and the State Bank of India typically have a larger demand for loans than they can supply, and small regional banks (such as the Greater Bombay Co-operative Bank and the AP Mahesh Cooperative Bank) frequently have more funds on hand than they can profitably lend to existing customers. Basically, they cannot generate enough good loans with the funds they have available. As a result, a very large bank may arrange a syndicated loan with a firm or country and then sell portions of it to a syndicate of other banks. With a syndicated loan, each bank has a separate loan agreement with the borrowers. Syndicated loans also benefit banks by allowing them to spread the risk of each loan across several banks.

The syndicate is generally composed of a lead arranger and participant lenders. As the name suggests, the lead arranger takes the lead, creating the relationship with the borrower and negotiating the specifics of the loan. The participant lenders are typically not involved in the negotiation process. The lead arranger works with the participant lenders to determine shares of the loan and generally lends the most. While all lenders receive interest and principal payments, the lead arranger also receives an up-front fee as compensation for its additional responsibilities.

A syndicated loan may be publicly traded. It may be a line of credit and be *undrawn*, or it may be drawn and used by a firm. Syndicated loans are always rated investment grade. However, a *leveraged* syndicated loan is rated speculative grade (i.e., it is *junk*).

We provide you an example of a long-term syndicated bank loan from India. In August 2020, Vedanta Ltd. tied up with the State Bank of India for a long-term syndicated loan facility worth ₹10,000 crore. While SBI acted as the facility agent along with a commitment of ₹5,000 crore as a lender, the SBICAP Trustee Company Ltd. acted as the security trustee with door to door tenor of seven years. A large number of banks across Asia participated in the syndication facility.

15.5 International Bonds

A **Eurobond** is a bond issued in multiple countries but denominated in a single currency, usually the issuer's home currency. For example, an American firm may issue a rupee-denominated bond in a number of foreign countries. Such bonds have become an important way to raise capital for many international companies and governments. Eurobonds are issued outside the restrictions that apply to domestic offerings and are syndicated and traded mostly from London. However, trading can and does take place anywhere there are buyers and sellers. Eurobonds had been trading for many years before the euro, the single currency across many European countries, was created in 1999. However, because the two terms are so similar, people mistakenly think Eurobonds must be denominated in euros. To avoid confusion, many refer to Eurobonds as *international bonds.*

Foreign bonds, unlike Eurobonds, are issued in a single country and are usually denominated in that country's currency. For example, a Canadian firm might issue yen-denominated bonds in Japan. Often, the country in which these bonds are issued will draw distinctions between them and bonds issued by domestic issuers–including different tax laws, restrictions on the amount issued, and tougher disclosure rules.

Foreign bonds often are nicknamed for the country where they are issued: Yankee bonds (United States), Samurai bonds (Japan), Rembrandt bonds (the Netherlands), Bulldog bonds (Great Britain), and dim sum bonds (Chinese yuan-denominated bonds issued in Hong Kong). Masala Bonds represent rupee-denominated bonds issued by Indian entities outside India. Partly because of tougher regulations and disclosure requirements, the foreign bond market hasn't grown in past years with the vigor of the Eurobond market.

15.6 Patterns of Financing

The previous sections of this chapter discussed some institutional details related to long-term financing. We now consider the relationship between long-term financing and investments. As we have seen in earlier chapters, firms want to spend on capital projects with positive NPVs. How can these firms get the cash to fund investments in positive NPV projects? First, firms generating positive cash flow internally can use that flow for positive NPV investments. In accounting terms, this cash flow is net income plus depreciation minus dividends. Second, firms can fund positive NPV capital spending through external financing–that is, by issuing debt and equity.

This relationship between investment and financing is described in Figure 15.1. The left-hand side of the figure indicates that cash flow can fund both capital spending and investment in net working capital. A similar figure for Indian firms would have historically used about 60 percent of cash flow on

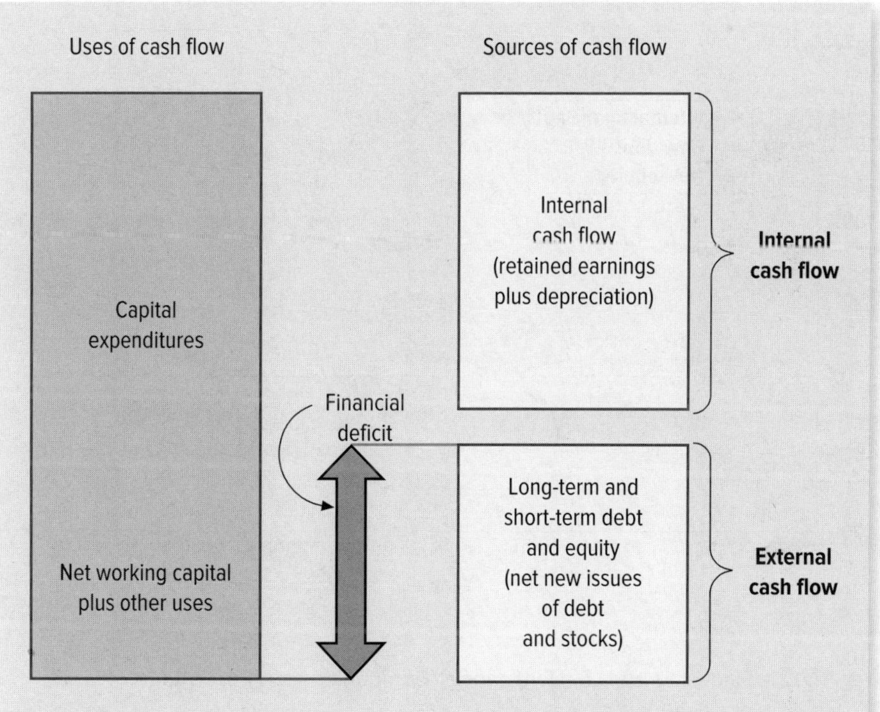

The deficit is the difference between uses of cash flow and internal financing.

Figure 15.1 The Long-Term Financial Deficit in the U.S. Nonfinancial corporations capital spending and about 40 percent on investment in net working capital. The right-hand side of the figure shows the two sources of cash flow: internal and external financing. In the figure, uses of cash flow exceed internal financing. Stocks and bonds must be issued to fill the *financial deficit.*

In practice, what has been the split between internal and external financing? Figure 15.2 breaks down total financing for U.S. businesses into internal financing, financing through new equity, and financing through new debt for each year from 1975 to 2020. Consider 2015, for example. Internal financing in the United States was about 94 percent of the total, new debt was about 37 percent of the total, and new equity was about negative 31 percent of the total. Notice that in this year, as in all the years, the three sources of funds must add to 100 percent. If you are wondering why net equity is a negative number, it is because companies repurchased more stock than they issued in that year.

The figure illustrates a number of points. First, internally generated cash flow has been the dominant source of financing. Second, this dominance has increased over the sample period, with internal financing actually exceeding 100 percent for a majority of the years from 2005 to 2020. A number above 100 percent implies that external financing is negative. In other words, companies are, in rupee terms, redeeming more stocks and bonds than they are issuing. Third, this redemption occurred in equity much more than in debt. New equity was negative in most years since 1994, indicating that the rupee amount of stock buybacks exceeded the rupee amount of stock issues throughout this period. By contrast, new debt financing was positive in every year but 1975, 1983, and 2009. One can view this as share buybacks being financed with new debt. Why do firms typically prefer to use internal financing over external financing, and debt over equity? We will offer an explanation in a subsequent chapter when we introduce pecking order theory.

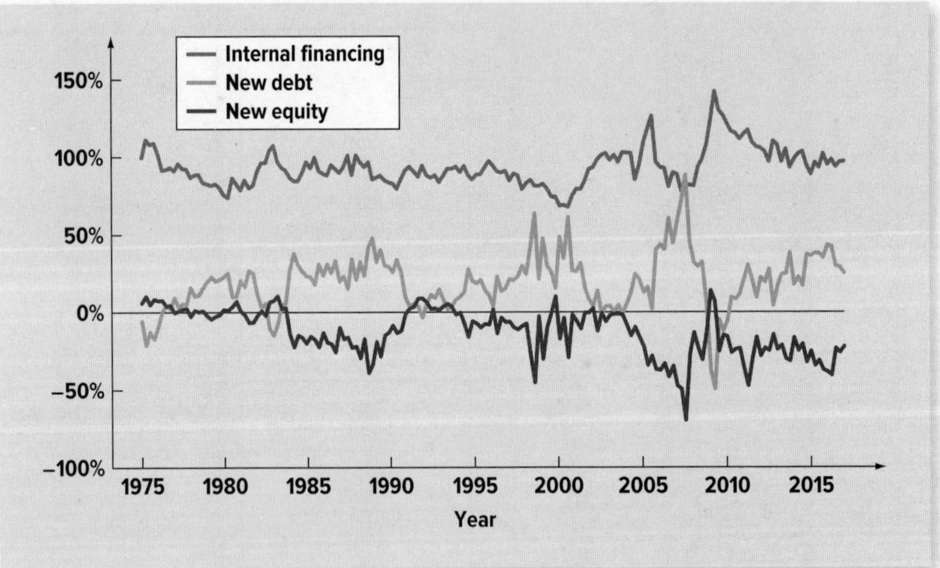

Figure 15.2 Financing by U.S. Nonfinancial Companies as a Percentage of Uses of Cash Flow

SOURCE: Board of Governors of the Federal Reserve System, "Flow of Funds Accounts of the United States," *Federal Reserve Statistical Release,* September 21, 2020, www.federalreserve.gov/releases/Z1/current/default.htm.

15.7 Recent Trends in Capital Structure

Figure 15.2 indicates that U.S. firms tended to issue debt while retiring stock. This pattern of financing raises the question: Did the capital structure of firms change over this time period? One might expect the answer to be yes because debt issuances and stock retirements should raise the ratio of debt to equity. However, look at Figure 15.3, where the ratio of total debt to the book value of equity is shown for each year from 1975 to 2020. The ratio was actually lower in 2020 than it was in 1975. This result is not surprising once retained earnings are considered. As long as net income exceeds dividends, retained earnings will be positive, raising the book value of equity.

Of course, equity can be measured in terms of market value, rather than book value. Figure 15.3 also shows the ratio of total debt to the market value of equity for U.S. firms. While the debt-market value ratio is also lower in 2020 than in 1975, the year-by-year pattern is somewhat different from the pattern for debt-to-book value. The debt-market value ratio rose significantly from 1999 to 2002 and again in 2008, reflecting the sharp drop in stock prices during those periods. Conversely, the debt-market value ratio fell during both the late 1990s and the period from 2008 to 2020, reflecting the sharp rise in stock prices during that period. As Figure 15.3 shows, leverage ratios are strongly affected by stock market movements when market values, rather than book values, of equity are used.

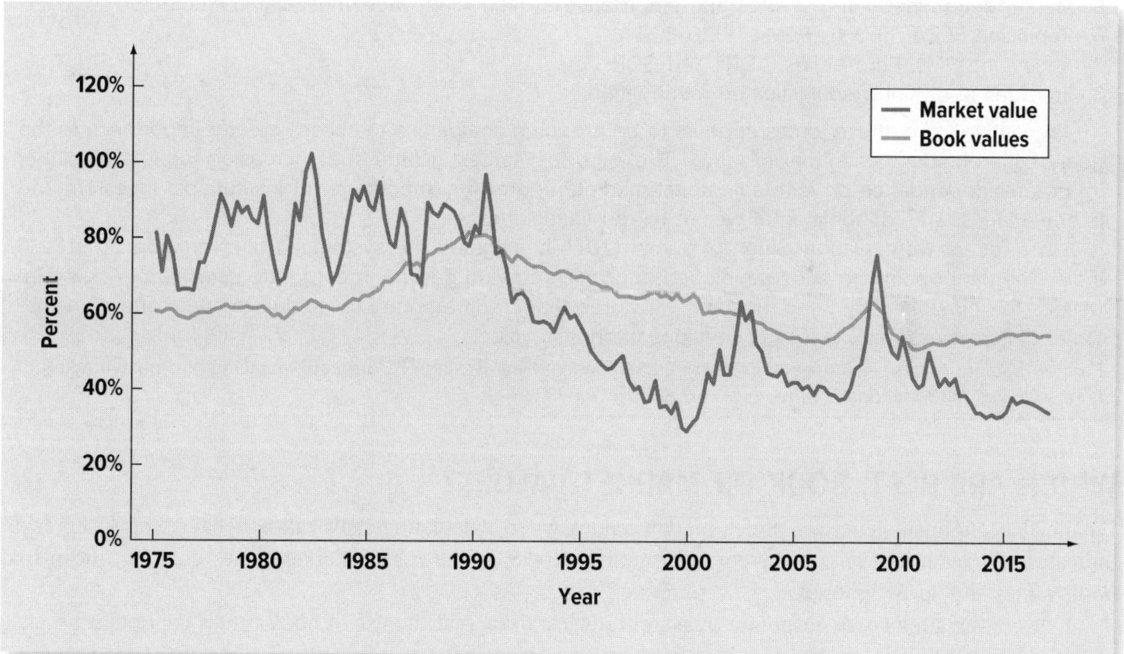

Figure 15.3 Debt-to-Equity Ratios: Total Debt as a Percentage of Book Value of Equity and Market Value of Equity for U.S. Nonfinancial Firms from 1975 to 2020

SOURCE: Board of Governors of the Federal Reserve System, "Flow of Funds Accounts of the United States," *Federal Reserve Statistical Release*, September 21, 2020, www.federalreserve.gov/releases/Z1/current/default.htm.

Financing of Indian Companies: The Changing Scenario

Traditionally, corporate sector in India is dominated by business group affiliates with close links with the promoter business house. For instance, Kotak Mahindra Bank belongs to the Uday Kotak Group. Similarly, JK Tyres belongs to the JK Singhania Group. Their earlier funding was primarily through institutional borrowings from state-owned development financial institutions like IFCI, ICICI, IDBI, and so on. This implied that there was a preponderance of loan capital in their financial structure and shareholders' equity played a rather marginal role. Business group companies also used to depend for their long-term financing from other business group affiliates (within), known as internal capital markets.

Reflecting the emerging economic and financial environment in the post-liberalization era, the role of the financial managers in India has changed and become more complex and demanding. The main elements of the changed economic and financial environment, inter alia, are the following:

1. Considerable relaxation in industrial licensing framework.
2. Abolition of the highly restrictive Monopolies and Restrictive Trade Practices (MRTP) Act and its replacement by the Competition Act 2002.
3. Abolition of Controller of Capital Issues (CCI) and the setting up of the SEBI, NSE, IRDA and many other institutional intermediaries.
4. Globalization, convertibility of rupee, liberalized foreign investments in India, Indian foreign investment abroad.
5. Market determined interest rates and emergence of highly innovative financial instruments.
6. Replacing FERA, 1973 by FEMA, 1999.
7. Access of AIMs, Euro-issues, ADRs and GDRs, etc.
8. Emergence of highly sophisticated money-market.

A confluence of these forces appears to be prodding companies to accord greater importance to the goal of shareholder wealth maximization. The important forces include – [a] increasing foreign exposure; [b] greater dependence on external capital market; [c] growing importance of institutional investors and intermediaries; and [d] abolition of wealth tax on financial assets.

In a recent work, Gaurav Singh Chauhan (2017) highlighted the systematic deleveraging of firms in India. The paper points to underdeveloped bond markets and decline in corporate investments as explanations for this unhealthy trend. Readers will agree that credit rationed firms, due to such form of institutional deficiencies, result in loss of precious economic value.

Further reading: Authors, information collation and Chauhan, Gaurav Singh. "Corporate financing and deleveraging of firms in India." *IIMB management review*, 29.3 (2017): 170–187.

WHICH ARE BEST: BOOK OR MARKET VALUES?

Financial economists generally prefer market values when calculating debt ratios because, as Chapter 14 indicates, market prices reflect current information. However, the use of market values does not mean that book values should be ignored.

Our conversations with corporate treasurers suggest to us that the use of book values is popular because of the volatility of the stock market. It is frequently claimed that the inherent volatility of the stock market makes market-based debt ratios move around too much. In addition, restrictions of debt in bond covenants are usually expressed in book values rather than market values. Moreover, firms such as Standard & Poor's and Moody's use debt ratios expressed in book values to measure creditworthiness.

A key fact is that whether we use book or market values, debt ratios for U.S. nonfinancial firms generally have been well below 100 percent of total equity in recent years; that is, firms generally use less debt than equity. This is opposite to the historical pattern of non-financial firms, primarily owned by corporate business houses in India.

RESEARCH IN EMERGING MARKET CONTEXT

Agur et al. (2019) conducted a study on the integration of emerging markets (EM) sovereign rupee-denominated and local-currency bond markets on an international level. Their findings suggest that the EM rupee-denominated debt markets are highly integrated and correlated with the US and EU interest rates. However, the local currency bond markets are not as globally integrated.

In a study conducted by Gubareva et al. (2022), it was discovered that EM financial securities were more resilient to financial turmoil caused by the COVID-19 pandemic than corporate and sovereign securities. The findings report that the pandemic significantly impacted the creditworthiness of sovereign countries and corporates.

References

Agur, I., Chan, M., Goswami, M., & Sharma, S. (2019). On international integration of emerging sovereign bond markets. *Emerging Markets Review*, *38*, 347–363.

Gubareva, M., Umar, Z., Sokolova, T., & Vo, X. V. (2022). Astonishing insights: emerging market debt spreads throughout the pandemic. *Applied Economics*, *54*(18), 2067–2076.

Summary and Conclusions

The basic sources of long-term financing are long-term debt, preference share, and equity share. This chapter described the essential features of each.

1. We emphasized that:
   a. Common shareholders have residual risk and return in a company.
   b. Common shareholders have voting rights.
   c. Dividends are not a business expense and firms cannot be forced into bankruptcy for nonpayment of a dividend.
2. Long-term debt involves contractual obligations set out in indentures. There are many kinds of debt, but the essential feature is that debt involves a stated amount that must be repaid. Interest payments on debt are considered a business expense and are tax deductible up to the limits established by the Tax Cuts and Jobs Act.
3. Preference share has some of the features of debt and some of the features of common equity. Holders of preference share have preference in liquidation and in dividend payments compared to holders of common equity.
4. Firms need financing for capital expenditures, working capital, and other long-term uses. Most of the financing is provided from internally generated cash flow.
5. For many years, U.S. firms have been retiring large amounts of equity. These share buybacks have been financed with new debt.

Concept Questions

1. **Bond Features** What are the main features of a corporate bond that would be listed in the indenture?
2. **Preference Share and Debt** What are the differences between preference share and debt?
3. **Preference share** Preference Share doesn't offer a corporate tax shield on the dividends paid. Why do we still observe some firms issuing preference share?

4. **Preference Share and Bond Yields** The yields on nonconvertible preference share are lower than the yields on corporate bonds. Why is there a difference? Which investors are the primary holders of preference share? Why?
5. **Corporate Financing** What are the main differences between corporate debt and equity? Why do some firms try to issue equity in the guise of debt?
6. **Call Provisions** A company is contemplating a long-term bond issue. It is debating whether to include a call provision. What are the benefits to the company from including a call provision? What are the costs? How do these answers change for a put provision?
7. **Proxy** What is a proxy?
8. **Preference Share** Do you think preference share is more like debt or equity? Why?
9. **Long-Term Financing** As was mentioned in the chapter, new equity issues are generally only a small portion of all new issues. At the same time, companies continue to issue new debt. Why do companies tend to issue little new equity but continue to issue new debt?
10. **Internal versus External Financing** What is the difference between internal financing and external financing?
11. **Internal versus External Financing** What factors influence a firm's choice of external versus internal equity financing?
12. **Classes of Stock** Several publicly traded companies have issued more than one class of stock. Why might a company issue more than one class of stock?
13. **Callable Bonds** Do you agree or disagree with the following statement: In an efficient market, callable and noncallable bonds will be priced in such a way that there will be no advantage or disadvantage to the call provision. Why?
14. **Bond Prices** If interest rates fall, will the price of noncallable bonds move up higher than that of callable bonds? Why or why not?
15. **Sinking Funds** Sinking funds have both positive and negative characteristics for bondholders. Why?

Questions and Problems

BASIC (Questions 1–7)

1. **Corporate Voting** The shareholders of the Pineapple Company need to elect seven new directors. There are 750,000 shares outstanding currently trading at ₹64 per share. You would like to serve on the board of directors; unfortunately, no one else will be voting for you. How much will it cost you to be certain that you can be elected if the company uses straight voting? How much will it cost you if the company uses cumulative voting?
2. **Cumulative Voting** An election is being held to fill four seats on the board of directors of a firm in which you hold stock. The company has 27,300 shares outstanding. If the election is conducted under cumulative voting and you own 500 shares, how many more shares must you buy to be assured of earning a seat on the board?
3. **Cumulative Voting** The shareholders of Solar Power Corp. need to elect five new directors to the board. There are 15.2 million shares of equity share outstanding and the current share price is ₹16.85. If the company uses cumulative voting procedures, how much will it cost to guarantee yourself one seat on the board of directors?
4. **Corporate Voting** Highway 65, Inc., is going to elect 12 board members next month. Marisol owns 11.6 percent of the total shares outstanding. How confident can she be of having one of her candidate friends elected under the cumulative voting rule? Will her friend be elected for certain if the voting procedure is changed to the staggering rule, under which shareholders vote on four board members at a time?
5. **Financial Leverage** Home Corp. has interest-bearing debt with a market value of ₹65 million. The company also has 2.1 million shares that sell for ₹43 per share. What is the debt-equity ratio for this company based on market values?
6. **Financial Leverage** Edgehill, Inc., has 355,000 bonds outstanding. The bonds have a par value of ₹1,000, a coupon rate of 5.4 percent paid semiannually, and 27 years to maturity. The current YTM on the bonds is 4.6 percent. The company also has 11 million shares of stock outstanding, with a market price of ₹76 per share. What is the company's market value debt-equity ratio?

7. **Financial Leverage** Fields, Inc., has the following book value balance sheet:

Assets		Total Debt and Equity	
Current assets	₹ 125,000,000	Total debt	₹ 170,000,000
		Equity	
		Equity share	₹ 15,000,000
		Capital surplus	70,000,000
		Accumulated retained earnings	100,000,000
Net fixed assets	₹ 230,000,000	Total shareholders' equity	₹ 185,000,000
Total assets	₹ 355,000,000	Total debt and shareholders' equity	₹ 355,000,000

a. What is the debt-equity ratio based on book values?
b. Suppose the market value of the company's debt is ₹180 million and the market value of equity is ₹590 million. What is the debt-equity ratio based on market values?
c. Which is more relevant, the debt-equity ratio based on book values or market values? Why?

8. **Valuing Callable Bonds** Assets, Inc., plans to issue ₹5 million of bonds with a coupon rate of 7.5 percent, a par value of ₹1,000, semiannual coupons, and 30 years to maturity. The current market interest rate on these bonds is 6.2 percent. In one year, the interest rate on the bonds will be either 9 percent or 6 percent with equal probability. Assume investors are risk-neutral.

INTERMEDIATE (Questions 8–11)

a. If the bonds are noncallable, what is the price of the bonds today?
b. If the bonds are callable one year from today at ₹1,080, will their price be greater or less than the price you computed in part (a)? Why?

9. **Valuing Callable Bonds** New Business Ventures, Inc., has an outstanding perpetual bond with a 9 percent coupon rate that can be called in one year. The bond makes annual coupon payments and has a par value of ₹1,000. The call premium is set at ₹150 over par value. There is a 60 percent chance that the interest rate in one year will be 11 percent and a 40 percent chance that the interest rate will be 7 percent. If the current interest rate is 9 percent, what is the current market price of the bond?

10. **Valuing Callable Bonds** Bandon Manufacturing intends to issue callable, perpetual bonds with annual coupon payments and a par value of ₹1,000. The bonds are callable at ₹1,140. One-year interest rates are 9 percent. There is a 60 percent probability that long-term interest rates one year from today will be 10 percent and a 40 percent probability that they will be 8 percent. Assume that if interest rates fall, the bonds will be called. What coupon rate should the bonds have in order to sell at par value?

11. **Valuing Callable Bonds** Williams Industries has decided to borrow money by issuing perpetual bonds with a coupon rate of 5.8 percent, payable annually, and a par value of ₹1,000. The one-year interest rate is 5.8 percent. Next year, there is a 35 percent probability that interest rates will increase to 7 percent and a 65 percent probability that they will fall to 4 percent.

a. What will the market value of these bonds be if they are noncallable?
b. If the company decides instead to make the bonds callable in one year, what coupon will be demanded by the bondholders for the bonds to sell at par? Assume that the bonds will be called if interest rates fall and that the call premium is equal to the annual coupon.
c. What will be the value of the call provision to the company?

12. **Treasury Bonds** The following Treasury bond quote appeared in *The Wall Street Journal* on May 11, 2004:

CHALLENGE (Question 12)

9.125	May 09	100.09375	100.12500	. . .	−2.15

Why would anyone buy this Treasury bond with a negative yield to maturity? How is this possible?

16

Capital Structure

BASIC CONCEPTS

In May 2020, Apple raised ₹8.5 billion in capital by selling bonds. In part because interest rates were so low, Apple couldn't resist another bite, selling ₹5.5 billion more bonds in August. ExxonMobil also dug into the market, issuing ₹9.5 billion worth of bonds in April. Overall, in the United States, corporate bond issuance surpassed ₹2.2 trillion for the year, an all-time record amount.

Indian corporate bond issuances in the domestic markets during November 2023 touched ₹10.97 billion, cumulatively touching ₹106 billion for 2023, the highest in any calendar year. The key factors driving this were lower interest rates and stability in the bond market, prompting the corporates to lock in the lower rates for more extended periods.

So, in issuing all this debt, companies succeeded in raising capital, but why did they choose to issue bonds instead of stock? A firm's choice of debt or equity is known as a capital structure decision, and the deductibility of interest expense is an important part of this decision. In this chapter, we discuss the basic ideas underlying capital structures and how firms decide on the optimal capital structure.

Please visit us at **rwjcorporatefinance.blogspot.com** for the latest developments in the world of corporate finance.

16.1 The Capital Structure Question and the Pie Theory

How should a firm choose its debt-equity ratio? We call our approach to the capital structure question the **pie model**. If you are wondering why we chose this name, take a look at Figure 16.1. The pie in question is the sum of the financial claims of the firm, which are debt and equity in this case. We define the value of the firm to be this sum. Hence, the value of the firm, V, is:

$$V = B + S \tag{16.1}$$

where B is the market value of the debt and S is the market value of the equity. Figure 16.1 presents two possible ways of slicing this pie between stock and debt: 40 percent–60 percent and 60 percent–40 percent. If the goal of the management of the firm is to make the firm as valuable as possible, then the firm should pick the debt-equity ratio that makes the pie–the total value–as big as possible.

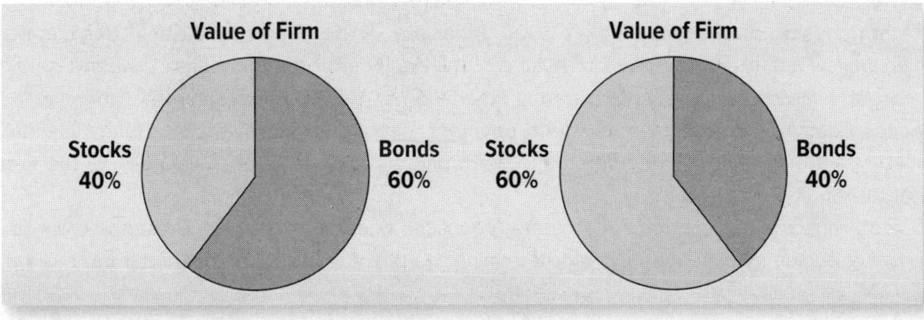

Figure 16.1 Two Pie Models of Capital Structure

This discussion begs two important questions:

1. Why should the stockholders in the firm care about maximizing the value of the entire firm?
2. What ratio of debt to equity maximizes the shareholders' interests?

We will examine each of the two questions in turn.

16.2 Maximizing Firm Value versus Maximizing Stockholder Interests

The following example illustrates that the capital structure that maximizes the value of the firm is the one that financial managers should choose for the shareholders.

EXAMPLE 16.1

Debt and Firm Value Suppose the market value of the Roshini Collections Company is ₹1,000. The company currently has no debt and each of Roshini Collections 100 shares of stock sells for ₹10. A company such as Roshini Collections' with no debt is called an *unlevered* company. Further suppose that plans to borrow ₹500 and pay the ₹500 proceeds to shareholders as an extra cash dividend of ₹5 per share. After the issuance of debt, the firm becomes *levered*. The investments of the firm will not change as a result of this transaction. What will the value of the firm be after the proposed restructuring?

Management recognizes that, by definition, only one of three outcomes can occur from restructuring. Firm value after restructuring can be (1) greater than the original firm value of ₹1,000, (2) equal to ₹1,000, or (3) less than ₹1,000. After consulting with investment bankers, management believes that restructuring will not change firm value more than ₹250 in either direction. It views firm values of ₹1,250, ₹1,000, and ₹750 as the relevant range. The original capital structure and these three possibilities under the new capital structure are:

	No Debt (Original Capital Structure)	Value of Debt plus Equity after Payment of Dividend (Three Possibilities)		
		I	II	III
Debt	₹ 0	₹ 500	₹ 500	₹500
Equity	1,000	750	500	250
Firm value	₹1,000	₹1,250	₹1,000	₹750

(continued)

Note that the value of equity is below ₹1,000 under any of the three possibilities. This can be explained in one of two ways. First, the table shows the value of the equity after the extra cash dividend is paid. Because cash is paid out, a dividend represents a partial liquidation of the firm. Consequently, there is less value in the firm for the equityholders after the dividend payment. Second, in the event of a future liquidation, stockholders will be paid only after bondholders have been paid in full. The debt is a burden of the firm, reducing the value of the equity.

Of course, management recognizes that there are infinite possible outcomes. These three are to be viewed as representative outcomes only. We now can determine the payoff to stockholders under the three possibilities:

	Payoff to Shareholders after Restructuring		
	I	II	III
Capital gains	–₹250	–₹500	–₹750
Dividends	500	500	500
Net gain or loss to stockholders	₹250	₹ 0	–₹250

No one can be sure ahead of time which of the three outcomes will occur. However, imagine that managers believe that Outcome I is most likely. They should definitely restructure the firm because the stockholders would gain ₹250. That is, although the price of the stock declines by ₹250 to ₹750, they receive ₹500 in dividends. The net gain is ₹250 (= –₹250 + 500). Also, notice that the value of the firm would rise by ₹250 (= ₹1,250 – 1,000).

Alternatively, imagine that managers believe that Outcome III is most likely. In this case, they should not restructure the firm because the stockholders would incur a ₹250 loss. That is, the stock falls by ₹750 to ₹250 and they receive ₹500 in dividends. Their net loss is –₹250 (= –₹750 + 500). Notice that the value of the firm would change by –₹250 (= ₹750 – 1,000).

Finally, imagine that the managers believe that Outcome II is most likely. Restructuring would not affect the stockholders' interest because the net gain to stockholders in this case is zero. Notice that the value of the firm is unchanged if Outcome II occurs.

This example explains why managers should attempt to maximize the value of the firm. In other words, it answers question (1) in Section 16.1. We find in this example the following wisdom:

Managers should choose the capital structure that they believe will have the highest firm value because this capital structure will be most beneficial to the firm's stockholders.[1]

Clearly, Roshini Collections should borrow ₹500 if it expects Outcome I. The crucial question in determining a firm's capital structure is: Which outcome is likely to occur? However, this example does not tell us which of the three outcomes is most likely to occur and it does not tell us whether debt should be added to Roshini Collections's capital structure. In other words, it does not answer question (2) in Section 16.1. This second question is treated in the next section.

At this point, a sharp student may realize that there is a trivial way to increase the size of the pie. If the firm issues new equity or debt, and invests the proceeds in a zero NPV project, the firm will have more real assets, and thereby grow in value. Does this mean that managers should always seek to grow the size of the firm by issuing more securities? The answer is no, because growth in this manner does not make any of the firm's investors better off. When we say that managers should choose the capital structure that maximizes the firm's value, we mean that managers should choose the optimal mix of debt and equity that will lead to the highest firm value, *holding the firm's real assets fixed.* If the manager instead issues equity or debt to invest in more real capital projects, the firm will grow in size, but investors will not be better off unless those projects had positive NPV.

[1]This result may not hold exactly in a more complex case where debt has a significant possibility of default. Issues of default are treated in the next chapter.

16.3 Financial Leverage and Firm Value: An Example

LEVERAGE AND RETURNS TO SHAREHOLDERS

Excel Master coverage online

The previous section shows that the capital structure producing the highest firm value is the one that maximizes shareholder wealth. In this section, we wish to determine that optimal capital structure. We begin by illustrating the effect of capital structure on returns to stockholders. We will use a detailed example that we encourage students to study carefully. Once we have this example under our belts, we will be ready to determine the optimal capital structure.

Karuna Kranti Corporation currently has no debt in its capital structure. The firm is considering issuing debt to buy back some of its equity. Both its current and proposed capital structures are presented in Table 16.1. The firm's assets are ₹8,000. There are 400 shares of the all-equity firm, implying a market value per share of ₹20. The proposed debt issue is for ₹4,000, leaving ₹4,000 in equity. The interest rate is 10 percent. We assume the stock price is constant here; we will discuss the effects of leverage on stock price later in this chapter.

The effect of economic conditions on earnings per share is shown in Table 16.2 for the current capital structure (all equity). Consider first the middle column, where earnings are expected to be ₹1,200. Because assets are ₹8,000 and assets equal equity for this all-equity firm, the return on equity (ROE) is 15 percent (= ₹1,200/₹8,000). Earnings per share (EPS) is ₹3.00 (= ₹1,200/400). Similar calculations yield EPS of ₹1.00 and ₹5.00 in the cases of recession and expansion, respectively.

The case of leverage is presented in Table 16.3. Because the firm does not change its collection of real assets, earnings before interest is the same as in Table 16.2. Debt is ₹4,000 here, so interest is ₹400 (= .10 × ₹4,000). Earnings after interest are ₹800 (= ₹1,200 – 400) in the middle (expected) case. Because equity is ₹4,000, ROE is 20 percent (= ₹800/₹4,000). Earnings per share are ₹4.00 (= ₹800/200). Similar calculations yield earnings of ₹0 and ₹8.00 for recession and expansion, respectively.

Tables 16.2 and 16.3 show that the effect of financial leverage depends on the company's earnings before interest. If earnings before interest are equal to ₹1,200, the return on equity (ROE) is higher under the proposed structure. If earnings before interest are equal to ₹400, the ROE is higher under the current structure.

Table 16.1 Financial Structure of Karuna Kranti Corporation

	Current	Proposed
Assets	₹8,000	₹8,000
Debt	₹ 0	₹4,000
Equity (market and book)	₹8,000	₹4,000
Interest rate	10%	10%
Market value/share	₹ 20	₹ 20
Shares outstanding	400	200

Table 16.2 Karuna Kranti's Current Capital Structure: No Debt

	Recession	Expected	Expansion
Earnings	₹400	₹1,200	₹2,000
Return on equity (ROE) = Earnings/Equity	5%	15%	25%
Earnings per share (EPS)	₹1.00	₹ 3.00	₹ 5.00

Table 16.3 Karuna Kranti's Proposed Capital Structure: Debt = ₹4,000

	Recession	Expected	Expansion
Earnings before interest (EBI)	₹400	₹1,200	₹2,000
Interest	400	400	400
Earnings after interest	₹ 0	₹ 800	₹1,600
Return on equity (ROE) = Earnings after interest/Equity	0%	20%	40%
Earnings per share (EPS)	₹ 0	₹ 4.00	₹ 8.00

This idea is represented in Figure 16.2. The solid line represents the case of no leverage. The line begins at the origin, indicating that earnings per share (EPS) would be zero if earnings before interest (EBI) was zero. The EPS rises in tandem with a rise in EBI.

The dotted line represents the case of ₹4,000 of debt. Here EPS is negative if EBI is zero. This follows because ₹400 of interest must be paid regardless of the firm's profits.

Now consider the slopes of the two lines. The slope of the dotted line (the line with debt) is steeper than the slope of the solid line. This occurs because the levered firm has fewer shares of stock outstanding than the unlevered firm. Therefore, any increase in EBI leads to a greater rise in EPS for the levered firm because the earnings increase is distributed over fewer shares of stock.

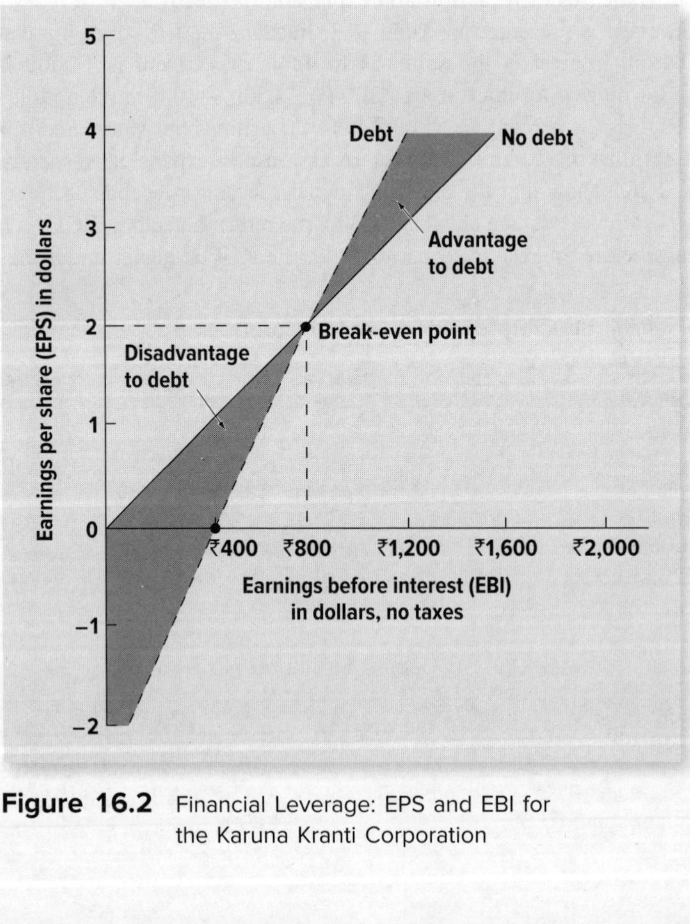

Figure 16.2 Financial Leverage: EPS and EBI for the Karuna Kranti Corporation

Table 16.4 Payoff and Cost to Shareholders of Karuna Kranti Corporation under the Proposed Structure and under the Current Structure with Homemade Leverage

	Recession	Expected	Expansion
Strategy A: Buy 100 Shares of Levered Equity			
EPS of levered equity (taken from last line of Table 16.3)	₹ 0	₹ 4	₹ 8
Earnings per 100 shares	₹ 0	₹ 400	₹ 800
Initial cost = 100 shares @ ₹20/share = ₹2,000			
Strategy B: Homemade Leverage			
Earnings per 200 shares in current unlevered Karuna Kranti	₹1 × 200 = ₹ 200	₹3 × 200 = ₹ 600	₹5 × 200 = ₹ 1,000
Interest at 10% on ₹2,000	200	200	200
Net earnings	₹ 0	₹ 400	₹ 800
Initial cost = 200 shares @ ₹20/share (Cost of stock) – ₹2,000 (Amount borrowed) = ₹2,000			

Investor receives the same payoff whether she (1) buys shares in a levered corporation or (2) buys shares in an unlevered firm and borrows on personal account. Her initial investment is the same in either case. The firm neither helps nor hurts her by adding debt to its capital structure.

Because the dotted line has a lower intercept but a steeper slope, the two lines must intersect. The break-even point occurs at ₹800 of EBI. Were earnings before interest to be ₹800, both firms would produce ₹2 of earnings per share (EPS). Because ₹800 is break-even, earnings above ₹800 lead to a greater EPS for the levered firm. Earnings below ₹800 lead to a greater EPS for the unlevered firm.

THE CHOICE BETWEEN DEBT AND EQUITY

Tables 16.2 and 16.3 and Figure 16.2 are important because they show the effect of leverage on earnings per share. Students should study the tables and figure until they feel comfortable with the calculation of each number in them. However, we have not yet presented the punch line. That is, we have not yet stated which capital structure is better for Karuna Kranti.

At this point, many students believe that leverage is beneficial because EPS is expected to be ₹4.00 with leverage and only ₹3.00 without leverage. However, leverage also creates risk. Note that in a recession, EPS is higher (₹1.00 versus ₹0) for the unlevered firm. A risk-averse investor might prefer the all-equity firm, whereas a risk-neutral (or less risk-averse) investor might prefer leverage. Given this ambiguity, which capital structure is better?

Modigliani and Miller (MM or M&M) have a convincing argument that a firm cannot change the total value of its outstanding securities by changing the proportions of its capital structure. In other words, the value of the firm is always the same under different capital structures. In still other words, no capital structure is any better or worse than any other capital structure for the firm's stockholders. This rather pessimistic result is the famous *MM Proposition I*.[2]

Their argument compares a simple strategy, which we call Strategy A, with a two-part strategy, which we call Strategy B. Both of these strategies for shareholders of Karuna Kranti are illuminated in Table 16.4. Let us now examine the first strategy.

Strategy A: Buy 100 shares of the levered equity

[2]The original paper is Franco Modigliani and Merton Miller, "The Cost of Capital, Corporation Finance and the Theory of Investment," *American Economic Review* 48, no. 3 (June 1958): 261–97.

The first line in the top panel of Table 16.4 shows EPS for the proposed levered equity in the three economic states. The second line shows the earnings in the three states for an individual buying 100 shares. The next line shows that the cost of these 100 shares is ₹2,000.

Let us now consider the second strategy, which has two parts to it.

Strategy B: Homemade leverage

1. Borrow ₹2,000 from either a bank or, more likely, a brokerage house. If the brokerage house is the lender, we say that this activity is *going on margin*.
2. Use the borrowed proceeds plus your own investment of ₹2,000 (a total of ₹4,000) to buy 200 shares of the current unlevered equity at ₹20 per share.

The bottom panel of Table 16.4 shows payoffs under Strategy B, which we call the *homemade leverage* strategy. First, observe the middle column, which indicates that 200 shares of the unlevered equity are expected to generate ₹600 of earnings. Assuming that the ₹2,000 is borrowed at a 10 percent interest rate, the interest expense is ₹200 (= .10 × ₹2,000). The net earnings are expected to be ₹400. A similar calculation generates net earnings of either ₹0 or ₹800 in recession or expansion, respectively.

Now let us compare these two strategies, both in terms of earnings per year and in terms of initial cost. The top panel of the table shows that Strategy A generates earnings of ₹0, ₹400, and ₹800 in the three states. The bottom panel of the table shows that Strategy B generates the same net earnings in the three states.

The top panel of the table shows that Strategy A involves an initial cost of ₹2,000. Similarly, the bottom panel shows an identical net cost of ₹2,000 for Strategy B.

This shows a very important result. Both the cost and the payoff from the two strategies are the same. We must conclude that Karuna Kranti is neither helping nor hurting its stockholders by restructuring. In other words, an investor is not receiving anything from corporate leverage that she could not receive on her own.

Note that, as shown in Table 16.1, the equity of the unlevered firm is valued at ₹8,000. Because the equity of the levered firm is ₹4,000 and its debt is ₹4,000, the value of the levered firm is also ₹8,000. Now suppose that, for whatever reason, the value of the levered firm were actually greater than the value of the unlevered firm. Here, Strategy A would cost more than Strategy B. In this case, an investor would prefer to borrow on his own account and invest in the stock of the unlevered firm. He would get the same net earnings each year as if he had invested in the stock of the levered firm. However, his cost would be less. The strategy would not be unique to our investor. Given the higher value of the levered firm, no rational investor would invest in the stock of the levered firm. Anyone desiring shares in the levered firm would get the same rupee return more cheaply by borrowing to finance a purchase of the unlevered firm's shares. The equilibrium result would be, of course, that the value of the levered firm would fall and the value of the unlevered firm would rise until they became equal. At this point, individuals would be indifferent between Strategy A and Strategy B.

This example illustrates the basic result of Modigliani-Miller (MM) and is, as we have noted, commonly called their Proposition I. We restate this proposition as follows:

MM Proposition I (no taxes): The value of the levered firm is the same as the value of the unlevered firm.

This is one of the most important results in all of corporate finance. In fact, it is generally considered the beginning point of modern managerial finance. Before MM, the effect of leverage on the value of the firm was considered complex and convoluted. Modigliani and Miller showed a blindingly simple result: If levered firms are priced too high, rational investors will borrow on their personal accounts to buy shares in unlevered firms. This substitution is often called *homemade leverage*. As long as individuals borrow (and lend) on the same terms as the firms, they can duplicate the effects of corporate leverage on their own.

The example of Karuna Kranti Corporation shows that leverage does not affect the value of the firm. Because we showed earlier that stockholders' welfare is directly related to the firm's value, the example indicates that changes in capital structure cannot affect the stockholders' welfare.

A KEY ASSUMPTION

The stark MM result that capital structure does not affect firm value only holds under certain assumptions that we will cover throughout the next few chapters. One key assumption is that individuals can borrow as cheaply as corporations. If, alternatively, individuals can borrow only at a higher rate, we easily can show that corporations can increase firm value by borrowing.

Is this assumption of equal borrowing costs a good one? Individuals who want to buy stock and borrow can do so by establishing a margin account with a broker. Under this arrangement, the broker lends the individual a portion of the purchase price. The individual might buy ₹10,000 of stock by investing ₹6,000 of her own funds and borrowing ₹4,000 from the broker. Should the stock be worth ₹9,000 on the next day, the individual's net worth or equity in the account would be ₹5,000 = ₹9,000 − 4,000.[3]

The broker fears that a sudden price drop will cause the equity in the individual's account to be negative, implying that the broker may not get the loan repaid in full. To guard against this possibility, stock exchange rules require that the individual make additional cash contributions (replenish her margin account) as the stock price falls. Because (1) the procedures for replenishing the account have developed over many years and (2) the broker holds the stock as collateral, there is little default risk to the broker.[4] In particular, if margin contributions are not made on time, the broker can sell the stock to satisfy the loan. Therefore, brokers generally charge low interest, with many rates being only slightly above the risk-free rate.

By contrast, corporations frequently borrow using illiquid assets (e.g., plant and equipment) as collateral. The costs to the lender of initial negotiation and ongoing supervision, as well as of working out arrangements in the event of financial distress, can be quite substantial. It is difficult to argue that individuals must borrow at higher rates than corporations.

16.4 Modigliani and Miller: Proposition II (No Taxes)

RISK TO EQUITYHOLDERS RISES WITH LEVERAGE

At a Karuna Kranti corporate meeting, a corporate officer said, "Well, maybe it does not matter whether the corporation or the individual levers–as long as some leverage takes place. Leverage benefits investors. After all, an investor's expected return rises with the amount of the leverage present." He then pointed out that, as shown in Tables 16.2 and 16.3, the expected return on unlevered equity is 15 percent, whereas the expected return on levered equity is 20 percent.

However, another officer replied, "Not necessarily. Though the expected return rises with leverage, the risk rises, as well." This point can be seen from an examination of Tables 16.2 and 16.3. With earnings before interest (EBI) varying between ₹400 and ₹2,000, earnings per share (EPS) for the stockholders of the unlevered firm vary between ₹1.00 and ₹5.00. EPS for the stockholders of the levered firm vary between ₹0 and

[3]We are ignoring the one-day interest charge on the loan.

[4]Had this text been published before October 19, 1987, when stock prices declined by more than 20 percent in a single day, we might have used the phrase "virtually no" risk instead of "little" risk.

₹8.00. This greater range for the EPS of the levered firm implies greater risk for the levered firm's stockholders. Levered stockholders have better returns in good times than do unlevered stockholders but worse returns in bad times. The two tables also show greater range for the ROE of the levered firm's stockholders. The earlier interpretation concerning risk applies here, as well.

The same insight can be taken from Figure 16.2. The slope of the line for the levered firm is greater than the slope of the line for the unlevered firm. This means that the levered stockholders have better returns in good times than do unlevered stockholders but worse returns in bad times, implying greater risk with leverage. The slope of the line measures the risk to stockholders because the slope indicates the responsiveness of ROE to changes in firm performance (earnings before interest).

PROPOSITION II: REQUIRED RETURN TO EQUITYHOLDERS RISES WITH LEVERAGE

Because levered equity has greater risk, it should have a greater expected return as compensation. In our example, the market requires a 15 percent expected return for the unlevered equity, but it requires a 20 percent expected return for the levered equity.

This type of reasoning allows us to develop *MM Proposition II*. Here MM argue that the expected return on equity is positively related to leverage because the risk to equityholders increases with leverage.

To develop this position, recall that the firm's weighted average cost of capital, WACC, in a world without taxes can be written as:[5]

$$\text{WACC} = \frac{S}{B+S} \times R_S + \frac{B}{B+S} \times R_B \tag{16.2}$$

where:

R_B = Cost of debt

R_S = Expected return on equity or stock, also called the cost of equity or the required return on equity

WACC = Firm's weighted average cost of capital

B = Value of the firm's bonds or debt

S = Value of the firm's stock or equity

Equation 16.2 is intuitive. It says that a firm's weighted average cost of capital is a weighted average of its cost of debt and its cost of equity. The weight applied to debt is the proportion of debt in the capital structure and the weight applied to equity is the proportion of equity in the capital structure. Calculations of WACC from Equation 16.2 for both the unlevered and the levered firm are presented in Table 16.5.

An implication of MM Proposition I is that WACC is a constant for a given firm, regardless of the capital structure.[6] For example, Table 16.5 shows that WACC for Karuna Kranti is 15 percent, with or without leverage.

Let us now define R_0 to be the *cost of capital for an all-equity firm*. For the Karuna Kranti Corp., R_0 is calculated as:

$$R_0 = \frac{\text{Expected earnings to unlevered firm}}{\text{Unlevered equity}} = \frac{₹1{,}200}{₹8{,}000} = .15, \text{ or } 15\%$$

[5]Because we do not have taxes here, the cost of debt is R_B, not $R_B(1 - T_C)$ as it was in Chapter 13.

[6]This statement holds in a world of no taxes. It does not hold in a world with taxes, a point to be brought out later in this chapter (see Figure 16.6).

Table 16.5 Cost of Capital Calculations for Karuna Kranti

$$\text{WACC} = \frac{B}{B+S} \times R_B + \frac{S}{B+S} \times R_S$$

$$\text{Unlevered firm: } \frac{0}{₹8{,}000} \times .10^* + \frac{₹8{,}000}{₹8{,}000} \times .15^{\dagger} = .15, \text{ or } 15\%$$

$$\text{Levered firm: } \frac{₹4{,}000}{₹8{,}000} \times .10^* + \frac{₹4{,}000}{₹8{,}000} \times .20^{\ddagger} = .15, \text{ or } 15\%$$

*The cost of debt is 10 percent.

†From the "Expected" column in Table 16.2, we learn that expected earnings for the unlevered firm are ₹1,200. From Table 16.1 we learned that equity for the unlevered firm is ₹8,000. Thus, R_S for the unlevered firm is:

$$\frac{\text{Expected earnings}}{\text{Equity}} = \frac{₹1{,}200}{₹8{,}000} = .15, \text{ or } 15\%$$

‡From the "Expected" column in Table 16.3, we learn that expected earnings after interest for the levered firm are ₹800. From Table 16.1 we learned that equity for the levered firm is ₹4,000. Thus, R_S for the levered firm is:

$$\frac{\text{Expected earnings after interest}}{\text{Equity}} = \frac{₹800}{₹4{,}000} = .20, \text{ or } 20\%$$

As can be seen from Table 16.5, WACC is equal to R_0 for Karuna Kranti. In fact, WACC must always equal R_0 in a world without corporate taxes.[7]

Proposition II states the expected return on equity, R_S, in terms of leverage. The exact relationship, derived by setting WACC = R_0 and then rearranging Equation 16.2, is:[8]

MM Proposition II (No Taxes):

$$R_S = R_0 + \frac{B}{S}(R_0 - R_B) \quad \textbf{(16.3)}$$

Equation 16.3 implies that the required return on equity is a linear function of the firm's debt-equity ratio. Examining Equation 16.3, we see that if R_0 exceeds the cost of debt, R_B, then the cost of equity rises with increases in the debt-equity ratio, B/S. Normally R_0 should exceed R_B. That is, because even unlevered equity is risky, it should have an expected return greater than that of less risky debt. Note that Equation 16.3 holds for Karuna Kranti in its levered state:

$$R_S = .15 + \frac{₹4{,}000}{₹4{,}000}(.15 - .10) = .20, \text{ or } 20\%$$

[7]We again emphasize that this statement holds in a world of no taxes. It does not hold in a world with taxes, a point to be brought out later in this chapter (see Figure 16.6).

[8]This can be derived from Equation 16.2 by setting WACC = R_0, yielding:

$$\frac{B}{B+S}R_B + \frac{S}{B+S}R_S = R_0$$

Multiplying both sides by $(B + S)/S$ yields:

$$\frac{B}{S}R_B + R_S = \frac{B+S}{S}R_0$$

We can rewrite the right side as:

$$\frac{B}{S}R_B + R_S = \frac{B}{S}R_0 + R_0$$

Moving $(B/S)R_B$ to the right side and rearranging yields:

$$R_S = R_0 + \frac{B}{S}(R_0 - R_B)$$

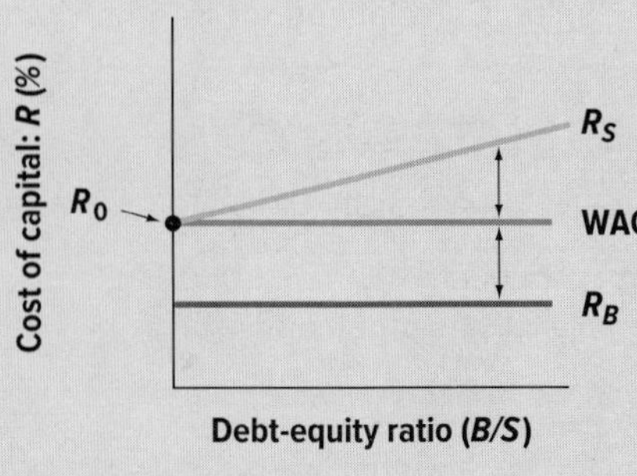

$R_S = R_0 + (R_0 - R_B)B/S$

R_S is the cost of equity.

R_B is the cost of debt.

R_0 is the cost of capital for an all-equity firm.

WACC is a firm's weighted average cost of capital. In a world with no taxes, WACC for a levered firm is equal to R_0.

R_0 is a single point, whereas R_S, R_B, and WACC are all entire lines.

The cost of equity capital, R_S, is positively related to the firm's debt-equity ratio. The firm's weighted average cost of capital, WACC, is invariant to the firm's debt-equity ratio.

Figure 16.3 The Cost of Equity, the Cost of Debt, and the Weighted Average Cost of Capital: MM Proposition II with No Corporate Taxes

Figure 16.3 graphs Equation 16.3. As you can see, we have plotted the relationship between the cost of equity, R_S, and the debt-equity ratio, B/S, as a straight line. What we witness in Equation 16.3 and illustrate in Figure 16.3 is the effect of leverage on the cost of equity. As the firm raises the debt-equity ratio, each rupee of equity is levered with additional debt. This raises the risk of equity and therefore the required return, R_S, on the equity.

Figure 16.3 also shows that WACC is unaffected by leverage, a point we have already made. It is important for students to realize that R_0, the cost of capital for an all-equity firm, is represented by a single dot on the graph. By contrast, WACC is an entire line.

EXAMPLE 16.2

MM Propositions I and II Sahay Motors, an all-equity firm, has expected earnings of ₹10 million per year in perpetuity. The firm pays all of its earnings out as dividends, so the ₹10 million also may be viewed as the stockholders' expected cash flow. There are 10 million shares outstanding, implying expected annual cash flow of ₹1 per share. The cost of capital for this unlevered firm is 10 percent. In addition, the firm will soon build a new plant for ₹4 million. The plant is expected to generate additional cash flow of ₹1 million per year. These figures can be described as follows:

Current Company	New Plant
Cash flow: ₹10 million	Initial outlay: ₹4 million
Number of outstanding shares: 10 million	Additional annual cash flow: ₹1 million

(continued)

The project's net present value is:

$$-₹4 \text{ million} + \frac{₹1 \text{ million}}{.1} = ₹6 \text{ million}$$

assuming that the project is discounted at the same rate as the firm as a whole. Before the market knows of the project, the market value balance sheet of the firm is:

SAHAY MOTORS **Balance Sheet (All Equity)**	
Old assets: $\frac{₹10 \text{ million}}{.1} = ₹100 \text{ million}$	Equity: ₹100 million (10 million shares of stock)

The value of the firm is ₹100 million because the cash flow of ₹10 million per year is capitalized (discounted) at 10 percent. A share of stock sells for ₹10 (= ₹100 million/10 million) because there are 10 million shares outstanding.

The market value balance sheet is a useful tool for financial analysis. Because students are often thrown off guard by it initially, we recommend extra study here. The key is that the market value balance sheet has the same form as the balance sheet that accountants use. That is, assets are placed on the left side, whereas liabilities and owners' equity are placed on the right side. In addition, the left and right sides must be equal. The difference between a market value balance sheet and the accountant's balance sheet is in the numbers. Accountants value items in terms of historical cost (original purchase price less depreciation), whereas financial analysts value items in terms of market value.

To raise money to cover the cost of building the new plant, the firm will issue ₹4 million of either equity or debt. Let's consider the effect of equity and debt financing.

Stock Financing Imagine that the firm announces that in the near future it will raise ₹4 million in equity to build a new plant. The stock price, and therefore the value of the firm, will rise to reflect the positive net present value of the plant. According to efficient markets, the increase occurs immediately. That is, the rise occurs on the day of the announcement of the new project, not on the date of either the onset of construction of the plant or the forthcoming stock offering. The market value balance sheet becomes this:

SAHAY MOTORS **Balance Sheet** **(After Announcement of Equity Issue to Construct Plant)**			
Old assets	₹100 million	Equity	₹106 million (10 million shares of stock)
NPV of plant:			
$-₹4 \text{ million} + \frac{₹1 \text{ million}}{.1} =$	6 million		
Total assets	₹106 million		

(continued)

Note that the NPV of the plant is included in the market value balance sheet. Because the new shares have not yet been issued, the number of outstanding shares remains 10 million. The price per share has now risen to ₹10.60 (= ₹106 million/10 million) to reflect news concerning the plant.

Shortly thereafter, ₹4 million of stock is issued or floated. Because the stock is selling at ₹10.60 per share, 377,359 (= ₹4 million/₹10.60) shares of stock are issued. Imagine that the funds are put in the bank temporarily before being used to build the plant. The market value balance sheet becomes this:

SAHAY MOTORS
Balance Sheet
(After Issuance of Stock but Before Construction Begins on Plant)

Old assets	₹100 million	Equity	₹110 million
NPV of plant	6 million		(10,377,359 shares of stock)
Proceeds from new issue of stock (currently placed in bank)	4 million		
Total assets	₹110 million		

The number of shares outstanding is now 10,377,359 because 377,359 new shares were issued. The price per share is ₹10.60 (= ₹110,000,000/10,377,359). Note that the price has not changed. This is consistent with efficient capital markets because the stock price should move only due to new information.

Of course, the funds are placed in the bank only temporarily. Shortly after the new issue, the ₹4 million is given to a contractor who builds the plant. To avoid problems in discounting, we assume that the plant is built immediately. The balance sheet then looks like this:

SAHAY MOTORS
Balance Sheet
(After Completion of the Plant)

Old assets	₹100 million	Equity	₹110 million
			(10,377,359 shares of stock)
PV of plant: $\frac{₹1\text{ million}}{.1} =$	10 million		
Total assets	₹110 million		

Though total assets do not change, the composition of the assets does change. The bank account has been emptied to pay the contractor. The present value of cash flows of ₹1 million a year from the plant is reflected as an asset worth ₹10 million. Because the building expenditures of ₹4 million have already been paid, they no longer represent a future cost. Hence, they no longer reduce the value of the plant. According to efficient capital markets, the price per share of stock remains ₹10.60.

Expected yearly cash flow from the firm is ₹11 million, ₹10 million of which comes from the old assets and ₹1 million from the new. The expected return to equityholders is:

$$R_S = \frac{₹11{,}000{,}000}{₹110{,}000{,}000} = .10, \text{ or } 10\%$$

Because the firm is all equity, $R_S = R_0 = 10$ percent.

(continued)

Debt Financing Alternatively, imagine the firm announces that in the near future it will borrow ₹4 million at 6 percent to build a new plant. This implies yearly interest payments of ₹240,000 (= ₹4,000,000 × .06). Again the stock price rises immediately to reflect the positive net present value of the plant. We have the following:

SAHAY MOTORS Balance Sheet (After Announcement of Debt Issue to Construct Plant)			
Old assets	₹100 million	Equity	₹106 million
NPV of plant:			(10 million shares of stock)
$-₹4 \text{ million} + \dfrac{₹1 \text{ million}}{.1}$	6 million		
Total assets	₹106 million		

The value of the firm is the same as in the equity financing case because (1) the same plant is to be built and (2) MM proved that debt financing is neither better nor worse than equity financing.

At some point ₹4 million of debt is issued. As before, the funds are placed in the bank temporarily. The market value balance sheet becomes this:

SAHAY MOTORS Balance Sheet (After Debt Issuance but Before Construction Begins on Plant)			
Old assets	₹100 million	Debt	₹4 million
NPV of plant	6 million	Equity	106 million
			(10 million shares of stock)
Proceeds from debt issue (currently invested in bank)	4 million		
Total assets	₹110 million	Debt plus equity	₹110 million

Note that debt appears on the right side of the balance sheet. The stock price is still ₹10.60 in accordance with our discussion of efficient capital markets.

Finally, the contractor receives ₹4 million and builds the plant. The market value balance sheet turns into this:

SAHAY MOTORS Balance Sheet (After Completion of the Plant)			
Old assets	₹100 million	Debt	₹4 million
PV of plant	10 million	Equity	106 million
			(10 million shares of stock)
Total assets	₹110 million	Debt plus equity	₹110 million

(continued)

The only change here is that the bank account has been depleted to pay the contractor. The equityholders expect yearly cash flow after interest of:

₹10,000,000	+	1,000,000	−	240,000	=	₹10,760,000
Cash flow on old assets		Cash flow on new assets		Interest: ₹4 million × .06		

The equityholders expect to earn a return of:

$$\frac{₹10{,}760{,}000}{₹106{,}000{,}000} = .1015, \text{ or } 10.15\%$$

This return of 10.15 percent for levered equityholders is higher than the 10 percent return for the unlevered equityholders. This result is sensible because, as we argued earlier, levered equity is riskier. In fact, the return of 10.15 percent should be exactly what MM Proposition II predicts. This prediction can be verified by plugging the values into:

$$R_S = R_0 + \frac{B}{S} \times (R_0 - R_B)$$

We obtain:

$$.10 + \frac{₹4{,}000{,}000}{₹106{,}000{,}000} \times (.10 - .06) = .1015, \text{ or } 10.15\%$$

This example was useful for two reasons. First, we wanted to introduce the concept of market value balance sheets, a tool that will prove useful elsewhere in the text. Among other things, this technique allows us to calculate the price per share of a new issue of stock. Second, the example illustrates three aspects of Modigliani and Miller:

1. The example is consistent with MM Proposition I because the value of the firm is ₹110 million after either equity or debt financing.
2. Students are often more interested in stock price than in firm value. We show that the stock price is always ₹10.60, regardless of whether debt or equity financing is used.
3. The example is consistent with MM Proposition II. The expected return to equityholders rises from 10 to 10.15 percent, just as MM Proposition II states. This rise occurs because the equityholders of a levered firm face more risk than do the equityholders of an unlevered firm.

MM: AN INTERPRETATION

The Modigliani-Miller results indicate that managers cannot change the value of a firm by repackaging the firm's securities. Though this idea was considered revolutionary when it was originally proposed in the late 1950s, the MM approach and proof have since met with wide acclaim.[9]

MM argue that the firm's overall cost of capital cannot be reduced as debt is substituted for equity, even though debt appears to be cheaper than equity. The reason for this is that as the firm adds debt, the remaining equity becomes more risky. As this risk rises, the cost of equity capital rises as a result. The increase in the cost of the remaining equity capital offsets the higher proportion of the firm financed by low-cost debt. In fact, MM prove that the two effects exactly offset each other, so that both the value of the firm and the firm's overall cost of capital are invariant to leverage.

[9]Both Merton Miller and Franco Modigliani were awarded separate Nobel Prizes, in part for their work on capital structure.

In Their Own Words

IN PROFESSOR MILLER'S WORDS . . .

The Modigliani-Miller results are not easy to understand fully. This point is related in a story told by Merton Miller.*

How difficult it is to summarize briefly the contribution of the [Modigliani-Miller] papers was brought home to me very clearly last October after Franco Modigliani was awarded the Nobel Prize in Economics in part–but, of course, only in part–for the work in finance. The television camera crews from our local stations in Chicago immediately descended upon me. "We understand," they said, "that you worked with Modigliani some years back in developing these M and M theorems and we wonder if you could explain them briefly to our television viewers."

"How briefly?" I asked.

"Oh, take ten seconds," was the reply.

Ten seconds to explain the work of a lifetime! Ten seconds to describe two carefully reasoned articles, each running to more than thirty printed pages and each with sixty or so long footnotes! When they saw the look of dismay on my face, they said, "You don't have to go into details. Just give us the main points in simple, commonsense terms."

"The main point of the first or, cost-of-capital article, was, in principle at least, simple enough to make. It said that in an economist's ideal world of complete and perfect capital markets and with full and symmetric information among all market participants, the total market value of all the securities issued by a firm was governed by the earning power and risk of its underlying real assets and was independent of how the mix of securities issued to finance it was divided between debt instruments and equity capital . . ."

Such a summary, however, uses too many shorthanded terms and concepts, like perfect capital markets, that are rich in connotations to economists but hardly so to the general public. So I thought, instead, of an analogy that we ourselves had invoked in the original paper . . .

"Think of the firm," I said, "as a gigantic tub of whole milk. The farmer can sell the whole milk as is. Or he can separate out the cream and sell it at a considerably higher price than the whole milk would bring. (That's the analogy of a firm selling low-yield and hence high-priced debt securities.) But, of course, what the farmer would have left would be skim milk with low butterfat content and that would sell for much less than whole milk. That corresponds to the levered equity. The M and M proposition says that if there were no costs of separation (and, of course, no government dairy support programs), the cream plus the skim milk would bring the same price as the whole milk."

The television people conferred among themselves and came back to inform me that it was too long, too complicated, and too academic.

"Don't you have anything simpler?" they asked. I thought of another way that the M and M proposition is presented these days, which emphasizes the notion of market completeness and stresses the role of securities as devices for 'partitioning' a firm's payoffs in each possible state of the world among the group of its capital suppliers.

"Think of the firm," I said, "as a gigantic pizza, divided into quarters. If now you cut each quarter in half into eighths, the M and M proposition says that you will have more pieces but not more pizza."

Again there was a whispered conference among the camera crew, and the director came back and said:

"Professor, we understand from the press releases that there were two M and M propositions. Can we try the other one?"

[Professor Miller tried valiantly to explain the second proposition, though this was apparently even more difficult to get across. After his attempt:]

Once again there was a whispered conversation. They shut the lights off. They folded up their equipment. They thanked me for giving them the time. They said that they'd get back to me. But I knew that I had somehow lost my chance to start a new career as a packager of economic wisdom for TV viewers in convenient ten-second bites. Some have the talent for it . . . and some just don't.

*Taken from *GSB Chicago, University of Chicago*, Autumn 1986.

MM use an interesting analogy to food. They consider a dairy farmer with two choices. On the one hand, he can sell whole milk. On the other hand, by skimming he can sell a combination of cream and lowfat milk. Though the farmer can get a high price for the cream, he gets a low price for the lowfat milk, implying no net

Summary of Modigliani-Miller Propositions without Taxes

Assumptions

- No taxes.
- No transaction costs.
- Individuals and corporations can borrow at same rate.
- No bankruptcy costs and other agency costs.
- No asymmetric information.
- Efficient capital markets.

Results

Proposition I: $V_L = V_U$ (Value of levered firm equals value of unlevered firm)

Proposition II: $R_S = R_0 + \frac{B}{S}(R_0 - R_B)$

Intuition

Proposition I: Through homemade leverage, individuals can either duplicate or undo the effects of corporate leverage.

Proposition II: The cost of equity rises with leverage because the risk to equity rises with leverage.

gain. In fact, imagine that the proceeds from the whole-milk strategy were less than those from the cream-lowfat milk strategy. Arbitrageurs would buy the whole milk, perform the skimming operation themselves, and resell the cream and low fat milk separately. Competition between arbitrageurs would tend to boost the price of whole milk until proceeds from the two strategies became equal. Thus, the value of the farmer's milk is invariant to the way in which the milk is packaged.

Food found its way into this chapter earlier when we viewed the firm as a pie. MM argue that the size of the pie does not change no matter how stockholders and bondholders divide it. MM say that a firm's capital structure is irrelevant; it is what it is by some historical accident. The theory implies that firms' debt-equity ratios could be anything. They are what they are because of whimsical and random managerial decisions about how much to borrow and how much stock to issue.

Although scholars are always fascinated with far-reaching theories, students are perhaps more concerned with real-world applications. Do real-world managers follow MM by treating capital structure decisions with indifference? Unfortunately for the theory, virtually all companies in certain industries, such as banking, choose high debt-equity ratios. Conversely, companies in other industries, such as pharmaceuticals, choose low debt-equity ratios. In fact, almost any industry has a debt-equity ratio to which companies in that industry tend to adhere. Companies do not appear to be selecting their degree of leverage in a frivolous or random manner. Because of this, financial economists (including MM themselves) have argued that real-world factors may have been left out of the theory.

As discussed previously, the Modigliani-Miller result requires the assumption that individuals and corporations can borrow at the same rate. In fact, there are a number of assumptions, some more unrealistic than others, underlying the MM theory:[10]

1. No taxes.
2. No transaction costs.
3. Individuals and corporations can borrow at the same rate.

[10]MM were aware of these issues, as can be seen in their original paper.

4. No bankruptcy costs and other agency costs.
5. No asymmetric information.
6. Efficient capital markets.

We turn to taxes in the next section. Bankruptcy costs, other agency costs, and asymmetric information will be treated in the next chapter. Finally, the Modigliani-Miller result requires that the firm's debt and equity are priced by efficient capital markets, as described in an earlier chapter. If not, firms could increase the size of the pie by selling overpriced securities and buying back underpriced securities. A summary of the main Modigliani-Miller results without taxes is presented in the nearby boxed section.

16.5 Taxes

THE BASIC INSIGHT

The previous part of this chapter showed that firm value is unrelated to debt in a world without taxes. We now show that in the presence of corporate taxes, the firm's value is positively related to its debt. The basic intuition can be seen from a pie chart, such as the one in Figure 16.4. Consider the all-equity firm on the left. Here both equityholders and the Income Tax Authorities have claims on the firm. The value of the all-equity firm is, of course, that part of the pie owned by the equityholders. The proportion going to taxes is a cost.

The pie on the right for the levered firm shows three claims: equityholders, debtholders, and taxes. The value of the levered firm is the sum of the value of the debt and the value of the equity. In selecting between the two capital structures in the picture, a financial manager should select the one with the higher value. Assuming that the total area is the same for both pies, value is maximized for the capital structure paying the least in taxes. In other words, the manager should choose the capital structure that the Income Tax Authorities hates the most.[11]

Our discussion here will assume that all interest paid is tax deductible. In reality, however, the Tax Cuts and Jobs Act of 2017 placed limits on the amount of interest that can be deducted. Specifically, for 2018 through 2021, the net interest deduction is limited to at most 30 percent of EBITDA. After 2021, it drops to 30 percent of EBIT. The term "net interest" means interest paid less interest earned (if any). Also, the limits aren't exactly based on EBITDA and EBIT because of some adjustments, but the differences will be minor in

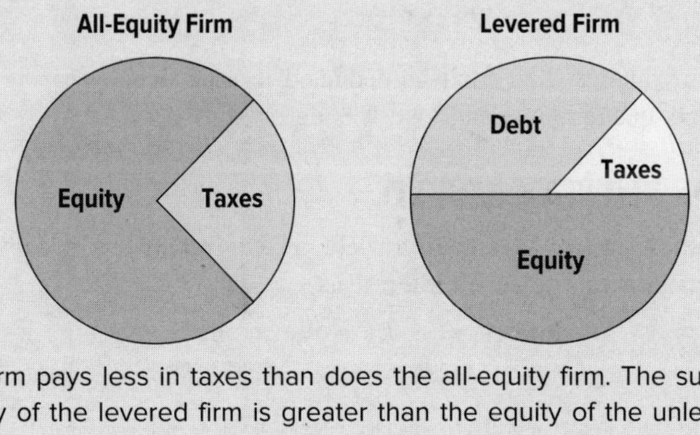

The levered firm pays less in taxes than does the all-equity firm. The sum of the debt plus the equity of the levered firm is greater than the equity of the unlevered firm.

Figure 16.4 Two Pie Models of Capital Structure under Corporate Taxes

[11]Under the MM propositions developed earlier, the two pies should be of the same size.

EXAMPLE 16.3

Taxes and Cash Flow The Lalali Services Company has a corporate tax rate, T_C, of 21 percent and expected earnings before interest and taxes (EBIT) of ₹1 million each year. Its entire earnings after taxes are paid out as dividends.

The firm is considering two alternative capital structures. Under Plan I, Lalali Services would have no debt in its capital structure. Under Plan II, the company would have ₹4,000,000 of debt, B. The cost of debt, R_B, is 10 percent.

The chief financial officer for Lalali Services makes the following calculations:

	Plan I	Plan II
Earnings before interest and corporate taxes (EBIT)	₹1,000,000	₹1,000,000
Interest ($R_B B$)	0	400,000
Earnings before taxes (EBT) = (EBIT − $R_B B$)	₹1,000,000	₹ 600,000
Taxes (21%)	210,000	126,000
Earnings after corporate taxes EAT = [(EBIT − $R_B B$) × (1 − T_C)]	₹ 790,000	₹ 474,000
Total cash flow to both stockholders and bondholders [EBIT × (1 − T_C) + $T_C R_B B$]	₹ 790,000	₹ 874,000

The most relevant numbers for our purposes are the two on the bottom line. Dividends, which are equal to earnings after taxes in this example, are the cash flow to stockholders and interest is the cash flow to bondholders.[12] Here we see that more cash flow reaches the owners of the firm (both stockholders and bondholders) under Plan II. The difference is ₹84,000 (= ₹874,000 − 790,000). It does not take us long to realize the source of this difference. The Income Tax Authorities receives less tax under Plan II (₹126,000) than it does under Plan I (₹210,000). The difference here is ₹84,000 (= ₹210,000 − 126,000).

This difference occurs because the way the Income Tax Authorities treats interest is different from the way it treats earnings going to stockholders.[13] Interest totally escapes corporate taxation, whereas earnings after interest but before corporate taxes (EBT) are taxed at the 21 percent rate.

most cases. Importantly, any interest that can't be deducted in a particular year can be carried forward and deducted later. Thus, the tax deductibility isn't lost; it is deferred.

PRESENT VALUE OF THE TAX SHIELD

The previous discussion shows a tax advantage to debt or, equivalently, a tax disadvantage to equity. We now want to value this advantage. The rupee interest is:

$$\text{Interest} = \underbrace{R_B}_{\text{Interest rate}} \times \underbrace{B}_{\text{Amount borrowed}}$$

[12]The reader may wonder why the "total cash flow to both stockholders and bondholders" in this example does not include adjustments for depreciation, capital spending, and working capital that we emphasized in Chapters 2 and 6. It is because we are implicitly assuming that depreciation is equal to capital spending. We also are assuming that the changes in net working capital are zero. These assumptions make sense because the projected cash flows for the Lalali Services Company are perpetual.

[13]Note that stockholders actually receive more under Plan I (₹790,000) than under Plan II (₹474,000). Students are often bothered by this because it seems to imply that stockholders are better off without leverage. However, remember that there are more shares outstanding in Plan I than in Plan II. A full-blown model would show that earnings per share are higher with leverage.

This interest is ₹400,000 (= .10 × ₹4,000,000) for Lalali Services. All this interest is tax deductible. That is, whatever the taxable income of Lalali Services would have been without the debt, the taxable income is now ₹400,000 less with the debt.

Because the corporate tax rate is 21 percent in our example, the reduction in corporate taxes is ₹84,000 (= .21 × ₹400,000). This number is identical to the reduction in corporate taxes calculated previously.

Algebraically, the reduction in corporate taxes is:

$$\underbrace{T_C}_{\text{Corporate tax rate}} \times \underbrace{R_B \times B}_{\text{Rupee amount of interest}} \tag{16.4}$$

That is, whatever the taxes that a firm would pay each year without debt, the firm will pay $T_C R_B B$ less with debt of B. Equation 16.4 is often called the *tax shield from debt.* Note that it is an annual amount.

Suppose the firm plans to maintain a fixed amount of debt B into perpetuity. As long as the firm expects to be in a positive tax bracket, we can assume that the tax shield from debt in Equation 16.4 has the same risk as the interest on the debt. Its value can be determined by discounting at the cost of debt, R_B. Assuming the cash flows are perpetual, the present value of the tax shield is:

$$\frac{T_C R_B B}{R_B} = T_C B$$

VALUE OF THE LEVERED FIRM

We have calculated the present value of the tax shield from debt. Our next step is to calculate the value of the levered firm. The annual aftertax cash flow of an unlevered firm is:

$$\text{EBIT} \times (1 - T_C)$$

where EBIT is earnings before interest and taxes. The value of an unlevered firm is the present value of $\text{EBIT} \times (1 - T_C)$:

$$V_U = \frac{\text{EBIT} \times (1 - T_C)}{R_0}$$

where:

V_U = Present value of an unlevered firm.

$\text{EBIT} \times (1 - T_C)$ = Firm cash flows after corporate taxes.

T_C = Corporate tax rate.

R_0 = The cost of capital to an all-equity firm. As can be seen from the formula, R_0 discounts aftertax cash flows.

As shown previously, leverage increases the value of the firm by the tax shield, which is $T_C B$ for perpetual debt. We add this tax shield to the value of the unlevered firm to get the value of the levered firm.

We can write this algebraically as follows:[14]

$$V_L = \frac{\text{EBIT} \times (1 - T_C)}{R_0} + \frac{T_C R_B B}{R_B} = V_U + T_C B \tag{16.5}$$

[14]This relationship holds when the debt level is assumed to be constant through time. A different formula would apply if the debt-equity ratio was assumed to be nonconstant over time. For a deeper treatment of this point, see James A. Miles and John R. Ezzell, "The Weighted Average Cost of Capital, Perfect Capital Markets, and Project Life: A Clarification," *Journal of Financial and Quantitative Analysis* 15, no. 3 (September 1980): 719–30.

Equation 16.5 is MM Proposition I under corporate taxes. The first term in Equation 16.5 is the value of the cash flows of the firm with no debt tax shield. In other words, this term is equal to V_U, the value of the all-equity firm. The value of the levered firm is the value of an all-equity firm plus $T_C B$, the tax rate times the value of the debt. $T_C B$ is the present value of the tax shield in the case of perpetual cash flows.[15] Because the tax shield increases with the amount of debt, the firm can raise its total cash flow and its value by substituting debt for equity.

Note that we continue to assume all interest is tax deductible in this discussion. If some portion of interest paid is not deductible, it will be carried forward and deducted at a later date. This delay reduces, but does not eliminate, the value of the tax shield and the tax advantage of debt financing.

EXAMPLE 16.4

MM with Corporate Taxes Devaki Airlines is currently an unlevered firm. The company expects to generate ₹126.6 in earnings before interest and taxes (EBIT) in perpetuity. The corporate tax rate is 21 percent, implying aftertax earnings of ₹100. All earnings after tax are paid out as dividends.

The firm is considering a capital restructuring to allow ₹200 of debt. Its cost of debt capital is 10 percent. Unlevered firms in the same industry have a cost of equity capital of 20 percent. What is the new value of Devaki Airlines?

The value of Devaki Airlines will be equal to:

$$V_L = \frac{\text{EBIT} \times (1 - T_C)}{R_0} + T_C B$$

$$= \frac{₹100}{.20} + .21 \times ₹200$$

$$= ₹500 + 42 = ₹542$$

The value of the levered firm is ₹542, which is greater than the unlevered value of ₹500. Because $V_L = B + S$, the value of levered equity, S, is equal to ₹542 − 200 = ₹342. The value of Devaki Airlines as a function of leverage is illustrated in Figure 16.5.

(continued)

[15]The following example calculates the present value if we assume the debt has a finite life. Suppose the Maxwell Company has ₹1 million in debt with an 8 percent coupon rate. If the debt matures in two years and the cost of debt capital, R_B, is 10 percent, what is the present value of the tax shields if the corporate tax rate is 21 percent? The debt is amortized in equal installments over two years.

Year	Loan Balance	Interest	Tax Shield	Present Value of Tax Shield
0	₹1,000,000			
1	500,000	₹80,000	.21 × ₹80,000	₹15,272.73
2	0	40,000	.21 × ₹40,000	6,942.15
				₹22,214.88

The present value of the tax saving is:

$$\text{PV} = \frac{.21 \times ₹80{,}000}{1.10} + \frac{.21 \times ₹40{,}000}{1.10^2} = ₹22{,}214.88$$

The Maxwell Company's value is higher than that of a comparable unlevered firm by ₹22,214.88.

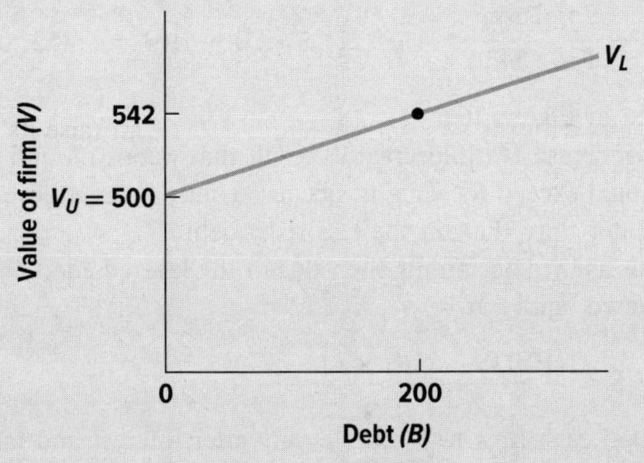

$$V_L = V_U + T_C B$$
$$= ₹500 + .21 \times ₹200$$
$$= ₹542$$

Debt reduces Devaki's tax burden. As a result, the value of the firm is positively related to debt.

Figure 16.5 The Effect of Financial Leverage on Firm Value: MM with Corporate Taxes in the Case of Devaki Airlines

EXPECTED RETURN AND LEVERAGE UNDER CORPORATE TAXES

MM Proposition II under no taxes posits a positive relationship between the expected return on equity and leverage. This result occurs because the risk of equity increases with leverage. The same intuition also holds in a world of corporate taxes. The exact formula in a world of corporate taxes is this:[16]

$$R_S = R_0 + \frac{B}{S} \times (1 - T_C) \times (R_0 - R_B) \tag{16.6}$$

[16]This relationship can be shown as follows: Given MM Proposition I under taxes, a levered firm's market value balance sheet can be written as:

$T_C B$ = Tax shield	S = Equity
V_u = Value of unlevered firm	B = Debt

The value of the unlevered firm is the value of the assets without benefit of leverage. The balance sheet indicates that the firm's value increases by $T_C B$ when debt of B is added. The expected cash flow from the left side of the balance sheet can be written as:

$$V_U R_0 + T_C B R_B \tag{a}$$

Because assets are risky, their expected rate of return is R_0. The tax shield has the same risk as the debt, so its expected rate of return is R_B.

The expected cash to bondholders and stockholders together is

$$S R_S + B R_B \tag{b}$$

Expression (b) reflects the fact that stock earns an expected return of R_S and debt earns the interest rate R_B.

Applying the formula to Devaki Airlines, we get:

$$R_s = .20 + \frac{₹200,200}{₹342,342} \times (1 - .21) \times (.20 - .10) = .2462, \text{ or } 24.62\%$$

This calculation is illustrated in Figure 16.6.

Whenever $R_0 > R_B$, R_S increases with leverage, a result that we also found in the no-tax case. As stated earlier in this chapter, R_0 should exceed R_B. That is, because equity (even unlevered equity) is risky, it should have an expected return greater than that on the less risky debt.

Let's check our calculations by determining the value of the levered equity in another way. The algebraic formula for the value of levered equity is:

$$S = \frac{(\text{EBIT} - R_B B) \times (1 - T_C)}{R_S}$$

The numerator is the expected cash flow to levered equity after interest and taxes. The denominator is the rate at which the cash flow to equity is discounted.

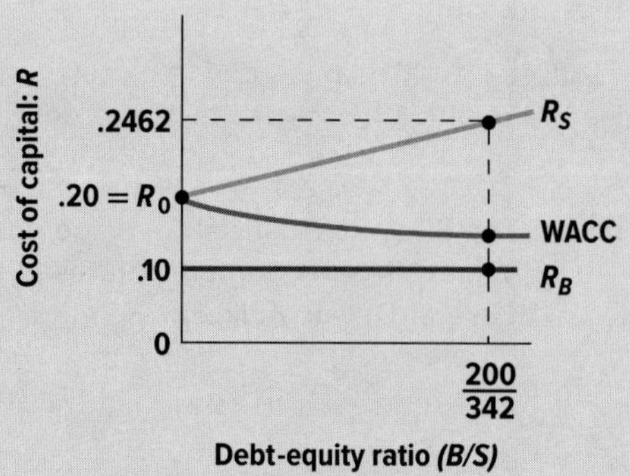

$$R_S = R_0 + (1 - T_C)(R_0 - R_B)B/S = .20 + \left(.79 \times .10 \times \frac{200}{342}\right)$$

$$= .2462, \text{ or } 24.62\%$$

Financial leverage adds risk to the firm's equity. As compensation, the cost of equity rises with the firm's risk. Note that R_0 is a single point, whereas R_S, R_B, and WACC are all entire lines.

Figure 16.6 The Effect of Financial Leverage on the Cost of Debt and Equity Capital

---

Because all cash flows are paid out as dividends in our no-growth perpetuity model, the cash flows going into the firm equal those going to stockholders. Hence (a) and (b) are equal:

$$SR_S + BR_B = V_U R_0 + T_C B R_B \qquad \text{(c)}$$

Dividing both sides of (c) by 5, subtracting BR_B from both sides, and rearranging yields

$$R_S = \frac{V_U}{S} \times R_0 - (1 - T_C) \times \frac{B}{S} R_B \qquad \text{(d)}$$

Because the value of the levered firm, V_L, equals $V_U + T_C B = B + S$, it follows that $V_U = S + (1 - T_C) \times B$. Thus (d) can be rewritten as:

$$R_S = \frac{S + (1 - T_C) \times B}{S} \times R_0 - (1 - T_C) \times \frac{B}{S} R_B \qquad \text{(e)}$$

Bringing the terms involving $(1 - T_C) \times (B/S)$ together produces Equation 16.6.

For Devaki Airlines, we get:

$$\frac{(₹126.6 - .10 \times ₹200)(1 - .21)}{.2462} = ₹342$$

This is the same result we obtained earlier.

THE WEIGHTED AVERAGE COST OF CAPITAL, WACC, AND CORPORATE TAXES

In Chapter 13, we defined the weighted average cost of capital (with corporate taxes) as follows (note that $V_L = S + B$):

$$\text{WACC} = \frac{S}{V_L}R_S + \frac{B}{V_L}R_B(1 - T_C)$$

Note that the cost of debt capital, R_B, is multiplied by $(1 - T_C)$ because interest is tax deductible at the corporate level. However, the cost of equity, R_S, is not multiplied by this factor because dividends are not deductible. In the no-tax case, WACC is unaffected by leverage. This result is reflected in Figure 16.3, which we discussed earlier. However, because debt is tax-advantaged relative to equity, it can be shown that WACC declines with leverage in a world with corporate taxes. This result can be seen in Figure 16.6.

For Devaki Airlines, WACC is equal to:

$$\text{WACC} = \left(\frac{₹342}{₹542}\right) \times .2462 + \left(\frac{₹200}{₹542}\right) \times .10 \times .79 = .1845, \text{ or } 18.45\%$$

Devaki Airlines has reduced its WACC from 20 percent (with no debt) to 18.45 percent with reliance on debt. This result is intuitive because it suggests that when a firm lowers its WACC, the firm's value will increase. Using the WACC approach, we can confirm that the value of Devaki Airlines is ₹542:

$$V_L = \frac{\text{EBIT} \times (1 - T_C)}{\text{WACC}} = \frac{₹100,100}{.1845} = ₹542542$$

STOCK PRICE AND LEVERAGE UNDER CORPORATE TAXES

At this point, students often believe the numbers–or at least are too intimidated to dispute them. However, they sometimes think we have asked the wrong question. "Why are we choosing to maximize the value of the firm?" they will say. "If managers are looking out for the stockholders' interest, why aren't they trying to maximize stock price?" If this question occurred to you, you have come to the right section.

Our response is twofold: First, we showed in the first section of this chapter that the capital structure that maximizes firm value is also the one that most benefits the interests of the stockholders.

However, that general explanation is not always convincing to students. As a second procedure, we calculate the stock price of Devaki Airlines both before and after the exchange of debt for stock. We do this by presenting a set of market value balance sheets. The market value balance sheet for the company in its all-equity form can be represented as follows:

DEVAKI AIRLINES Balance Sheet (All-Equity Firm)		
Physical assets	Equity	₹500
$\frac{₹126.6}{.20} \times (1 - .21) = ₹500$		(100 shares)

Assuming that there are 100 shares outstanding, each share is worth ₹5 (= ₹500/100). Suppose the company announces that it will issue ₹200 of debt to buy back ₹200 of stock. We know from our previous discussion that the value of the firm will rise to reflect the tax shield of debt. If we assume that capital markets efficiently price securities, the increase occurs immediately. That is, the rise occurs on the day of the announcement, not on the date of the debt-for-equity exchange. The market value balance sheet now becomes:

DEVAKI AIRLINES Balance Sheet (After Announcement of Debt Issue)			
Physical assets	₹500	Equity	₹542
			(100 shares)
Present value of tax shield:			
$T_C B = .21 \times ₹200 =$	42		
Total assets	₹542		

Note that the debt has not yet been issued. Therefore, only equity appears on the right side of the balance sheet. Each share is now worth ₹542/100 = ₹5.42, implying that the stockholders have benefited by ₹42. The equityholders gain because they are the owners of a firm that has improved its financial policy.

The introduction of the tax shield to the balance sheet is confusing to many students. Although physical assets are tangible, the intangible nature of the tax shield bothers some students. However, remember that an asset is any item with value. The tax shield has value because it reduces the stream of future taxes. The fact that one cannot touch the shield in the way that one can touch a physical asset is a philosophical, not financial, consideration.

At some point, the exchange of debt for equity occurs. Debt of ₹200 is issued and the proceeds are used to buy back shares. How many shares of stock are repurchased? Because shares are now selling at ₹5.42 each, the number of shares that the firm acquires is ₹200/₹5.42 = 36.90. This leaves 63.10 (= 100 − 36.90) shares of stock outstanding. The market value balance sheet is now:

DEVAKI AIRLINES Balance Sheet (After Exchange Has Taken Place)			
Physical assets	₹500	Equity	₹342
			(100 − 36.90 = 63.10 shares)
Present value of tax shield	42	Debt	200
Total assets	₹542	Debt plus equity	₹542

Each share of the stock is worth ₹342/63.1 = ₹5.42 after the exchange. Notice that the stock price does not change on the exchange date. As we mentioned, the stock price moves on the date of the announcement only. Because the shareholders participating in the exchange receive a price equal to the market price per share after the exchange, they do not care whether they exchange their stock.

This example was provided for two reasons. First, it shows that an increase in the value of the firm from debt financing leads to an increase in the price of the stock. In fact, the stockholders capture the entire ₹42 tax shield. Second, we wanted to provide more work with market value balance sheets.

A summary of the main results of Modigliani-Miller with corporate taxes is presented in the nearby boxed section.

Summary of Modigliani-Miller Propositions with Corporate Taxes

Assumptions

- Corporations are taxed at the rate T_C on earnings after interest.
- There are no transaction or bankruptcy costs.
- Individuals and corporations borrow at the same rate.

Results

Proposition I: $V_L = V_U + T_C B$ (for a firm with perpetual debt)

Proposition II: $R_S = R_0 + \frac{B}{S}(1 - T_C)(R_0 - R_B)$

Intuition

Proposition I: Because corporations can deduct interest payments but not dividend payments, corporate leverage lowers tax payments.

Proposition II: The cost of equity rises with leverage because the risk to equity rises with leverage.

RESEARCH IN EMERGING MARKET CONTEXT

Jadiyappa et al. (2016) researched the impact of capital structure on firms' leverage, debt maturity ratio, and debt specialization. They found that the leverage and debt maturity ratio were negatively affected, while debt specialization was positively affected. This impact was greater for priority firms, which were favourably regulated than for other firms. Bandopadhyay and Barua (2016) conducted empirical research in India, which showed that capital structure choice and corporate performance varied according to industry affiliation, business group ownership, firm-specific factors, macroeconomic policy, and business cycle. Rao et al. (2019) examined whether the theories of capital structure decisions apply equally to small and medium-sized enterprises (SMEs) in India. Their findings confirmed the applicability of the pecking order theory for SMEs in India. Additionally, profitability is the main variable for manufacturing SMEs, whereas profitability has no meaningful significance for service SMEs.

(continued)

References

Bandyopadhyay, A., & Barua, N. M. (2016). Factors determining capital structure and corporate performance in India: Studying the business cycle effects. *The Quarterly Review of Economics and Finance, 61,* 160–172.

Jadiyappa, N., Vanga, N. R., & Krishnankutty, R. (2016). Financial liberalization and capital structuring decisions of corporate firms: evidence from India. *Economics Letters, 149,* 33–37.

Rao, P., Kumar, S., & Madhavan, V. (2019). A study on factors driving the capital structure decisions of small and medium enterprises (SMEs) in India. *IIMB Management Review, 31*(1), 37–50.

Summary and Conclusions

1. We began our discussion of the capital structure decision by arguing that the particular capital structure that maximizes the value of the firm is also the one that provides the most benefit to the stockholders.
2. In a world of no taxes, the famous Proposition I of Modigliani and Miller proves that the value of the firm is unaffected by the debt-equity ratio. In other words, a firm's capital structure is a matter of indifference in that world. The authors obtain their results by showing that either a high or a low corporate ratio of debt-to-equity can be offset by homemade leverage. The result hinges on the assumption that individuals can borrow at the same rate as corporations, an assumption we believe to be quite plausible.
3. MM's Proposition II in a world without taxes states:

$$R_S = R_0 + \frac{B}{S}(R_0 - R_B)$$

   This implies that the expected rate of return on equity (also called the *cost of equity* or the *required return on equity*) is positively related to the firm's leverage. This makes intuitive sense because the risk of equity rises with leverage, a point illustrated by Figure 16.3.
4. Although the above work of MM is quite elegant, it does not explain the empirical findings on capital structure very well. MM imply that the capital structure decision is a matter of indifference, whereas the decision appears to be a weighty one in the real world. To achieve real-world applicability, we next considered corporate taxes.
5. In a world with corporate taxes but no bankruptcy costs, firm value is an increasing function of leverage. The formula for the value of the firm is:

$$V_L = V_U + T_C B$$

   Expected return on levered equity can be expressed as:

$$R_S = R_0 + (1 - T_C) \times (R_0 - R_B) \times \frac{B}{S}$$

   Here, value is positively related to leverage. This result implies that firms should have a capital structure almost entirely composed of debt. Because real-world firms select more moderate levels of debt, the next chapter considers modifications to the results of this chapter.

Concept Questions

1. **MM Assumptions** List the assumptions that lie behind the Modigliani-Miller theory in a world without taxes. Are these assumptions reasonable in the real world? Explain.
2. **MM Propositions** In a world with no taxes, no transaction costs, and no costs of financial distress, is the following statement true, false, or uncertain? If a firm issues equity to repurchase some of its debt, the price per share of the firm's stock will rise because the shares are less risky. Explain.
3. **MM Propositions** In a world with no taxes, no transaction costs, and no costs of financial distress, is the following statement true, false, or uncertain? Moderate borrowing will not increase the required return on a firm's equity. Explain.
4. **MM Propositions** What is the quirk in the tax code that makes a levered firm more valuable than an otherwise identical unlevered firm?
5. **Business Risk versus Financial Risk** Explain what is meant by business and financial risk. Suppose Firm A has greater business risk than Firm B. Is it true that Firm A also has a higher cost of equity capital? Explain.
6. **MM Propositions** How would you answer in the following debate?

   Q: Isn't it true that the riskiness of a firm's equity will rise if the firm increases its use of debt financing?

   A: Yes, that's the essence of MM Proposition II.

   Q: And isn't it true that, as a firm increases its use of borrowing, the likelihood of default increases, thereby increasing the risk of the firm's debt?

   A: Yes.

   Q: In other words, increased borrowing increases the risk of the equity and the debt?

   A: That's right.

   Q: Well, given that the firm uses only debt and equity financing, and given that the risks of both are increased by increased borrowing, does it not follow that increasing debt increases the overall risk of the firm and therefore decreases the value of the firm?

   A: ?
7. **Optimal Capital Structure** If we consider only the effects of taxes, what is the optimal capital structure?
8. **Financial Leverage** Why is the use of debt financing referred to as financial leverage?
9. **Homemade Leverage** What is homemade leverage?
10. **Capital Structure Goal** What is the basic goal of financial management with regard to capital structure?

Questions and Problems

BASIC (Questions 1–16)

1. **EBIT and Leverage** Fujita, Inc., has no debt outstanding and a total market value of ₹222,000. Earnings before interest and taxes, EBIT, are projected to be ₹18,000 if economic conditions are normal. If there is strong expansion in the economy, then EBIT will be 25 percent higher. If there is a recession, then EBIT will be 30 percent lower. The company is considering a

₹60,000 debt issue with an interest rate of 7 percent. The proceeds will be used to repurchase shares of stock. There are currently 7,400 shares outstanding. Ignore taxes for this problem. Assume the stock price is constant under all scenarios.

a. Calculate earnings per share, EPS, under each of the three economic scenarios before any debt is issued. Also calculate the percentage changes in EPS when the economy expands or enters a recession.
b. Repeat part (a) assuming that the company goes through with recapitalization. What do you observe?

2. **EBIT, Taxes, and Leverage** Repeat parts (a) and (b) in Problem 1 assuming the company has a tax rate of 21 percent, a market-to-book ratio of 1.0, and the stock price remains constant.

3. **ROE and Leverage** Suppose the company in Problem 1 has a market-to-book ratio of 1.0 and the stock price remains constant.

a. Calculate return on equity, ROE, under each of the three economic scenarios before any debt is issued. Also calculate the percentage changes in ROE for economic expansion and recession, assuming no taxes.
b. Repeat part (a) assuming the firm goes through with the proposed recapitalization.
c. Repeat parts (a) and (b) of this problem assuming the firm has a tax rate of 21 percent.

4. **Break-Even EBIT** Foundation Corporation is comparing two different capital structures, an all-equity plan (Plan I) and a levered plan (Plan II). Under Plan I, the company would have 145,000 shares of stock outstanding. Under Plan II, there would be 125,000 shares of stock outstanding and ₹716,000 in debt outstanding. The interest rate on the debt is 8 percent and there are no taxes.

a. If EBIT is ₹300,000, which plan will result in the higher EPS?
b. If EBIT is ₹600,000, which plan will result in the higher EPS?
c. What is the break-even EBIT?

5. **MM and Stock Value** In Problem 4, use MM Proposition I to find the price per share of equity under each of the two proposed plans. What is the value of the firm?

6. **Break-Even EBIT and Leverage** Dickson Corp. is comparing two different capital structures. Plan I would result in 12,700 shares of stock and ₹100,050 in debt. Plan II would result in 9,800 shares of stock and ₹226,200 in debt. The interest rate on the debt is 10 percent.

a. Ignoring taxes, compare both of these plans to an all-equity plan assuming EBIT will be ₹70,000. The all-equity plan would result in 15,000 shares of stock outstanding. Which of the three plans has the highest EPS? The lowest?
b. In part (a) what are the break-even levels of EBIT for each plan as compared to that for an all-equity plan? Is one higher than the other? Why?
c. Ignoring taxes, when will EPS be identical for Plans I and II?
d. Repeat parts (a), (b), and (c) assuming that the corporate tax rate is 21 percent. Are the break-even levels of EBIT different from before? Why or why not?

7. **Leverage and Stock Value** Ignoring taxes in Problem 6, what is the price per share of equity under Plan I? Plan II? What principle is illustrated by your answers?

8. **Homemade Leverage** Finch, Inc., is debating whether or not to convert its all-equity capital structure to one that is 30 percent debt. Currently there are 6,500 shares outstanding and the price per share is ₹51. EBIT is expected to remain at ₹41,000 per year forever. The interest rate on new debt is 8 percent and there are no taxes.

a. Allison, a shareholder of the firm, owns 100 shares of stock. What is her cash flow under the current capital structure, assuming the firm has a dividend payout rate of 100 percent?
b. What will Allison's cash flow be under the proposed capital structure of the firm? Assume that she keeps all 100 of her shares.

c. Suppose the company does convert, but Allison prefers the current all-equity capital structure. Show how she could unlever her shares of stock to recreate the original capital structure.
d. Using your answer to part (c), explain why the company's choice of capital structure is irrelevant.

9. **Homemade Leverage and WACC** ABC Co. and XYZ Co. are identical firms in all respects except for their capital structure. ABC is all-equity financed with ₹680,000 in stock. XYZ uses both stock and perpetual debt; its stock is worth ₹340,000 and the interest rate on its debt is 7 percent. Both firms expect EBIT to be ₹67,000. Ignore taxes.
   a. Rico owns ₹41,500 worth of XYZ's stock. What rate of return is he expecting?
   b. Show how Rico could generate exactly the same cash flows and rate of return by investing in ABC and using homemade leverage.
   c. What is the cost of equity for ABC? What is it for XYZ?
   d. What is the WACC for ABC? For XYZ? What principle have you illustrated?

10. **MM** Sugar Skull Corp. uses no debt. The weighted average cost of capital is 7.9 percent. If the current market value of the equity is ₹15.6 million and there are no taxes, what is EBIT?

11. **MM and Taxes** In the previous question, suppose the corporate tax rate is 22 percent. What is EBIT in this case? What is the WACC? Explain.

12. **Calculating WACC** Solar Industries has a debt-equity ratio of 1.25. Its WACC is 7.8 percent, and its cost of debt is 4.7 percent. The corporate tax rate is 21 percent.
    a. What is the company's cost of equity capital?
    b. What is the company's unlevered cost of equity capital?
    c. What would the cost of equity be if the debt-equity ratio were 2? What if it were 1? What if it were zero?

13. **Calculating WACC** Navarro Corp. has no debt but can borrow at 5.9 percent. The firm's WACC is currently 9.20 percent and the tax rate is 21 percent.
    a. What is the company's cost of equity?
    b. If the company converts to 25 percent debt, what will its cost of equity be?
    c. If the company converts to 50 percent debt, what will its cost of equity be?
    d. What is the company's WACC in part (b)? In part (c)?

14. **MM and Taxes** Fields & Co. expects its EBIT to be ₹125,000 every year forever. The company can borrow at 7 percent. The company currently has no debt and its cost of equity is 12 percent. If the tax rate is 24 percent, what is the value of the company? What will the value be if the company borrows ₹205,000 and uses the proceeds to repurchase shares?

15. **MM and Taxes** In Problem 14, what is the cost of equity after recapitalization? What is the WACC? What are the implications for the firm's capital structure decision?

16. **MM Proposition I** Levered, Inc., and Unlevered, Inc., are identical in every way except their capital structures. Each company expects to earn ₹16 million before interest per year in perpetuity, with each company distributing all its earnings as dividends. Levered's perpetual debt has a market value of ₹60 million and costs 8 percent per year. Levered has 1.8 million shares of stock outstanding that sell for ₹101 per share. Unlevered has no debt and 3.4 million shares outstanding, currently worth ₹72 per share. Neither firm pays taxes. Is Levered's stock a better buy than Unlevered's stock?

INTERMEDIATE (Questions 17–26)

17. **MM** Tool Manufacturing has an expected EBIT of ₹57,000 in perpetuity and a tax rate of 21 percent. The firm has ₹134,000 in outstanding debt at an interest rate of 5.35 percent and its unlevered cost of capital is 10.3 percent. What is the value of the company according to MM Proposition I with taxes? Should the company change its debt-equity ratio if the goal is to maximize the value of the company? Explain.

18. **Firm Value** Tempest Corporation expects an EBIT of ₹37,700 every year forever. The company currently has no debt and its cost of equity is 11 percent. The tax rate is 22 percent.

a. What is the current value of the company?
b. Suppose the company can borrow at 6 percent. What will the value of the company be if it takes on debt equal to 50 percent of its unlevered value? What if it takes on debt equal to 100 percent of its unlevered value?
c. What will the value of the company be if it takes on debt equal to 50 percent of its levered value? What if the company takes on debt equal to 100 percent of its levered value?

19. **MM Proposition I with Taxes** The Bellwood Company is financed entirely with equity. The company is considering a loan of ₹3.4 million. The loan will be repaid in equal installments over the next two years and has an interest rate of 8 percent. The company's tax rate is 24 percent. According to MM Proposition I with taxes, what would be the increase in the value of the company after the loan?

20. **MM Proposition I without Taxes** Alpha Corporation and Beta Corporation are identical in every way except their capital structures. Alpha Corporation, an all-equity firm, has 16,000 shares of stock outstanding, currently worth ₹35 per share. Beta Corporation uses leverage in its capital structure. The market value of Beta's debt is ₹80,000 and its cost of debt is 9 percent. Each firm is expected to have earnings before interest of ₹89,000 in perpetuity. Neither firm pays taxes. Assume that every investor can borrow at 9 percent per year.

a. What is the value of Alpha Corporation?
b. What is the value of Beta Corporation?
c. What is the market value of Beta Corporation's equity?
d. How much will it cost to purchase 20 percent of each firm's equity?
e. Assuming each firm meets its earnings estimates, what will be the rupee return to each position in part (d) over the next year?
f. Construct an investment strategy in which an investor purchases 20 percent of Alpha's equity and replicates both the cost and rupee return of purchasing 20 percent of Beta's equity.
g. Is Alpha's equity more or less risky than Beta's equity? Explain.

21. **Cost of Capital** Joylin, Inc., has equity with a market value of ₹15.4 million and debt with a market value of ₹5.9 million. Treasury bills that mature in one year yield 4 percent per year and the expected return on the market portfolio is 11 percent. The beta of the company's equity is 1.15. The firm pays no taxes.

a. What is the company's debt-equity ratio?
b. What is the firm's weighted average cost of capital?
c. What is the cost of capital for an otherwise identical all-equity firm?

22. **Homemade Leverage** The Day Company and the Knight Company are identical in every respect except that Day is unlevered. Financial information for the two firms appears here. All earnings streams are perpetuities. Neither firm pays taxes. Both firms distribute all earnings available to common stockholders immediately.

	Day	Knight
Projected operating income	₹ 325,000	₹ 325,000
Year-end interest on debt	—	48,000
Market value of stock	2,100,000	1,500,000
Market value of debt	—	800,000

a. An investor who can borrow at 6 percent per year wishes to purchase 5 percent of Knight's equity. Can he increase his rupee return by purchasing 5 percent of Day's equity if he borrows so that the initial net costs of the two strategies are the same?

b. Given the two investment strategies in (a), which will investors choose? When will this process cease?

23. **MM Propositions** Refi Corporation is planning to repurchase part of its common stock by issuing corporate debt. As a result, the firm's debt-equity ratio is expected to rise from 35 percent to 50 percent. The firm currently has ₹2.5 million worth of debt outstanding. The cost of this debt is 5.1 percent per year. The firm expects to have an EBIT of ₹920,000 per year in perpetuity and pays no taxes.

a. What is the market value of the firm before and after the repurchase announcement?
b. What is the expected return on the firm's equity before the announcement of the stock repurchase plan?
c. What is the expected return on the equity of an otherwise identical all-equity firm?
d. What is the expected return on the firm's equity after the announcement of the stock repurchase plan?

24. **Stock Value and Leverage** Warsaw Manufacturing, Inc., plans to announce that it will issue ₹1.9 million of perpetual debt and use the proceeds to repurchase common stock. The bonds will sell at par with a coupon rate of 5 percent. The company is currently all-equity and worth ₹6.7 million with 290,000 shares of common stock outstanding. After the sale of the bonds, the company will maintain the new capital structure indefinitely. The annual pretax earnings of ₹1.32 million are expected to remain constant in perpetuity. The tax rate is 21 percent.

a. What is the expected return on the company's equity before the announcement of the debt issue?
b. Construct the company's market value balance sheet before the announcement of the debt issue. What is the price per share of the firm's equity?
c. Construct the company's market value balance sheet immediately after the announcement of the debt issue.
d. What is the company's stock price per share immediately after the repurchase announcement?
e. How many shares will the company repurchase as a result of the debt issue? How many shares of common stock will remain after the repurchase?
f. Construct the market value balance sheet after the restructuring.
g. What is the required return on the company's equity after the restructuring?

25. **MM with Taxes** Dickson, Inc., has a debt-equity ratio of 2.3. The firm's weighted average cost of capital is 9 percent and its pretax cost of debt is 5.3 percent. The tax rate is 24 percent.

a. What is the company's cost of equity capital?
b. What is the company's unlevered cost of equity capital?
c. What would the company's weighted average cost of capital be if the firm's debt-equity ratio were .75? What if it were 1.3?

26. **ROE and Leverage** In Problem 2, suppose instead that you assume the company has a market-to-book ratio of 1.0 before recapitalization and the stock price changes according to MM. How would this affect your answer?

CHALLENGE (Questions 27–31)

27. **Weighted Average Cost of Capital** In a world of corporate taxes only, show that the WACC can be written as WACC = $R_0 \times [1 - T_C(B/V)]$.

28. **Cost of Equity and Leverage** Assuming a world of corporate taxes only, show that the cost of equity, R_S, is as given in the chapter by MM Proposition II with corporate taxes.

29. **Business and Financial Risk** Assume a firm's debt is risk-free, so that the cost of debt equals the risk-free rate, R_f. Define β_A as the firm's asset beta–that is, the systematic risk of the firm's assets. Define β_S to be the beta of the firm's equity. Use the capital asset pricing model, CAPM, along with MM Proposition II to show that $\beta_S = \beta_A \times (1 + B/S)$, where B/S is the debt-equity ratio. Assume the tax rate is zero.

30. **Stockholder Risk** Suppose a firm's business operations mirror movements in the economy as a whole very closely–that is, the firm's asset beta is 1.0. Use the result of the previous problem to find the equity beta for this firm for debt-equity ratios of 0, 1, 5, and 20. What does this tell you about the relationship between capital structure and shareholder risk? How is the shareholders' required return on equity affected? Explain.

31. **Unlevered Cost of Equity** Beginning with the cost of capital equation–that is:

$$\text{WACC} = \frac{S}{B+S}R_S + \frac{B}{B+S}R_B$$

show that the cost of equity capital for a levered firm can be written as follows:

$$R_S = R_0 + \frac{B}{S}(R_0 - R_B)$$

Excel Master It! Problem

Excel Master coverage online

The TL Corporation currently has no debt outstanding. Josh Culberson, the CFO, is considering restructuring the company by issuing debt and using the proceeds to repurchase outstanding equity. The company's assets are worth ₹40 million, the stock price is ₹25 per share, and there are 1,600,000 shares outstanding. In the expected state of the economy, EBIT is expected to be ₹3 million. If there is a recession, EBIT would fall to ₹1.8 million and in an expansion EBIT would increase to ₹4.3 million. If the company issues debt, it will issue a combination of short-term debt and long-term debt. The ratio of short-term debt to long-term debt will be 0.20. The short-term debt will have an interest rate of 3 percent and the long-term debt will have an interest rate of 8 percent.

a. On the next worksheet, fill in the values in each table. For the debt-equity ratio, create a spinner that changes the debt-equity ratio. The resulting debt-equity ratio should range from 0 to 10 at increments of 0.1.
b. Graph the EBIT and EPS for the TL Corporation on the same graph using a scatter plot.
c. What is the break-even EBIT between the current capital structure and the new capital structure?
d. To illustrate the new capital structure, you would like to create a pie chart. Another pie chart that is available is the pie of pie chart. Using the pie of pie chart, graph the equity and total debt in the main pie chart and the short-term debt and long-term debt in the secondary pie chart. Note, if you right-click on a data series in the chart and select Format Data Series, Series Options, then Split Series By, you can display the series by a customized choice. In the customization, you can select which data series you want displayed in the primary pie chart and the secondary pie chart.

Mini Case — STEPHENSON REAL ESTATE RECAPITALIZATION

Stephenson Real Estate Company was founded 25 years ago by the current CEO, Robert Stephenson. The company purchases real estate, including land and buildings, and rents the property to tenants. The company has shown a profit every year for the past 18 years, and the shareholders are satisfied with the company's management. Prior to founding Stephenson Real Estate, Robert was the founder and CEO of a failed alpaca farming operation. The resulting bankruptcy made him extremely averse to debt financing. As a result, the company is entirely equity financed, with 12 million shares of common stock outstanding. The stock currently trades at ₹53.80 per share.

Stephenson is evaluating a plan to purchase a tract of land in the southeastern United States for ₹49 million. The land will subsequently be leased to tenant farmers. This purchase is expected to increase Stephenson's annual pretax earnings by ₹11.5 million in perpetuity. Kim Weyand, the company's new CFO, has been put in charge of the project. Kim has determined that the company's current cost of capital is 10.5 percent. She feels that the company would be more valuable if it included debt in its capital structure, so she is evaluating whether the company should issue debt to entirely finance the project. Based on some conversations with investment banks, she thinks that the company can issue bonds at par value with a coupon rate of 7 percent. Based on her analysis, she also believes that a capital structure in the range of 70 percent equity/30 percent debt would be optimal. If the company goes beyond 30 percent debt, its bonds would carry a lower rating and a much higher coupon because the possibility of financial distress and the associated costs would rise sharply. Stephenson has a 21 percent corporate tax rate (state and federal).

1. If Stephenson wishes to maximize its total market value, would you recommend that it issue debt or equity to finance the land purchase? Explain.
2. Construct Stephenson's market value balance sheet before it announces the purchase.
3. Suppose Stephenson decides to issue equity to finance the purchase.
   a. What is the net present value of the project?
   b. Construct Stephenson's market value balance sheet after it announces that the firm will finance the purchase using equity. What would be the new price per share of the firm's stock? How many shares will Stephenson need to issue to finance the purchase?
   c. Construct Stephenson's market value balance sheet after the equity issue but before the purchase has been made. How many shares of common stock does Stephenson have outstanding? What is the price per share of the firm's stock?
   d. Construct Stephenson's market value balance sheet after the purchase has been made.
4. Suppose Stephenson decides to issue debt to finance the purchase.
   a. What will the market value of Stephenson be if the purchase is financed with debt?
   b. Construct Stephenson's market value balance sheet after both the debt issue and the land purchase. What is the price per share of the firm's stock?
5. Which method of financing maximizes the per-share stock price of Stephenson's equity?

17

Capital Structure

LIMITS TO THE USE OF DEBT

No matter how you look at it, 2020 was a tough year for brick-and-mortar retailers. By September, 27 big retailers had filed for bankruptcy, with varying outcomes. For example, both Neiman Marcus and JCPenney restructured debt and emerged from bankruptcy. Others, like Brooks Brothers and Lucky Brand, were acquired, while Stein Mart and Art Van Furniture closed for good.

The Indian market has also seen distressed sales of businesses, accelerated by the Covid-19 lock-downs. In November 2020, the online furniture retailer Urban Ladder was bought by Reliance Industries at a price ~80% lower than its peak valuation.

As these situations point out, there is a limit to the financial leverage a company can use, and the risk of too much leverage is bankruptcy. In this chapter, we discuss the costs associated with bankruptcies and how companies attempt to avoid this unhappy outcome.

The previous chapter began with the question, "How should a firm choose its debt-equity ratio?" We first presented the Modigliani-Miller (MM) result that, in a world without taxes, the value of the levered firm is the same as the value of the unlevered firm. In other words, the choice of the debt-equity ratio is unimportant here.

We next showed the MM result that, in a world with corporate taxes, the value of the firm increases with leverage, implying that firms should take on as much debt as possible. But this result leaves us with unanswered questions. Is this the whole story? Should financial managers really set their firms' debt-to-value ratios near 100 percent? If so, why do real-world companies have, as we show later in this chapter, rather modest levels of debt?

The current chapter bridges the gap between theory and practice. We show that there are good reasons for modest capital structures in practice, even in a world with taxes. We begin with the concept of bankruptcy costs. These costs increase with debt, offsetting the tax advantage of leverage.

Please visit us at **rwjcorporatefinance.blogspot.com** for the latest developments in the world of corporate finance.

17.1 Costs of Financial Distress

BANKRUPTCY RISK OR BANKRUPTCY COST?

As mentioned throughout the previous chapter, debt provides tax benefits to the firm. However, debt puts pressure on the firm because interest and principal payments are obligations. If these obligations are not met, the firm may risk some sort of financial distress. The ultimate distress is *bankruptcy*, where ownership of the firm's assets is legally transferred from the stockholders to the bondholders. These debt obligations are fundamentally different from stock obligations. Although stockholders like and expect dividends, they are not legally entitled to dividends in the way bondholders are legally entitled to interest and principal payments.

We show next that bankruptcy costs, or more generally financial distress costs, tend to offset the advantages to debt. We begin by looking at a simple example of bankruptcy. Taxes are ignored to focus only on the costs of debt.

EXAMPLE 17.1

Bankruptcy Costs The Singham Company plans to be in business for one more year. It forecasts a cash flow of either ₹100 or ₹50 in the coming year, each occurring with 50 percent probability. The firm has no other assets. Previously issued debt requires payments of ₹49 of interest and principal. The Marathe Company has identical cash flow prospects but has ₹60 of interest and principal obligations. The cash flows of these two firms can be represented as follows:

	Singham Company		Marathe Company	
	Boom Times (prob. 50%)	Recession (prob. 50%)	Boom Times (prob. 50%)	Recession (prob. 50%)
Cash flow	₹100	₹50	₹100	₹50
Payment of interest and principal on debt	49	49	60	50
Distribution to stockholders	₹ 51	₹ 1	₹ 40	₹ 0

For Singham Company in both boom times and recession and for Marathe Company in boom times, cash flow exceeds interest and principal payments. In these situations, the bondholders are paid in full and the stockholders receive any residual. However, the most interesting of the four columns involves Marathe Company in a recession. Here the bondholders are owed ₹60, but the firm has only ₹50 in cash. Because we assume that the firm has no other assets, the bondholders cannot be satisfied in full. Bankruptcy occurs, implying that the bondholders will receive all of the firm's cash and the stockholders will receive nothing. Importantly, the stockholders do not have to come up with the additional ₹10 (= ₹60 – 50). Corporations have limited liability in India, U.S.A., and most other countries, implying that bondholders cannot sue the stockholders for the extra ₹10.[1]

Let's compare the two companies in recession. The bondholders of Singham receive ₹49 and the stockholders receive ₹1, for a total of ₹50. The bondholders of Marathe receive ₹50 and the stockholders receive ₹0, also for a total of ₹50. There is an important point here. While Marathe goes bankrupt but Singham does not, the investors of both firms receive ₹50. In other words, bankruptcy does not reduce the firm's cash flows. One often hears that bankruptcy causes a reduction in value or cash flow. But in our example, it is a recession causing the reduction, not bankruptcy.

(continued)

[1]There are situations where the limited liability of corporations can be *pierced*. Typically, fraud or misrepresentation must be present.

However, we have left something out. Marathe's example is not realistic because it ignores an important cash flow. A more realistic set of numbers might be:

Marathe Company		
	Boom Times (prob. 50%)	Recession (prob. 50%)
Earnings	₹100	₹50
Debt repayment	60	35
Distribution to stockholders	₹ 40	₹ 0

Why do the bondholders receive only ₹35 in a recession? If cash flow is only ₹50, bondholders will be informed that they will not be paid in full. These bondholders are likely to hire lawyers to negotiate or even to sue the company. The firm is also likely to hire lawyers to defend itself. Further costs will be incurred if the case gets to a bankruptcy court. These fees are always paid before the bondholders get paid. In this example, we are assuming that bankruptcy costs total ₹15 (= ₹50 − 35).

Let's compare the example with bankruptcy costs to the example without these costs. Because of its greater leverage, Marathe Company faces the possibility of bankruptcy, while Singham Company does not. Nevertheless, as we saw earlier, total cash flow to investors is the same for both firms in a world without bankruptcy costs. However, once we introduce bankruptcy costs, total cash flow to investors becomes lower for the bankrupt company, Marathe. In a recession, Singham's bondholders receive ₹49 and the stockholders receive ₹1, for a total of ₹50. In a recession, Marathe's bondholders receive ₹35 and the stockholders receive ₹0, for a total of only ₹35. We can conclude the following:

Leverage increases the likelihood of bankruptcy. However, bankruptcy does not, by itself, lower the cash flows to investors. Rather, it is the costs associated with bankruptcy that lower cash flows.

Our pie example can provide an explanation. In a world without bankruptcy costs, the bondholders and the stockholders share the entire pie. However, bankruptcy costs eat up some of the pie in the real world, leaving less for the stockholders and bondholders.

17.2 Description of Financial Distress Costs

The preceding example showed that bankruptcy costs can lower the value of the firm. In fact, the same general result holds even if a legal bankruptcy is prevented. Thus, *financial distress costs* may be a better phrase than *bankruptcy costs.* Let's look at these costs in more detail.

DIRECT COSTS OF FINANCIAL DISTRESS: LEGAL AND ADMINISTRATIVE COSTS OF LIQUIDATION OR REORGANIZATION

As mentioned earlier, lawyers are involved throughout all the stages before and during bankruptcy. With fees often in the hundreds of rupees an hour, these costs can add up quickly. A wag once remarked that bankruptcies are to lawyers what blood is to sharks. In addition, administrative and accounting fees can substantially add to the total bill. And if a trial takes place, we must not forget expert witnesses. Each side may hire a number of these witnesses to testify about the fairness of a proposed settlement. Their fees can easily rival those of lawyers or accountants. (However, we personally look upon these witnesses kindly because they are frequently drawn from the ranks of finance professors.)

One well-publicized bankruptcy concerned a municipality, Orange County, California, not a corporation. This bankruptcy followed large bond trading losses in the county's financial portfolio. The *Los Angeles Times* stated:

> Orange County taxpayers lost ₹1.69 billion, and their government, one year ago today, sank into bankruptcy. Now they are spending millions more to get out of it.
>
> Accountants pore over fiscal ledgers at ₹325 an hour. Lawyers toil into the night–at ₹385 an hour. Financial advisers from one of the nation's most prominent investment houses labor for the taxpayers at ₹150,000 a month. Clerks stand by the photocopy machines, running up bills that sometimes exceed ₹3,000.
>
> Total so far: ₹29 million. And it's nowhere near over.
>
> The multipronged effort to lift Orange County out of the nation's worst municipal bankruptcy has become a money-eating machine, gobbling up taxpayer funds at a rate of ₹2.4 million a month. That's ₹115,000 a day.
>
> County administrators are not alarmed.
>
> They say Orange County's bankruptcy was an epic disaster that will require equally dramatic expenditures of taxpayer cash to help it survive. While they have refused to pay several thousand rupees worth of claimed expenses–lavish dinners, big hotel bills–they have rarely questioned the sky-high hourly fees. They predict the costs could climb much higher.
>
> Indeed, participants in the county's investment pool have agreed to create a separate ₹50 million fund to pay the costs of doing legal battle with Wall Street.[2]

Of course, Orange County got off cheaply when compared with Detroit, which spent ₹170 million to get out of bankruptcy. Bankruptcy costs in the private sector are often far larger than those in Orange County and Detroit. The direct costs of Enron's and WorldCom's bankruptcies were commonly estimated to exceed ₹1 billion and ₹600 million, respectively. The costs of Lehman Brothers' bankruptcy are larger still. The company emerged from bankruptcy in March 2012 as a liquidating trust, with the goal of selling off assets and paying creditors. The direct bankruptcy costs were eye-watering: Lehman spent more than ₹2.2 billion on lawyers, accountants, consultants, and examiners for its U.S. and European operations. This number is the sum of many large costs. For example, one law firm billed ₹200,000 for business meals, ₹439,000 for computerized and other research, ₹115,000 for local transportation, and ₹287,000 for copying charges at 10 cents per page. The other costs of the bankruptcy may have been even larger. Some experts estimated that because Lehman rushed into bankruptcy, it lost out on ₹75 billion that it could have earned if the sale of many of its assets had been better planned.

A number of academic studies have measured the direct costs of financial distress. Although large in absolute amount, these costs are actually small as a percentage of firm value. White, Altman, and Weiss estimate the direct costs of financial distress to be about 3 percent of the market value of the firm.[3] In a study of direct financial distress costs of 20 railroad bankruptcies, Warner finds that net financial distress costs were, on average, 1 percent of the market value of the firm seven years before bankruptcy and were somewhat larger percentages as bankruptcy approached (e.g., 2.5 percent of the market value of the firm three years before bankruptcy).[4] Lubben estimates the average cost of legal fees alone to be about 1.5 percent

[2]Dexter Filkins, "The High Cost of Going Bankrupt," *Los Angeles Times,* December 6, 1995, www.latimes.com/archives/la-xpm-1995-12-06-mn-10861-story.html.

[3]Michelle J. White, "Bankruptcy Costs and the New Bankruptcy Code," *Journal of Finance* 38, no. 2 (May 1983): 477–88; Edward I. Altman, "A Further Empirical Investigation of the Bankruptcy Cost Question," *Journal of Finance* 39, no. 4 (September 1984): 1067–89; and Lawrence A. Weiss, "Bankruptcy Resolution: Direct Costs and Violation of Priority of Claims," *Journal of Financial Economics* 27, no. 2 (October 1990): 285–314.

[4]Jerold B. Warner, "Bankruptcy Costs: Some Evidence," *Journal of Finance* 32, no. 2 (May 1977): 337–47.

of total assets for bankrupt firms.[5] Bris, Welch, and Zhu find bankruptcy expenses as measured against asset values to be in the 2 to 10 percent range.[6]

INDIRECT COSTS OF FINANCIAL DISTRESS

Impaired Ability to Conduct Business Bankruptcy harms relationships with customers and suppliers. Sales are frequently lost because of both fear of impaired service and loss of trust. For example, in 2008, both General Motors and Chrysler were experiencing significant financial difficulties, and many people felt that one or both companies would eventually file for bankruptcy (both later did). As a result of the bad news surrounding the companies, there was a loss of confidence in the companies' automobiles. A study showed that 75 percent of Americans would not purchase an automobile from a bankrupt company because the company might not honor the warranty and it might be difficult to obtain replacement parts. This concern resulted in lost potential sales for both companies, which only added to the financial distress. Chrysler actually found itself in a similar situation when it skirted insolvency in the 1970s. Many previously loyal Chrysler customers, fearing the loss of parts and servicing in a bankruptcy, switched to other manufacturers. As another example, gamblers avoided the Atlantis casino in Atlantic City after it became technically insolvent. Gamblers are a superstitious bunch. Many wondered, "If the casino itself cannot make money, how can I expect to make money there?" A particularly outrageous story concerned two unrelated stores both named Mitchells in New York City. When one Mitchells declared bankruptcy, customers stayed away from both stores. In time, the second store was forced to declare bankruptcy, as well.

In 2020, based on the rumors of possible bankruptcy, account holders of Yes Bank raided the bank branches and ATMs in most parts of the country, resulting in bank run. The Reserve Bank of India (RBI) had to intervene and arrange for additional liquidity to meet customer demands and also issue a statement on the bank's stability putting rumors to rest. Yes Bank was rescued by a Reserve Bank-led bailout plan under which SBI picked up 49 percent equity along with other large banks in India. Similar was the case with the Lakshmi Vilas Bank. However, RBI intervention was prompt in this case - and a total collapse and chaos was avoided.

Though these indirect costs clearly exist, it is quite difficult to measure them. Altman estimates that both direct and indirect costs of financial distress are frequently greater than 20 percent of firm value.[7] Andrade and Kaplan estimate total distress costs to be between 10 percent and 20 percent of firm value.[8] Bar-Or estimates expected future distress costs for firms that are currently healthy to be 8 to 10 percent of operating value, a number below the estimates of either Altman or Andrade and Kaplan.[9] However, unlike Bar-Or, these authors consider distress costs for firms already in distress, not expected distress costs for currently healthy firms.

Cutler and Summers examine the costs of the well-publicized Texaco bankruptcy.[10] In January 1984, Pennzoil reached what it believed to be a binding agreement to acquire three-sevenths of Getty Oil. However, less than a week later, Texaco acquired all of Getty at a higher per-share price. Pennzoil then sued Getty for breach of contract. Because Texaco had previously indemnified Getty against litigation, Texaco became liable for damages.

---

[5]Stephen J. Lubben, "The Direct Costs of Corporate Reorganization: An Empirical Examination of Professional Fees in Large Chapter 11 Cases," *American Bankruptcy Law Journal* 74 (Fall 2000): 509–22.

[6]Arturo Bris, Ivo Welch, and Ning Zhu, "The Costs of Bankruptcy: Chapter 7 Liquidation versus Chapter 11 Reorganization," *Journal of Finance* 61, no. 3 (June 2006): 1253–1303.

[7]Edward I. Altman, "A Further Empirical Investigation of the Bankruptcy Cost Question," *Journal of Finance* 39, no. 4 (September 1984): 1067–89.

[8]Gregor Andrade and Steven N. Kaplan, "How Costly Is Financial (Not Economic) Distress? Evidence from Highly Leveraged Transactions That Became Distressed," *Journal of Finance* 53, no. 5 (October 1998): 1443–93.

[9]Yuval Bar-Or, "An Investigation of Expected Financial Distress Costs," unpublished paper, Wharton School, University of Pennsylvania, 2000.

[10]David M. Cutler and Lawrence H. Summers, "The Costs of Conflict Resolution and Financial Distress: Evidence from the Texaco-Pennzoil Litigation," *RAND Journal of Economics* 19, no. 2 (Summer 1988): 157–72.

In November 1985, the Texas State Court awarded damages of ₹12 billion to Pennzoil, although this amount was later reduced. As a result, Texaco filed for bankruptcy. Cutler and Summers identify nine important events over the course of the litigation. They find that Texaco's market value (stock price times number of shares outstanding) fell a cumulative ₹4.1 billion over these events, whereas Pennzoil's rose only ₹682 million. Thus, Pennzoil gained about one-sixth of what Texaco lost, resulting in a net loss to the two firms of almost ₹3.5 billion.

What could explain this net loss? Cutler and Summers suggest that it is likely due to costs that Texaco and Pennzoil incurred from the litigation and subsequent bankruptcy. The authors argue that direct bankruptcy fees represent only a small part of these costs, estimating Texaco's aftertax legal expenses at about ₹165 million. Legal costs to Pennzoil were more difficult to assess because Pennzoil's lead lawyer, Joe Jamail, stated publicly that he had no set fee. However, using a clever statistical analysis, the authors estimate his fee was about ₹200 million. So, what drove the remaining costs?

Indirect costs of financial distress may be the culprit. An affidavit by Texaco stated that, following the lawsuit, some of its suppliers were demanding cash payments. Other suppliers halted or canceled shipments of crude oil. Certain banks restricted Texaco's use of futures contracts on foreign exchange. The affidavit stressed that these constraints were reducing Texaco's ability to run its business, leading to deterioration of its financial condition. Could these sorts of indirect costs explain the ₹3.5 billion disparity between Texaco's drop and Pennzoil's rise in market value? Unfortunately, although indirect costs likely played a large role here, there is no way to accurately estimate them.

Bankruptcy risk can also severely limit a firm's ability to hire and retain productive employees. No one likes to board a sinking ship, and workers at troubled companies may even consider jumping ship. A forward-looking employee will realize that advancement opportunities are low and layoff probabilities are high if the firm is in danger of bankruptcy. Thus, another indirect cost of financial distress comes in the form of increased labor costs. While it is difficult to quantify this labor cost exactly, we know that it is higher in more labor-intensive firms (relative to machines, humans worry more about layoffs and advancement opportunities). Using detailed Swedish labor data, researchers have also found that the most productive and skilled workers are the first to react to bankruptcy risk by jumping ship, suggesting that skill-intensive firms should be especially mindful of the effect of bankruptcy risk on their labor costs.[11]

AGENCY COSTS

When a firm has debt, conflicts of interest arise between stockholders and bondholders. Because of this, stockholders are tempted to pursue selfish strategies. These conflicts of interest, which are magnified when financial distress is incurred, impose **agency costs** on the firm. We describe three kinds of selfish strategies that stockholders use to hurt the bondholders and help themselves. These strategies are costly because they will lower the market value of the whole firm.

Selfish Investment Strategy 1: Incentive to Take Large Risks Firms near bankruptcy often take great chances because they believe that they are playing with someone else's money. Imagine a levered firm considering two mutually exclusive projects, a low-risk one and a high-risk one. There are two equally likely outcomes, recession and boom. The firm is in such dire straits that should a recession hit, it will come near to bankruptcy with one project and actually fall into bankruptcy with the other. The cash flows for the entire firm if the low-risk project is taken can be described as follows:

[11]Ramin P. Baghai, Rui C. Silva, Viktor Thell, and Vikrant Vig, "Talent in Distressed Firms: Investigating the Labor Costs of Financial Distress," *Journal of Finance*, forthcoming 2020.

Value of Entire Firm if Low-Risk Project Is Chosen

	Probability	Value of Firm	=	Stock	+	Bonds
Recession	.5	₹100	=	₹ 0	+	₹100
Boom	.5	200	=	100	+	100

If a recession occurs, the value of the firm will be ₹100; if a boom occurs, the value of the firm will be ₹200. The expected value of the firm is ₹150 (= .5 × ₹100 + .5 × ₹200).

The firm has promised to pay bondholders ₹100. Shareholders will obtain the difference between the total payoff and the amount paid to the bondholders. In other words, the bondholders have the prior claim on the payoffs and the shareholders have the residual claim.

Now suppose that the riskier project can be substituted for the low-risk project. The payoffs and probabilities are as follows:

Value of Entire Firm if High-Risk Project Is Chosen

	Probability	Value of Firm	=	Stock	+	Bonds
Recession	.5	₹ 50	=	₹ 0	+	₹ 50
Boom	.5	240	=	140	+	100

The expected value of the firm is ₹145 (= .5 × ₹50 + .5 × ₹240), which is lower than the expected value of the firm with the low-risk project. The low-risk project would be accepted if the firm were all equity. However, note that the expected value of the stock is ₹70 (= .5 × ₹0 + .5 × ₹140) with the high-risk project, but only ₹50 (= .5 × ₹0 + .5 × ₹100) with the low-risk project. Given the firm's present levered state, stockholders will select the high-risk project, even though the high-risk project has a lower NPV.

The key is that relative to the low-risk project, the high-risk project increases firm value in a boom and decreases firm value in a recession. The increase in value in a boom is captured by the stockholders because the bondholders are paid in full (they receive ₹100) regardless of which project is accepted. Conversely, the drop in value in a recession is lost by the bondholders because they are paid in full with the low-risk project but receive only ₹50 with the high-risk one. The stockholders will receive nothing in a recession anyway, whether the high-risk or low-risk project is selected. Financial economists argue that stockholders steal value from the bondholders by selecting high-risk projects.

A story illustrates why this strategy is sometimes referred to as *gambling for resurrection* or *risk shifting.* It seems that FedEx was near financial collapse within a few years of its inception. The founder, Frederick Smith, took ₹5,000 of corporate funds to Las Vegas in despair. He won at the gaming tables, providing enough capital to allow the firm to survive. Had he lost, the banks would have received ₹5,000 less when the firm reached bankruptcy.

Selfish Investment Strategy 2: Incentive toward Underinvestment Stockholders of a firm with a significant probability of bankruptcy often find that new investment helps the bondholders at the stockholders' expense. The simplest case might be a real estate owner facing imminent bankruptcy. If he takes ₹100,000 out of his own pocket to refurbish the building, he could increase the building's value

Table 17.1 Example Illustrating Incentive to Underinvest

	Firm without Project		Firm with Project Costing ₹1,000	
	Boom	**Recession**	**Boom**	**Recession**
Firm cash flows	₹5,000	₹2,400	₹6,700	₹4,100
Bondholders' claim	4,000	2,400	4,000	4,000
Stockholders' claim	₹1,000	₹ 0	₹2,700	₹ 100

The project has a positive NPV. However, much of its value is captured by bondholders. Rational managers, acting in the stockholders' interest, will reject the project.

by, say, ₹150,000. Though this investment has a positive net present value, he will turn it down if the increase in value cannot prevent bankruptcy. "Why," he asks, "should I use my own funds to improve the value of a building that the bank will soon repossess?"

The incentive to underinvest in positive NPV projects is sometimes referred to as a *debt overhang* problem. This idea is formalized by the following example. Consider the firm in Table 17.1, which must decide whether to accept or reject a new project. The project's cost is ₹1,000. The first two columns in the table show cash flows without the project. The firm receives cash inflows of ₹5,000 and ₹2,400 under a boom and a recession, respectively. However, the firm must pay principal and interest of ₹4,000, implying that the firm will default in a recession.

Alternatively, as indicated in the next two columns of the table, the firm could raise equity to invest in the new project. Assume that the project generates cash flow of ₹1,700 in either state, bringing the firm's cash flow to ₹6, 700 (= ₹5,000 + 1,700) in a boom and ₹4,100 (= ₹2,400 + 1,700) in a recession. Because the firm's cash flow of ₹4,100 in a recession exceeds the bondholders' claim of ₹4,000, bankruptcy is avoided. Because ₹1,700 is much greater than the project's cost of ₹1,000, the project has a positive NPV at any plausible interest rate. Clearly, an all-equity firm would accept the project.

However, the project hurts the stockholders of the levered firm. To see this, imagine the old stockholders contribute the ₹1,000 themselves.[12] Assuming that a boom and a recession are equally likely, the expected value of the stockholders' interest without the project is ₹500 (= .5 × ₹1,000 + .5 × ₹0). The expected value with the project is ₹1,400 (= .5 × ₹2,700 + .5 × ₹100). The stockholders' interest rises by only ₹900 (= ₹1,400 − 500) but costs ₹1,000.

Why does a project with a positive NPV hurt the stockholders? The key is that the stockholders contribute the full ₹1,000 investment, but the stockholders and bondholders share the benefits. The stockholders take the entire gain if a boom occurs. Conversely, the bondholders reap most of the cash flow from the project in a recession.

The discussion of Selfish Strategy 1 is quite similar to the discussion of Selfish Strategy 2. In both cases, an investment strategy for the levered firm is different from the one for the unlevered firm. Thus, leverage results in a distorted investment policy. Whereas the unlevered corporation always chooses projects with positive net present values, the levered firm may deviate from this policy.

Selfish Investment Strategy 3: Milking the Property Another strategy is to pay out extra dividends or other distributions to shareholders in times of financial distress, leaving less in the firm for the bondholders. This strategy goes by a variety of names, including *wealth transfer* and *milking the property* (a phrase

[12]The same qualitative results will be obtained if the ₹1,000 is raised from new stockholders. However, the math becomes much more difficult because we must determine how many new shares are issued.

taken from real estate). Selfish Strategies 2 and 3 are very similar. In Selfish Strategy 2, the firm chooses not to raise new equity. Selfish Strategy 3 goes one step further because equity is actually withdrawn through the dividend.

A famous example of a more creative wealth transfer from debt to equity involves the 1993 Marriott spinoff, in which Marriott Corporation announced that it would split into two companies, Marriott International and Host Marriott Corporation. Under the proposed split, existing stockholders would own claims to both new firms, while existing bondholders could only make a claim to the assets of Host Marriott Corporation. Thus, the original bondholders of Marriott Corporation lost their claim to assets transferred to the stockholders of Marriott International. Today, such wealth transfers are usually blocked by debt covenants, as we will describe in the next section.

Summary of Selfish Strategies The distortions discussed occur only when there is a significant probability of bankruptcy or financial distress. Distortions are unlikely to affect, say, utilities regulated by state commissions because financial distress is rare among these firms. By contrast, small firms in risky industries, such as tech, are more likely to experience financial distress and, in turn, to be affected by such distortions.

Who pays for the cost of selfish investment strategies? We argue that it is ultimately the stockholders. Rational bondholders know that when financial distress is imminent, they cannot expect help from stockholders. Rather, stockholders are likely to choose investment strategies that reduce the value of the bonds. Bondholders protect themselves accordingly by raising the interest rate that they require on the bonds. Because the stockholders must pay these high rates, they ultimately bear the costs of selfish strategies. For firms that face these distortions, debt will be difficult and costly to obtain. These firms will have low leverage ratios.

The relationship between stockholders and bondholders is very similar to the relationship between Sanjeev Kumar and Dev Anand, good friends and movie stars in the 1930s. Anand reportedly said that the good thing about Kumar was that you knew exactly where you stood with him. When you needed his help, you could always count on him to let you down.

17.3 Can Costs of Debt Be Reduced?

As U.S. senators are prone to say, "A billion here, a billion there. Pretty soon it all adds up." Each of the costs of financial distress we have mentioned is substantial in its own right; their sum may well impact debt financing. Managers have an incentive to reduce these costs. We now turn to some of the methods to do so. However, it should be mentioned at the outset that the methods here can, at most, reduce the costs of debt. They cannot eliminate them entirely.

PROTECTIVE COVENANTS

Because stockholders must pay higher interest rates as insurance against their own selfish strategies, they frequently make agreements with bondholders in hopes of lower rates. These agreements, called **protective covenants**, are incorporated as part of the loan document, or indenture, between stockholders and bondholders. The covenants must be taken seriously because a broken covenant can lead to default. Protective covenants can be classified into two types: negative covenants and positive covenants.

A **negative covenant** limits or prohibits actions that the company may take. Some typical negative covenants are:

1. Limitations are placed on the amount of dividends a company may pay.
2. The firm may not pledge any of its assets to other lenders.
3. The firm may not merge with another firm.

4. The firm may not sell or lease its major assets without approval by the lender.
5. The firm may not issue additional long-term debt.

A **positive covenant** specifies an action that the company agrees to take or a condition the company must abide by. Some examples are:

1. The company agrees to maintain its working capital at a minimum level.
2. The company must furnish periodic financial statements to the lender.

These lists of covenants are not exhaustive. The authors have seen loan agreements with more than 30 covenants.

Smith and Warner examined public issues of debt and found that 91 percent of the bond indentures included covenants that restricted the issuance of additional debt, 23 percent restricted dividends, 39 percent restricted mergers, and 36 percent limited the sale of assets.[13]

Protective covenants should reduce the costs of bankruptcy, ultimately increasing the value of the firm. Stockholders are likely to favor all reasonable covenants. To see this, consider three choices by stockholders to reduce bankruptcy costs:

1. *Issue no debt.* Because of the tax advantages to debt, this is a very costly way of avoiding conflicts.
2. *Issue debt with no restrictive and protective covenants.* In this case, bondholders will demand high interest rates to compensate for the unprotected status of their debt.
3. *Write protective and restrictive covenants into the loan contracts.* If the covenants are reasonable and are clearly written, the creditors may receive protection without large costs being imposed on the shareholders. With this protection, the creditors are likely to accept a lower interest rate than they would accept without the covenants.

Even if bond covenants reduce flexibility, they can increase the value of the firm. They can be the lowest-cost solution to the stockholder-bondholder conflict. A list of typical bond covenants and their uses appears in Table 17.2.

Table 17.2 Loan Covenants

Shareholder Action or Firm Circumstances	Covenant Type	Reason for Covenant
As firm approaches financial distress, shareholders may want firm to make high-risk investments.	Financial statement restrictions 1. Minimum working capital 2. Minimum interest coverage 3. Minimum net worth	High-risk investments transfer value from bondholders to stockholders when financial distress is a realistic possibility. Covenants reduce probability of financial distress.
Shareholders may attempt to transfer corporate assets to themselves.	Restrictions on asset disposition 1. Limit on dividends 2. Limit on sale of assets 3. Collateral and mortgages	Covenants limit the ability of shareholders to transfer assets to themselves and to underinvest.
Shareholders may attempt to increase risk of firm.	Restrictions on switching assets	Increased firm risk helps shareholders and hurts bondholders.
Shareholders may attempt to issue new debt of equal or greater priority.	Dilution restrictions 1. Limit on leasing 2. Limit on further borrowing	Covenants restrict dilution of the claim of existing bondholders.

[13]Clifford W. Smith Jr. and Jerold B. Warner, "On Financial Contracting: An Analysis of Bond Covenants," *Journal of Financial Economics* 7, no. 2 (June 1979): 117–61.

CONSOLIDATION OF DEBT

One reason bankruptcy costs are so high is that different creditors (and their lawyers) contend with each other. This problem can be alleviated by proper coordination between bondholders and stockholders. For example, perhaps one lender, or at most a few lenders, can shoulder the entire debt. Should financial distress occur, negotiating costs are minimized under this arrangement. In addition, bondholders can purchase stock. In this way, stockholders and debtholders are not pitted against each other because they are not separate entities. This appears to be the approach in Japan, where large banks generally take significant stock positions in the firms to which they lend money. Debt-equity ratios in Japan are far higher than those in the United States. To an extent, this problem was also there in India (till 1990s).

17.4 Integration of Tax Effects and Financial Distress Costs

Modigliani and Miller argue that the firm's value rises with leverage in the presence of corporate taxes. Because this relationship implies that all firms should choose maximum debt, the theory does not predict the behavior of firms in the real world.

Other authors have suggested that bankruptcy and related costs reduce the value of the levered firm. The integration of tax effects and distress costs appears in Figure 17.1. In the top graph of the figure, the diagonal straight line represents the value of the firm in a world without bankruptcy costs. The ∩-shaped curve represents the value of the firm with these costs. This curve rises as the firm moves from all equity to a small amount of debt. Here, the present value of the distress costs is minimal because the probability of distress is so small. However, as more and more debt is added, the present value of these costs rises at an increasing rate. At some point, the increase in the present value of these costs from an additional Rupee of debt equals the increase in the present value of the tax shield. This is the debt level that maximizes the value of the firm and is represented by B^* in Figure 17.1. In other words, B^* is the optimal amount of debt. Bankruptcy costs increase faster than the tax shield beyond this point, implying a reduction in firm value from further leverage.

In the bottom graph of Figure 17.1, the weighted average cost of capital falls as debt is added to the capital structure. After reaching B^*, the weighted average cost of capital rises. The optimal amount of debt produces the lowest weighted average cost of capital.

The optimal amount of debt was also affected by the Tax Cuts and Jobs Act (TCJA) of 2017. Because of the limits to the deductibility of interest, which we have discussed elsewhere, the tax advantage of debt was reduced for some some firms starting in 2018, which implies a lower level for B^*.

Our discussion implies that a firm's capital structure decision involves a trade-off between the tax benefits of debt and the costs of financial distress. In fact, this approach is frequently called the *trade-off* or the *static trade-off* theory of capital structure. The implication is that there is an optimal amount of debt for any individual firm. This amount of debt becomes the firm's target debt level. Because financial distress costs cannot be expressed in a precise way, no formula has yet been developed to determine a firm's optimal debt level exactly. However, the last section of this chapter offers some rules of thumb for selecting a debt-equity ratio in the real world. Our situation reminds us of a quote from John Maynard Keynes. He supposedly said that although most historians would agree that Queen Elizabeth I was both a better monarch and an unhappier woman than Queen Victoria, no one has yet been able to express the statement in a precise and rigorous formula.

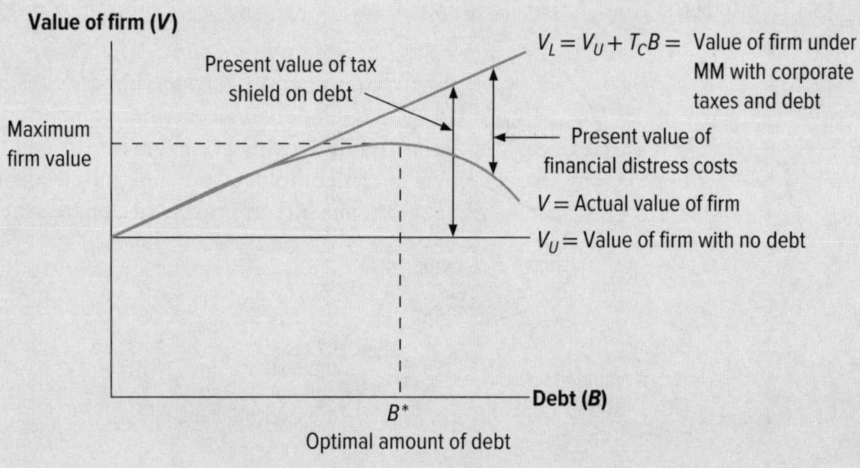

The tax shield increases the value of the levered firm. Financial distress costs lower the value of the levered firm. The two offsetting factors produce an optimal amount of debt at B^*.

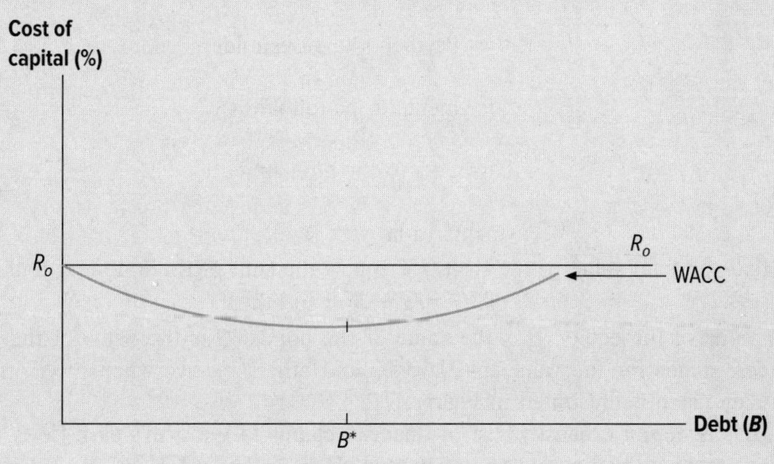

According to the static theory, the WACC falls initially because of the tax advantage of debt. Beyond Point B^*, it begins to rise because of financial distress costs.

Figure 17.1 The Optimal Amount of Debt and the Value of the Firm

PIE AGAIN

Now that we have considered bankruptcy costs, let's return to the pie approach of the previous chapter. The cash flows (CF) of the firm go to four different claimants: stockholders, bondholders, the government (in the form of taxes), and, during the bankruptcy process, lawyers (and others). We can express this idea algebraically as:

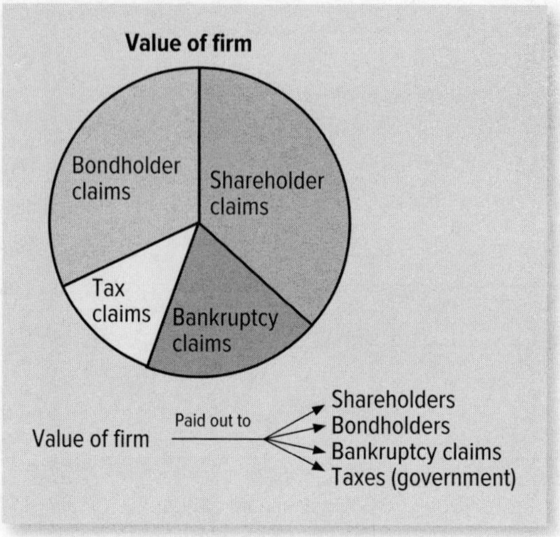

Figure 17.2 The Pie Model with Real-World Factors

$$\begin{gathered}\text{CF} = \text{Payments to stockholders} \\ + \\ \text{Payments to bondholders} \\ + \\ \text{Payments to the government} \\ + \\ \text{Payments to lawyers (and others)}\end{gathered}$$

It follows that the total value of the firm, V_T, equals the sum of the following four components:

$$V_T = S + B + G + L$$

where S is the value of the equity, B is the value of the bonds, G is the value of the government claims from taxes, and L stands for the value that lawyers and others receive when the firm is under financial distress. This relationship is illustrated in Figure 17.2.

Of course, this is not an exhaustive list of financial claims to the firm's cash flows. To give an unusual example, everyone reading this book has an economic claim to the cash flows of General Motors. After all, if you are injured in an accident, you might sue GM. Win or lose, GM will expend resources dealing with the matter. If you think this is far-fetched and unimportant, ask yourself how much GM might be willing to pay every man, woman, and child in the country to have them promise that they would never sue GM, no matter what happened. The law does not permit such payments, but that does not mean that a value to all of those potential claims does not exist. We guess that it would run into the billions of rupees, and, for GM or any other company, there should be a slice of the pie labeled *LS* for "potential lawsuits."

Figure 17.2 illustrates the essence of MM's intuition. While V_T is determined by the firm's cash flows, the firm's capital structure merely cuts V_T into slices. Capital structure does not affect the total value, V_T.

There is a difference between claims such as those of stockholders and bondholders on the one hand and those of government and potential litigants in lawsuits on the other. The first set of claims are **marketable claims** and the second set are **nonmarketable claims**. Marketable claims can be bought and sold in financial markets and the nonmarketable claims cannot. This distinction between marketable and nonmarketable claims is important. When stock is issued, stockholders pay cash to the firm for the privilege of later receiving dividends. Similarly, bondholders pay cash to the firm for the privilege of receiving interest in the future. However, the Income Tax Authorities pay nothing to the firm for the privilege of receiving taxes in the future. Similarly, lawyers pay nothing to the firm for the privilege of receiving fees from the firm in the future.

When we speak of the value of the firm, we are referring to the value of the marketable claims, V_M, and not the value of nonmarketable claims, V_N. What we have shown is that capital structure does not affect the total value:

$$\begin{aligned} V_T &= S + B + G + L \\ &= V_M + V_N \end{aligned}$$

But as we saw, the value of the marketable claims, V_M, can change with changes in the capital structure.

By the pie theory, any increase in V_M must imply an identical decrease in V_N. Rational financial managers will choose a capital structure to maximize the value of the marketable claims, V_M. Equivalently, rational managers will work to minimize the value of the nonmarketable claims, V_N. These are taxes and bankruptcy costs in the previous example, but they also include all the other nonmarketable claims such as the *LS* claim.

17.5 Signaling

The previous section pointed out that the corporate leverage decision involves a trade-off between a tax subsidy and financial distress costs. This idea was graphed in Figure 17.1, where the marginal tax subsidy exceeds the distress costs for low levels of debt. The reverse holds for high levels of debt. The firm's capital structure is optimized where the marginal subsidy to debt equals the marginal cost.

Let's explore this idea a little more. What is the relationship between a company's profitability and its debt level? A firm with low anticipated profits will likely take on a low level of debt. A small interest deduction is all that is needed to offset all of this firm's pretax profits. And too much debt would raise the firm's expected distress costs. A more successful firm would probably take on more debt. This firm could use the extra interest to reduce the taxes from its greater earnings. Being more financially secure, this firm would find its extra debt increasing the risk of bankruptcy only slightly. In other words, rational firms raise debt levels (and the associated interest payments) when profits are expected to increase.

How do investors react to an increase in debt? Rational investors are likely to infer a higher firm value from a higher debt level. These investors are likely to bid up a firm's stock price after the firm has, say, issued debt in order to buy back equity. We say that investors view debt as a signal of firm value.

Now we get to the incentives of managers to fool the public. Consider a firm whose level of debt is optimal. That is, the marginal tax benefit of debt equals the marginal distress costs of debt. Imagine that the firm's manager desires to increase the firm's current stock price, perhaps because he knows that many of his stockholders want to sell their stock soon. This manager might want to increase the level of debt to make investors think that the firm is more valuable than it really is. If the strategy works, investors will push up the price of the stock.

This implies that firms can fool investors by taking on some additional leverage. Now let's ask the big question: Are there benefits to extra debt but no costs, implying that all firms will take on as much debt as possible? The answer, fortunately, is that there are costs, as well. Imagine that a firm has issued extra debt to fool the public. At some point, the market will learn that the company is not that valuable after all. At this time, the stock price should actually fall below what it would have been had the debt never been increased. Why? Because the firm's debt level is now above the optimal level. That is, the marginal tax benefit of debt is below the marginal cost of debt. If the current stockholders plan to sell, say, half of their shares now and retain the other half, an increase in debt will help them on immediate sales but likely hurt them on later ones.

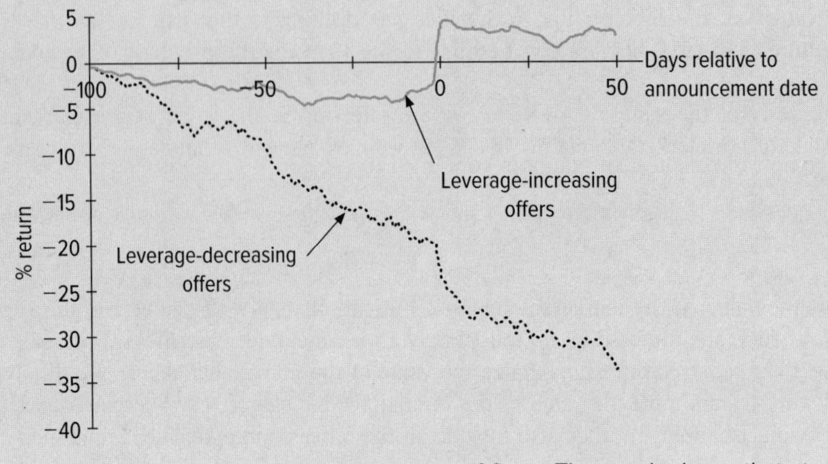

Exchange offers change the debt-equity ratios of firms. The graph shows that stock prices increase for firms whose exchange offers increase leverage. Conversely, stock prices decrease for firms whose offers decrease leverage.

Figure 17.3 Stock Returns at the Time of Announcements of Exchange Offers

SOURCE: Kshitij Shah, "The Nature of Information Conveyed by Pure Capital Structure Changes," *Journal of Financial Economics* 36, no. 1 (August 1994): 89–126.

Now here is the important point: We said that in a world where managers do not attempt to fool investors, valuable firms issue more debt than less valuable ones. It turns out that even when managers attempt to fool investors, the more valuable firms still will want to issue more debt than the less valuable firms. That is, while all firms will increase debt levels somewhat to fool investors, the costs of extra debt prevent the less valuable firms from issuing more debt than the more valuable firms issue. Investors still can treat debt level as a signal of firm value. In other words, investors still can view an announcement of debt as a positive sign for the firm.

You might argue that this example is too simplistic. Perhaps the stockholders of some firms want to sell most of their stock immediately, whereas the stockholders of other firms want to sell only a little of theirs now. It is impossible to tell here whether the firms with the most debt are the most valuable or merely the ones with the least skeptical stockholders. Because other objections can be brought up as well, signaling theory is best validated by empirical evidence. And fortunately, the empirical evidence tends to support the theory.

Consider the evidence concerning **exchange offers**. Firms can change their debt levels through exchange offers, of which there are two types. The first type of offer allows stockholders to exchange some of their stock for debt, thereby increasing leverage. The second type allows bondholders to exchange some of their debt for stock, decreasing leverage. Figure 17.3 shows the stock price behavior of firms that change their proportions of debt and equity via exchange offers. The solid line in the figure indicates that stock prices rise substantially on the date when an exchange offering increasing leverage is announced. (This date is referred to as Day 0 in the figure.) Conversely, the dotted line in the figure indicates that stock price falls substantially when an offer decreasing leverage is announced.

The market infers from an increase in debt that the firm is better off, leading to a stock price rise. Conversely, the market infers the reverse from a decrease in debt, implying a stock price fall. We say that managers signal information when they change leverage.

17.6 Shirking, Perquisites, and Bad Investments: A Note on Agency Cost of Equity

A previous section introduced the static trade-off model, where a rise in debt increases both the tax shield and the costs of distress. We now extend the trade-off model by considering an important agency cost of equity. A discussion of this cost of equity is contained in a well-known quote from Adam Smith:[14]

> The directors of such [joint-stock] companies, however, being the managers of other people's money than of their own, it cannot well be expected that they should watch over it with the same anxious vigilance with which the partners in a private copartnery frequently watch over their own. Like the stewards of a rich man, they are apt to consider attention to small matters as not for their master's honor, and very easily give themselves a dispensation from having it. Negligence and profusion, therefore, must always prevail, more or less, in the management of the affairs of such a company.

This elegant prose can be restated in modern vocabulary: An individual will work harder for a firm if she is one of its owners than if she is just an employee. In addition, the individual will work harder if she owns a large percentage of the company than if she owns a small percentage. This idea has an important implication for capital structure, which we illustrate with the following example.

EXAMPLE 17.2

Agency Costs Ms. Padmini is an owner-entrepreneur running a computer services firm worth ₹1 million. She currently owns 100 percent of the firm. Because of the need to expand, she must raise another ₹2 million. She can either issue ₹2 million of debt at 12 percent interest or issue ₹2 million in stock. The cash flows under the two alternatives are presented here:

	Debt Issue				Stock Issue			
Work Intensity	Cash Flow	Interest	Cash Flow to Equity	Cash Flow to Ms. Padmini (100% of equity)	Cash Flow	Interest	Cash Flow to Equity	Cash Flow to Ms. Padmini (33.33% of equity)
6-hour days	₹300,000	₹240,000	₹ 60,000	₹ 60,000	₹300,000	0	₹300,000	₹100,000
10-hour days	400,000	240,000	160,000	160,000	400,000	0	400,000	133,333

Like any entrepreneur, Ms. Padmini can choose the degree of intensity with which she works. In our example, she can work either a 6- or a 10-hour day. With the debt issue, the extra work brings her ₹100,000 (= ₹160,000 – 60,000) more income. However, let's assume that with a stock issue she retains only a one-third interest in the equity. Here, the extra work brings her merely ₹33,333 (= ₹133,333 - 100,000). Being human, she is likely to work harder if she issues debt. In other words, she has more incentive to *shirk* if she issues equity.

(continued)

[14]Adam Smith, 1776. *The Wealth of Nations,* 1776, Cannon edition (New York: Modern Library, 1937): 700, as quoted in Michael C. Jensen and William H. Meckling, "Theory of the Firm: Managerial Behavior, Agency Costs, and Ownership Structure," *Journal of Financial Economics* 3, no. 4 (October 1976): 305–60.

In addition, she is likely to obtain more *perquisites* (a big office, a company car, more expense account meals) if she issues stock. If she is a one-third stockholder, two-thirds of these costs are paid for by the other stockholders. If she is the sole owner, any additional perquisites reduce her equity stake alone.

Finally, she is more likely to take on capital budgeting projects with negative net present values. For example, she might be tempted to engage in *empire building,* by overpaying to acquire other firms or over-investing in internal projects. It might seem surprising that a manager with any equity interest at all would take on negative NPV projects because the stock price would clearly fall here. However, managerial salaries generally rise with firm size, providing managers with an incentive to accept some unprofitable projects after all the profitable ones have been taken on. That is, when an unprofitable project is accepted, the loss in stock value to a manager with only a small equity interest may be less than the increase in salary. In fact, it is our opinion that losses from accepting bad projects are far greater than losses from either shirking or excessive perquisites. Hugely unprofitable projects have bankrupted whole firms, something that even the largest expense account is unlikely to do.

As the firm issues more equity, our entrepreneur will likely increase leisure time, work-related perquisites, and unprofitable investments. These three items are called agency costs because managers of the firm are agents of the stockholders.[15]

This example is very applicable to a small company considering a large stock offering. Because a manager-owner will greatly dilute his or her share of the total equity in this case, a significant drop in work intensity or a significant increase in fringe benefits is possible. However, the example may be less applicable for a large corporation with many stockholders. Consider a large company such as Tata Motors issuing stock for the umpteenth time. The typical manager there already has such a small percentage stake in the firm that any temptation for negligence has probably been experienced before. An additional offering cannot be expected to increase this temptation.

In our example, who bears the burden of these agency costs: the current owner, that is, Ms. Padmini, or the new stockholders? The new stockholders do not bear these costs as long as they invest with their eyes open. Knowing that Ms. Padmini may work shorter hours, they will pay a lower price for the stock. Thus, it is the owner who is hurt by agency costs. However, Ms. Padmini can protect herself to some extent. As stockholders reduce bankruptcy costs through protective covenants, an owner may allow monitoring by new stockholders. Though proper reporting and surveillance may reduce the agency costs of equity, these techniques are unlikely to eliminate them.

It is commonly suggested that leveraged buyouts (LBOs) significantly reduce these costs of equity. In an LBO, a purchaser, usually a team of existing management, buys out the stockholders at a price above the current market. In other words, the company goes private: The stock is placed in the hands of only a few people. Because the managers now own a substantial chunk of the business, they are likely to work harder than when they were hired hands.[16]

[15]As previously discussed, *agency costs* are generally defined as the costs from the conflicts of interest among stockholders, bondholders, and managers.

[16]One professor we know introduces his classes to LBOs by asking the students three questions:

1. How many of you have ever owned a car?
2. How many of you have ever rented a car?
3. How many of you took better care of the car you owned than the car you rented?

As it is human nature to take better care of your own car, it is human nature to work harder when you own more of the company.

EFFECT OF AGENCY COSTS OF EQUITY ON DEBT-EQUITY FINANCING

The preceding discussion of the agency costs of equity should be viewed as an extension of the static trade-off model. That is, we stated in Section 17.4 that the change in the value of the firm when debt is substituted for equity is the difference between (1) the tax shield on debt and (2) the increase in the costs of financial distress (including the agency costs of debt). Now the change in the value of the firm is (1) the tax shield on debt plus (2) the reduction in the agency costs of equity minus (3) the increase in the costs of financial distress (including the agency costs of debt). The optimal debt-equity ratio would be higher in a world with agency costs of equity than in a world without these costs. However, because costs of financial distress are so significant, the costs of equity do not imply 100 percent debt financing.

FREE CASH FLOW

Any reader of murder mysteries knows that a criminal must have both motive and opportunity. The discussion thus far has been about motive. Managers with only a small ownership interest have an incentive for wasteful behavior because they bear only a small portion of the costs of, say, excessive expense accounts, and they reap all of the benefits.

Now let's talk about opportunity. A manager can pad his expense account only if the firm has the cash flow to cover it. We might expect to see more wasteful activity in a firm with a capacity to generate large cash flows than in one with a capacity to generate only small cash flows. This simple idea, which is formally called the *free cash flow hypothesis,* is backed by a fair amount of empirical research.[17] A frequently cited paper found that firms with high free cash flow are more likely to make bad acquisitions than firms with low free cash flow.[18]

The hypothesis has important implications for capital structure. Because dividends leave the firm, they reduce free cash flow. According to the free cash flow hypothesis, an increase in dividends should benefit the stockholders by reducing the ability of managers to pursue wasteful activities. Furthermore, because interest and principal also leave the firm, debt reduces free cash flow, as well. In fact, firms are legally obligated to pay interest and principal, implying that creditors can push the company into bankruptcy if these payments are withheld. By contrast, firms have no legal obligation to continue paying dividends. Thus, bond payments should have a greater effect than dividends on the free-spending ways of managers. Because of this, the free cash flow hypothesis argues that a shift from equity to debt will boost firm value.

In summary, the free cash flow hypothesis provides still another reason for firms to issue debt. We previously discussed the cost of equity; new equity dilutes the holdings of managers with equity interests, increasing their motive to waste corporate resources. We now state that debt reduces free cash flow because the firm must make interest and principal payments. The free cash flow hypothesis implies that debt reduces the opportunity for managers to waste resources.

17.7 The Pecking-Order Theory

Although the trade-off theory has dominated corporate finance circles for a long time, attention also is being paid to the *pecking-order theory.*[19] To understand this view of the world, let's put ourselves in the position of a corporate financial manager whose firm needs new capital. The manager faces a choice

[17]The seminal theoretical article is Michael C. Jensen, "Agency Costs of Free Cash Flow, Corporate Finance and Takeovers," *American Economic Review* 76, no. 2 (May 1986): 323–29.

[18]Larry Lang, René Stulz, and Ralph A. Walkling, "Managerial Performance, Tobin's Q and the Gains from Successful Tender Offers," *Journal of Financial Economics* 24, no. 1 (September 1989): 137–54.

[19]The pecking-order theory is generally attributed to Stewart C. Myers, "The Capital Structure Puzzle," *Journal of Finance* 39, no. 3 (July 1984): 574–92.

between issuing debt and issuing equity. Previously, we evaluated the choice in terms of tax benefits, distress costs, and agency costs. However, there is one consideration that we have so far neglected: timing.

Imagine the manager saying:

> I want to issue stock in one situation only—when it is overvalued. If the stock of my firm is selling at ₹50 per share, but I think that it is actually worth ₹60, I will not issue stock. I would actually be giving new stockholders a gift because they would receive stock worth ₹60 but would only have to pay ₹50 for it. More important, my current stockholders would be upset because the firm would be receiving ₹50 in cash but giving away something worth ₹60. So if I believe that my stock is undervalued, I would issue bonds. Bonds, particularly those with little or no risk of default, are likely to be priced correctly. Their value is determined primarily by the marketwide interest rate, which is publicly known.
>
> But suppose our stock is selling at ₹70. Now I'd like to issue stock. If I can get some fool to buy our stock for ₹70 while the stock is really worth only ₹60, I will be making ₹10 for our current shareholders.

Although this may strike you as a cynical view, it seems to square well with reality. Before the United States adopted insider trading and disclosure laws, many managers were alleged to have unfairly trumpeted their firm's prospects prior to equity issuance. And even today, managers seem more willing to issue equity after the price of their stock has risen versus when it has fallen. Timing might be an important motive in equity issuance, perhaps even more important than the motives in the trade-off model. After all, the firm in the preceding example immediately makes ₹10 by properly timing the issuance of equity. Ten rupees' worth of agency costs and bankruptcy cost reduction might take many years to realize.

The key that makes the example work is *asymmetric information*: The manager must know more about the firm's prospects than does the typical investor. If the manager's estimate of the true worth of the company is no better than the estimate of a typical investor, any attempts by the manager to time will fail. This assumption of asymmetry makes sense, as we expect managers to know more about their company than do outsiders because managers work at the company every day. (One caveat is that some managers are perpetually optimistic about their firm, blurring good judgment.)

But we are not done with this example yet; we must consider the investor. Imagine an investor saying:

> I make investments carefully because they involve my hard-earned money. However, even with all the time I put into studying stocks, I can't possibly know what the managers themselves know. After all, I've got a day job to be concerned with. So I watch what the managers do. If a firm issues stock, the firm was likely overvalued beforehand. If a firm issues debt, the firm was likely undervalued.

When we look at both issuers and investors, we see a kind of poker game, with each side trying to outwit the other. What should the issuing firm do in this poker game? Clearly, the firm should issue debt if the equity is undervalued. But what if the equity is overvalued? Here it gets tricky because a first thought is that the firm should issue equity. However, if a firm issues equity, investors will infer that the stock is overvalued. They will not buy it until the stock has fallen enough to eliminate any advantage from equity issuance. This mechanism is related to the signaling framework introduced in Section 17.5. Equity issuance sends a negative signal to investors that the manager believes the stock is overvalued. Smart investors will react to the signal by lowering their valuation of the stock.

In fact, it can be shown that only the most overvalued firms have any incentive to issue equity. Should even a moderately overpriced firm issue equity, investors will infer that this firm is among the most overpriced, causing the stock to fall more than is deserved. The end result is that virtually no one will issue equity.[20]

---

[20]For simplicity, we will not go into detail regarding the proof, but feel free to dig deeper by reading Stewart C. Myers, "The Capital Structure Puzzle," *Journal of Finance* 39, no. 3 (July 1984): 574–92.

The result that essentially all firms should issue debt is clearly an extreme one. It is as extreme as (1) the MM result that in a world without taxes, firms are indifferent to capital structure and (2) the MM result that in a world of corporate taxes but no financial distress costs, all firms should be 100 percent debt-financed. It may be true that finance folks take models to the extreme!

But as we can temper MM's conclusions by combining financial distress costs with corporate taxes, we can temper those of the pure pecking-order theory. This pure version assumes that timing is the financial manager's only consideration. In reality, a manager must consider taxes, financial distress costs, and agency costs, as well. Thus, a firm may issue debt only up to a point. If financial distress becomes a real possibility beyond that point, the firm may issue equity instead.

RULES OF THE PECKING ORDER

The previous discussion presented the basic ideas behind the pecking-order theory. What are the practical implications of the theory for financial managers? The theory provides the following two rules for the real world.

Rule #1: Use Internal Financing In our discussion, we have oversimplified by comparing equity to riskless debt. Managers cannot use special knowledge of their firm to determine if this type of debt is mispriced because the rate of interest is the same for all issuers of riskless debt. In reality, corporate debt has the possibility of default. Just as managers tend to issue equity when they think it is overvalued, managers also tend to issue debt when they think it is overvalued.

When would managers view their debt as overvalued? Probably in the same situations when they think their equity is overvalued. If the public thinks that the firm's prospects are rosy, but the managers see trouble ahead, these managers would view their debt–as well as their equity–as being overvalued. That is, the public might see the debt as nearly risk-free, whereas the managers see a strong possibility of default.

Investors are likely to price a debt issue with the same skepticism that they have when pricing an equity issue. The way managers get out of this box is to finance projects out of retained earnings. You don't have to worry about investor skepticism if you can avoid going to investors in the first place. So the first rule of the pecking order is this:

Use internal financing.

Rule #2: Issue Safe Securities First Although investors fear mispricing of both debt and equity, the fear is much greater for equity. Corporate debt still has relatively little risk compared to equity because if financial distress is avoided, investors receive a fixed return. The pecking-order theory implies that if outside financing is required, debt should be issued before equity. Only when the firm's debt capacity is reached should the firm consider equity.

Of course, there are many types of debt. Because convertible debt is more risky than straight debt, the pecking-order theory implies that managers should issue straight debt before issuing convertibles. So, the second rule of pecking-order theory is this:

Issue the safest securities first.

IMPLICATIONS

A number of implications associated with the pecking-order theory are at odds with those of the trade-off theory.

1. *There is no target amount of leverage.* According to the trade-off model, each firm balances the benefits of debt, such as the tax shield, with the costs of debt, such as distress costs. The optimal amount of leverage occurs where the marginal benefit of debt equals the marginal cost of debt.

By contrast, the pecking-order theory does not imply a target amount of leverage. Rather, each firm chooses its leverage ratio based on financing needs. Firms first fund projects out of retained earnings. This should lower the percentage of debt in the capital structure because profitable, internally funded projects raise both the book value and the market value of equity. Additional projects are funded with debt, clearly raising the debt level. However, at some point, the debt capacity of the firm becomes exhausted, giving way to equity issuance. Thus, the amount of leverage is determined by the existence of available projects. Firms do not pursue a target debt-equity ratio.

2. *Profitable firms use less debt.* Profitable firms generate cash internally, implying less need for outside financing. Because firms desiring outside capital turn to debt first, profitable firms end up relying on less debt. The trade-off model does not have this implication. Here the greater cash flow of more profitable firms creates greater debt capacity. These firms will use that debt capacity to capture the tax shield and the other benefits of leverage.
3. *Companies like financial slack.* The pecking-order theory is based on the difficulties of obtaining financing at a reasonable cost. A skeptical investing public thinks a stock is overvalued if the managers try to issue more of it, thereby leading to a stock price decline. Because this happens with bonds only to a lesser extent, managers rely first on bond financing. However, firms only can issue so much debt before encountering the potential costs of financial distress.

   Wouldn't it be easier to have the cash ahead of time? This is the idea behind financial slack. Because firms know that they will have to fund profitable projects at various times in the future, they accumulate cash today. They are then not forced to go to the capital markets when a project comes up. However, there is a limit to the amount of cash a firm will want to accumulate. As mentioned earlier in this chapter, too much free cash may tempt managers to pursue wasteful activities.

17.8 Personal Taxes

So far in this chapter, we have considered corporate taxes only. Because interest on debt is tax deductible whereas dividends on stock are not deductible, we argued that the tax code gives firms an incentive to issue debt. But corporations are not the only ones paying taxes; individuals must pay taxes on both the dividends and the interest that they receive. We cannot fully understand the effect of taxes on capital structure until all taxes, both corporate and personal, are considered.

THE BASICS OF PERSONAL TAXES

Let's begin by examining an all-equity firm that receives ₹1 of pretax earnings. If the corporate tax rate is T_C, the firm pays taxes of T_C, leaving itself with earnings after taxes of $1 - T_C$. Let's assume that this entire amount is distributed to the stockholders as dividends. If the personal tax rate on stock dividends is T_S, the stockholders pay taxes of $(1 - T_C) \times T_S$, leaving them with $(1 - T_C) \times (1 - T_S)$ after taxes.

Alternatively, imagine that the firm is financed with debt. Here, the entire ₹1 of earnings will be paid out as interest because interest is deductible at the corporate level. If the personal tax rate on interest is T_B, the bondholders pay taxes of T_B, leaving them with $1 - T_B$ after taxes.

THE EFFECT OF PERSONAL TAXES ON CAPITAL STRUCTURE

To explore the effect of personal taxes on capital structure, let's consider three questions:

1. Ignoring costs of financial distress, what is the firm's optimal capital structure if dividends and interest are taxed at the same personal rate–that is, $T_S = T_B$?

The firm should select the capital structure that gets the most cash into the hands of its investors. This is the same as selecting a capital structure that minimizes the total amount of taxes at both the corporate and personal levels.

As we have said, beginning with ₹1 of pretax corporate earnings, stockholders receive $(1 - T_C) \times (1 - T_S)$ and bondholders receive $1 - T_B$. We can see that if $T_S = T_B$, bondholders receive more than stockholders. The firm should issue debt, not equity, in this situation. Intuitively, income is taxed twice–once at the corporate level and once at the personal level–if it is paid to stockholders. Conversely, income is taxed only at the personal level if it is paid to bondholders.

Note that the assumption of no personal taxes, which we used in the previous chapter, is a special case of the assumption that both interest and dividends are taxed at the same rate. Without personal taxes, the stockholders receive $1 - T_C$ while the bondholders receive ₹1. As we stated in a previous chapter, firms should issue debt in a world without personal taxes.

2. Under what conditions will the firm be indifferent between issuing equity or debt?

   The firm will be indifferent if the cash flow to stockholders equals the cash flow to bondholders. That is, the firm is indifferent when:

$$(1 - T_C) \times (1 - T_S) = 1 - T_B \quad \textbf{(17.1)}$$

3. What should companies do in the real world?

   Although this is an important question, it is a hard one–perhaps too hard to answer definitively. Nevertheless, let's begin by working with the highest tax rates. As of 2018, the corporate tax rate was 21 percent. For investors in the highest marginal tax bracket, interest income was taxed at 37 percent. Investors in this highest bracket faced a 20 percent tax rate on dividends. For India, in FY2023, as per the Ministry of Finance, Government of India, these rates were - corporate tax rate of 25 percent, investors' interest income of 30 percent, and investors' dividend income of 30 percent.

   At these rates, the left side of Equation 17.1 becomes (1 − .21)(1 − .20), which equals .632, or 63.2 percent. The right side of the equation becomes (1 − .37), which equals .63, or 63 percent, so the difference is small once we consider personal taxes.

What we see is that the Tax Cuts and Jobs Act of 2017 has significantly reduced the tax advantage of debt once we consider personal taxes. Before 2018, the corporate tax rate was much higher, which created a much greater incentive to avoid taxes at the corporate level and pay them at the personal level. Thanks to the TCJA, the much lower corporate rate from 2018 forward has reduced, or even eliminated, that incentive.

Our conclusions here are based on the assumption that investors face the highest possible tax rates. In reality, tax-exempt institutions, such as pension funds and (most) university endowments, pay no personal taxes.[21] Individual investors who own stock or bonds in their retirement savings accounts also face no personal taxes during the accumulation period. More generally, we expect investors to tilt their portfolios toward tax-advantaged investments for which they face low tax rates. At the extreme, if we assume no personal taxes, so $T_S = T_B = 0$, then the left side of Equation 17.1 equals $1 - T_C$ and the right side equals 1. In other words, if investors face close-to-zero personal tax rates, then the only tax rate that matters is the corporate tax rate, and firms should issue debt.

[21]The Tax Cuts and Jobs Act created a tax that applies to the investment income of a small number of very large endowments held by private colleges and universities.

17.9 How Firms Establish Capital Structure

The theories of capital structure are among the most elegant and sophisticated in the field of finance. Financial economists should (and do!) pat themselves on the back for contributions in this area. However, the practical applications of the theories are scarce. Consider that our work on net present value produced an exact formula for evaluating projects. Prescriptions for capital structure under either the trade-off model or the pecking-order theory are vague by comparison. No exact formula is available for evaluating the optimal debt-equity ratio. Because of this, we turn to evidence from the real world.

The following empirical regularities are worth considering when formulating capital structure policy.

1. *Most nonfinancial corporations have low debt-asset ratios.* How much debt is used in the real world? Figure 17.4 shows the median debt-to-value ratio, defined as book value of debt to market value of the firm, in each of 39 different countries. This ratio ranges from slightly over 50 percent for Korea to slightly under 10 percent for Australia. The ratio for India is the seventh highest at about 36.5 percent. The ratio for U.S. companies is the fourth lowest.

   Should we view these ratios as being high or low? Because academics generally see corporate tax reduction as a chief motivation for debt, we might wonder if real-world companies issue enough debt to

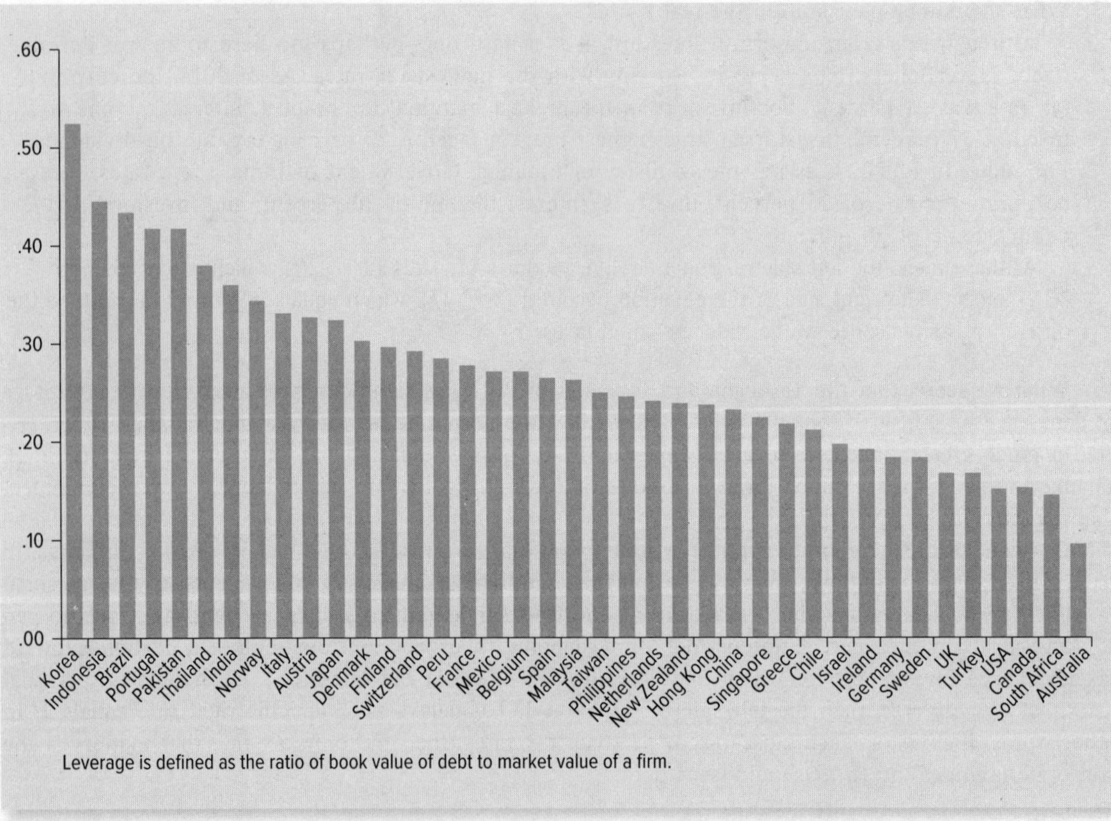

Figure 17.4 Median Leverage Ratio of Sample Firms in 39 Different Countries (1991–2006)

SOURCE: Joseph P. H. Fan, Sheridan Titman, and Garry Twite, "An International Comparison of Capital Structure and Debt Maturity Choices," *Journal of Financial and Quantitative Analysis* 47, no. 1 (February 2012): 23–56, Figure 1.

Table 17.3(a) Capital Structure Ratios for Selected U.S. Industries (medians)

Industry	Ratio of Debt to Total Capital*	Ratio of Debt to Equity	Number of Companies	SIC Code	Representative Companies
Electric utilities	45.9%	85.4%	13	491	American Electric Power, Southern Co.
Computer equipment	13.7	12.0	14	357	Apple, HP
Paper	45.7	84.2	14	26	Avery Dennison, International Paper
Petroleum refining	41.1	69.8	10	291	Chevron, ExxonMobil
Airlines	55.5	124.9	9	451	Delta, Southwest
Telephone communications	37.5	59.9	9	484	AT&T, T-Mobile
Motor vehicle equipment	34.7	53.2	23	371	Allison Transmission, Sorl Auto Parts
Fabric apparel	42.0	56.5	10	23	Hanes Brands, Under Armour
General merchandise stores	23.5	30.7	11	53	Costco, Rupee General
Eating places	51.9	107.9	22	5812	McDonald's, Papa John's
Drugs	10.5	11.7	49	283	Merck, Pfizer
Steel works	20.6	31.4	6	331	Insteel Industries, Steel Dynamics

*Debt is the book value of preferred stock and long-term debt, including amounts due in one year. Equity is the market value of outstanding shares. Total capital is the sum of debt and equity. Median values are shown.

greatly reduce, if not completely eliminate, corporate taxes. The empirical evidence suggests that this is not the case. For example, Federal corporate taxes in the United States for 2019 were more than ₹230 billion. It is clear that corporations do not issue debt up to the point where tax shelters are completely used up.[22] There are clearly limits to the amount of debt corporations can issue, perhaps because of the financial distress costs discussed earlier in this chapter.

2. *A number of firms use no debt.* In a fascinating study, Agrawal and Nagarajan examined approximately 100 firms on the New York Stock Exchange, none of which issued long-term debt.[23] They found that these firms are averse to leverage of any kind, including short-term debt. In addition, they have levels of cash and marketable securities well above their levered counterparts. Typically, the managers of these firms have high equity ownership. Furthermore, there is significantly greater family involvement in all-equity firms than in levered firms.

   Thus, a story emerges: Managers of all-equity firms are less diversified than the managers of similar, but levered, firms. Because of this, significant leverage represents an added risk that the managers of all-equity firms are loath to accept.

3. *There are differences in the capital structures of different industries.* There are significant interindustry differences in debt ratios that persist over time. As can be seen in Tables 17.3(a) and 17.3(b), debt ratios tend to be quite low in high-growth industries with ample future investment opportunities, such as the drug and electronics industries. This is true even when the need for external financing is great. Industries with large investments in tangible assets, such as building construction, tend to have high leverage.

[22] For further insight, see John R. Graham, "How Big Are the Tax Benefits of Debt?" *Journal of Finance* 55, no. 5 (October 2000): 1901–41.

[23] Anup Agrawal and Nandu J. Nagarajan, "Corporate Capital Structure, Agency Costs, and Ownership Control: The Case of All-Equity Firms," *Journal of Finance* 45, no. 4 (September 1990): 1325–31.

Table 17.3(b) Capital Structure Ratios for Selected Indian Nonfinancial Firms (Median) Three-year Average

Industry	Debt as a percentage of the Market Value of Equity and Debt
High Leverage	
Textiles & Apparel	77%
Food Processing	73%
Power Generation/Distribution	73%
Hotel, Resort & Restaurants	65%
Medium Leverage	
Footwear	49%
Telecommunication Equipment	38%
Metals - Castings/Forgings	35%
BPO/IT-enabled Services	35%
Low Leverage	
Information Tech. - Education	29%
Aquaculture	22%
Chemicals	16%
Online Services	1%

SOURCE: Authors' computations, period 2020–23.

We also observe sectors that have been seeing heavy competition, regulatory policy flip-flops and struggles such as textiles, real estate, and non-banking financial services in India have high debt ratios. Apart from the inability to repay past debt, the eroding value of equity (due to losses) leads to a rise in the debt as a percentage of the market value of equity and debt.

4. *Most corporations employ target debt-equity ratios.* Graham and Harvey asked 392 chief financial officers (CFOs) whether their firms use target debt-equity ratios, with the results presented in Figure 17.5.[24] As can be seen, the great majority of the firms use targets, though the strictness of the targets varies across companies. Only 19 percent of the firms avoid target ratios. Results elsewhere in the paper indicate that large firms are more likely than small firms to employ these targets. The CFOs did not specify what they meant by either flexible or strict targets. However, elsewhere in the study, the respondents indicated that, by and large, they did not rebalance in response to changes in their firm's stock price, suggesting flexibility in target ratios.

   How should companies establish target debt-equity ratios? While there is no mathematical formula for establishing a target ratio, we present three important factors affecting the ratio:

[24]John R. Graham and Campbell R. Harvey, "The Theory and Practice of Corporate Finance: Evidence from the Field," *Journal of Financial Economics* 60, no. 2-3 (May 2001): 187-243.

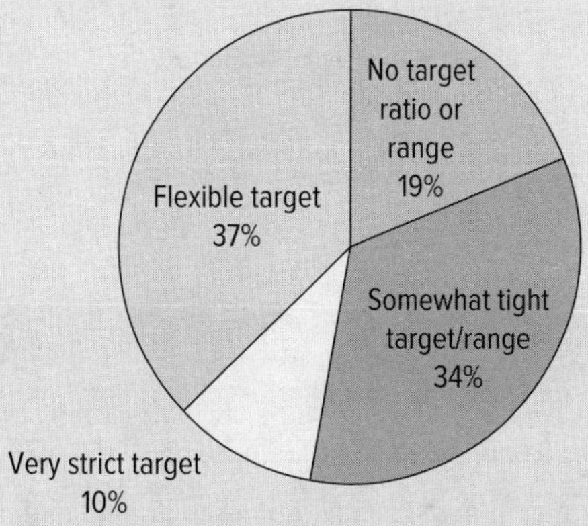

Survey responses of 392 CFOs concerning their use of target debt-equity ratios.

SOURCE: Figure 6 of John R. Graham and Campbell R. Harvey, "The Theory and Practice of Corporate Finance: Evidence from the Field," *Journal of Financial Economics* 60, no. 2–3 (May 2001): 187–243.

Figure 17.5 Survey Results on the Use of Target Debt-Equity Ratios

- *Taxes*: As we pointed out earlier, firms can deduct interest for tax purposes only to the extent allowed by the TCJA. Highly profitable firms are more likely to have larger target ratios than less profitable firms.[25]
- *Types of assets*: Financial distress is costly with or without formal bankruptcy proceedings. The costs of financial distress depend on the types of assets that the firm has. If a firm has a large investment in land, buildings, and other tangible assets, it will have smaller costs of financial distress than a firm with a large investment in research and development. Research and development typically has less resale value than land; most of its value disappears in financial distress. Therefore, firms with large investments in tangible assets are likely to have higher target debt-equity ratios than firms with large investments in research and development.
- *Uncertainty of operating income*: Firms with uncertain operating income have a high probability of experiencing financial distress, even without debt. These firms must finance mostly with equity. For example, pharmaceutical firms have uncertain operating income because no one can predict whether today's research will generate new, profitable drugs. Consequently, these firms issue little debt. By contrast, the operating income of firms in regulated industries, such as utilities, generally has low volatility. Relative to other industries, utilities use a great deal of debt.

5. *Capital structures of individual firms can vary significantly over time*. While Graham and Harvey report that most firms use target leverage ratios, another paper concludes that capital structures of individual firms often vary widely over time.[26] For example, consider Figure 17.6, which presents

[25]By contrast, the pecking-order theory argues that profitable firms will employ less debt because they can invest out of retained earnings. However, the pecking-order theory argues against the use of target ratios in the first place.

[26]Harry DeAngelo and Richard Roll, "How Stable Are Corporate Capital Structures?" *Journal of Finance* 70, no. 1 (February 2015): 373–418.

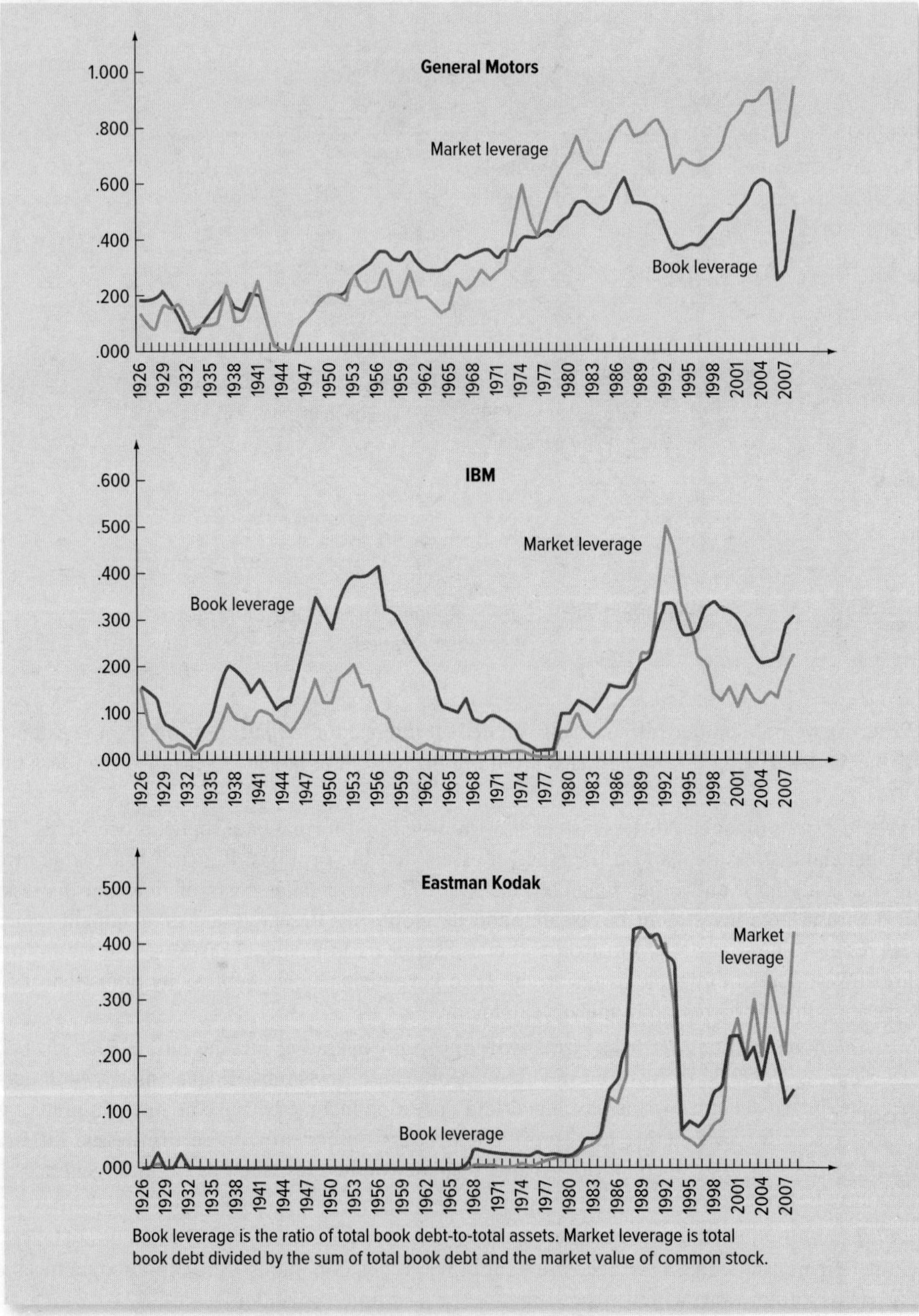

Figure 17.6 Leverage Ratios of General Motors, IBM, and Eastman Kodak over Time

SOURCE: Harry DeAngelo and Richard Roll, "How Stable Are Corporate Capital Structures?" *Journal of Finance* (February 2015).

leverage ratios for General Motors, IBM, and Eastman Kodak from 1926 to 2008. Both book leverage (total book value of debt divided by total assets) and market leverage (total book value of debt divided by total book debt plus market value of common stock) are shown. Regardless of the measure, all three companies display significant variations in leverage. Large variations in individual firm leverage over time are evidence that variations in individual firm investment opportunities and the need for financing are important determinants of capital structure, and such variations demonstrate the importance of financial slack (i.e., firms borrow money when they have projects worth spending it on).

One final note is in order. Because no formula supports them, the preceding points may seem too nebulous to assist financial decision making. In practice, many real-world firms base their capital structure decisions on industry averages and the need for a certain amount of financial slack. This may strike some as a cowardly approach, but it at least keeps firms from deviating far from accepted practice. After all, the existing firms in any industry are the survivors. Therefore, we should pay at least some attention to their decisions.

RESEARCH IN EMERGING MARKET CONTEXT

Chakrabarti and Chakrabarti (2019) studied Indian energy companies and found that firms' age, asset turnover ratio, liquidity, and size are significant determinants of capital structure. On the other hand, they found sales growth, non-debt tax shield, and tangibility ratio to be insignificant determinants.

Bajaj et al. (2020) compared Indian and Chinese firms and observed that Indian firms tend to revert to their target leverage ratios at a faster rate than Chinese firms. The inflation rate, bond market, and stock market development were significant factors impacting leverage in India, while bond market development significantly impacted leverage in China.

Jadiyappa et al. (2020) studied the impact of debt diversification on firm value. They found that such diversification practices decrease the value of firms due to less efficient monitoring by the creditors. They also revealed that the agency costs increase, particularly among business group-affiliated firms. Moreover, debt diversification creates a free rider problem among lenders that affects the agency costs of firms and their accounting performance.

References

Bajaj, Yukti, Smita Kashiramka, & Shveta Singh. "Capital structure dynamics: China and India (Chindia) perspective." *European Business Review* (2020).

Chakrabarti, Anindita, & Ahindra Chakrabarti. "The capital structure puzzle–evidence from Indian energy sector." *International Journal of Energy Sector Management* (2019).

Jadiyappa, Nemiraja, L. Emily Hickman, Pavana Jyothi, Narender Vunyale, & Bhanu Sireesha. "Does debt diversification impact firm value? Evidence from India." *International Review of Economics & Finance* 67 (2020): 362–377.

Summary and Conclusions

1. We mentioned in the last chapter that according to theory, firms should create all-debt capital structures under corporate taxation. Because firms generally employ moderate amounts of debt in the real world, the theory must have been missing something at that point. We stated in this chapter that costs of financial distress cause firms to restrain their issuance of debt. These costs are of two types: direct and indirect. Lawyers' and accountants' fees during the bankruptcy process are examples of direct costs. We mentioned four examples of indirect costs:

   Impaired ability to conduct business.
   Incentive to take on risky projects.
   Incentive toward underinvestment.
   Distribution of funds to stockholders prior to bankruptcy.
2. Because financial distress costs are substantial and the stockholders ultimately bear them, firms have an incentive to reduce costs. Protective covenants and debt consolidation are two common cost reduction techniques.
3. Because costs of financial distress can be reduced but not eliminated, firms will not finance entirely with debt. Figure 17.1 illustrates the relationship between firm value and debt. In the figure, firms select the debt-equity ratio at which firm value is maximized.
4. Signaling theory argues that profitable firms are likely to increase their leverage because the extra interest payments will offset some of the pretax profits. Rational stockholders will infer higher firm value from a higher debt level. Thus, investors view debt as a signal of firm value.
5. Managers owning a small proportion of a firm's equity can be expected to work less, maintain more lavish expense accounts, and accept more pet projects with negative NPVs than managers owning a large proportion of equity. Because new issues of equity dilute a manager's percentage interest in the firm, such agency costs are likely to increase when a firm's growth is financed through new equity rather than through new debt.
6. The pecking-order theory implies that managers prefer internal to external financing. If external financing is required, managers tend to choose the safest securities, such as debt. Firms may accumulate financial slack to avoid external equity.
7. The results so far have ignored personal taxes. If distributions to equityholders are taxed at a lower effective personal tax rate than are interest payments, the tax advantage to debt at the corporate level is partially offset.
8. Debt-equity ratios vary across industries. We present three factors determining the target debt-equity ratio:
   a. *Taxes*: Firms with high taxable income should rely more on debt than firms with low taxable income.
   b. *Types of assets*: Firms with a high percentage of intangible assets such as research and development should have low debt. Firms with primarily tangible assets should have higher debt.
   c. *Uncertainty of operating income*: Firms with high uncertainty of operating income should rely mostly on equity.

Concept Questions

1. **Bankruptcy Costs** What are the direct and indirect costs of bankruptcy? Briefly explain each.
2. **Stockholder Incentives** Do you agree or disagree with the following statement? A firm's stockholders will never want the firm to invest in projects with negative net present values. Why?
3. **Capital Structure Decisions** Due to large losses incurred in the past several years, a firm has ₹2 billion in tax loss carryforwards. This means that the next ₹2 billion of the firm's income will be free from

corporate income taxes. Security analysts estimate that it will take many years for the firm to generate ₹2 billion in earnings. The firm has a moderate amount of debt in its capital structure. The firm's CEO is deciding whether to issue debt or equity to raise the funds needed to finance an upcoming project. Which method of financing would you recommend? Why?

4. **Cost of Debt** What steps can stockholders take to reduce the costs of debt?

5. **MM and Bankruptcy Costs** How does the existence of financial distress costs and agency costs affect Modigliani and Miller's theory in a world where corporations pay taxes?

6. **Optimal Capital Structure** Is there an easily identifiable debt-equity ratio that will maximize the value of a firm? Why or why not?

7. **Observed Capital Structures** Refer to the observed capital structures given in Table 17.3 of the text. What do you notice about the types of industries with respect to their average debt-equity ratios? Are certain types of industries more likely to be highly leveraged than others? What are some possible reasons for this observed segmentation? Do the operating results and tax history of the firms play a role? How about their future earnings prospects? Explain.

8. **Bankruptcy and Corporate Ethics** As mentioned in the text, some firms have filed for bankruptcy because of actual or likely litigation-related losses. Is this a proper use of the bankruptcy process?

9. **Bankruptcy and Corporate Ethics** Firms sometimes use the threat of a bankruptcy filing to force creditors to renegotiate terms. Critics argue that, in such cases, the firm is using bankruptcy laws "as a sword rather than a shield." Is this an ethical tactic?

10. **Bankruptcy and Corporate Ethics** Continental Airlines once filed for bankruptcy, at least in part, as a means of reducing labor costs. Whether this move was ethical or proper was hotly debated. Give both sides of the argument.

Questions and Problems

BASIC (Questions 1–4)

1. **Firm Value** Maddux Corp. has EBIT of ₹725,000 per year that is expected to continue in perpetuity. The unlevered cost of equity for the company is 11 percent and the corporate tax rate is 24 percent. The company also has a perpetual bond issue outstanding with a market value of ₹1.6 million.
   a. What is the value of the company?
   b. The CFO of the company informs the company president that the value of the company is ₹4.9 million. Is the CFO correct?

2. **Agency Costs** Tom Scott is the owner, president, and primary salesperson for Scott Manufacturing. Because of this, the company's profits are driven by the amount of work Tom does. If he works 40 hours each week, the company's EBIT will be ₹455,000 per year; if he works a 50-hour week, the company's EBIT will be ₹560,000 per year. The company is currently worth ₹2.9 million. The company needs a cash infusion of ₹1.2 million and can issue equity or issue debt with an interest rate of 8 percent. Assume there are no corporate taxes.
   a. What are the cash flows to Tom under each scenario?
   b. Under which form of financing is Tom likely to work harder?
   c. What specific new costs will occur with each form of financing?

3. **Nonmarketed Claims** King, Inc., has debt outstanding with a face value of ₹4.3 million. The value of the firm if it were entirely financed by equity would be ₹17.9 million. The company also has 320,000 shares of stock outstanding that sell at a price of ₹44 per share. The corporate tax rate is 21 percent. What is the decrease in the value of the company due to expected bankruptcy costs?

4. **Capital Structure and Nonmarketed Claims** Suppose the president of the company in the previous problem stated that the company should increase the amount of debt in its capital structure because of the tax-advantaged status of its interest payments. His argument is that this action would increase the value of the company. How would you respond?

INTERMEDIATE (Questions 5–8)

5. **Capital Structure and Growth** Edwards Construction currently has debt outstanding with a market value of ₹87,000 and a cost of 11 percent. The company has EBIT of ₹9,570 that is expected to continue in perpetuity. Assume there are no taxes.

   a. What is the value of the company's equity? What is the debt-to-value ratio?
   b. What are the equity value and debt-to-value ratio if the company's growth rate is 3 percent?
   c. What are the equity value and debt-to-value ratio if the company's growth rate is 7 percent?

6. **Costs of Financial Distress** Steinberg Corporation and Dietrich Corporation are identical firms except that Dietrich is more levered. Both companies will remain in business for one more year. The companies' economists agree that the probability of the continuation of the current expansion is 80 percent for the next year and the probability of a recession is 20 percent. If the expansion continues, each firm will generate earnings before interest and taxes (EBIT) of ₹2.9 million. If a recession occurs, each firm will generate earnings before interest and taxes (EBIT) of ₹1.3 million. Steinberg's debt obligation requires the firm to pay ₹925,000 at the end of the year. Dietrich's debt obligation requires the firm to pay ₹1.35 million at the end of the year. Neither firm pays taxes. Assume a discount rate of 13 percent.

   a. What is the value today of Steinberg's debt and equity? What about that for Dietrich's debt and equity?
   b. Steinberg's CEO recently stated that Steinberg's value should be higher than Dietrich's because the firm has less debt and therefore less bankruptcy risk. Do you agree or disagree with this statement?

7. **Agency Costs** Fountain Corporation's economists estimate that a good business environment and a bad business environment are equally likely for the coming year. The managers of the company must choose between two mutually exclusive projects. Assume that the project the company chooses will be the firm's only activity and that the firm will close one year from today. The company is obligated to make a ₹4,200 payment to bondholders at the end of the year. The projects have the same systematic risk but different volatilities. Consider the following information pertaining to the two projects:

Economy	Probability	Low-Volatility Project Payoff	High-Volatility Project Payoff
Bad	.50	₹4,200	₹3,400
Good	.50	4,600	4,900

   a. What is the expected value of the company if the low-volatility project is undertaken? What if the high-volatility project is undertaken? Which of the two strategies maximizes the expected value of the firm?
   b. What is the expected value of the company's equity if the low-volatility project is undertaken? What is it if the high-volatility project is undertaken?
   c. Which project would the company's stockholders prefer? Explain.
   d. Suppose bondholders are fully aware that stockholders might choose to maximize equity value rather than total firm value and opt for the high-volatility project. To minimize this agency cost, the firm's bondholders decide to use a bond covenant to stipulate that the bondholders can demand a higher payment if the company chooses to take on the high-volatility project. What payment to bondholders would make stockholders indifferent between the two projects?

8. **Financial Distress** Good Time Company is a regional chain department store. It will remain in business for one more year. The probability of a boom year is 60 percent and the probability of a recession is 40 percent. It is projected that the company will generate a total cash flow of ₹112 million in a boom year and ₹43 million in a recession. The company's required debt payment at the end of the year is ₹65 million. The market value of the company's outstanding debt is ₹49 million. The company pays no taxes.

   a. What payoff do bondholders expect to receive in the event of a recession?
   b. What is the promised return on the company's debt?
   c. What is the expected return on the company's debt?

CHALLENGE (Questions 9–10)

9. **Personal Taxes, Bankruptcy Costs, and Firm Value** When personal taxes on interest income and bankruptcy costs are considered, the general expression for the value of a levered firm in a world in which the tax rate on equity distributions equals zero is:

$$V_L = V_U + \{1 - [(1 - T_C)/(1 - T_B)]\} \times B - C(B)$$

where:

V_L = Value of a levered firm
V_U = Value of an unlevered firm
B = Value of the firm's debt
T_C = Tax rate on corporate income
T_B = Personal tax rate on interest income
$C(B)$ = Present value of the costs of financial distress

   a. In their no-tax model, what do Modigliani and Miller assume about T_C, T_B, and $C(B)$? What do these assumptions imply about a firm's optimal debt-equity ratio?
   b. In their model with corporate taxes, what do Modigliani and Miller assume about T_C, T_B, and $C(B)$? What do these assumptions imply about a firm's optimal debt-equity ratio?
   c. Consider an all-equity firm that is certain to be able to use interest deductions to reduce its corporate tax bill. If the corporate tax rate is 25 percent, the personal tax rate on interest income is 20 percent, and there are no costs of financial distress, by how much will the value of the firm change if it issues ₹1 million in debt and uses the proceeds to repurchase equity?
   d. Consider another all-equity firm that does not pay taxes due to large tax loss carryforwards from previous years. The personal tax rate on interest income is 20 percent and there are no costs of financial distress. What would be the change in the value of this firm from adding ₹1 of perpetual debt rather than ₹1 of equity?

10. **Personal Taxes, Bankruptcy Costs, and Firm Value** Overnight Publishing Company (OPC) has ₹2.5 million in excess cash. The firm plans to use this cash either to retire all of its outstanding debt or to repurchase equity. The firm's debt is held by one institution that is willing to sell it back to OPC for ₹2.5 million. The institution will not charge OPC any transaction costs. Once OPC becomes an all-equity firm, it will remain unlevered forever. If OPC does not retire the debt, the company will use the ₹2.5 million in cash to buy back some of its stock on the open market. Repurchasing stock also has no transaction costs. The company will generate ₹1.3 million of annual earnings before interest and taxes in perpetuity regardless of its capital structure. The firm immediately pays out all earnings as dividends at the end of each year. OPC is subject to a corporate tax rate of 21 percent and the required rate of return on the firm's unlevered equity is 20 percent. The personal tax rate on interest income is 25 percent and there are no taxes on equity distributions. Assume there are no bankruptcy costs.

   a. What is the value of OPC if it chooses to retire all of its debt and become an unlevered firm?
   b. What is the value of OPC if it decides to repurchase stock instead of retiring its debt? (*Hint*: Use the equation for the value of a levered firm with personal tax on interest income from the previous problem.)
   c. Assume that expected bankruptcy costs have a present value of ₹400,000. How does this influence OPC's decision?

Mini Case — McKENZIE CORPORATION'S CAPITAL BUDGETING

Sam McKenzie is the founder and CEO of McKenzie Restaurants, Inc., a regional company. Sam is considering opening several new restaurants. Sally Thornton, the company's CFO, has been put in charge of the capital budgeting analysis. She has examined the potential for the company's expansion and determined that the success of the new restaurants will depend critically on the state of the economy over the next few years.

McKenzie currently has a bond issue outstanding with a face value of ₹26 million that is due in one year. Covenants associated with this bond issue prohibit the issuance of any additional debt. This restriction means that the expansion will be entirely financed with equity at a cost of ₹5.4 million. Sally has summarized her analysis in the following table, which shows the value of the company in each state of the economy next year, both with and without expansion:

Economic Growth	Probability	Without Expansion	With Expansion
Low	.30	₹22,000,000	₹29,000,000
Normal	.50	31,000,000	37,000,000
High	.20	48,000,000	54,000,000

1. What is the expected value of the company in one year, with and without expansion? Would the company's stockholders be better off with or without expansion? Why?
2. What is the expected value of the company's debt in one year, with and without the expansion?
3. One year from now, how much value creation is expected from the expansion? How much value is expected for stockholders? Bondholders?
4. If the company announces that it is not expanding, what do you think will happen to the price of its bonds? What will happen to the price of the bonds if the company does expand?
5. If the company opts not to expand, what are the implications for the company's future borrowing needs? What are the implications if the company does expand?
6. Because of the bond covenant, the expansion would have to be financed with equity. How would it affect your answer if the expansion were financed with cash on hand instead of new equity?

Appendix 17A Some Useful Formulas of Financial Structure

Appendix 17B The Miller Model and the Graduated Income Tax

To access the appendices for this chapter, please log on to www.mheducation.co.in.

18

Valuation and Capital Budgeting for the Levered Firm

In 2020, Tesla's yet-to-be-built Cybertruck factory was being sought by Austin, Texas, as well as Tulsa, Oklahoma. In an effort to land the plant, commissioners in Travis County, Texas, home of Austin, offered Tesla tax incentives of ₹14.7 million or more over the next 10 years. This was on top of the ₹46.6 million previously offered by the local school district. Incentives to build a plant were not new to Tesla: The company received about ₹1.4 billion in incentives to build its battery plant in Nevada in 2014.

When a corporation opens a major plant or considers relocation, municipalities often create packages loaded with subsidies such as these. Other common enticements include subsidized debt, educational training, and road and infrastructure creation.

Subsidies in India can take various forms. Smartphone contract manufacturers for Apple, Samsung, and other makers use the production-linked incentives (PLI) where firms receive cashback on the incremental sale of goods. States like Uttarakhand and Himachal Pradesh encourage firms to set up industrial units in their states by providing subsidies on investments made in plant and machinery.

With subsidized debt, a state or municipality guarantees the debt, which allows the company to borrow at a much lower interest rate. If the interest rate on the debt is lower than the company's normal cost of debt, how does the firm evaluate the financial benefits of this and other such subsidies? In this chapter, we illustrate how to evaluate projects using the adjusted present value and flow to equity approaches to valuation to answer this and related questions.

Please visit us at **rwjcorporatefinance.blogspot.com** for the latest developments in the world of corporate finance.

18.1 Adjusted Present Value Approach

In this chapter, we describe three approaches to valuation for the levered firm. In particular, we describe the adjusted present value (APV) approach, the flow to equity (FTE) approach, and the weighted average cost of capital (WACC) approach. The analysis of these approaches is relevant for entire firms as well as individual projects. As you may recognize, we have discussed the WACC approach in depth in a previous chapter. In this chapter, we will introduce the APV and FTE approaches, and show that each of the three approaches is logically consistent with the others and will give the same answer. However, at times, one approach might be easier to implement than another, and we suggest guidelines for selecting between the approaches. We start with the adjusted present value method.

The **adjusted present value (APV)** method is best described by the following formula:

$$\text{APV} = \text{NPV} + \text{NPVF}$$

In words, the value of a project to a levered firm (APV) is equal to the value of the project to an unlevered firm (NPV) plus the net present value of the financing side effects (NPVF). We can generally think of four side effects:

1. *The tax subsidy to debt*: This was discussed in Chapter 16, where we pointed out that for perpetual debt, the value of the tax subsidy is $T_C B$. (T_C is the corporate tax rate and B is the value of the debt.) The material about valuation under corporate taxes in Chapter 16 is actually an application of the APV approach.
2. *The costs of issuing new securities*: As we will discuss in detail in Chapter 20, investment bankers participate in the public issuance of corporate debt. These bankers must be compensated for their time and effort, a cost that lowers the value of the project.
3. *The costs of financial distress*: The possibility of financial distress, and bankruptcy in particular, arises with debt financing. As we discussed in a previous chapter, financial distress imposes costs, thereby lowering value.
4. *Subsidies to debt financing*: The interest on debt issued by state and local governments is not taxable to the investor. Because of this, the yield on tax-exempt debt is generally substantially below the yield on taxable debt. Frequently, corporations can obtain financing from a municipality at the tax-exempt rate because the municipality can borrow at that rate. As with any subsidy, this subsidy adds value.

Although each of the preceding four side effects is important, the tax deduction to debt almost certainly has the highest Rupee value in most actual situations. For this reason, the following example considers the tax subsidy but not the other three side effects.[1]

Consider a project of the R. R. Panda Co. with the following characteristics:

Cash inflows: ₹500,000 per year for the indefinite future.
Cash costs: ₹383,038 per year for the indefinite future.
Initial investment: ₹475,000
$T_C = 21\%$
$R_0 = 20\%$, where R_0 is the cost of capital for an all-equity-financed project.

If both the project and the firm are financed with only equity, the project's cash flow is as follows:

Cash inflows	₹500,000
Cash costs	383,038
Operating income	₹116,962
Corporate tax (21%)	24,562
Unlevered cash flow (UCF)	₹ 92,400

The distinction between present value and net present value is important for this example. The present value of a project is determined before the initial investment at Year 0 is subtracted. The initial investment is subtracted for the calculation of net present value.

We then need R_0, the cost of capital for an all-equity-financed project. Assuming an appropriate discount rate of 20 percent, the present value of the project is:

$$\frac{₹92{,}400}{.20} = ₹462{,}000$$

[1]The Brindavan Enterprises example in Section 18.6 handles both flotation costs and interest subsidies.

The net present value (NPV) of the project–that is, the value of the project if it were financed with only equity–is:

$$₹462,000 - 475,000 = -₹13,000$$

Because the NPV is negative, the project would be rejected by a firm that plans to finance with only equity.

Now imagine that the firm finances the project with exactly ₹121,900 in debt in perpetuity, so that the remaining investment of ₹353,100 (= ₹475,000 − 121,900) is financed with equity. The net present value of the project under leverage, which we call the adjusted present value, or the APV, is:

$$\text{APV} = \text{NPV} + T_C \times B$$
$$₹12,599 = -₹13,000 + .21 \times ₹121,900$$

That is, the value of the project when financed with leverage is equal to the value of the project when financed with all equity plus the tax shield from the debt. Because this number is positive, the project should be accepted.[2]

You may be wondering why we chose such a precise amount of debt. Actually, we chose it so that the ratio of debt to the present value of the project under leverage is 25 percent.[3]

In this example, debt is a fixed proportion of the present value of the project, not a fixed proportion of the initial investment of ₹475,000. This is consistent with the goal of a target debt-market-value ratio, which we find in the real world. For example, commercial banks typically lend to real estate developers a fixed percentage of the appraised market value of a project, not a fixed percentage of the initial investment.

18.2 Flow to Equity Approach

The **flow to equity (FTE)** approach is an alternative valuation approach. The formula calls for discounting the cash flow from the project to the equityholders of the levered firm at the cost of equity capital, R_S. For a perpetuity, this becomes:

$$\frac{\text{Cash flow from project to equityholders of the levered firm}}{R_S}$$

There are three steps to the FTE approach.

STEP 1: CALCULATING LEVERED CASH FLOW (LCF)[4]

Assuming an interest rate of 10 percent, the perpetual cash flow to equityholders in our R. R. Panda Co. example is:

[2]This example is meant to dramatize the potential importance of the tax benefits of debt. In practice, the firm will likely find the value of a project to an all-equity-financed firm to have a positive NPV.

[3]That is, the present value of the project after the initial investment has been made is ₹12,599 + 475,000 = ₹487,599. The debt-to-value ratio of the project is ₹121,900/₹487,599 = .25.

This level of debt can be calculated directly. Note that:

$$\text{Present value of levered project} = \text{Present value of unlevered project} + T_C \times B$$
$$V_{\text{With debt}} = ₹487,599 \qquad + .21 \times .25 \times V_{\text{With debt}}$$

Rearranging the last line, we have:

$$V_{\text{With debt}} \times (1 - .21 \times .25) = ₹462,000$$
$$V_{\text{With debt}} = ₹487,599$$

Debt is .25 of value: ₹121,900 = .25 × ₹487,599.

[4]We use the term levered cash flow (LCF) for simplicity. A more complete term would be distributable cash flow (a.k.a., free cash flow) from the project to the equityholders of a levered firm. Similarly, a more complete term for unlevered cash flow (UCF) would be distributable cash flow (a.k.a., free cash flow) from the project to the equityholders of an unlevered firm.

Cash inflows	₹500,000
Cash costs	383,038
Interest (.10 × ₹121,900)	12,190
Income after interest	₹104,772
Corporate tax (21%)	22,002
Levered cash flow (LCF)	₹ 82,770

Alternatively, we can calculate levered cash flow (LCF) directly from unlevered cash flow (UCF). The key here is that the difference between the cash flow that equityholders receive in an unlevered firm and the cash flow that equityholders receive in a levered firm is the aftertax interest payment. (Repayment of principal does not appear in this example because the debt is perpetual.) We write this algebraically as:

$$\text{UCF} - \text{LCF} = (1 - T_C)R_B B$$

The term on the right side of this expression is the aftertax interest payment. Because cash flow to the unlevered equityholders (UCF) is ₹92,400 and the aftertax interest payment is ₹9,630 (= .79 × .10 × ₹121,900), cash flow to the levered equityholders (LCF) is:

$$₹92{,}400 - 9{,}630 = ₹82{,}770$$

which is exactly the number we calculated earlier.

STEP 2: CALCULATING R_S

The next step is to calculate the discount rate, R_S. Note that we assumed that the discount rate on unlevered equity, R_0, is 20 percent. As we saw in an earlier chapter, the formula for R_S is:

$$R_S = R_0 + \frac{B}{S}(1 - T_C)(R_0 - R_B)$$

Note that our target debt-value ratio of 25 percent implies a target debt-equity ratio of 1/3. Applying the preceding formula to this example, we have:

$$R_S = .20 + \frac{1}{3}(.79)(.20 - .10) = .2263, \text{ or } 22.63\%$$

STEP 3: VALUATION

The present value of the project's LCF is:

$$\frac{\text{LCF}}{R_S} = \frac{₹82{,}770}{.2263} = ₹365{,}699$$

Because the initial investment is ₹475,000 and ₹121,900 is borrowed, the firm must advance the project ₹353,100 (= ₹475,000 − 121,900) out of its own cash reserves. The net present value of the project is the difference between the present value of the project's LCF and the investment not borrowed. The NPV is:

$$₹365{,}699 - 353{,}100 = ₹12{,}599$$

which is identical to the result found with the APV approach.

18.3 Weighted Average Cost of Capital Method

Finally, we can value a project or a firm using the **weighted average cost of capital (WACC)** method. Although this method was discussed in earlier chapters, it is worthwhile to review it here. The WACC approach begins with the insight that projects of levered firms are simultaneously financed with both debt and equity. The cost of capital is a weighted average of the cost of debt and the cost of equity. The cost of equity is R_S. Ignoring taxes, the cost of debt is the borrowing rate, R_B. However, with corporate taxes, the appropriate cost of debt is $(1 - T_C)R_B$, the aftertax cost of debt.

The formula for determining the weighted average cost of capital, WACC, is:

$$\text{WACC} = R_S \frac{S}{S+B} + R_B(1 - T_C)\frac{B}{S+B}$$

The weight for equity, $S/(S + B)$, and the weight for debt, $B/(S + B)$, are target ratios. Target ratios are generally expressed in terms of market values, not accounting, or book, values.

The formula calls for discounting the *unlevered* cash flow of the project (UCF) at the weighted average cost of capital. The net present value of the project can be written algebraically as:

$$\sum_{t=1}^{\infty} \frac{\text{UCF}_t}{(1 + \text{WACC})^t} - \text{Initial investment}$$

If the project is a perpetuity, the net present value is:

$$\frac{\text{UCF}}{\text{WACC}} - \text{Initial investment}$$

We previously stated that the target debt-value ratio of our project is 25 percent and the corporate tax rate is 21 percent, implying that the weighted average cost of capital is:

$$\text{WACC} = .75 \times .2263 + .25 \times .10 \times .79 = .1895, \text{ or } 18.95\%$$

Note that WACC, 18.95 percent, is lower than the cost of equity capital for an all-equity firm of 20 percent. This must always be the case because debt financing provides a tax subsidy that lowers the average cost of capital.

We previously determined the UCF of the project to be ₹92,400, implying that the present value of the project is:

$$\frac{₹92{,}400}{.1895} = ₹487{,}599$$

The initial investment is ₹475,000, so the NPV of the project is:

$$₹487{,}599 - 475{,}000 = ₹12{,}599$$

Note that all three approaches yield the same project valuation.

18.4 A Comparison of the APV, FTE, and WACC Approaches

In this chapter, we provide three approaches to valuation for projects of a levered firm. The adjusted present value (APV) approach first values the project on an all-equity basis. The project's aftertax cash flows under all-equity financing (called unlevered cash flows, or UCF) are placed in the numerator of the capital budgeting equation. The discount rate, assuming all-equity financing, appears in the denominator. At this point, the calculation is identical to that performed in the early chapters of this book. We then add the net present value of the debt. We point out that the net present value of the debt is likely to be the sum of four parameters: tax effects, flotation costs, bankruptcy costs, and interest subsidies.

The flow to equity (FTE) approach discounts the aftertax cash flow from a project going to the equityholders of a levered firm (LCF). LCF, which we've noted stands for levered cash flow, is the residual to equityholders after interest has been deducted. The discount rate is R_S, the cost of capital to the equityholders of a levered firm. For a firm with leverage, R_S must be greater than R_0, the cost of capital for an unlevered firm. This follows from our material in Chapter 16 showing that leverage raises the risk to the equityholders.

The last approach is the weighted average cost of capital method. This technique calculates the project's aftertax cash flows assuming all-equity financing (UCF). The UCF is placed in the numerator of the capital budgeting equation. The denominator, WACC, is a weighted average of the cost of equity capital and the cost of debt capital. The tax advantage of debt is reflected in the denominator because the cost of debt capital is determined net of corporate tax. The numerator does not reflect debt at all.

All three approaches perform the same task: valuation in the presence of debt financing. As illustrated in the previous sections, all three provide the same valuation estimate. However, as we saw before, the approaches are markedly different in technique. Because of this, students often ask questions of the following sort: "How can this be? How can the three approaches look so different and yet give the same answer?" We believe that the best way to handle questions like these is through the following two points:

1. *APV versus WACC*: Of the three approaches, APV and WACC display the greatest similarity. After all, both approaches put the unlevered cash flow (UCF) in the numerator. However, the APV approach discounts these flows at R_0, yielding the value of the unlevered project. Adding the present value of the tax shield gives the value of the project under leverage. The WACC approach discounts UCF at the WACC, which is lower than R_0.

   Both approaches adjust the basic NPV formula for unlevered firms to reflect the tax benefit of leverage. The APV approach makes this adjustment directly. It adds in the present value of the tax shield as a separate term. The WACC approach makes the adjustment in a more subtle way. Here, the discount rate is lowered below R_0. These two adjustments always have the same quantitative effect.
2. *Entity being valued*: The FTE approach appears at first glance to be far different from the other two. For both the APV and the WACC approaches, the initial investment is subtracted out in the final step (₹475,000 in our example). However, for the FTE approach, only the firm's contribution to the initial investment (₹353,100 = ₹475,000 − 121,900) is subtracted out. This occurs because, under the FTE approach, only the future cash flows to the levered equityholders (LCF) are valued. By contrast, future cash flows to the unlevered equityholders (UCF) are valued in both the APV and WACC approaches. Because LCFs are net of interest payments, whereas UCFs are not, the initial investment under the FTE approach is correspondingly reduced by debt financing. In this way, the FTE approach produces the same answer that the other two approaches do.

A SUGGESTED GUIDELINE

The net present value of our project is exactly the same under each of the three methods. In theory, this should always be the case.[5] However, one method is usually easier to calculate than than the others, and, in some cases, one or more of the methods are virtually impossible to calculate. We first consider when it is best to use the WACC and FTE approaches.

[5]Isik Inselbag and Howard Kaufold, "Two DCF Approaches for Valuing Companies under Alternative Financial Strategies (and How to Choose between Them)," *Journal of Applied Corporate Finance* 10, no. 1 (Spring 1997): 144–22.

If the risk of a project stays constant throughout its life, it is plausible to assume that R_0 remains constant throughout the project's life. This assumption of constant risk appears to be reasonable for most real-world projects. In addition, if the debt-value ratio remains constant over the life of the project, both R_S and WACC will remain constant. Under this latter assumption, either the FTE or the WACC approach is easy to apply. However, if the debt-value ratio varies from year to year, both R_S and WACC vary from year to year, as well. Using the FTE or the WACC approach when the denominator changes every year is computationally quite complex, and when computations become complex, the error rate rises. Both the FTE and WACC approaches present difficulties when the debt-value ratio changes over time.

In our R. R. Panda Co. valuation example, we considered a project that generates constant cash flows in perpetuity, so maintaining a constant level of debt is equivalent to maintaining a constant debt-equity ratio. That allowed us to apply a constant R_S and WACC over the life of the project. In general, it is easier to use the APV approach if the firm plans to maintain a certain level of debt in each future period because such a debt policy implies that the debt-equity ratio will not remain constant, so we would need to calculate a new R_S and WACC to discount each year's cash flows.

The APV approach is based on the level of debt in each future period. Consequently, when the debt level can be specified precisely for future periods, the APV approach is easy to use. However, when the debt level is uncertain, the APV approach becomes more problematic. When the debt-value ratio is constant, the debt level varies with the value of the project. Because the value of the project in a future year cannot be easily forecast, the level of debt cannot be easily forecast either.

We suggest the following guideline:

Use WACC or FTE if the firm's target debt-value ratio applies to the project over its life. Use APV if the project's level of debt is known over the life of the project.

There are a number of situations where the APV approach is preferred. In a leveraged buyout (LBO) the firm begins with a large amount of debt but rapidly pays down the debt over a number of years. Because the schedule of debt reduction in the future is known when the LBO is arranged, tax shields in every future year can be easily forecast. The APV approach is easy to use here. (An illustration of the APV approach applied to LBOs is provided in the Appendix to this chapter.) By contrast, the WACC and FTE approaches are virtually impossible to apply here because the debt-equity value cannot be expected to be constant over time. In addition, situations involving interest subsidies and flotation costs are much easier to handle with the APV approach. (The Brindavan Enterprises example in Section 18.6 applies the APV approach to subsidies and flotation costs.) Finally, the APV approach handles the lease-versus-buy decision much more easily than does either the FTE or the WACC approach. (A full treatment of the lease-versus-buy decision appears in a later chapter.)

The preceding examples are special cases. Typical capital budgeting situations are more suitable to either the WACC or the FTE approach than to the APV approach. Financial managers generally think in terms of target debt-value ratios. If a project does better than expected, both its value and its debt capacity will likely rise. The manager will increase debt correspondingly here. Conversely, the manager would be likely to reduce debt if the value of the project were to decline unexpectedly. Of course, because financing is a time-consuming task, the ratio cannot be adjusted daily or monthly. Rather, the adjustment can be expected to occur over the long run. As mentioned before, the WACC and FTE approaches are more appropriate than is the APV approach when a firm focuses on a target debt-value ratio.

Discussions with business executives have convinced us that the WACC is by far the most widely used method in the real world. However, we believe the APV approach can be very useful in cases like LBOs in which the firm has a specific plan in mind for the level of debt in future years.

The Three Methods of Valuation with Leverage

1. Adjusted present value (APV) method:

$$\sum_{t=1}^{\infty} \frac{UCF_t}{(1+R_0)^t} + \text{Additional effects of debt} - \text{Initial investment}$$

UCF_t = The project's cash flow at Date t to the equityholders of an unlevered firm.
R_0 = Cost of capital for project in an unlevered firm.

2. Flow to equity (FTE) method:

$$\sum_{t=1}^{\infty} \frac{LCF_t}{(1+R_S)^t} - (\text{Initial investment} - \text{Amount borrowed})$$

LCF_t = The project's cash flow at Date t to the equityholders of a levered firm.
R_S = Cost of equity capital with leverage.

3. Weighted average cost of capital (WACC) method:

$$\sum_{t=1}^{\infty} \frac{UCF_t}{(1+\text{WACC})^t} - \text{Initial investment}$$

WACC = Weighted average cost of capital.

Notes

1. The middle term in the APV formula implies that the value of a project with leverage is greater than the value of the project without leverage. Because WACC $< R_0$, the WACC formula implies that the value of a project with leverage is greater than the value of the project without leverage.
2. In the FTE method, cash flow after interest (LCF) is used. The initial investment is reduced by the amount borrowed.

Guidelines

1. Use WACC or FTE if the firm's target debt-value ratio applies to the project over its life.
2. Use APV if the project's level of debt is known over the life of the project.

18.5 Valuation When the Discount Rate Must Be Estimated

The previous sections of this chapter introduced APV, FTE, and WACC–the three basic approaches to valuation of a firm with leverage. However, one important detail remains. The example in Sections 18.1 through 18.3 assumed a discount rate. We now want to show how this rate is determined for firms with leverage, with an application to the three preceding approaches. The example in this section adds to the work in Chapters 9-13 on the discount rate for levered and unlevered firms along with that in Chapter 16 on the effect of leverage on the cost of capital.

EXAMPLE 18.1

Cost of Capital Wardha-Worli Enterprises (WWE) is a large conglomerate thinking of entering the widget business, where it plans to finance projects with a debt-value ratio of 25 percent (or a debt-equity ratio of 1/3). There is currently one firm in the widget industry, Aditya Widgets (AW). This firm is financed with 40 percent debt and 60 percent equity. The beta of AW's equity is 1.5. AW has a borrowing rate of 12 percent, and WWE expects to borrow for its widget venture at 10 percent. The corporate tax rate for both firms is 21 percent, the market risk premium is 8.5 percent, and the risk-free interest rate is 8 percent. What is the appropriate discount rate for WWE to use for its widget venture?

As shown in Sections 18.1–18.3, a corporation may use one of three capital budgeting approaches: APV, FTE, or WACC. The appropriate discount rates for these three approaches are R_0, R_S, and WACC, respectively. Because AW is WWE's only competitor in widgets, we look at AW's cost of capital to calculate R_0, R_S, and WACC for WWE's widget venture. The following four-step procedure will allow us to calculate all three discount rates:

1. *Determining AW's cost of equity capital*: First, we determine AW's cost of equity capital using the security market line:

$$\begin{aligned} R_S &= R_F + \beta \times [E(R_M) - R_F] \\ &= .08 + 1.5 \times .085 \\ &= .2075, \text{ or } 20.75\% \end{aligned}$$

2. *Determining AW's hypothetical all-equity cost of capital*: We must standardize the preceding number in some way because AW's and WWE's widget ventures have different target debt-value ratios. The easiest approach is to calculate the hypothetical cost of equity capital for AW, assuming all-equity financing. This can be determined from MM's Proposition II under taxes:

$$\begin{aligned} R_S &= R_0 + \frac{B}{S}(1 - T_C)(R_0 - R_B) \\ .2075 &= R_0 + \frac{.4}{.6}(1 - .21)(R_0 - .12) \end{aligned}$$

By solving the equation, we find that $R_0 = .1773$, or 17.73 percent. Of course, R_0 is less than R_S because the cost of equity capital would be less when the firm employs no leverage.

At this point, firms in the real world generally make the assumption that the business risk of their venture is about equal to the business risk of the firms already in the business. Applying this assumption to our problem, we assert that the discount rate of WWE's widget venture if all-equity-financed is also 17.73 percent.[6] This discount rate would be employed if WWE uses the APV approach because the APV approach calls for R_0, the project's cost of capital in a firm with no leverage.

3. *Determining R_S for WWE's widget venture*: Alternatively, WWE might use the FTE approach, where the discount rate for levered equity is determined like this:

$$\begin{aligned} R_S &= R_0 + \frac{B}{S}(1 - T_C)(R_0 - R_B) \\ &= .1733 + \frac{.2}{.6}(1 - .21)(.1733 - .10) \\ &= .1977, \text{ or } 19.77\% \end{aligned}$$

(continued)

[6]Alternatively, a firm might assume that its venture would be somewhat riskier because it is a new entrant. In this case, the firm might select a discount rate slightly higher than 17.73 percent. Of course, no exact formula exists for adjusting the discount rate upward.

Note that the cost of equity capital for WWE's widget venture, 19.77 percent, is less than the cost of equity capital for AW, 20.75 percent. This occurs because AW has a higher debt-equity ratio. (As mentioned, both firms are assumed to have the same business risk.)

4. *Determining WACC for WWE's widget venture*: Finally, WWE might use the WACC approach. Here is the appropriate calculation:

$$\begin{aligned}\text{WACC} &= \frac{B}{S+B}R_B(1-T_C) + R_S\frac{S}{S+B}\\ &= \frac{1}{4}(.10)(1-.21) + \frac{3}{4}(.1977)\\ &= .1680, \text{ or } 16.80\%\end{aligned}$$

The preceding example shows how the three discount rates, R_0, R_S, and WACC, are determined in the real world. These are the appropriate rates for the APV, FTE, and WACC approaches, respectively. Note that R_S for Aditya Widgets is determined first because the cost of equity capital can be determined from the beta of the firm's stock. As discussed in an earlier chapter, beta can be estimated easily for any publicly traded firm.

18.6 APV Example

As mentioned earlier in this chapter, firms generally set a target debt-equity ratio, allowing the use of WACC and FTE for capital budgeting. APV does not work as well here. However, as we also mentioned earlier, APV is the preferred approach when there are side benefits and side costs to debt. Because the analysis here can be tricky, we now devote an entire section to an example where, in addition to the tax subsidy to debt, both flotation costs and interest subsidies come into play.

EXAMPLE 18.2

APV Brindavan Enterprises is considering a ₹10 million project that will last five years, with straight-line depreciation of ₹2 million per year. The cash revenues less cash expenses per year are ₹3.5 million. The corporate tax rate is 21 percent. The risk-free rate is 10 percent and the unlevered cost of equity is 20 percent.

The cash flow projections each year are:

	Year 0	Year 1	Year 2	Year 3	Year 4	Year 5
Initial outlay	−₹10,000,000					
Depreciation tax shield		.21 × ₹2,000,000 = ₹420,000	₹ 420,000	₹ 420,000	₹ 420,000	₹ 420,000
Revenue less expenses		(1 − .21) × ₹3,500,000 = ₹2,765,000	₹2,765,000	₹2,765,000	₹ 2,765,000	₹ 2,765,000

(continued)

Because the APV of a project is the sum of its all-equity value plus the additional effects of debt, we will examine each in turn.

All-Equity Value Assuming the project is financed with all equity, the value of the project is:

$$-₹10{,}000{,}000 + \frac{₹420{,}000}{.10} \times \left[1 - \left(\frac{1}{1.10}\right)^5\right] + \frac{₹2{,}765{,}000}{.20} \times \left[1 - \left(\frac{1}{1.20}\right)^5\right] = -₹138{,}827$$

Initial cost + Depreciation tax shield + Present value of (Cash revenues − Cash expenses)

This calculation uses the techniques presented in the early chapters of this book. Notice that we have assumed that the depreciation tax shield is risk free, and therefore discounted it at the riskless rate of 10 percent. If the firm believes the depreciation tax shield is risky, it can use a higher discount rate to reflect the riskiness of the depreciation tax shield.[7] The revenues less expenses are discounted at the higher rate of 20 percent.

An all-equity firm would clearly reject this project because the NPV is −₹138,827. And equity flotation costs would only make the NPV more negative. However, debt financing may add enough value to the project to justify acceptance. We consider the effects of debt next.

Additional Effects of Debt Brindavan Enterprises can obtain a five-year, nonamortizing loan for ₹7,500,000 after flotation costs at the risk-free rate of 10 percent. Flotation costs are fees paid when stock or debt is issued. These fees may go to printers, lawyers, and investment bankers, among others. Brindavan Enterprises is informed that flotation costs will be 1 percent of the gross proceeds of its loan. The previous chapter indicates that debt financing alters the NPV of a typical project. We look at the effects of debt next.

Flotation Costs Given that flotation costs are 1 percent of the gross proceeds, we have:

$$₹7{,}500{,}000 = (1 - .01) \times \text{Gross proceeds} = .99 \times \text{Gross proceeds}$$

The gross proceeds are:

$$\frac{₹7{,}500{,}000}{1 - .01} = \frac{₹7{,}500{,}000}{.99} = ₹7{,}575{,}758$$

The flotation costs will be ₹75,758 (= .01 × ₹7,575,758). To check the calculation, note that net proceeds are ₹7,500,000 (= ₹7,575,758 − 75,758). In other words, Brindavan Enterprises receives only ₹7.5 million. The flotation costs of ₹75,758 are received by intermediaries such as investment bankers.

Flotation costs are paid immediately but are deducted from taxes by amortizing on a straight-line basis over the life of the loan. The cash flows from flotation costs are calculated as:

	Year 0	Year 1	Year 2	Year 3	Year 4	Year 5
Flotation costs	−₹75,758					
Deduction		$\frac{₹75{,}758}{5}$ = ₹15,152	₹15,152	₹15,152	₹15,152	₹15,152
Tax shield from flotation costs		.21 × ₹15,152 = ₹3,182	₹ 3,182	₹ 3,182	₹ 3,182	₹ 3,182

The relevant cash flows from flotation costs are in bold. When we discount at 10 percent, the tax shield has a net present value of:

$$₹3{,}182 \times \text{PVIFA}_{10\%,5} = ₹12{,}062$$

(*continued*)

[7]In practice, many firms instead discount the depreciation tax shield using the same discount rate they use to discount revenue less expenses. This approach is easy to implement, but fails to account for the fact that the depreciation tax shield is typically much less risky than revenue less expenses.

The net cost of flotation is:

$$-₹75{,}758 + 12{,}062 = -₹63{,}696$$

The net present value of the project after the flotation costs of debt but before the benefits of debt is:

$$-₹138{,}827 - 63{,}696 = -₹202{,}523$$

Tax Subsidy Interest must be paid on the gross proceeds of the loan, even though intermediaries receive the flotation costs. Because the gross proceeds of the loan are ₹7,575,758, annual interest is ₹757,576 (= ₹7,575,758 × .10). The interest cost after taxes is ₹598,485 [= ₹757,576 × (1 − .21)]. Because the loan is nonamortizing, the entire debt of ₹7,575,758 is repaid at Year 5. These terms are indicated here:

	Year 0	Year 1	Year 2	Year 3	Year 4	Year 5
Loan (gross proceeds)	₹7,575,758					
Interest paid		10% × ₹7,575,758 = ₹757,576	₹ 757,576	₹ 757,576	₹ 757,576	₹ 757,576
Aftertax interest		(1 − .21) × ₹757,576 = ₹598,485	₹ 598,485	₹ 598,485	₹ 598,485	₹ 598,485
Repayment of debt						₹ 7,575,758

The relevant cash flows are listed in the preceding table. They are (1) loan received, (2) annual interest cost after taxes, and (3) repayment of debt. Note that we include the gross proceeds of the loan as an inflow because the flotation costs have previously been subtracted.

In Chapter 16, we mentioned that the financing decision can be evaluated in terms of net present value. The net present value of the loan is the sum of the net present values of each of the three cash flows. This can be represented as follows:

$$\text{NPV (loan)} = +\ \text{Amount borrowed} - \text{Present value of aftertax interest payments} - \text{Present value of loan repayments} \quad \textbf{(18.1)}$$

The calculations for this example are:

$$₹603{,}080 = ₹7{,}575{,}758 - \frac{₹598{,}485}{.10} \times \left[1 - \left(\frac{1}{1.10}\right)^5\right] - \frac{₹7{,}575{,}758}{1.10^5} \quad \textbf{(18.1}'\textbf{)}$$

The NPV of the loan is positive, reflecting the interest tax shield.[8]

The adjusted present value of the project with this financing is:

$$\text{APV} = \text{All-equity value} - \text{Flotation costs of debt} + \text{NPV(loan)} \quad \textbf{(18.2)}$$

$$₹400{,}557 = -₹138{,}827 - 63{,}696 + 603{,}080 \quad \textbf{(18.2}'\textbf{)}$$

Though we previously saw that an all-equity firm would reject the project, a firm would accept the project if a ₹7.5 million (net) loan could be obtained.

Because the loan discussed was at the market rate of 10 percent, we have considered only two of the three additional effects of debt (flotation costs and tax subsidy) so far. We now examine another loan where the third effect arises.

(continued)

[8]The NPV(loan) must be zero in a no-tax world because interest provides no tax shield there. To check this intuition, we calculate:

$$\text{No-tax case: } 0 = +₹7{,}575{,}758 - \frac{₹757{,}576}{.10} \times \left[1 - \left(\frac{1}{1.10}\right)^5\right] - \frac{₹7{,}575{,}758}{1.10^5}$$

Nonmarket Rate Financing A number of companies are fortunate enough to obtain subsidized financing from a governmental authority. Suppose that the project of Brindavan Enterprises is deemed socially beneficial and the state of Madhya Pradesh grants the firm a ₹7.5 million loan at 8 percent interest. In addition, all flotation costs are absorbed by the state. Clearly, the company will choose this loan over the one we previously calculated. The cash flows from the loan under the subsidized terms are calculated as:

	Year 0	Year 1	Year 2	Year 3	Year 4	Year 5
Loan received	₹7,500,000					
Interest paid		.08 × ₹7,500,000 = ₹600,000	₹ 600,000	₹ 600,000	₹ 600,000	₹ 600,000
Aftertax interest		(1 − .21) × ₹600,000 = ₹474,000	₹ 474,000	₹ 474,000	₹ 474,000	₹ 474,000
Repayment of debt						₹ 7,500,000

The relevant cash flows are listed in the preceding table. Using Equation 18.1, the NPV of the loan is:

$$₹1{,}046{,}257 = ₹7{,}500{,}000 - \frac{₹474{,}000}{.10} \times \left[1 - \left(\frac{1}{1.10}\right)^5\right] - \frac{₹7{,}500{,}000}{1.10^5} \quad \textbf{(18.1'')}$$

Why do we discount the cash flows in Equation 18.1″ at 10 percent when the firm is borrowing at 8 percent? We discount at 10 percent because that is the fair, or market, rate. That is, 10 percent is the rate at which the firm could borrow without benefit of subsidization. The net present value of the subsidized loan is larger than the net present value of the earlier loan because the firm is now borrowing at the below-market rate of 8 percent. Note that the NPV of the loan calculation in Equation 18.1″ captures both the tax effect and the nonmarket rate effect.

The net present value of the project with subsidized debt financing is:

$$\text{APV} = \text{All-equity value} - \text{Flotation costs of debt} + \text{NPV (loan)} \quad \textbf{(18.2)}$$

$$₹907{,}430 = -₹138{,}827 - 0 + 1{,}046{,}257 \quad \textbf{(18.2'')}$$

The preceding example illustrates the adjusted present value (APV) approach. The approach begins with the present value of a project for the all-equity firm. Next, the effects of debt are added in. The approach has many beneficial components. It is intuitively appealing because individual components are calculated separately and added together in a simple way. And, if the debt from the project can be specified precisely, the present value of the debt can be calculated precisely.

18.7 Beta and Leverage

A previous chapter provides the formula for the relationship between the beta of the common stock and leverage of the firm in a world without taxes. We reproduce this formula here:

$$\beta_{\text{Equity}} = \beta_{\text{Asset}}\left(1 + \frac{\text{Debt}}{\text{Equity}}\right) \quad \textbf{(18.3)}$$

As pointed out earlier, this relationship holds under the assumption that the beta of debt is zero.

Because firms must pay corporate taxes in practice, it is worthwhile to provide the relationship in a world with corporate taxes. If we assume the debt tax shield is as risky as the debt, it can be shown that the relationship between the beta of the unlevered firm and the beta of the levered equity is:[9]

$$\beta_{\text{Equity}} = \beta_{\text{Unlevered firm}}\left(1 + \frac{(1 - T_C)\text{Debt}}{\text{Equity}}\right) \tag{18.4}$$

when (1) the corporation is taxed at the rate of T_C and (2) the debt has a zero beta.

Because $[1 + (1 - T_C)\text{Debt/Equity}]$ must be more than 1 for a levered firm, it follows that $\beta_{\text{Unlevered firm}} < \beta_{\text{Equity}}$. The corporate tax case of Equation 18.4 is quite similar to the no-tax case of Equation 18.3 because the beta of levered equity must be greater than the beta of the unlevered firm in either case. The intuition that leverage increases the risk of equity applies in both cases.

However, notice that the two equations are not equal. It can be shown that leverage increases the equity beta less rapidly under corporate taxes. This occurs because, under taxes, leverage creates a risk-free tax shield, thereby lowering the risk of the entire firm.

THE PROJECT IS NOT SCALE ENHANCING

Because the previous example was scale enhancing, we began with the beta of the firm's equity. If the project is not scale enhancing, we could begin with the equity betas of firms in the industry of the project. For each firm, we could calculate the hypothetical beta of the unlevered equity using Equation 18.5. The CAPM could then be used to determine the project's discount rate from the average of these betas.

---

[9]This result holds only if the beta of debt equals zero. To see this, note that:

$$V_U + T_C B = V_L = B + S \tag{a}$$

where:

V_U = Value of unlevered firm.
V_L = Value of levered firm.
B = Value of debt in a levered firm.
S = Value of equity in a levered firm.

As we stated in the text, the beta of the levered firm is a weighted average of the debt beta and the equity beta:

$$\frac{B}{B+S} \times \beta_B + \frac{S}{B+S} \times \beta_S$$

where β_B and β_S are the betas of the debt and the equity of the levered firm, respectively. Because $V_L = B + S$, we have:

$$\frac{B}{V_L} \times \beta_B + \frac{S}{V_L} \times \beta_S \tag{b}$$

The beta of the levered firm can also be expressed as a weighted average of the beta of the unlevered firm and the beta of the tax shield:

$$\frac{V_U}{V_U + T_C B} \times \beta_U + \frac{T_C B}{V_U + T_C B} \times \beta_B$$

where β_U is the beta of the unlevered firm. This follows from Equation (a). Because $V_L = V_U + T_C B$, we have:

$$\frac{V_U}{V_L} \times \beta_U + \frac{T_C B}{V_L} \times \beta_B \tag{c}$$

We can equate Equations (b) and (c) because both represent the beta of a levered firm. Equation (a) tells us that $V_U = S + (1 - T_C) \times B$. Under the assumption that $\beta_B = 0$, equating Equations (b) and (c) and using Equation (a) yields Equation 18.4.

The generalized formula for the levered beta (where β_B is not zero) is:

$$\beta_S = \beta_U + (1 - T_C)(\beta_U - \beta_B)\,\frac{B}{S}$$

and

$$\beta_U = \frac{S}{B(1 - T_C) + S}\beta_S + \frac{B(1 - T_C)}{B(1 - T_C) + S}\beta_B$$

EXAMPLE 18.3

Unlevered Betas B. Marandi Ltd., is considering a scale-enhancing project. The market value of the firm's debt is ₹100 million and the market value of the firm's equity is ₹200 million. The debt is considered risk-free. The corporate tax rate is 21 percent. Regression analysis indicates that the beta of the firm's equity is 2. The risk-free rate is 10 percent and the expected market premium is 8.5 percent. What would the project's discount rate be in the hypothetical case that B. Marandi Ltd., is all equity?

We can answer this question in two steps.

1. *Determining beta of hypothetical all-equity firm*: Rearranging Equation 18.4, we have this:

$$
\begin{aligned}
\beta_{\text{Unlevered firm}} &= \frac{\text{Equity}}{\text{Equity} + (1 - T_C) \times \text{Debt}} \times \beta_{\text{Equity}} \\
&= \frac{₹200{,}000{,}000}{₹200{,}000{,}000 + (1 - .21) \times ₹100{,}000{,}000} \times 2 \qquad \textbf{(18.5)} \\
&= 1.43
\end{aligned}
$$

2. *Determining discount rate*: We calculate the discount rate if the firm were all equity by applying the CAPM to the beta of the unlevered firm:

$$
\begin{aligned}
R_S &= R_F + \beta \times [E(R_M) - R_F] \\
&= .10 + 1.43 \times .085 \\
&= .2219, \text{ or } 22.19\%
\end{aligned}
$$

EXAMPLE 18.4

More Unlevered Betas The Nadeem Shravan Company, which currently manufactures staples, is considering a ₹1 million investment in a project in the aircraft adhesives industry. The corporation estimates unlevered aftertax cash flows (UCF) of ₹300,000 per year into perpetuity from the project. The firm will finance the project with a debt-value ratio of .5 (or, equivalently, a debt-equity ratio of 1.0).

The three competitors in this new industry are currently unlevered, with betas of 1.2, 1.3, and 1.4. Assuming a risk-free rate of 5 percent, a market risk premium of 9 percent, and a corporate tax rate of 21 percent, what is the net present value of the project?

We can answer this question in five steps.

1. *Calculating the average unlevered beta in the industry*: The average unlevered beta across all three existing competitors in the aircraft adhesives industry is:

$$\frac{1.2 + 1.3 + 1.4}{3} = 1.3$$

2. *Calculating the levered beta for Nadeem Shravan's new project*: Assuming the same unlevered beta for this new project as for the existing competitors, we have, from Equation 18.4:

$$
\begin{aligned}
\beta_{\text{Equity}} &= \left(1 + \frac{(1 - T_C)\ \text{Debt}}{\text{Equity}}\right)\beta_{\text{Unlevered firm}} \\
&= \left(1 + \frac{.79 \times 1}{1}\right) \times 1.3 \\
&= 2.33
\end{aligned}
$$

(continued)

3. *Calculating the cost of levered equity for the new project*: We calculate the discount rate by applying the CAPM to the levered beta:

$$R_S = R_F + \beta \times [E(R_M) - R_F]$$
$$= .05 + 2.33 \times .09$$
$$= .2594, \text{ or } 25.94\%$$

4. *Calculating the WACC for the new project*: The formula for determining the weighted average cost of capital is:

$$\text{WACC} = \frac{B}{V} R_B(1 - T_C) + R_S\frac{S}{V}$$
$$= \frac{1}{2} \times .05 \times .79 + .2594 \times \frac{1}{2}$$
$$= .1495, \text{ or } 14.95\%$$

5. *Determining the project's value:* Because the cash flows are perpetual, the NPV of the project is:

$$\text{NPV} = \frac{\text{Unlevered cash flows (UCF)}}{\text{WACC}} - \text{Initial investment}$$
$$= \frac{₹300{,}000}{.1495} - ₹1{,}000{,}000$$
$$= ₹1{,}007{,}159$$

RESEARCH IN EMERGING MARKET CONTEXT

Sarkar (2020) reports that the relationship between operating and financial leverage is not always a substitute, as traditional literature suggests. It is a complex relationship that may not follow a straightforward pattern.

Singh and Bansal (2016) show that financial and operating leverage negatively impacts the firm's performance indicators, such as Economic Value Added (EVA) and Tobin's Q.

Kim-Duc and Nam (2024) have developed a general framework that provides a consistent valuation between the Cost of Capital (CoC) and Adjusted Present Value (APV) methods, taking into account varying debt levels. The framework also considers the debt, trade-off between corporate income taxes (CIT) and personal income taxes (PIT), tax benefits and financial distress costs.

References

Kim-Duc, N., & Nam, P. K. (2024). Consistent valuation: extensions from bankruptcy costs and tax integration with time-varying debt. *Review of Quantitative Finance and Accounting*, *62*(2), 719–754.

Sarkar, S. (2020). The relationship between operating leverage and financial leverage. *Accounting & Finance*, *60*, 805–826.

Singh, Amit Kumar, and Preeti Bansal. "Impact Of Financial Leverage on Firm's Performance And Valuation: A Panel Data Analysis." *Indian Journal of Accounting 2* (2016): 73–80

Summary and Conclusions

Earlier chapters of this text showed how to value projects and entire firms with and without leverage. In the previous three chapters, we discussed how a firm determines the amount of leverage in its capital structure. We pointed out that the introduction of taxes and bankruptcy costs changes a firm's financing decisions. Most rational corporations should employ some debt in a world of this type. This chapter has discussed three methods for valuation by levered firms: (1) the adjusted present value (APV), (2) flow to equity (FTE), and (3) weighted average cost of capital (WACC) approaches.

Concept Questions

1. **APV** How is the APV of a project calculated?
2. **WACC and APV** What is the main difference between the WACC and APV methods?
3. **FTE** What is the main difference between the FTE approach and the other two approaches?
4. **Capital Budgeting** You are determining whether your company should undertake a new project and have calculated the NPV of the project using the WACC method when the CFO, a former accountant, notices that you did not use the interest payments in calculating the cash flows of the project. What should you tell him? If he insists that you include the interest payments in calculating the cash flows, what method can you use?
5. **Beta and Leverage** What are the two types of risk that are measured by a levered beta?

Questions and Problems

BASIC (Questions 1–9)

1. **NPV and APV** Benton is a rental car company that is trying to determine whether to add 25 cars to its fleet. The company fully depreciates all its rental cars over five years using the straight-line method. The new cars are expected to generate ₹225,000 per year in earnings before taxes and depreciation for five years. The company is entirely financed by equity and has a 21 percent tax rate. The required return on the company's unlevered equity is 14 percent and the new fleet will not change the risk of the company.

   a. What is the maximum price that the company should be willing to pay for the new fleet of cars if it remains an all-equity company?

   b. Suppose the company can purchase the fleet of cars for ₹700,000. Additionally, assume the company can issue ₹450,000 of five-year debt to finance the project at the risk-free rate of 8 percent. All principal will be repaid in one balloon payment at the end of the fifth year. What is the APV of the project?

2. **APV** Knotts, Inc., an all-equity firm, is considering an investment of ₹1.32 million that will be depreciated according to the straight-line method over its four-year life. The project is expected to generate earnings before taxes and depreciation of ₹470,000 per year for four years. The investment will not change the risk level of the firm. The company can obtain a four-year, 9.5 percent loan to finance the project from a local bank. All principal will be repaid in one balloon payment at the end of the fourth year. The bank will charge the firm ₹45,000 in flotation fees, which will be amortized over the four-year life of the loan. If the company financed the project entirely with equity, the firm's cost of capital would

be 14 percent. The corporate tax rate is 25 percent. Using the APV method, determine whether the company should undertake the project.

3. **FTE** Pompeii Pizza Club owns three identical restaurants popular for their specialty pizzas. Each restaurant has a debt-equity ratio of 40 percent and makes interest payments of ₹42,000 at the end of each year. The cost of the firm's levered equity is 19 percent. Each store estimates that annual sales will be ₹1.15 million; annual cost of goods sold will be ₹645,000; and annual general and administrative costs will be ₹385,000. These cash flows are expected to remain the same forever. The corporate tax rate is 22 percent.

   a. Use the flow to equity approach to determine the value of the company's equity.

   b. What is the total value of the company?

4. **WACC** If Smolinski, Inc., were an all-equity company, it would have a beta of 1.05. The company has a target debt-equity ratio of .40. The expected return on the market portfolio is 11 percent and Treasury bills currently yield 3.5 percent. The company has one bond issue outstanding that matures in 13 years, has a coupon rate of 5.6 percent, and makes semiannual payments. The bond currently sells for ₹1,060. The corporate tax rate is 21 percent.

   a. What is the company's cost of debt?

   b. What is the company's cost of equity?

   c. What is the company's weighted average cost of capital?

5. **Beta and Leverage** North Pole Fishing Equipment Corporation and South Pole Fishing Equipment Corporation would have identical equity betas of 1.05 if both were all-equity financed. The market value information for each company is shown here:

	North Pole	South Pole
Debt	₹1,900,000	₹3,700,000
Equity	₹3,700,000	₹1,900,000

   The expected return on the market portfolio is 11.3 percent and the risk-free rate is 3.2 percent. Both companies are subject to a corporate tax rate of 21 percent. Assume the beta of debt is zero.

   a. What is the equity beta of each company?

   b. What is the required rate of return on equity for each company?

6. **NPV of Loans** The CFO of Kendrick Enterprises is evaluating a 10-year, 5.8 percent loan with gross proceeds of ₹5.3 million. The interest payments on the loan will be made annually. Flotation costs are estimated to be 2.5 percent of gross proceeds and will be amortized using a straight-line schedule over the 10-year life of the loan. The company has a tax rate of 21 percent and the loan will not increase the risk of financial distress for the company.

   a. Calculate the net present value of the loan excluding flotation costs.

   b. Calculate the net present value of the loan including flotation costs.

7. **NPV for an All-Equity Company** Jimenez, Inc., is an all-equity firm. The cost of the company's equity is currently 11.2 percent and the risk-free rate is 3.4 percent. The company is currently considering a project that will cost ₹11.6 million and last six years. The company uses straight-line depreciation. The project will generate revenues minus expenses each year in the amount of ₹3.5 million. If the company has a tax rate of 23 percent, should it accept the project?

8. **WACC** National Electric Company (NEC) is considering a ₹41 million project in its power systems division. Tom Edison, the company's chief financial officer, has evaluated the project and determined

that the project's unlevered cash flows will be ₹3.1 million per year in perpetuity. Mr. Edison has devised two possibilities for raising the initial investment: issuing 10-year bonds or issuing common stock. The company's pretax cost of debt is 5.1 percent and its cost of equity is 10.3 percent. The company's target debt-to-value ratio is 60 percent. The project has the same risk as the company's existing businesses and will support the same amount of debt. The tax rate is 21 percent. Should NEC accept the project?

9. **WACC** Williams, Inc., has compiled the following information on its financing costs:

Type of Financing	Book Value	Market Value	Cost
Short-term debt	₹12,000,000	₹12,500,000	4.1%
Long-term debt	20,000,000	23,000,000	7.2
Common stock	9,000,000	54,000,000	13.8
Total	₹41,000,000	₹89,500,000	

The company is in the 21 percent tax bracket and has a target debt-equity ratio of 60 percent. The target short-term debt/long-term debt ratio is 20 percent.

a. What is the company's weighted average cost of capital using book value weights?
b. What is the company's weighted average cost of capital using market value weights?
c. What is the company's weighted average cost of capital using target capital structure weights?
d. What is the difference between WACCs? Which is the correct WACC to use for project evaluation?

INTERMEDIATE (Questions 10–14)

10. **APV** Triad Corporation has established a joint venture with Tobacco Road Construction, Inc., to build a toll road in North Carolina. The initial investment in paving equipment is ₹145 million. The equipment will be fully depreciated using the straight-line method over its economic life of 5 years. Earnings before interest, taxes, and depreciation collected from the toll road are projected to be ₹19.7 million per annum for 20 years starting from the end of the first year. The corporate tax rate is 21 percent. The required rate of return for the project under all-equity financing is 13 percent. The pretax cost of debt for the joint partnership is 8.5 percent. To encourage investment in the country's infrastructure, the U.S. government will subsidize the project with an ₹85 million, 15-year loan at an interest rate of 5 percent per year. All principal will be repaid in one balloon payment at the end of Year 15. What is the adjusted present value of this project?

11. **APV** For the company in the previous problem, what is the value of being able to issue subsidized debt instead of having to issue debt at the terms it would normally receive? Assume the face amount and maturity of the debt issue are the same.

12. **APV** Longhorn, Inc., has produced rodeo supplies for over 20 years. The company currently has a debt-equity ratio of 50 percent and the tax rate is 21 percent. The required return on the firm's levered equity is 14 percent. The company is planning to expand its production capacity. The equipment to be purchased is expected to generate the following unlevered cash flows:

Year	Cash Flow
0	–₹14,800,000
1	5,500,000
2	9,000,000
3	8,700,000

The company has arranged a debt issue of ₹8.7 million to partially finance the expansion. Under the loan, the company would pay interest of 7 percent at the end of each year on the outstanding balance at the beginning of the year. The company also would make year-end principal payments of ₹2.9 million per year, completely retiring the issue by the end of the third year. Using the adjusted present value method, should the company proceed with the expansion?

13. WACC First and Goal Corporation's stock returns have a covariance with the market portfolio of .0487. The standard deviation of the returns on the market portfolio is 20 percent and the expected market risk premium is 6.7 percent. The company has bonds outstanding with a total market value of ₹60 million and a yield to maturity of 6.5 percent. The company also has 4.1 million shares of common stock outstanding, each selling for ₹32. The company's CEO considers the firm's current debt-equity ratio optimal. The corporate tax rate is 21 percent and the risk-free rate is 3.1 percent. The company is considering the purchase of additional equipment that would cost ₹56 million. The expected unlevered cash flows from the equipment are ₹17.9 million per year for five years. Purchasing the equipment will not change the risk level of the firm.

   a. Use the weighted average cost of capital approach to determine whether the company should purchase the equipment.

   b. Suppose the company decides to fund the purchase of the equipment entirely with debt. What is the cost of capital for the project now? Explain.

14. **Beta and Leverage** Estefan Industries has a new project available that requires an initial investment of ₹4.9 million. The project will provide unlevered cash flows of ₹925,000 per year for the next 20 years. The company will finance the project with a debt-value ratio of .35. The company's bonds have a YTM of 5.9 percent. The companies with operations comparable to this project have unlevered betas of 1.09, 1.17, 1.28, and 1.20. The risk-free rate is 3.6 percent and the market risk premium is 7 percent. The tax rate is 21 percent. What is the NPV of this project?

CHALLENGE (Questions 15–18)

15. **APV, FTE, and WACC** Summers, Inc., is an unlevered firm with expected annual earnings before taxes of ₹20.5 million in perpetuity. The current required return on the firm's equity is 10.5 percent and the firm distributes all of its earnings as dividends at the end of each year. The company has 2.1 million shares of common stock outstanding and is subject to a corporate tax rate of 21 percent. The firm is planning a recapitalization under which it will issue ₹30 million of perpetual 5 percent debt and use the proceeds to buy back shares.

   a. Calculate the value of the company before the recapitalization plan is announced. What is the value of equity before the announcement? What is the price per share?

   b. Use the APV method to calculate the company value after the recapitalization plan is announced. What is the value of equity after the announcement? What is the price per share?

   c. How many shares will be repurchased? What is the value of equity after the repurchase has been completed? What is the price per share?

   d. Use the flow to equity method to calculate the value of the company's equity after the recapitalization.

16. **APV, FTE, and WACC** Bluegrass Mint Company has a debt-equity ratio of .35. The required return on the company's unlevered equity is 13.1 percent and the pretax cost of the firm's debt is 6.4 percent. Sales revenue for the company is expected to remain stable indefinitely at last year's level of ₹19.3 million. Variable costs amount to 60 percent of sales. The tax rate is 21 percent and the company distributes all its earnings as dividends at the end of each year.

   a. If the company were financed entirely by equity, how much would it be worth?

   b. What is the required return on the firm's levered equity?

c. Use the weighted average cost of capital method to calculate the value of the company. What is the value of the company's equity? What is the value of the company's debt?

d. Use the flow to equity method to calculate the value of the company's equity.

17. **APV, FTE, and WACC** Bruin Industries just issued ₹365,000 of perpetual 6 percent debt and used the proceeds to repurchase stock. The company expects to generate ₹151,000 of earnings before interest and taxes in perpetuity. The company distributes all its earnings as dividends at the end of each year. The firm's unlevered cost of capital is 10.5 percent and the corporate tax rate is 21 percent.

a. What is the value of the company as an unlevered firm?

b. Use the adjusted present value method to calculate the value of the company with leverage.

c. What is the required return on the firm's levered equity?

d. Use the flow to equity method to calculate the value of the company's equity.

18. **Projects That Are Not Scale Enhancing** Blue Angel, Inc., a private firm in the holiday gift industry, is considering a new project. The company currently has a target debt-equity ratio of .40, but the industry target debt-equity ratio is .35. The industry average beta is 1.15. The market risk premium is 7 percent and the risk-free rate is 4 percent. Assume all companies in this industry can issue debt at the risk-free rate. The corporate tax rate is 21 percent. The project requires an initial outlay of ₹825,000 and is expected to result in a ₹94,000 cash inflow at the end of the first year. The project will be financed at the company's target debt-equity ratio. Annual cash flows from the project will grow at a constant rate of 5 percent until the end of the fifth year and remain constant forever thereafter. Should the company invest in the project?

Mini Case THE LEVERAGED BUYOUT OF CHEEK PRODUCTS, INC.

Cheek Products, Inc. (CPI), was founded 53 years ago by Joe Cheek and originally sold snack foods such as potato chips and pretzels. Through acquisitions, the company has grown into a conglomerate with major divisions in the snack food, home security systems, cosmetics, and plastics industries. Additionally, the company has several smaller divisions. In recent years, the company has been underperforming, but the company's management doesn't seem to be aggressively pursuing opportunities to improve operations (or the stock price).

Meg Whalen is a financial analyst specializing in identifying potential buyout targets. She believes that two major changes are needed at CPI. First, she thinks that the company would be better off if it sold several divisions and concentrated on its core competencies in snack foods and home security systems. Second, the company is financed entirely with equity. Because the cash flows of the company are relatively steady, Meg thinks the company's debt-equity ratio should be 25 percent. She believes these changes would significantly enhance shareholder wealth, but she also believes that the existing board and company management are unlikely to take the necessary actions. As a result, Meg thinks the company is a good candidate for a leveraged buyout.

A leveraged buyout (LBO) is the acquisition by a small group of equity investors of a public or private company. Generally, an LBO is financed primarily with debt. The new shareholders service the heavy interest and principal payments with cash from operations and/or asset sales. Shareholders generally hope to reverse the LBO within three to seven years by way of a public offering or sale of the company to another firm. A buyout is therefore likely to be successful only if the firm generates enough cash to service the debt in the early years and if the company is attractive to other buyers a few years down the road.

Meg has suggested the potential LBO to her partners, Ben Feller and Brenton Flynn. Ben and Brenton have asked Meg to provide projections of the cash flows for the company. Meg has provided the following estimates (in millions):

	2022	2023	2024	2025	2026
Sales	₹2,419	₹2,713	₹2,923	₹2,992	₹3,114
Costs	643	844	888	960	1,011
Depreciation	427	454	473	496	506
EBT	₹1,349	₹1,415	₹1,562	₹1,536	₹1,597
Capital expenditures	₹ 246	₹ 213	₹ 267	₹ 271	₹ 267
Change in NWC	–₹ 107	–₹ 164	₹ 89	₹ 84	₹ 95
Asset sales	₹1,250	₹ 905			

At the end of five years, Meg estimates that the growth rate in cash flows will be 3.5 percent per year. The capital expenditures are for new projects and the replacement of equipment that wears out. Additionally, the company would realize cash flow from the sale of several divisions. Even though the company will sell these divisions, overall sales should increase because of a more concentrated effort on the remaining divisions.

After plowing through the company's financials and various pro forma scenarios, Ben and Brenton feel that, in five years, they will be able to sell the company to another party or take it public again. They also are aware that they will have to borrow a considerable amount of the purchase price. The interest payments on the debt for each of the next five years if the LBO is undertaken will be (in millions):

	2022	2023	2024	2025	2026
Interest payments	₹1,690	₹1,935	₹2,280	₹2,225	₹2,300

The company currently has a required return on assets of 14 percent. Because of the high debt level, the debt will carry a yield to maturity of 12.5 percent for the next five years. When the debt is refinanced in five years, they believe the new yield to maturity will be 8 percent.

CPI currently has 215 million shares of stock outstanding that sell for ₹29 per share. The corporate tax rate is 21 percent. If Meg, Ben, and Brenton decide to undertake the LBO, what is the most they should offer per share?

Appendix 18A The Adjusted Present Value Approach to Valuing Leveraged Buyouts

To access the appendix for this chapter, please log on to www.mheducation.co.in.

19

Dividends and Other Payouts

On September 25, 2020, security and aerospace company Lockheed Martin announced a broad plan to reward stockholders for the recent success of the firm's business. Under the plan, Lockheed would (1) boost its annual dividend by 8.3 percent, from ₹2.40 cents per share to ₹2.60 per share, and (2) repurchase about ₹1.3 billion of its common stock during the next year. Investors cheered, bidding up the stock price by about 3.2 percent on the day of the announcement. In India, in October 2023, Tata Consultancy Services announced a repurchase plan totaling 1.12 percent of the total outstanding shares at ₹4,150 apiece, i.e., a price that was 18 percent higher than the market trading price. Investors were pleased. Why were investors so pleased? To find out, this chapter explores these types of actions and their implications for shareholders.

Please visit us at **rwjcorporatefinance.blogspot.com** for the latest developments in the world of corporate finance.

19.1 Different Types of Payouts

The term *dividend* usually refers to a cash distribution of earnings. If a distribution is made from sources other than current or accumulated retained earnings, the term *distribution* rather than dividend is used. However, it is acceptable to refer to a distribution from earnings as a *dividend* and a distribution from capital as a *liquidating dividend.*

The most common type of dividend is in the form of cash. When public companies pay dividends, they usually pay **regular cash dividends** four times a year. Sometimes firms will pay a regular cash dividend and an *extra cash dividend.* Paying a cash dividend reduces corporate cash and retained earnings–except in the case of a liquidating dividend (where paid-in capital may be reduced).

Another type of dividend is paid out in shares of stock. This dividend is referred to as a **stock dividend** (also known as issue of bonus shares). It is not a true dividend because no cash leaves the firm. Rather, a stock dividend increases the number of shares outstanding, reducing the value of each share. A stock dividend is commonly expressed as a ratio; for example, with a 2 percent stock dividend, a shareholder receives 1 new share for every 50 currently owned.

When a firm declares a **stock split**, it increases the number of shares outstanding. Because each share is now entitled to a smaller percentage of the firm's cash flow, the stock price should fall. For example, if the managers of a firm whose stock is selling at ₹90 declare a three-for-one stock split, the price of a share of stock should fall to ₹30. A stock split strongly resembles a stock dividend except that it is usually much larger.

An alternative form of cash payout is a **stock repurchase**. As a firm may use cash to pay dividends, it may use cash to buy back shares of its stock. The shares are held by the company and accounted for as treasury stock.

19.2 Standard Method of Cash Dividend Payment

The decision to pay a dividend rests in the hands of the board of directors of the company. A dividend is distributable to shareholders of record on a specific date. When a dividend has been declared, it becomes a liability of the firm and cannot be easily rescinded by the company. The amount of the dividend is expressed as rupees per share (dividend per share), as a percentage of the market price (dividend yield), or as a percentage of earnings per share (dividend payout).

For a list of today's dividends in the U.S. markets, go to **www.thestreet.com/dividends/**.

For a list of today's dividends in the Indian markets, go to the Corporate Actions section of BSE **https://www.bseindia.com/corporates/corporates_act.html**

The mechanics of a dividend payment can be illustrated by the example in Figure 19.1 and the following chronology:

1. **Declaration date**: On January 15 (the declaration date), the board of directors passes a resolution to pay a dividend of ₹1 per share on February 16 to all holders of record on January 30.
2. **Date of record**: The company prepares a list on January 30 of all individuals believed to be stockholders as of this date. The word *believed* is important here: The dividend will not be paid to individuals whose notification of purchase is received by the company after January 30.
3. **Ex-dividend date**: To make sure that dividend checks go to the right people, brokerage firms and stock exchanges establish an *ex-dividend date.* This date is one business day before the date of record (discussed next). If you buy the stock before this date, you are entitled to the dividend. If you buy on this date or after, the previous owner will get the dividend. The ex-dividend date in our example is Thursday, January 29. Before this date, the stock is said to trade *cum dividend.*
4. **Date of payment**: The dividend checks are mailed to the stockholders on February 16.

Obviously, the ex-dividend date is important because an individual purchasing the security before the ex-dividend date will receive the current dividend, whereas another individual purchasing the security on or after this date will not receive the dividend. The stock price will therefore fall on the ex-dividend date (assuming no other events occur). It is worthwhile to note that this drop is an indication of efficiency, not inefficiency, because the market rationally attaches value to a cash dividend. This is illustrated in Figure 19.2.

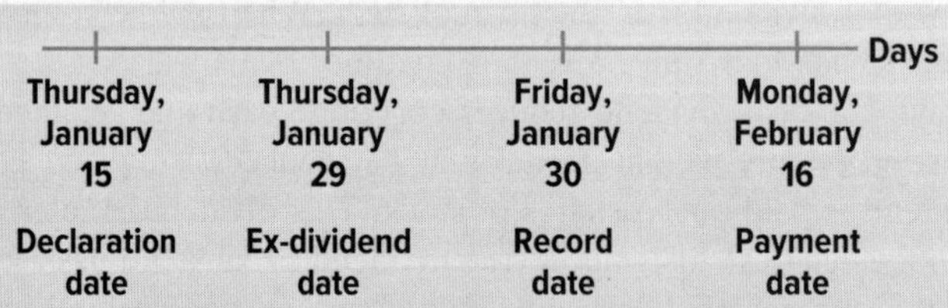

1. *Declaration date*: The board of directors declares a payment of dividends.
2. *Record date*: The declared dividends are distributable to shareholders of record on a specific date.
3. *Ex-dividend date*: A share of stock becomes ex dividend on the date the seller is entitled to keep the dividend; under T+2 Settlement rules in US, shares are traded ex dividend on and after the business day before the record date. In India, under the current T+1 settlement cycle, ex-dividend and Record date happen to be the same day.
4. *Payment date*: The dividend checks are mailed to shareholders of record.

Figure 19.1 Example of Procedure for Dividend Payment

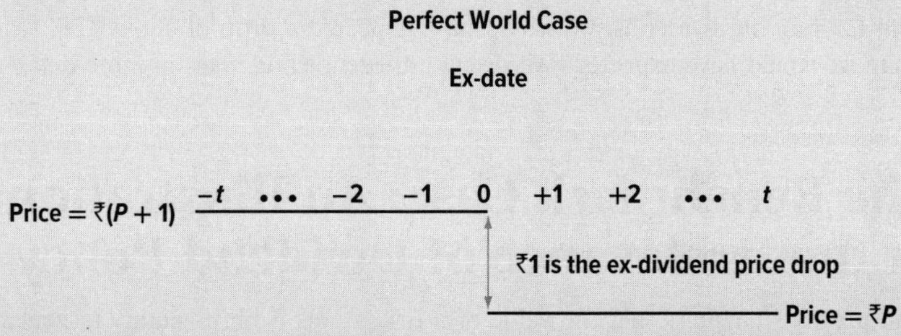

In a world without taxes, the stock price will fall by the amount of the dividend on the ex-date (Time 0). If the dividend is ₹1 per share, the price will be equal to P on the ex-date.

Before ex-date (−1)	Price = ₹(P + 1)
Ex-date (0)	Price = ₹P

Figure 19.2 Price Behavior around the Ex-Dividend Date for a ₹1 Cash Dividend

The amount of the price drop may depend on tax rates. Consider the case with no capital gains taxes. On the day before a stock goes ex dividend, a purchaser must decide either (1) to buy the stock immediately and pay tax on the forthcoming dividend or (2) to buy the stock tomorrow, thereby missing the dividend. If all investors are in the 20 percent tax bracket and the quarterly dividend is ₹1, the stock price should fall by ₹.80 on the ex-dividend date. That is, if the stock price falls by this amount on the ex-dividend date, purchasers will receive the same return from either strategy.

As an example of the price drop on the ex-dividend date, we examine the large dividend paid by aerospace company TransDigm Group in December 2019. The dividend was ₹32.50 per share at a time when the stock price was around ₹600, so the dividend was about 5 percent of the total stock price, a truly special dividend. The stock went ex dividend on December 27, 2019. The stock price chart here shows the change in TransDigm during December of that year.

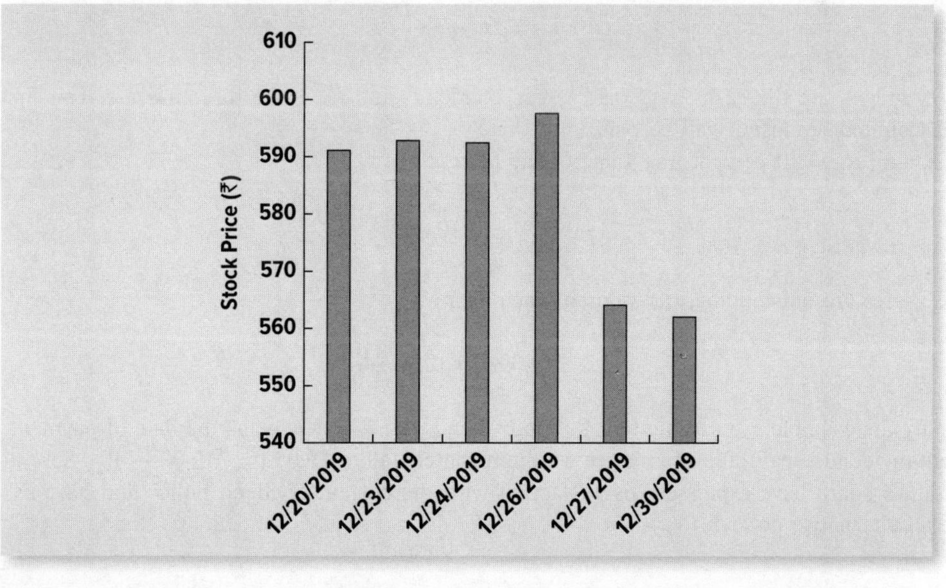

The stock closed at ₹597.78 on December 26 and opened at ₹568.00 on December 27–a drop of ₹29.78. With a 20 percent tax rate on dividends, we would have expected a drop of about ₹26, so the actual price dropped more than we would have expected. We discuss dividends and taxes in more detail in a subsequent section.

19.3 The Benchmark Case: An Illustration of the Irrelevance of Dividend Policy

We have stated in previous chapters that the value of a firm stems from its ability to generate and pay out its distributable (i.e., free) cash flow. Specially, we put forth the idea that the value of a share of stock should be equal to the present value of its future expected dividend payouts. This idea still stands. In this section, we discuss dividend policy, which we define as the timing of a firm's dividend payouts given the level of its distributable cash flow. A firm never dies with cash still left inside that could still be distributed to investors. Therefore, we assume that a firm pays out all of its distributable cash flow at some point over its life. For now, we will also assume that firms can only distribute cash via dividends (we will consider share repurchases in the next section).

A powerful argument can be made that the timing of dividends does not matter when cash flows do not change. In a world without taxes and other frictions, dividend policy is irrelevant for investors.

This idea will be illustrated with the Upasana Company. Upasana is an all-equity firm that started 10 years ago. The current financial managers know at the present time (Date 0) that the firm will dissolve in one year (Date 1). At Date 0, the managers are able to forecast cash flows with perfect certainty. The managers know that the firm will receive a cash flow of ₹10,000 immediately and another ₹10,000 next year. Upasana has no additional projects.

CURRENT POLICY: DIVIDENDS SET EQUAL TO CASH FLOW

At the present time, dividends (D) at each date are set equal to the available cash flow of ₹10,000. The value of the firm can be calculated by discounting these dividends. This value is expressed as:

$$V_0 = D_0 + \frac{D_1}{1 + R_S}$$

where D_0 and D_1 are the cash flows paid out in dividends and R_S is the discount rate. The first dividend is not discounted because it will be paid immediately.

Assuming $R_S = 10$ percent, the value of the firm is:

$$₹19{,}090.91 = ₹10{,}000 + \frac{₹10{,}000}{1.1}$$

If 1,000 shares are outstanding, the value of each share is:

$$₹19.09 = ₹10 + \frac{₹10}{1.1}$$

To simplify the example, we assume that the ex-dividend date is the same as the date of payment. After the imminent dividend is paid, the stock price will immediately fall to ₹9.09 (= ₹19.09 − 10). Several members of Upasana's board have expressed dissatisfaction with the current dividend policy and have asked you to analyze an alternative policy.

ALTERNATIVE POLICY: INITIAL DIVIDEND IS GREATER THAN CASH FLOW

Another policy is for the firm to pay a dividend of ₹11 per share immediately, which is a total dividend payout of ₹11,000. Because the available cash flow is only ₹10,000, the extra ₹1,000 must be raised in one of a few ways. Perhaps the simplest would be to issue ₹1,000 of stock now (at Date 0). Assume that stock is issued and the new stockholders will desire enough cash flow at Date 1 to let them earn the required 10 percent return on their Date 0 investment. The new stockholders will demand ₹1,100 of the Date 1 cash flow, leaving only ₹8,900 to the old stockholders. The dividends to the old stockholders will be these:

	Date 0	Date 1
Aggregate dividends to old stockholders	₹ 11,000	₹ 8,900
Dividends per share	₹ 11.00	₹ 8.90

The present value of the dividends per share is therefore:

$$₹19.09 = ₹11 + \frac{₹8.90}{1.1}$$

Students often find it instructive to determine the price at which the new stock is issued. Because the new stockholders are not entitled to the immediate dividend, they would pay ₹8.09 (= ₹8.90/1.1) per share. Thus, 123.60 (= ₹1,000/₹8.09) new shares are issued.

THE INDIFFERENCE PROPOSITION

Notice that the stock value is equal under either dividend policy. This leads to the initially surprising conclusion that the change in dividend policy did not affect the value of a share of stock as long as all distributable cash flow is paid out. However, on reflection, the result seems sensible. The new stockholders are parting with their money at Date 0 and receiving it back with the appropriate return at Date 1. In other words, they are taking on a zero NPV investment.

The indifference of investors toward dividend policy implies two other important indifference conditions. First, investors should be indifferent between dividends and *retained earnings.* Here, retained earnings just means that the firm plans to retain the cash inside the firm today instead of paying out the cash as a dividend today. The firm must eventually pay out all its cash, so retained earnings is equivalent to a policy in which the firm delays dividends. Since investors are indifferent to the timing of dividends, they are also indifferent between dividends and retained earnings.

Second, investors should be indifferent between dividends and capital gains. *Capital gains* refers to changes in the share price. When the firm pays out a dividend in a benchmark world, the share price drops by the amount of the dividend, so shareholders suffer a capital loss (or a negative capital gain). Investors are not worse off, however, because they also receive the cash dividend to make up for the capital loss. A firm strategy that favors capital gains over dividends is equivalent to a strategy in which a firm delays dividends. Again, since investors are indifferent to the timing of dividends, they are also indifferent between dividends and capital gains.

HOMEMADE DIVIDENDS

To illustrate the indifference investors have toward dividend policy in our example, we used present value equations. An alternative and perhaps more intuitively appealing explanation avoids the mathematics of discounted cash flows.

Suppose individual Investor X prefers dividends per share of ₹10 at both Dates 0 and 1. Would she be disappointed when informed that the firm's management is adopting the alternative dividend policy (dividends of ₹11 and ₹8.90 on the two dates, respectively)? Not necessarily: She could easily reinvest the ₹1 of unneeded funds received on Date 0, yielding an incremental return of ₹1.10 at Date 1. She would receive her desired net cash flow of ₹11 − 1 = ₹10 at Date 0 and ₹8.90 + 1.10 = ₹10 at Date 1.

Conversely, imagine Investor Z, who prefers ₹11 of cash flow at Date 0 and ₹8.90 of cash flow at Date 1, and finds that management will pay dividends of ₹10 at both Dates 0 and 1. He can sell off shares of stock at Date 0 to receive the desired amount of cash flow. That is, if he sells off shares (or fractions of shares) at Date 0 totaling ₹1, his cash flow at Date 0 becomes ₹10 + 1 = ₹11. Because a ₹1 sale of stock at Date 0 will reduce his dividends by ₹1.10 at Date 1, his net cash flow at Date 1 would be ₹10 − 1.10 = ₹8.90.

The example illustrates how investors can make **homemade dividends**. In this instance, corporate dividend policy is being undone by a potentially dissatisfied stockholder. This homemade dividend is illustrated by Figure 19.3. Here the firm's cash flows of ₹10 per share at both Dates 0 and 1 are represented by Point A. This point also represents the initial dividend payout. However, as we saw, the firm could alternatively pay out ₹11 per share at Date 0 and ₹8.90 per share at Date 1, a strategy represented by Point B. Similarly, by either issuing new stock or buying back old stock, the firm could achieve a dividend payout represented by any point on the diagonal line.

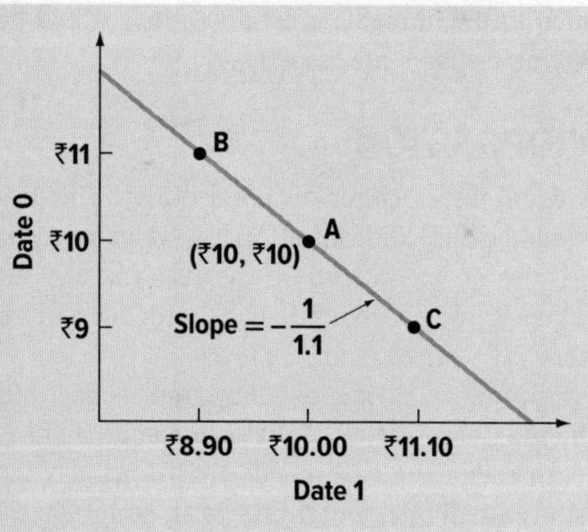

The graph illustrates both (1) how managers can vary dividend policy and (2) how individuals can undo the firm's dividend policy.

Managers varying dividend policy: A firm paying out all cash flows immediately is at Point A on the graph. The firm could achieve Point B by issuing stock to pay extra dividends or achieve Point C by buying back old stock with some of its cash.

Individuals undoing the firm's dividend policy: Suppose the firm adopts the dividend policy represented by Point B: dividends per share of ₹11 at Date 0 and ₹8.90 at Date 1. An investor can reinvest ₹1 of the dividends at 10 percent, which will place her at Point A. Suppose, alternatively, the firm adopts the dividend policy represented by Point A. An investor can sell off ₹1 of stock at Date 0, placing him at Point B. No matter what dividend policy the firm establishes, a shareholder can undo it.

Figure 19.3 Homemade Dividends: A Trade-off between Dividends per Share at Date 0 and Dividends per Share at Date 1

The previous paragraph describes the choices available to the managers of the firm. The same diagonal line also represents the choices available to the shareholder. For example, if the shareholder receives a per-share dividend distribution of (₹11, ₹8.90), he or she can either reinvest some of the dividends to move down and to the right on the graph or sell off shares of stock and move up and to the left.

The implications of the graph can be summarized in two sentences:

1. By varying dividend policy, managers can achieve any payout along the diagonal line in Figure 19.3.
2. Either by reinvesting excess dividends at Date 0 or by selling off shares of stock at this date, an individual investor can achieve any net cash payout along the diagonal line.

Because both the company and the individual investor can move only along the diagonal line, dividend policy in this model is irrelevant. The changes the managers make in dividend policy can be undone by an individual who, by either reinvesting dividends or selling off stock, can move to a desired point on the diagonal line.

A TEST

You can test your knowledge of this material by examining these true statements:

1. Dividends are relevant.
2. Dividend policy is irrelevant.

The first statement follows from common sense. Clearly, investors prefer higher dividends to lower dividends at any single date if the dividend level is held constant at every other date. In other words, if the dividend per share at a given date is raised while the dividend per share for each other date is held constant, the stock price will rise. This act can be accomplished by management decisions that improve productivity, increase tax savings, or strengthen product marketing. In fact, you may recall that in Chapter 9 we argued that the value of a firm's equity is equal to the discounted present value of all its future dividends.

The second statement is understandable once we realize that dividend policy cannot raise the dividend per share at one date while holding the dividend level per share constant at all other dates. Rather, dividend policy merely establishes the trade-off between dividends at one date and dividends at another date. As we saw in Figure 19.3, holding cash flows constant, an increase in Date 0 dividends can be accomplished only by a decrease in Date 1 dividends. The extent of the decrease is such that the present value of all dividends is unaffected.

DIVIDENDS AND INVESTMENT POLICY

The preceding argument shows that an increase in dividends through issuance of new shares neither helps nor hurts the stockholders. Similarly, a reduction in dividends through share repurchase neither helps nor hurts stockholders. The key to this result is understanding that the overall level of cash flows is assumed to be fixed and that we are not changing the available positive net present value projects.

What about reducing capital expenditures to increase dividends? Earlier chapters show that a firm should accept all positive net present value projects. To do otherwise would reduce the value of the firm. We have an important point:

Firms should never give up a positive NPV project to increase a dividend (or to pay a dividend for the first time).

This idea was implicitly considered by Miller and Modigliani. One of the assumptions underlying their dividend irrelevance proposition was this: "The investment policy of the firm is set ahead of time and is not altered by changes in dividend policy."[1]

[1]The original paper is Franco Modigliani and Merton H. Miller, "The Cost of Capital, Company Finance and the Theory of Investment," *American Economic Review* 48, no. 3 (June 1958): 261–97.

19.4 Repurchase of Stock

Instead of paying dividends, a firm may use cash to repurchase shares of its own stock. Share repurchases, also called buybacks, have taken on increased importance in recent years. Consider Figure 19.4, which shows the aggregate rupee amounts of dividends, repurchases, and earnings for large U.S. firms in the years from 2004 to 2020. As can be seen, the amount of repurchases was more than the amount of dividends up to 2008. However, the amount of dividends exceeded the amount of repurchases in late 2008 and throughout 2009, before reversing after 2009. Notice also from Figure 19.4 that there is "stickiness" to repurchases and dividend payouts. In late 2008 when aggregate corporate earnings turned negative, the level of dividends and share repurchases did not change much. More generally, the volatility of aggregate earnings has been greater than that of dividends and share repurchases.

Share repurchases are typically accomplished in one of three ways. First, companies may purchase their own stock, just as anyone would buy shares of a particular stock. In these *open market purchases*, the firm

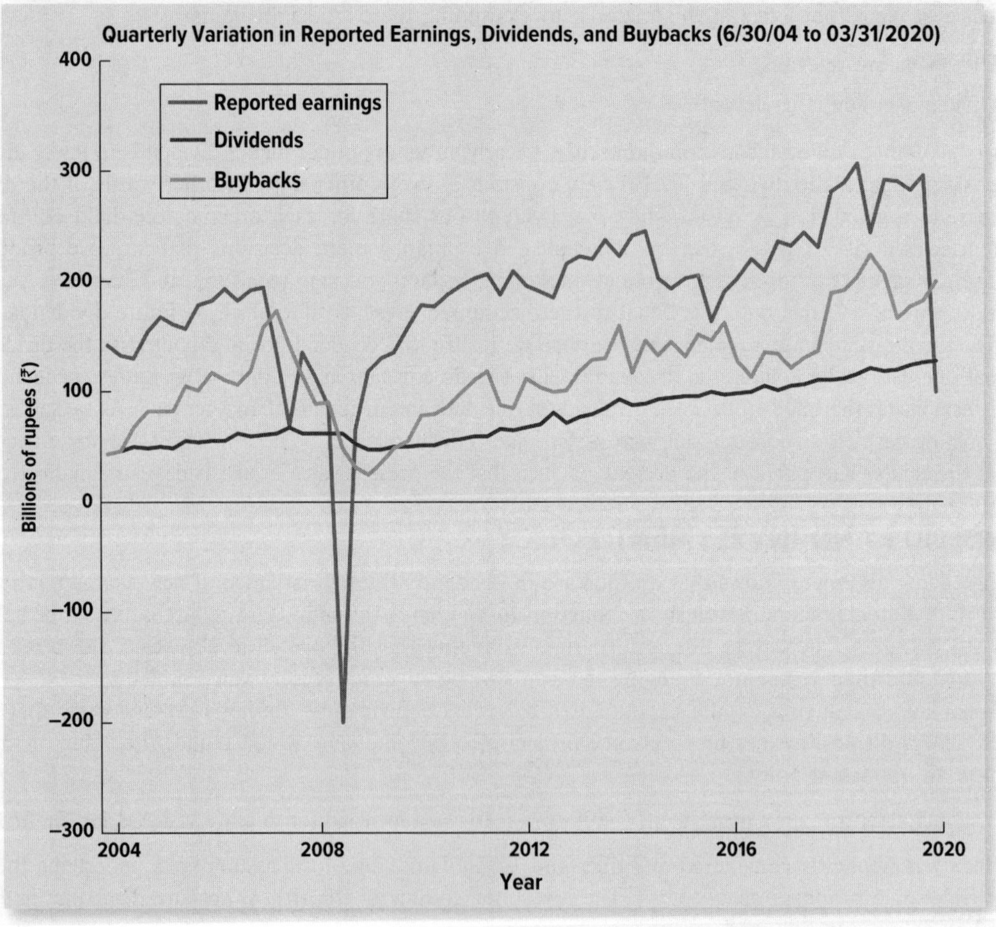

Figure 19.4 Earnings, Dividends, and Net Repurchases for Large U.S. Firms

SOURCE: S&P Dow Jones Indices, S&P.

does not reveal itself as the buyer. The seller does not know whether the shares were sold back to the firm or to another investor.

Second, the firm could institute a *tender offer*. Here, the firm announces to all of its stockholders that it is willing to buy a fixed number of shares at a specific price. Suppose Amar and Chameli (A&C), Inc., has 1 million shares of stock outstanding, with a stock price of ₹50 per share. The firm makes a tender offer to buy back 300,000 shares at ₹60 per share. A&C chooses a price above ₹50 to induce shareholders to sell–that is, tender–their shares. In fact, if the tender price is set high enough, shareholders may want to sell more than the 300,000 shares. In the extreme case where all outstanding shares are tendered, A&C will buy back 3 out of every 10 shares that a shareholder has. On the other hand, if shareholders do not tender enough shares, the offer can be canceled. A method related to a tender offer is the *Dutch auction*. Here the firm does not set a fixed price for the shares to be sold. Instead, the firm conducts an auction in which it bids for shares. The firm announces the number of shares it is willing to buy back at various prices, and shareholders indicate how many shares they are willing to sell at the various prices. The firm will then pay the lowest price that will achieve its goal.

Finally, firms may repurchase shares from specific individual stockholders, a procedure called a *targeted repurchase*. Suppose the International Biotechnology Company purchased approximately 10 percent of the outstanding stock of the Prime Robotics Company (P-R Co.) in April at around ₹38 per share. At that time, International Biotechnology announced to the Securities and Exchange Commission that it might eventually try to take control of P-R Co. In May, P-R Co. repurchased the International Biotechnology holdings at ₹48 per share, well above the market price at that time. This offer was not extended to other shareholders.

Companies engage in targeted repurchases for a variety of reasons. In some rare cases, a single large stockholder can be bought out at a price lower than that in a tender offer. The legal fees in a targeted repurchase also may be lower than those in a more typical buyback. In addition, the shares of large stockholders often are repurchased to avoid a takeover that is unfavorable to management.

We now consider an example of a repurchase presented in a theoretical world without taxes or other frictions. We next discuss real-world factors involved in the repurchase decision.

DIVIDEND VERSUS REPURCHASE: CONCEPTUAL EXAMPLE

Imagine that Tezaab Industries has excess cash of ₹300,000 (or ₹3 per share) and is considering an immediate payment of this amount as an extra dividend. The firm forecasts that, after the dividend, earnings will be ₹450,000 per year, or ₹4.50 for each of the 100,000 shares outstanding. Because the price-earnings ratio is 6 for comparable companies, the shares of the firm should sell for ₹27 (= ₹4.50 × 6) after the dividend is paid. These figures are presented in the top half of Table 19.1. Because the dividend is ₹3 per share, the stock would have sold for ₹30 a share before payment of the dividend.

Alternatively, the firm could use the excess cash to repurchase some of its own stock. Imagine that a tender offer of ₹30 per share is made. Here, 10,000 shares are repurchased so that the total number of shares remaining is 90,000. With fewer shares outstanding, the earnings per share will rise to ₹5 (= ₹450,000/90,000). The price-earnings ratio remains at 6 because both the business and financial risks of the firm are the same in the repurchase case as they were in the dividend case. The price of a share after the repurchase is ₹30 (= ₹5 × 6). These results are presented in the bottom half of Table 19.1.

If commissions, taxes, and other imperfections are ignored in our example, the stockholders are indifferent between a dividend and a repurchase. With dividends, each stockholder owns a share worth ₹27 and receives ₹3 in dividends, so that the total value is ₹30. This figure is the same as both the amount received by the selling stockholders and the value of the stock for the remaining stockholders in the repurchase case.

Table 19.1 Dividend versus Repurchase Example for Tezaab Industries

	For Entire Firm	Per Share
Extra Dividend		**(100,000 shares outstanding)**
Proposed dividend	₹ 300,000	₹ 3.00
Forecasted annual earnings after dividend	450,000	4.50
Market value of stock after dividend	2,700,000	27.00
Repurchase		**(90,000 shares outstanding)**
Forecasted annual earnings after repurchase	₹ 450,000	₹ 5.00
Market value of stock after repurchase	2,700,000	30.00

This example illustrates the important point that, in a perfect market, the firm is indifferent between a dividend payment and a share repurchase. The share price will remain constant in the case of a share repurchase, while the share price will fall in the case of a dividend payment. However, shareholders will be indifferent between the two because they will receive the cash dividend payment to exactly make up for the decline in share price in the case of a dividend payment. This result is quite similar to the indifference propositions established by MM for debt versus equity financing and for dividends versus capital gains.

You often may read in the popular financial press that a repurchase agreement is beneficial because earnings per share increase. Earnings per share do rise for Tezaab Industries if a repurchase is substituted for a cash dividend: The EPS is ₹4.50 after a dividend and ₹5 after the repurchase. This result holds because the drop in shares after a repurchase implies a reduction in the denominator of the EPS ratio.

However, the financial press frequently places undue emphasis on EPS figures in a repurchase agreement. Given the irrelevance propositions we have discussed, the increase in EPS here is not beneficial. Table 19.1 shows that, in a perfect capital market, the total value to the stockholder is the same under the dividend payment strategy as under the repurchase strategy.

DIVIDENDS VERSUS REPURCHASES: REAL-WORLD CONSIDERATIONS

We previously referred to Figure 19.4, which showed growth in share repurchases relative to dividends. In fact, most firms that pay dividends also repurchase shares of stock. This suggests that repurchasing shares of stock is not always a substitute for paying dividends but rather a complement to it. Recently, the number of U.S. industrial firms that pay dividends only or repurchase only is about the same as the number of firms paying both dividends and repurchasing shares. Why do some firms choose repurchases over dividends? Here are perhaps five of the most common reasons.

1. Flexibility Firms often view dividends as a commitment to their stockholders and are quite hesitant to reduce an existing dividend. Repurchases do not represent a similar commitment. A firm with a permanent increase in cash flow is likely to increase its dividend. Conversely, a firm whose cash flow increase is only temporary is likely to repurchase shares of stock.

2. Executive Compensation Executives are frequently given stock options as part of their overall compensation. Let's revisit the Tezaab Industries example of Table 19.1, where the firm's stock was selling at ₹30 when the firm was considering either a dividend or a repurchase. Further imagine that Tezaab had granted 1,000 stock options to its CEO, Abhijeet Singh, two years earlier. At that time, the stock price was, say, only ₹20. This means that Mr. Singh can buy 1,000 shares for ₹20 a share at any time between the grant of the options and their expiration, a procedure called *exercising* the options. His gain from exercising is directly proportional to the rise in the stock price above ₹20. As we saw in the example, the price of the stock would fall to ₹27 following a dividend but would remain at ₹30 following a repurchase. The CEO would clearly prefer a repurchase to a dividend because the difference between the stock price and the exercise price of ₹20 would be ₹10 (= ₹30 − 20) following the repurchase but only ₹7 (= ₹27 − 20) following the dividend. Existing stock options will always have greater value when the firm repurchases shares instead of paying a dividend because the stock price will be greater after a repurchase than after a dividend.

3. Offset to Dilution The exercise of employee stock options also increases the number of shares outstanding. In other words, exercise causes dilution of the stock. Firms frequently buy back shares of stock to offset this dilution. However, it is hard to argue that this is a valid reason for repurchase. As we showed in Table 19.1, repurchase is neither better nor worse for the stockholders than a dividend. Our argument holds whether or not stock options have been exercised previously.

4. Undervaluation Many companies buy back stock because they believe that a repurchase is their best investment. This occurs more frequently when managers believe that the stock price is temporarily depressed.

The fact that some companies repurchase their stock when they believe it is undervalued does not imply that the management of the company must be correct; only empirical studies can make this determination. So far, the evidence is mixed. However, the immediate stock market reaction to the announcement of a stock repurchase is usually quite favorable, because it signals that the manager believes the shares are worth more than the current market price.

5. Taxes Because taxes for both dividends and share repurchases are treated in depth in the next section, suffice it to say at this point that repurchases provide a tax advantage over dividends.

19.4A Repurchase of Shares in India

In India, repurchase of stock is commonly known as buyback of shares.[2] More than 40 companies in India announced buyback of shares in the calendar year 2023. IT behemoth TCS announced a share buyback of ₹ 17,000 crore at ₹ 4,150 a share. The buyback price was at a premium of about 18 percent to the prevailing price. As per trends, one can observe an increasing use of buyback as a means of financial restructuring by India Inc.

Under the buyback scheme, paid-up capital of the company can be reduced by cancelling the amount of shares purchased. Another option is to reissue the shares bought back after a period of 24 months from the date of last buyback of securities. Once the buyback is finalized, the companies are prohibited from issuing new shares for a 12-month duration, with the exception of bonus issues or fulfilling existing obligations such as conversion of warrants, stock option schemes or conversion of preference shares. The bought back shares do not qualify for any voting or dividend rights and for bonus or any rights issue before they are reissued. However, strong cash flows and reserves are a prerequisite for going in for buyback.

METHODS OF BUYBACK IN INDIA

The buyback of shares is often done in three ways.

[a] Open Offer Purchase - In an open offer, a company can buy its shares directly from the stock market through brokers. The company has to fix a maximum price for an open market offer, stipulate the number of shares it intends to purchase, and announce the closing date of the offer.

[2]In 1998, the Indian government gave in to the demand from the corporate sector for permitting buy-back. This demand became more intense after the new takeover code came into force last year. There were fears that many well-managed companies might be taken over, particularly where the percentage of promoter's holding is not very high. By a 1998 amendment to the Companies Act, 1956, government allowed a company to buyback its own shares (Section 77A). Even before 1998, buyback was possible either as reduction of capital (Section 100) or as a scheme of arrangement (Section 391), both with the court's approval. This section takes inputs from Securities and Exchange Board of India's (Buyback of Securities) Regulation, 1998, Chapter V, General Obligations; and SEBI Takeover Code, 1997.

[b] Tender Offer - In a tender offer, the offer is at a fixed price offer, i.e., the company fixes a particular price for the maximum number of shares it is willing to purchase. It also fixes an outer time limit for accepting the offer. The offer price is usually fixed at a premium in order to encourage shareholders to surrender their shares. Within this, firms can use the targeted buyback methods to repurchase shares from a select group of shareholders. But this method of buyback is rarely seen in the Indian context. The best example of such a buyback in the Indian context was the buyback of shares undertaken by the Great Eastern Shipping Company (GESCO) to protect itself from a hostile takeover bid led by the Abhishek H Dalmia group.[3]

[c] Book Building Offer- A method of buyback available but not used by companies often is to use the book building process to buyback shares. If the book building option is used, a draft prospectus has to be filed with SEBI. The prospectus should contain all the details of the offer, except the price at which the securities will be offered (a price band is specified). The prospectus is then circulated among institutional buyers by a leading merchant banker acting as the book runner. Institutional investors specify the price as well as the volume of shares they intend to sell. The book runner, on receiving the above information, determines the price at which the offer is to be made to the public.

Exhibit 19.1 summarizes the three methods.

Exhibit 19.1 Nuances of Share Buyback Methods

Buyback Method	Tender Offer	Open Offer	Book-Building
Price for buyback	Fixed Price	Market determined	Based on bidding price
Buy-back remains open for	15–30 days	12 months from the date of resolution	15–30 days
Prospectus required	No	No	Yes, filled with regulator
Can promoters participate in the buy-back	Yes	No	Yes

RESTRICTIONS ON BUYBACK BY INDIAN COMPANIES

The regulatory framework governing buybacks in India is primarily dictated by the Companies Act, 2013, and the Securities and Exchange Board of India (SEBI) (buy-back of securities) regulations, 2018. These regulations aim to ensure transparency and safeguard the interests of investors. The main requirements/features are: [a] Buyback should not exceed 25 percent of the total paid-up capital and free reserves of the company; [b] For upto 10 percent repurchase, approval of Board of directors is required. For upto 25 percent of repurchase, shareholder approval is needed; [c] The post-buyback debt-to-equity ratio should not be more than 2:1; [d] A declaration of solvency has to be filed with SEBI and Registrar Of Companies; [e] The shares bought back should be extinguished and physically destroyed; [f] The company must complete the buyback within 12 months of passing the resolution.

The regulations keep on evolving to protect the interests of small investors.

[3]Abhishek H Dalmia group of Delhi made a hostile bid for a 45 percent stake in the GESCO at ₹27 a share. The offer and counteroffers made by the Abhishek H Dalmia group and the promoters of GESCO pushed up the bidding cost. The Abhishek H Dalmia group ultimately sold its stake (around 3 million shares) at ₹54 per share for a consideration of ₹16.3 crore to the GESCO promoters. The Abhishek H Dalmia group had acquired these shares in Gesco for a consideration of ₹7.2 crores. Hence, the Dalmia group made cool gains in a short period.

STEPS INVOLVED IN A BUYBACK

The previous buyback guidelines imposed stringent rules for purchasing shares from the stock exchange. A company that had opted to buyback shares from the stock exchange is required to appoint a merchant banker and make a public announcement of the offer seven days before the commencement of the buyback. This public announcement, containing true and material information, had to be filed with SEBI two days prior. The announcement also needed to clearly specify the brokers and stock exchanges involved. Additionally, the company's directors were required to take full responsibility for the information in the document.

The company was also obligated to submit a copy of the special resolution passed at its general meeting with the stock exchange. This submission, including an explanatory memorandum, needed to be filed within seven days of the resolution being passed. The explanatory memorandum to the resolution had to specify have the buyback price, the quantity of shares intended for buyback, and detailed records of the company's transactions and holdings over the six months preceding the special resolution. This information included the number of shares acquired, the acquisition price, the dates of acquisition, the quantity of shares intended for buyback, and detailed records of the company's transactions and holdings over the six months preceding the special resolution. This information included the number of shares acquired, the acquisition price, and the dates of acquisition. Additionally, the resolution also had to be made public within two days of its passage. Furthermore, the buyback regulations mandated that the company open an escrow account and deposit the required amount before the offer date.

The company was obligated to conclude the share buyback within 12 months from the date of passing the special resolution. Additionally, upon completing the buyback offer, the company was required to publish an advertisement in a national daily within two days. This advertisement was to detail the quantity of shares purchased, their acquisition price, and the total amount invested in the buyback, and any resulting alterations in the company's capital structure and shareholder composition before and after the buyback.

FACTORS DRIVING REPURCHASE OF SHARES IN INDIA

As pointed out in Section 19.4, various theoretical issues and real-world considerations force companies to go in for repurchase of shares. A few of them, which are more specific to India, are listed below:

1. Unused cash: If they have huge cash reserves with not many new profitable projects to invest in and if the company thinks the market price of its share is undervalued. Example: Infosys Limited and Hindustan Unilever Limited.
2. Tax gains: Since dividends are taxed at a higher rate than capital gains, many companies prefer buyback to reward their investors instead of distributing cash dividends, as capital gains tax is generally lower. Example: Smartlink Holdings Limited.
3. Market perception: By buying their shares at a price higher than prevailing market price, a company attempts to signal that its share valuation should be higher. Example: NMDC Limited.
4. Escape monitoring of accounts and legal controls: The company can avoid market regulator's supervision by delisting its shares from the local exchange. It avoids any public scrutiny of its books of accounts. Example: Accelya Solutions India Limited and Kodak India Limited.
5. Show rosier financials: Companies try to use buyback method to show better financial ratios. For example, when a company uses its cash to buy stock, it reduces outstanding shares and also the assets on the balance sheet (because cash is an asset). Thus, return on assets (ROA) actually increases with reduction in assets, and return on equity (ROE) increases as there is less outstanding equity. Example: Ajanta Pharma Limited.
6. Increase promoter's stake: Some companies buyback stock to increase the promoter's holding. Example: Nestle India Limited, KIOCL.

Exhibit 19.2 lists the spate of buybacks and their methods that took place in the year 2023.

Exhibit 19.2 Select Share Buyback Details in the year 2023

Buyback Type	Tender Offer					Delisting	Book Building		
	Technocraft Industries Ltd	Zydus Lifesciences Ltd	Piramal Enterprises Ltd	Larsen & Toubro	Tata Consultancy Services	Shreyas Shipping Logistics Ltd	SENCO Gold Ltd	Tata Technologies Ltd	Cello World Ltd
Open Date	1-Feb-23	29-Feb-24	31-Aug-23	18-Sep-23	01-Dec-23	11-Oct-23	04-Jul-23	22-Nov-23	30-Oct-23
Close Date	14-Feb-23	07-Mar-24	06-Sep-23	25-Sep-23	07-Dec-23	17-Oct-23	6-Jul-23	24-Nov-23	01-Nov-23
Price	1000	1005	1250	3200	4150	400	301-317	475-500	61

19.5 Personal Taxes, Dividends, and Stock Repurchases

Section 19.3 asserted that in a world without taxes and other frictions, the timing of dividend payout does not matter if distributable cash flows do not change. Similarly, Section 19.4 concluded that the choice between a share repurchase and a dividend is irrelevant in a world of this type. This section examines the effect of taxes on both dividends and repurchases. Our discussion is facilitated by classifying firms into two types: those without sufficient cash to pay a dividend and those with sufficient cash to do so.

FIRMS WITHOUT SUFFICIENT CASH TO PAY A DIVIDEND

It is simplest to begin with a firm without cash that is owned by a single entrepreneur. If this firm should decide to pay a dividend of ₹100, it must raise capital. The firm might choose among a number of different stock and bond issues to pay the dividend. For simplicity, we assume that the entrepreneur contributes cash to the firm by issuing stock to himself. This transaction, diagrammed in the left side of Figure 19.5, would clearly be a *wash* in a world without taxes or other frictions. The ₹100 cash goes into the firm when stock is issued and is immediately paid out as a dividend. The entrepreneur neither benefits nor loses when the dividend is paid, a result consistent with Miller-Modigliani.

Now assume that dividends are taxed at the owner's personal tax rate of 15 percent. The firm still receives ₹100 upon issuance of stock. However, the entrepreneur does not get to keep the full ₹100 dividend. Instead the dividend payment is taxed, implying that the owner receives only ₹85 net after tax. The entrepreneur loses ₹15.

Though the example is clearly contrived and unrealistic, similar results can be reached for more plausible situations. Financial economists generally agree that in a world of personal taxes, firms should not issue stock to pay dividends.

The direct costs of issuance will add to this effect. Investment bankers must be paid when new capital is raised. Due to these costs, the net receipts due to the firm from a new issue are less than 100 percent of total capital raised. Because the size of new issues can be lowered by a reduction in dividends, we have another argument in favor of a low-dividend policy.

Of course, our advice not to finance dividends through new stock issues might need to be modified somewhat in the real world. A company with a large and steady cash flow for many years in the past might be paying a regular dividend. If the cash flow unexpectedly dried up for a single year, should new stock be issued so that dividends could be continued? Although our previous discussion would imply that new stock

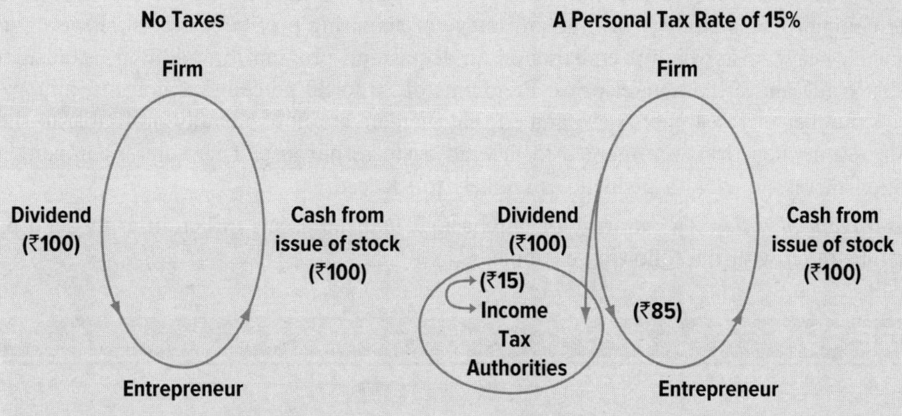

In the no-tax case, the entrepreneur receives the ₹100 in dividends that he gave to the firm when purchasing stock. The entire operation is called a *wash*; in other words, it has no economic effect. With taxes, the entrepreneur still receives ₹100 in dividends. However, assume he must pay ₹15 in taxes to the Income Tax Authorities. The entrepreneur loses and the Income Tax Authorities wins when a firm issues stock to pay a dividend.

Figure 19.5 Firm Issues Stock to Pay a Dividend

should not be issued, many managers might issue the stock anyway for practical reasons. In particular, stockholders appear to prefer dividend stability. Managers might be forced to issue stock to achieve this stability, knowing full well the adverse tax consequences.

FIRMS WITH SUFFICIENT CASH TO PAY A DIVIDEND

The previous discussion argued that in a world with personal taxes, a firm should not issue stock to pay a dividend. Does the tax disadvantage of dividends imply the stronger policy, "Never, under any circumstances, pay dividends in a world with personal taxes"?

We argue next that this prescription does not necessarily apply to firms with excess cash. To see this, imagine a firm with ₹1 million in extra cash after selecting all positive NPV projects and determining the level of prudent cash balances. The firm might consider the following alternatives to a dividend:

1. *Select additional capital budgeting projects.* Because the firm has taken all the available positive NPV projects already, it must invest its excess cash in negative NPV projects. This is clearly a policy at variance with the principles of corporate finance.

   In spite of our distaste for this policy, researchers have suggested that many managers purposely take on negative NPV projects in lieu of paying dividends.[4] The idea here is that managers would rather keep the funds in the firm because their prestige, pay, and perquisites often are tied to the firm's size. Although managers may help themselves here, they are hurting stockholders. We broached this subject in Chapter 17, and we will have more to say about it later in this chapter.

[4]See, for example, Michael C. Jensen, "Agency Costs of Free Cash Flow, Corporate Finance, and Takeovers," *American Economic Review* 76, no. 2 (May 1986): 323–29.

2. *Acquire other companies.* To avoid the payment of dividends, a firm might use excess cash to acquire another company. This strategy has the advantage of acquiring profitable assets. However, a firm often incurs heavy costs when it embarks on an acquisition program. In addition, acquisitions are invariably made above the market price. Premiums of 20 to 80 percent are not uncommon. Because of this, a number of researchers have argued that mergers are not generally profitable to the acquiring company, even when firms are merged for a valid business purpose. Therefore, a company making an acquisition merely to avoid a dividend is unlikely to succeed.
3. *Purchase financial assets.* The strategy of purchasing financial assets in lieu of a dividend payment can be illustrated with the following example.

EXAMPLE 19.1

Dividends and Taxes The Raghuvanshi Electric Company has ₹1,000 of extra cash. It can retain the cash and invest it in Treasury bills yielding 10 percent or it can pay the cash to shareholders as a dividend. Shareholders also can invest in Treasury bills with the same yield. Suppose the corporate tax rate is 21 percent and the personal tax rate is 28 percent for all individuals. Further suppose the maximum tax rate on dividends is 15 percent. How much cash will investors have after five years under each policy?

If dividends are paid now, shareholders will receive:

$$₹1{,}000 \times (1 - .15) = ₹850$$

today after taxes. Because their return after personal tax on Treasury bills is 7.2 percent [= .10 × (1 − .28)], shareholders will have:

$$₹850 \times 1.072^5 = ₹1{,}203.35$$

in five years. Note that interest income is taxed at the personal tax rate (28 percent in this example), but dividends are taxed at the lower rate of 15 percent.

If Raghuvanshi Electric Company retains the cash to invest in Treasury bills, its aftertax interest rate will be 7.9 percent [= .10 × (1 − .21)]. At the end of five years, the firm will have:

$$₹1{,}000 \times 1.079^5 = ₹1{,}462.54$$

If these proceeds are then paid as a dividend, the stockholders will receive:

$$₹1{,}462.54 \times (1 - .15) = ₹1{,}243.16$$

after personal taxes at Year 5. The aftertax value received by stockholders will be greater if the firm pays the dividend in Year 5.

This example shows that for a firm with extra cash, the dividend payout decision will depend on personal and corporate tax rates. If personal tax rates are higher than corporate tax rates, a firm will have an incentive to reduce dividend payouts. However, if personal tax rates are lower than corporate tax rates, a firm will have an incentive to pay out any excess cash as dividends.

In the United States in 2020, the highest tax rate for individuals was 37 percent and the corporate tax rate was 21 percent. Because many investors face tax rates above the corporate tax rate, it appears that firms have an incentive to hoard cash.

Similar peculiarities exist in Indian tax legislation, encouraging businesses to invest their capital in other dividend-paying companies instead of disbursing dividends. If the receiving business distributes the dividend amount to its shareholders, any dividends received from domestic companies are not included in the income of the receiving firm. However, dividends from overseas companies are not free from taxation upon receipt. For individuals, the dividends received are taxed at the applicable tax rate.

4. *Repurchase shares.* The example we described in the previous section showed that investors are indifferent between share repurchases and dividends in a world without taxes and transaction costs. However, under current tax law, stockholders generally prefer a repurchase to a dividend.

   As an example, consider an individual receiving a dividend of ₹1 on each of 100 shares of a stock. With a 15 percent tax rate, that individual would pay taxes of ₹15 on the dividend. Selling shareholders would pay lower taxes if the firm repurchased ₹100 of existing shares. This occurs because taxes are paid only on the profit from a sale. The individual's gain on a sale would be only ₹40 if the shares sold for ₹100 were originally purchased for, say, ₹60. The capital gains tax would be ₹6 (= .15 × ₹40), a number below the tax on dividends of ₹15. Note that the tax from a repurchase is less than the tax on a dividend even though the same 15 percent tax rate applies to both the repurchase and the dividend.

   The key point here is that a taxable investor who receives a dividend must pay taxes on it. With a repurchase, that same investor can choose whether or not to participate. An investor with a large potential capital gain can choose not to sell and vice versa. Of all the alternatives to dividends mentioned in this section, the strongest case can be made for repurchases. In fact, academics have long wondered why firms ever pay a dividend instead of repurchasing stock. There have been at least two possible reasons for avoiding repurchases. First, Grullon and Michaely point out that, in the long ago past, the Securities and Exchange Commission (SEC) had accused some firms undergoing share repurchase programs of illegal price manipulation.[5] However, these authors indicate that SEC Rule 10b-18, adopted in 1982, provides guidelines for firms to avoid the charge of price manipulation. These guidelines are relatively easy to follow, so firms should not have to worry about this charge today. In fact, Grullon and Michaely believe that the large increase in buyback programs in recent decades is at least partially the result of 10b-18. Second, the Income Tax Authorities can penalize firms repurchasing their own stocks if the only reason for doing so is to avoid the taxes that would be levied on dividends. However, this threat has not materialized with the growth in corporate repurchases. These two reasons do not seem to justify the avoidance of repurchases.

SUMMARY OF PERSONAL TAXES

This section suggests that because of personal taxes, firms have an incentive to reduce dividends. They might increase capital expenditures, acquire other companies, or purchase financial assets. However, due to financial considerations and legal constraints, rational firms with large cash flows will likely exhaust these activities with plenty of cash left over for dividends.

It is harder to explain why firms pay dividends instead of repurchasing shares. The tax savings from repurchases can be significant and fear of either the SEBI or the SEC or the Income Tax Authorities seems overblown. Academics are of two minds here. Some argue that companies were slow to grasp the benefits from repurchases. However, because the idea has firmly caught on, the trend toward replacement of dividends with repurchases could continue. Others argue that companies have paid dividends all along for good reasons. We consider potential benefits of dividends in the next section.

[5]See Gustavo Grullon and Roni Michaely, "Dividends, Share Repurchases, and the Substitution Hypothesis," *Journal of Finance* 57, no. 4 (August 2002): 1649–84.

19.6 Real-World Factors Favoring a High-Dividend Policy

The previous section pointed out that because individuals pay taxes on dividends, financial managers might seek ways to reduce dividends. While we discussed the problems with taking on more capital budgeting projects, acquiring other firms, and hoarding cash, we stated that a share repurchase has many of the benefits of a dividend with less of a tax disadvantage. This section considers reasons why a firm might still choose to pay its shareholders high dividends.

DESIRE FOR CURRENT INCOME

It has been argued that many individuals desire current income. The classic example is the group of retired people and others living on a fixed income. The argument further states that these individuals would bid up the stock price should dividends rise and bid down the stock price should dividends fall.

This argument does not hold in perfect capital markets because an individual preferring high current cash flow but holding low-dividend securities could easily sell off shares to provide the necessary funds. Thus, in a world of no transaction costs, a high current-dividend policy would be of no value to the stockholder.

However, the current income argument is relevant in the real world. Stock sales involve brokerage fees and other transaction costs–direct cash expenses that could be avoided by an investment in high-dividend securities. In addition, stock sales are time-consuming, further leading investors to buy high-dividend securities.

To put this argument in perspective, remember that financial intermediaries such as mutual funds can perform repackaging transactions at low cost. Such intermediaries could buy low-dividend stocks and, by a controlled policy of realizing gains, pay their investors at a higher rate.

BEHAVIORAL FINANCE

Suppose it turned out that the transaction costs in selling no-dividend securities could not account for the preference of investors for dividends. Would there still be a reason for high dividends? We introduced the topic of behavioral finance in Chapter 14, pointing out that the ideas of behaviorists represent a strong challenge to the theory of efficient capital markets. It turns out that behavioral finance also has an argument for high dividends.

The basic idea here concerns *self-control*. Although we cannot review all that psychology has to say about self-control, let's focus on one example–losing weight. Suppose Ali Mohammad, a college student, got back from the Christmas break more than a few pounds heavier than he would like. Everyone would probably agree that diet and exercise are the two ways to lose weight. But how should Ali put this approach into practice? (We'll focus on exercise, though the same principle would apply to his diet.) One way–let's call it the economists' way–would involve trying to make rational decisions. Each day Ali would balance the costs and the benefits of exercising. Perhaps he would choose to exercise on most days because losing the weight is important to him. However, when he is too busy with exams, he might rationally choose not to exercise because he cannot afford the time. And he wants to be socially active. So he may rationally choose to avoid exercise on days when parties and other social commitments become too time-consuming.

At first glance, this seems sensible. The problem is that he must make a choice every day, and there may be too many days when his lack of self-control gets the better of him. He may tell himself that he doesn't have the time to exercise on a particular day because he is starting to find exercise boring, not because he really doesn't have the time. Before long, he is avoiding exercise on most days–and overeating in reaction to the guilt from not exercising!

Is there an alternative? One way would be to set rigid rules. Perhaps Ali decides to exercise five days a week no matter what. This is not necessarily the best approach for everyone, but there is no question that many of us (perhaps most of us) live by a set of rules. Shefrin and Statman suggest some typical rules:[6]

- Jog at least two miles a day.
- Do not consume more than 1,200 calories per day.
- Save at least 2 percent of every paycheck for children's college education and never withdraw from this fund.
- Never touch a drop of alcohol.

What does this have to do with dividends? Investors also must deal with self-control. Suppose a retiree wants to consume ₹20,000 a year from savings, in addition to Social Security and her pension. On one hand, she could buy stocks with a dividend yield high enough to generate ₹20,000 in dividends. On the other hand, she could place her savings in no-dividend stocks, selling off ₹20,000 each year for consumption. Though these two approaches seem equivalent financially, the second one may allow for too much leeway. If lack of self-control gets the better of her, she might sell off too much, leaving little for her later years. Better, perhaps, to short-circuit this possibility by investing in dividend-paying stocks with a firm personal rule of never "dipping into principal." Although behaviorists do not claim that this approach is for everyone, they argue that enough people think this way to explain why firms pay dividends even though, as we said earlier, dividends are tax disadvantaged.

Does behavioral finance argue for increased stock repurchases as well as increased dividends? The answer is no because investors will sell the stock that firms repurchase. As we have said, selling stock involves too much leeway. Investors might sell too many shares of stock, leaving little for later years. The behaviorist argument may explain why companies pay dividends in a world with personal taxes.

AGENCY COSTS

Although stockholders, bondholders, and management start firms for mutually beneficial reasons, one party later may gain at the other's expense. Take the potential conflict between bondholders and stockholders. Bondholders would like stockholders to leave as much cash as possible in the firm so that this cash would be available to pay the bondholders during times of financial distress. Conversely, stockholders would like to keep this extra cash for themselves. That's where dividends come in. Managers, acting on behalf of the stockholders, may pay dividends to keep the cash away from the bondholders. In other words, a dividend can be viewed as a wealth transfer from bondholders to stockholders. There is empirical evidence for this view of things. DeAngelo and DeAngelo find that firms in financial distress are reluctant to cut dividends.[7] Of course, bondholders know about the propensity of stockholders to transfer money out of the firm. To protect themselves, bondholders frequently create loan agreements stating that dividends can be paid only if the firm has earnings, cash flow, and working capital above specified levels.

Although managers may be looking out for stockholders in any conflict with bondholders, managers may pursue selfish goals at the expense of stockholders in other situations. As we discussed in a previous chapter, managers might pad expense accounts, take on pet projects with negative NPVs, or not work hard. Managers find it easier to pursue these selfish goals when the firm has plenty of free cash flow. After all, one cannot squander funds if the funds are not available in the first place. And that is where dividends come in. Several scholars have suggested that the board of directors can use dividends to reduce agency costs.[8] By paying dividends equal to the amount of "surplus" cash flow, a firm can reduce management's ability to squander the firm's resources.

[6] Hersh M. Shefrin and Meir Statman, "Explaining Investor Preference for Cash Dividends," *Journal of Financial Economics* 13, no. 2 (June 1984): 253–82.

[7] Harry DeAngelo and Linda DeAngelo, "Dividend Policy and Financial Distress: An Empirical Investigation of Troubled NYSE Firms," *Journal of Finance* 45, no. 5 (December 1990): 1415–31.

[8] Michael Rozeff, "How Companies Set Their Dividend Payout Ratios," in *The Revolution in Corporate Finance,* eds. Joel M. Stern and Donald H. Chew (New York: Basil Blackwell, 1986). See also Robert S. Hansen, Raman Kumar, and Dilip K. Shome, "Dividend Policy and Corporate Monitoring: Evidence from the Regulated Electric Utility Industry," *Financial Management* 23, no. 1 (Spring 1994): 16–22.

This discussion suggests a reason for increased dividends, but the same argument applies to share repurchases, as well. Managers, acting on behalf of stockholders, can as easily keep cash from bondholders through repurchases as through dividends. And the board of directors, also acting on behalf of stockholders, can reduce the cash available to spendthrift managers as easily through repurchases as through dividends. The presence of agency costs is not an argument for dividends over repurchases. Rather, agency costs imply firms may increase either dividends or share repurchases rather than hoard large amounts of cash.

The COVID-19 pandemic raised concerns about another potential agency motive for paying out cash instead of retaining cash inside the firm. In April 2020, a group of large restaurant chains led by KFC, Wendy's, and Papa John's asked the government for ₹145 billion in relief funds to help them survive the pandemic-induced shutdown. However, these restaurant chains had been highly profitable in recent years. If they had saved those profits for a rainy day instead of paying out to investors via dividends or share repurchases, they would have been able to keep on paying their bondholders and employees during the shutdown without needing a government bailout. Angry pundits alleged that firms may pay out dividends on purpose so that they can demand government aid in times of crisis.

INFORMATION CONTENT OF DIVIDENDS AND DIVIDEND SIGNALING

Information Content While there are many things researchers do not know about dividends, we know one thing for sure: The stock price of a firm generally rises when the firm announces a dividend increase and generally falls when a dividend reduction is announced. For example, Asquith and Mullins estimate that stock prices rise about 3 percent following announcements of dividend initiations.[9] Michaely, Thaler, and Womack find that stock prices fall about 7 percent following announcements of dividend omissions.[10]

The question is how we should interpret this empirical evidence. Consider the following three positions on dividends:

1. From the homemade dividend argument of MM, dividend policy is irrelevant, given that future earnings (and cash flow) are held constant.
2. Because of tax effects, a firm's stock price is negatively related to the current dividend when future earnings (or cash flow) are held constant.
3. Because of stockholders' desire for current income, a firm's stock price is positively related to its current dividend, even when future earnings (or cash flow) are held constant.

At first glance, the empirical evidence that stock prices rise when dividend increases are announced may seem consistent with Position 3 and inconsistent with Positions 1 and 2. In fact, many writers have said this. However, other authors have countered that the observation itself is consistent with all three positions. They point out that companies do not like to cut a dividend. Firms will raise the dividend only when future earnings, cash flow, and so on are expected to rise enough so that the dividend is not likely to be reduced later to its original level. A dividend increase is management's *signal* to the market that the firm is expected to do well.

It is the expectation of good times, and not only the stockholders' affinity for current income, that raises the stock price. The rise in the stock price following the dividend signal is called the **information content effect** of the dividend. To summarize, imagine that the stock price is unaffected or even negatively affected by the level of dividends, given that future earnings (or cash flow) are held constant. Nevertheless, the information content effect implies that the stock price may rise when dividends are raised if dividends simultaneously cause stockholders to increase their expectations of future earnings and cash flow.

[9] Paul Asquith and David W. Mullins, "The Impact of Initiating Dividend Payments on Shareholders' Wealth," *Journal of Business* 56, no. 1 (January 1983): 77–96.

[10] Roni Michaely, Richard Thaler, and Kent Womack, "Price Reactions to Dividend Initiations and Omissions: Overreaction or Drift?" *Journal of Finance* 50, no. 2 (June 1995): 573–608.

Dividend Signaling We argued that the market infers a rise in earnings and cash flows from a dividend increase, leading to a higher stock price. Conversely, the market infers a decrease in cash flows from a dividend reduction, leading to a fall in stock price. This raises an interesting corporate strategy: Could management increase dividends just to make the market think that cash flows will be higher, even when management knows that cash flows will not rise?

While this strategy may seem dishonest, academics take the position that managers frequently attempt the strategy. Academics begin with the following accounting identity for an all-equity firm:

$$\text{Cash flow} = \text{Capital expenditures} + \text{Dividends}^{11} \tag{19.1}$$

Equation 19.1 must hold if a firm is neither issuing nor repurchasing stock. That is, the cash flow from the firm must go somewhere. If it is not paid out in dividends, it must be used in some expenditure. Whether the expenditure involves a capital budgeting project or a purchase of Treasury bills, it is still an expenditure.

Imagine that we are in the middle of the year and investors are trying to make some forecast of cash flow over the entire year. These investors may use Equation 19.1 to estimate cash flow. Suppose the firm announces that current dividends will be ₹50 million and the market believes that capital expenditures are ₹80 million. The market would then determine cash flow to be ₹130 million (= ₹50 + 80).

Now, suppose that the firm had, alternatively, announced a dividend of ₹70 million. The market might assume that cash flow remains at ₹130 million, implying capital expenditures of ₹60 million (= ₹130 − 70). Here, the increase in dividends would hurt stock price because the market anticipates valuable capital expenditures will be crowded out. Alternatively, the market might assume that capital expenditures remain at ₹80 million, implying the estimate of cash flow to be ₹150 million (= ₹70 + 80). The stock price would likely rise here because stock prices usually increase with cash flow. In general, academics believe that models where investors assume capital expenditures remain the same are more realistic. Thus, an increase in dividends raises the stock price.

Now we come to the incentives of managers to fool the public. Suppose you are a manager who wants to boost the stock price, perhaps because you are planning to sell some of your personal holdings of the company's stock immediately. You might increase dividends so that the market would raise its estimate of the firm's cash flow, thereby also boosting the current stock price.

If this strategy is appealing, would anything prevent you from raising dividends without limit? The answer is yes because there is also a cost to raising dividends. That is, the firm will have to forgo some of its profitable projects. Remember that cash flow in Equation 19.1 is a constant, so an increase in dividends is obtained only by a reduction in capital expenditures. At some point, the market will learn that cash flow has not increased, but instead profitable capital expenditures have been cut. Once the market absorbs this information, the stock price should fall below what it would have been had dividends never been raised. If you plan to sell, say, half of your shares and retain the other half, an increase in dividends should help you on the immediate sale but hurt you when you sell your remaining shares years later. So your decision on the level of dividends will be based, among other things, on the timing of your personal stock sales.

This is a simplified example of dividend signaling, where the manager sets dividend policy based on maximum benefit for herself.[12] Alternatively, a given manager may have no desire to sell his shares immediately but knows that, at any one time, plenty of ordinary shareholders will want to do so. For the benefit

[11]The correct representation of Equation 19.1 involves cash flow, not earnings. However, with little loss of understanding, we could discuss dividend signaling in terms of earnings, not cash flow.

[12]Papers examining fully developed models of signaling include Sudipto Bhattacharya, "Imperfect Information, Dividend Policy, and 'The Bird in the Hand' Fallacy," *Bell Journal of Economics* 10, no. 1 (Spring 1979): 259–70; Sudipto Bhattacharya, "Nondissipative Signaling Structures and Dividend Policy," *Quarterly Journal of Economics* 95, no. 1 (August 1980): 1–24; Stephen A. Ross, "The Determination of Financial Structure: The Incentive-Signalling Approach," *Bell Journal of Economics* 8, no. 1 (Spring 1977): 23–40; and Merton H. Miller and Kevin Rock, "Dividend Policy under Asymmetric Information," *Journal of Finance* 40, no. 4 (September 1985): 1031–51.

of shareholders in general, a manager will always be aware of the trade-off between current and future stock prices. And this, then, is the essence of signaling with dividends. It is not enough for a manager to set dividend policy to maximize the true (or intrinsic) value of the firm. He also must consider the effect of dividend policy on the current stock price, even if the current stock price does not reflect true value.

19.7 The Clientele Effect: A Resolution of Real-World Factors?

In the previous two sections, we pointed out that the existence of personal taxes favors a low-dividend policy, whereas other factors favor high dividends. The financial profession had hoped that it would be easy to determine which of these sets of factors dominates. Unfortunately, after years of research, no one has been able to conclude which of the two is more important. This is surprising: We might be skeptical that the two sets of factors would cancel each other out so perfectly.

However, one particular idea, known as the **clientele effect**, implies that the two sets of factors are likely to cancel each other out after all. To understand this idea, let's separate investors in high tax brackets from those in low tax brackets. Individuals in high tax brackets likely prefer either no or low dividends. Low tax bracket investors generally fall into three categories. First, there are individual investors in low brackets. They are likely to prefer some dividends if they desire current income. Second, pension funds pay no taxes on either dividends or capital gains. Because they face no tax consequences, pension funds also will prefer dividends if they have a preference for current income. Finally, companies can exclude at least 50 percent of their dividend income but cannot exclude any of their capital gains. Thus, companies are likely to prefer high-dividend stocks, even without a preference for current income.

Suppose that 40 percent of all investors prefer high dividends and 60 percent prefer low dividends, yet only 20 percent of firms pay high dividends while 80 percent pay low dividends. Here, the high-dividend firms will be in short supply, implying that their stock should be bid up while the stock of low-dividend firms should be bid down.

However, the dividend policies of all firms need not be fixed in the long run. In this example, we would expect enough low-dividend firms to increase their payout so that 40 percent of the firms pay high dividends and 60 percent of the firms pay low dividends. After this adjustment, no firm will gain from changing its dividend policy. Once payouts of companies conform to the desires of stockholders, no single firm can affect its market value by switching from one dividend strategy to another.

Clienteles are likely to form in the following way:

Group	Stocks
Individuals in high tax brackets	Zero- to low-payout stocks
Individuals in low tax brackets	Low- to medium-payout stocks
Tax-free institutions	Medium-payout stocks
Companies	High-payout stocks

To see if you understand the clientele effect, consider the following statement: "In a world where many investors like high dividends, a firm can boost its share price by increasing its dividend payout ratio." True or false?

The statement is likely to be false. As long as there are already enough high-dividend firms to satisfy dividend-loving investors, a firm will not be able to boost its share price by paying high dividends. A firm can boost its stock price only if an unsatisfied clientele exists.

Our discussion of clienteles followed from the fact that tax brackets vary across investors. If shareholders care about taxes, stocks should attract clienteles based on dividend yield. Is there any evidence that this is the case?

Consider Figure 19.6. Here, Graham and Kumar rank common stocks by their dividend yields (the ratio of dividend to stock price) and place them into five portfolios, called quintiles.[13] The bottom quintile contains the 20 percent of stocks with the lowest dividend yields; the next quintile contains the 20 percent of stocks with the next lowest dividend yields; and so on. The figure shows the weight of each quintile in the portfolios of low-, medium-, and high-income investors. As can be seen, relative to low-income investors, high-income investors put a greater percentage of their assets into low-dividend securities. Conversely, again relative to low-income investors, high-income investors put a smaller percentage of their assets into high-dividend securities.

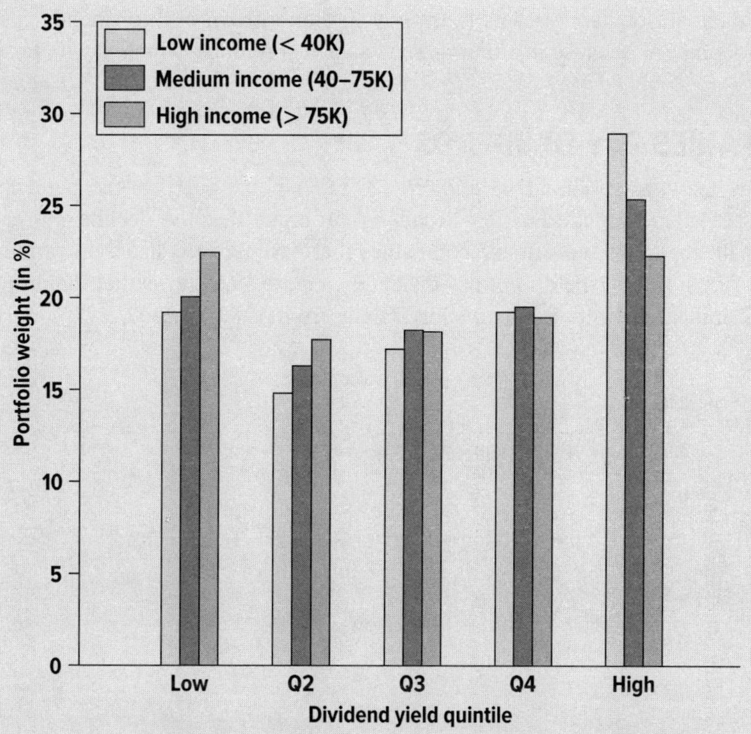

All stocks are ranked on their dividend yields and placed into five quintile portfolios. The figure shows the weight of each quintile in the portfolios of low-, medium-, and high-income investors. Relative to those with lower income, high-income investors place a greater percentage of their assets in low-dividend stocks and a smaller percentage in high-dividend stocks.

Figure 19.6 Preferences of Investors for Dividend Yield

SOURCE: Adapted from Figure 2 of John R. Graham and Alok Kumar, "Do Dividend Clienteles Exist? Evidence on Dividend Preferences of Retail Investors," *Journal of Finance* 61, no. 3 (June 2006): 1305–36.

[13]John R. Graham and Alok Kumar, "Do Dividend Clienteles Exist? Evidence on Dividend Preferences of Retail Investors," *Journal of Finance* 61, no. 3 (June 2006): 1305-36.

19.8 What We Know and Do Not Know about Dividend Policy

CORPORATE DIVIDENDS ARE SUBSTANTIAL

We pointed out earlier in the chapter that dividends are tax disadvantaged relative to capital gains because dividends are taxed upon payment whereas taxes on capital gains are deferred until sale. Nevertheless, unlike Indian economy, dividends in the U.S. economy are substantial. Consider Figure 19.7, which shows the ratio of aggregate dividends to aggregate earnings for all U.S. firms from 1980 to 2019. The ratio was approximately 70 percent in 2019.

We might argue that the taxation on dividends is actually minimal, perhaps because dividends are paid primarily to individuals in low tax brackets (currently the tax rate on cash dividends is substantially lower than for ordinary income) or because institutions such as pension funds, which pay no taxes, are the primary recipients.

FEWER COMPANIES PAY DIVIDENDS

Although dividends are substantial, Fama and French (FF) point out that the percentage of companies paying dividends has fallen over the last few decades.[14] FF argue that the decline was caused primarily by an explosion of small, currently unprofitable companies that have recently listed on various stock exchanges. For the most part, firms of this type do not pay dividends. Figure 19.8 shows that the proportion of dividend payers among U.S. industrial firms dropped substantially from 1980 to 2002.

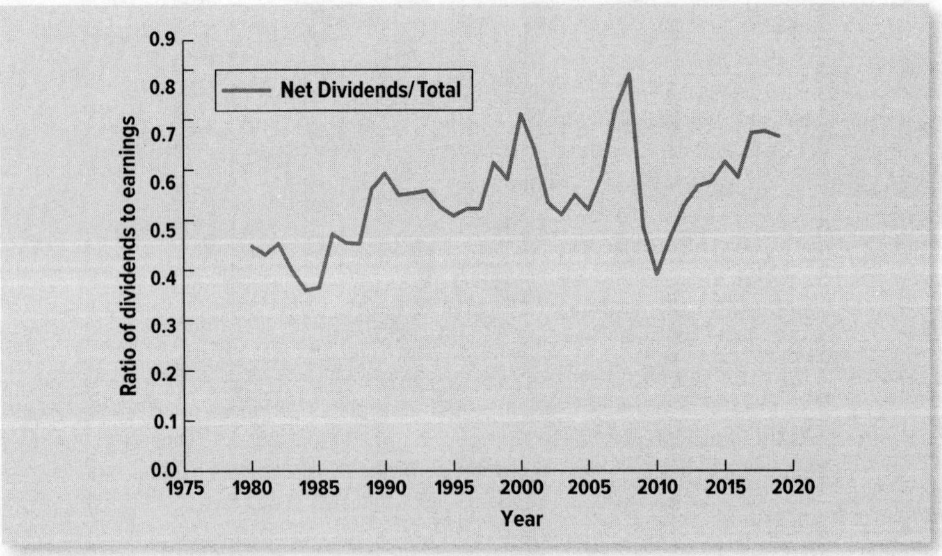

Figure 19.7 Ratio of Aggregate Dividends to Aggregate Earnings for All U.S. Firms: 1980 to 2019

SOURCE: The Bureau of Economic Analysis, November 2020.

[14]Eugene F. Fama and Kenneth R. French, "Disappearing Dividends: Changing Firm Characteristics or Lower Propensity to Pay?" *Journal of Financial Economics* 60, no. 1 (April 2001): 3–43.

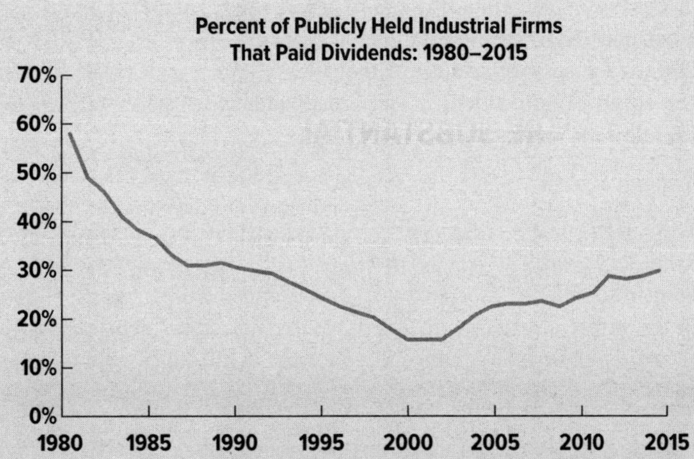

This figure reports the proportion of U.S. industrial firms that paid dividends over the years from 1980 to 2015. The proportion dropped significantly from 1980 to 2002, with a rebound over the next several years.

Figure 19.8 Proportion of Dividend Payers among All Publicly Held U.S. Industrial Firms: 1980–2015

SOURCE: Harry DeAngelo, Linda DeAngelo, and Douglas J. Skinner, "Corporate Payout Policy," *Foundations and Trends in Finance* 3, no. 2–3 (2008): 95–287. Data updated by DeAngelo, DeAngelo, and Skinner.

This figure, presented in a paper by DeAngelo, DeAngelo, and Skinner, also shows an increase in the proportion of dividend payers from 2002 to 2015.[15] One obvious potential explanation is the cut in the maximum tax rate on dividends to 15 percent, signed into law in May 2003.

Figure 19.8 does not imply that dividends across all firms declined from 1980 to 2015. DeAngelo, DeAngelo, and Skinner point out that while small firms have shied away from dividends, the largest firms have substantially increased their dividends over recent decades.[16] This increase has created such concentration in dividends that the 25 top dividend-paying firms accounted for more than 50 percent of aggregate dividends in the United States in 2020.[17] DeAngelo and colleagues suggest that "Industrial firms exhibit a two-tier structure in which a small number of firms with very high earnings generates the majority of earnings and dominates the dividend supply, while the majority of firms has at best a modest impact on aggregate earnings and dividends."

COMPANIES SMOOTH DIVIDENDS

In 1956, John Lintner made two important observations concerning dividend policy that still ring true.[18] First, real-world companies typically set long-term target ratios of dividends to earnings. A firm is likely to set a low target ratio if it has many positive NPV projects relative to available cash flow and a high ratio if it has few positive NPV projects. Second, managers know that only part of any change in earnings is

[15]Harry DeAngleo, Linda DeAngelo, and Douglas J. Skinner, "Corporate Payout Policy," *Foundations and Trends in Finance* 3, no. 2-3 (2008): 95-287. Data updated by the authors.

[16]Harry DeAngleo, Linda DeAngelo, and Douglas J. Skinner, "Are Dividends Disappearing? Dividend Concentration and the Consolidation of Earnings," *Journal of Financial Economics* 72, no. 3 (June 2004): 425-56.

[17]In 2020, about 80 percent of S&P 500 companies paid cash dividends.

[18]John Lintner, "Distribution of Incomes of Companies among Dividends, Retained Earnings, and Taxes," *American Economic Review* 46, no. 2 (May 1956): 97-113.

likely to be permanent. Because managers need time to assess the permanence of any earnings rise, dividend changes appear to lag earnings changes by a number of periods.

Taken together, Lintner's observations suggest that two parameters describe dividend policy: the target payout ratio (t) and the speed of adjustment of current dividends to the target (s). Dividend changes will tend to conform to the following model:

$$\text{Dividend change} \equiv D_1 - D_0 = s \times (t\text{EPS}_1 - D_0) \qquad \textbf{(19.2)}$$

where D_1 and D_0 are dividends in the next year and dividends in the current year, respectively. EPS_1 is earnings per share in the next year.

The limiting cases in Equation 19.2 occur when $s = 1$ and $s = 0$. If $s = 1$, the actual change in dividends will be equal to the target change in dividends. Here, full adjustment occurs immediately. If $s = 0$ then $D_1 = D_0$. In other words, there is no change in dividends at all. Real-world companies can be expected to set s between 0 and 1.

EXAMPLE 19.2

Dividend Smoothing Sathavahana Ispat Limited (SIL), has a target payout ratio of .30. Last year's earnings per share were ₹10, and in accordance with the target, SIL paid dividends of ₹3 per share last year. However, earnings have jumped to ₹20 this year. Because the managers do not believe that this increase is permanent, they do not plan to raise dividends all the way to ₹6 (= .30 × ₹20). Rather, their speed of adjustment coefficient, s, is .5, implying that the *increase* in dividends from last year to this year will be:

$$.5 \times (₹6 - 3) = ₹1.50$$

That is, the increase in dividends is the product of the speed of adjustment coefficient, .50, times the difference between what dividends would be with full adjustment [₹6 (= .30 × ₹20)] and last year's dividends. Dividends will increase by ₹1.50, so dividends this year will be ₹4.50 (= ₹3 + 1.50).

Now, suppose that earnings stay at ₹20 next year. The increase in dividends next year will be:

$$.5 \times (₹6 - 4.50) = ₹.75$$

In words, the increase in dividends from this year to next year will be the speed of adjustment coefficient (.50) times the difference between what dividends would have been next year with full adjustment (₹6) and this year's dividends (₹4.50). Because dividends will increase by ₹.75, dividends next year will be ₹5.25 (= ₹4.50 + .75). In this way, dividends will slowly rise every year if earnings in all future years remain at ₹20. However, dividends will reach ₹6 only at infinity.

An implication of Lintner's model is that the dividends-to-earnings ratio rises when a company begins a period of bad times, and the ratio falls when a company starts a period of good times. Thus, dividends display less variability than do earnings. In other words, firms smooth dividends.

The Pros and Cons of Paying Dividends

Pros	Cons
1. Dividends may appeal to investors who desire stable cash flow but do not want to incur the transaction costs from periodically selling shares of stock.	1. Dividends are taxed upon payment whereas taxes on capital gains are deferred until sale.

Pros	Cons
2. Behavioral finance argues that investors with limited self-control can meet current consumption needs with high-dividend stocks while adhering to the policy of never dipping into principal.	2. Dividends can reduce internal sources of financing. Dividends may force the firm to forgo positive NPV projects or to rely on costly external equity financing.
3. Managers, acting on behalf of stockholders, can pay dividends in order to keep cash from bondholders.	3. Once established, dividend cuts are hard to make without adversely affecting a firm's stock price.
4. The board of directors, acting on behalf of stockholders, can use dividends to reduce the cash available to spendthrift managers.	
5. Managers may increase dividends to signal their optimism concerning future cash flow.	

SOME SURVEY EVIDENCE ABOUT DIVIDENDS

A study surveyed a large number of financial executives regarding dividend policy. One of the questions asked was this: "Do these statements describe factors that affect your company's dividend decisions?" Tables 19.2(a) and 19.2(b) shows some of the results.

As shown in Tables 19.2(a) and 19.2(b), financial managers are very disinclined to cut dividends. Moreover, they are very conscious of their previous dividends and desire to maintain a relatively steady dividend. In contrast, the cost of external capital and the desire to attract "prudent man" investors (those with fiduciary duties) are less important.

Table 19.3 is drawn from the same survey, but here the responses are to the question, "How important are the following factors to your company's dividend decisions?" Not surprisingly given the responses in Tables 19.2(a) and 19.2(b) and our earlier discussion, the highest priority is maintaining a consistent dividend policy. The next several items are also consistent with our previous analysis. Financial managers are

Table 19.2(a) Survey Responses on Dividend Decisions in the U.S.A.*

Policy Statements	Percentage Who Agree or Strongly Agree
1. We try to avoid reducing dividends per share.	93.8%
2. We try to maintain a smooth dividend from year to year.	89.6
3. We consider the level of dividends per share that we have paid in recent quarters.	88.2
4. We are reluctant to make dividend changes that might have to be reversed in the future.	77.9
5. We consider the change or growth in dividends per share.	66.7
6. We consider the cost of raising external capital to be smaller than the cost of cutting dividends.	42.8
7. We pay dividends to attract investors subject to "prudent man" investment restrictions.	41.7

*Survey respondents were asked the question, "Do these statements describe factors that affect your company's dividend decisions?"

SOURCE: Adapted from Table 4 of Alon Brav, John R. Graham, Campbell R. Harvey, and Roni Michaely, "Payout Policy in the 21st Century," *Journal of Financial Economics* 77, no. 3 (September 2005): 483–527.

Table 19.2(b) Survey Responses on Dividend Decisions in India

Policy Statements	Percentage Who Agree or Strongly Agree
(a) Dividend change follows shift in long-term earnings	85.20%
(b) Has long-term target dividend payout ratio	81.50%
(c) Focus more on absolute level of dividends than dividend changes	67.90%
(d) Responsive to shareholders preferences regarding dividends	82.70%
(e) Willing to rescind dividend increase in the event of growth opportunities	56.80%
(f) Cash dividends as residual after financing desired investments from earnings	46.90%
(g) Dividend payout ratio affects the market value of the firm	71.60%
(h) Dividends provide signaling mechanism of the future prospects of the firm	71.60%
(i) Investors have different relative risk perceptions of dividends and retained earnings	64.20%
(j) Investors are indifferent between receiving dividends and capital gains	64.20%
(k) Share buyback programme should replace dividend payments of the firm	53.10%
(l) Dividend payments subject the firm to the scrutiny of the investors	49.40%
(m) Dividend payments provide a bonding mechanism to encourage managers to act in the best interests of the shareholders	55.60%

Further Reading: Manoj Anand, Corporate Finance Practices in India: A Survey, Vikalpa, Vol. 24(4), Oct. 2002.

very concerned about earnings stability and future earnings levels in making dividend decisions, and they consider the availability of good investment opportunities. Survey respondents also believed that attracting both institutional and individual (retail) investors was relatively important.

In contrast to our discussion in the earlier part of this chapter of taxes and flotation costs, the financial managers in this survey did not think that personal taxes paid on dividends by shareholders are very important. And even fewer think that equity flotation costs are relevant.

Table 19.3 Survey Responses on Dividend Decisions in the U.S.A.*

Policy Statements	Percentage Who Think This Is Important or Very Important
1. Maintaining consistency with our historic dividend policy.	84.1%
2. Stability of future earnings.	71.9
3. A sustainable change in earnings.	67.1
4. Attracting institutional investors to purchase our stock.	52.5
5. The availability of good investment opportunities for our firm to pursue.	47.6
6. Attracting retail investors to purchase our stock.	44.5
7. Personal taxes our stockholders pay when receiving dividends.	21.1
8. Flotation costs to issuing new equity.	9.3

*Survey respondents were asked the question, "How important are the following factors to your company's dividend decisions?"

SOURCE: Adapted from Table 5 of Alon Brav, John R. Graham, Campbell R. Harvey, and Roni Michaely, "Payout Policy in the 21st Century," *Journal of Financial Economics* 77, no. 3 (September 2005): 483–527.

19.9 Putting It All Together

Much of what we have discussed in this chapter (and much of what we know about dividends from decades of research) can be pulled together and summarized in the following six points:[19]

1. Aggregate dividend and stock repurchases are massive, and they have increased steadily in nominal and real terms over the years.
2. Cash dividends and repurchases are heavily concentrated among a relatively small number of large, mature firms.
3. Managers are very reluctant to cut dividends, normally doing so only due to firm-specific problems.
4. Managers smooth dividends, raising them slowly and incrementally as earnings grow.
5. Stock prices react to unanticipated changes in dividends.
6. The magnitude of stock repurchases tends to vary with transitory earnings.

The challenge now is to fit these six pieces into a reasonably coherent picture. With regard to payouts in general, meaning the combination of stock repurchases and cash dividends, a simple life cycle theory fits Points 1 and 2. The key ideas are straightforward. First, relatively young firms with less available cash generally should not make cash distributions. They need the cash to fund positive NPV projects (and flotation costs discourage the raising of outside cash).

As a firm survives and matures, it begins to generate free cash flow (which, you will recall, is internally generated cash flow beyond that needed to fund profitable investment activities). Significant free cash flow can lead to agency problems if it is not distributed. Managers may become tempted to pursue empire building or otherwise spend the excess cash in ways not in the shareholders' best interests. Firms come under shareholder pressure to make distributions rather than hoard cash. And, consistent with what we observe, we expect large firms with a history of profitability to make large distributions.

The life cycle theory says that firms trade off the agency costs of excess cash retention against the potential future costs of external equity financing. A firm should begin making distributions when it generates sufficient internal cash flow to fund its investment needs now and into the foreseeable future.

The more complex issue concerns the type of distribution, cash dividends versus repurchase. The tax argument in favor of repurchases is a clear and strong one. Repurchases are a much more flexible option (and managers greatly value financial flexibility), so the question is: Why would firms ever choose a cash dividend?

If we are to answer this question, we have to ask a different question. What can a cash dividend accomplish that a share repurchase cannot? One answer is that when a firm makes a commitment to pay a cash dividend now and into the future, it sends a two-part signal to the markets. As we already have discussed, one signal is that the firm anticipates being profitable, with the ability to make the payments on an ongoing basis. Note that a firm cannot benefit by trying to fool the market in this regard because the firm would ultimately be punished when it couldn't make the dividend payment (or couldn't make it without relying on external financing). A cash dividend may let a firm distinguish itself from less profitable rivals.

A second, and more subtle, signal takes us back to the agency problem of free cash flow. By committing to pay cash dividends now and in the future, the firm signals that it won't be hoarding cash (or at least not as much cash), thereby reducing agency costs and enhancing shareholder wealth.

[19]This list is distilled in part from a longer list in Harry DeAngelo and Linda DeAngelo, "Payout Policy Pedagogy: What Matters and Why," *European Financial Management* 13, no. 1 (January 2007): 11–27.

This two-part signaling story is consistent with Points 3–5 in the previous section, but an obvious objection remains. Why don't firms commit to a policy of setting aside whatever money would be used to pay dividends and use it instead to buy back shares? After all, either way, a firm is committing to pay out cash to shareholders.

A fixed repurchase strategy suffers from two drawbacks. The first is verifiability. A firm could announce an open market repurchase and then not do it. By suitably fudging its books, it would be some time before the deception was discovered. It would be necessary for shareholders to develop a monitoring mechanism, meaning some sort of way for stockholders to know for sure that the repurchase was in fact done. Such a mechanism wouldn't be difficult to build (it could be a simple trustee relationship such as we observe in the bond markets), but it currently does not exist. Of course, a tender offer repurchase needs little or no verification, but such offers have expenses associated with them. The beauty of a cash dividend is that it needs no monitoring. A firm is forced to cut and mail checks four times a year, year in and year out.

Characteristics of a Sensible Payout Policy

- Over time, pay out all free cash flow.
- Avoid cutting positive NPV projects to pay dividends or buy back shares.
- Do not initiate dividends until the firm is generating substantial free cash flow.
- Set the current regular dividend consistent with a long-run target payout ratio.
- Set the level of dividends low enough to avoid expensive future external financing.
- Use repurchases to distribute transitory cash flow increases.

A second objection to a fixed repurchase strategy is more controversial. Suppose managers, as insiders, are better able than stockholders to judge whether their stock price is too high or too low. (Note that this idea does not conflict with semistrong market efficiency if inside information is the reason.) In this case, a fixed repurchase commitment forces management to buy back stock even in circumstances when the stock is overvalued. In other words, it forces management into making negative NPV investments.

More research on the cash dividend versus share repurchase question is needed, but the historical trend seems to be favoring continued growth in repurchases relative to dividends. Total corporate payouts seem to be relatively stable over time, but repurchases are becoming a larger portion of that total. Most recently, aggregate repurchases have passed aggregate dividends.

One aspect of aggregate cash dividends that has not received much attention is that there may be a strong legacy effect. Before 1982, the regulatory status of stock repurchases was somewhat murky, creating a significant disincentive. In 1982, the SEC, after years of debate, created a clear set of guidelines for firms to follow, thereby making repurchases much more attractive.

The legacy effect arises because many of the giant firms that pay such a large portion of aggregate dividends were paying dividends before (and perhaps long before) 1982. To the extent that these firms are unwilling to cut their dividends, aggregate cash dividends will be large, but only because of a *lock-in* effect for older firms. If locked-in legacy payers account for much of the aggregate dividend, what we should observe is (1) a sharply reduced tendency for maturing firms to initiate dividends and (2) a growth in repurchases relative to cash dividends over time. We actually do see evidence of both of these trends; however, legacy effects alone can't account for all cash dividend payers.

19.10 Bonus Shares and Stock Splits

Another type of dividend is paid out in shares of stock. This type of dividend is called a stock dividend. A stock dividend is not a true dividend because it is not paid in cash. The effect of a stock dividend is to increase the number of shares that each owner holds. Because there are more shares outstanding, each is worth less.

Information on upcoming stock splits is available on the splits calendars at **www.investmenthouse.com** and **finance.yahoo.com**.

A stock dividend is commonly expressed as a percentage; a 20 percent stock dividend means that a shareholder receives one new share for every five currently owned (a 20 percent increase). Because every shareholder receives 20 percent more stock, the total number of shares outstanding rises by 20 percent. As we will see in a moment, the result is that each share of stock is worth about 20 percent less.

A stock split is essentially the same thing as a stock dividend, except that a split is expressed as a ratio instead of a percentage. When a split is declared, each share is split up to create additional shares. For example, in a three-for-one stock split, each old share is split into three new shares.

SOME DETAILS ABOUT STOCK SPLITS AND STOCK DIVIDENDS

Stock splits and stock dividends have essentially the same impacts on the company and the shareholder: They increase the number of shares outstanding and reduce the value per share. The accounting treatment is not the same, however, and it depends on two things: (1) whether the distribution is a stock split or a stock dividend and (2) the size of the stock dividend if it is called a dividend.

By convention, stock dividends of less than 20 to 25 percent are called *small stock dividends.* The accounting procedure for such a dividend is discussed next. A stock dividend greater than this range of 20 to 25 percent is called a *large stock dividend.* Large stock dividends are not uncommon. For example, in August 2020, Tesla underwent a five-for-one stock split in the form of a 400 percent stock dividend. Except for some relatively minor accounting differences, this has the same effect as a five-for-one stock split.

Example of a Small Stock Dividend The Chattisgarhi Co., a consulting firm specializing in difficult accounting problems, has 10,000 shares of stock outstanding, each selling at ₹66. The total market value of the equity is ₹66 × 10,000 = ₹660,000. With a 10 percent stock dividend, each stockholder receives one additional share for each 10 owned, and the total number of shares outstanding after the dividend is 11,000.

Before the stock dividend, the equity portion of Chattisgarhi's balance sheet might look like this:

Common stock (₹1 par, 10,000 shares outstanding)	₹ 10,000
Capital in excess of par value	200,000
Retained earnings	290,000
Total owners' equity	₹ 500,000

A seemingly arbitrary accounting procedure is used to adjust the balance sheet after a small stock dividend. Because 1,000 new shares are issued, the common stock account is increased by ₹1,000 (1,000 shares at ₹1 par value each), for a total of ₹11,000. The market price of ₹66 is ₹65 greater than the par value, so the "excess" of ₹65 × 1,000 shares = ₹65,000 is added to the capital surplus account (capital in excess of par value), producing a total of ₹265,000.

Total owners' equity is unaffected by the stock dividend because no cash has come in or gone out, so retained earnings are reduced by the entire ₹66,000, leaving ₹224,000. The net effect of these machinations is that Chattisgarhi's equity accounts now look like this:

Common stock (₹1 par, 11,000 shares outstanding)	₹ 11,000
Capital in excess of par value	265,000
Retained earnings	224,000
Total owners' equity	₹ 500,000

Example of a Stock Split A stock split is conceptually similar to a stock dividend, but it is commonly expressed as a ratio. In a three-for-two split, each shareholder receives one additional share of stock for each two held originally, so a three-for-two split amounts to a 50 percent stock dividend. Again, no cash is paid out and the percentage of the entire firm that each shareholder owns is unaffected.

The accounting treatment of a stock split is a little different from (and simpler than) that of a stock dividend. Suppose Chattisgarhi decides to declare a two-for-one stock split. The number of shares outstanding will double to 20,000 and the par value will be halved to ₹.50 per share. The owners' equity after the split is represented as follows:

Common stock (₹.50 par, 20,000 shares outstanding)	₹ 10,000
Capital in excess of par value	200,000
Retained earnings	290,000
Total owners' equity	₹ 500,000

Note that for all three of the categories, the figures on the right are completely unaffected by the split. The only changes are in the par value per share and the number of shares outstanding. Because the number of shares has doubled, the par value of each is cut in half.

For a list of recent stock splits, try **finance.yahoo.com/calendar/splits/**.

Example of a Large Stock Dividend In our example, if a 100 percent stock dividend were declared, 10,000 new shares would be distributed, so 20,000 shares would be outstanding. At a ₹1 par value per share, the common stock account would rise by ₹10,000, for a total of ₹20,000. The retained earnings account would be reduced by ₹10,000, leaving ₹280,000. The result would be the following:

Common stock (₹1 par, 20,000 shares outstanding)	₹ 20,000
Capital in excess of par value	200,000
Retained earnings	280,000
Total owners' equity	₹ 500,000

STOCK SPLITS AND STOCK DIVIDENDS IN INDIA

In India, stock dividends are commonly known as bonus shares, and hence issue of stock dividends is known as *issue of bonus shares.* While the concept of small stock dividends is not popular in India, large stock dividends are quite popular among Indian companies especially when the companies are doing well and/or their share prices have crossed beyond the popular trading range. Relatively, stock splits are a recent phenomenon among Indian companies. It is done to increase liquidity in the stock trading and/or bring the price of a share to a more tradable range. Exhibits 19.3 and 19.4 give a few recent examples of bonus issues and stock splits in India.

Exhibit 19.3 Examples of Bonus Issues in India

Company Name	Ex Date	Bonus Record Date	Bonus Ratio
Standard Capital Markets	Dec 29, 2023	Dec 29, 2023	02:01
Paul Merchants Ltd	Dec 19, 2023	Dec 19, 2023	
Alphalogic Industries Ltd	Dec 01, 2023	Dec 01, 2023	01:01
Sonata Software Ltd	Dec 12, 2023	Dec 12, 2023	
Axita Cotton Ltd	Dec 22, 2023	Dec 25, 2023	01:03
Alphalogic Techsys Ltd	Dec 22, 2023	Dec 22, 2023	

Exhibit 19.4 Examples of Stock Splits in India

Company Name	Split Date	Old Face Value (par value)	New Face Value (par value)
Manorama Industries	07-03-2024	10	2
Trishakti Ind	16-01-2024		
Cochin Shipyard	10-01-2024	10	5
Pearl Global Industries	05-01-2024		
Nestle India Ltd	05-01-2024	10	1
Tiger Logistics	04-03-2024		

All the companies in the Exhibit above are either large-sized companies going through a phase of good times *or* small-sized companies looking at increasing the liquidity of their stocks by increase in the floating stock.

VALUE OF STOCK SPLITS AND STOCK DIVIDENDS

The laws of logic tell us that stock splits and stock dividends can (1) leave the value of the firm unaffected, (2) increase its value, or (3) decrease its value. Unfortunately, the issues are complex enough that we cannot easily determine which of the three relationships holds.

The Benchmark Case A strong case can be made that stock dividends and splits do not change either the wealth of any shareholder or the wealth of the firm as a whole. In our preceding example, the equity had a total market value of ₹660,000. With the small stock dividend, the number of shares increased to 11,000, so it seems that each would be worth ₹660,000/11,000 = ₹60.

A shareholder who had 100 shares worth ₹66 each before the dividend would have 110 shares worth ₹60 each afterward. The total value of the stock is ₹6,600 either way; so the stock dividend doesn't really have any economic effect.

After the stock split, there are 20,000 shares outstanding, so each should be worth ₹660,000/20,000 = ₹33. In other words, the number of shares doubles and the price halves. From these calculations, it appears that stock dividends and splits are just paper transactions.

Although these results are relatively obvious, there are reasons that are often given to suggest that there may be some benefits to these actions. The typical financial manager is aware of many real-world complexities, and, for that reason, the stock split or stock dividend decision is not treated lightly in practice.

Popular Trading Range Proponents of stock dividends and stock splits frequently argue that a security has a proper **trading range**. When the security is priced above this level, many investors do not have the funds to buy the common trading unit of 100 shares, called a *round lot.* Although securities can be purchased in *odd-lot* form (fewer than 100 shares), the commissions are greater. Firms will split the stock to keep the price in this trading range.

For example, in early 2003, Microsoft announced a two-for-one stock split. This was the ninth split for Microsoft since the company went public in 1986. The stock had split three-for-two on two occasions and two-for-one a total of seven times. So for every share of Microsoft you owned in 1986 when the company first went public, you would own 288 shares as of the most recent stock split in 2003. Similarly, since Walmart went public in 1970, it has split its stock two-for-one nine times; Apple has split four-for-one once, seven-for-one once, and two-for-one three times since going public in 1987. For a really long split history, consider Procter & Gamble (P&G), which has split five-for-one twice, 1.5-to-one once, and two-for-one eight times since 1920. Each share of P&G purchased prior to the company's first stock split would have become 9,600 shares along the way.

Although this argument of a trading range is a popular one, its validity is questionable for a number of reasons. Mutual funds, pension funds, and other institutions have steadily increased their trading activity since World War II and now handle a sizable percentage of total trading volume (e.g., on the order of 80 percent of NYSE trading volume). Because these institutions buy and sell in huge amounts, the individual share price is of little concern. Commissions charged for trades by individual investors have also dropped dramatically in recent years, and some online discount brokerage firms now offer commission-free trading, and even the ability to buy fractional shares.

Furthermore, we sometimes observe share prices that are quite large that do not appear to cause problems. To take an extreme case, consider the Swiss chocolatier Lindt. In November 2020, Lindt shares were selling for around 82,500 Swiss francs each, or about ₹91,800. A round lot would have cost a cool ₹9.18 million. This is fairly expensive, but also consider Berkshire-Hathaway, the company run by legendary investor Warren Buffett. In late 2020, each share in the company sold for about ₹320,000.

Finally, there is evidence that stock splits actually may decrease the liquidity of the company's shares. Following a two-for-one split, the number of shares traded should more than double if liquidity is increased by the split. This doesn't appear to happen, possibly because some investors follow a naïve behavioral rule of always trading 100 shares (or some other fixed number of shares) both before and after the split. If investors fail to at least double the number of shares traded after a split, liquidity (measured in terms of total rupees traded per day) will decrease after a split.

REVERSE SPLITS

A less frequently encountered financial maneuver is the **reverse split**. For example, in September 2020, Superconductor Technologies announced a 1-for-10 reverse stock split, and, in August 2020, TOP Ships announced a 1-for-25 reverse split. In a 1-for-25 reverse split, each investor exchanges 25 old shares for 1 new share. The par value is increased by a factor of 25 in the process. In what is one of the biggest reverse splits ever (in terms of market cap), banking giant Citigroup announced in March 2011

To hear reverse stock split horror story, listen to **tinyurl.com/y2bv78ja** that it would do a 1-for-10 reverse split, thereby reducing the number of its shares outstanding from 29 billion to 2.9 billion. As with stock splits and stock dividends, a case can be made that a reverse split has no real effect.

Given real-world imperfections, three related reasons are cited for reverse splits. First, transaction costs to shareholders may be less after the reverse split. Second, the liquidity and marketability of a company's stock might be improved when its price is raised to the popular trading range. Third, stocks selling at prices below a certain level are not considered respectable, meaning that investors underestimate these firms' earnings, cash flow, growth, and stability. Some financial analysts argue that a reverse split can achieve instant respectability. As was the case with stock splits, none of these reasons is particularly compelling, especially not the third one.

There are two other reasons for reverse splits. First, stock exchanges have minimum price per share requirements. A reverse split may bring the stock price up to such a minimum. In 2001–2002, in the wake of a bear market, this motive became an increasingly important one. In 2001, 106 companies asked their shareholders to approve reverse splits. There were 111 reverse splits in 2002 and 75 in 2003, but only 14 by midyear 2004. The most common reason for these reverse splits is that Nasdaq begins the delisting process for a company whose stock price drops below ₹1 per share for 30 days. Many companies, particularly internet-related technology companies, found themselves in danger of being delisted and used reverse splits to boost their stock prices. Second, companies sometimes perform reverse splits and, at the same time, buy out any stockholders who end up with less than a certain number of shares.

For example, in September 2020, Westell Technologies shareholders approved a reverse/forward split. In this case, the company first did a 1-for-1,000 reverse stock split and then repurchased all shares held by stockholders with less than one share of stock, thereby eliminating smaller shareholders. After the reverse split, the number of shareholders was reduced to less than 300, allowing the company to delist, saving a considerable amount on administrative expenses. What made the proposal especially imaginative was that immediately after the reverse split, the company did a 1,000-for-1 ordinary split to restore the stock to its original cost!

RESEARCH IN EMERGING MARKET CONTEXT

In recent years, several studies have been conducted to understand the dividend policy of Indian firms. Dixit et al. (2020) found that the life-cycle theory can explain the dividend policy of these firms, but there is no evidence to support the signaling and catering theories. Additionally, Jacob and Jijo (2018) discovered that institutional investors tend to have larger holdings in dividend-paying firms and prefer dividend-payers over non-payers. However, for smaller firms, these investors prefer non-payers. Ranajee et al. (2018) observed that payout levels increase over time, and business group firms tend to pay higher dividends compared to standalone firms. The payout ratio is also determined by firm leverage, profitability, non-promoter holdings, and growth prospects. Pathak and Ranajee (2020) reported that better earnings quality is associated with larger dividend payments for Indian firms, and dividend payment decreases with poor earnings quality. In particular, earnings manipulation is done to increase earnings, especially for business group-affiliated firms. Finally, Varma et al. (2018) found

(continued)

that tender offer buyback is used more predominantly for capital structure corrections, while in the case of open market repurchase in India, dividend substitution and capital structure correction act as the key drivers.

References

Dixit, B. K., Gupta, N., & Saurabh, S. (2020). Dividend policy in India: reconciling theory and evidence. *Managerial Finance, 46*(11), 1437–1453.

Jacob, C., & Jijo Lukose PJ (2018). Institutional ownership and dividend payout in emerging markets: Evidence from India. *Journal of Emerging Market Finance, 17*(1_suppl), S54–S82.

Pathak, R. & Ranajee, R (2020). Earnings quality and corporate payout policy linkages: An Indian context. *The North American Journal of Economics and Finance, 51,* 100855.

Ranajee, R., Pathak, R., & Saxena, A. (2018). To pay or not to pay: what matters the most for dividend payments?. *International Journal of Managerial Finance, 14*(2), 230–244.

Varma, U., Singh, H., & Munjal, A. (2018). Corporate restructuring through Share buybacks: An Indian experience. *Australasian Accounting, Business and Finance Journal, 12*(2), 117–133.

Summary and Conclusions

1. The dividend policy of a firm is irrelevant in a perfect capital market because the shareholder can effectively undo the firm's dividend strategy. If a shareholder receives a greater dividend than desired, he or she can reinvest the excess. Conversely, if the shareholder receives a smaller dividend than desired, he or she can sell off extra shares of stock. This argument is due to MM and is similar to their homemade leverage concept, discussed in a previous chapter.
2. Stockholders will be indifferent between dividends and share repurchases in a perfect capital market.
3. Because dividends in the United States are taxed, companies should not issue stock to pay out a dividend.
4. Also because of taxes, firms have an incentive to reduce dividends. For example, they might consider increasing capital expenditures, acquiring other companies, or purchasing financial assets. However, due to financial considerations and legal constraints, rational firms with large cash flows will likely exhaust these activities with plenty of cash left over for dividends.
5. In a world with personal taxes, a strong case can be made for repurchasing shares instead of paying dividends.
6. Nevertheless, there are a number of justifications for dividends even in a world with personal taxes:
   a. Investors in no-dividend stocks incur transaction costs when selling off shares for current consumption.
   b. Behavioral finance argues that investors with limited self-control can meet current consumption needs via high-dividend stocks while adhering to a policy of "never dipping into principal."
   c. Managers, acting on behalf of stockholders, can pay dividends to keep cash from bondholders. The board of directors, also acting on behalf of stockholders, can use dividends to reduce the cash available to spendthrift managers.
7. The stock market reacts positively to increases in dividends (or an initial payment) and negatively to decreases in dividends. This suggests that there is information content in dividend payments.
8. High- (low-) dividend firms should arise to meet the demands of dividend-preferring (capital gains-preferring) investors. Because of these clienteles, it is not clear that a firm can create value by changing its dividend policy.

Concept Questions

1. **Dividend Policy Irrelevance** How is it possible that dividends are so important, but at the same time dividend policy is irrelevant?

2. **Stock Repurchases** What is the impact of a stock repurchase on a company's debt ratio? Does this suggest another use for excess cash?

3. **Dividend Policy** It is sometimes suggested that firms should follow a "residual" dividend policy. With such a policy, the main idea is that a firm should focus on meeting its investment needs and maintaining its desired debt-equity ratio. Having done so, a firm pays out any leftover, or residual, income as dividends. What do you think would be the chief drawback to a residual dividend policy?

4. **Dividend Chronology** On Tuesday, December 8, Hometown Power Co.'s board of directors declares a dividend of 75 cents per share payable on Tuesday, January 16, to shareholders of record as of Tuesday, January 2. When is the ex-dividend date? If a shareholder buys stock before that date, who gets the dividends on those shares: the buyer or the seller?

5. **Alternative Dividends** Some companies, like one British company that offers its large shareholders free crematorium use, pay dividends in kind (i.e., offer their services to shareholders at below-market cost). Should mutual funds invest in stocks that pay these dividends in kind? (The fundholders do not receive these services.)

6. **Dividends and Stock Price** If increases in dividends tend to be followed by (immediate) increases in share prices, how can it be said that dividend policy is irrelevant?

7. **Dividends and Stock Price** Last month, Central Virginia Power Company, which had been having trouble with cost overruns on a nuclear power plant that it had been building, announced that it was "temporarily suspending dividend payments due to the cash flow crunch associated with its investment program." The company's stock price dropped from ₹28.50 to ₹25 when this announcement was made. How would you interpret this change in the stock price? (That is, what would you say caused it?)

8. **Dividend Reinvestment Plans** The DRK Company has recently developed a dividend reinvestment plan, or DRIP. The plan allows investors to reinvest cash dividends automatically in DRK in exchange for new shares of stock. Over time, investors in DRK will be able to build their holdings by reinvesting dividends to purchase additional shares of the company.

   More than 1,000 companies offer dividend reinvestment plans. Most companies with DRIPs charge no brokerage or service fees. In fact, the shares of DRK will be purchased at a 10 percent discount from the market price. A consultant for DRK estimates that about 75 percent of DRK's shareholders will take part in this plan. This is somewhat higher than the average. Evaluate DRK's dividend reinvestment plan. Will it increase shareholder wealth? Discuss the advantages and disadvantages involved here.

9. **Dividend Policy** For initial public offerings of common stock, 2020 was a relatively slow year, with about ₹61.7 billion raised by the process. Relatively few of the 163 firms involved paid cash dividends. Why do you think that most chose not to pay cash dividends?

10. **Investment and Dividends** The Phew Charitable Trust pays no taxes on its capital gains or on its dividend income or interest income. Would it be irrational for it to have low-dividend, high-growth stocks in its portfolio? Would it be irrational for it to have municipal bonds in its portfolio? Explain.

Use the following information to answer the next two questions:

Historically, the U.S. tax code treated dividend payments made to shareholders as ordinary income. Dividends were taxed at the investor's marginal tax rate, which was as high as 38.6 percent in 2002. Capital gains were taxed at a capital gains tax rate, which was the same for most investors and fluctuated through the years. In 2002, the capital gains tax rate stood at 20 percent. In an effort to stimulate the economy, President George W. Bush presided over a tax plan overhaul that included changes in dividend and capital gains tax rates. The new tax plan, which was implemented in 2003, called for a 15 percent tax rate on both dividends and capital gains for investors in higher tax brackets. For lower-tax-bracket investors, the tax rate on dividends and capital gains was set at 5 percent through 2007, dropping to zero in 2008.

11. **Ex-Dividend Stock Prices** How do you think this tax law change affects ex-dividend stock prices?
12. **Stock Repurchases** How do you think this tax law change affects the relative attractiveness of stock repurchases compared to dividend payments?
13. **Dividends and Stock Value** The growing perpetuity model expresses the value of a share of stock as the present value of the expected dividends from that stock. How can you conclude that dividend policy is irrelevant when this model is valid?
14. **Bird-in-the-Hand Argument** The bird-in-the-hand argument, which states that a dividend today is safer than the uncertain prospect of a capital gain tomorrow, is often used to justify high dividend payout ratios. Explain the fallacy behind this argument.
15. **Dividends and Income Preference** The desire for current income is not a valid explanation of preference for high current dividend policy because investors can always create homemade dividends by selling a portion of their stocks. Is this statement true or false? Why?
16. **Dividends and Clientele** Cap Henderson owns Neotech stock because its price has been steadily rising over the past few years and he expects this performance to continue. Cap is trying to convince Sarah Jones to purchase some Neotech stock, but she is reluctant because Neotech has never paid a dividend. She depends on steady dividends to provide her with income.
    a. What preferences are these two investors demonstrating?
    b. What argument should Cap use to convince Sarah that Neotech stock is the stock for her?
    c. Why might Cap's argument not convince Sarah?
17. **Dividends and Taxes** Your aunt is in a high tax bracket and would like to minimize the tax burden of her investment portfolio. She is willing to buy and sell to maximize her aftertax returns, and she has asked for your advice. What would you suggest she do?
18. **Dividends versus Capital Gains** If the market places the same value on ₹1 of dividends as on ₹1 of capital gains, then firms with different payout ratios will appeal to different clienteles of investors. One clientele is as good as another; therefore, a firm cannot increase its value by changing its dividend policy. Yet empirical investigations reveal a strong correlation between dividend payout ratios and other firm characteristics. For example, small, rapidly growing firms that have recently gone public almost always have payout ratios that are zero; all earnings are reinvested in the business. Explain this phenomenon if dividend policy is irrelevant.
19. **Dividend Irrelevancy** In spite of the theoretical argument that dividend policy should be irrelevant, the fact remains that many investors like high dividends. If this preference exists, a firm can boost its share price by increasing its dividend payout ratio. Explain the fallacy in this argument.
20. **Dividends and Stock Price** Empirical research has found that there have been significant increases in stock price on the day an initial dividend (i.e., the first time a firm pays a cash dividend) is announced. What does this finding imply about the information content of initial dividends?

Questions and Problems

BASIC (Questions 1–10)

1. **Dividends and Taxes** Gatto, Inc., has declared a ₹5.85 per share dividend. Suppose capital gains are not taxed, but dividends are taxed at 15 percent. New Income Tax Authorities regulations require that taxes be withheld at the time the dividend is paid. The company's stock sells for ₹78.35 per share, and the stock is about to go ex dividend. What do you think the ex-dividend price will be?

2. **Stock Dividends** The owners' equity accounts for Vulcano International are shown here:

Common stock (₹.50 par value)	₹ 20,000
Capital surplus	210,000
Retained earnings	587,300
Total owners' equity	₹817,300

a. If the company's stock currently sells for ₹42 per share and a 10 percent stock dividend is declared, how many new shares will be distributed? Show how the equity accounts would change.
b. If the company declared a 25 percent stock dividend, how would the accounts change?

3. **Stock Splits** For the company in Problem 2, show how the equity accounts will change if:

a. The company declares a 4-for-1 stocsk split. How many shares are outstanding now? What is the new par value per share?
b. The company declares a 1-for-5 reverse stock split. How many shares are outstanding now? What is the new par value per share?

4. **Stock Splits and Stock Dividends** Stockton Mineral Operations, Inc. (SMO), currently has 540,000 shares of stock outstanding that sell for ₹83 per share. Assuming no market imperfections or tax effects exist, what will the share price be after:

a. SMO has a 5-for-3 stock split?
b. SMO has a 15 percent stock dividend?
c. SMO has a 42.5 percent stock dividend?
d. SMO has a 4-for-7 reverse stock split?

Determine the new number of shares outstanding in parts (a) through (d).

5. **Regular Dividends** The balance sheet for Quinn Corp. is shown here in market value terms. There are 12,000 shares of stock outstanding.

Market Value Balance Sheet			
Cash	₹ 49,300	Equity	₹404,300
Fixed assets	355,000		
Total	₹404,300	Total	₹404,300

The company has declared a dividend of ₹1.45 per share. The stock goes ex dividend tomorrow. Ignoring any tax effects, what is the stock selling for today? What will it sell for tomorrow? What will the balance sheet look like after the dividends are paid?

6. **Share Repurchase** In the previous problem, suppose the company has announced it is going to repurchase ₹17,400 worth of stock. What effect will this transaction have on the equity of the company? How many shares will be outstanding? What will the price per share be after the repurchase? Ignoring tax effects, show how the share repurchase is effectively the same as a cash dividend.

7. **Stock Dividends** The market value balance sheet for Murray Manufacturing is shown here. The company has declared a stock dividend of 25 percent. The stock goes ex dividend tomorrow (the chronology for a

stock dividend is similar to that for a cash dividend). There are 11,000 shares of stock outstanding. What will the ex-dividend price be?

Market Value Balance Sheet			
Cash	₹ 134,000	Debt	₹ 116,000
Fixed assets	652,000	Equity	670,000
Total	₹ 786,000	Total	₹ 786,000

8. **Stock Dividends** The company with the common equity accounts shown here has declared a stock dividend of 15 percent when the market value of its stock is ₹64 per share. What effects on the equity accounts will the distribution of the stock dividend have?

Common stock (₹1 par value)	₹ 225,000
Capital surplus	535,000
Retained earnings	2,968,500
Total owners' equity	₹ 3,728,500

9. **Stock Splits** In the previous problem, suppose the company instead decides on a four-for-one stock split. The firm's 75 cent per share cash dividend on the new (postsplit) shares represents an increase of 10 percent over last year's dividend on the presplit stock. What effect does this have on the equity accounts? What was last year's dividend per share?

10. **Dividends and Stock Price** The Mann Company belongs to a risk class for which the appropriate discount rate is 10 percent. The company currently has 235,000 outstanding shares selling at ₹106 each. The firm is contemplating the declaration of an ₹8 dividend at the end of the fiscal year that just began. Assume there are no taxes on dividends. Answer the following questions based on the Miller and Modigliani model, which is discussed in the text.

    a. What will be the price of the stock on the ex-dividend date if the dividend is declared?
    b. What will be the price of the stock at the end of the year if the dividend is not declared?
    c. If the company makes ₹3.7 million of new investments at the beginning of the period, earns net income of ₹1.675 million, and pays the dividend at the end of the year, how many shares of new stock must the firm issue to meet its funding needs?
    d. Is it realistic to use the MM model in the real world to value stock? Why or why not?

INTERMEDIATE (Questions 11–16)

11. **Homemade Dividends** You own 1,000 shares of stock in Avondale Company. You will receive a dividend of ₹3.45 per share in one year. In two years, the company will pay a liquidating dividend of ₹62 per share. The required return on the company's stock is 15 percent. What is the current share price of your stock (ignoring taxes)? If you would rather have equal dividends in each of the next two years, show how you can accomplish this by creating homemade dividends. (*Hint*: Dividends will be in the form of an annuity.)

12. **Homemade Dividends** In the previous problem, suppose you want only ₹1,500 total in dividends the first year. What will your homemade dividend be in two years?

13. **Stock Repurchase** Erna Company is evaluating an extra dividend versus a share repurchase. In either case, ₹53,500 would be spent. Current earnings are ₹1.79 per share and the stock currently sells for ₹64 per share. There are 9,000 shares outstanding. Ignore taxes and other imperfections in answering parts (a) and (b).

    a. Evaluate the two alternatives in terms of the effect on the price per share of the stock and shareholder wealth.

b. What will be the effect on the company's EPS and PE ratio under the two different scenarios?
c. In the real world, which of these actions would you recommend? Why?

14. **Dividends and Firm Value** The net income of Progressive Company is ₹165,000. The company has 35,000 outstanding shares and a 100 percent payout policy. The expected value of the firm one year from now is ₹2.1 million. The appropriate discount rate for the company is 12 percent and the dividend tax rate is zero.

a. What is the current value of the firm assuming the current dividend has not yet been paid?
b. What is the ex-dividend price of the company's stock if the board follows its current policy?
c. At the dividend declaration meeting, several board members claimed that the dividend is too meager and is probably depressing the company's price. They proposed that the company sell enough new shares to finance a ₹7.50 dividend.
  i. Comment on the claim that the low dividend is depressing the stock price. Support your argument with calculations.
  ii. If the proposal is adopted, at what price will the new shares sell? How many will be sold?

15. **Dividend Policy** Mahomes Co. has a current period cash flow of ₹1.2 million and pays no dividends. The present value of the company's future cash flows is ₹15.9 million. The company is entirely financed with equity and has 475,000 shares outstanding. Assume the dividend tax rate is zero.

a. What is the share price of the company's stock?
b. Suppose the board of directors of the company announces its plan to pay out 50 percent of its current cash flow as cash dividends to its shareholders. How can Jeff Miller, who owns 1,000 shares of the company's stock, achieve a zero payout policy on his own?

16. **Dividend Smoothing** The Sharpe Co. just paid a dividend of ₹2.30 per share of stock. Its target payout ratio is 40 percent. The company expects to have earnings per share of ₹6.95 one year from now.

a. If the adjustment rate is .3 as defined in the Lintner model, what is the dividend one year from now?
b. If the adjustment rate is .6 instead, what is the dividend one year from now?
c. Which adjustment rate is more conservative? Why?

CHALLENGE (Questions 17–20)

17. **Expected Return, Dividends, and Taxes** The Gecko Company and the Gordon Company are two firms whose business risk is the same but that have different dividend policies. Gecko pays no dividend, whereas Gordon has an expected dividend yield of 2.9 percent. Suppose the capital gains tax rate is zero, whereas the dividend tax rate is 35 percent. Gecko has an expected earnings growth rate of 11 percent annually and its stock price is expected to grow at this same rate. If the aftertax expected returns on the two stocks are equal (because they are in the same risk class), what is the pretax required return on Gordon's stock?

18. **Dividends and Taxes** As discussed in the text, in the absence of market imperfections and tax effects, we would expect the share price to decline by the amount of the dividend payment when the stock goes ex dividend. Once we consider the role of taxes, however, this is not necessarily true. One model has been proposed that incorporates tax effects into determining the ex-dividend price:[20]

$$(P_0 - P_X)/D = (1 - T_P)/(1 - T_G)$$

Here P_0 is the price just before the stock goes ex, P_X is the ex-dividend share price, D is the amount of the dividend per share, T_P is the relevant marginal personal tax rate on dividends, and T_G is the effective marginal tax rate on capital gains.

a. If $T_P = T_G = 0$, how much will the share price fall when the stock goes ex?
b. If $T_P = 15$ percent and $T_G = 0$, how much will the share price fall?
c. If $T_P = 15$ percent and $T_G = 30$ percent, how much will the share price fall?

[20] Edwin J. Elton and Martin J. Gruber, "Marginal Stockholder Tax Rates and the Clientele Effect," *Review of Economics and Statistics* 52, no. 1 (February 1970): 68–74.

d. Suppose the only owners of stock are companies. Recall that companies get at least a 50 percent exemption from taxation on the dividend income they receive, but they do not get such an exemption on capital gains. If the company's income and capital gains tax rates are both 21 percent, by how much does this model predict the share price will fall?

e. What does this problem tell you about real-world tax considerations and the dividend policy of the firm?

19. **Dividends versus Reinvestment** National Business Machine Co. (NBM) has ₹5 million of extra cash after taxes have been paid. NBM has two choices to make use of this cash. One alternative is to invest the cash in financial assets. The resulting investment income will be paid out as a special dividend at the end of three years. In this case, the firm can invest in Treasury bills yielding 2.5 percent or in 4.3 percent preferred stock. Assume Income Tax Authorities regulations allow the company to exclude from taxable income 50 percent of the dividends received from investing in another company's stock. Another alternative is to pay out the cash now as dividends. This would allow the shareholders to invest on their own in Treasury bills with the same yield, or in preferred stock. The corporate tax rate is 21 percent. Assume the investor has a 31 percent personal income tax rate, which is applied to interest income and preferred stock dividends. Also assume the personal dividend tax rate is 15 percent on common stock dividends. Should the cash be paid today or in three years? Which of the two options generates the highest aftertax income for the shareholders?

20. **Dividends versus Reinvestment** After completing its capital spending for the year, Carlson Manufacturing has ₹1,000 of extra cash. Carlson's managers must choose between investing the cash in Treasury bonds that yield 3 percent or paying the cash out to investors who would invest in the bonds themselves.

a. If the corporate tax rate is 21 percent, what personal tax rate would make the investors equally willing to receive the dividend or to let Carlson invest the money?

b. Is the answer to part (a) reasonable? Why or why not?

c. Suppose the only investment choice is a preferred stock that yields 6 percent. The corporate dividend exclusion of 50 percent applies. What personal tax rate will make the stockholders indifferent to the outcome of Carlson's dividend decision?

d. Is this a compelling argument for a low dividend payout ratio? Why or why not?

Mini Case ELECTRONIC TIMING, INC.

Electronic Timing, Inc. (ETI), is a small company founded 15 years ago by electronics engineers Tom Miller and Jessica Kerr. ETI manufactures integrated circuits to capitalize on the complex mixed-signal design technology and has recently entered the market for frequency timing generators, or silicon timing devices, which provide the timing signals or "clocks" necessary to synchronize electronic systems. Its clock products originally were used in PC video graphics applications, but the market subsequently expanded to include motherboards, PC peripheral devices, and other digital consumer electronics, such as digital television boxes and game consoles. ETI also designs and markets custom application-specific integrated circuits (ASICs) for industrial customers. The ASICs's design combines analog and digital, or mixed-signal, technology. In addition to Tom and Jessica, Rami Nafal, who provided capital for the company, is the third primary owner. Each owns 25 percent of the one million shares outstanding. Several other individuals, including current employees, own the remaining company shares.

Recently, the company designed a new computer motherboard. The company's new design is both more efficient and less expensive to manufacture, and the ETI design is expected to become standard in many personal computers. After investigating the possibility of manufacturing the new motherboard, ETI determined that the costs involved in building a new plant would be prohibitive. The owners also decided that they were unwilling to bring in another large outside owner. Instead, ETI sold the design to an outside firm. The sale of the motherboard design was completed for an aftertax payment of ₹30 million.

1. Tom believes the company should use the extra cash to pay a special one-time dividend. How will this proposal affect the stock price? How will it affect the value of the company?
2. Jessica believes that the company should use the extra cash to pay off debt and upgrade and expand its existing manufacturing capability. How would Jessica's proposals affect the company?
3. Rami is in favor of a share repurchase. He argues that a repurchase will increase the company's PE ratio, return on assets, and return on equity. Are his arguments correct? How will a share repurchase affect the value of the company?
4. Another option discussed by Tom, Jessica, and Rami would be to begin a regular dividend payment to shareholders. How would you evaluate this proposal?
5. One way to value a share of stock is the dividend growth, or growing perpetuity, model. Consider the following: The dividend payout ratio is 1 minus *b*, where *b* is the retention, or plowback, ratio. So, the dividend next year will be the earnings next year, E_1, times 1 minus the retention ratio. The most commonly used equation to calculate the sustainable growth rate is the return on equity times the retention ratio. Substituting these relationships into the dividend growth model, we get the following equation to calculate the price of a share of stock today:

$$P_0 = \frac{E_1(1 - b)}{R_S - \text{ROE} \times b}$$

   What are the implications of this result in terms of whether the company should pay a dividend or upgrade and expand its manufacturing capability? Explain.
6. Does the question of whether the company should pay a dividend depend on whether the company is organized as a company or an LLC?

INVESTIGATING INDIA INC. IN PRACTICE

Surya Prakash wanted to learn more about corporate finance in real life. You are to help him in the same. Exhibits 19.2, 19.3 and 19.4 share real-life illustrations of select share buybacks, bonus issues and stock splits, respectively, in the years 2023 and 2024. Pick two companies of your choice from each exhibit and see their share price movements and other corporate maneuvers (before, at that time and after these announcements/moves). Can you see any inkling of the corporate finance dividend-based theories in practice? Discuss on the findings of your investigations.

20

PART V: LONG-TERM FINANCING

Raising Capital

On September 16, 2020, in one of the most anticipated IPOs of the year, cloud database company Snowflake, went public. Assisted by investment banks Morgan Stanley, Goldman Sachs, JPMorgan, and a host of others, the company offered 28 million shares of stock at a price of ₹120 per share. The first trade on the New York Stock Exchange was at ₹245 per share, a 104 percent jump from the initial stock price. The stock quickly rose to ₹319, before closing at ₹253.93. What made Snowflake's stock offering particularly unique was that the company sold Class A shares, with limited voting rights, in the IPO. The company also had Class B shares that controlled 98.5 percent of the voting power. The Class B stock was held entirely by the company's founder and earlier investors. There has been a lot of activities in raising equity capital in Indian markets as well. Roughly, 240 companies raised ₹576 billion in equity financing in the calendar year 2023. Within the first two months of 2024, 48 companies have raised ₹117 billion in equity financing. The IPO's high subscription rate indicates that investors are willing to provide the companies with funds for growth. In this chapter, we will examine the process by which companies such as Snowflake sell stock to the public, the costs of doing so, and the role of investment banks in the process.

The Indian government promoted the establishment of SME exchanges in order to facilitate the equity fund raising process for small and medium-sized businesses. The first SME company on the BSE SME platform was listed in 2012. Subsequently, NSE adopted a comparable name for the SME platform, NSE EMERGE. Following an 11-year journey, 483 businesses were able to raise equity on the BSE SME platform, while 269 businesses raised financing on NSE EMERGE.

Businesses large and small have one thing in common: They need long-term capital. This chapter describes how they get it. We pay particular attention to what is probably the most important stage in a company's financial life cycle—the IPO. Such offerings are the process by which companies convert from being privately owned to publicly owned. For many people, starting a company, growing it, and taking it public is the ultimate entrepreneurial dream.

This chapter examines how firms access capital in the real world. The financing method is generally tied to the firm's life cycle. Startup firms often are financed via venture capital. As firms grow, they may want to "go public." A firm's first public offering is called an IPO, which stands for initial public offering. Later offerings are called SEOs, for seasoned equity offerings. This chapter follows the life cycle of the firm, covering venture capital, IPOs, and SEOs. Debt financing is discussed toward the end of the chapter.

Please visit us at **rwjcorporatefinance.blogspot.com** for the latest developments in the world of corporate finance.

20.1 Entrepreneurship: Early-Stage Financing and Venture Capital

One day, you and a friend have a great idea for a new computer software product that will help users communicate using the next-generation meganet. Filled with entrepreneurial zeal, you call the product Megacomm and set about bringing it to market.

Working nights and weekends, you are able to create a prototype of your product. It doesn't actually work, but at least you can show it around to illustrate your idea. To actually develop the product, you need to hire programmers, buy computers, rent office space, and so on. Unfortunately, because you are both MBA students, your combined assets are insufficient to fund a pizza party, much less a startup company. You need what is often referred to as OPM–other people's money.

Your first thought might be to approach a bank for a loan. You would probably discover, however, that banks generally are not interested in making loans to startup companies with no assets (other than an idea) run by fledgling entrepreneurs with no track record. While you could go on the hit TV show *Shark Tank* in search of funds, very few people are able to get a bite at this source of financing. Instead your search for capital would likely lead you to the **venture capital (VC)** market.

One group of potential investors goes by the name of **angel investors**, or **angels**. They may be friends and family, with little knowledge of your product's industry and little experience backing startup companies. However, some angels are more knowledgeable individuals or groups of individuals who have invested in a number of previous ventures.

ENTREPRENUERSHIP

Entrepreneurs create new businesses, which means they bear most of the risk but can also reap much of the reward. And though most entrepreneurs will never reach the same level, Bill Gates of Microsoft and Steve Jobs of Apple are the ultimate success stories, as both companies were started in the founders' garages. Unlike traditional professions, there is no set path to success for an entrepreneur, but sweat equity and a broad skill set are important.

Entrepreneurship has grown to the point that many colleges offer degrees on the subject, but there are other sources of help. Most large cities have entrepreneur centers, and there are also seed investor groups for entrepreneurs. One of the best-known is Y Combinator (YC). YC funds a large number of startups in a "boot camp" style, bringing entrepreneurs together. Networking and information sharing can be important determinants of success, especially at this point in a company's life. Several well-known companies that were funded by YC include Airbnb, Dropbox, and DoorDash.

For more Y Combinator, check out: **www.ycombinator.com/**.

VENTURE CAPITAL

The term *venture capital* does not have a precise meaning, but it generally refers to financing for new, often high-risk, ventures. So-called angels are usually individuals who invest their own money, but they tend to focus on smaller deals. Venture capital firms specialize in pooling funds from various sources and investing them. The underlying sources of funds for such firms include individuals, pension funds, insurance companies, large corporations, and even university endowments. The broad term *private equity* is often used to label the rapidly growing area of equity financing for nonpublic companies.

Venture capitalists share some common characteristics, of which three are particularly important:[1]

1. *VCs are financial intermediaries that raise funds from outside investors.* VC firms are typically organized as limited partnerships. As with any limited partnership, limited partners invest with the general partner, who makes the investment decisions. The limited partners are frequently institutional investors, such as pension plans, endowments, and corporations. Wealthy individuals and families are often limited partners, as well.

   This characteristic separates VCs from angels because angels typically invest their own money. In addition, corporations sometimes set up internal venture capital divisions to fund fledgling firms. However, Metrick and Yasuda point out that, because these divisions invest the funds of their corporate parent, rather than the funds of others, they are not–in spite of their name–venture capitalists.

2. *VCs play an active role in overseeing, advising, and monitoring the companies in which they invest.* Members of venture capital firms frequently join the board of directors. The principals in VC firms are generally quite experienced in business. By contrast, while entrepreneurs at the helm of startup companies may be bright, creative, and knowledgeable about their products, they often lack much business experience.
3. *VCs generally do not want to own the investment forever.* Rather, VCs look for an exit strategy, such as taking the investment public (a topic we discuss in the next section) or selling it to another company. Corporate venture capital does not share this characteristic because corporations are frequently content to have the investment stay on the books of the internal VC division indefinitely.

This last characteristic is quite important in determining the nature of typical VC investments. A firm must be a certain size to either go public or be easily sold. Because the investment is generally small initially, it must possess great growth potential; many businesses do not. Imagine an individual who wants to open a gourmet restaurant. If the owner is a true "foodie" with no desire to expand beyond one location, it is unlikely the restaurant will ever become large enough to go public. By contrast, firms in high-tech fields often have significant growth potential and many VC firms specialize in this area.

The venture capital market serves as an important source of funds for new companies. Figure 20.1 shows the cash flows for a new company during its early life. At the start of a company's life, cash flows are negative while the product is being developed. Often, there are very large cash outflows during this stage. When the product is being rolled out to market, cash flows are still negative until growth and expansion occur.

Venture capitalists and venture capital firms recognize that many or even most new ventures will not fly, but the occasional one will. The potential profits are enormous in such cases. To limit their risk, venture capitalists generally provide financing in stages. At each stage, enough money is invested to reach the next milestone or planning stage.

For more on funding stages, including a list of angel investor groups, check out **www.fundz.net/**.

STAGES OF FINANCING

Venture capital firms often specialize in different stages. Some specialize in very early "seed money," or ground floor, financing. In contrast, financing in the later stages might come from venture capitalists specializing in so-called "mezzanine-level financing," where *mezzanine level* refers to the level just above the ground floor.

A *seed*, or *angel, round* is the initial investment. At this stage, while the company may have a product available, it is often in the beta stage. Companies use the money from a seed round to adapt the product for market demand and prove the product is viable. Product pricing is also a key goal during this period. Although seed round investors may receive equity directly, financing is often provided in the form of convertible notes or *advisory shares*. Advisory shares are vested over time, which encourages the angel investor to stay involved in the company.

For more on the VC industry, check out **nvca.org**.

[1]These characteristics are discussed in depth in Andrew Metric and Ayako Yasuda, *Venture Capital and the Finance of Innovation*, 2nd ed. (Hoboken, NJ: John Wiley and Sons, 2011).

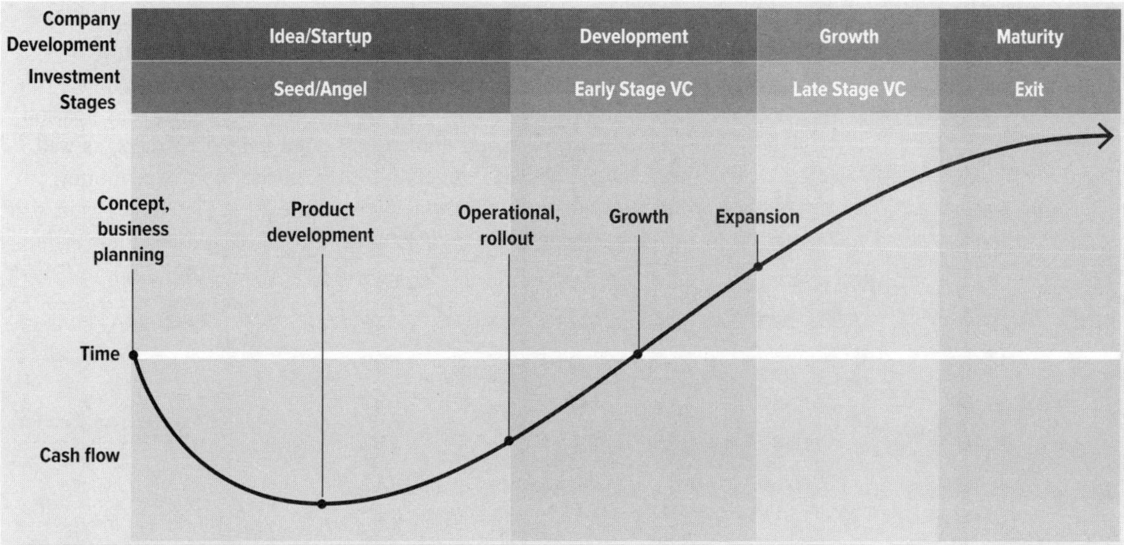

Figure 20.1 Cash Flows for a Startup

SOURCE: *National Venture Capital Association Yearbook* 2020 (Pitchbook Data, Inc.).

Although there are seed money VC firms, an important source of investment at this stage is often friends and family. As we discuss in a subsequent section, funding may also come from websites such as Kickstarter.

Early-stage venture capital is generally classified as *Series A* or *Series B*. Series A funding is the next stage after seed funding. Series A funding generally covers the salaries of the people involved, market research, and finalizing the product. Receiving a seed round investment is not a guarantee of further venture capital investment as less than 10 percent of companies advance to Series A funding. Although all forms of financing may be used, preferred stock is commonly used in this round.

Series B funding is used to ignite growth in the company. The company will have a product on the market, but financing is needed to expand production and grow market share. Often, the goal of this Series B funding is to generate a net profit. This is also the first stage at which common stock is the most popular form of financing.

Late-stage rounds are generally classified as *Series C*, *Series D*, and so on. Many companies never make it to these stages as Series B funding may be sufficient. A Series C round is used to grab a greater market share, fund acquisitions, or develop more products. Late-stage funding can also be used to set the company up to be acquired or go public. For companies looking to go public in the next year or so, *bridge financing* is often used. Bridge financing is used to cover the expenses of an IPO and is often provided by an investment bank.

More recently, *growth equity* has become more common as a form of venture capital in the later stage of a company's growth. Growth equity provides funds for mature companies for which a buyout or IPO would not make sense at the time. Growth equity allows a company to stay private longer than historically was the case. Growth equity is often associated, but not limited to, *unicorns*, which are private companies that have a value exceeding ₹1 billion. Table 20.1 shows the number of deals for the past 10 years by VC stage. As you can see, in a given year there are many more angel rounds than growth equity rounds.

Although you might think that much of the venture capital investment occurs during the early stages of a company, as you can see in Table 20.2, most of the investment by rupee amount occurs in later stages. This is due to the large financing requirements for larger, fast growing companies.

Table 20.1 Venture Capital Deals by Round

	Angel and Seed	Early VC	Later VC	Growth Equity
2010	1,746	2,129	1,588	551
2011	2,618	2,453	1,751	643
2012	3,557	2,630	1,771	670
2013	4,668	2,852	1,893	695
2014	5,491	3,172	2,057	891
2015	5,783	3,250	2,040	1,001
2016	4,790	3,016	1,888	885
2017	4,956	3,384	2,052	1,021
2018	4,622	3,731	2,295	1,217
2019	4,760	3,882	2,717	1,217

SOURCE: *National Venture Capital Association Yearbook* 2020 (Pitchbook Data, Inc.).

Table 20.2 Venture Capital Investment by Funding Stage in 2019 (billions)

Angel and Seed	₹ 9.6
Early VC	43.2
Later VC	80.7
Growth Equity	66.4

SOURCE: *National Venture Capital Association Yearbook* 2020 (Pitchbook Data, Inc.).

The fact that financing is available in stages and is contingent on specified goals being met is a powerful motivating force for the firm's founders. Often, the founders receive relatively little in the way of salary and have substantial portions of their personal assets tied up in the business. At each stage of financing, the value of the founders' stake grows and the probability of success rises.

In addition to providing financing, venture capitalists often actively participate in running the firm, providing the benefit of experience with previous startups as well as general business expertise. This is especially true when the firm's founders have little or no hands-on experience in running a company.

SOME VENTURE CAPITAL REALITIES

Although there is a large venture capital market, the truth is that access to venture capital is very limited. Venture capital companies receive huge numbers of unsolicited proposals, the vast majority of which end up unread in the circular file. In fact, the National Venture Capital Association (NVCA) estimates that only one company is funded for every 100 proposals received. Venture capitalists rely heavily on informal networks of lawyers, accountants, bankers, and other venture capitalists to help identify potential investments. As a result, personal contacts are important in gaining access to the venture capital market; it is very much an "introduction" market.

Venture capitalists tend to be specialized, investing in particular industries. In fact, if you look at Table 20.3, you will see that most of venture capital investment in first stage financing is in software and health care.

Table 20.3 Venture Capital Flow by Sector in 2019: First Round

	Number of Deals	Capital Raised (millions)
Commercial services	317	₹1,097.7
Consumer goods and recreation	161	521.6
Energy	31	54.0
Health care devices	105	551.1
Health care services	205	538.3
IT hardware	70	205.8
Media	110	239.9
Other	820	2,608.1
Pharma and biotech	208	2,893.3
Software	903	2,585.9

SOURCE: *National Venture Capital Association Yearbook* 2020 (Pitchbook Data, Inc.).

Another simple fact about venture capital is that it is quite expensive. In a typical deal, the venture capitalist will demand (and get) 40 percent or more of the equity in the company. Venture capitalists frequently hold voting preferred stock, giving them various priorities in the event the company is sold or liquidated. The venture capitalist will typically demand (and get) several seats on the company's board of directors and may even appoint one or more members of senior management.

The internet is a tremendous source of venture capital information, both for suppliers and demanders of capital. For example, the site at **www.dealflow.com** prompts you to search the firm's database as either an entrepreneur (capital seeker) or a venture capitalist (capital supplier).

VENTURE CAPITAL FIRMS

Venture capital funds operate much like a mutual fund, pooling money from investors. VC firms raise investment pools, then managers make investments for investors. There are about 1,000 VC firms and 2,000 VC funds. The largest funds launched in 2019 are shown in Table 20.4.

Table 20.4 Largest VC Funds Launched in 2019

Investor Name	Fund Name	Fund Size (M)	Close Date	Fund State
TCV	TCV X	₹3,200.0	January 31, 2019	California
Andreessen Horowitz	Andreessen Horowitz LSV Fund I	₹2,238.9	July 17, 2019	California
Norwest Venture Partners	Norwest Venture Partners XV	₹2,000.0	November 14, 2019	California
Founders Fund	The Founders Fund VII	₹1,496.4	November 20, 2019	California
Vivo Capital	Vivo Capital Fund IX	₹1,430.0	October 30, 2019	California
Sapphire Ventures	Sapphire Ventures Fund IV	₹1,400.0	December 18, 2019	California
Lightspeed Venture Partners	Lightspeed Venture Partners Select III	₹1,361.8	June 21, 2019	California
Bond Capital (San Francisco)	Bond Capital Fund	₹1,250.0	May 1, 2019	California
Sequoia Capital	Sequoia Capital US Growth Fund VIII	₹998.5	December 6, 2019	California
Andreessen Horowitz	Andreessen Horowitz Fund VI	₹840.0	July 17, 2019	California

SOURCE: *National Venture Capital Association Yearbook* 2020 (Pitchbook Data, Inc.).

Table 20.5 Top States by VC Raised in 2019

	Number of Funds	Capital Raised (M)
California	123	₹31,513.4
Massachusetts	28	₹ 7,515.5
New York	40	₹ 4,583.5
Connecticut	2	₹910.0
Ohio	7	₹894.1
Illinois	10	₹721.1
Washington	10	₹689.1
Texas	9	₹546.3
Pennsylvania	4	₹417.0
District of Columbia	2	₹365.0

SOURCE: *National Venture Capital Association Yearbook* 2020 (Pitchbook Data, Inc.)

Large VC firms are responsible for much of the later-stage investment in startups. For example, SoftBank, one of the largest VC firms, invested about ₹18.5 billion in WeWork, although SoftBank lost much of its investment as WeWork was valued at only ₹2.9 billion by the middle of 2020.

Although VC investment is available around the world, to find the center of the VC world, we suggest you head to Sand Hill Road in Menlo Park, California, in the famous Silicon Valley. Table 20.5 shows the total amount of venture capital managed by VC firms in each state. As you can see, California had the largest amount of VC funds raised in 2019 by a substantial margin.

Learn more about crowdfunding at the Crowdfunding Professional Association website, **www.cfpa.org.**

CROWDFUNDING

On April 5, 2012, the Jumpstart Our Business Startups (JOBS) Act was signed into law. A provision of this act allows companies to raise money through *crowdfunding*, which is the practice of raising small amounts of capital from a large number of people, typically via the internet. Crowdfunding was first used to underwrite the U.S. tour of British rock band Marillion. The JOBS Act allows companies to sell equity by crowdfunding. Originally, the JOBS Act allowed a company to issue up to ₹1 million in securities in a 12-month period, although this limit was later raised to a maximum of ₹50 million.

Check out two of the more well-known project and charitable crowdfunding websites **www.kickstarter.com** and **www.gofundme.com.**

In May 2016, Regulation CF (also known as Title III of the JOBS Act) kicked in, which allows small investors access to new crowdfunding "portals." Previously, investors in crowdfunding had to be "accredited." For an individual, this requirement translates to more than ₹1 million in net worth or more than ₹200,000 in income for two of the past three years. Regulation CF allows investors with less than ₹107,000 in income or assets to invest at least ₹2,200 per year, up to a maximum of ₹5,350.

To sell securities through Regulation CF, a company must file a form with the SEC. This filing makes the company eligible to list its securities on a crowdfunding portal that is approved by FINRA (the Financial Industry Regulatory Authority), the same agency we mentioned earlier in the textbook for bond price reporting. Crowdfunding portals are already specializing. For example, there are portals that specialize in only accredited investors, all investors, or real estate investors, to name just a few.

INITIAL COIN OFFERINGS

See upcoming ICOs at **icodrops.com.**

In addition to sales of traditional debt and equity, a company can raise funds by selling *tokens*. These tokens often grant the holder the right to use the company's service in the future. For example, a company building a railroad may issue a token that can be used as a train ticket after the railroad is built.

Token sales occur on digital currency platforms and can be easily transferred on the platform or converted to U.S. rupees on specialized token exchanges. This liquidity has made tokens a popular means of funding since their introduction in 2015. Tokens are now purchased by both customers and investors who may never use the token for the service being offered.

The initial sale of a token on a digital currency platform is often called an **initial coin offering** or **ICO** (to sound like IPO). Many startup companies are now choosing to raise funds through an ICO rather than the traditional venture capital channels. The most common platform for issuing new tokens is Ethereum, but there are many competitors. In 2019, there were 109 ICOs with a total value of about ₹371 million, down significantly from the 1,253 ICOs and ₹7.8 billion raised in 2018.

Token sales are most popular among companies that are building services based on blockchain technology. This technology is at the heart of bitcoin and other cryptocurrencies. A blockchain is a timestamped ledger of transactions that is kept among a network of users without centralized control. It is similar to a traditional database, except that cryptography is used to make it infeasible to change the data once it is added to the chain. Many industries, including finance, are now updating their recordkeeping infrastructure with blockchain technology.

The SEC has some warnings about ICOs at **tinyurl.com/y5fawdjq.**

Token sales can also serve as an effective marketing tool. This is especially true if the business benefits from network effects, because the potential for price appreciation in the tokens attracts new customers. The increase in customers increases the value of the service, which in turn increases the value of the tokens. For example, Civic is building a blockchain-based identity platform, and its currency is used to purchase identity verification services from trusted parties. The company raised ₹33 million in June 2017 through an ICO of the CVC token. The total value of the tokens in January 2018 was about ₹462 million, although in an indication of the volatility of tokens, the value dropped to less than ₹40 million by late 2020.

RESEARCH ON VC-PE INVESTMENTS IN INDIA

In the last decade, the Indian Venture Capital and Private Equity (VC and PE) industry has witnessed a dramatic increase in the number of enterprises funded. As of 2020, over 950 funds have supported over 4,700 enterprises across a wide range of industries, including the northern, southern, and western regions of the country (Sabarinathan, 2019).

Chinchwadkar and Shekhar (2016) track the evolution of the regulatory environment for the PE industry in India, from the SEBI (Venture Capital Funds) Regulations 1996 to the SEBI (Alternative Investment Funds) (Amendment) Regulations 2013, which govern the industry today. The study concludes that a regulator should not create regulations in isolation; they must take inputs from varied stakeholders to develop effective regulations.

Katti and Raithatha's (2018) empirical results find evidence of value erosion due to the presence of VC investors. They justify, through the opportunistic behavior of the investor, having an easy route to exit the investment through the secondary market in case of the firm's expected underperformance. The study also reveals that VC investors' origin influences firm performance.

(continued)

Mishra and Bag (2020) find that the success of a VC deal hinges not only on the final outcome, such as post-company valuation and realised revenue, but also on several observable contractual characteristics which include syndication, use of convertible security and ownership percentage with noticeable deal features.

Dominic and Gopalaswamy (2019) studied VC market liquidity and stated that the exit probability is just 30 percent for the whole Indian VC market. Strategic sales and secondary sales have a high probability of exit for a longer time.

Rajan (2010) reviews the Indian VC-PE industry's (recent) high growth rates. He highlights the following areas of concern for long-run success:(a) First, an ecosystem must be created that encourages early-stage investment. (b) Second, the short-duration outlook of VC-PE investment does not allow hand-holding and participation in value-adding partnerships. Hence, it does not bode well. (c) Third, the time intervals between successive funding rounds should increase.

Further readings: (a) Sabarinathan, G. "Angel Investments in India–Trends, Prospects and Issues." *IIMB Management Review* 31, no. 2 (2019): 200–214. (b) Rajan, A Thillai, "A life-cycle analysis of VC-PE investments in India", *The Journal of Private Equity,* Winter 2010, pp. 72–82. (c) Chinchwadkar, Rohan, and Vidhu Shekhar. "Evolution of Private Equity Regulations in Emerging Markets: A Case of India." *The Journal of Private Equity* 20, no. 1 (2016): 38–44. (d) Katti, Supriya, and Mehul Raithatha. "Impact of venture capital investment on firm performance: An Indian Evidence." *Global Business Review* 21, no. 4 (2020): 1011–1024. (e) Mishra, Sarita, and Dinabandhu Bag. "Deriving successful venture capital deal profile through decision tree analysis in Indian context." *World Journal of Entrepreneurship, Management and Sustainable Development* (2020). (f) Dominic, James, and Arun Kumar Gopalaswamy. "Is the venture capital market liquid? Evidence from India." *Global Finance Journal* 41 (2019): 146–157.

20.2 The Public Issue

If firms wish to attract a large set of investors, they will issue public securities. There are a lot of regulations for public issues, with perhaps the most important established in the 1930s. The Securities Act of 1933 regulates new interstate securities issues and the Securities Exchange Act of 1934 regulates securities that are already outstanding. The Securities and Exchange Board of India (SEBI) in India and the Securities and Exchange Commission (SEC) in the USA administer both Acts.

In 1988, the Government of India established the SEBI as an autonomous body. It was given statutory form in 1992 with the SEBI Act, 1992. The Securities Contracts (Regulation) Act, 1956 (SCRA) and the SEBI Act, 1992 set forth the guidelines for all new securities issues. The SCRA of 1956 and the Securities Laws (Amendment) Bill, 1999 are the basis for regulating outstanding securities. The SEBI administers both the Acts.

The basic steps for issuing securities are:

1. In any issue of securities to the public, management first must obtain approval from the board of directors.
2. The firm must prepare a **registration statement** and file it with the SEBI (for India) or the SEC (for U.S.A.) This statement contains a great deal of financial information, including a financial history, details of the existing business, proposed financing, and plans for the future. It easily can run to 50 or more pages. The document is required for all public issues of securities with two principal exceptions:

   a. Loans that mature within nine months.

   b. Issues that involve less than ₹5 million.

The second exception is known as the *small-issues exemption*. Issues of less than ₹5 million are governed by **Regulation A**, for which only a brief offering statement–rather than the full registration statement–is needed. In India, the second exemption is not available.

3. The SEBI (for India) or the SEC (for U.S.A.) studies the registration statement during a *waiting period*. During this time, the firm may distribute copies of a preliminary prospectus. The preliminary prospectus is called a **red herring** because bold red letters are printed on the cover. A **prospectus** contains much of the information put into the registration statement and is given to potential investors by the firm. The company cannot sell the securities during the waiting period. However, oral offers can be made.

   A registration statement will become effective on the 20th day after its filing unless the SEBI (in India)/SEC (in US) sends a *letter of comment* suggesting changes. After the changes are made, the 20-day waiting period starts anew.
4. The registration statement does not initially contain the price of the new issue. On the effective date of the registration statement, a price is determined and a full-fledged selling effort gets under way. A final prospectus must accompany the delivery of securities or confirmation of sale, whichever comes first.
5. **Tombstone** advertisements are used during and after the waiting period. An example is reproduced in Figure 20.2.

The tombstone contains the name of the issuer (the World Wrestling Federation, now known as World Wrestling Entertainment). It provides some information about the issue and lists the investment banks (the underwriters) involved with selling the issue. The role of the investment banks in selling securities is discussed more fully in the following pages.

The investment banks on the tombstone are divided into groups called *brackets* based on their participation in the issue, and the names of the banks are listed alphabetically within each bracket. The brackets are often viewed as a kind of pecking order. In general, the higher the bracket, the greater is the underwriter's prestige. In recent years, the use of printed tombstones has declined, in part as a cost-saving measure.

DIRECT LISTING

While firms usually use underwriters to help their stock become publicly traded, it is not required. If it wishes to do so, and it meets the requirements of the stock exchange, a company can do a **direct listing**, also known as a *direct public offering*, or DPO. In this case, the firm arranges for its stock to be listed on the exchange without marketing and other help from an underwriter. While direct listings were uncommon for large firms, they have become more common in recent years. For example, software platform company Palantir, with a valuation well into the billions of rupees, completed one on the NYSE in 2020. Previously, music streaming service Spotify and enterprise software company Slack also went public via direct listings. Among other things, a direct listing is much less expensive because there are no underwriting fees and other associated costs. Such fees are discussed in detail in a subsequent section, and they can be substantial.

In a major shift, in late 2020, the SEC changed its rules to allow companies to sell new shares as a part of a DPO. Previously, the only shares that could be offered were existing shares held by company founders, investors, and employees. By allowing companies to offer newly created shares, the SEC has made it much easier for firms to bypass the traditional, often costly, underwriting process.

SPECIAL-PURPOSE ACQUISITION COMPANIES

Special-purpose acquisition companies (SPACs), or "blank check" companies, have become much more popular recently. In fact, in 2020, there were almost 250 SPAC IPOs compared to fewer than 170 ordinary

This announcement is neither an offer to sell nor a solicitation of an offer to buy any of these securities.
The offering is made only by the Prospectus.

New Issue

11,500,000 Shares

World Wrestling Federation Entertainment, Inc.

Class A Common Stock

Price ₹17.00 Per Share

Copies of the Prospectus may be obtained in any State in which this announcement is circulated from only such of the Underwriters, including the undersigned, as may lawfully offer these securities in such State.

U.S. Offering

9,200,000 Shares

This portion of the underwriting is being offered in the United States and Canada.

Bear, Stearns & Co., Inc.

Credit Suisse First Boston

Merrill Lynch & Co.

Wit Capital Corporation

Allen & Company Incorporated   Banc of America Securities LLC   Deutsche Banc Alex. Brown

Donaldson, Lufkin & Jenrette   A.G. Edwards & Sons, Inc.   Hambrecht & Quist   ING Barings

Prudential Securities   SG Cowen   Wassertein Perella Securities, Inc.   Advest, Inc.

Axiom Capital Management, Inc.   Blackford Securities Corp.   J.C. Bradford & Co.

Joseph Charles & Assoc., Inc.   Chatsworth Securities LLC   Gabelli & Company, Inc.

Gaines, Berland, Inc.   Jefferies & Company, Inc.   Josephthal & Co., Inc.   Neuberger Berman, LLC

Raymond James & Associates, Inc.   Sanders Morris Mundy

Tucker Anthony Cleary Gull   Wachovia Securities, Inc.

International Offering

2,300,000 Shares

This portion of the underwriting is being offered outside of the United States and Canada.

Bear, Stearns International Limited

Credit Suisse First Boston

Merrill Lynch International

Figure 20.2 An Example of a Tombstone Advertisement

IPOs. An SPAC is created to raise funds in order to finance a merger or acquisition within a set time frame. Although the opportunity may not be identified, SPACs have gone public recently with specific target firms in mind before the IPO. For example, online gambling company DraftKings was acquired by Diamond Eagle Acquisition after Diamond Eagle's IPO. Diamond Eagle was created specifically to take DraftKings public. The key advantages of an SPAC are that it is cheaper and less time consuming than a traditional IPO.

The SPAC trend accelerated in the first half of 2021. There were over 200 by early March. In fact, on Monday, March 2 alone, there were 15 SPAC IPOs. During the last week of February, 50 SPACs filed preliminary paperwork, implying an annual pace of about 2,600 per year.

A reverse merger is related to an SPAC, but is used less often. In a reverse merger, a privately traded company acquires a publicly traded company, which results in the combined company being publicly traded.

DUAL-CLASS STOCK IPOS

In another chapter, we discussed the unequal voting rights associated with "dual-class" stock. In the past several years, dual-class IPOs have become much more common. In 2020, about 42 percent of tech IPOs that went public had more than one share class. For example, when DoorDash went public on December 9, 2020, its three cofounders retained 75 percent of the stock voting rights. Other IPOs with large voting rights granted to founders included Airbnb (43 percent) and Palantir (49.99 percent).

Proponents of unequal voting rights argue that it allows visionary management room to experiment and build a stronger business. Of course, others claim that unequal voting rights reduce the accountability of management to shareholders. Note that there can be truth to both of these statements.

20.3 Alternative Issue Methods

When a company decides to issue a new security, it can sell it as a public issue or a private issue. If it is a public issue, the firm is required to register the issue with the SEBI (in India)/SEC (in US). If the issue is sold to fewer than 35 investors, it can be treated as a private issue. A registration statement is not required in this case.[2]

There are two kinds of public issues: the *general cash offer* and the *rights offer*. Cash offers are sold to all interested investors and rights offers are sold to existing shareholders. Equity is sold by both the cash offer and the rights offer, though almost all debt is sold by the cash offer.

A company's first public equity issue is referred to as an **initial public offering (IPO)**. All initial public offerings are cash offers because, if the firm's existing shareholders wanted to buy the shares, the firm would not need to sell them publicly. A **seasoned equity offering (SEO)** refers to a new issue where the company's securities have been previously issued. A seasoned equity offering of common stock may be made by either a cash offer or a rights offer.

> IPO information is widely available. Try IPO Scoop at **www.iposcoop.com.**

These methods of issuing new securities are shown in Table 20.6 and discussed in the next few sections.

[2]However, regulation significantly restricts the resale of unregistered equity securities. For example, the purchaser may be required to hold the securities for at least one year (or more). Many of the restrictions were significantly eased in 1990 for very large institutional investors. The private placement of bonds is discussed in a later section.

Table 20.6 The Methods of Issuing New Securities

Method	Type	Definition
Public		
Traditional negotiated cash offer	Firm commitment cash offer	Company negotiates an agreement with an investment banker to underwrite and distribute the new shares. A specified number of shares are bought by underwriters and sold at a higher price.
	Best-efforts cash offer	Company has investment bankers sell as many of the new shares as possible at the agreed-upon price. There is no guarantee concerning how much cash will be raised.
	Dutch auction cash offer	Company has investment bankers auction shares to determine the highest offer price obtainable for a given number of shares to be sold.
Privileged subscription	Direct rights offer	Company offers the new stock directly to its existing shareholders.
	Standby rights offer	Like the direct rights offer, this contains a privileged subscription arrangement with existing shareholders. The net proceeds are guaranteed by the underwriters.
Nontraditional cash offer	Shelf cash offer	Qualifying companies can authorize all the shares they expect to sell over a two-year period and sell them when needed.
	Competitive firm cash offer	Company can elect to award the underwriting contract through a public auction instead of negotiation.
Private	Direct placement	Securities are sold directly to the purchaser, who, at least until recently, generally could not resell the securities for at least two years.

20.4 The Cash Offer

As mentioned, stock is sold to interested investors in a **cash offer**. If the cash offer is a public one, **investment banks** are usually involved. Investment banks are financial intermediaries that perform a wide variety of services. In addition to aiding in the sale of securities, they may facilitate mergers and other corporate reorganizations and act as brokers to both individual and institutional clients. You may well have heard of large Wall Street investment banking houses such as Goldman Sachs and Morgan Stanley.

For corporate issuers, investment bankers perform services such as the following:

Formulating the method used to issue the securities.

Pricing the new securities.

Selling the new securities.

There are three basic methods of issuing securities for cash:

1. *Firm commitment*: Under this method, the investment bank (or a group of investment banks) buys the securities for less than the offering price and accepts the risk of not being able to sell them. Because this function involves risk, we say that the investment banker *underwrites* the securities in a firm commitment. In other words, when participating in a firm commitment offering, the investment banker acts as an *underwriter*. Because firm commitments are so prevalent, we will use *investment banker* and *underwriter* interchangeably in this chapter.

   To minimize the risks here, a number of investment banks may form an underwriting group, or **syndicate**, to share the risk and to help sell the issue. In such a group, one or more managers arrange or comanage the deal. The manager is designated as the lead manager or principal manager, with responsibility for all aspects of the issue. The other investment bankers in the syndicate serve primarily to sell the issue to their clients.

The difference between the underwriter's buying price and the offering price is called the *gross spread* or *underwriting discount*. It is the basic compensation received by the underwriter. Sometimes the underwriter will get noncash compensation in the form of warrants or stock in addition to the spread.

Firm commitment underwriting is really a purchase-sale arrangement and the syndicate's fee is the spread. The issuer receives the full amount of the proceeds less the spread and all the risk is transferred to the underwriter. If the underwriter cannot sell all of the issue at the agreed-upon offering price, it may need to lower the price on the unsold shares. However, because the offering price usually is not set until the underwriters have investigated how receptive the market is to the issue, this risk is usually minimal. This is particularly true with seasoned new issues because the price of the new issue can be based on prior trades in the security.

Because the offering price is usually set just before selling begins, the issuer doesn't know precisely what its net proceeds will be until that time. To determine the offering price, the underwriter will meet with potential buyers, typically large institutional buyers such as mutual funds. Often, the underwriter and company management will do presentations in multiple cities, pitching the stock in what is known as a *road show*. Potential buyers provide information about the price they would be willing to pay and the number of shares they would purchase at a particular price. This process of soliciting information about buyers and the prices and quantities they would demand is known as **bookbuilding**. As we will see, despite the bookbuilding process, underwriters frequently get the price wrong, or so it seems.

2. *Best efforts*: The underwriter bears risk with a firm commitment because it buys the entire issue. Conversely, the syndicate avoids this risk under a best-efforts offering because it does not purchase the shares. Instead, it merely acts as an agent, receiving a commission for each share sold. The syndicate is legally bound to use its best efforts to sell the securities at the agreed-upon offering price. Beyond this, the underwriter does not guarantee any particular amount of money to the issuer. This form of underwriting has become relatively rare.
3. *Dutch auction underwriting*: With a **Dutch auction** underwriting, the underwriter does not set a fixed price for the shares to be sold. Instead, the underwriter conducts an auction in which investors bid for shares. The offer price is determined from the submitted bids. A Dutch auction also is known by the more descriptive name *uniform price auction*. This approach is relatively new in the IPO market and has not been widely used there, but is very common in the bond markets. It is the sole way that the U.S. Treasury sells its notes, bonds, and bills to the public.

To understand a Dutch or uniform price auction, consider a simple example. Suppose the Rial Company wants to sell 400 shares to the public. The company receives five bids as follows:

Bidder	Quantity	Price
A	100 shares	₹16
B	100 shares	14
C	100 shares	12
D	200 shares	12
E	200 shares	10

Bidder A is willing to buy 100 shares at ₹16 each, Bidder B is willing to buy 100 shares at ₹14, and so on. The Rial Company examines the bids to determine the highest price that will result in all 400 shares being sold. At ₹14, A and B would be the only bidders interested at that price and would buy only 200 shares between them, so that price is too high. Working our way down, all 400 shares won't be sold until we hit a price of ₹12, so ₹12 will be the offer price in the IPO. Bidders A through D will receive shares, while Bidder E will not.

There are two additional important points in our example. First, all the winning bidders will pay ₹12–even Bidders A and B, who actually bid higher prices. The fact that all successful bidders pay the same price is the reason for the name "uniform price auction." The idea in such an auction is to encourage bidders to bid aggressively by providing some protection against submitting a high bid.

Second, notice that at the ₹12 offer price, there are actually bids for 500 shares, which exceeds the 400 shares Rial wants to sell. There has to be some sort of allocation. How this is done varies a bit; but in the IPO market the approach has been to compute the ratio of shares offered to shares bid at the offer price or better, which, in our example, is 400/500 = .8, and allocate bidders that percentage of their bids. In other words, Bidders A through D would each receive 80 percent of the shares they bid at a price of ₹12 per share.

The period after a new issue is initially sold to the public is called the *aftermarket*. During this period, the members of the underwriting syndicate generally do not sell shares of the new issue for less than the offer price.

In most offerings, the principal underwriter is permitted to buy shares if the market price falls below the offering price. The purpose is to *support* the market and *stabilize* the price from temporary downward pressure. If the issue remains unsold after a time (e.g., 30 days), members may leave the group and sell their shares at whatever price the market will allow.

Many underwriting contracts contain a **Green Shoe provision**, which gives the members of the underwriting group the option to purchase additional shares at the offering price.[3] The stated reason for the Green Shoe option is to cover excess demand and oversubscription. Green Shoe options usually last for about 30 days and involve 15 percent of the newly issued shares. The Green Shoe option is a benefit to the underwriting syndicate and a cost to the issuer. If the market price of the new issue goes above the offering price within 30 days, the underwriters can buy shares from the issuer and immediately resell the shares to the public. ICICI Bank in India is a good example of a firm always offering securities having a green shoe option. It went in for a public issue raising ₹8,750 crore. The issue had a green shoe option of ₹1,313 crore.

Almost all underwriting agreements contain *lockups*. Such arrangements specify how long insiders must wait after an IPO before they can sell some of their stock. Typically, lockup periods are set at 180 days. Because of this provision, insiders must maintain a significant economic interest in the company for six months following the IPO. Lockups are also important because it is not unusual for the number of locked-up insider shares to exceed the number of shares held by the public. When the lockup period ends, insiders may sell a large number of shares, thereby depressing share price.

Beginning well before an offering and extending for 40 calendar days following an IPO, the SEBI (in India)/SEC (in US) requires that a firm and its managing underwriters observe a *quiet period*. This means that all communication with the public must be limited to ordinary announcements and other purely factual

[3]The Green Shoe Corp. was the first firm to allow this provision.

In Their Own Words

ROBERT S. HANSEN ON THE ECONOMIC RATIONALE FOR THE FIRM COMMITMENT OFFER

Underwriters provide four main functions: certification, monitoring, marketing, and risk bearing.

Certification assures investors that the offer price is fair. Investors have concerns about whether the offer price is unfairly above the stock's intrinsic value. Certification increases issuer value by reducing investor doubt about fairness, making a better offer price possible.

Monitoring of issuing firm management and performance builds value because it adds to shareholders' ordinary monitoring. Underwriters provide collective monitoring on behalf of both capital suppliers and current shareholders. Individual shareholder monitoring is limited because the shareholder bears the entire cost, whereas all owners collectively share the benefit, pro rata. By contrast, in underwriter monitoring, all stockholders share both the costs and benefits, pro rata.

Due diligence and legal liability for the proceeds give investors assurance. However, what makes certification and monitoring credible is the lead bank's reputation in competitive capital markets, where they are disciplined over time. Evidence that irreputable behavior is damaging to a bank's future abounds. Capital market participants punish poorly performing banks by refusing to hire them. The participants pay banks for certification and meaningful monitoring in "quasi-rents" in the spread, which represent the fair cost of "renting" the reputations.

Marketing is finding long-term investors who can be persuaded to buy the securities at the offer price. This would not be needed if demand for new shares were "horizontal." There is much evidence that issuers and syndicates repeatedly invest in costly marketing practices, such as expensive road shows, to identify and expand investor interest. Another is organizing members to avoid redundant pursuit of the same customers. Lead banks provide trading support in the issuer's stock for several weeks after the offer.

Underwriting risk is like the risk of selling a put option. The syndicate agrees to buy all new shares at the offer price and resell them at that price or at the market price, whichever is lower. Thus, once the offer begins, the syndicate is exposed to potential losses on unsold inventory should the market price fall below the offer price. The risk is likely to be small because offerings are typically well prepared for quick sale.

Robert S. Hansen was the Francis Martin Chair in Business Finance and Economics at Tulane University. He passed away unexpectedly in 2019.

matters. The SEBI's (in India)/SEC's (in US) logic is that all relevant information should be contained in the prospectus. An important result of this requirement is that the underwriters' analysts are prohibited from making recommendations to investors. As soon as the quiet period ends, however, the managing underwriters typically publish research reports, usually accompanied by a favorable "buy" recommendation.

Firms that don't stay quiet can have their IPOs delayed. For example, just before Google's IPO, an interview with cofounders Sergey Brin and Larry Page appeared in *Playboy*. The interview almost caused a postponement of the IPO, but Google was able to amend its prospectus in time. **Salesforce.com**'s IPO was delayed because an interview with CEO Marc Benioff appeared in *The New York Times*. **Salesforce.com** finally went public two months later.

INVESTMENT BANKS

Investment banks are at the heart of new security issues. They provide advice, market the securities (after investigating the market's receptiveness to the issue), and underwrite the proceeds. They accept the risk that the market price may fall between the date the offering price is set and the time the issue is sold.

An investment banker's success depends on reputation. A good reputation can help investment bankers retain customers and attract new ones. In other words, financial economists argue that each investment bank has a reservoir of *reputation capital.* One measure of this reputation capital is the pecking order among investment banks, which, as we mentioned earlier, even extends to the brackets of the tombstone ad in Figure 20.2. MBA students are aware of this order because they know that accepting a job with a top-tier firm is universally regarded as more prestigious than accepting a job with a lower-tier firm.

Investment banks put great importance in their relative rankings and view downward movement in their placement with much distaste. This jockeying for position may seem as unimportant as the currying of royal favor in the court of Louis XVI. However, in any industry where reputation is so important, the firms in the industry must guard theirs with great vigilance.

A firm can offer its securities to the underwriter on either a competitive or a negotiated basis. In a **competitive offer**, the issuing firm sells its securities to the underwriter with the highest bid. In a **negotiated offer**, the issuing firm works with one underwriter. Because the firm generally does not negotiate with many underwriters concurrently, negotiated deals may suffer from lack of competition.

Whereas competitive bidding occurs frequently in other areas of commerce, it may surprise you that negotiated deals in investment banking occur with all but the largest issuing firms. Investment bankers point out that they must expend much time and effort learning about the issuer before setting an issue price and a fee schedule. Except in the case of large issues, underwriters could not, it is argued, commit this time without the near certainty of receiving the contract.

Studies generally show that issuing costs are higher in negotiated deals than in competitive ones. However, many financial economists point out that the underwriter gains a great deal of information about the issuing firm through negotiation–information likely to increase the probability of a successful offering.

THE OFFERING PRICE

Determining the correct offering price is the most difficult task the lead investment bank faces in an initial public offering. The issuing firm faces a potential cost if the offering price is set too high or too low. If the issue is priced too high, it may be unsuccessful and have to be withdrawn. If the issue is priced below the true market price, the issuer's existing shareholders will experience an opportunity loss. The process of determining the best offer price is called bookbuilding. In bookbuilding, potential investors commit to buying a certain number of shares at various prices.

Underpricing is fairly common. For example, Ritter examined 13,509 firms that went public between 1960 and 2020 in the United States. He found that the average IPO rose in price 17.2 percent in the first day of trading following issuance (see Table 20.7). These figures are not annualized!

Underpricing obviously helps new shareholders earn a higher return on the shares they buy. However, the existing shareholders of the issuing firm are not helped by underpricing. To them, it is an indirect cost of issuing new securities. Consider Chinese online retailer Alibaba's IPO in September 2014. The stock was priced at ₹68 in the IPO and rose to a first-day high of ₹99.70, before closing at ₹93.89, a gain of about 38.1 percent. Based on these numbers, Alibaba was underpriced by about ₹25.89 per share. Because Alibaba sold 320.1 million shares, the company missed out on an additional ₹8.3 billion (= ₹25.89 × 320.1 million), a record amount "left on the table." The previous record of ₹5.1 billion was held by Visa, set in its 2008 IPO.

Table 20.7 Number of Offerings, Average First-Day Return, and Gross Proceeds of Initial Public Offerings: 1960–2020

Year	Number of Offerings*	Average First-Day Return, %[†]	Gross Proceeds (millions)[‡]
1960–1969	2,661	21.2%	₹ 7,988
1970–1979	1,536	7.1	₹ 6,663
1980–1989	2,365	6.9	₹ 60,881
1990–1999	4,193	21.1	₹ 294,826
2001–2009	1,332	21.3	₹ 295,045
2010–2020	1,417	11.7	₹ 371,389
1960–2020	13,509	17.2%	₹1,037,798

SOURCE: Professor Jay R. Ritter, University of Florida.

*The number of offerings excludes IPOs with an offer price of less than ₹5.00, ADRs, best efforts, units, and Regulation A offers (small issues, raising less than ₹1.5 million during the 1980s), real estate investment trusts (REITs), partnerships, and closed-end funds. Banks, S&Ls, and non-CRSP-listed IPOs are included.

[†]First-day returns are computed as the percentage return from the offering price to the first closing market price.

[‡]Gross proceeds data are from Securities Data Co., and they exclude overallotment options but include the international tranche, if any. No adjustments for inflation have been made.

BOOK BUILDING NORMS IN INDIA

SEBI allowed IPOs in India to use the book building process from 1995 onwards. Book building process has become much more straightforward to conduct with the help of vast IT infrastructure provided by NSE/BSE.

Rules governing book building are covered in Chapter XI of the Securities and Exchange Board of India (Disclosure and Investor Protection) Guidelines 2000. It defines book building as "a process undertaken by which a demand for the securities proposed to be issued by a corporate body is elicited and built up, and the price for such securities is assessed for the determination of the quantum of such securities to be issued using a notice, circular, advertisement, document or information memoranda or offer document." In book building, the underwriters do road shows and take non-binding orders from investors before setting the issue price.

For issuers who prioritize price accuracy, auctions may result in insufficient evaluation and excessive uncertainty. Conversely, for issuers aiming to minimize underpricing, auctions can lead to excessive resource allocation for evaluation, resulting in lower average bid prices. With book building, the underwriter coordinates the number of investors that will participate, guaranteeing that enough (but not too many) are involved. Book building allows the underwriter to manage the participation of investors–ensuring an optimal balance–while also.

An example from private sector: InterGlobe Aviation Ltd., owner of the popular low flying carrier Indigo Airlines, came out with a public issue of ₹3,130 crore. The face value of the shares offered was ₹10 each. The price band for the bidding was between ₹700 and ₹765. Individual and institutional investors actively participated in the bidding and the issue was oversubscribed 6.14 times. After the bidding was over, the price was fixed at ₹765. Based on this price, the company decided to issue 39,464,562 equity shares, at an issue price of ₹765.

(continued)

An example from the public sector: Mazagon Dock Shipbuilders Limited, India's leading defence public sector undertaking shipyard under the Ministry of Defence, came out with a public issue of ₹444 crore. The face value of the shares offered was ₹10 each. The price band for the bidding was between ₹135 and ₹145. Individual and institutional investors actively participated in the bidding, and the issue was oversubscribed 157 times. After the bidding was over, the price was fixed at ₹145. Based on this price, the company decided to issue 30,599,017 equity shares at an issue price of ₹145.

UNDERPRICING: A POSSIBLE EXPLANATION

There are several possible explanations for underpricing, but so far there is no agreement among scholars as to which explanation is correct. We now provide two well-known explanations for underpricing. The first explanation begins with the observation that when the price of a new issue is too low, the issue is often *oversubscribed*. This means investors will not be able to buy all of the shares they want and the underwriters will allocate the shares among investors. The average investor will find it difficult to get shares in an oversubscribed offering because there will not be enough shares to go around. Although initial public offerings have positive initial returns on average, a significant fraction of them have price drops. An investor submitting an order for all new issues may be allocated more shares in issues that go down in price than in issues that go up in price.

Consider this tale of two investors. Smt. Sebastian knows precisely what companies are worth when their shares are offered. Shri. Atmaram knows only that prices usually rise in the first month after the IPO. Armed with this information, Shri. Atmaram decides to buy 1,000 shares of every IPO. Does Shri. Atmaram actually earn an abnormally high average return across all initial offerings?

The answer is no, and at least one reason is Smt. Sebastian. Because knows that Company Vasudha Limited is underpriced, she invests all her money in its IPO. When the issue is oversubscribed, the underwriters must allocate the shares between Smt. Sebastian and Shri. Atmaram. If they do this on a pro rata basis and if Smt. Sebastian has bid for, say, twice as many shares as Shri. Atmaram, she will get two shares for each one Shri. Atmaram receives. The net result is that when an issue is underpriced, Shri. Atmaram cannot buy as much of it as he wants.

Smt. Sebastian also knows that Company Prathama Limited is overpriced. In this case, she avoids its IPO altogether, and Shri. Atmaram ends up with a full 1,000 shares. To summarize, Shri. Atmaram receives fewer shares when more knowledgeable investors swarm to buy an underpriced issue, but he gets all he wants when the smart money avoids the issue.

This is called the *winner's curse* and it is one possible reason why IPOs have such a large average return. When the average investor wins and gets his allocation, it is because those who knew better avoided the issue. To counteract the winner's curse and attract the average investor, underwriters underprice issues.[4]

Perhaps a simpler explanation for underpricing is risk. Although IPOs, on average, have positive initial returns, a significant fraction experience price drops. A price drop would cause the underwriter a loss on his own holdings. In addition, the underwriter risks being sued by angry customers for selling overpriced securities. Underpricing mitigates both problems.

[4]This explanation was first suggested in Kevin Rock, "Why New Issues Are Underpriced," *Journal of Financial Economics* 15, no. 12 (January-February 1986): 187–212.

In Their Own Words

JAY RITTER ON IPO UNDERPRICING AROUND THE WORLD

In every country, initial public offerings (IPOs) are underpriced on average, although the magnitude varies across countries and across time.

In general, countries with developed capital markets have more moderate underpricing than in emerging markets. Furthermore, as a country's capital markets become more developed, extreme underpricing tends to disappear. There are exceptions, however, to the general pattern. In Japan, small companies tend to have severe underpricing. Although the equally weighted average first-day return in Japan is 46.8 percent, during 2015-2016 the average for IPOs raising more than ₹20 million was about 10 percent, whereas the average for those raising smaller amounts was more than 100%.

In some countries, government regulations lead to severe underpricing because regulators limit the price-to-earnings ratio at which a company can sell its shares. The high average initial return on IPOs sold in China can be attributed to these regulations. After regulators imposed a limit of 23 on the price-to-earnings ratio, the average initial return jumped from 35 percent during 2009-2012 to 375 percent in 2014-2016. A similar situation existed in India till 1991. In those days, the offer price of shares was controlled by the CCI, i.e., the Controller of Capital Issues. The decade of the 1990s started with SEBI removing the control on pricing of premiums. In calendar year 2023, the average first day returns of IPOs in India had been about 27.85 percent on the Main board (non-SME).

The following table gives a summary of the average first-day returns on IPOs in many countries, with the figures for earlier years, when commercial databases were less widely available, collected from studies done by a variety of authors.

Country	Sample Size	Time Period	Avg. Initial Return
Argentina	30	1991–2018	5.7%
Australia	2,069	1976–2018	19.8%
Austria	106	1971–2018	6.2%
Belgium	154	1984–2017	11.0%
Brazil	303	1979–2018	30.3%
Bulgaria	9	2004–2007	36.5%
Canada	758	1971–2017	6.4%
Chile	86	1982–2018	6.9%
China	3,798	1990–2019	169.5%
Cyprus	73	1997–2012	20.3%
Denmark	173	1984–2017	7.4%
Egypt	74	1990–2017	9.4%
Finland	209	1971–2018	14.2%
France	834	1983–2017	9.7%
Germany	779	1978–2014	23.0%
Greece	373	1976–2013	50.8%
Hong Kong	2,042	1980–2017	44.5%
India	3,145	1990–2017	85.2%
Indonesia	643	1990–2019	46.3%
Iran	279	1991–2004	22.4%
Ireland	38	1991–2013	21.6%
Israel	348	1990–2006	13.8%
Italy	413	1985–2018	13.1%
Japan	3,756	1970–2019	46.8%
Jordan	53	1999–2008	149.0%
Malaysia	562	1980–2018	51.0%
Mauritius	40	1989–2005	15.2%

Country	Sample Size	Time Period	Avg. Initial Return
Mexico	149	1987–2017	13.3%
Morocco	33	2000–2011	33.3%
Netherlands	212	1982–2017	13.3%
New Zealand	269	1979–2018	15.9%
Nigeria	125	1989–2017	12.8%
Norway	266	1984–2018	6.7%
Pakistan	80	2000–2013	22.1%
Philippines	173	1987–2018	17.3%
Poland	350	1991–2019	11.7%
Portugal	33	1992–2017	11.5%
Russia	64	1999–2013	3.3%
Saudi Arabia	80	2003–2011	239.8%
Singapore	687	1973–2017	25.8%
South Africa	342	1980–2018	17.2%
South Korea	2,007	1980–2018	55.2%
Spain	199	1986–2018	9.2%
Sri Lanka	134	1987–2018	28.9%
Sweden	405	1980–2015	25.9%
Switzerland	164	1983–2018	25.2%
Taiwan	1,915	1980–2019	37.2%
Thailand	697	1987–2018	40.0%
Tunisia	38	2001–2014	21.7%
Turkey	404	1990–2014	9.6%
United Arab Emirates	24	2003–2010	270.1%
United Kingdom	5,185	1959–2016	15.8%
United States	13,509	1960–2020	17.2%
Vietnam	167	2005–2017	33.3%

RESEARCH ON INITIAL PUBLIC OFFERINGS IN INDIA

Shette, Kuntluru, and Korivi (2016) reported that the earnings and market performance of IPO companies are considerably higher in the year of the IPO, compared to the years following the IPO. Additionally, the quality of earnings during the IPO-year is lower than in the post-IPO years. The findings also indicate that opportunistic earnings management during the IPO year has a significant negative impact on the long-term adjusted earnings and market performance. Das, Saha, and Kundu (2016) observed that the price-to-book value ratio, age of the IPO firm, and aftermarket corporate measures, such as bonus issue and stock split, have a substantial predictive power in explaining the long-run performance. Sahoo and Raj (2022) discovered that the qualitative information pertaining to market leadership, well-established brand image, and a modern, scalable information technology infrastructure significantly affects underpricing.

Studying the Indian SME exchanges, Bhattacharya (2017) reports that IPO performance is driven by the market timing or due to high allocation to market makers. In the post listing period, the allocation to market makers and demand from retail investors drives the liquisity. Further, IPO timing and underwriter reputation significantly predict the long-term performance of SME IPOs. Arora and Singh's (2019) study on SME listed firms revealed that underwriter reputation helps reduce information asymmetry and signals firm quality to investors. They report that underwriter reputation plays a significant role in positively influencing investors' perception and assisting them in making investment decisions.

Further readings: (a) Shette, R., Kuntluru, S., & Korivi, S. R. (2016). Opportunistic earnings management during initial public offerings: evidence from India. *Review of Accounting and Finance,* 15(3), 352–371. (b) Das, G., Saha, M., & Kundu, A. (2016). Analyzing long-run performance of select initial public offerings using monthly returns: Evidence from India. *Vision,* 20(3), 237–248. (c) Sahoo, S., & Raj, R. (2022). Disclosed qualitative factors and underpricing: empirical evidence from Indian IPO market. *Pacific Accounting Review, 34*(5), 687–707. (d) Bhattacharya, A. (2017). Innovations in new venture financing: Evidence from Indian SME IPOs. *Global Finance Journal, 34,* 72–88. (e) Arora, N., & Singh, B. (2019). Impact of auditor and underwriter reputation on underpricing of SME IPOs in India. *Management and Labour Studies,* 44(2), 193–208.

EVIDENCE ON UNDERPRICING

Figure 20.3 provides a more general illustration of the underpricing phenomenon. What is shown is the month-by-month history of underpricing for SEC-registered IPOs.[5] The period covered is 1960 through 2020. Figure 20.4 presents the number of offerings in each month for the same period.

Figure 20.3 shows that underpricing can be quite dramatic, exceeding 100 percent in some months. In such months, the average IPO more than doubled in value, sometimes in a matter of hours. Also, the degree of underpricing varies through time and periods of severe underpricing ("hot-issue" markets) are followed by periods of little underpricing ("cold-issue" markets). For example, in the 1960s, the average IPO was underpriced by 21.2 percent. In the 1970s, the average underpricing was much smaller (7.1 percent) and the amount of underpricing was actually very small or even negative for much of that time. Underpricing in the 1980s ran about 6.9 percent. For 1990–1999, IPOs were underpriced by 21.1 percent; they were underpriced by 21.3 percent in 2000–2009 and they were underpriced by 11.7 percent in 2010–2020.

From Figure 20.4, it is apparent that the number of IPOs is also highly variable through time. Further, there are pronounced cycles in both the degree of underpricing and the number of IPOs. Comparing Figures 20.3 and 20.4, we see that increases in the number of new offerings tend to follow periods of significant underpricing by roughly six months. This probably occurs because companies decide to go public when they perceive that the market is highly receptive to new issues.

[5]The discussion in this section draws on Roger G. Ibbotson, Jody L. Sindelar, and Jay R. Ritter, "The Market's Problems with the Pricing of Initial Public Offerings," *Journal of Applied Corporate Finance* 7, no. 1 (Spring 1994): 66–74.

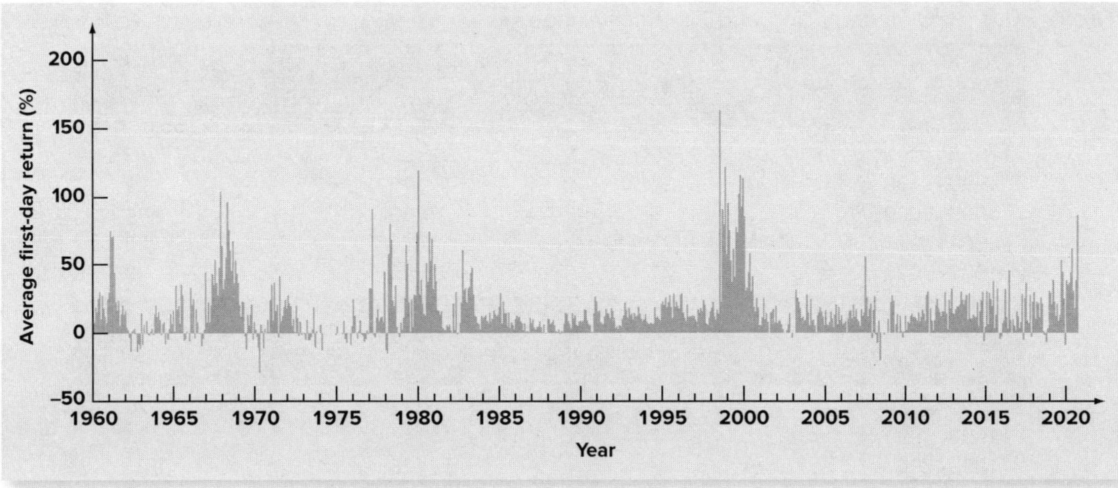

Figure 20.3 Average Initial Returns by Month for SEC-Registered Initial Public Offerings: 1960–2020

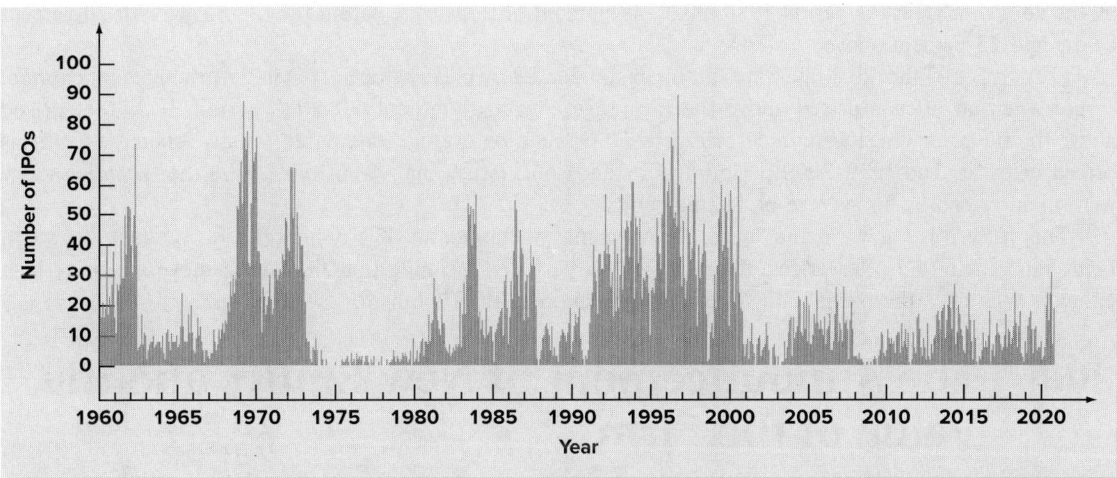

Figure 20.4 Number of Offerings by Month for SEC-Registered Initial Public Offerings: 1960–2020

THE PARTIAL ADJUSTMENT PHENOMENON

When a company files its registration statement with the SEBI (in India)/SEC (in US), at some point in the process it will indicate a range of stock prices between which it expects to offer shares. This range is called the "file price range," or words to that effect. A file price range of ₹10 to ₹12 is common, but many others exist. The Snowflake IPO we discussed to open the chapter is a good example. The company indicated a preliminary price range of ₹75-₹85, but the final offer price was ₹120, and the stock soared on the first day of trading.

Just before a company's shares are sold to investors, the final IPO offer price is determined. As shown in Section A of Table 20.8, that price can be above, within, or below the price range originally indicated

Table 20.8 IPO Underpricing and File Price Range

A: Percentage of IPOs Relative to File Price Range	Below	Within	Above
1980–1989	30%	57%	13%
1990–1998	27	49	24
1999–2000	18	38	44
2001–2020	33	45	22
1980–2020	28	49	23
B: Average First-Day Returns Relative to File Price Range	**Below**	**Within**	**Above**
1980–1989	0%	6%	20%
1990–1998	4	11	31
1999–2000	8	26	122
2001–2020	3	13	42
1980–2020	3	12	50

by the company. Over the period 1980-2020, 49 percent of IPOs were within the file range, with 28 percent below and 23 percent above.

Section B of Table 20.8 illustrates an interesting and very clear pattern. IPO underpricing is much more severe when an offer is priced above the file range. Again over the 1980-2020 period, IPOs that priced above the file price range were underpriced by 50 percent, on average, compared to only 3 percent for firms priced below it. The 1999-2000 period again stands out. Issues that "went off" above the file price range were underpriced by an average of 122 percent!

This pattern is known as the "partial adjustment" phenomenon. The name refers to the fact that when firms raise their IPO offer prices, they only do so partially, meaning that they don't move the price high enough. Why does the partial adjustment phenomenon exist? The answer is unknown.

20.5 The Announcement of New Equity and the Value of the Firm

As mentioned, when firms return to the equity markets for additional funds, they arrange for a seasoned equity offering (SEO). The basic processes for an SEO and an IPO are the same. However, something curious happens on the announcement day of an SEO. It seems reasonable that long-term financing is used to fund positive net present value projects. Consequently, when the announcement of external equity financing is made, one might think that the firm's stock price would go up. As we mentioned in an earlier chapter, precisely the opposite actually happens. The firm's stock price tends to decline on the announcement of a new issue of common stock. Plausible reasons for this strange result include:

1. *Managerial information*: If managers have superior information about the market value of the firm, they may know when the firm is overvalued. If they do, they might attempt to issue new shares of stock when the market value exceeds the correct value. This will benefit existing shareholders. However, the potential new shareholders are not stupid. They will infer overvaluation from the new issue, thereby bidding down the stock price on the announcement date of the issue.

2. *Debt capacity*: We argued in an earlier chapter that a firm likely chooses its debt-equity ratio by balancing the tax shield from the debt against the cost of financial distress. When the managers of a firm have special information that the probability of financial distress has risen, the firm is more likely to raise capital through stock than through debt. If the market infers this chain of events, the stock price should fall on the announcement date of an equity issue.
3. *Issue costs*: As we discuss in the next section, there are substantial costs associated with selling securities.

Whatever the reason, a drop in stock price following the announcement of a new issue is an example of an indirect cost of selling securities. This drop might typically be on the order of 3 percent for an industrial corporation (and somewhat smaller for a public utility); so, for a large company, it can represent a substantial amount of money. We label this drop the *abnormal return* in our discussion of the costs of new issues that follows.

To give a couple of recent examples, in May 2020, e-commerce company Shopify announced a secondary offering. Its stock fell about 3.6 percent on the day of the announcement. And in September 2020, security company ADT announced a secondary offering. Its stock dropped 13.3 percent on the day of the announcement.

20.6 The Cost of New Issues

Issuing securities to the public is not free. The costs fall into six categories:

1. Gross spread, or underwriting discount:	The spread is the difference between the price the issuer receives and the price offered to the public.
2. Other direct expenses:	These are costs incurred by the issuer that are not part of the compensation to underwriters. They include filing fees, legal fees, and taxes–all reported in the prospectus.
3. Indirect expenses:	These costs are not reported in the prospectus and include the time management spends on the new issue.
4. Abnormal returns:	In a seasoned issue of stock, the price typically drops by about 3 percent upon the announcement of the issue. The drop protects new shareholders from buying overpriced stock.
5. Underpricing:	For initial public offerings, the stock typically rises substantially after the issue date. This underpricing is a cost to the firm because the stock is sold for less than its efficient price in the aftermarket.
6. Green Shoe option:	The Green Shoe option gives the underwriters the right to buy additional shares at the offer price to cover overallotments. This option is a cost to the firm because the underwriter will buy additional shares only when the offer price is below the price in the aftermarket.

Research indicates the direct costs for an IPO can be very large, particularly for smaller issues (less than ₹10 million).[6] On a smaller IPO, for example, the total direct costs amount to 25.22 percent of the amount raised. This means that if a company sells ₹10 million in stock, it will net only about ₹7.5 million; the other ₹2.5 million goes to cover the underwriter spread and other direct expenses. On issues over ₹500 million, a company can be expected to pay 5.5 percent in direct costs. Typical underwriter spreads on an IPO range

[6]Inmoo Lee, Scott Lochhead, Jay Ritter, and Quanshui Zhao, "The Costs of Raising Capital," *Journal of Financial Research* 19 (Spring 1996), updated by the authors.

from about 5 percent up to 10 percent or so, but for well over half of the IPOs studied, the spread is exactly 7 percent; so this is, by far, the most common spread.

Overall, four clear patterns emerge. First, with the possible exception of straight debt offerings (about which we will have more to say later), there are substantial economies of scale. The underwriter spreads are smaller on larger issues, and the other direct costs fall sharply as a percentage of the amount raised–a reflection of the mostly fixed nature of such costs. Second, the costs associated with selling debt are substantially less than the costs of selling equity. Third, IPOs have higher expenses than SEOs, but the difference is not as great as might originally be guessed. Finally, straight bonds are cheaper to float than convertible bonds.

As we have previously discussed, the underpricing of IPOs is an additional cost to the issuer. In general, larger firms issuing over ₹200 million are expected to have much lower underpricing. Overall, across all size groups, the total direct costs amount to about 10 percent of the amount raised, and the underpricing amounts to about 19 percent.

Finally, with regard to debt offerings, there are two general patterns in direct costs: First, there are substantial economies of scale here as well. Second, investment-grade issues have much lower direct costs, particularly for straight bonds. Recall from a previous chapter that bonds carry different credit ratings. Higher-rated bonds are said to be investment grade, whereas lower-rated bonds are noninvestment grade, or junk, bonds. A straight bond issue less than ₹10 million can be expected to cost about 1.90 percent if it is investment grade, but 5.27 percent with a junk bond rating. A straight bond issue over ₹500 million would be expected to cost only .08 percent, while a similar junk bond issue would cost about 2.63 percent.

THE COSTS OF GOING PUBLIC: A CASE STUDY

On January 30, 2020, Black Diamond Therapeutics, the Massachusetts-based oncology medicine company, went public via an IPO. Black Diamond issued 10,586,316 shares of stock at a price of ₹19 each. The lead underwriters on the IPO were JPMorgan Chase, Jefferies, and Cowen, assisted by a syndicate of other investment banks. Even though the IPO raised a gross sum of ₹201.1 million, Black Diamond only got to keep ₹184.4 million after expenses. The biggest expense was the 7 percent underwriter spread, which is the usual spread for an offering of that size. Black Diamond sold each of the 10.59 million shares to the underwriters for ₹17.67, and the underwriters in turn sold the shares to the public for ₹19 each.

But wait–there's more. Black Diamond spent ₹23,914 in SEC registration fees and ₹28,135 in FINRA filing fees. The company also spent ₹125,000 in exchange listing fees, ₹1.3 million in legal fees, ₹950,000 on accounting to obtain the necessary audits, ₹4,000 for a transfer agent to physically transfer the shares and maintain a list of shareholders, ₹150,000 for printing and engraving expenses, ₹10,000 for Blue Sky fees, and finally, ₹98,951 in miscellaneous expenses.

As Black Diamond's outlays show, an IPO can be a costly undertaking! In the end, Black Diamond's expenses totaled ₹16.77 million, of which ₹14.08 million went to the underwriters and ₹2.69 million went to other parties. All told, the total direct cost to Black Diamond was 8.97 percent of the issue proceeds raised by the company. In Black Diamond's case, the stock more than doubled on the first day of trading, closing at ₹39.48, so the indirect costs were much larger.

20.7 Rights

When new shares of common stock are offered to the general public in a seasoned equity offering, the proportionate ownership of existing shareholders is likely to be reduced. However, if a preemptive right is contained in the firm's articles of incorporation, the firm first must offer any new issue of common stock to existing shareholders. This assures that each owner can keep his proportionate share.

An issue of common stock to existing stockholders is called a *rights offering*. Here each shareholder is issued an *option* to buy a specified number of new shares from the firm at a specified price within a specified time, after which the rights expire. A firm whose stock is selling at ₹30 may let current stockholders buy a fixed number of shares at ₹10 per share within two months. The terms of the option are evidenced by certificates known as *share warrants* or *rights*. Such rights often are traded on securities exchanges or over the counter. Rights offerings are very common in Europe and India but not in the United States.

THE MECHANICS OF A RIGHTS OFFERING

We illustrate the mechanics of a rights offering by considering Narmada Power Company. Narmada Power has 1 million shares outstanding and the stock is selling at ₹20 per share, implying a market capitalization of ₹20 million. The company plans to raise ₹5 million of new equity funds by a rights offering.

The process of issuing rights differs from the process of issuing shares of stock for cash. Existing stockholders are notified that they have been given one right for each share of stock they own. Exercise occurs when a shareholder sends payment to the firm's subscription agent (usually a bank) and turns in the required number of rights. Shareholders of Narmada Power will have several choices: (1) subscribe for the full number of entitled shares, (2) sell the rights, or (3) do nothing and let the rights expire.

SUBSCRIPTION PRICE

Narmada Power must first determine the **subscription price**, which is the price that existing shareholders are allowed to pay for a share of stock. A rational shareholder will subscribe to the rights offering only if the subscription price is below the market price of the stock on the offer's expiration date. If the stock price at expiration is ₹13 and the subscription price is ₹15, no rational shareholder will subscribe. Why pay ₹15 for something worth ₹13? Narmada Power chooses a price of ₹10, which is well below the current market price of ₹20. As long as the market price does not fall by half before expiration, the rights offering will succeed.

NUMBER OF RIGHTS NEEDED TO PURCHASE A SHARE

Narmada Power wants to raise ₹5 million in new equity. With a subscription price of ₹10, it will issue 500,000 new shares. This number can be determined by dividing the total amount to be raised by the subscription price:

$$\text{Number of new shares} = \frac{\text{Funds to be raised}}{\text{Subscription price}} = \frac{₹5{,}000{,}000}{₹10} = 500{,}000 \text{ shares}$$

Because stockholders typically get one right for each share of stock they own, Narmada Power will issue 1 million rights. To determine how many rights must be exercised to get one share of stock, we can divide the number of existing (or old) shares of stock by the number of new shares:

$$\begin{array}{r}\text{Number of rights needed}\\ \text{to buy a share of stock}\end{array} = \frac{\text{"Old" shares}}{\text{"New" shares}} = \frac{1{,}000{,}000}{500{,}000} = 2 \text{ rights}$$

A shareholder must give up two rights plus ₹10 to receive a share of new stock. If all the stockholders do this, Narmada Power will raise the required ₹5 million.

Given that Narmada Power wants to raise ₹5 million, the number of new shares and the number of rights needed to buy one new share follow from the subscription price, as indicated below:

Subscription Price	Number of New Shares	Number of Rights Needed to Buy One Share of Stock
₹20	250,000 (= ₹5,000,000/₹20)	4 (= 1,000,000/250,000)
10	500,000 (= ₹5,000,000/₹10)	2 (= 1,000,000/500,000)
5	1,000,000 (= ₹5,000,000/₹5)	1 (= 1,000,000/1,000,000)

As can be seen, a lower subscription price leads the firm both to issue more shares and to reduce the number of rights needed to buy one share.

EFFECT OF RIGHTS OFFERING ON PRICE OF STOCK

Rights clearly have value. In the case of Narmada Power, the right to buy a share of stock worth ₹20 for ₹10 is valuable.

Suppose a shareholder of Narmada Power owns two shares of stock just before the rights offering. This situation is depicted in Table 20.9. Initially, the price of Narmada Power is ₹20 per share, so the shareholder's total holding is worth 2 × ₹20 = ₹40. A stockholder with two shares will receive two rights. The Narmada Power rights offer gives shareholders with two rights the opportunity to purchase one additional share for ₹10. The holding of the shareholder who exercises these rights and buys the new share would increase to three shares. The value of the new holding would be ₹40 + 10 = ₹50 (the ₹40 initial value plus the ₹10 paid to the company). Because the stockholder now holds three shares, the price per share would drop to ₹50/3 = ₹16.67.

The difference between the old share price of ₹20 and the new share price of ₹16.67 reflects the fact that the old shares carried rights to subscribe to the new issue. The difference must be equal to the value

Table 20.9 The Value to the Individual Shareholder of Narmada Power's Rights

Initial Position of Shareholder	
Number of shares	2
Share price	₹20
Value of holding	₹40
Terms of Offer	
Subscription price	₹10
Number of rights issued	2
Number of rights for a share	2
Shareholder Position after Offer	
Number of shares	3
Share price	₹16.67
Value of holding	₹50
Value of a Right	
Old price − New price	₹20 − 16.67 = ₹3.33
$\frac{\text{New price} - \text{Subscription price}}{\text{Number of rights for a share}}$	(₹16.67 − 10)/2 = ₹3.33

of one right–that is, ₹20 − 16.67 = ₹3.33. We also can calculate the value of a right in another way. The rights offer lets an individual pay ₹10 for a share worth ₹16.67, generating a gain of ₹6.67. Because the individual needs two rights for this transaction, a rational individual would be willing to pay as much as ₹3.33 (= ₹6.67/2) for a single right.

As we learned of an ex-dividend date in the previous chapter, there is an **ex-rights date** here. An individual buying the stock prior to the ex-rights date will receive the rights when they are distributed. An individual buying the stock on or after the ex-rights date will not receive the rights. In our example, the price of the stock prior to the ex-rights date is ₹20. An individual buying on or after the ex-rights date is not entitled to the rights. The price on or after the ex-rights date is ₹16.67.

Table 20.10 shows what happens to Narmada Power. If all shareholders exercise their rights, the number of shares will increase to 1.5 million (= 1 million + .5 million) and the value of the firm will increase to ₹25 million (= ₹20 million + 5 million). After the rights offering, the value of each share will drop to ₹16.67 (= ₹25 million/1.5 million).

An investor holding no shares of Narmada Power stock who wants to subscribe to the new issue can do so by buying rights. An outside investor buying two rights will pay ₹3.33 × 2 = ₹6.67. If the investor exercises the rights at a subscription cost of ₹10, the total cost would be ₹10 + 6.67 = ₹16.67. In return for this expenditure, the investor will receive a share of the new stock, which is worth ₹16.67.

Of course, outside investors also can buy Narmada Power stock directly at ₹16.67 per share. In an efficient stock market, it will make no difference whether new stock is obtained via rights or via direct purchase.

EFFECTS ON SHAREHOLDERS

Shareholders can either sell their rights or exercise them, though it makes no difference which alternative is chosen. To see this, consider an investor owning two shares. She will be granted two rights. She can sell the two rights for ₹3.33 each, obtaining ₹3.33 × 2 = ₹6.67 in cash. Because the two shares are each worth ₹16.67, her holdings are valued at:

Shares	= 2 × ₹16.67 =	₹33.33
Sold rights	= 2 × ₹ 3.33 =	6.67
Total	=	₹40.00

Table 20.10 Narmada Power Company Rights Offering

Initial Position	
Number of shares	1 million
Share price	₹20
Value of firm	₹20 million
Terms of Offer	
Subscription price	₹10
Number of rights issued	1 million
Number of rights for a share	2
After Offer	
Number of shares	1.5 million
Value of firm	₹25 million
Share price	₹16.67

Alternatively, if the shareholder exercises her rights, she ends up with three shares worth a total of ₹16.67 × 3 = ₹50. In other words, by spending ₹10, the value of her holdings are worth ₹10 more than the ₹40 value from selling her rights and holding on to her shares. The individual is indifferent between exercising and selling the rights.

It is obvious that after the rights offering, the new market price of the firm's stock will be lower than the price before the rights offering. As we have seen, however, stockholders have not suffered a loss from the offering. The stock price decline is very much like that in a stock split, a device described in Chapter 19. The lower the subscription price, the greater is the price decline resulting from a rights offering. Because shareholders receive rights equal in value to the price drop, the rights offering does *not* hurt stockholders.

There is one last issue. How do we set the subscription price in a rights offering? If you think about it, you will see that the subscription price really should not matter. It has to be below the market price of the stock for the rights to have value; but beyond this, the price is arbitrary. In principle, it could be as low as we cared to make it as long as it is not zero.

THE UNDERWRITING ARRANGEMENTS

Undersubscription can occur if investors throw away rights or if bad news causes the market price of the stock to fall below the subscription price. To ensure against these possibilities, rights offerings are typically arranged by **standby underwriting**. Here the underwriter makes a firm commitment to purchase the unsubscribed portion of the issue at the subscription price less a take-up fee. The underwriter usually receives a **standby fee** as compensation for this risk-bearing function.

In practice, the subscription price is usually set well below the current market price, making the probability of a rights failure quite small. Though a small percentage (less than 10 percent) of shareholders fail to exercise valuable rights, shareholders are usually allowed to purchase unsubscribed shares at the subscription price. This **oversubscription privilege** makes it unlikely that the corporate issuer would need to turn to its underwriter for help.

20.8 The Rights Puzzle

Smith calculated the issuance costs from three alternative methods: an equity issue with underwriting, a rights issue with standby underwriting, and a pure rights issue.[7] His results suggest that a pure rights issue is the cheapest of the three alternatives, with total costs as a percentage of proceeds being 6.17 percent, 6.05 percent, and 2.45 percent for the three alternatives, respectively.

If corporate executives are rational, they will raise equity in the cheapest manner. The preceding evidence suggests that issues of pure rights should dominate. Surprisingly, almost all new equity issues in the United States are sold without rights. Conversely, rights offerings are quite common elsewhere in the world. The avoidance of rights offerings in the United States is generally viewed as an anomaly in the finance profession, though a few explanations have been advanced:

1. Underwriters increase the stock price through their selling effort and enhanced public confidence. However, Smith could find no evidence of this in an examination of 52 rights offerings and 344 underwritten offerings.
2. Because the underwriter buys the shares at the agreed-upon price, it is providing insurance to the firm. That is, the underwriter loses if it is unable to sell all the shares to the public. However, the

[7]Clifford W. Smith, "Alternative Methods for Raising Capital," *Journal of Financial Economics* 5, no. 3 (December 1977): 273–307; Myron Slovin, Marie Sushka, and Kam Wah Lai, "Alternative Flotation Methods, Adverse Selection, and Ownership Structure: Evidence from Seasoned Equity Issuance in the U.K.," *Journal of Financial Economics* 57, no. 2 (August 2000): 157–90.

potential economic loss is probably not large. In most cases, the offer price is set within 24 hours of the offering, by which time the underwriter has usually made a careful assessment of the market for the shares.

3. The underwriter certifies that the offering price is consistent with the true value of the issue, providing investors the comfort to purchase the stock.[8] This certification occurs because the underwriting firm obtains special access to the firm and is willing to put its reputation for correct pricing on the line.
4. Other arguments include (a) the proceeds of underwritten issues are available sooner than are the proceeds from a rights offer, (b) underwriters provide a wider distribution of ownership than would be possible with a rights offering, (c) consulting advice from investment bankers may be beneficial, (d) stockholders find exercising rights a nuisance, and (e) the risk that the market price might fall below the subscription price is significant.

All of the preceding arguments are pieces of the puzzle, but none seems very convincing. Further research on the topic is needed.

20.9 Dilution

A subject that comes up quite a bit in discussions involving the issuance of stock is **dilution**. Dilution refers to a loss in existing shareholders' value. There are several kinds:

1. Dilution of percentage ownership.
2. Dilution of stock price.
3. Dilution of book value.
4. Dilution of earnings per share.

Is dilution bad? Though the word "dilution" definitely has a negative connotation, we argue below that only dilution of stock price is unambiguously bad.

DILUTION OF PERCENTAGE OWNERSHIP

The first type of dilution can arise whenever a firm sells shares to the general public. For example, Keshav Maitreya owns 5,000 shares of Mirza Shoe Company. Mirza Shoe currently has 50,000 shares of stock outstanding; each share gets one vote. Keshav controls 10 percent (= 5,000/50,000) of the votes and receives 10 percent of the dividends.

If Mirza Shoe issues 50,000 new shares of common stock to the public via a general cash offer, Keshav's ownership in Mirza Shoe may be diluted. If she does not participate in the new issue, her ownership will drop to 5 percent (= 5,000/100,000). Notice that, if the equity offering is used to fund a positive NPV project, the value of Keshav's shares should rise. However, even in this case, she will now own a smaller percentage of the firm.

Because a rights offering would ensure Keshav an opportunity to maintain her proportionate 10 percent share, dilution of the ownership of existing shareholders can be avoided by using a rights offering.

[8] James Booth and Richard Smith, "The Certification Role of the Investment Banker in New Issue Pricing," *Midland Corporate Finance Journal*, Spring 1986.

DILUTION OF STOCK PRICE

To address stock price dilution, let's consider Urvashi Sattu Manufacturing (USM), an all-equity firm with 1 million shares outstanding and earnings of ₹1,000,000 (or ₹1 per share) each year into perpetuity. If the discount rate is 20 percent, the price per share is ₹5 (= ₹1/.20). The market value of the equity is ₹5 million (= ₹5 × 1 million). For simplicity, we ignore taxes.

Now imagine that USM decides to accept a project costing ₹2 million and generating earnings in perpetuity of ₹600,000 per year. The present value of the project is:

$$-₹2,000,000 + ₹600,000/.20 = ₹1,000,000$$

If the project is accepted, the earnings of the firm will increase to ₹1,600,000. Once the firm publicly announces the project, the discounted cash flow of the firm rises to:

$$₹1,600,000/.20 - ₹2,000,000 = ₹6,000,000$$

With a million shares outstanding, the stock price becomes ₹6.

Of course, new shares must be issued to raise the ₹2 million. With a stock price of ₹6, the firm must issue 333,333 (= ₹2,000,000/₹6) additional shares. We can derive the ₹6 stock price in another way. Once the ₹2 million investment has been spent–that is, the project has been funded–the present value of the firm becomes ₹1,600,000/.20 = ₹8,000,000. The price per share can be calculated as ₹8,000,000/1,333,333 = ₹6 . The basic results of this example are presented in the first two columns of Table 20.11.

Why does the share price rise in this example? Because the net present value of the project is positive. Suppose the project still costs ₹2 million but generates only ₹200,000 per year. The project has a negative NPV, lowering the stock price. The relevant numbers here are presented in the third column of Table 20.11.

We can tell whether old shareholders in USM experienced price dilution by looking at whether the share price declines after the new issue. The stock price rises if the firm issues stock to fund a project with a positive NPV. Conversely, the stock price falls if the project has a negative NPV. These conclusions are consistent with the fifth row of Table 20.11.

In this simple example, we have assumed that the stock price always reflects the firm's true market value (including the new project) divided by the number of shares. In reality, this may not always be the case. If new shares are issued for less than those shares are worth in terms of market value, and the firm does not make up for the difference by using the issuance proceeds to finance a positive NPV project, then old shareholders will experience price dilution. For an extreme example, let's consider USM prior to the arrival of the new project opportunity, when it had a market value of ₹5 million and 1 million shares outstanding worth ₹5 per share. Suppose the CEO of USM issues herself 100,000 shares as compensation. In return, she provides managerial services to USM that turn out to be completely worthless. The market value of the firm would remain the same at ₹5 million, but the share price would fall to ₹4.55 [= ₹5,000,000/(1,000,000 + 100,000)].

Table 20.11 New Issues and Dilution: The Case of Urvashi Sattu Manufacturing

	Initial	Positive NPV Project	Negative NPV Project	Zero NPV Project
Number of shares in firm	1,000,000	1,333,333	1,500,000	1,400,000
Annual earnings	₹1,000,000	₹1,600,000	₹1,200,000	₹1,400,000
Firm market value at announcement	₹5,000,000	₹6,000,000	₹4,000,000	₹5,000,000
Firm market value after funding		₹8,000,000	₹6,000,000	₹7,000,000
Price per share	₹5	₹6	₹4	₹5
Book value	₹10,000,000	₹12,000,000	₹12,000,000	₹12,000,000
Book value per share	₹10	₹9	₹8	₹8.57

DILUTION OF BOOK VALUE

We have not mentioned book value yet in this example. Let's now assume that the firm initially has a book value of ₹10 million, implying book value per share of ₹10. Why would the firm have a book value above the market value of ₹5 million? Most likely the firm is not doing well, perhaps because of poor management or bad industry prospects.

As a baseline case here, imagine the firm accepts a project with earnings each year into perpetuity of ₹400,000. The NPV of this project is:

$$-₹2{,}000{,}000 + ₹400{,}000/.20 = ₹0$$

The price remains at ₹5 per share, implying the firm must issue 400,000 (= ₹2,000,000/₹5) new shares. Because the book value of the project equals its cost of ₹2,000,000, the book value of the firm rises to ₹12 million. With 400,000 shares issued, the book value per share falls to ₹8.57 (= ₹12 million/1.4 million). These numbers are displayed in the last column of Table 20.11.

Why does the book value per share drop? The original book value per share of ₹10 was well above the price, or market value, per share of ₹5. Because the project has an NPV of zero, the market value of the cash inflows from the project is equal to the book value, or cost, of the project, which is ₹2 million. By combining the book-to-market ratio of 2 for the existing firm with the book-to-market ratio of 1 for the project, the book-to-market ratio falls when the new project is funded. Because the market value per share stays the same at ₹5, the book value per share must fall.

Now, a manager might be upset with this decline in book value per share, but is it really anything to worry about? No, because the price per share has remained at ₹5, implying that the shareholders have been unaffected. The general rule still holds that managers should accept projects with positive NPVs because they boost stock prices and reject projects with negative NPVs. What happens to book value is largely irrelevant.

Admittedly, we have examined the special case of a project with a zero NPV. If the project had a positive NPV, the resulting book value per share would have been higher than ₹8.57 because fewer shares would have to be issued. Conversely, if the project had a negative NPV, the resulting book value per share would have been lower. We can see this in Table 20.11 with the book value per share being ₹9 for the positive NPV project and ₹8 per share for the negative NPV project. But again, change in book value is irrelevant.

DILUTION OF EARNINGS PER SHARE

Does EPS rise and fall in tandem with stock price? Not necessarily, and it is easy to come up with examples that show the difference. Again consider USM with initial EPS of ₹1. Suppose that the firm accepts a project that costs ₹2 million, as before. However, now imagine that the project generates just one cash flow, a payment of ₹5,184,000 three years from today. The net present value of this project is:

$$-₹2{,}000{,}000 + ₹5{,}184{,}000/1.20^3 = ₹1{,}000{,}000$$

The firm's value rises to ₹6 million (= ₹5 million + 1 million) and the price per share rises to ₹6. However, earnings per share in the first year fall below ₹1. Why? Because new shares must be issued to fund the project, but the project does not generate any earnings in the first year. The general rule here is that a project with big growth in earnings over time may reduce EPS initially, even if the NPV is positive. This is an important point because managerial compensation is frequently based on EPS. Managers compensated on EPS are inadvertently incentivized to avoid a project with low initial earnings, even if the project has a positive net present value, but this is not good for the stockholders. Again, from the shareholders' perspective, managers should accept projects with positive NPVs and reject projects with negative NPVs. The immediate impact on EPS, like the impact on book value per share, is not as important.

CONCLUSION

This example has focused on the impact of new issues of equity on dilution. We examined dilution of percentage ownership, stock price, book value per share, and earnings per share. We concluded that only the impact of new issues on stock price per share is relevant to a firm's stockholders.[9] Dilution of the other variables is irrelevant to the stockholders.

20.10 Shelf Registration

To simplify the procedure for issuing securities, the SEBI (in India)/SEC (in US) currently allows **shelf registration**. Shelf registration permits a corporation to register an offering that it reasonably expects to sell within the next two years. A master registration statement is filed at the time of registration. The company is permitted to sell the issue whenever it wants over those two years as long as it distributes a short-form statement. For example, in June 2020, Ballard Power announced a shelf registration of up to ₹750 million in common stock, preferred stock, warrants, and debt.

Not all companies are allowed shelf registration. The major qualifications are as follows:

1. The company must be rated *investment grade*.
2. The firm cannot have defaulted on its debt in the past three years.
3. The aggregate market value of the firm's outstanding stock must be more than ₹150 million.
4. The firm must not have violated the Securities Exchange Act of 1934 in the past three years.

Shelf registration allows firms to use the *dribble method* of new equity issuance. With dribbling, a company registers the issue and hires an underwriter to be its selling agent. The company sells shares in small amounts from time to time via a stock exchange. Companies that have used dribble programs include Wells Fargo & Company, Pacific Gas and Electric, and The Southern Company.

The rule has been controversial. Several arguments have been made against shelf registration:

1. The timeliness of disclosure is reduced with shelf registration because the master registration statement may have been prepared up to two years before the actual issue occurs.
2. Some investment bankers have argued that shelf registration will cause a market overhang because registration informs the market of future issues. It has been suggested that this overhang will depress market prices.

SHELF REGISTRATION IN INDIA

Shelf registration is a process which can facilitate frequent and quick issuance of securities (especially debt securities), and is available in India only to specifically designated Public Financial Institutions (PFIs) and not to all corporate issuers. In the past, ICICI, among others, had made use of the Shelf registration to raise debt securities.

Shelf registration in India is allowed through an umbrella prospectus, whereby a company files one consolidated offer document with the securities market regulator, i.e., SEBI for the entire amount it proposes to raise over the next twelve months allowing the company to make more than one offering within the stipulated period.

(continued)

[9] In a rights offering, one should consider the impact on stock price prior to the ex-rights date.

In the recent past, there has been increasing pressure on SEBI to extend shelf-registration to all types of corporate issuers. On the other hand, SEBI is wary of its misuse resulting in a systemic failure and hence has not given a green signal to all types of corporate issuers.

20.11 Issuing Long-Term Debt

The general procedures followed in a public issue of bonds are the same as those for stocks. The issue must be registered with the SEBI (in India)/SEC (in US), there must be a prospectus, and so on. The registration statement for a public issue of bonds, however, is different from the one for common stock. For bonds, the registration statement must indicate an indenture.

Another important difference is that more than 50 percent of all debt is issued privately. There are two basic forms of direct private long-term financing: term loans and private placement.

Term loans are direct business loans. These loans have maturities between one and five years. Most term loans are repayable during the life of the loan. The lenders include commercial banks, insurance companies, and other lenders that specialize in corporate finance. **Private placements** are similar to term loans except that the maturity is longer.

The important differences between direct private long-term financing and public issues of debt are:

1. A direct long-term loan avoids the cost of the regulator (SEC or SEBI as the case may be) registration.
2. Direct placement is likely to have more restrictive covenants.
3. It is easier to renegotiate a term loan or a private placement in the event of a default. It is harder to renegotiate a public issue because hundreds of holders are usually involved.
4. Life insurance companies and pension funds dominate the private placement segment of the bond market. Commercial banks are significant participants in the term loan market.
5. The costs of distributing bonds are lower in the private market.

The interest rates on term loans and private placements are usually higher than those on an equivalent public issue. This difference reflects the trade-off between a higher interest rate and more flexible arrangements in the event of financial distress, as well as the lower costs associated with private placements.

An additional, and very important, consideration is that the flotation costs associated with selling debt are much less than the comparable costs associated with selling equity.

20.12 Capital Issues in India

Table 20.12 captures the trends in the new capital issues in India by non-government companies. We have observed the periodical figures fluctuating lately with no visible trends whatsoever. The size of the capital issues, along with their numbers in India, largely depends on the moods of the capital market - which lately have been linked to the flow of foreign institutional investment and inflows in mutual funds. In the last two decades, the constant divestment process of the Government of India from the state-owned companies, i.e., public sector units such as Coal India Limited, added to these figures.

Table 20.12 Trends in New Capital Issues in India by Non-Government Companies

	Ordinary Shares		Preference Shares		Debentures		Total	
Year	No. of Issues	Amount (₹ in Crores)	No. of Issues	Zero NPV Project	No. of Issues	Amount (₹ in Crores)	No. of Issues	Amount (₹ in Crores)
1981–82	357	305	73	3	73	290	503	598
1986–87	424	1007	94	1	94	1573	612	2581
1991–92	366	1916	145	2	145	4275	656	6193
1996–97	801	6101	32	75	32	4233	865	10409
2001–02	6	860	-	-	13	4832	19	5692
2006–07	114	29756	-	-	3	850	117	30603
2011–12	49	8152	-	-	14	7528	63	15680
2016–17	116	30358	-	-	16	29547	132	59905
2017–18	214	67993	-	-	7	4953	221	72946
2018–19	129	16754	-	-	25	36680	154	53432
2019–20	73	65509	-	-	34	14984	107	80493
2020–21	74	102062	-	-	16	5806	90	107868
2021–22	164	138894	-	-	28	11589	192	150484
2022–23	237	45266	-	-	34	9221	271	54487

SOURCE: Reserve Bank of India "New Capital Issues by Non-Government Public Limited Companies" www.rbi.org.in

Table 20.13 gives a sample list of new security issues in India, the specifics of the method, and the type of issues.

Table 20.13 Examples of Issuing New Securities in India

Method and Type of Issue	Company	Details
Public offering – traditional firm commitment cash offer	South Asian Petrochemicals Limited	₹74 crore offer of 50 lac equity shares and 69.5 lac debentures
Public offering – Dutch auction cash offer	Government of India GILT bonds*	NA
Privileged subscription – standby rights offer	Tata Motors Limited*	1:5 rights offer for ₹1,300 crore; offer of convertible debentures and non-convertible debentures with warrants
Nontraditional offer – shelf cash offer (as per its ADR norms)	ICICI Bank Limited*	Public-offer for ₹8,750 crore with up to 5% reserved for existing retail shareholders
Nontraditional offer – competitive firm cash offer	NTPC Limited*	Offer of 8668.3 lac equity shares (underwriters selected through tender process)
Private – direct placement	Crest Communications Limited	16.5 lac equity shares for ₹48.2 crore
Privileged subscription – direct rights offer	Deepak Fertilizers & Petrochemicals Ltd.	3:20 rights offer for ₹178.12 crore; offer of 1.34 crore equity shares
Public offering – best efforts cash offer	IRCTC	2.016 crore shares for ₹645.12 crore

NOTE: * indicates not a perfect example of the method and type of issue. We provide the nearest example.

RESEARCH IN EMERGING MARKET CONTEXT

Qualified Institutional Placement (QIP) is a private equity placement where institutional buyers are the only ones allowed to participate. A study by Katti et al. (2021) found that QIPs in India are issued at a premium, as opposed to private placement discounts that are common in most other economies. The researchers attributed this to the certification effect of business group affiliations, which includes signaling through promoters' ownership and monitoring by existing institutional investors.

Another study by Ghalke et al. (2022) found that small and medium-sized enterprises (SMEs) that raise funds on the SME platform use the money from initial public offerings (IPOs) to rebalance their accounts after a period of heavy investment, rather than for growth finance.

Furthermore, Nikbakht et al. (2021) discovered that reputable investment banks play a crucial role in preventing Indian IPO firms from manipulating pre-IPO earnings. Also, harder-to-value firms, such as those with extensive research and development, are more likely to engage in pre-IPO earnings management.

References

Ghalke, A., Kumar, S., & Rao, S. N. (2022). SME financing through public equity: review of the Indian SME exchanges. *Indian Growth and Development Review, 15*(1), 85–97.

Katti, S., Verma, N., Phani, B. V., & Ghosh, C. (2021). Price premium of private placement: evidence from India. *International Journal of Managerial Finance, 17*(5), 757–782.

Nikbakht, E., Sarkar, S., Smith, G. C., & Spieler, A. C. (2021). Pre-IPO earnings management: Evidence from India. *Journal of International Accounting, Auditing and Taxation, 44*, 100400.

Sony, B., & Bhaduri, S. (2021). Choice between rights issue and private placements of equity and the role of information asymmetry. *Managerial Finance, 48*(3), 409–428.

Summary and Conclusions

1. Venture capital is a common source of financing in startup and privately held firms. Venture capital is particularly important in financing high-tech enterprises. Venture capital financing was at its peak during the internet bubble around the turn of the century.
2. A company's first public equity issue is called an initial public offering (IPO). IPOs are generally underpriced. That is, the stock price in the aftermarket is normally above the issue price.
3. A seasoned equity offering (SEO) refers to a new issue when the company's securities have already been publicly traded. On average, the stock price of the issuing company falls upon the announcement of an SEO.
4. The underwriter bears risk with a firm commitment because it buys the entire issue. Conversely, the investment banker avoids this risk under a best-efforts offering because it does not purchase the shares. Firm commitment underwriting is far more prevalent for large issues than is best-efforts underwriting.
5. Rights offerings are cheaper than general cash offers and eliminate the problem of underpricing. Yet most new equity issues in the United States are underwritten general cash offers.
6. While dilution in stock price hurts stockholders, dilution of percentage interest, book value per share, and EPS–by themselves–do not.
7. Shelf registration allows a corporation to register an offering that it reasonably expects to sell within two years.

Concept Questions

1. **Debt versus Equity Offering Size** In the aggregate, debt offerings are much more common than equity offerings and typically much larger as well. Why?

2. **Debt versus Equity Flotation Costs** Why are the costs of selling equity so much larger than the costs of selling debt?

3. **Bond Ratings and Flotation Costs** Why do noninvestment-grade bonds have much higher direct costs than investment-grade issues?

4. **Underpricing in Debt Offerings** Why is underpricing not a great concern with bond offerings?

Use the following information to answer the next three questions. Zipcar, the car-sharing company, went public in April 2011. Assisted by the investment bank Goldman Sachs, Zipcar sold 9.68 million shares at ₹18 each, thereby raising a total of ₹174.24 million. By the end of the first day of trading, the stock had zipped to ₹28 per share, down from a high of ₹31.50. Based on the end-of-day numbers, Zipcar shares were apparently underpriced by about ₹10 each, meaning that the company missed out on an additional ₹96.8 million.

5. **IPO Pricing** The Zipcar IPO was underpriced by about 56 percent. Should Zipcar be upset at Goldman over the underpricing?

6. **IPO Pricing** In the previous question, how would it affect your thinking to know that the company was incorporated about 10 years earlier, had only ₹186 million in revenues in 2010, and had never earned a profit? Additionally, the viability of the company's business model was still unproven.

7. **IPO Pricing** In the previous two questions, how would it affect your thinking to know that in addition to the 9.68 million shares offered in the IPO, Zipcar had an additional 30 million shares outstanding? Of those 30 million shares, 14.1 million shares were owned by four venture capital firms and 15.5 million shares were owned by the 12 directors and executive officers.

8. **Cash Offer versus Rights Offer** Ren-Stimpy International is planning to raise fresh equity capital by selling a large new issue of common stock. Ren-Stimpy is currently a publicly traded corporation and is trying to choose between an underwritten cash offer and a rights offering (not underwritten) to current shareholders. Ren-Stimpy management is interested in minimizing the selling costs and has asked you for advice on the choice of issue methods. What is your recommendation and why?

9. **IPO Underpricing** In 1980, a certain assistant professor of finance bought 12 initial public offerings of common stock. He held each of these for approximately one month and then sold them. The investment rule he followed was to submit a purchase order for every firm commitment initial public offering of oil and gas exploration companies. There were 22 of these offerings and he submitted a purchase order for approximately ₹1,000 in stock for each of the companies. With 10 of these, no shares were allocated to this assistant professor. With 5 of the 12 offerings that were purchased, fewer than the requested number of shares were allocated.

   The year 1980 was very good for oil and gas exploration company owners: On average, for the 22 companies that went public, the stocks were selling for 80 percent above the offering price a month after the initial offering date. The assistant professor looked at his performance record and found that the ₹8,400 invested in the 12 companies had grown to ₹10,000, representing a return of only about 20 percent (commissions were negligible). Did he have bad luck or should he have expected to do worse than the average initial public offering investor? Explain.

10. **IPO Pricing** The following material represents the cover page and summary of the prospectus for the initial public offering of the Pest Investigation Control Corporation (PICC), which is going public

tomorrow with a firm commitment initial public offering managed by the investment banking firm of Erlanger and Ritter.

Answer the following questions:

a. Assume that you know nothing about PICC other than the information contained in the prospectus. Based on your knowledge of finance, what is your prediction for the price of PICC tomorrow? Provide a short explanation of why you think this will occur.

b. Assume that you have several thousand rupees to invest. When you get home from class tonight, you find that your stockbroker, whom you have not talked to for weeks, has called. She has left a message that PICC is going public tomorrow and that she can get you several hundred shares at the offering price if you call her back first thing in the morning. Discuss the merits of this opportunity.

PROSPECTUS **PICC**

200,000 shares

PEST INVESTIGATION CONTROL CORPORATION

Of the shares being offered hereby, all 200,000 are being sold by the Pest Investigation Control Corporation ("the Company"). Before the offering, there has been no public market for the shares of PICC, and no guarantee can be given that any such market will develop.

These securities have not been approved or disapproved by the SEC, nor has the commission passed judgment upon the accuracy or adequacy of this prospectus. Any representation to the contrary is a criminal offense.

	Price to Public	Underwriting Discount	Proceeds to Company*
Per share	₹11.00	₹1.10	₹9.90
Total	₹2,200,000	₹220,000	₹1,980,000

*Before deducting expenses estimated at ₹27,000 and payable by the company.

This is an initial public offering. The common shares are being offered, subject to prior sale, when, as, and if delivered to and accepted by the Underwriters and subject to approval of certain legal matters by their Counsel and by Counsel for the Company. The Underwriters reserve the right to withdraw, cancel, or modify such offer and to reject offers in whole or in part.

Erlanger and Ritter, Investment Bankers

July 13, 2022

Prospectus Summary

The Company	The Pest Investigation Control Corporation (PICC) breeds and markets toads and tree frogs as ecologically safe insect-control mechanisms.
The Offering	200,000 shares of common stock, no par value.
Listing	The Company will seek listing on Nasdaq and will trade over the counter.
Shares Outstanding	As of June 30, 2022, 400,000 shares of common stock were outstanding. After the offering, 600,000 shares of common stock will be outstanding.
Use of Proceeds	To finance expansion of inventory and receivables and general working capital, and to pay for country club memberships for certain finance professors.

Selected Financial Information
(amounts in thousands except per-share data)

	Fiscal Year Ended June 30				As of June 30, 2022	
	2020	2021	2022		Actual	As Adjusted for This Offering
Revenues	₹60.00	₹120.00	₹240.00	Working capital	₹ 8	₹1,961
Net earnings	3.80	15.90	36.10	Total assets	511	2,464
Earnings per share	.01	.04	.09	Stockholders' equity	423	2,376

11. **Competitive and Negotiated Offers** What are the comparative advantages of a competitive offer and a negotiated offer, respectively?

12. **Seasoned Equity Offers** What are the possible reasons why the stock price typically drops on the announcement of a seasoned new equity issue?

13. **Raising Capital** Megabucks Industries is planning to raise fresh equity capital by selling a large new issue of common stock. Megabucks, a publicly traded corporation, is trying to choose between an underwritten cash offer and a rights offering (not underwritten) to current shareholders. Megabucks' management is interested in maximizing the wealth of current shareholders and has asked you for advice on the choice of issue methods. What is your recommendation? Why?

14. **Shelf Registration** Explain why shelf registration has been used by many firms instead of syndication.

15. **IPOs** Every IPO is unique, but what are the basic empirical regularities in IPOs?

Questions and Problems

BASIC (Questions 1–9)

1. **Rights Offerings** Hassinah, Inc., is proposing a rights offering. Presently there are 435,000 shares outstanding at ₹71 each. There will be 50,000 new shares offered at ₹64 each.
   a. What is the new market value of the company?
   b. How many rights are associated with one of the new shares?
   c. What is the ex-rights price?
   d. What is the value of a right?
   e. Why might a company have a rights offering rather than a general cash offer?

2. **Rights Offering** The Clifford Corporation has announced a rights offer to raise ₹25 million for a new journal, the *Journal of Financial Excess*. This journal will review potential articles after the author pays a nonrefundable reviewing fee of ₹5,000 per page. The stock currently sells for ₹48 per share and there are 2.7 million shares outstanding.
   a. What is the maximum possible subscription price? What is the minimum?

b. If the subscription price is set at ₹41 per share, how many shares must be sold? How many rights will it take to buy one share?
c. What is the ex-rights price? What is the value of a right?
d. Show how a shareholder with 1,000 shares before the offering and no desire (or money) to buy additional shares is not harmed by the rights offer.

3. **Rights** The Tennis Shoe Co. has concluded that additional equity financing will be needed to expand operations and that the needed funds will be best obtained through a rights offering. It has correctly determined that as a result of the rights offering, the share price will fall from ₹56 to ₹54.30 (₹56 is the rights-on price; ₹54.30 is the ex-rights price, also known as the *when-issued* price). The company is seeking ₹17.5 million in additional funds with a per-share subscription price equal to ₹41. How many shares are there currently before the offering? (Assume that the increment to the market value of the equity equals the gross proceeds from the offering.)

4. **IPO Underpricing** The Woods Co. and the Koepka Co. have both announced IPOs at ₹40 per share. One of these is undervalued by ₹12, and the other is overvalued by ₹5, but you have no way of knowing which is which. You plan to buy 1,000 shares of each issue. If an issue is underpriced, it will be rationed, and only half your order will be filled. If you *could* get 1,000 shares in Woods and 1,000 shares in Koepka, what would your profit be? What profit do you actually expect? What principle have you illustrated?

5. **Calculating Flotation Costs** The Meadows Corporation needs to raise ₹75 million to finance its expansion into new markets. The company will sell new shares of equity via a general cash offering to raise the needed funds. If the offer price is ₹23 per share and the company's underwriters charge a spread of 7 percent, how many shares need to be sold?

6. **Calculating Flotation Costs** In the previous problem, if the SEC filing fee and associated administrative expenses of the offering are ₹1.9 million, how many shares need to be sold?

7. **Calculating Flotation Costs** The Telwar Co. has just gone public. Under a firm commitment agreement, the company received ₹25.11 for each of the 30 million shares sold. The initial offering price was ₹27 per share, and the stock rose to ₹32.49 per share in the first few minutes of trading. The company paid ₹1.4 million in direct legal and other costs and ₹375,000 in indirect costs. What was the flotation cost as a percentage of funds raised?

8. **Price Dilution** Damron, Inc., has 250,000 shares of stock outstanding. Each share is worth ₹81, so the company's market value of equity is ₹20,250,000. Suppose the firm issues 40,000 new shares at the following prices: ₹81, ₹76, and ₹68. What effect will each of these alternative offering prices have on the existing price per share?

9. **Stock Offerings** The Chen Company has 70,000 shares of stock that each sells for ₹55. Suppose the company issues 9,000 shares of new stock at the following prices: ₹55, ₹30, and ₹20. What is the effect of each of the alternative offering prices on the existing price per share?

INTERMEDIATE (Questions 10–18)

10. **Dilution** Marker, Inc., wishes to expand its facilities. The company currently has 5 million shares outstanding and no debt. The stock sells for ₹64 per share, but the book value per share is ₹19. Net income is currently ₹12.2 million. The new facility will cost ₹28 million, and it will increase net income by ₹775,000.

a. Assuming a constant price-earnings ratio, what will the effect be of issuing new equity to finance the investment? To answer, calculate the new book value per share, the new total earnings, the new EPS, the new stock price, and the new market-to-book ratio. What is going on here?
b. What would the new net income for the company have to be for the stock price to remain unchanged?

11. **Dilution** The all-equity firm Metallica Heavy Metal Mining (MHMM) Corporation wants to diversify its operations. Some recent financial information for the company is shown here:

Stock price	₹75
Number of shares	64,000
Total assets	₹9,400,000
Total liabilities	₹4,100,000
Net income	₹980,000

MHMM is considering an investment that has the same PE ratio as the firm. The cost of the investment is ₹1.5 million, and it will be financed with a new equity issue. The return on the investment will equal MHMM's current ROE. What will happen to the book value per share, the market value per share, and the EPS? What is the NPV of this investment? Does dilution take place?

12. **Dilution** In the previous problem, what would the ROE on the investment have to be if we wanted the price after the offering to be ₹75 per share? (Assume the PE ratio remains constant.) What is the NPV of this investment? Does any dilution take place?

13. **Rights** A company's stock currently sells for ₹93 per share. Last week the firm issued rights to raise new equity. To purchase a new share, a stockholder must remit ₹20 and three rights.
    a. What is the ex-rights stock price?
    b. What is the price of one right?
    c. When will the price drop occur? Why will it occur then?

14. **Rights** Cheung Corp.'s stock is currently selling at ₹43 per share. There are 1.3 million shares outstanding. The firm is planning to raise ₹2.9 million to finance a new project. What are the ex-rights stock price, the value of a right, and the appropriate subscription prices under the following scenarios?
    a. Two shares of outstanding stock are entitled to purchase one additional share of the new issue.
    b. Four shares of outstanding stock are entitled to purchase one additional share of the new issue.
    c. How does the stockholders' wealth change from part (a) to part (b)?

15. **Rights** Bell Buckle Mfg. is considering a rights offer. The company has determined that the ex-rights price would be ₹71. The current price is ₹76 per share, and there are 29 million shares outstanding. The rights offer would raise a total of ₹95 million. What is the subscription price?

16. **Value of a Right** Show that the value of a right can be written as

$$\text{Value of a right} = P_{RO} - P_X = (P_{RO} - P_S)/(N + 1)$$

where P_{RO}, P_S, and P_X stand for the rights-on price, the subscription price, and the ex-rights price, respectively, and N is the number of rights needed to buy one new share at the subscription price.

17. **Selling Rights** Nougat Corp. wants to raise ₹5.1 million via a rights offering. The company currently has 530,000 shares of common stock outstanding that sell for ₹55 per share. Its underwriter has set a subscription price of ₹30 per share and will charge the company a spread of 6 percent. If you currently own 5,000 shares of stock in the company and decide not to participate in the rights offering, how much money can you get by selling your rights?

18. **Valuing a Right** Knight Inventory Systems, Inc., has announced a rights offer. The company has announced that it will take four rights to buy a new share in the offering at a subscription price of ₹35. At the close of business the day before the ex-rights day, the company's stock sells for ₹60 per share. The next morning, you notice that the stock sells for ₹53 per share and the rights sell for ₹3 each. Are the stock and/or the rights correctly priced on the ex-rights day? Describe a transaction in which you could use these prices to create an immediate profit.

19. **Understanding a Prospectus in India** Dhandapani Finance Limited is a publicly listed non-banking financial services company. It offers various financial services like hire purchase, leasing services, and bills

discounting. Its competitors include Cholamandalam DBS Finance, Mahindra & Mahindra Financial Services, and SREI Infrastructure Finance, among others. In the online resources for the book, we have made available the draft prospectus of this company (Log on to www.mheducation.co.in). The document contains 100 pages. After going through the same, answer the following queries: [a] What is the method of financing and the type of issue? [b] Does the issue have any underwriter? If so, mention the names of underwriters. [c] Who is the lead manager for this issue? Are there any other syndicate members who are part of managing the issue? [d] Based on the draft prospectus, mention the brief details of the issue including the purpose of the issue.

Mini Case EAST COAST YACHTS GOES PUBLIC

Larissa Warren and Dan Ervin have been discussing the future of East Coast Yachts. The company has been experiencing fast growth, and the future looks like clear sailing. However, the fast growth means that the company's growth can no longer be funded by internal sources, so Larissa and Dan have decided the time is right to take the company public. To this end, they have entered into discussions with the investment bank of Crowe & Mallard. The company has a working relationship with Robin Perry, the underwriter who assisted with the company's previous bond offering. Crowe & Mallard have helped numerous small companies in the IPO process, so Larissa and Dan feel confident with this choice.

Robin begins by telling Larissa and Dan about the process. Although Crowe & Mallard charged an underwriter fee of 4 percent on the bond offering, the underwriter fee is 7 percent on all initial stock offerings of the size of East Coast Yachts' initial offering. Robin tells Larissa and Dan that the company can expect to pay about ₹2.2 million in legal fees and expenses, ₹15,000 in SEC registration fees, and ₹20,000 in other filing fees. Additionally, to be listed on the Nasdaq, the company must pay ₹100,000. There are also transfer agent fees of ₹8,500 and engraving expenses of ₹525,000. The company also should expect to pay ₹75,000 for other expenses associated with the IPO.

Finally, Robin tells Larissa and Dan that to file with the SEC, the company must provide three years' worth of audited financial statements. She is unsure of the costs of the audit. Dan tells Robin that the company provides audited financial statements as part of its bond indenture and the company pays ₹325,000 per year for the outside auditor.

1. At the end of the discussion, Dan asks Robin about the Dutch auction IPO process. What are the differences in the expenses to East Coast Yachts if it uses a Dutch auction IPO versus a traditional IPO? Should the company go public with a Dutch auction or use a traditional underwritten offering?
2. During the discussion of the potential IPO and East Coast Yachts' future, Dan states that he feels the company should raise ₹75 million. However, Larissa points out that if the company needs more cash soon, a secondary offering close to the IPO would be potentially problematic. Instead, she suggests that the company should raise ₹100 million in the IPO. How can we calculate the optimal size of the IPO? What are the advantages and disadvantages of increasing the size of the IPO to ₹100 million?
3. After deliberation, Larissa and Dan have decided that the company should use a firm commitment offering with Crowe & Mallard as the lead underwriter. The IPO will be for ₹90 million. Ignoring underpricing, how much will the IPO cost the company as a percentage of the funds received?
4. Many of the employees of East Coast Yachts have shares of stock in the company because of an existing employee stock purchase plan. To sell the stock, the employees can tender their shares to be sold in the IPO at the offering price, or the employees can retain their stock and sell it in the secondary market after East Coast Yachts goes public (once the 180-day lockup period expires). Larissa asks you to advise the employees about which option is best. What would you suggest to the employees?

21

Leasing

Have you ever flown on General Electric (GE) Airlines? Probably not; but with about 1,700 planes, GE Capital Aviation Services (GECAS), part of GE, owns one of the largest aircraft fleets in the world. In fact, this financing arm of GE owns more than ₹38 billion in assets, generated about ₹6.8 billion in profits during 2019, and has more than 225 customers in 75 countries. Why does GECAS own so many planes? It turns out more than 40 percent of all commercial jetliners worldwide are leased, which is what GECAS does. But why is GECAS in the business of buying assets, only to lease them out? And why don't the companies that lease from GECAS purchase the assets themselves? This chapter answers these and other questions associated with leasing.

Please visit us at **rwjcorporatefinance.blogspot.com** for the latest developments in the world of corporate finance.

21.1 Types of Leases

THE BASICS

A *lease* is a contractual agreement between a lessee and lessor. The agreement establishes that the lessee has the right to use an asset and in return must make periodic payments to the lessor, the owner of the asset. The lessor is either the asset's manufacturer or an independent leasing company. If the lessor is an independent leasing company, it must buy the asset from a manufacturer. Then the lessor delivers the asset to the lessee, and the lease goes into effect.

As far as the lessee is concerned, it is the use of the asset that is most important, not who owns the asset. The use of an asset can be obtained by a lease contract. Because the user also can buy the asset, leasing and buying involve alternative financing arrangements for the use of an asset. This is illustrated in Figure 21.1.

The specific example in Figure 21.1 happens often in the computer industry. Firm U, the lessee, might be a hospital, a law firm, or any other firm that uses computers. The lessor is an independent leasing company that purchased the equipment from a manufacturer such as IBM or Apple. Leases of this type are called **direct leases**. In the figure, the lessor issued both debt and equity to finance the purchase.

Of course, a manufacturer like Boeing could lease its own airplanes, though we do not show this situation in the example. Leases of this type are called **sales-type leasing**. In this case, Boeing would compete with the independent leasing company.

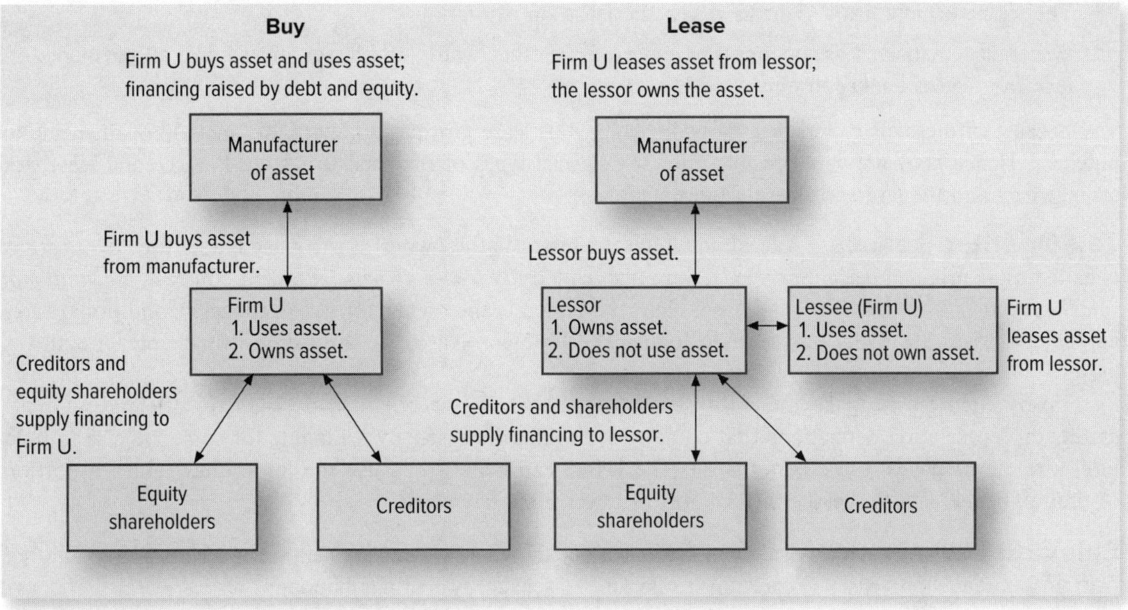

Figure 21.1 Buying versus Leasing

OPERATING LEASES

Years ago, a lease where the lessee received an operator along with the equipment was called an **operating lease**. Though the operating lease defies an exact definition today, this form of leasing has several important characteristics:

1. Operating leases are usually not fully amortized. This means that the payments required under the terms of the lease are not enough to recover the full cost of the asset for the lessor. This occurs because the term, or life, of the operating lease is usually less than the economic life of the asset. The lessor expects to recover the costs of the asset by renewing the lease or by selling the asset for its residual value.
2. Operating leases usually require the lessor to maintain and insure the leased assets.
3. Perhaps the most interesting feature of an operating lease is the cancellation option. This option gives the lessee the right to cancel the lease contract before the expiration date. If the option to cancel is exercised, the lessee must return the equipment to the lessor. The value of a cancellation clause depends on whether future technological or economic conditions are likely to make the value of the asset to the lessee less than the value of the future lease payments under the lease.

To leasing practitioners, the preceding characteristics constitute an operating lease. However, accountants use the term in a slightly different way, as we will see shortly.

FINANCIAL LEASES

Financial leases are the exact opposite of operating leases, as is seen from their important characteristics:

1. Financial leases do not provide for maintenance or service by the lessor.
2. Financial leases are fully amortized.

3. The lessee usually has a right to renew the lease on expiration.
4. Generally, financial leases cannot be canceled. In other words, the lessee must make all payments or face the risk of bankruptcy.

Because of these characteristics, particularly (2), this lease provides an alternative method of financing to purchase. Hence, its name is a sensible one. Two special types of financial leases are the sale and leaseback arrangement and the leveraged lease arrangement.

Tax-Oriented Leases A lease in which the lessor is the owner of the leased asset for tax purposes is called a **tax-oriented lease**. Such leases are also called *tax leases* or *true leases*. In contrast, a *conditional sales agreement lease* is not a true lease. Here the lessee is the owner for tax purposes. Conditional sales agreement leases are really just secured loans. The financial leases we discuss in this chapter are all tax leases.

Tax-oriented leases make the most sense when the lessee is not in a position to efficiently use tax credits or depreciation deductions that come with owning the asset. By arranging for someone else to hold title, a tax lease passes these benefits on. The lessee can benefit because the lessor may return a portion of the tax benefits to the lessee in the form of lower lease payments.

Sale and Leaseback A **sale and leaseback** occurs when a company sells an asset it owns to another firm and immediately leases it back. In a sale and leaseback, two things happen:

1. The lessee receives cash from the sale of the asset.
2. The lessee makes periodic lease payments, thereby retaining use of the asset.

For example, in January 2020, Bed Bath & Beyond posted a ₹250 million gain from the sale and leaseback of company-owned real estate. The 2.1 million square feet of space sold to Oak Street Real Estate Capital, LLC, included the company's headquarters, a distribution facility, and an undisclosed number of its roughly 1,500 stores. The stock price jumped 2 percent on the news. In December 2023, Air India Express, the wholly-owned Low-Cost Carrier (LCC) subsidiary of Air India, carried out a sale and leaseback arrangement for 10 of its B737-8s. The LCC had received its first aircraft in November 2023, with the remaining nine were scheduled for delivery by March 31, 2024. The sale and leaseback arrangement provided the LCC with immediate cash, thereby improving its liquidity position and increasing fleet flexibility. Such sale and leaseback arrangements are quite common in the aviation world.

Leveraged Leases A **leveraged lease** is a three-sided arrangement among the lessee, the lessor, and the lenders:

1. As in other leases, the lessee uses the assets and makes periodic lease payments.
2. As in other leases, the lessor purchases the assets, delivers them to the lessee, and collects the lease payments. However, the lessor puts up no more than 40 to 50 percent of the purchase price.
3. The lenders supply the remaining financing and receive interest payments from the lessor. The arrangement on the right side of Figure 21.1 would be a leveraged lease if the bulk of the financing was supplied by creditors.

The lenders in a leveraged lease typically use a *nonrecourse loan*. This means that the lessor is not obligated to the lender in case of a default. However, the lender is protected in two ways:

1. The lender has a first lien on the asset.
2. In the event of loan default, the lease payments are made directly to the lender.

The lessor puts up only part of the funds but gets the lease payments and all the tax benefits of ownership. These lease payments are used to pay the debt service of the nonrecourse loan. The lessee benefits because, in a competitive market, the lease payment is lowered when the lessor saves taxes.

21.2 Accounting and Leasing

Before November 1976, a firm could arrange to use an asset through a lease and not disclose the asset or the lease contract on the balance sheet. Lessees needed to report information on leasing activity only in the footnotes of their financial statements. Thus, leasing led to **off-balance sheet financing**.

In November 1976, the Financial Accounting Standards Board (FASB) issued its *Statement of Financial Accounting Standards No. 13* (FAS 13), "Accounting for Leases." Under FAS 13, certain leases are classified as capital leases. For a capital lease, the present value of the lease payments appears on the right side of the balance sheet. The identical value appears on the left side of the balance sheet as an asset. Operating leases are not disclosed on the balance sheet except in the footnotes. Exactly what constitutes a financial or operating lease for accounting purposes will be discussed in a moment.

Starting in 2019, companies were required to disclose operating leases on their balance sheets, which was a major change. The implication is that most leases are now reported on the balance sheet, so off-balance sheet financing has largely been eliminated (at least from leasing activities).

The accounting implications of this distinction are illustrated in Table 21.1. Imagine a firm that, years ago, issued ₹100,000 of equity to purchase land. It now wants to use a ₹100,000 truck, which it can either purchase or lease. The balance sheet reflecting the purchase of the truck is shown at the top of the table assuming the truck is financed entirely with debt. Alternatively, imagine that the firm leases the truck. If the lease is judged to be an operating one, the middle balance sheet is created. Here, neither the lease liability nor the truck appears on the balance sheet. The bottom balance sheet reflects a capital lease. The truck is shown as an asset and the lease is shown as a liability.

Under the old (pre-2019) rules, if the firm uses an operating lease, then the balance sheet will look like the one in Part B of the table. Neither the truck nor the lease obligations appear. Under the new rules, the balance sheet will look more like Part C of the table. There, the truck is shown as an asset, and the value of the lease payments is shown as a liability.[1]

Table 21.1 Examples of Balance Sheets under FAS 13

Balance Sheet			
A. Truck is purchased with debt (the company owns a ₹100,000 truck):			
Truck	₹100,000	Debt	₹100,000
Land	100,000	Equity	100,000
Total assets	₹200,000	Total debt and equity	₹200,000
B. Operating lease (the company has an operating lease for the truck):			
Truck	₹ 0	Debt	₹ 0
Land	100,000	Equity	100,000
Total assets	₹100,000	Total debt and equity	₹100,000
C. Capital lease (the company has a capital lease for the truck):			
Assets under capital lease	₹100,000	Obligations under capital lease	₹100,000
Land	100,000	Equity	100,000
Total assets	₹200,000	Total debt and equity	₹200,000

[1]In the capital lease balance sheet, we have made the simplifying assumption that the present value of the lease payments under the capital lease is equal to the cost of the truck. In general, the lessee must report the lesser of the present value of the lease payment stream or the cost of the equipment under lease.

Because firms had an incentive prior to 2019 to classify a lease as an operating lease, FAS 13 states that a lease must be classified as a capital one if at least one of the following four criteria is met:

1. The present value of the lease payments is at least 90 percent of the fair market value of the asset at the start of the lease.
2. The lease transfers ownership of the property to the lessee by the end of the term of the lease.
3. The lease term is 75 percent or more of the estimated economic life of the asset.
4. The lessee can purchase the asset at a price below fair market value when the lease expires. This is frequently called a *bargain purchase price option.*

These rules capitalize leases that are similar to purchases. The first two rules capitalize leases where the asset is likely to be purchased at the end of the lease period. The last two rules capitalize long-term leases.

Some firms have tried to cook the books by exploiting this classification scheme. Suppose a trucking firm wants to lease a ₹200,000 truck that it expects to use for 15 years. A clever financial manager could try to negotiate a lease contract for 10 years with lease payments having a present value of ₹178,000. These terms would get around Criteria 1 and 3. If Criteria 2 and 4 could be circumvented, the arrangement would be an operating lease and would not show up on the balance sheet.

Why would it matter if the lease liability is disclosed but kept off the balance sheet? Recall from our discussion of behavioral finance in an earlier chapter that investors may pay less attention to disclosures of liabilities in the footnotes. The rule change in 2019 seems to recognize that the same information conveyed in the footnotes of disclosure documents does not have the same impact as direct disclosure of the lease liability on the balance sheet.

21.2a Indian Accounting Standard (Ind AS) 116 on Leases

In 2009, the Ministry of Corporate Affairs, Government of India, issued the converged Indian Accounting Standards (Ind ASs), with Ind AS 17 covering the Leases. In 2019, the Ministry of Corporate Affairs (MCA) notified Ind AS 116, the new leases accounting standard replacing the earlier accounting guidance in Ind AS-17, 'Leases'. The objectives of Ind AS 116 are to prescribe, for lessees and lessors, the appropriate accounting policies and disclosures in relation to finance leases and operating leases.

Unlike past practices, Ind AS 116 eliminated the classification of leases as a finance lease or operating lease. It introduces a single on-balance sheet accounting model wherein reporting of the operating leases will be on-balance sheet as if the company has borrowed funds to purchase a stake in the leased asset. Hence, the assets taken on lease would be recognized as assets having a corresponding lease liability, claiming depreciation and interest expense on the lease liability.

A lessor shall classify each lease as either an operating lease or a finance lease. A lease is considered a finance lease if it transfers substantially all the risks and rewards associated with ownership of the underlying asset. Conversely, a lease is classified as an operating lease if it does not transfer substantially all the risks and rewards associated with ownership of the underlying asset. Ind AS 116 applies to all leases, including sub-lease. The standard is applicable to hire purchase transactions as well.

21.3 Taxes, the Income Tax Authorities, and Leases

The lessee can deduct lease payments for income tax purposes if the lease is qualified by the Internal Revenue Service (in the U.S.A.) or the Income Tax Authority (in India). Because tax shields are critical to the economic viability of any lease, all interested parties generally obtain an opinion from the Income Tax Authorities before agreeing to a major lease transaction. The opinion of the Income Tax Authorities will reflect the following guidelines:

1. The term of the lease must be less than 30 years. If the term is greater than 30 years, the transaction will be regarded as a conditional sale.
2. The lease should not have an option to acquire the asset at a price below its fair market value. This type of bargain option would give the lessee the asset's residual scrap value, implying an equity interest.
3. The lease should not have a schedule of payments that is very high at the start of the lease term and thereafter very low. Early balloon payments would be evidence that the lease was being used to avoid taxes and not for a legitimate business purpose.
4. The lease payments must provide the lessor with a fair market rate of return. The profit potential of the lease to the lessor should be separate from the deal's tax benefits.
5. The lease should not limit the lessee's right to issue debt or pay dividends while the lease is operative.
6. Renewal options must be reasonable and reflect the fair market value of the asset. This requirement can be met by granting the lessee the first option to meet a competing outside offer.

The reason the Income Tax Authorities is concerned about lease contracts is that many times they appear to be set up solely to avoid taxes. To see how this could happen, suppose a firm plans to purchase a ₹1 million bus that has a five-year class life. Depreciation expense would be ₹200,000 per year, assuming straight-line depreciation. Now suppose the firm can lease the bus for ₹500,000 per year for two years and buy the bus for ₹1 at the end of the two-year term. The present value of the tax benefits from acquiring the bus would clearly be less than if the bus were leased. The speedup of lease payments would greatly benefit the firm and give it a form of accelerated depreciation. If the tax rates of the lessor and lessee are different, leasing can be a form of tax avoidance.

21.4 The Cash Flows of Leasing

In this section, we identify the basic cash flows used in evaluating a lease. Consider the decision confronting the Wadia Company, which manufactures pipe. Business has been expanding, and Wadia currently has a five-year backlog of pipe orders for the Barauni-Malda Pipeline.

The International Boring Machine Corporation (IBMC) makes a pipe-boring machine that can be purchased for ₹10,000. Wadia has determined that it needs a new machine, and the IBMC model will save Wadia ₹6,000 per year in reduced electricity bills for the next five years. These savings are known with certainty because Wadia has a long-term electricity purchase agreement with State Power Distribution Firms.

Wadia has a corporate tax rate of 21 percent. For simplicity, we assume that five-year straight-line depreciation is used for the pipe-boring machine and the machine will be worthless after five years.

Falguni Leasing Corporation has offered to lease the same pipe-boring machine to Wadia for ₹2,500 per year for five years. With the lease, Wadia would remain responsible for maintenance, insurance, and operating expenses.[2]

Sanjay Surana, a recently hired MBA, has been asked to calculate the incremental cash flows from leasing the IBMC machine in lieu of buying it. He has prepared Table 21.2, which shows the direct cash

[2] We have assumed that lease payments are made at the end of each year. In practice, most leases require lease payments to be made at the beginning of the year.

Table 21.2 Cash Flows to Wadia from Using the IBMC Pipe-Boring Machine: Buy versus Lease

	Year 0	Year 1	Year 2	Year 3	Year 4	Year 5
Buy						
Cost of machine	–₹ 10,000					
Aftertax operating savings						
[₹4,740 = ₹6,000 × (1 – .21)]		₹4,740	₹4,740	₹4,740	₹4,740	₹4,740
Depreciation tax benefit*		420	420	420	420	420
Total	–₹ 10,000	₹5,160	₹5,160	₹5,160	₹5,160	₹5,160
Lease						
Lease payments		–₹2,500	–₹2,500	–₹2,500	–₹2,500	–₹ 2,500
Tax benefits of lease payments						
(₹525 = ₹2,500 × .21)		525	525	525	525	525
Aftertax operating savings		4,740	4,740	4,740	4,740	4,740
Total		₹2,765	₹2,765	₹2,765	₹2,765	₹2,765

*Depreciation is straight-line. Because the depreciable base is ₹10,000, depreciation expense per year is ₹10,000/5 = ₹2,000.
The depreciation tax benefit per year is equal to:
Tax rate × Depreciation expense per year = .21 × ₹2,000 = ₹420

flow consequences of buying the pipe-boring machine and also signing the lease agreement with Falguni Leasing.

To simplify matters, Sanjay has prepared Table 21.3, which subtracts the direct cash flows of buying the pipe-boring machine from those of leasing it. Noting that only the net advantage of leasing is relevant to Wadia, he concludes the following from his analysis:

1. Operating costs are not directly affected by leasing. Wadia will save ₹4,740 (after taxes) from use of the IBMC boring machine regardless of whether the machine is owned or leased. This cash flow stream does not appear in Table 21.3.
2. If the machine is leased, Wadia will save the ₹10,000 it would have used to purchase the machine. This saving shows up as an initial cash *inflow* of ₹10,000 in Year 0.
3. If Wadia leases the pipe-boring machine, it will no longer own this machine and must give up the depreciation tax benefits. These lost tax benefits show up as an *outflow*.

Table 21.3 Incremental Cash Flow Consequences for Wadia from Leasing Instead of Purchasing

Lease Minus Buy	Year 0	Year 1	Year 2	Year 3	Year 4	Year 5
Lease						
Lease payments		–₹2,500	–2,500	–2,500	–2,500	–2,500
Tax benefits of lease payments		525	525	525	525	525
Buy (minus)						
Cost of machine	(–₹10,000)					
Lost depreciation tax benefit		–420	–420	–420	–420	–420
Total	₹ 10,000	–₹2,395	–2,395	–2,395	–2,395	–2,395

The bottom line presents the cash flows from leasing relative to the cash flows from purchasing. The cash flows would be exactly the opposite if we considered the purchase relative to the lease.

4. If Wadia chooses to lease the machine, it must pay ₹2,500 per year for five years. The first payment is due at the end of the first year. (This is a break: Often the first payment is due immediately.) The lease payments are tax deductible and, as a consequence, generate tax benefits of ₹525 (= .21 × ₹2,500).

The net cash flows have been placed in the bottom line of Table 21.3. These numbers represent the cash flows from leasing relative to the cash flows from the purchase. It is arbitrary that we express the cash flows in this way. We could have expressed the cash flows from the purchase relative to the cash flows from leasing. These cash flows would look like this:

	Year 0	Year 1	Year 2	Year 3	Year 4	Year 5
Net cash flows from purchase alternative relative to lease alternative	−₹10,000	₹2,395	₹2,395	₹2,395	₹2,395	₹2,395

Of course, the cash flows here are the opposite of those in the bottom line of Table 21.3. Depending on our purpose, we may look at either the purchase relative to the lease or vice versa. You should become comfortable with either viewpoint.

Now that we have the cash flows, we can make our decision by discounting the cash flows properly. However, because the discount rate is tricky, we take a detour in the next section before moving back to the Wadia case. In this next section, we show that cash flows in the lease-versus-buy decision should be discounted at the aftertax cost of debt.

A NOTE ABOUT TAXES

Sanjay has assumed that Wadia can use the tax benefits of the depreciation allowances and the lease payments. This may not always be the case. If Wadia were losing money (or had loss carryforwards), it would not pay taxes, and the tax shelters would be worthless (unless they could be shifted to someone else). As we mentioned before, this is one circumstance under which leasing may make a great deal of sense. If this were the case, the relevant entries in Table 21.2 would have to be changed to reflect a zero tax rate.

21.5 A Detour for Discounting and Debt Capacity with Corporate Taxes

The analysis of leases is difficult, and both financial practitioners and academics have made conceptual errors. These errors revolve around taxes. We hope to avoid their mistakes by beginning with the simplest type of example: a loan for one year. Though this example is unrelated to our lease-versus-buy situation, principles developed here will apply directly to lease-buy analysis.

PRESENT VALUE OF RISKLESS CASH FLOWS

Consider a corporation that lends ₹100 for a year. If the interest rate is 10 percent, the firm will receive ₹110 at the end of the year. Of this amount, ₹10 is interest and the remaining ₹100 is the original principal. A corporate tax rate of 21 percent implies taxes on the interest of ₹2.10 (= .21 × ₹10). The firm ends up with ₹107.90 (= ₹110 − 2.10) after taxes on a ₹100 investment.

Now consider a company that borrows ₹100 for a year. With a 10 percent interest rate, the firm must pay ₹110 to the bank at the end of the year. However, the borrowing firm can take the ₹10 of interest as a tax deduction. The corporation pays ₹2.10 (= .21 × ₹10) less in taxes than it would have paid had it not borrowed the money at all. Considering this reduction in taxes, the firm must repay ₹107.90 (= ₹110 − 2.10) on a ₹100 loan. The cash flows from both lending and borrowing are displayed in Table 21.4.

The previous two paragraphs show a very important result: The firm could not care less whether it received ₹100 today or ₹107.90 next year.[3] If it received ₹100 today, it could lend it out, thereby receiving ₹107.90 after corporate taxes at the end of the year. Conversely, if it knows today that it will receive ₹107.90 at the end of the year, it could borrow ₹100 today. The aftertax interest and principal payments on the loan would be paid with the ₹107.90 that the firm will receive at the end of the year. Because of this interchangeability, we say that a payment of ₹107.90 next year has a present value of ₹100. Because ₹100 = ₹107.90/1.079, a riskless cash flow should be discounted at the aftertax interest rate of .079 [= .10 × (1 − .21)].

Of course, the preceding discussion is a specific example. The general principle is this:

In a world with corporate taxes, the firm should discount riskless cash flows at the aftertax riskless rate of interest.

Table 21.4 Lending and Borrowing in a World with Corporate Taxes (interest rate is 10 percent and corporate tax rate is 21 percent)

Date 0		Date 1	
Lending example			
Lend ₹100		Receive	₹100.00 of principal
		Receive	₹ 10.00 of interest
	7.9% lending rate →	Pay	₹ 2.10 (= .21 × ₹10) in taxes
			₹107.90
Aftertax lending rate is 7.9%.			
Borrowing example			
Borrow ₹100		Pay	₹100.00 of principal
		Pay	₹ 10.00 of interest
	7.9% borrowing rate →	Receive	₹ 2.10 (= .21 × ₹10) as a tax rebate
			₹107.90
Aftertax borrowing rate is 7.9%.			

General principle: In a world with corporate taxes, riskless cash flows should be discounted at the aftertax riskless interest rate.

[3]For simplicity, assume that the firm received ₹100, or ₹107.90 after corporate taxes. The pretax inflows would be ₹126.58 [= ₹100/(1 − .21)] or ₹136.58 [= ₹107.90/(1 − .21)], respectively.

OPTIMAL DEBT LEVEL AND RISKLESS CASH FLOWS

In addition, our example can illustrate a related point concerning optimal debt level. Consider a firm that has determined that the current level of debt in its capital structure is optimal. Immediately following that determination, it is surprised to learn that it will receive a guaranteed payment of ₹107.90 in one year from a tax-exempt government lottery. This future windfall is an asset that, like any asset, should raise the firm's optimal debt level. How much does this payment raise the firm's optimal level?

Our analysis implies that the firm's optimal debt level must be ₹100 more than it previously was. That is, the firm could borrow ₹100 today, perhaps paying the entire amount out as a dividend. It would owe the bank ₹110 at the end of the year. Because it receives a tax rebate of ₹2.10 (= .21 × ₹10), its net repayment will be ₹107.90. The borrowing of ₹100 today is fully offset by next year's government lottery proceeds of ₹107.90. In other words, the lottery proceeds act as an irrevocable trust that can service the increased debt. Note that we do not need to know the optimal debt level before the lottery was announced. We are merely saying that whatever this pre-lottery optimal level was, the optimal debt level is ₹100 more after the lottery announcement.

Of course, this is just one example. The general principle is:[4]

In a world with corporate taxes, we determine the increase in the firm's optimal debt level by discounting a future guaranteed aftertax inflow at the aftertax riskless interest rate.

Conversely, suppose that a second, unrelated firm is surprised to learn that it must pay ₹107.90 next year to the government for back taxes. Clearly, this additional liability impinges on the second firm's debt capacity. By the previous reasoning, it follows that the second firm's optimal debt level must be lowered by exactly ₹100.

21.6 NPV Analysis of the Lease-versus-Buy Decision

Our detour leads to a simple method for evaluating leases: Discount all cash flows at the aftertax interest rate. From the bottom line of Table 21.3, Wadia's incremental cash flows from leasing versus purchasing are:

	Year 0	Year 1	Year 2	Year 3	Year 4	Year 5
Net cash flows from lease alternative relative to purchase alternative	₹10,000	−₹2,395	−₹2,395	−₹2,395	−₹2,395	−₹2,395

Let us assume that Wadia can either borrow or lend at the interest rate of 6.329114 percent. If the corporate tax rate is 21 percent, the correct discount rate is the aftertax rate of 5 percent [= .06329114 × (1 − .21)].When 5 percent is used to compute the NPV of the lease, we have:

$$\text{NPV} = ₹10{,}000 - ₹2{,}395 \times \text{PVIFA}_{5\%,\,5} = -₹369.10 \qquad \textbf{(21.1)}$$

Because the net present value of the incremental cash flows from leasing relative to purchasing is negative, Wadia prefers to purchase. The NPV we have computed here is often called the **net advantage to leasing**

[4]This principle holds for riskless or guaranteed cash flows only. Unfortunately, there is no easy formula for determining the increase in optimal debt level from a risky cash flow.

(NAL). Surveys indicate that the NAL approach is the most popular means of lease analysis in the real world.

Equation 21.1 is the correct approach to lease-versus-buy analysis. Students are often bothered by two things. First, they question whether the cash flows in Table 21.3 are truly riskless. We examine this issue next. Second, they feel that this approach lacks intuition. We address this concern a little later.

THE DISCOUNT RATE

Because we discounted at the aftertax riskless rate of interest, we have implicitly assumed that the cash flows in the Wadia example are riskless. Is this appropriate?

A lease payment is like the debt service on a secured bond issued by the lessee, and the discount rate should be the same as the interest rate on such debt. In general, this rate will be slightly higher than the riskless rate considered in the previous section. The various tax shields could be somewhat riskier than the lease payments for two reasons. First, the value of the depreciation tax benefits depends on the ability of Wadia to generate enough taxable income to use them. Second, the corporate tax rate may change in the future, just as it fell in 1986, increased in 1993, and fell again in 2018. For these two reasons, a firm might be justified in discounting the depreciation tax benefits at a rate higher than that used for the lease payments. Our experience is that real-world companies discount both the depreciation shield and lease payments at the same rate. This implies that financial practitioners view these two risks as minor. We adopt the real-world convention of discounting the two flows at the same rate. This rate is the aftertax interest rate on secured debt issued by the lessee.

At this point, some students still question why we use the aftertax interest rate on debt instead of the WACC as the discount rate in lease-versus-buy analysis. If fact, the aftertax interest rate on debt is equivalent to the WACC assuming that the project (leasing rather than buying) is financed fully with debt.

21.7 Debt Displacement and Lease Valuation

THE BASIC CONCEPT OF DEBT DISPLACEMENT

The previous analysis allows us to calculate the right answer in a simple manner. This clearly must be viewed as an important benefit. However, the analysis has little intuitive appeal. To remedy this, we hope to make lease-buy analysis more intuitive by considering the issue of debt displacement.

A firm that purchases equipment will generally issue debt to finance the purchase. The debt becomes a liability of the firm. A lessee incurs a liability equal to the present value of all future lease payments. Because of this, we argue that leases displace debt. The balance sheets in Table 21.5 illustrate how leasing might affect debt.

Suppose a firm initially has ₹100,000 of assets and a 150 percent optimal debt-equity ratio. The firm's debt is ₹60,000 and its equity is ₹40,000. As in the Wadia case, suppose the firm must use a new ₹10,000 machine. The firm has two alternatives:

1. *The firm can purchase the machine.* If it does, it will finance the purchase with a secured loan and with equity. The debt capacity of the machine is assumed to be the same as for the firm as a whole.
2. *The firm can lease the asset and get 100 percent financing.* That is, the present value of the future lease payments will be ₹10,000.

If the firm finances the machine with both secured debt and new equity, its debt will increase by ₹6,000 and its equity by ₹4,000. Its optimal debt-equity ratio of 150 percent will be maintained.

Table 21.5 Debt Displacement Elsewhere in the Firm When a Lease Is Instituted

Assets		Liabilities	
Initial situation			
Current	₹ 50,000	Debt	₹ 60,000
Fixed	50,000	Equity	40,000
Total	₹100,000	Total	₹100,000
Buy with secured loan			
Current	₹ 50,000	Debt	₹ 66,000
Fixed	50,000	Equity	44,000
Machine	10,000		
Total	₹110,000	Total	₹110,000
Lease			
Current	₹ 50,000	Lease	₹ 10,000
Fixed	50,000	Debt	56,000
Machine	10,000	Equity	44,000
Total	₹110,000	Total	₹110,000

This example shows that leases reduce the level of debt elsewhere in the firm. Though the example illustrates a point, it is not meant to show a precise method for calculating debt displacement.

Conversely, consider the lease alternative. Because the lessee views the lease payment as a liability, the lessee thinks in terms of a liability-equity ratio, not a debt-equity ratio. As mentioned, the present value of the lease liability is ₹10,000. If the leasing firm is to maintain a liability-equity ratio of 150 percent, debt elsewhere in the firm must fall by ₹4,000 when the lease is instituted. Because debt must be repurchased, net liabilities rise by only ₹6,000 (= ₹10,000 – 4,000) when ₹10,000 of assets are placed under lease.[5]

Debt displacement is a hidden cost of leasing. If a firm leases, it will not use as much regular debt as it would otherwise. The benefits of debt capacity will be lost–particularly the lower taxes associated with interest expense.

OPTIMAL DEBT LEVEL IN THE WADIA EXAMPLE

The previous section showed that leasing displaces debt. Though the section illustrated a point, it was not meant to show the precise method for calculating debt displacement. Here we describe the precise method for calculating the difference in optimal debt levels between the purchase and lease alternatives in the Wadia example.

From the last line of Table 21.3, we know these cash flows from the purchase alternative relative to the cash flows from the lease alternative:[6]

	Year 0	Year 1	Year 2	Year 3	Year 4	Year 5
Net cash flows from purchase alternative relative to lease alternative	–₹10,000	₹2,395	₹2,395	₹2,395	₹2,395	₹2,395

[5]Growing firms in the real world will not generally repurchase debt when instituting a lease. Rather, they will issue less debt in the future than they would have without the lease.

[6]The last line of Table 21.3 presents the cash flows from the lease alternative relative to the purchase alternative. As we pointed out earlier, our cash flows are reversed because we are now presenting the cash flows from the purchase alternative relative to the lease alternative.

An increase in the optimal debt level at Year 0 occurs because the firm learns at that time of guaranteed cash flows beginning at Year 1. Our detour into discounting and debt capacity told us to calculate this increased debt level by discounting the future riskless cash inflows at the aftertax interest rate.[7] The additional debt level of the purchase alternative relative to the lease alternative is:

$$₹10{,}369.10 = \frac{₹2{,}395}{1.05} + \frac{₹2{,}395}{1.05^2} + \frac{₹2{,}395}{1.05^3} + \frac{₹2{,}395}{1.05^4} + \frac{₹2{,}395}{1.05^5}$$

That is, whatever the optimal amount of debt would be under the lease alternative, the optimal amount of debt would be ₹10,369.10 more under the purchase alternative.

This result can be stated in another way. Imagine there are two identical firms except that one firm purchases the boring machine and the other leases it. From Table 21.3, we know that the purchasing firm generates ₹2,395 more cash flow after taxes in each of the five years than does the leasing firm. Further imagine that the same bank lends money to both firms. The bank should lend the purchasing firm more money because it has a greater cash flow each period. How much extra money should the bank lend the purchasing firm so that the incremental loan can be paid off by the extra cash flows of ₹2,395 per year? The answer is exactly ₹10,369.10–the increase in the optimal debt level we calculated earlier.

To see this, let us work through the example year by year. Because the purchasing firm borrows ₹10,369.10 more at Year 0 than does the leasing firm, the purchasing firm will pay interest of ₹656.27 (= ₹10,369.10 × .06329114) at Year 1 on the additional debt. The interest allows the firm to reduce its taxes by ₹137.82 (= ₹656.27 × .21), leaving an aftertax outflow of ₹518.45 (= ₹656.27 – 137.82) at Year 1.

We know from Table 21.3 that the purchasing firm generates ₹2,395 more cash at Year 1 than does the leasing firm. Because the purchasing firm has the extra ₹2,395 coming in at Year 1 but must pay interest on its loan, how much of the loan can the firm repay at Year 1 and still have the same cash flow as the leasing firm? The purchasing firm can repay ₹1,876.55 (= ₹2,395 – 518.45) of the loan at Year 1 and still have the same net cash flow that the leasing firm has. After the repayment, the purchasing firm will have a remaining balance of ₹8,492.55 (= ₹10,369.10 – 1,876.55) at Year 1. For each of the five years, this sequence of cash flows is displayed in Table 21.6. The outstanding balance goes to zero over the five years. The annual cash flow of ₹2,395, which represents the extra cash from purchasing instead of leasing, fully amortizes the loan of ₹10,369.10.

Table 21.6 Calculation of Increase in Optimal Debt Level if Wadia Purchases Instead of Leases

	Year 0	Year 1	Year 2	Year 3	Year 4	Year 5
Outstanding balance of loan	₹10,369.10	₹8,492.55*	₹6,522.18	₹4,453.29	₹2,280.95	₹ 0
Interest		656.27	537.50	412.80	281.85	144.36
Tax deduction on interest		137.82	112.88	86.69	59.19	30.32
Aftertax interest expense		₹ 518.45	₹ 424.63	₹ 326.11	₹ 222.66	₹ 114.05
Extra cash that purchasing firm generates over leasing firm (from Table 21.3)		₹2,395.00	₹2,395.00	₹2,395.00	₹2,395.00	₹2,395.00
Repayment of loan		₹1,876.55†	₹1,970.37	₹2,068.89	₹2,172.34	₹2,280.95

Assume that there are two otherwise identical firms: one leases and the other purchases. The purchasing firm can borrow ₹10,369.10 more than the leasing firm. The extra cash flow each year of ₹2,395 from purchasing instead of leasing can be used to pay off the loan in five years.

*₹8,492.55 = ₹10,369.10 – 1,876.55.

†₹1,876.55 = ₹2,395 – 518.45.

[7] Though our detour considered only riskless cash flows, the cash flows in a leasing example are not necessarily riskless. As we explained earlier, we adopt the real-world convention of discounting at the aftertax interest rate on secured debt issued by the lessee.

Our analysis of debt capacity has two purposes. First, we want to show the additional debt capacity from purchasing. We just completed this task. Second, we want to determine whether the lease is preferred to the purchase. This decision rule follows easily from our discussion. By leasing the equipment and having ₹10,369.10 less debt than under the purchasing alternative, the firm has exactly the same cash flows in Years 1 to 5 that it would have through a levered purchase. We can ignore cash flows beginning in Year 1 when comparing the lease alternative to the purchase-with-debt alternative. However, the cash flows differ between the alternatives at Year 0:

1. *The purchase cost at Year 0 of ₹10,000 is avoided by leasing.* This should be viewed as a cash inflow under the leasing alternative.
2. *The firm borrows ₹10,369.10 less at Year 0 under the lease alternative than it can under the purchase alternative.* This should be viewed as a cash outflow under the leasing alternative.

Because the firm borrows ₹10,369.10 less by leasing but saves only ₹10,000 on the equipment, the lease alternative requires an extra cash outflow at Year 0 relative to the purchase alternative of −₹369.10 (= ₹10,000 − 10,369.10). Because cash flows in later years from leasing are identical to those from purchasing with debt, the firm should purchase.

Two Methods for Calculating Net Present Value of Lease Relative to Purchase*

Method 1: Discount all cash flows at the aftertax interest rate:

$$-₹369.10 = ₹10{,}000 - ₹2{,}395 \times \text{PVIFA}_{5\%,\,5}$$

Method 2: Compare purchase price with reduction in optimal debt level under leasing alternative:

−₹369.10 =	₹10,000 −	10,369.10
	Purchase price	Reduction in optimal debt level if leasing

*Because we are calculating the NPV of the lease relative to the purchase, a negative value indicates that the purchase alternative is preferred.

This is exactly the same answer we got when, earlier in this chapter, we discounted all cash flows at the aftertax interest rate. Of course, this is no coincidence: The increase in the optimal debt level also is determined by discounting all cash flows at the aftertax interest rate. The accompanying box presents both methods. The numbers in the box are in terms of the NAL of the lease relative to the purchase. A negative NAL indicates that the purchase alternative should be taken.

21.8 Does Leasing Ever Pay? The Base Case

We previously looked at the lease-buy decision from the point of view of the potential lessee, Wadia. Let's now look at the decision from the point of view of the lessor, Falguni Leasing. This firm faces three cash flows, which are displayed in Table 21.7. First, Falguni purchases the machine for ₹10,000 at Year 0. Second, because the asset is depreciated straight-line over five years, the depreciation expense at the end of each of the five years is ₹2,000 (= ₹10,000/5). The yearly depreciation tax shield is ₹420 (= ₹2,000 × .21). Third, because the yearly lease payment is ₹2,500, the aftertax lease payment is ₹1,975 [= ₹2,500 × (1 − .21)].

Table 21.7 Cash Flows to Falguni Leasing as Lessor of IBMC Pipe-Boring Machine

	Year 0	Year 1	Year 2	Year 3	Year 4	Year 5
Cash for machine	–₹10,000					
Depreciation tax benefit (₹420 = ₹2,000 × .21)		₹ 420	₹ 420	₹ 420	₹ 420	₹ 420
Aftertax lease payment [₹1,975 = ₹2,500 × (1 – .21)]		1,975	1,975	1,975	1,975	1,975
Total	–₹10,000	₹2,395	₹2,395	₹2,395	₹2,395	₹2,395

These cash flows are the opposite of the cash flows to Wadia, the lessee (see the bottom line of Table 21.3).

Now examine the total cash flows to Falguni Leasing displayed in the bottom line of Table 21.7. Those of you with a good memory will notice something interesting. These cash flows are exactly the opposite of those of Wadia displayed in the bottom line of Table 21.3. Those of you with a healthy sense of skepticism may be thinking something interesting: "If the cash flows of the lessor are exactly the opposite of those of the lessee, the combined cash flow of the two parties must be zero each year. There does not seem to be any joint benefit to this lease. Because the net present value to the lessee was –₹369.10, the NAL to the lessor must be ₹369.10. The joint NAL is ₹0 (= –₹369.10 + 369.10). There does not appear to be any way for the NAL of both the lessor and the lessee to be positive at the same time. Because one party would inevitably lose money, the leasing deal could never fly."

This is one of the most important results of leasing. Though Table 21.7 concerns one particular leasing deal, the principle can be generalized. As long as (1) both parties are subject to the same interest and tax rates and (2) transaction costs are ignored, there can be no leasing deal that benefits both parties. However, there is a lease payment for which both parties would calculate an NAL of zero. Given that payment, Wadia would be indifferent to whether it leased or bought, and Falguni Leasing would be indifferent to whether it leased or not.[8]

A student with an even healthier sense of skepticism might be thinking, "This textbook appears to be arguing that leasing is not beneficial. Yet we know that leasing occurs frequently in the real world. Maybe, just maybe, the textbook is wrong." Although we will not admit to being wrong (what authors would?!), we freely admit that our explanation is incomplete at this point. The next section considers factors that give benefits to leasing.

21.9 Reasons for Leasing

Proponents of leasing make many claims about why firms should lease assets rather than buy them. Some of the reasons given to support leasing are good, and some are not. Here we discuss good reasons for leasing and those we think are not good.

GOOD REASONS FOR LEASING

Leasing is a good choice if at least one of the following is true:

1. Taxes will be reduced by leasing.
2. The lease contract will reduce certain types of uncertainty.

[8]The break-even lease payment is ₹2,392.09 in our example. Both the lessor and lessee can solve for this as follows:

$$₹10{,}000 = ₹420 \times \text{PVIFA}_{5\%,\,5} + L \times (1 - .21) \times \text{PVIFA}_{5\%,\,5}$$

In this case, L = ₹2,392.09.

3. Transaction costs will be higher for buying an asset and financing it with debt or equity than for leasing the asset.

Tax Advantages The most important reason for long-term leasing is tax reduction. If the corporate income tax were repealed, long-term leasing would probably disappear. The tax advantages of leasing exist because firms are in different tax brackets.

Should a user in a low tax bracket purchase, he will receive little tax benefit from depreciation and interest deductions. Should the user lease, the lessor will receive the depreciation shield and the interest deductions. In a competitive market, the lessor must charge a low lease payment to reflect these tax shields. The user is likely to lease rather than purchase.

In our example with Wadia and Falguni Leasing, the value of the lease to Falguni was ₹369.10:

$$₹369.10 = -₹10,000 + ₹2,395 \times \text{PVIFA}_{5\%,\ 5}$$

Of course the value of the lease to Wadia was exactly the opposite (–₹369.10). Because the lessor's gains came at the expense of the lessee, no deal could be arranged.

However, if Wadia pays no taxes and the lease payments are reduced to ₹2,393 from ₹2,500, both Falguni and Wadia will find positive NPVs in leasing. Wadia can rework Table 21.3 with $T_C = 0$, finding that its cash flows from leasing are now these:

	Year 0	Year 1	Year 2	Year 3	Year 4	Year 5
Cost of machine	₹10,000					
Lease payment		–₹2,393	–₹2,393	–₹2,393	–₹2,393	–₹2,393

The NAL to Wadia is:

$$\begin{aligned} \text{NAL} &= ₹10,000 - ₹2,393 \times \text{PVIFA}_{6.329114\%,\ 5} \\ &= ₹9.43 \end{aligned}$$

Notice that the discount rate is the interest rate of 6.329114 percent because tax rates are zero. In addition, the full lease payment of ₹2,393–and not some lower aftertax number–is used because there are no taxes. Finally, note that depreciation is ignored, also because no taxes apply.

Given a lease payment of ₹2,393, the cash flows to Falguni Leasing look like this:

	Year 0	Year 1	Year 2	Year 3	Year 4	Year 5
Cost of machine	–₹10,000					
Depreciation tax shield (₹420 = ₹2,000 × .21)		₹ 420	₹ 420	₹ 420	₹ 420	₹ 420
Aftertax lease payment [₹1,890.47 = ₹2,393 × (1 – .21)]		1,890.47	1,890.47	1,890.47	1,890.47	1,890.47
Total		₹2,310.47	₹2,310.47	₹2,310.47	₹2,310.47	₹2,310.47

The NAL to Falguni is:

$$\begin{aligned} \text{NAL} &= -₹10,000 + ₹2,310.47 \times \text{PVIFA}_{5\%,\ 5} \\ &= -₹10,000 + 10,003.13 \\ &= ₹3.13 \end{aligned}$$

As a consequence of different tax rates, the lessee (Wadia) gains ₹9.43 and the lessor (Falguni) gains ₹3.13. Both the lessor and the lessee can gain if their tax rates are different because the lessor uses the depreciation and interest tax shields that cannot be used by the lessee. The Income Tax Authorities loses tax revenue and some of the tax gains of the lessor are passed on to the lessee in the form of lower lease payments.

Because both parties can gain when tax rates differ, the lease payment is agreed upon through negotiation. Before negotiation begins, each party needs to know the *reservation* payment of both parties. This is the payment that will make one party indifferent to whether it enters the lease deal. In other words, this is the payment that makes the NAL equal to zero. These payments are calculated next.

Reservation Payment of Lessee We now solve for L_{MAX}, the payment that makes the value of the lease to the lessee zero. When the lessee is in a zero tax bracket, its cash flows, in terms of L_{MAX}, are as follows:

	Year 0	Year 1	Year 2	Year 3	Year 4	Year 5
Cost of machine	₹10,000					
Lease payment		$-L_{MAX}$	$-L_{MAX}$	$-L_{MAX}$	$-L_{MAX}$	$-L_{MAX}$

This table implies that:

$$\text{Value of lease} = ₹10{,}000 - L_{MAX} \times \text{PVIFA}_{6.329114\%,\ 5}$$

The value of the lease equals zero when:

$$L_{MAX} = \frac{₹10{,}000}{\text{PVIFA}_{6.329114\%,\ 5}} = ₹2{,}395.26$$

After performing this calculation, the lessor knows that the maximum payment the lessee will accept is ₹2,395.26.

Reservation Payment of Lessor We now solve for L_{MIN}, the payment that makes the value of the lease to the lessor zero. The cash flows to the lessor, in terms of L_{MIN}, are these:

	Year 0	Year 1	Year 2	Year 3	Year 4	Year 5
Cost of machine	−₹10,000					
Depreciation tax shield (₹420 = ₹2,000 × .21)		₹420	₹420	₹420	₹420	₹420
Aftertax lease payment (T_C = .21)		$L_{MIN} \times .79$	$L_{MIN} \times .79$	$L_{MIN} \times .79$	$L_{MIN} \times .79$	$L_{MIN} \times .79$

This table implies that:

$$\text{Value of lease} = -₹10{,}000 + ₹420 \times \text{PVIFA}_{5\%,\ 5} + L_{MIN} \times .79 \times \text{PVIFA}_{5\%,\ 5}$$

The NAL equals zero when:

$$\begin{aligned} L_{MIN} &= \frac{₹10{,}000}{.79 \times \text{PVIFA}_{5\%,5}} - \frac{₹420}{.79} \\ &= ₹2{,}923.73 - 531.65 \\ &= ₹2{,}392.09 \end{aligned}$$

After performing this calculation, the lessee knows that the lessor will never agree to a lease payment below ₹2,392.09.

A Reduction of Uncertainty We have noted that the lessee does not own the property when the lease expires. The value of the property at this time is called the *residual value*, and the lessor has a firm claim to it. When the lease contract is signed, there may be substantial uncertainty about what the residual value of the asset will be. Under a lease contract, this residual risk is borne by the lessor. Conversely, the user bears this risk when purchasing.

It is common sense that the party best able to bear a particular risk should do so. If the user has little risk aversion, she will not suffer by purchasing. However, if the user is highly averse to risk, she should find a third-party lessor more capable of assuming this burden.

This latter situation frequently arises when the user is a small or newly formed firm. Because the risk of the entire firm is likely to be quite high and because the principal stockholders are likely to be undiversified, the firm desires to minimize risk wherever possible. A potential lessor, such as a large, publicly held financial institution, is far more capable of bearing the risk. Conversely, this situation is not expected to happen when the user is a blue chip corporation. That potential lessee is more able to bear risk.

Transaction Costs The costs of changing an asset's ownership are generally greater than the costs of writing a lease agreement. Consider the choice that confronts a person who lives in Kanpur but must do business in Chennai for two days. It would clearly be cheaper to rent a hotel room for two nights than it would be to buy a condominium for two days and then to sell it.

Leases generate agency costs, as well. For example, the lessee might misuse or overuse the asset because she has no interest in the asset's residual value. This cost will be implicitly paid by the lessee through a high lease payment. Although the lessor can reduce these agency costs through monitoring, monitoring itself is costly. Leasing is most beneficial when the transaction costs of purchase and resale outweigh the agency costs and monitoring costs of a lease.

BAD REASONS FOR LEASING

Leasing and Accounting Income Leasing can have a significant effect on the appearance of the firm's financial statements. If a firm is successful at keeping its leases off the books, the balance sheet and, potentially, the income statement can be made to look better. As a consequence, accounting-based performance measures such as return on assets, or ROA, can appear to be higher. As we have mentioned, changes in lease accounting in 2019 made keeping leases off the books much more difficult.

One Hundred Percent Financing It is often claimed that leasing provides 100 percent financing, whereas secured equipment loans require an initial down payment. However, we argued earlier that leases tend to displace debt elsewhere in the firm. Our earlier analysis suggests that leases do not permit a greater level of total liabilities than do purchases with borrowing.

Other Reasons There are, of course, many special reasons that some companies find advantages in leasing. In one celebrated case, the U.S. Navy leased a fleet of tankers instead of asking Congress for appropriations. Thus, leasing may be used to circumvent capital expenditure control systems set up by bureaucratic firms. This is alleged to be a relativ ely common occurrence in hospitals. Likewise, many school districts lease buses and modular classrooms and pay for them out of their operating budgets when they are unable to gain approval for a bond issue to raise funds.

Some Indian Examples of Leasing

1. Tata Steel Limited, India's second-largest steel firm, wanted to replace its mining equipment for its West Bokaro mines. The cost of the equipment was around ₹100 crore. Tata Steel opted for leasing. GE Capital, SREI Intl. and IL&FS bade for the lease deal. Finally, Tata Steel decided to give the deal to IL&FS. The leasing period was 60 months, and the EMI came out to be ₹2.296 crore. The advance payment to the supplier was ₹5 crore, and ₹1 crore was paid upfront as lease management fees.
2. Air India invited global tenders for five aircraft on lease, enabling it to sell its four old aircraft. Singapore Airlines won this bid to provide the aircraft. This was structured as a 'dry lease' for 2 years, with monthly payments and involved a 15% upfront advance payment to Singapore Airlines. 'Dry lease' is the lease of the aircraft only, without crew. 'Wet lease' means a lease of an aircraft, including its crew. In a wet lease, the lessor provides the aircraft, one or more complete crews (including engineers) including their salaries and allowances, all maintenance for the aircraft itself and, usually, third-party liability cover. The deal involved the lessor (Singapore Airlines) charging for the aircraft hourly, with a minimum number of hours per month guaranteed by the lessee (Air India). For example, the lessor may charge US ₹1000 per hour but will want a minimum of 100 hours per month paid, irrespective of whether the lessee clocks 100 hours of travel in that month.

21.10 Some Unanswered Questions

Our analysis suggests that the primary advantage of long-term leasing results from the differential tax rates of the lessor and the lessee. Other valid reasons for leasing are lower contracting costs and risk reduction. There are several questions our analysis has not specifically answered.

ARE THE USES OF LEASES AND DEBT COMPLEMENTARY?

Ang and Peterson find that firms with high debt tend to lease frequently, as well.[9] This result should not be puzzling. The corporate attributes that provide high debt capacity also may make leasing advantageous. Even though leasing displaces debt (i.e., leasing and borrowing are substitutes) for an individual firm, high debt and high leasing can be positively associated when we look at a number of firms.

WHY ARE LEASES OFFERED BY BOTH MANUFACTURERS AND THIRD-PARTY LESSORS?

The offsetting effects of taxes can explain why both manufacturers and third-party lessors offer leases.

1. For manufacturer lessors, the basis for determining depreciation is the manufacturer's cost. For third-party lessors, the basis is the sales price that the lessor paid to the manufacturer. Because the sales price is generally greater than the manufacturer's cost, this is an advantage to third-party lessors.
2. The manufacturer must recognize a profit for tax purposes when selling the asset to the third-party lessor. The manufacturer's profit for some equipment can be deferred if the manufacturer becomes the lessor. This provides an incentive for manufacturers to lease.

[9] James Ang and Pamela P. Peterson, "The Leasing Puzzle," *Journal of Finance* 39, no. 4 (September 1984): 1055–65.

WHY ARE SOME ASSETS LEASED MORE THAN OTHERS?

Certain assets appear to be leased more frequently than others. Smith and Wakeman have looked at nontax incentives affecting leasing.[10] Their analysis suggests many asset and firm characteristics that are important in the lease-versus-buy decision. The following are among the things they mention:

The more sensitive the value of an asset is to use and maintenance decisions, the more likely it is that the asset will be purchased instead of leased. They argue that ownership provides a better incentive to minimize maintenance costs than does leasing.

Price discrimination opportunities may be important. Leasing may be a way of circumventing laws against charging too low a price.

[10]Clifford W. Smith Jr. and L. MacDonald Wakeman, "Determinants of Corporate Leasing Policy," *Journal of Finance* 40, no. 3 (July 1985): 895–908.

RESEARCH IN EMERGING MARKET CONTEXT

Zhang et al. (2019) discovered that a lower level of financial leasing can enhance the impact of bank loans on economic growth. However, as the lease financing level increases, bank loans' effect on economic growth becomes limited. Therefore, countries must balance financial leasing and bank lending based on their specific economic and financial infrastructure to maximize the role of different financing tools in promoting the economy.

In fact, leasing is an important aspect of the circular business model. However, a study by Agrawal et al. (2021) found that combining leasing with modularity, a circular product design strategy, does not always result in lower environmental or social welfare costs than leasing or selling modular products separately.

References

Vishal Agrawal, Atalay Atasu, Sezer Ülkü (2021). Leasing, Modularity, and the Circular Economy. *Management Science 67*(11):6782–6802.

Zhang, Y., Zhai, L., & Sun, H. (2019). Does the level of financial leasing matter in the impact of bank lending on economic growth: Evidence from the global market (2006–2016). *Finance Research Letters, 30*, 352–359.

Summary and Conclusions

A large fraction of America's equipment is leased rather than purchased. This chapter both described the institutional arrangements surrounding leases and showed how to evaluate leases financially.

1. Leases can be separated into two types: financial and operating. Financial leases are generally longer-term, fully amortized, and not cancelable without a hefty termination payment. Operating leases are usually shorter-term, partially amortized, and cancelable.
2. When a firm purchases an asset with debt, both the asset and the liability appear on the firm's balance sheet. If a lease meets at least one of a number of criteria, it must be capitalized. This means that the present value of the lease appears as both an asset and a liability. A lease escapes capitalization if it does not meet any of these criteria.

Leases not meeting the criteria are called operating leases, though the accountant's definition differs somewhat from the practitioner's definition. Operating leases are reported on the balance sheet beginning in 2019.

3. Firms generally lease for tax purposes. To protect its interests, the Income Tax Authorities allows financial arrangements to be classified as leases only if a number of criteria are met.
4. We showed that risk-free cash flows should be discounted at the aftertax risk-free rate. Because both lease payments and depreciation tax shields are nearly riskless, all relevant cash flows in the lease-versus-buy decision should be discounted at a rate near this aftertax rate. We use the real-world convention of discounting at the aftertax interest rate on the lessee's secured debt.
5. To further explain this topic, we presented an alternative method in the hopes of increasing the reader's intuition. Relative to a lease, a purchase generates debt capacity. This increase in debt capacity can be calculated by discounting the difference between the cash flows of the purchase and the cash flows of the lease by the aftertax interest rate. The increase in debt capacity from a purchase is compared to the extra outflow at Year 0 from a purchase.
6. If the lessor is in the same tax bracket as the lessee, the cash flows to the lessor are exactly the opposite of the cash flows to the lessee. Thus, the sum of the value of the lease to the lessee plus the value of the lease to the lessor must be zero. Although this suggests that leases are never advantageous, there are actually at least three good reasons for leasing:
   a. Differences in tax brackets between the lessor and lessee.
   b. Shift of risk bearing to the lessor.
   c. Minimization of transaction costs.

Concept Questions

1. **Leasing versus Borrowing** What are the key differences between leasing and borrowing? Are they perfect substitutes?
2. **Leasing and Taxes** Taxes are an important consideration in the leasing decision. Which is more likely to lease: A profitable corporation in a high tax bracket or a less profitable one in a low tax bracket? Why?
3. **Leasing and IRR** What are some of the potential problems with looking at IRRs when evaluating a leasing decision?
4. **Leasing** Comment on the following remarks:
   a. Leasing reduces risk and can reduce a firm's cost of capital.
   b. Leasing provides 100 percent financing.
   c. If the tax advantages of leasing were eliminated, leasing would disappear.
5. **Income Tax Authorities Criteria** Discuss the Income Tax Authorities criteria for determining whether a lease is tax deductible. In each case, give a rationale for the criterion.
6. **Sale and Leaseback** Why might a firm choose to engage in a sale and leaseback transaction? Give two reasons.
7. **Leasing Cost** Explain why the aftertax borrowing rate is the appropriate discount rate to use in lease evaluation.

   Refer to the following example for Questions 8–10. In September 2020, Australia's Regional Express Ltd. announced that it had leased six Boeing 737-800 aircraft to fly the Sydney-Melbourne route.
8. **Leasing versus Purchase** Why wouldn't Regional Express Ltd. purchase the planes if they were obviously needed for the company's operations?

9. **Reasons to Lease** Why would the lessors be willing to buy planes from Boeing and then lease the planes to Regional Express Ltd.? How is this different from lending money to Regional Express Ltd. to buy the planes?

10. **Leasing** What do you suppose happens to the plane at the end of the lease period?

Questions and Problems

BASIC (Questions 1–8)

Use the following information to work Problems 1–6. You work for a nuclear research laboratory that is contemplating leasing a diagnostic scanner (leasing is a common practice with expensive, high-tech equipment). The scanner costs ₹4.3 million and would be depreciated straight-line to zero over four years. Because of radiation contamination, it will actually be completely valueless in four years. You can lease it for ₹1.275 million per year for four years.

1. **Lease or Buy** Assume that the tax rate is 21 percent. You can borrow at 8 percent before taxes. Should you lease or buy?

2. **Leasing Cash Flows** What are the cash flows from the lease from the lessor's viewpoint? Assume a 21 percent tax rate.

3. **Finding the Break-Even Payment** What would the lease payment have to be for both the lessor and the lessee to be indifferent about the lease?

4. **Taxes and Leasing Cash Flows** Assume that your company does not contemplate paying taxes for the next several years. What are the cash flows from leasing in this case?

5. **Setting the Lease Payment** In the previous question, over what range of lease payments will the lease be profitable for both parties?

6. **MACRS Depreciation and Leasing** Rework Problem 1 assuming that the scanner will be depreciated as 3-year property under MACRS (see Chapter 6 for the depreciation allowances).

7. **Lease or Buy** Kaleidescope Entertainment is considering buying a machine that costs ₹625,000. The machine will be depreciated over five years by the straight-line method and will be worthless after five years. The company can lease the machine with year-end payments of ₹155,000. The company can issue bonds at an interest rate of 7 percent. If the corporate tax rate is 21 percent, should the company buy or lease?

8. **Setting the Lease Payment** Quartz Corporation is a relatively new firm. Quartz has experienced enough losses during its early years to provide it with at least eight years of tax loss carryforwards, so Quartz's effective tax rate is zero. Quartz plans to lease equipment from New Leasing Company. The term of the lease is five years. The purchase cost of the equipment is ₹725,000. New Leasing Company is in the 23 percent tax bracket. Each firm can borrow at 9 percent.
   a. What is Quartz's reservation price?
   b. What is New Leasing Company's reservation price?
   c. Explain why these reservation prices determine the negotiating range of the lease.

INTERMEDIATE (Questions 9–16)

Use the following information to work Problems 9–11. The Wildcat Oil Company is trying to decide whether to lease or buy a new computer-assisted drilling system for its oil exploration business. Management has decided that it must use the system to stay competitive; it will provide ₹2.8 million in annual pretax cost savings. The system costs ₹8.78 million and will be depreciated straight-line to zero over five years. Wildcat's tax rate is 21 percent and the firm can borrow at 7 percent. Lambert Leasing Company has offered to lease the drilling equipment to Wildcat for payments of ₹1.95 million per year. Lambert's policy is to require its lessees to make payments at the start of the year.

9. **Lease or Buy** What is the NAL for Wildcat? What is the maximum lease payment that would be acceptable to the company?

10. **Leasing and Salvage Value** Suppose it is estimated that the equipment will have an aftertax residual value of ₹900,000 at the end of the lease. What is the maximum lease payment acceptable to Wildcat now?

11. **Deposits in Leasing** Many lessors require a security deposit in the form of a cash payment or other pledged collateral. Suppose Lambert requires Wildcat to pay a ₹600,000 security deposit at the inception of the lease. If the lease payment is still ₹1.95 million, is it advantageous for Wildcat to lease the equipment now?

12. **Debt Capacity** Montclair Manufacturing is considering leasing some equipment. The annual lease payment would be ₹420,000 per year for six years. The appropriate interest rate is 6 percent and the company is in the 21 percent tax bracket. How would signing the lease affect the debt capacity for the company?

13. **Setting the Lease Price** An asset costs ₹825,000 and will be depreciated in a straight-line manner over its three-year life. It will have no salvage value. The corporate tax rate is 22 percent and the appropriate interest rate is 7 percent.
    a. What set of lease payments will make the lessee and the lessor equally well off?
    b. Show the general condition that will make the value of a lease to the lessor the negative of the value to the lessee.
    c. Assume that the lessee pays no taxes and the lessor is in the 22 percent tax bracket. For what range of lease payments does the lease have a positive NPV for both parties?

14. **Lease or Buy** Wolfson Corporation has decided to purchase a new machine that costs ₹2.1 million. The machine will be depreciated on a straight-line basis and will be worthless after four years. The corporate tax rate is 24 percent. The Sur Bank has offered Wolfson a four-year loan for ₹2.1 million. The repayment schedule is four yearly principal repayments of ₹525,000 and an interest charge of 9 percent on the outstanding balance of the loan at the beginning of each year. Both principal repayments and interest are due at the end of each year. Cal Leasing Corporation offers to lease the same machine to Wolfson. Lease payments of ₹640,000 per year are due at the beginning of each of the four years of the lease.
    a. Should Wolfson lease the machine or buy it with bank financing?
    b. What is the annual lease payment that will make Wolfson indifferent to whether it leases the machine or purchases it?

15. **Setting the Lease Price** An asset costs ₹745,000 and will be depreciated in a straight-line manner over its three-year life. It will have no salvage value. The lessor can borrow at 6 percent and the lessee can borrow at 9 percent. The corporate tax rate is 21 percent for both companies.
    a. How does the fact that the lessor and lessee have different borrowing rates affect the calculation of the NAL?
    b. What set of lease payments will make the lessee and the lessor equally well off?
    c. Assume that the lessee pays no taxes and the lessor is in the 21 percent tax bracket. For what range of lease payments does the lease have a positive NPV for both parties?

16. **Automobile Lease Payments** Automobiles are often leased, and several terms are unique to auto leases. Suppose you are considering leasing a car. The price you and the dealer agree on for the car is ₹49,500. This is the base capitalized cost. Other costs added to the capitalized cost price include the acquisition (bank) fee, insurance, or extended warranty. Assume these costs are ₹850. Capitalization cost reductions include any down payment, credit for trade-in, or dealer rebate. Assume you make a down payment of ₹5,000, and there is no trade-in or rebate. If you drive 10,000 miles per year, the lease-end residual value for this car will be ₹28,500 after three years. The lease or "money" factor, which is the interest rate on the loan, is the APR of the loan divided by 2,400.[11] The lease factor the dealer quotes you is .00185.

[11]The money factor of 2,400 is the product of three numbers: 2, 12, and 100. The 100 is used to convert the APR, expressed as a percentage, to a decimal number. The 12 converts this rate to a monthly rate. Finally, the monthly rate is applied to the sum of the net capitalization cost plus the residual. If we divide this sum by 2, the result is the average anticipated book value. Thus, the end result of the calculation using the money factor is to multiply a monthly rate by the average book value to get a monthly payment.

The monthly lease payment consists of three parts: a depreciation fee, a finance fee, and sales tax. The depreciation fee is the net capitalization cost minus the residual value, divided by the term of the lease. The net capitalization cost is the cost of the car minus any cost reductions plus any additional costs. The finance fee is the net capitalization cost plus the residual, times the money factor, and the monthly sales tax is the depreciation payment plus the finance fee, times the tax rate. What APR is the dealer quoting you? What is your monthly lease payment for a 36-month lease if the sales tax is 7 percent?

CHALLENGE (Questions 17–18)

17. **Lease versus Borrow** Return to the case of the diagnostic scanner discussed in Problems 1 through 6. Suppose the entire ₹4.3 million purchase price of the scanner is borrowed. The rate on the loan is 8 percent and the loan will be repaid in equal installments. Create a lease-versus-buy analysis that explicitly incorporates the loan payments. Show that the NPV of leasing instead of buying is not changed from what it was in Problem 1. Why is this so?

18. **Lease or Buy** High electricity costs have made Farmer Corporation's chicken-plucking machine economically worthless. Only two machines are available to replace it. The International Plucking Machine (IPM) model is available only on a lease basis. The lease payments will be ₹80,000 for five years, due at the beginning of each year. This machine will save Farmer ₹29,000 per year through reductions in electricity costs. As an alternative, Farmer can purchase a more energy-efficient machine from Basic Machine Corporation (BMC) for ₹365,000. This machine will save ₹32,000 per year in electricity costs. A local bank has offered to finance the machine with a loan. The interest rate on the loan will be 10 percent on the remaining balance and will require five annual principal payments of ₹73,000. Farmer has a target debt-asset ratio of 67 percent and a tax rate of 21 percent. After five years, both machines will be worthless. The machines will be depreciated on a straight-line basis.

   a. Should Farmer lease the IPM machine or purchase the more efficient BMC machine?
   b. Does your answer depend on the form of financing for direct purchase?
   c. How much debt is displaced by this lease?

19. **Cost of Lease:** In Section 21.9, we detailed a lease deal done by Tata Steel with IL&FS Limited for replacement of mining equipment in West Bokaro mines. With the details provided, estimate the cost of lease for Tata Steel Limited. How would you approach the problem when given the task to compare the deal with its option of equipment credit with a manufacturer?

Mini Case THE DECISION TO LEASE OR BUY AT WARF COMPUTERS

Warf Computers has decided to proceed with the manufacture and distribution of the virtual keyboard (VK) the company has developed. To undertake this venture, the company needs to obtain equipment for the production of the microphone for the keyboard. Because of the required sensitivity of the microphone and its small size, the company needs specialized equipment for production.

Nick Warf, the company president, has found a vendor for the equipment. Clapton Acoustical Equipment has offered to sell Warf Computers the necessary equipment at a price of ₹7.93 million. Because of the rapid development of new technology, the equipment falls in the three-year MACRS depreciation class. At the end of four years, the market value of the equipment is expected to be ₹1.02 million.

Alternatively, the company can lease the equipment from Hendrix Leasing. The lease contract calls for four annual payments of ₹1.924 million, due at the beginning of each year. Additionally, Warf Computers must make a security deposit of ₹520,000 that will be returned when the lease expires. Warf Computers can issue bonds with a yield of 11 percent and the company has a marginal tax rate of 21 percent.

1. Should Warf buy or lease the equipment?
2. Nick mentions to James Hendrix, the president of Hendrix Leasing, that although the company will need the equipment for four years, he would like a lease contract for two years instead. At the end of the two

years, the lease could be renewed. Nick also would like to eliminate the security deposit, but he would be willing to increase the lease payments to ₹2,307,500 for each of the two years. When the lease is renewed in two years, Hendrix would consider the increased lease payments in the first two years when calculating the terms of the renewal. The equipment is expected to have a market value of ₹4.2 million in two years. What is the NAL of the lease contract under these terms? Why might Nick prefer this lease? What are the potential ethical issues concerning the new lease terms?

3. In the leasing discussion, James informs Nick that the contract could include a purchase option for the equipment at the end of the lease. Hendrix Leasing offers three purchase options:
   a. An option to purchase the equipment at the fair market value.
   b. An option to purchase the equipment at a fixed price. The price will be negotiated before the lease is signed.
   c. An option to purchase the equipment at a price of ₹500,000.

   How would the inclusion of a purchase option affect the value of the lease?
4. James also informs Nick that the lease contract can include a cancellation option. The cancellation option would allow Warf Computers to cancel the lease on any anniversary date of the contract. In order to cancel the lease, Warf Computers would be required to give 30 days' notice prior to the anniversary date. How would the inclusion of a cancellation option affect the value of the lease?

Appendix 21A APV Approach to Leasing

To access the appendix for this chapter, please log on to www.mheducation.co.in.

22

PART VI: OPTIONS, FUTURES, AND CORPORATE FINANCE

Options and Corporate Finance

On December 2, 2020, the closing stock prices for cell phone company Verizon, consumer food company General Mills, and biofuel company Renewable Energy were ₹61.36, ₹60.22, and ₹59.66, respectively. Each company had a call option trading on the Chicago Board Options Exchange with a ₹60 strike price and an expiration date of April 21, 2021—140 days away. You might expect that the prices on these call options would be similar, but they weren't. Verizon's options sold for ₹2.97, General Mills' options traded at ₹3.50, and Renewable Energy's options traded at ₹10.40. Why would options on these three similarly priced stocks be priced so differently when the strike prices and the time to expiration were exactly the same? A big reason is that the volatility of the underlying stock is an important determinant of an option's underlying value, and these three stocks had very different volatilities. In this chapter, we explore this issue—and many others—in much greater depth using the Nobel Prize–winning Black-Scholes option pricing model.

Please visit us at **rwjcorporatefinance.blogspot.com** for the latest developments in the world of corporate finance.

22.1 Options

An **option** is a contract giving its owner the right to buy or sell an asset at a fixed price on or before a given date. An option on a building might give the buyer the right to buy the building for ₹1 million on or anytime before the Saturday prior to the third Wednesday in January 2026. Options are a unique type of financial contract because they give the buyer the right, but not the *obligation*, to do something. The buyer uses the option only if it is advantageous to do so; otherwise the option can be thrown away.

The Options Industry Council has a web page with lots of educational material at **www.optionseducation.org**.

There is a special vocabulary associated with options. Here are some important definitions:

1. *Exercising the option*: The act of buying or selling the underlying asset via the option contract.
2. *Strike, or exercise, price*: The fixed price in the option contract at which the holder can buy or sell the underlying asset.
3. *Expiration date*: The maturity date of the option; after this date, the option is dead.
4. *American and European options*: An American option may be exercised anytime up to the expiration date. A European option differs from an American option in that it can be exercised only on the expiration date.

22.2 Call Options

The most common type of option is a **call option**. A call option gives the owner the right to buy an asset at a fixed price during a particular period. There is no restriction on the kind of asset, but the most common ones traded on exchanges are options on stocks and bonds.

For example, call options on IBM stock can be purchased on the Chicago Board Options Exchange. IBM does not issue (i.e., sell) call options on its common stock. Instead, individual investors are the original buyers and sellers of call options on IBM common stock. Suppose it is April 1. A representative call option on IBM stock enables an investor to buy 100 shares of IBM on or before September 19 (options expire on the Saturday after the third Friday of the month) at an exercise price of ₹100. This is a valuable option if there is some probability that the price of IBM common stock will exceed ₹100 on or before September 19.

THE VALUE OF A CALL OPTION AT EXPIRATION

What is the value of a call option contract on common stock at expiration? The answer depends on the value of the underlying stock at expiration.

Let's continue with the IBM example. Suppose the stock price is ₹130 at expiration. The buyer of the call option has the right to buy the underlying stock at the exercise price of ₹100.[1] In other words, he has the right to exercise the call. Having the right to buy something for ₹100 when it is worth ₹130 is obviously a good thing. The value of this right is ₹30 (= ₹130 − 100) on the expiration day.[2]

The call would be worth even more if the stock price was higher on the expiration day. If IBM were selling for ₹150 on the date of expiration, the call would be worth ₹50 (= ₹150 − 100) at that time. In fact, the call's value increases ₹1 for every ₹1 rise in the stock price.

If the stock price is greater than the exercise price, we say that the call is *in the money*. Of course, it is also possible that the value of the common stock will turn out to be less than the exercise price, in which case we say that the call is *out of the money*. The holder will not exercise in this case. If the stock price at the expiration date is ₹90, no rational investor would exercise. Why pay ₹100 for stock worth only ₹90? Because the option holder has no obligation to exercise the call, she can walk away from the option. As a consequence, if IBM's stock price is less than ₹100 on the expiration date, the value of the call option will be ₹0. In this case, the value of the call option is not the difference between IBM's stock price and ₹100, as it would be if the holder of the call option had the obligation to exercise the call.

Here is the payoff of this call option at expiration:

	Payoff on the Expiration Date	
	If Stock Price Is Less Than ₹100	If Stock Price Is Greater Than ₹100
Call option value	₹0	Stock price − ₹100

Figure 22.1 plots the value of the call option at expiration against the value of IBM's stock. This is referred to as the *hockey stick diagram* of call option values. If the stock price is less than ₹100, the call is out of the money and worthless. If the stock price is greater than ₹100, the call is in the money and its value rises one-for-one with increases in the stock price. Notice that the call can never have a negative value. It is a *limited liability instrument*, which means that all the holder can lose is the initial amount she paid for it.

[1]We use *buyer*, *owner*, and *holder* interchangeably.

[2]This example assumes that the call lets the holder purchase one share of stock at ₹100. In reality, one call option contract would let the holder purchase 100 shares. The profit would then equal ₹3,000 [= (₹130 − 100) × 100].

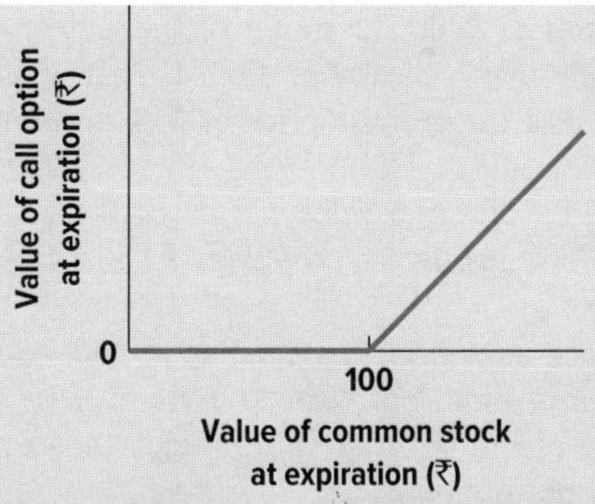

A call option gives the owner the right to buy an asset at a fixed price during a particular time period. If, at the expiration date, IBM's stock price is greater than the exercise price of ₹100, the call's value is:

Stock price − ₹100

If IBM's stock price is less than ₹100 at this time, the value of the call is zero.

Figure 22.1 The Value of a Call Option on the Expiration Date

EXAMPLE 22.1

Call Option Payoffs Suppose Mr. Sukhiram holds a one-year call option on RNRL common stock. It is a European call option and can be exercised at ₹150. Assume that the expiration date has arrived. What is the value of the RNRL call option on the expiration date? If RNRL is selling for ₹200 per share, Mr. Sukhiram can exercise the option—purchase RNRL at ₹150—and then immediately sell the share at ₹200. Mr. Sukhiram will have made ₹50 (= ₹200 − 150). The price of this call option must be ₹50 at expiration.

Instead, assume that RNRL is selling for ₹100 per share on the expiration date. If Mr. Sukhiram still holds the call option, he will throw it out. The value of the RNRL call option on the expiration date will be zero in this case.

22.3 Put Options

A **put option** can be viewed as the opposite of a call option. Just as a call gives the holder the right to buy the stock at a fixed price, a put gives the holder the right to *sell* the stock for a fixed exercise price.

THE VALUE OF A PUT OPTION AT EXPIRATION

The circumstances that determine the value of the put are the opposite of those for a call option because a put option gives the holder the right to sell shares. Let us assume that the exercise price of the put is

₹50 and the stock price at expiration is ₹40. The owner of this put option has the right to sell the stock for *more* than it is worth, something that is clearly profitable. That is, he can buy the stock at the market price of ₹40 and immediately sell it at the exercise price of ₹50, generating a profit of ₹10 (= ₹50 – 40). The value of the option at expiration must be ₹10.

The profit would be greater still if the stock price was lower. If the stock price were only ₹30, the value of the option would be ₹20 (= ₹50 – 30). In fact, for every ₹1 that the stock price declines at expiration, the value of the put rises by ₹1.

However, suppose that the stock at expiration is trading at ₹60–or any price above the exercise price of ₹50. The owner of the put option would not want to exercise here. It is a losing proposition to sell a stock for ₹50 when it trades in the open market at ₹60. Instead, the owner of the put will walk away from the option. That is, he will let the put option expire.

Here is the payoff of this put option:

	Payoff on the Expiration Date	
	If Stock Price Is Less Than ₹50	If Stock Price Is Greater Than ₹50
Put option value	₹50 – Stock price	₹0

Figure 22.2 plots the values of a put option for all possible values of the underlying stock. It is helpful to compare Figure 22.2 to Figure 22.1 for the call option. The call option is valuable when the stock price is above the exercise price and the put option is valuable when the stock price is below the exercise price.

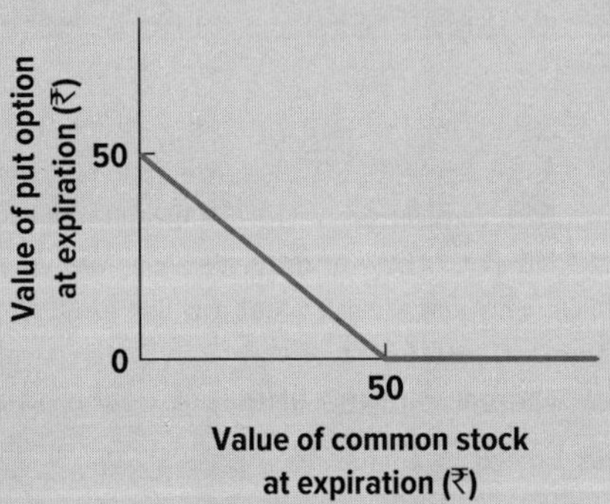

A put option gives the owner the right to sell an asset at a fixed price during a particular period. If the stock price is greater than the exercise price of ₹50, the put value is zero. If the stock price is less than ₹50, the put value is:

₹50 – Stock price

Figure 22.2 The Value of a Put Option on the Expiration Date

EXAMPLE 22.2

Put Option Payoffs Ms. Dukhiram believes that BPCL will fall from its current ₹160 per-share price. She buys a put. Her put option contract gives her the right to sell a share of BPCL stock at ₹150 one year from now. If the price of BPCL is ₹200 on the expiration date, she will tear up the put option contract because it is worthless. That is, she will not want to sell stock worth ₹200 for the exercise price of ₹150.

On the other hand, if BPCL is selling for ₹100 on the expiration date, she will exercise the option. In this case, she can buy a share of BPCL in the market for ₹100 per share and turn around and sell the share at the exercise price of ₹150. Her profit will be ₹50 (= ₹150 − 100). Therefore, the value of the put option on the expiration date will be ₹50.

22.4 Selling Options

Check out these option exchanges:
www.bseindia.com
www.nseindia.com
www.cboe.com
www.nasdaq.com
www.cmegroup.com
www.euronext.com

An investor who sells (or *writes*) a call on common stock must deliver shares of the common stock if required to do so by the call option holder. Notice that the seller is obligated to do so.

If, at the expiration date, the price of the common stock is greater than the exercise price, the holder will exercise the call and the seller must give the holder shares of stock in exchange for the exercise price. The seller loses the difference between the stock price and the exercise price. Assume that the stock price is ₹60 and the exercise price is ₹50. Knowing that exercise is imminent, the option seller buys stock in the open market at ₹60. Because she is obligated to sell at ₹50, she loses ₹10 (= ₹50 − 60). Conversely, if at the expiration date, the price of the common stock is below the exercise price, the call option will not be exercised and the seller's liability is zero.

Why would the seller of a call place himself in such a precarious position? After all, the seller loses money if the stock price ends up above the exercise price, and merely avoids losing money if the stock price ends up below the exercise price. The answer is that the seller is paid to take this risk. On the day that the option transaction takes place, the seller receives the price that the buyer pays.

Now let's look at the seller of puts. An investor who sells a put on common stock agrees to purchase shares of common stock if the put holder should so request. The seller loses on this deal if the stock price falls below the exercise price. Assume that the stock price is ₹40 and the exercise price is ₹50. The holder of the put will exercise in this case. In other words, she will sell the underlying stock at the exercise price of ₹50. This means that the seller of the put must buy the underlying stock at the exercise price of ₹50. Because the stock is worth only ₹40, the loss here is ₹10 (= ₹40 − 50).

The values of the *sell-a-call* and *sell-a-put* positions are depicted in Figure 22.3. The graph on the left side of the figure shows that the seller of a call loses nothing when the stock price at the expiration date is below ₹50. However, the seller loses a Rupee for every Rupee that the stock rises above ₹50. The graph in the center of the figure shows that the seller of a put loses nothing when the stock price at expiration date is above ₹50. However, the seller loses a Rupee for every Rupee that the stock falls below ₹50.

It is worthwhile to spend a few minutes comparing the graphs in Figure 22.3 to those in Figures 22.1 and 22.2. The graph of selling a call (the graph on the left side of Figure 22.3) is the mirror image

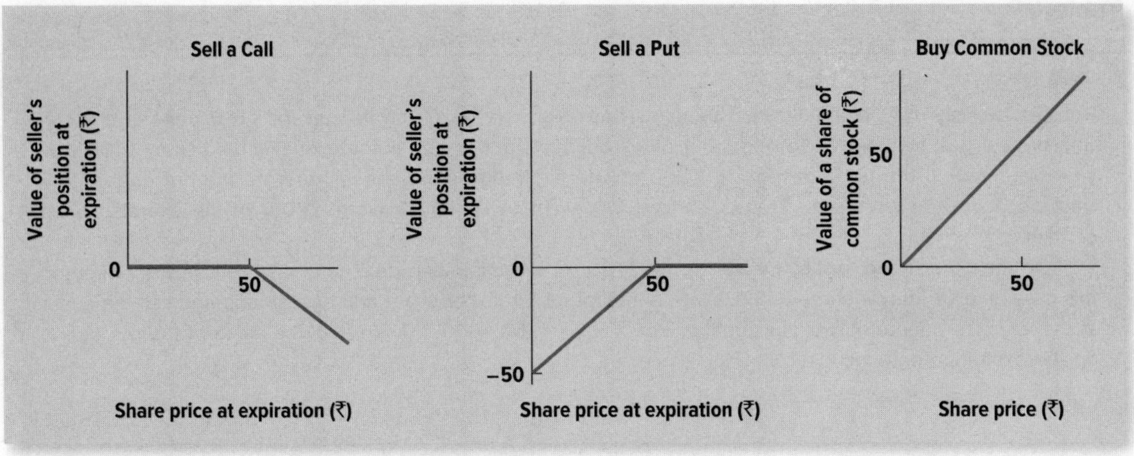

Figure 22.3 The Payoffs to Sellers of Calls and Puts and to Buyers of Common Stock

of the graph of buying a call (Figure 22.1).[3] This occurs because options are a zero-sum game. The seller of a call loses what the buyer makes. Similarly, the graph of selling a put (the middle graph in Figure 22.3) is the mirror image of the graph of buying a put (Figure 22.2). Again, the seller of a put loses what the buyer makes.

Figure 22.3 also shows the value at expiration of buying common stock. Notice that buying the stock is the same as buying a call option on the stock with an exercise price of zero. This is not surprising. If the exercise price is zero, the call holder can buy the stock for nothing, which is really the same as owning it.

22.5 Option Quotes

Now that we understand the definitions for calls and puts, let's see how these options are quoted. Table 22.1(a) presents information about United States Steel options expiring in January 2022, obtained from **finance.yahoo.com**. At the time of these quotes, United States Steel stock was selling for ₹15.57.

On the left in the table are the available strike prices. The top half of the table presents call option quotes; put option quotes are in the bottom section. The second column contains ticker symbols, which uniquely indicate the underlying stock, the type of option, the expiration date, and the strike price. Next, we have the most recent prices on the options ("Last"), the bid and ask prices, and the change from the previous day ("Change"). Note that option prices are quoted on a per-option basis, but trading actually occurs in standardized contracts, where each contract calls for the purchase (for calls) or sale (for puts) of 100 shares. Thus, the call option with a strike price of ₹17 last traded at ₹3.65 per option, or ₹365 per contract. Volume shows the number of contracts traded this day and Open Interest is the number of contracts currently outstanding.

For more about option ticker symbols in the U.S.A., go to the "Symbol Directory" link under "Tools & Resources" at **www.cboe.com.**

For more about option ticker symbols in India, go to the "Derivatives Watch" link under "Markets > Derivatives" at **www.bseindia.com.**

[3]Actually, because of differing exercise prices, the two graphs are not quite mirror images of each other. The exercise price in Figure 22.1 is ₹100 and the exercise price in Figure 22.3 is ₹50.

Table 22.1(a) Information about the Options of United States Steel

Calls for January 21, 2022

Contract Name	Last Trade Date	Strike ^	Last Price	Bid	Ask	Change	% Change	Volume	Open Interest	Implied Volatility
X220121C00003000	2020-12-02 1:29PM EST	3.00	12.45	12.50	12.70	+0.35	+2.89%	2	643	72.66%
X220121C00005000	2020-12-02 11:06AM EST	5.00	10.72	10.75	10.95	-0.03	-0.28%	3	1,322	78.32%
X220121C00008000	2020-12-02 1:36PM EST	8.00	8.25	8.40	8.55	+0.10	+1.23%	27	9,135	72.95%
X220121C00010000	2020-12-02 3:33PM EST	10.00	6.95	7.00	7.15	+0.30	+4.51%	70	6,642	69.29%
X220121C00012000	2020-12-02 3:52PM EST	12.00	5.90	5.80	5.95	+0.47	+8.66%	69	10,644	66.94%
X220121C00015000	2020-12-02 3:57PM EST	15.00	4.44	4.35	4.55	+0.38	+9.36%	119	12,875	65.19%
X220121C00017000	2020-12-02 3:55PM EST	17.00	3.65	3.50	3.75	+0.36	+10.94%	134	2,830	63.23%
X220121C00020000	2020-12-02 3:12PM EST	20.00	2.70	2.63	2.75	+0.30	+12.50%	60	8,322	61.69%
X220121C00022000	2020-12-02 3:56PM EST	22.00	2.19	2.14	2.37	+0.23	+11.73%	102	2,242	61.69%
X220121C00025000	2020-12-02 3:46PM EST	25.00	1.65	1.65	1.70	+0.21	+14.58%	84	6,187	60.57%

Puts for January 21, 2022

Contract Name	Last Trade Date	Strike ^	Last Price	Bid	Ask	Change	% Change	Volume	Open Interest	Implied Volatility
X220121P00003000	2020-12-02 12:16PM EST	3.00	0.10	0.10	0.12	-0.06	-37.50%	3	9,573	90.63%
X220121P00005000	2020-12-02 2:56PM EST	5.00	0.32	0.28	0.36	-0.08	-20.00%	5,902	84,786	81.25%
X220121P00008000	2020-12-02 12:16PM EST	8.00	0.92	0.86	0.95	+0.01	+1.10%	34	20,273	72.95%
X220121P00010000	2020-12-02 3:53PM EST	10.00	1.50	1.50	1.55	-0.03	-1.96%	53	7,754	69.78%
X220121P00012000	2020-12-02 2:42PM EST	12.00	2.42	2.27	2.36	+0.08	+3.42%	52	821	67.19%
X220121P00015000	2020-12-02 3:57PM EST	15.00	3.80	3.75	3.90	-0.04	-1.04%	48	917	64.31%
X220121P00017000	2020-12-01 10:40AM EST	17.00	5.12	4.90	5.05	+0.22	+4.49%	11	210	62.04%
X220121P00020000	2020-12-02 2:10PM EST	20.00	7.25	6.90	7.20	+0.02	+0.28%	201	2,039	60.67%
X220121P00022000	2020-12-02 12:10PM EST	22.00	8.55	8.50	8.70	-2.84	-24.93%	191	52	60.43%
X220121P00025000	2020-12-01 10:36AM EST	25.00	10.95	10.90	11.20	0.00	-	2	1,029	59.72%

We also see how these options are quoted in Indian markets. They are primarily traded in the National Stock Exchange (NSE). Table 22.1(b) presents information about Dr. Reddy's Laboratories Limited options traded on 28 March 2024, obtained from **www.nseindia.com**. At the time of these quotes, Dr. Reddy's Laboratories was selling at ₹6,195.25.

Note that option prices are quoted on a per-option basis, but trading actually occurs in standardized contracts, where each contract calls for the purchase (for calls) or sale (for puts) of 125 shares in the case of Dr. Reddy's Laboratories. Thus, the call option expiring on March 25 with a strike price of ₹6,125 last traded at ₹142.20 per option, or ₹17,775 per contract. The final two columns contain volume and the open interest, which is the number of contracts of Dr. Reddy's Laboratories currently outstanding at the NSE. The trading volumes in derivatives markets indicate that near month contracts are more popular than

Table 22.1(b): Information about the Options of Dr. Reddy's Laboratories (as on March 28, 2024)

Call Options

Expiry Date	25-Apr-24	25-Apr-24	25-Apr-24	28-Mar-24	28-Mar-24	28-Mar-24	25-Apr-24	28-Mar-24	25-Mar-24	28-Apr-24
Strike	6,200.00	6,100.00	6,150.00	6,200.00	6,300.00	6,150.00	6,500.00	6,400.00	6,300.00	6,250.00
Open Interest	653	183	127	125	349	126	304	1392	184	77
Volume (Contracts)	2,839	1,837	1,461	1,400	1,185	1,165	1,026	942	878	643
Prev. Close	117.65	161.50	142.20	6.70	1.70	12.05	41.65	1.10	85.75	3.25
%Chng	23.25	23.59	20.01	–10.45	–97.06	99.17	24.85	–95.45	22.74	–58.46

Put Options

Expiry Date	28-Mar-24	28-Mar-24	28-Mar-24	25-Apr-24	28-Mar-24	28-Mar-24	25-Apr-24	28-Mar-24	28-Mar-24	25-Apr-24
Strike	6,100.00	6,000.00	6,050.00	6,100.00	6,200.00	6,150.00	6,000.00	5,950.00	5,900.00	5,900.00
Open Interest	213	207	108	630	143	133	268	135	672	281
Volume (Contracts)	637	595	589	583	385	358	317	286	250	215
Prev. Close	57	10.95	22.85	152.40	146.90	99.95	105.45	3.5	0.9	68.45
%Chng	–94.74	–89.04	–91.90	–35.50	–70.80	–91.60	–41.49	–72.86	–94.44	–47.41

not-so-near month contracts, call options are more popular than put options, and contracts on indexes are more popular than individual securities.

22.6 Combinations of Options

Puts and calls can serve as building blocks for more complex option contracts. Figure 22.4 illustrates the payoff from buying a put option on a stock and simultaneously buying the stock.

Excel Master coverage online

If the share price is greater than the exercise price, the put option is worthless and the value of the combined position is equal to the value of the common stock. If, instead, the exercise price is greater than the share price, the decline in the value of the shares will be exactly offset by the rise in the value of the put.

The strategy of buying a put and buying the underlying stock is called a *protective put*. It is as if we are buying insurance for the stock. The stock can always be sold at the exercise price, regardless of how far the market price of the stock falls.

Note that the combination of buying a put and buying the underlying stock has the same shape in Figure 22.4 as the call purchase in Figure 22.1. To pursue this point, consider the graph for buying a call, which is shown at the far left of Figure 22.5. This graph is the same as Figure 22.1, except that the exercise price is ₹50 here. Now let's try the strategy of:

(Leg A) Buying a call.

(Leg B) Buying a risk-free, zero coupon bond (i.e., a T-bill) with a face value of ₹50 that matures on the same day that the option expires.

We have drawn the graph of Leg A of this strategy at the far left of Figure 22.5, but what does the graph of Leg B look like? It looks like the middle graph of the figure. That is, anyone buying this zero coupon bond will be guaranteed to receive ₹50, regardless of the price of the stock at expiration.

What does the graph of simultaneously buying both Leg A and Leg B of this strategy look like? It looks like the far right graph of Figure 22.5. That is, the investor receives a guaranteed ₹50 from the bond, regardless of what happens to the stock. In addition, the investor receives a payoff from the call of ₹1 for every ₹1 that the price of the stock rises above the exercise price of ₹50.

The far right graph of Figure 22.5 looks exactly like the far right graph of Figure 22.4. An investor gets the same payoff from the strategy of Figure 22.4 and the strategy of Figure 22.5, regardless of what happens to the price of the underlying stock. In other words, the investor gets the same payoff from:

1. Buying a put and buying the underlying stock.
2. Buying a call and buying a risk-free, zero coupon bond.

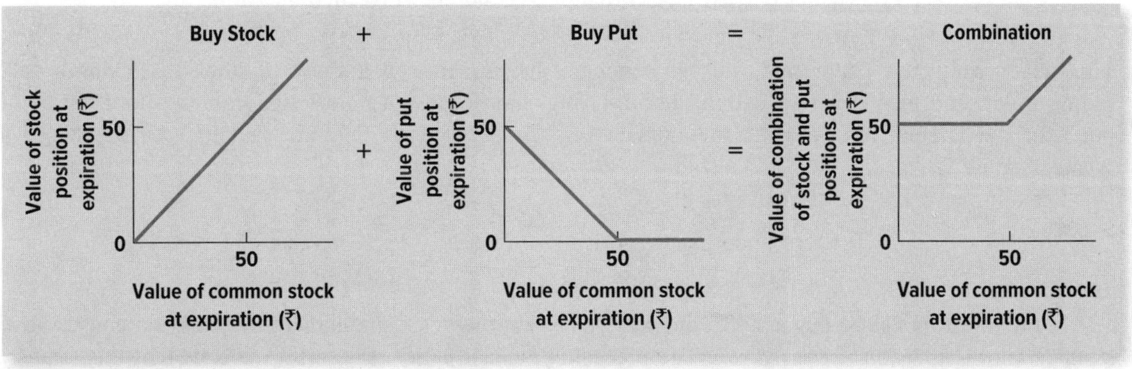

Figure 22.4 Payoff to the Combination of Buying a Put and Buying the Underlying Stock

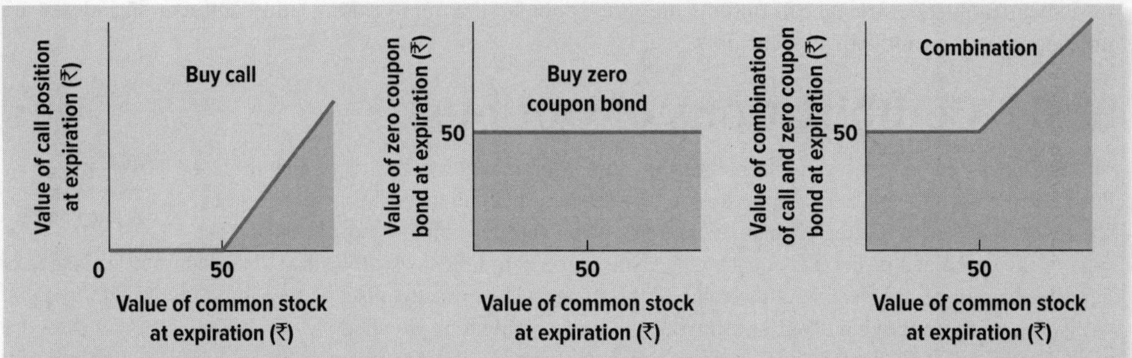

The graph of buying a call and buying a zero coupon bond is the same as the graph of buying a put and buying the stock in Figure 22.4.

Figure 22.5 Payoff to the Combination of Buying a Call and Buying a Zero Coupon Bond

If investors have the same payoffs from the two strategies, the two strategies must have the same cost. Otherwise, all investors will choose the strategy with the lower cost and avoid the strategy with the higher cost. This leads to the following interesting result:

$$\text{Price of underlying stock} + \text{Price of put} = \text{Price of call} + \text{Present value of exercise price} \quad \textbf{(22.1)}$$
$$\text{Cost of first strategy} = \text{Cost of second strategy}$$

This relationship is known as **put-call parity** and is one of the most fundamental relationships concerning options. It says that there are two ways of buying a protective put. You can buy a put and buy the underlying stock simultaneously. Here, your total cost is the price of the underlying stock plus the price of the put. Or you can buy a call and buy a zero coupon bond. Here, your total cost is the price of the call plus the price of the zero coupon bond. The price of the zero coupon bond is equal to the present value of the exercise price–that is, the present value of ₹50 in our example.

Equation 22.1 is a very precise relationship. It holds only if the put and the call have both the same exercise price and the same expiration date. In addition, the maturity date of the zero coupon bond must be the same as the expiration date of the options.

To see how fundamental put-call parity is, let's rearrange the formula, yielding:

$$\text{Price of underlying stock} = \text{Price of call} - \text{Price of put} + \text{Present value of exercise price}$$

This relationship now states that you can replicate the purchase of a share of stock by buying a call, selling a put, and buying a zero coupon bond. (Note that because a minus sign comes before "Price of put," the put is sold, not bought.) Investors in this three-legged strategy are said to have purchased a *synthetic* stock.

Let's do one more transformation:

$$\text{Price of underlying stock} - \text{Price of call} = -\text{Price of put} + \text{Present value of exercise price}$$

Many investors like to buy a stock and write a call on the stock simultaneously. This is a conservative strategy known as *selling a covered call.* The preceding put-call parity relationship tells us that this strategy

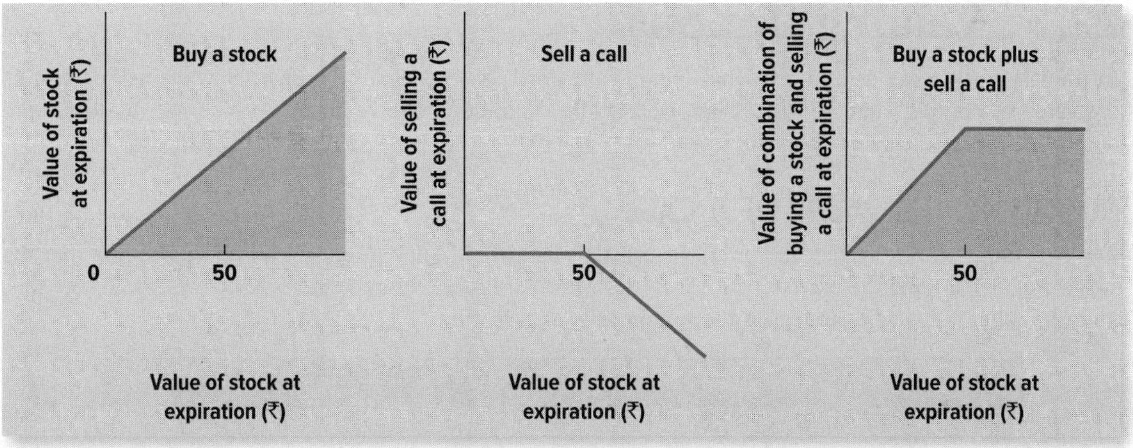

Figure 22.6 Payoff to the Combination of Buying a Stock and Selling a Call

is equivalent to selling a put and buying a zero coupon bond. Figure 22.6 develops the graph for the covered call. You can verify that the covered call can be replicated by selling a put and simultaneously buying a zero coupon bond.

Of course, there are other ways of rearranging the basic put-call relationship. For each rearrangement, the strategy on the left side is equivalent to the strategy on the right side. The beauty of put-call parity is that it shows how any strategy in options can be achieved in two different ways.

To test your understanding of put-call parity, suppose shares of stock in Bhubhaneswari Plantations Limited are selling for ₹80. A three-month call option with an ₹85 strike price goes for ₹6. The risk-free rate is .5 percent per month. What's the value of a three-month put option with an ₹85 strike price?

We can rearrange the put-call parity relationship to solve for the price of the put as follows:

$$\begin{aligned}\text{Price of put} &= -\text{Price of underlying stock} + \text{Price of call} + \text{Present value of strike price}\\ &= -₹80 + ₹6 + ₹85/1.005^3\\ &= ₹9.74\end{aligned}$$

As shown, the value of the put is ₹9.74.

EXAMPLE 22.3

A Synthetic T-Bill Suppose shares of stock in Kanchenganga Brewers are selling for ₹110. A call option on Kanchenganga with one year to maturity and a ₹110 strike price sells for ₹15. A put with the same terms sells for ₹5. What's the risk-free rate?

To answer, we need to use put-call parity to determine the price of a risk-free, zero coupon bond:

Price of underlying stock + Price of put − Price of call = Present value of exercise price

Plugging in the numbers, we get:

$$₹110 + 5 - 15 = ₹100$$

Because the present value of the ₹110 strike price is ₹100, the implied risk-free rate is 10 percent.

22.7 Valuing Options

In the last section, we determined what options are worth on the expiration date. Now we will determine the value of options when you buy them well before expiration.[4] We begin by considering the lower and upper bounds on the value of a call.

BOUNDING THE VALUE OF A CALL

Lower Bound Consider an American call that is in the money prior to expiration. Assume that the stock price is ₹60 and the exercise price is ₹50. In this case, the option cannot sell below ₹10. To see this, note the following simple strategy if the option sells at, say, ₹9:

		Transaction	
Today	(1)	Buy call.	–₹ 9
Today	(2)	Exercise call—that is, buy underlying stock at exercise price.	–₹50
Today	(3)	Sell stock at current market price.	+₹60
		Arbitrage profit	+₹ 1

The type of profit that is described in this transaction is an *arbitrage* profit. Arbitrage profits come from transactions that have no risk or cost and cannot occur regularly in normal, well-functioning financial markets. The excess demand for these options would quickly force the option price up to at least ₹10 (= ₹60 – 50).

Of course, the price of the option is likely to be above ₹10. Investors will rationally pay more than ₹10 because of the possibility that the stock will rise above ₹60 before expiration. Suppose the call actually sells for ₹12. In this case, we say that the *intrinsic value* of the option is ₹10, meaning it must always be worth at least this much. The remaining ₹12 – 10 = ₹2 is called the *time premium*, and it represents the extra amount that investors are willing to pay because of the possibility that the stock price will rise before the option expires.

Upper Bound Is there an upper boundary for the option price as well? It turns out that the upper boundary is the price of the underlying stock. That is, an option to buy common stock cannot have a greater value than the common stock itself. A call option can be used to buy common stock with a payment of the exercise price. It would be foolish to buy stock this way if the stock could be purchased directly at a lower price. The upper and lower bounds are represented in Figure 22.7.

THE FACTORS DETERMINING CALL OPTION VALUES

The previous discussion indicated that the price of a call option must fall somewhere in the shaded region of Figure 22.7. We now will determine more precisely where in the shaded region it should be. The factors that determine a call's value can be broken into two sets. The first set contains the features of the option contract. The two basic contract features are the exercise price and the expiration date. The second set of factors affecting the call price concerns characteristics of the stock and the market.

Exercise Price An increase in the exercise price reduces the value of the call. Imagine that there are two calls on a stock selling at ₹60. The first call has an exercise price of ₹50 and the second one has an exercise price of ₹40. Which call would you rather have? Clearly, you would rather have the call with an exercise price of ₹40 because that one is ₹20 (= ₹60 – 40) in the money. In other words, the call with an exercise price of ₹40 should sell for more than an otherwise identical call with an exercise price of ₹50.

[4]Our discussion in this section is of American options because they are more commonly traded in the real world. As necessary, we will indicate differences for European options.

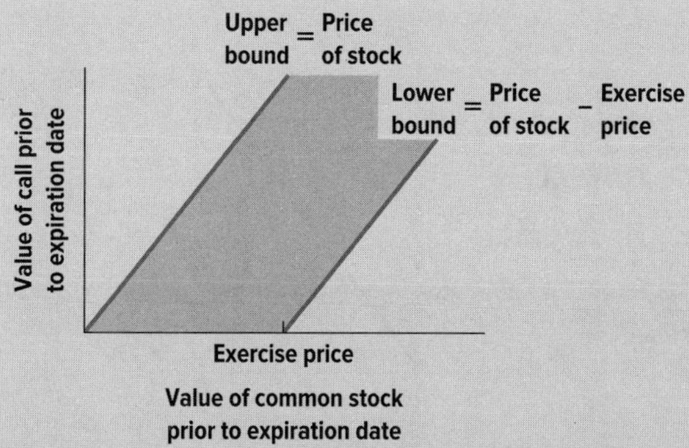

Figure 22.7 The Upper and Lower Boundaries of Call Option Values

Expiration Date The value of an American call option must be at least as great as the value of an otherwise identical option with a shorter term to expiration. Consider two American calls: One has a maturity of nine months and the other expires in six months. Obviously, the nine-month call has the same rights as the six-month call, and it also has an additional three months within which these rights can be exercised. It cannot be worth less and will generally be more valuable.[5]

Stock Price Other things being equal, the higher the stock price, the more valuable the call option will be. If a stock is worth ₹80, a call with an exercise price of ₹100 isn't worth very much. If the stock soars to ₹120, the call becomes much more valuable.

There is a good discussion of options at **www.nasdaqtrader.com**.

Now consider Figure 22.8, which shows the relationship between the call price and the stock price prior to expiration. The curve indicates that the call price increases as the stock price increases. It can be shown that the relationship is represented not by a straight line, but by a *convex* curve. That is, the increase in the call price for a given change in the stock price is greater when the stock price is high than when the stock price is low.

There are two special points regarding the curve in Figure 22.8:

1. *The stock is worthless*. The call must be worthless if the underlying stock is worthless. If the stock has no chance of attaining any value, it is not worthwhile to pay the exercise price to obtain the stock.
2. *The stock price is very high relative to the exercise price*. In this situation the owner of the call knows that she will end up exercising the call. She can view herself as the owner of the stock now with one difference: She must pay the exercise price at expiration.

Thus, the value of her position–that is, the value of the call–is:

$$\text{Stock price} - \text{Present value of exercise price}$$

These two points on the curve are summarized in the bottom half of Table 22.2.

[5]This relationship need not hold for a European call option. Consider a firm with two otherwise identical European call options, one expiring at the end of May and the other expiring a few months later. Further assume that a huge dividend is paid in early June. If the first call is exercised at the end of May, its holder will receive the underlying stock. If he does not sell the stock, he will receive the large dividend shortly thereafter. However, the holder of the second call will receive the stock through exercise after the dividend is paid. Because the market knows that the holder of this option will miss the dividend, the value of the second call option could be less than the value of the first.

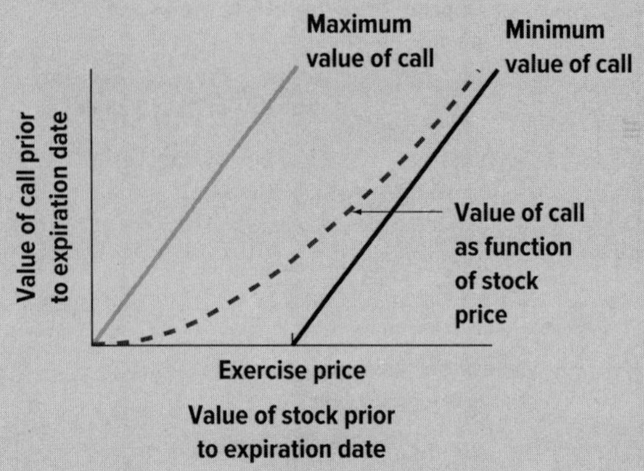

The call price is positively related to the stock price. In addition, the change in the call price for a given change in the stock price is greater when the stock price is high than when it is low.

Figure 22.8 Value of an American Call as a Function of Stock Price

The Key Factor: The Variability of the Underlying Asset The greater the variability of the underlying asset, the more valuable the call option will be. Consider the following example. Suppose that just before the call expires, the stock price will be either ₹100 with probability .5 or ₹80 with probability .5. What will be the value of a call with an exercise price of ₹110? Clearly, it will be worthless because no matter what happens to the stock, its price will always be below the exercise price.

Table 22.2 Factors Affecting American Option Values

Increase in	Call Option*	Put Option*
Value of underlying asset (stock price)	+	–
Exercise price	–	+
Stock volatility	+	+
Interest rate	+	–
Time to expiration	+	+

In addition to the preceding, we have presented the following four relationships for American calls:

1. The call price can never be greater than the stock price (*upper bound*).
2. The call price can never be less than either zero or the difference between the stock price and the exercise price (*lower bound*).
3. The call is worth zero if the stock is worth zero.
4. When the stock price is much greater than the exercise price, the call price tends toward the difference between the stock price and the present value of the exercise price.

*The signs (+, –) indicate the effect of the variables on the value of the option. For example, the two +s for stock volatility indicate that an increase in volatility will increase both the value of a call and the value of a put.

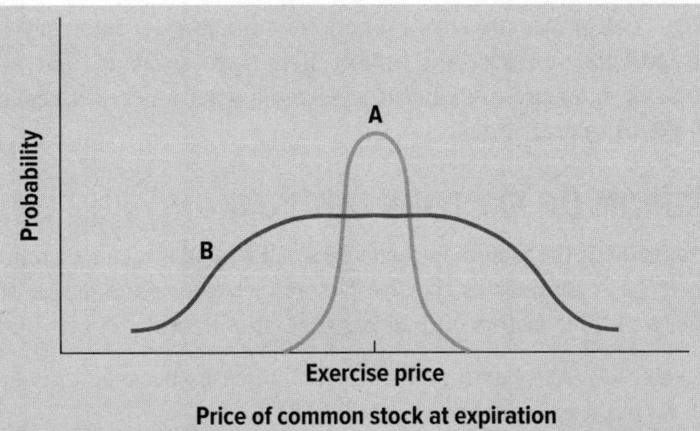

The call on Stock B is worth more than the call on Stock A because Stock B is more volatile. At expiration, a call that is deep in the money is more valuable than a call that is only slightly in the money. However, at expiration, a call way out of the money is worth zero, as is a call only slightly out of the money.

Figure 22.9 Distribution of Common Stock Price at Expiration for Both Security A and Security B; Options on the Two Securities Have the Same Exercise Price

For an option-oriented site focusing on volatilities, visit **www.ivolatility.com**.

What happens if the stock is more variable? Suppose we add ₹20 to the best case and take ₹20 away from the worst case. Now the stock has a one-half chance of being worth ₹60 and a one-half chance of being worth ₹120. We have spread the stock returns, but, of course, the expected value of the stock has stayed the same:

$$(.5 \times ₹80) + (.5 \times ₹100) = ₹90 = (.5 \times ₹60) + (.5 \times ₹120)$$

Notice that the call option has value now because there is a one-half chance that the stock price will be ₹120, or ₹10 above the exercise price of ₹110. This illustrates an important point. There is a fundamental distinction between holding an option on an underlying asset and holding the underlying asset. If investors in the marketplace are risk-averse, a rise in the variability of the stock will decrease its market value. However, the holder of a call receives payoffs from the positive tail of the probability distribution. As a consequence, a rise in the variability of the underlying stock increases the market value of the call.

This result also can be seen from Figure 22.9. Consider two stocks, A and B, each of which has returns that are normally distributed. For each security, the figure illustrates the probability of different stock prices on the expiration date. As can be seen from the figure, Stock B has more volatility than does Stock A. This means that Stock B has a higher probability of both abnormally high returns and abnormally low returns. Let us assume that options on each of the two securities have the same exercise price. To option holders, a return much below average on Stock B is no worse than a return only moderately below average on Stock A. In either situation, the option expires out of the money. However, to option holders, a return much above average on Stock B is better than a return only moderately above average on Stock A. Because a call's price at the expiration date is the difference between the stock price and the exercise price, the value of the call on B at expiration will be higher in this case.

The Interest Rate Call prices are also a function of the level of interest rates. Buyers of calls do not pay the exercise price until they exercise the option, if they do so at all. The ability to delay payment is more valuable when interest rates are high and less valuable when interest rates are low. Thus, the value of a call is positively related to interest rates.

A QUICK DISCUSSION OF FACTORS DETERMINING PUT OPTION VALUES

Given our extended discussion of the factors influencing a call's value, we can examine the effect of these factors on puts very easily. Table 22.2 summarizes the five factors influencing the prices of both American calls and American puts. The effects of three factors on puts are the opposite of the effects of these three factors on calls:

1. The put's market value *decreases* as the stock price increases because puts are in the money when the stock sells below the exercise price.
2. The value of a put with a high exercise price is *greater* than the value of an otherwise identical put with a low exercise price for the reason given in (1).
3. A high interest rate *adversely* affects the value of a put. The ability to sell a stock at a fixed exercise price sometime in the future is worth less if the present value of the exercise price is reduced by a high interest rate.

The effects of the other two factors on puts are the same as the effects of these factors on calls:

4. The value of an American put with a distant expiration date is greater than an otherwise identical put with an earlier expiration.[6] The longer time to maturity gives the put holder more flexibility, just as it did in the case of a call.
5. Volatility of the underlying stock increases the value of the put. The reasoning is similar to that for a call. At expiration, a put that is way in the money is more valuable than a put only slightly in the money. However, at expiration, a put way out of the money is worth zero, just as is a put only slightly out of the money.

22.8 An Option Pricing Formula

We have explained qualitatively that the value of a call option is a function of five variables:

Excel Master coverage online

1. The current price of the underlying asset, which for stock options is the price of a share of common stock.
2. The exercise price.
3. The time to the expiration date.
4. The variance of the underlying asset.
5. The risk-free interest rate.

It is time to replace the qualitative model with a precise option valuation model. The model we choose is the famous Black-Scholes option pricing model. You can put numbers into the Black-Scholes model and get values back.

The Black-Scholes model is represented by a rather imposing formula. A derivation of the formula is not possible in this textbook, as many students will be happy to learn. However, some appreciation for the achievement, as well as some intuitive understanding, is in order.

[6]Though this result must hold in the case of an American put, it need not hold for a European put.

In the early chapters of this book, we showed how to discount capital budgeting projects using the net present value formula. We also used this approach to value stocks and bonds. Why, students sometimes ask, can't the same NPV formula be used to value puts and calls? This is a good question: The earliest attempts at valuing options used NPV. Unfortunately, the attempts were unsuccessful because no one could determine the appropriate discount rate. An option is generally riskier than the underlying stock, but no one knew exactly how much riskier.

Black and Scholes attacked the problem by pointing out that a strategy of borrowing to finance a stock purchase duplicates the risk of a call. Then, knowing the price of a stock, we can determine the price of a call such that its return is identical to that of the stock-with-borrowing alternative.

We illustrate the intuition behind the Black-Scholes approach by considering a simple example where a combination of a call and a stock eliminates all risk. This example works because we let the future stock price be one of only two values. Hence, the example is called a *two-state*, or *binomial option, model.* By eliminating the possibility that the stock price can take on other values, we are able to duplicate the call exactly.

A TWO-STATE OPTION MODEL

Consider the following example. Suppose the current market price of a stock is ₹50 and the stock will either be ₹60 or ₹40 at the end of the year. Further, imagine a call option on this stock with a one-year expiration date and a ₹50 exercise price. Investors can borrow at 10 percent. Our goal is to determine the value of the call.

To value the call correctly, we need to examine two strategies. The first is to buy the call. The second is to:

1. Buy one-half a share of stock.
2. Borrow ₹18.18, implying a payment of principal and interest at the end of the year of ₹20 (= ₹18.18 × 1.10).

As you will see shortly, the cash flows from the second strategy match the cash flows from buying a call. (A little later we will show how we came up with the exact fraction of a share of stock to buy and the exact borrowing amount.) Because the cash flows match, we say that we are duplicating the call with the second strategy.

At the end of the year, the future payoffs are set out as follows:

	Future Payoffs	
Initial Transactions	**If Stock Price Is ₹60**	**If Stock Price Is ₹40**
1. Buy a call	₹60 − 50 = ₹10	₹ 0
2. Buy $\frac{1}{2}$ share of stock	$\frac{1}{2}$ × ₹60 = ₹30	$\frac{1}{2}$ × ₹40 = ₹20
Borrow ₹18.18 at 10%	−(₹18.18 × 1.10) = −₹20	−₹20
Total from stock and borrowing strategy	₹10	₹ 0

Note that the future payoff structure of the "buy-a-call" strategy is duplicated by the strategy of "buy stock and borrow." That is, under either strategy, an investor would end up with ₹10 if the stock price rose and ₹0 if the stock price fell. These two strategies are equivalent as far as traders are concerned.

If two strategies always have the same cash flows at the end of the year, how must their initial costs be related? The two strategies must have the same initial cost. Otherwise, there will be an arbitrage possibility. We can easily calculate this cost for our strategy of buying stock and borrowing:

Buy $\frac{1}{2}$ share of stock	$\frac{1}{2}$ × ₹50 =	₹25.00
Borrow ₹18.18		−18.18
		₹ 6.82

Because the call option provides the same payoffs at expiration as does the strategy of buying stock and borrowing, the call must be priced at ₹6.82. This is the value of the call option in a market without arbitrage profits.

We left two issues unexplained in the preceding example.

Determining the Delta How did we know to buy one-half share of stock in the duplicating strategy? Actually, the answer is easier than it might first appear. The call price at the end of the year will be either ₹10 or ₹0, whereas the stock price will be either ₹60 or ₹40. Thus, the call price has a potential swing of ₹10 (= ₹10 − 0) next period, whereas the stock price has a potential swing of ₹20 (= ₹60 − 40). We can write this in terms of the following ratio:

$$\text{Delta} = \frac{\text{Swing of call}}{\text{Swing of stock}} = \frac{₹10 - 0}{₹60 - 40} = \frac{1}{2}$$

As indicated, this ratio is called the *delta* of the call. In words, a ₹1 swing in the price of the stock gives rise to a ₹.50 swing in the price of the call. Because we are trying to duplicate the call with the stock, it seems sensible to buy one-half share of stock instead of buying one call. In other words, the risk of buying one-half share of stock should be the same as the risk of buying one call.

Determining the Amount of Borrowing How did we know how much to borrow? Buying one-half share of stock brings us either ₹30 or ₹20 at expiration, which is exactly ₹20 more than the payoffs of ₹10 and ₹0, respectively, from the call. To duplicate the call through a purchase of stock, we also should borrow enough money so that we have to pay back exactly ₹20 of interest and principal. This amount of borrowing is the present value of ₹20, which is ₹18.18 (= ₹20/1.10).

Now that we know how to determine both the delta and the borrowing, we can write the value of the call as follows:

$$\begin{array}{ccccccc} \text{Value of call} & = & \text{Stock price} & \times & \text{Delta} & - & \text{Amount borrowed} \\ ₹6.82 & = & ₹50 & \times & \frac{1}{2} & - & ₹18.18 \end{array} \qquad \textbf{(22.2)}$$

We will find this intuition useful in explaining the Black-Scholes model.

Risk-Neutral Valuation Before leaving this simple example, we should comment on a remarkable feature. We found the exact value of the option without even knowing the probability that the stock would go up or down! If an optimist thought the probability of an up move was high and a pessimist thought it was low, they would still agree on the option value. How can that be? The answer is that the current ₹50 stock price already balances the views of the optimists and the pessimists. The option reflects that balance because its value depends on the stock price.

This insight provides us with another approach to valuing the call. If we don't need the probabilities of the two states to value the call, perhaps we can select *any* probabilities we want and still come up with the right answer. Suppose we selected probabilities such that the expected return on the stock is equal to the risk-free rate of 10 percent. We know that the stock return given a rise in the stock's price is 20 percent (= ₹60/₹50 − 1) and the stock return given a fall in the stock's price is −20 percent (= ₹40/₹50 − 1). We can solve for the probability of a rise necessary to achieve an expected return of 10 percent as follows:

$$.10 = \text{Probability of a rise} \times .20 + (1 - \text{Probability of rise}) \times -.20$$

Solving this formula, we find that the probability of a rise is .75 and the probability of a fall is .25. If we apply these probabilities to the call, we can value it as:

$$\text{Value of call} = ₹6.82 = \frac{.75 \times ₹10 + .25 \times ₹0}{1.10}$$

which is the same value we got from the duplicating approach.

Why did we select probabilities such that the expected return on the stock is 10 percent? We wanted to work with the special case where investors are *risk-neutral.* This case occurs when the expected return on any asset (including both the stock and the call) is equal to the risk-free rate. In other words, this case occurs when investors demand no additional compensation beyond the risk-free rate, regardless of the risk of the asset in question.

What would have happened if we had assumed that the expected return on the stock was greater than the risk-free rate? The value of the call would still be ₹6.82. However, the calculations would be more difficult. If we assumed that the expected return on the stock was 11 percent, we would have had to derive the expected return on the call. Although the expected return on the call would have been higher than 11 percent, it would have taken a lot of work to determine the expected return precisely. Why do any more work than you have to? Because we can't think of any good reason, we (and most other financial economists) choose to assume risk neutrality.

Thus, the preceding material allows us to value a call in the following two ways:

1. Determine the cost of a strategy duplicating the call. This strategy involves an investment in a fractional share of stock financed by partial borrowing.
2. Calculate the probabilities of a rise and a fall in stock prices under the assumption of risk neutrality. Use these probabilities in conjunction with the risk-free rate to discount the payoffs of the call at expiration.

THE BLACK-SCHOLES MODEL

The preceding example illustrates the duplicating strategy. Unfortunately, a strategy such as this will not work in the real world over, say, a one-year time frame because there are many more than two possibilities for next year's stock price. However, the number of possibilities is reduced as the period is shortened. Is there a time period over which the stock price can only have two outcomes? Academics argue that the assumption that there are only two possibilities for the stock price over the next infinitesimal instant is quite plausible.[7]

In our opinion, the fundamental insight of Black and Scholes is to shorten the time period. They show that a specific combination of stock and borrowing can indeed duplicate a call over an infinitesimal time horizon. Because the price of the stock will change over the first instant, another combination of stock and borrowing is needed to duplicate the call over the second instant and so on. By adjusting the combination from moment to moment, they can continually duplicate the call. It may boggle the mind that a formula can (1) determine the duplicating combination at any moment and (2) value the

There's a Black-Scholes calculator (and a lot more) at **www.cmegroup.com**.

[7]A full treatment of this assumption can be found in John C. Hull, *Options, Futures and Other Derivatives* (Upper Saddle River, NJ: Prentice Hall, 2017).

option based on this duplicating strategy. Suffice it to say that their dynamic strategy allows them to value a call in the real world, just as we showed how to value the call in the two-state model.

This is the basic intuition behind the Black-Scholes model. Because the actual derivation of their formula is far beyond the scope of this text, we present the formula itself:

Black-Scholes Model

$$C = S\mathrm{N}(d_1) - Ee^{-Rt}\mathrm{N}(d_2)$$

where:

$$d_1 = \left[\ln(S/E) + (R + \sigma^2/2)t\right]/\sqrt{\sigma^2 t}$$

$$d_2 = d_1 - \sqrt{\sigma^2 t}$$

This formula for the value of a call, C, is one of the most complex in finance. However, it involves only five parameters:

1. S = Current stock price
2. E = Exercise price of call
3. R = Annual risk-free rate of return, continuously compounded
4. σ^2 = Variance (per year) of the continuous return on the stock
5. t = Time (in years) to expiration date

In addition, there is this statistical concept:

$\mathrm{N}(d)$ = Probability that a standardized, normally distributed, random variable will be less than or equal to d

Rather than discuss the formula in its algebraic state, we illustrate the formula with an example.

EXAMPLE 22.4

Black-Scholes Consider Pushpanjali Equipment Company (PEC). On April 19, the PEC April 49 call option had a closing value of ₹4. The stock itself was selling at ₹50. On April 19, the option had 199 days to expiration (maturity date = November 4). The annual risk-free interest rate, continuously compounded, was 7 percent.

This information defines three variables directly:

1. The stock price, S, is ₹50.
2. The exercise price, E, is ₹49.
3. The risk-free rate, R, is .07.

In addition, the time to maturity, t, can be calculated quickly: The formula calls for t to be expressed in years.

4. We express the 199-day interval in years as t = 199/365.

In the real world, an option trader would know S and E exactly. Traders generally view Indian Treasury bills as riskless, so a current quote from **www.rbi.org.in**, or a similar source, would be obtained for the interest rate. The trader also would know (or could count) the number of days to expiration exactly. The fraction of a year to expiration, t, could be calculated quickly.

(continued)

The problem comes in determining the variance of the stock's return. The formula calls for the variance between the purchase date of April 19 and the expiration date. Unfortunately, this represents the future, so the correct value for variance is not available. Instead, traders frequently estimate variance from past data, just as we calculated variance in an earlier chapter. In addition, some traders may use intuition to adjust their estimate. For example, if anticipation of an upcoming event is likely to increase the volatility of the stock, the trader might adjust her estimate of variance upward to reflect this. (This problem was severe during and after the recession of 2008. The stock market was quite risky in the aftermath, so estimates using pre-recession data were too low.)

The preceding discussion was intended merely to mention the difficulties in variance estimation, not to present a solution. For our purposes, we assume that a trader has come up with an estimate of variance:

5. The variance of PEC stock has been estimated to be .09 per year.

Using these five parameters, we calculate the Black-Scholes value of the PEC call option in three steps:

Step 1: *Calculate d_1 and d_2.* These values can be determined by a straightforward, albeit tedious, insertion of our parameters into the basic formula. We have:

$$\begin{aligned} d_1 &= \left[\ln\left(\frac{S}{E}\right) + \left(R + \sigma^2/2\right)t\right]/\sqrt{\sigma^2 t} \\ &= \left[\ln\left(\frac{50}{49}\right) + (.07 + .09/2) \times \frac{199}{365}\right]/\sqrt{.09 \times \frac{199}{365}} \\ &= [.0202 + .0627]/.2215 = .3742 \\ d_2 &= d_1 - \sqrt{\sigma^2 t} \\ &= .1527 \end{aligned}$$

Step 2: *Calculate* $N(d_1)$ *and* $N(d_2)$. We can best understand the values $N(d_1)$ and $N(d_2)$ by examining Figure 22.10. The figure shows the normal distribution with an expected value of 0 and a standard deviation of 1. This is frequently called the *standard normal distribution*. We mentioned in an earlier chapter that the probability that a drawing from this distribution will be between −1 and +1 (within one standard deviation of its mean) is 68.26 percent.

Now let us ask a different question: What is the probability that a drawing from the standardized normal distribution will be below a particular value? The probability that a drawing will be below 0 is clearly 50 percent because the normal distribution is symmetric. Using statistical terminology, we say that the *cumulative probability* of 0 is 50 percent. Statisticians also say that N(0) = 50 percent. It turns out that:

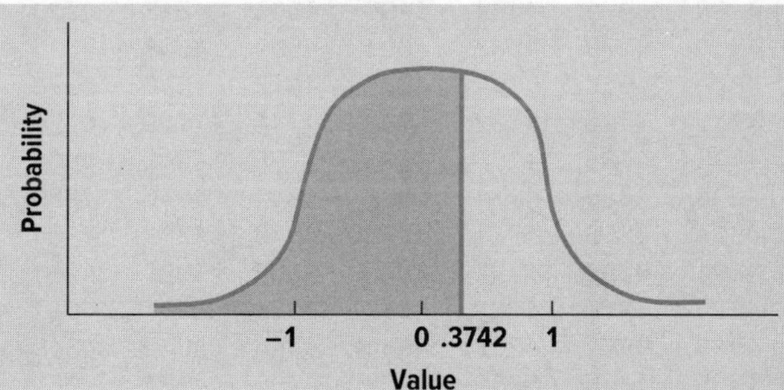

The shaded area represents cumulative probability. Because the probability is .6459 that a drawing from the standard normal distribution will be below .3742, we say that N(.3742) = .6459. That is, the cumulative probability of .3742 is .6459.

Figure 22.10 Graph of Cumulative Probability

$$N(d_1) = N(.3742) = .6459$$
$$N(d_2) = N(.1527) = .5607$$

The first value means that there is a 64.59 percent probability that a drawing from the standardized normal distribution will be below .3742. The second value means that there is a 56.07 percent probability that a drawing from the standardized normal distribution will be below .1527. More generally, N(*d*) is the probability that a drawing from the standardized normal distribution will be below *d*. In other words, N(*d*) is the cumulative probability of *d*. Note that d_1 and d_2 in our example are slightly above zero, so $N(d_1)$ and $N(d_2)$ are slightly greater than .50.

Perhaps the easiest way to determine $N(d_1)$ and $N(d_2)$ is from the Excel function NORMSDIST. In our example, NORMSDIST(.3742) and NORMSDIST(.1527) are .6459 and .5607, respectively.

We also can determine the cumulative probability from Table 22.3. Consider *d* = .37. This can be found in the table as .3 on the vertical and .07 on the horizontal. The value in the table for *d* = .37 is .1443. This

Table 22.3 Cumulative Probabilities of the Standard Normal Distribution Function

d	.00	.01	.02	.03	.04	.05	.06	.07	.08	.09
.0	.0000	.0040	.0080	.0120	.0160	.0199	.0239	.0279	.0319	.0359
.1	.0398	.0438	.0478	.0517	.0557	.0596	.0636	.0675	.0714	.0753
.2	.0793	.0832	.0871	.0910	.0948	.0987	.1026	.1064	.1103	.1141
.3	.1179	.1217	.1255	.1293	.1331	.1368	.1406	.1443	.1480	.1517
.4	.1554	.1591	.1628	.1664	.1700	.1736	.1772	.1808	.1844	.1879
.5	.1915	.1950	.1985	.2019	.2054	.2088	.2123	.2157	.2190	.2224
.6	.2257	.2291	.2324	.2357	.2389	.2422	.2454	.2486	.2517	.2549
.7	.2580	.2611	.2642	.2673	.2704	.2734	.2764	.2794	.2823	.2852
.8	.2881	.2910	.2939	.2967	.2995	.3023	.3051	.3078	.3106	.3133
.9	.3159	.3186	.3212	.3238	.3264	.3289	.3315	.3340	.3365	.3389
1.0	.3413	.3438	.3461	.3485	.3508	.3531	.3554	.3577	.3599	.3621
1.1	.3643	.3665	.3686	.3708	.3729	.3749	.3770	.3790	.3810	.3830
1.2	.3849	.3869	.3888	.3907	.3925	.3944	.3962	.3980	.3997	.4015
1.3	.4032	.4049	.4066	.4082	.4099	.4115	.4131	.4147	.4162	.4177
1.4	.4192	.4207	.4222	.4236	.4251	.4265	.4279	.4292	.4306	.4319
1.5	.4332	.4345	.4357	.4370	.4382	.4394	.4406	.4418	.4429	.4441
1.6	.4452	.4463	.4474	.4484	.4495	.4505	.4515	.4525	.4535	.4545
1.7	.4554	.4564	.4573	.4582	.4591	.4599	.4608	.4616	.4625	.4633
1.8	.4641	.4649	.4656	.4664	.4671	.4678	.4686	.4693	.4699	.4706
1.9	.4713	.4719	.4726	.4732	.4738	.4744	.4750	.4756	.4761	.4767
2.0	.4772	.4778	.4783	.4788	.4793	.4798	.4803	.4808	.4812	.4817
2.1	.4821	.4826	.4830	.4834	.4838	.4842	.4846	.4850	.4854	.4857
2.2	.4861	.4864	.4868	.4871	.4875	.4878	.4881	.4884	.4887	.4890
2.3	.4893	.4896	.4898	.4901	.4904	.4906	.4909	.4911	.4913	.4916
2.4	.4918	.4920	.4922	.4925	.4927	.4929	.4931	.4932	.4934	.4936
2.5	.4938	.4940	.4941	.4943	.4945	.4946	.4948	.4949	.4951	.4952
2.6	.4953	.4955	.4956	.4957	.4959	.4960	.4961	.4962	.4963	.4964
2.7	.4965	.4966	.4967	.4968	.4969	.4970	.4971	.4972	.4973	.4974
2.8	.4974	.4975	.4976	.4977	.4977	.4978	.4979	.4979	.4980	.4981
2.9	.4981	.4982	.4982	.4983	.4984	.4984	.4985	.4985	.4986	.4986
3.0	.4987	.4987	.4987	.4988	.4988	.4989	.4989	.4989	.4990	.4990

N(*D*) represents areas under the standard normal distribution function. Suppose that $D_1 = .24$. The table implies a cumulative probability of .5000 + .0948 = .5948. If D_1 is equal to .2452, we must estimate the probability by interpolating between N(.25) and N(.24).

(*continued*)

value is not the cumulative probability of .37. We must first make an adjustment to determine cumulative probability. That is:

$$N(.37) = .50 + .1443 = .6443$$
$$N(-.37) = .50 - .1443 = .3557$$

Unfortunately, our table handles only two significant digits, whereas our value of .3742 has four significant digits. Hence, we must interpolate to find N(.3742). Because N(.37) = .6443 and N(.38) = .6480, the difference between the two values is .0037 (= .6480 – .6443). Because .3742 is 42 percent of the way between .37 and .38, we interpolate as:[8]

$$N(.3742) = .6443 + .42 \times .0037 = .6459$$

Step 3: *Calculate C.* We have:

$$\begin{aligned} C &= S \times [N(d_1)] - Ee^{-Rt} \times [N(d_2)] \\ &= ₹50 \times [N(d_1)] - ₹49 \times [e^{-.07\times(199/365)}] \times [N(d_2)] \\ &= (₹50 \times .6459) - (₹49 \times .9626 \times .5607) \\ &= ₹32.295 - 26.445 \\ &= ₹5.85 \end{aligned}$$

The estimated price of ₹5.85 is greater than the ₹4 actual price, implying that the call option is underpriced. A trader believing in the Black-Scholes model would buy a call. Of course, the Black-Scholes model is fallible. Perhaps the disparity between the model's estimate and the market price reflects error in the trader's estimate of variance.

The previous example stressed the calculations involved in using the Black-Scholes formula. Is there any intuition behind the formula? Yes, and that intuition follows from the stock purchase and borrowing strategy in our binomial example. The first line of the Black-Scholes equation is:

$$C = SN(d_1) - Ee^{-Rt}N(d_2)$$

which is exactly analogous to Equation 22.2:

$$\text{Value of call} = \text{Stock price} \times \text{Delta} - \text{Amount borrowed} \quad \textbf{(22.2)}$$

We presented this equation in the binomial example. It turns out that $N(d_1)$ is the delta in the Black-Scholes model. $N(d_1)$ is .6459 in the previous example. In addition, $Ee^{-Rt}N(d_2)$ is the amount that an investor must borrow to duplicate a call. In the previous example, this value is ₹26.45 (= ₹49 × .9626 × .5607). The model tells us that we can duplicate the call of the preceding example by both:

Another good options calculator can be found at **www.option-price.com/index.php**.

1. Buying .6459 shares of stock.
2. Borrowing ₹26.45.

It is no exaggeration to say that the Black-Scholes formula is among the most important contributions in finance. It allows anyone to calculate the value of an option given a few parameters. The attraction of the formula is that four of the parameters are observable: the current price of stock, *S*; the exercise price, *E*; the interest rate, *R*; and the time to expiration date, *t*. Only one of the parameters must be estimated: the variance of return, σ^2.

[8]This method is called *linear interpolation*. It is only one of a number of possible methods of interpolation.

To see how truly attractive this formula is, note what parameters are not needed. First, the investor's risk aversion does not affect value. The formula can be used by anyone, regardless of willingness to bear risk. Second, it does not depend on the expected return on the stock! Investors with different assessments of the stock's expected return will nevertheless agree on the call price. As in the two-state example, this is because the call depends on the stock price, and that price already balances investors' divergent views.

22.9 Stocks and Bonds as Options

The previous material in this chapter described, explained, and valued publicly traded options. This is important material to any finance student because much trading occurs in these listed options. The study of options has another purpose for the student of corporate finance, which we will explore in this section.

You may have heard the one-liner about the elderly gentleman who was surprised to learn that he had been speaking prose all of his life. The same can be said about the corporate finance student and options. Although options were formally defined for the first time in this chapter, many corporate policies discussed earlier in the text were actually options in disguise. Though it is beyond the scope of this chapter to recast all of corporate finance in terms of options, the rest of the chapter considers three examples of implicit options:

1. Stocks and bonds as options.
2. Capital structure decisions as options.
3. Capital budgeting decisions as options.

We begin by illustrating the implicit options in stocks and bonds.

This example is similar to the bankruptcy examples presented in our chapters about capital structure. Our new insight is that the relationship between the common stock and the firm can be expressed in

EXAMPLE 22.5

Stocks and Bonds as Options The Popatlal Company has been awarded the concessions at next year's Olympic Games in Antarctica. Because the firm's principals live in Antarctica and because there is no other concession business on that continent, their enterprise will disband after the games. The firm has issued debt to help finance this venture. Interest and principal due on the debt next year will be ₹800, at which time the debt will be paid off in full. The firm's cash flows next year are forecast as follows:

	Popatlal's Cash Flow Schedule			
	Very Successful Games	Moderately Successful Games	Moderately Unsuccessful Games	Outright Failure
Cash flow before interest and principal	₹1,000	₹850	₹700	₹550
− Interest and principal	800	800	700	550
Cash flow to stockholders	₹ 200	₹ 50	₹ 0	₹ 0

As can be seen, the principals forecast four equally likely scenarios. If either of the first two scenarios occurs, the bondholders will be paid in full. The extra cash flow goes to the stockholders. However, if either of the last two scenarios occurs, the bondholders will not be paid in full. Instead, they will receive the firm's entire cash flow, leaving the stockholders with nothing.

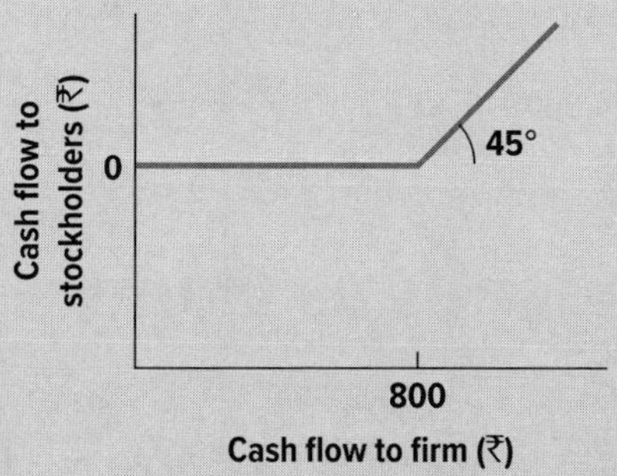

The stockholders can be viewed as having a call option on the firm. If the cash flows of the firm exceed ₹800, the stockholders pay ₹800 in order to receive the firm's cash flows. If the cash flows of the firm are less than ₹800, the stockholders do not exercise their option. They walk away from the firm, receiving nothing.

Figure 22.11 Cash Flow to Stockholders of Popatlal Company as a Function of Cash Flow to Firm

terms of options. We consider call options first because the intuition is easier. The put option scenario is treated next.

THE FIRM EXPRESSED IN TERMS OF CALL OPTIONS

The Stockholders We now show that stock can be viewed as a call option on the firm. To illustrate this, Figure 22.11 graphs the cash flow to the stockholders as a function of the cash flow to the firm. The stockholders receive nothing if the firm's cash flows are less than ₹800; here, all of the cash flows go to the bondholders. However, the stockholders earn a Rupee for every Rupee that the firm receives above ₹800. The graph looks exactly like the call option graphs that we considered earlier in this chapter.

But what is the underlying asset upon which the stock is a call option? The underlying asset is the firm itself. That is, we can view the bondholders as owning the firm. However, the stockholders have a call option on the firm with an exercise price of ₹800.

If the firm's cash flow is above ₹800, the stockholders would choose to exercise this option. In other words, they would buy the firm from the bondholders for ₹800. Their net cash flow is the difference between the firm's cash flow and their ₹800 payment. This would be ₹200 (= ₹1,000 – 800) if the games are very successful and ₹50 (= ₹850 – 800) if the games are moderately successful.

Should the value of the firm's cash flows be less than ₹800, the stockholders would not choose to exercise their option. Instead, they would walk away from the firm, as any call option holder would do. The bondholders would then receive the firm's entire cash flow.

This view of the firm is a novel one and students are frequently bothered by it on first exposure. However, we encourage students to keep looking at the firm in this way until the view becomes second nature to them.

The Bondholders What about the bondholders? Our earlier cash flow schedule showed that they would get the entire cash flow of the firm if the firm generates less cash than ₹800. Should the firm earn more than ₹800, the bondholders would receive only ₹800. That is, they are entitled only to interest and principal. This schedule is graphed in Figure 22.12.

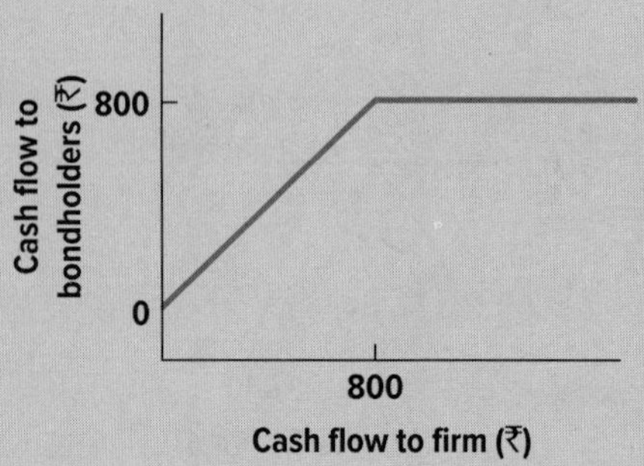

The bondholders can be viewed as owning the firm but writing a call option on the firm to the stockholders, as well. If the cash flows of the firm exceed ₹800, the call is exercised against the bondholders. The bondholders give up the firm and receive ₹800. If the cash flows are less than ₹800, the call expires. The bondholders receive the cash flows of the firm in this case.

Figure 22.12 Cash Flow to Bondholders of Popatlal Company as a Function of Cash Flow to Firm

In keeping with our view that the stockholders have a call option on the firm, what does the bondholders' position consist of? The bondholders' position can be described by two claims:

1. They own the firm.
2. They have written a call on the firm with an exercise price of ₹800.

As we mentioned before, the stockholders walk away from the firm if cash flows are less than ₹800. The bondholders retain ownership in this case. However, if the cash flows are greater than ₹800, the stockholders exercise their option. They call the stock away from the bondholders for ₹800.

THE FIRM EXPRESSED IN TERMS OF PUT OPTIONS

The preceding analysis expresses the positions of the stockholders and the bondholders in terms of call options. We now can express the situation in terms of put options.

The Stockholders The stockholders' position can be expressed by three claims:

1. They own the firm.
2. They owe ₹800 in interest and principal to the bondholders.

If the debt were risk-free, these two claims would fully describe the stockholders' situation. However, because of the possibility of default, we have a third claim, as well:

3. The stockholders own a put option on the firm with an exercise price of ₹800. The group of bondholders is the seller of the put.

Now consider two possibilities.

Cash Flow Is Less Than ₹800 Because the put has an exercise price of ₹800, the put is in the money. The stockholders *put*–that is, sell–the firm to the bondholders. Normally, the holder of a put receives the exercise price when the asset is sold. However, the stockholders already owe ₹800 to the bondholders. The debt of ₹800 is canceled–and no money changes hands–when the stock is delivered to the bondholders. Because the stockholders give up the stock in exchange for extinguishing the debt, the stockholders end up with nothing if the cash flow is below ₹800.

Cash Flow Is Greater Than ₹800 Because the put is out of the money here, the stockholders do not exercise. The stockholders retain ownership of the firm but pay ₹800 to the bondholders as interest and principal.

The Bondholders

The bondholders' position can be described by two claims:

1. The bondholders are owed ₹800.
2. They have sold a put option on the firm to the stockholders with an exercise price of ₹800.

Cash Flow Is Less Than ₹800 As mentioned before, the stockholders will exercise the put in this case. This means that the bondholders are obligated to pay ₹800 for the firm. Because they are owed ₹800, the two obligations offset each other. The bondholders end up with the firm in this case.

Cash Flow Is Greater Than ₹800 Here, the stockholders do not exercise the put. The bondholders merely receive the ₹800 that is due them.

Expressing the bondholders' position in this way is illuminating. With a riskless default-free bond, the bondholders are owed ₹800. Thus, we can express the risky bond in terms of a riskless bond and a put:

$$\begin{matrix}\text{Value of risky} \\ \text{bond}\end{matrix} = \begin{matrix}\text{Value of} \\ \text{default-free bond}\end{matrix} - \begin{matrix}\text{Value of} \\ \text{put option}\end{matrix}$$

That is, the value of the risky bond is the value of the default-free bond less the value of the stockholders' option to sell the company for ₹800.

A RESOLUTION OF THE TWO VIEWS

We have argued that the positions of the stockholders and the bondholders can be viewed either in terms of calls or in terms of puts. These two viewpoints are summarized in Table 22.4.

We have found from experience that it is generally harder for students to think of the firm in terms of puts than in terms of calls. It would be helpful if there were a way to show that the two viewpoints

Table 22.4 Positions of Stockholders and Bondholders in Popatlal Company in Terms of Calls and Puts

Stockholders	Bondholders
Positions viewed in terms of call options	
1. Stockholders own a call on the firm with an exercise price of ₹800.	1. Bondholders own the firm. 2. Bondholders have sold a call on the firm to the stockholders.
Positions viewed in terms of put options	
1. Stockholders own the firm. 2. Stockholders owe ₹800 in interest and principal to bondholders. 3. Stockholders own a put option on the firm with an exercise price of ₹800.	1. Bondholders are owed ₹800 in interest and principal. 2. Bondholders have sold a put on the firm to the stockholders.

are equivalent. Fortunately, there is *put-call parity*. In an earlier section, we presented the put-call parity relationship as Equation 22.1, which we now repeat:

$$\text{Price of underlying stock} + \text{Price of put} = \text{Price of call} + \text{Present value of exercise price} \quad \textbf{(22.1)}$$

Using the results of this section, Equation 22.1 can be rewritten like this:

$$\text{Value of call on firm} = \text{Value of firm} + \text{Value of put on firm} - \text{Value of default-free bond}$$

$$\text{Stockholders' position in terms of call options} = \text{Stockholders' position in terms of put options} \quad \textbf{(22.3)}$$

Going from Equation 22.1 to Equation 22.3 involves a few steps. First, we treat the firm, not the stock, as the underlying asset in this section. (In keeping with common convention, we refer to the *value* of the firm and the *price* of the stock.) Second, the exercise price is now ₹800, which is the principal and interest on the firm's debt. Taking the present value of this amount at the riskless rate yields the value of a default-free bond. Third, the order of the terms in Equation 22.1 is rearranged in Equation 22.3.

Note that the left side of Equation 22.3 is the stockholders' position in terms of call options, as shown in Table 22.4. The right side of Equation 22.3 is the stockholders' position in terms of put options, as shown in the same table. Put-call parity shows that viewing the stockholders' position in terms of call options is equivalent to viewing the stockholders' position in terms of put options.

Now let's rearrange the terms in Equation 22.3 to yield the following:

$$\text{Value of firm} - \text{Value of call on firm} = \text{Value of default-free bond} - \text{Value of put on firm}$$

$$\text{Bondholders' position in terms of call options} = \text{Bondholders' position in terms of put options} \quad \textbf{(22.4)}$$

The left side of Equation 22.4 is the bondholders' position in terms of call options, as shown in Table 22.4. (The minus sign on this side of the equation indicates that the bondholders are *writing* a call.) The right side of the equation is the bondholders' position in terms of put options, as shown in Table 22.4. Put-call parity shows that viewing the bondholders' position in terms of call options is equivalent to viewing the bondholders' position in terms of put options.

A NOTE ABOUT LOAN GUARANTEES

In the Popatlal example given earlier, the bondholders bore the risk of default. Of course, bondholders generally ask for an interest rate that is high enough to compensate them for bearing risk. When firms experience financial distress, they can no longer attract new debt at moderate interest rates. Firms experiencing distress have frequently sought loan guarantees from the government. Our framework can be used to understand these guarantees.

If the firm defaults on a guaranteed loan, the government must make up the difference. In other words, a government guarantee converts a risky bond into a riskless bond. What is the value of this guarantee?

Recall that with option pricing:

$$\text{Value of default-free bond} = \text{Value of risky bond} + \text{Value of put option}$$

This equation shows that the government is assuming an obligation that has a cost equal to the value of a put option.

This analysis differs from that of both politicians and company spokespeople. They generally say that the guarantee will cost the taxpayers nothing because the guarantee enables the firm to attract debt, thereby staying solvent. However, it should be pointed out that although solvency may be a strong possibility, it is never a certainty. When the guarantee is made, the government's obligation has a cost in terms of present value. To say that a government guarantee costs the government nothing is like saying a put on the stock of Microsoft has no value because the stock is likely to rise in price.

Actually, the U.S. government has had good fortune with loan guarantees. Its biggest guarantees before the 2008 financial crisis were to the Lockheed Corporation in 1971 and the Chrysler Corporation in 1980. Both firms nearly ran out of cash and defaulted on loans. In both cases, the U.S. government came to the rescue by agreeing to guarantee new loans. Under the guarantees, if Lockheed and Chrysler had defaulted on new loans, the lenders could have obtained the full value of their claims from the U.S. government. From the lender's point of view, the loans became as risk-free as Treasury bonds. These guarantees enabled Lockheed and Chrysler to borrow large amounts of cash and get through a difficult time. As it turned out, neither firm defaulted.

Who benefits from a typical loan guarantee?

1. If existing risky bonds are guaranteed, all gains accrue to the existing bondholders. The stockholders gain nothing because the limited liability of corporations absolves the stockholders of any obligation in bankruptcy.
2. If new debt is issued and guaranteed, the new debtholders do not gain. Rather, in a competitive market, they must accept a low interest rate because of the debt's low risk. The stockholders gain here because they are able to issue debt at a low interest rate. In addition, some of the gains accrue to the old bondholders because the firm's value is greater than would otherwise be true. Therefore, if shareholders want all the gains from loan guarantees, they should renegotiate or retire existing bonds before the guarantee is in place. This happened in the Chrysler case.

22.10 Options and Corporate Decisions: Some Applications

In this section we explore the implications of options analysis in two key areas: capital budgeting and mergers. We start with mergers and show a very surprising result. We then go on to show that the net present value rule has some important wrinkles in a leveraged firm.

MERGERS AND DIVERSIFICATION

Elsewhere in this book, we discuss mergers and acquisitions. There we mention that diversification is frequently cited as a reason for two firms to merge. Is diversification a good reason to merge? It might seem so. After all, in an earlier chapter, we spent a lot of time explaining why diversification is valuable for investors in their own portfolios because of the elimination of unsystematic risk.

To investigate this issue, let's consider two companies, Sunny Day Activewear (SDA) and Rainy Day Activewear (RDA). For obvious reasons, SDA has high cash flows if the weather is sunny while RDA has high cash flows if the weather is rainy. Both companies have risky cash flows that depend on the weather. If the two companies were to merge, the combined company would have a much more stable cash flow. In other words, a merger would diversify away some of the risk and, in fact, make bankruptcy much less likely.

Notice that the operations of the two firms are very different, so the proposed merger is a purely financial merger. This means that there are no *synergies* or other value-creating possibilities except, possibly, gains from risk reduction. Here is some premerger information:

	Sunny Day Activewear	Rainy Day Activewear
Market value of assets	₹30 million	₹10 million
Face value of pure discount debt	₹12 million	₹ 4 million
Debt maturity	3 years	3 years
Asset return standard deviation	50%	60%

The risk-free rate, continuously compounded, is 5 percent. Given this, we can view the equity in each firm as a call option and calculate the following using Black-Scholes to determine equity values (check these for practice):

	Sunny Day Activewear	Rainy Day Activewear
Market value of equity	₹20.424 million	₹7.001 million
Market value of debt	₹ 9.576 million	₹2.999 million

If you check these, you may get slightly different answers if you use Table 22.3 (we used a spreadsheet). Notice that we calculated the market value of debt using the balance sheet identity.

After the merger, the combined firm's assets will be the sum of the premerger values (₹30 + 10 = ₹40 million) because no value was created or destroyed. Similarly, the total face value of the debt is now ₹16 million. However, we will assume that the combined firm's asset return standard deviation is 40 percent. This is lower than for either of the two individual firms because of the diversification effect.

So, what is the impact of this merger? To find out, we compute the postmerger value of the equity. Based on our discussion, here is the relevant information:

	Combined Firm
Market value of assets	₹40 million
Face value of pure discount debt	₹16 million
Debt maturity	3 years
Asset return standard deviation	40%

Once again, we can calculate equity and debt values:

	Combined Firm
Market value of equity	₹26.646 million
Market value of debt	₹13.354 million

What we notice is that this merger is a terrible idea, at least for the stockholders! Before the merger, the stock in the two separate firms was worth a total of ₹20.424 + 7.001 = ₹27.425 million, compared to only ₹26.646 million postmerger; so the merger vaporized ₹27.425 − 26.646 = ₹.779 million, or almost ₹800,000, in equity.

Where did the ₹800,000 in equity go? It went to the bondholders. Their bonds were worth ₹9.576 + 2.999 = ₹12.575 million before the merger and ₹13.354 million after, a gain of exactly ₹.779 million. This merger neither created nor destroyed value, but it shifted it from the stockholders to the bondholders.

Our example shows that pure financial mergers are a bad idea, and it also shows why. The diversification works in the sense that it reduces the volatility of the firm's return on assets. This risk reduction benefits the bondholders by making default less likely. This is sometimes called the *coinsurance* effect. Essentially, by merging, the firms insure each other's bonds. The bonds are less risky and rise in value. If the bonds increase in value and there is no net increase in asset values, then the equity must decrease in value. Pure financial mergers are good for creditors but not for stockholders.

Another way to see this is that because the equity is a call option, a reduction in return variance on the underlying asset has to reduce its value. The reduction in value in the case of a purely financial merger has an interesting interpretation. The merger makes default (and bankruptcy) less likely to happen. That is obviously a good thing from a bondholder's perspective, but why is it a bad thing from a stockholder's perspective? The answer is simple: The right to go bankrupt is a valuable stockholder option. A purely financial merger reduces the value of that option.

OPTIONS AND CAPITAL BUDGETING

We now consider two issues regarding capital budgeting. What we will show is that, for a leveraged firm, the shareholders might prefer a lower NPV project to a higher one. We then show that they might even prefer a *negative* NPV project to a positive NPV project.

As usual, we will illustrate these points first with an example. Here is the basic background information for the firm:

Market value of assets	₹20 million
Face value of pure discount debt	₹40 million
Debt maturity	5 years
Asset return standard deviation	50%

The risk-free rate is 4 percent. As we have now done several times, we can calculate equity and debt values:

Market value of equity	₹ 5.744 million
Market value of debt	₹14.256 million

This firm has a fairly high degree of leverage: The debt-equity ratio based on market values is ₹14.256/₹5.744 = 2.48, or 248 percent. This is high, but not unheard of. Notice also that the option here is out of the money; as a result, the delta is .547.

The firm has two mutually exclusive investments under consideration. The projects affect both the market value of the firm's assets and the firm's asset return standard deviation as follows:

	Project A	Project B
NPV	₹ 4	₹ 2
Market value of firm's assets (₹20 + NPV)	₹24	₹22
Firm's asset return standard deviation	40%	60%

Which project is better? It is obvious that Project A has the higher NPV, but by now you are wary of the change in the firm's asset return standard deviation. One project reduces it; the other increases it. To see which project the stockholders like better, we have to go through our now familiar calculations:

	Project A	Project B
Market value of equity	₹ 5.965	₹ 8.751
Market value of debt	₹18.035	₹13.249

There is a dramatic difference between the two projects. Project A benefits both the stockholders and the bondholders, but most of the gain goes to the bondholders. Project B has a huge impact on the value of equity, plus it reduces the value of the debt. Clearly the stockholders prefer B.

What are the implications of our analysis? Basically, we have discovered two things. First, when the equity has a delta significantly smaller than 1.0, any value created will go partially to the bondholders. Second, stockholders have a strong incentive to increase the variance of the return on the firm's assets. More specifically, stockholders will have a strong preference for variance-increasing projects as opposed to variance-decreasing ones, even if that means a lower NPV.

Let's do one final example. Here is a different set of numbers:

Market value of assets	₹20 million
Face value of pure discount debt	₹100 million
Debt maturity	5 years
Asset return standard deviation	50%

The risk-free rate is 4 percent, so the equity and debt values are these:

Market value of equity	₹ 2.012 million
Market value of debt	₹17.988 million

Notice that the change from our previous example is that the face value of the debt is now ₹100 million, so the option is far out of the money. The delta is only .24, so most of any value created will go to the bondholders.

The firm has an investment under consideration that must be taken now or never. The project affects both the market value of the firm's assets and the firm's asset return standard deviation as follows:

Project NPV	−₹ 1 million
Market value of firm's assets (₹20 million + NPV)	₹19 million
Firm's asset return standard deviation	70%

The project has a negative NPV, but it increases the standard deviation of the firm's return on assets. If the firm takes the project, here is the result:

Market value of equity	₹ 4.834 million
Market value of debt	₹14.166 million

This project more than doubles the value of the equity! Once again, what we are seeing is that stockholders have a strong incentive to increase volatility, particularly when the option is far out of the money. What is happening is that the shareholders have relatively little to lose because bankruptcy is the likely outcome. As a result, there is a strong incentive to go for a long shot, even if that long shot has a negative NPV. It's a bit like using your very last Rupee on a lottery ticket. It's a bad investment, but there aren't a lot of other options!

This example illustrates a conflict of interest between stockholders and bondholders that we discussed in an earlier chapter. Because stockholders hold a call option, they have incentives to take large risks and gamble for resurrection. Such risk taking hurts bondholders, who have sold a call option and therefore prefer less volatility.

22.11 Investment in Real Projects and Options

Let us quickly review the material about capital budgeting presented earlier in the text. We first considered projects where forecasts for future cash flows were made at Year 0. The expected cash flow in each future period was discounted at an appropriate risky rate, yielding an NPV calculation. For independent projects, a positive NPV meant acceptance and a negative NPV meant rejection. This approach treated risk through the discount rate.

We later considered decision tree analysis, an approach that handles risk in a more sophisticated way. We pointed out that the firm will make investment and operating decisions on a project over its entire life. We value a project today, assuming that future decisions will be optimal. However, we do not yet know what these decisions will be because much information remains to be discovered. The firm's ability to delay its investment and operating decisions until the release of information is an option. We now illustrate this option through an example.

EXAMPLE 22.6

Options and Capital Budgeting Essar Oil Corporation is considering the purchase of an oil field in a remote part of Kashmir. The seller has listed the property for ₹10,000 and is eager to sell immediately. Initial drilling costs are ₹500,000. Essar anticipates that 10,000 barrels of oil can be extracted each year for many decades. Because the termination date is so far in the future and so hard to estimate, the firm views the cash flow stream from the oil as a perpetuity. With oil prices at ₹50 per barrel and extraction costs at ₹46 a barrel, the firm anticipates a net margin of ₹4 per barrel. Because oil prices are expected to rise at the inflation rate, the firm assumes that its cash flow per barrel will always be ₹4 in real terms. The appropriate real discount rate is 10 percent. For simplicity, we will ignore taxes. Should Essar buy the property?

The NPV of the oil field to Essar is:

$$-₹110{,}000 = -₹10{,}000 - ₹500{,}000 + \frac{₹4 \times 10{,}000}{.10}$$

According to this analysis, Essar should not purchase the land.

Though this approach uses the standard capital budgeting techniques of this and other textbooks, it is actually inappropriate for this situation. To see this, consider the analysis of Abhishek Gehlot, a consultant to Essar. He agrees that the price of oil is *expected* to rise at the rate of inflation. However, he points out that the

(*continued*)

next year will be quite perilous for oil prices. On the one hand, OPEC is considering a long-term agreement that would raise oil prices to ₹65 per barrel in real terms for many years in the future. On the other hand, Nag Motors recently indicated that cars using a mixture of sand and water for fuel are currently being tested. Abhishek argues that oil will be priced at ₹35 per barrel in real terms for many years should this development prove successful. Full information about both these developments will be released in exactly one year.

Should oil prices rise to ₹65 a barrel, the NPV of the project would be:

$$₹1{,}390{,}000 = -₹10{,}000 - 500{,}000 + \frac{(₹65 - 46) \times 10{,}000}{.10}$$

However, should oil prices fall to ₹35 a barrel, the NPV of the oil field will be even more negative than it is today.

Abhishek makes two recommendations to Essar's board. He argues that:

1. The land should be purchased.
2. The drilling decision should be delayed until information about both OPEC's new agreement and Nag Motors' new automobile is released.

Abhishek explains his recommendations to the board by first assuming that the land has already been purchased. He argues that under this assumption, the drilling decision should be delayed. Second, he investigates his assumption that the land should have been purchased in the first place. This approach of examining the second decision (whether to drill) after assuming that the first decision (to buy the land) has been made also was used in our earlier presentation on decision trees. Let us now work through Abhishek's analysis.

Assume the land has already been purchased. If the land has already been purchased, should drilling begin immediately? If drilling begins immediately, the NPV is −₹110,000. If the drilling decision is delayed until new information is released in a year, the optimal choice can be made at that time.

If oil prices drop to ₹35 a barrel, Essar should not drill. Instead, the firm should walk away from the project, losing nothing beyond its ₹10,000 purchase price for the land. If oil prices rise to ₹65, drilling should begin.

Abhishek points out that by delaying, the firm will invest the ₹500,000 of drilling costs only if oil prices rise. By delaying, the firm saves ₹500,000 in the case where oil prices drop. Abhishek concludes that once the land is purchased, the drilling decision should be delayed.[9]

Should the land have been purchased in the first place? We now know that if the land has been purchased, it is optimal to defer the drilling decision until the release of information. Given that we know this optimal decision concerning drilling, should the land be purchased in the first place? Without knowing the exact probability that oil prices will rise, Abhishek is nevertheless confident that the land should be purchased. The NPV of the project at ₹65 per barrel oil prices is ₹1,390,000, whereas the cost of the land is only ₹10,000. Abhishek believes that an oil price rise is possible, though by no means probable. Even so, he argues that the high potential return is clearly worth the risk.

This example presents an approach that is similar to our decision tree analysis of the Solar Equipment Company in a previous chapter. Our purpose in this section is to discuss this type of decision in an option framework. When Essar purchases the land, it is actually purchasing a call option. That is, once the land has been purchased, the firm has an option to buy an active oil field at an exercise price of ₹500,000. As it turns out, one should generally not exercise a call option immediately.[10] In this case, the firm should delay exercise until relevant information concerning future oil prices is released.

[9]Actually, there are three separate effects here. First, the firm avoids drilling costs in the case of low oil prices by delaying the decision. This is the effect discussed by Abhishek. Second, the present value of the ₹500,000 payment is less when the decision is delayed, even if drilling eventually takes place. Third, the firm loses one year of cash inflows through delay.

The first two effects support delaying the decision. The third effect supports immediate drilling. In this example, the first effect greatly outweighs the other two effects. Thus, Abhishek avoided the second and third effects in his presentation.

[10]Actually, it can be shown that a call option on a stock that pays no dividend should never be exercised before expiration. However, for a dividend-paying stock, it may be optimal to exercise prior to the ex-dividend date. The analogy applies to our example of an option in real assets.

This section points out a serious deficiency in classical capital budgeting: Net present value calculations typically ignore the flexibility that real-world firms have. In our example, the standard techniques generated a negative NPV for the land purchase. Yet, by allowing the firm the option to change its investment policy according to new information, the land purchase easily can be justified.

We encourage the reader to look for hidden options in projects. Because options are beneficial, managers are shortchanging their firm's projects if capital budgeting calculations ignore flexibility.

The firm would receive cash flows from oil earlier if drilling begins immediately. This is equivalent to the benefit from exercising a call on a stock prematurely in order to capture the dividend. However, in our example, this dividend effect is far outweighed by the benefits from waiting.

RESEARCH IN EMERGING MARKET CONTEXT

Banerjee et al. (2018) studied the Indian markets during a period of short-sale constraint, where institutional short-selling was either curtailed or banned outright. They investigated the effects of option listings and delistings and found a strong positive impact on listings/relisting, signalling a favourable market perception of the event. However, they also found a negative impact on delistings. Over long horizons, volatility was higher in both listed and delisted periods.

Dixit and Singh (2019) conducted an empirical study on the NSE Nifty 50 indices to investigate the impact of introducing short-selling and a well-functioning security lending and borrowing market on the overpricing of Nifty 50 index put options. Their results suggest that introducing short-selling significantly reduced the overpricing of Nifty 50 index put options.

Chakrabarti (2020) conducted a study on the response of options to market-wide volatility shocks. The study found that risk aversion premiums exhibited correlated patterns in the market index and individual stock options, resulting in a common relationship. The results remained consistent even after the inclusion of market-specific and stock-specific factors.

References

Banerjee, P., Chatrath, A., Christie-David, R., & Maitra, D. (2018). The effects of options listing and delisting in a short-sale-constrained market: Evidence from the Indian equities markets. *Global Finance Journal*, *35*, 157–169.

Chakrabarti, P. (2021). Co-movement of volatility risk premium: evidence from single stock options market in India. *Applied Economics Letters*, *28*(14), 1181–1186.

Dixit, A., & Singh, S. (2019). Options pricing and short-selling in the underlying: Evidence from India. *Journal of Futures Markets*, *39*(10), 1250–1268.

Summary and Conclusions

This chapter serves as an introduction to options.

1. The most familiar options are puts and calls. These options give the holder the right to sell or buy shares of common stock at a given exercise price. American options can be exercised any time up to and including the expiration date. European options can be exercised only on the expiration date.
2. We showed that a strategy of buying a stock and buying a put is equivalent to a strategy of buying a call and buying a zero coupon bond. From this, the put-call parity relationship was established:

$$\text{Value of stock} + \text{Value of put} - \text{Value of call} = \text{Present value of exercise price}$$

3. The value of an option depends on five factors:
   a. The price of the underlying asset.
   b. The exercise price.
   c. The expiration date.
   d. The variability of the underlying asset.
   e. The interest rate on risk-free bonds.

   The Black-Scholes model can determine the intrinsic price of an option from these five factors.
4. Much of corporate financial theory can be presented in terms of options. In this chapter, we pointed out that:
   a. Common stock can be represented as a call option on the firm.
   b. Stockholders enhance the value of their call by increasing the risk of their firm.
   c. Real projects have hidden options that enhance value.

Concept Questions

1. **Options** What is a call option? A put option? Under what circumstances might you want to buy each? Which one has greater potential profit? Why?
2. **Options** Complete the following sentence for each of these investors:
   a. A buyer of call options.
   b. A buyer of put options.
   c. A seller (writer) of call options.
   d. A seller (writer) of put options.

   "The (buyer/seller) of a (put/call) option (pays/receives) money for the (right/obligation) to (buy/sell) a specified asset at a fixed price for a fixed length of time."
3. **American and European Options** What is the difference between an American option and a European option?
4. **Intrinsic Value** What is the intrinsic value of a call option? Of a put option? How do we interpret these values?
5. **Option Pricing** You notice that shares of stock in the Patel Corporation are going for ₹50 per share. Call options with an exercise price of ₹35 per share are selling for ₹10. What's wrong here? Describe how you can take advantage of this mispricing if the option expires today.
6. **Options and Stock Risk** If the risk of a stock increases, what is likely to happen to the price of call options on the stock? To the price of put options? Why?
7. **Option Risk** True or false: The unsystematic risk of a share of stock is irrelevant for valuing the stock because it can be diversified away; therefore, it is also irrelevant for valuing a call option on the stock. Explain.
8. **Option Pricing** Suppose a certain stock currently sells for ₹30 per share. If a put option and a call option are available with ₹30 exercise prices, which do you think will sell for more? Explain.
9. **Option Price and Interest Rates** Suppose the interest rate on T-bills suddenly and unexpectedly rises. All other things being the same, what is the impact on call option values? On put option values?
10. **Contingent Liabilities** When you take out an ordinary student loan, it is usually the case that whoever holds that loan is given a guarantee by the U.S. government, meaning that the government will make up any payments you skip. This is one example of the many loan guarantees made by the U.S. government. Such guarantees don't show up in calculations of government spending or in official deficit figures. Why not? Should they show up?
11. **Options and Expiration Dates** What is the impact of lengthening the time to expiration on an option's value? Explain.

12. **Options and Stock Price Volatility** What is the impact of an increase in the volatility of the underlying stock's return on an option's value? Explain.

13. **Insurance as an Option** An insurance policy is considered analogous to an option. From the policyholder's point of view, what type of option is an insurance policy? Why?

14. **Equity as a Call Option** It is said that the equityholders of a levered firm can be thought of as holding a call option on the firm's assets. Explain what is meant by this statement.

15. **Option Valuation and NPV** You are the CEO of Titan Industries and have just been awarded a large number of employee stock options. The company has two mutually exclusive projects available. The first project has a large NPV and will reduce the total risk of the company. The second project has a small NPV and will increase the total risk of the company. You have decided to accept the first project when you remember your employee stock options. How might this affect your decision?

16. **Put-Call Parity** You find a put and a call with the same exercise price and maturity. What do you know about the relative prices of the put and call? Prove your answer and provide an intuitive explanation.

17. **Put-Call Parity** A put and a call have the same maturity and strike price. If they have the same price, which one is in the money? Prove your answer and provide an intuitive explanation.

18. **Put-Call Parity** One thing put-call parity tells us is that given any three of a stock, a call, a put, and a T-bill, the fourth can be synthesized or replicated using the other three. How can we replicate a share of stock using a call, a put, and a T-bill?

Questions and Problems

BASIC (Questions 1–17)

1. **Two-State Option Pricing Model** T-bills currently yield 3.4 percent. Stock in Deadwood Manufacturing is currently selling for ₹67 per share. There is no possibility that the stock will be worth less than ₹60 per share in one year.

   a. What is the value of a call option with a ₹55 exercise price? What is the intrinsic value?
   b. What is the value of a call option with a ₹45 exercise price? What is the intrinsic value?
   c. What is the value of a put option with a ₹55 exercise price? What is the intrinsic value?

2. **Understanding Option Quotes** Use the option quote information shown here to answer the questions that follow. The stock is currently selling for ₹85.

Option and NY Close	Expiration	Strike Price	Calls		Puts	
			Vol.	Last	Vol.	Last
RWJ						
	Mar	80	230	2.80	160	.80
	Apr	80	170	6.00	127	1.40
	Jul	80	139	8.50	43	3.90
	Oct	80	60	10.20	11	3.65

   a. Are the call options in the money? What is the intrinsic value of an RWJ Corp. call option?
   b. Are the put options in the money? What is the intrinsic value of an RWJ Corp. put option?
   c. Two of the options are clearly mispriced. Which ones? At a minimum, what should the mispriced options sell for? Explain how you could profit from the mispricing in each case.

3. **Calculating Payoffs** Use the option quote information shown here to answer the questions that follow. The stock is currently selling for ₹40.

Option and NY Close	Expiration	Strike Price	Calls		Puts	
			Vol.	Last	Vol.	Last
Macrosoft						
	Feb	38	85	2.35	37	.24
	Mar	38	61	3.15	22	.93
	May	38	22	4.87	11	2.44
	Aug	38	3	6.15	3	3.56

a. Suppose you buy 10 contracts of the February 38 call option. How much will you pay, ignoring commissions?

b. In part (a), suppose that Macrosoft stock is selling for ₹43 per share on the expiration date. How much is your options investment worth? What if the terminal stock price is ₹39? Explain.

c. Suppose you buy 10 contracts of the August 38 put option. What is your maximum gain? On the expiration date, Macrosoft is selling for ₹32 per share. How much is your options investment worth? What is your net gain?

d. In part (c), suppose you sell 10 of the August 38 put contracts. What is your net gain or loss if Macrosoft is selling for ₹34 at expiration? For ₹41? What is the break-even price–that is, the terminal stock price that results in a zero profit?

4. **Two-State Option Pricing Model** The price of Chive Corp. stock will be either ₹57 or ₹84 at the end of the year. Call options are available with one year to expiration. T-bills currently yield 4 percent.

a. Suppose the current price of the stock is ₹65. What is the value of the call option if the exercise price is ₹50 per share?

b. Suppose the exercise price is ₹60 in part (a). What is the value of the call option now?

5. **Two-State Option Pricing Model** The price of Cilantro, Inc., stock will be either ₹60 or ₹80 at the end of the year. Call options are available with one year to expiration. T-bills currently yield 6 percent.

a. Suppose the current price of the stock is ₹70. What is the value of the call option if the exercise price is ₹50 per share?

b. Suppose the exercise price is ₹55 in part (a). What is the value of the call option now?

6. **Put-Call Parity** A stock is currently selling for ₹73 per share. A call option with an exercise price of ₹70 sells for ₹5.27 and expires in three months. If the risk-free rate of interest is 2.6 percent per year, compounded continuously, what is the price of a put option with the same exercise price?

7. **Put-Call Parity** A put option that expires in six months with an exercise price of ₹45 sells for ₹4.84. The stock is currently priced at ₹43, and the risk-free rate is 3.5 percent per year, compounded continuously. What is the price of a call option with the same exercise price?

8. **Put-Call Parity** A put option and a call option with an exercise price of ₹65 and three months to expiration sell for ₹5.27 and ₹1.04, respectively. If the risk-free rate is 3.1 percent per year, compounded continuously, what is the current stock price?

9. **Put-Call Parity** A put option and call option with an exercise price of ₹50 expire in four months and sell for ₹5.99 and ₹8.64, respectively. If the stock is currently priced at ₹52.27, what is the annual continuously compounded rate of interest?

10. **Black-Scholes** What are the prices of a call option and a put option with the following characteristics?

Stock price	= ₹58
Exercise price	= ₹60
Risk-free rate	= 2.7% per year, compounded continuously
Maturity	= 4 months
Standard deviation	= 47% per year

11. **Black-Scholes** What are the prices of a call option and a put option with the following characteristics?

Stock price	= ₹58
Exercise price	= ₹55
Risk-free rate	= 4% per year, compounded continuously
Maturity	= 5 months
Standard deviation	= 53% per year

12. **Delta** What are the deltas of a call option and a put option with the following characteristics? What does the delta of the option tell you?

Stock price	= ₹74
Exercise price	= ₹70
Risk-free rate	= 4.3% per year, compounded continuously
Maturity	= 9 months
Standard deviation	= 46% per year

13. **Black-Scholes and Asset Value** You own a lot in Key West, Florida, that is currently unused. Similar lots have recently sold for ₹1.35 million. Over the past five years, the price of land in the area has increased 7 percent per year, with an annual standard deviation of 5 percent. A buyer has recently approached you and wants an option to buy the land in the next 12 months for ₹1.6 million. The risk-free rate of interest is 5 percent per year, compounded continuously. How much should you charge for the option?

14. **Black-Scholes and Asset Value** In the previous problem, suppose you wanted the option to sell the land to the buyer in one year. Assuming all the facts are the same, describe the transaction that would occur today. What is the price of the transaction today?

15. **Time Value of Options** You are given the following information concerning options on a particular stock:
   a. What is the intrinsic value of the call option? Of the put option?
   b. What is the time value of the call option? Of the put option?
   c. Does the call or the put have the larger time value component? Would you expect this to be true in general?

Stock price	= ₹64
Exercise price	= ₹60
Risk-free rate	= 2% per year, compounded continuously
Maturity	= 6 months
Standard deviation	= 57% per year

16. **Risk-Neutral Valuation** A stock is currently priced at ₹84. The stock will either increase or decrease by 18 percent over the next year. There is a call option on the stock with a strike price of ₹80 and one year until expiration. If the risk-free rate is 8 percent, what is the risk-neutral value of the call option?

17. **Risk-Neutral Valuation** In the previous problem, assume the risk-free rate is only 5 percent. What is the risk-neutral value of the option now? What happens to the risk-neutral probabilities of a stock price increase and a stock price decrease?

INTERMEDIATE (Questions 18–29)

18. **Black-Scholes** A call option matures in six months. The underlying stock price is ₹75, and the stock's return has a standard deviation of 20 percent per year. The risk-free rate is 4 percent per year, compounded continuously. If the exercise price is ₹0, what is the price of the call option?

19. **Black-Scholes** A call option has an exercise price of ₹70 and matures in six months. The current stock price is ₹73, and the risk-free rate is 5 percent per year, compounded continuously. What is the price of the call if the standard deviation of the stock is 0 percent per year?

20. **Black-Scholes** A stock is currently priced at ₹47. A call option with an expiration of one year has an exercise price of ₹50. The risk-free rate is 12 percent per year, compounded continuously, and the standard deviation of the stock's return is infinitely large. What is the price of the call option?

21. **Equity as an Option** Sunburn Sunscreen has a zero coupon bond issue outstanding with a ₹10,000 face value that matures in one year. The current market value of the firm's assets is ₹10,900. The standard deviation of the return on the firm's assets is 31 percent per year, and the annual risk-free rate is 6 percent per year, compounded continuously. Based on the Black-Scholes model, what is the market value of the firm's equity and debt?

22. **Equity as an Option and NPV** Suppose the firm in the previous problem is considering two mutually exclusive investments. Project A has an NPV of ₹2,400 and Project B has an NPV of ₹2,800. As a result of taking Project A, the standard deviation of the return on the firm's assets will increase to 49 percent per year. If Project B is taken, the standard deviation will fall to 26 percent per year.

    a. What is the value of the firm's equity and debt if Project A is undertaken? If Project B is undertaken?
    b. Which project would the stockholders prefer? Can you reconcile your answer with the NPV rule?
    c. Suppose the stockholders and bondholders are, in fact, the same group of investors. Would this affect your answer to part (b)?
    d. What does this problem suggest to you about stockholder incentives?

23. **Equity as an Option** Frostbite Thermalwear has a zero coupon bond issue outstanding with a face value of ₹20,000 that matures in one year. The current market value of the firm's assets is ₹23,100. The standard deviation of the return on the firm's assets is 38 percent per year, and the annual risk-free rate is 6 percent per year, compounded continuously. Based on the Black-Scholes model, what is the market value of the firm's equity and debt? What is the firm's continuously compounded cost of debt?

24. **Mergers and Equity as an Option** Suppose Sunburn Sunscreen and Frostbite Thermalwear in the previous problems have decided to merge. Because the two companies have seasonal sales, the combined firm's return on assets will have a standard deviation of 21 percent per year.

    a. What is the combined value of equity in the two existing companies? The value of debt?
    b. What is the value of the new firm's equity? The value of debt?
    c. What was the gain or loss for shareholders? For bondholders?
    d. What happened to shareholder value here?

25. **Equity as an Option and NPV** A company has a single zero coupon bond outstanding that matures in five years with a face value of ₹16.5 million. The current value of the company's assets is ₹15.1 million, and the standard deviation of the return on the firm's assets is 41 percent per year. The risk-free rate is 6 percent per year, compounded continuously.

    a. What is the current market value of the company's equity?
    b. What is the current market value of the company's debt?
    c. What is the company's continuously compounded cost of debt?

d. The company has a new project available. The project has an NPV of ₹2.2 million. If the company undertakes the project, what will be the new market value of equity? Assume volatility is unchanged.

e. Assuming the company undertakes the new project and does not borrow any additional funds, what is the new continuously compounded cost of debt? What is happening here?

26. **Two-State Option Pricing Model** Ken is interested in buying a European call option written on Southeastern Airlines, Inc., a non-dividend-paying common stock, with a strike price of ₹55 and one year until expiration. Currently, the company's stock sells for ₹57 per share. Ken knows that, in one year, the company's stock will be trading at either ₹67 per share or ₹46 per share. Ken is able to borrow and lend at the risk-free EAR of 2.5 percent.

a. What should the call option sell for today?

b. If no options currently trade on the stock, is there a way to create a synthetic call option with identical payoffs to the call option just described? If there is, how would you do it?

c. How much does the synthetic call option cost? Is this greater than, less than, or equal to what the actual call option costs? Does this make sense?

27. **Two-State Option Pricing Model** Rob wishes to buy a European put option on BioLabs, Inc., a non-dividend-paying common stock, with a strike price of ₹60 and six months until expiration. The company's common stock is currently selling for ₹57 per share and Rob expects that the stock price will either rise to ₹67 or fall to ₹48 in six months. Rob can borrow and lend at the risk-free EAR of 5 percent.

a. What should the put option sell for today?

b. If no options currently trade on the stock, is there a way to create a synthetic put option with identical payoffs to the put option just described? If there is, how would you do it?

c. How much does the synthetic put option cost? Is this greater than, less than, or equal to what the actual put option costs? Does this make sense?

28. **Two-State Option Pricing Model** Maverick Manufacturing, Inc., must purchase gold in three months for use in its operations. Maverick's management has estimated that if the price of gold were to rise above ₹1,940 per ounce, the firm would go bankrupt. The current price of gold is ₹1,820 per ounce. The firm's chief financial officer believes that the price of gold will either rise to ₹2,035 per ounce or fall to ₹1,670 per ounce over the next three months. Management wishes to eliminate any risk of the firm going bankrupt. Maverick can borrow and lend at the risk-free EAR of 6.50 percent.

a. Should the company buy a call option or a put option on gold? To avoid bankruptcy, what strike price and time to expiration would the company like this option to have?

b. How much should such an option sell for in the open market?

c. If no options currently trade on gold, is there a way for the company to create a synthetic option with identical payoffs to the option just described? If there is, how would the firm do it?

d. How much does the synthetic option cost? Is this greater than, less than, or equal to what the actual option costs? Does this make sense?

29. **Black-Scholes and Collar Cost** An investor is said to take a position in a "collar" if she buys the asset, buys an out-of-the-money put option on the asset, and sells an out-of-the-money call option on the asset. The two options should have the same time to expiration. Suppose Marie wishes to purchase a collar on Riggs, Inc., a non-dividend-paying common stock, with six months until expiration. She would like the put to have a strike price of ₹55 and the call to have a strike price of ₹80. The current price of the stock is ₹68 per share. Marie can borrow and lend at the continuously compounded risk-free rate of 7 percent per year, and the annual standard deviation of the stock's return is 50 percent. Use the Black-Scholes model to calculate the total cost of the collar that Marie is interested in buying. What is the effect of the collar?

CHALLENGE (Questions 30–38)

30. **Debt Valuation and Time to Maturity** Zoso Industries has a zero coupon bond issue that matures in two years with a face value of ₹50,000. The current value of the company's assets is ₹34,600, and the standard deviation of the return on assets is 60 percent per year.

a. Assume the risk-free rate is 5 percent per year, compounded continuously. What is the value of a risk-free bond with the same face value and maturity as the company's bond?

b. What price would the bondholders have to pay for a put option on the company's assets with a strike price equal to the face value of the debt?

c. Using the answers from parts (a) and (b), what is the value of the company's debt? What is the continuously compounded yield on the company's debt?

d. From an examination of the value of the assets of the company, and the fact that the debt must be repaid in two years, it seems likely that the company will default on its debt. Management has approached bondholders and proposed a plan whereby the company would repay the same face value of debt, but the repayment would not occur for five years. What is the value of the debt under the proposed plan? What is the new continuously compounded yield on the debt? Explain why this occurs.

31. Debt Valuation and Asset Variance Marshall Corp. has a zero coupon bond that matures in five years with a face value of ₹75,000. The current value of the company's assets is ₹71,000, and the standard deviation of its return on assets is 34 percent per year. The risk-free rate is 7 percent per year, compounded continuously.

a. What is the value of a risk-free bond with the same face value and maturity as the current bond?

b. What is the value of a put option on the company's assets with a strike price equal to the face value of the debt?

c. Using the answers from parts (a) and (b), what is the value of the company's debt? What is the continuously compounded yield on the company's debt?

d. Assume the company can restructure its assets so that the standard deviation of its return on assets increases to 43 percent per year. What happens to the value of the debt? What is the new continuously compounded yield on the debt? Reconcile your answers in parts (c) and (d).

e. What happens to bondholders if the company restructures its assets? What happens to shareholders? How does this create an agency problem?

32. Two-State Option Pricing and Corporate Valuation Strudler Real Estate, Inc., a construction firm financed by both debt and equity, is undertaking a new project. If the project is successful, the value of the firm in one year will be ₹198 million, but if the project is a failure, the firm will be worth only ₹120 million. The current value of the company is ₹163 million, a figure that includes the prospects for the new project. The company has zero coupon bonds due in one year with a face value of ₹150 million. Treasury bills that mature in one year have an EAR of 7 percent. The company pays no dividends.

a. Use the two-state option pricing model to find the current value of the company's debt and equity.

b. Suppose the company has 500,000 shares of common stock outstanding. What is the price per share of the company's equity?

c. Compare the market value of the company's debt to the present value of an equal amount of debt that is riskless with one year until maturity. Is the firm's debt worth more than, less than, or the same as the riskless debt? Does this make sense? What factors might cause these two values to be different?

d. Suppose that in place of the preceding project, the company's management decides to undertake a project that is even more risky. The value of the company will either increase to ₹217 million or decrease to ₹105 million by the end of the year. Surprisingly, management concludes that the value of the company today will remain at exactly ₹163 million if this risky project is substituted for the less risky one. Use the two-state option pricing model to determine the values of the firm's debt and equity if the company plans on undertaking this new project. Which project do bondholders prefer?

33. Black-Scholes and Dividends In addition to the five factors discussed in the chapter, dividends also affect the price of an option. The Black-Scholes option pricing model with dividends is:

$$C = S \times e^{-dt} \times \mathrm{N}(d_1) - E \times e^{-Rt} \times \mathrm{N}(d_2)$$

$$d_1 = \left[\ln(S/E) + \left(R - d + \sigma^2/2\right) \times t\right]/(\sigma \times \sqrt{t})$$

$$d_2 = d_1 - \sigma \times \sqrt{t}$$

All of the variables are the same as for the Black-Scholes model without dividends except for the variable d, which is the continuously compounded dividend yield on the stock.

a. What effect do you think the dividend yield will have on the price of a call option? Explain.

b. A stock is currently priced at ₹94 per share, the standard deviation of its return is 50 percent per year, and the risk-free rate is 4 percent per year, compounded continuously. What is the price of a call option with a strike price of ₹90 and a maturity of six months if the stock has a dividend yield of 2 percent per year?

34. Put-Call Parity and Dividends The put-call parity condition is altered when dividends are paid. The dividend-adjusted put-call parity formula is:

$$S \times e^{-dt} + P = E \times e^{-Rt} + C$$

where d is again the continuously compounded dividend yield.

a. What effect do you think the dividend yield will have on the price of a put option? Explain.

b. From the previous question, what is the price of a put option with the same strike price and time to expiration as the call option?

35. Put Delta In the chapter we noted that the delta for a put option is $N(d_1) - 1$. Is this the same thing as $-N(-d_1)$? (*Hint*: Yes, but why?)

36. Black-Scholes Put Pricing Model Use the Black-Scholes model for pricing a call, put-call parity, and the previous question to show that the Black-Scholes model for directly pricing a put can be written as follows:

$$P = E \times e^{-Rt} \times N(-d_2) - S \times N(-d_1)$$

37. Black-Scholes A stock is currently priced at ₹50. The stock will never pay a dividend. The risk-free rate is 12 percent per year, compounded continuously, and the standard deviation of the stock's return is 60 percent. A European call option on the stock has a strike price of ₹100 and no expiration date, meaning that it has an infinite life. Based on Black-Scholes, what is the value of the call option? Do you see a paradox here? Do you see a way out of the paradox?

38. Delta You purchase one call and sell one put with the same strike price and expiration date. What is the delta of your portfolio? Why?

39. Options Quotes The following data on NIFTY BANKEX, i.e., NSE's banking index has been taken from the Business Standard Newspaper dated March 15, 2024.[11]

Instrument No.	1	2
INSTRUMENT FEATURES	**Call option**	**Put option**
Expiry Date	20-03-2024	20-03-2024
Strike Price	46,500	46,500
Premium Open/High/Low (₹)	500/626/309	339.95/546.55/260.25
Traded Qty. (Contracts)	35,33,945	43,81,690
Notional Value (₹Crores)	2,129.75	2,593.91
Open Interest	1,06,441	1,19,501

Based on the above information, answer the following questions:

a. 'On the above date, the NIFTY BANKEX closed below its open price' - Yes or No? Discuss.

[11]Ignore transaction costs and time value of money for this section (unless asked).

b. If it is known that (i) NIFTY BANKEX on 15-03-2024 closed at 46,594, and (ii) on the above date, Raghuvir invested a total of ₹2000 in either of the above two instruments purchasing 4 contracts (ignore the lot size of Bankex), compute the maximum profit and maximum loss Raghuvir would have incurred.

c. If the NIFTY BANKEX on that day traded between 46,360 and 46,617, how much would a protected put on the above date would have cost?

d. Based on the above information, can we state that 'the average premium of call option was more than put option' - Yes or No? Discuss.

e. It is known that a web-trading site charges 0.15% as brokerage on 'buying of all types of options.' Brokerage is computed on the underlying value of the contract. Gaurik Shah buys 1 call contract of the above description at ₹309/-. For this trade, how much would Gaurik Shah will be charged?

f. A competing web-trading site charges ₹20/contract traded as brokerage on 'buying of all types of options.' Radhakrishnan Pillai buys 1 call contract of the above description at ₹309/-. For this trade, how much would Radhakrishnan Pillai will be charged?

Excel Master It! Problem

Excel Master coverage online

In addition to spinners and scroll bars, there are numerous other controls in Excel. For this assignment, you need to build a Black-Scholes Option Pricing Model spreadsheet using several of these controls.

a. Buttons are always used in sets. Using buttons permits you to check an option, and the spreadsheet will use that input. In this case, you need to create two buttons, one for a call option and one for a put option. When using the spreadsheet, if you click the call option, the spreadsheet will calculate a call price, and if you click the put option, it will calculate the price of a put. Notice on the next spreadsheet that cell B20 is empty. This cell should change names. The names should be "Call option price" and "Put option price." In the price cell, only the price for the call option or put option is displayed, depending on which button is selected. For the button, use the button under Form Controls.

b. A Combo Box uses a drop-down menu with values entered by the spreadsheet developer. One advantage of a Combo Box is that the user can choose values from the drop-down menu or enter another value if he or she chooses. In this case, you want to create a Combo Box for the stock price and a separate Combo Box for the strike price. On the right-hand side of the spreadsheet, we have values for the drop-down menu. These values should be created in an array before the Combo Box is inserted. To create an ActiveX Combo Box, go to Developer, Insert, and select Combo Box from the ActiveX Controls menu. After you draw the Combo Box, right-click on the box, select Properties, and enter the LinkedCell, which is the cell where you want the output displayed, and the ListFillRange, which is the range that contains the list of values you want displayed in the drop-down menu.

c. In contrast to a Combo Box, a List Box permits the user to scroll through a list of possible values that are predetermined by the spreadsheet developer. No other values can be entered. You need to create a List Box for the interest rate using the interest rate array on the right-hand side of the spreadsheet. To insert a List Box, go to Developer, Insert, and choose the List Box from the ActiveX Controls. To enter the linked cell and array of values, you will need to go to the Properties for the List Box. To do this, right-click on the List Box and select Properties from the menu. We should note here that to edit both the Combo Box and List Box, you will need to make sure that Design Mode is checked on the Developer tab.

CLISSOLD INDUSTRIES OPTIONS

You are currently working for Clissold Industries. The company, which went public five years ago, engages in the design, production, and distribution of lighting equipment and specialty products worldwide. Because of recent events, Mal Clissold, the company president, is concerned about the company's risk, so he asks for your input.

In your discussion with Mal, you explain that the CAPM proposes that the market risk of the company's stock is the determinant of its expected return. Even though Mal agrees with this, he argues that his portfolio consists entirely of Clissold Industry stock and options, so he is concerned with the total risk, or standard deviation, of the company's stock. Furthermore, even though he has calculated the standard deviation of the company's stock for the past five years, he would like an estimate of the stock's volatility moving forward.

Mal states that you can find the estimated volatility of the stock for future periods by calculating the implied standard deviation of option contracts on the company stock. When you examine the factors that affect the price of an option, all of the factors except the standard deviation of the stock are directly observable in the market. Mal states that because you can observe all of the option factors except the standard deviation, you can solve the Black-Scholes model and find the implied standard deviation.

To help you find the implied standard deviation of the company's stock, Mal has provided you with the following option prices on four call options that expire in six months. The risk-free rate is 4 percent and the current stock price is ₹53.

Strike rice	Option Price
₹50	₹12.78
55	10.14
60	7.99
65	5.81

1. How many different volatilities would you expect to see for the stock?
2. Unfortunately, solving for the implied standard deviation is not as easy as Mal suggests. In fact, there is no direct solution for the standard deviation of the stock even if we have all the other variables for the Black-Scholes model. Mal still would like you to estimate the implied standard deviation of the stock. To do this, set up a spreadsheet using the Solver function in Excel to calculate the implied volatilities for each of the options.
3. Are all of the implied volatilities for the options the same? (*Hint*: No.) What are the possible reasons that can cause different volatilities for these options?
4. After you discuss the importance of volatility on option prices, your boss mentions that he has heard of the VIX. What is the VIX and what does it represent? You might need to visit the Chicago Board Options Exchange (CBOE) at **www.cboe.com** to help with your answer.
5. When you are on the CBOE website, look for the option quotes for the VIX. What does the implied volatility of a VIX option represent?

Options and Corporate Finance: Extensions and Applications

In 2020, the stock market took a nose dive when the COVID-19 lockdowns occurred, and we have already discussed the quick market rebound. But what is less well-known is how the market rebound affected the value of employee stock options for executives who had options granted early in the year. For example, Peloton stock went on a ride, and the options granted to President William Lynch gained more than ₹64 million in value by October. Over the same time period, options granted to Dick's Sporting Goods CEO Edward Stack gained ₹60 million in value. Since 2021, ESOPs have gained traction, and ESOP cashouts have led to ₹1.46 billion of wealth in the hands of startup employees since the beginning of 2021, according to data from Qapita. This was despite a 62 percent drop in cashout events in 2023.

Over the years, many new-age companies, like PhonePe, Swiggy and others, have been rewarding employees with ESOPs and repurchasing them at a lucrative price, eventually generating wealth for employees, especially those who joined an organization early. In this chapter, we discuss employee stock options, as well as the options seen in capital budgeting.

Please visit us at **rwjcorporatefinance.blogspot.com** for the latest developments in the world of corporate finance.

23.1 Executive Stock Options

WHY OPTIONS?

Executive compensation is usually made up of a base salary plus some or all of the following elements:

1. Long-term compensation.
2. Annual bonuses.
3. Retirement contributions.
4. Options.
5. Restricted stock units.

The options component is often the biggest part of total compensation for many top executives, although the use of restricted stock units has grown in recent years.

In this section, we will discuss how to estimate the market value of executive stock options using the Black-Scholes option pricing formula. To value an option, we need to know its exercise price. For tax reasons discussed below, the exercise price of executive stock options is almost always equal to the price of the underlying stock on the day the option is granted. We will also explain why executives may value an option grant at less than its market value.

Options in the stock of the company are increasingly being granted to executives as an alternative to increases in base pay. Some of the reasons given for using options are these:

1. Options make executives share the same interests as the stockholders. By aligning interests, executives are more likely to make decisions for the benefit of the stockholders.
2. Options allow the company to lower the executives' base pay. This removes pressure on morale caused by disparities between the salaries of executives and those of other employees.
3. Options put an executive's pay at risk, rather than guaranteeing it, regardless of the performance of the firm.
4. Options are a tax-efficient way to pay employees. Under current tax law, if an executive is given options to purchase company stock and the options are "at the money," they are not considered part of taxable income to the employee. The options are taxed only when and if they are eventually exercised.

The Securities and Exchange Board of India notified the SEBI (Share Based Employee Benefits and Sweat Equity) Regulations, 2021 ("New SEBI ESOP Regulations") on August 13, 2021. The New SEBI ESOP Regulations govern all share-based employee benefit schemes dealing in securities, including employee stock options, employee share purchase, stock appreciation rights, general employee benefits and retirement benefits (**"Share Based Benefit Schemes"**). The New SEBI ESOP Regulations cover regulations on sweat equity shares.

EXAMPLE 23.1

Options at Starbucks Stock options are not always restricted to the highest-ranking executives. Starbucks, the coffee chain, has pushed options down to the lowest-level employees. To quote its founder, Howard Schultz, "Even though we were a private company, we would grant stock options to every employee companywide, from the top managers to the baristas, in proportion to their level of base pay. They could then, through their efforts, help make Starbucks more successful every year, and if Starbucks someday went public, their options could eventually be worth a good sum of money." When Starbucks eventually went public, employees indeed reaped rewards from the stock options granted.

VALUING EXECUTIVE COMPENSATION

The complexity of the total compensation package often makes valuation a difficult task. The economic value of the options depends on factors such as the volatility of the underlying stock and the exact terms of the option grant.

To estimate the economic value of the employee stock, the Black-Scholes option pricing formula is often used. Of course, we are missing many features of the particular plans, and the best we can hope for is a rough estimate. Simple matters such as requiring the executive to hold the option for a fixed period, the freeze-out period, before exercising can significantly diminish the value of a standard option. Equally important, the Black-Scholes formula has to be modified if the stock pays dividends and is no longer applicable if the volatility of the stock is changing randomly over time. Intuitively, a call option on a dividend-paying stock is worth less than a call on a stock that pays no dividends: All other things being equal, the dividends will lower the stock price.

Suppose a company computes the fair market value of the options. Assume that the options are in the money and that they are worth ₹25 each. Suppose, too, that the CEO holds 1 million such options for a total value of ₹25 million. This is the amount that the options would trade at in the financial markets and that traders and investors would be willing to pay for them.[1] If the company were very large, it would not be unreasonable for it to view this as the cost of granting the options to the CEO. Of course, in return, the company would expect the CEO to improve the value of the company to its shareholders by at least this amount. As we have seen, perhaps the main purpose of options is to align the interests of management with those of the shareholders of the firm. However, the ₹25 million is not necessarily a fair measure of what the options are worth to the CEO.

From the employees' perspective, stock options often have a hidden cost. Suppose that the CEO of ABC has options on 1 million shares with an exercise price of ₹30 per share, and the current price of ABC stock is ₹50 per share. If the options were exercised today, they would be worth ₹20 million (an underestimation of their market value). In addition, suppose the CEO owns ₹5 million in company stock and has ₹5 million in other assets. The CEO clearly has a very undiversified personal portfolio. By the standards of modern portfolio theory, having 25/30, or about 83 percent, of her personal wealth in one stock and its options is unnecessarily risky.

Although the CEO is wealthy by most standards, shifts in stock price impact the CEO's economic well-being. If the price drops from ₹50 per share to ₹30 per share, the current exercise value of the options on 1 million shares drops from ₹20 million down to zero. Ignoring the fact that if the options had more time to mature they might not lose all of this value, we nevertheless have a rather startling decline in the CEO's net worth from ₹30 million to ₹8 million (= ₹5 million in other assets plus stock that is now worth ₹3 million). But that is the purpose of giving the options and the stock holdings to the CEO–namely, to make the CEO's fortunes rise and fall with those of the company. It is why the company requires the executive to hold the options for at least a freeze-out period rather than letting the executive sell them immediately to realize their value.

The implication is that when options are a large portion of an executive's net worth, the total value of the position to the executive is less than the market value. As a purely financial matter, an executive might be happier with ₹5 million in cash rather than ₹20 million in options. At least the executive could then diversify her personal portfolio.

ESOPs in India: A Few Examples

Infosys Technologies Limited

Infosys, the IT services giant, issued ESOPs to employees regularly from 1994 onwards. It can easily be called the company which pioneered the ESOPs revolution in India.

ACC Limited

ACC, the cement giant, has an employee stock option scheme (ESOS) from 2001 onwards. Remarkably, the organization, in a period of two decades, has had three different ESOS formulas for arriving at the exercise price, sometimes at market price on the date of issue and most other times at a discount of over 20 percent.

Lupin Limited

Lupin, the pharmaceutical giant, held on to talented employees by introducing attractive ESOP packages under the label 'Partners in Progress' covering about 30 percent of its managerial staff.

[1] We ignore warrant dilution in this example. See Chapter 24 for a discussion of warrant dilution.

Restricted stock units (RSUs) are a growing form of employee compensation. RSUs are shares of stock granted to employees. The stock is "restricted" because it is subject to a vesting schedule, which can be based on length of employment or on performance goals. RSUs are often also governed by other limits on transfers or sales that the company can impose. Only after vesting do the shares have voting and dividend rights. RSUs have less leverage than stock options and are almost always worth something even if the stock price drops dramatically.

A drawback of executive stock options and RSUs is that they incentivize executives to focus on temporarily maximizing stock prices around dates when they plan to exercise options or sell stock. Such a focus can come at the expense of maximizing long-term shareholder value. Perhaps in response to this critique, it has become increasingly common for boards to tie grants of stock options and RSUs to performance-vesting provisions on top of traditional time-vesting provisions.[2] Under a performance-vesting provision, whether the option or RSU vests (can be exercised or sold) depends on whether the firm reaches a variety of accounting performance targets such as earnings per share or return on assets. These performance-vesting provisions provide another way to motivate managers to improve firm performance according to a variety of metrics, beyond share price at a certain date. Since these vesting provisions limit the ability of executives to exercise options or sell stock, they are another reason executives may value their equity compensation at less than market value.

23.2 Valuing a Startup

Rishi Singh was not your typical MBA student. Since childhood, he'd had one ambition: to open a restaurant that sells alligator meat. He went to business school because he realized that although he knew 101 ways to cook alligator, he didn't have the business skills necessary to run a restaurant. He was extremely focused, with each course at graduate school being important to him only to the extent that it could further his dream.

While taking his school's course in entrepreneurship, he began to develop a business plan for his restaurant, which he now called Alligator Tandoor. He thought about marketing, he thought about raising capital, and he thought about dealing with future employees. He even devoted a great deal of time to designing the physical layout of the restaurant. Against the professor's advice in his entrepreneurship class, he designed the restaurant in the shape of an alligator, where the front door went through the animal's mouth. Of course, his business plan would not be complete without financial projections. After much thought, he came up with the projections shown in Table 23.1.

The table starts with sales projections, which rise from ₹300,000 in the first year to a steady state of ₹1 million a year. Cash flows from operations are shown in the next line, although we leave out the intermediate calculations needed to move from Line (1) to Line (2). After subtracting working capital, the table shows net cash flows in Line (4). Net cash flows are negative initially, as is quite common in startups, but they become positive by Year 3. However, the rest of the table presents the unfortunate truth. The cash flows from the restaurant yield a present value of ₹582,562, assuming a discount rate of 20 percent. Unfortunately, the cost of the building is greater, at ₹700,000, implying a negative net present value of –₹117,438.

The projections indicate that Rishi's lifelong dream may not come to pass. He cannot expect to raise the capital needed to open his restaurant; if he did obtain the funding, the restaurant would likely go under anyway. Rishi checked and rechecked the numbers, hoping in vain to discover either a numerical error or a cost-saving omission that would move his venture from the red to the black. In fact, Rishi saw that, if anything, his forecasts were generous: A 20 percent discount rate and an infinite-lived building are on the optimistic side.

[2] J. Carr Bettis, John Bizjak, and Jeffrey Coles, "Performance-Vesting Provisions in Executive Compensation," *Journal of Accounting and Economics* 66, no. 1: 194–221.

Table 23.1 Financial Projections for Alligator Tandoor

	Year 1	Year 2	Year 3	Year 4	All Future Years
(1) Sales	₹300,000	₹600,000	₹900,000	₹1,000,000	₹1,000,000
(2) Cash flows from operations	−100,000	−50,000	75,000	250,000	250,000
(3) Increase in working capital	50,000	20,000	10,000	10,000	0
(4) Net cash flows [(2) − (3)]	−₹150,000	−₹ 70,000	₹ 65,000	₹ 240,000	₹ 250,000
Present value of net cash flows in Years 1–4 (discounted at 20%)			−₹ 20,255		
Present value of terminal value	₹250,000/.20 × 1/1.20^4 =		₹602,816		
Present value of restaurant			582,562		
− Cost of building			700,000		
Net present value of restaurant			−₹117,438		

It wasn't until Rishi took a course in corporate strategy that he saw the hidden value in his venture. In that course, his instructor repeatedly stated the importance of positioning a firm to take advantage of new opportunities. Although Rishi didn't see the connection at first, he finally realized the implications for Alligator Tandoor. His financial projections were based on expectations. There was a 50 percent probability that alligator meat would be more popular than he thought, in which case actual cash flows would exceed projections. And there was a 50 percent probability that the meat would be less popular, in which case the actual cash flows would fall short of projections.

If the restaurant did poorly, it would probably fold in a few years because he would not want to keep losing money forever. However, if the restaurant did well, he would be in a position to expand. With alligator meat being popular in one locale, it would likely prove popular in other locales, as well. He noticed two options: the option to abandon under bad conditions and the option to expand under good conditions. Although both options can be valued according to the principles of the previous chapter, we focus on the option to expand in this example.

Rishi reasoned that as much as he personally liked alligator meat, consumer resistance in some regions of the country would doom Alligator Tandoor. So he developed a strategy of catering only to those regions where alligator meat is somewhat popular already. He forecasts that although he could expand quickly if the first restaurant proved successful, the market would limit him to 30 additional restaurants.

Rishi believes that this expansion would occur about four years from now. He believes that he will need three years of operating the first restaurant to (1) get the initial restaurant running smoothly and (2) have enough information to place an accurate value on the restaurant. If the first restaurant is successful enough, he will need another year to obtain outside capital. He will be ready to build the 30 additional units around the fourth year.

Rishi will value his enterprise, including the option to expand, according to the Black-Scholes model. From Table 23.1, we see that each unit costs ₹700,000, implying a total cost over the 30 additional units of ₹21,000,000 (= 30 × ₹700,000). The present value of the cash inflows from these 30 units is ₹17,476,852 (= 30 × ₹582,562), according to the table. However, because the expansion will occur around the fourth year, this present value calculation is provided from the point of view of four years in the future. The present value as of today is ₹8,428,266 (= ₹17,476,852/1.20^4), assuming a discount rate of 20 percent per year. Rishi views his potential restaurant business as an option, where the exercise price is ₹21,000,000 and the value of the underlying asset is ₹8,428,266. The option is currently out of the money, a result that follows from the negative value of a typical restaurant, as calculated in Table 23.1. Of course, Rishi is hoping that the option will move into the money within four years.

Table 23.2 Valuing a Startup Firm (Alligator Tandoor) as an Option

Facts

1. The value of a single restaurant is negative, as indicated by the net present value calculation in Table 23.1 of –₹117,438. The restaurant would not be funded if there were no possibility of expansion.
2. If the pilot restaurant is successful, Rishi Singh plans to create 30 additional restaurants around Year 4. This leads to the following observations:
   a. The total cost of 30 units is ₹21,000,000 (= 30 × ₹700,000).
   b. The present value of future cash flows as of Year 4 is ₹17,476,852 (= 30 × ₹582,562).
   c. The present value of these cash flows today is ₹8,428,266 (= ₹17,476,852/1.20^4).
   We assume that cash flows from the project are discounted at 20 percent per year.
   The business is essentially a call option, where the exercise price is ₹21,000,000 and the underlying asset is worth ₹8,428,266.
3. Rishi Singh estimates the standard deviation of the annual return on Alligator Tandoor's stock to be 50 percent.
   Parameters of the Black-Scholes model:

$$\begin{aligned} S \text{ (stock price)} &= ₹8{,}428{,}266 \\ E \text{ (exercise price)} &= ₹21{,}000{,}000 \\ t \text{ (time to maturity)} &= 4 \text{ years} \\ \sigma \text{ (standard deviation)} &= 50\% \\ R \text{ (continuously compounded interest rate)} &= 3.5\% \end{aligned}$$

Calculation from the Black-Scholes model:

$$C = SN(d_1) - Ee^{-Rt}N(d_2)$$

$$d_1 = \left[\ln(S/E) + \left(R + \tfrac{1}{2}\sigma^2\right)t\right] / \sqrt{\sigma^2 t}$$

$$d_2 = d_1 - \sqrt{\sigma^2 t}$$

$$d_1 = \left[\ln\frac{8{,}428{,}266}{21{,}000{,}000} + \left(.035 + \frac{.50^2}{2}\right)4\right] / \sqrt{.50^2 \times 4} = -.27293$$

$$d_2 = -.27293 - \sqrt{.50^2 \times 4} = -1.27293$$

$$N(d_1) = N(-.27293) = .3925$$

$$N(d_2) = N(-1.27293) = .1015$$

$$C = ₹8{,}428{,}266 \times .3925 - ₹21{,}000{,}000 \times e^{-.035\times 4} \times .1015 = ₹1{,}454{,}274$$

Value of business including cost of pilot restaurant = ₹1,454,274 – 117,438
= ₹1,336,836

Rishi needs three additional parameters to use the Black-Scholes model: R, the continuously compounded interest rate; t, the time to maturity; and σ, the standard deviation of the underlying asset. Rishi uses the yield on a four-year zero coupon bond, which is 3.5 percent, as the estimate of the interest rate. The time to maturity is four years. The estimate of standard deviation is a little trickier because there is no historical data on alligator restaurants. Rishi finds that the average annual standard deviation of the returns on publicly traded restaurants is 35 percent. Because Alligator Tandoor is a new venture, he reasons that the risk here would be somewhat greater. He finds that the average annual standard deviation for restaurants that have gone public in the last few years is 45 percent. Rishi's restaurant is newer still, so he uses a standard deviation of 50 percent.

There is now enough data to value Rishi's venture. The value according to the Black-Scholes model shown in Table 23.2 is ₹1,454,274. Of course, Rishi must start his pilot restaurant before he can take advantage of this option. The net value of the call option plus the negative net present value of the pilot restaurant is ₹1,336,836 (= ₹1,454,274 – 117,438). Because this value is large and positive, Rishi decides to stay with his dream of Alligator Tandoor. He knows that the probability that the restaurant will fail is greater than 50 percent. Nevertheless, the option to expand is important enough that his restaurant business has value. And if he needs outside capital, he probably can attract the necessary investors.

This finding leads to the appearance of a paradox. If Rishi approaches investors to invest in a single restaurant with no possibility of expansion, he will probably not be able to attract capital. After all, Table 23.1 shows a net present value of –₹117,438. However, if Rishi thinks bigger, he will likely be able to attract all the capital he needs. But this is really not a paradox at all. By thinking bigger, Rishi is offering investors the option–not the obligation–to expand.

This example may seem farfetched, but business situations involving options are very commonplace and worth understanding. Embedded options are at the heart of business. There are two possible outcomes for virtually every business idea. On the one hand, the business may fail, in which case the managers will probably try to shut it down in the most cost-efficient way. On the other hand, the business may prosper, in which case the managers will try to expand. Virtually every business has both the option to abandon and the option to expand. Though those in the finance field are typically strong supporters of the net present value approach to capital budgeting, some argue that it is an incomplete approach if it does not take options into account, and we will admit, they are probably not wrong. If virtually all projects have embedded options, only an approach such as the one we have outlined can be appropriate. Ignoring the options is likely to lead to serious undervaluation.

23.3 More about the Binomial Model

Earlier in this chapter, we examined two applications of options: executive compensation and the startup decision. In both cases, we valued an option using the Black-Scholes model. Although this model is justifiably well known, it is not the only approach to option valuation. As mentioned in the previous chapter, the two-state, or binomial, model is an alternative and–in some situations–a superior approach to valuation. The rest of this chapter examines two applications of the binomial model.

HEATING OIL

Two-Date Example Consider Amitabh Bachchan, owner of a typical heating oil distributor, whose business consists of buying heating oil at the wholesale level and reselling the oil to homeowners at a somewhat higher price. Most of her revenue comes from sales during the winter. Today, September 1, heating oil sells for ₹2.00 per gallon. Of course, this price is not fixed. Rather, oil prices will vary from September 1 until December 1, the time when her customers will probably make their big winter purchases of heating oil. Let's simplify the situation by assuming that Amitabh believes that oil prices will either be at ₹2.74 or ₹1.46 on December 1. Figure 23.1 portrays this possible price movement. This potential price range represents a great deal of uncertainty because Amitabh has no idea which of the two possible prices actually will occur. However, this price variability does not translate into that much risk because she can pass price changes on to her customers. That is, she will charge her customers more if she ends up paying ₹2.74 per gallon than if she ends up paying ₹1.46 per gallon.

Of course, Amitabh is avoiding risk by passing on that risk to her customers. Her customers accept the risk, perhaps because they are each too small to negotiate a better deal. This is not the case with CESC,

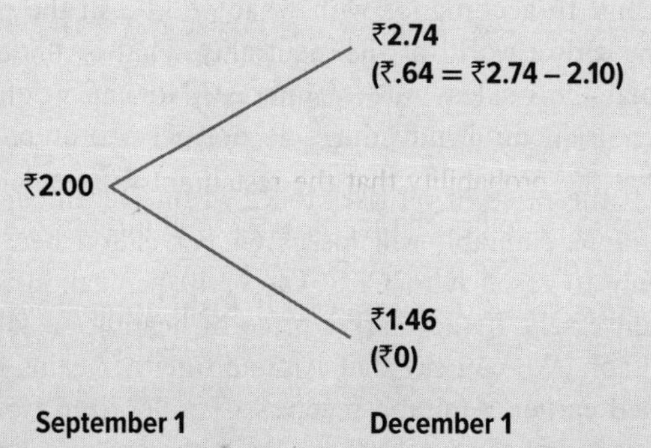

The price of heating oil on December 1 will be either ₹2.74 or ₹1.46. Because the price on September 1 is ₹2.00, we say that $u = 1.37$ (= ₹2.74/₹2.00) and $d = .73$ (= ₹1.46/₹2.00). The loss per gallon to Amitabh (or, equivalently, the gain per gallon to CESC) of ₹.64 in the up state or ₹0 in the down state is shown in parentheses.

Figure 23.1 Movement of Heating Oil Prices from September 1 to December 1 in a Two-Date Example

a large electric utility in her area. CESC approaches Amitabh with the following proposition. The utility would like to be able to buy up to 6 million gallons of oil from her at ₹2.10 per gallon on December 1.

Although this arrangement represents a lot of oil, both Amitabh and CESC know that Amitabh can expect to lose money on it. If prices rise to ₹2.74 per gallon, the utility will happily buy all 6 million gallons at only ₹2.10 per gallon, clearly creating a loss for the distributor. However, if oil prices decline to ₹1.46 per gallon, the utility will not buy any oil. After all, why should CESC pay ₹2.10 per gallon to Amitabh when the utility can buy all the oil it wants at ₹1.46 per gallon in the open market? In other words, CESC is asking for a call option on heating oil. To compensate Amitabh for the risk of loss, the two parties agree that CESC will pay her ₹1 million up front for the right to buy up to 6 million gallons of oil at ₹2.10 per gallon.

Is this a fair deal? Although small distributors may evaluate a deal like this by gut feel, we can evaluate it more quantitatively by using the binomial model described in the previous chapter. In that chapter, we pointed out that option problems can be handled most easily by assuming risk-neutral pricing. In this approach, we first note that oil will either rise 37 percent (= ₹2.74/₹2.00 − 1) or fall −27 percent (= ₹1.46/₹2.00 − 1) from September 1 to December 1. We can think of these two numbers as the possible returns on heating oil. In addition, we introduce two new terms, u and d. We define u as $1 + .37 = 1.37$ and d as $1 - .27 = .73$.[3] Using the methodology of the previous chapter, we value the contract in the following two steps.

Step 1: Determining the Risk-Neutral Probabilities We determine the probability of a price rise such that the expected return on oil exactly equals the risk-free rate. Assuming an 8 percent annual interest rate, which implies a 2 percent rate over the next three months, we can solve for the probability of a rise as follows:[4]

$$.02 = \text{Probability of rise} \times .37 + (1 - \text{Probability of rise}) \times (-.27)$$

Solving this equation, we find that the probability of a rise is approximately 45 percent, implying that the probability of a fall is 55 percent. In other words, if the probability of a price rise is 45 percent, the expected

[3] As we will see later, u and d are consistent with a standard deviation of the annual return on heating oil of 63 percent.

[4] For simplicity, we ignore both storage costs and a convenience yield.

return on heating oil is 2 percent. In accordance with what we said in the previous chapter, these are the probabilities that are consistent with a world of risk neutrality. That is, under risk neutrality, the expected return on any asset would equal the riskless rate of interest. No one would demand an expected return above this riskless rate because risk-neutral individuals do not need to be compensated for bearing risk.

Step 2: Valuing the Contract If the price of oil rises to ₹2.74 on December 1, CESC will want to buy oil from Amitabh at ₹2.10 per gallon. Amitabh will lose ₹.64 per gallon because she buys oil in the open market at ₹2.74 per gallon, only to resell it to CESC at ₹2.10 per gallon. This loss of ₹.64 is shown in parentheses in Figure 23.1. Conversely, if the market price of heating oil falls to ₹1.46 per gallon, CESC will not buy any oil from Amitabh. We can say that Amitabh neither gains nor loses if the price drops to ₹1.46. In addition, as mentioned earlier, Amitabh receives ₹1 million up front.

Given these numbers, the value of the contract to Amitabh can be calculated as:

$$\underbrace{[.45 \times (₹2.10 - 2.74) \times 6{,}000{,}000 + .55 \times 0]/1.02}_{\text{Value of the call option}} + ₹1{,}000{,}000 = -₹705{,}882 \quad \textbf{(23.1)}$$

As in the previous chapter, we are valuing an option using risk-neutral pricing. The cash flows of −₹.64 (= ₹2.10 − 2.74) and ₹0 per gallon are multiplied by their risk-neutral probabilities. The entire first term in Equation 23.1 is then discounted at 2 percent because the cash flows in that term occur on December 1. The ₹1,000,000 is not discounted because Amitabh receives it today, September 1. Because the present value of the contract is negative, Amitabh would be wise to reject the contract.

As stated before, the distributor has sold a call option to CESC. The first term in the preceding equation, which equals −₹1,705,882, can be viewed as the value of this call option. It is a negative number because the equation looks at the option from Amitabh's point of view. Therefore, the value of the call option would be ₹1,705,882 to CESC. On a per-gallon basis, the value of the option to CESC is:

$$[.45(₹2.74 - 2.10) + .55 \times 0]/1.02 = ₹.284 \quad \textbf{(23.2)}$$

Equation 23.2 shows that CESC will gain ₹.64 (= ₹2.74 − 2.10) per gallon in the up state because CESC can buy heating oil worth ₹2.74 for only ₹2.10 under the contract. By contrast, the contract is worth nothing to CESC in the down state because the utility will not pay ₹2.10 for oil selling for only ₹1.46 in the open market. Using risk-neutral pricing, the formula tells us that the value of the call option on one gallon of heating oil is ₹.284.

Three-Date Example Although the preceding example captures a number of aspects of the real world, it has one deficiency. It assumes that the price of heating oil can take on only two values on December 1. This is clearly not plausible: Oil can take on essentially any value, in reality. Although this deficiency seems glaring at first glance, it actually is easily correctable. All we have to do is introduce more intervals over the three-month period of our example.

For example, Figure 23.2 shows the price movement of heating oil over two intervals of 1½ months each.[5] As shown in the figure, the price will be either ₹2.50 or ₹1.60 on October 15. We refer to ₹2.50 as the price in the *up state* and ₹1.60 as the price in the *down state*. Heating oil has returns of 25 percent (= ₹2.50/₹2.00 − 1) and −20 percent (= ₹1.60/₹2.00 − 1) in the two states.

We assume the same variability as we move forward from October 15 to December 1. That is, given a price of ₹2.50 on October 15, the price on December 1 will be either ₹3.13 (= ₹2.50 × 1.25) or ₹2 (= ₹2.50 × .80). Similarly, given a price of ₹1.60 on October 15, the price on December 1 will be either ₹2 (= ₹1.60 × 1.25) or ₹1.28 (= ₹1.60 × .80). This assumption of constant variability is quite plausible

[5]Though it is not apparent at first glance, we will see later that the price movement in Figure 23.2 is consistent with the price movement in Figure 23.1.

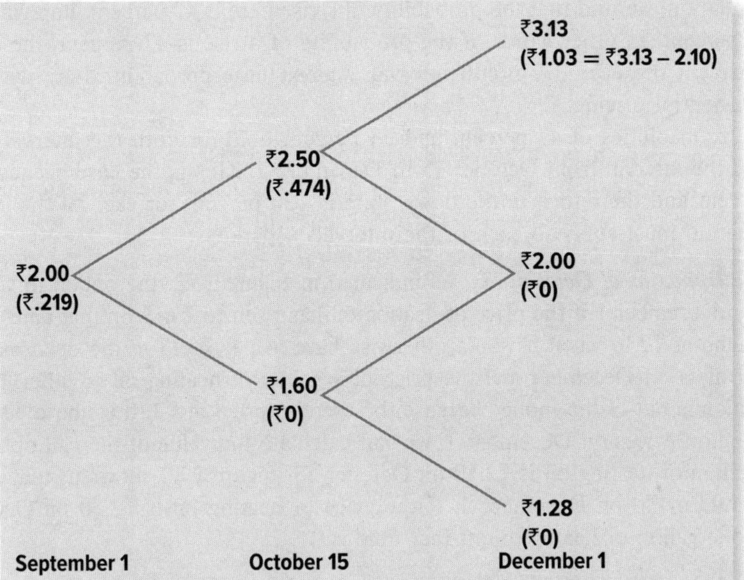

The figure shows the prices of a gallon of heating oil on three dates, given $u = 1.25$ and $d = .80$. There are three possible prices for heating oil on December 1. For each one of these three prices, we calculate the price on December 1 of a call option on a gallon of heating oil with an exercise price of ₹2.10. These numbers are in parentheses. Call prices at earlier dates are determined by the binomial model and also are shown in parentheses.

Figure 23.2 Movement of Heating Oil Prices in a Three-Date Model

because the rate of new information impacting heating oil (or most commodities or assets) is likely to be similar from month to month.

Note that there are three possible prices on December 1, but there are two possible prices on October 15. Also, note that there are two paths to a price of ₹2 on December 1. The price could rise to ₹2.50 on October 15 before falling back down to ₹2 on December 1. Alternatively, the price could fall to ₹1.60 on October 15 before going back up to ₹2 on December 1. In other words, the model has symmetry, where an up movement followed by a down movement yields the same price on December 1 as a down movement followed by an up movement.

How do we value CESC's option in this three-date example? We employ the same procedure that we used in the two-date example, although we now need an extra step because of the extra date.

Step 1: Determining the Risk-Neutral Probabilities As we did in the two-date example, we determine what the probability of a price rise would be such that the expected return on heating oil exactly equals the riskless rate. However, in this case we work with an interval of 1½ months. Assuming an 8 percent annual rate of interest, which implies a 1 percent rate over a 1½-month interval, we can solve for the probability of a rise like this:[6]

$$.01 = \text{Probability of rise} \times .25 + (1 - \text{Probability of rise}) \times (-.20)$$

[6] For simplicity, we ignore interest compounding.

Solving the equation, we find that the probability of a rise here is 47 percent, implying that the probability of a fall is 53 percent. In other words, if the probability of a rise is 47 percent, the expected return on heating oil is 1 percent per each 1½-month interval. Again, these probabilities are determined under the assumption of risk-neutral pricing.

Note that the probabilities of 47 percent and 53 percent hold for both the interval from September 1 to October 15 and the interval from October 15 to December 1. This is the case because the return in the up state is 25 percent and the return in the down state is –20 percent for each of the two intervals. Thus, the preceding equation must apply to each of the intervals separately.

Step 2: Valuing the Option as of October 15 As indicated in Figure 23.2, the option to CESC will be worth ₹1.03 per gallon on December 1 if the price of heating oil has risen to ₹3.13 on that date. That is, CESC can buy oil from Amitabh at ₹2.10 when it would otherwise have to pay ₹3.13 in the open market. However, the option will be worthless on December 1 if the price of a gallon of heating oil is either ₹2 or ₹1.28 on that date. Here, the option is out of the money because the exercise price of ₹2.10 is above either ₹2 or ₹1.28.

Using these option prices on December 1, we can calculate the value of the call option on October 15. If the price of a gallon of heating oil is ₹2.50 on October 15, Figure 23.2 shows us that the call option will be worth either ₹1.03 or ₹0 on December 1. If the price of heating oil is ₹2.50 on October 15, the value of the option on one gallon of heating oil at that time is:

$$(.47 \times ₹1.03 + .53 \times 0)/1.01 = ₹.474$$

Here we are valuing an option using the same risk-neutral pricing approach that we used in the earlier two-date example. This value of ₹.474 is shown in parentheses in Figure 23.2.

We also want to value the option on October 15 if the price at that time is ₹1.60. However, the value here is clearly zero, as indicated by this calculation:

$$(.47 \times ₹0 + .53 \times ₹0)/1.01 = ₹0$$

This is obvious once we look at Figure 23.2. We see from the figure that the call must end up out of the money on December 1 if the price of heating oil is ₹1.60 on October 15. The call must have zero value on October 15 if the price of heating oil is ₹1.60 on that date.

Step 3: Valuing the Option on September 1 In the previous step, we saw that the price of the call on October 15 would be ₹.474 if the price of a gallon of heating oil was ₹2.50 on that date. Similarly, the price of the option on October 15 would be ₹0 if oil was selling at ₹1.60 on that date. From these values, we can calculate the call option value on September 1:

$$(.47 \times ₹.474 + .53 \times ₹0)/1.01 = ₹.219$$

Notice that this calculation is completely analogous to the calculation of the option value in the previous step, as well as the calculation of the option value in the two-date example that we presented earlier. In other words, the same approach applies regardless of the number of intervals used. As we will see later, we can move to many intervals, which produces greater realism, yet still maintain the same basic methodology.

The previous calculation has given us the value to CESC of its option on one gallon of heating oil. Now we are ready to calculate the value of the contract to Amitabh. Given the calculations from the previous equation, the contract's value can be written as:

$$-₹.219 \times 6{,}000{,}000 + ₹1{,}000{,}000 = -₹312{,}943$$

That is, Amitabh is giving away an option worth ₹.219 for each of the 6 million gallons of heating oil. In return, she is receiving only ₹1,000,000 up front. Overall, she is losing ₹312,943. Of course, the value of the contract to CESC is the opposite, so the value to the utility is ₹312,943.

Extension to Many Dates We have looked at the contract between CESC and Amitabh using both a two-date example and a three-date example. The three-date case is more realistic because more possibilities for price movements are allowed here. However, why stop at 3 dates? Moving to 4 dates, 5 dates, 50 dates, 500 dates, and so on should give us even more realism. Note that, as we move to more dates, we are merely shortening the interval between dates without increasing the overall time period of three months (September 1 to December 1).

Imagine a model with 90 dates over the three months. Here, each interval is approximately one day long because there are about 90 days in a 3-month period. The assumption of two possible outcomes in the binomial model is more plausible over a one-day interval than it is over a 1½-month interval, let alone a 3-month interval. Of course, we could probably achieve greater realism still by going to an interval of, say, one hour or one minute.

How do we adjust the binomial model to accommodate increases in the number of intervals? It turns out that two simple formulas relate u and d to the standard deviation of the return on the underlying asset:[7]

$$u = e^{\sigma/\sqrt{n}} \text{ and } d = 1/u$$

where σ is the standard deviation of the annualized return on the underlying asset (heating oil, in this case) and n is the number of intervals over a year.

When we created the heating oil example, we assumed that the annualized standard deviation of the return on heating oil was 63 percent. Because there are four quarters in a year, $u = e^{.63/\sqrt{4}} = 1.37$ and $d = 1/1.37 = .73$, as shown in the two-date example of Figure 23.1. In the three-date example of Figure 23.2, where each interval is 1½ months long, $u = e^{.63/\sqrt{8}} = 1.25$ and $d = 1/1.25 = .80$. Thus, the binomial model can be applied in practice if the standard deviation of the return of the underlying asset can be estimated.

We stated earlier that the value of the call option on a gallon of heating oil was estimated to be ₹.284 in the two-date model and ₹.219 in the three-date model. How does the value of the option change as we increase the number of intervals while keeping the time period constant at three months (from September 1 to December 1)? We have calculated the value of the call for various time intervals in Table 23.3.[8] The realism increases with the number of intervals because the restriction of only two possible outcomes is more plausible over a short interval than over a long one. Thus, the value of the call when the number of intervals is 99 or infinity is likely more realistic than this value when the number of intervals is, say, 1 or 2.

However, a very interesting phenomenon can be observed from the table. Although the value of the call changes as the number of intervals increases, convergence occurs quite rapidly. The call's value with 4 intervals is almost identical to the value with 99 intervals. Thus, a small number of intervals appears applicable for the binomial model. Six intervals in a three-month period implies that each interval is two weeks long. Of course, the assumption that heating oil can take on only one of two prices in two weeks is unrealistic. The paradox is that this unrealistic assumption still produces a realistic call price.

What happens when the number of intervals goes to infinity, implying that the length of the interval goes to zero? It can be proved mathematically that we end up with the value of the Black-Scholes model. This value also is presented in Table 23.3. We can argue that the Black-Scholes model is the best approach to value the heating oil option. It is also quite easy to apply. We can use a calculator to value options with Black-Scholes, whereas we must generally use a computer program for the binomial model. However, as shown in Table 23.3, the values from the binomial model, even with relatively few intervals, are quite close to the Black-Scholes values. Although Black-Scholes may save us time, it does not materially affect our estimate of value.

[7] See John C. Hull, *Options, Futures, and Other Derivatives,* 10th ed. (Upper Saddle River, NJ: Prentice Hall, 2017), for a derivation of these formulas.

[8] In this discussion, we have used both *intervals* and *dates*. To keep the terminology straight, remember that the number of intervals is always one less than the number of dates. For example, if a model has two dates, it has only one interval.

Table 23.3 Value of a Call on One Gallon of Heating Oil

Number of Intervals*	Call Value
1	₹.284
2	.219
3	.244
4	.226
6	.223
10	.229
20	.228
30	.228
40	.227
50	.227
99	.226
Black-Scholes Infinity	.226

In this example, the value of the call according to the binomial model varies as the number of intervals increases. However, the value of the call converges rapidly to the Black-Scholes value. The binomial model, even with only a few intervals, appears to be a good approximation of Black-Scholes.

*The number of intervals is always one less than the number of dates.

At this point, it seems as if the Black-Scholes model is preferable to the binomial model. Who wouldn't want to save time and still get a slightly more accurate value? As we will see, there are plenty of situations where the binomial model is preferred to the Black-Scholes model. One such situation is presented in the next section.

23.4 Shutdown and Reopening Decisions

Some of the earliest and most important examples of real options have occurred in the natural resources and mining industries.

VALUING A GOLD MINE

The Waqt Indian Sona gold mine was founded in 1882 on one of the richest veins of gold in the West. Thirty years later, by 1912, the mine had been played out; occasionally, however, depending on the price of gold, it was reopened. Currently, gold is not actively mined at Waqt Indian Sona, but its stock is still traded on the exchange under the ticker symbol WAQT. WAQT has no debt and, with about 20 million outstanding shares, its market value (stock price times number of shares outstanding) exceeds ₹6 billion. WAQT owns about 160 acres of land surrounding the mine and has a 100-year government lease to mine gold there. However, land in the desert has a market value of only a few thousand rupees. WAQT holds cash securities and other assets worth about ₹30 million. What could possibly explain why a company with ₹30 million in assets and a closed gold mine with no cash flow has the market value that WAQT has?

The answer lies in the options that WAQT implicitly owns in the form of a gold mine. Assume that the current price of gold is about ₹1,300 per ounce and the cost of extraction and processing at the mine is about ₹1,400 per ounce. It is no wonder that the mine is closed. Every ounce of gold extracted costs

₹1,400 and can be sold for only ₹1,300, for a loss of ₹100 per ounce. Presumably, if the price of gold were to rise, the mine could be opened. It costs ₹20 million to open the mine; when it is opened, production is 50,000 ounces per year. Geologists believe that the amount of gold in the mine is essentially unlimited, and WAQT has the right to mine it for the next 100 years. Under the terms of its lease, WAQT cannot stockpile gold and each year must sell all the gold it mines that year. Closing the mine, which costs ₹10 million, requires equipment to be shuttered and some environmental precautions to be put in place. We will refer to the ₹20 million required to open the mine as the entry fee, or investment, and the ₹10 million to close it as the closing or abandonment cost. We cannot avoid the abandonment cost by keeping the mine open and not operating.

From a financial perspective, WAQT is really a package of options on the price of gold disguised as a company and a mine. The basic option is a call on the price of gold where the exercise price is the ₹1,400 extraction cost. The option is complicated by having an exercise fee of ₹20 million–the opening cost–whenever it is exercised and a closing fee of ₹10 million when it is abandoned. It is also complicated by the fact that it is a perpetual option with no final maturity.

THE ABANDONMENT AND OPENING DECISIONS

Before valuing the option implicit in WAQT, it is useful to see what we can say by applying common sense. To begin with, the mine should be opened only when the price of gold is sufficiently above the extraction cost of ₹1,400 per ounce. Because it costs ₹20 million to open the mine, the mine should not be opened whenever the price of gold is only slightly above ₹1,400. At a gold price of, say, ₹1,401, the mine wouldn't be opened because the one-rupee profit per ounce translates into ₹50,000 per year (= 50,000 ounces × ₹1/ounce). This would not begin to cover the ₹20 million opening costs. More significantly, though, the mine probably would not be opened if the price rose to ₹1,450 per ounce, even though a ₹50 profit per ounce–₹2,500,000 per year–would pay the ₹20 million opening costs at any reasonable discount rate. The reason is that here, as in all option problems, volatility (in this case the volatility of gold) plays a significant role. Because the gold price is volatile, the price has to rise sufficiently above ₹1,400 per ounce to make it worth opening the mine. If the price at which the mine is opened is too close to the extraction price of ₹1,400 per ounce, say at ₹1,450 per ounce, we would open the mine every time the price jogged above ₹1,450. Unfortunately, we would then find ourselves operating at a loss or facing a closing decision whenever gold jogged back down ₹50 per ounce (only about 3 percent) to ₹1,400.

The estimated volatility of the return on gold is about 25 percent per year. This means that a single annual standard deviation movement in the gold price is 25 percent of ₹1,300, or ₹325 per year. Surely with this amount of random movement in the gold price, a threshold of, for example, ₹1,405 is much too low at which to open the mine. Similar logic applies to the closing decision. If the mine is open, we will clearly keep it open as long as the gold price is above the extraction cost of ₹1,400 per ounce because we are profiting on every ounce of gold mined. But we also won't close the mine down because the gold price drops below ₹1,400 per ounce. We will tolerate a running loss because gold may later rise back above ₹1,400. If, alternatively, we closed the mine, we would pay the ₹10 million abandonment cost, only to pay another ₹20 million to reopen the mine if the price rose again.

To summarize, if the mine is currently closed, then it will be opened–at a cost of ₹20 million–whenever the price of gold rises sufficiently above the extraction cost of ₹1,400 per ounce. If the mine is currently operating, then it will be closed down–at a cost of ₹10 million–whenever the price of gold falls sufficiently below the extraction cost of ₹1,400 per ounce. WAQT's problem is to find these two threshold prices at which it opens a closed mine and closes an open mine. We call these prices p_{open} and p_{close}, respectively, where:

$$p_{open} > ₹1{,}400/\text{ounce} > p_{close}$$

In other words, WAQT will open the mine if the gold price option is sufficiently in the money and will close it when the option is sufficiently out of the money.

We know that the more volatile the gold price, the further away p_{open} and p_{close} will be from ₹1,400 per ounce. We also know that the greater the cost of opening the mine, the higher p_{open} will be, and the greater the cost of abandoning the mine, the lower p_{close} will be. Interestingly, we also should expect that p_{open} will be higher if the abandonment cost is increased. After all, if it costs more to abandon the mine, WAQT will need to be more assured that the price will stay above the extraction cost when it decides to open the mine. Otherwise, WAQT will face the costly choice between abandonment and operating at a loss if the price falls below ₹1,400 per ounce. Similarly, raising the cost of opening the mine will make WAQT more reluctant to close an open mine. As a result, p_{close} will be lower.

The preceding arguments have enabled us to reduce the problem of valuing WAQT to two stages. First, we have to determine the threshold prices, p_{open} and p_{close}. Second, given the best choices for these thresholds, we must determine the value of a gold option that is exercised for a cost of ₹20 million when the gold price rises above p_{open} and is shut down for a cost of ₹10 million whenever the gold price is below p_{close}.

When the mine is open–that is, when the option is exercised–the annual cash flow is equal to the difference between the gold price and the extraction cost of ₹1,400 per ounce times 50,000 ounces. When the mine is shut down, it generates no cash flow.

The following diagram describes the decisions available at each point in time:

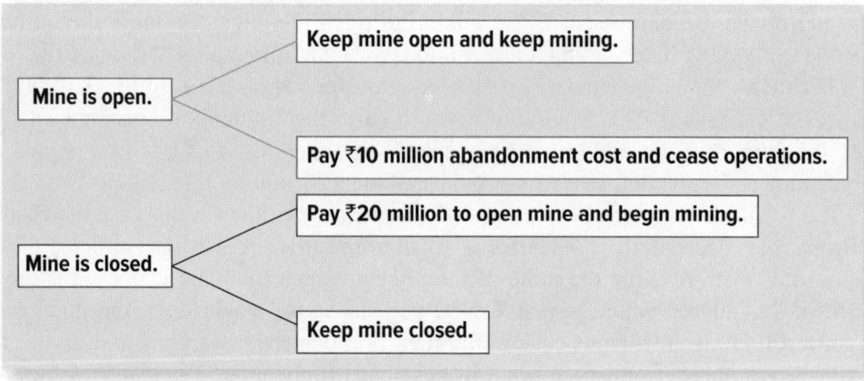

How do we determine the critical values for p_{open} and p_{close} and then the value of the mine? It is possible to get a good approximation by using the tools we have currently developed.

VALUING THE SIMPLE GOLD MINE

Here is what has to be done both to determine p_{open} and p_{close} and to value the mine.

Step 1 Find the risk-free interest rate and the volatility. We assume a semiannual interest rate of 3.4 percent and a volatility of 25 percent per year for gold.

Step 2 Construct a binomial tree and fill it in with gold prices. Suppose that we set the steps of the tree six months apart. If the annual volatility is 25 percent, u is equal to $e^{.25/\sqrt{2}}$, which is approximately equal to 1.19. The other parameter, d, is .84 (= 1/1.19). Figure 23.3 illustrates the tree. Starting at the current price of ₹1,300, the first 19 percent increase takes the price to ₹1,551 in six months. The first 16 percent decrease takes the price to ₹1,089. Subsequent steps are up 19 percent or down 16 percent from the previous price. The tree extends for the 100-year life of the lease, or 200 six-month steps.

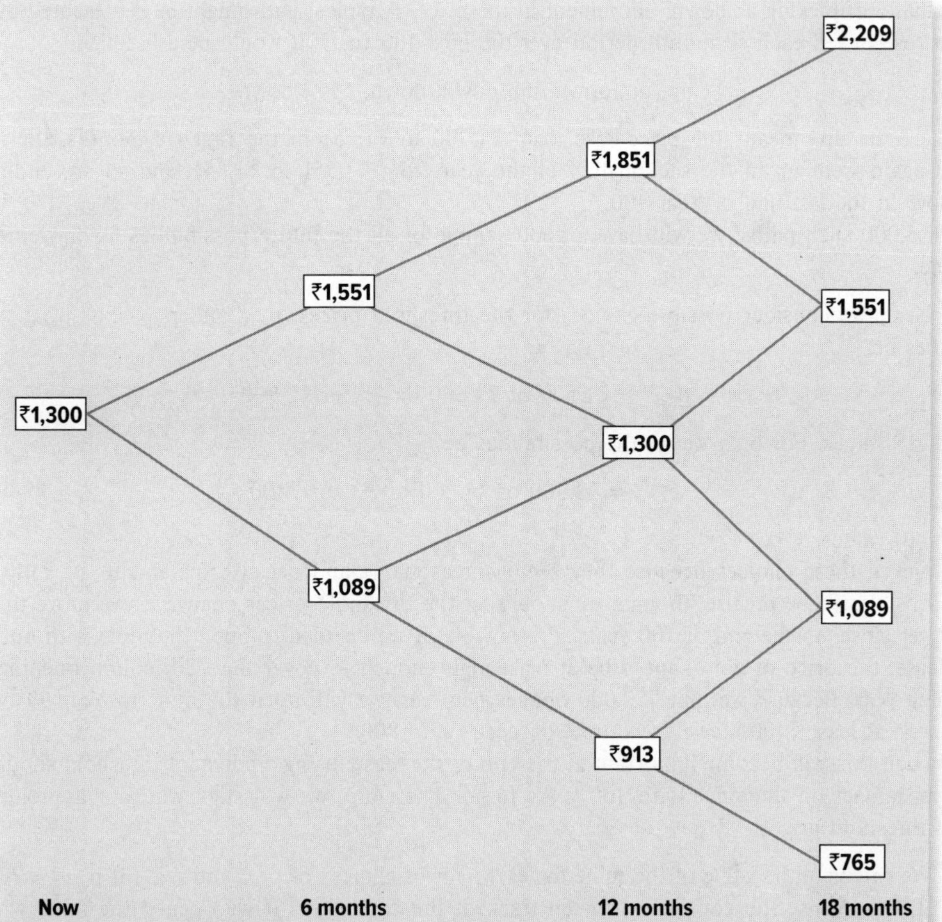

Steps of the binomial tree are six months apart. For each step, *u* is equal to 1.19 and *d* is equal to .84. Note that *u* and *d* are rounded to two decimal points.

Figure 23.3 A Binomial Tree for Gold Prices

Using our analysis from the previous section, we now compute the risk-adjusted probabilities for each step. Given a semiannual interest rate of 3.4 percent, we have:

$$3.4\% = \text{Probability of a rise} \times .19 + (1 - \text{Probability of a rise}) \times -.16$$

Solving this equation gives us .55 for the probability of a rise, implying that the probability of a fall is .45. These probabilities are the same for each six-month interval. In other words, if the probability of a rise is .55, the expected return on gold is 3.4 percent per each six-month interval. These probabilities are determined under the assumption of risk-neutral pricing. In other words, if investors are risk-neutral, they will be satisfied with an expected return equal to the risk-free rate because the extra risk of gold will not concern them.

Step 3 Now we turn the computer on and let it simulate, say, 5,000 possible paths through the tree. At each node, the computer has a .55 probability of picking an "up" movement in the price and a corresponding

.45 probability of picking a "down" movement in the price. A typical path might be represented by whether the price rose or fell each six-month period over the next 100 years; it would be a list like:

up, up, down, up, down, down, . . . , down

where the first "up" means the price rose from ₹1,300 to ₹1,551 in the first six months, the next "up" means it again went up in the second half of the year from ₹1,551 to ₹1,851, and so on, ending with a down move in the last half of Year 100.

With 5,000 such paths, we will have a good sample of all the future possibilities for movement in the gold price.

Step 4 Next, we consider possible choices for the threshold prices, p_{open} and p_{close}. For p_{open}, we let the possibilities be:

$$p_{open} = ₹1{,}500 \text{ or } ₹1{,}600 \text{ or } \ldots \text{ or } ₹2{,}900$$

a total of 15 values. For p_{close} we let the possibilities be:

$$p_{close} = ₹1{,}300 \text{ or } ₹1{,}200 \text{ or } \ldots \text{ or } ₹400$$

a total of 10 values.

We picked these choices because they seemed reasonable and because increments of ₹100 for each seemed sensible. To be precise, though, we should let the threshold prices change as we move through the tree and get closer to the end of 100 years. Presumably, if we decided to open the mine with one year left on the lease, the price of gold should be at least high enough to cover the ₹20 million opening costs in the coming year. Because we mine 50,000 ounces per year, we will open the mine in Year 99 only if the gold price is at least ₹400 above the extraction cost, or ₹1,800.

Although this will become important at the end of the lease, using a constant threshold shouldn't have too big an impact on the value with 100 years to go. Therefore, we will stick with our approximation of constant threshold prices.

Step 5 We calculate the value of the mine for each pair of choices of p_{open} and p_{close}. If p_{open} = ₹2,200 and p_{close} = ₹1,100, we use the computer to keep track of the cash flows if we opened the mine whenever it was previously closed and the gold price rose to ₹2,200, and closed the mine whenever it was previously open and the gold price fell to ₹1,100. We do this for each of the 5,000 paths we simulated in Step 3.

Consider the path illustrated in Figure 23.4:

up, up, down, up, up, down, down, down, down

As can be seen from the figure, the price reaches a peak of ₹2,209 in 2½ years, only to fall to ₹1,089 over the following four six-month intervals. If p_{open} = ₹2,200 and p_{close} = ₹1,100, the mine will be opened when the price reaches ₹2,209, necessitating a cost of ₹20 million. However, the firm can sell 25,000 ounces of gold at ₹2,209 per ounce at that time, producing a cash flow of ₹20.234 million [= 25,000(₹2,209 − 1,400)]. When the price falls to ₹1,851 six months later, the firm sells another 25,000 ounces, yielding a cash flow of ₹11.284 million [= 25,000(₹1,851 − 1,400)]. The price continues to fall, reaching ₹1,300 a year later. Here, the firm experiences a cash outflow because production costs are ₹1,400 per ounce. Next, the price falls to ₹1,089. Because this price is below p_{close} of ₹1,100, the mine is closed at a cost of ₹10 million. Of course, the price of gold will fluctuate in further years, leading to the possibility of future mine openings and closings.

This path is just a possibility. It may or may not occur in any simulation of 5,000 paths. For each of the 5,000 paths that the computer simulated, we have a sequence of semiannual cash flows using a p_{open} of ₹2,200 and a p_{close} of ₹1,100. We calculate the present value of each of these cash flows, discounting at the

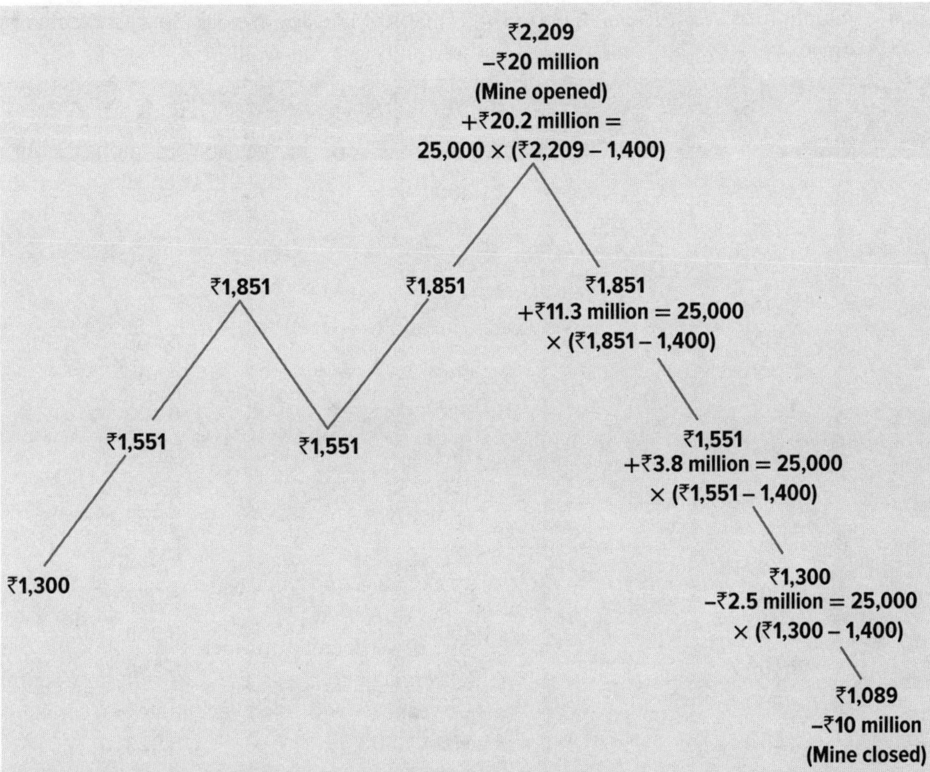

Imagine that this path is one of the 5,000 simulated price paths for gold. Because p_{open} = ₹2,200 and p_{close} = ₹1,100, the mine is opened when the price reaches ₹2,209. The mine is closed when the price reaches ₹1,089.

Figure 23.4 A Possible Path for the Price of Gold

interest rate of 3.4 percent. Summing across all the cash flows, we have the present value of the gold mine for one path.

We then take the average present value of the gold mine across all the 5,000 simulated paths. This number is the expected value of the mine from following a policy of opening the mine whenever the gold price hits ₹2,200 and closing it at a price of ₹1,100.

Step 6 The final step is to compare the different expected discounted cash flows from Step 5 for the range of possible choices for p_{open} and p_{close} and to pick the highest one. This is the best estimate of the expected value of the mine. The values for p_{open} and p_{close} corresponding to this estimate are the points at which to open a closed mine and to shut an open one.

As mentioned in Step 4, there are 15 different values for p_{open} and 10 different values for p_{close}, implying 150 (= 15 × 10) different pairs. Consider Table 23.4, which shows the present values associated with the 20 best pairs. The table indicates that the best pair is p_{open} = ₹2,900 and p_{close} = ₹1,200, with a present value of ₹6.629 billion. This number represents the average present value across 5,000 simulations, all assuming the preceding values of p_{open} and p_{close}. The next best pair is p_{open} = ₹2,200 and p_{close} = ₹1,300, with a present value of ₹6.557 billion. The third best pair has a somewhat lower present value, and so on.

Table 23.4 Valuation of Waqt Indian Sona (WAQT) Gold Mine for the 20 Best Choices of p_{open} and p_{close}

p_{open}	p_{close}	Estimated Value of Gold Mine (in millions)
₹2,900	₹1,200	₹6,629
2,200	1,300	6,557
2,000	1,000	6,428
2,000	1,200	6,288
1,800	1,400	6,168
2,900	500	6,140
2,800	500	6,103
2,900	900	6,055
3,000	1,100	6,054
2,600	900	6,050
2,600	600	6,038
3,000	500	6,033
1,900	1,400	5,958
2,100	700	5,939
2,300	500	5,934
2,200	1,400	5,928
1,800	800	5,895
2,300	600	5,892
2,400	1,100	5,862
1,900	500	5,855

For our simulation, WAQT opens the mine whenever the gold price rises above p_{open} and closes the mine whenever the gold price falls below p_{close}.

Of course, our estimate of the value of the mine is ₹6.629 billion, the present value of the best pair of choices. The market capitalization (Price × Number of shares outstanding) of WAQT should reach this value if the market makes the same assumptions that we did. Note that the value of the firm is quite high using an option framework. However, as stated earlier, WAQT would appear worthless if a regular discounted cash flow approach were used. This occurs because the initial gold price of ₹1,300 is below the extraction cost of ₹1,400.

This example is not easy, neither in concepts nor in implementation. However, the extra work involved in mastering this example is worth it because the example illustrates the type of modeling that actually occurs in corporate finance departments in the real world.

Furthermore, the example illustrates the benefits of the binomial approach. We merely calculate the cash flows associated with each of a number of simulations, discount the cash flows from each simulation, and average present values across the simulations. Because the Black-Scholes model is not amenable to simulations, it cannot be used for this type of problem. In addition, there are a number of other situations where the binomial model is more appropriate than is the Black-Scholes model. For example, it is well known that the Black-Scholes model cannot properly handle options with dividend payments prior to the expiration date. This model also does not adequately handle the valuation of an American put. By contrast, the binomial model can easily handle both of these situations.

Thus, any student of corporate finance would benefit from being well versed in both models. The Black-Scholes model should be used whenever appropriate because it is simpler to use than is the binomial model. However, for the more complex situations where the Black-Scholes model breaks down, the binomial model becomes a necessary tool.

RESEARCH IN EMERGING MARKET CONTEXT

Hazra et al. (2019) studied iron ore mine planning parameters using Stochastic NPV methods. They aimed to include the uncertainties of metal prices and ore grade. They concluded that Real Option Valuation (ROV) is the best method for mine planning. This is because it considers uncertainties of parameters as well as management flexibilities in the mining project. The results showed that exercising the options of continue, deferral, and expansion can result in 10 percent higher NPV than the stochastic NPV.

Gupta (2021) states that India's Paris Agreement targets involve replacing fossil fuels with renewables to produce energy. He studied the problem of replacing coal with wind and solar power as a real option problem with coal price uncertainty. The author suggests that policies to boost wind and solar power investment have significant value.

References

Gupta, S. D. (2021). Using real options to value capacity additions and investment expenditures in renewable energies in India. *Energy Policy*, *148*, 111916.

Hazra, T., Samanta, B., & Dey, K. (2019). Real option valuation of an Indian iron ore deposit through system dynamics model. *Resources Policy*, *60*, 288–299.

Summary and Conclusions

Real options, which are pervasive in business, are not captured by net present value analysis. Chapter 7 valued real options via decision trees. Given the work on options in the previous chapter, we are now able to value real options according to the Black-Scholes model and the binomial model.

In this chapter, we described and valued four different types of options:

1. Executive stock options, which are technically not real options.
2. The embedded option in a startup company.
3. The option in simple business contracts.
4. The option to shut down and reopen a project.

We tried to keep the presentation simple and straightforward from a mathematical point of view. The binomial approach to option pricing in Chapter 22 was extended to many periods. This adjustment brings us closer to the real world because the assumption of only two prices at the end of an interval is more plausible when the interval is short.

Concept Questions

1. **Employee Stock Options** Why do companies issue options to executives if they cost the company more than they are worth to the executive? Why not give cash and split the difference? Wouldn't that make both the company and the executive better off?
2. **Real Options** What are the two options that many businesses have?
3. **Project Analysis** Why does a strict NPV calculation typically understate the value of a company or project?
4. **Real Options** Utility companies often face a decision to build new plants that burn coal, oil, or both. If the prices of both coal and oil are highly volatile, how valuable is the decision to build a plant that can burn either coal or oil? What happens to the value of this option as the correlation between coal and oil prices increases?
5. **Real Options** Your company owns a vacant lot in a suburban area. What is the advantage of waiting to develop the lot?
6. **Real Options** Star Mining buys a gold mine, but the cost of extraction is currently too high to make the mine profitable. In option terminology, what type of option(s) does the company have on this mine?
7. **Real Options** You are discussing real options with a colleague. During the discussion, the colleague states, "Real option analysis makes no sense because it says that a real option on a risky venture is worth more than a real option on a safe venture." How should you respond to this statement?
8. **Real Options and Capital Budgeting** Your company currently uses traditional capital budgeting techniques, including net present value. After hearing about the use of real option analysis, your boss decides that your company should use real option analysis in place of net present value. How would you evaluate this decision?
9. **Insurance as an Option** Insurance, whether purchased by a corporation or an individual, is in essence an option. What type of option is an insurance policy?
10. **Real Options** How would the analysis of real options change if a company has competitors?

Questions and Problems

BASIC (Questions 1–5)

1. **Employee Stock Options** Cheryl Levin is the chief executive officer of Mountainbrook Trading Company. The board of directors has just granted Cheryl 35,000 at-the-money European call options on the company's stock, which is currently trading at ₹50 per share. The stock pays no dividends. The options will expire in five years and the standard deviation of the returns on the stock is 53 percent. Treasury bills that mature in five years currently yield a continuously compounded interest rate of 6 percent.
   a. Use the Black-Scholes model to calculate the value of the stock options.
   b. You are Cheryl's financial adviser. She must choose between the previously mentioned stock option package and an immediate ₹750,000 bonus. If she is risk-neutral, which would you recommend?
   c. How would your answer to part (b) change if Cheryl were risk-averse and could not sell the options prior to expiration?
2. **Employee Stock Options** Jared Lazarus has just been named the new chief executive officer of BluBell Fitness Centers, Inc. In addition to an annual salary of ₹350,000, his 3-year contract

states that his compensation will include 25,000 at-the-money European call options on the company's stock that expire in three years. The current stock price is ₹53 per share and the standard deviation of the returns on the firm's stock is 57 percent. The company does not pay a dividend. Treasury bills that mature in three years yield a continuously compounded interest rate of 5 percent. Assume that the annual salary payments occur at the end of the year and that these cash flows should be discounted at a rate of 7 percent. Using the Black-Scholes model to calculate the value of the stock options, determine the total value of the compensation package on the date the contract is signed.

3. **Binomial Model** Gasworks, Inc., has been approached to sell up to 5 million gallons of gasoline in three months at a price of ₹1.85 per gallon. Gasoline is currently selling on the wholesale market at ₹1.63 per gallon and has a standard deviation of 61 percent. If the risk-free rate is 6 percent per year, what is the value of this option?

4. **Real Options** J&R Construction Company is an international conglomerate with a real estate division that owns the right to erect an office building on a parcel of land in downtown Sacramento over the next year. This building would cost ₹60 million to construct. Due to low demand for office space in the downtown area, such a building is worth approximately ₹53.5 million today. If demand increases, the building would be worth ₹65.5 million a year from today. If demand decreases, the same office building would be worth only ₹50.2 million in a year. The company can borrow and lend at the risk-free annual effective rate of 4.8 percent. A local competitor in the real estate business has recently offered ₹1.8 million for the right to build an office building on the land. Should the company accept this offer? Use a two-state model to value the real option.

5. **Real Options** Jet Black is an international conglomerate with a petroleum division and is currently competing in an auction to win the right to drill for crude oil on a large piece of land in one year. The current market price of crude oil is ₹40 per barrel and the land is believed to contain 750,000 barrels of oil. If found, the oil would cost ₹60 million to extract. Treasury bills that mature in one year yield a continuously compounded interest rate of 4 percent and the standard deviation of the returns on the price of crude oil is 50 percent. Use the Black-Scholes model to calculate the maximum bid that the company should be willing to make at the auction.

INTERMEDIATE (Questions 6–8)

6. **Real Options** Sardano and Sons is a large, publicly held company that is considering leasing a warehouse. One of the company's divisions specializes in manufacturing steel, and this particular warehouse is the only facility in the area that suits the firm's operations. The current price of steel is ₹650 per ton. If the price of steel falls over the next six months, the company will purchase 1,750 tons of steel and produce 175,000 steel rods. Each steel rod will cost ₹7 to manufacture and the company plans to sell the rods for ₹15 each. It will take only a matter of days to produce and sell the steel rods. If the price of steel rises or remains the same, it will not be profitable to undertake the project and the company will allow the lease to expire without producing any steel rods. Treasury bills that mature in six months yield a continuously compounded interest rate of 4.5 percent and the standard deviation of the returns on steel is 38 percent. Use the Black-Scholes model to determine the maximum amount that the company should be willing to pay for the lease.

7. **Real Options** Wet for the Summer, Inc., manufactures filters for swimming pools. The company is deciding whether to implement a new technology in its pool filters. One year from now, the company will know whether the new technology is accepted in the market. If the demand for the new filters is high, the present value of the cash flows in one year will be ₹19.4 million. If the demand is low, the value of the cash flows in one year will be ₹10.1 million. The value of the project today under these assumptions is ₹14.1 million and the risk-free rate is 6 percent. Suppose that, in one year, if the demand for the new technology is low, the company can sell the technology for ₹11.9 million. What is the value of the option to abandon?

8. **Binomial Model** There is a European put option on a stock that expires in two months. The stock price is ₹76 and the standard deviation of the stock returns is 60 percent. The option has a strike price of ₹80

and the risk-free interest rate is an annual percentage rate of 5 percent. What is the price of the put option today using one-month steps?

9. **Binomial Model** In the previous problem, assume that the exercise style on the option is American rather than European. What is the price of the option now? (*Hint*: How will you find the value of the option if it can be exercised early? When would you exercise the option early?) CHALLENGE (Questions 9–10)

10. **Real Options** You are in discussions to purchase an option on an office building with a strike price of ₹57 million. The building is currently valued at ₹55 million. The option will allow you to purchase the building either six months from today or one year from today. Six months from today, accrued rent payments from the building in the amount of ₹900,000 will be made to the owners. If you exercise the option in six months, you will receive the accrued rent payment; otherwise, the payment will be made to the current owners. A second accrued rent payment of ₹900,000 will be paid one year from today with the same payment terms. The standard deviation of the value of the building is 30 percent and the risk-free rate is an annual percentage rate of 6 percent. What is the price of the option today using 6-month steps? (*Hint*: The value of the building in six months will be reduced by the accrued rent payment if you do not exercise the option at that time.)

11. **ESOPs in India** Sonu Sood completed his MBA from a premier business school in India and had joining offers from two reputed financial firms. A mid-sized investment bank which recently came up with an IPO was offering him to pay a fixed component of ₹15 lakh annually and an ESOP giving him an opportunity to own 3000 shares. The lock-in period for the ESOP was 3 years. He got another offer from a large-sized investment bank, which was offering him a similar profile and offered him to pay ₹20 lakh annually. However, this firm did not offer him any ESOPs. Sonu felt that since the profiles offered at the two banks were almost similar, he needed to find a value of the ESOP option that was being offered by the mid-sized investment bank. He did some data mining to find that the present price of the stock of this mid-sized I-bank was ₹779 (Yearly High - ₹1800 and Yearly Low - ₹560). He found that the implied volatility of stocks of large-sized I-bank is around 25%, for a mid-sized I-bank is 30% and for a small-sized I-bank is around 50%. You are required to find out which of the two offers he should choose. Assume the risk-free rate to be 6% p.a.

12. **Modeling Insurance** Rubina Dilaik, aged 34 and a working professional, took a pure risk insurance plan from Life Insurance Corporation (LIC) of India. The LIC insurance product was known as Anmol Jeevan. The product involved Rubina to pay ₹3,055 at the start of every year. In an unfortunate scenario of death of the insured person during the term of the policy (i.e., the one-year period), LIC would have paid her a sum assured of ₹10 lakh. In all other scenarios, the customer (i.e., the insured person) would have got a zero sum from LIC, i.e., on maturity, the insurance product value was 'nil'. What type of option is this product, i.e., LIC Anmol Jeevan? Can you attempt modeling this insurance product?

EXOTIC CUISINE'S EMPLOYEE STOCK OPTIONS

As a newly minted MBA, you've taken a management position with Exotic Cuisine, Inc., a restaurant chain that just went public last year. The company's restaurants specialize in exotic main dishes, using ingredients such as alligator, buffalo, and ostrich. A concern you had going in was that the restaurant business is very risky. However, after some due diligence, you discovered a common misperception about the restaurant industry. It is widely thought that 90 percent of new restaurants close within three years; however, recent evidence suggests the failure rate is closer to 60 percent over three years. So, it is a risky business, although not as risky as you originally thought.

During your interview process, one of the benefits mentioned was employee stock options. Upon signing your employment contract, you received options with a strike price of ₹40 for 10,000 shares of company stock. As is fairly common, your stock options have a 3-year vesting period and a 10-year expiration, meaning that you cannot exercise the options for three years and you lose them if you leave before they vest. After the 3-year vesting period, you can exercise the options at any time prior to expiration. Thus, the employee stock options are European (and subject to forfeit) for the first three years and American afterward. Of course, you cannot sell the options, nor can you enter into any sort of hedging agreement. If you leave the company after the options vest, you must exercise within 90 days or forfeit.

Exotic Cuisine stock is currently trading at ₹27.15 per share, a slight increase from the initial offering price last year. There are no market-traded options on the company's stock. Because the company has been traded for only about a year, you are reluctant to use the historical returns to estimate the standard deviation of the stock's return. However, you have estimated that the average annual standard deviation for restaurant company stocks is about 55 percent. Because Exotic Cuisine is a newer restaurant chain, you decide to use a 60 percent standard deviation in your calculations. The company is relatively young and you expect that all earnings will be reinvested back into the company for the near future. Therefore, you expect no dividends will be paid for at least the next 10 years. A 3-year Treasury note currently has a yield of 3.8 percent, and a 10-year Treasury note has a yield of 4.4 percent.

1. You're trying to value your options. What minimum value would you assign? What is the maximum value you would assign?
2. Suppose that in three years the company's stock is trading at ₹60. At that time, should you keep the options or exercise them immediately? What are some of the important determinants in making such a decision?
3. Your options, like most employee stock options, are not transferable or tradable. Does this have a significant effect on the value of the options? Why?
4. Why do you suppose employee stock options usually have a vesting provision? Why must they be exercised shortly after you depart the company even after they vest?
5. A controversial practice with employee stock options is repricing. What happens is that a company experiences a stock price decrease, which leaves employee stock options far out of the money or *underwater*. In such cases, many companies have *repriced* or *restruck* the options, meaning that the company leaves the original terms of the option intact but lowers the strike price. Proponents of repricing argue that because the option is very unlikely to end in the money because of the stock price decline, the motivational force is lost. Opponents argue that repricing is in essence a reward for failure. How do you evaluate this argument? How does the possibility of repricing affect the value of an employee stock option at the time it is granted?
6. As we have seen, much of the volatility in a company's stock price is due to systematic or marketwide risks. Such risks are beyond the control of a company and its employees. What are the implications for employee stock options? In light of your answer, can you recommend an improvement over traditional employee stock options?

Warrants and Convertibles

In November 2020, German airline company Lufthansa announced that it had sold a new bond issue. The company sold €600 million (₹727 million) worth of 2 percent coupon bonds due in 2025. The bonds were sold near par value, so the yield to maturity might seem surprisingly low, particularly given the bond's CCC+ credit rating on subordinated debt. So how was Lufthansa able to issue bonds with such a low promised yield?

The answer is these bonds were convertible into shares of the company's equity share at a price of €12.96 per share. Lufthansa shares were trading at €9.25 when the bonds were issued, so conversion was not immediately profitable, but it could prove to be very lucrative at some point in the future if the stock price were to rise. So, in essence, these convertible bonds are low coupon bonds with an attached call option held by the bondholders.

How do we value a financial instrument that is a combination of a bond and call options? This chapter explores this and other issues.

Please visit us at **rwjcorporatefinance.blogspot.com** for the latest developments in the world of corporate finance.

24.1 Warrants

Warrants are securities that give holders the right, but not the obligation, to buy shares of equity share directly from a company at a fixed price for a given period. Each warrant specifies the number of shares of stock that the holder can buy, the exercise price, and the expiration date.

From the preceding description of warrants, it is clear that they are similar to call options. The differences in contractual features between warrants and the call options that trade on the Chicago Board Options Exchange *or* the National Stock Exchange *or* the Bombay Stock Exchange are minimal. A major difference is that warrants have longer maturity periods.[1] Some warrants are actually perpetual, meaning that they never expire.

Warrants are referred to as *equity kickers* because they are usually issued in combination with privately placed bonds.[2] In most cases, warrants are attached to the bonds when issued. The loan agreement will state whether the warrants are detachable from the bond–that is, whether they can be sold separately. Usually, the warrant can be detached immediately.

[1] Warrants are usually protected against stock splits and dividends in the same way that call options are.
[2] Warrants also are issued with publicly distributed bonds and new issues of equity share.

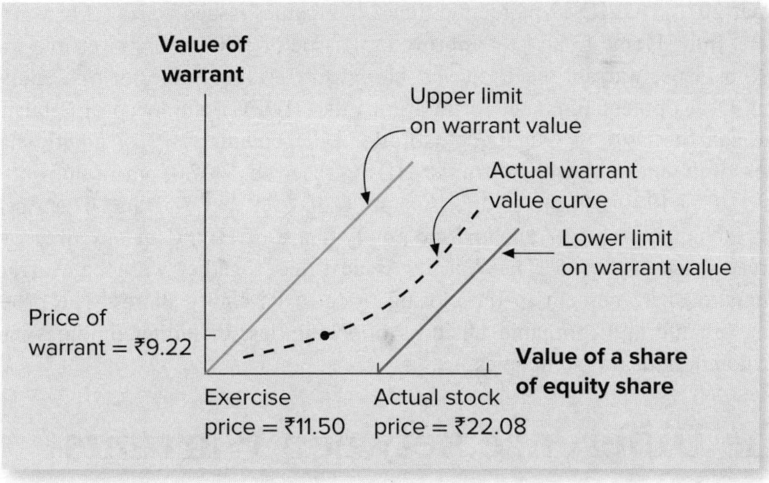

Figure 24.1 RIDE Warrants on December 2, 2020

For example, electric truck company Lordstown Motors (RIDE) issued warrants on March 19, 2019. Each stockholder received .333 warrants for every share of stock owned, and each warrant gave the holder the right to purchase one share of stock at an exercise price of ₹11.50. The warrants expired in five years. On December 2, 2020, RIDE stock closed at ₹22.08 and the price of a warrant was ₹9.22.

The relationship between the value of RIDE's warrants and its stock price can be viewed as similar to the relationship between a call option and the stock price, described in a previous chapter. Figure 24.1 depicts the relationship for RIDE's warrants. The lower limit on the value of the warrants is zero if RIDE's stock price is below ₹11.50 per share. If the price of RIDE's stock rises above ₹11.50 per share, the lower limit is the stock price minus ₹11.50. The upper limit is the price of RIDE's stock. A warrant to buy one share of stock cannot sell at a price above the price of the underlying stock.

The price of RIDE's warrants on December 2, 2020, was higher than the lower limit. The height of the warrant price above the lower limit will depend on the following:

1. The variance of RIDE's stock returns.
2. The time to expiration date.
3. The risk-free rate of interest.
4. The stock price of RIDE.
5. The exercise price.

These are the same factors that determine the value of a call option.

In India, warrants are a popular mechanism for *raising capital* and (importantly) for *raising promoters, stake* in the company. For example, Garware Marine Industries Ltd. issued 3,50,000 warrants of ₹10/- each at a price of ₹25/- (inclusive of premium of ₹15/- per warrant) to promoters, entitling them (warrant holders) to convert into 3,50,000 equity shares at a price of ₹25/- per share.[3] The funds raised from the warrants were to be utilized for part funding the capital expenditure plans and repayment of existing debts.

[3] The issue price computed as per SEBI guidelines was ₹24.7 per warrant. The issue details also stated [a] issue of 4,70,000 warrants issued at a price of ₹25 (inclusive of premium of ₹15 per warrant) to non-promoters, which will entitle the warrant holders to convert into 4,70,000 equity shares at a price of ₹25 per share; [b] the conversion period of the warrants shall not exceed 18 months from the date of the issue; [c] the warrants (and the related new shares issued) shall be locked in for a period of three years from the date of their allotment.

During the year 2020, COVID-19 pandemic times, companies issued warrants or warrant-related instruments. For instance, India Home Loan Ltd. approved the issue of 16,00,000 convertible warrants to promoters at a price of ₹76.75 per warrant, each convertible into or exchangeable for one equity share of ₹76.75 per share. Housing Development Finance Corporation Ltd. (HDFC), the low-profile business group, raised ₹14,000 crore through the issue of Qualified Institutions Placement (QIP) of equity shares and non-convertible debentures simultaneously with warrants. HDFC received ₹307.03 crore upfront through the issue and allotment of 1,70,57,400 warrants at an issue price of ₹180 per warrant. The warrants entitled the warrant holder to exchange each warrant for one equity share of HDFC at any time over the next three years at a pre-agreed price of ₹2,165. The Warrant Issue Price, together with the Warrant Exercise Price, represented a premium of 32 percent to the closing price of its equity shares. The proceeds of the issue were for financing organic and inorganic business opportunities, including funding expansion plans for HDFC's subsidiary and associate companies.

24.2 The Difference between Warrants and Call Options

From the holder's point of view, warrants are similar to call options on equity share. A warrant, like a call option, gives its holder the right to buy equity share at a specified price. Warrants usually have an expiration date, though in most cases they are issued with longer lives than call options. From the firm's point of view, however, a warrant is very different from a call option on the company's equity share.

The most important difference between call options and warrants is that call options are issued by individuals and warrants are issued by firms. When a warrant is exercised, a firm must issue new shares of stock. Each time a warrant is exercised, the number of shares outstanding increases.

Suppose the Bismillah Chemicals issues a warrant giving holders the right to buy one share of equity share at ₹25. If the warrant is exercised, Bismillah must print one new stock certificate. In exchange for the stock certificate, it receives ₹25 from the holder.

In contrast, when a call option is exercised, there is no change in the number of shares outstanding. Suppose Ms. Padmini holds a call option on the equity share of the Bismillah Chemicals. The call option gives Ms. Padmini the right to buy one share of the equity share of the Bismillah Chemicals for ₹25. If Ms. Padmini chooses to exercise the call option, a seller, say Mr. Narad, is obligated to give her one share of Bismillah's equity share in exchange for ₹25. If Mr. Narad does not already own a share, he must buy one in the stock market. The call option is a side bet between buyers and sellers on the value of the Bismillah Chemicals's equity share. When a call option is exercised, one investor gains and the other loses. The total number of shares outstanding of the Bismillah Chemicals remains constant, and no new funds are made available to the company.

EXAMPLE 24.1

Warrants and Firm Value To see how warrants affect the value of the firm, imagine that Mr. Gautam Goud and Ms. Rabri Devi are two investors who have together purchased six ounces of platinum. At the time they bought the platinum, Mr. Gautam Goud and Ms. Rabri Devi each contributed half of the cost, which we will assume was ₹3,000 for six ounces, or ₹500 an ounce (they each contributed ₹1,500). They incorporated, printed two stock certificates, and named the firm the GR Company. Each certificate represents a one-half claim to the platinum. Mr. Gautam Goud and Ms. Rabri Devi each own one certificate. They have formed a company with platinum as its only asset.

(continued)

A Call Is Issued Suppose Mr. Gautam Goud later decides to sell to Ms. Jennifer D'Souza a call option issued on Mr. Gautam Goud's share. The call option gives Ms. Jennifer D'Souza the right to buy Mr. Gautam Goud's share for ₹1,800 within the next year. If the price of platinum rises above ₹600 per ounce, the firm will be worth more than ₹3,600, and each share will be worth more than ₹1,800. If Ms. Jennifer D'Souza decides to exercise her option, Mr. Gautam Goud must turn over his stock certificate and receive ₹1,800.

How would the firm be affected by the exercise? The number of shares will remain the same. There will still be two shares, now owned by Ms. Rabri Devi and Ms. Jennifer D'Souza. If the price of platinum rises to ₹700 an ounce, each share will be worth ₹2,100 (= ₹4,200/2). If Ms. Jennifer D'Souza exercises her option at this price, she will gain ₹300.

A Warrant Is Issued Instead This story changes if a warrant is issued. Suppose that Mr. Gautam Goud does not sell a call option to Ms. Jennifer D'Souza. Instead, Mr. Gautam Goud and Ms. Rabri Devi have a stockholders' meeting. They vote that GR Company will issue a warrant and sell it to Ms. Jennifer D'Souza. The warrant will give Ms. Jennifer D'Souza the right to receive a share of the company at an exercise price of ₹1,800.[4] If Ms. Jennifer D'Souza decides to exercise the warrant, the firm will issue another stock certificate and give it to Ms. Jennifer D'Souza in exchange for ₹1,800.

From Ms. Jennifer D'Souza's perspective, the call option and the warrant seem to be the same. The exercise prices of the warrant and the call are the same: ₹1,800. It is still advantageous for Ms. Jennifer D'Souza to exercise the warrant when the price of platinum exceeds ₹600 per ounce. However, we will show that Ms. Jennifer D'Souza actually makes less in the warrant situation due to dilution.

The GR Company also must consider dilution. Suppose the price of platinum increases to ₹700 an ounce and Ms. Jennifer D'Souza exercises her warrant. Two things will occur:

1. Ms. Jennifer D'Souza will pay ₹1,800 to the firm.
2. The firm will print one stock certificate and give it to Ms. Jennifer D'Souza. The stock certificate will represent a one-third claim on the value of the firm.

Because Ms. Jennifer D'Souza contributes ₹1,800 to the firm, the value of the firm increases. It is now worth:

$$\begin{aligned}\text{New value of firm} &= \text{Value of platinum} + \text{Contribution to the firm by Ms. Jennifer D'Souza}\\ &= ₹4{,}200 \qquad\qquad + \qquad\qquad ₹1{,}800\\ &= ₹6{,}000\end{aligned}$$

Because Ms. Jennifer D'Souza has a one-third claim on the firm's value, her share is worth ₹2,000 (= ₹6,000/3). By exercising the warrant, Ms. Jennifer D'Souza gains ₹2,000 – 1,800 = ₹200. This is illustrated in Table 24.1.

Dilution Why does Ms. Jennifer D'Souza gain only ₹200 in the warrant case but ₹300 in the call option case? The key is share price dilution, as we discussed in an earlier chapter. GR Company has issued another share in exchange for less than market value, leading to a decline in the share price. In the call option case, she contributes ₹1,800 and receives one of the two outstanding shares. That is, she receives a share worth ₹2,100 (= 1/2 × ₹4,200). Her gain is ₹300 (= ₹2,100 – 1,800). We rewrite this gain like this:

$$\frac{₹4{,}200}{2} - ₹1{,}800 = ₹300 \qquad \textbf{(24.1)}$$

(continued)

[4] The sale of the warrant brings cash into the firm. We assume that the sale proceeds immediately leave the firm through a cash dividend to Mr. Gautam Goud and Ms. Rabri Devi. This simplifies the analysis because the firm with warrants then has the same total value as the firm without warrants.

Table 24.1 Effect of Call Option and Warrant on the GR Company*

	Price of Platinum per Share	
Value of Firm if	**₹700**	**₹600**
No warrant		
Mr. Gautam Goud's share	₹2,100	₹1,800
Ms. Rabri Devi's share	2,100	1,800
Firm	₹4,200	₹3,600
Call option		
Mr. Gautam Goud's claim	₹ 0	₹1,800
Ms. Rabri Devi's claim	2,100	1,800
Ms. Jennifer D'Souza's claim	2,100	0
Firm	₹4,200	₹3,600
Warrant		
Mr. Gautam Goud's share	₹2,000	₹1,800
Ms. Rabri Devi's share	2,000	1,800
Ms. Jennifer D'Souza's share	2,000	0
Firm	₹6,000	₹3,600

*If the price of platinum is ₹700, the value of the firm is equal to the value of six ounces of platinum plus the excess rupees paid into the firm by Ms. Jennifer D'Souza. This amount is ₹4,200 + 1,800 = ₹6,000.

In the warrant case, she contributes ₹1,800 and receives a newly created share. She now owns one of the three outstanding shares. Because the ₹1,800 remains in the firm, her share is worth ₹2,000 [= (₹4,200 + 1,800)/3]. Her gain is ₹200 (= ₹2,000 − 1,800). We rewrite this gain as follows:

$$\frac{₹4{,}200 + 1{,}800}{2 + 1} - ₹1{,}800 = ₹200 \quad \textbf{(24.2)}$$

Warrants also affect accounting numbers. Warrants and (as we will see) convertible bonds cause the number of shares to increase. This causes the firm's net income to be spread over more shares, thereby decreasing earnings per share. Firms with significant amounts of warrants and convertible issues must report earnings on a *primary* basis and a *fully diluted* basis.

HOW THE FIRM CAN HURT WARRANT HOLDERS

Suppose that the platinum firm owned by Mr. Gautam Goud and Ms. Rabri Devi has issued a warrant to Ms. Jennifer D'Souza that is in the money and about to expire. One way that Mr. Gautam Goud and Ms. Rabri Devi can hurt Ms. Jennifer D'Souza is to pay themselves a large dividend. This could be funded by selling a substantial amount of platinum. The value of the firm would fall, and the warrant would be worth much less.

24.3 Warrant Pricing and the Black-Scholes Model

We now wish to express the gains from exercising a call and a warrant in more general terms. The gain on a call can be written like this:

$$\frac{\text{Firm's value net of debt}}{N} - \text{Exercise price} \tag{24.3}$$

Equation 24.3 generalizes Equation 24.1. We define the *firm's value net of debt* to be the total firm value less the value of the debt. The total firm value is ₹4,200 in our example, and there is no debt. The N stands for the number of shares outstanding, which is two in our example. The ratio on the left is the value of a share of stock. The gain on a warrant can be written as follows:

$$\frac{\text{Firm's value net of debt} + \text{Exercise price} \times N_w}{N + N_w} - \text{Exercise price} \tag{24.4}$$

Equation 24.4 generalizes Equation 24.2. The numerator of the left term is the firm's value net of debt after the warrant is exercised. It is the sum of the firm's value net of debt prior to the warrant's exercise plus the proceeds the firm receives from the exercise. The proceeds equal the product of the exercise price multiplied by the number of warrants. The number of warrants appears as N_w. (Our analysis uses the plausible assumption that all warrants that are in the money will be exercised.) Note that $N_w = 1$ in our numerical example. The denominator, $N + N_w$, is the number of shares outstanding after the exercise of the warrants. The ratio on the left is the value of a share of stock after exercise. By rearranging terms, we can rewrite Equation 24.4 as:[5]

$$\frac{N}{N + N_w} \times \left(\frac{\text{Firm's value net of debt}}{N} - \text{Exercise price}\right) \tag{24.5}$$

Equation 24.5 relates the gain on a warrant to the gain on a call. Note that the term within parentheses is Equation 24.3. The gain from exercising a warrant is a proportion of the gain from exercising a call in a firm without warrants. The proportion $N/(N + N_w)$ is the ratio of the number of shares in the firm without warrants to the number of shares after all the warrants have been exercised. This ratio must always be less than one. Thus, the gain on a warrant must be less than the gain on an identical call in a firm without warrants. Note that $N/(N + N_w) = 2/3$ in our example, which explains why Ms. Jennifer D'Souza gains ₹300 on her call yet gains only ₹200 on her warrant.

The preceding implies that the Black-Scholes model must be adjusted for warrants. When a call option is issued to Ms. Jennifer D'Souza, we know that the exercise price is ₹1,800 and the time to expiration is one year. Though we have not provided the price of the stock, the variance of the stock, or the interest rate, we easily could provide these data for a real-world situation. Thus, we could use the Black-Scholes model to value Ms. Jennifer D'Souza's call.

[5] To derive Equation 24.5, we separate "Exercise price" in Equation 24.4. This yields:

$$\frac{\text{Firm's value net of debt}}{N + N_w} - \frac{N}{N + N_w} \times \text{Exercise price}$$

By rearranging terms, we can obtain Equation 24.5.

Suppose that the warrant is to be issued tomorrow to Ms. Jennifer D'Souza. We know the number of warrants to be issued, the warrant's expiration date, and the exercise price. Using our assumption that the warrant proceeds are immediately paid out as a dividend, we could use the Black-Scholes model to value the warrant. We would first calculate the value of an identical call. The warrant price is the call price multiplied by the ratio $N/(N + N_w)$.

24.4 Convertible Bonds

A **convertible bond** is similar to a bond with warrants. The most important difference is that a bond with warrants can be separated into distinct securities and a convertible bond cannot. A convertible bond gives the holder the right to exchange it for a given number of shares of stock anytime up to and including the maturity date of the bond.

Preferred stock can frequently be converted into equity share. A convertible preferred stock is the same as a convertible bond except that it has an infinite maturity date.

EXAMPLE 24.2

Convertibles Going back to the Lufthansa convertible bonds, Lufthansa raised €600 million by issuing convertible subordinated debentures with a 2 percent coupon rate due in 2025. Each bond had a par value of €100,000 and was convertible into 7,716.049 shares of Lufthansa equity share any time before maturity. The number of shares received for each bond (7,716.049 in this example) is called the **conversion ratio**.

Bond traders also speak of the **conversion price** of the bond. This price is calculated as the ratio of the face value of the bond to the conversion ratio. Because the face value of each Lufthansa bond was €100,000, the conversion price was €12.96 (= €100,000/7,716.049). If a bondholder chose to convert, she would give up a bond with a face value of €100,000 and receive 7,716.049 shares of Lufthansa equity share in return. The conversion is equivalent to paying €12.96 for each share of Lufthansa equity share received.

When Lufthansa issued its convertible bonds, its equity share was trading at €9.25 per share. The conversion price of €12.96 was 40 percent higher than the actual equity share price. This 40 percent is referred to as the **conversion premium**. It reflects the fact that the conversion option in Lufthansa convertible bonds was out of the money, meaning that immediate conversion would be unprofitable. This conversion premium is typical.

Convertibles are almost always protected against stock splits and stock dividends. If Lufthansa's equity share were split two-for-one, the conversion ratio would increase from 7,716.049 to 15,432.098.

Conversion ratio, conversion price, and conversion premium are well-known terms in the real world. For that reason alone, students should master these concepts. However, conversion price and conversion premium implicitly assume that the bond is selling at par. If the bond is selling at another price, the terms have little meaning. By contrast, conversion ratio can have a meaningful interpretation regardless of the price of the bond.

To give an example of these ideas, consider convertible bonds issued by offshore driller Transocean. The bonds were offered for sale in December 2007 and will mature in 2037. The conversion ratio on the bonds is 5.931. This ratio means that the conversion price was ₹1,000/5.931 = ₹168.61. In December 2020,

Transocean's stock was selling for about ₹2, so this price implied a conversion premium of 8,330 percent. We should note that the conversion premium was much lower in 2007 when the convertible bond was issued.

24.5 The Value of Convertible Bonds

The value of a convertible bond can be described in terms of three components: straight bond value, conversion value, and option value. We examine these three components next.

STRAIGHT BOND VALUE

The straight bond value is what the convertible bonds would sell for if they could not be converted into equity share. It will depend on the general level of interest rates and on the default risk. The convertible bonds issued by Lufthansa were rated CCC+, and CCC+ rated bonds were priced to yield 4.6 percent per six months. The semiannual coupons were €1,000, the principal amount was €100,000, and the maturity was five years. The straight bond value of the Lufthansa convertible bonds can be determined by discounting the €1,000 semiannual coupon payment and principal amount at 4.6 percent:

$$\begin{aligned}\text{Straight bond value} &= €1{,}000 \times \text{PVIFA}_{4.6\%,\ 10} + \frac{€100{,}000}{1.046^{10}} \\ &= €7{,}873.96 + 63{,}779.80 \\ &= €71{,}653.76\end{aligned}$$

The straight bond value of a convertible bond is a minimum value. The price of Lufthansa's convertible bonds could not have gone lower than the straight bond value.

Figure 24.2 illustrates the relationship between straight bond value and stock price. In Figure 24.2 we have been somewhat dramatic and implicitly assumed that the convertible bond is default free. In this case, the straight bond value does not depend on the stock price, so it is graphed as a straight line.

CONVERSION VALUE

The value of convertible bonds depends on conversion value. **Conversion value** is what the bonds would be worth if they were immediately converted into equity share at current prices. Typically, we compute conversion value by multiplying the number of shares of equity share that will be received when the bond is converted by the current price of the equity share.

When the bonds were issued, each Lufthansa convertible bond could have been converted into 7,716.049 shares of Lufthansa equity share. Lufthansa equity share was selling for €9.25. Thus, the conversion value was 7,716.049 × €9.25 = €71,373.45. A convertible cannot sell for less than its conversion value. Arbitrage prevents this from happening. If Lufthansa's convertible sold for less than ₹71,373.45, investors would have bought the bonds and converted them into equity share and sold the stock. The profit would have been the difference between the value of the stock sold and the bond's conversion value.

Thus, convertible bonds have two minimum values: the straight bond value and the conversion value. The conversion value is determined by the value of the firm's underlying equity share. This is illustrated in Figure 24.2. As the value of equity share rises and falls, the conversion value rises and falls with it. If the price of Lufthansa's equity share increased by €1, the conversion value of its convertible bonds increased by €7,716.049.

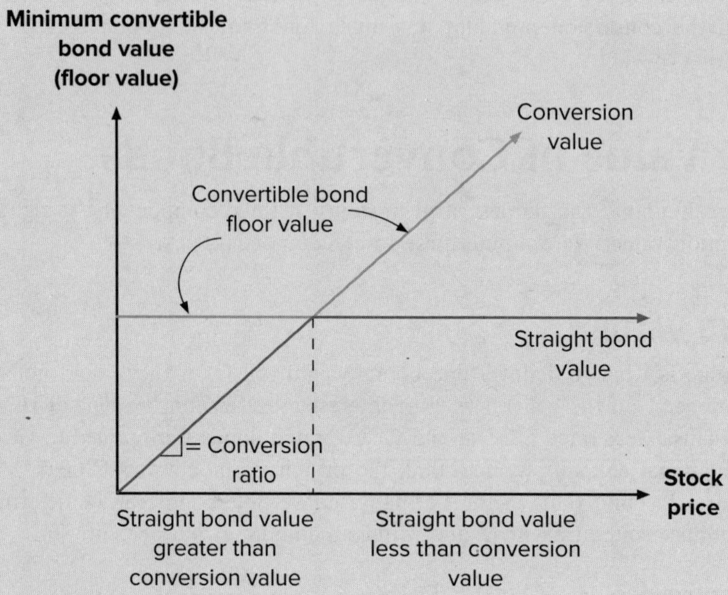

As shown, the minimum, or floor, value of a convertible bond is either its straight bond value or its conversion value, whichever is greater.

Figure 24.2 Minimum Value of a Convertible Bond versus the Value of the Stock for a Given Interest Rate

OPTION VALUE

The value of a convertible bond will generally exceed both the straight bond value and the conversion value.[6] This occurs because holders of convertibles need not convert immediately. Instead, by waiting, they can take advantage of whichever is greater in the future: the straight bond value or the conversion value. This option to wait has value, and it raises the value over both the straight bond value and the conversion value.

When the value of the firm is low, the value of convertible bonds is most significantly influenced by their underlying value as straight debt. However, when the value of the firm is very high, the value of convertible bonds is mostly determined by their underlying conversion value. This is illustrated in Figure 24.3.

The bottom portion of the figure implies that the value of a convertible bond is the maximum of its straight bond value or its conversion value, plus its option value:

$$\text{Value of convertible bond} = \text{The greater of (Straight bond value, Conversion value)} + \text{Option value}$$

[6]The most plausible exception is when conversion would provide the investor with a dividend much greater than the interest available prior to conversion. The optimal strategy here could very well be to convert immediately, implying that the market value of the bond would exactly equal the conversion value. Other exceptions occur when the firm is in default or the bondholders are forced to convert.

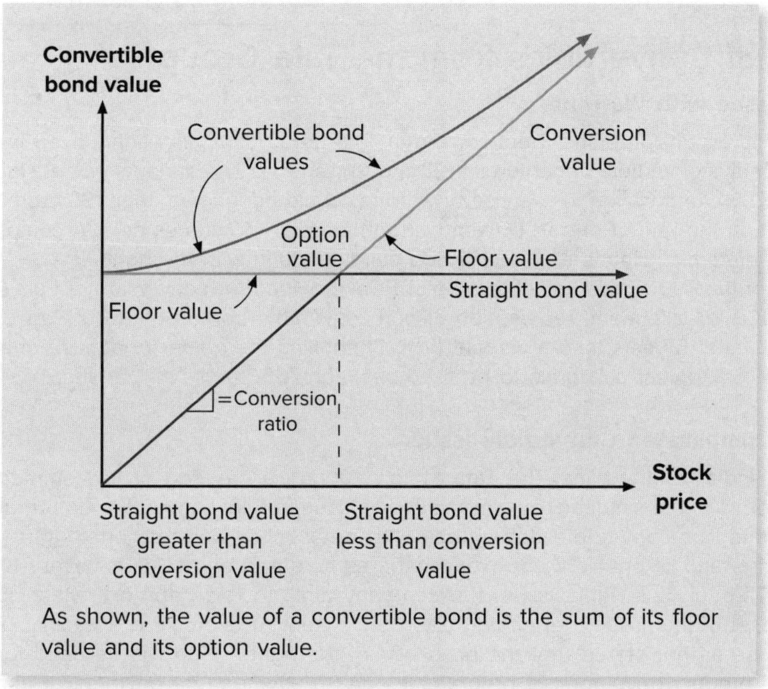

Figure 24.3 Value of a Convertible Bond versus the Value of the Stock for a Given Interest Rate

EXAMPLE 24.3

Conversion Suppose the Moulton Company has outstanding 1,000 shares of equity share and 100 bonds. Each bond has a face value of ₹1,000 at maturity. They are discount bonds and pay no coupons. At maturity, each bond can be converted into 10 shares of newly issued equity share.

What circumstances will make it advantageous for the holders of Moulton convertible bonds to convert to equity share at maturity?

If the holders of the convertible bonds convert, they will receive $100 \times 10 = 1{,}000$ shares of equity share. Because there were already 1,000 shares, the total number of shares outstanding becomes 2,000 upon conversion. Converting bondholders own 50 percent of the value of the firm, V. If they do not convert, they will receive ₹100,000 or V, whichever is less. The choice for the holders of the Moulton bonds is obvious: They should convert if 50 percent of V is greater than ₹100,000. This will be true whenever V is greater than ₹200,000. This is illustrated as follows:

Payoff to Convertible Bondholders and Stockholders of the Moulton Company

	(1) $V \leq 100{,}000$	(2) ₹100,000 $< V \leq$ ₹200,000	(3) $V >$ ₹200,000
Decision:	Bondholders will not convert	Bondholders will not convert	Bondholders will convert
Convertible bondholders	V	₹100,000	$.5V$
Stockholders	0	$V -$ ₹100,000	$.5V$

Examples of Convertibles from the Tata Group

Trent's PCD Issue with Warrants

To part-finance its expansion plans, Trent Limited (a Tata group company) announced its plans to float a rights issue of partly-convertible debentures (PCDs) with warrants. The announcement stated that the PCD issue will raise ₹118 crore, while the exercise of warrants could bring in another ₹90 crore. The rights offer was being made at the rate of one PCD (with warrant) for every 10 shares held. A company release said there was no preferential allotment of such PCDs planned along with the rights issue.

The terms of the ₹900 (face value) three-part PCD provided for conversion of Part A into one share at a price of ₹400, on allotment; redemption of non-convertible portion of ₹500 (Part B) with a yield to maturity of 5.5%, after 5 years; and a warrant (Part C) entitling the holder to acquire one equity share in the third, fourth or fifth year at a price to be fixed between ₹650 and 700 per share.

Tata Motors Complicated Convertible Issue

Pink papers in India reported that the Tata Motors, during a meeting of its committee of directors, approved the terms of the simultaneous and unlinked issue of fully convertible debentures with detachable warrants and non-convertible debentures with detachable warrants on a rights basis. This has been done in the ratio of one FCD for every 4 shares held and one NCD for every 10 shares held of the company. Through this rights issue, the company aims to raise approximately up to ₹979 crore from the proposed rights issue, depending upon the extent of exercise of warrants by the investors. The news release further stated that the proceeds of the rights issue will be used for capital expenditure and new product development programmes and repayment/pre-payment of expensive borrowings of the company.

The FCDs will have a face value of ₹65 and be compulsorily converted into 1 ordinary share on March 31, at value 65 per share. The FCD will carry an interest of 7 percent on the face value. Every five FCDs will have one detachable and tradable equity warrant which can be exercised and converted into one ordinary share at a price of ₹120 after 18 months from the date of allotment.

The NCDs will have a face value of ₹100 and carry an interest of 11 percent per annum payable annually. The NCD will be redeemed in three installments of ₹30, ₹35 and ₹35 each at the end of the 4th, 5th and 6th year, respectively, from the date of allotment and would also have a put and call option at the end of 24 months from the date of allotment. Every two NCDs will have one detachable and tradable equity warrant which can be exercised and converted into one ordinary share at a price of ₹120 after 18 months from the date of allotment.

24.6 Issuing Warrants and Convertibles in Efficient Markets

Probably there is no other area of corporate finance where real-world practitioners get as confused as they do on the reasons for issuing convertible debt. To separate fact from fantasy, we present a rather structured argument. We first compare convertible debt to straight debt. Then we compare convertible debt to equity. For each comparison, we ask in what situations is the firm better off with convertible debt and in what situations is it worse off? We will show that in an efficient market without taxes or other frictions, a firm is neither better nor worse off if it chooses to issue warrants or convertibles.

CONVERTIBLE DEBT VERSUS STRAIGHT DEBT

Convertible debt pays a lower interest rate than does otherwise identical straight debt. If the interest rate is 10 percent on straight debt, the interest rate on convertible debt might be 9 percent. Investors will accept a lower interest rate on a convertible because of the potential gain from conversion.

Imagine a firm that seriously considers both convertible debt and straight debt, finally deciding to issue convertibles. When would this decision have benefited the firm and when would it have hurt the firm? We consider two situations.

The Stock Price Later Rises So That Conversion Is Indicated The firm clearly likes to see the stock price rise. However, it would have benefited even more had it previously issued straight debt instead of a convertible. Although the firm paid out a lower interest rate than it would have with straight debt, it was obligated to sell the convertible holders a chunk of the equity at a below-market price.

The Stock Price Later Falls or Does Not Rise Enough to Justify Conversion The firm hates to see the stock price fall. However, as long as the stock price does fall, the firm is glad that it had previously issued convertible debt instead of straight debt. This is because the interest rate on convertible debt is lower. Because conversion does not take place, our comparison of interest rates is all that is needed.

Summary Compared to straight debt, the firm is worse off having issued convertible debt if the underlying stock subsequently does well. The firm is better off having issued convertible debt if the underlying stock subsequently does poorly. In an efficient market, we cannot predict future stock prices. Thus, we cannot argue that convertibles either dominate or are dominated by straight debt.

CONVERTIBLE DEBT VERSUS EQUITY SHARE

Next, imagine a firm that seriously considers both convertible debt and equity share but finally decides to issue convertibles. When would this decision benefit the firm and when would it hurt the firm? We consider our two situations.

The Stock Price Later Rises So That Conversion Is Indicated The firm is better off having previously issued a convertible instead of equity. To see this, consider the Lufthansa convertible bond. The firm could have issued stock for €9.25. Instead, by issuing a convertible, the firm will effectively receive substantially more for a share upon conversion.

The Stock Price Later Falls or Does Not Rise Enough to Justify Conversion No firm wants to see its stock price fall. However, given that the price did fall, the firm would have been better off if it had previously issued stock instead of a convertible. The firm would have benefited by issuing stock above its future market price. That is, the firm would have received more than the subsequent worth of the stock. However, the drop in stock price did not affect the value of the convertible much because the straight bond value serves as a floor.

Summary Compared with equity, the firm is better off having issued convertible debt if the underlying stock subsequently does well. The firm is worse off having issued convertible debt if the underlying stock subsequently does poorly. We cannot predict future stock prices in an efficient market. Thus, we cannot argue that issuing convertibles is better or worse than issuing equity. The preceding analysis is summarized in Table 24.2.

Table 24.2 The Case For and Against Convertible Bonds (CBs)

	If Firm Subsequently Does Poorly	If Firm Subsequently Prospers
Convertible bonds (CBs)	No conversion because of low stock price.	Conversion because of high stock price.
Compared to: Straight bonds	CBs provide cheap financing because coupon rate is lower.	CBs provide expensive financing because bonds are converted, which dilutes existing equity.
Equity share	CBs provide expensive financing because firm could have issued equity share at high prices.	CBs provide cheap financing because firm issues stock at high prices when bonds are converted.

Modigliani-Miller (MM) pointed out that, abstracting from taxes and other frictions, the firm is indifferent to whether it issues stock or issues debt. The MM relationship is a quite general one. Their theory could be adjusted to show that the firm is indifferent to whether it issues convertibles or issues other instruments. To save space (and the patience of students) we have omitted a full-blown proof of MM in a world with convertibles. However, our results are perfectly consistent with MM. Now we turn to the real-world view of convertibles.

THE "FREE LUNCH" STORY

The preceding discussion suggests that issuing a convertible bond is no better and no worse than issuing other instruments. Unfortunately, many corporate executives fall into the trap of arguing that issuing convertible debt is actually better than issuing alternative instruments. This is a "free lunch" type of explanation, of which we are quite critical.

EXAMPLE 24.4

Are Convertibles Always Better? The stock price of Rameshwar Company is ₹20. Suppose this company can issue subordinated debentures at 10 percent. It also can issue convertible bonds at 6 percent with a conversion value of ₹800. The conversion value means that the holders can convert a convertible bond into 40 (= ₹800/₹20) shares of equity share.

A company treasurer who believes in free lunches might argue that convertible bonds should be issued because they represent a cheaper source of financing than both subordinated bonds and equity share. The treasurer will point out that if the company does poorly and the price does not rise above ₹20, the convertible bondholders will not convert the bonds into equity share. In this case the company will have obtained debt financing at below-market rates by attaching worthless equity kickers. On the other hand, if the firm does well and the price of its equity share rises to ₹25 or above, convertible holders will convert. The company will issue 40 shares. The company will receive a bond with a face value of ₹1,000 in exchange for issuing 40 shares of equity share, implying a conversion price of ₹25. The company will have issued equity share at ₹25 per share, or 25 percent above the ₹20 equity share price prevailing when the convertible bonds were issued. This enables it to lower its cost of equity capital. The treasurer happily points out, regardless of whether the company does well or poorly, convertible bonds are the cheapest form of financing.

Although this argument may sound quite plausible at first, there is a flaw. The treasurer is comparing convertible financing with straight debt when the stock subsequently falls. However, the treasurer compares convertible financing with equity share when the stock subsequently rises. This is an unfair mixing of

(continued)

comparisons. By contrast, our analysis in Table 24.2 was fair because we examined both stock increases and decreases when comparing a convertible with each alternative instrument. We found that no single alternative dominated convertible bonds in both up and down markets.

THE "EXPENSIVE LUNCH" STORY

Suppose we stand the treasurer's argument on its head by comparing (1) convertible financing with straight debt when the stock rises and (2) convertible financing with equity when the stock falls.

From Table 24.2, we see that convertible debt is more expensive than straight debt when the stock subsequently rises. The firm's obligation to sell convertible holders a chunk of equity at a below-market price more than offsets the lower interest rate on a convertible.

Also from Table 24.2, we see that convertible debt is more expensive than equity when the stock subsequently falls. Had the firm issued stock, it would have received a price higher than its subsequent worth. Therefore, the expensive lunch story implies that convertible debt is an inferior form of financing. Of course, we dismiss both the free lunch and the expensive lunch arguments.

A RECONCILIATION

In an efficient financial market, there is neither a free lunch nor an expensive lunch. Convertible bonds can be neither cheaper nor more expensive than other instruments. A convertible bond is a package of straight debt and an option to buy equity share. The difference between the market value of a convertible bond and the value of a straight bond is the price investors pay for the call option feature. In an efficient market, this is a fair price.

Television Eighteen's ZCSPCD Offer

On 19th January of a certain year, Television Eighteen's shares closed on the BSE at ₹68.75. The company had recently announced that its shareholders can subscribe to the rights offer of Zero Coupon Secured Partly Convertible Debentures (ZCSPCD). The company stated that the rights offer presented investors an opportunity to reduce the cost of acquisition of their original holdings.

TV 18 operated the CNBC India channel. It held a 100 percent stake in Television Eighteen Mauritius (TEM) which, in turn, has a 49 percent stake in CNBC India. TV 18 sold content to TEM, which received subscription revenues and sold 50 percent of the advertising time to Indian advertisers. TEM passed the subscription and advertising revenues to CNBC India after adjusting for the cost of content and a profit margin. TEM wanted to fund its share of CNBC India's losses.

At the end of July of the same year, TV 18 had to recover ₹67.65 crore from TEM. This included loans given to TEM to finance the losses of CNBC India. With an equity investment of ₹17.18 crore, TV 18's total exposure to TEM worked out to a little more than 80 percent of its net worth. The exposure to TEM only increased given that the objective of the rights offer was to increase the financial support to TEM. Cash recoveries from TEM commenced meaningfully only when CNBC India started breaking even. Analysts agreed that the pay-offs would depend on CNBC India — which was making losses at that time. And they will be significant if the venture breaks even.

The shareholders are offered one ZCSPCD, at ₹150, for every 13 shares held. Subscription to one ZCSPCD will lead to allotment of two shares at ₹10 each a day before the completion of 12 months after allotment. Investors will receive ₹24.38 per ZCSPCD at the end of the third, fourth and fifth years. At the end of the sixth year, they will receive ₹89.38. In all, the investors would receive ₹162.52 over the 6 years and 2 equity shares at face value of 10 allocated at year 1.

In general, if a company prospers, issuing convertible bonds will turn out to be worse than issuing straight bonds and better than issuing equity share. In contrast, if a company does poorly, convertible bonds will turn out to be better than issuing straight bonds and worse than issuing equity share.

24.7 Why Are Warrants and Convertibles Issued?

Research shows that firms that issue convertible bonds are different from other firms. Some of the differences are:

1. The bond ratings of firms using convertibles are lower than those of other firms.[7]
2. Convertibles tend to be used by smaller firms with high growth rates and more financial leverage.[8]
3. Convertibles are usually subordinated and unsecured.

The kind of company that uses convertibles provides clues to why they are issued. Here are some explanations that make sense. Note that all of these explanations involve a breakdown in efficient markets. If markets are not perfectly efficient, firms can benefit by issuing one type of security over another.

MATCHING CASH FLOWS

If financing is costly (i.e., it costs the firm more than fair market value), it makes sense to issue securities whose cash flows match those of the firm. A young, risky, and (it hopes) growing firm might prefer to issue convertibles or bonds with warrants because these will have lower initial interest costs. When the firm is successful, the convertibles (or warrants) will be converted. This causes expensive dilution, but it occurs when the firm can most afford it.

RISK SYNERGY

Another argument for convertible bonds and bonds with warrants is that they are useful when it is very costly to assess the risk of the issuing company. Suppose you are evaluating a new product by a startup company. The new product is a genetically engineered virus that may increase the yields of corn crops in northern climates. It also may cause cancer. This type of product is difficult to value properly. Thus, the risk of the company is very hard to determine: It may be high or it may be low. If you could be sure the risk of the company was high, you would price the bonds for a high yield, say 15 percent. If it was low, you would price them at a lower yield, say 10 percent.

Convertible bonds and bonds with warrants can protect somewhat against mistakes of risk evaluation. Convertible bonds and bonds with warrants have two components: straight bonds and call options on the

Table 24.3 A Hypothetical Case of the Yields on Convertible Bonds*

	Firm Risk	
	Low	High
Straight bond yield	10%	15%
Convertible bond yield	6	7

*The yields on straight bonds reflect the risk of default. The yields on convertibles are not as sensitive to default risk.

[7] Eugene F. Brigham, "An Analysis of Convertible Debentures: Theory and Some Empirical Evidence," *Journal of Finance* 21, no. 1 (1966): 35–54.
[8] Wayne H. Mikkelson, "Convertible Calls and Security Returns," *Journal of Financial Economics* 9, no. 3 (September 1981): 237–64.

company's underlying stock. If the company turns out to be a low-risk company, the straight bond component will have high value and the call option will have low value. However, if the company turns out to be a high-risk company, the straight bond component will have low value and the call option will have high value. This is illustrated in Table 24.3.

However, although risk has effects on value that cancel each other out in convertibles and bonds with warrants, the market and the buyer nevertheless must make an assessment of the firm's potential to value securities, and it is not clear that the effort involved is that much less than is required for a straight bond.

AGENCY COSTS

Convertible bonds can resolve agency problems associated with raising money. In a previous chapter, we showed that straight bonds are like risk-free bonds minus a put option on the assets of the firm. This creates an incentive for creditors to force the firm into low-risk activities. In contrast, holders of equity share have incentives to adopt high-risk projects. High-risk projects with negative NPVs transfer wealth from bondholders to stockholders. If these conflicts cannot be resolved, the firm may be forced to pass up profitable investment opportunities. Because convertible bonds have an equity component, less expropriation of wealth can occur when convertible debt is issued instead of straight debt.[9] In other words, convertible bonds mitigate agency costs. One implication is that convertible bonds have less-restrictive debt covenants than do straight bonds in the real world. Casual empirical evidence seems to bear this out.

BACKDOOR EQUITY

A popular theory of convertibles views them as *backdoor equity*.[10] The basic story is that young, small, high-growth firms cannot usually issue debt on reasonable terms due to high financial distress costs. However, the owners may be unwilling to issue equity if current stock prices are too low.

Lewis, Rogalski, and Seward examine the risk-shifting and backdoor-equity theories of convertible bond debt.[11] They find evidence for both theories.

24.8 Conversion Policy

There is one aspect of convertible bonds that we have omitted so far. Firms are frequently granted a call option on the bond. The typical arrangements for calling a convertible bond are simple. When the bond is called, the holder has about 30 days to choose between the following:

1. Converting the bond to equity share at the conversion ratio.
2. Surrendering the bond and receiving the call price in cash.

What should bondholders do? It should be obvious that if the conversion value of the bond is greater than the call price, conversion is better than surrender; and if the conversion value is less than the call price, surrender is better than conversion. If the conversion value is greater than the call price, the call is said to **force conversion**.

What should financial managers do? Calling the bonds does not change the value of the firm as a whole. However, an optimal call policy can benefit the stockholders at the expense of the bondholders.

[9] Amir Barnea, Robert A. Haugen, and Lemma Senbet, *Agency Problems and Financial Contracting*, Prentice Hall Foundations of Science Series (New York: Prentice Hall, 1985): Chapter VI.

[10] Jeremy C. Stein, "Convertible Bonds as Backdoor Equity Financing," *Journal of Financial Economics* 32, no. 1 (August 1992): 3–21. See also Craig M. Lewis, Richard J. Rogalski, and James K. Seward, "Understanding the Design of Convertible Debt," *Journal of Applied Corporate Finance* 11, no. 1 (Spring 1998): 45–53.

[11] Craig M. Lewis, Richard J. Rogalski, and James K. Seward, "Is Convertible Debt a Substitute for Straight Debt or for Common Equity?" *Financial Management* 28, no. 3 (Autumn 1999): 5–27.

Because we are speaking about dividing a pie of fixed size, the optimal call policy is simple: Do whatever the bondholders do not want you to do.

Bondholders would love the stockholders to call the bonds when the bonds' market value is below the call price. Shareholders would be giving bondholders extra value. Alternatively, should the value of the bonds rise above the call price, the bondholders would love the stockholders not to call the bonds because bondholders would be allowed to hold onto a valuable asset.

There is only one policy left. This is the policy that maximizes shareholder value and minimizes bondholder value:

Call the bond when its value is equal to the call price.

It is puzzling that firms do not always call convertible bonds when the conversion value reaches the call price. Ingersoll examined the call policies of 124 firms between 1968 and 1975.[12] In most cases he found that the company waited to call the bonds until the conversion value was much higher than the call price. The median company waited until the conversion value of its bonds was 44 percent higher than the call price. This is not even close to our optimal strategy. Why?

One reason is that if firms attempt to implement the optimal strategy, it may not be truly optimal. Recall that bondholders have 30 days to decide whether to convert bonds to equity share or to surrender bonds for the call price in cash. In 30 days, the stock price could drop, forcing the conversion value below the call price. If so, the convertible is out of the money and the firm is giving away money. The firm would be giving up cash for equity share worth much less. Because of this possibility, firms in the real world usually wait until the conversion value is substantially above the call price before they trigger the call.[13] This is sensible.

[12] Jonathan Ingersoll, "An Examination of Corporate Call Policies on Convertible Securities," *Journal of Finance* 32, no. 2 (May 1977): 463–78. See also Milton Harris and Artur Raviv, "A Sequential Signalling Model of Convertible Debt Call Policy," *Journal of Finance* 40, no. 5 (December 1985): 1263–81. Harris and Raviv describe a signal equilibrium that is consistent with Ingersoll's result. They show that managers with favorable information will delay calls to avoid depressing stock prices.

[13] See Paul Asquith, "Convertible Bonds Are Not Called Late," *Journal of Finance* 50, no. 4 (September 1995): 1275–89. On the other hand, the stock market usually reacts negatively to the announcement of a call. For example, see Ajai K. Singh, Arnold R. Cowan, and Nandkumar Nayar, "Underwritten Calls of Convertible Bonds," *Journal of Financial Economics* 29, no. 1 (March 1991): 173–96; and Michael A. Mazzeo and William T. Moore, "Liquidity Costs and Stock Price Response to Convertible Security Calls," *Journal of Business* 65, no. 3 (July 1992): 353–69.

Ederington, Caton, and Campbell tested various theories about when it is optimal to call convertibles. They found evidence consistent with the preceding 30-day "safety margin" theory. They also found that calls of in-the-money convertibles are highly unlikely if dividends to be received (after conversion) exceed the company's interest payment. See Louis H. Ederington, Gary L. Caton, and Cynthia J. Campbell, "To Call or Not to Call Convertible Debt," *Financial Management* 26, no. 1 (Spring 1997): 22–31.

RESEARCH IN EMERGING MARKET CONTEXT

Kim et al. (2023) conducted a study to investigate whether companies issuing convertible bonds differ from those issuing bonds with warrants. They found that younger firms with more growth opportunities, larger size, high leverage, low profitability, low credit rating, and low ownership concentrations are likelier to issue hybrid securities instead of straight debt or equity. Additionally, they found that firms with more growth opportunities, larger size, low profitability, and higher ownership concentrations prefer to issue convertible bonds rather than bonds with warrants.

Burlacu and Jimenez-Garcès (2022) studied "backdoor equity financing" using callable convertible bonds. They found that the call feature does not solve the firm's financing problem because a standard convertible bond has the same functions. These findings challenge the belief that the call option in convertible bonds is essential to avoid financial distress costs.

References

Burlacu, R., & Jimenez-Garcès, S. (2022). Why do firms issue callable convertible bonds? A critique of the "backdoor equity financing" theory. *Journal of Banking & Finance, 144,* 106636.

Kim, W. S., Oh, S., & Kiymaz, H. (2023). Motives and market reactions to convertible bonds and bonds with warrants issuance in an emerging market. *International Journal of Finance & Economics, 28*(3), 2449–2474.

Summary and Conclusions

1. A warrant gives the holder the right to buy shares of equity share at an exercise price for a given period. Typically, warrants are issued in a package with privately placed bonds. Afterwards, they become detached and trade separately.
2. A convertible bond is a combination of a straight bond and a call option. The holder can give up the bond in exchange for shares of stock.
3. Convertible bonds and warrants are like call options. However, there are some important differences:
   a. Warrants and convertible securities are issued by corporations. Call options are traded between individual investors.
      i. Warrants are usually issued privately and are combined with a bond. In most cases, the warrants can be detached immediately after the issue. In some cases, warrants are issued with preferred stock, with equity share, or in executive compensation programs.
      ii. Convertibles are usually bonds that can be converted into equity share.
      iii. Call options are sold separately by individual investors (called writers of call options).
   b. Warrants and call options are exercised for cash. The holder of a warrant gives the company cash and receives new shares of the company's stock. The holder of a call option gives another individual cash in exchange for shares of stock. When someone converts a bond, it is exchanged for equity share. As a consequence, bonds with warrants and convertible bonds have different effects on corporate cash flow and capital structure.
   c. Warrants and convertibles cause dilution to the existing shareholders. When warrants are exercised and convertible bonds converted, the company must issue new shares of equity share. The percentage ownership of the existing shareholders will decline. New shares are not issued when call options are exercised.
4. Many arguments, both plausible and implausible, are given for issuing convertible bonds and bonds with warrants. One plausible rationale for such bonds has to do with risk. Convertibles and bonds with warrants are associated with risky companies. Lenders can do several things to protect themselves from high-risk companies:
   a. They can require high yields.
   b. They can lend less, or not at all, to firms whose risk is difficult to assess.
   c. They can impose severe restrictions on such debt.

   Another useful way to protect against risk is to issue bonds with equity kickers. This gives the lenders the chance to benefit from risks and reduces the conflicts between bondholders and stockholders concerning risk.
5. A certain puzzle particularly vexes financial researchers: Convertible bonds usually have call provisions. Companies appear to delay calling convertibles until the conversion value greatly exceeds the call price. From the shareholders' standpoint, the optimal call policy would be to call the convertibles when the conversion value equals the call price.

Concept Questions

1. **Warrants and Options** What is the primary difference between a warrant and a traded call option?
2. **Warrants** Explain the following limits on the prices of warrants:
   - **a.** If the stock price is below the exercise price of the warrant, the lower bound on the price of a warrant is zero.
   - **b.** If the stock price is above the exercise price of the warrant, the lower bound on the price of a warrant is the difference between the stock price and the exercise price.
   - **c.** An upper bound on the price of any warrant is the current value of the firm's stock.
3. **Convertible Bonds and Stock Volatility** Suppose you are evaluating a callable, convertible bond. If the stock price volatility increases, how will this affect the price of the bond?
4. **Convertible Bond Value** What happens to the price of a convertible bond if interest rates increase?
5. **Dilution** What is dilution, and why does it occur when warrants are exercised?
6. **Warrants and Convertibles** What is wrong with the simple view that it is cheaper to issue a bond with a warrant or a convertible feature because the required coupon is lower?
7. **Warrants and Convertibles** Why do firms issue convertible bonds and bonds with warrants?
8. **Convertible Bonds** Why will convertible bonds not be voluntarily converted to stock before expiration?
9. **Convertible Bonds** When should a firm force conversion of convertibles? Why?
10. **Warrant Valuation** A warrant with six months until expiration entitles its owner to buy 10 shares of the issuing firm's equity share for an exercise price of ₹31 per share. If the current market price of the stock is ₹15 per share, will the warrant be worthless?

Questions and Problems

BASIC (Questions 1–9)

1. **Conversion Price** A convertible bond with a par value of ₹1,000 has a conversion ratio of 15.7. What is the conversion price?
2. **Conversion Ratio** A convertible bond with a par value of ₹1,000 has a conversion price of ₹27.35. What is the conversion ratio of the bond?
3. **Conversion Premium** Agawal, Inc., recently issued bonds with a conversion ratio of 15.2 and a par value of ₹1,000. If the stock price at the time of the bond issue was ₹46.34, what was the conversion premium?
4. **Convertible Bonds** Wilder Home Products, Inc., recently issued ₹2 million worth of 3 percent convertible debentures. Each convertible bond has a face value of ₹1,000. Each convertible bond can be converted into 18.4 shares of equity share anytime before maturity. The stock price is ₹34.86 and the market value of each bond is ₹980.
   - **a.** What is the conversion ratio?
   - **b.** What is the conversion price?
   - **c.** What is the conversion premium?
   - **d.** What is the conversion value?
   - **e.** If the stock price increases by ₹2, what is the new conversion value?
5. **Warrant Value** A warrant gives its owner the right to purchase three shares of equity share at an exercise price of ₹64 per share. The current market price of the stock is ₹71. What is the minimum value of the warrant?

6. **Convertible Bond Value** An analyst has recently informed you that at the issuance of a company's convertible bonds, one of the two following sets of relationships existed:

	Scenario A	Scenario B
Face value of bond	₹1,000	₹1,000
Straight value of convertible bond	900	950
Market value of convertible bond	1,000	900

Assume the bonds are available for immediate conversion. Which of the two scenarios do you believe is more likely? Why?

7. **Convertible Bond Value** Muscles Fitness Center, Inc., issued convertible bonds with a conversion price of ₹70. The bonds are available for immediate conversion. The current price of the company's equity share is ₹67 per share. The current market price of the convertible bonds is ₹975. The convertible bonds' straight value is unknown.

   a. What is the minimum price for the convertible bonds?
   b. Explain the difference between the current market price of each convertible bond and the value of the equity share into which it can be immediately converted.

8. **Convertible Bonds** You own a callable, convertible bond with a conversion ratio of 23.17 and a par value of ₹1,000. The stock is currently selling for ₹54 per share. The issuer of the bond has announced a call at a call price of 110. What are your options here? What should you do?

9. **Warrant Value** General Modems has five-year warrants that currently trade in the open market. Each warrant gives its owner the right to purchase one share of equity share for an exercise price of ₹65.

   a. Suppose the stock is currently trading for ₹62 per share. What is the lower limit on the price of the warrant? What is the upper limit?
   b. Suppose the stock is currently trading for ₹73 per share. What is the lower limit on the price of the warrant? What is the upper limit?

INTERMEDIATE (Questions 10 13)

10. **Convertible Bonds** Vital Silence Corp. has just issued a 30-year callable, convertible bond with a coupon rate of 5 percent and annual coupon payments. The bond has a conversion price of ₹78. The company's stock is selling for ₹24 per share. The owner of the bond will be forced to convert if the bond's conversion value is ever greater than or equal to ₹1,100. The required return on an otherwise identical nonconvertible bond is 7 percent. Assume a par value of ₹1,000.

    a. What is the minimum value of the bond?
    b. If the stock price were to grow by 10 percent per year forever, how long would it take for the bond's conversion value to exceed ₹1,100?

11. **Convertible Bonds** Rob Stevens is the chief executive officer of Isner Construction, Inc., and owns 800,000 shares of stock. The company currently has 4.8 million shares of stock and convertible bonds with a face value of ₹35 million outstanding. The convertible bonds have a conversion price of ₹38 and the stock is currently selling for ₹46.

    a. What percentage of the firm's equity share does Rob own?
    b. If the company decides to call the convertible bonds and force conversion, what percentage of the firm's equity share will Rob own? He does not own any convertible bonds.

12. **Warrants** Through Fire, Inc., an all-equity firm, has 12 shares of stock outstanding. Yesterday, the firm's assets consisted of 13 ounces of platinum, currently worth ₹1,030 per ounce. Today, the company issued Janet Wu a warrant for its fair value of ₹1,030. The warrant gives Janet the right to buy a single share of the firm's stock for ₹1,050 and can be exercised only on its expiration date one year from today. The firm used the proceeds from the issuance to immediately purchase an additional ounce of platinum.

a. What was the price of a single share of stock before the warrant was issued?
b. What was the price of a single share of stock immediately after the warrant was issued?
c. Suppose platinum is selling for ₹1,070 per ounce on the warrant's expiration date in one year. What will be the value of a single share of stock on the warrant's expiration date?

13. **Warrants** The capital structure of Ricketti Enterprises, Inc., consists of 25 million shares of equity share and 1.7 million warrants. Each warrant gives its owner the right to purchase one share of equity share for an exercise price of ₹24. The current stock price is ₹32 and each warrant is worth ₹9. What is the new stock price if all warrant holders decide to exercise today?

CHALLENGE (Questions 14–16)

14. **Convertible Calculations** You have been hired to value a new 25-year callable, convertible bond. The bond has a 4.9 percent coupon rate, payable annually. The conversion price is ₹135 and the stock currently sells for ₹36.47. The stock price is expected to grow at 12 percent per year. The bond is callable at ₹1,150, but based on prior experience, it won't be called unless the conversion value is ₹1,250. The required return on this bond is 9 percent. What value would you assign to this bond?

15. **Warrant Value** Superior Clamps, Inc., has a capital structure consisting of 7 million shares of equity share and 900,000 warrants. Each warrant gives its owner the right to purchase one share of newly issued equity share for an exercise price of ₹25. The warrants are European and will expire one year from today. The market value of the company's assets is ₹165 million and the annual variance of the returns on the firm's assets is .20. Treasury bills that mature in one year yield a continuously compounded interest rate of 7 percent. The company does not pay a dividend. Use the Black-Scholes model to determine the value of a single warrant.

16. **Warrant Value** Omega Airline's capital structure consists of 2.7 million shares of equity share and zero coupon bonds with a face value of ₹18 million that mature in six months. The firm just announced that it will issue warrants with an exercise price of ₹95 and six months until expiration to raise the funds to pay off its maturing debt. Each warrant can be exercised only at expiration and gives its owner the right to buy a single newly issued share of equity share. The firm will place the proceeds from the warrant issue immediately into Treasury bills. The market value balance sheet shows that the firm will have assets worth ₹240 million after the announcement. The company does not pay dividends. The standard deviation of the returns on the firm's assets is 50 percent and Treasury bills with a six-month maturity yield 6 percent. How many warrants must the company issue today to be able to use the proceeds from the sale to pay off the firm's debt obligation in six months?

17. **Convertible Bond Value:** Refer to the box in Section 24.6 discussing Television Eighteen's ZCSPCD offer. Poornima holds 100 shares; how much does she need to invest? Can we state that the amount needed for investment would be nearly 17% of the market value of the 100 shares?

18. **Convertible Offer Details:** Refer to the box in Section 24.6 discussing Television Eighteen's ZCSPCD offer. Can we state that the shareholders will get the chance to subscribe to two shares for every 13 shares held? Can we also state that the shareholders will get the above chance with a lock-in-period of 12 months? Discuss.

S&S AIR'S CONVERTIBLE BOND

Chris Guthrie was recently hired by S&S Air, Inc., to assist the company with its short-term financial planning and to evaluate the company's performance. Chris graduated from college five years ago with a finance degree. He has been employed in the finance department of a Fortune 500 company since then.

S&S Air was founded 10 years ago by two friends, Mark Sexton and Todd Story. The company has manufactured and sold light airplanes over this period, and the company's products have received high reviews for safety and reliability. The company has a niche market in that it sells primarily to individuals who own and fly their own airplanes. The company has two models: the Birdie, which sells for ₹53,000, and the Eagle, which sells for ₹78,000.

S&S Air is not publicly traded, but the company needs new funds for investment opportunities. In consultation with Tonisha Jones of underwriter Raines and Warren, Chris decided that a convertible bond issue with a 20-year maturity is the way to go. He met with the owners, Mark and Todd, and presented his analysis of the convertible bond issue. Because the company is not publicly traded, Chris looked at comparable publicly traded companies and determined that the average PE ratio for the industry is 17.5. Earnings per share for the company are ₹1.75. With this in mind, Chris concluded that the conversion price should be ₹45 per share.

Several days later, Todd, Mark, and Chris met again to discuss the potential bond issue. Both Todd and Mark have researched convertible bonds and have questions for Chris. Todd begins by asking Chris if the convertible bond issue will have a lower coupon rate than a comparable bond without a conversion feature. Chris replies that to sell the bond at par value, the convertible bond issue would require a 5 percent coupon rate with a conversion value of ₹680.56, while a plain vanilla bond would have an 8 percent coupon rate. Todd nods in agreement, and he explains that the convertible bonds are a win-win form of financing. He states that if the value of the company stock does not rise above the conversion price, the company has issued debt at a cost below the market rate (5 percent instead of 8 percent). If the company's stock does rise to the conversion value, the company has effectively issued stock at above the current value.

Mark immediately disagrees, arguing that convertible bonds are a no-win form of financing. He argues that if the value of the company stock rises to ₹45, the company is forced to sell stock at the conversion price. This means the new shareholders (those who bought the convertible bonds) benefit from a bargain price. Put another way, if the company prospers, it would have been better to have issued straight debt so that the gains would not be shared.

Chris has gone back to Tonisha for help. As Tonisha's assistant, you've been asked to prepare another memo answering the following questions:

1. Why do you think Chris is suggesting a conversion price of ₹45? Given that the company is not publicly traded, does it even make sense to talk about a conversion price?
2. What is the floor value of the S&S Air convertible bond?
3. What is the conversion ratio of the bond?
4. What is the conversion premium of the bond?
5. What is the value of the option?
6. Is there anything wrong with Todd's argument that it is cheaper to issue a bond with a convertible feature because the required coupon is lower?
7. Is there anything wrong with Mark's argument that a convertible bond is a bad idea because it allows new shareholders to participate in gains made by the company?
8. How can you reconcile the arguments made by Todd and Mark?
9. During the debate, a question comes up concerning whether the bonds should have an ordinary (not make-whole) call feature. Chris confuses everybody by stating, "The call feature lets S&S Air force conversion, thereby minimizing the problem Mark has identified." What is he talking about? Is he making sense?

Derivatives and Hedging Risk

Natural disasters are, of course, a major risk for property and casualty insurance companies. For example, the 2011 tsunami in Japan was estimated to have cost ₹360 billion, and Hurricane Katrina in the U.S. caused more than ₹125 billion in damages in 2005. So how do insurance and reinsurance companies handle this risk? One way is to issue catastrophe, or "cat," bonds. With a cat bond, the issuer pays the coupon like any other bond; however, if a "trigger" is hit, the issuer may not have to pay the remaining coupons or repay the principal. During 2020, companies issued about ₹14.2 billion in cat bonds and other insurance-linked securities, raising the total to about ₹45.3 billion in cat bonds outstanding. During 2020, there were about ₹188 million in losses on cat bonds. To give you an idea of the wide range of triggers on cat bonds, about ₹132 million of the losses were pandemic losses due to COVID-19. As we will see in this chapter, there are a variety of sophisticated financial tools available to deal with risks, including futures, options, and swaps.

Please visit us at **rwjcorporatefinance.blogspot.com** for the latest developments in the world of corporate finance.

25.1 Derivatives, Hedging, and Risk

The name *derivatives* is self-explanatory. A derivative is a financial instrument whose payoffs and values are derived from, or depend on, something else. Often, we speak of the thing that the derivative depends on as the *primitive* or the *underlying*. In Chapter 22 we studied how options work. An option is a derivative. The value of a stock option depends on the value of the underlying stock on which it is written. Actually, options are quite complicated examples of derivatives. The vast majority of derivatives are simpler than options. Most derivatives are forward or futures agreements or what are called *swaps*, and we will study each of these in some detail.

Why do firms use derivatives? The answer is that derivatives are tools for changing the firm's risk exposure. Someone once said that derivatives are to finance what scalpels are to surgery. By using derivatives, the firm can cut away unwanted portions of risk exposure and even transform the exposures into quite different forms. A central point in finance is that risk is undesirable. In our chapters about risk and return, we pointed out that individuals would choose risky securities only if the expected return compensated for the risk. Similarly, a firm will accept a project with high risk only if the return on the project compensates for this risk. Not surprisingly, then, firms are usually looking for ways to reduce their risk. When the firm reduces its risk exposure with the use of derivatives, it is said to be **hedging**. Hedging offsets the firm's risk, such as the risk in a project, by one or more transactions in the financial markets.

Derivatives also can be used to change or even increase the firm's risk exposure. When this occurs, the firm is **speculating** on the movement of some economic variables–those that underlie the derivative. If a derivative is purchased that will rise in value if interest rates rise, and if the firm has no offsetting exposure to interest rate changes, then the firm is speculating that interest rates will rise and give it a profit on its derivatives position. Using derivatives to translate an opinion about whether interest rates or some other economic variable will rise or fall is the opposite of hedging–it is risk enhancing. Speculating on your views on the economy and using derivatives to profit if that view turns out to be correct is not necessarily wrong, but the speculator always should remember that sharp tools cut deeply: If the opinions on which the derivatives position is based turn out to be incorrect, then the consequences can prove costly. Efficient market theory teaches how difficult it is to predict what markets will do. Most of the poor experiences with derivatives have occurred not from their use as instruments for hedging and offsetting risk, but rather from speculation.

SHOULD FIRMS ALWAYS HEDGE AWAY RISKS?

Suppose an airline's cash flows depend on the price of jet fuel. Jet fuel prices will either be low or high next year. Because the airline uses jet fuel as an input, the airline will have high cash flows next year if fuel prices are low. On the other hand, if fuel costs are high, the airline's cash flows will be low. Suppose the airline can hedge away risk associated with jet fuel prices by trading in the futures market. By hedging, the airline can earn the expected value of next year's cash flows, while removing all cash flow risk. Should the airline hedge?

Students are frequently surprised to learn that it may not be optimal for firms to hedge away all cash flow risk, even if they can do so at very low cost. First, there is no need for firms to hedge if markets are perfectly efficient and investors face no frictions or transaction costs. If markets are perfectly efficient, firms can always raise financing from new investors at a fair price, so low cash flows will not limit their ability to invest in positive-NPV projects. If the firm's investors don't like the risk attached to the firm's cash flows, then the investors can hedge away the risk on their own.

Admittedly, asking the stockholders in an airline to hedge fuel price risk on their own is unrealistic. In the real world, firms are likely to be more sophisticated than individual investors. Firms may have more information about what risks to hedge and face lower transaction costs.

However, even in the real world, there is a compelling reason some firms should optimally choose to live with risk rather than hedging it all way. Returning to our airline example, most airlines will want to expand operations when jet fuel costs are low. If fuel costs are high, airlines may be operating at a loss, and most would prefer to limit investments or even contract. Without hedging, the airline's cash flow needs for investment are already naturally matched with its incoming cash flow.

For this reason, most airlines choose to hedge away only a portion of their exposure to jet fuel to guard against bankruptcy. If airlines hedged away all risk, they would always have the same medium level of cash flow and would not have enough cash on hand to invest aggressively if fuel prices drop.

Of course, not all airlines follow the same strategy. While most mature airlines would prefer to contract if fuel costs rise, upstarts like Southwest Airlines followed a strategy of grabbing market share during tough times. Therefore, it made sense for Southwest to hedge more aggressively in the 2000s, because its strategy of increasing market share required greater investments during periods with high fuel prices.

This key insight was first proposed by Froot, Scharfstein, and Stein in their model of optimal hedging.[1] They advised that firms should hedge against bad shocks only to the extent that they need cash during bad

[1] Kenneth A. Froot, David S. Scharfstein, and Jeremy C. Stein, "Risk Management: Coordinating Corporate Investment and Financing Policies," *Journal of Finance* 48 no. 5 (1993): 1629–58.

times. If the firm's cash flows are already matched to investment and other cash flow needs, then the firm could be worse off by hedging away all cash flow risk.

25.2 Forward Contracts

Let's now turn to forward contracts, which are commonly used in hedging. You have probably been dealing in forward contracts your whole life without knowing it. Suppose you walk into a shoe store on February 1 to buy the newest and best running shoes, Sprightly Flyers. The cashier tells you that the shoes are currently sold out, but he takes your phone number, saying that he will reorder them for you. He says the shoes will cost ₹200. If you agree on February 1 to pick up and pay ₹200 for the shoes when called, you and the cashier have engaged in a **forward contract**. That is, you have agreed both to pay for the shoes and to pick them up when the store notifies you. Because you are agreeing to buy the shoes at a later date, you are buying a forward contract on February 1. In commodity parlance, you will be taking delivery when you pick up the shoes. The shoes are called the **deliverable instrument**.

The cashier, acting on behalf of the shoe store, is selling, or writing, a forward contract. The shoe store has agreed to turn the shoes over to you at the predetermined price of ₹200 as soon as the shoes arrive. The act of turning the shoes over to you is called **making delivery**. Table 25.1 illustrates the shoe purchase. Note that the agreement takes place on February 1. The price and the conditions for sale are set at that time. In this case, the sale will occur when the shoes arrive. In other cases, an exact date of sale would be given. However, no cash changes hands on February 1; cash changes hands only when the shoes arrive.

Though forward contracts may have seemed exotic to you before you began this chapter, you can see that they are quite commonplace. Dealings in your personal life probably have involved forward contracts. Similarly, forward contracts occur all the time in business. Every time a firm orders an item that cannot be delivered immediately, a forward contract takes place. Sometimes, particularly when the order is small, an oral agreement will suffice. Other times, particularly when the order is large, a written agreement is necessary.

Note that a forward contract is not an option. Both the buyer and the seller are obligated to perform under the terms of the contract. Conversely, the buyer of an option chooses whether to exercise the option.

A forward contract should be contrasted with a **cash transaction**–that is, a transaction where exchange is immediate. Had the shoe been on the shoe store's shelf, your purchase of it would constitute a cash transaction.

Table 25.1 Illustration of Shoe Purchase as a Forward Contract

February 1	Date When Shoes Arrives
Buyer	
Buyer agrees to:	Buyer:
1. Pay the purchase price of ₹200.	1. Pays purchase price of ₹200.
2. Receive shoes when shoes arrive.	2. Receives shoes.
Seller	
Seller agrees to:	Seller:
1. Give up shoes when shoes arrive.	1. Gives up shoes.
2. Accept payment of ₹200 when shoes arrive.	2. Accepts payment of ₹200.

25.3 Futures Contracts

A variant of the forward contract takes place on financial exchanges. Contracts on exchanges are usually called **futures contracts**. There are a number of futures exchanges in the United States and elsewhere, and more are being established. The CME Group is among the largest, combining the old Chicago Mercantile Exchange (CME) and the Multi-Commodity Exchange of India (MCX). However, the two are still separate trading platforms. The New York Mercantile Exchange (NYM) now also is owned by the CME. Another notable exchange is the London International Financial Futures and Options Exchange (LIFFE).

Alike, there exist a number of futures exchanges in India. In terms of trading volume, the National Stock Exchange of India in Mumbai is the largest stock futures trading exchange in the world. Bombay Stock Exchange also has a stock futures trading platform. Futures exchanges for commodities include National Commodity and Derivatives Exchange (NCDEX) and Multi-Commodity Exchange (MCX). NCDEX focuses itself on Indian agricultural commodities and MCX focuses itself on mirror products of popular global commodities (such as, Crude Oil and Gold).

Table 25.2(a) gives a partial *Wall Street Journal* listing for selected futures contracts. Taking a look at the corn contracts in the table, note that the contracts trade on the CBT, one contract calls for the delivery of 5,000 bushels of corn, and prices are quoted in cents per bushel. The months in which the contracts mature are given in the first column.

For the oats contract with a March maturity, the first number in the row is the opening price (295.00 cents per bushel), the next number is the high price for the day (301.75), and the following number is the low price for the day (295.00). The *settlement price* is the fourth number (300.75), and it essentially is the closing price for the day. For purposes of marking to market, this is the figure used. The change, listed next, is the movement in the settlement price since the previous trading session (4.25 cents). Finally, the *open interest* (3,710), the number of contracts outstanding at the end of the day, is shown.

To see how large futures trading can be, look at the CBT Treasury notes contracts (under the interest rate heading). One contract is for Treasury notes with a face, or par, value of ₹100,000. The total open interest for these two months (there are more contract months available that are not shown) is about 3,186,722 contracts. The total face value outstanding is ₹318.7 billion for this one type of contract!

In the Indian context, most trading in futures contracts occurs on the NSE. Among all the equity exchanges, NSE ranks first in the world in terms of number of contracts traded. Table 25.2(b) gives a partial NSE listing from the leading pink paper for selected single-stock futures contracts. Looking at the contracts of Kotak Bank, note that the contracts trade at the NSE; one contract calls for the delivery of 400 shares of Kotak Bank, and prices are quoted at per share basis.

For the Kotak Bank contract with an April maturity, the first number is the opening price (₹1800 per share), the next number is the high price for the day (₹1800), and the following number is the low price for the day (₹1782.65). The closing price is the fourth number (₹1789.60), essentially the *settlement price* for the day. This figure is used for marking to market. The next column volume (14,961 contracts) represents the number of contracts traded during the day. The last column, open interest (95,884 contracts), is the number of contracts outstanding at the end of the day.

Though we are discussing a futures contract, let us work with a forward contract first. Suppose, on a Thursday, you wrote a forward contract for September wheat at ₹4.07. From our discussion of forward contracts, this would mean that you would agree to turn over an agreed-upon number of wheat bushels for ₹4.07 per bushel on some specified date later in the month of September.

A futures contract differs somewhat from a forward contract. First, the seller can choose to deliver the wheat on any day during the delivery month–that is, the month of September. This gives the seller leeway that he would not have with a forward contract. When the seller decides to deliver, he notifies the exchange

Table 25.2(a)
Futures Contracts Quote, December 4, 2020

Futures Contracts

Metal & Petroleum Futures

	Open	Contract High	hi lo	Low	Settle	Chg	Open interest
Copper-High (CMX)-25,000 lbs.; $ per lb.							
Dec	3.4800	3.5055	▲	3.4580	**3.4790**	0.0040	4,633
March'21	3.4935	3.5230	▲	3.4695	**3.4905**	0.0015	167,647
Gold (CMX)-100 troy oz.; $ per troy oz.							
Dec	1829.20	1842.00		1825.30	**1836.80**	11.10	15,718
Jan'21	1830.50	1844.00		1824.00	**1838.40**	10.80	2,428
Feb	1833.90	1847.40		1826.70	**1841.10**	10.90	396,152
April	1837.00	1850.70		1830.50	**1844.70**	10.80	69,763
June	1839.50	1852.90		1832.90	**1847.10**	10.80	31,294
Aug	1843.60	1854.40		1836.10	**1849.00**	10.60	8,469
Palladium (NYM) - 50 troy oz.; $ per troy oz.							
Dec	2360.00	2360.00		2225.10	**2302.10**	–95.30	102
March'21	2417.60	2431.60		2228.00	**2317.90**	–90.30	9,561
Platinum (NYM)-50 troy oz.; $ per troy oz.							
Dec	...	...		...	**1037.00**	26.60	1
Jan'21	1020.20	1042.10		1005.00	**1038.60**	26.50	48,031
Silver (CMX)-5,000 troy oz.; $ per troy oz.							
Dec	24.100	24.340		23.935	**24.087**	0.062	3,337
March'21	24.220	24.420		23.850	**24.137**	0.057	127,183
Crude Oil, Light Sweet (NYM)-1,000 bbls.; $ per bbl.							
Jan	44.99	45.84		44.66	**45.64**	0.36	377,052
Feb	45.14	45.98		44.84	**45.79**	0.35	205,147
March	45.24	46.07		44.98	**45.91**	0.34	192,213
April	45.42	46.13		45.07	**45.96**	0.32	97,163
June	45.46	46.08		45.06	**45.93**	0.29	214,184
Dec	44.86	45.18		44.46	**45.00**	0.01	282,937
NY Harbor ULSD (NYM)-42,000 gal.; $ per gal.							
Jan	1.3612	1.3984		1.3541	**1.3933**	.0271	110,717
Feb	1.3721	1.4049		1.3633	**1.3999**	.0246	49,764
Gasoline-NY RBOB (NYM)-42,000 gal.; $ per gal.							
Jan	1.2376	1.2664		1.2239	**1.2617**	.0218	125,665
Feb	1.2447	1.2749		1.2357	**1.2705**	.0191	46,848
Natural Gas (NYM)-10,000 MMBtu.; $ per MMBtu.							
Jan	2.760	2.768		2.484	**2.507**	–.273	298,896
Feb	2.756	2.769		2.486	**2.515**	–.263	96,590
March	2.706	2.711		2.441	**2.476**	–.247	195,204
April	2.637	2.644		2.393	**2.434**	–.223	86,784
May	2.636	2.649		2.405	**2.449**	–.210	54,769
Oct	2.761	2.792		2.560	**2.614**	–.184	92,144

Agriculture Futures

	Open	Contract High	hi lo	Low	Settle	Chg	Open interest
Corn (CBT)-5,000 bu.; cents per bu.							
Dec	419.25	423.25		417.75	**422.50**	3.50	6,680
March'21	424.00	427.50		422.00	**426.50**	2.75	900,392
Oats (CBT)-5,000 bu.; cents per bu.							
Dec	...	...		...	**303.75**	9.25	44
March'21	295.00	301.75		295.00	**300.75**	4.25	3,710
Soybeans (CBT)-5,000 bu.; cents per bu.							
Jan	1154.25	1170.75		1152.00	**1168.25**	15.25	297,028
March	1156.00	1172.50		1154.00	**1170.25**	15.50	261,969
Soybean Meal (CBT)-100 tons; $ per ton.							
Dec	389.80	394.00		389.40	**392.80**	3.30	2,204
Jan'21	385.60	391.00		384.70	**390.00**	4.40	125,693
Soybean Oil (CBT)-60,000 lbs.; cents per lb.							
Dec	37.81	38.72		37.81	**38.68**	1.21	1,218
Jan'21	37.09	37.80		36.88	**37.73**	.81	142,999
Rough Rice (CBT)-2,000 cwt.; $ per cwt.							
Jan	12.41	12.42		12.31	**12.33**	–.13	8,267
March	12.61	12.61		12.50	**12.52**	–.12	810
Wheat (CBT)-5,000 bu.; cents per bu.							
Dec	573.50	576.00		568.00	**571.75**	–6.25	161
March'21	588.50	591.00		579.75	**584.50**	–4.00	196,463
Wheat (KC)-5,000 bu.; cents per bu.							
Dec	...	...		...	**545.00**	–5.50	78
March'21	553.50	556.25		544.75	**549.75**	–4.00	123,486
Cattle-Feeder (CME)-50,000 lbs.; cents per lb.							
Jan	141.725	142.000		139.225	**139.800**	–2.000	19,379
March	140.925	141.100		138.600	**139.325**	–1.650	10,095
Cattle-Live (CME)-40,000 lbs.; cents per lb.							
Dec	110.600	110.600		108.950	**109.600**	–1.100	19,012
Feb'21	113.750	113.750		111.675	**112.575**	–1.350	112,256
Hogs-Lean (CME)-40,000 lbs.; cents per lb.							
Dec	66.425	66.450		65.850	**66.025**	–.325	16,568
Feb'21	67.875	68.050		66.725	**66.925**	–.950	84,333
Lumber (CME)-110,000 bd. ft., $ per 1,000 bd. ft.							
Jan	657.50	663.40		653.60	**660.00**	11.00	1,846
March	626.90	638.50		626.00	**636.00**	16.00	735
Milk (CME)-200,000 lbs., cents per lb.							
Dec	15.14	15.50		15.14	**15.45**	.26	4,864
Jan'21	15.60	16.06		15.50	**15.98**	.34	3,509
Cocoa (ICE-US)-10 metric tons; $ per ton.							
Dec	2,897	2,897		2,897	**2,897**	–10	80
March'21	2,648	2,726		2,630	**2,651**	13	95,344
Coffee (ICE-US)-37,500 lbs.; cents per lb.							
Dec	117.65	117.65		117.65	**117.65**	.80	136
March'21	119.65	121.00		118.60	**120.05**	.95	116,177
Sugar-World (ICE-US)-112,000 lbs.; cents per lb.							
March	14.62	14.89		14.58	**14.71**	.11	413,003
May	14.03	14.19		13.94	**14.04**	.07	223,217
Sugar-Domestic (ICE-US)-112,000 lbs.; cents per lb.							
Jan	28.50	28.50		28.50	**28.50**	...	1,610
March	28.51	28.51		28.51	**28.51**	–.38	3,359
Cotton (ICE-US)-50,000 lbs.; cents per lb.							
Dec	69.85	69.85		69.25	**69.42**	–.57	64
March'21	71.60	71.98		71.07	**71.11**	–.49	133,285
Orange Juice (ICE-US)-15,000 lbs.; cents per lb.							
Jan	125.85	127.50		125.30	**126.80**	1.15	6,289
March	127.40	128.20		126.55	**127.95**	1.20	3,942

Interest Rate Futures

	Open	Contract High	hi lo	Low	Settle	Chg	Open interest
Ultra Treasury Bonds (CBT) - $100,000; pts 32nds of 100%							
Dec	...	...		...	**213-290**	1-19.0	30,469
March'21	211-050	212-180		210-210	**212-060**	1-19.0	1,003,784
Treasury Bonds (CBT)-$100,000; pts 32nds of 100%							
Dec	...	...		...	**171-290**	22.0	51,139
March'21	172-140	173-040		172-050	**172-280**	23.0	1,109,512
Treasury Notes (CBT)-$100,000; pts 32nds of 100%							
Dec	137-305	138-065		137-275	**138-025**	7.5	79,375
March'21	137-165	137-260		137-140	**137-210**	7.5	3,107,347
5 Yr. Treasury Notes (CBT)-$100,000; pts 32nds of 100%							
Dec	125-150	125-185		125-140	**125-167**	2.7	81,914
March'21	125-242	125-282		125-230	**125-262**	3.2	3,043,284
2 Yr. Treasury Notes (CBT)-$200,000; pts 32nds of 100%							
Dec	110-126	110-133		110-126	**110-132**	.7	40,276
March'21	110-122	110-130		110-120	**110-126**	.6	1,805,095
30 Day Federal Funds (CBT)-$5,000,000; 100 - daily avg.							
Dec	99.9125	99.9150		99.9125	**99.9125**		120,495
Jan'21	99.9200	99.9200		99.9150	**99.9150**		150,645
10 Yr. Del. Int. Rate Swaps (CBT)-$100,000; pts 32nds of 100%							
Dec	...	...		...	**100-235**	8.0	157,513
Eurodollar (CME)-$1,000,000; pts of 100%							
Dec	99.7575	99.7625		99.7525	**99.7625**	.0050	1,103,367
March'21	99.7900	99.8050		99.7900	**99.8000**	.0050	1,133,884
June	99.8000	99.8100		99.7950	**99.8050**	.0050	847,506
Dec	99.7500	99.7550		99.7450	**99.7500**	.0050	824,964

Currency Futures

	Open	Contract High	hi lo	Low	Settle	Chg	Open interest
Japanese Yen (CME)-¥12,500,000; $ per 100¥							
Dec	.9578	.9647		.9567	**.9620**	.0054	181,520
March'21	.9589	.9661		.9582	**.9634**	.0054	3,971
Canadian Dollar (CME)-CAD 100,000; $ per CAD							
Dec	.7742	.7781	▲	.7727	**.7779**	.0041	136,425
March'21	.7746	.7784	▲	.7731	**.7782**	.0041	7,640
British Pound (CME)-£62,500; $ per £							
Dec	1.3374	1.3502	▲	1.3353	**1.3450**	.0091	144,781
March'21	1.3382	1.3512	▲	1.3366	**1.3461**	.0091	5,864
Swiss Franc (CME)-CHF 125,000; $ per CHF							
Dec	1.1179	1.1249	▲	1.1171	**1.1221**	.0058	51,043
March'21	1.1215	1.1282	▲	1.1206	**1.1255**	.0058	1,165
Australian Dollar (CME)-AUD 100,000; $ per AUD							
Dec	.7414	.7451	▲	.7399	**.7448**	.0046	129,494
March'21	.7419	.7456	▲	.7405	**.7453**	.0045	2,845
Mexican Peso (CME)-MXN 500,000; $ per MXN							
Dec	.05001	.05030		.04988	**.05020**	.00032	145,745
March'21	.04957	.04984		.04943	**.04974**	.00032	3,882
Euro (CME)-€125,000; $ per €							
Dec	1.2116	1.2177	▲	1.2103	**1.2145**	.0043	622,031
March'21	1.2146	1.2205	▲	1.2132	**1.2174**	.0042	29,764

Index Futures

	Open	Contract High	hi lo	Low	Settle	Chg	Open interest
Mini DJ Industrial Average (CBT)-$5 x index							
Dec	29886	30092		29755	**29932**	64	88,990
March'21	29782	29990		29659	**29830**	62	7,438
S&P 500 Index (CME)-$250 x index							
Dec	3668.40	3673.40	▲	3658.30	**3664.60**	–2.70	32,600
March'21	...	...		...	**3656.80**	–2.70	26
Mini S&P 500 (CME)-$50 x index							
Dec	3671.00	3682.00	▲	3655.25	**3664.50**	–2.75	2,494,833
March'21	3663.25	3674.00	▲	3647.50	**3656.75**	–2.75	133,159
Mini S&P Midcap 400 (CME)-$100 x index							
Dec	2194.20	2216.20		2183.40	**2202.70**	12.20	53,476
March'21	2191.00	2210.00		2186.70	**2198.90**	11.60	2
Mini Nasdaq 100 (CME)-$20 x index							
Dec	12472.00	12540.25	▲	12444.00	**12462.25**	8.00	238,420
March'21	12474.50	12535.00	▲	12443.00	**12459.50**	8.25	6,117
Mini Russell 2000 (CME)-$50 x index							
Dec	1842.30	1860.80		1830.30	**1847.20**	9.70	550,108
Mini Russell 1000 (CME)-$50 x index							
Dec	2046.30	2070.60	▲	2057.50	**2060.80**	1.30	9,047
U.S. Dollar Index (ICE-US)-$1,000 x index							
Dec	91.07	91.10	▼	90.51	**90.72**	–.40	35,676
March'21	91.03	91.03	▼	90.44	**90.65**	–.41	1,773

Source: FactSet

SOURCE: *The Wall Street Journal*, December 4, 2020, www.wsj.com.

Table 25.2(b) Data on Stock Futures contracts traded on NSE, April 9 2024
Published on the next day in *popular financial* newspapers

Symbol	Volume (Contracts)	Open Interest (Contracts)	Open	High	Low	Close
HDFC BANK	38,177	3,00,307	1,558.20	1,558.20	1,545.10	1,550.95
RELIANCE	24,514	1,64,370	2,982.60	2,984.35	2,937.75	2,940.70
ICICI BANK	43,967	1,10,112	1,093.35	1,115.30	1,091.35	1,107.75
INFY	40,580	1,09,231	1,495.35	1,519.00	1,491.45	1,501.95
KOTAK BANK	14,961	95,884	1,800.00	1,800.00	1,782.65	1,789.60
AXIS BANK	34,112	87,768	1,090.20	1,092.40	1,073.00	1,081.95
TCS	23,571	82,500	3,981.95	4,021.70	3,930.00	3,952.65
SBIN	18,593	59,703	771.1	775.7	763.7	766.8

clearinghouse that he wants to do so. The clearinghouse then notifies an individual who bought a September wheat contract to stand ready to accept delivery within the next few days. Though each exchange selects the buyer in a different way, the buyer is generally chosen in a random fashion. Because there are so many buyers at any one time, the buyer selected by the clearinghouse to take delivery almost certainly did not originally buy the contract from the seller now making delivery.

Second, futures contracts are traded on an exchange, whereas forward contracts are generally traded off an exchange. Because of this, there is generally a liquid market in futures contracts. A buyer can net out her futures position with a sale. A seller can net out his futures position with a purchase. If a buyer of a futures contract does not subsequently sell her contract, she must take delivery.

Third, and most important, the prices of futures contracts are **marked to market** daily. Suppose the price falls to ₹4.05 on Friday's close. Because all buyers lost 2 cents per bushel on that day, they each must turn over the 2 cents per bushel to their brokers within 24 hours, and the brokers subsequently remit the proceeds to the clearinghouse. All sellers gained 2 cents per bushel on that day, so they each receive 2 cents per bushel from their brokers. Their brokers are subsequently compensated by the clearinghouse. Because there is a buyer for every seller, the clearinghouse must break even every day.

Now suppose that the price rises to ₹4.12 on the close of the following Monday. Each buyer receives 7 cents (= ₹4.12 − 4.05) per bushel, and each seller must pay 7 cents per bushel. Finally, suppose that on Monday a seller notifies his broker of his intention to deliver.[2] The delivery price will be ₹4.12, which is Monday's close.

There are clearly many cash flows in futures contracts. However, after all the dust settles, the net price to the buyer must be the price at which she bought originally. That is, an individual buying at Thursday's closing price of ₹4.07 and being called to take delivery on Monday pays 2 cents per bushel on Friday, receives 7 cents per bushel on Monday, and takes delivery at ₹4.12. Her net outflow per bushel is −₹4.07 (= −₹.02 + .07 − 4.12), which is the price at which she contracted on Thursday. (Our analysis ignores the time value of money.) Conversely, an individual selling at Thursday's closing price of ₹4.07 and notifying his broker concerning delivery the following Monday receives 2 cents per bushel on Friday, pays 7 cents per bushel on Monday, and makes delivery at ₹4.12. His net inflow per bushel is ₹4.07 (= ₹.02 − .07 + 4.12), which is the price at which he contracted on Thursday.

These details are presented in a nearby box. For simplicity, we assumed that the buyer and seller who initially transact on Thursday's close meet in the delivery process.[3] The point in the example is that the

[2] He will deliver on Wednesday, two days later.

[3] As pointed out earlier, this is actually very unlikely to occur in the real world.

buyer's net payment of ₹4.07 per bushel is the same as if she purchased a forward contract for ₹4.07. Similarly, the seller's net receipt of ₹4.07 per bushel is the same as if he sold a forward contract for ₹4.07 per bushel. The only difference is the timing of the cash flows. The buyer of a forward contract knows that he will make a single payment of ₹4.07 on the expiration date. He will not need to worry about any other cash flows in the interim. Conversely, though the cash flows to the buyer of a futures contract will also net to exactly ₹4.07, the pattern of cash flows is unknown ahead of time.

The mark-to-market provision on futures contracts has two related effects. The first concerns differences in net present value. A large price drop immediately following purchase means an immediate payment for the buyer of a futures contract. Though the net outflow of ₹4.07 is still the same as under a forward contract, the present value of the cash outflows is greater to the buyer of a futures contract. Of course, the present value of the cash outflows is less to the buyer of a futures contract if a price rise follows purchase.[4] Though this effect could be substantial in certain theoretical circumstances, it appears to be of quite limited importance in the real world.[5]

Second, the firm must have extra liquidity to handle a sudden outflow prior to expiration. This added risk may make the futures contract less attractive.

Students frequently ask, "Why in the world would managers of the commodity exchanges ruin perfectly good contracts with these bizarre mark-to-market provisions?" Actually, the reason is a very good one. Consider

Illustration of Example Involving Marking to Market in Futures Contracts

Both buyer and seller originally transact at Thursday's closing price. Delivery takes place at Monday's closing price.*

	Thursday, September 19	Friday, September 20	Monday, September 23	Delivery (Notification Given by Seller on Monday)
Closing price	₹4.07	₹4.05	₹4.12	
Buyer	Buyer purchases futures contract at closing price of ₹4.07/bushel.	Buyer must pay 2 cents/bushel to clearinghouse within one business day.	Buyer receives 7 cents/bushel from clearinghouse within one business day.	Buyer pays ₹4.12 per bushel and receives grain within two business days.
Buyer's net payment of −₹4.07 (= −₹.02 + .07 − 4.12) is the same as if buyer purchased a forward contract for ₹4.07/bushel.				
Seller	Seller sells futures contract at closing price of ₹4.07/bushel.	Seller receives 2 cents/bushel from clearinghouse within one business day.	Seller pays 7 cents/bushel to clearinghouse within one business day.	Seller receives ₹4.12 per bushel and delivers grain within two business days.
Seller's net receipt of ₹4.07 (= ₹.02 − .07 + 4.12) is the same as if seller sold a forward contract for ₹4.07/bushel.				

*For simplicity, we assume that buyer and seller both (1) initially transact at the same time and (2) meet in the delivery process. This is actually very unlikely to occur in the real world because the clearinghouse assigns the buyer to take delivery in a random manner.

[4] The direction is reversed for the seller of a futures contract. However, the general point that the net present value of cash flows may differ between forward and futures contracts holds for sellers, as well.

[5] See John C. Cox, Jonathan E. Ingersoll, and Stephen A. Ross, "The Relationship between Forward and Future Prices," *Journal of Financial Economics* (1981).

the forward contract in Table 25.1 concerning the shoe store. Suppose the public quickly loses interest in these shoes. By the time the shoe store calls the buyer, other stores may have dropped the price of the shoes to ₹175. Because the forward contract was for ₹200, the buyer has an incentive not to take delivery on the forward contract. Conversely, should the shoes become a hot item selling at ₹225, the shoe store may not call the buyer.

As indicated, forward contracts have a big flaw. Whichever way the price of the deliverable instrument moves, one party has an incentive to default. There are many cases where defaults have occurred in the real world. One famous case concerned Coca-Cola. When the company began in the early twentieth century, Coca-Cola made an agreement to supply its bottlers and distributors with cola syrup at a constant price forever. Of course, subsequent inflation would have caused Coca-Cola to lose large sums of money had it honored the contract. After much legal effort, Coke and its bottlers put an *inflation escalator clause* in the contract. Another famous case concerned Westinghouse. It seems the firm had promised to deliver uranium to certain utilities at a fixed price. The price of uranium skyrocketed in the 1970s, making Westinghouse lose money on every shipment. Westinghouse defaulted on its agreement. The utilities took Westinghouse to court but did not recover amounts anything near what Westinghouse owed them.

Mark-to-market provisions minimize the chance of default on a futures contract. If the price rises, the seller has an incentive to default on a forward contract. However, after paying the clearinghouse, the seller of a futures contract has little reason to default. If the price falls, the same argument can be made for the buyer. Because changes in the value of the underlying asset are recognized daily, there is no accumulation of loss and the incentive to default is reduced.

Because of this default issue, forward contracts generally involve individuals and institutions who know and can trust each other. But as W. C. Fields said, "Trust everybody, but cut the cards." Lawyers earn a handsome living writing supposedly airtight forward contracts, even among friends. The genius of the

Derivatives Trading in India: Focus on Equity Markets

The economic liberalization of the early nineties facilitated the introduction of derivatives based on interest rates and foreign exchange. The derivatives trading on stock exchanges commenced in the year 2000 on NSE, with futures trading on S&P CNX NIFTY Index. The ban on commodity futures trading was lifted in the early 2000s. This move resulted in the formation of three commodities exchanges in India, namely, NCDEX, MCX, and NMCE. Later, in 2018, the NMCE ceased to exist as it was merged with ICEX. Lately, even corporates have been allowed to write agri-options in an atmosphere of high volatility. Recently, NSE launched its first agricultural commodity futures contract in December 2020. Derivatives on stock indexes and individual stocks have grown rapidly since they were launched. In particular, single stock futures have become hugely popular. Lately, index options have become increasingly popular.

In the context of institutional investors, the Over-The-Counter (OTC) markets are the preferred choice for trading interest rate futures. These markets thrive on instruments like interest rate swaps and forward rate agreements. Interestingly, foreign exchange derivatives, despite their longer history, remain less active than interest rate derivatives in India. Among OTC instruments, currency forwards and swaps stand out as the most popular. Importers, exporters, and banks utilize the rupee forward market to hedge their foreign currency exposure. While turnover and liquidity in this market have been on the rise, trading primarily occurs in shorter maturity contracts—typically one year or less. The most commonly traded forward contracts have durations of one month, three months, or six months, with the three-month contract being particularly prevalent.

Meanwhile, derivatives trading on equity exchanges (primarily NSE) had a meteoric pace. We find that the trading volume in the F&O segment indicates that the near-month contracts are more popular than not-so-near contracts, futures contracts are more popular than options, and call options are more popular than put options. We also observe that contracts on individual securities are less popular than those on indices.

mark-to-market system is that it can prevent default where it is most likely to occur–among investors who do not know each other. Textbooks on futures contracts from decades ago usually include a statement such as, "No major default has ever occurred on the commodity exchanges." No textbook published after the Hunt Brothers defaulted on silver contracts in the 1970s can make that claim. Nevertheless, the extremely low default rate in futures contracts is truly awe-inspiring.

25.4 Hedging

Now that we have determined how futures contracts work, let us talk about hedging. There are two types of hedges, long and short. We discuss the short hedge first.

EXAMPLE 25.1

Futures Hedging In June, Renju Abraham anticipates a harvest of 50,000 bushels of wheat at the end of September. He has two alternatives:

1. *Write futures contracts against his anticipated harvest.* The September wheat contract on the Multi-Commodity Exchange of India (MCX) is trading at ₹3.75 a bushel on June 1. He executes the following transaction:

Date of Transaction	Transaction	Price per Bushel
June 1	Write 10 September futures contracts	₹3.75

He notes that transportation costs to the designated delivery point in Lucknow are 30 cents/bushel. His net price per bushel is ₹3.45 = ₹3.75 − .30.

2. *Harvest the wheat without writing a futures contract.* Alternatively, Bernard could harvest the wheat without the benefit of a futures contract. The risk would be quite great here because no one knows what the cash price in September will be. If prices rise, he will profit. Conversely, he will lose if prices fall.

We say that Strategy 2 is an unhedged position because there is no attempt to use the futures markets to reduce risk. Conversely, Strategy 1 involves a hedge. That is, a position in the futures market offsets the risk of a position in the physical—that is, in the actual—commodity.

Though hedging may seem quite sensible to you, it should be mentioned that not everyone hedges. Bernard might reject hedging for at least three reasons.

First, he may be uninformed about hedging. We have found that not everyone in business understands the hedging concept. Many executives have told us that they do not want to use futures markets for hedging their inventories because the risks are too great. However, we disagree. While there are large price fluctuations in these markets, hedging actually reduces the risk that an individual holding inventories bears.

Second, Bernard may have a special insight or some special information that commodity prices will rise. He would not be wise to lock in a price of ₹3.75 if he expects the cash price in September to be well above this price.

Third, Bernard may want to invest aggressively in new farming operations if wheat prices rise and scale back operations if prices fall. Without hedging, his cash flow is naturally matched with his investment goals.

(continued)

Following the insights of the Froot, Scharfstein, and Stein model described earlier in this chapter, Bernard decides not to hedge away all his cash flow risk.

The hedge of Strategy 1 is called a **short hedge** because Bernard reduces his risk by selling a futures contract. The short hedge is very common in business. It occurs whenever someone either anticipates receiving inventory or is holding inventory. Bernard is anticipating the harvest of grain. A manufacturer of soybean meal and oil may hold large quantities of raw soybeans that are already paid for. However, the prices to be received for meal and oil are unknown because no one knows what the market prices will be when the meal and oil are produced. The manufacturer may write futures contracts in meal and oil to lock in sales prices. An oil company may hold large inventories of petroleum to be processed into heating oil. The firm could sell futures contracts in heating oil to lock in the sales price. A mortgage banker may assemble mortgages slowly before selling them in bulk to a financial institution. Movements of interest rates affect the value of the mortgages while they are in inventory. The mortgage banker could sell Treasury bond futures contracts to offset this interest rate risk.

EXAMPLE 25.2

More Hedging On April 1, Malleshwari Chemical agreed to sell petrochemicals to the U.S. government in the future. The delivery dates and prices have been determined. Because oil is a basic ingredient in the production process, Malleshwari Chemical will need to have large quantities of oil on hand. The firm can get the oil in one of two ways:

1. *Buy the oil as the firm needs it.* This is an unhedged position because, as of April 1, the firm does not know the prices it will later have to pay for the oil. Oil is quite a volatile commodity, so Malleshwari Chemical is bearing a good bit of risk. The key to this risk bearing is that the sales price to the U.S. government already has been fixed. Thus, Malleshwari Chemical cannot pass on increased costs to the consumer.
2. *Buy futures contracts.*[6] The firm can buy futures contracts with expiration months corresponding to the dates the firm needs inventory. The futures contracts lock in the purchase price to Malleshwari Chemical. Because there is a crude oil futures contract for every month, selecting the correct futures contract is not difficult. Many other commodities have only five contracts per year, frequently necessitating buying contracts one month away from the month of production.

As mentioned earlier, Malleshwari Chemical is interested in hedging the risk of fluctuating oil prices because it cannot pass any cost increases on to the consumer. Suppose, alternatively, that Malleshwari Chemical was not selling petrochemicals on a fixed contract to the U.S. government. Instead, imagine that the petrochemicals were to be sold to private industry at currently prevailing prices. The price of petrochemicals should move directly with oil prices because oil is a major component of petrochemicals. Because cost increases are likely to be passed on to the consumer, Malleshwari Chemical would probably not want to hedge in this case. Instead, the firm is likely to choose Strategy 1, buying the oil as it is needed. If oil prices increase between April 1 and, say, September 1, Malleshwari Chemical, of course, will find that its inputs have become quite costly. However, in a competitive market, its revenues are likely to rise, as well.

(continued)

[6] Alternatively, the firm could buy the oil on April 1 and store it. This would eliminate the risk of price movement because the firm's oil costs would be fixed upon the immediate purchase. However, this strategy would be inferior to Strategy 2 in the common case where the difference between the futures contract quoted on April 1 and the April 1 cash price is less than the storage costs.

Strategy 2 is called a **long hedge** because one purchases a futures contract to reduce risk. In other words, one takes a long position in the futures market. In general, a firm institutes a long hedge when it is committed to a fixed sales price. One class of situations involves actual written contracts with customers, such as the one Malleshwari Chemical had with the U.S. government. Alternatively, a firm may find that it cannot easily pass on costs to consumers or does not want to pass on these costs. For example, a group of students opened a small meat market called *What's Your Beef* near the University of Pennsylvania in the late 1970s.[7] This was a time of volatile consumer prices, especially food prices. Knowing that their fellow students were particularly budget-conscious, the owners vowed to keep food prices constant regardless of price movements in either direction. They accomplished this by purchasing futures contracts in various agricultural commodities.

25.5 Interest Rate Futures Contracts

In this section, we consider interest rate futures contracts. Our examples deal with futures contracts on Treasury bonds because of their high popularity. We first price Treasury bonds and Treasury bond forward contracts. Differences between futures and forward contracts are explored. Hedging examples are provided next.

PRICING OF TREASURY BONDS

As mentioned earlier in the text, a Treasury bond pays semiannual interest over its life. In addition, the face value of the bond is paid at maturity. Consider a 20-year, 8 percent coupon bond that was issued on March 1. The first payment is to occur in six months–that is, on September 1. The value of the bond can be determined as follows:

Pricing of Treasury Bond

$$P_{TB} = \frac{₹40}{1 + R_1} + \frac{₹40}{(1 + R_2)^2} + \frac{₹40}{(1 + R_3)^3} + \cdots + \frac{₹40}{(1 + R_{39})^{39}} + \frac{₹1,040}{(1 + R_{40})^{40}} \quad \textbf{(25.1)}$$

Because an 8 percent coupon bond pays interest of ₹80 a year, the semiannual coupon is ₹40. Principal and the semiannual coupon are both paid at maturity. As we mentioned in a previous chapter, the price of the Treasury bond, P_{TB}, is determined by discounting each payment on the bond at the appropriate spot rate. Because the payments are semiannual, each spot rate is expressed in semiannual terms. That is, imagine a horizontal term structure where the effective annual yield is 8 percent for all maturities. Because each spot rate, R, is expressed in semiannual terms, each spot rate is $\sqrt{1.08} - 1 = .0392$, or 3.92 percent. Coupon payments occur every six months, so there are 40 spot rates over the 20-year period.

PRICING OF FORWARD CONTRACTS

Now imagine a forward contract where, on March 1, you agree to buy a new 20-year, 8 percent coupon Treasury bond in six months (on September 1). As with typical forward contracts, you will pay for the bond on September 1, not March 1. The cash flows from both the Treasury bond issued on March 1 and the forward contract that you purchase on March 1 are presented in Figure 25.1. The cash flows on the Treasury bond begin exactly six months earlier than do the cash flows on the forward contract. The Treasury bond is purchased with cash on March 1 (Date 0). The first coupon payment occurs on September 1 (Date 1). The last

[7]Ordinarily, an unusual firm name in this textbook is a tip-off that it is fictional. This, however, is a true story.

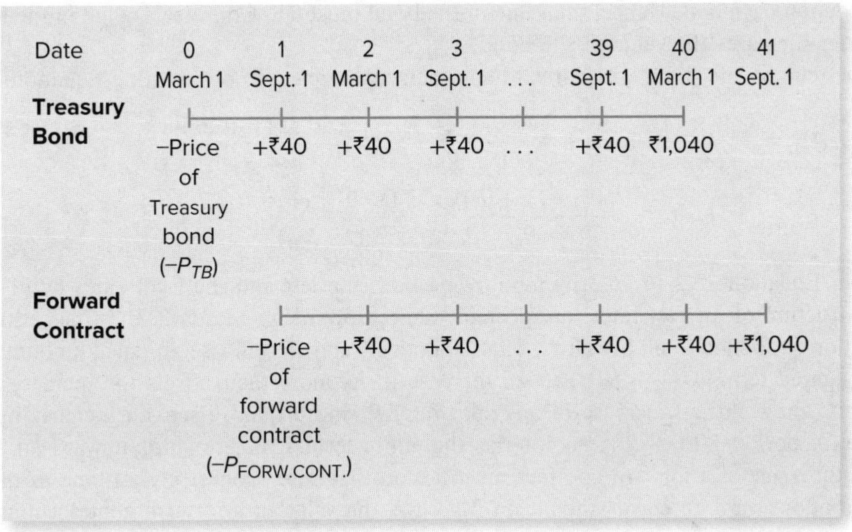

Figure 25.1 Cash Flows for Both a Treasury Bond and a Forward Contract on a Treasury Bond

coupon payment occurs at Date 40, along with the face value of ₹1,000. The forward contract compels you to pay $P_{FORW.CONT.}$, the price of the forward contract, on September 1 (Date 1). You receive a new Treasury bond at that time. The first coupon payment you receive from the bond occurs on March 1 of the following year (Date 2). The last coupon payment occurs at Date 41, along with the face value of ₹1,000.

Given the 40 spot rates, Equation 25.1 showed how to price a Treasury bond. How do we price the forward contract on a Treasury bond? As we saw earlier in the text that net present value analysis can be used to price bonds, we will now show that net present value analysis can be used to price forward contracts. Given the cash flows for the forward contract in Figure 25.1, thc price of the forward contract must satisfy the following equation:

$$\frac{P_{FORW.CONT.}}{1+R_1} = \frac{₹40}{(1+R_2)^2} + \frac{₹40}{(1+R_3)^3} + \frac{₹40}{(1+R_4)^4} + \cdots + \frac{₹40}{(1+R_{40})^{40}} + \frac{₹1{,}040}{(1+R_{41})^{41}} \quad \textbf{(25.2)}$$

The right side of Equation 25.2 discounts all the cash flows from the delivery instrument (the Treasury bond issued on September 1) back to Date 0 (March 1). Because the first cash flow occurs at Date 2 (March 1 of the subsequent year), it is discounted by $1/(1 + R_2)^2$. The last cash flow of ₹1,040 occurs at Date 41, so it is discounted by $1/(1 + R_{41})^{41}$. The left side represents the cost of the forward contract as of Date 0. Because the actual outpayment occurs at Date 1, it is discounted by $1/(1 + R_1)$.

Students often ask, "Why are we discounting everything back to Date 0 when we are actually paying for the forward contract on September 1?" The answer is that we apply the same techniques to Equation 25.2 that we apply to all capital budgeting problems: We want to put everything in today's (Date 0's) rupees. Given that the spot rates are known in the marketplace, traders should have no more trouble pricing a forward contract by Equation 25.2 than they would have pricing a Treasury bond by Equation 25.1.

Forward contracts are similar to the underlying bonds themselves. If the entire term structure of interest rates unexpectedly shifts upward on March 2, the Treasury bond issued the previous day should fall in value. This can be seen from Equation 25.1. A rise in each of the spot rates lowers the present value of each of the coupon payments. Hence, the value of the bond must fall. Conversely, a fall in the term structure of interest rates increases the value of the bond.

The same relationship holds with forward contracts, as we can see by rewriting Equation 25.2 like this:

$$P_{\text{FORW.CONT.}} = \frac{₹40 \times (1 + R_1)}{(1 + R_2)^2} + \frac{₹40 \times (1 + R_1)}{(1 + R_3)^3} + \frac{₹40 \times (1 + R_1)}{(1 + R_4)^4} + \cdots + \frac{₹40 \times (1 + R_1)}{(1 + R_{40})^{40}} + \frac{₹1{,}040 \times (1 + R_1)}{(1 + R_{41})^{41}} \tag{25.3}$$

We went from Equation 25.2 to 25.3 by multiplying both the left and the right sides by $(1 + R_1)$. If the entire term structure of interest rates unexpectedly shifts upward on March 2, the first term on the right side of Equation 25.3 should fall in value.[8] That is, both R_1 and R_2 will rise an equal amount. However, R_2 enters as a squared term, $1/(1 + R_2)^2$, so an increase in R_2 more than offsets the increase in R_1. As we move farther to the right, an increase in any spot rate, R_i, more than offsets an increase in R_1. Here, R_i enters as the ith power, $1/(1 + R_i)^i$. As long as the entire term structure shifts upward an equal amount on March 2, the value of a forward contract must fall on that date. Conversely, as long as the entire term structure shifts downward an equal amount on March 2, the value of a forward contract must rise.

FUTURES CONTRACTS

The previous discussion concerned a forward contract in U.S. Treasury bonds–that is, a forward contract where the deliverable instrument is a U.S. Treasury bond. What about a futures contract on a Treasury bond?[9] We mentioned earlier that futures contracts and forward contracts are quite similar, though there are a few differences between the two. First, futures contracts are generally traded on exchanges, whereas forward contracts are not traded on exchanges. In this case, the Treasury bond futures contract is traded on the Multi-Commodity Exchange of India. Second, futures contracts generally allow the seller a period of time in which to deliver, whereas forward contracts generally call for delivery on a particular day. The seller of a Treasury bond futures contract can choose to deliver on any business day during the delivery month.[10] Third, futures contracts are subject to the mark-to-the-market convention, whereas forward contracts are not. Traders in Treasury bill futures contracts must adhere to this convention. Fourth, there is generally a liquid market for futures contracts, allowing contracts to be quickly netted out. That is, a buyer can sell his futures contract at any time and a seller can buy back her futures contract at any time. Conversely, because forward markets are generally quite illiquid, traders cannot easily net out their positions. The popularity of the Treasury bond futures contract has produced liquidity even higher than that on other futures contracts. Positions in that contract can be netted out quite easily.

This discussion is not intended to be an exhaustive list of differences between the Treasury bond forward contract and the Treasury bond futures contract. Rather, it is intended to show that both contracts share fundamental characteristics. Though there are differences, the two instruments should be viewed as variations of the same species, not different species. The pricing of Equation 25.3, which is exact for the forward contract, should be a decent approximation for the futures contract.

HEDGING IN INTEREST RATE FUTURES

Now that we have the basic institutional details under our belts, we are ready for examples of hedging using either futures contracts or forward contracts on Treasury bonds. Because the T-bond futures contract is

[8] We are assuming that each spot rate shifts by the same amount. Suppose that on March 1 $R_1 = 5\%$, $R_2 = 5.4\%$, and $R_3 = 5.8\%$. Assuming that all rates increase by ½% on March 2, R_1 becomes 5.5% (= 5% + ½%), R_2 becomes 5.9%, and R_3 becomes 6.3%.

[9] Futures contracts on bonds are also called *interest rate futures contracts*.

[10] Delivery occurs two business days after the seller notifies the clearinghouse of her intention to deliver.

extremely popular, whereas the forward contract is traded sporadically, our examples use the futures contract.

EXAMPLE 25.3

Interest Rate Hedging Irfan Khan owns a mortgage banking company. On March 1, she made a commitment to lend a total of ₹1 million to various homeowners on May 1. The loans are 20-year mortgages carrying a 12 percent coupon, the going interest rate on mortgages at the time, so the mortgages are made at par. Though homeowners would not use the term, we could say that she is buying a *forward contract* on a mortgage. That is, she agrees on March 1 to give ₹1 million to her borrowers on May 1 in exchange for principal and interest from them every month for the next 20 years.

Like many mortgage bankers, she has no intention of paying the ₹1 million out of her own pocket. Rather, she intends to sell the mortgages to an insurance company. The insurance company will actually lend the funds and will receive principal and interest over the next 20 years. Irfan does not currently have an insurance company in mind. She plans to visit the mortgage departments of insurance companies over the next 60 days to sell the mortgages to one or many of them. She sets April 30 as a deadline for making the sale because the borrowers expect the funds on the following day.

Suppose Irfan sells the mortgages to the Insurance Company on April 15. What price will Aradhana pay for the bonds?

You may think the insurance company will obviously pay ₹1 million for the loans. However, suppose interest rates have risen above 12 percent by April 15. The insurance company will buy the mortgage at a discount. Suppose the insurance company agrees to pay only ₹940,000 for the mortgages. Because the mortgage banker agreed to lend a full ₹1 million to the borrowers, the mortgage banker must come up with the additional ₹60,000 (= ₹1,000,00 – 940,000) out of her own pocket.

Alternatively, suppose interest rates fall below 12 percent by April 15. The mortgages can be sold at a premium under this scenario. If the insurance company buys the mortgages at ₹1.05 million, the mortgage banker will have made an unexpected profit of ₹50,000 (= ₹1,050,000 – 1,000,000).

Because Irfan is unable to forecast interest rates, this risk is something that she would like to avoid. The risk is summarized in Table 25.3.

Seeing the interest rate risk, students at this point may ask, "What does the mortgage banker get out of this loan to offset her risk bearing?" Irfan wants to sell the mortgages to the insurance company so that she can get two fees. The first is an *origination fee*, which is paid to the mortgage banker by the insurance company

Table 25.3 Effects of Changing Interest Rates on Irfan Khan, Mortgage Banker

	Mortgage Interest Rate on April 15	
	Above 12%	**Below 12%**
Sale Price to Aradhana **Insurance Company**	Below ₹1 million (we assume ₹940,000).	Above ₹1 million (we assume ₹1.05 million).
Effect on Mortgage Banker	She loses because she must lend the full ₹1 million to borrowers.	She gains because she lends only ₹1 million to borrowers.
Rupee **Gain or Loss**	Loss of ₹60,000 (= ₹1,000,000 – 940,000).	Gain of ₹50,000 (= ₹1,050,000 – 1,000,000).

The interest rate on March 1, the date when the loan agreement was made with the borrowers, was 12 percent. April 15 is the date the mortgages were sold to Aradhana Insurance Company.

(*continued*)

on April 15—that is, on the date the loan is sold. An industry standard in certain locales is 1 percent of the value of the loan, which is ₹10,000 (= .01 × ₹1 million). In addition, Irfan will act as a collection agent for the insurance company. For this service, she will receive a small portion of the outstanding balance of the loan each month. If she is paid .03 percent of the loan each month, she will receive ₹300 (= .0003 × ₹1 million) in the first month. As the outstanding balance of the loan declines, she will receive less.

Though Irfan will earn profitable fees on the loan, she bears interest rate risk. She loses money if interest rates rise after March 1 and she profits if interest rates fall after March 1. To hedge this risk, she writes June Treasury bond futures contracts on March 1. As with mortgages, Treasury bond futures contracts fall in value if interest rates rise. Because she writes the contract, she makes money on these contracts if they fall in value. Therefore, with an interest rate rise, the loss she endures on the mortgages is offset by the gain she earns in the futures market. Conversely, Treasury bond futures contracts rise in value if interest rates fall. Because she writes the contracts, she suffers losses on them when rates fall. With an interest rate fall, the profit she makes on the mortgages is offset by the loss she suffers in the futures markets.

The details of this hedging transaction are presented in Table 25.4. The column on the left is labeled "Cash Markets" because the deal in the mortgage market is transacted off an exchange. The column on the right shows the offsetting transactions in the futures market. Consider the first row. The mortgage banker enters into a forward contract on March 1. She simultaneously writes Treasury bond futures contracts. Ten contracts are written because the deliverable instrument on each contract is ₹100,000 of Treasury bonds. The total is ₹1 million (= 10 × ₹100,000), which is equal to the value of the mortgages. Irfan would prefer to write May Treasury bond futures contracts. Here, Treasury bonds would be delivered on the futures contract during the same month that the loan is funded. Because there is no May T-bond futures contract, Irfan achieves the closest match through a June contract.

If held to maturity, the June contract would obligate the mortgage banker to deliver Treasury bonds in June. Interest rate risk ends in the cash market when the loans are sold. Interest rate risk must be terminated in the futures market at that time. Irfan nets out her position in the futures contracts as soon as the loan is sold to Aradhana Insurance.

Table 25.4 Illustration of Hedging Strategy for Irfan Khan, Mortgage Banker

	Cash Markets	Futures Markets
March 1	Mortgage banker makes forward contracts to lend ₹1 million at 12 percent for 20 years. The loans are to be funded on May 1. No cash changes hands on March 1.	Mortgage banker writes 10 June Treasury bond futures contracts.
April 15	Loans are sold to Aradhana Insurance Company. Mortgage banker will receive sale price from Aradhana on the May 1 funding date.	Mortgage banker buys back all the futures contracts.
If interest rates rise:	Loans are sold at a price below ₹1 million. Mortgage banker loses because she receives less than the ₹1 million she must give to borrowers.	Each futures contract is bought back at a price below the sales price, resulting in profit. Mortgage banker's profit in futures market offsets loss in cash market.
If interest rates fall:	Loans are sold at a price above ₹1 million. Mortgage banker gains because she receives more than the ₹1 million she must give to borrowers.	Each futures contract is bought back at a price above the sales price, resulting in loss. Mortgage banker's loss in futures market offsets gain in cash market.

As our example shows, risk is clearly reduced via an offsetting transaction in the futures market. However, is risk totally eliminated? Risk would be totally eliminated if losses in the cash markets were exactly offset by gains in the futures markets and vice versa. This is unlikely to happen because mortgages and Treasury bonds are not identical instruments. First, mortgages may have different maturities than Treasury bonds. Second, Treasury bonds have a different payment stream than do mortgages. Principal is paid only at maturity on T-bonds, whereas principal is paid every month on mortgages. Because mortgages pay principal continuously, these instruments have a shorter *effective* maturity than do Treasury bonds of equal maturity.[11] Third, mortgages have default risk whereas Treasury bonds do not. The term structure applicable to instruments with default risk may change even when the term structure for risk-free assets remains constant. Fourth, mortgages may be paid off early and hence have a shorter *expected* maturity than Treasury bonds of equal maturity.

Because mortgages and Treasury bonds are not identical instruments, they are not identically affected by interest rates. If Treasury bonds are less volatile than mortgages, financial consultants may advise Irfan to write more than 10 T-bond futures contracts. Conversely, if these bonds are more volatile, the consultant may state that fewer than 10 futures contracts are needed. An optimal ratio of futures to mortgages will reduce risk as much as possible. However, because the price movements of mortgages and Treasury bonds are not perfectly correlated, Irfan's hedging strategy cannot eliminate all risk.

The preceding strategy is called a *short hedge* because Irfan sells futures contracts to reduce risk. Though it involves an interest rate futures contract, this short hedge is analogous to short hedges in agricultural and metallurgical futures contracts. We argued at the beginning of this chapter that individuals and firms institute short hedges to offset inventory price fluctuations. Once Irfan makes a contract to lend money to borrowers, the mortgages effectively become her inventory. She writes a futures contract to offset the price fluctuations of her inventory.

We now consider an example where a mortgage banker institutes a *long hedge.*

EXAMPLE 25.4

Short versus Long Hedging Sanghamitra Bhattacharya is another mortgage banker. Her firm faces problems similar to those facing Irfan's firm. However, she tackles the problems through the use of **advance commitments**, a strategy that is the opposite of Irfan's. That is, Sanghamitra promises to deliver loans to a financial institution before she lines up borrowers. On March 1, her firm agreed to sell mortgages to No-State Insurance Co. The agreement specifies that she must turn over 12 percent coupon mortgages with a face value of ₹1 million to No-State by May 1. No-State is buying the mortgages at par, implying that they will pay Sanghamitra ₹1 million on May 1. As of March 1, Sanghamitra had not signed up any borrowers. Over the next two months, she will seek out individuals who want mortgages beginning May 1.

As with Irfan, changing interest rates will affect Sanghamitra. If interest rates fall before she signs up a borrower, the borrower will demand a premium on a 12 percent coupon loan. That is, the borrower will receive more than par on May 1.[12] Because Sanghamitra receives par from the insurance company, she must make up the difference.

Conversely, if interest rates rise, a 12 percent coupon loan will be made at a discount. That is, the borrower will receive less than par on May 1. Because Sanghamitra receives par from the insurance company, the difference is pure profit to her.

(continued)

[11] Alternatively, we can say that mortgages have shorter duration than do Treasury bonds of equal maturity. A precise definition of duration is provided later in this chapter.

[12] Alternatively, the mortgage would still be at par if a coupon rate below 12 percent were used. However, this is not done because the insurance company wants to buy only 12 percent mortgages.

Table 25.5 Illustration of Advance Commitment for Sanghamitra Bhattacharya, Mortgage Banker

	Cash Markets	Futures Markets
March 1	Mortgage banker makes a forward contract (advance commitment) to deliver ₹1 million of mortgages to No-State Insurance. The insurance company will pay par to Ms. Bhattacharya for the loans on May 1. The borrowers are to receive their funding from the mortgage banker on May 1. The mortgages are to be 12 percent coupon loans for 20 years.	Mortgage banker buys 10 June Treasury bond futures contracts.
April 15	Mortgage banker signs up borrowers for 12 percent coupon, 20-year mortgages. She promises that the borrowers will receive funds on May 1.	Mortgage banker sells all futures contracts.
If interest rates rise:	Mortgage banker issues mortgages to borrowers at a discount. Mortgage banker gains because she receives par from the insurance company.	Futures contracts are sold at a price below purchase price, resulting in loss. Mortgage banker's loss in futures market offsets gain in cash market.
If interest rates fall:	Loans to borrowers are issued at a premium. Mortgage banker loses because she receives only par from insurance company.	Futures contracts are sold at a price above purchase price, resulting in gain. Mortgage banker's gain in futures market offsets loss in cash market.

The details are provided in Table 25.5. As did Irfan, Sanghamitra finds the risk burdensome. Therefore, she offsets her advance commitment with a transaction in the futures markets. Because she loses in the cash market when interest rates fall, she buys futures contracts to reduce the risk. When interest rates fall, the value of her futures contracts increases. The gain in the futures market offsets the loss in the cash market. Conversely, she gains in the cash markets when interest rates rise. The value of her futures contracts decreases when interest rates rise, offsetting her gain.

We call this a *long hedge* because Sanghamitra offsets risk in the cash markets by buying a futures contract. Though it involves an interest rate futures contract, this long hedge is analogous to long hedges in agricultural and metallurgical futures contracts. We argued at the beginning of this chapter that individuals and firms institute long hedges when their finished goods are to be sold at a fixed price. Once Sanghamitra makes the advance commitment with No-State Insurance, she has fixed her sales price. She buys a futures contract to offset the price fluctuation of her raw materials—that is, her mortgages.

25.6 Duration Hedging

The last section concerned the risk of interest rate changes. We now want to explore this risk in a more precise manner. In particular, we want to show that the concept of duration is a prime determinant of interest rate risk. We begin by considering the effect of interest rate movements on bond prices.

THE CASE OF ZERO COUPON BONDS

Imagine a world where the interest rate is 10 percent across all maturities. A one-year pure discount bond pays ₹110 at maturity. A five-year pure discount bond pays ₹161.05 at maturity. Both of these bonds are worth ₹100, as given by the following:[13]

Value of 1-Year Pure Discount Bond

$$₹100 = \frac{₹110}{1.10}$$

Value of 5-Year Pure Discount Bond

$$₹100 = \frac{₹161.05}{1.10^5}$$

Which bond will change more when interest rates move? To find out, we calculate the value of these bonds when interest rates are either 8 or 12 percent. The results are presented in Table 25.6. As can be seen, the five-year bond has greater price swings than does the one-year bond. That is, both bonds are worth ₹100 when interest rates are 10 percent. The five-year bond is worth more than the one-year bond when interest rates are 8 percent and worth less than the one-year bond when interest rates are 12 percent. We state that the five-year bond is subject to more price volatility. This point, which was mentioned in an earlier section of the chapter, is not difficult to understand. The interest rate term in the denominator, $1 + R$, is taken to the fifth power for a five-year bond and only to the first power for the one-year bond. Thus, the effect of a changing interest rate is magnified for the five-year bond. The general rule is this:

The percentage price changes of long-term pure discount bonds are greater than the percentage price changes of short-term pure discount bonds.

THE CASE OF TWO BONDS WITH THE SAME MATURITY BUT WITH DIFFERENT COUPONS

The previous example concerned pure discount bonds of different maturities. We now want to see the effect of different coupons on price volatility. To show the effect of differing maturities, we consider two bonds with the same maturity but with different coupons.

Table 25.6 Value of a Pure Discount Bond as a Function of Interest Rate

Interest Rate	1-Year Pure Discount Bond	5-Year Pure Discount Bond
8%	$₹101.85 = \frac{₹110}{1.08}$	$₹109.61 = \frac{₹161.05}{1.08^5}$
10%	$₹100.00 = \frac{₹110}{1.10}$	$₹100.00 = \frac{₹161.05}{1.10^5}$
12%	$₹\ 98.21 = \frac{₹110}{1.12}$	$₹\ 91.38 = \frac{₹161.05}{1.12^5}$

For a given interest rate change, a 5-year pure discount bond fluctuates more in price than does a 1-year pure discount bond.

[13] Alternatively, we could have chosen bonds that pay ₹100 at maturity. Their values would be ₹90.91 (= ₹100/1.10) and ₹62.09 (= ₹100/1.10^5). However, our comparisons to come are made easier if both have the same initial price.

Table 25.7 Value of Coupon Bonds at Different Interest Rates

Interest Rate	5-Year, 10% Coupon Bond
8%	$₹107.99 = \frac{₹10}{1.08} + \frac{₹10}{1.08^2} + \frac{₹10}{1.08^3} + \frac{₹10}{₹1.08^4} + \frac{₹110}{1.08^5}$
10%	$₹100.00 = \frac{₹10}{1.10} + \frac{₹10}{1.10^2} + \frac{₹10}{1.10^3} + \frac{₹10}{1.10^4} + \frac{₹110}{1.10^5}$
12%	$₹92.79 = \frac{₹10}{1.12} + \frac{₹10}{1.12^2} + \frac{₹10}{1.12^3} + \frac{₹10}{1.12^4} + \frac{₹110}{1.12^5}$
Interest Rate	**5-Year, 1% Coupon Bond**
8%	$₹72.05 = \frac{₹1}{1.08} + \frac{₹1}{1.08^2} + \frac{₹1}{1.08^3} + \frac{₹1}{1.08^4} + \frac{₹101}{1.08^5}$
10%	$₹65.88 = \frac{₹1}{1.10} + \frac{₹1}{1.10^2} + \frac{₹1}{1.10^3} + \frac{₹1}{1.10^4} + \frac{₹101}{1.10^5}$
12%	$₹60.35 = \frac{₹1}{1.12} + \frac{₹1}{1.12^2} + \frac{₹1}{1.12^3} + \frac{₹1}{1.12^4} + \frac{₹101}{1.12^5}$

Consider a five-year, 10 percent coupon bond and a five-year, 1 percent coupon bond. When interest rates are 10 percent, the bonds are priced like this:

Value of 5-Year, 10 Percent Coupon Bond

$$₹100 = \frac{₹10}{1.10} + \frac{₹10}{1.10^2} + \frac{₹10}{1.10^3} + \frac{₹10}{1.10^4} + \frac{₹110}{1.10^5}$$

Value of 5-Year, 1 Percent Coupon Bond

$$₹65.88 = \frac{₹1}{1.10} + \frac{₹1}{1.10^2} + \frac{₹1}{1.10^3} + \frac{₹1}{1.10^4} + \frac{₹101}{1.10^5}$$

Which bond will change more in percentage terms if interest rates change?[14] To find out, we first calculate the value of these bonds when interest rates are either 8 or 12 percent. The results are presented in Table 25.7. As we would expect, the 10 percent coupon bond always sells for more than the 1 percent coupon bond. Also, as we would expect, each bond is worth more when the interest rate is 8 percent than when the interest rate is 12 percent.

We calculate percentage price changes for both bonds as the interest rate changes from 10 to 8 percent and from 10 to 12 percent:

	10% Coupon Bond	1% Coupon Bond
Interest rate changes from 10% to 8%:	$\frac{₹107.99}{₹100} - 1 = .0799$, or 7.99%	$\frac{₹72.05}{₹65.88} - 1 = .0936$, or 9.36%
Interest rate changes from 10% to 12%:	$\frac{₹92.79}{₹100} - 1 = -.0721$, or −7.21%	$\frac{₹60.35}{₹65.88} - 1 = -.0840$, or −8.40%

[14] The bonds are at different prices initially. Thus, we are concerned with percentage price changes, not absolute price changes.

As we can see, the 1 percent coupon bond has a greater percentage price increase than does the 10 percent coupon bond when the interest rate falls. Similarly, the 1 percent coupon bond has a greater percentage price decrease than does the 10 percent coupon bond when the interest rate rises. We say that the percentage price changes on the 1 percent coupon bond are greater than are the percentage price changes on the 10 percent coupon bond.

DURATION

The question, of course, is "Why?" We can answer this question only after we have explored a concept called **duration**. We begin by noticing that any coupon bond is actually a combination of pure discount bonds. For example, the five-year, 10 percent coupon bond is made up of five pure discount bonds:

1. A pure discount bond paying ₹10 at the end of Year 1.
2. A pure discount bond paying ₹10 at the end of Year 2.
3. A pure discount bond paying ₹10 at the end of Year 3.
4. A pure discount bond paying ₹10 at the end of Year 4.
5. A pure discount bond paying ₹110 at the end of Year 5.

Similarly, the five-year, 1 percent coupon bond is made up of five pure discount bonds. Because the price volatility of a pure discount bond is determined by its maturity, we would like to determine the average maturity of the five pure discount bonds that make up a five-year coupon bond. This leads us to the concept of duration.

We calculate average maturity in three steps. For the 10 percent coupon bond, we have these:

1. *Calculate present value of each payment.* We do this as follows:

Year	Payment	Present Value of Payment by Discounting at 10%
1	₹ 10	₹ 9.091
2	10	8.264
3	10	7.513
4	10	6.830
5	110	68.301
		₹100.00

2. *Express the present value of each payment in relative terms.* We calculate the relative value of a single payment as the ratio of the present value of the payment to the value of the bond. The value of the bond is ₹100. We obtain these values:

Year	Payment	Present Value of Payment	Relative Value = $\frac{\text{Present Value of Payment}}{\text{Value of Bond}}$
1	₹ 10	₹ 9.091	₹9.091/₹100 = .09091
2	10	8.264	.08264
3	10	7.513	.07513
4	10	6.830	.06830
5	110	68.301	.68301
		₹100.00	1.0

The bulk of the relative value, 68.301 percent, occurs at Year 5 because the principal is paid back at that time.

3. *Weight the maturity of each payment by its relative value:*

$$\begin{aligned} 4.1699 \text{ years} = {} & 1 \text{ year} \times .09091 + 2 \text{ years} \times .08264 + 3 \text{ years} \times .07513 \\ & + 4 \text{ years} \times .06830 + 5 \text{ years} \times .68301 \end{aligned}$$

There are many ways to calculate the average maturity of a bond. We have calculated it by weighting the maturity of each payment by the payment's present value. We find that the *effective maturity* of the bond is 4.1699 years. *Duration* is a commonly used word for effective maturity. Note that duration is expressed in units of time.[15]

Because the five-year, 10 percent coupon bond has a duration of 4.1699 years, its percentage price fluctuations should be the same as those of a zero coupon bond with a duration of 4.1699 years.[16] It turns out that the five-year, 1 percent coupon bond has a duration of 4.8740 years. Because the 1 percent coupon bond has a higher duration than the 10 percent bond, the 1 percent coupon bond should be subject to greater price fluctuations. This is exactly what we found earlier. In general, we say the following:

The percentage price changes of a bond with high duration are greater than the percentage price changes of a bond with low duration.

A final question: Why does the 1 percent bond have a greater duration than the 10 percent bond, even though they both have the same five-year maturity? As mentioned earlier, duration is an average of the maturity of the bond's cash flows weighted by the present value of each cash flow. The 1 percent coupon bond receives only ₹1 in each of the first four years. The weights applied to Years 1 through 4 in the duration formula will be lower. Conversely, the 10 percent coupon bond receives ₹10 in each of the first four years. The weights applied to Years 1 through 4 in the duration formula will be higher.

MATCHING LIABILITIES WITH ASSETS

Earlier in this chapter, we argued that firms can hedge risk by trading in futures. Because some firms are subject to interest rate risk, we showed how they can hedge with interest rate futures contracts. Firms also may hedge interest rate risk by matching liabilities with assets. This ability to hedge follows from our discussion of duration.

[15]The mathematical formula for duration is:

$$\text{Duration} = \frac{\text{PV}(C_1)1 + \text{PV}(C_2)2 + \cdots + \text{PV}(C_t)t}{\text{PV}}$$

and:

$$\text{PV} = \text{PV}(C_1) + \text{PV}(C_2) + \cdots + \text{PV}(C_t)$$

$$\text{PV}(C_t) = \frac{C_t}{(1 + R)^t}$$

where C_t is the cash to be received in Time t, and R is the current discount rate. Also, note that in our numerical example, we discounted each payment by the interest rate of 10 percent. This was done because we wanted to calculate the duration of the bond before a change in the interest rate occurred. After a change in the rate to, say, 8 or 12 percent, all three of our steps would need to reflect the new interest rate. In other words, the duration of a bond is a function of the current interest rate.

[16]Actually, this relationship exactly holds only in the case of a one-time shift in a flat yield curve, where the change in the spot rate is identical for all maturities.

EXAMPLE 25.5

Using Duration The Physical Bank of Guwahati has the following market value balance sheet:

PHYSICAL BANK OF GUWAHATI
Market Value Balance Sheet

	Market Value	Duration
Assets		
Overnight money	₹ 35 million	0
Accounts receivable-backed loans	500 million	3 months
Inventory loans	275 million	6 months
Industrial loans	40 million	2 years
Mortgages	150 million	14.8 years
	₹ 1,000 million	
Liabilities and Owners' Equity		
Checking and savings accounts	₹ 400 million	0
Certificates of deposit	300 million	1 year
Long-term financing	200 million	10 years
Equity	100 million	
	₹ 1,000 million	

The bank has ₹1,000 million of assets and ₹900 million of liabilities. Its equity is the difference between the two: ₹100 million (= ₹1,000 million – 900 million). Both the market value and the duration of each individual item are provided in the balance sheet. Both overnight money and checking and savings accounts have a duration of zero. This is because the interest paid on these instruments adjusts immediately to changing interest rates in the economy.

The bank's managers think that interest rates are likely to move quickly in the coming months. Because they do not know the direction of the movement, they are worried that their bank is vulnerable to changing rates. They call in a consultant, Lambodar Upadhyay, to determine a hedging strategy.

Lambodar first calculates the duration of the assets and the duration of the liabilities:[17]

Duration of Assets

$$2.56 \text{ years} = 0 \text{ years} \times \frac{₹35 \text{ million}}{₹1{,}000 \text{ million}} + \tfrac{1}{4} \text{ year} \times \frac{₹500 \text{ million}}{₹1{,}000 \text{ million}}$$

$$+ \tfrac{1}{2} \text{ year} \times \frac{₹275 \text{ million}}{₹1{,}000 \text{ million}} + 2 \text{ years} \times \frac{₹40 \text{ million}}{₹1{,}000 \text{ million}} \qquad \textbf{(25.4)}$$

$$+ 14.8 \text{ years} \times \frac{₹150 \text{ million}}{₹1{,}000 \text{ million}}$$

(continued)

[17] Note that the duration of a group of items is an average of the duration of the individual items weighted by the market value of each item. This is a simplifying step that greatly increases duration's practicality.

Duration of Liabilities

$$2.56 = 0 \text{ years} \times \frac{₹400 \text{ million}}{₹900 \text{ million}} + 1 \text{ year} \times \frac{₹300 \text{ million}}{₹900 \text{ million}} + 10 \text{ years} \times \frac{₹200 \text{ million}}{₹900 \text{ million}} \quad \textbf{(25.5)}$$

The duration of the assets, 2.56 years, equals the duration of the liabilities. Because of this, Lambodar argues that the firm is immune to interest rate risk.

To be on the safe side, the bank calls in a second consultant, Saradha Govindarajan. Saradha argues that it is incorrect to match durations because assets total ₹1,000 million and liabilities total only ₹900 million. If both assets and liabilities have the same duration, the price change on a rupee of assets should be equal to the price change on a rupee of liabilities. However, the total price change will be greater for assets than for liabilities because there are more assets than liabilities in this bank. The firm will be immune to interest rate risk only when the duration of the liabilities is greater than the duration of the assets. Saradha states that the following relationship must hold if the bank is to be **immunized**—that is, immune to interest rate risk:

$$\begin{matrix}\text{Duration of} \\ \text{assets}\end{matrix} \times \begin{matrix}\text{Market value of} \\ \text{assets}\end{matrix} = \begin{matrix}\text{Duration of} \\ \text{liabilities}\end{matrix} \times \begin{matrix}\text{Market value} \\ \text{of liabilities}\end{matrix} \quad \textbf{(25.6)}$$

She says that the bank should not equate the duration of the liabilities with the duration of the assets. Rather, using Equation 25.6, the bank should match the duration of the liabilities to the duration of the assets. She suggests two ways to achieve this match.

1. *Increase the duration of the liabilities without changing the duration of the assets.* Saradha argues that the duration of the liabilities could be increased to:

$$\text{Duration of assets} \times \frac{\text{Market value of assets}}{\text{Market value of liabilities}} = 2.56 \text{ years} \times \frac{₹1{,}000 \text{ million}}{₹900 \text{ million}}$$

$$= 2.84 \text{ years}$$

Equation 25.6 then becomes:

$$2.56 \times ₹1 \text{ billion} = 2.84 \times ₹900 \text{ million}$$

2. *Decrease the duration of the assets without changing the duration of the liabilities.* Alternatively, Saradha points out that the duration of the assets could be decreased to:

$$\text{Duration of liabilities} \times \frac{\text{Market value of liabilities}}{\text{Market value of assets}} = 2.56 \text{ years} \times \frac{₹900 \text{ million}}{₹1{,}000 \text{ million}}$$

$$= 2.30 \text{ years}$$

Equation 25.6 then becomes:

$$2.30 \times ₹1 \text{ billion} = 2.56 \times ₹900 \text{ million}$$

Though we agree with Saradha's analysis, the bank's current mismatch was small in this example. Huge mismatches have occurred for real-world financial institutions, particularly savings and loans. S&Ls have frequently invested large portions of their assets in mortgages. The durations of these mortgages would clearly be above 10 years. Many of the funds available for mortgage lending were financed by short-term credit, especially savings accounts. The duration of such instruments is quite small. A thrift institution in this situation faces a large amount of interest rate risk because any increase in interest rates would greatly reduce the value of the mortgages. Because an interest rate rise would reduce the value of the liabilities only slightly, the equity of the firm would fall. As interest rates rose over much of the 1960s and 1970s, many S&Ls found that the market value of their equity approached zero.

Duration and the accompanying immunization strategies are useful in other areas of finance. For example, a firm may have established a pension fund to meet obligations to retirees. If the assets of a pension fund are invested in bonds and other fixed-income securities, the duration of the assets can be computed. Similarly, the firm views the obligations to retirees as analogous to interest payments on debt. The duration of these liabilities can be calculated, as well. The manager of a pension fund would commonly choose pension assets so that the duration of the assets is matched with the duration of the liabilities. In this way, changing interest rates would not affect the net worth of the pension fund.

Life insurance companies receiving premiums today are legally obligated to provide death benefits in the future. Actuaries view these future benefits as analogous to interest and principal payments of fixed-income securities. The duration of these expected benefits can be calculated. Insurance firms frequently invest in bonds where the duration of the bonds is matched to the duration of the future death benefits.

The business of a leasing company is quite simple. The firm issues debt to purchase assets, which are then leased. The lease payments have a duration, as does the debt. Leasing companies frequently structure debt financing so that the duration of the debt matches the duration of the lease. If a firm did not do this, the market value of its equity could be eliminated by a quick change in interest rates.

25.7 Swap Contracts

Swaps are close cousins to forwards and futures contracts. Swaps are arrangements between two counterparties to exchange cash flows over time. There is enormous flexibility in the forms that swaps can take, but the three basic types are **interest rate swaps**, **currency swaps**, and **credit default swaps**. Often these are combined when interest received in one currency is swapped for interest in another currency.

INTEREST RATE SWAPS

Like other derivatives, swaps are tools that firms can use to easily change their risk exposures and their balance sheets.[18] Consider a firm that has borrowed and carried on its books an obligation to repay a 10-year loan for ₹100 million of principal with a 9 percent coupon rate paid annually. Ignoring the possibility of calling the loan, the firm expects to have to pay coupons of ₹9 million every year for 10 years and a balloon payment of ₹100 million at the end of the 10 years. Suppose, though, that the firm is uncomfortable with having this large fixed obligation on its books. Perhaps the firm is in a cyclical business where its revenues vary and could conceivably fall to a point where it would be difficult to make the debt payment.

Suppose, too, that the firm earns a lot of its revenue from financing the purchase of its products. Typically, a manufacturer might help its customers finance their purchase of its products through a leasing or credit subsidiary. Usually these loans are for relatively short periods and are financed at some premium over the prevailing short-term rate of interest. This puts the firm in the position of having revenues that move up and down with interest rates while its costs are relatively fixed.

What the firm would really prefer is to have a floating-rate loan rather than a fixed-rate loan. That way, when interest rates rise, the firm would have to pay more on the loan, but it would be making more on its product financing. An interest rate swap is ideal in this situation.

Of course, the firm also could go into the capital markets and borrow ₹100 million at a variable interest rate and then use the proceeds to retire its outstanding fixed-rate loan. Although this is possible, it is generally quite expensive, requiring the underwriting of a new loan and the repurchase of the existing loan. The ease of entering a swap is its inherent advantage.

[18] Under current accounting rules, most derivatives do not usually show up on firms' balance sheets because they do not have a historical cost (i.e., the amount a dealer would pay on the initial transaction day).

This particular swap would be one that exchanged its fixed obligation for an agreement to pay a floating rate. Every year it would agree to pay a coupon based on whatever the prevailing interest rate was at the time in exchange for an agreement from a counterparty to pay the firm's fixed coupon.

A common reference point for floating-rate commitments is called LIBOR. LIBOR stands for the London Interbank Offered Rate, and it is the rate that most international banks charge one another for rupee-denominated loans in the London market. LIBOR is commonly used as the reference rate for a floating-rate commitment and, depending on the creditworthiness of the borrower, the rate can vary from LIBOR to LIBOR plus one point (or more) over LIBOR.

If we assume that our firm has a credit rating that requires it to pay LIBOR plus 50 basis points, then, in a swap, it would be exchanging its fixed 9 percent obligation for the obligation to pay whatever the prevailing LIBOR rate is plus 50 basis points. Table 25.8 displays how the cash flows on this swap would work. In the table, we have assumed that LIBOR starts at 8 percent and rises for three years to 11 percent and then drops to 7 percent. As the table shows, the firm would owe a coupon of 8.5% × ₹100 million = ₹8.5 million in Year 1, ₹9.5 million in Year 2, ₹10.5 million in Year 3, and ₹11.5 million in Year 4. The steep drop to 7 percent lowers the annual payments to ₹7.5 million thereafter. In return, the firm receives the fixed payment of ₹9 million each year. Actually, rather than swapping the full payments, the cash flows would be netted. Because the firm is paying variable and receiving fixed–which it uses to pay its lender–in the first year, for example, the firm owes ₹8.5 million and is owed by its counterparty, who is paying fixed, ₹9 million. Net, the firm would receive a payment of ₹.5 million. Because the firm has to pay its lender ₹9 million but gets a net payment from the swap of ₹.5 million, it really pays out only the difference, or ₹8.5 million. In each year, then, the firm would effectively pay only LIBOR plus 50 basis points.

Notice, too, that the entire transaction can be carried out without any need to change the terms of the original loan. In effect, by swapping, the firm has found a counterparty that is willing to pay its fixed obligation in return for the firm paying a floating obligation.

We should note that in October 2020, LIBOR itself was swapped for the Secured Overnight Financing Rate (SOFR) on exchange-traded swaps at the Chicago Mercantile Exchange. SOFR is the interest rate based on transactions in the Treasury repurchase market where investors offer banks overnight loans backed by their bond assets. The LIBOR scandal in 2012 caused regulators and market participants alike to search for another reference interest rate that was less susceptible to manipulation. In the U.S., SOFR has become that reference interest rate. For now, at least, you are likely to see floating rate instruments based on either one of these rates.

CURRENCY SWAPS

FX stands for foreign exchange, and currency swaps are sometimes called FX swaps. Currency swaps are swaps of obligations to pay cash flows in one currency for obligations to pay cash flows in another currency.

Table 25.8 Fixed-for-Floating Swap: Cash Flows (in millions)

	Coupons									
Year	**1**	**2**	**3**	**4**	**5**	**6**	**7**	**8**	**9**	**10**
A. Swap										
Fixed obligation	₹9	₹9	₹9	₹9	₹9	₹9	₹9	₹9	₹9	₹9
LIBOR floating	−8.5	−9.5	−10.5	−11.5	−7.5	−7.5	−7.5	−7.5	−7.5	−7.5
B. Original loan										
Fixed obligation	−₹9	−₹9	−₹9	−₹9	−₹9	−₹9	−₹9	−₹9	−₹9	−₹109
Net effect	−8.5	−9.5	−10.5	−11.5	−7.5	−7.5	−7.5	−7.5	−7.5	−107.5

Currency swaps arise as a natural vehicle for hedging risk in international trade. Suppose a U.S. firm sells a broad range of its product line in the German market. Every year the firm can count on receiving revenue from Germany in euros. We will study international finance later in this book, but, for now, we can observe that because exchange rates fluctuate, this subjects the firm to considerable risk.

If the firm produces its products in the United States and exports them to Germany, then the firm has to pay its workers and its suppliers in rupees. But it is receiving some of its revenues in euros. The exchange rate between rupees and euros changes over time. As the euro rises in value, the German revenues are worth more rupees, but as it falls, they are worth fewer rupees. Suppose the firm can count on selling 100 million euros of goods each year in Germany. If the exchange rate is 2 euros for each rupee, then the firm will receive ₹50 million. But if the exchange rate were to rise to 3 euros for each rupee, the firm would receive only ₹33.333 million for its 100 million euros. The firm would like to protect itself against these currency swings.

To do so, the firm can enter a currency swap. We will learn more about exactly what the terms of such a swap might be, but, for now, we can assume that the swap is for five years at a fixed term of 100 million euros for ₹50 million each year. Now, no matter what happens to the exchange rate between euros and rupees over the next five years, as long as the firm makes 100 million euros each year from the sale of its products, it will swap this for ₹50 million each year.

CREDIT DEFAULT SWAPS

A credit default swap (CDS) is like insurance against value loss due to a firm defaulting on a bond. As in other swaps, a person involved in a CDS is called a counterparty. There are always two counterparties in a CDS. In a typical CDS, Counterparty 1 pays Counterparty 2 a periodic payment. In exchange, Counterparty 2 agrees to pay par for a particular bond issue if default occurs. Counterparty 1 is called the protection buyer and Counterparty 2 is called the protection seller. The periodic payment is called the CDS spread.

Suppose the Mizuno Company wants to borrow ₹200 million from United Pacific Bank and is willing to pay a spread of 50 basis points (bps) over LIBOR. United Pacific Bank is interested but cannot justify such a large loan to one company and the attendant credit risks. United Pacific can agree to the loan and buy protection for a 40 basis point CDS spread. Midland Insurance Company agrees to be the counterparty to United Pacific and, in case Mizuno defaults, will pay the par amount. In exchange, Midland Insurance will receive ₹800,000 per year (= 40 bps × ₹200 million) for a specified term, say, five years.

In this simple example, the terms of the CDS are clear and precise. In practice, there is no organized exchange or template. Each counterparty will attempt to negotiate the best possible agreement.

Swap Pricing We have not addressed the question of how the market sets prices for swaps–either interest rate swaps, credit default swaps, or currency swaps. In the fixed-for-floating example and in the currency swap, we quoted some terms. We won't go into great detail on exactly how it is done, but we can stress the most important points.

Swaps, like forwards and futures, are essentially zero-sum transactions, which is to say that, in both cases, the market sets prices at a fair level and neither party has any substantial bargain or loss at the moment the deal is struck. In the currency swap, the swap rate is some average of the market expectation of what the exchange rate will be over the life of the swap. In the interest rate swap, the rates are set as the fair floating and fixed rates for the creditor, taking into account the creditworthiness of the counterparties. We actually can price swaps fairly once we know how to price forward contracts. In our interest rate swap example, the firm swapped LIBOR plus 50 basis points for a 9 percent fixed rate, all on a principal amount of ₹100 million. This is equivalent to a series of forward contracts extending over the life of the swap. In Year 1, having made the swap, the firm is in the same position that it would be if it had sold a forward contract entitling the buyer to receive LIBOR plus 50 basis points on ₹100 million in return for a fixed payment of ₹9 million (9 percent of ₹100 million). Similarly, the currency swap also can be viewed as a series of forward contracts. In a credit default swap, the swap rate is a market expectation of the default rate for a particular bond over a particular time.

EXOTICS

Up to now we have dealt with the meat and potatoes of the derivatives markets: swaps, options, forwards, and futures. **Exotics** are the complicated blends of these that often produce surprising results for buyers.

One of the more interesting types of exotics is called an *inverse floater*. In our fixed-for-floating swap, the floating payments fluctuated with LIBOR. An inverse floater is one that fluctuates inversely with some rate such as LIBOR. For example, the floater might pay an interest rate of 20 percent minus LIBOR. If LIBOR is 9 percent, then the inverse pays 11 percent, and if LIBOR rises to 12 percent, the payments on the inverse would fall to 8 percent. Clearly, the purchaser of an inverse profits from the inverse if interest rates fall.

Both floaters and inverse floaters have supercharged versions called *superfloaters* and *superinverses* that fluctuate more than one for one with movements in interest rates. As an example of a superinverse floater, consider a floater that pays an interest rate of 30 percent minus twice LIBOR. When LIBOR is 10 percent, the inverse pays:

$$30\% - 2 \times 10\% = 30\% - 20\% = 10\%$$

And if LIBOR falls by 3 percent to 7 percent, then the return on the inverse rises by 6 percent from 10 percent to 16 percent:

$$30\% - 2 \times 7\% = 30\% - 14\% = 16\%$$

Sometimes derivatives are combined with options to bound the impact of interest rates. The most important of these instruments are called *caps* and *floors*. A cap is so named because it puts an upper limit, or a cap, on the impact of a rise in interest rates. A floor, conversely, provides a floor below which the interest rate impact is insulated.

To illustrate the impact of these, consider a firm that is borrowing short term and is concerned that interest rates might rise. Using LIBOR as the reference interest rate, the firm might purchase a 7 percent cap. The cap pays the firm the difference between LIBOR and 7 percent on some principal amount, provided that LIBOR is greater than 7 percent. As long as LIBOR is below 7 percent, the holder of the cap receives no payments.

By purchasing the cap, the firm has assured itself that even if interest rates rise above 7 percent, it will not have to pay more than a 7 percent rate. Suppose that interest rates rise to 9 percent. While the firm is borrowing short term and paying 9 percent rates, this is offset by the cap, which is paying the firm the difference between 9 percent and the 7 percent limit. For any LIBOR rate above 7 percent, the firm receives the difference between LIBOR and 7 percent, and, as a consequence, it has capped its cost of borrowing at 7 percent.

On the other side, consider a financial firm that is in the business of lending short term and is concerned that interest rates–and consequently its revenues–might fall. The firm could purchase a floor to protect itself from such declines. If the limit on the floor is 7 percent, then the floor pays the difference between 7 percent and LIBOR whenever LIBOR is below 7 percent, and nothing if LIBOR is above 7 percent. Thus, if interest rates were to fall to, say, 5 percent while the firm is receiving only 5 percent from its lending activities, the floor is paying it the difference between 7 percent and 5 percent, or an additional 2 percent. By purchasing the floor, the firm has assured itself of receiving no less than 7 percent from the combination of the floor and its lending activities.

We have only scratched the surface of what is available in the world of derivatives. Derivatives are designed to meet marketplace needs, and the only binding limitation is the human imagination. Nowhere should the buyer's warning *caveat emptor* be taken more seriously than in the derivatives markets, and this is especially true for the exotics. If swaps are the meat and potatoes of the derivatives markets, then caps and floors are the meat and potatoes of the exotics. As we have seen, they have obvious value as hedging instruments. But much attention has been focused on truly exotic derivatives, some of which appear to have arisen more as the residuals that were left over from more straightforward deals. We won't examine these in any detail, but suffice it to say that some of these are so volatile and unpredictable that market participants have dubbed them "toxic waste."

25.8 Actual Use of Derivatives

Because derivatives do not usually appear in financial statements, it is much more difficult to observe the use of derivatives by firms compared to, say, bank debt. Much of our knowledge of corporate derivative use comes from academic surveys. Most surveys report that the use of derivatives appears to vary widely among large, publicly traded firms. Large firms are far more likely to use derivatives than are small firms. Table 25.9 shows that for firms that use derivatives, foreign currency and interest rate derivatives are the most frequently used.

Table 25.9 Derivative Usage: Survey Results

Percentage of Companies Using Derivatives

2010	71%
2009	79

In Which Asset Classes Do You Use Derivatives?

	2010	2009
Interest rates	65%	68%
Currencies	62	58
Credit	13	13
Energy	19	13
Commodities	23	22
Equities	13	9

Do You Expect Your Use of Derivatives to Change?

	2010		2009	
	Increase	Decrease	Increase	Decrease
Interest rates	19%	15%	13%	20%
Currencies	20	8	31	6
Credit	4	4	2	13
Energy	11	7	5	9
Commodities	16	6	12	10
Equities	6	7	7	6

Do You Use an Integrated Risk Management Strategy or Do You Hedge Transactions or Specific Currency Exposures?

	2010	2009
Hedge total risk	31.8%	21.1%
Hedge transactions	34.1	47.4
Hedge specific currency exposures	34.1	31.6

SOURCE: Adapted from *Treasury & Risk*, March 2010 and March 2011.

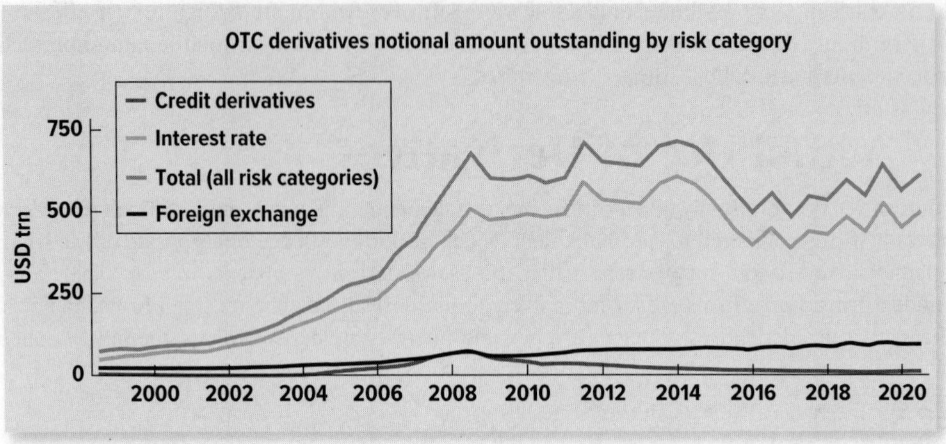

Figure 25.2 OTC Derivatives by Category

SOURCE: BIS OTC derivative statistics, Table D5.1.

The prevailing view is that derivatives can be very helpful in reducing the variability of firm cash flows, which, in turn, reduces the various costs associated with financial distress. Therefore, it is somewhat puzzling that large firms use derivatives more often than small firms because large firms tend to have less cash flow variability than small firms. Also, some surveys report that firms occasionally use derivatives when they want to speculate about future prices and not just to hedge risks.

However, most of the evidence is consistent with the theory that derivatives are most frequently used by firms where financial distress costs are high and access to the capital markets is constrained.

To give you an idea of the growth in derivatives, Figure 25.2 shows the notional amount of foreign exchange, interest rate, and credit derivatives. In 1999, there was about ₹72 trillion in notional value of these derivatives outstanding. A high of ₹710 trillion was reached in 2014. By mid-2020, the notional value had dipped to about ₹607 trillion. The growth and decline of credit derivatives is interesting in that there was a rapid growth around the financial crisis of 2008, before a decline and then a slight uptick in recent years.

25.9 An Overview of Corporate Hedging in India

'Given the volatility of the rupee against the dollar, metal companies have now begun to hedge their risks in the commodity market here.'

This line, as part of pink papers, are common after the RBI allowed metal companies with no underlying exposure abroad to hedge their risk.

This section looks at corporate hedging in India, especially concerning the foreign exchange risks they face, the relevant guidelines and the behaviour of Indian firms with respect to their preferences for specific instruments.

HEDGING GUIDELINES FOR FOREIGN EXCHANGE DERIVATIVES

When it comes to foreign exchange derivatives related to the domestic currency, residents can utilize foreign exchange forward contracts, foreign currency-rupee swap instruments, and currency options– both cross-currency and foreign currency-rupee options. In cases where derivatives involve only foreign currency, a variety of products such as Interest Rate Swaps, Forward Contracts and Options are allowed. The RBI has also formulated guidelines to simplify documentation requirements for the Small and Medium Enterprises (SME) sector. Although these financial products serve various purposes, their fundamental prerequisite is an underlying exposure to foreign exchange risk. In other words, derivatives are primarily used for hedging purposes.

Authorized dealer banks can also enter forward contracts with a few conditions. Authorized dealers can use innovative products like cross-currency options, interest rate swaps (IRS) and currency swaps, caps/collars and forward rate agreements (FRAs) in the international foreign exchange market.

HEDGING INSTRUMENTS FOR INDIAN FIRMS[19]

Then last decade has witnessed amplified volatility in the INR-USD exchange rates in the backdrop of the increased dollar-inflows into the Indian stock markets. A summary of the foreign exchange risk hedging behaviour of select Indian firms is given in Table 25.10.

Table 25.10 indicates that all the firms have their earnings tied to either the US dollar, Euro or Pound, underscoring their global and diverse nature of transactions. Forward contracts are commonly used, and among these firms, Reliance Industries depends heavily on them for hedging requirements. Forward contracts can be customized according to a firm's precise requirements, which make them popular. Tailoring allows firms to precisely match their exposures, unlike exchange-traded derivatives such as futures, which are standardized and may not offer exact matching.

Table 25.10 Evidence of Derivatives use for Hedging FX Risk by Indian Firms

Company	Instruments	Currencies Involved & Nature of Exposure
Reliance Industries	Currency Swaps Options Contracts Forward Contracts	Earnings in all businesses are linked to USD. The key input, crude oil is purchased in USD. All export revenues are in foreign currency and local prices are based on import parity prices as well
Maruti Suzuki	Forward Contracts Currency swaps	INR-JPY & US $-INR Import/Royalty payable in Yen and Exports Receivables in dollars. USD-INR for Interest rate and forex risk.
Mahindra and Mahindra	Forward Contracts Currency Swaps	INR-JPY, INR-EUR $-INR as Trade payables in Yen and Euro and export receivables in dollars. JPY-INR for Interest rate and foreign exchange risk.
Arvind Mills	Forward Contracts Option Contracts	$-INR, GBP-INR, INR-$, as most of the revenue is either in dollars or linked to dollars due to export.
Infosys	Forward Contracts Options Contracts Range Barrier Options	$-INR, INR-$, Eur-INR as most of the revenue is in these currencies.
Tata Consultancy Services	Forward Contracts Option Contracts	Eur-INR, GBP-INR, $-INR as revenues largely denominated in foreign currency, predominantly US$, GBP, and Euro. Other currencies include Australian $, Canadian $, South African Rand, and Swiss Franc
Dr. Reddy's Labs	Forward Contracts Options Contracts	$-INR, Eur-$ as exposed on receivables and loans payable. Exposure is mostly in USD

NOTE:

1. $-INR Forward contracts denote selling of USD forwards to convert revenues to INR. INR-$ Forward contracts denote buying of USD forwards to meet USD payment obligations.
2. $-INR Option contracts are Put options to sell USD. INR-$ are Call options to buy USD.

[19] Further reading: Sivakumar, A., & Sarkar, R. (2018). Corporate hedging for foreign exchange risk in India. Industrial and Management Engineering Department, Indian Institute of Technology, Kanpur, 58.

Reliance Industries, Maruti Suzuki and Mahindra & Mahindra are firms that employ currency swaps. The use of swaps as a hedging strategy indicates that these firms have longer planning horizons compared to other companies. Given their inherent characteristics–such as extended gestation periods and substantial initial capital investments–it is understandable why they adopt longer-term planning approaches.

TCS has shifted its hedging strategy from forwards to options for managing its exposure to the US Dollar. This trend is observed among several Indian firms due to the significant volatility in the USD-INR exchange rate. Options provide greater profit potential in volatile conditions, offering unlimited upside while mitigating downside risk. In contrast, forwards carry risk if exchange rate expectations are incorrect, potentially resulting in missed profits. For example, Hexaware Technologies and a few more software companies often take losses in their quarterly results to cover the potential exposure due to similar instruments.

Infosys employs range barrier options as a strategy to mitigate the impact of volatile dollar exchange rates. Given their reliance on exports and limited domestic market, software firms need flexible hedging solutions during periods of high volatility. Additionally, their planning horizons tend to be shorter compared to capital-intensive companies.

RESEARCH IN EMERGING MARKET CONTEXT

Mahadevan and Lakshminarayana (2020) conducted a study to explore the relationship between corporate hedging theories and the use of foreign currency loans by companies listed in India. The study found that companies in the manufacturing sector were more likely to use foreign currency loans than those in the services sector. The study also identified variables such as debt to net worth, export to sales, and revenue (log of revenue) as significant factors influencing companies' likelihood of raising foreign currency loans. Interestingly, the interest coverage ratio hurt the likelihood of companies opting for foreign currency loans.

Pradhan and Hiremath's (2021) study on Indian firms found that companies with dollar debt lack a natural hedge against exchange rate volatility. Mandatory hedging and offshore derivatives markets are essential to combat this issue. Additionally, providing accessible domestic credit can reduce reliance on external commercial borrowings.

References

Pradhan, A. K., & Hiremath, G. S. (2021). Effects of foreign currency debt on investment of the firms in emerging economy. *International Journal of Finance & Economics*, *26*(4), 4993–5004.

Mahadevan, S., & Lakshminarayana, G. S. (2020). Corporate Hedging Theories and Usage of Foreign Currency Loans: A Logit Model Approach. *Investment Management and Financial Innovations, 17*(4), 367–377.

Summary and Conclusions

1. Firms hedge to reduce risk. This chapter showed a number of hedging strategies. The Froot, Scharfstein, and Stein model explains why some firms should optimally choose to live with risk rather than hedge all the risk away.
2. A forward contract is an agreement by two parties to sell an item for cash at a later date. The price is set at the time the agreement is signed. However, cash changes hands on the date of delivery. Forward contracts are generally not traded on organized exchanges.

3. Futures contracts are also agreements for future delivery. They have certain advantages, such as liquidity, that forward contracts do not. An unusual feature of futures contracts is the mark-to-the-market convention. If the price of a futures contract falls on a particular day, every buyer of the contract must pay money to the clearinghouse. Every seller of the contract receives money from the clearinghouse. Everything is reversed if the price rises. The mark-to-the-market convention prevents defaults on futures contracts.

4. We divided hedges into two types: short hedges and long hedges. An individual or firm that sells a futures contract to reduce risk is instituting a short hedge. Short hedges are generally appropriate for holders of inventory. An individual or firm that buys a futures contract to reduce risk is instituting a long hedge. Long hedges are typically used by firms with contracts to sell finished goods at a fixed price.

5. An interest rate futures contract employs a bond as the deliverable instrument. Because of their popularity, we worked with Treasury bond futures contracts. We showed that Treasury bond futures contracts can be priced using the same type of net present value analysis that is used to price Treasury bonds themselves.

6. Many firms face interest rate risk. They can reduce this risk by hedging with interest rate futures contracts. As with other commodities, a short hedge involves the sale of a futures contract. Firms that are committed to buying mortgages or other bonds are likely to institute short hedges. A long hedge involves the purchase of a futures contract. Firms that have agreed to sell mortgages or other bonds at a fixed price are likely to institute long hedges.

7. Duration measures the average maturity of all the cash flows of a bond. Bonds with high duration have high price variability. Firms frequently try to match the duration of their assets with the duration of their liabilities.

8. Swaps are agreements to exchange cash flows over time. The first major type is an interest rate swap in which one pattern of coupon payments, say, fixed payments, is exchanged for another, say, coupons that float with LIBOR. The second major type is a currency swap, in which an agreement is struck to swap payments denominated in one currency for payments in another currency over time.

Concept Questions

1. **Hedging Strategies** If a firm is selling futures contracts on lumber as a hedging strategy, what must be true about the firm's exposure to lumber prices?

2. **Hedging Strategies** If a firm is buying call options on pork belly futures as a hedging strategy, what must be true about the firm's exposure to pork belly prices?

3. **Forwards and Futures** What is the difference between a forward contract and a futures contract? Why do you think that futures contracts are much more common? Are there any circumstances under which you might prefer to use forwards instead of futures? Explain.

4. **Hedging Commodities** Bubbling Crude Corporation, a large Texas oil producer, would like to hedge against adverse movements in the price of oil because this is the firm's primary source of revenue. What should the firm do? Provide at least two reasons it probably will not be possible to achieve a completely flat risk profile with respect to oil prices.

5. **Sources of Risk** A company produces an energy-intensive product and uses natural gas as the energy source. The competition primarily uses oil. Explain why this company is exposed to fluctuations in both oil and natural gas prices.

6. **Hedging Commodities** If a textile manufacturer wanted to hedge against adverse movements in cotton prices, it could buy cotton futures contracts or buy call options on cotton futures contracts. What would be the pros and cons of the two approaches?

7. **Option** Explain why a put option on a bond is conceptually the same as a call option on interest rates.

8. **Hedging Interest Rates** A company has a large bond issue maturing in one year. When it matures, the company will float a new issue. Current interest rates are attractive and the company is concerned that rates next year will be higher. What are some hedging strategies that the company might use in this case?

9. **Swaps** Explain why a swap is effectively a series of forward contracts. Suppose a firm enters a swap agreement with a swap dealer. Describe the nature of the default risk faced by both parties.

10. **Swaps** Suppose a firm enters a fixed-for-floating interest rate swap with a swap dealer. Describe the cash flows that will occur as a result of the swap.

11. **Transaction versus Economic Exposure** What is the difference between transactions and economic exposure? Which can be hedged more easily? Why?

12. **Hedging Exchange Rate Risk** If a U.S. company exports its goods to Japan, how would it use a futures contract on Japanese yen to hedge its exchange rate risk? Would it buy or sell yen futures? Does the way the exchange rate is quoted in the futures contract matter?

13. **Hedging Strategies** For the following scenarios, describe a hedging strategy using futures contracts that might be considered.

    a. A public utility is concerned about rising costs.
    b. A candy manufacturer is concerned about rising costs.
    c. A corn farmer fears that this year's harvest will be at record high levels across the country.
    d. A manufacturer of photographic film is concerned about rising costs.
    e. A natural gas producer believes there will be excess supply in the market this year.
    f. A bank derives all its income from long-term, fixed-rate residential mortgages.
    g. A stock mutual fund invests in large, blue-chip stocks and is concerned about a decline in the stock market.
    h. A U.S. importer of Swiss army knives will pay for its order in six months in Swiss francs.
    i. A U.S. exporter of construction equipment has agreed to sell some cranes to a German construction firm. The U.S. firm will be paid in euros in three months.

14. **Swaps** In September 2020, Unilever and JP Morgan entered into a ₹500 million 10-year swap, the first swap to use SOFR as the reference interest rate. The interest rate swap effectively converted ₹500 million of fixed-rate debt for a floating rate based on SOFR. Why would Unilever use a swap agreement? In other words, why didn't the company go ahead and issue floating-rate bonds since the net effect of issuing fixed-rate bonds and then doing a swap is to create a floating-rate bond?

15. **Hedging Strategies** William Santiago is interested in entering the import/export business. During a recent visit with his financial advisers, he said, "If we play the game right, this is the safest business in the world. By hedging all of our transactions in the foreign exchange futures market, we can eliminate all of our risk." Do you agree with Mr. Santiago's assessment of hedging? Why or why not?

16. **Hedging Strategies** Kevin Nomura is a Japanese student who is planning a one-year stay in the United States. He expects to arrive in the United States in eight months. He is worried about depreciation of the yen relative to the rupee over the next eight months and wishes to take a position in foreign exchange futures to hedge this risk. What should Mr. Nomura's hedging position be? Assume the exchange rate between Japanese and U.S. currencies is quoted as yen/rupee.

Questions and Problems

BASIC (Questions 1–8)

1. **Futures Quotes** Refer to Table 25.2(a) in the text to answer this question. Suppose you purchase a March 2021 cocoa futures contract on December 4, 2020, at the last price of the day. What will your profit or loss be if cocoa prices turn out to be ₹3,014 per metric ton at expiration?

2. **Futures Quotes** Refer to Table 25.2(a) in the text to answer this question. Suppose you sell five March 2021 silver futures contracts on December 4, 2020, at the last price of the day. What will your profit or loss be if silver prices turn out to be ₹24.83 per ounce at expiration? What if silver prices are ₹23.16 per ounce at expiration?

3. **Put and Call Payoffs** Suppose a financial manager buys call options on 50,000 barrels of oil with an exercise price of ₹65 per barrel. She simultaneously sells a put option on 50,000 barrels of oil with the same exercise price of ₹65 per barrel. Consider her gains and losses if oil prices are ₹60, ₹62, ₹65, ₹68, and ₹70. What do you notice about the payoff profile?

4. **Marking to Market** You are long 10 gold futures contracts, established at an initial settle price of ₹1,810 per ounce, where each contract represents 100 ounces. Over the subsequent four trading days, gold settles at ₹1,816, ₹1,812, ₹1,807, and ₹1,813, respectively. Compute the cash flows at the end of each trading day and your total profit or loss at the end of the trading period.

5. **Marking to Market** You are short 25 gasoline futures contracts, established at an initial settle price of ₹1.34 per gallon, where each contract represents 42,000 gallons. Over the subsequent four trading days, gasoline settles at ₹1.37, ₹1.32, ₹1.36, and ₹1.39, respectively. Compute the cash flows at the end of each trading day and your total profit or loss at the end of the trading period.

6. **Duration** What is the duration of a bond with three years to maturity and a coupon of 5.3 percent paid annually if the bond sells at par?

7. **Duration** What is the duration of a bond with four years to maturity and a coupon of 7.1 percent paid annually if the bond sells at par?

8. **Duration** Blue Steel Community Bank has the following market value balance sheet:

Asset or Liability	Market Value (in millions)	Duration (in years)
Federal funds deposits	₹ 43	0
Accounts receivable	555	.20
Short-term loans	340	.65
Long-term loans	103	5.25
Mortgages	498	12.85
Checking and savings deposits	605	0
Certificates of deposit	395	1.60
Long-term financing	285	9.80
Equity	254	N/A

a. What is the duration of the assets?
b. What is the duration of the liabilities?
c. Is the bank immune to interest rate risk?

INTERMEDIATE (Questions 9–15)

9. **Hedging with Futures** Refer to Table 25.2(a) in the text to answer this question. Suppose today is December 4, 2020, and your firm produces breakfast cereal and needs 180,000 bushels of corn in March 2021 for an upcoming promotion. You would like to lock in your costs today because you are concerned that corn prices might go up between now and March.

   a. How could you use corn futures contracts to hedge your risk exposure? What price would you effectively be locking in based on the closing price of the day?

   b. Suppose corn prices are ₹4.53 per bushel in March. What is the profit or loss on your futures position? Explain how your futures position has eliminated your exposure to price risk in the corn market.

10. **Interest Rate Swaps** ABC Company and XYZ Company need to raise funds to pay for capital improvements at their manufacturing plants. ABC Company is a well-established firm with an excellent credit rating in the debt market; it can borrow funds either at an 11 percent fixed rate or at LIBOR + 1 percent floating rate. XYZ Company is a fledgling startup firm without a strong credit history. It can borrow funds either at a 10 percent fixed rate or at LIBOR + 3 percent floating rate.

    a. Is there an opportunity here for ABC and XYZ to benefit by means of an interest rate swap?

    b. Suppose you've been hired at a bank that acts as a dealer in the swaps market and your boss has shown you the borrowing rate information for your clients, ABC and XYZ. Describe how you could bring these two companies together in an interest rate swap that would make both firms better off while netting your bank a 2 percent profit.

11. **Duration** Ted and Alice Hansel have a son who will begin college 12 years from today. School expenses of ₹55,000 will need to be paid at the beginning of each of the four years that their son plans to attend college. What is the duration of this liability to the couple if they can borrow and lend at the market interest rate of 5.3 percent?

12. **Duration** What is the duration of a bond with two years to maturity if the bond has a coupon rate of 4.8 percent paid semiannually and the market interest rate is 4.3 percent?

13. **Forward Pricing** The forward price (F) of a contract on an asset with neither carrying costs nor convenience yield is the current spot price of the asset (S_0) multiplied by 1 plus the appropriate interest rate between the initiation of the contract and the delivery date of the asset. Derive this relationship by comparing the cash flows that result from the following two strategies:

    Strategy 1: Buy silver on the spot market today and hold it for one year. (*Hint*: Do not use any of your own money to purchase the silver.)

    Strategy 2: Take a long position in a silver forward contract for delivery in one year. Assume that silver is an asset with neither carrying costs nor convenience yield.

14. **Forward Pricing** You enter into a forward contract to buy a 10-year, zero coupon bond that will be issued in one year. The face value of the bond is ₹1,000 and the 1-year and 11-year spot interest rates are 6 percent and 8 percent, respectively.

    a. What is the forward price of your contract?

    b. Suppose both the 1-year and 11-year spot rates unexpectedly shift downward by 2 percent. What is the new price of the forward contract?

15. **Forward Pricing** This morning you agreed to buy a one-year Treasury bond in six months. The bond has a face value of ₹1,000. Use the spot interest rates listed here to answer the following questions:

Time	EAR
6 months	3.61%
12 months	4.05
18 months	4.73
24 months	5.42

a. What is the forward price of this contract?

b. Suppose shortly after you purchased the forward contract all rates increased by 30 basis points. For example, the six-month rate increased from 3.61 percent to 3.91 percent. What is the price of a forward contract otherwise identical to yours given these changes?

16. **Financial Engineering** Suppose there were call options and forward contracts available on coal, but no put options. Show how a financial engineer could synthesize a put option using the available contracts. What does your answer tell you about the general relationship between puts, calls, and forwards? CHALLENGE (Question 16)

WILLIAMSON MORTGAGE, INC.

Jennifer Williamson recently received her MBA and has decided to enter the mortgage brokerage business. Rather than work for someone else, she has decided to open her own shop. Her cousin, Jerry, has approached her about a mortgage for a house he is building. The house will be completed in three months and he will need the mortgage at that time. Jerry wants a 25-year, fixed-rate mortgage in the amount of ₹500,000 with monthly payments.

Jennifer has agreed to lend Jerry the money in three months at the current market rate of 5.5 percent. Because Jennifer is just starting out, she does not have ₹500,000 available for the loan, so she approaches Max Cabell, the president of MC Insurance Corporation, about purchasing the mortgage from her in three months. Max has agreed to purchase the mortgage in three months, but he is unwilling to set a price on the mortgage. Instead, he has agreed in writing to purchase the mortgage at the market rate in three months. There are Treasury bond futures contracts available for delivery in three months. A Treasury bond contract is for ₹100,000 in face value of Treasury bonds.

1. What is the monthly mortgage payment on Jerry's mortgage?
2. What is the most significant risk Jennifer faces in this deal?
3. How can Jennifer hedge this risk?
4. Suppose that, in the next three months, the market rate of interest rises to 6.2 percent.
   a. How much will Max be willing to pay for the mortgage?
   b. What will happen to the value of Treasury bond futures contracts? Will the long or short position increase in value?
5. Suppose that, in the next three months, the market rate of interest falls to 4.6 percent.
   a. How much will Max be willing to pay for the mortgage?
   b. What will happen to the value of Treasury bond futures contracts? Will the long or short position increase in value?
6. Are there any possible risks Jennifer faces in using Treasury bond futures contracts to hedge her interest rate risk?

Short-Term Finance and Planning

In the early part of the 2020 COVID-19 lockdowns, auto dealers were offering unprecedented discounts such as no payments for 90 days and 0 percent loans for as long as seven years. In May 2020, car sales were down 30 percent from the previous year, but that was an improvement from April's year-over-year sales drop of 50 percent. The discounts worked as one Toyota dealer reported 200 cars on its lot, down from the normal level of 550 vehicles.

Industrywide, auto inventories were dropping all over the country. For example, it was estimated that there were only 44 days' sales of inventory for large pickup trucks such as the Ford F-150 and Chevrolet Silverado. While in normal times this might be a minor issue, because of auto plant shutdowns, the days' sales in inventory was dropping by one day as each day passed.

To this point, we have described many of the decisions of long-term finance, such as those of capital budgeting, dividend policy, and financial structure. In this chapter, we begin to discuss short-term finance. Short-term finance is primarily concerned with the analysis of decisions that affect current assets and current liabilities.

Frequently, the term *net working capital* is associated with short-term financial decision making. As we have described in previous chapters, net working capital is the difference between current assets and current liabilities. Often, short-term financial management is called *working capital management*. These terms mean the same thing.

There is no universally accepted definition of short-term finance. The most important difference between short-term and long-term finance is in the timing of cash flows. Short-term financial decisions typically involve cash inflows and outflows that occur within a year. These decisions include when a firm orders raw materials, pays in cash, and anticipates selling finished goods in one year for cash. In contrast, long-term financial decisions are involved when a firm purchases a special machine that will reduce operating costs over, say, the next five years.

What types of questions fall under the general heading of short-term finance? To name a few:

1. What is a reasonable level of cash to keep on hand (in a bank) to pay bills?
2. How much should the firm borrow in the short term?
3. How much credit should be extended to customers?

This chapter introduces the basic elements of short-term financial decisions. First, we discuss the short-term operating activities of the firm. We then identify some alternative short-term financial policies. Finally, we outline the basic elements in a short-term financial plan and describe short-term financing instruments.

Please visit us at **rwjcorporatefinance.blogspot.com** for the latest developments in the world of corporate finance.

26.1 Tracing Cash and Net Working Capital

In this section, we examine the components of cash and net working capital as they change from one year to the next. We already have discussed various aspects of this subject in Chapters 2 and 3. We briefly review some of that discussion as it relates to short-term financing decisions. Our goal is to describe the short-term operating activities of the firm and their impact on cash and net working capital.

Interested in a career in short-term finance? Visit **www.treasury-management.com**.

To begin, recall that *current assets* are cash and other assets that are expected to convert to cash within the year. Current assets are presented on the balance sheet in order of their accounting liquidity–the ease with which they can be converted to cash and the time it takes to convert them. Four of the most important items found in the current asset section of a balance sheet are cash and cash equivalents, marketable securities, accounts receivable, and inventories.

Analogous to their investment in current assets, firms use several kinds of short-term debt called *current liabilities*. Current liabilities are obligations that are expected to require cash payment within one year (or within the operating period if it is longer than one year). Three major current liabilities are accounts payable, expenses payable (including accrued wages and taxes), and notes payable.

Because we want to focus on changes in cash, we start off by defining cash in terms of the other elements of the balance sheet. This lets us isolate the cash account and explore the impact on cash from the firm's operating and financing decisions. The basic balance sheet identity can be written as:

$$\text{Net working capital} + \text{Fixed assets} = \text{Long-term debt} + \text{Equity} \qquad \textbf{(26.1)}$$

Net working capital is cash plus other current assets, less current liabilities:

$$\text{Net working capital} = (\text{Cash} + \text{Other current assets}) - \text{Current liabilities} \qquad \textbf{(26.2)}$$

If we substitute this for net working capital in the basic balance sheet identity and rearrange things a bit, we see that cash is:

$$\begin{aligned}\text{Cash} = {} & \text{Long-term debt} + \text{Equity} + \text{Current liabilities} \\ & - \text{Current assets other than cash} - \text{Fixed assets}\end{aligned} \qquad \textbf{(26.3)}$$

This tells us in general terms that some activities naturally increase cash and some activities decrease it. We can list these various activities, along with an example of each, as follows:

Activities That Increase Cash

Increasing long-term debt (borrowing over the long term)

Increasing equity (selling some stock)

Increasing current liabilities (getting a 90-day loan)

Decreasing current assets other than cash (selling some inventory for cash)

Decreasing fixed assets (selling some property)

Activities That Decrease Cash

Decreasing long-term debt (paying off a long-term debt)

Decreasing equity (repurchasing some stock)

Decreasing current liabilities (paying off a 90-day loan)

Increasing current assets other than cash (buying some inventory for cash)

Increasing fixed assets (buying some property)

Notice that our two lists are exact opposites. For example, floating a long-term bond issue increases cash (at least until the money is spent). Paying off a long-term bond issue decreases cash.

Activities that increase cash are called *sources of cash*. Those activities that decrease cash are called *uses of cash*. Looking back at our list, we see that sources of cash always involve increasing a liability (or equity) account or decreasing an asset account. This makes sense because increasing a liability means that we have raised money by borrowing it or by selling an ownership interest in the firm. A decrease in an asset means that we have sold or otherwise liquidated an asset. In either case, there is a cash inflow.

Uses of cash are the reverse. A use of cash involves decreasing a liability by paying it off, perhaps, or increasing assets by purchasing something. Both of these activities require that the firm spend some cash.

EXAMPLE 26.1

Sources and Uses Here is a quick check of your understanding of sources and uses: If accounts payable go up by ₹100, does this indicate a source or a use? What if accounts receivable go up by ₹100?

Accounts payable are what we owe our suppliers. This is a short-term debt. If it rises by ₹100, we have effectively borrowed the money, which is a source of cash. Receivables are what our customers owe to us, so an increase of ₹100 in accounts receivable means that we have loaned the money; this is a use of cash.

26.2 The Operating Cycle and the Cash Cycle

The primary concern in short-term finance is the firm's short-run operating and financing activities. For a typical manufacturing firm, these short-run activities might consist of the following sequence of events and decisions:

Event	Decision
1. Buying raw materials	1. How much inventory to order
2. Paying cash	2. Whether to borrow or draw down cash balances
3. Manufacturing the product	3. What choice of production technology to use
4. Selling the product	4. Whether credit should be extended to a particular customer
5. Collecting cash	5. How to collect

These activities create patterns of cash inflows and cash outflows. These cash flows are both unsynchronized and uncertain. They are unsynchronized because the payment of cash for raw materials does not happen at the same time as the receipt of cash from selling the product. They are uncertain because future sales and costs cannot be precisely predicted.

DEFINING THE OPERATING AND CASH CYCLES

We can start with a simple case. One day, call it Day 0, we purchase ₹1,000 worth of inventory on credit. We pay the bill 30 days later, and, after 30 more days, someone buys the ₹1,000 in inventory for ₹1,400. Our buyer does not actually pay for another 45 days. We can summarize these events chronologically as follows:

Day	Activity	Cash Effect
0	Acquire inventory	None
30	Pay for inventory	−₹1,000
60	Sell inventory on credit	None
105	Collect on sale	+₹1,400

The Operating Cycle There are several things to notice in our example. First, the entire cycle, from the time we acquire some inventory to the time we collect the cash, takes 105 days. This is called the **operating cycle**.

As we illustrate, the operating cycle is the length of time it takes to acquire inventory, sell it, and collect for it. This cycle has two distinct components. The first part is the time it takes to acquire and sell the inventory. This period, a 60-day span in our example, is called the *inventory period.* The second part is the time it takes to collect on the sale, 45 days in our example. This is called the *accounts receivable period.*

Based on our definitions, the operating cycle is the sum of the inventory and accounts receivable periods:

$$\begin{aligned}\text{Operating cycle} &= \text{Inventory period} + \text{Accounts receivable period}\\ 105 \text{ days} &= 60 \text{ days} + 45 \text{ days}\end{aligned} \tag{26.4}$$

What the operating cycle describes is how a product moves through the current asset accounts. The product begins life as inventory, it is converted to a receivable when it is sold, and it is finally converted to cash when we collect from the sale. Notice that, at each step, the asset is moving closer to cash.

The Cash Cycle The second thing to notice is that the cash flows and other events that occur are not synchronized. Suppose we don't pay for the inventory until 30 days after we acquire it. The intervening 30-day period is called the *accounts payable period.* Next, we spend cash on Day 30, but we don't collect until Day 105. Somehow, we have to arrange to finance the ₹1,000 for 105 − 30 = 75 days. This period is called the **cash cycle**.

The cash cycle, therefore, is the number of days that pass before we collect the cash from a sale, measured from when we actually pay for the inventory. Notice that, based on our definitions, the cash cycle is the difference between the operating cycle and the accounts payable period:

$$\begin{aligned}\text{Cash cycle} &= \text{Operating cycle} - \text{Accounts payable period}\\ 75 \text{ days} &= 105 \text{ days} - 30 \text{ days}\end{aligned} \tag{26.5}$$

Figure 26.1 depicts the short-term operating activities and cash flows of a typical manufacturing firm by way of a cash flow time line. As shown, the cash flow time line presents the operating cycle and the cash cycle in graphical form. The need for short-term financial management is suggested by the gap between the cash inflows and the cash outflows. This is related to the lengths of the operating cycle and the accounts payable period.

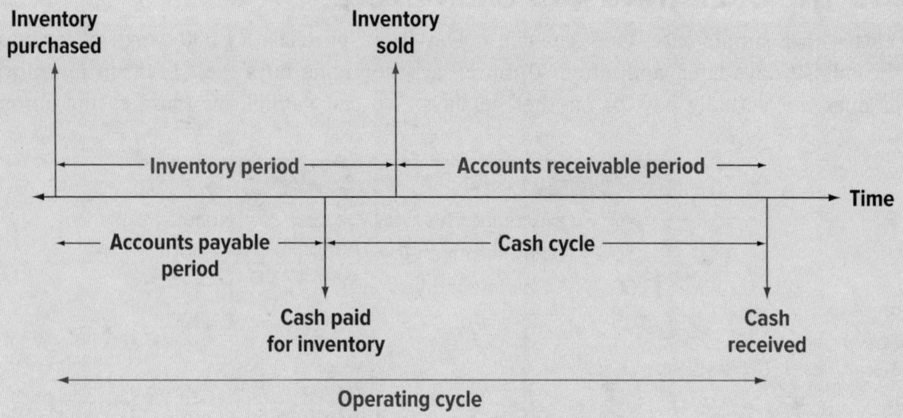

The operating cycle is the time period from inventory purchase until the receipt of cash. (The operating cycle may not include the time from placement of the order until arrival of the stock.) The cash cycle is the time period from when cash is paid out to when cash is received.

Figure 26.1 Cash Flow Time Line and the Short-Term Operating Activities of a Typical Manufacturing Firm

The gap between short-term inflows and outflows can be filled either by borrowing or by holding a liquidity reserve in the form of cash or marketable securities. Alternatively, the gap can be shortened by changing the inventory, receivable, and payable periods. These are all managerial options that we discuss in the following sections.

THE OPERATING CYCLE AND THE FIRM'S ORGANIZATION CHART

Before we examine the operating and cash cycles in greater detail, it is useful for us to take a look at the people involved in managing a firm's current assets and liabilities. As Table 26.1 illustrates, short-term financial management in a large corporation involves a number of different financial and nonfinancial managers. Examining Table 26.1, we see that selling on credit involves at least three different entities: the credit manager, the marketing manager, and the controller. Of these three, only two are responsible to the vice president of finance (the marketing function is usually associated with the vice president of marketing). Thus, there is the potential for conflict, particularly if different managers concentrate on only part of the picture. For example, if marketing is trying to land a new account, it may seek more liberal credit terms as an inducement. However, this may increase the firm's investment in receivables or its exposure to bad-debt risk, and conflict can result.

CALCULATING THE OPERATING AND CASH CYCLES

In our example, the lengths of time that made up the different periods were obvious. If all we have is financial statement information, we will have to do a little more work. We illustrate these calculations next.

Table 26.1 Managers Who Deal with Short-Term Financial Problems

Title of Manager	Duties Related to Short-Term Financial Management	Assets/Liabilities Influenced
Cash manager	Collection, concentration, disbursement; short-term investments; short-term borrowing; banking relations	Cash, marketable securities, short-term loans
Credit manager	Monitoring and control of accounts receivable; credit policy decisions	Accounts receivable
Marketing manager	Credit policy decisions	Accounts receivable
Purchasing manager	Decisions on purchases, suppliers; may negotiate payment terms	Inventory, accounts payable
Production manager	Setting of production schedules and materials requirements	Inventory, accounts payable
Payables manager	Decisions on payment policies and on whether to take discounts	Accounts payable
Controller	Accounting information on cash flows; reconciliation of accounts payable; application of payments to accounts receivable	Accounts receivable, accounts payable

To begin, we need to determine various things such as how long it takes, on average, to sell inventory and how long it takes, on average, to collect receivables. We start by gathering some balance sheet information such as the following (in thousands):

Item	Beginning	Ending	Average
Inventory	₹2,000	₹3,000	₹2,500
Accounts receivable	1,600	2,000	1,800
Accounts payable	750	1,000	875

Also, from the most recent income statement, we might have the following figures (in thousands):

Net sales	₹11,500
Cost of goods sold	8,200

We now need to calculate some financial ratios. We discussed these in some detail in Chapter 3; here, we define them and use them as needed.

The Operating Cycle First of all, we need the inventory period. We spent ₹8.2 million on inventory (our cost of goods sold). Our average inventory was ₹2.5 million. Thus, we turned our inventory over 3.28 (= ₹8.2/₹2.5) times during the year:[1]

$$\text{Inventory turnover} = \frac{\text{Cost of goods sold}}{\text{Average inventory}}$$

$$= \frac{₹8.2 \text{ million}}{₹2.5 \text{ million}} = 3.28 \text{ times}$$

[1]Notice that in calculating inventory turnover here, we use the average inventory instead of using the ending inventory as we did in Chapter 3. Both approaches are used in the real world. To gain some practice using average figures, we will stick with this approach in calculating various ratios throughout this chapter.

Loosely speaking, this tells us that we bought and sold off our inventory 3.28 times during the year. This means that, on average, we held our inventory for:

$$\text{Inventory period} = \frac{365 \text{ days}}{\text{Inventory turnover}}$$
$$= \frac{365}{3.28} = 111.3 \text{ days}$$

So, the inventory period is about 111 days. On average, in other words, inventory sat for about 111 days before it was sold.[2]

Similarly, receivables averaged ₹1.8 million and sales were ₹11.5 million. Assuming that all sales were credit sales, the receivables turnover is:[3]

$$\text{Receivables turnover} = \frac{\text{Credit sales}}{\text{Average accounts receivable}}$$
$$= \frac{₹11.5 \text{ million}}{₹1.8 \text{ million}} = 6.4 \text{ times}$$

If we turn over our receivables 6.4 times a year, then the receivables period is:

$$\text{Receivables period} = \frac{365 \text{ days}}{\text{Receivables turnover}}$$
$$= \frac{365}{6.4} = 57.1 \text{ days}$$

The receivables period is also called the *days' sales in receivables*, or the *average collection period*. Whatever it is called, it tells us that our customers took an average of 57 days to pay.

The operating cycle is the sum of the inventory and receivables periods:

$$\text{Operating cycle} = \text{Inventory period} + \text{Accounts receivable period}$$
$$= 111 \text{ days} + 57 \text{ days} = 168 \text{ days}$$

This tells us that, on average, 168 days elapse between the time we acquire inventory and, having sold it, collect for the sale.

The Cash Cycle We now need the payables period. From the information given earlier, we know that average payables were ₹875,000 and cost of goods sold was ₹8.2 million. Our payables turnover is:

$$\text{Payables turnover} = \frac{\text{Cost of goods sold}}{\text{Average payables}}$$
$$= \frac{₹8.2 \text{ million}}{₹.875 \text{ million}} = 9.4 \text{ times}$$

[2]This measure is conceptually identical to the days' sales in inventory figure we discussed in Chapter 3.

[3]If less than 100 percent of our sales were credit sales, then we would need a little more information, namely, credit sales for the year. See Chapter 3 for more discussion of this measure.

The payables period is:

$$\text{Payables period} = \frac{365 \text{ days}}{\text{Payables turnover}}$$
$$= \frac{365}{9.4} = 38.9 \text{ days}$$

We took an average of 39 days to pay our bills.

Finally, the cash cycle is the difference between the operating cycle and the payables period:

$$\text{Cash cycle} = \text{Operating cycle} - \text{Accounts payable period}$$
$$= 168 \text{ days} - 39 \text{ days} = 129 \text{ days}$$

So, on average, there is a 129-day delay between the time we pay for merchandise and the time we collect on the sale.

EXAMPLE 26.2

The Operating and Cash Cycles You have collected the following information for the Brahmaputra Company:

Item	Beginning	Ending
Inventory	₹5,000	₹7,000
Accounts receivable	1,600	2,400
Accounts payable	2,700	4,800

Credit sales for the year just ended were ₹50,000 and cost of goods sold was ₹30,000. How long does it take Brahmaputra to collect on its receivables? How long does merchandise stay around before it is sold? How long does Brahmaputra take to pay its bills?

We can first calculate the three turnover ratios:

$$\text{Inventory turnover} = ₹30{,}000/₹6{,}000 = 5 \text{ times}$$
$$\text{Receivables turnover} = ₹50{,}000/₹2{,}000 = 25 \text{ times}$$
$$\text{Payables turnover} = ₹30{,}000/₹3{,}750 = 8 \text{ times}$$

We use these to get the various periods:

$$\text{Inventory period} = 365/5 = 73 \text{ days}$$
$$\text{Receivables period} = 365/25 = 14.6 \text{ days}$$
$$\text{Payables period} = 365/8 = 45.6 \text{ days}$$

All told, Brahmaputra collects on a sale in 14.6 days, inventory sits around for 73 days, and bills get paid after about 46 days. The operating cycle here is the sum of the inventory and receivables periods: 73 + 14.6 = 87.6 days. The cash cycle is the difference between the operating cycle and the payables period: 87.6 − 45.6 = 42 days.

INTERPRETING THE CASH CYCLE

Our examples show that the cash cycle depends on the inventory, receivables, and payables periods. The cash cycle increases as the inventory and receivables periods get longer. It decreases if the company is able to defer payment of payables and thereby lengthen the payables period.

Most firms have a positive cash cycle, and they require financing for inventories and receivables. The longer the cash cycle, the more financing is required. Also, changes in the firm's cash cycle often are monitored as an early warning measure. A lengthening cycle can indicate that the firm is having trouble moving inventory or collecting on its receivables. Such problems can be masked, at least partially, by an increased payables cycle, so both cycles should be monitored.

The link between the firm's cash cycle and its profitability can be seen easily by recalling that one of the basic determinants of profitability and growth for a firm is its total asset turnover, which is defined as Sales/Total assets. In Chapter 3, we saw that the higher this ratio is, the greater are the firm's accounting return on assets, ROA, and return on equity, ROE. All else the same, the shorter the cash cycle, the lower is the firm's investment in inventories and receivables. As a result, the firm's total assets are lower and total turnover is higher.

A LOOK AT OPERATING AND CASH CYCLES

In 2020, The Hackett Group published its survey of working capital for various industries. The results of this survey highlight the marked differences in cash and operating cycles across industries. The table below shows four different industries and the median operating and cash cycles for each. Of these, the food and staples retail industry has both the shortest operating cycle and shortest cash cycle.

	Receivables Period (days)	Inventory Period (days)	Operating Cycle (days)	Payables Period (days)	Cash Cycle (days)
Aerospace and Defense	64	74	138	48	90
Beverages	37	71	108	79	29
Food and Staples Retail	5	38	43	29	14
Homebuilding	4	345	349	19	330

SOURCE: 2020 Working Capital Survey, The Hackett Group.

The aerospace and defense and beverages industries have similar inventory periods, but the beverages industry has a much smaller receivables period and a shorter operating cycle. The beverages industry also has a longer payables period, resulting in a cash cycle of 29 days, much shorter than the aerospace and defense industry. The homebuilding industry is much different than the other industries. Its inventory period is almost a year due to construction time and the time needed to close the sale. As a result, the cash conversion cycle is also almost a year in this industry.

We've seen that operating and cash cycles can vary quite a bit across industries, but these cycles also can be different for companies within the same industry. Below you will find the operating and cash cycles for selected consumer durables companies. As you can see, there are differences. Although each of the companies shown has a similar inventory period, Sleep Number has a receivables period of only four days and a payables period of 84 days, resulting in a cash conversion cycle of −26 days. Because of its longer receivables period and shorter payables period, Tempur Sealy's cash conversion cycle is 46 days.

	Receivables Period (days)	Inventory Period (days)	Operating Cycle (days)	Payables Period (days)	Cash Cycle (days)
Sleep Number	4	54	58	84	−26
Whirlpool	39	54	93	100	−7
Tempur Sealy	44	56	100	54	46

When you look at the operating and cash cycles, consider that each is really a financial ratio. As with any financial ratio, firm and industry characteristics will have an effect, so take care in your interpretation. In looking at Whirlpool and Tempur Sealy, we note both companies' longer receivables periods. Is that a bad thing? Maybe not. These companies have a different business model compared to Sleep Number and, as a result, aren't really comparable when it comes to receivables periods.

Even in India, due to different products and services, the cash cycle varies across industries. The Exhibit 26.1 below illustrates this point by comparing the current assets and current liabilities of eight different companies. In this list, Tata Consultancy Services (TCS) has the highest amount of account receivables. Does this mean Tata Consultancy Services is less efficient? Probably not, but the relatively high account receivables levels are likely consistent with the industry. The projects in the IT industry last a long time, and the payments are received upon completion of each project milestone. In contrast, the account receivables for Matrimony.com is nil as the subscription charges are collected upfront.

Exhibit 26.1 Current Assets and Current Liabilities as a percentage of Total Assets for Selected Indian Companies

Short-Term Financial & Working Capital Items	EIH	Maruti Suzuki India	Aditya Birla Fashion and Retail	Tata Consultancy Services	Andhra Petro	Matrimony .com	Sumedha Fiscal	Barak Valley
Cash and near cash	0%	0%	3%	8%	1%	28%	11%	1%
Accounts receivable	5%	3%	9%	25%	2%	0%	12%	5%
Inventories	1%	5%	24%	0%	10%	0%	9%	6%
Other current assets	10%	6%	13%	26%	4%	7%	19%	15%
Total current assets	17%	14%	49%	60%	17%	36%	51%	27%
Accounts payable	4%	12%	23%	6%	3%	8%	0%	9%
Other short-term liabilities	7%	10%	10%	18%	6%	21%	6%	14%
Current liabilities	12%	22%	24%	24%	9%	28%	6%	23%

26.3 Some Aspects of Short-Term Financial Policy

The policy that a firm adopts for short-term finance will be composed of at least two elements:

1. *The size of the firm's investment in current assets*: This is usually measured relative to the firm's level of total operating revenues. A flexible or accommodative short-term financial policy would maintain a high ratio of current assets to sales. A restrictive short-term financial policy would entail a low ratio of current assets to sales.
2. *The financing of current assets*: This is measured as the proportion of short-term debt to long-term debt. A restrictive short-term financial policy means a high proportion of short-term debt relative to long-term financing, and a flexible policy means less short-term debt and more long-term debt.

THE SIZE OF THE FIRM'S INVESTMENT IN CURRENT ASSETS

Flexible short-term financial policies include:

1. Keeping large balances of cash and marketable securities.
2. Making large investments in inventory.
3. Granting liberal credit terms, which results in a high level of accounts receivable.

Restrictive short-term financial policies are:

1. Keeping low cash balances and no investment in marketable securities.
2. Making small investments in inventory.
3. Allowing no credit sales and no accounts receivable.

Determining the optimal investment level in short-term assets requires an identification of the different costs of alternative short-term financing policies. The objective is to trade off the costs of restrictive policies against those of the flexible ones to arrive at the best compromise.

Current asset holdings are highest with a flexible short-term financial policy and lowest with a restrictive policy. Flexible short-term financial policies are costly in that they require higher cash outflows to finance cash and marketable securities, inventory, and accounts receivable. However, future cash inflows are highest with a flexible policy. Sales are stimulated by the use of a credit policy that provides liberal financing to customers. A large amount of inventory on hand (or "on the shelf") provides a quick delivery service to customers and increases in sales.[4] In addition, the firm can probably charge higher prices for the quick delivery service and the liberal credit terms of flexible policies. A flexible policy also may result in fewer production stoppages because of inventory shortages.[5]

Managing current assets can be thought of as involving a trade-off between costs that rise with the level of investment and costs that fall with the level of investment. Costs that rise with the level of investment in current assets are called **carrying costs**. Costs that fall with increases in the level of investment in current assets are called **shortage costs**.

Carrying costs are generally of two types. First, because the rate of return on current assets is low compared to that of other assets, there is an opportunity cost. Second, there is the cost of maintaining the economic value of the item. The cost of warehousing inventory belongs here.

[4]This is true of some types of finished goods.
[5]This is true of inventory of raw materials but not of finished goods.

Shortage costs are incurred when the investment in current assets is low. If a firm runs out of cash, it will be forced to sell marketable securities. If the firm cannot readily sell marketable securities, it may need to borrow or default on an obligation. (This general situation is called *cash-out.*) If a firm has no inventory (a *stockout*) or if it cannot extend credit to its customers, it will lose customers.

There are two kinds of shortage costs:

1. *Trading, or order, costs*: Order costs are the costs of placing an order for more cash (*brokerage costs*) or more inventory (*production setup costs*).
2. *Costs related to safety reserves*: These are the costs of lost sales, lost customer goodwill, and disruption of production schedules.

Figure 26.2 illustrates the basic nature of carrying costs and shortage costs. The total costs of investing in current assets are determined by adding the carrying costs and the shortage costs. The minimum point on the total cost curve (CA*) reflects the optimal balance of current assets. The curve is generally quite flat at the optimum, and it is difficult, if not impossible, to find the precise optimal balance of shortage and carrying costs. Usually, we are content with a choice near the optimum.

If carrying costs are low or shortage costs are high, the optimal policy calls for substantial current assets. In other words, the optimal policy is a flexible one. This is illustrated in the middle graph of Figure 26.2.

If carrying costs are high or shortage costs are low, the optimal policy is a restrictive one. That is, the optimal policy calls for modest current assets. This is illustrated in the bottom graph of the figure.

Opler, Pinkowitz, Stulz, and Williamson examine the determinants of holdings of cash and marketable securities by publicly traded firms.[6] They find evidence that firms behave according to the static trade-off model described earlier. Their study focuses only on liquid assets (i.e., cash and marketable securities), so that carrying costs are the opportunity costs of holding liquid assets and shortage costs are the risks of not having cash when investment opportunities are good.

Characteristics of Firms with High Holdings of Liquid Assets	Characteristics of Firms with Low Holdings of Liquid Assets
High-growth opportunities	Low-growth opportunities
High-risk investments	Low-risk investments
Small firms	Large firms
Low-credit firms	High-credit firms

Firms will hold more liquid assets (i.e., cash and marketable securities) to ensure that they can continue investing when cash flow is low relative to positive NPV investment opportunities. Firms that have good access to capital markets will hold less liquid assets.

SOURCE: Tim Opler, Lee Pinkowitz, René Stulz, and Rohan Williamson, "The Determinants and Implications of Corporate Cash Holdings," *Journal of Financial Economics* 52, no. 1 (April 1999): 3–46.

[6]Tim Opler, Lee Pinkowitz, René Stulz, and Rohan Williamson, "The Determinants and Implications of Corporate Cash Holdings," *Journal of Financial Economics* 52, no. 1 (April 1999): 3–46.

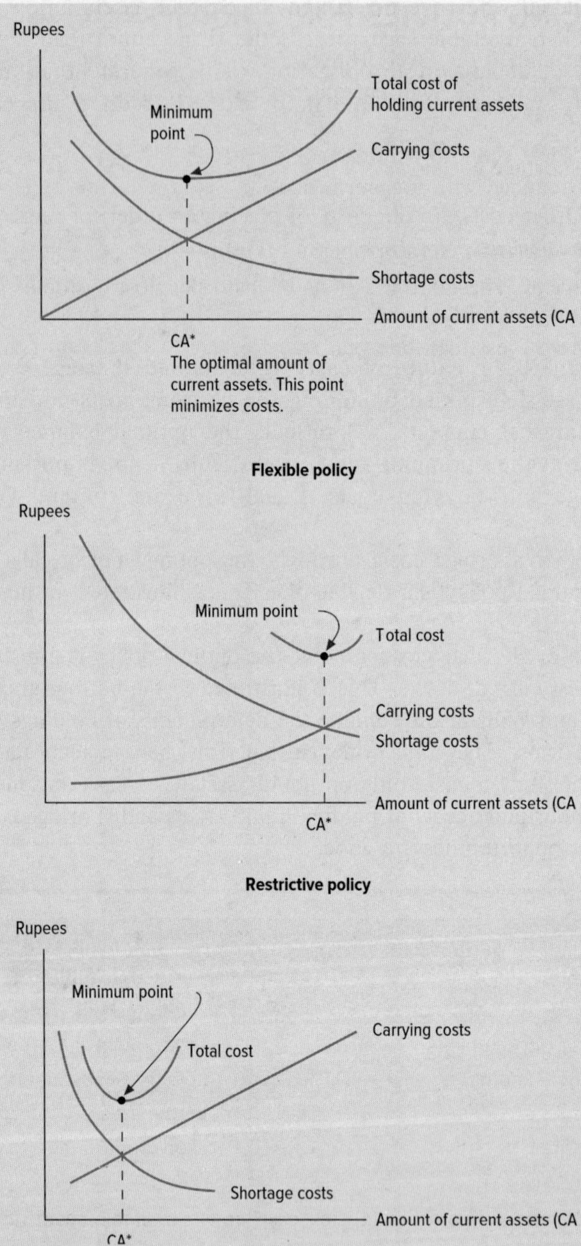

Carrying costs increase with the level of investment in current assets. They include both opportunity costs and the costs of maintaining the asset's economic value. *Shortage costs* decrease with increases in the level of investment in current assets. They include trading costs and the costs of running out of the current asset (e.g., being short on cash).

Figure 26.2 Carrying Costs and Shortage Costs

ALTERNATIVE FINANCING POLICIES FOR CURRENT ASSETS

In the previous section, we examined the level of investment in current assets. Now we turn to the level of current liabilities, assuming the investment in current assets is optimal.

An Ideal Model In an ideal economy, short-term assets can always be financed with short-term debt, and long-term assets can be financed with long-term debt and equity. In this economy, net working capital is always zero.

Imagine the simple case of a grain elevator operator. Grain elevator operators buy crops after harvest, store them, and sell them during the year. They have high inventories of grain after the harvest and end with low inventories just before the next harvest.

Bank loans with maturities of less than one year are used to finance the purchase of grain. These loans are paid with the proceeds from the sale of grain.

The situation is shown in Figure 26.3. Long-term assets are assumed to grow over time, whereas current assets increase at the end of the harvest and then decline during the year. Short-term assets end at zero just before the next harvest. These assets are financed by short-term debt, and long-term assets are financed with long-term debt and equity. Net working capital–current assets minus current liabilities–is always zero.

Different Strategies for Financing Current Assets Current assets cannot be expected to drop to zero in the real world because a long-term rising level of sales will result in some permanent investment in current assets. A growing firm can be thought of as having a permanent requirement for both current assets and long-term assets. This total asset requirement will exhibit balances over time reflecting (1) a secular growth trend, (2) a seasonal variation around the trend, and (3) unpredictable day-to-day and month-to-month fluctuations. This is depicted in Figure 26.4. (We have not tried to show the unpredictable day-to-day and month-to-month variations in the total asset requirement.)

Now let us look at how this asset requirement is financed. First, consider the strategy (Strategy F in Figure 26.5) where long-term financing covers more than the total asset requirement, even at seasonal peaks.

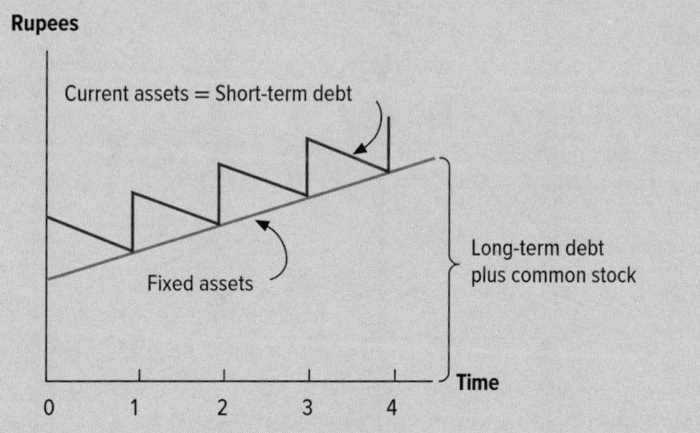

In an ideal world, net working capital is always zero because short-term assets are financed with short-term debt.

Figure 26.3 Financing Policy for an Ideal Economy

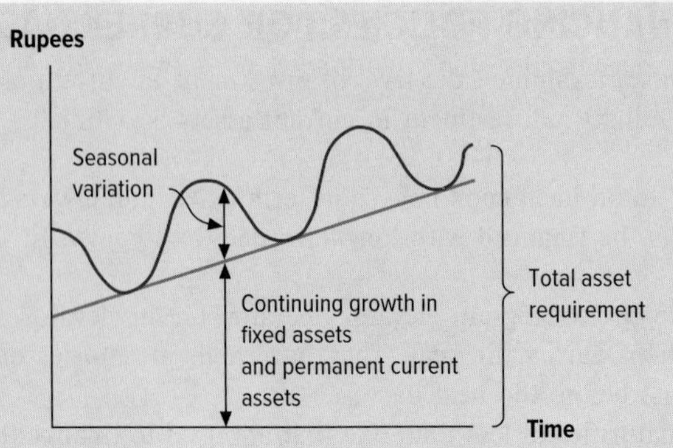

Figure 26.4 The Total Asset Requirement over Time

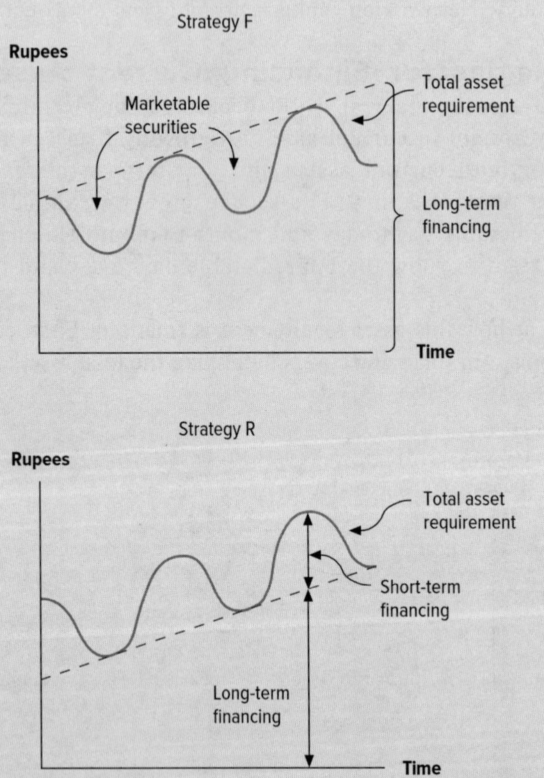

Strategy F always implies a short-term cash surplus and a large investment in cash and marketable securities.
Strategy R uses long-term financing for continuing asset requirements only, and short-term borrowing for seasonal variations.

Figure 26.5 Alternative Asset Financing Policies

The firm will have excess cash available for investment in marketable securities when the total asset requirement falls from peaks. Because this approach implies chronic short-term cash surpluses and a large investment in net working capital, it is considered a flexible strategy.

When long-term financing does not cover the total asset requirement, the firm must borrow short term to make up the deficit. This restrictive strategy is labeled Strategy R in Figure 26.5.

WHICH IS BEST?

What is the most appropriate amount of short-term borrowing? There is no definitive answer. Several considerations must be included in a proper analysis:

1. *Cash reserves*: The flexible financing strategy implies surplus cash and little short-term borrowing. This strategy reduces the probability that a firm will experience financial distress. Firms may not need to worry as much about meeting recurring short-term obligations. However, investments in cash and marketable securities are zero net present value investments at best.
2. *Maturity hedging*: Most firms finance inventories with short-term bank loans and fixed assets with long-term financing. Firms tend to avoid financing long-lived assets with short-term borrowing. This type of maturity mismatching would necessitate frequent financing and is inherently risky because short-term interest rates are more volatile than long-term rates.
3. *Term structure*: Short-term interest rates are normally lower than long-term interest rates. This implies that, on average, it is more costly to rely on long-term borrowing than on short-term borrowing.

26.4 Cash Budgeting

Excel Master coverage online

The cash budget is a primary tool of short-term financial planning. It allows the financial manager to identify short-term financial needs (and opportunities). It will tell the manager the required borrowing for the short term. It is the way of identifying the cash flow gap on the cash flow time line. The idea of the cash budget is simple: It records estimates of cash receipts and disbursements. We illustrate cash budgeting with the following example of Fun Toys.

EXAMPLE 26.3

Cash Collections All of Fun Toys' cash inflows come from the sale of toys. Cash budgeting for Fun Toys starts with a sales forecast for the next year by quarter:

	First Quarter	Second Quarter	Third Quarter	Fourth Quarter
Sales (in millions)	₹100	₹200	₹150	₹100

Fun Toys' fiscal year starts on July 1. Fun Toys' sales are seasonal and are usually very high in the second quarter due to holiday sales. But Fun Toys sells to department stores on credit and sales do not

(continued)

generate cash immediately. Instead, cash comes later from collections on accounts receivable. Fun Toys has a 90-day collection period and 100 percent of sales are collected the following quarter. In other words:

$$\text{Collections} = \text{Last quarter's sales}$$

This relationship implies that:

$$\text{Accounts receivable at end of last quarter} = \text{Last quarter's sales} \quad \textbf{(26.6)}$$

We assume that sales in the fourth quarter of the previous fiscal year were ₹100 million. From Equation 26.6 we know that accounts receivable at the end of the fourth quarter of the previous fiscal year were ₹100 million and collections in the first quarter of the current fiscal year are ₹100 million.

The first-quarter sales of the current fiscal year of ₹100 million are added to the accounts receivable, but ₹100 million of collections are subtracted. Therefore, Fun Toys ended the first quarter with accounts receivable of ₹100 million. The basic relation is:

$$\text{Ending accounts receivable} = \text{Starting accounts receivable} + \text{Sales} - \text{Collections}$$

Table 26.2 shows cash collections for Fun Toys for the next four quarters. Though collections are the only source of cash here, this need not always be the case. Other sources of cash could include sales of assets, investment income, and long-term financing.

Table 26.2 Sources of Cash (in millions)

	First Quarter	Second Quarter	Third Quarter	Fourth Quarter
Sales	₹100	₹200	₹150	₹100
Cash collections	−100	−100	−200	−150
Starting receivables	100	100	200	150
Ending receivables	₹100	₹200	₹150	₹100

CASH OUTFLOW

Next, we consider cash disbursements. They can be put into four basic categories, as shown in Table 26.3.

1. *Payments of accounts payable*: These are payments for goods or services, such as raw materials. These payments will generally be made after purchases. Purchases will depend on the sales forecast. In the case of Fun Toys, assume that:

$$\text{Payments} = \text{Last quarter's purchases}$$
$$\text{Purchases} = 1/2 \text{ next quarter's sales forecast}$$

2. *Wages, taxes, and other expenses*: This category includes all other normal costs of doing business that require actual cash expenditures.

3. *Capital expenditures*: These are payments of cash for long-lived assets. Fun Toys plans a major capital expenditure in the fourth quarter.
4. *Long-term financing*: This category includes interest and principal payments on long-term outstanding debt and dividend payments to shareholders.

The total forecast outflow appears in the last line of Table 26.3.

THE CASH BALANCE

The net cash balance appears in Table 26.4, and a large net cash outflow is forecast in the second quarter. This large outflow is not caused by an inability to earn a profit. Rather, it results from delayed collections on sales. This results in a cumulative cash shortfall of ₹30 million in the second quarter.

Fun Toys had established a minimum operating cash balance equal to ₹5 million to facilitate transactions, protect against unexpected contingencies, and maintain compensating balances at its commercial banks. This means that it has a cash shortfall in the second quarter equal to ₹35 million.

Table 26.3 Disbursement of Cash (in millions)

	First Quarter	Second Quarter	Third Quarter	Fourth Quarter
Sales	₹100	₹200	₹150	₹100
Purchases	100	75	50	50
Uses of cash				
Payments of accounts payable	50	100	75	50
Wages, taxes, and other expenses	20	40	30	20
Capital expenditures	0	0	0	100
Long-term financing expenses: interest and dividends	10	10	10	10
Total uses of cash	₹ 80	₹150	₹115	₹180

Table 26.4 The Cash Balance (in millions)

	First Quarter	Second Quarter	Third Quarter	Fourth Quarter
Total cash receipts	₹100	₹100	₹200	₹150
Total cash disbursements	80	150	115	180
Net cash flow	₹20	–₹50	₹85	–₹30
Cumulative excess cash balance	20	–30	55	25
Minimum cash balance	5	5	5	5
Cumulative finance surplus (deficit) requirement	₹15	–₹35	₹50	₹20

26.5 The Short-Term Financial Plan

Fun Toys has a short-term financing problem. It cannot meet the forecast cash outflows in the second quarter from internal sources. Its financing options include (1) unsecured bank borrowing, (2) secured borrowing, and (3) other sources.

UNSECURED LOANS

The most common way to finance a temporary cash deficit is to arrange a short-term unsecured bank loan. Firms that use short-term bank loans usually ask their bank for either a noncommitted or a committed *line of credit*. A *noncommitted* line of credit is an informal arrangement that allows firms to borrow up to a previously specified limit without going through the normal paperwork. The interest rate on the line of credit is usually set equal to the bank's prime lending rate plus an additional percentage.

Committed lines of credit are formal legal arrangements and usually involve a commitment fee paid by the firm to the bank (usually, the fee is approximately .25 percent of the total committed funds per year). For larger firms, the interest rate is often tied to the London Interbank Offered Rate (LIBOR), the Secured Overnight Financing Rate (SOFR), or to the bank's cost of funds, rather than the prime rate. Midsized and smaller firms often are required to keep compensating balances in the bank.

Compensating balances are deposits the firm keeps with the bank in low-interest or non-interest-bearing accounts. Compensating balances are commonly on the order of 2 to 5 percent of the amount used. By leaving these funds with the bank without receiving interest, the firm increases the effective interest earned by the bank on the line of credit. For example, if a firm borrowing ₹100,000 must keep ₹5,000 as a compensating balance, the firm effectively receives only ₹95,000. A stated interest rate of 10 percent implies yearly interest payments of ₹10,000 (= ₹100,000 × .10). The effective interest rate is 10.53 percent (= ₹10,000/₹95,000).

SECURED LOANS

Banks and other finance companies often require *security* for a loan. Security for short-term loans usually consists of accounts receivable or inventories.

Under **accounts receivable financing**, receivables are either *assigned* or *factored*. Under assignment, the lender not only has a lien on the receivables but also has recourse to the borrower (recourse implies the lender can collect assets or pursue legal action if the borrower fails to pay). Factoring involves the sale of accounts receivable. The purchaser, who is called a *factor*, must then collect on the receivables. The factor assumes the full risk of default on bad accounts.

As the name implies, an **inventory loan** uses inventory as collateral. Some common types of inventory loans are:

1. *Blanket inventory lien*: The blanket inventory lien gives the lender a lien against all the borrower's inventories.
2. *Trust receipt*: Under this arrangement, the borrower holds the inventory in trust for the lender. The document acknowledging the loan is called the trust receipt. Proceeds from the sale of inventory are remitted immediately to the lender.
3. *Field warehouse financing*: In field warehouse financing, a public warehouse company supervises the inventory for the lender.

Purchase order financing (or PO financing) is a popular form of factoring used by small and midsized companies. In a typical scenario, a small business receives a firm order from a customer but doesn't have sufficient funds to pay the supplier that manufactured the product. With PO financing, the factor pays the supplier. When the sale is completed and the seller is paid, the factor is repaid. A typical interest rate on purchase order factoring is 3.5 percent for the first 30 days, then 1.25 percent every 10 days after, an annual interest rate above 40 percent.

OTHER SOURCES

A variety of other sources of short-term funds are employed by corporations. The most important of these are the issuance of **commercial paper** and financing through **banker's acceptances**. Commercial paper consists of short-term notes issued by large, highly rated firms. Typically, these notes are of short maturity, ranging up to 270 days (beyond that limit, the firm must file a registration statement with the SEBI/SEC). Because the firm issues these directly and because it usually backs the issue with a special bank line of credit, the rate the firm obtains is often significantly below the prime rate the bank would charge it for a direct loan.

A banker's acceptance is an agreement by a bank to pay a sum of money. These agreements typically arise when a seller sends a bill or draft to a customer. The customer's bank *accepts* this bill and notes the acceptance on it, which makes it an obligation of the bank. In this way, a firm that is buying something from a supplier can effectively arrange for the bank to pay the outstanding bill. Of course, the bank charges the customer a fee for this service.

Purchase order financing is used when a company has a large purchase order. Fulfilling the purchase order can be problematic because the invoice will often not be paid for 60–90 days. Purchase order financing allows for the supplier to be paid upfront. A finance company essentially makes a loan, with the loan collateral based on the purchase order itself. Because of this structure, the lending requirements for purchase order financing are different from a traditional loan.

Recently, a new form of credit has become available, buy now, pay later (BNPL). In a BNPL transaction, a company purchases materials from a supplier. The supplier is paid relatively quickly by the BNPL finance company, often the same day. However, the purchasing company pays off the purchase over 90 days or so, often with no interest.

26.6 The Short–Term Financing Alternatives in India

In this section, we discuss the commonly available short-term financing alternatives for firms in India with a brief overview of them.

Overdraft It is the simplest and most popular form of Working Capital Finance. In this method of Working Capital Finance, the borrower is required to maintain a current account in the bank. The bank sanctions a limit up to which the borrower can overdraw. The overdrawn amount is repaid by depositing money back into the current account when the firm collects its receivables. The borrower pays the interest at the specified rate only when the amount is overdrawn. The most advantageous point of this form of finance is that the firm does not need to seek the approval of the bank every time it requires money.

Cash Credit It refers to a system of financing where a borrower is provided a credit limit, which he could utilize to run day-to-day business. The limits are decided based on the overall cash requirement of the business. The calculation is based on the total operating cycle and the gap between payments and receipt of cash.

Working Capital Loan This refers to the working capital limit of a borrower extended to him in the form of a short-term loan. For many Indian manufacturing companies, this loan component covers the permanent part of the working capital needed. In contrast, the cash credit component caters to the fluctuating part of the limit. The interest is charged on the loan component irrespective of utilization when such a term loan is availed.

Commercial Papers In India, Commercial Papers (CP) can be issued for a minimum period of 30 days to a maximum of 180 days. CPs are issued with a face value. However, the issue price is less than the face, but the redemption is at the face value. The discount on the issue is the interest portion. The discount is based on the amount of funds involved, the period, and the firm's credibility. CPs are issued in denominations of ₹5 lakh, but there is a cap of ₹25 lakh per investor. Reliance Industries is one of the active players in the CP market. Investors in CPs include mutual funds, institutional investors, and corporate bodies looking to place any short-term excess funds.

Inter-Corporate Deposits This is a popular method of financing the working capital needs. Companies facing a resource crunch generally borrow funds for a short period, not more than 6 months, from other companies having surplus liquidity. The interest rate on Inter-Corporate Deposits (ICDs) varies according to the amount of finance involved and the period for which finance is required. A financier arranges it, and, generally, the deal is struck based on the personal connections of the lenders, borrowers and financiers. One advantage of this system is that it can be arranged easily and quickly. Since ICDs are not covered under the Deposit Regulations of the Companies Act, there are no formal legal responsibilities involved.

Bills Financing Bills are negotiable instruments through which the buyer agrees to pay the drawer (payee) the value of the goods after a specified period. When an entrepreneur sells products on credit, they can draw a bill on the purchaser and, upon the purchaser's acceptance, obtain credit against the bill from their bank. Bank financing against bills can take the form of either discounting or purchasing. In discounting, the bank credits the client's account with the bill amount, minus a discount to cover interest charges for the remaining days until maturity, and then collects the bill as the client's agent. In purchasing, the bank takes ownership of the bill and claims it in its own right.

Factoring It is similar to invoice discounting, involving the sale of a business's accounts receivables to a third party at a price lower than their realizable value. This purchasing party is commonly known as a factor. Factoring services are offered by both banks and other financial institutions. Various types of factoring exist, including with recourse and without recourse, among others.

New and Unconventional Working Capital Loans in India

The following is a list of unconventional financing options available for small and medium enterprises from a large Indian bank:

(i) **Dealer financing:** It is structured as a direct line of credit to the dealers and channel partners specifically to be used for purchases from the company or as a revolving line for discounting bills raised by the company on the dealers.

(ii) **Trade receivables securitization:** This product leverages on the long-term relationships that companies have for clients or explicit off take agreements. The product can be structured as a long-term loan with escrow of the receivables originating from supplies to these customers or as a securitization of these future trade receivables.

(continued)

(iii) **Export receivables securitization:** Export receivables of a company can be used to raise funds internationally at rates which are better compared to those of a normal loan. For many companies in the developing countries like India, Pakistan, and Sri Lanka, the poor sovereign rating prevents access to international capital markets. Securitization of export receivables can be used to pierce this ceiling of sovereign rating.

(iv) **Brand financing:** This product creates a structure for funding the company against security of its brands. The structures could be a loan to the company with security of the brands, loan to a company to fund purchase of a brand, or a sale and lease back of the brands by the lender. Bankers reveal that this product has not been successful in the market.

(v) **Vendor financing:** This product can be structured as a direct line of credit to the vendors specifically to be used for supplies to the company or as revolving line for discounting bills raised by the vendors on the company.

(vi) **EPC contractor financing:** EPC financing is a product offered to clients who take up contracts / sub-contracts on various projects. It is not restricted to engineering and procurement type contracts, and can be useful for contract specific financing, with the primary recourse being the contract assets and with limited recourse to general balance sheet assets.

Working Capital Assessment Norms in India

Like many countries, the Reserve Bank of India mandated the method and quantum of short-term finance that a bank in India could grant to a firm until 1994. This control was exercised on the lines suggested by the Tandon committee. Depending on the size of credit required, the committee proposed three methods of lending, out of which the RBI accepted two methods for implementation:

- According to the first method, the borrower can be allowed maximum bank finance up to 75% of the working capital gap (working capital gap denotes the difference between total current assets required and the amount of finance available in the shape of current liabilities other than short term bank borrowings). The balance of 25% is to be brought by the borrower as a surplus of long-term funds over the long-term outlay.
- As per the second method, the borrower's contribution has to be 25% of the total current assets build-up instead of the working capital gap.

Other significant recommendations included – no-slip back in the current ratio, classification guidelines for current assets and current liabilities, identification of excess borrowing, and bifurcation of limits into loan and demand components. Usually, the borrower would not be allowed deviations from norms except in the case of bunched receipt of raw material, power cuts, strikes, transport delays, accumulation of finished goods due to non-availability of shipping space for exports, and buildup of finished goods stocks due to failure on the part of purchasers.

The post-liberalization of the economy brought major revisions to the norms for assessing working capital limits. All instructions relating to *maximum permissible bank finance* were withdrawn by RBI in 1997. The most important feature of the revised guidelines was the freedom given to the banks to apply. Each business has its peculiar characteristics, and not all businesses work alike. Tandon committees' main weakness was that they had specified the same set of parameters for judging all standard business units. This aspect was taken into account, and new limits for firms exceeding ₹1 crore were specified as follows:

The desired current ratio would be 1.33. The banks are free to apply 'Prudential Norms' to determine credit requirements while evaluating the proposal. However, the fact that Tandon Committee

(continued)

recommendations have been successful needs to be appreciated. So, the banks must consider the experiences gained under the Tandon Committee regime and suitably modify their assessment in tune with the new recommendations and the post-liberalization era. While assessing Working Capital requirements for assessing limits more than ₹1 crore, the following have to be taken care of:

- *Study of Past Performance and Establishing Past Trends*
- *Assessing the reasonableness of the projections for the Following Year*
- *Pruning down the built of Current Assets and Current Liabilities to a Need-Based Level.*

Further reading: *http://www.bankingindiaupdate.com and http://www.banknetindia.com*

RESEARCH IN EMERGING MARKET CONTEXT

According to a study by Baker et al. (2017), 55% of firms in India follow a moderate approach in financing their activities. This approach involves a trade-off between liquidity and profitability. The study shows that firms in India prefer an informal working capital management (WCM) approach and consider receivables as the most important component. Firms rely heavily on centralized cash management to manage inventory and use material requirement planning (MRP) and enterprise resource planning (ERP).

Chauhan and Banerjee (2018) found no evidence of systematic target-following behaviour of working capital for Indian manufacturing firms. The authors imply that even though optimal working capital might exist, emerging market firms may not be able to actively pursue it due to several financial constraints and managerial considerations. The results indicate that varying firm-specific characteristics do not influence the lack of target-following tendency, and it seems to be a systematic feature across firms in India.

Prasad et al. (2019) found that CEO duality, one of the nine board indicators of corporate governance, improves the working capital management of Indian non-financial firms. The study also suggests that additional information disclosure of the proactive indicators affects the WCM of Indian non-financial firms.

References

Baker, H. K., Kumar, S., Colombage, S., & Singh, H. P. (2017). Working capital management practices in India: survey evidence. *Managerial Finance*, *43*(3), 331–353.

Chauhan, G. S., & Banerjee, P. (2017). Financial constraints and optimal working capital–evidence from an emerging market. *International Journal of Managerial Finance*, *14*(1), 37–53.

Prasad, P., Sivasankaran, N., Saravanan, P., & Kannadhasan, M. (2019). Does corporate governance influence the working capital management of firms: evidence from India. *International Journal of Corporate Governance*, *10*(1), 42–80.

Summary and Conclusions

1. This chapter introduced the management of short-term finance. Short-term finance involves short-lived assets and liabilities. We traced and examined the short-term sources and uses of cash as they appear on the firm's financial statements. We saw how current assets and current liabilities arise in the short-term operating activities and the cash cycle of the firm. From an accounting perspective, short-term finance involves net working capital.

2. Managing short-term cash flows involves the minimization of costs. The two major costs are carrying costs (the interest and related costs incurred by overinvesting in short-term assets such as cash) and shortage costs (the cost of running out of short-term assets). The objective of managing short-term finance and short-term financial planning is to find the optimal trade-off between these costs.
3. In an ideal economy, a firm could perfectly predict its short-term uses and sources of cash and net working capital could be kept at zero. In the real world, net working capital provides a buffer that lets the firm meet its ongoing obligations. The financial manager seeks the optimal level of each of the current assets.
4. The financial manager can use the cash budget to identify short-term financial needs. The cash budget tells the manager what borrowing is required or what lending will be possible in the short term. The firm has a number of possible ways of acquiring funds to meet short-term shortfalls, including unsecured and secured loans.

Concept Questions

1. **Operating Cycle** What are some of the characteristics of a firm with a long operating cycle?
2. **Cash Cycle** What are some of the characteristics of a firm with a long cash cycle?
3. **Sources and Uses** For the year just ended, you have gathered the following information about the Holly Corporation:
   a. A ₹200 dividend was paid.
   b. Accounts payable increased by ₹500.
   c. Fixed asset purchases were ₹900.
   d. Inventories increased by ₹625.
   e. Long-term debt decreased by ₹1,200.

   Label each as a source or use of cash and describe its effect on the firm's cash balance.
4. **Cost of Current Assets** Grohl Manufacturing, Inc., has recently installed a just-in-time (JIT) inventory system. Describe the effect this is likely to have on the company's carrying costs, shortage costs, and operating cycle.
5. **Operating and Cash Cycles** Is it possible for a firm's cash cycle to be longer than its operating cycle? Explain why or why not.
6. **Shortage Costs** What are the costs of shortages? Describe them.
7. **Reasons for Net Working Capital** In an ideal economy, net working capital is always zero. Why might net working capital be positive in a real economy?

Use the following information to answer Questions 8–12: Last month, BlueSky Airline announced that it would stretch out its bill payments to 45 days from 30 days. The reason given was that the company wanted to "control costs and optimize cash flow." The increased payables period will be in effect for all of the company's 4,000 suppliers.

8. **Operating and Cash Cycles** What impact did this change in payables policy have on BlueSky's operating cycle? Its cash cycle?
9. **Operating and Cash Cycles** What impact did the announcement have on BlueSky's suppliers?
10. **Corporate Ethics** Is it ethical for large firms to unilaterally lengthen their payables periods, particularly when dealing with smaller suppliers?
11. **Payables Period** Why don't all firms increase their payables periods to shorten their cash cycles?
12. **Payables Period** BlueSky lengthened its payables period to "control costs and optimize cash flow." Exactly what is the cash benefit to BlueSky from this change?

Questions and Problems

BASIC (Questions 1–11)

1. **Changes in the Cash Account** Indicate the impact of the following corporate actions on cash, using the letter *I* for an increase, *D* for a decrease, or *N* when no change occurs.
   - **a.** A dividend is paid with funds received from a sale of debt.
   - **b.** Real estate is purchased and paid for with short-term debt.
   - **c.** Inventory is bought on credit.
   - **d.** A short-term bank loan is repaid.
   - **e.** Next year's taxes are prepaid.
   - **f.** Preferred stock is redeemed.
   - **g.** Sales are made on credit.
   - **h.** Interest on long-term debt is paid.
   - **i.** Payments for previous sales are collected.
   - **j.** The accounts payable balance is reduced.
   - **k.** A dividend is paid.
   - **l.** Production supplies are purchased and paid with a short-term note.
   - **m.** Utility bills are paid.
   - **n.** Cash is paid for raw materials purchased for inventory.
   - **o.** Marketable securities are sold.

2. **Cash Equation** Cori's Corp. has an equity value of ₹14,735. Long-term debt is ₹8,300. Net working capital, other than cash, is ₹2,850. Fixed assets are ₹18,440. How much cash does the company have? If current liabilities are ₹2,325, what are current assets?

3. **Changes in the Operating Cycle** Indicate the effect that the following will have on the operating cycle. Use the letter *I* to indicate an increase, the letter *D* for a decrease, and the letter *N* for no change.
   - **a.** Receivables average goes up.
   - **b.** Credit repayment times for customers are increased.
   - **c.** Inventory turnover goes from 3 times to 6 times.
   - **d.** Payables turnover goes from 6 times to 11 times.
   - **e.** Receivables turnover goes from 7 times to 9 times.
   - **f.** Payments to suppliers are accelerated.

4. **Changes in Cycles** Indicate the impact of the following on the cash and operating cycles, respectively. Use the letter *I* to indicate an increase, the letter *D* for a decrease, and the letter *N* for no change.
   - **a.** The terms of cash discounts offered to customers are made less favorable.
   - **b.** The cash discounts offered by suppliers are increased; thus, payments are made earlier.
   - **c.** An increased number of customers begin to pay in cash instead of with credit.
   - **d.** Fewer raw materials than usual are purchased.
   - **e.** A greater percentage of raw material purchases are paid for with credit.
   - **f.** More finished goods are produced for inventory instead of for order.

5. **Calculating Cash Collections** The Morning Jolt Coffee Company has projected the following quarterly sales amounts for the coming year:

	Q1	Q2	Q3	Q4
Sales	₹750	₹810	₹890	₹980

a. Accounts receivable at the beginning of the year are ₹335. The company has a 45-day collection period. Calculate cash collections in each of the four quarters by completing the following:

	Q1	Q2	Q3	Q4
Beginning receivables				
Sales				
Cash collections				
Ending receivables				

b. Rework part (a) assuming a collection period of 60 days.
c. Rework part (a) assuming a collection period of 30 days.

6. **Calculating Cycles** Consider the following financial statement information for the Newk Corporation: Calculate the operating and cash cycles. How do you interpret your answer?

Item	Beginning		Ending
Inventory	₹12,435		₹15,615
Accounts receivable	6,120		6,287
Accounts payable	7,930		9,140
Net sales		₹143,187	
Cost of goods sold		79,218	

7. **Calculating Payments** Sexton Products has projected the following sales for the coming year:

	Q1	Q2	Q3	Q4
Sales	₹740	₹665	₹785	₹890

Sales in the year following this one are projected to be 15 percent greater in each quarter.

a. Calculate payments to suppliers assuming that the company places orders during each quarter equal to 30 percent of projected sales for the next quarter. Assume that the company pays immediately. What is the payables period in this case?
b. Rework part (a) assuming a 90-day payables period.
c. Rework part (a) assuming a 60-day payables period.

8. **Calculating Payments** The Bandon Pine Corporation's purchases from suppliers in a quarter are equal to 75 percent of the next quarter's forecast sales. The payables period is 60 days. Wages, taxes, and other expenses are 20 percent of sales, and interest and dividends are ₹110 per quarter. No capital expenditures are planned.

Here are the projected quarterly sales:

	Q1	Q2	Q3	Q4
Sales	₹1,925	₹2,460	₹2,120	₹1,850

Sales for the first quarter of the following year are projected at ₹1,950. Calculate the company's cash outlays by completing the following:

	Q1	Q2	Q3	Q4
Payment of accounts				
Wages, taxes, and other expenses				
Long-term financing expenses (interest and dividends)				
Total				

9. **Calculating Cash Collections** The following is the sales budget for Lemonis, Inc., for the first quarter of 2022:

	January	February	March
Sales budget	₹185,000	₹203,000	₹225,000

Credit sales are collected as follows:

65 percent in the month of the sale.
20 percent in the month after the sale.
15 percent in the second month after the sale.

The accounts receivable balance at the end of the previous quarter was ₹81,000 (₹59,000 of which were uncollected December sales).

a. Compute the sales for November.
b. Compute the sales for December.
c. Compute the cash collections from sales for each month from January through March.

10. **Calculating the Cash Budget** Here are some important figures from the budget of Nashville Nougats, Inc., for the second quarter of 2022:

	April	May	June
Credit sales	₹357,400	₹342,500	₹402,600
Credit purchases	125,100	157,300	195,500
Cash disbursements			
Wages, taxes, and expenses	51,200	64,700	77,300
Interest	12,400	12,400	12,400
Equipment purchases	84,500	131,000	0

The company predicts that 5 percent of its credit sales will never be collected, 35 percent of its sales will be collected in the month of the sale, and the remaining 60 percent will be collected in the following month. Credit purchases will be paid in the month following the purchase.

In March 2022, credit sales were ₹245,300 and credit purchases were ₹149,300. Using this information, complete the following cash budget:

	April	May	June
Beginning cash balance	₹125,000		
Cash receipts			
Cash collections from credit sales			
Total cash available			
Cash disbursements			
Purchases			

	April	May	June
Wages, taxes, and expenses			
Interest			
Equipment purchases			
Total cash disbursements			
Ending cash balance			

11. **Sources and Uses** Here are the most recent balance sheets for Country Kettles, Inc. Excluding accumulated depreciation, determine whether each item is a source or a use of cash and the amount:

COUNTRY KETTLES, INC. Balance Sheet		
	2021	2022
Assets		
Cash	₹ 40,414	₹ 39,291
Accounts receivable	93,041	97,621
Inventories	80,925	94,833
Property, plant, and equipment	199,474	209,207
Less: Accumulated depreciation	60,830	66,419
Total assets	₹353,024	₹374,533
Liabilities and Equity		
Accounts payable	₹ 65,489	₹ 67,885
Accrued expenses	8,359	7,497
Long-term debt	34,074	37,180
Common stock	21,000	25,300
Accumulated retained earnings	224,102	236,671
Total liabilities and equity	₹353,024	₹374,533

INTERMEDIATE (Questions 12–15)

12. **Cash Budgeting** The sales budget for your company in the coming year is based on a quarterly growth rate of 10 percent, with the first-quarter sales projection at ₹165 million. In addition to this basic trend, the seasonal adjustments for the four quarters are, in millions, 0, –₹12, –₹6, and ₹18, respectively. Generally, 50 percent of the sales can be collected within the quarter and 45 percent in the following quarter; the rest of the sales are bad debt. The bad debts are written off in the second quarter after the sales are made. The beginning accounts receivable balance is ₹84 million. Assuming all sales are on credit, compute the cash collections from sales for each quarter.

13. **Calculating the Cash Budget** Wildcat, Inc., has estimated sales (in millions) for the next four quarters as follows:

	Q1	Q2	Q3	Q4
Sales	₹170	₹185	₹200	₹225

Sales for the first quarter of the year after this one are projected at ₹180 million. Accounts receivable at the beginning of the year were ₹71 million. Wildcat has a 45-day collection period.

Wildcat's purchases from suppliers in a quarter are equal to 45 percent of the next quarter's forecast sales, and suppliers are normally paid in 36 days. Wages, taxes, and other expenses run about 25 percent of sales. Interest and dividends are ₹14 million per quarter.

Wildcat plans a major capital outlay in the second quarter of ₹85 million. Finally, the company started the year with a ₹54 million cash balance and wishes to maintain a ₹30 million minimum balance.

a. Complete a cash budget for Wildcat by filling in the following:

WILDCAT, INC. Cash Budget (in millions)				
	Q1	**Q2**	**Q3**	**Q4**
Beginning cash balance	₹54			
Net cash inflow				
Ending cash balance				
Minimum cash balance	30			
Cumulative surplus (deficit)				

b. Assume that Wildcat can borrow any needed funds on a short-term basis at a rate of 3 percent per quarter and can invest any excess funds in short-term marketable securities at a rate of 2 percent per quarter. Prepare a short-term financial plan by filling in the following schedule. What is the net cash cost (total interest paid minus total investment income earned) for the year?

WILDCAT, INC. Short-Term Financial Plan (in millions)				
	Q1	**Q2**	**Q3**	**Q4**
Target cash balance	₹30			
Net cash inflow				
New short-term investments				
Income from short-term investments				
Short-term investments sold				
New short-term borrowing				
Interest on short-term borrowing				
Short-term borrowing repaid				
Ending cash balance				
Minimum cash balance	30			
Cumulative surplus (deficit)				
Beginning short-term investments				
Ending short-term investments				
Beginning short-term debt				
Ending short-term debt				

14. Cash Management Policy Rework Problem 13 assuming the following:

a. Wildcat maintains a minimum cash balance of ₹40 million.

b. Wildcat maintains a minimum cash balance of ₹20 million.

Based on your answers in parts (a) and (b), do you think the firm can boost its profit by changing its cash management policy? Should other factors be considered as well? Explain.

15. Short-Term Finance Policy Cleveland Compressor and Pnew York Pneumatic are competing manufacturing firms. Their financial statements are printed here.

a. How are the current assets of each firm financed?

b. Which firm has the larger investment in current assets? Why?

c. Which firm is more likely to incur carrying costs and which is more likely to incur shortage costs? Why?

CLEVELAND COMPRESSOR
Balance Sheet

	2021	2022
Assets		
Current assets:		
Cash	₹ 16,339	₹ 13,862
Net accounts receivable	25,778	23,887
Inventory	43,287	54,867
Total current assets	₹ 85,404	₹ 92,616
Fixed assets:		
Plant, property, and equipment	99,615	101,543
Less: Accumulated depreciation	(31,957)	(34,331)
Net fixed assets	₹ 67,658	₹ 67,212
Prepaid expenses	1,791	1,914
Other assets	13,138	13,052
Total assets	₹167,991	₹174,794
Liabilities and Equity		
Current liabilities:		
Accounts payable	₹ 4,893	₹ 6,494
Notes payable	11,617	10,483
Accrued expenses	7,227	7,422
Other taxes payable	8,460	9,924
Total current liabilities	32,197	34,323
Long-term debt	22,036	22,036
Total liabilities	₹ 54,233	₹ 56,359
Equity:		
Common stock	38,000	38,000
Paid-in capital	12,000	12,000
Retained earnings	63,758	68,435
Total equity	113,758	118,435
Total liabilities and equity	₹167,991	₹174,794

CLEVELAND COMPRESSOR Income Statement 2022	
Income:	
Sales	₹ 162,749
Other income	1,002
Total income	₹ 163,751
Operating expenses:	
Cost of goods sold	103,570
Selling and administrative expenses	28,495
Depreciation	2,274
Total expenses	₹ 134,339
Pretax earnings	29,412
Taxes	14,890
Net earnings	₹ 14,522
Dividends	₹ 9,845
Retained earnings	4,677

PNEW YORK PNEUMATIC Balance Sheet	2021	2022
Assets		
Current assets:		
Cash	₹ 3,307	₹ 5,794
Net accounts receivable	22,133	26,177
Inventory	44,661	46,463
Total current assets	₹70,101	₹78,434
Fixed assets:		
Plant, property, and equipment	31,116	31,842
Less: Accumulated depreciation	(18,143)	(19,297)
Net fixed assets	₹12,973	₹12,545
Prepaid expenses	688	763
Other assets	1,385	1,601
Total assets	₹85,147	₹93,343
Liabilities and Equity		
Current liabilities:		
Accounts payable	₹ 5,019	₹ 6,008
Bank loans	645	3,722
Accrued expenses	3,295	4,254
Other taxes payable	4,951	5,688
Total current liabilities	₹13,910	₹19,672
Equity:		
Common stock	20,576	20,576
Paid-in capital	5,624	5,624
Retained earnings	46,164	48,598
Less: Treasury stock	(1,127)	(1,127)
Total equity	₹71,237	₹ 73,671
Total liabilities and equity	₹85,147	₹ 93,343

PNEW YORK PNEUMATIC Income Statement 2022	
Income:	
Sales	₹91,374
Other income	1,067
Total income	₹92,441
Operating expenses:	
Cost of goods sold	59,042
Selling and administrative expenses	18,068
Depreciation	1,154
Total expenses	₹78,264
Pretax earnings	14,177
Taxes	6,838
Net earnings	₹ 7,339
Dividends	₹ 4,905
Retained earnings	2,434

Excel Master It! Problem

Heidi Pedersen, the treasurer for Wood Products, Inc., has been asked by Justin Wood, the president, to prepare a memo detailing the company's ending cash balance for the next three months. Below, you will see the relevant estimates for this period.

Excel Master coverage online

	July	August	September
Credit sales	₹1,275,800	₹1,483,500	₹1,096,300
Credit purchases	765,480	890,160	657,780
Cash disbursements:			
Wages, taxes, and expenses	348,600	395,620	337,150
Interest	29,900	29,900	29,900
Equipment	0	158,900	96,300
Credit sales collections:			
Collected in month of sale	35%		
Collected month after sale	60%		
Never collected	5%		
June credit sales:	₹ 1,135,020		
June credit purchases	₹ 681,012		
Beginning cash balance	₹ 425,000		

All credit purchases are paid in the month after the purchase.

a. Complete the cash budget for Wood Products for the next three months.

b. Heidi knows that the cash budget will become a standard report completed before each quarter. To help reduce the time preparing the report each quarter, she would like a memo with the appropriate information in Excel linked to the memo. Prepare a memo to Justin that will automatically update when the values are changed in Excel.

Mini Case

KEAFER MANUFACTURING WORKING CAPITAL MANAGEMENT

You have recently been hired by Keafer Manufacturing to work in its established treasury department. Keafer Manufacturing is a small company that produces highly customized cardboard boxes in a variety of sizes for different purchasers. Adam Keafer, the owner of the company, works primarily in the sales and production areas of the company. Currently, the company basically puts all receivables in one pile and all payables in another, and a part-time bookkeeper periodically comes in and attacks the piles. Because of this disorganized system, the finance area needs work, and that's what you've been brought in to do.

The company currently has a cash balance of ₹210,000 and it plans to purchase new machinery in the third quarter at a cost of ₹390,000. The purchase of the machinery will be made with cash because of the discount offered for a cash purchase. Adam wants to maintain a minimum cash balance of ₹135,000 to guard against unforeseen contingencies. All of Keafer's sales to customers and purchases from suppliers are made with credit and no discounts are offered or taken.

The company had the following sales each quarter of the year just ended:

	Q1	Q2	Q3	Q4
Gross sales	₹1,102,000	₹1,141,000	₹1,125,000	₹1,063,000

After some research and discussions with customers, you're projecting that sales will be 8 percent higher in each quarter next year. Sales for the first quarter of the following year are also expected to grow at 8 percent. You calculate that Keafer currently has an accounts receivable period of 57 days and an accounts receivable balance of ₹675,000. However, 10 percent of the accounts receivable balance is from a company that has just entered bankruptcy, and it is likely that this portion will never be collected.

You've also calculated that Keafer typically orders supplies each quarter in the amount of 50 percent of the next quarter's projected gross sales and suppliers are paid in 53 days, on average. Wages, taxes, and other costs run about 25 percent of gross sales. The company has a quarterly interest payment of ₹185,000 on its long-term debt. Finally, the company uses a local bank for its short-term financial needs. It currently pays 1.2 percent per quarter on all short-term borrowing and maintains a money market account that pays .5 percent per quarter on all short-term deposits.

Adam has asked you to prepare a cash budget and short-term financial plan for the company under the current policies. He also has asked you to prepare additional plans based on changes in several inputs.

1. Use the numbers given to complete the cash budget and short-term financial plan.
2. Rework the cash budget and short-term financial plan assuming Keafer changes to a minimum cash balance of ₹90,000.
3. Rework the sales budget assuming an 11 percent growth rate in sales and a 5 percent growth rate in sales. Assume a ₹135,000 target cash balance.
4. Assuming the company maintains its target cash balance at ₹135,000, what sales growth rate would result in a zero need for short-term financing? To answer this question, you may need to set up a spreadsheet and use the "Solver" function.

27

Cash Management

When news breaks about a firm's bank accounts, it's usually because the company is running low on cash. However, that wasn't the case for many companies in the middle of 2020. In June, the cash holdings at nonfinancial companies reached ₹2.1 trillion, a record amount. This amount was a 30 percent increase over the same period one year prior. Two of the largest cash balances were held by AT&T and Delta, each with over ₹15 billion. Of course, financial firms can hold even larger cash balances. For example, at the same time, investment bank Goldman Sachs held about ₹153 billion in cash. Why would firms like these hold such large quantities of cash? We examine cash management in this chapter to find out.

The basic objective of cash management is to keep the investment in cash as low as possible while still keeping the firm operating efficiently and effectively. This goal usually reduces to the dictum, "Collect early and pay late." Accordingly, we discuss ways of accelerating collections and managing disbursements.

In addition, firms must invest temporarily idle cash in short-term marketable securities. As we discuss in various places, these securities can be bought and sold in the financial markets. As a group, they have very little default risk, and most are highly marketable. There are different types of these so-called money market securities, and we discuss a few of the most important ones.

Please visit us at **rwjcorporatefinance.blogspot.com** for the latest developments in the world of corporate finance.

27.1 Reasons for Holding Cash

John Maynard Keynes, in his classic work *The General Theory of Employment, Interest, and Money*, identified three motives for liquidity: the speculative motive, the precautionary motive, and the transaction motive. We discuss these next.

THE SPECULATIVE AND PRECAUTIONARY MOTIVES

The **speculative motive** is the need to hold cash in order to be able to take advantage of bargain purchases that might arise, attractive interest rates, favorable exchange rate fluctuations (in the case of international firms), or other profitable investments that may arise.

For most firms, reserve borrowing ability and marketable securities can be used to satisfy speculative motives. Thus, there might be a speculative motive for maintaining liquidity, but not necessarily for holding cash per se. Think of it this way: If you have a credit card with a very large credit limit, then you can probably take advantage of any unusual bargains that come along without carrying any cash.

This is also true, to a lesser extent, for precautionary motives. The **precautionary motive** is the need for a safety supply to act as a financial reserve. Once again, there probably is a precautionary motive for maintaining liquidity. However, given that the value of money market instruments is relatively certain and that instruments such as T-bills are extremely liquid, there is no real need to hold substantial amounts of cash for precautionary purposes.

THE TRANSACTION MOTIVE

Cash is needed to satisfy the **transaction motive**, which is the need to have cash on hand to pay bills. Transaction-related needs come from the normal disbursement and collection activities of the firm. The disbursement of cash includes the payment of wages and salaries, trade debts, taxes, and dividends.

Cash is collected from product sales, the selling of assets, and new financing. The cash inflows (collections) and outflows (disbursements) are not perfectly synchronized, and some level of cash holdings is necessary to serve as a buffer.

As electronic funds transfers and other high-speed, "paperless" payment mechanisms continue to develop, even the transaction demand for cash may all but disappear. Even if it does, however, there will still be a demand for liquidity and a need to manage it efficiently.

COMPENSATING BALANCES

Compensating balances are another reason to hold cash. As we discussed in the previous chapter, cash balances are kept at commercial banks to compensate for banking services the firm receives. A minimum compensating balance requirement may impose a lower limit on the level of cash a firm holds.

COSTS OF HOLDING CASH

When a firm holds cash in excess of some necessary minimum, it incurs an opportunity cost. The opportunity cost of excess cash (held in currency or bank deposits) is the interest income that could be earned by the next best use, such as investment in marketable securities.

Given the opportunity cost of holding cash, why would a firm hold cash in excess of its compensating balance requirements? The answer is that a cash balance must be maintained to provide the liquidity necessary for transaction needs–paying bills. If the firm maintains too small a cash balance, it may run out of cash. If this happens, the firm may have to raise cash on a short-term basis. This could involve selling marketable securities or borrowing.

Activities such as selling marketable securities and borrowing involve various costs. As we've discussed, holding cash has an opportunity cost. To determine the appropriate cash balance, the firm must weigh the benefits of holding cash against these costs. We discuss this subject in more detail in the sections that follow.

CASH MANAGEMENT VERSUS LIQUIDITY MANAGEMENT

Before we move on, we should note that it is important to distinguish between true cash management and a more general subject, liquidity management. The distinction is a source of confusion because the word *cash* is used in practice in two different ways. First of all, it has its literal meaning, actual cash on hand. However, financial managers frequently use the word to describe a firm's holdings of cash along with its marketable securities, and marketable securities are sometimes called *cash equivalents*, or *near-cash*. In our discussion of various firms' cash positions at the beginning of the chapter, what was actually being described was their total cash and cash equivalents.

The distinction between liquidity management and cash management is straightforward. Liquidity management concerns the optimal quantity of liquid assets a firm should have on hand, and it is one particular aspect of the current asset management policies we discussed in our previous chapter. Cash management is much more closely related to optimizing mechanisms for collecting and disbursing cash, and it is this subject that we primarily focus on in this chapter.

In general, the firm needs to balance the benefits of holding cash to meet transactions and avoid insolvency against the opportunity costs of lower returns. A sensible cash management policy is to have enough cash on hand to meet the obligations that may arise in the ordinary course of business and to invest some excess cash in marketable securities for precautionary purposes. All other excess cash should be invested in the business or paid out to investors.[1]

27.2 Understanding Float

As you no doubt know, the amount of money you have according to your chequebook can be very different from the amount of money that your bank thinks you have. The reason is that some of the cheques you have written haven't yet been presented to the bank for payment. The same thing is true for a business. The cash balance that a firm shows on its books is called the firm's *book*, or *ledger*, *balance*. The balance shown in its bank account as available to spend is called its *available*, or *collected*, *balance*. The difference between the available balance and the ledger balance, called the **float**, represents the net effect of cheques in the process of *clearing* (moving through the banking system).

DISBURSEMENT FLOAT

Cheques written by a firm generate *disbursement float*, causing a decrease in the firm's book balance but no change in its available balance. Suppose Ganesha Motor Industries. (GMI), currently has ₹100,000 on deposit with its bank. On June 8, it buys some raw materials and pays with a cheque for ₹100,000. The company's book balance is immediately reduced by ₹100,000 as a result.

GMI's bank, however, will not find out about this cheque until it is presented to GMI's bank for payment on, say, June 14. Until the cheque is presented, the firm's available balance is greater than its book balance by ₹100,000. In other words, before June 8, GMI has a zero float:

$$\begin{aligned}\text{Float} &= \text{Firm's available balance} - \text{Firm's book balance}\\ &= ₹100{,}000 - 100{,}000\\ &= ₹0\end{aligned}$$

GMI's position from June 8 to June 14 is:

$$\begin{aligned}\text{Disbursement float} &= \text{Firm's available balance} - \text{Firm's book balance}\\ &= ₹100{,}000 - 0\\ &= ₹100{,}000\end{aligned}$$

[1]There is some evidence that corporate governance has some role in the cash holdings of U.S. firms. Jarrad Harford, Sattar A. Mansi, and William F. Maxwell, "Corporate Governance and Firm Cash Holdings in the US," *Journal of Financial Economics* 87, no. 3 (March 2008): 535-55, find that firms with weaker corporate governance systems have smaller cash reserves. The combination of excess cash and weak governance leads to more capital spending and more acquisitions.

While the cheque is clearing, GMI has a balance with the bank of ₹100,000. It can obtain the benefit of this cash during this period. For example, the available balance could be temporarily invested in marketable securities and thus earn some interest. We will return to this subject a little later.

COLLECTION FLOAT AND NET FLOAT

Cheques received by the firm create *collection float*. Collection float increases book balances but does not immediately change available balances. Suppose GMI receives a cheque from a customer for ₹100,000 on October 8. Assume, as before, that the company has ₹100,000 deposited at its bank and a zero float. It deposits the cheque and increases its book balance by ₹100,000 to ₹200,000. However, the additional cash is not available to GMI until its bank has presented the cheque to the customer's bank and received ₹100,000. This will occur on, say, October 14. In the meantime, the cash position at GMI will reflect a collection float of ₹100,000. We can summarize these events. Before October 8, GMI's position is:

$$\begin{aligned} \text{Float} &= \text{Firm's available balance} - \text{Firm's book balance} \\ &= ₹100{,}000 - 100{,}000 \\ &= ₹0 \end{aligned}$$

GMI's position from October 8 to October 14 is:

$$\begin{aligned} \text{Collection float} &= \text{Firm's available balance} - \text{Firm's book balance} \\ &= ₹100{,}000 - 200{,}000 \\ &= -₹100{,}000 \end{aligned}$$

In general, a firm's payment (disbursement) activities generate disbursement float and its collection activities generate collection float. The net effect–that is, the sum of the total collection and disbursement floats–is the net float. The net float at a point in time is the overall difference between the firm's available balance and its book balance. If the net float is positive, then the firm's disbursement float exceeds its collection float, and its available balance exceeds its book balance. If the available balance is less than the book balance, then the firm has a net collection float.

A firm should be concerned with its net float and available balance more than with its book balance. If a financial manager knows that a cheque written by the company will not clear for several days, that manager will be able to keep a lower cash balance at the bank than might be possible otherwise. This can generate a great deal of money.

Take the case of Walmart. The average daily sales of Walmart are about ₹1.50 billion. If Walmart's collections could be sped up by a single day, then Walmart could free up ₹1.50 billion for investing. At a relatively modest .01 percent daily rate, the interest earned would be on the order of ₹150,000 *per day.*

EXAMPLE 27.1

Staying Afloat Suppose you have ₹5,000 on deposit. One day, you write a cheque for ₹1,000 to pay for books and you deposit ₹2,000. What are your disbursement, collection, and net floats?

After you write the ₹1,000 cheque, you show a balance of ₹4,000 on your books, but the bank shows ₹5,000 while the cheque is clearing. The difference is a disbursement float of ₹1,000.

After you deposit the ₹2,000 cheque, you show a balance of ₹6,000. Your available balance doesn't rise until the cheque clears. This results in a collection float of –₹2,000. Your net float is the sum of the collection and disbursement floats, or –₹1,000.

Overall, you show ₹6,000 on your books. The bank shows a ₹7,000 balance, but only ₹5,000 is available because your deposit has not been cleared. The discrepancy between your available balance and your book balance is the net float (–₹1,000), and it is bad for you. If you write another cheque for ₹5,500, there may not be sufficient available funds to cover it and it might bounce. This is why financial managers have to be more concerned with available balances than book balances.

FLOAT MANAGEMENT

Float management involves controlling the collection and disbursement of cash. The objective of cash collection is to speed up collections and reduce the lag between the time customers pay their bills and the time the cash becomes available. The objective of cash disbursement is to control payments and minimize the firm's costs associated with making payments.

For a real-world example of float management services, visit **www.fiserv.com**.

Total collection or disbursement times can be broken down into three parts: mailing time, processing delay, and availability delay:

1. *Mailing time* is the part of the collection and disbursement processes during which cheques are trapped in the postal system.
2. *Processing delay* is the time it takes the receiver of a cheque to process the payment and deposit it in a bank for collection.
3. *Availability delay* refers to the time required to clear a cheque through the banking system.

Speeding up collections involves reducing one or more of these components. Slowing disbursements involves increasing one of them. We will describe some procedures for managing collection and disbursement times later. First, we need to discuss how float is measured.

Measuring Float The size of the float depends on both the rupees and the time delay involved. Suppose you mail a cheque for ₹500 to another state each month. It takes five days in the mail for the cheque to reach its destination (the mailing time) and one day for the recipient to get over to the bank (the processing delay). The recipient's bank holds out-of-state cheques for three days (availability delay). The total delay is $5 + 1 + 3 = 9$ days.

In this case, what is your average daily disbursement float? There are two equivalent ways of calculating the answer. First, you have a ₹500 float for nine days, so we say that the total float is 9 × ₹500 = ₹4,500. Assuming 30 days in the month, the average daily float is ₹4,500/30 = ₹150.

Alternatively, your disbursement float is ₹500 for nine days out of the month and zero the other 21 days (again, assuming 30 days in a month). Your average daily float is:

$$\begin{aligned}\text{Average daily float} &= (9 \times ₹500 + 21 \times ₹0)/30 \\ &= 9/30 \times ₹500 + 21/30 \times ₹0 \\ &= ₹4{,}500/30 \\ &= ₹150\end{aligned}$$

This means that, on an average day, your book balance is ₹150 less than your available balance, representing a ₹150 average disbursement float.

Things are only a little more complicated when there are multiple disbursements or receipts. To illustrate, suppose Concepts, Inc., receives two items each month as follows:

Amount	Processing and availability delay	Total float
Item 1: ₹5,000,000	× 9	= ₹45,000,000
Item 2: ₹3,000,000	× 5	= ₹15,000,000
Total: ₹8,000,000		₹60,000,000

The average daily float is equal to:

$$\text{Average daily float} = \frac{\text{Total float}}{\text{Total days}} = \frac{₹60 \text{ million}}{30} = ₹2 \text{ million} \qquad \textbf{(27.1)}$$

So, on an average day, there is ₹2 million that is uncollected and unavailable.

Another way to see this is to calculate the average daily receipts and multiply by the weighted average delay. Average daily receipts are:

$$\text{Average daily receipts} = \frac{\text{Total receipts}}{\text{Total days}} = \frac{₹8 \text{ million}}{30} = ₹266{,}666.67$$

Of the ₹8 million total receipts, ₹5 million, or ⅝ of the total, is delayed for nine days. The other ⅜ is delayed for five days. The weighted average delay is:

$$\begin{aligned}\text{Weighted average delay} &= (5/8) \times 9 \text{ days} + (3/8) \times 5 \text{ days}\\ &= 5.625 + 1.875\\ &= 7.50 \text{ days}\end{aligned}$$

The average daily float is:

$$\begin{aligned}\text{Average daily float} &= \text{Average daily receipts} \times \text{Weighted average delay}\\ &= ₹266{,}666.67 \times 7.50 \text{ days} \qquad (27.2)\\ &= ₹2 \text{ million}\end{aligned}$$

Some Details In measuring float, there is an important difference to note between collection and disbursement float. We defined *float* as the difference between the firm's available cash balance and its book balance. With a disbursement, the firm's book balance goes down when the cheque is *mailed*, so the mailing time is an important component in disbursement float. However, with a collection, the firm's book balance isn't increased until the cheque is *received*, so mailing time is not a component of collection float.

This doesn't mean that mailing time is not important. The point is that when collection *float* is calculated, mailing time should not be considered. As we will discuss, when total collection time is considered, the mailing time is a crucial component.

Also, when we talk about availability delay, how long it actually takes a cheque to clear isn't really crucial. What matters is how long we must wait before the bank grants availability—that is, use of the funds. Banks actually use availability schedules to determine how long a cheque is held based on time of deposit and other factors. Beyond this, availability delay can be a matter of negotiation between the bank and a customer. In a similar vein, for outgoing cheques, what matters is the date our account is debited, not when the recipient is granted availability.

Cost of the Float The basic cost of collection float to the firm is the opportunity cost of not being able to use the cash. At a minimum, the firm could earn interest on the cash if it were available for investing.

Suppose the Laddu Corporation has average daily receipts of ₹1,000 and a weighted average delay of three days. The average daily float is 3 × ₹1,000 = ₹3,000. This means that, on a typical day, there is ₹3,000 that is not earning interest. Suppose Laddu could eliminate the float entirely. What would be the benefit? If it costs ₹2,000 to eliminate the float, what is the NPV of doing so?

Figure 27.1 illustrates the situation for Laddu. Assume Laddu starts with a zero float. On a given day, Day 1, Laddu receives and deposits a cheque for ₹1,000. The cash will become available three days later on Day 4. At the end of the day on Day 1, the book balance is ₹1,000 more than the available balance, so the float is ₹1,000. On Day 2, the firm receives and deposits another cheque. It will collect three days later on Day 5. At the end of Day 2, there are two uncollected cheques, and the books show a ₹2,000 balance. The bank, however, still shows a zero available balance, so the float is ₹2,000. The same sequence occurs on Day 3, and the float rises to a total of ₹3,000.

On Day 4, Laddu again receives and deposits a cheque for ₹1,000. However, it also collects ₹1,000 from the Day 1 cheque. The change in book balance and the change in available balance are identical, +₹1,000, so the float stays at ₹3,000. The same thing happens every day after Day 4; the float therefore stays at ₹3,000 forever.[2]

Figure 27.2 illustrates what happens if the float is eliminated entirely on some Day *t* in the future. After the float is eliminated, daily receipts are still ₹1,000. The firm collects the same day because the float is eliminated, so daily collections are also still ₹1,000. As Figure 27.2 illustrates, the only change occurs the first day. On that day, as usual, Laddu collects ₹1,000 from the sale made three days before. Because

	Day 1	Day 2	Day 3	Day 4	Day 5	...
Beginning float	₹ 0	₹1,000	₹2,000	₹3,000	₹3,000	...
Cheques received	1,000	1,000	1,000	1,000	1,000	...
Cheques cleared (cash available)	− 0	− 0	− 0	− 1,000	− 1,000	...
Ending float	₹1,000	₹2,000	₹3,000	₹3,000	₹3,000	...

Figure 27.1 Buildup of the Float

	Day *t*	Day *t* + 1	Day *t* + 2	...
Beginning float	₹3,000	₹ 0	₹ 0	...
Cheques received	1,000	1,000	1,000	...
Cheques cleared (cash available)	− 4,000	− 1,000	− 1,000	...
Ending float	₹ 0	₹ 0	₹ 0	...

Figure 27.2 Effect of Eliminating the Float

[2]This permanent float is sometimes called the *steady-state float.*

the float is gone, it also collects on the sales made two days before, one day before, and that same day, for an additional ₹3,000. Total collections on Day *t* are ₹4,000 instead of ₹1,000.

What we see is that Laddu generates an extra ₹3,000 on Day *t* by eliminating the float. On every subsequent day, Laddu receives ₹1,000 in cash as it did before the float was eliminated. The only change in the firm's cash flows from eliminating the float is this extra ₹3,000 that comes in immediately. No other cash flows are affected, so Laddu is ₹3,000 richer.

In other words, the PV of eliminating the float is equal to the total float. Laddu could pay this amount out as a dividend, invest it in interest-bearing assets, or do anything else with it. If it costs ₹2,000 to eliminate the float, then the NPV is ₹3,000 – 2,000 = ₹1,000, so Laddu should do it.

EXAMPLE 27.2

Reducing the Float: Part I Instead of eliminating the float, suppose Laddu can reduce it to one day. What is the maximum Laddu should be willing to pay for this?

If Laddu can reduce the float from three days to one day, then the amount of the float will fall from ₹3,000 to ₹1,000. From our immediately preceding discussion, we see right away that the PV of doing this is equal to the ₹2,000 float reduction. Laddu should be willing to pay up to ₹2,000.

EXAMPLE 27.3

Reducing the Float: Part II Look back at Example 27.2. A large bank is willing to provide the float reduction service for ₹175 per year, payable at the end of each year. The relevant discount rate is 8 percent. Should Laddu hire the bank? What is the NPV of the investment? How do you interpret this discount rate? What is the most per year that Laddu should be willing to pay?

The PV to Laddu is still ₹2,000. The ₹175 would have to be paid out every year forever to maintain the float reduction, so the cost is perpetual and its PV is ₹175/.08 = ₹2,187.50. The NPV is ₹2,000 – 2,187.50 = –₹187.50; therefore, the service is not a good deal.

Ignoring the possibility of bounced cheques, the discount rate here corresponds most closely to the cost of short-term borrowing. The reason is that Laddu could borrow ₹1,000 from the bank every time a cheque was deposited and pay it back three days later. The cost would be the interest that Laddu would have to pay.

The most Laddu would be willing to pay is whatever charge results in an NPV of zero. This zero NPV occurs when the ₹2,000 benefit exactly equals the PV of the costs—that is, when ₹2,000 = C/.08, where C is the annual cost. Solving for C, we find that C = .08 × ₹2,000 = ₹160 per year.

Ethical and Legal Questions The cash manager must work with collected bank cash balances and not the firm's book balance (which reflects cheques that have been deposited but not collected). If this is not done, a cash manager could be drawing on uncollected cash as a source of funds for short-term investing. Most banks charge a penalty rate for the use of uncollected funds. However, banks may not have good enough accounting and control procedures to be fully aware of the use of uncollected funds. This raises some ethical and legal questions for the firm.

ELECTRONIC DATA INTERCHANGE AND CHEQUE 21: THE END OF FLOAT?

Electronic data interchange (EDI) is a general term that refers to the growing practice of direct, electronic information exchange between all types of businesses. One important use of EDI, often called *financial EDI*, or *FEDI*, is to electronically transfer financial information and funds between parties, thereby eliminating paper invoices, paper cheques, mailing, and handling. For example, it is now possible to arrange to have your checking account directly debited each month to pay many types of bills, and corporations now routinely directly deposit paycheque into employee accounts. More generally, EDI allows a seller to send a bill electronically to a buyer, thereby avoiding the mail. The buyer can then authorize payment, which also occurs electronically. Its bank then transfers the funds to the seller's account at a different bank. The net effect is that the length of time required to initiate and complete a business transaction is shortened considerably, and much of what we normally think of as float is sharply reduced or eliminated. As the use of FEDI increases (which it will), float management will evolve to focus much more on issues surrounding computerized information exchange and funds transfers.

One of the drawbacks of EDI (and FEDI) is that it is expensive and complex to set up. However, with the growth of the internet, a new form of EDI has emerged: e-commerce. For example, networking giant Cisco Systems books millions in orders each day on its website from resellers around the world. Firms also are linking to critical suppliers and customers via "extranets," which are business networks that extend a company's internal network. Because of security concerns and lack of standardization, don't look for e-commerce and extranets to eliminate the need for EDI anytime soon. In fact, these are complementary systems that will most likely be used in tandem as the future unfolds.

On October 29, 2004, the Cheque Clearing for the 21st Century Act, also known as Cheque 21, took effect. Before Cheque 21, a bank receiving a cheque was required to send the physical cheque to the customer's bank before payment could be made. Now a bank can transmit an electronic image of the cheque to the customer's bank and receive payment immediately. Previously, an out-of-state cheque might take three days to clear. But with Cheque 21, the clearing time is typically one day, and often a cheque can clear the same day it is written. Thus, Cheque 21 has significantly reduced float.

In India, RBI introduced a new cheque-clearing system in the year 2013, known as the Cheque Truncation System (CTS). It is a MICR-based clearing system that helps eliminate the physical movement of cheques. This has resulted in fewer days in clearing and reduced fraud and manual errors. Most importantly, it enables better reconciliation to banks.

27.3 Cash Collection and Concentration

From our previous discussion, we know that collection delays work against the firm. All other things being the same, a firm will adopt procedures to speed up collections and thereby decrease collection times. In addition, even after cash is collected, firms need procedures to funnel, or concentrate, that cash where it can be best used. We discuss some common collection and concentration procedures next.

COMPONENTS OF COLLECTION TIME

Based on our previous discussion, we can depict the basic parts of the cash collection process as follows. The total time in this process is made up of mailing time, cheque-processing delay, and the bank's availability delay.

The amount of time that cash spends in each part of the cash collection process depends on where the firm's customers and banks are located and how efficient the firm is in collecting cash.

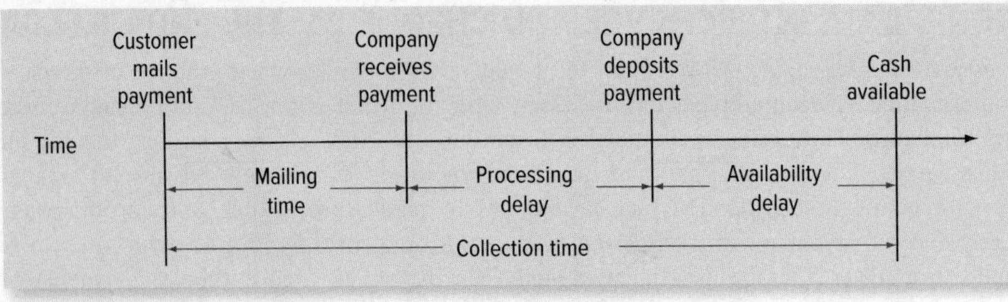

CASH COLLECTION

How a firm collects from its customers depends in large part on the nature of the business. The simplest case would be a business such as a restaurant chain. Most of its customers will pay with cash, credit card, or payment apps at the point of sale (this is called *over-the-counter collection*), so there is no problem with mailing delay. Normally, the funds will be deposited in a local bank and the firm will have some means (discussed later) of gaining access to the funds.

When some or all of the payments a company receives are cheques that arrive through the mail, all three components of collection time become relevant. The firm may choose to have all the cheques mailed to one location; more commonly, the firm might have a number of different mail collection points to reduce mailing times. Also, the firm may run its collection operation itself or might hire an outside firm that specializes in cash collection. We discuss these issues in more detail in the following pages.

Other approaches to cash collection exist. One that is becoming more common is the preauthorized payment arrangement. With this arrangement, the payment amounts and payment dates are fixed in advance. When the agreed-upon date arrives, the amount is automatically transferred from the customer's bank account to the firm's bank account, which sharply reduces or even eliminates collection delays. The same approach is used by firms that have online terminals, meaning that when a sale is rung up, the money is immediately transferred to the firm's accounts.

LOCKBOXES

When a firm receives its payments by mail, it must decide where the cheques will be mailed and how the cheques will be picked up and deposited. Careful selection of the number and locations of collection points can greatly reduce collection times. Many firms use special post office boxes called **lockboxes** to intercept payments and speed up cash collection.

Figure 27.3 illustrates a lockbox system. The collection process is started by customers mailing their cheques to a post office box instead of sending them to the firm. The lockbox is maintained by a local bank. A large corporation may actually maintain more than 20 lockboxes around the country.

In the typical lockbox system, the local bank collects the lockbox cheques several times a day. The bank deposits the cheques directly to the firm's account. Details of the operation are recorded (in some computer-usable form) and sent to the firm.

A lockbox system reduces mailing time because cheques are received at a nearby post office instead of at corporate headquarters. Lockboxes also reduce processing time because the corporation doesn't have to open the envelopes and deposit cheques for collection. All in all, a bank lockbox system should enable a firm to get its receipts processed, deposited, and cleared faster than if it were to receive cheques at its headquarters and deliver them itself to the bank for deposit and clearing.

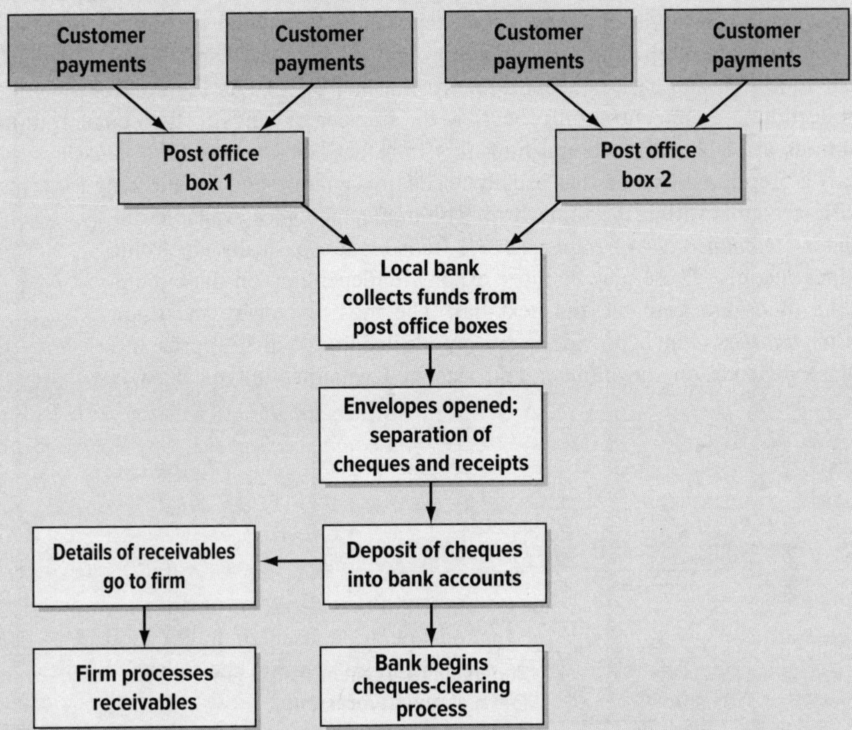

The flow starts when a corporate customer mails remittances to a post office box instead of to the corporation. Several times a day, the bank collects the lockbox receipts from the post office. The cheques are then put into the company bank accounts.

Figure 27.3 Overview of Lockbox Processing

Some firms have turned to what are called *electronic lockboxes* as an alternative to traditional lockboxes. In one version of an electronic lockbox, customers use the telephone or the internet to access their account–say, their credit card account at a bank–review their bill, and authorize payment without paper ever having changed hands on either end of the transaction. Clearly, an electronic lockbox system is far superior to traditional bill payment methods, at least from the biller's perspective. Look for systems like this to continue to grow in popularity.

CASH CONCENTRATION

As we discussed earlier, a firm will typically have a number of cash collection points; as a result, cash collections may end up in many different banks and bank accounts. From here the firm needs procedures to move the cash into its main accounts. This is called **cash concentration**. By routinely pooling its cash, the firm greatly simplifies its cash management by reducing the number of accounts that must be tracked. Also, by having a larger pool of funds available, a firm may be able to negotiate or otherwise obtain a better rate on any short-term investments.

In setting up a concentration system, firms will typically use one or more *concentration banks*. A concentration bank pools the funds obtained from local banks contained within some geographic region. Concentration systems are often used in conjunction with lockbox systems. Figure 27.4 illustrates how an integrated cash collection and cash concentration system might look. As Figure 27.4 illustrates, a key part of the cash collection and concentration process is the transfer of funds to the concentration bank. There are several options available for accomplishing this transfer. The cheapest is a *depository transfer cheque* (*DTC*), which is a preprinted cheque that usually needs no signature and is valid only for transferring funds between specific accounts within the same firm. The money becomes available one to two days later. *Automated clearinghouse* (*ACH*) transfers are basically electronic versions of paper cheques. These may be more expensive, depending on the circumstances, but the funds are available the next day. The most expensive means of transfer are *wire transfers,* which provide same-day availability. Which approach a firm will choose depends on the number and size of payments. A typical ACH

The Association for Financial Professionals has current info about cash management, **www.afponline.org**.

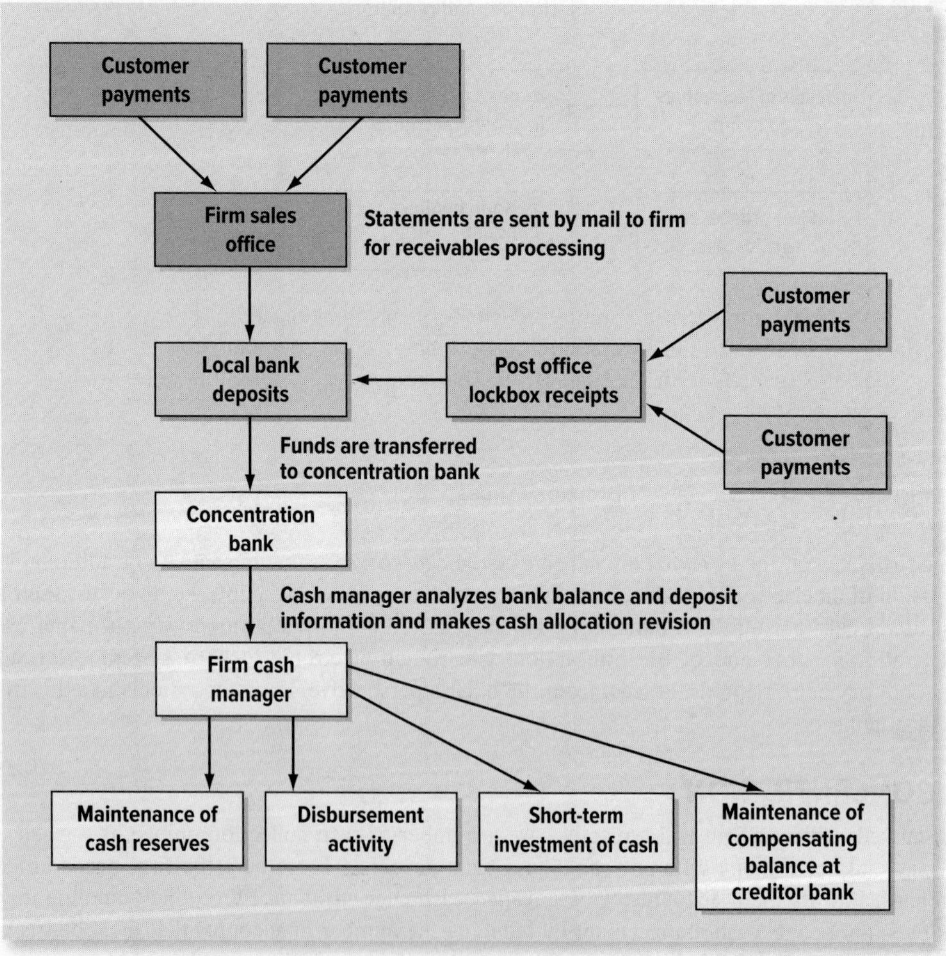

Figure 27.4 Lockboxes and Concentration Banks in a Cash Management System

transfer might be ₹200, whereas a typical wire transfer would be several million rupees. Firms with a large number of collection points and relatively small payments will choose the cheaper route, whereas firms that receive smaller numbers of relatively large payments may choose more expensive procedures.

In India, RBI monitors all wire transfers under Section 35A of the Banking Regulation Act, 1949. Two wire services are available 24×7×365 – Real Time Gross Settlement System (RTGS) or National Electronic Funds Transfer (NEFT). These are in addition to the proprietary wire systems of a few banks, such as State Bank Electronic Payment System (STEPS).

While NEFT and RTGS were introduced by RBI, IMPS (Immediate Mobile Payment Service) was introduced by National Payments Corporation of India (NPCI). In 2016, the introduction of UPI (Unified Payment Interface) revolutionized digital payments in India. Unlike NEFT, RTGS, and IMPS, UPI allows users to transfer money instantly between bank accounts using a single identifier, eliminating the need for bank account details or IFSC codes.

ACCELERATING COLLECTIONS: AN EXAMPLE

The decision of whether or not to use a bank cash management service incorporating lockboxes and concentration banks depends on where a firm's customers are located and the speed of the Indian postal system. Suppose Aditya Industries, located in Indore, is considering a lockbox system. Its collection delay is currently eight days.

Atlantic does business in the southwestern part of the country (Karnataka, Maharashtra, and Andhra Pradesh). The proposed lockbox system would be located in Hyderabad and operated by Canara Bank. Canara Bank has analyzed Atlantic's cash-gathering system and has concluded that it can decrease collection time by two days. Specifically, the bank has come up with the following information on the proposed lockbox system:

$$\begin{aligned} \text{Reduction in mailing time} &= 1.0 \text{ day} \\ \text{Reduction in clearing time} &= .5 \text{ days} \\ \text{Reduction in firm processing time} &= .5 \text{ days} \\ \text{Total} &= 2.0 \text{ days} \end{aligned}$$

The following is also known:

$$\begin{aligned} \text{Daily interest on Treasury bills} &= .025\% \\ \text{Average number of daily payments to lockboxes} &= 2{,}000 \\ \text{Average size of payment} &= ₹600 \end{aligned}$$

The cash flows for the current collection operation are shown in the following cash flow time chart:

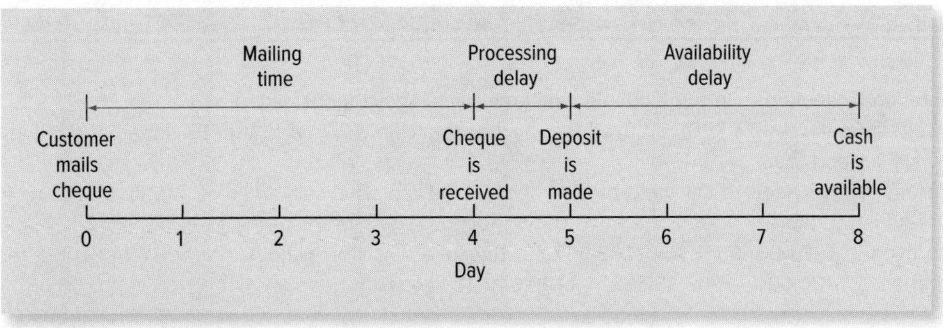

The cash flows for the lockbox collection operation will be as follows:

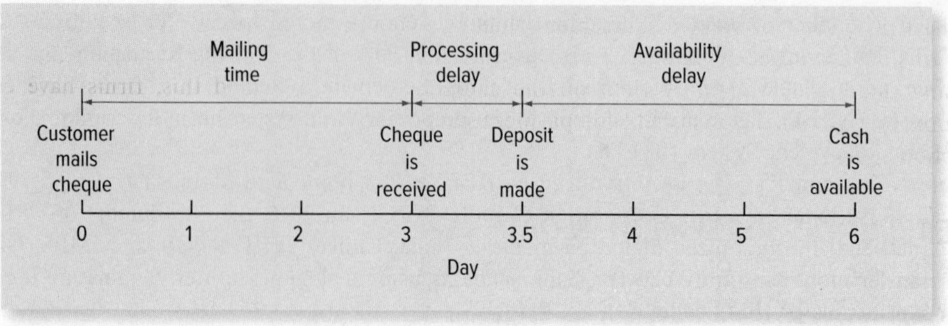

Canara Bank has agreed to operate this lockbox system for a fee of 25 cents per cheque processed. Should Atlantic give the go-ahead?

We first need to determine the benefit of the system. The average daily collections from the southwestern region are ₹1.2 million (= 2,000 × ₹600). The collection time will be decreased by two days, so the lockbox system will increase the collected bank balance by ₹1.2 million × 2 = ₹2.4 million. In other words, the lockbox system releases ₹2.4 million to the firm by reducing processing, mailing, and clearing time by two days. From our earlier discussion, we know that this ₹2.4 million is the PV of the proposal.

To calculate the NPV, we need to determine the PV of the costs. There are several different ways to proceed. First, at 2,000 cheques per day and ₹.25 per cheque, the daily cost is ₹500. This cost will be incurred every day forever. At an interest rate of .025 percent per day, the PV is therefore ₹500/.00025 = ₹2 million. The NPV is ₹2.4 million − 2 million = ₹400,000, and the system appears to be desirable.

Alternatively, Atlantic could invest the ₹2.4 million at .025 percent per day. The interest earned would be ₹2.4 million × .00025 = ₹600 per day. The cost of the system is ₹500 per day, so running it obviously generates a profit in the amount of ₹100 per day. The PV of ₹100 per day forever is ₹100/.00025 = ₹400,000, as we calculated before.

Finally, each cheque is for ₹600 and is available two days sooner if the system is used. The interest on ₹600 for two days is 2 × ₹600 × .00025 = ₹.30. The cost is 25 cents per cheque, so Atlantic makes a nickel (= ₹.30 − .25) on every cheque. With 2,000 cheques per day, the profit is ₹.05 × 2,000 cheques = ₹100 per day, as we previously calculated.

EXAMPLE 27.4

Accelerating Collections In our example concerning the Aditya Industries' proposed lockbox system, suppose Canara Bank wants a ₹20,000 fixed fee (paid annually) in addition to the 25 cents per cheque. Is the system still a good idea?

To answer, we need to calculate the PV of the fixed fee. The daily interest rate is .025 percent. The annual rate is therefore $1.00025^{365} - 1 = .09553$, or 9.553%. The PV of the fixed fee (which is paid each year forever) is ₹20,000/.09553 = ₹209,357.52. Because the NPV without the fee is ₹400,000, the NPV with the fee is ₹400,000 − 209,357.52 = ₹190,642.48. It's still a good idea.

27.4 Managing Cash Disbursements

From the firm's point of view, disbursement float is desirable, so the goal in managing disbursement float is to slow down disbursements. To do so, the firm may develop strategies to increase mail float, processing float, and availability float on the cheques it writes. Beyond this, firms have developed procedures for minimizing cash held for payment purposes. We discuss the most common of these in this section.

INCREASING DISBURSEMENT FLOAT

As we have seen, slowing down payments comes from the time involved in mail delivery, cheque processing, and collection of funds. Disbursement float can be increased by writing a cheque on a geographically distant bank. For example, a Chandigarh supplier might be paid with cheques drawn on a Hyderabad bank. This will increase the time required for the cheque to clear through the banking system. Mailing cheques from remote post offices is another way firms slow down disbursement.

Tactics for maximizing disbursement float are debatable on both ethical and economic grounds. First, as we discuss in some detail in the next chapter, payment terms frequently offer a substantial discount for early payment. The discount is usually much larger than any possible savings from "playing the float game." In such cases, increasing mailing time will be of no benefit if the recipient dates payments based on the date received (as is common) as opposed to the postmark date.

Beyond this, suppliers are unlikely to be fooled by attempts to slow down disbursements. The negative consequences of poor relations with suppliers can be costly. In broader terms, intentionally delaying payments by taking advantage of mailing times or unsophisticated suppliers may amount to avoiding paying bills when they are due–an unethical business procedure.

CONTROLLING DISBURSEMENTS

We have seen that maximizing disbursement float is probably a poor business practice. However, a firm will still wish to tie up as little cash as possible in disbursements. Firms have therefore developed systems for efficiently managing the disbursement process. The general idea in such systems is to have no more than the minimum amount necessary to pay bills on deposit in the bank. We discuss some approaches to accomplishing this goal next.

Zero-Balance Accounts With a **zero-balance account (ZBA)** system, the firm, in cooperation with its bank, maintains a master account and a set of subaccounts. When a cheque written on one of the subaccounts must be paid, the necessary funds are transferred in from the master account. Figure 27.5 illustrates how such a system might work. In this case, the firm maintains two disbursement accounts, one for suppliers and one for payroll. As shown, if the firm does not use zero-balance accounts, then each of these accounts must have a safety stock of cash to meet unanticipated demands. If the firm does use zero-balance accounts, then it can keep one safety stock in a master account and transfer the funds to the two subsidiary accounts as needed. The key is that the total amount of cash held as a buffer is smaller under the zero-balance arrangement, which frees up cash to be used elsewhere.

Controlled Disbursement Accounts With a **controlled disbursement account** system, almost all payments that must be made in a given day are known in the morning. The bank informs the firm of the total, and the firm transfers (usually by wire) the amount needed.

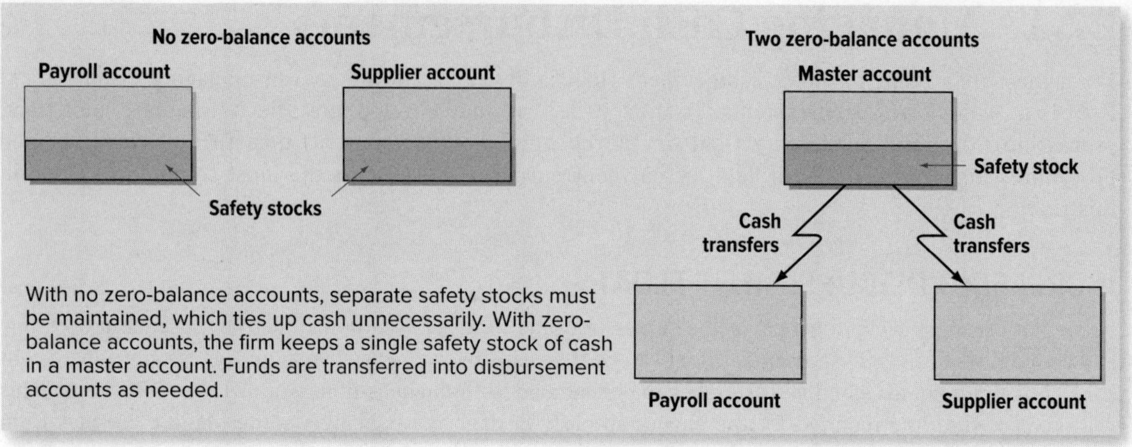

Figure 27.5 Zero-Balance Accounts

27.5 Investing Idle Cash

If a firm has a temporary cash surplus, it can invest in short-term securities. As we have mentioned at various times, the market for short-term financial assets is called the *money market*. The maturity of short-term financial assets that trade in the money market is one year or less.

Most large firms manage their own short-term financial assets, carrying out transactions through banks and dealers. Some large firms and many small firms use money market mutual funds. These are funds that invest in short-term financial assets for a management fee. The management fee is compensation for the professional expertise and diversification provided by the fund manager.

Among the many money market mutual funds, some specialize in corporate customers. In addition, banks offer arrangements in which the bank takes all excess available funds at the close of each business day and invests them for the firm.

TEMPORARY CASH SURPLUSES

Firms have temporary cash surpluses for various reasons. Two of the most important are the financing of seasonal or cyclical activities of the firm and the financing of planned or possible expenditures.

Seasonal or Cyclical Activities Some firms have a predictable cash flow pattern. They have surplus cash flows during part of the year and deficit cash flows the rest of the year. For example, Golf Galaxy, a retail golf store, has a seasonal cash flow pattern influenced by the golf season.

A firm such as Golf Galaxy may buy marketable securities when surplus cash flows occur and sell marketable securities when deficits occur. Of course, bank loans are another short-term financing device. The use of bank loans and marketable securities to meet temporary financing needs is illustrated in Figure 27.6. In this case, the firm is following a compromise working capital policy in the sense we discussed in the previous chapter.

Planned or Possible Expenditures Firms frequently accumulate temporary investments in marketable securities to provide the cash for a plant construction program, dividend payment, or other large

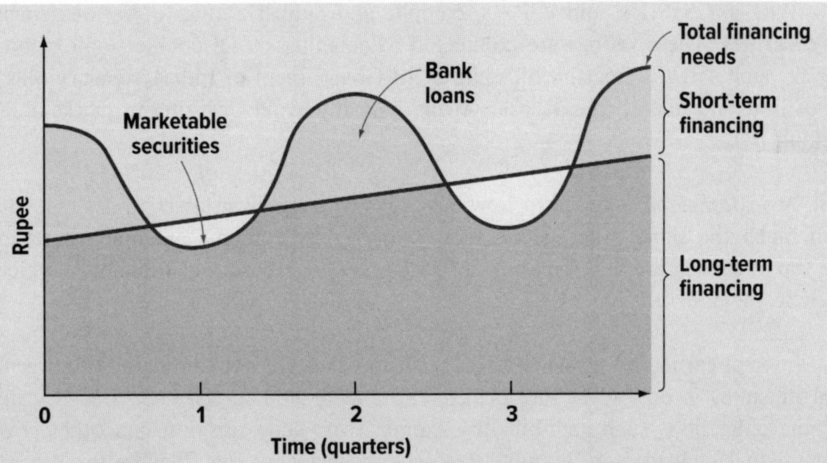

Time 1: A surplus cash flow exists. Seasonal demand for assets is low. The surplus cash flow is invested in short-term marketable securities.

Time 2: A deficit cash flow exists. Seasonal demand for assets is high. The financial deficit is financed by selling marketable securities and by bank borrowing.

Figure 27.6 Seasonal Cash Demands

expenditure. Thus, firms may issue bonds and stocks before the cash is needed, investing the proceeds in short-term marketable securities and then selling the securities to finance the expenditures. Also, firms may face the possibility of having to make a large cash outlay. An obvious example would involve the possibility of losing a large lawsuit. Firms may build up cash surpluses against such a contingency.

CHARACTERISTICS OF SHORT-TERM SECURITIES

Given that a firm has some temporarily idle cash, a variety of short-term securities are available for investing. The most important characteristics of these short-term marketable securities are their maturity, default risk, marketability, and taxability.

Maturity From Chapter 8, we know that for a given change in the level of interest rates, the prices of longer-maturity securities will change more than those of shorter-maturity securities. As a consequence, firms that invest in long-term securities are accepting greater risk than firms that invest in securities with short-term maturities.

We called this type of risk *interest rate risk*. Firms often limit their investments in marketable securities to those maturing in less than 90 days to avoid the risk of losses in value from changing interest rates. Of course, the expected return on securities with short-term maturities is usually less than the expected return on securities with longer maturities.

Default Risk *Default risk* refers to the probability that interest and principal will not be paid in the promised amounts on the due dates (or will not be paid at all). In Chapter 8, we observed that various financial reporting agencies, such as Moody's Investors Service and Standard and Poor's, compile and in

India such as CARE's, CRISIL's, and ICRA's, compile and publish ratings of various corporate and other publicly held securities. These ratings are connected to default risk. Of course, some securities have negligible default risk, such as U.S. Treasury bills and (GoI Government of India) Treasury bills in India. Given the purposes of investing idle corporate cash, firms typically avoid investing in marketable securities with significant default risk.

Marketability *Marketability* refers to how easy it is to convert an asset to cash, so marketability and liquidity mean much the same thing. Some money market instruments are much more marketable than others. At the top of the list are U.S. Treasury in USA and GoI Treasury in India bills, which can be bought and sold very cheaply and very quickly.

Taxability Interest earned on money market securities that are not some kind of government obligation (either federal or state) is taxable at the local, state, and federal levels. U.S. Treasury in USA and GoI Treasury in India obligations such as T-bills are exempt from state taxation, but other government-backed debt is not. Municipal securities are exempt from federal taxes, but they may be taxed at the state level.

SOME DIFFERENT TYPES OF MONEY MARKET SECURITIES

Money market securities are generally highly marketable and short term. They usually have low risk of default. They are issued by the U.S. government in USA and Government of India in India (e.g., U.S. Treasury in USA and GoI Treasury in India bills), domestic and foreign banks (e.g., certificates of deposit), and business corporations (e.g., commercial paper). There are many types in all, and we illustrate only a few of the most common here.

U.S. Treasury in USA and GoI Treasury in India bills are obligations of the U.S. government in USA and Government of India in India that mature in 30, 90, or 180 days. Bills are sold by auction every week.

Short-term tax-exempts are short-term securities issued by states, municipalities, local housing agencies, and urban renewal agencies. Because these are all considered municipal securities, they are exempt from federal taxes. RANs, BANs, and TANs, for example, are revenue, bond, and tax anticipation notes, respectively. In other words, they represent short-term borrowing by municipalities in anticipation of cash receipts.

Short-term tax-exempts have more default risk than U.S. Treasury in USA and GoI Treasury in India issues and are less marketable. Because the interest is exempt from federal income tax, the pretax yield on tax-exempts is lower than that on comparable securities such as Treasury bills. Also, corporations face restrictions on holding tax-exempts as investments.

Commercial paper consists of short-term securities issued by finance companies, banks, and corporations. Typically, commercial paper is unsecured. Maturities range from a few weeks to 270 days.

There is no especially active secondary market in commercial paper. As a consequence, the marketability can be low; however, firms that issue commercial paper often will repurchase it directly before maturity. The default risk of commercial paper depends on the financial strength of the issuer. Moody's and S&P publish in USA and CARE's and CRISIL's publish quality ratings for commercial paper. These ratings are similar to the bond ratings we discussed in Chapter 8.

Check out short-term rates online at **www.bloomberg.com**.

Certificates of deposit (CDs) are short-term loans to commercial banks. The most common are jumbo CDs–those in excess of ₹100,000. There are active markets in CDs of 3-month, 6-month, 9-month, and 12-month maturities.

Repurchase agreements (repos) are sales of government securities (e.g., U.S. Treasury in USA and GoI Treasury in India bills) by a bank or securities dealer with an agreement to repurchase. Typically, an investor buys some Treasury securities from a bond dealer and simultaneously agrees to sell them back at a later date at a specified higher price. Repurchase agreements usually involve a very short term–overnight to a few days.

A corporate stockholder receiving either common or preferred dividends is granted a 50 percent (or more) dividend exclusion (reduced from 70 percent or more prior to the 2017 Tax Cuts and Jobs Act). This tax break creates a strong incentive for firms to invest idle cash in preferred stock, which offer relatively high dividend yields. A problem is that the dividend is fixed with ordinary preferred stock, so the price can fluctuate more than is desirable in a short-term investment. Money market preferred stock (also known as auction rate preferred) features a floating dividend. The dividend is reset fairly often (usually every 49 days); so this type of preferred has much less price volatility than ordinary preferred, and it is a popular short-term investment.

A NOTE ON MONEY MARKET INSTRUMENTS IN INDIA[3]

The money market is where liquid and short-term borrowing and lending occur. The lending of funds in this market constitutes short-term investments. Ideally, all bank notes, current accounts, cheque accounts, etc. belong to the money market. The short term is the term from the date when trading takes place to the date of redemption of the loan represented by the instrument (commonly referred to as the "term to maturity").

There are two types of instruments issued and traded in the money market, namely:

- **Instruments Paying Interest**: Examples of the same include Negotiable certificates of deposit; Short-term government securities; and Instruments issued by private sector (with a short-maturity).
- **Instruments Not Paying Interest**: Examples of the same include Bankers' Acceptances (Bas); Treasury bills (TBs); Commercial paper.

We elaborate below a few instruments that are quite popular money market instruments among large Indian firms:

- **Certificate of Deposit (CD)/Commercial Paper (CP)**: A negotiable interest-bearing debt of specific maturity, usually less than a year, for large sums. A CD/CP is a liquid instrument, that is, it can be traded in the secondary market. In India, a CD is issued by financial institutions and banks. On the other hand, CP is issued by any non-financial firm in India.
- **Interest rate swap**: An Interest Rate Swap (IRS) is a financial contract between two parties exchanging or swapping a stream of interest payments for a 'notional principal' amount on multiple occasions during a specified period. Such contracts generally involve exchanging a 'fixed to floating rate of interest' or 'floating to floating rate of interest'.
- **Forward Rate Agreement**: A Forward Rate Agreement (FRA) is a financial contract between two parties to exchange interest payments for a 'notional principal' amount on the settlement date for a specified period from the start date to the maturity date.
- **Intercorporate Deposit**: A short-term deposit made by one company with another. The period usually does not exceed six months and could be as short as one or a few days. These deposits are essentially 'Brokered Deposits', given the extensive involvement of brokers.

[3]Further readings: http://www.eagletraders.com/books/afm/afm3.html, www.debtonnet.com/cp/cpguideline.pdf,http://www.sbidfhi.com/xready.html, and http://pnbgilts.com/icds1.asp

RESEARCH IN EMERGING MARKET CONTEXT

Ranajee and Pathak (2020) report that cash levels are significantly higher during crisis periods for Indian firms. Promoter holding is observed to be a strong predictor of CCH. A firm's age and growth prospects do not determine cash levels for Indian firms. Business group-affiliated firms are less likely to engage in cash accumulation as opposed to firms that are large and financially constrained and have high promoter stakes.

Gupta and Bedi (2020) find that Indian corporate cash holdings and promoter ownership are negatively related to varying relations across different types of promoters. Cash holdings have a U-shaped relation with promoter ownership of foreign corporates. The authors also find a negative relation with non-promoter corporate ownership.

Chauhan, Pathak, and Kumar (2018) examined the effect of bank-appointed directors on CCH and found that firms with bank-appointed directors accumulate less cash. The bank-appointed directors have been found to reduce the sensitivity of investment cash flow. Importantly, they find that the benefits of a banker on a corporate board are concentrated only in standalone firms' CCH.

Dasgupta and Pathak's (2021) results support the idea of the "theory of law and finance" that legal tradition is a key factor determining corporate behaviour and policy. In particular, they observe that firms operating in civil law systems hold significantly higher cash than their peers from common law systems. In developed countries where civil law tradition prevails, firms hold reasonably higher cash, and contrarily, if the firm belongs to a high investor protection country with civil law traditions, the cash holdings get substantially reduced.

References

Chauhan, Y., Pathak, R., & Kumar, S. (2018). Do bank-appointed directors affect corporate cash holding?. *International Review of Economics & Finance*, *53*, 39–56.

Dasgupta, R., & Pathak, R. (2021). Does the legal origin affect corporate cash holding?. *International Journal of Emerging Markets*, *16*(8), 1964–1983.

Gupta, C. P., & Bedi, P. (2020). Corporate cash holdings and promoter ownership. *Emerging Markets Review*, *44*, 100718.

Pathak, R. & Ranajee, R. (2020). Earnings quality and corporate payout policy linkages: An Indian context. *The North American Journal of Economics and Finance*, *51*, 100855.

Summary and Conclusions

In this chapter, we have examined cash and liquidity management. We saw the following:

1. A firm holds cash to conduct transactions and to compensate banks for the various services they render.
2. The difference between a firm's available balance and its book balance is the firm's net float. The float reflects the fact that some cheques have not cleared and are thus uncollected. The financial manager always must work with collected cash balances and not with the company's book balance. To do otherwise is to use the bank's cash without the bank knowing it, which raises ethical and legal questions.
3. The firm can use a variety of procedures to speed up the collection of cash and slow down the disbursement of payments. Some methods to speed up the collection are the use of lockboxes, concentration banking, and wire transfers.

4. Because of seasonal and cyclical activities, to help finance planned expenditures, or as a contingency reserve, firms temporarily hold a cash surplus. The money market offers a variety of possible vehicles for "parking" this idle cash.

Concept Questions

1. **Cash Management** Is it possible for a firm to have too much cash? Why would shareholders care if a firm accumulates large amounts of cash?
2. **Cash Management** What options are available to a firm if it believes it has too much cash? How about too little?
3. **Agency Issues** Are stockholders and creditors likely to agree on how much cash a firm should keep on hand?
4. **Cash Management versus Liquidity Management** What is the difference between cash management and liquidity management?
5. **Short-Term Investments** Why is a preferred stock with a dividend tied to short-term interest rates an attractive short-term investment for corporations with excess cash?
6. **Collection and Disbursement Floats** Which would a firm prefer: a net collection float or a net disbursement float? Why?
7. **Float** Suppose a firm has a book balance of ₹2 million. At the automatic teller machine (ATM), the cash manager finds out that the bank balance is ₹2.5 million. What is the situation here? If this is an ongoing situation, what ethical dilemma arises?
8. **Short-Term Investments** For each of the short-term marketable securities given here, provide an example of the potential disadvantages the investment has for meeting a corporation's cash management goals:
   a. U.S. Treasury bills.
   b. Ordinary preferred stock.
   c. Negotiable certificates of deposit (NCDs).
   d. Commercial paper.
   e. Revenue anticipation notes.
   f. Repurchase agreements.
9. **Agency Issues** It is sometimes argued that excess cash held by a firm can aggravate agency problems (discussed in Chapter 1) and, more generally, reduce incentives for shareholder wealth maximization. How would you describe the issue here?
10. **Use of Excess Cash** One option a firm usually has with any excess cash is to pay its suppliers more quickly. What are the advantages and disadvantages of this use of excess cash?
11. **Use of Excess Cash** Another option usually available is to reduce the firm's outstanding debt. What are the advantages and disadvantages of this use of excess cash?
12. **Float** An unfortunately common practice goes like this (Warning: Don't try this at home): Suppose you are out of money in your checking account; however, your local grocery store, as a convenience to you as a customer, will cash a cheque for you, so you cash a cheque for ₹200. Of course, this cheque will bounce unless you do something. To prevent this, you go to the grocery the next day and cash another cheque for ₹200. You take this ₹200 and deposit it. You repeat this process every day and, in doing so, make sure that no cheques bounce. Eventually, a windfall arrives (perhaps in the form of money from home) and you are able to cover your outstanding cheques.

    To make it interesting, suppose you are absolutely certain that no cheques will bounce along the way. Assuming this is true, and ignoring any question of legality (what we have described is probably illegal cheque kiting), is there anything unethical about this? If you say yes, then why? In particular, who is harmed?

Questions and Problems

BASIC (Questions 1–10)

1. **Calculating Float** In a typical month, the Montrose Corporation receives 90 cheques totaling ₹85,000. These are delayed four days on average. What is the average daily float? Assume 30 days in a month.

2. **Calculating Net Float** Each business day, on average, a company writes cheques totaling ₹19,500 to pay its suppliers. The usual clearing time for the cheques is four days. Meanwhile, the company is receiving payments from its customers each day, in the form of cheques, totaling ₹24,600. The cash from the payments is available to the firm after two days.

   a. Calculate the company's disbursement float, collection float, and net float.
   b. How would your answer to part (a) change if the collected funds were available in one day instead of two?

3. **Costs of Float** Purple Feet Wine, Inc., receives an average of ₹18,600 in cheques per day. The delay in clearing is typically three days. The current interest rate is .017 percent per day.

   a. What is the company's float?
   b. What is the most the company should be willing to pay today to eliminate its float entirely?
   c. What is the highest daily fee the company should be willing to pay to eliminate its float entirely?

4. **Float and Weighted Average Delay** Your neighbor goes to the post office once a month and picks up two cheques, one for ₹8,450 and one for ₹4,200. The larger cheque takes four days to clear after it is deposited; the smaller one takes three days. Assume 30 days in a month.

   a. What is the total float for the month?
   b. What is the average daily float?
   c. What are the average daily receipts and weighted average delay?

5. **NPV and Collection Time** Your firm has an average receipt size of ₹135. A bank has approached you concerning a lockbox service that will decrease your total collection time by two days. You typically receive 4,900 cheques per day. The daily interest rate is .016 percent. If the bank charges a fee of ₹185 per day, should the lockbox project be accepted? What would the net annual savings be if the service were adopted?

6. **Using Weighted Average Delay** A mail-order firm processes 5,800 cheques per day. Of these, 60 percent are for ₹49 and 40 percent are for ₹84. The ₹49 cheques are delayed two days on average; the ₹84 cheques are delayed three days on average. Assume 30 days in a month.

   a. What is the average daily collection float? How do you interpret your answer?
   b. What is the weighted average delay? Use the result to calculate the average daily float.
   c. How much should the firm be willing to pay to eliminate the float?
   d. If the interest rate is 7 percent per year, calculate the daily cost of the float.
   e. How much should the firm be willing to pay to reduce the weighted average float by 1.5 days?

7. **Value of Lockboxes** Paper Submarine Manufacturing is investigating a lockbox system to reduce its collection time. It has determined the following:

Average number of payments per day	435
Average value of payment	₹845
Variable lockbox fee (per transaction)	₹.15
Daily interest rate on money market securities	.068%

The total collection time will be reduced by three days if the lockbox system is adopted.

a. What is the PV of adopting the system?
b. What is the NPV of adopting the system?
c. What is the net cash flow per day from adopting? Per cheque?

8. **Lockboxes and Collections** It takes Cookie Cutter Modular Homes, Inc., about six days to receive and deposit cheques from customers. The company's management is considering a lockbox system to reduce the firm's collection times. It is expected that the lockbox system will reduce receipt and deposit times to three days total. Average daily collections are ₹205,000, and the required rate of return is 4 percent per year. Assume 365 days per year.

a. What is the reduction in the outstanding cash balance as a result of implementing the lockbox system?
b. What is the daily rupee return that could be earned on these savings?
c. What is the maximum monthly charge the company should pay for this lockbox system if the payment is due at the end of the month? What if the payment is due at the beginning of the month?

9. **Value of Delay** Every two weeks, No More Pencils, Inc., disburses cheques that average ₹124,000 and take seven days to clear. How much interest can the company earn annually if it delays transfer of funds from an interest-bearing account that pays .009 percent per day for these seven days? Ignore the effects of compounding interest.

10. **NPV and Reducing Float** No More Books Corporation has an agreement with Floyd Bank whereby the bank handles ₹3.4 million in collections per day and requires a ₹320,000 compensating balance. No More Books is contemplating canceling the agreement and dividing its eastern region so that two other banks will handle its business. Banks A and B will each handle ₹1.7 million of collections per day, and each requires a compensating balance of ₹175,000. No More Books's financial management expects that collections will be accelerated by one day if the eastern region is divided. Should the company proceed with the new system? What will be the annual net savings? Assume that the T-bill rate is 2.5 percent annually.

INTERMEDIATE (Questions 11–12)

11. **Lockboxes and Collection Time** Bird's Eye Treehouses, Inc., a Kentucky company, has determined that a majority of its customers are located in the Pennsylvania area. Therefore, it is considering using a lockbox system offered by a bank located in Pittsburgh. The bank has estimated that use of the system will reduce collection time by 1.5 days. Based on the following information, should the lockbox system be adopted?

Average number of payments per day	825
Average value of payment	₹745
Variable lockbox fee (per transaction)	₹.15
Effective annual rate on money market securities	5.5%

How would your answer change if there were a fixed charge of ₹5,000 per year in addition to the variable charge?

12. **Calculating Transactions Required** Cow Chips, Inc., a large fertilizer distributor based in California, is planning to use a lockbox system to speed up collections from its customers located on the East Coast. A Philadelphia-area bank will provide this service for an annual fee of ₹6,500 plus 10 cents per transaction. The estimated reduction in collection and processing time is one day. If the average customer payment in this region is ₹2,900, how many customers each day, on average, are needed to make the system profitable for Cow Chips? Treasury bills are currently yielding 4 percent per year, and there are 365 days per year.

Mini Case CASH MANAGEMENT AT RICHMOND CORPORATION

Richmond Corporation was founded 20 years ago by its president, Daniel Richmond. The company originally began as a mail-order company but has grown rapidly in recent years, in large part due to its website. Because of the wide geographical dispersion of the company's customers, it currently employs a lockbox system with collection centers in San Francisco, St. Louis, Atlanta, and Boston.

Steve Dennis, the company's treasurer, has been examining the current cash collection policies. On average, each lockbox center handles ₹185,000 in payments each day. The company's current policy is to invest these payments in short-term marketable securities daily at the collection center banks. Every two weeks the investment accounts are swept and the proceeds are wire-transferred to Richmond's headquarters in Dallas to meet the company's payroll. The investment accounts each pay .068 percent per day and the wire transfers cost .20 percent of the amount transferred.

Steve has been approached by Third National Bank, located just outside Dallas, about the possibility of setting up a concentration banking system for Richmond Corporation. Third National will accept the lockbox centers' daily payments via automated clearinghouse (ACH) transfers in lieu of wire transfers. The ACH-transferred funds will not be available for use for one day. Once cleared, the funds will be deposited in a short-term account, which will yield .075 percent per day. Each ACH transfer will cost ₹200. Daniel has asked Steve to determine which cash management system will be the best for the company. Steve has asked you, his assistant, to answer the following questions:

1. What is Richmond Corporation's total net cash flow from the current lockbox system that is available to meet payroll?
2. Under the terms outlined by Third National Bank, should the company proceed with the concentration banking system?
3. What cost of ACH transfers would make the company indifferent between the two systems?

Appendix 27A Determining the Target Cash Balance

Appendix 27B Adjustable Rate Preferred Stock, Auction Rate Preferred Stock, and Floating-Rate Certificates of Deposit

To access the appendix for this chapter, please log on to www.mheducation.co.in.

28

Credit and Inventory Management

Managing inventory is an important part of any business, but shortages can occur due to a variety of factors. For example, when Popeyes Louisiana Kitchen brought out a new chicken sandwich to compete with rival Chick-fil-A, the sandwich was so popular that the company sold out in two weeks. It took two months before the company could get the sandwich back into restaurants. However, excess inventory can also cause problems. In 2020, the COVID-19 lockdown caused bars to close ahead of St. Patrick's Day and the NCAA basketball tournament, two of the busiest times for bars. As a result, more than 10 million gallons of beer had to be destroyed. The final cost of stale beer was expected to top ₹1 billion. And restaurant closures led to problems in other industries as producers disposed of excess meat, vegetables, and milk, and other products. In this chapter, we discuss, among other things, how companies arrive at an optimal inventory level.

Please visit us at **rwjcorporatefinance.blogspot.com** for the latest developments in the world of corporate finance.

28.1 Credit and Receivables

When a firm sells goods and services, it can demand cash on or before the delivery date, or it can extend credit to customers and allow some delay in payment. The next few sections provide an idea of what is involved in the firm's decision to grant credit to its customers. Granting credit is making an investment in a customer–an investment tied to the sale of a product or service.

Why do firms grant credit? Not all do, but the practice is extremely common. The obvious reason is that offering credit is a way of stimulating sales. The costs associated with granting credit are not trivial. First, there is the chance that the customer will not pay. Second, the firm has to bear the costs of carrying the receivables. The credit policy decision thus involves a trade-off between the benefits of increased sales and the costs of granting credit.

From an accounting perspective, when credit is granted, an account receivable is created. Such receivables include credit to other firms, called *trade credit*, and credit granted to consumers, called *consumer credit*. About one-sixth of all assets of U.S. industrial firms and nearly one-fifth of all assets of Indian industrial firms are in the form of accounts receivable, and so receivables obviously represent a major investment of financial resources by Indian businesses.

COMPONENTS OF CREDIT POLICY

If a firm decides to grant credit to its customers, then it must establish procedures for extending credit and collecting. In particular, the firm will have to deal with the following components of credit policy:

1. *Terms of sale*: The terms of sale establish how the firm proposes to sell its goods and services. A basic decision is whether the firm will require cash or will extend credit. If the firm does grant credit to a customer, the terms of sale will specify (perhaps implicitly) the credit period, the cash discount and discount period, and the type of credit instrument.
2. *Credit analysis*: In granting credit, a firm determines how much effort to expend trying to distinguish between customers who will pay and customers who will not pay. Firms use a number of devices and procedures to determine the probability that customers will not pay; put together, these are called credit analysis.
3. *Collection policy*: After credit has been granted, the firm has the potential problem of collecting the cash, for which it must establish a collection policy.

In the next several sections, we will discuss these components of credit policy that collectively make up the decision to grant credit.

THE CASH FLOWS FROM GRANTING CREDIT

In a previous chapter, we described the accounts receivable period as the time it takes to collect on a sale. There are several events that occur during this period. These events are the cash flows associated with granting credit, and they can be illustrated with a cash flow diagram:

The Cash Flows of Granting Credit

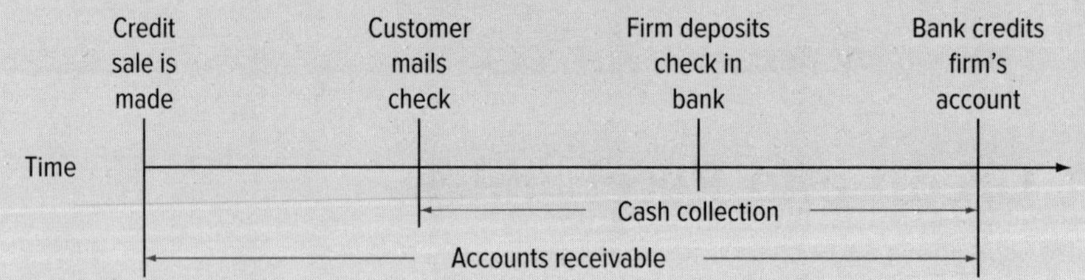

As our time line indicates, the typical sequence of events when a firm grants credit is as follows: (1) The credit sale is made, (2) the customer sends a check to the firm, (3) the firm deposits the check, and (4) the firm's account is credited for the amount of the check.

Based on our discussion in the previous chapter, it is apparent that one of the factors influencing the receivables period is float. One way to reduce the receivables period is to speed up the check mailing, processing, and clearing. Because we cover this subject elsewhere, we will ignore float in the subsequent discussion and focus on what is likely to be the major determinant of the receivables period: credit policy.

THE INVESTMENT IN RECEIVABLES

The investment in accounts receivable for any firm depends on the amount of credit sales and the average collection period. If a firm's average collection period, ACP, is 30 days, then, at any given time, there will be 30 days' worth of sales outstanding. If credit sales run ₹1,000 per day, the firm's accounts receivable then will be equal to 30 days × ₹1,000 per day = ₹30,000, on average.

As our example illustrates, a firm's receivables generally will be equal to its average daily sales multiplied by its average collection period:

For more on accounts receivable management, visit **www.insidearm.com**.

$$\text{Accounts receivable} = \text{Average daily sales} \times \text{ACP} \tag{28.1}$$

A firm's investment in accounts receivable depends on factors that influence credit sales and collections.

We have seen the average collection period in various places, including Chapters 3 and 26. Recall that we use the terms *days' sales in receivables*, *receivables period*, and *average collection period* interchangeably to refer to the length of time it takes for the firm to collect on a sale.

28.2 Terms of the Sale

As we described previously, the terms of a sale are made up of three distinct elements:

1. The period for which credit is granted (the credit period).
2. The cash discount and the discount period.
3. The type of credit instrument.

Within a given industry, the terms of sale are usually fairly standard, but these terms vary quite a bit across industries. In many cases, the terms of sale are remarkably archaic and literally date to previous centuries. Organized systems of trade credit that resemble current practice can be traced easily to the great fairs of medieval Europe, and they almost surely existed long before then.

THE BASIC FORM

The easiest way to understand the terms of sale is to consider an example. Terms such as 2/10, net 60 are common. This means that customers have 60 days from the invoice date (discussed a bit later) to pay the full amount; however, if payment is made within 10 days, a 2 percent cash discount can be taken.

Consider a buyer who places an order for ₹1,000, and assume that the terms of the sale are 2/10, net 60. The buyer has the option of paying ₹1,000 × (1 − .02) = ₹980 in 10 days or paying the full ₹1,000 in 60 days. If the terms are stated as net 30, then the customer has 30 days from the invoice date to pay the entire ₹1,000, and no discount is offered for early payment.

For more about the credit process for small businesses, visit the National Association of Credit Management at **www.nacm.org**.

In general, credit terms are interpreted in the following way:

<take this discount off the invoice price>/<if you pay in this many days>,

<or pay the full invoice amount in this many days>

Thus, 5/10, net 45 means take a 5 percent discount from the full price if you pay within 10 days, or else pay the full amount in 45 days.

THE CREDIT PERIOD

The **credit period** is the basic length of time for which credit is granted. The credit period varies widely from industry to industry, but it is almost always between 30 and 120 days. If a cash discount is offered, then the credit period has two components: the net credit period and the cash discount period.

The net credit period is the length of time the customer has to pay. The cash discount period is the time during which the discount is available. With 2/10, net 30, the net credit period is 30 days and the cash discount period is 10 days.

The Invoice Date The invoice date is the beginning of the credit period. An **invoice** is a written account of merchandise shipped to the buyer. For individual items, by convention, the invoice date is usually the shipping date or the billing date, not the date on which the buyer receives the goods or the bill.

Many other arrangements exist. For example, the terms of sale might be ROG, for *receipt of goods*. In this case, the credit period starts when the customer receives the order. This might be used when the customer is in a remote location.

With EOM dating, all sales made during a particular month are assumed to be made at the end of that month. This is useful when a buyer makes purchases throughout the month, but the seller bills only once a month.

Terms of 2/10, EOM tell the buyer to take a 2 percent discount if payment is made by the 10th of the month; otherwise the full amount is due. Confusingly, the end of the month is sometimes taken to be the 25th day of the month. MOM, for middle of month, is another variation.

Seasonal dating is sometimes used to encourage sales of seasonal products during the off-season. A product sold primarily in the summer (e.g., saffron kulfi) can be shipped in January with credit terms of 2/10, net 30. However, the invoice might be dated May 1 so that the credit period actually begins at that time. This practice encourages buyers to order early.

Length of the Credit Period Several factors influence the length of the credit period. Two important ones are the buyer's inventory period and operating cycle. All else equal, the shorter these are, the shorter the credit period will be.

From Chapter 26, the operating cycle has two components: the inventory period and the receivables period. The buyer's inventory period is the time it takes the buyer to acquire inventory (from us), process it, and sell it. The buyer's receivables period is the time it then takes the buyer to collect on the sale. Note that the credit period we offer is effectively the buyer's payables period.

By extending credit, we finance a portion of our buyer's operating cycle and thereby shorten that buyer's cash cycle (see Figure 26.1). If our credit period exceeds the buyer's inventory period, then we are financing not only the buyer's inventory purchases, but part of the buyer's receivables, as well.

Furthermore, if our credit period exceeds our buyer's operating cycle, then we are effectively providing financing for aspects of our customer's business beyond the immediate purchase and sale of our merchandise. The reason is that the buyer effectively has a loan from us even after the merchandise is resold, and the buyer can use that credit for other purposes. For this reason, the length of the buyer's operating cycle is often cited as an appropriate upper limit to the credit period.

There are a number of other factors that influence the credit period. Many of these also influence our customer's operating cycles; so, once again, these are related subjects. Among the most important are these:

1. *Perishability and collateral value*: Perishable items have relatively rapid turnover and relatively low collateral value. Credit periods are thus shorter for such goods. A food wholesaler selling fresh fruit and produce might use net 7 days. Alternatively, jewelry might be sold for 5/30, net 4 months.
2. *Consumer demand*: Products that are well established generally have more rapid turnover. Newer or slow-moving products often will have longer credit periods associated with them to entice buyers. Also, as we have seen, sellers may choose to extend much longer credit periods for off-season sales (when customer demand is low).

3. *Cost, profitability, and standardization*: Relatively inexpensive goods tend to have shorter credit periods. The same is true for relatively standardized goods and raw materials. These all tend to have lower markups and higher turnover rates, both of which lead to shorter credit periods. However, there are exceptions. Auto dealers, for example, generally pay for cars as they are received.
4. *Credit risk*: The greater the credit risk of the buyer, the shorter the credit period is likely to be (if credit is granted at all).
5. *Size of the account*: If an account is small, the credit period may be shorter because small accounts cost more to manage and the customers are less important.
6. *Competition*: When the seller is in a highly competitive market, longer credit periods may be offered as a way of attracting customers.
7. *Customer type*: A single seller might offer different credit terms to different buyers. A food wholesaler might supply groceries, bakeries, and restaurants. Each group would probably have different credit terms. More generally, sellers often have both wholesale and retail customers, and they frequently quote different terms to the two types.

CASH DISCOUNTS

As we have seen, **cash discounts** are often part of the terms of sale. The practice of granting discounts for cash purchases in the United States dates to the Civil War and is widespread today. One reason discounts are offered is to speed up the collection of receivables. This will have the effect of reducing the amount of credit being offered, and the firm must trade this off against the cost of the discount.

Notice that when a cash discount is offered, the credit is essentially free during the discount period. The buyer pays for the credit only after the discount expires. With 2/10, net 30, a rational buyer either pays in 10 days to make the greatest possible use of the free credit or pays in 30 days to get the longest possible use of the money in exchange for giving up the discount. By giving up the discount, the buyer effectively gets 30 − 10 = 20 days' credit.

Another reason for cash discounts is that they are a way of charging higher prices to customers that have had credit extended to them. In this sense, cash discounts are a convenient way of charging for the credit granted to customers.

Cost of the Credit

In our examples, it might seem that the discounts are rather small. With 2/10, net 30, early payment gets the buyer only a 2 percent discount. Does this provide a significant incentive for early payment? The answer is yes because the implicit interest rate is extremely high.

To see why the discount is important, we will calculate the cost to the buyer of not paying early. To do this, we will find the interest rate that the buyer is effectively paying for the trade credit. Suppose the order is for ₹1,000. The buyer can pay ₹980 in 10 days or wait another 20 days and pay ₹1,000. It's obvious that the buyer is effectively borrowing ₹980 for 20 days and that the buyer pays ₹20 in interest on the "loan." What's the interest rate?

This interest is ordinary discount interest, which we discussed in Chapter 4. With ₹20 in interest on ₹980 borrowed, the rate is ₹20/₹980 = .020408, or 2.0408 percent. This is relatively low, but remember that this is the rate per 20-day period. There are 365/20 = 18.25 such periods in a year; so, by not taking the discount, the buyer is paying an effective annual rate (EAR) of:

$$\text{EAR} = 1.020408^{18.25} - 1 = .4459, \text{ or } 44.59\%$$

From the buyer's point of view, this is an expensive source of financing!

Given that the interest rate is so high here, it is unlikely that the seller benefits from early payment. Ignoring the possibility of default by the buyer, the decision of a customer to forgo the discount almost surely works to the seller's advantage.

Trade Discounts While cash discounts are typically offered to the buyer on the invoice in return for early payment, *trade discounts* are offered on the list price that the customer sees at the time of purchase. Cash discounts and trade discounts differ in how they are presented to customers and in their accounting, but their real effects on required payment amounts and timing are similar. Both reward the customer for payment before a certain date. With our 2/10, EOM terms applied to a trade discount, the buyer takes a 2 percent discount if the invoice is paid by the 10th, but the bill is considered due on the 10th, and overdue after that. Thus, the credit period and the discount period are effectively the same, and there is no reward for paying before the due date.

The Cash Discount and the ACP To the extent that a cash discount encourages customers to pay early, it will shorten the receivables period and, all other things being equal, reduce the firm's investment in receivables.

Suppose a firm currently has terms of net 30 and an ACP of 30 days. If it offers terms of 2/10, net 30, then perhaps 50 percent of its customers (in terms of volume of purchases) will pay in 10 days. The remaining customers still will take an average of 30 days to pay. What will the new ACP be? If the firm's annual sales are ₹15 million (before discounts), what will happen to the investment in receivables?

If half of the customers take 10 days to pay and half take 30, then the new ACP will be:

$$\text{New ACP} = .50 \times 10 \text{ days} + .50 \times 30 \text{ days} = 20 \text{ days}$$

The ACP falls from 30 days to 20 days. Average daily sales are ₹15 million/365 = ₹41,095.89 per day. Receivables will fall by ₹41,095.89 × 10 = ₹410,959.

CREDIT INSTRUMENTS

The **credit instrument** is the basic evidence of indebtedness. Most trade credit is offered on *open account.* This means that the only formal instrument of credit is the invoice, which is sent with the shipment of goods and which the customer signs as evidence that the goods have been received. Afterward, the firm and its customers record the exchange on their books of account.

At times, the firm may require that the customer sign a *promissory note.* This is a basic IOU and might be used when the order is large, when there is no cash discount involved, or when the firm anticipates a problem in collections. Promissory notes are not common, but they can eliminate possible controversies later about the existence of debt.

One problem with promissory notes is that they are signed after delivery of the goods. One way to obtain a credit commitment from a customer before the goods are delivered is to arrange a *commercial draft.* Typically, the firm draws up a commercial draft calling for the customer to pay a specific amount by a specified date. The draft is then sent to the customer's bank with the shipping invoices.

If immediate payment is required on the draft, it is called a *sight draft.* If immediate payment is not required, then the draft is a *time draft.* When the draft is presented and the buyer "accepts" it, meaning that the buyer promises to pay it in the future, then it is called a *trade acceptance* and is sent back to the selling firm. The seller can then keep the acceptance or sell it to someone else. If a bank accepts the draft, meaning that the bank is guaranteeing payment, then the draft becomes a *banker's acceptance.* This arrangement is common in international trade, and banker's acceptances are actively traded in the money market.

A firm also can use a conditional sales contract as a credit instrument. With such an arrangement, the firm retains legal ownership of the goods until the customer has completed payment. Conditional sales contracts usually are paid in installments and have an interest cost built into them.

OTHER CREDIT INSTRUMENTS IN INDIA[1]

Export financing: This financial instrument is offered in the case of goods exported (say, carpets) from India to arbitrage on lower interest rates abroad. To mitigate the disadvantage of higher domestic interest rates faced by exporters, such as carpet manufacturers, banks provide concessional financing for exports. Export financing can be broadly classified into:

- **Pre-shipment credit:** This type of financing is provided to cover costs associated with the purchase, processing, packing, and shipping of goods. Pre-shipment credit is available in rupees and foreign currency, depending upon the requirement.
- **Post-shipment credit:** Post-shipment credit is provided to finance the exporter after the dispatch of goods until the realization of sales proceeds from the foreign buyer as per the terms of the transaction or the letter of credit received from the foreign buyer's banker.

Forfaiting: Forfaiting is an extension of factoring services in international trade. It enables an exporter to discount his export receivables with an agency called forfaiter. It also frees the exporter from the commercial and political risks inherent in international trade, as forfaiting is mainly done without recourse. In India, the Export-Import Bank of India (commonly known as Exim Bank) acts as the nodal agency for forfaiting contracts. Exhibit 28.1 showcases the flow chart of a forfaiting transaction.

Exhibit 28.1 A Flow Chart of a Forfaiting Transaction

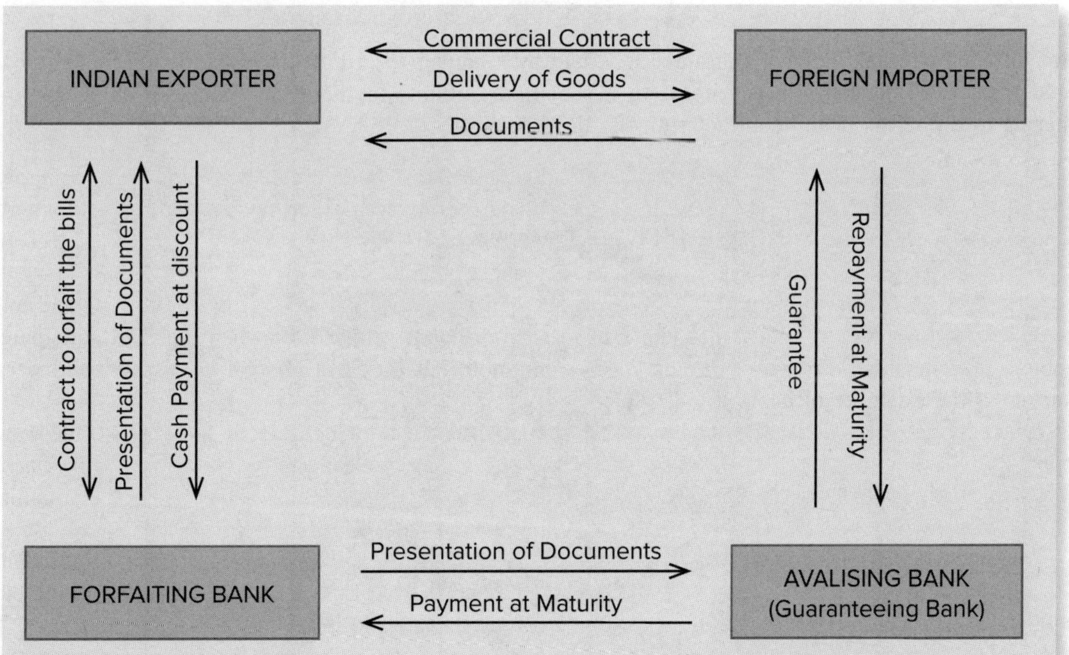

[1]This sub-section is based on discussion with industry experts.

Non-Fund (fee) based Instruments / Documentary Credit Instruments: These are commercial documents guaranteeing payment by the bank to the beneficiary, which is usually the merchandise seller, against the underlying transaction.

Letter of Credit: When a bank issues a letter of credit, it commits to paying the seller if the required documents are presented according to the agreement. It could be issued either for domestic transaction or for international trade.[2] The most important feature of this form of finance is that it is a non-fund based arrangement, as funds are not involved in the issue of the letter of credit. It is a contingent liability for the bank.

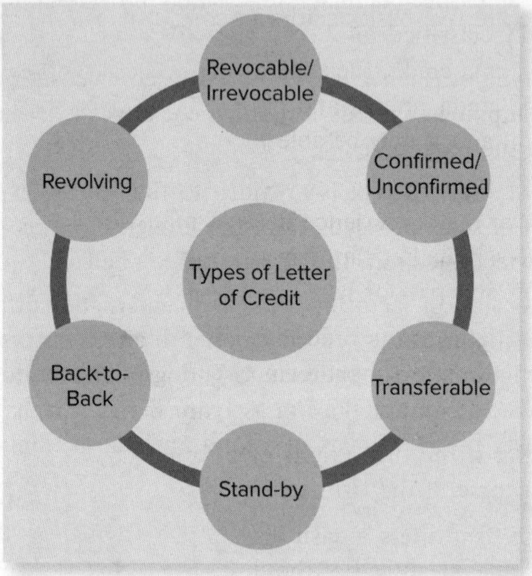

Letter of Guarantee: A letter of guarantee is issued by a banker to a third party indicating that the bank would meet the financial consequences (to a specified amount) in the event of failure of its client in adhering to the terms of the contract with the third party.

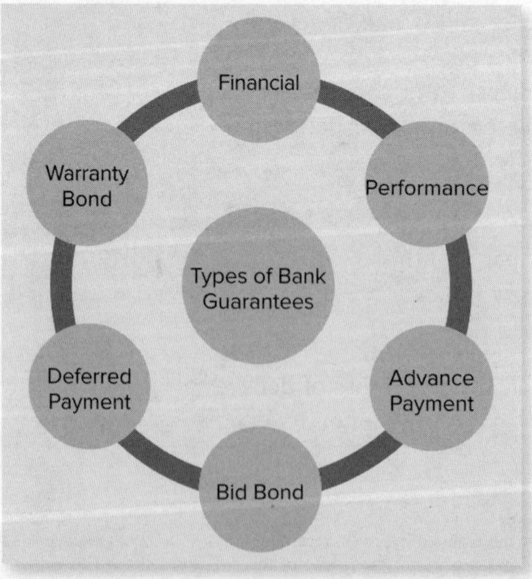

[2]Typically employed for international trade because of the long gestation periods involved in global trade.

28.3 Analyzing Credit Policy

In this section, we take a closer look at the factors that influence the decision to grant credit. Granting credit makes sense only if the NPV from doing so is positive. Thus, we need to look at the NPV of the decision to grant credit.

CREDIT POLICY EFFECTS

In evaluating credit policy, there are five basic factors to consider:

1. *Revenue effects*: If the firm grants credit, then there will be a delay in revenue collections as some customers take advantage of the credit offered and pay later. However, the firm may be able to charge a higher price if it grants credit and it may be able to increase the quantity sold. Total revenues thus may increase.
2. *Cost effects*: Although the firm may experience delayed revenues if it grants credit, it still will incur the costs of sales immediately. Whether the firm sells for cash or credit, it still will have to acquire or produce the merchandise (and pay for it).
3. *The cost of debt*: When the firm grants credit, it must arrange to finance the resulting receivables. As a result, the firm's cost of short-term borrowing is a factor in the decision to grant credit.[3]
4. *The probability of nonpayment*: If the firm grants credit, some percentage of the credit buyers will not pay. This can't happen, of course, if the firm sells for cash.
5. *The cash discount*: When the firm offers a cash discount as part of its credit terms, some customers will choose to pay early to take advantage of the discount.

EVALUATING A PROPOSED CREDIT POLICY

To illustrate how credit policy can be analyzed, we will start with a relatively simple case. Lepakshi Software has been in existence for two years and is one of several successful firms that develop computer programs. Currently, Lepakshi sells for cash only.

Lepakshi is evaluating a request from some major customers to change its current policy to net one month (30 days). To analyze this proposal, we define the following:

P = Price per unit
v = Variable cost per unit
Q = Current quantity sold per month
Q' = Quantity sold under new policy
R = Monthly required return

For now, we ignore discounts and the possibility of default. Also, we ignore taxes because they don't affect our conclusions.

[3]The cost of short-term debt is not necessarily the required return on receivables, although it commonly is assumed to be. As always, the required return on an investment depends on the risk of the investment, not the source of the financing. The buyer's cost of short-term debt is closer in spirit to the correct rate. We will maintain the implicit assumption that the seller and the buyer have the same short-term debt cost. In any case, the time periods in credit decisions are relatively short, so a relatively small error in the discount rate will not have a large effect on our estimated NPV.

NPV of Switching Policies To illustrate the NPV of switching credit policies, suppose we have the following for Lepakshi:

$$P = ₹49$$
$$v = ₹20$$
$$Q = 100$$
$$Q' = 110$$

If the required return, R, is 2 percent per month, should Lepakshi make the switch?

Currently, Lepakshi has monthly sales of $P \times Q = ₹4{,}900$. Variable costs each month are $v \times Q = ₹2{,}000$, so the monthly cash flow from this activity is:

$$\begin{aligned} \text{Cash flow with old policy} &= (P - v)Q \\ &= (₹49 - 20) \times 100 \\ &= ₹2{,}900 \end{aligned} \tag{28.2}$$

This is not the total cash flow for Lepakshi, of course, but it is all that we need to look at because fixed costs and other components of cash flow are the same whether or not the switch is made.

If Lepakshi does switch to net 30 days on sales, then the quantity sold will rise to $Q' = 110$. Monthly revenues will increase to $P \times Q'$ and costs will be $v \times Q'$. The monthly cash flow under the new policy will be:

$$\begin{aligned} \text{Cash flow with new policy} &= (P - v)Q' \\ &= (₹49 - 20) \times 110 \\ &= ₹3{,}190 \end{aligned} \tag{28.3}$$

Going back to Chapter 6, we know that the relevant incremental cash flow is the difference between the new and old cash flows:

$$\begin{aligned} \text{Incremental cash inflow} &= (P - v)(Q' - Q) \\ &= (₹49 - 20) \times (110 - 100) \\ &= ₹290 \end{aligned}$$

This says that the benefit each month of changing policies is equal to the gross profit per unit sold, $P - v = ₹29$, multiplied by the increase in sales, $Q' - Q = 10$. The present value of the future incremental cash flows is:

$$\text{PV} = [(P - v)(Q' - Q)]/R \tag{28.4}$$

For Lepakshi, this present value works out to be:

$$\text{PV} = (₹29 \times 10)/.02 = ₹14{,}500$$

Notice that we have treated the monthly cash flow as a perpetuity because the same benefit will be realized each month, forever.

Now that we know the benefit of switching, what's the cost? There are two components to consider. First, because the quantity sold will rise from Q to Q', Lepakshi will have to produce $Q' - Q$ more units at a cost of $v(Q' - Q) = ₹20 \times (110 - 100) = ₹200$. Second, the sales that would have been collected this month under the current policy ($P \times Q = ₹4{,}900$) will not be collected. Under the new policy, the sales made this month won't be collected until 30 days later. The cost of the switch is the sum of these two components:

$$\text{Cost of switching} = PQ + v(Q' - Q) \tag{28.5}$$

For Lepakshi, this cost would be $₹4{,}900 + 200 = ₹5{,}100$.

Putting it all together, we see that the NPV of the switch is:

$$\text{NPV of switching} = -[PQ + v(Q' - Q)] + [(P - v)(Q' - Q)]/R \tag{28.6}$$

For Lepakshi, the cost of switching is ₹5,100. As we saw earlier, the benefit is ₹290 per month, forever. At 2 percent per month, the NPV is:

$$\begin{aligned} \text{NPV} &= -₹5{,}100 + ₹290/.02 \\ &= -₹5{,}100 + 14{,}500 \\ &= ₹9{,}400 \end{aligned}$$

Therefore, the switch is very profitable.

EXAMPLE 28.1

We'd Rather Fight Than Switch Suppose a company is considering a switch from all cash to net 30, but the quantity sold is not expected to change. What is the NPV of the switch? Explain.

In this case, $Q' - Q$ is zero, so the NPV is $-PQ$. What this says is that the effect of the switch is to postpone one month's collections forever, with no benefit from doing so.

A Break-Even Application Based on our discussion thus far, the key variable for Lepakshi is $Q' - Q$, the increase in unit sales. The projected increase of 10 units is only an estimate, so there is some forecasting risk. Under the circumstances, it's natural to wonder what increase in unit sales is necessary to break even.

Earlier, the NPV of the switch was defined as:

$$\text{NPV} = -[PQ + v(Q' - Q)] + [(P - v)(Q' - Q)]/R$$

We can calculate the break-even point explicitly by setting the NPV equal to zero and solving for $(Q' - Q)$:

$$\begin{aligned} \text{NPV} = 0 &= -[PQ + v(Q' - Q)] + [(P - v)(Q' - Q)]/R \\ Q' - Q &= PQ/[(P - v)/R - v] \end{aligned} \tag{28.7}$$

For Lepakshi, the break-even sales increase is:

$$\begin{aligned} Q' - Q &= ₹4{,}900/(₹29/.02 - ₹20) \\ &= 3.43 \text{ units} \end{aligned}$$

This tells us that the switch is a good idea as long as Lepakshi is confident that it can sell at least 3.43 more units per month.

28.4 Optimal Credit Policy

So far, we've discussed how to compute net present values for a switch in credit policy. We have not discussed the optimal amount of credit or the optimal credit policy. In principle, the optimal amount of credit is determined by the point at which the incremental cash flows from increased sales are exactly equal to the incremental costs of carrying the increase in investment in accounts receivable.

For business reports on credit, visit **www.creditworthy.com**.

THE TOTAL CREDIT COST CURVE

The trade-off between granting credit and not granting credit isn't hard to identify, but it is difficult to quantify precisely. As a result, we can only describe an optimal credit policy.

To begin, the carrying costs associated with granting credit come in three forms:

1. The required return on receivables.
2. The losses from bad debts.
3. The costs of managing credit and credit collections.

We already have discussed the first and second of these. The third cost, the cost of managing credit, consists of the expenses associated with running the credit department. Firms that don't grant credit have no such department and no such expense. These three costs all will increase as credit policy is relaxed.

If a firm has a very restrictive credit policy, then all of the associated costs will be low. In this case, the firm will have a shortage of credit, so there will be an opportunity cost. This opportunity cost is the extra potential profit from credit sales that are lost because credit is refused. This forgone benefit comes from two sources: the increase in quantity sold, Q' minus Q, and (potentially) a higher price. The opportunity costs go down as credit policy is relaxed.

The sum of the carrying costs and the opportunity costs of a particular credit policy is called the total *credit cost curve*. We have drawn such a curve in Figure 28.1. As shown, there is a point where the total credit cost is minimized. This point corresponds to the optimal amount of credit or, equivalently, the optimal investment in receivables.

If the firm extends more credit than this minimum, the additional net cash flow from new customers will not cover the carrying costs of the investment in receivables. If the level of receivables is below this amount, then the firm is forgoing valuable profit opportunities.

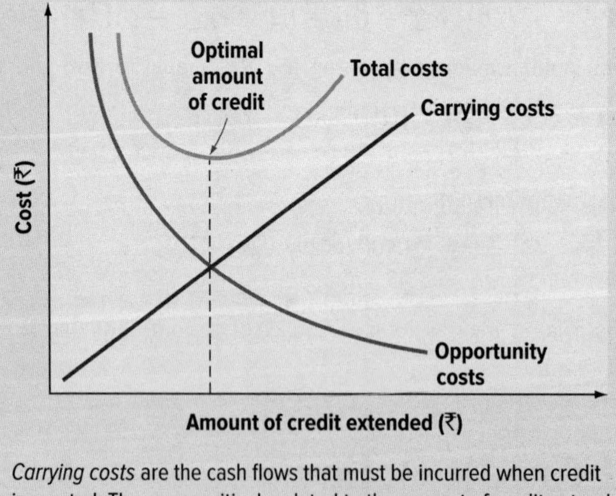

Carrying costs are the cash flows that must be incurred when credit is granted. They are positively related to the amount of credit extended. *Opportunity costs* are the lost sales resulting from refusing credit. These costs go down when credit is granted.

Figure 28.1 The Costs of Granting Credit

In general, the costs and benefits from extending credit will depend on the characteristics of particular firms and industries. All other things being equal, it is likely that firms with (1) excess capacity, (2) low variable operating costs, and (3) repeat customers will extend credit more liberally than other firms. See if you can explain why each of these characteristics contributes to a more liberal credit policy.

ORGANIZING THE CREDIT FUNCTION

Firms that grant credit have the expense of running a credit department. In practice, firms often choose to contract out all or part of the credit function to a factor, an insurance company, or a captive finance company. Chapter 26 discusses factoring, an arrangement in which the firm sells its receivables. Depending on the specific arrangement, the factor may have full responsibility for credit checking, authorization, and collection. Smaller firms may find such an arrangement cheaper than running a credit department.

Firms that manage internal credit operations are self-insured against default. An alternative is to buy credit insurance through an insurance company. The insurance company offers coverage up to a preset rupee limit for accounts. As you would expect, accounts with a higher credit rating merit higher insurance limits. This type of insurance is particularly important for exporters, and government insurance is available for certain types of exports.

Large firms often extend credit through a **captive finance company**, which is a wholly owned subsidiary that handles the credit function for the parent company. Ford Motor Credit (FMC) is a well-known example. Ford sells to car dealers, who in turn sell to customers. FMC finances the dealers' inventory of cars and also finances customers who buy the cars.

Why would a firm choose to set up a separate company to handle the credit function? There are a number of reasons, but a primary one is to separate the production and financing of the firm's products for management, financing, and reporting. The finance subsidiary can borrow in its own name, using its receivables as collateral, and the subsidiary often carries a better credit rating than the parent. This may allow the firm to achieve a lower overall cost of debt than could be obtained if production and financing were commingled.

28.5 Credit Analysis

Thus far, we have focused on establishing credit terms. Once a firm decides to grant credit to its customers, it must then establish guidelines for determining who will and who will not be allowed to buy on credit. *Credit analysis* refers to the process of deciding whether or not to extend credit to a particular customer. It usually involves two steps: gathering relevant information and determining creditworthiness.

Credit analysis is important because potential losses on receivables can be substantial. On their balance sheets, companies report the amount of receivables they expect not to collect. In late 2020, IBM reported that ₹354 million of accounts receivable were doubtful, and Microsoft reported ₹610 million as an allowance for losses.

WHEN SHOULD CREDIT BE GRANTED?

Imagine that a firm is trying to decide whether or not to grant credit to a customer. This decision can get complicated. Note that the answer depends on what will happen if credit is refused. Will the customer pay cash? Or will the customer not make the purchase at all? To avoid being bogged down by this and other difficulties, we will use some special cases to illustrate the key points.

A One-Time Sale We start by considering the simplest case. A new customer wishes to buy one unit on credit at a price of P per unit. If credit is refused, the customer will not make the purchase.

Furthermore, we assume that, if credit is granted, then, in one month, the customer will either pay up or default. The probability of the second of these events is π. In this case, the probability (π) can be interpreted as the percentage of *new* customers who will not pay. Our business does not have repeat customers, so this is strictly a one-time sale. Finally, the required return on receivables is R per month and the variable cost is v per unit.

The analysis here is straightforward. If the firm refuses credit, then the incremental cash flow is zero. If it grants credit, then it spends v (the variable cost) this month and expects to collect $(1 - \pi)P$ next month. The NPV of granting credit is:

$$\text{NPV} = -v + (1 - \pi)P/(1 + R) \tag{28.8}$$

For Lepakshi Software, this NPV is:

$$\text{NPV} = -₹20 + (1 - \pi) \times ₹49/1.02$$

With, say, a 20 percent rate of default, this works out to be:

$$\text{NPV} = -₹20 + .80 \times ₹49/1.02 = ₹18.43$$

Therefore, credit should be granted. Notice that we have divided by $(1 + R)$ here instead of by R because we now assume that this is a one-time transaction.

Our example illustrates an important point. In granting credit to a new customer, a firm risks its variable cost (v). It stands to gain the full price (P). For a new customer, then, credit may be granted even if the default probability is high. The break-even probability in this case can be determined by setting the NPV equal to zero and solving for π:

$$\begin{aligned} \text{NPV} = 0 &= -₹20 + (1 - \pi) \times ₹49/1.02 \\ 1 - \pi &= ₹20/₹49 \times 1.02 \\ \pi &= .584, \text{ or } 58.4\% \end{aligned}$$

Lepakshi should extend credit as long as there is a 1 − .584 = .416, or 41.6 percent chance or better of collecting. This explains why firms with higher markups tend to have looser credit terms.

This percentage (58.4 percent) is the maximum acceptable default probability for a new customer. If a returning, cash-paying customer wanted to switch to a credit basis, the analysis would be different and the maximum acceptable default probability would be much lower.

The important difference is that, if we extend credit to a returning customer, we risk the total sales price (P) because this is what we collect if we don't extend credit. If we extend credit to a new customer, we risk only our variable cost.

Repeat Business A second, very important factor to keep in mind is the possibility of repeat business. We can illustrate this by extending our one-time sale example. We make one important assumption: A new customer who does not default the first time around will remain a customer forever and never default.

If the firm grants credit, it spends v this month. Next month, it gets nothing if the customer defaults or it gets P if the customer pays. If the customer pays, then the customer will buy another unit on credit and the firm will spend v again. The net cash inflow for the month is $P - v$. In every subsequent month, this same $P - v$ will occur as the customer pays for the previous month's order and places a new one.

It follows from our discussion that, in one month, the firm will receive ₹0 with probability π. With probability $(1 - \pi)$, however, the firm will have a permanent new customer. The value of a new customer is equal to the present value of $(P - v)$ every month forever:

$$\text{PV} = (P - v)/R$$

The NPV of extending credit is therefore:

$$\text{NPV} = -v + (1 - \pi)(P - v)/R \tag{28.9}$$

For Lepakshi, this is:

$$\begin{aligned}\text{NPV} &= -₹20 + (1 - \pi) \times (₹49 - 20)/.02 \\ &= -₹20 + (1 - \pi) \times ₹1{,}450\end{aligned}$$

Even if the probability of default is 90 percent, the NPV is:

$$\text{NPV} = -₹20 + .10 \times ₹1{,}450 = ₹125$$

Lepakshi should extend credit unless default is a virtual certainty. The reason is that it costs only ₹20 to find out who is a good customer and who is not. A good customer is worth ₹1,450, however, so Lepakshi can afford quite a few defaults.

Our repeat business example probably exaggerates the acceptable default probability, but it does illustrate that it often will turn out that the best way to do credit analysis is to extend credit to almost anyone. It also points out that the possibility of repeat business is a crucial consideration. In such cases, the important thing is to control the amount of credit initially offered to any one customer so that the possible loss is limited. The amount can be increased with time. Most often, the best predictor of whether or not someone will pay in the future is whether or not they have paid in the past.

Web-surfing students should peruse the Dun & Bradstreet home page. This major supplier of credit information can be found at **www.dnb.com**.

CREDIT INFORMATION

If a firm wants credit information about customers, there are a number of sources. Information sources commonly used to assess creditworthiness include the following:

1. *Financial statements*: A firm can ask a customer to supply financial statements such as balance sheets and income statements. Minimum standards and rules of thumb based on financial ratios like the ones we discussed in Chapter 3 then can be used as a basis for extending or refusing credit.
2. *Credit reports about the customer's payment history with other firms*: Quite a few organizations sell information about the credit strength and credit history of business firms. The best-known and largest firm of this type is Dun & Bradstreet, which provides subscribers with credit reports on individual firms. Experian is another well-known credit-reporting firm. Ratings and information are available for a huge number of firms, including very small ones. Equifax, Transunion, and Experian are the major suppliers of consumer credit information.
3. *Banks*: Banks will generally provide some assistance to their business customers in acquiring information about the creditworthiness of other firms.

4. *The customer's payment history with the firm*: The most obvious way to obtain information about the likelihood of customers not paying is to examine whether they have settled past obligations (and how quickly).

Recent developments in fintech have allowed firms to much more effectively collect and analyze credit information about their customers. For example, Ant Group, a Chinese fintech firm, has experienced explosive growth since it launched as Alipay in 2004. As of 2021, Ant Group is preparing to go public with an estimated valuation of ₹150 to ₹300 billion. Among other activities, Ant Group provides merchants with e-commerce services and helps merchants collect digital payments from customers. Because Ant Group handles payments and collections for other businesses, it is able to provide credit to these businesses with the benefit of knowing detailed information about their creditworthiness.

CREDIT EVALUATION AND SCORING

There are no magical formulas for assessing the probability that a customer will not pay. In very general terms, the classic **five *C*s of credit** are the basic factors to be evaluated:

1. *Character*: The customer's willingness to meet credit obligations.
2. *Capacity*: The customer's ability to meet credit obligations out of operating cash flows.
3. *Capital*: The customer's financial reserves.
4. *Collateral*: An asset pledged in the case of default.
5. *Conditions*: General economic conditions in the customer's line of business.

Credit scoring is the process of calculating a numerical rating for a customer based on information collected; credit is then granted or refused based on the result. A firm might rate a customer on a scale of 1 (very poor) to 10 (very good) on each of the five *C*s of credit using all the information available about the customer. A credit score could then be calculated by totaling these ratings. Based on experience, a firm might choose to grant credit only to customers with a score above, say, 30.

Firms such as credit card issuers have developed statistical models for credit scoring. Usually, all of the legally relevant and observable characteristics of a large pool of customers are studied to find their historic relation to defaults. Based on the results, it is possible to determine the variables that best predict whether a customer will pay and then calculate a credit score based on those variables.

Because credit-scoring models and procedures determine who is and who is not creditworthy, it is not surprising that they have been the subject of government regulation. In particular, the kinds of background and demographic information that can be used in the credit decision are limited.

28.6 Collection Policy

Collection policy is the final element in credit policy. Collection policy involves monitoring receivables to spot trouble and obtaining payment on past-due accounts.

MONITORING RECEIVABLES

To keep track of payments by customers, most firms will monitor outstanding accounts. First of all, a firm normally will keep track of its average collection period (ACP) through time. If a firm is in a seasonal business, the ACP will fluctuate during the year; but unexpected increases in the ACP are a cause for concern. Either customers in general are taking longer to pay or some percentage of accounts receivable are seriously overdue.

The **aging schedule** is a second basic tool for monitoring receivables. To prepare one, the credit department classifies accounts by age.[4] Suppose a firm has ₹100,000 in receivables. Some of these accounts are only a few days old, but others have been outstanding for quite some time. The following is an example of an aging schedule:

Aging Schedule

Age of Account	Amount	Percentage of Total Value of Accounts Receivable
0–10 days	₹ 50,000	50%
11–60 days	25,000	25
61–80 days	20,000	20
Over 80 days	5,000	5
	₹100,000	100%

If this firm has a credit period of 60 days, then 25 percent of its accounts are late. Whether or not this is serious depends on the nature of the firm's collections and customers. It is often the case that accounts beyond a certain age are almost never collected. Monitoring the age of accounts is very important in such cases.

Firms with seasonal sales will find the percentages on the aging schedule changing during the year. If sales in the current month are very high, then total receivables also will increase sharply. This means that the older accounts, as a percentage of total receivables, become smaller and might appear less important. Some firms have refined the aging schedule so that they have an idea of how it should change with peaks and valleys in their sales.

COLLECTION EFFORT

A firm usually goes through the following sequence of procedures for customers whose payments are overdue:

1. It sends out a delinquency letter informing the customer of the past-due status of the account.
2. It makes a telephone call to the customer.
3. It employs a collection agency.
4. It takes legal action against the customer.

At times, a firm may refuse to grant additional credit to customers until arrearages are cleared up. This may antagonize a normally good customer, which points to a potential conflict between the collections department and the sales department.

In probably the worst case, the customer files for bankruptcy. When this happens, the credit-granting firm is just another unsecured creditor. The firm can wait, or it can sell its receivable. For example, when retailer JCPenney filed for bankruptcy in 2020, it owed more than ₹5 billion, including debt to large suppliers. The largest debts owed to vendors were the ₹32 million owed to Nike and ₹14.2 million owed to Alfred Dunner.

28.7 Inventory Management

Like receivables, inventories represent a significant investment for many firms. For a typical manufacturing operation, inventories often will exceed 15 percent of assets. For a retailer, inventories could represent more than 25 percent of assets. From our discussion in Chapter 26, we know that a firm's operating

[4]Aging schedules also are used elsewhere in business such as in inventory tracking.

cycle is made up of its inventory period and its receivables period. This is one reason for considering credit and inventory policy in the same chapter. Beyond this, both credit policy and inventory policy are used to drive sales, and the two must be coordinated to ensure that the process of acquiring inventory, selling it, and collecting on the sale is a smooth one. For example, changes in credit policy designed to stimulate sales must be accompanied by planning for adequate inventory.

THE FINANCIAL MANAGER AND INVENTORY POLICY

Despite the size of a typical firm's investment in inventories, the financial manager of a firm will not normally have primary control over inventory management. Instead, other functional areas such as purchasing, production, and marketing will usually share decision-making authority regarding inventory. Inventory management has become an increasingly important specialty in its own right, and financial management often will only have input into the decision. For this reason, we will look at some basics of inventory and inventory policy.

Visit the Society for Inventory Management Benchmarking Analysis at **www.simba.org**.

INVENTORY TYPES

For a manufacturer, inventory is normally classified into one of three categories. The first category is *raw materials*. This is whatever the firm uses as a starting point in its production process. Raw materials might be something as basic as iron ore for a steel manufacturer or something as sophisticated as disk drives for a computer manufacturer.

The second type of inventory is *work-in-progress*, which is just what the name suggests–unfinished product. How big this portion of inventory is depends in large part on the length of the production process. For an airframe manufacturer, for example, work-in-progress can be substantial. The third and final type of inventory is *finished goods*–that is, products ready to ship or sell.

Keep in mind three things concerning inventory types. First, the names for the different types can be a little misleading because one company's raw materials can be another's finished goods. Going back to our steel manufacturer, iron ore would be a raw material and steel would be the final product. An auto body panel stamping operation will have steel as its raw material and auto body panels as its finished goods, and an automobile assembler will have body panels as raw materials and automobiles as finished products.

The second thing to keep in mind is that the various types of inventory can be quite different in terms of their liquidity. Raw materials that are commodity-like or relatively standardized can be easy to convert to cash. Work-in-progress, on the other hand, can be quite illiquid and have little more than scrap value. As always, the liquidity of finished goods depends on the nature of the product.

Finally, a very important distinction between finished goods and other types of inventories is that the demand for an inventory item that becomes a part of another item is usually termed *derived* or *dependent demand* because the firm's need for these inventory types depends on its need for finished items. In contrast, the firm's demand for finished goods is not derived from demand for other inventory items, so it is sometimes said to be *independent*.

INVENTORY COSTS

As we discussed in Chapter 26, two basic types of costs are associated with current assets in general and with inventory in particular. The first of these is *carrying costs*. Here, carrying costs represent all of the direct and opportunity costs of keeping inventory on hand. These include:

1. Storage and tracking costs.
2. Insurance and taxes.
3. Losses due to obsolescence, deterioration, or theft.
4. The opportunity cost of capital on the invested amount.

The sum of these costs can be substantial, ranging roughly from 20 to 40 percent of inventory value per year.

The other type of costs associated with inventory is *shortage costs*. Shortage costs are costs associated with having inadequate inventory on hand. The two components of shortage costs are restocking costs and costs related to safety reserves. Depending on the firm's business, restocking or order costs are either the costs of placing an order with suppliers or the costs of setting up a production run. The costs related to safety reserves are opportunity losses such as lost sales and loss of customer goodwill that result from having inadequate inventory.

A basic trade-off exists in inventory management because carrying costs increase with inventory levels, whereas shortage or restocking costs decline with inventory levels. The basic goal of inventory management thus is to minimize the sum of these two costs. We consider ways to reach this goal in the next section.

28.8 Inventory Management Techniques

As we described earlier, the goal of inventory management is usually framed as cost minimization. Three techniques are discussed in this section, ranging from the relatively simple to the very complex.

THE ABC APPROACH

The ABC approach is a simple approach to inventory management in which the basic idea is to divide inventory into three (or more) groups. The underlying rationale is that a small portion of inventory in terms of quantity might represent a large portion in terms of inventory value. This situation would exist for a manufacturer that uses some relatively expensive, high-tech components and some relatively inexpensive basic materials in producing its products.

Figure 28.2 illustrates an ABC comparison of items in terms of the percentage of inventory value represented by each group versus the percentage of items represented. As Figure 28.2 shows, the A Group constitutes only 10 percent of inventory by item count, but it represents more than half of the value of inventory. The A Group items are thus monitored closely and inventory levels are kept relatively low. At the other end, basic inventory items, such as nuts and bolts, also exist, but because these are crucial and inexpensive, large quantities are ordered and kept on hand. These would be C Group items. The B Group is made up of in-between items.

THE ECONOMIC ORDER QUANTITY MODEL

The economic order quantity (EOQ) model is the best-known approach for explicitly establishing an optimal inventory level. The basic idea is illustrated in Figure 28.3, which plots the various costs associated with holding inventory (on the vertical axis) against inventory levels (on the horizontal axis). As shown, inventory carrying costs rise and restocking costs decrease as inventory levels increase. From our general discussion in Chapter 26 and our discussion of the total credit cost curve in this chapter, the general shape of the total inventory cost curve is familiar. With the EOQ model, we will attempt to specifically locate the minimum total cost point, Q^*.

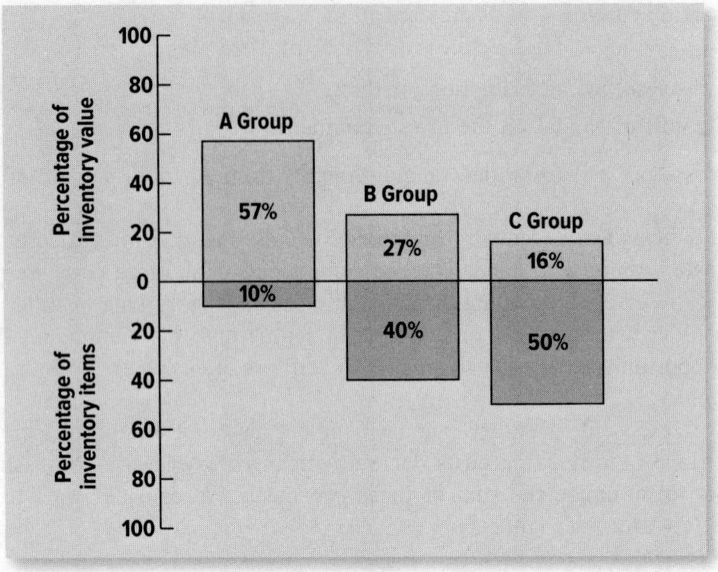

Figure 28.2 ABC Inventory Analysis

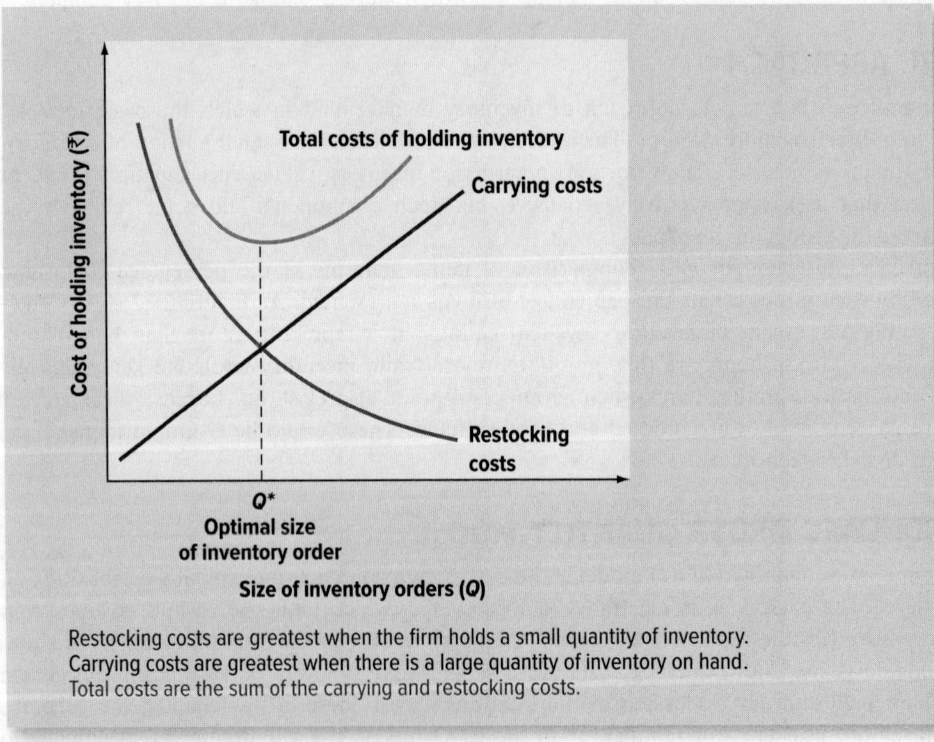

Figure 28.3 Costs of Holding Inventory

In our discussion that follows, an important point to keep in mind is that the actual cost of the inventory itself is not included. The reason is that the total amount of inventory the firm needs in a given year is dictated by sales. What we are analyzing here is how much the firm should have on hand at any particular time. More precisely, we are trying to determine what order size the firm should use when it restocks its inventory.

Inventory Depletion To develop the EOQ, we will assume that the firm's inventory is sold off at a steady rate until it hits zero. At that point, the firm restocks its inventory back to some optimal level. Suppose the Madhu Company starts out today with 3,600 units of a particular item in inventory. Annual sales of this item are 46,800 units, which is 900 per week. If Madhu sells 900 units of inventory each week, all the available inventory will be sold after four weeks, and Madhu will restock by ordering (or manufacturing) another 3,600 and start over. This selling and restocking process produces a sawtooth pattern for inventory holdings; this pattern is illustrated in Figure 28.4. As the figure shows, Madhu always starts with 3,600 units in inventory and ends up at zero. On average, then, inventory is half of 3,600, or 1,800 units.

The Carrying Costs As Figure 28.3 illustrates, carrying costs are normally assumed to be directly proportional to inventory levels. Suppose we let Q be the quantity of inventory that Madhu orders each time (3,600 units); we will call this the *restocking quantity*. Average inventory then would

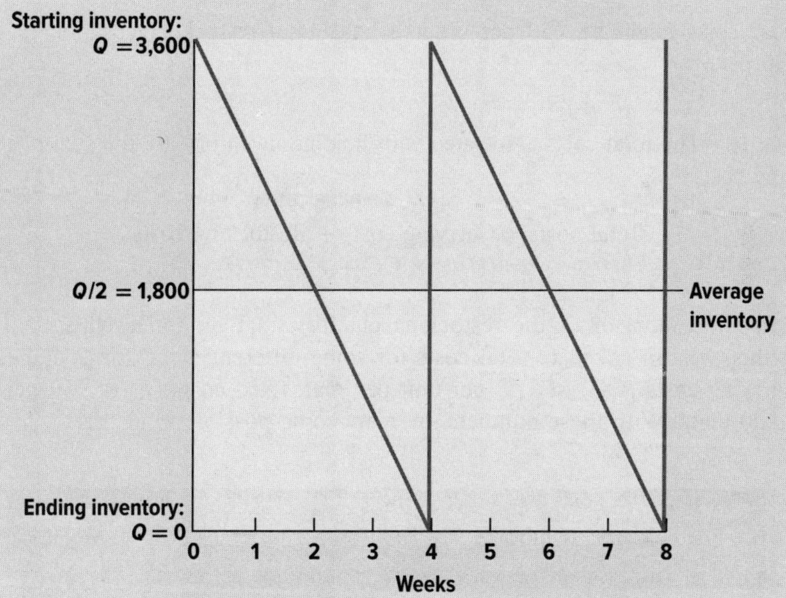

The Madhu Company starts with inventory of 3,600 units. The quantity drops to zero by the end of the fourth week. The average inventory is $Q/2 = 3{,}600/2 = 1{,}800$ over the period.

Figure 28.4 Inventory Holdings for the Madhu Company

be $Q/2$, or 1,800 units. If we let CC be the carrying cost per unit per year, Madhu's total carrying costs will be:

$$\begin{aligned}\text{Total carrying costs} &= \text{Average inventory} \times \text{Carrying costs per unit} \\ &= (Q/2) \times \text{CC}\end{aligned} \tag{28.10}$$

In Madhu's case, if carrying costs were ₹.75 per unit per year, total carrying costs would be the average inventory of 1,800 multiplied by ₹.75, or ₹1,350 per year.

The Shortage Costs For now, we will focus only on the restocking costs. In essence, we will assume that the firm never actually runs short on inventory, so that costs relating to safety reserves are not important. We will return to this issue later.

Restocking costs are normally assumed to be fixed. In other words, every time we place an order, fixed costs are associated with that order (remember that the cost of the inventory itself is not considered here). Suppose we let T be the firm's total unit sales per year. If the firm orders Q units each time, then it will need to place a total of T/Q orders. For Madhu, annual sales are 46,800 and the order size is 3,600. Madhu thus places a total of 46,800/3,600 = 13 orders per year. If the fixed cost per order is F, the total restocking cost for the year would be:

$$\begin{aligned}\text{Total restocking cost} &= \text{Fixed cost per order} \times \text{Number of orders} \\ &= F \times (T/Q)\end{aligned} \tag{28.11}$$

For Madhu, order costs might be ₹50 per order, so the total restocking cost for 13 orders would be ₹50 × 13 = ₹650 per year.

The Total Costs The total costs associated with holding inventory are the sum of the carrying costs and the restocking costs:

$$\begin{aligned}\text{Total costs} &= \text{Carrying costs} + \text{Restocking costs} \\ &= (Q/2) \times \text{CC} + F \times (T/Q)\end{aligned} \tag{28.12}$$

Our goal is to find the value of Q, the restocking quantity, that minimizes this cost. To see how we might go about this, we can calculate total costs for some different values of Q. For the Madhu Company, we had carrying costs (CC) of ₹.75 per unit per year, fixed costs (F) of ₹50 per order, and total sales (T) of 46,800 units. With these numbers, here are some possible total costs (check some of these for practice):

Restocking Quantity (Q)	Carrying Costs (Q/2 × CC)	+	Restocking Costs (F × T/Q)	=	Total Costs
500	₹ 187.50		₹4,680.00		₹4,867.50
1,000	375.00		2,340.00		2,715.00
1,500	562.50		1,560.00		2,122.50
2,000	750.00		1,170.00		1,920.00
2,500	**937.50**		**936.00**		**1,873.50**
3,000	1,125.00		780.00		1,905.00
3,500	1,312.50		668.57		1,981.07

Inspecting the numbers, we see that total costs start out at almost ₹5,000 and decline to just under ₹1,900. The cost-minimizing quantity is about 2,500.

To find the exact cost-minimizing quantity, we can look back at Figure 28.3. What we notice is that the minimum point occurs right where the two lines cross. At this point, carrying costs and restocking costs are the same. For the particular types of costs we have assumed here, this will always be true; so we can find the minimum point by setting these costs equal to each other and solving for Q^*:

$$\begin{aligned} \text{Carrying costs} &= \text{Restocking costs} \\ (Q^*/2) \times \text{CC} &\doteq F \times (T/Q^*) \end{aligned} \tag{28.13}$$

With a little algebra, we get:

$$Q^{*2} = \frac{2T \times F}{\text{CC}} \tag{28.14}$$

To solve for Q^*, we take the square root of both sides to find:

$$Q^* = \sqrt{\frac{2T \times F}{\text{CC}}} \tag{28.15}$$

This reorder quantity, which minimizes the total inventory cost, is called the **economic order quantity (EOQ)**. For the Madhu Company, the EOQ is:

$$\begin{aligned} Q^* &= \sqrt{\frac{2T \times F}{\text{CC}}} \\ &= \sqrt{\frac{(2 \times 46{,}800) \times ₹50}{.75}} \\ &= \sqrt{6{,}240{,}000} \\ &= 2{,}498 \text{ units} \end{aligned}$$

For Madhu, the economic order quantity is 2,498 units. At this level, verify that the restocking costs and carrying costs are both ₹936.75.

EXAMPLE 28.2

Carrying Costs Thalaivar Shoes begins each period with 100 pairs of hiking boots in stock. This stock is depleted each period and reordered. If the carrying cost per pair of boots per year is ₹3, what are the total carrying costs for the hiking boots?

Inventories always start at 100 items and end up at zero, so average inventory is 50 items. At an annual cost of ₹3 per item, total carrying costs are ₹150.

EXAMPLE 28.3

Restocking Costs In Example 28.2, suppose Thalaivar sells a total of 600 pairs of boots in a year. How many times per year does Thalaivar restock? Suppose the restocking cost is ₹20 per order. What are total restocking costs?

Thalaivar orders 100 items each time. Total sales are 600 items per year, so Thalaivar restocks six times per year, or about every two months. The restocking costs would be 6 orders × ₹20 per order = ₹120.

EXAMPLE 28.4

The EOQ Based on our previous two examples, what size orders should Thalaivar place to minimize costs? How often will Thalaivar restock? What are the total carrying and restocking costs? The total costs?

We know that the total number of pairs of boots ordered for the year (*T*) is 600. The restocking cost (*F*) is ₹20 per order and the carrying cost (CC) is ₹3 per unit per year. We can calculate the EOQ for Thalaivar as follows:

$$\begin{aligned} \text{EOQ} &= \sqrt{\frac{2T \times F}{\text{CC}}} \\ &= \sqrt{\frac{(2 \times 600) \times ₹20}{3}} \\ &= \sqrt{8{,}000} \\ &= 89.44 \text{ units} \end{aligned}$$

Because Thalaivar sells 600 pairs per year, it will restock 600/89.44 = 6.71 times. The total restocking costs will be ₹20 × 6.71 = ₹134.16. Average inventory will be 89.44/2 = 44.72. The carrying costs will be ₹3 × 44.72 = ₹134.16, the same as the restocking costs. The total costs are ₹268.33.

EXTENSIONS TO THE EOQ MODEL

Thus far, we have assumed that a company will let its inventory run down to zero and then reorder. In reality, a company will wish to reorder before its inventory goes to zero for two reasons. First, by always having at least some inventory on hand, the firm minimizes the risk of a stockout and the resulting losses of sales and customers. Second, when a firm does reorder, there will be some time lag before the inventory arrives. To finish our discussion of the EOQ, we consider two extensions: safety stocks and reorder points.

Safety Stocks A *safety stock* is the minimum level of inventory that a firm keeps on hand. Inventories are reordered whenever the level of inventory falls to the safety stock level. The top of Figure 28.5 illustrates how a safety stock can be incorporated into an EOQ model. Notice that adding a safety stock means that the firm does not run its inventory all the way down to zero. Other than this, the situation here is identical to that described in our earlier discussion of the EOQ.

Reorder Points To allow for delivery time, a firm will place orders before inventories reach a critical level. The *reorder points* are the times at which the firm will actually place its inventory orders. These points are illustrated in the middle of Figure 28.5. As shown, the reorder points occur some fixed number of days (or weeks or months) before inventories are projected to reach zero.

One of the reasons that a firm will keep a safety stock is to allow for uncertain delivery times. We can therefore combine our reorder point and safety stock discussions in the bottom part of Figure 28.5. The result is a generalized EOQ model in which the firm orders in advance of anticipated needs and also keeps a safety stock of inventory.

MANAGING DERIVED-DEMAND INVENTORIES

The third type of inventory management technique is used to manage derived-demand inventories. As we described earlier, demand for some inventory types is derived from, or dependent on, other inventory needs. A good example is given by the auto manufacturing industry, in which the demand for finished products depends

A. Safety stocks

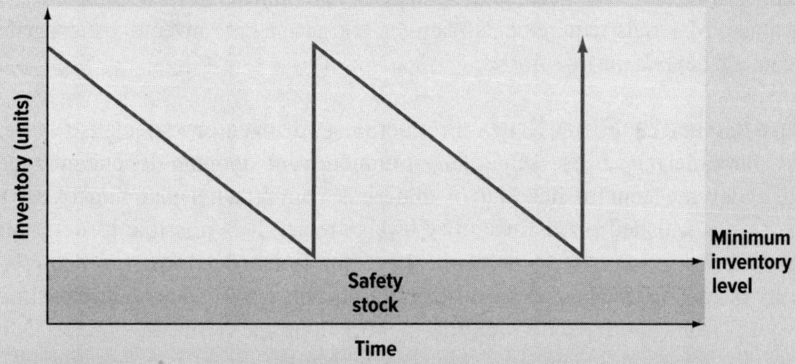

With a safety stock, the firm reorders when inventory reaches a minimum level.

B. Reorder points

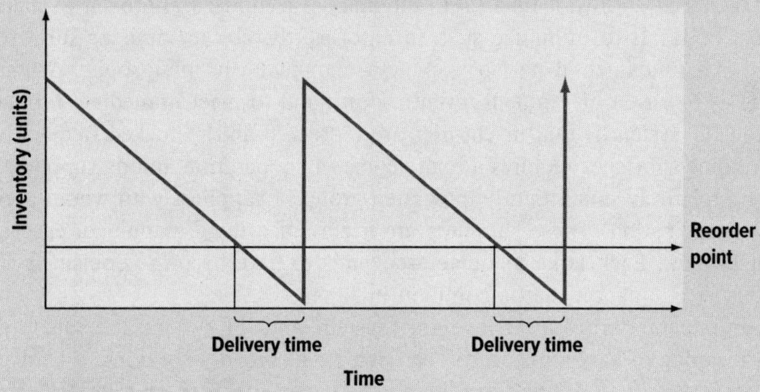

When there are lags in delivery or production times, the firm reorders when inventory reaches the reorder point.

C. Combined reorder points and safety stocks

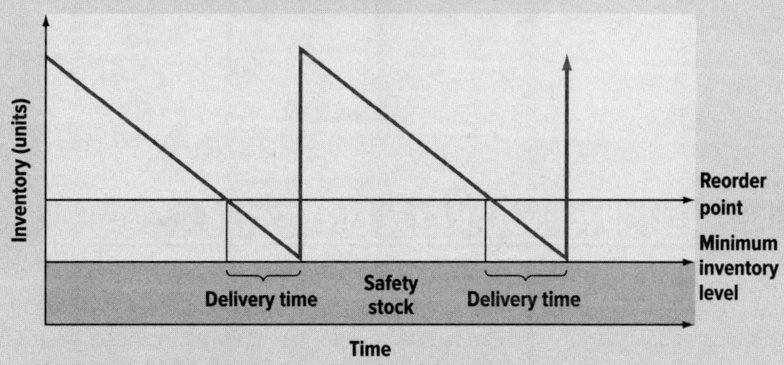

By combining safety stocks and reorder points, the firm maintains a buffer against unforeseen events.

Figure 28.5 Safety Stocks and Reorder Points

on consumer demand, marketing programs, and other factors related to projected unit sales. The demand for inventory items such as tires, batteries, headlights, and other components is then completely determined by the number of autos planned. Materials requirements planning and just-in-time inventory management are two methods for managing demand-dependent inventories.

Materials Requirements Planning Production and inventory specialists have developed computer-based systems for ordering and/or scheduling production of demand-dependent types of inventories. These systems fall under the general heading of **materials requirements planning (MRP)**. The basic idea behind MRP is that, once finished goods inventory levels are set, it is possible to determine what levels of work-in-progress inventories must exist to meet the need for finished goods. From there, it is possible to calculate the quantity of raw materials that must be on hand. This ability to schedule backward from finished goods inventories stems from the dependent nature of work-in-progress and raw materials inventories. MRP is particularly important for complicated products for which a variety of components are needed to create the finished product.

Just-in-Time Inventory **Just-in-time (JIT) inventory** is a modern approach to managing dependent inventories. The goal of JIT is to minimize such inventories, thereby maximizing turnover. The approach began in Japan and is a fundamental part of Japanese manufacturing philosophy. As the name suggests, the basic goal of JIT is to have only enough inventory on hand to meet immediate production needs.

The result of the JIT system is that inventories are reordered and restocked frequently. Making such a system work and avoiding shortages requires a high degree of cooperation among suppliers. Japanese manufacturers often have a relatively small, tightly integrated group of suppliers with whom they work closely to achieve the needed coordination. These suppliers are a part of a large manufacturer's (such as Toyota's) industrial group, or *keiretsu*. Each large manufacturer tends to have its own keiretsu. It also helps to have suppliers located nearby, a situation that is common in Japan.

The *kanban* is an integral part of a JIT inventory system, and JIT systems are sometimes called *kanban systems*. The literal meaning of kanban is "card" or "sign"; but, broadly speaking, a kanban is a signal to a supplier to send more inventory. A kanban can literally be a card attached to a bin of parts. When a worker pulls that bin, the card is detached and routed back to the supplier, who then supplies a replacement bin.

A JIT inventory system is an important part of a larger production planning process. A full discussion of it would necessarily shift our focus away from finance to production and operations management, so we will leave it here.

RESEARCH IN EMERGING MARKET CONTEXT

Panda and Nanda (2018) find a convex relationship between Working Capital Financing (WCF) and profitability among chemical, construction, and consumer goods firms. Firms in these sectors can finance a larger portion of their working capital requirements through short-term debt without negatively impacting profitability. The authors find a concave relationship pattern for firms in the machinery, metal, and textile industries, implying that increasing debt financing of working capital requirements would increase profitability for the firms who have financed the lower portion of their working capital by short-term bank borrowing.

Seth et al. (2020) empirically investigate the relationship between working capital management (WCM) efficiency and exogenous variables of the Indian manufacturing sector along with its sub-industries involved in export activities. Industry-wise results showed a significant relationship between leverage, net fixed asset ratio, profitability, asset turnover ratio, total asset growth rate and productivity with cash conversion cycle (CCC).

Yao and Deng (2018) report that managers can be motivated to manipulate their working capital management due to their compensation incentives. The report states a negative relationship between managerial risk-taking incentives and accounts receivable, as well as a negative relationship between vega and the market value of accounts receivable to shareholders. As a result, equity holders should be cautious when CEOs change their accounts receivable management policy.

References

Panda, A. K., & Nanda, S. (2018). Working capital financing and corporate profitability of Indian manufacturing firms. *Management Decision*, *56*(2), 441–457.

Seth, H., Chadha, S., Ruparel, N., Arora, P. K., & Sharma, S. K. (2020). Assessing working capital management efficiency of Indian manufacturing exporters. *Managerial Finance*, *46*(8), 1061–1079.

Yao, H., & Deng, Y. (2018). Managerial incentives and accounts receivable management policy.–*Managerial Finance*, *44*(7), 865–884.

Summary and Conclusions

This chapter has covered the basics of credit and inventory policy. The major topics we discussed include:

1. The components of credit policy: We discussed the terms of sale, credit analysis, and collection policy. Under the general subject of terms of sale, the credit period, the cash discount and discount period, and the credit instrument were described.
2. Credit policy analysis: We developed the cash flows from the decision to grant credit and showed how the credit decision can be analyzed in an NPV setting. The NPV of granting credit depends on five factors: revenue effects, cost effects, the cost of debt, the probability of nonpayment, and the cash discount.
3. Optimal credit policy: The optimal amount of credit the firm should offer depends on the competitive conditions under which the firm operates. These conditions will determine the carrying costs associated with granting credit and the opportunity costs of the lost sales resulting from refusing to offer credit. The optimal credit policy minimizes the sum of these two costs.
4. Credit analysis: We looked at the decision to grant credit to a particular customer. We saw that two considerations are very important: the cost relative to the selling price and the possibility of repeat business.
5. Collection policy: Collection policy determines the method of monitoring the age of accounts receivable and dealing with past-due accounts. We described how an aging schedule can be prepared and the procedures a firm might use to collect on past-due accounts.
6. Inventory types: We described the different inventory types and how they differ in terms of liquidity and demand.
7. Inventory costs: The two basic inventory costs are carrying and restocking costs. We discussed how inventory management involves a trade-off between these two costs.
8. Inventory management techniques: We described the ABC approach and the EOQ model approach to inventory management. We also briefly touched on materials requirements planning (MRP) and just-in-time (JIT) inventory management.

Concept Questions

1. **Credit Instruments** Describe each of the following:
   a. Sight draft.
   b. Time draft.
   c. Banker's acceptance.
   d. Promissory note.
   e. Trade acceptance.
2. **Trade Credit Forms** In what form is trade credit most commonly offered? What is the credit instrument in this case?
3. **Receivables Costs** What costs are associated with carrying receivables? What costs are associated with not granting credit? What do we call the sum of the costs for different levels of receivables?
4. **Five *Cs* of Credit** What are the five *Cs* of credit? Explain why each is important.
5. **Credit Period Length** What are some of the factors that determine the length of the credit period? Why is the length of the buyer's operating cycle often considered an upper bound on the length of the credit period?
6. **Credit Period Length** In each of the following pairings, indicate which firm would probably have a longer credit period and explain your reasoning.
   a. Firm A sells a miracle cure for baldness; Firm B sells toupees.
   b. Firm A specializes in products for landlords; Firm B specializes in products for renters.
   c. Firm A sells to customers with an inventory turnover of 10 times; Firm B sells to customers with an inventory turnover of 20 times.
   d. Firm A sells fresh fruit; Firm B sells canned fruit.
   e. Firm A sells and installs carpeting; Firm B sells rugs.
7. **Inventory Types** What are the different inventory types? How do the types differ? Why are some types said to have dependent demand, whereas other types are said to have independent demand?
8. **Just-in-Time Inventory** If a company moves to a JIT inventory management system, what will happen to inventory turnover? What will happen to total asset turnover? What will happen to return on equity (ROE)? (*Hint*: Remember the DuPont equation from Chapter 3.)
9. **Inventory Costs** If a company's inventory carrying costs are ₹5 million per year and its fixed order costs are ₹8 million per year, do you think the firm keeps too much inventory on hand or too little? Why?
10. **Inventory Period** At least part of Dell's corporate profits can be traced to its inventory management. Using just-in-time inventory, Dell typically maintains an inventory of three to four days' sales. Competitors such as HP, Inc., and IBM have attempted to match Dell's inventory policies but lag far behind. In an industry where the price of PC components continues to decline, Dell clearly has a competitive advantage. Why would you say that it is to Dell's advantage to have such a short inventory period? If doing this is valuable, why don't all other PC manufacturers switch to Dell's approach?

Questions and Problems

BASIC (Questions 1–12)

1. **Cash Discounts** You place an order for 250 units of inventory at a unit price of ₹190. The supplier offers terms of 1/10, net 30.
   a. How long do you have to pay before the account is overdue? If you take the full period, how much should you remit?

b. What is the discount being offered? How quickly must you pay to get the discount? If you do take the discount, how much should you remit?
c. If you don't take the discount, how much interest are you paying implicitly? How many days' credit are you receiving?

2. **Size of Accounts Receivable** The Caccamisse Corporation has annual sales of ₹29 million. The average collection period is 34 days. What is the average investment in accounts receivable as shown on the balance sheet? Assume 365 days per year.

3. **ACP and Accounts Receivable** Kyoto Joe, Inc., sells earnings forecasts for Japanese securities. Its credit terms are 2/10, net 30. Based on experience, 65 percent of all customers will take the discount. Assume 365 days per year.

   a. What is the average collection period for the company?
   b. If the company sells 980 forecasts every month at a price of ₹1,670 each, what is its average balance sheet amount in accounts receivable?

4. **Size of Accounts Receivable** Sweetens Cove, Inc., has weekly credit sales of ₹23,400, and the average collection period is 31 days. What is the average accounts receivable figure?

5. **Terms of Sale** A firm offers terms of 1/10, net 30. What effective annual interest rate does the firm earn when a customer does not take the discount? Without doing any calculations, explain what will happen to this effective rate if:

   a. The discount is changed to 2 percent.
   b. The credit period is increased to 45 days.
   c. The discount period is increased to 14 days.

6. **ACP and Receivables Turnover** Benton, Inc., has an average collection period of 24 days. Its average daily investment in receivables is ₹49,300. What are annual credit sales? What is the receivables turnover? Assume 365 days per year.

7. **Size of Accounts Receivable** Essence of Skunk Fragrances, Ltd., sells 9,300 units of its perfume collection each year at a price per unit of ₹415. All sales are on credit with terms of 1/10, net 40. The discount is taken by 45 percent of the customers. What is the amount of the company's accounts receivable? In reaction to sales by its main competitor, Sewage Spray, Essence of Skunk is considering a change in its credit policy to terms of 2/10, net 30 to preserve its market share. How will this change in policy affect accounts receivable? Assume 365 days per year.

8. **Size of Accounts Receivable** The Paa Ko Corporation sells on credit terms of net 30. Its accounts are, on average, four days past due. If annual credit sales are ₹7.2 million, what is the company's balance sheet amount in accounts receivable? Assume 365 days per year.

9. **Evaluating Credit Policy** Air Spares is a wholesaler that stocks engine components and test equipment for the commercial aircraft industry. A new customer has placed an order for eight high-bypass turbine engines, which increase fuel economy. The variable cost is ₹1.325 million per unit, and the credit price is ₹1.74 million each. Credit is extended for one period, and based on historical experience, payment for about 1 out of every 200 such orders is never collected. The required return is 1.8 percent per period.

   a. Assuming that this is a one-time order, should it be filled? The customer will not buy if credit is not extended.
   b. What is the break-even probability of default in part (a)?
   c. Suppose that customers who don't default become repeat customers and place the same order every period forever. Further assume that repeat customers never default. Should the order be filled? What is the break-even probability of default?
   d. Describe in general terms why credit terms will be more liberal when repeat orders are a possibility.

10. **Credit Policy Evaluation** Red Hawk, Inc., is considering a change in its cash-only sales policy. The new terms of sale would be net one month. Based on the following information, determine if the company should proceed or not. Describe the buildup of receivables in this case. The required return is .95 percent per month.

	Current Policy	New Policy
Price per unit	₹485	₹485
Cost per unit	₹365	₹365
Unit sales per month	920	975

11. **EOQ** Queen Manufacturing uses 3,900 switch assemblies per week and then reorders another 3,900. If the relevant carrying cost per switch assembly is ₹6.25, and the fixed order cost is ₹1,400, is the company's inventory policy optimal? Why or why not?

12. **EOQ** The Trektronics store begins each week with 380 phasers in stock. This stock is depleted each week and reordered. If the carrying cost per phaser is ₹31 per year and the fixed order cost is ₹325, what is the total carrying cost? What is the restocking cost? Should the company increase or decrease its order size? Describe an optimal inventory policy for the company in terms of order size and order frequency.

INTERMEDIATE (Questions 13–16)

13. **EOQ Derivation** Prove that when carrying costs and restocking costs are as described in the chapter, the EOQ must occur at the point where the carrying costs and restocking costs are equal.

14. **Credit Policy Evaluation** The Branson Corporation is considering a change in its cash-only policy. The new terms would be net one period. Based on the following information, determine if the company should proceed or not. The required return is 2.3 percent per period.

	Current Policy	New Policy
Price per unit	₹83	₹86
Cost per unit	₹47	₹47
Unit sales per month	2,960	3,045

15. **Credit Policy Evaluation** Fitzgerald Corp. currently has an all-cash credit policy. It is considering making a change in the credit policy by going to terms of net 30 days. Based on the following information, what do you recommend? The required return is .85 percent per month.

	Current Policy	New Policy
Price per unit	₹127	₹129
Cost per unit	₹94	₹96
Unit sales per month	1,320	1,340

16. **Credit Policy** The Silver Spokes Bicycle Shop has decided to offer credit to its customers during the spring selling season. Sales are expected to be 125 bicycles. The average cost to the shop of a bicycle is

₹750. The owner knows that only 96 percent of the customers will be able to make their payments. To identify the remaining 4 percent, the company is considering subscribing to a credit agency. The initial charge for this service is ₹1,000, with an additional charge of ₹8.95 per individual report. Should she subscribe to the agency?

CHALLENGE (Questions 17–22)

17. **Break-Even Quantity** In Problem 14, what is the break-even quantity for the new credit policy?

18. **Credit Markup** In Problem 14, what is the break-even price per unit that should be charged under the new credit policy? Assume that the sales figure under the new policy is 3,310 units and all other values remain the same.

19. **Credit Markup** In Problem 15, what is the break-even price per unit under the new credit policy? Assume all other values remain the same.

20. **Safety Stocks and Order Points** Saché, Inc., expects to sell 700 of its designer suits every week. The store is open seven days a week and expects to sell the same number of suits every day. The company has an EOQ of 500 suits and a safety stock of 100 suits. Once an order is placed, it takes three days for Saché to get the suits in. How many orders does the company place per year? Assume that it is Monday morning before the store opens and a shipment of suits has just arrived. When will Saché place its next order?

21. **Evaluating Credit Policy** Solar Engines manufactures solar engines for tractor-trailers. Given the fuel savings available, new orders for125 units have been made by customers requesting credit. The variable cost is ₹14,800 per unit, and the credit price is ₹16,100 each. Credit is extended for one period. The required return is 1.9 percent per period. If Solar Engines extends credit, it expects that 30 percent of the customers will be repeat customers and place the same order every period forever and the remaining customers will be one-time orders. Should credit be extended?

22. **Evaluating Credit Policy** In the previous problem, assume that the probability of default is 15 percent. Should the orders be filled now? Assume the number of repeat customers is affected by the defaults. In other words, 30 percent of the customers who do not default are expected to be repeat customers.

23. **Credit Period** Prosenjit Monitors Limited (PML), manufacturers of computer monitors, is considering liberalization of existing credit terms to four of their large customers - TCS, Wipro, Infosys, and Cognizant. The credit period and likely quantity of monitors that will be lifted (per year) by the customers are as follows:

Credit Period (Days)	TCS	Wipro	Infosys	Cognizant
0	500	1000	-	-
30	500	1500	500	-
60	500	2000	1000	200
90	500	2500	1500	400

The selling price per monitor is ₹9,000/-. The expected contribution is 15% of the selling price. The cost of carrying debtors averages 15% per annum. You are required to help Prosenjit in solving the following problem:

a. Determine the credit period to be allowed to each customer.

b. What other problems Prosenjit might face in allowing the credit period as determined in (a) above?

Mini Case CREDIT POLICY AT BRAAM INDUSTRIES

Tricia Haltiwinger, the president of Braam Industries, has been exploring ways of improving the company's financial performance. Braam Industries manufactures and sells office equipment to retailers. The company's growth has been relatively slow in recent years, but with an expansion in the economy, it appears that sales may increase more quickly in the future. Tricia has asked Andrew Preston, the company's treasurer, to examine Braam's credit policy to see if a different credit policy can help increase profitability.

The company currently has a policy of net 30. As with any credit sales, default rates are always of concern. Because of Braam's screening and collection process, the default rate on credit is currently only 2.1 percent. Andrew has examined the company's credit policy in relation to other vendors and has determined that three options are available.

The first option is to relax the company's decision on when to grant credit. The second option is to increase the credit period to net 45 and the third option is a combination of the relaxed credit policy and the extension of the credit period to net 45. On the positive side, each of the three policies under consideration would increase sales. The three policies have the drawbacks that default rates would increase, the administrative costs of managing the firm's receivables would increase, and the receivables period would increase. The credit policy change would impact all four of these variables in different degrees. Andrew has prepared the following table outlining the effect on each of these variables:

	Annual Sales (in millions)	Default Rate (% of sales)	Administrative Costs (% of sales)	Receivables Period
Current policy	₹113	2.10%	1.60%	38 days
Option 1	129	2.60	2.40	41
Option 2	127	2.20	1.90	51
Option 3	130	2.50	2.10	49

Braam's variable costs of production are 45 percent of sales and the relevant interest rate is a 6 percent effective annual rate. Which credit policy should the company use? Also, notice that in Option 2 the default rate and administrative costs are below those in Option 3. Is this plausible? Why or why not?

Appendix 28A More about Credit Policy Analysis

To access the appendix for this chapter, please log on to www.mheducation.co.in.

29

PART VIII: SPECIAL TOPICS

Mergers, Acquisitions, and Divestitures

In June 2020, Just Eat Takeaway delivered when it agreed to purchase Grubhub for ₹7.3 billion. Just Eat Takeaway is a European food delivery service. The acquisition of Grubhub gave the company an immediate presence in the U.S. food delivery market. And, in January 2020, Visa announced that it was acquiring Plaid for ₹5.3 billion. Plaid enables customers to share bank accounts with more than 11,000 financial institutions and 2,600 fintech developers. The acquisition would give Visa an immediate opportunity in the fintech markets.

How do companies like Just Eat Takeaway and Visa determine whether an acquisition is a good idea? This chapter explores reasons that mergers should take place—and, just as important, reasons they should not.

Please visit us at **rwjcorporatefinance.blogspot.com** for the latest developments in the world of corporate finance.

29.1 The Basic Forms of Acquisitions

Acquisitions follow one of three basic forms: (1) merger or consolidation, (2) acquisition of stock, and (3) acquisition of assets.

MERGER OR CONSOLIDATION

A **merger** refers to the absorption of one firm by another. The acquiring firm retains its name and identity, and it acquires all of the assets and liabilities of the acquired firm. After a merger, the acquired firm ceases to exist as a separate business entity.

A **consolidation** is the same as a merger except that an entirely new firm is created. In a consolidation, both the acquiring firm and the acquired firm terminate their previous legal existence and become part of the new firm.

EXAMPLE 29.1

Merger Basics Suppose Firm A acquires Firm B in a merger. Further, suppose Firm B's shareholders are given one share of Firm A's stock in exchange for two shares of Firm B's stock. From a legal standpoint, Firm A's shareholders are not directly affected by the merger. However, Firm B's shares cease to exist. In a consolidation, the shareholders of Firm A and Firm B exchange their shares for shares of a new firm (e.g., Firm C).

Because of the similarities between mergers and consolidations, we shall refer to both types of reorganization as mergers. Here are two important points about mergers and consolidations:

1. A merger is legally straightforward and does not cost as much as other forms of acquisition. It avoids the necessity of transferring title of each individual asset of the acquired firm to the acquiring firm.
2. The stockholders of each firm must approve a merger.[1] Typically, two-thirds of share owners must vote in favor for it to be approved. In addition, shareholders of the acquired firm have *appraisal rights*. This means that they can demand that the acquiring firm purchase their shares at a fair value. Often, the acquiring firm and the dissenting shareholders of the acquired firm cannot agree on a fair value, which results in expensive legal proceedings.

In India, most mergers have been for either of two reasons- one is by force of the lenders and/or regulators, and the second is a within-business group exercise. Indian banking space is one of the best examples for the first reason. In November 2020, the Lakshmi Vilas Bank (LVB) was merged with DBS Group Holdings following an amalgamation plan spearheaded by the RBI, to rescue the troubled LVB. For the second reason, a classic illustration is the merger of Ambani group entities, Reliance Petroleum Limited and Reliance Industries Limited, resulting in the largest private firm in India, Reliance Industries Limited. In 2023, HDFC Bank acquired mortgage lender HDFC Ltd., causing its subsidiaries to shift to HDFC Bank.

ACQUISITION OF STOCK

A second way to acquire another firm is to purchase the firm's voting stock in exchange for cash, shares of stock, or other securities. This process may start as a private offer from the management of one firm to another. At some point, the offer is taken directly to the selling firm's stockholders, often by a tender offer. A **tender offer** is a public offer to buy shares of a target firm. It is made by one firm directly to the shareholders of another firm. The offer is communicated to the target firm's shareholders by public announcements such as newspaper advertisements. Sometimes a general mailing is used in a tender offer. However, a general mailing is difficult because the names and addresses of the stockholders of record are not usually available.

The following factors are involved in choosing between an acquisition of stock and a merger:

1. In an acquisition of stock, shareholder meetings need not be held and a vote is not required. If the shareholders of the target firm do not like the offer, they are not required to accept it and need not tender their shares.
2. In an acquisition of stock, the bidding firm can deal directly with the shareholders of a target firm via a tender offer. The target firm's management and board of directors are bypassed.
3. Target managers often resist acquisition. In such cases, acquisition of stock circumvents the target firm's management. Resistance by the target firm's management often makes the cost of acquisition of stock higher than the cost by merger.
4. Frequently, a minority of shareholders will hold out in a tender offer and, thus, the target firm cannot be completely absorbed.
5. Complete absorption of one firm by another requires a merger. Many acquisitions of stock end with a formal merger.

In 2019, Ruchi Soya was acquired by Baba Ramdev's Patanjali Ayurveda-led consortium via an insolvency resolution process. In 2020, GSK Consumer was acquired by Hindustan Unilever and Uber Eats was acquired by Zomato. A classic case of hostile acquisition is India Cements' acquisition of Raasi Cements. The hostility

[1]Mergers between corporations require compliance with state laws. In virtually all states, the shareholders of each corporation must give their assent.

of the acquisition can be gauged from the fact that a tender offer to acquire shares of Raasi Cements was made at more than 12 times the price Raasi Cements used to be traded two years before the acquisition.[2] In the year 2022, NDTV was taken over by the Adani Group through AMG Media Networks Limited (AMNL).

ACQUISITION OF ASSETS

One firm can acquire another by buying all of its assets. The selling firm does not necessarily vanish because its "shell" can be retained. A formal vote of the target stockholders is required in an acquisition of assets. An advantage here is that although the acquirer is often left with minority shareholders in an acquisition of stock, this does not happen in an acquisition of assets. Minority shareholders often present problems, such as holdouts. However, asset acquisition involves transferring title to individual assets, which can be costly.

There are a few such cases in the Indian market.

In December 2017, Adani Transmission acquired Reliance Infrastructure's Mumbai power distribution business. In this case, Adani acquired specific assets from Reliance Infrastructure. On the other hand, in September 2023, Nirma acquired a majority stake in Glenmark Life Sciences (GLS) by buying a 75% stake in GLS. Subsequently, in February 2024, Nirma made an open offer to buy out the remaining minority shareholders.

A CLASSIFICATION SCHEME

Financial analysts have typically classified acquisitions into three types:

1. *Horizontal acquisition*: Here, both the acquirer and acquired are in the same industry. Just Eat Takeaway's acquisition of Grubhub, which we mentioned at the beginning of the chapter, would be a horizontal acquisition.
2. *Vertical acquisition*: A vertical acquisition involves firms at different steps of the production process. The Visa acquisition of Plaid was a vertical acquisition. Another vertical acquisition was the 2020 Salesforce acquisition of Vlocity. Vlocity provides cloud and mobile-based software built natively on the Salesforce platform.
3. *Conglomerate acquisition*: The acquiring firm and the acquired firm are not related to each other. Conglomerate acquisitions are popular in the technology arena. For example, by early 2020, Alphabet had acquired more than 238 companies since 2003. And while you may be familiar with Google's Android OS for cell phones, you may not be aware that Google acquired Android in 2005. In recent times, the Indian market has seen many horizontal acquisitions such as Zomato acquiring Uber Eats, Myntra acquiring Jabong, Hindalco acquiring Aleris and FirstCry acquiring BabyOye. On the other hand, LIC's acquisition of IDBI Bank is an example of vertical acquisition. Similar is the case of HDFC acquiring Apollo Munich Health Insurance. Barak Valley Cements' acquisition of tea gardens and plantation estates can be termed a conglomerate acquisition.

A NOTE ABOUT TAKEOVERS

Takeover is a general and imprecise term referring to the transfer of control of a firm from one group of shareholders to another.[3] A firm that has decided to take over another firm is usually referred to as the **bidder**. The bidder offers to pay cash or securities to obtain the stock or assets of another company. If the

[2]India Cements paid a final acquisition price of ₹286 per share of Raasi Cements (1998). In 1996, Raasi Cements was trading in the range of ₹16–28. The above hostile takeover is also a typical case of leveraged buyout in India wherein the assets of the target company are used as security for the loan raised by the acquirer (herein, India Cements) for the purpose of acquiring the target (herein, Raasi Cements).

[3]*Control* usually can be defined as having a majority vote on the board of directors.

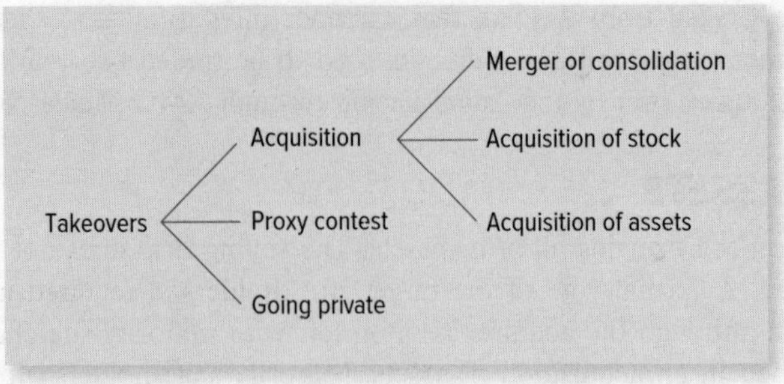

Figure 29.1 Varieties of Takeovers

offer is accepted, the **target firm** will give up control over its stock or assets to the bidder in exchange for *consideration* (i.e., its stock, its debt, or cash).[4]

Takeovers can occur by acquisitions, proxy contests, and going-private transactions. Thus, takeovers encompass a broader set of activities than acquisitions, as depicted in Figure 29.1.

If a takeover is achieved by acquisition, it will be by merger, tender offer for shares of stock, or purchase of assets. In mergers and tender offers, the acquiring firm buys the voting equity share of the acquired firm.

Proxy contests can result in takeovers, as well. Proxy contests occur when a group of shareholders attempts to gain seats on the board of directors. A *proxy* is written authorization for one shareholder to vote the stock of another shareholder. In a proxy contest, an insurgent group of shareholders solicits proxies from other shareholders.

In *going-private transactions*, a small group of investors purchases all the equity shares of a public firm. The group usually includes members of incumbent management and some outside investors. The shares of the firm are delisted from stock exchanges and can no longer be purchased in the open market.

29.2 Synergy

The previous section discussed the basic forms of acquisition. We now examine why firms are acquired. Although the previous section pointed out that acquisitions and mergers have different definitions, these differences will be unimportant in this, and many of the following, sections. Unless otherwise stated, we will refer to acquisitions and mergers synonymously.

Much of our thinking here can be organized around the following four questions:

1. Is there a rational reason for mergers? Yes—in a word, **synergy**.

   Suppose Firm A is contemplating acquiring Firm B. The standalone value of Firm A is V_A and the value of Firm B is V_B. (It is reasonable to assume that for public companies, V_A and V_B can be determined by observing the market prices of the outstanding securities.) The difference between the value of the combined firm (V_{AB}) and the sum of the values of the firms as separate entities is the synergy from the acquisition:

$$\text{Synergy} = V_{AB} - (V_A + V_B)$$

   In words, synergy occurs if the value of the combined firm after the merger is greater than the sum of the value of the acquiring firm and the value of the acquired firm before the merger.

2. Where does this magic force, synergy, come from?

[4]Audra L. Boone and J. Harold Mulherin, "How Are Firms Sold?" *Journal of Finance* 62, no. 2 (April 2007): 847–75; look closely at the takeover process and the chain of negotiations and competitive bidding.

Increases in cash flow create value. We define ΔCF_t as the difference between the cash flows at Date t of the combined firm and the sum of the cash flows of the two separate firms. From the chapters about capital budgeting, we know that the cash flow in any period t can be written as:

$$\Delta CF_t = \Delta Rev_t - \Delta Costs_t - \Delta Taxes_t - \Delta Capital\ requirements_t$$

where ΔRev_t is the incremental revenue of the acquisition; $\Delta Costs_t$ is the incremental costs of the acquisition; $\Delta Taxes_t$ is the incremental acquisition taxes; and $\Delta Capital\ requirements_t$ is the incremental new investment required in working capital and fixed assets.

It follows from our classification of incremental cash flows that the possible sources of synergy fall into four basic categories: revenue enhancement, cost reduction, lower taxes, and lower capital requirements.[5] Improvements in at least one of these four categories create synergy. Each of these categories will be discussed in detail in the next section.

In addition, reasons often are provided for mergers where improvements are not expected in any of these four categories. These "bad" reasons for mergers will be discussed in Section 29.4.

3. How are these synergistic gains shared? In general, the acquiring firm pays a premium for the acquired, or target, firm. If the stock of the target is selling for ₹50, the acquirer might need to pay ₹60 a share, implying a premium of ₹10, or 20 percent. The gain to the target in this example is ₹10. Suppose that the synergy from the merger is ₹30. The gain to the acquiring firm, or bidder, would be ₹20 (= ₹30 − 10). The bidder would actually lose if the synergy were less than the premium of ₹10. A more detailed treatment of these gains or losses will be provided in Section 29.6.
4. Are there other motives for a merger besides synergy? Yes.

   As we have said, synergy is the source of benefit to stockholders. However, the managers are likely to view a potential merger differently. Even if the synergy from the merger is less than the premium paid to the target, the managers of the acquiring firm still may benefit. For example, the revenues of the combined firm after the merger will almost certainly be greater than the revenues of the bidder before the merger. The managers may receive higher compensation once they are managing a larger firm. Even beyond the increase in compensation, managers generally experience greater prestige and power when managing a larger firm. Conversely, the managers of the target could lose their jobs after the acquisition. They might very well oppose the takeover even if their stockholders would benefit from the premium. These issues will be discussed in more detail in Section 29.9.

29.3 Sources of Synergy

In this section, we discuss sources of synergy.[6]

REVENUE ENHANCEMENT

A combined firm may generate greater revenues than two separate firms. Increased revenues can come from marketing gains, strategic benefits, and market power.

---

[5]Many reasons are given by firms to justify mergers and acquisitions. When two firms merge, the boards of directors of the two firms adopt an *agreement of merger*. The agreement of merger of Sirius and XM Radio is typical. It lists the economic benefits that shareholders can expect from the merger: (1) Operating cost savings across the board, including general and administrative costs, sales and marketing costs, subscriber acquisition costs, research and development costs, product development, manufacturing, inventory costs, and programming operating infrastructure. (2) Additional shareholder value in the longer term due to savings on satellite fleet, terrestrial infrastructure, and other capital cost redundancies. (3) Greater appeal to large national advertisers that have a significant number of media alternatives. (4) Advertising sales expense savings. (5) Enhanced operating leverage resulting in accelerated free cash flow generation.

[6]Matthew Rhodes-Kropf and David T. Robinson, "The Market for Mergers and the Boundaries of the Firm," *Journal of Finance* 63, no. 3 (June 2008): 1169–1211, address a related question of who buys whom. Contrary to conventional wisdom, they argue that it does not appear that firms with relatively high market value tend to buy firms with relatively low values. Instead, they show firms tend to pair with other firms having similar ratios.

Marketing Gains It frequently is claimed that, due to improved marketing, mergers and acquisitions can increase operating revenues. Improvements can be made in the following areas:

1. Ineffective media programming and advertising efforts.
2. A weak distribution network.
3. An unbalanced product mix.

Strategic Benefits Some acquisitions promise a *strategic* benefit, which is more like an option than a standard investment opportunity. Imagine that a sewing machine company acquires a computer company. The firm will be well-positioned if technological advances allow computer-driven sewing machines in the future.

Michael Porter has used the word *beachhead* to denote the strategic benefits from entering a new industry.[7] He uses the example of Procter & Gamble's acquisition of the Charmin Paper Company as a beachhead that allowed Procter & Gamble to develop a highly interrelated cluster of paper products–disposable diapers, paper towels, feminine hygiene products, and bathroom tissue.

Market or Monopoly Power One firm may acquire another to reduce competition. If so, prices can be increased, generating monopoly profits. However, mergers that reduce competition do not benefit society and the U.S. Department of Economic Affairs, Government of India or the Competition Commission of India may challenge them. In India, the Competition Commission of India (CCI) or the Government of India (Ministry of Finance) monitors such merger deals and acts if they feel that the deal would lead to monopolies.

Cross-Selling A combined firm may be able to sell additional products or services to existing customers. Up-selling or bundling of products are related strategies to increase revenue. For example, the merger of Bank of America with Merrill Lynch in 2013 allowed Merrill Lynch brokers to cross-sell banking services to their investment clients.

COST REDUCTION

A combined firm may operate more efficiently than two separate firms. Often, lower costs are cited as a primary reason for a merger. A merger can increase operating efficiency in the ways we discuss next.

Economy of Scale Economy of scale means that the average cost of production falls as the level of production increases. Figure 29.2 illustrates the relation between cost per unit and size for a typical firm. As can be seen, average cost first falls and then rises. In other words, the firm experiences economies of scale until optimal firm size is reached. Diseconomies of scale arise after that.

Though the precise nature of economies of scale is unknown, it is one obvious benefit of horizontal mergers. The phrase *spreading overhead* is frequently used in connection with economies of scale. This refers to sharing central facilities such as corporate headquarters, top management, and computer systems.

Economies of Vertical Integration Operating economies can be gained from vertical combinations as well as from horizontal combinations. The main purpose of vertical acquisitions is to make coordination of closely related operating activities easier. This is probably why most forest product firms that

[7]Michael Porter, *Competitive Advantage* (New York: Free Press, 1988).

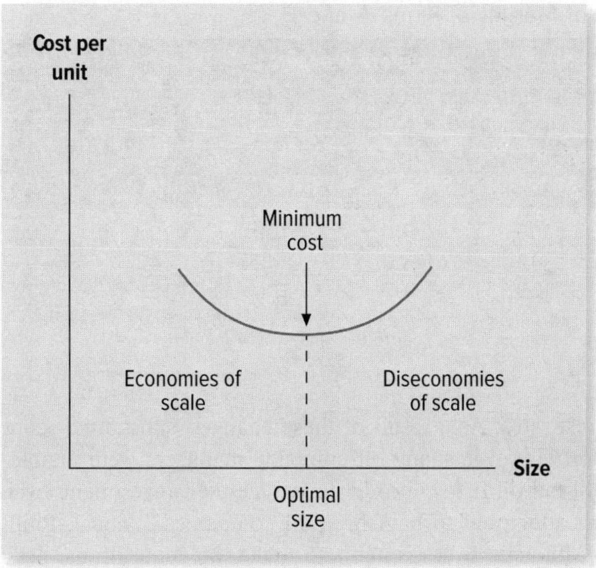

Figure 29.2 Economies of Scale and the Optimal Size of the Firm

cut timber also own sawmills and hauling equipment. Because petroleum is used to make plastics and other chemical products, the DuPont-Conoco merger was motivated by DuPont's need for a steady supply of oil. Economies of vertical integration probably explain why most airline companies own airplanes. They also may explain why some airline companies have purchased hotels and car rental companies.

Technology Transfer Technology transfer is another reason for a merger. An automobile manufacturer might well acquire an aircraft company if aerospace technology can improve automotive quality. This technology transfer was the motivation behind the merger of Google and Android.

Complementary Resources Some firms acquire others to improve usage of existing resources. A ski equipment store merging with a tennis equipment store will smooth sales over both the winter and summer seasons, thereby making better use of store capacity.

Elimination of Inefficient Management A change in management often can increase firm value. Some managers overspend on perquisites and pet projects, making them ripe for takeover. For example, the leveraged buyout of RJR Nabisco was instituted primarily to halt the profligate behavior of CEO Ross Johnson. Alternatively, incumbent managers may not understand changing market conditions or new technology, making it difficult for them to abandon old strategies. Although the board of directors should replace these managers, the board often is unable to act independently. A merger may be needed to make the necessary replacements.

Michael C. Jensen cites the oil industry as an example of managerial inefficiency.[8] In the late 1970s, changes in the oil industry included expectations of lower oil prices, increased exploration and development

[8]Michael C. Jensen, "Agency Costs of Free Cash Flow, Corporate Finance, and Takeovers," *American Economic Review* 76, no. 2 (May 1986): 323–29.

Table 29.1 Tax Effect of Merger of Firms A and B

	Before Merger				After Merger	
	Firm A		Firm B		Firm AB	
	If State 1	If State 2	If State 1	If State 2	If State 1	If State 2
Taxable income	₹200	–₹100	–₹100	₹200	₹100	₹100
Taxes	42	0	0	42	21	21
Net income	₹158	–₹100	–₹100	₹158	₹ 79	₹ 79

Neither firm will be able to deduct its losses prior to the merger. The merger allows the losses from A to offset the taxable profits from B—and vice versa.

costs, and higher real interest rates. As a result of these changes, substantial reductions in exploration and development were called for. However, many oil company managers were unable to downsize their firms. Acquiring companies sought out oil firms in order to reduce their investment levels. For example, T. Boone Pickens of Mesa Petroleum attempted to buy three oil companies–Unocal, Phillips, and Getty–to install more frugal management. Although he was unable to make the acquisitions, his attempts spurred existing management to reduce expenditures on exploration and development, generating huge gains to the shareholders of these firms, including himself.

Mergers and acquisitions can be viewed as part of the labor market for top management. Michael Jensen and Richard Ruback have used the phrase "market for corporate control," in which alternative management teams compete for the right to manage corporate activities.[9]

TAX GAINS

Tax reduction may be a powerful incentive for some acquisitions. This reduction can come from:

1. The use of tax losses.
2. The use of unused debt capacity.
3. The use of surplus funds.

Net Operating Losses A firm with a profitable division and an unprofitable one will have a low tax bill because the loss in one division offsets the income in the other. However, if the two divisions are actually separate companies, the profitable firm will not be able to use the losses of the unprofitable one to offset its income. Thus, in the right circumstances, a merger can lower taxes.

Consider Table 29.1, which shows pretax income, taxes, and aftertax income for Firms A and B. Firm A earns ₹200 in State 1 but loses money in State 2. The firm pays taxes in State 1 but is not entitled to a tax rebate in State 2. Conversely, Firm B turns a profit in State 2 but not in State 1. This firm pays taxes only in State 2. The table shows that the combined tax bill of the two separate firms is always ₹42, regardless of which situation occurs.

However, the last two columns of the table show that after a merger, the combined firm will pay taxes of only ₹21. Taxes drop after the merger because a loss in one division offsets the gain in the other.

[9]Michael C. Jensen and Richard S. Ruback, "The Market for Corporate Control," *Journal of Financial Economics* 11, no. 1-4 (April 1983): 5–50.

The message of this example is that firms need taxable profits to take advantage of potential losses. These losses often are referred to as *net operating losses*, or *NOL* for short. Mergers can sometimes bring losses and profits together. However, there are two qualifications to the previous example:

1. Federal tax laws permit firms that experience alternating periods of profits and losses to equalize their taxes by carryforward provisions. The accounting rules are complicated, but, generally, a firm that has a loss can carry the loss forward for 20 years. A merger to exploit unused tax shields must offer tax savings over and above what can be accomplished by firms via carryovers.[10]
2. The Income Tax Authorities may disallow an acquisition if the principal purpose of the acquisition is to avoid federal tax. This is one of the catch-22s of the Internal Revenue Code.

Debt Capacity There are at least two cases where mergers allow for increased debt and a larger tax shield. In the first case, the target has too little debt and the acquirer can infuse the target with the missing debt. In the second case, both the target and acquirer have optimal debt levels. A merger leads to risk reduction, generating greater debt capacity and a larger tax shield. We treat each case in turn.

Case 1: Unused Debt Capacity In Chapter 17, we pointed out that every firm has a certain amount of debt capacity. This debt capacity is beneficial because greater debt leads to a greater tax shield. More formally, every firm can borrow a certain amount before the marginal costs of financial distress equal the marginal tax shield. This debt capacity is a function of many factors, perhaps the most important being the risk of the firm. Firms with high risk generally cannot borrow as much as firms with low risk. For example, a utility or a supermarket, both firms with low risk, can have higher debt-to-value ratios than a technology firm.

Some firms, for whatever reason, have less debt than is optimal. Perhaps the managers are risk-averse, or perhaps the managers don't know how to assess debt capacity properly. Is it bad for a firm to have too little debt? The answer is yes. As we have said, the optimal level of debt occurs when the marginal cost of financial distress equals the marginal tax shield. Too little debt reduces firm value.

This is where mergers come in. A firm with little or no debt is an inviting target. An acquirer could raise the target's debt level after the merger to create a bigger tax shield.

Case 2: Increased Debt Capacity Let's move back to the principles of modern portfolio theory, as presented in Chapter 11. Consider two stocks in different industries, where both stocks have the same risk or standard deviation. A portfolio of these two stocks has lower risk than that of either stock separately. In other words, the two-stock portfolio is somewhat diversified, whereas each stock by itself is completely undiversified.[11]

Now, rather than considering an individual buying both stocks, consider a merger between the two underlying firms. Because the risk of the combined firm is less than that of either one separately, banks should be willing to lend more money to the combined firm than the total of what they would lend to the two firms separately. In other words, the risk reduction that the merger generates leads to greater debt capacity.

Imagine that each firm can borrow ₹100 on its own before the merger. Perhaps the combined firm after the merger will be able to borrow ₹250. Debt capacity has increased by ₹50 (= ₹250 − 200).

[10]Under the 1986 Tax Reform Act, a corporation's ability to carry forward net operating losses (and other tax credits) is limited when more than 50 percent of the stock changes hands over a three-year period.

[11]Although diversification is most easily explained by considering stocks in different industries, the key is that the returns on the two stocks are less than perfectly correlated–a relationship that should occur even for stocks in the same industry.

In Their Own Words

MICHAEL C. JENSEN ON MERGERS AND ACQUISITIONS

Economic analysis and evidence indicate that takeovers, leveraged buyouts (LBOs), and corporate restructurings are playing an important role in helping the economy adjust to major competitive changes in the last two decades. The competition among alternative management teams and organizational structures for control of corporate assets has enabled vast economic resources to move more quickly to their highest-valued use. In the process, substantial benefits for the economy as a whole as well as for shareholders have been created. Overall gains to selling-firm shareholders from mergers, acquisitions, leveraged buyouts, and other corporate restructurings in the 12-year period 1977–1988 totaled over ₹500 billion in 1988 Rupees. I estimate gains to buying-firm shareholders to be at least ₹50 billion for the same period. These gains equaled 53 percent of the total cash dividends (valued in 1988 Rupees) paid to investors by the entire corporate sector in the same period.

Mergers and acquisitions are a response to new technologies or market conditions that require a strategic change in a company's direction or use of resources. Compared to current management, a new owner is often better able to accomplish major change in the existing organizational structure. Alternatively, leveraged buyouts bring about organizational change by creating entrepreneurial incentives for management and by eliminating the centralized bureaucratic obstacles to maneuverability that are inherent in large public corporations.

When managers have a substantial ownership interest in the organization, the conflicts of interest between shareholders and managers over the payout of the company's free cash flow are reduced. Management's incentives are focused on maximizing the value of the enterprise, rather than building empires—often through poorly conceived diversification acquisitions—without regard to shareholder value. Finally, the required repayment of debt replaces management's discretion in paying dividends and the tendency to over-retain cash. Substantial increases in efficiency are thereby created.

Michael C. Jensen is Jesse Isidor Straus Professor of Business Administration, Emeritus, at Harvard University. An outstanding scholar and researcher, he is famous for his pathbreaking analysis of the modern corporation and its relations with its stockholders.

Remember that debt generates a tax shield. If debt rises after the merger, taxes will fall. That is, because of the greater interest payments after the merger, the tax bill of the combined firm should be less than the sum of the tax bills of the two separate firms before the merger. In other words, the increased debt capacity from a merger can reduce taxes.

To summarize, we first considered the case where the target had too little leverage. The acquirer could infuse the target with more debt, generating a greater tax shield. Next, we considered the case where both the target and acquirer began with optimal debt levels. A merger leads to more debt even here. That is, the risk reduction from the merger creates greater debt capacity and a greater tax shield.

Surplus Funds Another quirk in the tax law involves surplus funds. Consider a firm that has *free cash flow*. That is, it has cash flow available after payment of all taxes and after all positive net present value projects have been funded. In this situation, aside from purchasing securities, the firm can either pay dividends or buy back shares.

We already have seen in our previous discussion of dividend policy that an extra dividend will increase the income tax paid by some investors. Investors pay lower taxes in a share repurchase.[12] However, a share repurchase is not a legal option if the sole purpose is to avoid taxes on dividends.

Instead, the firm might make acquisitions with its excess funds. Here, the shareholders of the acquiring firm avoid the taxes they would have paid on a dividend, and no taxes are paid on dividends remitted from the acquired firm.[13]

[12]A dividend is taxable to all tax-paying recipients. A repurchase creates a tax liability only for those who choose to sell (and do so at a profit).

[13]The situation is actually a little more complex: The target's shareholders must pay taxes on their capital gains. These stockholders likely will demand a premium from the acquirer to offset this tax.

REDUCED CAPITAL REQUIREMENTS

Earlier, we stated that due to economies of scale, mergers can reduce operating costs. It follows that mergers can reduce capital requirements, as well. Accountants typically divide capital into two components: fixed capital and working capital.

When two firms merge, the managers likely will find duplicate facilities. If both firms had their own headquarters, all executives in the merged firm could be moved to one headquarters building, allowing the other headquarters to be sold. Some plants might be redundant, as well. Or two merging firms in the same industry might consolidate their research and development, permitting some R&D facilities to be sold.

The same goes for working capital. The inventory-to-sales ratio and the cash-to-sales ratio often decrease as firm size increases. A merger permits these economies of scale to be realized, allowing a reduction in working capital.

29.4 Two Financial Side Effects of Acquisitions

EARNINGS GROWTH

An acquisition can create the appearance of earnings growth, perhaps fooling investors into thinking that the firm is worth more than it really is. Let's consider two companies, Hindusthan Resources, Ltd., and Bharat Enterprises, as depicted in the first two columns of Table 29.2. As can be seen, earnings per share are ₹1 for both companies. However, Hindusthan sells for ₹25 per share, implying a price-earnings (PE) ratio of 25 (= ₹25/₹1). By contrast, Bharat sells for ₹10, implying a PE ratio of 10. This means that an investor in Hindusthan pays ₹25 to get ₹1 in earnings, whereas an investor in Bharat receives the same ₹1 in earnings on only a ₹10 investment. Are investors getting a better deal with Bharat? Not necessarily. Perhaps Hindusthan's earnings are expected to grow faster than are Bharat's earnings. If this is the case, an investor in Hindusthan will expect to receive high earnings in later years, making up for low earnings in the short term. In fact, Chapter 9 argues that the primary determinant of a firm's PE ratio is the market's expectation of the firm's growth rate in earnings.

Now let's imagine that Hindusthan acquires Bharat, with the merger creating no value. If the market is smart, it will realize that the combined firm is worth the sum of the values of the separate firms. In this case, the market value of the combined firm will be ₹3,500, which is equal to the sum of the values of the separate firms before the merger.

Table 29.2 Financial Positions of Hindusthan Resources Ltd. and Bharat Enterprises

	Hindusthan Resources before Merger	Bharat Enterprises before Merger	Hindusthan Resources after Merger	
			The Market Is "Smart"	The Market Is "Fooled"
Earnings per share	₹ 1.00	₹ 1.00	₹ 1.43	₹ 1.43
Price per share	₹ 25.00	₹ 10.00	₹ 25.00	₹ 35.71
Price-earnings ratio	25	10	17.5	25
Number of shares	100	100	140	140
Total earnings	₹ 100	₹ 100	₹ 200	₹ 200
Total value	₹2,500	₹1,000	₹3,500	₹5,000

Exchange ratio: 1 share in Hindusthan for 2.5 shares in Bharat.

At these values, Hindusthan will acquire Bharat by exchanging 40 of its shares for 100 shares of Bharat, so that Hindusthan will have 140 shares outstanding after the merger.[14] Hindusthan's stock price remains at ₹25 (= ₹3,500/140). With 140 shares outstanding and ₹200 of earnings after the merger, Hindusthan earns ₹1.43 (= ₹200/140) per share after the merger. Its PE ratio becomes 17.5 (= ₹25/₹1.43), a drop from 25 before the merger. This scenario is represented by the third column of Table 29.2. Why has the PE dropped? The combined firm's PE will be an average of Hindusthan's high PE and Bharat's low PE before the merger. This is common sense once you think about it. Hindusthan's PE should drop when it takes on a new division with low growth.

Let us now consider the possibility that the market is fooled. As we said, the acquisition enables Hindusthan to increase its earnings per share from ₹1 to ₹1.43. If the market is fooled, it might mistake the 43 percent increase in earnings per share for true growth. In this case, the price-earnings ratio of Hindusthan may not fall after the merger. Suppose the price-earnings ratio of Hindusthan remains at 25. The total value of the combined firm will increase to ₹5,000 (= ₹25 × ₹200) and the stock price per share of Hindusthan will increase to ₹35.71 (= ₹5,000/140). This is reflected in the last column of the table.

This is earnings growth magic. Can we expect this magic to work in the real world? Managers of previous generations certainly thought so, with firms such as Lipton India, Goodricke Tea, Brooke Bond India, Modi Cements, Graphite India and Carbon Everflow all trying to play the P/E-multiple game in the 1990s. While some investors may naively use price-earnings ratios to value firms, such tricks are unlikely to fool the market in the long run.

Carbon Everflow and Graphite India merger

Graphite India Limited and Carbon Everflow Limited were two companies in the same sector, i.e., graphite electrodes and other graphite products. The same business group, K K Bangur Group, owned both companies. Among the two, Graphite India was the larger player. On a certain day, to the market' s surprise, K K Bangur group announced merger of Graphite India into Carbon Everflow Limited. The figures listing various scenarios below tell the reason behind the move:

Financials before and after merger: Potential Scenarios

	Graphite India	Carbon Everflow	Merge Carbon Everflow into Graphite India	Merge Graphite India into Carbon Everflow	If markets are intelligent then P/E ratio will also adjust automatically
Sales (in ₹ Crore)	265	145	410	410	410
PAT (in ₹ Crore)	19.16	10.47	29.63	29.63	29.63
Share Capital (in ₹ Crore)	1.21	1.25	2.10	2.94	2.94
EPS	15.87	8.38	14.11	10.08	10.08
Market Price (in ₹)	28.00	20.00	24.83	24.09	20.00
P/E Ratio	1.76	2.39	1.76	2.39	1.98
Market Capitalization (in ₹ Crore)	34	25	52	71	59

[14]This ratio implies a fair exchange because a share of Bharat is selling for 40 percent (= ₹10/₹25) of the price of a share of Hindusthan.

Probably, the promoters, Bangur's thought that the earnings growth magic would work, i.e., the market would discount the merged entity at a higher P/E ratio of 2.4, resulting in higher share price. But if markets were efficient, then the P/E ratio of the merged entity would also adjust automatically (as shown in the last column).

So, many of you would be eager to know about what happened to share prices after the merger. Of course, markets could not be fooled. The P/E ratio of the merged entity was corrected appropriately.

DIVERSIFICATION

Diversification is often mentioned as a benefit of one firm acquiring another. Earlier in this chapter, we noted that U.S. Steel included diversification as a benefit in its acquisition of Marathon Oil. At the time of the merger, U.S. Steel was a cash-rich company, with more than 20 percent of its assets in cash and marketable securities. It is not uncommon to see firms with surplus cash articulating a need for diversification.

However, we argue that diversification, by itself, may not produce increases in value. To see this, recall that part of a business's variability of return can be attributed to what is specific to the business and called unsystematic risk.

As you recall from Chapter 11 in our discussion of the CAPM, conceptually, unsystematic risk can be diversified away through mergers. However, the investor does not need widely diversified companies such as General Electric to eliminate unsystematic risk. Shareholders can diversify more easily than corporations by purchasing equity share in different corporations. For example, the shareholders of U.S. Steel could have purchased shares in Marathon if they believed there would be diversification gains in doing so. Thus, diversification through conglomerate merger may not benefit shareholders.[15]

Diversification can produce gains to the acquiring firm if one of three things is true:

1. Diversification decreases the unsystematic risk at lower costs than by investors' adjustments to personal portfolios. This seems very unlikely.
2. Diversification reduces risk and thereby increases debt capacity. This possibility was mentioned earlier in the chapter.
3. Internal capital or labor allocations are better for diversified firms than would be true for nondiversified firms.

Otherwise, one should be cautious in accepting diversification as a benefit in a merger or acquisition.

29.5 A Cost to Stockholders from Reduction in Risk

We considered two financial side effects of mergers in the previous section. Merging for either of these two reasons will not necessarily destroy value. Rather, it is unlikely that merging for these two reasons will increase value. In this section, we examine a by-product of acquisitions that could actually destroy value, at least from the stockholders' point of view. As we will see, mergers increase the safety of bonds, raising the value of these bonds and hurting the stockholders.

In Chapter 11, we considered an individual adding one security after another, all of equal risk, to a portfolio. We saw that as long as the securities were less than perfectly positively correlated with each other, the risk of this portfolio fell as the number of securities rose. In a word, this risk reduction reflected

[15]In fact, a number of scholars have argued that diversification can *reduce* firm value by weakening corporate focus, a point to be developed in a later section of this chapter.

diversification. Diversification also happens in a merger. When two firms merge, the volatility of their combined value is usually less than their volatilities as separate entities.

However, there is a surprising result here. Whereas an individual benefits from portfolio diversification, diversification from a merger actually may hurt the stockholders. The reason is that the bondholders are likely to gain from the merger because their debt is now "insured" by two firms, not one. It turns out that this gain to the bondholders is at the stockholders' expense.

THE BASE CASE

Consider an example where Firm A acquires Firm B. Panel I of Table 29.3 shows the net present values of Firm A and Firm B prior to the merger in the two possible states of the economy. Because the probability of each state is .50, the market value of each firm is the average of its values in the two states. The market value of Firm A is:

$$.5 \times ₹80 + .5 \times ₹20 = ₹50$$

Now imagine that the merger of the two firms generates no synergy. The combined Firm AB will have a market value of ₹75 (= ₹50 + 25), the sum of the values of Firm A and Firm B. Further imagine that the stockholders of Firm B receive stock in AB equal to Firm B's stand-alone market value of ₹25. In other words, Firm B receives no premium. Because the value of AB is ₹75, the stockholders of Firm A have a value of ₹50 (= ₹75 − 25) after the merger–exactly what they had before the merger. The stockholders of both Firms A and B are indifferent to the merger.

BOTH FIRMS HAVE DEBT

Alternatively, imagine that Firm A has debt with a face value of ₹30 in its capital structure, as shown in Panel II of Table 29.3. Without a merger, Firm A will default on its debt in State 2 because the value of Firm A in this state is ₹20, less than the face value of the debt of ₹30. As a consequence, Firm A cannot pay the full value of the debt claim; the bondholders receive only ₹20 in this state. The creditors take the possibility of default into account, valuing the debt at ₹25 (= .5 × ₹30 + .5 × ₹20).

Firm B's debt has a face value of ₹15. Firm B will default in State 1 because the value of the firm in this state is ₹10, less than the face value of the debt of ₹15. The value of Firm B's debt is ₹12.50 (= .5 × ₹10 + .5 × ₹15). It follows that the sum of the value of Firm A's debt and the value of Firm B's debt is ₹37.50 (= ₹25 + 12.50).

Now let's see what happens after the merger. Firm AB is worth ₹90 in State 1 and ₹60 in State 2, implying a market value of ₹75 (= .5 × ₹90 + .5 × ₹60). The face value of the debt in the combined firm is ₹45 (= ₹30 + 15). Because the value of the firm is greater than ₹45 in either state, the bondholders always get paid in full. Thus, the value of the debt is its face value of ₹45. This value is ₹7.50 greater than the sum of the values of the two debts before the merger, which we found to be ₹37.50. Therefore, the merger benefits the bondholders.

What about the stockholders? Because the equity of Firm A was worth ₹25 and the equity of Firm B was worth ₹12.50 before the merger, let's assume that Firm AB issues two shares to Firm A's stockholders for every share issued to Firm B's stockholders. Firm AB's equity is ₹30, so Firm A's shareholders get shares worth ₹20 and Firm B's shareholders get shares worth ₹10. Firm A's stockholders lose ₹5 (= ₹20 − 25) from the merger. Similarly, Firm B's stockholders lose ₹2.50 (= ₹10 − 12.50). The total loss to the stockholders of both firms is ₹7.50, exactly the gain to the bondholders from the merger.

There are a lot of numbers in this example. The point is that the bondholders gain ₹7.50 and the stockholders lose ₹7.50 from the merger. Why does this transfer of value occur? To see what is going on, notice that when the two firms are separate, Firm B does not guarantee Firm A's debt. That is, if Firm A

Table 29.3 Stock-Swap Mergers

	NPV		
	State 1	**State 2**	**Market Value**
Probability	.5	.5	
I. Base case (no debt in either firm's capital structure)			
Values before merger:			
Firm A	₹80	₹20	₹50
Firm B	₹10	₹40	₹25
Values after merger:*			
Firm AB	₹90	₹60	₹75
II. Debt with face value of ₹30 in Firm A's capital structure Debt with face value of ₹15 in Firm B's capital structure			
Values before merger:			
Firm A	₹80	₹20	₹50
Debt	30	20	25
Equity	50	0	25
Firm B	₹10	₹40	₹25
Debt	10	15	12.50
Equity	0	25	12.50
Values after merger:†			
Firm AB	₹90	₹60	₹75
Debt	45	45	45
Equity	45	15	30

Values of both Firm A's debt and Firm B's debt rise after the merger. Values of both Firm A's stock and Firm B's stock fall after the merger.

*Stockholders in Firm A receive ₹50 of stock in Firm AB. Stockholders in Firm B receive ₹25 of stock in Firm AB. Stockholders in both firms are indifferent to the merger.

†Stockholders in Firm A receive stock in Firm AB worth ₹20. Stockholders in Firm B receive stock in Firm AB worth ₹10. Gains and losses from the merger are:

Loss to stockholders in Firm A: ₹20 − 25 = −₹5

Loss to stockholders in Firm B: ₹10 − 12.50 = −₹2.50

Combined gain to bondholders in both firms: ₹45.00 − 37.50 = ₹7.50

defaults on its debt, Firm B does not help the bondholders of Firm A. However, after the merger, the bondholders can draw on the cash flows from both A and B. When one of the divisions of the combined firm fails, creditors can be paid from the profits of the other division. This mutual guarantee, which is called the *coinsurance effect*, makes the debt less risky and more valuable than before.

There is no net benefit to the firm as a whole. The bondholders gain the coinsurance effect and the stockholders lose the coinsurance effect. Some general conclusions emerge from the preceding analysis:

1. Mergers can help bondholders. The size of the gain to bondholders depends on the reduction in the probability of bankruptcy after the combination. That is, the less risky the combined firm is, the greater are the gains to bondholders.
2. Stockholders are hurt by the amount that bondholders gain.
3. Conclusion 2 applies to mergers without synergy. In practice, much depends on the size of the synergy.

HOW CAN SHAREHOLDERS REDUCE THEIR LOSSES FROM THE COINSURANCE EFFECT?

The coinsurance effect raises bondholder values and lowers shareholder values. However, there are at least two ways in which shareholders can reduce or eliminate the coinsurance effect. First, the shareholders of Firm A could retire its debt before the merger announcement date and reissue an equal amount of debt after the merger. Because debt is retired at the low premerger price, this type of refinancing transaction can neutralize the coinsurance effect to the bondholders.

Also, note that the debt capacity of the combined firm is likely to increase because the acquisition reduces the probability of financial distress. The shareholders' second alternative is to issue more debt after the merger. An increase in debt following the merger will have two effects, even without the prior action of debt retirement. The interest tax shield from new corporate debt raises firm value, as discussed in an earlier section of this chapter. In addition, an increase in debt after the merger raises the probability of financial distress, thereby reducing or eliminating the bondholders' gain from the coinsurance effect.

29.6 The NPV of a Merger

Firms typically use NPV analysis when making acquisitions. The analysis is relatively straightforward when the consideration is cash. The analysis becomes more complex when the consideration is stock.

CASH

Suppose Firm A and Firm B have values as separate entities of ₹500 and ₹100, respectively. They are both all-equity firms. If Firm A acquires Firm B, the merged Firm AB will have a combined value of ₹700 due to synergies of ₹100. The board of Firm B has indicated that it will sell Firm B if it is offered ₹150 in cash.

Should Firm A acquire Firm B? Assuming that Firm A makes the acquisition with cash, its value after the acquisition is:[16]

$$\begin{aligned}\text{Value of Firm A after the acquisition} &= \text{Value of combined firm} - \text{Cash paid}\\ &= ₹700 - 150\\ &= ₹550\end{aligned}$$

Because Firm A was worth ₹500 prior to the acquisition, the NPV to Firm A's stockholders is:

$$₹50 = ₹550 - 500 \qquad \textbf{(29.1)}$$

Assuming that there are 25 shares in Firm A, each share of the firm is worth ₹20 (= ₹500/25) prior to the merger and ₹22 (= ₹550/25) after the merger. These calculations are displayed in the first and third columns of Table 29.4. Looking at the rise in stock price, we conclude that Firm A should make the acquisition.

We spoke earlier of both the synergy and the premium of a merger. We also can value the NPV of a merger to the acquirer:

$$\text{NPV of a merger to acquirer} = \text{Synergy} - \text{Premium}$$

[16]The analysis will be essentially the same if new stock is issued. However, the analysis will differ if new debt is issued to fund the acquisition because of the tax shield to debt. An adjusted present value (APV) approach would be necessary here.

Table 29.4 Cost of Acquisition: Cash versus Equity Share

	Before Acquisition		After Acquisition: Firm A		
	(1)	(2)	(3)	(4)	(5)
	Firm A	Firm B	Cash*	Equity Share† Exchange Ratio (.75:1)	Equity Share† Exchange Ratio (.6818:1)
Market value (V_A, V_B)	₹500	₹100	₹550	₹700	₹700
Number of shares	25	10	25	32.5	31.818
Price per share	₹ 20	₹ 10	₹ 22	₹ 21.54	₹ 22

*Value of Firm A after acquisition: Cash

$V_A = V_{AB} - \text{Cash}$

₹550 = ₹700 − 150

†Value of Firm A after acquisition: Equity share

$V_A = V_{AB}$

₹700 = ₹700

Because the value of the combined firm is ₹700 and the premerger values of A and B were ₹500 and ₹100, respectively, the synergy is ₹100 [= ₹700 − (₹500 + 100)]. The premium is ₹50 (= ₹150 − 100). The NPV of the merger to the acquirer is:

$$\text{NPV of merger to Firm A} = ₹100 - 50 = ₹50$$

One caveat is in order. This textbook has consistently argued that the market value of a firm is the best estimate of its true value. However, we must adjust our analysis when discussing mergers. If the true price of Firm A without the merger is ₹500, the market value of Firm A may actually be above ₹500 when merger negotiations take place. This happens because the market price reflects the possibility that the merger will occur. If the probability is 60 percent that the merger will take place, the market price of Firm A will be:

$$\begin{array}{cccccccc} & \text{Market value of Firm A with merger} & \times & \text{Probability of merger} & + & \text{Market value of Firm A without merger} & \times & \text{Probability of no merger} \\ ₹530 = & ₹550 & \times & .60 & + & ₹500 & \times & .40 \end{array}$$

The managers would underestimate the NPV from the merger in Equation 29.1 if the market price of Firm A were used. Thus, managers face the difficult task of valuing their own firm without the acquisition.

EQUITY SHARE

Of course, Firm A could purchase Firm B with equity share instead of cash. Unfortunately, the analysis is not as straightforward here. To handle this scenario, we need to know how many shares are outstanding in Firm B. We assume that there are 10 shares outstanding, as indicated in Column 2 of Table 29.4.

Suppose Firm A exchanges 7.5 of its shares for the entire 10 shares of Firm B. We call this an exchange ratio of .75:1. The value of each share of Firm A's stock before the acquisition is ₹20. Because 7.5 × ₹20 = ₹150, this exchange appears to be the equivalent of purchasing Firm B in cash for ₹150.

This is incorrect: The true cost to Firm A is greater than ₹150. To see this, note that Firm A has 32.5 (= 25 + 7.5) shares outstanding after the merger. Firm B shareholders own 23 percent (= 7.5/32.5) of the combined firm. Their holdings are valued at ₹161.54 (= .23 × ₹700). Because these stockholders receive stock in Firm A worth ₹161.54, the cost of the merger to Firm A's stockholders must be ₹161.54, not ₹150.

This result is shown in Column 4 of Table 29.4. The value of each share of Firm A's stock after a stock-for-stock transaction is only ₹21.54 (= ₹700/32.5). We found out earlier that the value of each share is ₹22 after a cash-for-stock transaction. The difference is that the cost of the stock-for-stock transaction to Firm A is higher.

This nonintuitive result occurs because the exchange ratio of 7.5 shares of Firm A for 10 shares of Firm B was based on the premerger prices of the two firms. However, because the stock of Firm A rises after the merger, Firm B stockholders receive more than ₹150 in Firm A stock.

What should the exchange ratio be so that Firm B stockholders receive only ₹150 of Firm A's stock? We begin by defining α, the proportion of the shares in the combined firm that Firm B's stockholders own. Because the combined firm's value is ₹700, the value of Firm B stockholders after the merger is:

$$\text{Value of Firm B Stockholders after Merger:}$$
$$\alpha \times ₹700$$

Setting α × ₹700 = ₹150, we find that α = 21.43 percent. In other words, Firm B's stockholders will receive ₹150 if they receive 21.43 percent of the firm after the merger.

Now we determine the number of shares issued to Firm B's shareholders. The proportion, α, that Firm B's shareholders have in the combined firm can be expressed as follows:

$$\alpha = \frac{\text{New shares issued}}{\text{Old shares} + \text{New shares issued}} = \frac{\text{New shares issued}}{25 + \text{New shares issued}}$$

Plugging our value of α into the equation yields:

$$.2143 = \frac{\text{New shares issued}}{25 + \text{New shares issued}}$$

Solving for the unknown, we have:

$$\text{New shares} = 6.818 \text{ shares}$$

Total shares outstanding after the merger are 31.818 (= 25 + 6.818). Because 6.818 shares of Firm A are exchanged for 10 shares of Firm B, the exchange ratio is .6818:1.

Results at the exchange ratio of .6818:1 are displayed in Column 5 of Table 29.4. Because there are now 31.818 shares, each share of equity share is worth ₹22 (= ₹700/31.818), exactly what it is worth in the cash-for-stock transaction. Given that the board of Firm B will sell its firm for ₹150, this is the fair exchange ratio, not the ratio of .75:1 mentioned earlier.

CASH VERSUS EQUITY SHARE

In this section, we have examined both cash deals and stock-for-stock deals. Our analysis leads to the following question: When do bidders want to pay with cash and when do they want to pay with stock? There is no easy formula: The decision hinges on a few variables, with perhaps the most important being the price of the bidder's stock.

In the example of Table 29.4, Firm A's market price per share prior to the merger was ₹20. Let's now assume that, at the time, Firm A's managers believed the "true" price was ₹15. In other words, the managers believed that their stock was overvalued. Is it likely for managers to have a different view than that of the market? Yes–managers often have more information than does the market. After all, managers deal with customers, suppliers, and employees daily and are likely to obtain private information.

Now imagine that Firm A's managers are considering acquiring Firm B with either cash or stock. The overvaluation would have no impact on the merger terms in a cash deal; Firm B still would receive ₹150 in cash. However, the overvaluation would have a big impact on a stock-for-stock deal. Although Firm B receives ₹150 worth of Firm A's stock as calculated at market prices, Firm A's managers know that the true value of the stock is less than ₹150.

How should Firm A pay for the acquisition? Clearly, Firm A has an incentive to pay with stock because it would end up giving away less than ₹150 of value. This conclusion might seem rather cynical because Firm A is, in some sense, trying to cheat Firm B's stockholders. However, both theory and empirical evidence suggest that firms are more likely to acquire with stock when their own stocks are overvalued.[17]

The story is not quite this simple. Just as the managers of Firm A think strategically, Firm B's managers will likely think this way as well. Suppose that in the merger negotiations, Firm A's managers push for a stock-for-stock deal. This might tip off Firm B's managers that Firm A is overpriced. Perhaps Firm B's managers will ask for better terms than Firm A is currently offering. Alternatively, Firm B may resolve to accept cash or not to sell at all.

And as Firm B learns from the negotiations, the market learns also. Empirical evidence shows that the acquirer's stock price generally falls upon the announcement of a stock-for-stock deal.[18]

However, this discussion does not imply that mistakes are never made. For example, consider the stock-for-stock merger in January 2001 between AOL, an internet service provider, and Time Warner (TW), a media firm. Although the deal was presented as a merger of equals and the combined company was called Time Warner, AOL appears, in retrospect, to have been the acquirer. The merger was one of the biggest of all time, with a combined market capitalization between the two firms of about ₹350 billion at the time of the announcement in January 2000. (The delay of about a year between merger announcement and merger completion was due to regulatory review.) It also is considered one of the worst deals of all time, with Time Warner getting acquired by Charter Communications for only about ₹79 billion in 2016. Interestingly, AOL was purchased by Verizon in 2015.

AOL was in a precarious position at the time of the 2001 merger, providing narrow-band internet service when consumers were hungering for broadband. Also, at least in retrospect, internet stocks were greatly overpriced. The deal allowed AOL to offer its inflated stock as currency for a company not in the technology industry and, therefore, not nearly as overpriced, if overpriced at all. Had TW looked at the deal in this way, it might have called it off. Alternatively, it could have demanded cash, though it is unlikely that AOL had the financial resources to pay in this way.

As TW's managers did not understand all the implications of the merger right away, it appears that the market did not either. TW's stock price rose more than 25 percent relative to the market in the week following the merger announcement.

29.7 Friendly versus Hostile Takeovers

Mergers are generally initiated by the acquiring, not the target, firm. The acquirer must decide to purchase another firm, select the tactics to effectuate the merger, determine the highest price it is willing to pay, set an initial bid price, and make contact with the target firm. Often the CEO of the acquiring firm calls the CEO of the target and proposes a merger. Should the target be receptive, a merger eventually occurs. Of

[17]The basic theoretical ideas are presented in Stewart C. Myers and Nicholas S. Majluf, "Corporate Financing and Investment Decisions When Firms Have Information That Investors Do Not Have," *Journal of Financial Economics* 13, no. 2 (June 1984): 187–221.

[18]For example, see Gregor Andrade, Mark Mitchell, and Erik Stafford, "New Evidence and Perspectives on Mergers," *Journal of Economic Perspectives* 15, no. 2 (Spring 2001): 103–20; and Randall Heron and Erik Lie, "Operating Performance and the Method of Payment in Takeovers," *Journal of Financial and Quantitative Analysis* 37, no. 1 (March 2002): 137–55.

course, there may be many meetings, with negotiations over price, terms of payment, and other parameters. The target's board of directors generally has to approve the acquisition. Sometimes the bidder's board also must give its approval. Finally, an affirmative vote by the stockholders is needed. But when all is said and done, an acquisition that proceeds in this way is viewed as *friendly*.

Of course, not all acquisitions are friendly. The target's management may resist the merger, in which case the acquirer must decide whether to pursue the merger and, if so, what tactics to use. Facing resistance, the acquirer may begin by purchasing some of the target's stock in secret. This position often is called a *toehold*. The Williams Act, passed in 1968 and one of the landmark pieces of legislation of the era, requires that the acquirer file a Schedule 13D with the Securities and Exchange Commission (SEC) within 10 days of obtaining a 5 percent holding in the target's stock. Similarly, the provision also exists in the Indian context, created under the aegis of the Securities and Exchange Board of India (SEBI). The acquirer must provide detailed information, including its intentions and its position in the target, on this schedule. Secrecy ends at this point because the acquirer must state that it plans to acquire the target. The price of the target's shares probably will rise after the filing, with the new stock price reflecting the possibility that the target will be bought out at a premium. Acquirers, however, often will make the most of this 10-day delay, buying as much stock as possible at the low prefiling price during this period.

Although the acquirer may continue to purchase shares in the open market, an acquisition is unlikely to be effectuated in this manner. Rather, the acquirer is more likely at some point to make a *tender offer* (an offer made directly to the stockholders to buy shares at a premium above the current market price). The tender offer may specify that the acquirer will purchase all shares that are tendered–that is, turned in to the acquirer. Alternatively, the offer may state that the acquirer will purchase all shares up to, say, 50 percent of the number of shares outstanding. If more shares are tendered, prorating will occur. If, in the extreme case, all of the shares are tendered, each stockholder will be allowed to sell one share for every two shares tendered. The acquirer also may say that it will accept the tendered shares only if a minimum number of shares have been tendered.

Under the Williams Act, a tender offer must be held open for at least 20 days. This delay gives the target time to respond. The target may want to notify its stockholders not to tender their shares. It may release statements to the press criticizing the offer. The target also may encourage other firms to enter the bidding process.

At some point, the tender offer ends, at which time the acquirer finds out how many shares have been tendered. The acquirer does not necessarily need 100 percent of the shares to obtain control of the target. In some companies, a holding of 20 percent or so may be enough for control. In others, the percentage needed for control is much higher. Control is a vague term, but you might think of it operationally as control over the board of directors. Stockholders elect members of the board, who, in turn, appoint managers. If the acquirer receives enough stock to elect a majority of the board members, these members can appoint the managers whom the acquirer wants, and effective control often can be achieved with less than a majority. As long as some of the original board members vote with the acquirer, a few new board members can gain the acquirer a working majority.

Sometimes, once the acquirer gets working control, it proposes a merger to obtain the few remaining shares that it does not already own. The transaction is now friendly because the board of directors will approve it. Mergers of this type are often called *cleanup* mergers.

A tender offer is not the only way to gain control of a *hostile* target. Alternatively, the acquirer may continue to buy more shares in the open market until control is achieved. This strategy, often called a *street sweep*, is infrequently used, perhaps because of the difficulty of buying enough shares to obtain control. Also, as mentioned, tender offers often allow the acquirer to return the tendered shares if fewer shares than the desired number are tendered. By contrast, shares purchased in the open market cannot be returned.

Another means to obtain control is a *proxy fight*–a procedure involving corporate voting. Elections for seats on the board of directors are generally held at the annual stockholders' meeting. After purchasing shares in the target company, the acquirer nominates a slate of candidates to run against the current directors. The acquirer generally hires a proxy solicitor, who contacts shareholders prior to the stockholders' meeting, making a pitch for the new candidates. Should the acquirer's candidates win a majority of the seats on the board, the acquirer will control the firm. And as with tender offers, effective control often can be achieved with less than a majority. The acquirer may want to change a few specific policies of the firm, such as the firm's capital budgeting program or its diversification plan. Or it may want to replace management. If some of the original board members are sympathetic to the acquirer's plans, a few new board members can give the acquirer a working majority.

For example, Land & Buildings Investment Management founder Jonathan Litt has engaged in several proxy battles with mall owner Taubman Properties. With mall traffic declining, Litt disagreed with the company's decisions regarding several key properties. Litt lost a proxy fight in 2017 for a seat on the board of directors, but he won a seat in 2018. Then, in 2019, Litt promised another proxy fight if Taubman did not sell several of its properties.

Whereas mergers end up with the acquirer owning all of the target's stock, the victor in a proxy fight does not gain additional shares. The reward to the proxy victor is share price appreciation if the victor's policies prove effective. In fact, the threat of a proxy fight may raise share prices because management may improve operations to head off the fight. Of course, a proxy fight also can cause a loss in value if the activist's actions are viewed negatively. For example, in April 2017, Innoviva avoided a proxy fight with activist investor Elliott Management by agreeing to support two of Elliott's nominees for its board. Innoviva's stock price dropped about 10 percent on the day of the announcement. In India, mergers and acquisitions are regulated under the Indian Companies Act, 2013 and SEBI Act[19]. With the enactment of the Competition Act in 2002, mergers and acquisitions also came within the ambit of this legislation[20]. Different necessities have given rise to these three legislations to regulate these combinations. The Companies Act tries to protect the interests of the secured creditors. Provisions of the Companies Act, 2013 allow schemes of combinations to be effectuated pursuant to the prior approval of the courts. On the other hand, SEBI Act aims to safeguard the interests of investors. Acquisitions of 25% or more shares trigger an open offer under SEBI takeover code[21].

The Competition Act's objective is much broader since it aims to protect the appreciable adverse effect on trade-related competition in the relevant market in India. For example, in 2020, Indigo Airlines intended to acquire a controlling stake in Air India. However, the combined entity's domestic market share may have caused monopoly issues, such as barriers to entry to other competitors (competitors may not have a market to trade), a rise in passenger fares, or poor quality of service. Hence, Indigo was deterred from going ahead with the merger plans.

Summarizing, the Companies Act and SEBI Act aim to safeguard the interests of private entities. On the other hand, the Competition Act scrutinizes the impact of combinations on the market as a whole, along with its players, including consumers.

29.8 Defensive Tactics

Target firm managers frequently resist takeover attempts. Actions to defeat a takeover may benefit the target shareholders if the bidding firm raises its offer price or another firm makes a bid. Alternatively, resistance may reflect self-interest at the shareholders' expense. That is, the target managers might fight a takeover to

[19]Norms were created under the SEBI Substantial Acquisition of Shares and Takeovers Regulations, 1997. There are multiple amendments to it. The SEBI website www.sebi.gov.in details out the same.

[20]Earlier, mergers and acquisitions used to come under the Monopolies and Restrictive Trade Practice (MRTP) Act.

[21]If the bidder already holds more than 25% shareholding, then any additional 5% increase in shareholding triggers an open offer. When an individual's or entity's stake purchase exceeds 5% for the first time, or 2% if already holding more than 5%, they must publicly announce share purchase.

preserve their jobs. Sometimes management resists while simultaneously improving corporate policies. Stockholders can benefit in this case, even if the takeover fails.

In this section, we describe various ways in which target managers resist takeovers. A company is said to be *in play* if one or more suitors are currently interested in acquiring it. It is useful to separate defensive tactics before a company is in play from tactics after the company is in play.

DETERRING TAKEOVERS BEFORE BEING IN PLAY

Corporate Charters The corporate charter refers to the articles of incorporation and corporate bylaws governing a firm.[22] Among other provisions, the charter establishes conditions allowing a takeover. Firms frequently amend charters to make acquisitions more difficult. As examples, consider the following two amendments:

1. *Classified board*: In an unclassified board of directors, stockholders elect all of the directors each year. In a classified, or staggered, board, only a fraction of the board is elected each year, with terms running for multiple years. For example, one-third of the board might stand for election each year, with terms running for three years. Classified boards increase the time an acquirer needs to obtain a majority of seats on the board. In the previous example, the acquirer can gain control of only one-third of the seats in the first year after acquisition. Another year must pass before the acquirer is able to control two-thirds of the seats. Therefore, the acquirer may not be able to change management as quickly as it would like. However, some argue that classified boards are not necessarily effective because the old directors often choose to vote with the acquirer. The use of classified boards has been declining in recent years. In 2005, about 53 percent of the companies in the S&P 500 had classified boards. That percentage declined to less than 10 percent by 2019.
2. *Supermajority provisions*: Corporate charters determine the percentage of voting shares needed to approve important transactions such as mergers. A supermajority provision in the charter means that this percentage is above 50 percent. Two-thirds' majorities are common, though the number can be much higher. A supermajority provision clearly increases the difficulty of acquisition in the face of hostile management. Many charters with supermajority provisions have what is known as a *board out* clause, as well. Here, supermajority does not apply if the board of directors approves the merger. This clause makes sure that the provision hinders only hostile takeovers.

Golden Parachutes This colorful term refers to generous severance packages provided to management in the event of a takeover. The argument is that golden parachutes will deter takeovers by raising the cost of acquisition. However, some authorities point out that the deterrence effect is likely to be unimportant because a severance package, even a generous one, is probably a small part of the cost of acquiring a firm. In addition, some argue that golden parachutes actually *increase* the probability of a takeover. The reasoning here is that management has a natural tendency to resist any takeover because of the possibility of job loss. A large severance package softens the blow of a takeover, reducing management's inclination to resist.

Poison Pills The poison pill is a sophisticated defensive tactic that Martin Lipton, a well-known New York attorney, developed in the early 1980s. Since then a number of variants have surfaced, so

[22]Ronald W. Masulis, Cong Wang, and Fei Xie, "Corporate Governance and Acquirer Returns," *Journal of Finance* 62, no. 4 (August 2007): 1851–89, find that acquirer firms with more antitakeover provisions receive lower stock market returns than they would otherwise receive.

there is no single definition of a poison pill. For example, in October 2013, famed auction house Sotheby's enacted a poison pill to ward off hedge fund Third Point, which was run by activist investor Dan Loeb. Sotheby's poison pill was somewhat unique in that it kicked in if an activist investor acquired more than 10 percent of the company's stock or a passive investor acquired more than 20 percent of the company's stock. If either of these events happened, every shareholder except the shareholder causing the poison pill to become active would be given the right to buy new stock at half price. At the time, Sotheby's had about 69 million shares outstanding. If Third Point acquired more than 10 percent of the stock (6.9 million shares), every shareholder except Third Point could have bought a new share for every one previously held. If all shareholders exercised this option, Sotheby's would have had to issue 62.1 million (= .90 × 69 million) new shares, bringing its total to 131.1 million. The stock price would drop sharply because the company would be selling shares at half price. The bidder's percentage of the firm would drop from 10 percent to 5.3 percent (= 6.9 million/131.1 million). Dilution of this magnitude causes some critics to argue that poison pills are insurmountable.

Ownership Structures Complex ownership structures are common across Asian business groups. As in other Asian countries, one popular way of deterring takeovers in India is by creating a complicated ownership structure involving a mix of cross-holdings and/or pyramidal structures, resulting in enhanced control. The interrelation of ownership structure, corporate strategy, and external forces for the large business groups and conglomerates from India ensures no chance of takeover battles.[23] As a quick point, we can say that till date, there has been no publicly available study (or literature work or transparency in terms of publicly available documentation) that could capture the complex ownership structure of investment firms of the largest Indian business groups (excepting the House of Tatas).

DETERRING A TAKEOVER AFTER THE COMPANY IS IN PLAY

Greenmail and Standstill Agreements Managers may arrange a *targeted repurchase* to forestall a takeover attempt. In a targeted repurchase, a firm buys back its own stock from a potential bidder, usually at a substantial premium, with the provision that the seller promises not to acquire the company for a specified period. Critics of such payments label them *greenmail.*

A *standstill agreement* occurs when the acquirer, for a fee, agrees to limit its holdings in the target. As part of the agreement, the acquirer often promises to offer the target a right of first refusal in the event that the acquirer sells its shares. This promise prevents the block of shares from falling into the hands of another would-be acquirer.

Greenmail has been a colorful part of the financial lexicon since its first application in the late 1970s. Since then, pundits have commented numerous times on either its ethical or unethical nature. Greenmail has declined in recent years, perhaps for two reasons. First, Congress has imposed a tax on the profits from greenmail. Second, the law on greenmail is currently unsettled, causing recipients to worry about potential lawsuits.

White Knight and White Squire A firm facing an unfriendly merger offer might arrange to be acquired by a friendly suitor, commonly referred to as a *white knight*. The white knight might be favored because it is willing to pay a higher purchase price. Alternatively, it might promise not to lay off employees, fire managers, or sell off divisions. White knights often can increase the amount paid to the target firm.

[23]Further reading: Kakani, Ram Kumar and Tejas Vishwas Joshi, "The Tata Group after the JRD Period: Management and Ownership Structure", XLRI Jamshedpur Working Paper # 06-03, URL: http://ssrn.com/abstract=889394.

EXAMPLE 29.2

Takeover Defenses Suppose on April 2, 2021, Namaskar Industries Limited, had 28 million shares outstanding and the company's stock price closed the day before at ₹49.25 per share on the Bombay Stock Exchange. Further suppose that on April 2, Namaskar's board of directors made two decisions:

1. The board approved management's agreement with the Koirala family of Nepal to buy, for ₹51 a share, the Koirala's 2.6 million shares in Namaskar. This was part of a greenmail agreement ending the Koirala family's attempt to control Namaskar.
2. The board authorized the company to repurchase 7.5 million shares (27 percent of the outstanding shares) of its stock. The board simultaneously established an employee stock ownership plan to be funded with 4.9 million shares of Namaskar stock.

These two actions made Namaskar invulnerable to unfriendly takeover attempts. In effect, the company was selling about 20 percent of its stock to the employee stock ownership plan. Earlier, Namaskar had put in place a provision that said 80 percent of the stockholders have to approve a takeover. Namaskar's stock price fell by ₹.25 over the next two days. Because this move can probably be explained by random error, there is no evidence that Namaskar's actions reduced shareholder value.

For example, in 2019, Japanese hotel company UNIZO Holdings received a hostile bid of ¥3,100 per share from travel agency H.I.S. In response, UNIZO found a white knight in SoftBank, which made a tender offer of ¥4,000 per share to help fight off the bid. Before SoftBank could conclude the tender offer, Chitocea Investment made another tender offer for ¥5,100 per share.

Management instead may wish to avoid any acquisition at all. A third party, termed a *white squire*, might be invited to make a significant investment in the firm, under the condition that it vote with management and not purchase additional shares.

Leveraged Recapitalizations Firm management often will issue debt to pay out a dividend or repurchase shares–a transaction called a *leveraged recapitalization* (or "recap" for short). These transactions fend off takeovers in a number of ways. First, the stock price may rise, perhaps because of the increased tax shield from greater debt, thereby making the acquisition more expensive (and thus less attractive) to the bidder. Of course, the price will rise only if the firm's debt level before the recapitalization was below the optimum level, so a levered recapitalization is not recommended for every target. Consultants point out that firms with low debt and stable cash flows are ideal candidates for such recaps.

Second, as part of the recapitalization, management may issue new securities that give management greater voting control than it had before the recap. The increase in control makes a hostile takeover more difficult.

Third, firms with a lot of cash on their balance sheets often are seen as attractive targets. As part of the recap, the firm may also use existing cash reserves to pay a dividend or buy back stock, reducing the firm's appeal as a takeover candidate.

Exclusionary Self-Tenders An *exclusionary self-tender* is the opposite of a targeted repurchase. Here, the firm makes a tender offer for a given amount of its own stock while excluding targeted stockholders.

In a particularly celebrated case, Unocal made a tender offer for 29 percent of its shares while excluding its largest shareholder, Mesa Partners II (led by T. Boone Pickens). Unocal's self-tender was for ₹72 per share, which was ₹16 over the prevailing market price. It was designed to defeat Mesa's attempted takeover of Unocal by transferring wealth, in effect, from Mesa to Unocal's other stockholders.

Asset Restructurings In addition to altering capital structure, firms may sell off existing assets or buy new ones to avoid takeover. Targets generally sell, or divest, assets for two reasons. First, a target firm may have assembled a hodgepodge of assets in different lines of business, with the various segments fitting together poorly. Value might be increased by placing these divisions into separate firms. Academics often emphasize the concept of *corporate focus* or *pure plays*. The idea here is that firms function best by focusing on those few businesses that they really know. A rise in stock price following a divestiture will reduce the target's appeal to a bidder. As with a recap, the stock price increase indicates that a value-increasing strategy (in this case, increasing corporate focus) that could have been implemented after the merger has already been implemented.

The second reason is that a bidder might be interested in a specific division of the target. The target can reduce the bidder's interest by selling off this division. Although the strategy may fend off a merger, it can hurt the target's stockholders if the division is worth more to the target than to the division's buyer. Authorities frequently talk of selling off the *crown jewels* or pursuing a *scorched earth policy*.

While some targets divest existing assets, others buy new ones. Two reasons are generally given here. First, the bidder may like the target as is. The addition of an unrelated business makes the target less appealing to the acquirer. However, a bidder always can sell off the new business, so the purchase is likely not a strong defense. Second, antitrust legislation is designed to prohibit mergers that reduce competition. Antitrust law is enforced by both the Department of Economic Affairs, Government of India (DEA) and the Competition Commission of India (CCI). A target may purchase a company, knowing that this new division will pose antitrust problems for the bidder. However, this strategy might not be effective because, in its filings with the DEA and the CCI, the bidder can state its intention to sell off the unrelated business.

29.9 Have Mergers Added Value?

In Section 29.2, we stated that synergy occurs if the value of the combined firm after the merger is greater than the sum of the value of the acquiring firm and the value of the acquired firm before the merger. Section 29.3 provided a number of sources of synergy in mergers, implying that mergers can create value. We now want to know whether mergers actually create value in practice. This is an empirical question and must be answered by empirical evidence.

There are a number of ways to measure value creation, but many academics favor *event studies*. These studies estimate abnormal stock returns on, and around, the merger announcement date. An *abnormal return* is usually defined as the difference between an actual stock return and the return on a market index or control group of stocks. This control group is used to net out the effect of marketwide or industrywide influences.

Consider Table 29.5, where returns around the announcement days of mergers are reported. The average abnormal percentage return across all mergers from 1980 to 2001 is 1.35 percent. This number combines the returns on both the acquiring company and the acquired company. Because 1.35 percent is positive, the market believes that mergers, on average, create value. The other three returns in the first column are positive, as well, implying value creation in the different subperiods. Many other academic studies have provided similar results. It appears from this column that the synergies we mentioned in Section 29.3 show up in the real world.

However, the next column tells us something different. Across all mergers from 1980 to 2001, the aggregate Rupee change around the day of merger announcement is −₹79 billion. This means that the market is, on average, reducing the combined stock value of the acquiring and acquired companies around

Table 29.5 Percentage and Rupee Returns for Mergers

	Gain or Loss to Merger (Both Acquired and Acquiring Firms)		Gain or Loss to Acquiring Firms	
Time Period	Abnormal Percentage Return	Aggregate Rupee Gain or Loss	Abnormal Percentage Return	Aggregate Rupee Gain or Loss
1980–2001	1.35%	–₹79 billion	1.10%	–₹220 billion
1980–1990	2.41	12 billion	.64	– 4 billion
1991–2001	1.04	– 90 billion	1.20	– 216 billion
1998–2001	.29	–134 billion	.69	– 240 billion

SOURCE: Adapted from Sara B. Moeller, Frederik P. Schlingemann, and René M. Stulz, "Wealth Destruction on a Massive Scale? A Study of Acquiring-Firm Returns in the Recent Merger Wave," *Journal of Finance* 60, no. 2 (April 2005): 757–82, Table 1.

the merger announcement date. Though the difference between the two columns may seem confusing, there is an explanation. Although most mergers have created value, mergers involving the very largest firms have lost value. The abnormal percentage return is an unweighted average in which the returns on all mergers are treated equally. A positive return here reflects all those small mergers that created value. However, losses in a few large mergers cause the aggregate Rupee change to be negative.

But there is more. The rest of the second column indicates that the aggregate Rupee losses occurred only in the 1998 to 2001 period. While there were losses of –₹134 billion in this period, there were gains of ₹12 billion from 1980 to 1990. And interpolation of the table indicates that there were gains of ₹44 billion (= ₹134 – 90) from 1991 through 1997. It appears that some large mergers lost a great deal of value from 1998 to 2001.

The results in a table such as Table 29.5 should have important implications for public policy because Congress is always wondering whether mergers are to be encouraged or discouraged. However, the results in that table are, unfortunately, ambiguous. On the one hand, you could focus on the first column, saying that mergers create value, on average. Proponents of this view might argue that the great losses in the few large mergers were flukes, not likely to occur again. On the other hand, we cannot easily ignore the fact that over the entire period, mergers destroyed more value than they created. A proponent of this position might quote the old adage, "Except for World War I and World War II, the 20th century was quite peaceful."

Before we move on, some final thoughts are in order. Readers may be bothered that abnormal returns are taken only around the time of the acquisition, well before all of the acquisition's impact is revealed. Academics look at long-term returns, but they have a special fondness for short-term returns. If markets are efficient, the short-term return provides an unbiased estimate of the total effect of the merger. Long-term returns, while capturing more information about a merger, also reflect the impact of many unrelated events.

RETURNS TO BIDDERS

The preceding results combined returns on both bidders and targets. Investors want to separate the bidders from the targets. Columns 3 and 4 of Table 29.5 provide returns for acquiring companies alone. The third column shows that abnormal percentage returns for bidders have been positive for the entire sample period and for each of the individual subperiods–a result similar to that for bidders and targets combined. The fourth column indicates aggregate Rupee losses, suggesting that large mergers did worse than small ones. The time pattern for these aggregate Rupee losses to bidders is presented in Figure 29.3. Again, the large losses occurred from 1998 to 2001, with the greatest loss in 2000.

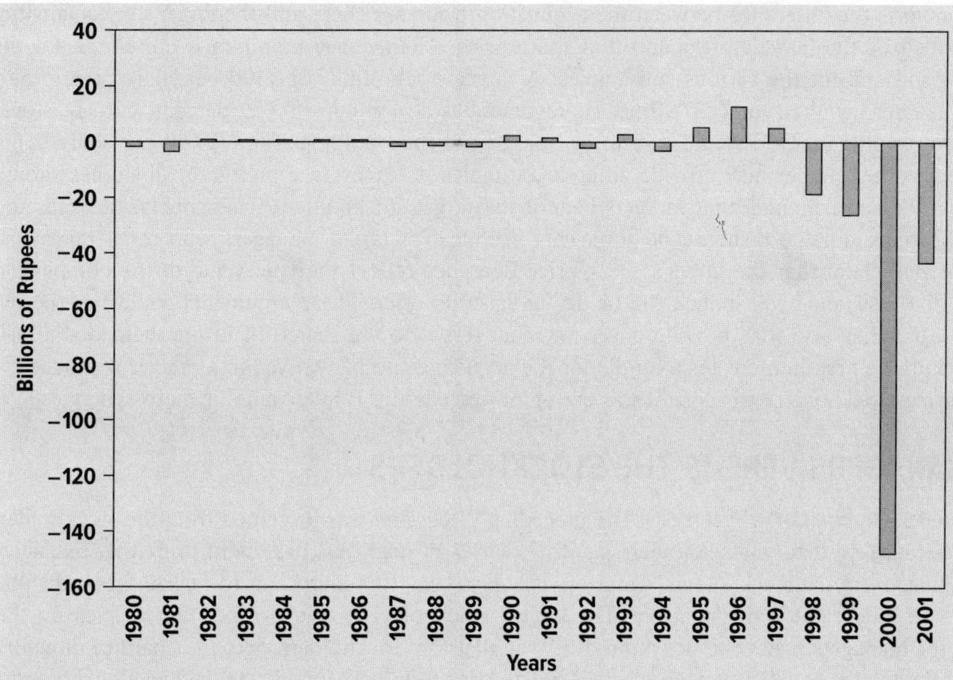

The graph shows the aggregate Rupee gain or loss across all acquiring firms each year from 1980 to 2001.

Figure 29.3 Yearly Aggregate Rupee Gain or Loss for the Shareholders of Acquiring Firms

SOURCE: Sara B. Moeller, Frederik P. Schlingemann, and René M. Stulz, "Wealth Destruction on a Massive Scale? A Study of Acquiring-Firm Returns in the Recent Merger Wave," *Journal of Finance* 60, no. 2 (April 2005): 757–82, Figure 1.

Let's fast-forward a few decades and imagine that you are the CEO of a company. In that position you will certainly be faced with potential acquisitions. Does the evidence in Table 29.5 and Figure 29.3 encourage you to make acquisitions or not? Again, the evidence is ambiguous. On the one hand, you could focus on the averages in Column 3 of the table, likely increasing your appetite for acquisitions. On the other hand, Column 4 of the table, as well as the figure, might give you pause.

TARGET COMPANIES

Although the evidence presented for both the combined entity and the bidder alone is ambiguous, the evidence for targets is crystal clear. Acquisitions benefit the target's stockholders. Consider the following chart, which shows the median merger premium over different periods in the United States:[24]

Time Period	1973–1998	1973–1979	1980–1989	1990–1998
Premium	37.9%	47.2%	37.7%	34.5%

[24]Gregor Andrade, Mark Mitchell, and Erik Stafford, "New Evidence and Perspectives on Mergers," *Journal of Economic Perspectives* 15, no. 2 (Spring 2001): 103–20, Table 1.

The premium is the difference between the acquisition price per share and the target's pre-acquisition share price, divided by the target's pre-acquisition share price. The average premium is quite high for the entire sample period and for the various subsamples. A target stock selling at ₹100 per share before the acquisition that is later acquired for ₹137.90 per share generates a premium of 37.9 percent. Clearly, stockholders of any firm trading at ₹100 would love to be able to sell their holdings for ₹137.90 per share.

Though other studies may provide different estimates of the average premium, all studies show positive premiums. We can conclude that mergers benefit the target stockholders. This conclusion leads to at least two implications. First, we should be somewhat skeptical of target managers who resist takeovers. These managers may claim that the target's stock price does not reflect the true value of the company. Or they may say that resistance will induce the bidder to raise its offer. These arguments could be true in certain situations, but they also may provide cover for managers who are scared of losing their jobs after acquisition. Second, the premium creates a hurdle for the acquiring company. Even in a merger with true synergies, the acquiring stockholders will lose if the premium exceeds the Rupee value of these synergies.

THE MANAGERS VERSUS THE STOCKHOLDERS

Managers of Bidding Firms The preceding discussion was presented from the stockholders' point of view. Because, in theory, stockholders pay the salaries of managers, we might think that managers would look at things from the stockholders' point of view. However, it is important to realize that individual stockholders have little clout with managers. The typical stockholder is not in a position to pick up the phone and give the managers a piece of her mind. It is true that the stockholders elect the board of directors, which monitors the managers. However, an elected director has little contact with individual stockholders.

It is fair to ask whether managers are held fully accountable for their actions. This question is at the heart of what economists call *agency theory*. Researchers in this area often argue that managers work less hard, get paid more, and make worse business decisions than they would if stockholders had more control over them. And there is a special place in agency theory for mergers. Managers frequently receive bonuses for acquiring other companies. In addition, their pay is often positively related to the size of their firm. Finally, managers' prestige also is tied to firm size. Because firm size increases with acquisitions, managers are disposed to look favorably on acquisitions, perhaps even ones with a negative NPV.

A fascinating study compared companies where managers received a lot of options on their own company's stock as part of their compensation package with companies where the managers did not.[25] Because option values rise and fall in tandem with the firm's stock price, managers receiving options have an incentive to forgo mergers with negative NPVs. The paper reported that the acquisitions by firms where managers receive lots of options (termed *equity-based compensation* in the paper) create more value than the acquisitions by firms where managers receive few or no options.

Agency theory also may explain why the biggest merger failures have involved large firms. Managers owning a small fraction of their firm's stock have less incentive to behave responsibly because the great majority of any losses are borne by other stockholders. Managers of large firms likely have a smaller percentage interest in their firm's stock than do managers of small firms (a large percentage of a large firm is too costly to acquire). Thus, the merger failures of large acquirers may be due to the small percentage ownership of the managers.

An earlier chapter of this text discussed the free cash flow hypothesis. The idea here is that managers can spend only what they have. Managers of firms with low cash flow are likely to run out of cash before they run out of good (positive NPV) investments. Conversely, managers of firms with high cash flow are likely to have cash on hand even after all the good investments are taken. Managers are rewarded for growth,

[25]Sudip Datta, Mai Iskandar-Datta, and Kartik Raman, "Executive Compensation and Corporate Acquisition Decisions," *Journal of Finance* 56, no. 6 (December 2001): 2299–2336.

so managers with cash flow above that needed for good projects have an incentive to spend the remainder on bad (negative NPV) projects. A paper tested this conjecture, finding that "cash-rich firms are more likely than other firms to attempt acquisitions. . . . [C]ash-rich bidders destroy seven cents in value for every Rupee of cash reserves held. . . . [C]onsistent with the stock return evidence, mergers in which the bidder is cash-rich are followed by abnormal declines in operating performance."[26]

The previous discussion has considered the possibility that some managers are unscrupulous–more interested in their own welfare than in the welfare of their stockholders. However, one paper entertained the idea that other managers were more fools than unscrupulous. Malmendier and Tate classified certain CEOs as overconfident, either because they refused to exercise stock options on their own company's stock when it was rational to do so or because the press portrayed them as confident or optimistic.[27] The authors find that these overconfident managers are more likely to make acquisitions than are other managers. In addition, the stock market reacts more negatively to announcements of acquisitions when the acquiring CEO is overconfident.

Managers of Target Firms Our discussion has focused on the managers of acquiring firms, finding that these managers sometimes make more acquisitions than they should. However, that is only half of the story. Stockholders of target firms may have as hard a time controlling their managers. While there are many ways that managers of target firms can put themselves ahead of their stockholders, two seem to stand out. First, we said earlier that because premiums are positive, takeovers are beneficial to the target's stockholders. However, if managers may be fired after their firms are acquired, they may resist these takeovers.[28] Tactics employed to resist takeover, generally called defensive tactics, were discussed in an earlier section of this chapter. Second, managers who cannot avoid takeover may bargain with the bidder, getting a good deal for themselves at the expense of their shareholders.

Consider Wulf's fascinating work on *mergers of equals* (MOEs).[29] Some deals are announced as MOEs, primarily because both firms have equal ownership in and equal representation on the board of directors of the merged entity. AOL and Time Warner, Daimler-Benz and Chrysler, Morgan Stanley and Dean Witter, and Fleet Financial Group and BankBoston are generally held out as examples of MOEs. Nevertheless, authorities point out that in any deal, one firm is typically "more equal" than the other. That is, the target and the bidder usually can be distinguished in practice. For example, Daimler-Benz is commonly classified as the bidder and Chrysler as the target in their merger.

Wulf finds that targets get a lower percentage of the merger gains, as measured by abnormal returns around the announcement date, in MOEs than in other mergers. And the percentage of the gains going to the target is negatively related to the representation of the target's officers and directors on the postmerger board. These and other findings lead Wulf to conclude: "They [the findings of the paper] suggest that CEOs trade power for premium in merger of equals transactions."

29.10 The Tax Forms of U.S. Acquisitions

If one firm buys another, the transaction may be taxable or tax-free. In a *taxable acquisition*, the shareholders of the acquired firm are considered to have sold their shares and their realized capital gains or losses will be taxed. In a taxable transaction, the *appraised value* of the assets of the selling firm may be revalued, as we explain next.

[26]Jarrad Harford, "Corporate Cash Reserves and Acquisitions,"*Journal of Finance* 54, no. 6 (December 1999): 1969–97.

[27]Ulrike Malmendier and Geoffrey Tate, "Who Makes Acquisitions? CEO Overconfidence and the Market's Reaction," *Journal of Financial Economics* 89, no. 1 (July 2008): 20–43.

[28]However, as stated earlier, managers may resist takeovers to raise the offer price, not to prevent the merger.

[29]Julie Wulf, "Do CEOs in Mergers Trade Power for Premium? Evidence from 'Mergers of Equals,'" *Journal of Law, Economics, & Organization* 20, no. 1 (April 2004): 60–101.

In a *tax-free acquisition*, the selling shareholders are considered to have exchanged their old shares for new ones of equal value and thus have experienced no capital gains or losses. In a tax-free acquisition, the assets are not revalued.

EXAMPLE 29.3

Taxes Suppose that 15 years ago Bill Evans started the Samurai Machinery (SM) Corp., which purchased plant and equipment costing ₹80,000. These have been the only assets of SM and the company has no debts. Bill is the sole proprietor of SM and owns all the shares. For tax purposes, the assets of SM have been depreciated using the straight-line method over 10 years and have no salvage value. The annual depreciation expense has been ₹8,000 (= ₹80,000/10). The machinery has no accounting value today (i.e., it has been written off the books). However, because of inflation, the fair market value of the machinery is ₹200,000. As a consequence, the S. A. Steel Company has bid ₹200,000 for all of the outstanding stock of Samurai.

Tax-Free Transaction If Bill Evans receives *shares* of S. A. Steel worth ₹200,000, the Income Tax Authorities will treat the sale as a tax-free transaction. Bill will not have to immediately pay taxes on any gain received from the stock, although he will pay capital gains taxes when he chooses to sell the stock. In addition, S. A. Steel will be allowed the same depreciation deduction that Samurai Machinery was allowed. Because the asset already has been fully depreciated, S. A. Steel will receive no depreciation deduction.

Taxable Transaction If S. A. Steel pays ₹200,000 in cash for Samurai Machinery, the transaction will be taxable with the following consequences:

1. In the year of the merger, Bill Evans must pay taxes on the difference between the merger price of ₹200,000 and his initial contribution to the firm of ₹80,000. His taxable income is ₹120,000 (= ₹200,000 − 80,000).
2. S. A. Steel may elect to *write up* the value of the machinery. In this case, S. A. Steel will be able to depreciate the machinery from an initial tax basis of ₹200,000. If S. A. Steel depreciates straight-line over 10 years, depreciation will be ₹20,000 (= ₹200,000/10) per year.

   If S. A. Steel elects to write up the machinery, S. A. Steel must treat the ₹200,000 write-up as taxable income immediately.[30]
3. Should S. A. Steel not elect the write-up, there is no increase in depreciation. Depreciation remains zero in this example. In addition, because there is no write-up, S. A. Steel does not need to recognize any additional taxable income.

   Because the tax benefits from depreciation occur slowly over time and the taxable income is recognized immediately, the acquirer generally elects not to write up the value of the machinery in a taxable transaction.

Because the write-up is not allowed for tax-free transactions and is generally not chosen for taxable ones, the only real tax difference between the two types of transactions concerns the taxation of the selling shareholders. These individuals can defer taxes under a tax-free situation but must pay taxes immediately under a taxable situation, so the tax-free transaction has better tax consequences. The tax implications for both types of transactions are displayed in Table 29.6.

[30]Technically, Samurai Machinery pays this tax. However, because Samurai is now a subsidiary of S. A. Steel, S. A. Steel is the effective taxpayer.

Table 29.6 The Tax Consequences of S. A. Steel Company's Acquisition of Samurai Machinery

	Type of Acquisition	
Buyer or Seller	**Taxable Acquisition**	**Tax-Free Acquisition**
Bill Evans (Seller)	Immediate tax on ₹120,000 (= ₹200,000 – 80,000)	Capital gains tax not paid until Evans sells shares of S. A. Steel
S. A. Steel (Buyer)	S. A. Steel may elect to write up assets: 1. Assets of Samurai are written up to ₹200,000 (with a useful life of 10 years). Annual depreciation expense is ₹20,000. 2. Immediate tax on ₹200,000 write-up of assets. Alternatively, S. A. Steel may elect not to write up assets. Here there is neither additional depreciation nor immediate tax. Typically acquirers elect not to write up assets.	No additional depreciation

S. A. Steel acquires Samurai Machinery for ₹200,000, which is the market value of Samurai's equipment. The book value of the equipment is ₹0. Bill Evans started Samurai Steel 15 years ago with a contribution of ₹80,000.

The tax consequences of a tax-free acquisition are better than the tax consequences of a taxable acquisition because the seller pays no immediate tax on a tax-free acquisition.

29.11 Accounting for Acquisitions

Earlier in this textbook, we mentioned that firms keep two distinct sets of books: the stockholders' books and the tax books. The previous section concerned the effects of acquisitions on the tax books. We now consider the stockholders' books. When one firm acquires another, the buyer uses the purchase method to account for the acquisition.

Purchase accounting requires that the assets of the acquired firm be reported at their fair market value on the books of the acquiring firm. This allows the acquiring firm to establish a new cost basis for the acquired assets.

In a purchase, an accounting term called **goodwill** is created. Goodwill is the excess of the purchase price over the sum of the fair market values of the individual assets acquired.

EXAMPLE 29.4

Acquisitions and Accounting Suppose Firm A acquires Firm B, creating a new firm, Firm AB. Firm A's and Firm B's financial positions at the date of the acquisition are shown in Table 29.7. The book value of Firm B on the date of the acquisition is ₹10 million. This is the sum of ₹8 million in buildings and ₹2 million in cash. However, an appraiser states that the sum of the fair market values of the individual buildings is ₹14 million. With ₹2 million in cash, the sum of the market values of the individual assets in Firm B is ₹16 million. This represents the value to be received if the firm is liquidated by selling off the individual assets separately. However, in business, the whole is often worth more than the sum of the parts. Firm A pays ₹19 million in cash for Firm B. This difference of ₹3 million (= ₹19 million – 16 million) is goodwill. It represents the increase in value from keeping the firm as an ongoing business. Firm A issued ₹19 million in new debt to finance the acquisition.

The total assets of Firm AB increase to ₹39 million. The buildings of Firm B appear in the new balance sheet at their current market value. That is, the market value of the assets of the acquired firm becomes part

(continued)

of the book value of the new firm. However, the assets of the acquiring firm (Firm A) remain at their old book value. They are not revalued upward when the new firm is created.

The excess of the purchase price over the sum of the fair market values of the individual assets acquired is ₹3 million. This amount is reported as goodwill. Financial analysts generally ignore goodwill because it has no cash flow consequences. Each year, the firm must assess the value of its goodwill. If the value goes down (this is called *impairment* in accounting speak), the amount of goodwill on the balance sheet must be decreased accordingly. Otherwise, no amortization is required.

Table 29.7 Accounting for Acquisitions: Purchase (in millions)

Firm A				Firm B				Firm AB			
Cash	₹ 4	Equity	₹20	Cash	₹ 2	Equity	₹10	Cash	₹ 6	Debt	₹19
Land	16			Land	0			Land	16	Equity	20
Buildings	0			Buildings	8			Buildings	14		
								Goodwill	3		
Total	₹20		₹20	Total	₹10		₹10	Total	₹39		₹39

When the purchase method is used, the assets of the acquired firm (Firm B) appear in the combined firm's books at their fair market value.

29.12 Going Private and Leveraged Buyouts

Going-private transactions and leveraged buyouts have much in common with mergers, and it is worthwhile to discuss them in this chapter. A publicly traded firm *goes private* when a private group, usually composed of existing management, purchases its stock. As a consequence, the firm's stock is taken off the market (if it is an exchange-traded stock, it is delisted) and is no longer traded. In going-private transactions, shareholders of publicly held firms are forced to accept cash for their shares.

Going-private transactions are frequently called *leveraged buyouts* (LBOs). In a leveraged buyout, the cash offer price is financed with large amounts of debt. Part of the appeal of LBOs is that the arrangement calls for little equity capital. This equity capital is generally supplied by a small group of investors, some of whom are likely to be managers of the firm being purchased.

The selling stockholders are invariably paid a premium above market price in an LBO, as in a merger. As with a merger, the acquirer profits only if the synergy created is greater than the premium. Synergy is quite plausible in a merger of two firms, and we delineated a number of types of synergy earlier in the chapter. However, it is more difficult to explain synergy in an LBO because only one firm is involved.

Two reasons are generally given for value creation in an LBO. First, the extra debt provides a tax deduction, which, as earlier chapters suggested, leads to an increase in firm value. Most LBOs center around firms with stable earnings and with low to moderate debt. The LBO may increase the firm's debt to its optimum level.

The second source of value comes from increased efficiency and often is explained in terms of "the carrot and the stick." Managers become owners under an LBO, giving them an incentive to work hard. This incentive is commonly referred to as the carrot, and the carrots in some LBOs have been huge. For example, consider the LBO of Nashville-based hospital company HCA. In 2007, an investment consortium led by

KKR, Bain Capital LLC, and Dr. Thomas Frist, who co-founded HCA in 1968, purchased HCA for ₹33 billion. Because of the leveraged nature of the transaction, the investment group only put up about ₹5.3 billion and borrowed the rest. In 2010, HCA paid a dividend of ₹4.3 billion to the LBO investors. Then, in 2011, the company went public again, raising about ₹3.79 billion. In the IPO, the LBO investment group received about ₹1 billion, which meant that all of the capital the group had invested in HCA had been returned. Of course, this was not all the investors received. After the LBO, they still held about ₹11 billion in HCA stock! And this was not the first LBO for HCA. In 1989, a group including Dr. Frist's son took HCA private in an LBO valued at ₹5.1 billion. When they took the company public in 1992, they earned an 800 percent gain.

Interest payments from the high level of debt constitute the stick. Large interest payments easily can turn a profitable firm before an LBO into an unprofitable one after the LBO. Management must make changes, through either revenue increases or cost reductions, to keep the firm in the black. Agency theory, a topic mentioned earlier in this chapter, suggests that managers can be wasteful with a large free cash flow. Interest payments reduce this cash flow, forcing managers to curb the waste.

Though it is easy to measure the additional tax shields from an LBO, it is difficult to measure the gains from increased efficiency. Nevertheless, this increased efficiency is considered at least as important as the tax shield in explaining the LBO phenomenon.

Academic research suggests that LBOs have, on average, created value. First, premiums are positive, as they are with mergers, implying that selling stockholders benefit. Second, studies indicate that LBOs that eventually go public generate high returns for the management group. Finally, other studies show that operating performance increases after the LBO. However, we cannot be completely confident of value creation because researchers have difficulty obtaining data about LBOs that do not go public. If these LBOs generally destroy value, the sample of firms going public would be a biased one. Regardless of the average performance of firms undertaking an LBO, we can be sure of one thing: Because of the great leverage involved, the risk is huge.

29.13 Divestitures

This chapter has primarily been concerned with acquisitions, but it is also worthwhile to consider their opposite–**divestitures**. Divestitures come in a number of different varieties, the most important of which we discuss next.

SALE

The most basic type of divestiture is the *sale* of a division, business unit, segment, or set of assets to another company. The buyer generally, but not always, pays in cash. A number of reasons are provided for sales. First, in an earlier section of this chapter, we considered asset sales as a defense against hostile takeovers. It was pointed out in that section that sales often improve corporate focus, leading to greater overall value for the seller. This same rationale applies when the selling company is not in play. Second, asset sales provide needed cash to liquidity-poor firms. Third, it often is argued that the scarcity of data about individual business segments makes large, diversified firms hard to value. Investors may discount the firm's overall value because of this lack of transparency. Sell-offs streamline a firm, making it easier to value. However, this argument is inconsistent with market efficiency because it implies that large, diversified firms sell below their true value. Fourth, firms may want to sell unprofitable divisions. However, unprofitable divisions are likely to have low values to anyone. A division should be sold only if its value is greater to the buyer than to the seller.

There has been a fair amount of research on sell-offs, with academics reaching two conclusions. First, event studies show that returns on the seller's stock are positive around the time of the announcement of sale, suggesting that sell-offs create value to the seller. Second, acquisitions often are sold off down the road. For example, Kaplan and Weisbach found that more than 40 percent of acquisitions were later divested, a result that does not reflect well on mergers.[31] The average time between acquisition and divestiture was about seven years.

SPIN-OFF

In a *spin-off*, a parent firm turns a division into a separate entity and distributes shares in this entity to the parent's stockholders. Spin-offs differ from sales in at least two ways. First, the parent firm receives no cash from a spin-off: Shares are sent for free to the stockholders. Second, the initial stockholders of the spun-off division are the same as the parent's stockholders. By contrast, the buyer in a divestiture is most likely another firm. However, because the shares of the division are publicly traded after the spin-off, the identities of the stockholders will change over time.

At least five reasons are generally given for a spin-off. First, as with a divestiture, the spin-off may increase corporate focus. Second, because the spun-off division is now publicly traded, the Securities and Exchange Commission requires additional information to be disseminated–so investors may find it easier to value the parent and subsidiary after the spin-off. Third, corporations often compensate executives with shares of stock in addition to cash. The stock acts as an incentive: Good performance from managers leads to stock price increases. However, prior to the spin-off, executives can receive stock only in the parent company. If the division is small relative to the entire firm, price movement in the parent's stock will be less related to the performance of the manager's division than to the performance of the rest of the firm. Thus, divisional managers may see little relation between their effort and stock appreciation. However, after the spin-off, the manager can be given stock in the subsidiary. The manager's effort should directly impact price movement in the subsidiary's stock. Fourth, a spin-off may relieve debt overhang. As explained in a previous chapter, debt overhang occurs when a firm chooses not to invest in positive NPV projects because the firm is at risk of bankruptcy and is unable to raise additional financing. A spin-off can separate a division with good growth prospects from the rest of the troubled firm and allow that division to raise additional financing. Fifth, the tax consequences from a spin-off are generally better than from a sale because the parent receives no cash from a spin-off.

One example of spinoff in India is of Flipkart. The retail giant spun out its digital payments firm, PhonePe, thus forming a new wholly-owned subsidiary in December 2020. In July 2023, Reliance Industries spun-off its financial services business and renamed it Jio Financial Services (JFS) at around $20 billion.

CARVE-OUT

In a *carve-out*, the firm turns a division into a separate entity and then sells shares in the division to the public. Generally, the parent retains a large interest in the division. This transaction is similar to a spin-off, and the first four benefits listed for a spin-off apply to a carve-out, as well. However, the big difference is that the firm receives cash from a carve-out, but not from a spin-off. The receipt of cash can be both good and bad. On the one hand, many firms need cash. Michaely and Shaw find that large, profitable firms are more likely to use carve-outs, whereas small, unprofitable firms are more likely to use spin-offs.[32] One interpretation is that firms generally prefer the cash that comes with a carve-out. However, small and unprofitable

[31] Steven N. Kaplan and Michael S. Weisbach, "The Success of Acquisitions: Evidence from Divestitures," *Journal of Finance* 47, no. 1 (March 1992): 107–38.
[32] Roni Michaely and Wayne H. Shaw, "The Choice of Going Public: Spin-Offs vs. Carve-Outs," *Financial Management* 24, no. 3 (Autumn 1995): 5–21.

firms have trouble issuing stock. They must resort to a spin-off, where stock in the subsidiary is merely given to their own stockholders.

Unfortunately, there is also a dark side to cash, as developed in the free cash flow hypothesis. That is, firms with cash exceeding that needed for profitable capital budgeting projects may spend it on unprofitable ones. Allen and McConnell find that the stock market reacts positively to announcements of carve-outs if the cash is used to reduce debt.[33] The market reacts neutrally if the cash is used for investment projects.

Bharti Infratel is an example of an equity carveout. Bharti Airtel separated the mobile tower business into a separate entity and sold the shares to the public in December 2012 to raise capital. Even after the IPO, Bharti Airtel continued to be the majority shareholder.

TRACKING STOCKS

A parent corporation issues tracking stock to "track" the performance of a specific division of the corporation. For example, if the tracking stock pays dividends, the size of the dividend depends on the division's performance. However, although "trackers" trade separately from the parent's stock, the division stays with the parent. By contrast, the subsidiary separates from the parent in a spin-off.

The first tracking stock was tied to the performance of EDS, a subsidiary of General Motors. Later, large firms such as Walt Disney and Sony issued trackers. However, few companies have issued tracking stocks in recent years, and parents have pulled most of those issued in earlier times.

Perhaps the biggest problem with tracking stocks is their lack of clearly defined property rights. An optimistic accountant can increase the earnings of a particular division, leading to a larger dividend. A pessimistic accountant will have the reverse effect. Although accountants affect the earnings of regular companies, a change in earnings will not directly impact dividends.

[33]Jeffrey W. Allen and John J. McConnell, "Equity Carve-Outs and Managerial Discretion," *Journal of Finance* 53, no. 1 (February 1998): 163-86.

RESEARCH IN EMERGING MARKET CONTEXT

According to Ladkani and Banerjee's (2018) study, mergers and acquisitions (M&A) deals in India create shareholder wealth during deal announcements, regardless of the payment method used. The study also posits that the deal's relative size significantly impacts the abnormal return observed during such announcements. Acquirers with high promoter holdings tend to be less willing to offer stock when acquiring a majority stake. Conversely, larger deals, deals for listed target firms, and deals in the information technology sector opted for share swaps.

Sahu and Agarwal's (2017) study concentrated on the Indian pharmaceutical sector and identified export and import intensity, firm size, and research and development intensity as the primary determinants of M&As. The study concludes that M&As positively impact the profit margin in the post-M&A scenario.

Chidambaram, Krishnakumar, and Sethi (2018) conducted a study that found increased domestic and cross-border acquisition activity by Indian firms. The authors discovered that larger, younger firms, firms with cash on hand, firms with low leverage, and relatively overvalued firms are more likely to make an acquisition. Industry competition is a significant determining factor of acquisition activity, with companies in more competitive sectors more likely to acquire.

(continued)

Col and Sen's (2019) research indicates that the ownership and board characteristics of Indian acquirers change after acquiring targets in developed markets. The authors also found that changes in governance were more pronounced when the target countries had better investor protection. They reported a higher valuation for Indian acquirer firms following the acquisitions.

References

Chidambaran, N. K., Krishnakumar, D., & Sethi, M. (2018). Cross-border vs. domestic acquisitions: Evidence from India. *Journal of Economics and business*, *95*, 3–25.

Col, B., & Sen, K. (2019). The role of corporate governance for acquisitions by the emerging market multinationals: Evidence from India. *Journal of Corporate Finance*, *59*, 239–254.

Ladkani, R. M., & Banerjee, A. (2018). Emerging market bidder returns and the choice of payment method in mergers and acquisitions: Evidence from India. *Journal of emerging market finance*, *17*(3), 386–411.

Sahu, S. K., & Agarwal, N. (2017). Inter-firm differences in mergers and acquisitions: a study of the pharmaceutical sector in India. *Journal of Economic Studies*, *44*(5), 861–878.

Summary and Conclusions

1. One firm can acquire another in several different ways. The three legal forms of acquisition are merger and consolidation, acquisition of stock, and acquisition of assets. Mergers and consolidations are the least costly from a legal standpoint, but they require a vote of approval by the shareholders. Acquisition of stock does not require a shareholder vote and is usually done via a tender offer. However, it is difficult to obtain 100 percent control with a tender offer. Acquisition of assets is comparatively costly because it requires the more difficult transfer of asset ownership.
2. The synergy from an acquisition is defined as the value of the combined firm (V_{AB}) less the value of the two firms as separate entities (V_A and V_B):

$$\text{Synergy} = V_{AB} - (V_A + V_B)$$

   The shareholders of the acquiring firm will gain if the synergy from the merger is greater than the premium.
3. The possible benefits of an acquisition come from the following:
   a. Revenue enhancement.
   b. Cost reduction.
   c. Lower taxes.
   d. Reduced capital requirements.
4. Stockholders may not benefit from a merger that is done only to achieve diversification or earnings growth. And the reduction in risk from a merger actually may help bondholders and hurt stockholders.
5. A merger is said to be friendly when the managers of the target support it. A merger is said to be hostile when the target managers do not support it. Some of the most colorful language of finance stems from defensive tactics in hostile takeover battles. *Poison pills*, *golden parachutes*, *crown jewels*, and *greenmail* are terms that describe various antitakeover tactics.
6. The empirical research on mergers and acquisitions is extensive. On average, the shareholders of acquired firms fare very well. The effect of mergers on acquiring stockholders is less clear.
7. Mergers and acquisitions involve complicated tax and accounting rules. Mergers and acquisitions can be taxable or tax-free transactions. In a taxable transaction, each selling shareholder must pay taxes on the

stock's capital appreciation. Should the acquiring firm elect to write up the assets, additional tax implications arise. However, acquiring firms do not generally elect to write up the assets for tax purposes. The selling stockholders do not pay taxes at the time of a tax-free acquisition. The purchase method is used to account for mergers and acquisitions.

8. In a *going-private* transaction, a buyout group, usually including the firm's management, buys all the shares of the other stockholders. The stock is no longer publicly traded. A *leveraged buyout* is a going-private transaction financed by extensive leverage.

Concept Questions

1. **Merger Accounting** Explain the purchase accounting method for mergers. What is the effect on cash flows? On EPS?
2. **Merger Concepts** Indicate whether you think the following claims regarding takeovers are true or false. In each case, provide a brief explanation for your answer.
   - **a.** By merging competitors, takeovers have created monopolies that will raise product prices, reduce production, and harm consumers.
   - **b.** Managers act in their own interests at times and in reality may not be answerable to shareholders. Takeovers may reflect runaway management.
   - **c.** In an efficient market, takeovers would not occur because market prices would reflect the true value of corporations. Thus, bidding firms would not be justified in paying premiums above market prices for target firms.
   - **d.** Traders and institutional investors, having extremely short time horizons, are influenced by their perceptions of what other market traders will think of stock prospects and do not value takeovers based on fundamental factors. Thus, they will sell shares in target firms despite the true value of the firms.
   - **e.** Mergers are a way of avoiding taxes because they allow the acquiring firm to write up the value of the assets of the acquired firm.
   - **f.** Acquisitions analysis frequently focuses on the total value of the firms involved. An acquisition, however, will usually affect relative values of stocks and bonds, as well as their total value.
3. **Merger Rationale** Explain why diversification *per se* is probably not a good reason for merger.
4. **Corporate Split** No matter how you look at it, Dow Chemical had busy years in 2014 and 2015. In 2014, Dow announced that it was planning to sell its subsidiaries Angus Chemical Company, Sodium Borohydride, and AgroFresh. Dow also had recently completed the sale of a portion of its North America rail car fleet. Additionally, the company was in the process of a planned carveout of its U.S. Gulf Coast chlor-alkali/chlor-vinyl, global chlorinated organics, and epoxy businesses that would be completed in 2015. Why might a company split off a division? Is there a possibility of reverse synergy?
5. **Poison Pills** Are poison pills good or bad for stockholders? How do you think acquiring firms are able to get around poison pills?
6. **Merger and Taxes** Describe the advantages and disadvantages of a taxable merger as opposed to a tax-free exchange. What is the basic determinant of tax status in a merger? Would an LBO be taxable or nontaxable? Explain.
7. **Economies of Scale** What does it mean to say that a proposed merger will take advantage of available economies of scale? Suppose Eastern Power Co. and Western Power Co. are located in different time zones. Both operate at 60 percent of capacity except for peak periods, when they operate at 100 percent of capacity. The peak periods begin at 9:00 A.M. and 5:00 P.M. local time and last about 45 minutes. Explain why a merger between Eastern and Western might make sense.

8. **Hostile Takeovers** What types of actions might the management of a firm take to fight a hostile acquisition bid from an unwanted suitor? How do the target firm shareholders benefit from the defensive tactics of their management team? How are the target firm shareholders harmed by such actions? Explain.

9. **Merger Offers** Suppose a company in which you own stock has attracted two takeover offers. Would it ever make sense for your company's management to favor the lower offer? Does the form of payment affect your answer at all?

10. **Merger Profit** Acquiring firm stockholders seem to benefit little from takeovers. Why is this finding a puzzle? What are some of the reasons offered for it?

Questions and Problems

BASIC (Questions 1–8)

1. **Calculating Synergy** Pearl, Inc., has offered ₹197 million cash for all of the equity share in Jam Corporation. Based on recent market information, Jam is worth ₹178 million as an independent operation. If the merger makes economic sense for Pearl, what is the minimum estimated value of the synergistic benefits from the merger?

2. **Balance Sheets for Mergers** Consider the following premerger information about Firm X and Firm Y:

	Firm X	Firm Y
Total earnings	₹95,000	₹12,000
Shares outstanding	20,000	9,000
Per-share values:		
Market	₹ 63	₹ 15
Book	₹ 6	₹ 2

Assume that Firm X acquires Firm Y by issuing long-term debt to purchase all the shares outstanding at a merger premium of ₹5 per share. Assuming that neither firm has any debt before the merger, construct the postmerger balance sheet for Firm X assuming the use of the purchase accounting method.

3. **Balance Sheets for Mergers** Assume that the following balance sheets are stated at book value. Suppose that Meat Co. purchases Loaf, Inc. The fair market value of Loaf's fixed assets is ₹11,500 versus the ₹8,300 book value shown. Meat pays ₹18,400 for Loaf and raises the needed funds through an issue of long-term debt. Construct the postmerger balance sheet under the purchase accounting method.

Meat Co.			
Current assets	₹21,600	Current liabilities	₹ 7,320
Net fixed assets	51,600	Long-term debt	16,420
		Equity	49,460
Total	₹73,200	Total	₹73,200

Loaf, Inc.			
Current assets	₹ 4,700	Current liabilities	₹ 1,800
Net fixed assets	8,300	Long-term debt	3,120
		Equity	8,080
Total	₹13,000	Total	₹13,000

4. **Balance Sheets for Mergers** Silver Enterprises has acquired All Gold Mining in a merger transaction. Construct the balance sheet for the new corporation if the merger is treated as a purchase of interests for accounting purposes. The market value of All Gold Mining's fixed assets is ₹12,100; the market values for current and other assets are the same as the book values. Assume that Silver Enterprises issues ₹20,800 in new long-term debt to finance the acquisition. The following balance sheets represent the premerger book values for both firms:

Silver Enterprises			
Current assets	₹ 7,400	Current liabilities	₹ 4,030
Other assets	2,080	Long-term debt	10,600
Net fixed assets	23,910	Equity	18,760
Total	₹33,390	Total	₹33,390

All Gold Mining			
Current assets	₹ 2,080	Current liabilities	₹ 2,070
Other assets	800	Long-term debt	0
Net fixed assets	9,620	Equity	10,510
Total	₹12,580	Total	₹12,580

5. **Cash versus Stock Payment** Penn Corp. is analyzing the possible acquisition of Teller Company. Both firms have no debt. Penn believes the acquisition will increase its total aftertax annual cash flows by ₹1.45 million indefinitely. The current market value of Teller is ₹31.5 million, and that of Penn is ₹53 million. The appropriate discount rate for the incremental cash flows is 10 percent. Penn is trying to decide whether it should offer 40 percent of its stock or ₹44.5 million in cash to Teller's shareholders.

   a. What is the cost of each alternative?
   b. What is the NPV of each alternative?
   c. Which alternative should Penn choose?

6. **EPS, PE, and Mergers** The shareholders of Bread Company have voted in favor of a buyout offer from Butter Corporation. Information about each firm is given here:

	Bread	Butter
Price-earnings ratio	7.2	14.4
Shares outstanding	73,000	146,000
Earnings	₹210,000	₹630,000

Bread's shareholders will receive one share of Butter stock for every three shares they hold in Bread.

   a. What will the EPS of Butter be after the merger? What will the PE ratio be if the NPV of the acquisition is zero?
   b. What must Butter feel is the value of the synergy between these two firms? Explain how your answer can be reconciled with the decision to go ahead with the takeover.

7. **Merger Rationale** Cholern Electric Company (CEC) is a public utility that provides electricity to the central Colorado area. Recent events at its Mile-High Nuclear Station have been discouraging. Several shareholders have expressed concern over last year's financial statements.

Income Statement Last Year (in millions)		Balance Sheet End of Year (in millions)	
Revenue	₹110	Assets	₹400
Fuel	50	Debt	300
Other expenses	30	Equity	100
Interest	30		
Net income	₹ 0		

Recently, a wealthy group of individuals has offered to purchase half of CEC's assets at fair market price. Management recommends that this offer be accepted because "[w]e believe our expertise in the energy industry can be better exploited by CEC if we sell our electricity generating and transmission assets and enter the telecommunications business. Although telecommunications is a riskier business than providing electricity as a public utility, it is also potentially very profitable."

Should the management approve this transaction? Why or why not?

8. **Cash versus Stock as Payment** Consider the following premerger information about a bidding firm (Firm B) and a target firm (Firm T). Assume that both firms have no debt outstanding.

	Firm B	Firm T
Shares outstanding	6,400	1,500
Price per share	₹53	₹19

Firm B has estimated that the value of the synergistic benefits from acquiring Firm T is ₹17,000.

a. If Firm T is willing to be acquired for ₹23 per share in cash, what is the NPV of the merger?
b. What will the price per share of the merged firm be assuming the conditions in part (a)?
c. In part (a), what is the merger premium?
d. Suppose Firm T is agreeable to a merger by an exchange of stock. If B offers one of its shares for every two of T's shares, what will the price per share of the merged firm be?
e. What is the NPV of the merger assuming the conditions in part (d)?

9. **Cash versus Stock as Payment** In the previous problem, are the shareholders of Firm T better off with the cash offer or the stock offer? At what exchange ratio of B shares to T shares would the shareholders in T be indifferent between the two offers?

INTERMEDIATE (Questions 9–14)

10. **Effects of a Stock Exchange** Consider the following premerger information about Firm A and Firm B:

	Firm A	Firm B
Total earnings	₹5,850	₹1,900
Shares outstanding	1,600	400
Price per share	₹ 56	₹ 59

Assume that Firm A acquires Firm B via an exchange of stock at a price of ₹61 for each share of B's stock. Both A and B have no debt outstanding.

a. What will the earnings per share, EPS, of Firm A be after the merger?
b. What will Firm A's price per share be after the merger if the market incorrectly analyzes this reported earnings growth (i.e., the price-earnings ratio does not change)?

c. What will the price-earnings ratio of the postmerger firm be if the market correctly analyzes the transaction?

d. If there are no synergy gains, what will the share price of A be after the merger? What will the price-earnings ratio be? What does your answer for the share price tell you about the amount A bid for B? Was it too high? Too low? Explain.

11. **Merger NPV** Show that the NPV of a merger can be expressed as the value of the synergistic benefits, ΔV, less the merger premium.

12. **Merger NPV** Fly-By-Night Couriers is analyzing the possible acquisition of Flash-in-the-Pan Delivery. Neither firm has debt. The forecasts of Fly-By-Night show that the purchase would increase its annual aftertax cash flow by ₹345,000 indefinitely. The current market value of Flash-in-the-Pan is ₹8.1 million. The current market value of Fly-By-Night is ₹19 million. The appropriate discount rate for the incremental cash flows is 8 percent. Fly-By-Night is trying to decide whether it should offer 35 percent of its stock or ₹11.5 million in cash to Flash-in-the-Pan.

a. What is the synergy from the merger?

b. What is the value of Flash-in-the-Pan to Fly-By-Night?

c. What is the cost to Fly-By-Night of each alternative?

d. What is the NPV to Fly-By-Night of each alternative?

e. What alternative should Fly-By-Night use?

13. **Merger NPV** Harrods PLC has a market value of £85 million and 4.5 million shares outstanding. Selfridge Department Store has a market value of £30 million and 1.8 million shares outstanding. Harrods is contemplating acquiring Selfridge. Harrods's CFO concludes that the combined firm with synergy will be worth £130 million, and Selfridge can be acquired at a premium of £3.1 million.

a. If Harrods offers 900,000 shares of its stock in exchange for the 1.8 million shares of Selfridge, what will the stock price of Harrods be after the acquisition?

b. What exchange ratio between the two stocks would make the value of the stock offer equivalent to a cash offer of £33.1 million?

14. **Mergers and Shareholder Value** Bentley Corp. and Rolls Manufacturing are considering a merger. The possible states of the economy and each company's value in that state are shown here:
Bentley currently has a bond issue outstanding with a face value of ₹150,000. Rolls is an all-equity company.

State	Probability	Bentley	Rolls
Boom	.65	₹348,000	₹312,000
Recession	.35	132,000	95,000

a. What is the value of each company before the merger?

b. What are the values of each company's debt and equity before the merger?

c. If the companies continue to operate separately, what are the total value of the companies, the total value of the equity, and the total value of the debt?

d. What would be the value of the merged company? What would be the value of the merged company's debt and equity?

e. Is there a transfer of wealth in this case? Why?

f. Suppose that the face value of Bentley's debt was ₹90,000. Would this affect the transfer of wealth?

CHALLENGE (Questions 15–16)

15. **Calculating NPV** BQ, Inc., is considering making an offer to purchase iReport Publications. The vice president of finance has collected the following information:

	BQ	iReport
Price-earnings ratio	14.5	9.2
Shares outstanding	1,400,000	195,000
Earnings	₹4,300,000	₹705,000
Dividends	₹1,075,000	₹375,000

BQ also knows that securities analysts expect the earnings and dividends of iReport to grow at a constant rate of 5 percent each year. BQ management believes that the acquisition of iReport will provide the firm with some economies of scale that will increase this growth rate to 7 percent per year.

a. What is the value of iReport to BQ?
b. What would BQ's gain be from this acquisition?
c. If BQ were to offer ₹38 in cash for each share of iReport, what would the NPV of the acquisition be?
d. What's the most BQ should be willing to pay in cash per share for the stock of iReport?
e. If BQ were to offer 205,000 of its shares in exchange for the outstanding stock of iReport, what would the NPV be?
f. Should the acquisition be attempted? If so, should it be as in part (c) or as in part (e)?
g. BQ's outside financial consultants think that the 7 percent growth rate is too optimistic and a 6 percent rate is more realistic. How does this change your previous answers?

16. **Mergers and Shareholder Value** The Chocolate Ice Cream Company and the Vanilla Ice Cream Company have agreed to merge and form Fudge Swirl Consolidated. Both companies are exactly alike except that they are located in different towns. The end-of-period value of each firm is determined by the weather, as shown below. There will be no synergy to the merger.

State	Probability	Value
Rainy	.1	₹230,000
Warm	.4	450,000
Hot	.5	905,000

The weather conditions in each town are independent of those in the other. Furthermore, each company has an outstanding debt claim of ₹450,000. Assume that no premiums are paid in the merger.

a. What are the possible values of the combined company?
b. What are the possible values of end-of-period debt and stock after the merger?
c. Show that the bondholders are better off and the stockholders are worse off in the combined firm than they would have been if the firms had remained separate.

Mini Case — THE BIRDIE GOLF–HYBRID GOLF MERGER

Birdie Golf, Inc., has been in merger talks with Hybrid Golf Company for the past six months. After several rounds of negotiations, the offer under discussion is a cash offer of ₹282 million for Hybrid Golf. Both companies have niche markets in the golf club industry, and the companies believe a merger will result in significant synergies due to economies of scale in manufacturing and marketing, as well as significant savings in general and administrative expenses.

Bryce Bichon, the financial officer for Birdie, has been instrumental in the merger negotiations. Bryce has prepared the following pro forma financial statements for Hybrid Golf assuming the merger takes place. The financial statements include all synergistic benefits from the merger:

	2019	2020	2021	2022	2023w
Sales	₹409,600,000	₹460,800,000	₹512,000,000	₹576,000,000	₹640,000,000
Production costs	287,400,000	322,500,000	358,400,000	404,500,000	451,200,000
Depreciation	38,400,000	40,900,000	42,300,000	42,500,000	43,900,000
Other expenses	40,900,000	46,100,000	51,200,000	57,900,000	63,100,000
EBIT	₹ 42,900,000	₹ 51,300,000	₹ 60,100,000	₹ 71,100,000	₹ 81,800,000
Interest	9,730,000	11,260,000	12,300,000	12,800,000	13,800,000
Taxable income	₹ 33,170,000	₹ 40,040,000	₹ 47,800,000	₹ 58,300,000	₹ 68,000,000
Taxes (25%)	8,292,500	10,010,000	11,950,000	14,575,000	17,000,000
Net income	₹ 24,877,500	₹ 30,030,000	₹ 35,850,000	₹ 43,725,000	₹ 51,000,000

Bryce also is aware that the Hybrid Golf division will require investments each year for continuing operations, along with sources of financing. The following table outlines the required investments and sources of financing:

	2019	2020	2021	2022	2023
Investments:					
Net working capital	₹10,200,000	₹12,800,000	₹12,800,000	₹15,400,000	₹15,400,000
Fixed assets	7,700,000	13,800,000	9,300,000	31,400,000	3,900,000
Total	₹17,900,000	₹26,600,000	₹22,100,000	₹46,800,000	₹19,300,000
Sources of financing:					
New debt	₹17,900,000	₹ 9,200,000	₹ 8,200,000	₹15,000,000	₹ 6,100,000
Profit retention	0	17,400,000	13,900,000	31,800,000	13,200,000
Total	₹17,900,000	₹26,600,000	₹22,100,000	₹46,800,000	₹19,300,000

The management of Birdie Golf feels that the capital structure at Hybrid Golf is not optimal. If the merger takes place, Hybrid Golf will immediately increase its leverage with a ₹57 million debt issue, which would be followed by a ₹76 million dividend payment to Birdie Golf. This will increase Hybrid's debt-equity ratio from .50 to 1.00. Birdie Golf also will be able to use a ₹12.8 million tax loss carryforward in both 2020 and 2021 from Hybrid Golf's previous operations. The total value of Hybrid Golf is expected to be ₹460.8 million in five years, and the company will have ₹153.6 million in debt at that time.

Stock in Birdie Golf currently sells for ₹94 per share, and the company has 11.6 million shares of stock outstanding. Hybrid Golf has 5.2 million shares of stock outstanding. Both companies can borrow at an 8 percent interest rate. The risk-free rate is 6 percent, and the expected return on the market is 13 percent.

Bryce believes the current cost of capital for Birdie Golf is 11 percent. The beta for Hybrid Golf stock at its current capital structure is 1.30.

Bryce has asked you to analyze the financial aspects of the potential merger. Specifically, he has asked you to answer the following questions:

1. Suppose Hybrid shareholders will agree to a merger price of ₹63.25 per share. Should Birdie proceed with the merger?
2. What is the highest price per share that Birdie should be willing to pay for Hybrid?
3. Suppose Birdie is unwilling to pay cash for the merger but will consider a stock exchange. What exchange ratio would make the merger terms equivalent to the original merger price of ₹63.25 per share?
4. What is the highest exchange ratio Birdie would be willing to pay and still undertake the merger?

30

Financial Distress

In November 2020, a judge approved a deal to allow JCPenney to emerge from bankruptcy. Under the reorganization, a group of lenders agreed to forgive ₹1 billion in debt in exchange for 160 properties and six distribution centers. Mall operators Simon Property Group and Brookfield Property Partners acquired the company's retail operations for ₹1.75 billion. Current shareholders would receive nothing for their shares. In August 2020, J. Crew received court approval on its bankruptcy plan. Under the terms of the plan, ₹1.6 billion in debt would be converted to equity, trade creditors would receive partial payment from a ₹71 million pool, and shareholders would receive nothing. In May 2023, GoFirst (previously GoAir) Airlines filed for bankruptcy protection due to huge revenue losses caused by faulty engines supplied by Pratt & Whitney, grounding nearly half of its fleet of 56 planes.

These bankruptcies are examples of companies experiencing significant financial distress, which is the subject of this chapter. A firm with insufficient cash flow to make contractually required financial obligations, such as interest payments, is in financial distress. A firm that defaults on a required payment may be forced to liquidate its assets, but, more often, a defaulting firm will reorganize its financial structure. Financial restructuring involves replacing old financial claims with new ones and takes place with private workouts or legal bankruptcy. Private workouts are voluntary arrangements to restructure a company's debt, such as postponing a payment or reducing the size of the payment. If a private workout is not possible, formal bankruptcy is usually required.

Please visit us at **rwjcorporatefinance.blogspot.com** for the latest developments in the world of corporate finance.

30.1 What Is Financial Distress?

Financial distress is surprisingly hard to define precisely. This is true partly because of the variety of events befalling firms under financial distress. The list of events is almost endless, but here are some examples:

- Dividend reductions
- Plant closings
- Losses
- Layoffs
- CEO resignations
- Plummeting stock prices

Financial distress is a situation where a firm's operating cash flows are insufficient to satisfy current obligations (such as trade credits or interest expenses) and the firm is forced to take corrective action.[1]

[1]This definition is close to the one used by Karen Wruck, "Financial Distress, Reorganization, and Organizational Efficiency," *Journal of Financial Economics* 27, no. 2 (October 1990): 419–44.

Financial distress may lead a firm to default on a contract, and it may involve financial restructuring between the firm, its creditors, and its equity investors. Usually the firm is forced to take actions that it would not have taken if it had sufficient cash flow.

Our definition of financial distress can be expanded somewhat by linking it to insolvency. Insolvency is defined in *Black's Law Dictionary* as:[2]

> Inability to pay one's debts; lack of means of paying one's debts. Such a condition of a woman's (or man's) assets and liabilities that the former made immediately available would be insufficient to discharge the latter.

This definition has two general themes: stocks and flows.3 These two ways of thinking about insolvency are depicted in Figure 30.1. Stock-based insolvency occurs when a firm has negative net worth, so the value of its assets is less than the value of its debts. Flow-based insolvency occurs when operating cash flow is insufficient to meet current obligations. Flow-based insolvency refers to the inability to pay one's debts. Insolvency may lead to bankruptcy. Some of the largest U.S. bankruptcies are in Table 30.1.

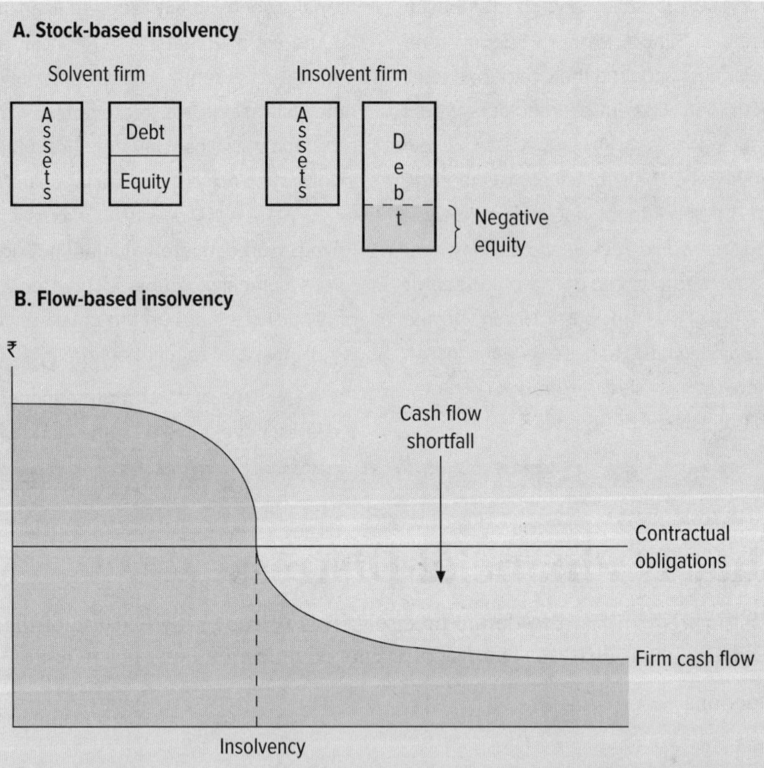

Stock-based insolvency occurs when the value of the assets of a firm is less than the value of the debts. This implies negative equity. Flow-based insolvency occurs when firm cash flows are insufficient to cover contractually required payments.

Figure 30.1 Insolvency

[2]Taken from Henry Campbell Black, *Black's Law Dictionary,* 5th ed. (St. Paul, MN: West Publishing Co., 1979).

[3]Edward Altman was one of the first to distinguish between stock-based insolvency and flow-based insolvency. See Edward I. Altman and Edith Hotchkiss, *Corporate Financial Distress and Bankruptcy: A Complete Guide to Predicting & Avoiding Distress and Profiting from Bankruptcy,* 3rd ed. (New York : John Wiley & Sons, 2005).

Table 30.1 Large U.S. Bankruptcies: 2008 through 2020

Firm	Liabilities (in millions)	Bankruptcy Date
1. Lehman Brothers Holdings, Inc.	₹613,000	09/15/08
2. General Motors Corp.	172,810	06/01/09
3. CIT Group, Inc.	64,901	11/01/09
4. Chrysler, LLC	55,200	04/30/09
5. Energy Futures Holdings Corp.	49,701	04/29/14
6. MF Global Holdings Ltd.	39,684	10/31/11
7. AMR Corp.	29,552	11/29/11
8. General Growth Properties	27,294	04/22/09
9. Thornburg Mortgage, Inc.	24,700	05/01/09
10. Hertz Global Holdings, Inc.	24,355	05/22/20

SOURCE: Edward I. Altman, NYU Salomon Center, Stern School of Business.

Bankruptcy cases in India started right from the pre-Independence days. Post-independence, the Government tried to counter the sickness with some ad-hoc measures. RBI monitored the industrial sickness. A cursory glance over the list of distressed companies over time reveals all types of companies. It includes companies with household names and famous products (Kingfisher Airlines, Mafatlals); financial service providers (Dewan Housing Finance Corporation, Yes Bank, Lakshmi Vilas Bank); companies with some of the largest asset base in their time (Bangurs, Suzlon); companies with thousands of employees (Jet Airways, Satyam Computers); companies with once enviable reputation in the stock exchanges (Silverline Technologies, Unitech); companies with seemingly unassailable positions in their markets (Tata Tele, Arvind Mills); companies which were darlings of financial institutions and banks (Essar Steel, Modi Tyres); and companies which issued shares at a high premium (IVRCL, Shree Rama Multi-Tech, Vardhaman Financial Services).

However, during the post-liberalization period 1990–2015, the rearrangement of a debtor's financial commitment was done using a consensual process without too much supervision. It led to the involvement of lenders (and, in some cases, even creditors). It was often triggered by an actual or potential default. The typical steps included - (a) entering into a standstill agreement, (b) negotiation on the restructuring package, (c) approval of the restructuring package, (d) negotiation/implementation of the restructuring package wherein restructuring may include interest funding, conversion of debt to equity/convertible preference shares and such. However, the incoming of the new Insolvency and Bankruptcy Code (IBC) in 2016 changed things. We'll know more about it in the following few sections.

30.2 What Happens in Financial Distress?

General Motors (GM) lost money in 2005 and 2007, with its accounting shareholder equity turning negative in 2006. Then, in June 2008, GM reported second quarter net income of negative ₹15 million. During this time, a steady loss in market share to rivals such as Toyota, BMW, and Honda was accompanied by a plummet in stock price from ₹50 in 2003 to about ₹1 in 2009. Automobile customers had good reason to worry about buying cars from GM. GM struggled to increase sales, cut costs, attempted to sell assets (e.g., the Hummer line), drew down bank debt, and arranged for more long-term financing. GM was clearly a firm experiencing financial distress. GM filed for bankruptcy on June 1, 2009. GM emerged from bankruptcy six weeks later and shares of GM were sold in the world's largest IPO (at the time) in November 2010. Most of the shares were owned by the U.S. Treasury in what had been one of the biggest "bailouts" of a private firm by the U.S. Treasury. Of course, many firms experiencing financial distress and bankruptcy do not fare as well as GM.

Firms deal with financial distress in several ways, such as these:

1. Selling major assets.
2. Merging with another firm.
3. Reducing capital spending and research and development.
4. Issuing new securities.
5. Negotiating with banks and other creditors.
6. Exchanging debt for equity.
7. Filing for bankruptcy.

Items (1), (2), and (3) concern the firm's assets. Items (4), (5), (6), and (7) involve the right side of the firm's balance sheet and are examples of financial restructuring. Financial distress may involve both asset restructuring and financial restructuring (i.e., changes on both sides of the balance sheet).

Some firms may actually benefit from financial distress by restructuring their assets. For example, managers can use financial distress to increase their bargaining power against labor unions and other groups representing workers. While this strategy has questionable ethical implications, the threat of mass layoffs appears to be an effective way to demand concessions from labor representatives. A levered recapitalization can also change a firm's behavior and force a firm to dispose of unrelated businesses. A firm going through a levered recapitalization will add a great deal of debt and, as a consequence, its cash flow may not be sufficient to cover required payments and it may be forced to sell its noncore businesses. For some firms, financial distress may bring about new organizational forms and new operating strategies. However, in this chapter, we focus on financial restructuring.

Financial restructuring may occur in a private workout or a bankruptcy reorganization under Chapter 11 of the U.S. bankruptcy code. Figure 30.2 shows how large public firms move through financial distress. Approximately half of the financial restructurings have been done via private workouts. Most large public firms (approximately 83 percent) that file for Chapter 11 bankruptcy are able to reorganize and continue to do business.[4]

Financial distress can serve as a firm's "early warning" system for trouble. Firms with more debt will experience financial distress earlier than firms with less debt. However, firms that experience financial distress earlier will have more time for private workouts and reorganization. Firms with low leverage will experience financial distress later and, in many instances, be forced to liquidate.

30.3 Bankruptcy Liquidation and Reorganization

Firms that cannot or choose not to make contractually required payments to creditors have two basic options: liquidation or reorganization. This section discusses bankruptcy liquidation and reorganization.[5]

[4]However, less than 20 percent of all firms (public or private) going through a Chapter 11 bankruptcy are successfully reorganized.

[5]One of the most important choices a bankrupt firm must make is whether to liquidate or reorganize. Arturo Bris, Ivo Welch, and Ning Zhu, "The Costs of Bankruptcy: Chapter 7 Liquidation versus Chapter 11 Reorganization," *Journal of Finance* 61, no. 3 (June 2006): 1253–1303, examines this choice. They find:

- Very small firms (i.e., with assets less than ₹100,000) are more likely to liquidate than reorganize compared to large firms.
- Firms with a large number of secured creditors are more likely to try to reorganize.
- Firms with an unsecured creditor, especially a bank, are more likely to choose liquidation.
- Firms that have large negative equity are more likely to try to reorganize.

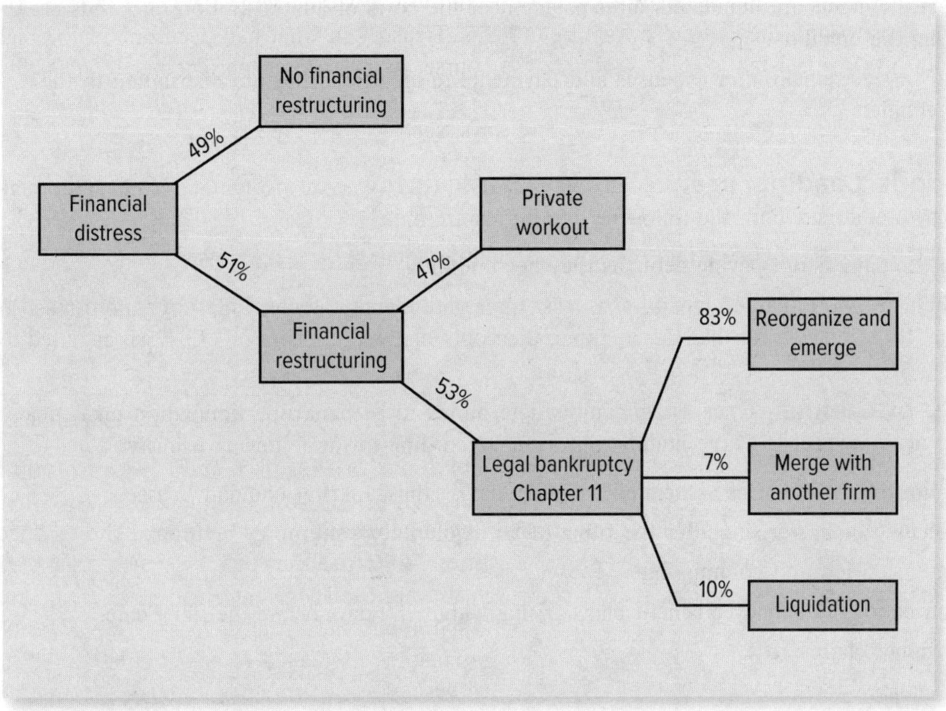

Figure 30.2 What Happens in Financial Distress with Large Public Firms

SOURCES: Karen H. Wruck, "Financial Distress, Reorganization, and Organizational Efficiency," *Journal of Financial Economics* 27, no. 2 (October 1990): 419–44, Figure 2. See also Stuart C. Gilson, John Kose, and Larry H. P. Lang, "Troubled Debt Restructurings," *Journal of Financial Economics* 27, no. 2 (October 1990): 315–53; and Lawrence A. Weiss, "Bankruptcy Resolution: Direct Costs and Violation of Priority of Claims," *Journal of Financial Economics* 27, no. 2 (October 1990): 285–314.

Liquidation means termination of the firm as a going concern; it involves selling the assets of the firm for salvage value. The proceeds, net of transactions costs, are distributed to creditors in order of established priority.

Reorganization is the option of keeping the firm a going concern; it sometimes involves issuing new securities to replace old securities.

Liquidation and formal reorganization may be done by bankruptcy. *Bankruptcy* is a legal proceeding and can be done voluntarily, with the company filing the petition, or involuntarily, with the creditors filing the petition.

BANKRUPTCY LIQUIDATION

Chapter 7 of the Bankruptcy Reform Act of 1978 deals with "straight" liquidation. The following sequence of events is typical:

1. A petition is filed in a federal court. A company may file a voluntary petition, or involuntary petitions may be filed against the company.
2. A bankruptcy trustee is elected by the creditors to take over the assets of the debtor company. The trustee will attempt to liquidate the assets.

3. When the assets are liquidated, after payment of the costs of administration, proceeds are distributed among the creditors.
4. If any assets remain after expenses and payments to creditors, they are distributed to the shareholders.

Conditions Leading to Involuntary Bankruptcy An involuntary bankruptcy petition may be filed by creditors if both the following conditions are met:

1. The company is not paying debts as they become due.
2. If there are more than 12 creditors, at least three with claims totaling ₹13,475 or more must join in the filing. If there are fewer than 12 creditors, then only one with a claim of ₹13,475 is required to file.

Priority of Claims Once a company is determined to be bankrupt, liquidation takes place. The distribution of the proceeds of the liquidation occurs according to the following priority:

1. Administration expenses associated with liquidating the bankrupt company's assets.
2. Unsecured claims arising after the filing of an involuntary bankruptcy petition.
3. Wages, salaries, and commissions.
4. Contributions to employee benefit plans arising within 180 days before the filing date.
5. Consumer claims.
6. Tax claims.
7. Secured and unsecured creditors' claims.
8. Preferred stockholders' claims.
9. Common stockholders' claims.

The priority rule in liquidation is the **absolute priority rule (APR)**.

One qualification to this list concerns secured creditors. Liens on property are outside APR ordering. However, if the secured property is liquidated and provides cash insufficient to cover the amount owed them, the secured creditors join with unsecured creditors in dividing the remaining liquidating value. In contrast, if the secured property is liquidated for proceeds greater than the secured claim, the net proceeds are used to pay unsecured creditors and others.

EXAMPLE 30.1

APR The Shakti Drugs Corporation is to be liquidated. Its liquidating value is ₹2.7 million. Bonds worth ₹1.5 million are secured by a mortgage on the Shakti Drugs Corporation corporate headquarters building, which is sold for ₹1 million; ₹200,000 is used to cover administrative costs and other claims (including unpaid wages, pension benefits, consumer claims, and taxes). After paying ₹200,000 to the administrative priority claims, the amount available to pay secured and unsecured creditors is ₹2.5 million. This is less than the amount of unpaid debt of ₹4 million.

Under APR, all creditors must be paid before shareholders, and the mortgage bondholders have first claim on the ₹1 million obtained from the sale of the headquarters building.

(continued)

The trustee has proposed the following distribution:

Type of Claim	Prior Claim	Cash Received under Liquidation
Bonds (secured by mortgage)	₹ 1,500,000	₹1,500,000
Subordinated debentures	2,500,000	1,000,000
Common stockholders	10,000,000	0
Total	₹14,000,000	₹2,500,000

Calculation of the Distribution	
Cash received from sale of assets available for distribution	₹2,500,000
Cash paid to secured bondholders on sale of mortgaged property	1,000,000
Available to bond and debenture holders	₹1,500,000
Total claims remaining (₹4,000,000 less payment of ₹1,000,000 on secured bonds)	₹3,000,000
Distribution of remaining ₹1,500,000 to cover total remaining claims of ₹3,000,000	

Type of Claim Remaining	Claim on Liquidation Proceeds	Cash Received
Bonds	₹ 500,000	₹ 500,000
Debentures	2,500,000	1,000,000
Total	₹3,000,000	₹1,500,000

BANKRUPTCY REORGANIZATION

Corporate reorganization takes place under Chapter 11 of the Federal Bankruptcy Reform Act of 1978, as amended by the Bankruptcy Abuse Prevention and Consumer Protection Act of 2005.[6] The general objective of a proceeding under Chapter 11 is to plan to restructure the company with some provision for repayment of creditors. A typical sequence of events follows:

1. A voluntary petition can be filed by the company, or an involuntary petition can be filed by three or more creditors (or one creditor if the total creditors are fewer than 12–see the previous subsection). The involuntary petition must allege that the company is not paying its debts.
2. Usually, a federal judge approves the petition and a time for filing proofs of claims of creditors and of shareholders is set.
3. In most cases, the company (the "debtor in possession") continues to run the business.[7]
4. For 120 days only, the company can file a reorganization plan. If it does, the company is given 180 days from the filing date to gain acceptance of the plan.

[6]Do bankruptcy codes matter? The answer is yes for Sergei A. Davydenko and Julian R. Franks ["Do Bankruptcy Codes Matter? A Study of Defaults in France, Germany, and the U.K.," *Journal of Finance* 63, no. 2 (April 2008): 565-608]. They find that the different bankruptcy codes of France, Germany, and the U.K. produce different outcomes of financial distress situations even though banks make significant adjustments in response to creditors' friendly or unfriendly codes.

[7]In Chapter 11 bankruptcies, the firm (now called "debtor in possession") continues to operate. In many cases, the firm will seek to borrow new money and use the proceeds to pay off secured creditors and to continue to operate until a reorganization plan is approved.

In Their Own Words

EDWARD I. ALTMAN ON CORPORATE FINANCIAL DISTRESS AND BANKRUPTCY

Financial distress of private and public entities throughout the world is a frequent occurrence with important implications for their many stakeholders. While the role of corporate bankruptcy laws is clear–either to provide a legal procedure that permits firms which have temporary liquidity problems to restructure and successfully emerge as continuing entities or to provide an orderly process to liquidate assets for the benefit of creditors before asset values are dissipated–bankruptcy laws differ markedly from country to country. It is generally agreed upon that the U.S. Chapter 11 provisions under the Bankruptcy Reform Act of 1978 provide the most protection for bankrupt firms' assets and result in a greater likelihood of successful reorganization than is found in other countries where liquidation and sale of the assets for the benefit of creditors is more likely the result. But the U.S. code's process is usually lengthy (averaging close to two years, except where a sufficient number of creditors agree in advance via a prepackaged Chapter 11) and expensive, and the reorganized entity is not always successful in avoiding subsequent distress. If the reorganization is unsuccessful, then liquidation under Chapter 7 will usually ensue.

Bankruptcy processes in the industrialized world outside the United States strongly favor senior creditors who obtain control of the firm and seek to enforce greater adherence to debt contracts. The U.K. process, for example, is speedy and less costly, but the reduced costs can result in undesirable liquidations, unemployment, and underinvestment. The new bankruptcy code in Germany attempts to reduce the considerable power of secured creditors but it is still closer to the U.K. system. In the United States, creditors and owners can negotiate "violations" to the "absolute priority rule"–this "rule" holds that more senior creditors must be paid in full, prior to any payments to more junior creditors or to owners. (However, the so-called violations to absolute priority have empirically been shown to be relatively small–such as under 10 percent of firm value.) Finally, the U.S. system gives the court the right to sanction postpetition debt financing, usually with superpriority status over existing claims, thereby facilitating the continuing operation of the firm. Recently, France had a similar successful experience.

A measure of performance of the U.S. bankruptcy system is the proportion of firms that emerge successfully. The results in the United States of late are somewhat mixed, with close to 83 percent of large firms emerging but probably less than 20 percent of smaller entities. And a not insignificant number of firms suffer subsequent distress and may file again.

Regardless of the location, one of the objectives of bankruptcy and other distressed workout arrangements

5. Creditors and shareholders are divided into classes. A class of creditors accepts the plan if two-thirds of the class (in rupee amount) and one-half of the class (in number) have indicated approval.[8]
6. After acceptance by creditors, the plan is confirmed by the court.
7. Payments in cash, property, and securities are made to creditors and shareholders. The plan may provide for the issuance of new securities.

Recently, Section 363 of the bankruptcy code has been in the news. In a traditional Chapter 11 filing, the bankruptcy plan is described to creditors and shareholders in a prospectus-like disclosure. The plan then must be approved in a vote by the interested parties. A Section 363 bankruptcy is more like an auction. An initial bidder, known as a "stalking horse," bids on all or part of the bankrupt corporation's assets. Other bidders are then invited into the process in an attempt to produce the highest possible bid. The main advantage of a Section 363 bankruptcy is speed. Because a traditional bankruptcy requires the approval of interested parties, it is not uncommon for the process to take several years, while a Section 363 bankruptcy is generally

[8]We are describing the standard events in a bankruptcy reorganization. Petitions are almost always accepted, and the general rule is that a reorganization plan will be accepted by the court if all of the creditor classes accept it and it will be rejected if all of the creditor classes reject it. However, if one or more (but not all) of the classes accept it, the plan may be eligible for a *cram down* procedure. A cram down takes place if the bankruptcy court finds a plan fair and equitable and accepts the plan for all creditors.

is that creditors and other suppliers of capital clearly know their rights and expected recoveries in the event of a distressed situation. When these are not transparent and/or are based on outdated processes with arbitrary and possibly corrupt outcomes, then the entire economic system suffers and growth is inhibited. Such is the case in several emerging market countries. Revision of these outdated systems should be a priority.

In addition to the comparative benefits of different national restructuring systems, a number of intriguing theoretical and empirical issues are related to the distressed firm. Among these are corporate debt capacity, manager-creditor-owner incentives, ability to predict distress, data and computations for default rate estimation, investment in securities of distressed firms, and post-reorganization performance assessment.

Corporate distress has a major impact on creditor-debtor relationships and, combined with business risk and tax considerations, affects the capital structure of companies. One key question is how costly are the *expected* distress costs compared to the *expected* tax benefits of using leverage–the so-called trade-off theory. Most analysts agree that the sum of direct (e.g., legal fees) and indirect costs is in the range of 10–20 percent of firm value.

Whether the taking of excess risk and overinvestment are examples of agency conflicts between managers and creditors rests upon one's view as to who are the true residual owners of a distressed firm–the existing equityholders or creditors who will more than likely be the new owners of a reorganized entity. Existing management has the exclusive right to file the first plan of reorganization within 120 days of filing, with exclusivity extensions possible. Their incentives and influence can be biased, however, and not always in accord with other stakeholders, primarily creditors. Limiting this exclusivity would appear to be desirable to speed up the process and restrict managerial abuse.

Distress prediction models have intrigued researchers and practitioners for more than 50 years. Models have evolved from univariate financial statement ratios to multivariate statistical classification models, to contingent claim and market value-based approaches, and finally to using artificial intelligence techniques. Most large financial institutions have one or more of these types of models in place as more sophisticated credit risk management frameworks are being introduced, sometimes combined with aggressive credit asset portfolio strategies. Increasingly, private credit assets are being treated as securities with estimates of default and recovery, as they are critical inputs to their valuation.

Perhaps the most intriguing by-product of corporate distress is the development of a relatively new class of investors known as *vultures.* These money managers specialize in securities of distressed and defaulted companies.

Edward I. Altman is Max L. Heine Professor of Finance, NYU Stern School of Business. He is widely recognized as one of the world's experts on bankruptcy and credit analysis, as well as the distressed debt and high-yield bond markets.

much quicker. For example, in the middle of 2009, both General Motors and Chrysler sped through the bankruptcy process in less than 45 days because of Section 363 auctions.

EXAMPLE 30.2

Chapter 11 Suppose Shakti Drugs Co. decides to reorganize under Chapter 11. Generally, senior claims are honored in full before various other claims receive anything. Assume that the *going concern* value of Shakti Drugs Co. is ₹3 million and that its balance sheet is as shown:

Assets	₹3,000,000
Liabilities	
Mortgage bonds	1,500,000
Subordinated debentures	2,500,000
Stockholders' equity	−1,000,000

(continued)

The firm has proposed the following reorganization plan:

Old Security	Old Claim	New Claim with Reorganization Plan
Mortgage bonds	₹1,500,000	₹1,500,000
Subordinated debentures	2,500,000	1,500,000

The firm also has proposed a distribution of new securities under a new claim with this reorganization plan:

Old Security	Received under Proposed Reorganization Plan
Mortgage bonds	₹1,000,000 in 9% senior debentures ₹500,000 in 11% subordinated debentures
Debentures	₹1,000,000 in 8% preferred stock ₹500,000 in common stock

However, it will be difficult for the firm to convince secured creditors (mortgage bonds) to accept unsecured debentures of equal face value. In addition, the company may wish to allow the old stockholders to retain some participation in the firm. Needless to say, this would be a violation of the absolute priority rule, and the holders of the debentures would not be happy.

BANKRUPTCY, LIQUIDATION, AND REORGANIZATION IN INDIA

In India, bankruptcy in the legal sense occurs when the firm cannot pay its bills or when its liabilities exceed the fair market value of its assets. However, creditors generally try to avoid forcing a firm into bankruptcy if it shows potential for future success. Indian law presently provides three routes to debt restructuring. First, an out-of-court restructuring option. Second, the IBC, under the aegis of the National Company Law Tribunal (NCLT). Third, a scheme of arrangement under the Companies Act, 2013, through the NCLT. The third route is sparingly used in practice.

Section 53 of the new code has established an order of priority among creditors, determining the sequence in which outstanding debts will be repaid. This is:

1. Interim Resolution Professional and liquidation costs;
2. Workmens dues (for 24 months), and secured creditor dues, if the security has been relinquished;
3. Employees dues (for 12 months);
4. Unsecured financial creditors;
5. Government dues, and unpaid dues to secured creditor, if the security has been realized;
6. Remaining debts and dues (which include, unsecured operational debts);
7. Preference shareholders;
8. Equity shareholders.

Insolvency and restructuring matters in India are primarily regulated by the Insolvency and Bankruptcy Code (IBC), 2016. It governs insolvency and liquidation proceedings for all limited liability entities, except financial services entities[9] (say, pension fund). IBC also governs insolvency and bankruptcy proceedings for individuals and partnerships.

The Companies Act, 2013 deals with voluntary schemes of arrangement and compromise between a company and its creditors (regarding company debts). In addition, India's central banking regulator, the RBI, issues circulars and notifications to banks and non-banking finance companies from time to time under the Banking (Regulation Act), 1948, setting out directions for resolving or restructuring distressed loans outside the IBC framework.

Before the enactment of the IBC, the jurisdiction regime was deemed debtor-friendly. However, the code has shifted the regime from debtor-in-control to creditor-in-possession. Once a debtor enters insolvency, its board of directors is suspended, and management is transferred to an independent insolvency resolution professional (RP) appointed by the bankruptcy tribunal. Creditors have the authority to replace the insolvency professional and will oversee the proceedings under their overall supervision. This change has made the insolvency and restructuring process more creditor-friendly.

We conclude by restating that the Supreme Court, National Company Law Tribunals (NCLTs) and National Company Law Appellate Tribunal (NCLAT) have the following sacrosanct order of objectives: "getting a resolution" (highest priority); "maximization of value of assets of the Corporate Debtor," and "promoting entrepreneurship, availability of credit and balancing the interests" (least priority).

In other words, it aimed to provide a comprehensive framework for resolving distressed companies and individuals. Further, to strengthen the IBC process, the Insolvency and Bankruptcy Code (Amendment) Act, 2023, is introduced, highlighting several noteworthy changes. The introduction of the Insolvency and Bankruptcy Board of India (Insolvency Resolution Process for Corporate Persons) (Second Amendment) Regulations, 2023, aims to facilitate the smooth functioning of the corporate insolvency resolution process. Key additions to the regulations include provisions for cooperation with the Resolution Professional (RP), submission and verification of claims, roles and obligations of authorized representatives, increased fees for authorized representatives, transfer of debt among creditors, audit of the corporate debtor, requests for resolution plans, a model timeline for the CIRP, and timelines for filing forms.

30.4 Private Workout or Bankruptcy: Which Is Best?

A firm that defaults on its debt payments will need to restructure its financial claims. The firm will have two choices: formal bankruptcy or **private workout**. The previous section described two types of formal bankruptcies: bankruptcy liquidation and bankruptcy reorganization. This section compares private workouts with bankruptcy reorganizations. Both types of financial restructuring involve exchanging new financial claims for old financial claims. Usually, senior debt is replaced with junior debt and junior debt is replaced with equity. Much academic research has described what happens in private workouts and formal bankruptcies.[10]

- Historically, half of financial restructurings have been private, but recently, formal bankruptcies have dominated.
- Firms that emerge from private workouts experience stock price increases that are much greater than those for firms emerging from formal bankruptcies.

[9]As yet, there is also no special regime for financial services entities. The IBC allows the government, in consultation with the financial services regulators, to notify financial service providers (FSPs). The government recently notified rules to establish a generic framework for insolvency and liquidation proceedings for systemically important FSPs.

[10]For example, see Stuart Gilson, "Managing Default: Some Evidence on How Firms Choose between Workouts and Chapter 11," *Journal of Applied Corporate Finance,* 4, no. 2 (Summer 1991): 62–70; and Stuart C. Gilson, John Kose, and Larry H. P. Lang, "Troubled Debt Restructurings: An Empirical Study of Private Reorganization of Firms in Default," *Journal of Financial Economics,* 27, no. 2 (October 1990): 315–53; and Lawrence A. Weiss, "Bankruptcy Resolution," *Journal of Financial Economics* 27, no. 2 (October 1990): 285–314.

- The direct costs of private workouts are much less than the costs of formal bankruptcies.
- Top management usually loses pay, and sometimes jobs, in both private workouts and formal bankruptcies.

These facts, when taken together, seem to suggest that a private workout is much better than a formal bankruptcy. We then ask: Why do firms ever use formal bankruptcies to restructure?

Absolute Priority Rule (APR)

The absolute priority rule states that senior claims are fully satisfied before junior claims receive anything.

Deviation from Rule

Equityholders	Expectation: No payout Reality: Payout in 81 percent of cases
Unsecured creditors	Expectation: Full payout after secured creditors Reality: Violation in 78 percent of cases
Secured creditors	Expectation: Full payout Reality: Full payout in 92 percent of cases

Reasons for Violations

- Creditors want to avoid the expense of litigation. Debtors are given a 120-day opportunity to cause delay and harm value.
- Managers often own equity and demand to be compensated.
- Bankruptcy judges like consensual plans and pressure parties to compromise.

SOURCE: Lawrence A. Weiss, "Bankruptcy Resolution: Direct Costs and Violation of Priority of Claims," *Journal of Financial Economics* 27, no. 2 (October 1990): 285–314.

THE MARGINAL FIRM

For the average firm, a formal bankruptcy is more costly than a private workout, but for other firms, formal bankruptcy is better. Formal bankruptcy allows firms to issue debt that is senior to all previously incurred debt. This new debt is *debtor in possession* (DIP) debt. For firms that need a temporary injection of cash, DIP debt makes bankruptcy reorganization an attractive alternative to a private workout. There are some tax advantages to bankruptcy. Firms do not lose tax carryforwards in bankruptcy and the tax treatment of the cancellation of indebtedness is better in bankruptcy. Also, interest on prebankruptcy unsecured debt stops accruing in formal bankruptcy.

HOLDOUTS

Bankruptcy is usually better for the equity investors than it is for the creditors. Using DIP debt and stopping prebankruptcy interest from accruing on unsecured debt help the stockholders and hurt the creditors. As a consequence, equity investors usually can hold out for a better deal in bankruptcy. The absolute priority rule, which favors creditors over equity investors, is usually violated in formal bankruptcies. One study found that in 81 percent of bankruptcies, the equity investor obtained some compensation.[11] Under Chapter 11, the creditors often are forced to give up some of their seniority rights to get management and the equity investors to agree to a deal.

COMPLEXITY

A firm with a complicated capital structure will have more trouble putting together a private workout. Firms with secured creditors and trade creditors usually will use formal bankruptcy because it is too hard to reach an agreement with many different types of creditors.

LACK OF INFORMATION

There is an inherent conflict of interest between equity investors and creditors, and the conflict is accentuated when both have incomplete information about the circumstances of financial distress. When a firm initially experiences a cash flow shortfall, it may not know whether the shortfall is permanent or temporary. If the shortfall is permanent, creditors will push for a formal reorganization or liquidation. However, if the cash flow shortfall is temporary, formal reorganization or liquidation may not be necessary. Equity investors will push for this viewpoint. This conflict of interest cannot be resolved easily.

These last two points are especially important. They suggest that financial distress will be more expensive (cheaper) if complexity is high (low) and information is incomplete (complete). Complexity and lack of information make cheap workouts less likely.

30.5 Prepackaged Bankruptcy

On May 1, 2019, Pennsylvania-based Sungard Availability Services Capital filed for a "prepackaged" bankruptcy. Under the terms of the plan, the company's debt would be reduced from ₹1.25 billion to ₹300 million, and existing creditors would be granted shares of the company's new stock. The bankruptcy was called the fastest ever: The company filed the plan just before 9 P.M. on May 1, 2019, and the judge signed the order confirming the exit by 6 P.M. the next day!

Firms typically file bankruptcy to seek protection from their creditors, essentially admitting that they cannot meet their financial obligations as they are presently structured. Once in bankruptcy, the firm attempts to reorganize its financial picture so that it can survive. A key to this process is that the creditors must ultimately give their approval to the restructuring plan. The time a firm spends in Chapter 11 depends on many things, but it usually depends most on the time it takes to get creditors to agree to a plan of reorganization.

A *prepackaged bankruptcy* (or just "prepack") is a combination of a private workout and legal bankruptcy.[12] Prior to filing bankruptcy, the firm approaches its creditors with a plan for reorganization. The two sides negotiate a settlement and agree on the details of how the firm's finances will be restructured in bankruptcy. Then, the firm puts together the necessary paperwork for the bankruptcy court before filing for bankruptcy. A filing is a prepack if the firm walks into court and, at the same time, files a reorganization plan complete with the documentation of the approval of its creditors, which is exactly what Sungard did.

---

[11] Lawrence A. Weiss, "Bankruptcy Resolution: Direct Costs and Violation of Priority of Claims," *Journal of Financial Economics* 27 (1990). However, William Beranek, Robert Boehmer, and Brooke Smith, "Much Ado about Nothing: Absolute Priority Deviations in Chapter 11," *Financial Management* 25, no. 3 (Autumn 1996): 102–09, find that 33.8 percent of bankruptcy reorganizations leave the stockholders with nothing. They also point out that deviations from the absolute priority rule are to be expected because the bankruptcy code allows creditors to waive their rights if they perceive a waiver to be in their best interests. A response can be found in Allan C. Eberhart and Lawrence A. Weiss, "The Importance of Deviations from the Absolute Priority Rule in Chapter 11 Bankruptcy Proceedings," *Financial Management* 27, no. 4 (Winter 1998): 106–10.

[12] John J. McConnell and Henri Servaes, "The Economics of Prepackaged Bankruptcy," *Journal of Applied Corporate Finance* 4, no. 2 (Summer 1991): 93–98, describe prepackaged bankruptcy.

The key to the prepackaged reorganization process is that both sides have something to gain and something to lose. If bankruptcy is imminent, it may make sense for the creditors to expedite the process even though they are likely to take a financial loss in the restructuring. Sungard's bankruptcy was painful for both stockholders and bondholders. Under the terms of the agreement, stockholders were wiped out entirely and lenders exchanged ₹800 million in debt for equity in the company.

In another example of a prepack, Atlantic City casino Revel filed a prepack bankruptcy on February 19, 2013. Debt holders who put up ₹1.155 billion in February 2011 would own 82 percent of the company's equity when it emerged from bankruptcy. On May 21, 2013, the company formally emerged from Chapter 11 bankruptcy. As an aside, in 2010, investment bank Morgan Stanley walked away from its entire ₹932 million investment in the company, so all-in-all, the Revel proved to be an expensive bet. The bankruptcy ultimately proved to be unsuccessful as the casino closed in September 2014.

Prepackaged bankruptcy arrangements require that most creditors reach agreement privately. Prepackaged bankruptcy doesn't seem to work when there are thousands of reluctant trade creditors.[13]

The main benefit of prepackaged bankruptcy is that it forces holdouts to accept a bankruptcy reorganization. If a large fraction of a firm's creditors can agree privately to a reorganization plan, the holdout problem may be avoided. It makes a reorganization plan in formal bankruptcy easier to put together.[14]

A study by McConnell, Lease, and Tashjian reports that prepackaged bankruptcies offer many of the advantages of formal bankruptcies, but they are also more efficient. The study suggests that the time spent and the direct costs of resolving financial distress are less in a prepackaged bankruptcy than in a formal bankruptcy.[15]

In India, private workout is a popular arrangement between a technically insolvent or bankrupt firm and its creditors, enabling it to bypass many of the costs and delays involved in legal bankruptcy proceedings. After waiting for long, SPIC Petrochemicals attempted to use this route to come out of bankruptcy. Essar Steel worked out an extension arrangement whereby the firm's creditors received payment in full, though not immediately. In its voluntary settlement, Siemens went in for a pro-rata cash settlement of creditor claims, in which a uniform percentage of each rupee owed is paid. On the other hand, in its private arrangement, Modi Rubber went for a creditor control arrangement in which the creditor committee replaced the operating management and operated the firm until all claims had been satisfied.

30.6 Predicting Corporate Bankruptcy: The Z-Score Model

Many potential lenders use credit scoring models to assess the creditworthiness of prospective borrowers. The general idea is to find factors that enable the lenders to discriminate between good and bad credit risks. To put it more precisely, lenders want to identify attributes of the borrower that can be used to predict default or bankruptcy.

---

[13]Sris Chatterjee, Upinder S. Dhillon, and Gabriel G. Ramirez, "Resolution of Financial Distress: Debt Restructurings via Chapter 11, Prepackaged Bankruptcies, and Workouts." *Financial Management* 25, no. 1 (Spring 1996): 5–18, find that firms using prepackaged bankruptcy arrangements are smaller and in better financial shape, and have greater short-term liquidity problems than firms using private workouts or Chapter 11.

[14]During bankruptcy, a proposed plan can be crammed down on a class of creditors. A bankruptcy court can force creditors to participate in a reorganization if it can be shown that the plan is "fair and equitable."

[15]John J. McConnell, Ronald C. Lease, and Elizabeth Tashjian. "Prepacks as a Mechanism for Resolving Financial Distress: The Evidence," *Journal of Applied Corporate Finance* 8, no. 4 (Winter 1996): 99–106.

Edward Altman, a professor at New York University, has developed the following model using financial statement ratios and multiple discriminant analyses to predict bankruptcy for publicly traded manufacturing firms:

$$\begin{aligned}Z = 3.3 \frac{\text{EBIT}}{\text{Total assets}} &+ 1.2 \frac{\text{Net working capital}}{\text{Total assets}} \\ + 1.0 \frac{\text{Sales}}{\text{Total assets}} &+ .6 \frac{\text{Market value of equity}}{\text{Book value of debt}} \\ + 1.4 \frac{\text{Accumulated retained earnings}}{\text{Total assets}}\end{aligned}$$

where Z is an index of bankruptcy.

A score of Z less than 2.675 indicates that a firm has a 95 percent chance of becoming bankrupt within one year. However, Altman's results show that, in practice, scores between 1.81 and 2.99 should be thought of as a gray area. In actual use, bankruptcy would be predicted if $Z \leq 1.81$ and nonbankruptcy if $Z \geq 2.99$. Altman shows that bankrupt firms and nonbankrupt firms have very different financial profiles one year before bankruptcy.[16] These financial ratios are the key intuition behind the Z-score model and are depicted in Table 30.2.

Altman's original Z-score model requires a firm to have publicly traded equity and be a manufacturer. He uses a revised model to make it applicable for private firms and nonmanufacturers. The resulting model is this:

$$\begin{aligned}Z = 6.56 \frac{\text{Net working capital}}{\text{Total assets}} &+ 3.26 \frac{\text{Accumulated retained earnings}}{\text{Total assets}} \\ + 1.05 \frac{\text{EBIT}}{\text{Total assets}} &+ 6.72 \frac{\text{Book value of equity}}{\text{Total liabilities}}\end{aligned}$$

where

$Z < 1.23$ indicates a bankruptcy prediction,

$1.23 \leq Z \leq 2.90$ indicates a gray area, and

$Z > 2.90$ indicates no bankruptcy.

Table 30.2 Financial Statement Ratios One Year before Bankruptcy: Manufacturing Firms

	Average Ratios One Year before Bankruptcy of:	
	Bankrupt Firms	**Nonbankrupt Firms**
$\frac{\text{Net working capital}}{\text{Total assets}}$	−6.1%	41.4%
$\frac{\text{Accumulated retained earnings}}{\text{Total assets}}$	−62.6%	35.5%
$\frac{\text{EBIT}}{\text{Total assets}}$	−31.8%	15.4%
$\frac{\text{Market value of equity}}{\text{Total liabilities}}$	40.1%	247.7%
$\frac{\text{Sales}}{\text{Assets}}$	150%	190%

SOURCE: Edward I. Altman, *Corporate Financial Distress and Bankruptcy* (New York: John Wiley & Sons, 1993), Table 3.1, 109.

[16]Although these are the original values proposed by Altman, in a more recent interview, he stated that a negative Z-score was now an indicator of potential bankruptcy. (See www.stern.nyu.edu/experience-stern/news-events/professor-edward-altman-discusses-his-z-score-research-and-today-s-credit-markets).

EXAMPLE 30.3

Bharat Composite Company is attempting to increase its line of credit with Bank of Baroda. The director of credit management of Bank of Baroda uses the Z-score model to determine creditworthiness. Bharat Composite Company is not an actively traded firm and market prices are not always very reliable, so the revised Z-score model can be used.

The balance sheet and income statement of Bharat Composite Company for 2022 are in Tables 2.1 and 2.2 (Chapter 2).

The first step is to determine the value of each of the financial statement variables and apply them in the revised Z-score model:

(in millions)

$$\frac{\text{Net working capital}}{\text{Total assets}} = \frac{₹271}{₹1{,}879} = .144$$

$$\frac{\text{Accumulated retained earnings}}{\text{Total assets}} = \frac{₹390}{₹1{,}879} = .208$$

$$\frac{\text{EBIT}}{\text{Total assets}} = \frac{₹159}{₹1{,}879} = .085$$

$$\frac{\text{Book value of equity}}{\text{Total liabilities}} = \frac{₹805}{₹1{,}074} = .750$$

The next step is to calculate the revised Z-score:

$$Z = 6.56 \times .144 + 3.26 \times .208 + 1.05 \times .085 + 6.72 \times .750$$
$$= 6.75$$

Finally, we determine that the Z-score is above 2.9, and we conclude that Bharat Composite is a good credit risk.

RESEARCH IN EMERGING MARKET CONTEXT

Charalambakis and Garrett (2016) conducted a study on predicting financial distress in Indian firms. They found that a model based on profitability and financial risk accurately predicted financial distress. The study also revealed that when combined with accounting information, market-based variables such as excess returns, market capitalization and return volatility did not impact the probability of financial distress for Indian firms. The authors suggest that a bankruptcy forecast model that works for a developed economy like the UK may not be suitable for an emerging economy like India.

Agrawal and Maheshwari (2019) found industry beta, a sensitivity variable for industry factors, statistically significant in predicting defaults. The study highlighted the importance of a firm's sensitivity to uncertainties in the relevant industry, which affects each firm differently. A higher sensitivity leads to an increased probability of default.

Bawa et al. (2019) examined the determinants of non-performing assets (NPA) of Indian scheduled commercial banks using a comprehensive list of 31 financial indicators. The study found that operational capability and intermediation costs are essential in identifying NPAs and should be monitored carefully.

(continued)

Gopalakrishnan and Mohapatra (2020) used large cross-country firm-level data to study the effects of a stronger insolvency regime on firms' default risk. The authors found that a stronger insolvency regime moderates the adverse effects of economic shocks on firms' default risk. They also explored various channels through which improved creditor rights influence firms' default risk, including dependence on external finance, corporate leverage, and managerial ethics.

References

Agrawal, K., & Maheshwari, Y. (2019). Efficacy of industry factors for corporate default prediction. *IIMB Management Review*, *31*(1), 71–77.

Bawa, J. K., Goyal, V., Mitra, S. K., & Basu, S. (2019). An analysis of NPAs of Indian banks: Using a comprehensive framework of 31 financial ratios. *IIMB Management Review*, *31*(1), 51–62.

Charalambakis, E. C., & Garrett, I. (2016). On the prediction of financial distress in developed and emerging markets: Does the choice of accounting and market information matter? A comparison of UK and Indian firms. *Review of Quantitative Finance and Accounting*, *47*, 1–28.

Gopalakrishnan, B., & Mohapatra, S. (2020). Insolvency regimes and firms' default risk under economic uncertainty and shocks. *Economic Modelling*, *91*, 180–197.

Summary and Conclusions

This chapter examined what happens when firms experience financial distress.

1. Financial distress is a situation where a firm's operating cash flow is insufficient to cover contractual obligations. Financially distressed firms often are forced to take corrective action and undergo financial restructuring. Financial restructuring involves exchanging new financial claims for old ones.
2. Financial restructuring can be accomplished with a private workout or formal bankruptcy and can involve liquidation or reorganization. However, liquidation is not as common.
3. Corporate bankruptcy involves Chapter 7 liquidation or Chapter 11 reorganization. An essential feature of the U.S. bankruptcy code is the absolute priority rule. The absolute priority rule states that senior creditors are paid in full before junior creditors receive anything. However, in practice, the absolute priority rule often is violated.
4. A newer form of financial restructuring is prepackaged bankruptcy. It is a hybrid of a private workout and formal bankruptcy.
5. Firms experiencing financial distress can be identified by abnormal financial statements. The Z-score model captures some of these differences.

Concept Questions

1. **Financial Distress** Define financial distress using the stock-based and flow-based approaches.
2. **Financial Distress** What are some benefits of financial distress?
3. **Prepackaged Bankruptcy** What is prepackaged bankruptcy? What is the main benefit of prepackaged bankruptcy?

4. **Financial Distress** Why doesn't financial distress always cause firms to go under?
5. **Liquidation versus Reorganization** What is the difference between liquidation and reorganization?
6. **APR** What is the absolute priority rule?
7. **DIP Loans** What are DIP loans? Where do DIP loans fall in the APR?
8. **Bankruptcy Ethics** Firms sometimes use the threat of a bankruptcy filing to force creditors to renegotiate terms. Critics argue that in such cases, the firm is using bankruptcy laws "as a sword rather than a shield." Is this an ethical tactic?
9. **Bankruptcy Ethics** Several firms have entered bankruptcy, or threatened to enter bankruptcy, at least in part as a means of reducing labor costs. Whether this move is ethical, or proper, is hotly debated. Is this an ethical use of bankruptcy?
10. **Bankruptcy versus Private Workouts** Why do so many firms file for legal bankruptcy when private workouts are so much less expensive?

Questions and Problems

BASIC (Questions 1–2)

1. When the Beacon Computer Company filed for bankruptcy under Chapter 7 of the U.S. bankruptcy code, it had the following balance sheet information:

Liquidating Value		Claims	
		Trade credit	₹ 4,900
		Secured mortgage notes	7,600
		Senior debentures	13,000
		Junior debentures	16,000
Total assets	₹35,600	Equity	−5,900

Assuming there are no legal fees associated with the bankruptcy, as a trustee, what distribution of liquidating value do you propose?

2. When the Master Printing Company filed for bankruptcy, it filed under Chapter 11 of the U.S. bankruptcy code. Key information is shown here:

Assets		Claims	
		Mortgage bonds	₹27,000
		Senior debentures	12,100
		Junior debentures	8,500
Going concern value	₹37,500	Book equity	−10,100

As a trustee, what reorganization plan would you accept?

INTERMEDIATE (Questions 3–4)

3. **Z-Score** Fair-to-Midland Manufacturing, Inc. (FMM), has applied for a loan at True Credit Bank. Jon Fulkerson, the credit analyst at the bank, has gathered the following information from the company's financial statements:

Total assets	₹115,000
EBIT	7,900
Net working capital	4,100
Book value of equity	23,000
Accumulated retained earnings	19,600
Sales	112,000

The stock price of FMM is ₹31 per share and there are 7,800 shares outstanding. What is the Z-score for this company?

4. **Z-Score** Jon Fulkerson also has received a credit application from Seether, LLC, a private company. An abbreviated portion of the financial information provided by the company is shown below:

Total assets	₹78,000
EBIT	8,600
Net working capital	3,900
Book value of equity	15,000
Accumulated retained earnings	26,000
Total liabilities	55,000

What is the Z-score for this company?

Appendix A

Mathematical Tables

Table A.1
Present Value of \$1 to Be Received after t Periods $= 1/(1 + r)^t$

Table A.2
Present Value of an Annuity of \$1 per Period for t Periods $= [1 - 1/(1 + r)^t]/r$

Table A.3
Future Value of \$1 at the End of t Periods $= (1 + r)^t$

Table A.4
Future Value of an Annuity of \$1 per Period for t Periods $= [(1 + r)^t - 1]/r$

Table A.5
Future Value of \$1 with a Continuously Compounded Rate r for t Periods: Values of e^{rt}

Table A.6
Present Value of \$1 with a Continuous Discount Rate r for t Periods: Values of e^{-rt}

Table A.1 Present Value of $1 to Be Received after t Periods = $1/(1 + r)^t$

Interest Rate *t*									
Period	1%	2%	3%	4%	5%	6%	7%	8%	9%
1	.9901	.9804	.9709	.9615	.9524	.9434	.9346	.9259	.9174
2	.9803	.9612	.9426	.9246	.9070	.8900	.8734	.8573	.8417
3	.9706	.9423	.9151	.8890	.8638	.8396	.8163	.7938	.7722
4	.9610	.9238	.8885	.8548	.8227	.7921	.7629	.7350	.7084
5	.9515	.9057	.8626	.8219	.7835	.7473	.7130	.6806	.6499
6	.9420	.8880	.8375	.7903	.7462	.7050	.6663	.6302	.5963
7	.9327	.8706	.8131	.7599	.7107	.6651	.6227	.5835	.5470
8	.9235	.8535	.7894	.7307	.6768	.6274	.5820	.5403	.5019
9	.9143	.8368	.7664	.7026	.6446	.5919	.5439	.5002	.4604
10	.9053	.8203	.7441	.6756	.6139	.5584	.5083	.4632	.4224
11	.8963	.8043	.7224	.6496	.5847	.5268	.4751	.4289	.3875
12	.8874	.7885	.7014	.6246	.5568	.4970	.4440	.3971	.3555
13	.8787	.7730	.6810	.6006	.5303	.4688	.4150	.3677	.3262
14	.8700	.7579	.6611	.5775	.5051	.4423	.3878	.3405	.2992
15	.8613	.7430	.6419	.5553	.4810	.4173	.3624	.3152	.2745
16	.8528	.7284	.6232	.5339	.4581	.3936	.3387	.2919	.2519
17	.8444	.7142	.6050	.5134	.4363	.3714	.3166	.2703	.2311
18	.8360	.7002	.5874	.4936	.4155	.3503	.2959	.2502	.2120
19	.8277	.6864	.5703	.4746	.3957	.3305	.2765	.2317	.1945
20	.8195	.6730	.5537	.4564	.3769	.3118	.2584	.2145	.1784
21	.8114	.6598	.5375	.4388	.3589	.2942	.2415	.1987	.1637
22	.8034	.6468	.5219	.4220	.3418	.2775	.2257	.1839	.1502
23	.7954	.6342	.5067	.4057	.3256	.2618	.2109	.1703	.1378
24	.7876	.6217	.4919	.3901	.3101	.2470	.1971	.1577	.1264
25	.7798	.6095	.4776	.3751	.2953	.2330	.1842	.1460	.1160
30	.7419	.5521	.4120	.3083	.2314	.1741	.1314	.0994	.0754
40	.6717	.4529	.3066	.2083	.1420	.0972	.0668	.0460	.0318
50	.6080	.3715	.2281	.1407	.0872	.0543	.0339	.0213	.0134

Period	10%	12%	14%	15%	16%	18%	20%	24%	28%	32%	36%
1	.9091	.8929	.8772	.8696	.8621	.8475	.8333	.8065	.7813	.7576	.7353
2	.8264	.7972	.7695	.7561	.7432	.7182	.6944	.6504	.6104	.5739	.5407
3	.7513	.7118	.6750	.6575	.6407	.6086	.5787	.5245	.4768	.4348	.3975
4	.6830	.6355	.5921	.5718	.5523	.5158	.4823	.4230	.3725	.3294	.2923
5	.6209	.5674	.5194	.4972	.4761	.4371	.4019	.3411	.2910	.2495	.2149
6	.5645	.5066	.4556	.4323	.4104	.3704	.3349	.2751	.2274	.1890	.1580
7	.5132	.4523	.3996	.3759	.3538	.3139	.2791	.2218	.1776	.1432	.1162
8	.4665	.4039	.3506	.3269	.3050	.2660	.2326	.1789	.1388	.1085	.0854
9	.4241	.3606	.3075	.2843	.2630	.2255	.1938	.1443	.1084	.0822	.0628
10	.3855	.3220	.2697	.2472	.2267	.1911	.1615	.1164	.0847	.0623	.0462
11	.3505	.2875	.2366	.2149	.1954	.1619	.1346	.0938	.0662	.0472	.0340
12	.3186	.2567	.2076	.1869	.1685	.1372	.1122	.0757	.0517	.0357	.0250
13	.2897	.2292	.1821	.1625	.1452	.1163	.0935	.0610	.0404	.0271	.0184
14	.2633	.2046	.1597	.1413	.1252	.0985	.0779	.0492	.0316	.0205	.0135
15	.2394	.1827	.1401	.1229	.1079	.0835	.0649	.0397	.0247	.0155	.0099
16	.2176	.1631	.1229	.1069	.0930	.0708	.0541	.0320	.0193	.0118	.0073
17	.1978	.1456	.1078	.0929	.0802	.0600	.0451	.0258	.0150	.0089	.0054
18	.1799	.1300	.0946	.0808	.0691	.0508	.0376	.0208	.0118	.0068	.0039
19	.1635	.1161	.0829	.0703	.0596	.0431	.0313	.0168	.0092	.0051	.0029
20	.1486	.1037	.0728	.0611	.0514	.0365	.0261	.0135	.0072	.0039	.0021
21	.1351	.0926	.0638	.0531	.0443	.0309	.0217	.0109	.0056	.0029	.0016
22	.1228	.0826	.0560	.0462	.0382	.0262	.0181	.0088	.0044	.0022	.0012
23	.1117	.0738	.0491	.0402	.0329	.0222	.0151	.0071	.0034	.0017	.0008
24	.1015	.0659	.0431	.0349	.0284	.0188	.0126	.0057	.0027	.0013	.0006
25	.0923	.0588	.0378	.0304	.0245	.0160	.0105	.0046	.0021	.0010	.0005
30	.0573	.0334	.0196	.0151	.0116	.0070	.0042	.0016	.0006	.0002	.0001
40	.0221	.0107	.0053	.0037	.0026	.0013	.0007	.0002	.0001	*	*
50	.0085	.0035	.0014	.0009	.0006	.0003	.0001	*	*	*	*

*The factor is zero to four decimal places.

Table A.2 Present Value of an Annuity of $1 per Period for t Periods = $[1 - 1/(1 + r)^t]/r$

Number of Periods	1%	2%	3%	4%	5%	6%	7%	8%	9%
	Interest Rate								
1	.9901	.9804	.9709	.9615	.9524	.9434	.9346	.9259	.9174
2	1.9704	1.9416	1.9135	1.8861	1.8594	1.8334	1.8080	1.7833	1.7591
3	2.9410	2.8839	2.8286	2.7751	2.7232	2.6730	2.6243	2.5771	2.5313
4	3.9020	3.8077	3.7171	3.6299	3.5460	3.4651	3.3872	3.3121	3.2397
5	4.8534	4.7135	4.5797	4.4518	4.3295	4.2124	4.1002	3.9927	3.8897
6	5.7955	5.6014	5.4172	5.2421	5.0757	4.9173	4.7665	4.6229	4.4859
7	6.7282	6.4720	6.2303	6.0021	5.7864	5.5824	5.3893	5.2064	5.0330
8	7.6517	7.3255	7.0197	6.7327	6.4632	6.2098	5.9713	5.7466	5.5348
9	8.5660	8.1622	7.7861	7.4353	7.1078	6.8017	6.5152	6.2469	5.9952
10	9.4713	8.9826	8.5302	8.1109	7.7217	7.3601	7.0236	6.7101	6.4177
11	10.3676	9.7868	9.2526	8.7605	8.3064	7.8869	7.4987	7.1390	6.8052
12	11.2551	10.5753	9.9540	9.3851	8.8633	8.3838	7.9427	7.5361	7.1607
13	12.1337	11.3484	10.6350	9.9856	9.3936	8.8527	8.3577	7.9038	7.4869
14	13.0037	12.1062	11.2961	10.5631	9.8986	9.2950	8.7455	8.2442	7.7862
15	13.8651	12.8493	11.9379	11.1184	10.3797	9.7122	9.1079	8.5595	8.0607
16	14.7179	13.5777	12.5611	11.6523	10.8378	10.1059	9.4466	8.8514	8.3126
17	15.5623	14.2919	13.1661	12.1657	11.2741	10.4773	9.7632	9.1216	8.5436
18	16.3983	14.9920	13.7535	12.6593	11.6896	10.8276	10.0591	9.3719	8.7556
19	17.2260	15.6785	14.3238	13.1339	12.0853	11.1581	10.3356	9.6036	8.9501
20	18.0456	16.3514	14.8775	13.5903	12.4622	11.4699	10.5940	9.8181	9.1285
21	18.8570	17.0112	15.4150	14.0292	12.8212	11.7641	10.8355	10.0168	9.2922
22	19.6604	17.6580	15.9369	14.4511	13.1630	12.0416	11.0612	10.2007	9.4424
23	20.4558	18.2922	16.4436	14.8568	13.4886	12.3034	11.2722	10.3741	9.5802
24	21.2434	18.9139	16.9355	15.2470	13.7986	12.5504	11.4693	10.5288	9.7066
25	22.0232	19.5235	17.4131	15.6221	14.0939	12.7834	11.6536	10.6748	9.8226
30	25.8077	22.3965	19.6004	17.2920	15.3725	13.7648	12.4090	11.2578	10.2737
40	32.8347	27.3555	23.1148	19.7928	17.1591	15.0463	13.3317	11.9246	10.7574
50	39.1961	31.4236	25.7298	21.4822	18.2559	15.7619	13.8007	12.2335	10.9617

Number of Periods	10%	12%	14%	15%	16%	18%	20%	24%	28%	32%
1	.9091	.8929	.8772	.8696	.8621	.8475	.8333	.8065	.7813	.7576
2	1.7355	1.6901	1.6467	1.6257	1.6052	1.5656	1.5278	1.4568	1.3916	1.3315
3	2.4869	2.4018	2.3216	2.2832	2.2459	2.1743	2.1065	1.9813	1.8684	1.7663
4	3.1699	3.0373	2.9137	2.8550	2.7982	2.6901	2.5887	2.4043	2.2410	2.0957
5	3.7908	3.6048	3.4331	3.3522	3.2743	3.1272	2.9906	2.7454	2.5320	2.3452
6	4.3553	4.1114	3.8887	3.7845	3.6847	3.4976	3.3255	3.0205	2.7594	2.5342
7	4.8684	4.5638	4.2883	4.1604	4.0386	3.8115	3.6046	3.2423	2.9370	2.6775
8	5.3349	4.9676	4.6389	4.4873	4.3436	4.0776	3.8372	3.4212	3.0758	2.7860
9	5.7590	5.3282	4.9464	4.7716	4.6065	4.3030	4.0310	3.5655	3.1842	2.8681
10	6.1446	5.6502	5.2161	5.0188	4.8332	4.4941	4.1925	3.6819	3.2689	2.9304
11	6.4951	5.9377	5.4527	5.2337	5.0286	4.6560	4.3271	3.7757	3.3351	2.9776
12	6.8137	6.1944	5.6603	5.4206	5.1971	4.7932	4.4392	3.8514	3.3868	3.0133
13	7.1034	6.4235	5.8424	5.5831	5.3423	4.9095	4.5327	3.9124	3.4272	3.0404
14	7.3667	6.6282	6.0021	5.7245	5.4675	5.0081	4.6106	3.9616	3.4587	3.0609
15	7.6061	6.8109	6.1422	5.8474	5.5755	5.0916	4.6755	4.0013	3.4834	3.0764
16	7.8237	6.9740	6.2651	5.9542	5.6685	5.1624	4.7296	4.0333	3.5026	3.0882
17	8.0216	7.1196	6.3729	6.0472	5.7487	5.2223	4.7746	4.0591	3.5177	3.0971
18	8.2014	7.2497	6.4674	6.1280	5.8178	5.2732	4.8122	4.0799	3.5294	3.1039
19	8.3649	7.3658	6.5504	6.1982	5.8775	5.3162	4.8435	4.0967	3.5386	3.1090
20	8.5136	7.4694	6.6231	6.2593	5.9288	5.3527	4.8696	4.1103	3.5458	3.1129
21	8.6487	7.5620	6.6870	6.3125	5.9731	5.3837	4.8913	4.1212	3.5514	3.1158
22	8.7715	7.6446	6.7429	6.3587	6.0113	5.4099	4.9094	4.1300	3.5558	3.1180
23	8.8832	7.7184	6.7921	6.3988	6.0442	5.4321	4.9245	4.1371	3.5592	3.1197
24	8.9847	7.7843	6.8351	6.4338	6.0726	5.4509	4.9371	4.1428	3.5619	3.1210
25	9.0770	7.8431	6.8729	6.4641	6.0971	5.4669	4.9476	4.1474	3.5640	3.1220
30	9.4269	8.0552	7.0027	6.5660	6.1772	5.5168	4.9789	4.1601	3.5693	3.1242
40	9.7791	8.2438	7.1050	6.6418	6.2335	5.5482	4.9966	4.1659	3.5712	3.1250
50	9.9148	8.3045	7.1327	6.6605	6.2463	5.5541	4.9995	4.1666	3.5714	3.1250

Table A.3 Future Value of $1 at the End of t Periods = $(1 + r)^t$

	Interest Rate								
Period	1%	2%	3%	4%	5%	6%	7%	8%	9%
1	1.0100	1.0200	1.0300	1.0400	1.0500	1.0600	1.0700	1.0800	1.0900
2	1.0201	1.0404	1.0609	1.0816	1.1025	1.1236	1.1449	1.1664	1.1881
3	1.0303	1.0612	1.0927	1.1249	1.1576	1.1910	1.2250	1.2597	1.2950
4	1.0406	1.0824	1.1255	1.1699	1.2155	1.2625	1.3108	1.3605	1.4116
5	1.0510	1.1041	1.1593	1.2167	1.2763	1.3382	1.4026	1.4693	1.5386
6	1.0615	1.1262	1.1941	1.2653	1.3401	1.4185	1.5007	1.5869	1.6771
7	1.0721	1.1487	1.2299	1.3159	1.4071	1.5036	1.6058	1.7138	1.8280
8	1.0829	1.1717	1.2668	1.3686	1.4775	1.5938	1.7182	1.8509	1.9926
9	1.0937	1.1951	1.3048	1.4233	1.5513	1.6895	1.8385	1.9990	2.1719
10	1.1046	1.2190	1.3439	1.4802	1.6289	1.7908	1.9672	2.1589	2.3674
11	1.1157	1.2434	1.3842	1.5395	1.7103	1.8983	2.1049	2.3316	2.5804
12	1.1268	1.2682	1.4258	1.6010	1.7959	2.0122	2.2522	2.5182	2.8127
13	1.1381	1.2936	1.4685	1.6651	1.8856	2.1329	2.4098	2.7196	3.0658
14	1.1495	1.3195	1.5126	1.7317	1.9799	2.2609	2.5785	2.9372	3.3417
15	1.1610	1.3459	1.5580	1.8009	2.0789	2.3966	2.7590	3.1722	3.6425
16	1.1726	1.3728	1.6047	1.8730	2.1829	2.5404	2.9522	3.4259	3.9703
17	1.1843	1.4002	1.6528	1.9479	2.2920	2.6928	3.1588	3.7000	4.3276
18	1.1961	1.4282	1.7024	2.0258	2.4066	2.8543	3.3799	3.9960	4.7171
19	1.2081	1.4568	1.7535	2.1068	2.5270	3.0256	3.6165	4.3157	5.1417
20	1.2202	1.4859	1.8061	2.1911	2.6533	3.2071	3.8697	4.6610	5.6044
21	1.2324	1.5157	1.8603	2.2788	2.7860	3.3996	4.1406	5.0338	6.1088
22	1.2447	1.5460	1.9161	2.3699	2.9253	3.6035	4.4304	5.4365	6.6586
23	1.2572	1.5769	1.9736	2.4647	3.0715	3.8197	4.7405	5.8715	7.2579
24	1.2697	1.6084	2.0328	2.5633	3.2251	4.0489	5.0724	6.3412	7.9111
25	1.2824	1.6406	2.0938	2.6658	3.3864	4.2919	5.4274	6.8485	8.6231
30	1.3478	1.8114	2.4273	3.2434	4.3219	5.7435	7.6123	10.063	13.268
40	1.4889	2.2080	3.2620	4.8010	7.0400	10.286	14.974	21.725	31.409
50	1.6446	2.6916	4.3839	7.1067	11.467	18.420	29.457	46.902	74.358
60	1.8167	3.2810	5.8916	10.520	18.679	32.988	57.946	101.26	176.03

Period	10%	12%	14%	15%	16%	18%	20%	24%	28%	32%	36%
1	1.1000	1.1200	1.1400	1.1500	1.1600	1.1800	1.2000	1.2400	1.2800	1.3200	1.3600
2	1.2100	1.2544	1.2996	1.3225	1.3456	1.3924	1.4400	1.5376	1.6384	1.7424	1.8496
3	1.3310	1.4049	1.4815	1.5209	1.5609	1.6430	1.7280	1.9066	2.0972	2.3000	2.5155
4	1.4641	1.5735	1.6890	1.7490	1.8106	1.9388	2.0736	2.3642	2.6844	3.0360	3.4210
5	1.6105	1.7623	1.9254	2.0114	2.1003	2.2878	2.4883	2.9316	3.4360	4.0075	4.6526
6	1.7716	1.9738	2.1950	2.3131	2.4364	2.6996	2.9860	3.6352	4.3980	5.2899	6.3275
7	1.9487	2.2107	2.5023	2.6600	2.8262	3.1855	3.5832	4.5077	5.6295	6.9826	8.6054
8	2.1436	2.4760	2.8526	3.0590	3.2784	3.7589	4.2998	5.5895	7.2058	9.2170	11.703
9	2.3579	2.7731	3.2519	3.5179	3.8030	4.4355	5.1598	6.9310	9.2234	12.166	15.917
10	2.5937	3.1058	3.7072	4.0456	4.4114	5.2338	6.1917	8.5944	11.806	16.060	21.647
11	2.8531	3.4785	4.2262	4.6524	5.1173	6.1759	7.4301	10.657	15.112	21.199	29.439
12	3.1384	3.8960	4.8179	5.3503	5.9360	7.2876	8.9161	13.215	19.343	27.983	40.037
13	3.4523	4.3635	5.4924	6.1528	6.8858	8.5994	10.699	16.386	24.759	36.937	54.451
14	3.7975	4.8871	6.2613	7.0757	7.9875	10.147	12.839	20.319	31.691	48.757	74.053
15	4.1772	5.4736	7.1379	8.1371	9.2655	11.974	15.407	25.196	40.565	64.359	100.71
16	4.5950	6.1304	8.1372	9.3576	10.748	14.129	18.488	31.243	51.923	84.954	136.97
17	5.0545	6.8660	9.2765	10.761	12.468	16.672	22.186	38.741	66.461	112.14	186.28
18	5.5599	7.6900	10.575	12.375	14.463	19.673	26.623	48.039	86.071	148.02	253.34
19	6.1159	8.6128	12.056	14.232	16.777	23.214	31.948	59.568	108.89	195.39	344.54
20	6.7275	9.6463	13.743	16.367	19.461	27.393	38.338	73.864	139.38	257.92	468.57
21	7.4002	10.804	15.668	18.822	22.574	32.324	46.005	91.592	178.41	340.45	637.26
22	8.1403	12.100	17.861	21.645	26.186	38.142	55.206	113.57	228.36	449.39	866.67
23	8.9543	13.552	20.362	24.891	30.376	45.008	66.247	140.83	292.30	593.20	1178.7
24	9.8497	15.179	23.212	28.625	35.236	53.109	79.497	174.63	374.14	783.02	1603.0
25	10.835	17.000	26.462	32.919	40.874	62.669	95.396	216.54	478.90	1033.6	2180.1
30	17.449	29.960	50.950	66.212	85.850	143.37	237.38	634.82	1645.5	4142.1	10143.
40	45.259	93.051	188.88	267.86	378.72	750.38	1469.8	5455.9	19427.	66521.	*
50	117.39	289.00	700.23	1083.7	1670.7	3927.4	9100.4	46890.	*	*	*
60	304.48	897.60	2595.9	4384.0	7370.2	20555.	56348.	*	*	*	*

*FVIV > 99,999.

Table A.4 Future Value of an Annuity of \$1 per Period for t Periods = $[(1 + r)^t - 1]/r$

	Interest Rate								
Number of Periods	**1%**	**2%**	**3%**	**4%**	**5%**	**6%**	**7%**	**8%**	**9%**
1	1.0000	1.0000	1.0000	1.0000	1.0000	1.0000	1.0000	1.0000	1.0000
2	2.0100	2.0200	2.0300	2.0400	2.0500	2.0600	2.0700	2.0800	2.0900
3	3.0301	3.0604	3.0909	3.1216	3.1525	3.1836	3.2149	3.2464	3.2781
4	4.0604	4.1216	4.1836	4.2465	4.3101	4.3746	4.4399	4.5061	4.5731
5	5.1010	5.2040	5.3091	5.4163	5.5256	5.6371	5.7507	5.8666	5.9847
6	6.1520	6.3081	6.4684	6.6330	6.8019	6.9753	7.1533	7.3359	7.5233
7	7.2135	7.4343	7.6625	7.8983	8.1420	8.3938	8.6540	8.9228	9.2004
8	8.2857	8.5830	8.8932	9.2142	9.5491	9.8975	10.260	10.637	11.028
9	9.3685	9.7546	10.159	10.583	11.027	11.491	11.978	12.488	13.021
10	10.462	10.950	11.464	12.006	12.578	13.181	13.816	14.487	15.193
11	11.567	12.169	12.808	13.486	14.207	14.972	15.784	16.645	17.560
12	12.683	13.412	14.192	15.026	15.917	16.870	17.888	18.977	20.141
13	13.809	14.680	15.618	16.627	17.713	18.882	20.141	21.495	22.953
14	14.947	15.974	17.086	18.292	19.599	21.015	22.550	24.215	26.019
15	16.097	17.293	18.599	20.024	21.579	23.276	25.129	27.152	29.361
16	17.258	18.639	20.157	21.825	23.657	25.673	27.888	30.324	33.003
17	18.430	20.012	21.762	23.698	25.840	28.213	30.840	33.750	36.974
18	19.615	21.412	23.414	25.645	28.132	30.906	33.999	37.450	41.301
19	20.811	22.841	25.117	27.671	30.539	33.760	37.379	41.446	46.018
20	22.019	24.297	26.870	29.778	33.066	36.786	40.995	45.762	51.160
21	23.239	25.783	28.676	31.969	35.719	39.993	44.865	50.423	56.765
22	24.472	27.299	30.537	34.248	38.505	43.392	49.006	55.457	62.873
23	25.716	28.845	32.453	36.618	41.430	46.996	53.436	60.893	69.532
24	26.973	30.422	34.426	39.083	44.502	50.816	58.177	66.765	76.790
25	28.243	32.030	36.459	41.646	47.727	54.865	63.249	73.106	84.701
30	34.785	40.568	47.575	56.085	66.439	79.058	94.461	113.28	136.31
40	48.886	60.402	75.401	95.026	120.80	154.76	199.64	259.06	337.88
50	64.463	84.579	112.80	152.67	209.35	290.34	406.53	573.77	815.08
60	81.670	114.05	163.05	237.99	353.58	533.13	813.52	1253.2	1944.8

Number of Periods	**10%**	**12%**	**14%**	**15%**	**16%**	**18%**	**20%**	**24%**	**28%**	**32%**	**36%**
1	1.0000	1.0000	1.0000	1.0000	1.0000	1.0000	1.0000	1.0000	1.0000	1.0000	1.0000
2	2.1000	2.1200	2.1400	2.1500	2.1600	2.1800	2.2000	2.2400	2.2800	2.3200	2.3600
3	3.3100	3.3744	3.4396	3.4725	3.5056	3.5724	3.6400	3.7776	3.9184	4.0624	4.2096
4	4.6410	4.7793	4.9211	4.9934	5.0665	5.2154	5.3680	5.6842	6.0156	6.3624	6.7251
5	6.1051	6.3528	6.6101	6.7424	6.8771	7.1542	7.4416	8.0484	8.6999	9.3983	10.146
6	7.7156	8.1152	8.5355	8.7537	8.9775	9.4420	9.9299	10.980	12.136	13.406	14.799
7	9.4872	10.089	10.730	11.067	11.414	12.142	12.916	14.615	16.534	18.696	21.126
8	11.436	12.300	13.233	13.727	14.240	15.327	16.499	19.123	22.163	25.678	29.732
9	13.579	14.776	16.085	16.786	17.519	19.086	20.799	24.712	29.369	34.895	41.435
10	15.937	17.549	19.337	20.304	21.321	23.521	25.959	31.643	38.593	47.062	57.352
11	18.531	20.655	23.045	24.349	25.733	28.755	32.150	40.238	50.398	63.122	78.998
12	21.384	24.133	27.271	29.002	30.850	34.931	39.581	50.895	65.510	84.320	108.44
13	24.523	28.029	32.089	34.352	36.786	42.219	48.497	64.110	84.853	112.30	148.47
14	27.975	32.393	37.581	40.505	43.672	50.818	59.196	80.496	109.61	149.24	202.93
15	31.772	37.280	43.842	47.580	51.660	60.965	72.035	100.82	141.30	198.00	276.98
16	35.950	42.753	50.980	55.717	60.925	72.939	87.442	126.01	181.87	262.36	377.69
17	40.545	48.884	59.118	65.075	71.673	87.068	105.93	157.25	233.79	347.31	514.66
18	45.599	55.750	68.394	75.836	84.141	103.74	128.12	195.99	300.25	459.45	700.94
19	51.159	64.440	78.969	88.212	98.603	123.41	154.74	244.03	385.32	607.47	954.28
20	57.275	72.052	91.025	102.44	115.38	146.63	186.69	303.60	494.21	802.86	1298.8
21	64.002	81.699	104.77	118.81	134.84	174.02	225.03	377.46	633.59	1060.8	1767.4
22	71.403	92.503	120.44	137.63	157.41	206.34	271.03	469.06	812.00	1401.2	2404.7
23	79.543	104.60	138.30	159.28	183.60	244.49	326.24	582.63	1040.4	1850.6	3271.3
24	88.497	118.16	158.66	184.17	213.98	289.49	392.48	723.46	1332.7	2443.8	4450.0
25	98.347	133.33	181.87	212.79	249.21	342.60	471.98	898.09	1706.8	3226.8	6053.0
30	164.49	241.33	356.79	434.75	530.31	790.95	1181.9	2640.9	5873.2	12941.	28172.3
40	442.59	767.09	1342.0	1779.1	2360.8	4163.2	7343.9	22729.	69377.	*	*
50	1163.9	2400.0	4994.5	7217.7	10436.	21813.	45497.	*	*	*	*
60	3034.8	7471.6	18535.	29220.	46058.	*	*	*	*	*	*

*FVIFA > 99,999.

Table A.5 Future Value of $1 with a Continuously Compounded Rate *r* for *t* Periods: Values of e^{rt}

	Continuously Compounded Rate (*r*)													
Period	1%	2%	3%	4%	5%	6%	7%	8%	9%	10%	11%	12%	13%	14%
1	1.0101	1.0202	1.0305	1.0408	1.0513	1.0618	1.0725	1.0833	1.0942	1.1052	1.1163	1.1275	1.1388	1.1503
2	1.0202	1.0408	1.0618	1.0833	1.1052	1.1275	1.1503	1.1735	1.1972	1.2214	1.2461	1.2712	1.2969	1.3231
3	1.0305	1.0618	1.0942	1.1275	1.1618	1.1972	1.2337	1.2712	1.3100	1.3499	1.3910	1.4333	1.4770	1.5220
4	1.0408	1.0833	1.1275	1.1735	1.2214	1.2712	1.3231	1.3771	1.4333	1.4918	1.5527	1.6161	1.6820	1.7507
5	1.0513	1.1052	1.1618	1.2214	1.2840	1.3499	1.4191	1.4918	1.5683	1.6487	1.7333	1.8221	1.9155	2.0138
6	1.0618	1.1275	1.1972	1.2712	1.3499	1.4333	1.5220	1.6161	1.7160	1.8221	1.9348	2.0544	2.1815	2.3164
7	1.0725	1.1503	1.2337	1.3231	1.4191	1.5220	1.6323	1.7507	1.8776	2.0138	2.1598	2.3164	2.4843	2.6645
8	1.0833	1.1735	1.2712	1.3771	1.4918	1.6161	1.7507	1.8965	2.0544	2.2255	2.4109	2.6117	2.8292	3.0649
9	1.0942	1.1972	1.3100	1.4333	1.5683	1.7160	1.8776	2.0544	2.2479	2.4596	2.6912	2.9447	3.2220	3.5254
10	1.1052	1.2214	1.3499	1.4918	1.6487	1.8221	2.0138	2.2255	2.4596	2.7183	3.0042	3.3201	3.6693	4.0552
11	1.1163	1.2461	1.3910	1.5527	1.7333	1.9348	2.1598	2.4109	2.6912	3.0042	3.3535	3.7434	4.1787	4.6646
12	1.1275	1.2712	1.4333	1.6161	1.8221	2.0544	2.3164	2.6117	2.9447	3.3201	3.7434	4.2207	4.7588	5.3656
13	1.1388	1.2969	1.4770	1.6820	1.9155	2.1815	2.4843	2.8292	3.2220	3.6693	4.1787	4.7588	5.4195	6.1719
14	1.1503	1.3231	1.5220	1.7507	2.0138	2.3164	2.6645	3.0649	3.5254	4.0552	4.6646	5.3656	6.1719	7.0993
15	1.1618	1.3499	1.5683	1.8221	2.1170	2.4596	2.8577	3.3201	3.8574	4.4817	5.2070	6.0496	7.0287	8.1662
16	1.1735	1.3771	1.6161	1.8965	2.2255	2.6117	3.0649	3.5966	4.2207	4.9530	5.8124	6.8210	8.0045	9.3933
17	1.1853	1.4049	1.6653	1.9739	2.3396	2.7732	3.2871	3.8962	4.6182	5.4739	6.4883	7.6906	9.1157	10.8049
18	1.1972	1.4333	1.7160	2.0544	2.4596	2.9447	3.5254	4.2207	5.0531	6.0496	7.2427	8.6711	10.3812	12.4286
19	1.2092	1.4623	1.7683	2.1383	2.5857	3.1268	3.7810	4.5722	5.5290	6.6859	8.0849	9.7767	11.8224	14.2963
20	1.2214	1.4918	1.8221	2.2255	2.7183	3.3201	4.0552	4.9530	6.0496	7.3891	9.0250	11.0232	13.4637	16.4446
21	1.2337	1.5220	1.8776	2.3164	2.8577	3.5254	4.3492	5.3656	6.6194	8.1662	10.0744	12.4286	15.3329	18.9158
22	1.2461	1.5527	1.9348	2.4109	3.0042	3.7434	4.6646	5.8124	7.2427	9.0250	11.2459	14.0132	17.4615	21.7584
23	1.2586	1.5841	1.9937	2.5093	3.1582	3.9749	5.0028	6.2965	7.9248	9.9742	12.5535	15.7998	19.8857	25.0281
24	1.2712	1.6161	2.0544	2.6117	3.3201	4.2207	5.3656	6.8210	8.6711	11.0232	14.0132	17.8143	22.6464	28.7892
25	1.2840	1.6487	2.1170	2.7183	3.4903	4.4817	5.7546	7.3891	9.4877	12.1825	15.6426	20.0855	25.7903	33.1155
30	1.3499	1.8221	2.4596	3.3204	4.4817	6.0496	8.1662	11.0232	14.8797	20.0855	27.1126	36.5982	49.4024	66.6863
35	1.4191	2.0138	2.8577	4.0552	5.7546	8.1662	11.5883	16.4446	23.3361	33.1155	46.9931	66.6863	94.6324	134.2898
40	1.4918	2.2255	3.3201	4.9530	7.3891	11.0232	16.4446	24.5235	36.5982	54.5982	81.4509	121.5104	181.2722	270.4264
45	1.5683	2.4596	3.8574	6.0496	9.4877	14.8797	23.3361	36.5982	57.3975	90.0171	141.1750	221.4064	347.2344	544.5719
50	1.6487	2.7183	4.4817	7.3891	12.1825	20.0855	33.1155	54.5982	90.0171	148.4132	244.6919	403.4288	665.1416	1096.633
55	1.7333	3.0042	5.2070	9.0250	15.6426	27.1126	46.9931	81.4509	141.1750	244.6919	424.1130	735.0952	1274.106	2208.348
60	1.8221	3.3201	6.0496	11.0232	20.0855	36.5982	66.6863	121.5104	221.4064	403.4288	735.0952	1339.431	2440.602	4447.067

	Continuously Compounded Rate (*r*)													
Period	15%	16%	17%	18%	19%	20%	21%	22%	23%	24%	25%	26%	27%	28%
1	1.1618	1.1735	1.1853	1.1972	1.2092	1.2214	1.2337	1.2461	1.2586	1.2712	1.2840	1.2969	1.3100	1.3231
2	1.3499	1.3771	1.4049	1.4333	1.4623	1.4918	1.5220	1.5527	1.5841	1.6161	1.6487	1.6820	1.7160	1.7507
3	1.5683	1.6161	1.6653	1.7160	1.7683	1.8221	1.8776	1.9348	1.9937	2.0544	2.1170	2.1815	2.2479	2.3164
4	1.8221	1.8965	1.9739	2.0544	2.1383	2.2255	2.3164	2.4109	2.5093	2.6117	2.7183	2.8292	2.9447	3.0649
5	2.1170	2.2255	2.3396	2.4596	2.5857	2.7183	2.8577	3.0042	3.1582	3.3201	3.4903	3.6693	3.8574	4.0552
6	2.4596	2.6117	2.7732	2.9447	3.1268	3.3201	3.5254	3.7434	3.9749	4.2207	4.4817	4.7588	5.0351	5.3656
7	2.8577	3.0649	3.2871	3.5254	3.7810	4.0552	4.3492	4.6646	5.0028	5.3656	5.7546	6.1719	6.6194	7.0993
8	3.3201	3.5966	3.8962	4.2207	4.5722	4.9530	5.3656	5.8124	6.2965	6.8210	7.3891	8.0045	8.6711	9.3933
9	3.8574	4.2207	4.6182	5.0531	5.5290	6.0496	6.6194	7.2427	7.9248	8.6711	9.4877	10.3812	11.3589	12.4286
10	4.4817	4.9530	5.4739	6.0496	6.6859	7.3891	8.1662	9.0250	9.9742	11.0232	12.1825	13.4637	14.8797	16.4446
11	5.2070	5.8124	6.4883	7.2427	8.0849	9.0250	10.0744	11.2459	12.5535	14.0132	15.6426	17.4615	19.4919	21.7584
12	6.0496	6.8210	7.6906	8.6711	9.7767	11.0232	12.4286	14.0132	15.7998	17.8143	20.0855	22.6464	25.5337	28.7892
13	7.0287	8.0045	9.1157	10.3812	11.8224	13.4637	15.3329	17.4615	19.8857	22.6464	25.7903	29.3708	33.4483	38.0918
14	8.1662	9.3933	10.8049	12.4286	14.2963	16.4446	18.9158	21.7584	25.0281	28.7892	33.1155	38.0918	43.8160	50.4004
15	9.4877	11.0232	12.0871	14.8797	17.2878	20.0855	23.3361	27.1126	31.5004	36.5982	42.5211	49.4024	57.3975	66.6863
16	11.0232	12.9358	15.1803	17.8143	20.9052	24.5325	28.7892	33.7844	39.6464	46.5255	54.5982	64.0715	75.1886	88.2347
17	12.8071	15.1803	17.9933	21.3276	25.2797	29.9641	35.5166	42.0980	49.8990	59.1455	70.1054	83.0963	98.4944	116.7459
18	14.8797	17.8143	21.3276	25.5337	30.5694	36.5982	43.8160	52.4573	62.8028	75.1886	90.0171	107.7701	129.0242	154.4700
19	17.2878	20.9052	25.2797	30.5694	36.9661	44.7012	54.0549	65.3659	79.0436	95.5835	115.5843	139.7702	169.0171	204.3839
20	20.0855	24.5325	29.9641	36.5982	44.7012	54.5982	66.6863	81.4509	99.4843	121.5104	148.4132	181.2722	221.4064	270.4264
21	23.3361	28.7892	35.5166	43.8160	54.0549	66.6863	82.2695	101.4940	125.2110	154.4700	190.5663	235.0974	290.0345	357.8092
22	27.1126	33.7844	42.0980	52.4573	65.3659	81.4509	101.4940	126.4694	157.5905	196.3699	244.6919	304.9049	379.9349	473.4281
23	31.5004	39.6464	49.8990	62.8028	79.0436	99.4843	125.2110	157.5905	198.3434	249.6350	314.1907	395.4404	497.7013	626.4068
24	36.5982	46.5255	59.1455	75.1886	95.5835	121.5104	154.4700	196.3699	249.6350	317.3483	403.4288	512.8585	651.9709	828.8175
25	42.5211	54.5982	70.1054	90.0171	115.5843	148.4132	190.5663	244.6919	314.1907	403.4288	518.0128	665.1416	854.0588	1096.633
30	90.0171	121.5104	164.0219	221.4064	298.8674	403.4288	544.5719	735.0952	992.2747	1339.431	1808.042	2440.602	3294.468	4447.067
35	190.5663	270.4264	383.7533	544.5719	772.7843	1096.633	1556.197	2208.348	3133.795	4447.067	6310.688	8955.293	12708.17	18033.74
40	403.4288	601.8450	897.8473	1339.431	1998.196	2980.958	4447.067	6634.244	9897.129	14764.78	22026.47	32859.63	49020.80	73130.44
45	854.0588	1339.431	2100.646	3294.468	5166.754	8103.084	12708.17	19930.37	31257.04	49020.80	76879.92	120571.7	189094.1	296558.6
50	1808.042	2980.958	4914.769	8103.084	13359.73	22026.47	36315.50	59874.14	98715.77	162754.8	268337.3	442413.4	729416.4	1202604.
55	3827.626	6634.244	11498.82	19930.37	34544.37	59874.14	103777.0	179871.9	311763.4	540364.9	936589.2	1623346.	2813669.	4876801.
60	8103.084	14764.78	26903.19	49020.80	89321.72	162754.8	296558.6	540364.9	984609.1	1794075.	3269017.	5956538.	10853520.	19776403.

Table A.6 Present Value of $1 with a Continuous Discount Rate r for t Periods: Values of e^{-rt}

	Continuous Discount Rate (r)																
Period	1%	2%	3%	4%	5%	6%	7%	8%	9%	10%	11%	12%	13%	14%	15%	16%	17%
1	.9900	.9802	.9704	.9608	.9512	.9418	.9324	.9231	.9139	.9048	.8958	.8869	.8781	.8694	.8607	.8521	.8437
2	.9802	.9608	.9418	.9231	.9048	.8869	.8694	.8521	.8353	.8187	.8025	.7866	.7711	.7558	.7408	.7261	.7118
3	.9704	.9418	.9139	.8869	.8607	.8353	.8106	.7866	.7634	.7408	.7189	.6977	.6771	.6570	.6376	.6188	.6005
4	.9608	.9231	.8869	.8521	.8187	.7866	.7558	.7261	.6977	.6703	.6440	.6188	.5945	.5712	.5488	.5273	.5066
5	.9512	.9048	.8607	.8187	.7788	.7408	.7047	.6703	.6376	.6065	.5769	.5488	.5220	.4966	.4724	.4493	.4274
6	.9418	.8869	.8353	.7866	.7408	.6977	.6570	.6188	.5827	.5488	.5169	.4868	.4584	.4317	.4066	.3829	.3606
7	.9324	.8694	.8106	.7558	.7047	.6570	.6126	.5712	.5326	.4966	.4630	.4317	.4025	.3753	.3499	.3263	.3042
8	.9231	.8521	.7866	.7261	.6703	.6188	.5712	.5273	.4868	.4493	.4148	.3829	.3535	.3263	.3012	.2780	.2576
9	.9139	.8353	.7634	.6977	.6376	.5827	.5326	.4868	.4449	.4066	.3716	.3396	.3104	.2837	.2592	.2369	.2165
10	.9048	.8187	.7408	.6703	.6065	.5488	.4966	.4493	.4066	.3679	.3329	.3012	.2725	.2466	.2231	.2019	.1827
11	.8958	.8025	.7189	.6440	.5769	.5169	.4630	.4148	.3716	.3329	.2982	.2671	.2393	.2144	.1920	.1720	.1541
12	.8869	.7866	.6977	.6188	.5488	.4868	.4317	.3829	.3396	.3012	.2671	.2369	.2101	.1864	.1653	.1466	.1300
13	.8781	.7711	.6771	.5945	.5220	.4584	.4025	.3535	.3104	.2725	.2393	.2101	.1845	.1620	.1423	.1249	.1097
14	.8694	.7558	.6570	.5712	.4966	.4317	.3753	.3263	.2837	.2466	.2144	.1864	.1620	.1409	.1225	.1065	.0926
15	.8607	.7408	.6376	.5488	.4724	.4066	.3499	.3012	.2592	.2231	.1920	.1653	.1423	.1225	.1054	.0907	.0781
16	.8521	.7261	.6188	.5273	.4493	.3829	.3263	.2780	.2369	.2019	.1720	.1466	.1249	.1065	.0907	.0773	.0659
17	.8437	.7118	.6005	.5066	.4274	.3606	.3042	.2567	.2165	.1827	.1541	.1300	.1097	.0926	.0781	.0659	.0556
18	.8353	.6977	.5827	.4868	.4066	.3396	.2837	.2369	.1979	.1653	.1381	.1153	.0963	.0805	.0672	.0561	.0469
19	.8270	.6839	.5655	.4677	.3867	.3198	.2645	.2187	.1809	.1496	.1237	.1023	.0846	.0699	.0578	.0478	.0396
20	.8187	.6703	.5488	.4493	.3679	.3012	.2466	.2019	.1653	.1353	.1108	.0907	.0743	.0608	.0498	.0408	.0334
21	.8106	.6570	.5326	.4317	.3499	.2837	.2299	.1864	.1511	.1225	.0993	.0805	.0652	.0529	.0429	.0347	.0282
22	.8025	.6440	.5169	.4148	.3329	.2671	.2144	.1720	.1381	.1108	.0889	.0714	.0573	.0460	.0369	.0296	.0238
23	.7945	.6313	.5016	.3985	.3166	.2516	.1999	.1588	.1262	.1003	.0797	.0633	.0503	.0400	.0317	.0252	.0200
24	.7866	.6188	.4868	.3829	.3012	.2369	.1864	.1466	.1153	.0907	.0714	.0561	.0442	.0347	.0273	.0215	.0169
25	.7788	.6065	.4724	.3679	.2865	.2231	.1738	.1353	.1054	.0821	.0639	.0498	.0388	.0302	.0235	.0183	.0143
30	.7408	.5488	.4066	.3012	.2231	.1653	.1225	.0907	.0672	.0498	.0369	.0273	.0202	.0150	.0111	.0082	.0061
35	.7047	.4966	.3499	.2466	.1738	.1225	.0863	.0608	.0429	.0302	.0213	.0150	.0106	.0074	.0052	.0037	.0026
40	.6703	.4493	.3012	.2019	.1353	.0907	.0608	.0408	.0273	.0183	.0123	.0082	.0055	.0037	.0025	.0017	.0011
45	.6376	.4066	.2592	.1653	.1054	.0672	.0429	.0273	.0174	.0111	.0071	.0045	.0029	.0018	.0012	.0007	.0005
50	.6065	.3679	.2231	.1353	.0821	.0498	.0302	.0183	.0111	.0067	.0041	.0025	.0015	.0009	.0006	.0003	.0002
55	.5769	.3329	.1920	.1108	.0639	.0369	.0213	.0123	.0071	.0041	.0024	.0014	.0008	.0005	.0003	.0002	.0001
60	.5488	.3012	.1653	.0907	.0498	.0273	.0150	.0082	.0045	.0025	.0014	.0007	.0004	.0002	.0001	.0001	.0000

	Continuous Discount Rate (*r*)																	
Period	18%	19%	20%	21%	22%	23%	24%	25%	26%	27%	28%	29%	30%	31%	32%	33%	34%	35%
1	.8353	.8270	.8187	.8106	.8025	.7945	.7866	.7788	.7711	.7634	.7558	.7483	.7408	.7334	.7261	.7189	.7118	.7047
2	.6977	.6839	.6703	.6570	.6440	.6313	.6188	.6065	.5945	.5827	.5712	.5599	.5488	.5379	.5273	.5169	.5066	.4966
3	.5827	.5655	.5488	.5326	.5169	.5016	.4868	.4724	.4584	.4449	.4317	.4190	.4066	.3946	.3829	.3716	.3606	.3499
4	.4868	.4677	.4493	.4317	.4148	.3985	.3829	.3679	.3535	.3396	.3263	.3135	.3012	.2894	.2780	.2671	.2567	.2466
5	.4066	.3867	.3679	.3499	.3329	.3166	.3012	.2865	.2725	.2592	.2466	.2346	.2231	.2122	.2019	.1920	.1827	.1738
6	.3396	.3198	.3012	.2837	.2671	.2516	.2369	.2231	.2101	.1979	.1864	.1755	.1653	.1557	.1466	.1381	.1300	.1225
7	.2837	.2645	.2466	.2299	.2144	.1999	.1864	.1738	.1620	.1511	.1409	.1313	.1225	.1142	.1065	.0993	.0926	.0863
8	.2369	.2187	.2019	.1864	.1720	.1588	.1466	.1353	.1249	.1153	.1065	.0983	.0907	.0837	.0773	.0714	.0659	.0608
9	.1979	.1809	.1653	.1511	.1381	.1262	.1153	.1054	.0963	.0880	.0805	.0735	.0672	.0614	.0561	.0513	.0469	.0429
10	.1653	.1496	.1353	.1225	.1108	.1003	.0907	.0821	.0743	.0672	.0608	.0550	.0498	.0450	.0408	.0369	.0334	.0302
11	.1381	.1237	.1108	.0993	.0889	.0797	.0714	.0639	.0573	.0513	.0460	.0412	.0369	.0330	.0296	.0265	.0238	.0213
12	.1154	.1023	.0907	.0805	.0714	.0633	.0561	.0498	.0442	.0392	.0347	.0308	.0273	.0242	.0215	.0191	.0169	.0150
13	.0963	.0846	.0743	.0652	.0573	.0503	.0442	.0388	.0340	.0299	.0263	.0231	.0202	.0178	.0156	.0137	.0120	.0106
14	.0805	.0699	.0608	.0529	.0460	.0400	.0347	.0302	.0263	.0228	.0198	.0172	.0150	.0130	.0113	.0099	.0086	.0074
15	.0672	.0578	.0498	.0429	.0369	.0317	.0273	.0235	.0202	.0174	.0150	.0129	.0111	.0096	.0082	.0071	.0061	.0052
16	.0561	.0478	.0408	.0347	.0296	.0252	.0215	.0183	.0156	.0133	.0113	.0097	.0082	.0070	.0060	.0051	.0043	.0037
17	.0469	.0396	.0334	.0282	.0238	.0200	.0169	.0143	.0120	.0102	.0086	.0072	.0061	.0051	.0043	.0037	.0031	.0026
18	.0392	.0327	.0273	.0228	.0191	.0159	.0133	.0111	.0093	.0078	.0065	.0054	.0045	.0038	.0032	.0026	.0022	.0018
19	.0327	.0271	.0224	.0185	.0153	.0127	.0105	.0087	.0072	.0059	.0049	.0040	.0033	.0028	.0023	.0019	.0016	.0013
20	.0273	.0224	.0183	.0150	.0123	.0101	.0082	.0067	.0055	.0045	.0037	.0030	.0025	.0020	.0017	.0014	.0011	.0009
21	.0228	.0185	.0150	.0122	.0099	.0080	.0065	.0052	.0043	.0034	.0028	.0023	.0018	.0015	.0012	.0010	.0008	.0006
22	.0191	.0153	.0123	.0099	.0079	.0063	.0051	.0041	.0033	.0026	.0021	.0017	.0014	.0011	.0009	.0007	.0006	.0005
23	.0159	.0127	.0101	.0080	.0063	.0050	.0040	.0032	.0025	.0020	.0016	.0013	.0010	.0008	.0006	.0005	.0004	.0003
24	.0133	.0105	.0082	.0065	.0051	.0040	.0032	.0025	.0019	.0015	.0012	.0009	.0007	.0006	.0005	.0004	.0003	.0002
25	.0111	.0087	.0067	.0052	.0041	.0032	.0025	.0019	.0015	.0012	.0009	.0007	.0006	.0004	.0003	.0003	.0002	.0002
30	.0045	.0033	.0025	.0018	.0014	.0010	.0007	.0006	.0004	.0003	.0002	.0002	.0001	.0001	.0001	.0001	.0000	.0000
35	.0018	.0013	.0009	.0006	.0005	.0003	.0002	.0002	.0001	.0001	.0001	.0000	.0000	.0000	.0000	.0000	.0000	.0000
40	.0007	.0005	.0003	.0002	.0002	.0001	.0001	.0000	.0000	.0000	.0000	.0000	.0000	.0000	.0000	.0000	.0000	.0000
45	.0003	.0002	.0001	.0001	.0001	.0000	.0000	.0000	.0000	.0000	.0000	.0000	.0000	.0000	.0000	.0000	.0000	.0000
50	.0001	.0001	.0000	.0000	.0000	.0000	.0000	.0000	.0000	.0000	.0000	.0000	.0000	.0000	.0000	.0000	.0000	.0000
55	.0001	.0000	.0000	.0000	.0000	.0000	.0000	.0000	.0000	.0000	.0000	.0000	.0000	.0000	.0000	.0000	.0000	.0000
60	.0000	.0000	.0000	.0000	.0000	.0000	.0000	.0000	.0000	.0000	.0000	.0000	.0000	.0000	.0000	.0000	.0000	.0000

Appendix B

Solutions to Selected End-of-Chapter Problems

CHAPTER 2

2.2 $121,660; $91,660
2.6 $1,127,000
2.10 $1,549,000
2.14 a. $110,225
b. $19,600
c. $14,350
d. $2,475
2.16 $1,300; $0

CHAPTER 3

3.2 1.63 times; 13.69%; $88,313.40
3.6 11.83%
3.10 9.04%
3.14 23.58 days
3.16 8.95 times

CHAPTER 4

4.2 a. $2,671.39
b. $4,253.74
c. $4,351.41
4.4 7.26%; 9.42%; 13.07%; 10.86%
4.10 a. $12,514.89
b. $6,340.25
c. $9,943.50
d. $10,453.31
4.14 $588,235.29; 4.21%
4.18 EAR = 176.68%
4.22 5.07%
4.26 $2,961,734.39
4.30 $531,028.71
4.34 $2,840,931.41
4.38 $309,171.80
4.42 $10,677.92; 13.73%
4.44 $179,859.81
4.52 $18,969.69
4.56 $19,326.90
4.60 EAR = 17.10%
4.64 APR = 36.53%; EAR = 43.31%

CHAPTER 5

5.2 2.28 years; 4.31 years; Never
5.6 15.11%; 19.52%
5.10 a. 11.51%
d. −$285.58; $1,369.06
5.14 a. 1.23 years; 1.48 years
b. $288.62; $366.87
c. 37.51%; 27.04%
d. 17.02%
5.18 a. 1.86 years; 1.53 years
b. $610,798.66; $488,760.86
c. 26.84%; 42.20%
d. 14.78%
5.22 48.18%; −41.51%

CHAPTER 6

6.2 $1,584.57
6.6 $221,767.55
6.10 $1,628,841.60
6.14 $64,268.07
6.17 $101,078.23
6.22 $3,933,333.33
6.28 $708,930.67
6.32 $4,910,413.48; 28.39%

CHAPTER 7

7.2 NPV_{Best} = $3,658,261.89
NPV_{Worst} = −$1,631,509.50
7.6 Go to market NPV = $19,100,000
Test market NPV = $20,458,558.56
7.10 9,805.98 units
7.14 Payback = 3.96 years
NPV = $10,421,358.80
IRR = 17.22%
7.20 a. 726.53
b. 1,075.56

CHAPTER 8

8.2 a. $1,000
b. $823.34
c. $1,235.56
8.6 3.71%
8.10 2.70%; 2.65%
8.12 2.48%
8.20 6.02%; 5.83%; 5.91%

CHAPTER 9

9.2 9.35%
9.6 $4.03
9.8 4.09%
9.13 $65.46
9.18 $3.55
9.22 $6.02
9.26 a. $85.05
b. $89.22
c. 4.90%

CHAPTER 10

10.2 2.23%; 12.16%
10.6 3.11%; 3.50%
10.10 a. 6.11%
b. 5.50%
10.14 7.48%
10.20 Arithmetic average = 8.33%
Geometric average = 7.20%

CHAPTER 11

11.2 10.06%
11.6 $E(R) = 9.62\%$
$\sigma_A = 15.29\%$
11.10 1.18
11.14 11.26%
11.19 2.50%

CHAPTER 12

12.2 a. 4.28%
b. 14.53%
12.5 $F_1 = 6.49\%$
$F_2 = 5.64\%$

CHAPTER 13

13.2 5.30%; 4.19%
13.6 9.38%
13.10 a. 6.31%
b. 13.39%
13.14 b. 4.29%
c. $44,925,373
13.18 .8790
13.22 $13,425,240

CHAPTER 15

15.2 4,961
15.6 .48
15.9 $954.96

CHAPTER 16

16.2 a. $1.35; $1.92; $2.40
b. $1.23; $2.02; $2.68
16.6 a. $4.72; $4.83; $4.67
b. $65,250
c. $65,250
d. $3.73; $3.82; $3.69
Break-even EBIT = $65,250
16.10 $1,232,400
16.14 $V_U = \$791,666.67$
$V = \$840,866.67$

CHAPTER 17

17.3 $423,000
17.8 a. $43,000,000
b. 32.65%
c. 14.69%

CHAPTER 18

18.2 $35,926.37
18.6 a. $479,657.71
b. $367,832.61
18.10 $20,441,354.03
18.13 $13,021,897.91

CHAPTER 19

19.2 a. New shares issued = 4,000
b. New shares issued = 10,000
19.6 11,484; $33.69
19.10 a. $98
b. $106
c. 34,906
19.14 a. $2,040,000
b. $53.57
c-1. $2,040,000
c-2. 1,919.83

CHAPTER 20

20.2 a. $48
b. 609,756; 4.43
c. $46.71; $1.29
d. 48,000; 48,000
20.6 3,595,138
20.12 20.42%
20.15 $28.10

CHAPTER 21

21.2 −$58,646.08
21.6 $33,392.96

21.10 $2,219,253.83
21.14 a. −$94,942.71
b. $605,604.52

CHAPTER 22

22.4 a. $16.92
b. $9.06
22.6 $1.82
22.10 Call = $5.63; Put = $7.10
22.14 $296,928.02
22.18 $75.00
22.22 Project A: Equity = $4,646.93; Debt = $8,653.07
Project B: Equity = $4,380.51; Debt = $9,319.49
22.26 a. $6.93
b. .57; Borrow $25.64
c. $6.93
22.34 $10.44

CHAPTER 23

23.2 $1,482,236.42
23.6 $279,908.38
23.10 $6,547,526

CHAPTER 24

24.2 36.56
24.5 $21
24.10 a. $751.82
b. 13.37 years
24.14 $764.54

CHAPTER 25

25.2 −$17,325; $24,425
25.6 2.85154 years
25.9 $47,700
25.14 a. $454.62
b. $547.86

CHAPTER 26

26.2 Cash = $1,745
Current assets = $6,920
26.6 Operating cycle = 80.43 days
Cash cycle = 41.11 days
26.10 Ending cash balance = $99,870; $100,985; $200,395

CHAPTER 27

27.2 a. Disbursement float = $78,000
Collection float = −$49,200
Net float = $28,800
b. Disbursement float = $78,000
Collection float = −$24,600
Net float = $53,400
27.6 a. $30,856
b. 2.53 days
c. $30,856
d. $5.72
e. $12,586
27.10 $3,370,000; $84,250

CHAPTER 28

28.2 $2,701,369.86
28.6 15.21 times; $749,770.83
28.10 $228,461.84
28.14 $280,542.39
28.18 $81.01

CHAPTER 29

29.2 Assets = $300,000
29.6 EPS = $4.93; PE = 12.60
29.10 a. $3.81
b. $58.31
c. 14.71
d. $55.61; 14.61

CHAPTER 30

30.4 3.363

CHAPTER 31

31.2 £ = $134.96
SF/£ = 1.1986
£/SF = .8343
31.6 Great Britain = 2.14%
Japan = 5.20%
Switzerland = 2.77%
31.10 Kr/$ = 9.2264
31.14 $1,116,909.24

Glossary

Absolute priority rule (APR) Establishes priority of claims under liquidation.

Accounts receivable financing A secured short-term loan that involves either the assigning of receivables or the factoring of receivables.

Adjusted present value (APV) Net present value adjusted for taxes, financial distress costs, and other financial side effects.

Advance commitment A promise to sell an asset before the seller has lined up purchase of the asset.

Agency costs Costs of conflicts of interest among stockholders, bondholders, and managers.

Agency problem A conflict of interest between a principal and an agent.

Aging schedule A compilation of accounts receivable by the age of account.

Allocated cost A cost arising from use of a resource that is used in multiple projects.

American depositary receipt (ADR) A security issued in the United States to represent shares of a foreign stock. Enables the stock to be traded in the United States.

Angel investors Individuals providing initial capital to startups.

Annual percentage rate (APR) The annual interest rate without consideration of compounding. Also called the stated annual interest rate.

Annuity A level stream of equal dollar payments that lasts for a fixed time.

Annuity due An annuity for which the cash flows occur at the beginning of the period.

Arithmetic average return The return earned in an average year over a multiyear period.

Asked price The price at which a dealer is willing to sell a security. Also called the ask price.

Asset beta The sensitivity of the value of the firm's assets to changes in the market. Also called unlevered beta.

Average Usually refers to the arithmetic mean.

Average tax rate Tax bill divided by taxable income.

Balance sheet A statement showing a firm's accounting value on a particular date. It reflects the fact that assets must be equal to the sum of liabilities and equity.

Banker's acceptance Agreement by a bank to pay a given sum of money at a future date.

Bearer form A form of bond without record of the owner's name. Whoever holds the bond (the bearer) is the owner.

Benchmark An index or average whose movement is considered a general indicator of the direction of the overall market. Used as a comparison for a portfolio's performance.

Beta A measure of the sensitivity of a security's return to systematic risk.

Beta coefficient The amount of systematic risk present in a particular risky asset relative to that in an average risky asset.

Bid price What a dealer is willing to pay for a security.

Bid-ask spread The difference between the bid and ask prices.

Bidder A firm or person that has made an offer to take over a firm.

Bookbuilding The process of soliciting information about price and quantity for a new security offering.

Break-even analysis Analysis of the level of sales at which a project would earn zero profit.

Broker An entity that brings security buyers and sellers together but does not maintain an inventory.

Bubble theory (of speculative markets) Security prices sometimes move wildly above their fundamental values.

Call option The right–but not the obligation–to buy the underlying asset at a stated price within a specified time.

Call premium The difference between the call price of a bond and its stated value.

Call protected Describes a bond that is not allowed to be called at the current date.

Call provision A written agreement between an issuing corporation and its bondholders that gives the corporation the option to redeem the bond at a specified price before the maturity date.

Capital asset pricing model (CAPM) An equilibrium asset pricing theory that shows that the equilibrium expected return on all risky assets is a function of their covariance with the market portfolio.

Capital budgeting The decision-making process for accepting or rejecting projects.

Capital gain The positive change in the value of an asset. A negative capital gain is a capital loss.

Capital gains yield The rate at which the value of an investment grows.

Capital intensity ratio The ratio of total assets to sales. Measures the amount of assets needed to generate $1 of sales.

Capital market line (CML) The efficient set of all assets, both risky and riskless, that provides the investor with the best possible opportunities.

Capital rationing The case where funds are limited to a fixed dollar amount and must be allocated among competing projects.

Capital structure The mix of the various debt and equity capital maintained by a firm.

Captive finance company A wholly owned subsidiary that handles the credit function for the parent company.

Carrying costs Costs that increase with increases in the level of investment in assets (usually refers to current assets).

Cash concentration Process a firm follows to move cash into its main accounts after collection.

Cash cycle In general, the time between cash disbursement and cash collection. In net working capital management, it can be thought of as the operating cycle less the average accounts payable period.

Cash discount A discount given for a cash purchase. Often offered to speed up the collection of receivables.

Cash flow Cash generated by the firm and paid to creditors and shareholders. It can be classified as (1) cash flow from operations, (2) cash flow from changes in fixed assets, and (3) cash flow from changes in net working capital.

Cash offer A public equity issue that is sold to all interested investors.

Cash transaction A transaction where exchange is immediate. Contrasted with a forward contract, which calls for future delivery of an asset at an agreed-upon price.

Change in net working capital The change in difference between current assets and current liabilities from one period to the next.

Characteristic line The line relating the expected return on a security to different returns on the market.

Clean price The quoted price on a bond.

Clientele effect Argument that stocks attract clienteles based on dividend yield or taxes.

Commercial paper Short-term, unsecured promissory notes issued by corporations, usually with investment-grade credit. Their maturity ranges up to 270 days.

Common stock Equity claims held by the residual owners of the firm who are the last to receive any distribution of earnings or assets.

Common-size statements Financial statements expressed in percentages instead of total dollars to allow for comparison.

Compensating balance Deposit that the firm keeps with the bank in a low-interest or non-interest-bearing account to compensate the bank for loans or services.

Competitive offer Method of selecting an investment bank for a new issue by offering the securities to the underwriter with the highest bid.

Compound interest Interest that is earned both on the initial principal and on interest earned on the initial principal in previous periods.

Compound value Value of a sum after investing it over one or more periods. Also called future value (FV).

Compounding Process of reinvesting each interest payment to earn more interest. Compounding is based on the idea that interest itself becomes principal and therefore also earns interest in subsequent periods.

Consolidation A merger in which an entirely new firm is created.

Continuous compounding Interest compounded continuously rather than at fixed intervals.

Contribution margin Amount that each additional sale contributes to the profit of the whole project.

Controlled disbursement account Allows a bank to determine total payments on an account in a given day and request that amount from a firm.

Conversion premium Difference between the conversion price and the current stock price divided by the current stock price.

Conversion price The ratio of the face value of a bond to the conversion ratio.

Conversion ratio The number of shares per bond that a bondholder would receive if the bond was converted.

Conversion value What a convertible bond would be worth if it was immediately converted into the common stock at the current price.

Convertible bond A bond that may be converted into another form of security, typically common stock, at the option of the holder at a specified price for a specified period of time.

Corporation Form of business organization that is created as a distinct "legal person" composed of one or more actual individuals or legal entities.

Correlation A standardized statistical measure of the dependence of two random variables. Defined as the covariance divided by the standard deviations of the two variables.

Coupon The stated interest payment on a debt instrument.

Coupon rate The annual coupon a bond pays divided by its face value.

Covariance A statistical measure of the degree to which random variables move together.

Credit default swap A derivative investment that provides insurance against loss due to a bond default.

Credit instrument Device by which a firm offers credit, such as an invoice or a promissory note.

Credit period The length of time for which credit is granted.

Credit scoring Determining the probability of default when granting customers credit.

Cross-rate The exchange rate between two foreign currencies that are both quoted in some third currency.

Cumulative voting A procedure whereby a shareholder may cast all of his or her votes for one member of the board of directors.

Currency swap Agreement to pay cash flows in one currency and receive them in another.

Current yield A bond's annual coupon divided by its current market price.

Date of payment Date that dividend checks are mailed. Also called payment date.

Date of record Date on which holders of record in a firm's stock ledger are designated as the recipients of either dividends or stock rights. Also called record date.

Dealer An entity that maintains an inventory and stands ready to buy and sell at any time.

Debenture An unsecured bond, usually with maturity of 10 years or more. A debt obligation backed by the general credit of the issuing corporation.

Debt displacement The amount of borrowing that leasing displaces. Firms that do a lot of leasing will be forced to cut back on borrowing.

Declaration date Date on which the board of directors passes a resolution to pay a dividend of a specified amount to all qualified holders of record on a specified date.

Default risk premium The portion of a nominal interest rate or bond yield that represents compensation for the possibility of default.

Deferred call A provision that prohibits the company from calling the bond before a certain date. During this period, the bond is said to be call protected.

Deliverable instrument The asset in a forward contract that will be delivered in the future at an agreed-upon price.

Depreciation tax shield Portion of an investment that can be deducted from taxable income.

Designated market marker (DMM) A person assigned by a security exchange to maintain a fair and orderly market for a group of securities.

Dilution Loss in existing shareholders' value. There are several kinds of dilution: (1) dilution of ownership, (2) dilution of stock price, (3) dilution of book value, and (4) dilution of earnings.

Direct lease A lease under which a lessor buys equipment from a manufacturer and leases it to a lessee.

Direct listing A security offering in which the company offers securities directly to investors, bypassing underwriters.

Dirty price The price of a bond including accrued interest.

Discounted payback period The length of time it takes for a project's discounted cash flows to equal its initial investment.

Discounting Calculating the present value of a future amount. The process is the opposite of compounding.

Divestiture The sale of assets, operations, divisions, and/or segments to a third party.

Dividend Payment made by a firm to its owners, either in cash or in stock. Also called the income component of the return on an investment in stock.

Dividend payout ratio Amount of cash paid to shareholders expressed as a percentage of earnings.

Dividend yield Dividends per share of common stock divided by market price per share.

DMM's post A fixed place on the exchange where the DMM operates.

DuPont identity States that return on equity (ROE) can be expressed as the product of profit margin, total asset turnover, and the equity multiplier (one plus the debt-equity ratio).

Duration The weighted average time of an asset's cash flows, often called *effective maturity*.

Dutch auction A security offering in which the underwriter sets the offer price through an auction. Also called a uniform price auction.

Economic order quantity (EOQ) Approach for explicitly establishing the reorder quantity that minimizes the total inventory cost.

Effective annual rate (EAR) The interest rate if it were compounded once per time period rather than several times per period.

Effective annual yield (EAY) The interest rate if it were compounded once per time period rather than several times per period.

Efficient frontier Graph representing a set of portfolios that maximize expected return at each level of portfolio risk. Also called the efficient set.

Efficient market hypothesis (EMH) States that prices of securities fully reflect available information. Investors buying bonds and stocks should expect to obtain an equilibrium rate of return. Firms should expect to receive the fair value for the securities they sell.

Efficient set Graph representing a set of portfolios that maximize expected return at each level of portfolio risk. Also called the efficient frontier.

Electronic communications network (ECN) A type of website that allows investors to trade directly with one another.

Empirical models Models based less on theory and more on regularities and relationships in market history.

Erosion Cash flow transferred to a new project from customers and sales of other products of the firm.

Eurobond An international bond sold primarily in countries other than the country in whose currency the issue is denominated.

Eurocurrency Money deposited in a financial center outside of the country whose currency is involved.

Ex-dividend date An individual purchasing a stock on or after its ex-dividend date will not receive the current dividend.

Ex-rights date An individual purchasing a stock on or after its ex-rights date will not receive the rights.

Exchange offers Occur when a firm offers to exchange stock for debt, or vice versa.

Exchange rate Price of one country's currency for another country's currency.

Exchange rate risk Risk that arises from holding currencies other than an entity's home currency when future exchange rates are uncertain.

Exotics Complicated blends of derivative instruments.

Face value The principal value of a bond that is repaid at the end of the term. Also referred to as par value or principal.

Factor model A model in which each stock's return is generated by common factors derived from systematic sources of risk.

Feasible set The best possible expected return–standard deviation pairs that can be constructed from a set of assets. Also called an opportunity set.

Financial distress Events preceding and including bankruptcy such as violation of loan contracts.

Financial lease A long-term, noncancelable lease that generally requires the lessee to pay all maintenance fees.

Financial ratio Relationships determined from a firm's financial information and used for comparison purposes.

Fisher effect The real rate of interest is invariant to the rate of inflation.

Five Cs of credit The five basic credit factors to be evaluated: character, capacity, capital, collateral, and conditions.

Fixed cost A cost that is not dependent on the amount of goods or services produced during the period.

Float The difference between bank cash and book cash. Represents the net effect of checks in the process of collection or clearing.

Floor broker NYSE members who execute customer buy and sell orders.

Flow to equity (FTE) A valuation approach that emphasizes cash flows to equity.

Forced conversion If the conversion value of a convertible is greater than the call price, the call can be used to force conversion.

Foreign bond An international bond issued by foreign borrowers in another nation's capital market and traditionally denominated in that nation's currency.

Foreign exchange market Market in which arrangements are made to exchange foreign currencies.

Forward contract An arrangement calling for future delivery of an asset at an agreed-upon price.

Forward exchange rate A future day's exchange rate between two major currencies.

Forward trade An agreement to buy or sell based on exchange rates established today for settlement in the future.

Free cash flow Cash flow that is free to distribute to creditors and stockholders because it is not needed for working capital or fixed asset investments.

Frequency distribution The organization of data to show how often certain values or ranges of values occur.

Future value (FV) Value of a sum after investing it over one or more periods.

Futures contract Obliges traders to purchase or sell an asset at an agreed-upon price on a specified future date. Futures differ from forward contracts in their standardization, exchange trading, margin requirements, and daily settling (mark to market).

Generally accepted accounting principles (GAAP) A common set of accounting concepts, standards, and procedures by which financial statements are prepared.

Geometric average return The average compound return earned per year over a multiyear period.

Gilts British and Irish government securities.

Goodwill The excess of the purchase price over the sum of the fair market values of the individual assets acquired.

Green Shoe provision A contract provision that gives the underwriter the option to purchase additional shares at the offering price to cover overallotments.

Growing annuity A finite number of growing cash flows.

Growing perpetuity A constant stream of cash flows without end that is expected to rise indefinitely.

Growth stock portfolio A portfolio that has an average PE ratio much in excess of the market average PE.

Hedging Taking a position in two or more securities that are negatively correlated (taking opposite trading positions) to reduce risk.

Holding period return The rate of return over a given period.

Homemade dividends An individual investor can undo corporate dividend policy by reinvesting excess dividends or selling off shares of stock to receive a desired cash flow.

Homogeneous expectations Idea that all individuals have the same beliefs concerning future expected returns, variances, and covariances.

Immunized Immune to interest rate risk.

Income statement Financial report that summarizes a firm's performance over a specified time period.

Incremental IRR IRR on the incremental investment from choosing a large project instead of a smaller project.

Indenture Written agreement between the corporate debt issuer and the lender. Sets forth maturity date, interest rate, and other terms. Also called deed of trust.

Independent project A project whose acceptance or rejection is independent of the acceptance or rejection of other projects.

Inflation premium The portion of a nominal interest rate that represents compensation for expected future inflation.

Inflation risk Risk faced by investors due to uncertainty about future inflation.

Information content effect The rise in the stock price following the dividend signal.

Initial coin offering (ICO) The initial sale of a token on a digital currency platform.

Initial public offering (IPO) The original sale of a company's securities to the public. Also called an unseasoned new issue.

Inside quotes The highest bid quotes and the lowest ask quotes for a security.

Interest rate parity (IRP) The interest rate differential between two countries is driven by the difference between the forward exchange rate and the spot exchange rate of the two countries' currencies.

Interest rate risk premium The compensation required by bondholders for bearing interest rate risk.

Interest rate swap Agreement to exchange one series of interest payments for another.

Internal growth rate The maximum growth rate that can be achieved with no external financing of any kind.

Internal rate of return (IRR) The discount rate at which the net present value of an investment is zero. It is a method of evaluating capital expenditure proposals.

International Fisher effect (IFE) States that real interest rates are equal from country to country.

Inventory loan A secured short-term loan using inventory as collateral. The three basic forms are a blanket inventory lien, a trust receipt, and field warehouse financing.

Investment banks Financial intermediaries that perform a variety of services including aiding in the sale of securities, facilitating mergers and other corporate reorganizations, acting as brokers to both individual and institutional clients, and trading for their own accounts.

Invoice Bill written by a seller of goods or services and submitted to the purchaser.

Just-in-time (JIT) inventory An inventory management approach that emphasizes minimizing inventory and maximizing turnover.

Leveraged lease Tax-oriented leasing arrangement that involves one or more third-party lenders.

Liquidation Termination of the firm as a going concern. Involves selling the assets of the firm and distributing cash to creditors and equity holders in order of established priority.

Liquidity premium The portion of a nominal interest rate or bond yield that represents compensation for lack of liquidity.

Lockbox Post office box set up to intercept payments. The most widely used device to speed up the collection of cash.

London Interbank Offered Rate (LIBOR) Rate the most creditworthy banks charge one another for large loans of Eurodollars overnight in the London market.

Long hedge Protecting the future cost of a purchase by purchasing a futures contract to protect against changes in the price of an asset.

Making delivery Refers to the seller of a forward contract actually turning over to the buyer the asset agreed upon in the contract.

Marginal tax rate Tax rate on the next dollar of income.

Marked to market Describes the daily settlement of obligations on futures positions.

Market model A one-factor model for returns where the factor is an index of the returns on the whole market.

Market portfolio In concept, a value-weighted index of all securities. In practice, a proxy such as the S&P 500 is used.

Marketable claims Claims that can be bought and sold in financial markets, such as those of stockholders and bondholders.

Materials requirements planning (MRP) A system for planning the levels of work-in-progress and raw materials a firm needs based on projected finished goods needs.

Maturity The specified date on which the face value of a bond is paid.

Mean The sum of the values observed divided by the total number of observations–sometimes referred to as the average.

Member The owner of a trading license on the NYSE.

Merger The absorption of one firm by another.

Monte Carlo simulation An exercise that generates possible outcomes for a project based on a model of the underlying factors that drive project performance.

Mutually exclusive investments Investments where the acceptance of one project precludes the acceptance of one or more alternative projects.

Negative covenant Part of the indenture or loan agreement that limits or prohibits actions that the company may take.

Negotiated offer The issuing firm negotiates a deal with one underwriter to offer a new issue rather than taking competitive bids.

Net advantage to leasing (NAL) The NPV that is calculated when deciding whether to lease or buy an asset.

Net present value (NPV) The present value of future cash flows discounted at the appropriate market interest rate minus the present value of the cost of the investment.

Net working capital Current assets minus current liabilities.

Nominal cash flow A cash flow expressed in actual currency.

Noncash item Expense against revenue that does not directly affect cash flow such as depreciation and deferred tax.

Nonmarketable claims Claims that cannot be easily bought and sold in the financial markets, such as those of the government and litigants in lawsuits.

Normal distribution Symmetric bell-shaped frequency distribution that can be completely defined by its mean and standard deviation.

Note Unsecured debt, usually with maturity of less than 10 years.

NVP rule Accept a project with a positive NPV and reject a project with a negative NPV.

Off-balance sheet financing Financing that is not shown as a liability on a company's balance sheet.

Operating cash flow Earnings before interest plus depreciation minus taxes. Cash generated from operations less capital spending and working capital requirements.

Operating cycle The time interval between the arrival of inventory stock and the date when cash is collected from receivables.

Operating lease Type of lease where the period of contract is less than the life of the equipment and the lessor pays all maintenance and servicing costs.

Operating leverage The degree to which a company's costs of operation are fixed as opposed to variable. The larger the fixed costs compared to variable costs, the larger the operating leverage.

Opportunity cost Most valuable alternative that is given up. The discount rate used in NPV computation is an opportunity interest rate.

Opportunity set The possible expected return-standard deviation pairs that can be constructed from a set of assets. Also called a feasible set.

Option A right–but not an obligation–to do something.

Order flow The flow of customer orders to buy and sell stocks.

Over-the-counter (OTC) market An informal network of brokers and dealers who negotiate sales of securities (not a formal exchange).

Oversubscription privilege Allows shareholders to purchase unsubscribed shares in a rights offering at the subscription price.

Par value The principal amount of a bond that is repaid at the end of the term. For stock, it is a relatively unimportant value except for bookkeeping purposes.

Partnership Form of business organization in which two or more co-owners form a business.

Payback period The length of time it takes for a project to return its initial investment.

Payout ratio Proportion of net income paid out in cash dividends.

Percentage of sales approach A financial planning protocol that specifies balance sheet and income statement items as a proportion of sales.

Perpetuity A constant stream of cash flows without end.

Pie model of capital structure A visual depiction of the firm that shows its full value as a circle with different claims dividing it into portions. Claims may be either marketable (stockholders) or nonmarketable (government).

Political risk Changes in value that arise as a consequence of political actions.

Portfolio Combined holding of more than one stock, bond, real estate asset, or other asset by an investor.

Positive covenant Part of the indenture or loan agreement that specifies an action that the company must undertake.

Precautionary motive The need for a safety supply of cash to act as a financial reserve.

Preferred stock A type of stock whose holders are given certain priority over common stockholders in the payment of dividends. Usually the dividend rate is fixed at the time of issue and no voting rights are given.

Present value (PV) The current value of future cash discounted at the appropriate interest rate.

Present value factor Factor used to calculate the present value of an amount to be received in a future period.

Primary market Where new issues of securities are offered to the public.

Principle of diversification Spreading an investment across a number of assets will eliminate some, but not all, of the risk.

Private placement The direct sale of a bond or other security to a limited number of investors.

Private workout Financial restructuring that takes place in lieu of formal bankruptcy.

Profitability index A method used to evaluate projects. It is the ratio of the present value of the future expected cash flows after initial investment divided by the initial investment.

Prospectus The legal document that must be given to every investor who contemplates purchasing registered securities in an offering. It describes the details of the company and the particular offering.

Protective covenant A part of the indenture or loan agreement that limits or requires certain actions by a company during the term of the loan to protect the lender's interest.

Proxy A grant of authority by the shareholder to transfer his or her voting rights to someone else.

Purchase accounting Method of reporting acquisitions that requires that the assets of the acquired firm be reported at their fair market value on the books of the acquiring firm.

Purchasing power parity (PPP) The idea that the exchange rate adjusts to keep purchasing power constant among currencies.

Put option The right–but not the obligation–to sell the underlying asset at a stated price within a specified time.

Put-call parity The value of a European call equals the value of the underlying stock and a put minus the cost of investing in a risk-free asset such that the asset is worth the option strike price at expiration.

Random walk A statistical model where stock price changes from day to day are random; the changes are independent of each other and have the same probability distribution.

Real cash flow A cash flow is expressed in terms of purchasing power, not actual dollars.

Real option The option to perform an action in managing a business or as part of a project.

Red herring The first document released by an underwriter of a new issue to prospective investors.

Registered form A form of bond issuance wherein a registrar records who initially owns the bonds and updates records for changes in ownership.

Registration statement Discloses all the pertinent information concerning a corporation that wants to make a public offering. The statement is filed with the Securities and Exchange Commission.

Regular cash dividend Cash payment by a firm to its shareholders, usually four times a year.

Regulation A The securities regulation that exempts small public offerings (those valued at less than $5 million) from most registration requirements.

Reorganization Financial restructuring of a failed firm. Both the firm's asset structure and its financial structure are changed to reflect their true values, and claims are settled.

Restricted stock units (RSUs) Shares of stock granted to employees by the company for compensation or bonus purposes.

Retention ratio Retained earnings divided by net income. Also called the plowback ratio.

Return on equity (ROE) Net income divided by total equity. Measures the profit per dollar of book equity.

Reverse split A procedure whereby the number of outstanding stock shares is reduced; for example, two outstanding shares are combined to create only one.

Sale and leaseback An arrangement whereby a firm sells its existing assets to a financial company, which then leases them back to the firm. This is often done to generate cash.

Sales-type lease An arrangement wherein a firm leases its own equipment.

Scenario analysis Analysis of the effect on a project of different scenarios with each scenario involving many variable changes.

Seasoned equity offering (SEO) A new public stock issue after the company's stock has been previously issued publically. Also called a seasoned new issue.

Secondary markets Where already-existing securities are bought and sold on the exchanges or in the over-the-counter market.

Secured Overnight Financing Rate (SOFR) Interest rate based on transactions in the Treasury repurchase market where investors offer banks overnight loans backed by their bond assets.

Security market line (SML) A straight line that shows the equilibrium relationship between systematic risk and expected rates of return.

Semistrong form efficiency Theory that the market is efficient with respect to all publicly available information.

Sensitivity analysis Analysis of the effect on the project when there is some change in a critical variable such as sales or costs.

Separation principle The principle that portfolio choice can be separated into two independent tasks: (1) determination of the optimal risky portfolio, which is a purely technical problem, and (2) the personal choice of the best mix of the risky portfolio and the risk-free asset.

Serial correlation The correlation between a variable and the lagged value of the same variable.

Sharpe ratio The risk premium of an asset divided by its standard deviation.

Shelf registration An SEC procedure that allows a firm to file a master registration statement summarizing planned financing for a two-year period and then file short statements when the firm wishes to sell any of the approved master statement securities during that period.

Short hedge Protecting the value of an asset held by selling a futures contract.

Short sale A way for an investor to bet that the price of an asset will decrease.

Shortage costs Costs that fall with increases in the level of investment in current assets.

Simple interest Interest calculated by considering only the original principal amount.

Sinking fund An account managed by the bond trustee for the purpose of repaying the bonds.

Sole proprietorship A business owned by a single individual that pays no corporate income tax but has unlimited liability for business debts and obligations.

Speculating Extremely high-risk investing.

Speculative motive The need to hold cash in order to be able to take advantage of future opportunities.

Spot exchange rate Exchange rate between two currencies for immediate delivery.

Spot trade An agreement today for settlement in two business days.

Stakeholder Anyone, other than stock- or bondholders, who has a potential claim on the cash flow of the firm.

Standard deviation The square root of the variance. The standard statistical measure of the spread of a sample.

Standby fee Amount paid to an underwriter who agrees to purchase any stock that is not subscribed to by a public investor in a rights offering.

Standby underwriting An agreement wherein an underwriter agrees to purchase any stock that is not purchased by a public investor.

Stock dividend Payment of a dividend in the form of stock rather than cash. A stock dividend comes from treasury stock, increases the number of shares outstanding, and reduces the value of each share.

Stock repurchase Occurs when a firm repurchases its own shares.

Stock split Increases the number of outstanding shares of stock while making no change in shareholders' equity.

Straight voting A shareholder may cast all of his or her votes for each candidate for the board of directors.

Strong form efficiency Theory that the market is efficient with respect to all available information, public or private.

Subscription price Price that existing shareholders pay for a share of stock in a rights offering.

Sunk cost A cost that has already occurred and cannot be reversed. Such costs should be ignored when deciding whether to accept or reject a project.

Supplemental liquidity providers (SLPs) Investment firms that are active participants in stocks assigned to them. Their job is to make a one-sided market (i.e., offering to either buy or sell). They trade purely for their own accounts.

Sustainable growth rate The maximum growth rate that can be achieved with no external equity financing while maintaining a constant debt-equity ratio.

Swap Agreement between two counterparties to exchange cash flows over time.

Syndicate A group of investment banking companies that agree to cooperate in a joint venture to underwrite an offering of securities for resale to the public.

Synergy (1) When the value of a combined firm after a merger is greater than the sum of the values of the firms premerger. (2) The positive incremental net gain associated with the combination of two firms through a merger or acquisition.

Systematic risk A risk that affects a large number of assets, each to a greater or lesser degree. Also called market risk or common risk.

Target firm A firm that is the object of a takeover by another firm.

Tax-oriented lease A financial lease in which the lessor is the owner for tax purposes. Also called a true lease or a tax lease.

Taxability premium The portion of a nominal interest rate or bond yield that represents compensation for unfavorable tax status.

Tender offer Public offer to buy shares of a target firm.

Term loans Direct business loans of typically one to five years.

Term structure of interest rates The relationship between nominal interest rates on default-free, pure discount securities and time to maturity; that is, the pure time value of money.

Tombstone An advertisement that announces a public offering of securities. It identifies the issuer, the type of security, the underwriters, and where additional information is available.

Total cash flow of the firm Total cash inflow minus total cash outflow.

Trading range Idea that investors prefer when the price of a firm's stock falls within certain bounds. An incentive to perform stock splits.

Transaction motive The need to hold cash that arises from normal disbursement and collection activities of the firm.

Treasury yield curve Plot of Treasury yields relative to maturity.

Unbiased forward rate (UFR) States that the forward rate is equal to the expected spot rate.

Uncovered interest parity (UIP) States that the expected currency spot rate is a function of the current spot rate and the interest rates in the countries.

Unsystematic risk Any risk that specifically affects a single asset or a small group of assets. Also called unique, idiosyncratic, or diversifiable risk.

Value additivity (VA) property The value of the firm is the sum of the values of the firm's different projects, divisions, and entities.

Value portfolio Portfolio of common stocks that has an average PE ratio substantially less than that of the market index.

Variable cost A cost that varies directly with volume and is zero when production is zero.

Variance The average squared deviation from the mean.

Venture capital (VC) Financing for new, often high-risk, ventures.

Weak form efficiency Theory that the market is efficient with respect to historical price information.

Weighted average cost of capital (WACC) The weighted average cost of a firm's common equity, preferred stock, and debt.

Yield to maturity (YTM) The discount rate that equates the present value of the interest payments and par value of a bond with the current price of a bond.

Zero coupon bonds Bonds with no coupons.

Zero-balance account (ZBA) A checking account in which a zero balance is maintained by a transfer of funds from a master account in an amount only large enough to cover checks presented.

Index

X

Y

Z